PATENT ENFORCEMENT IN THE US, GERMANY AND JAPAN

PATENT ENFORCEMENT IN THE US, GERMANY AND JAPAN

by

Toshiko Takenaka

Washington Research Foundation/W. Hunter Simpson Professor of Technology Law, School of Law, University of Washington

Christoph Rademacher

Associate Professor, Waseda University, Tokyo

Jan Krauss

Patent Attorney, Boehmert & Boehmert, Munich

Jochen Pagenberg

Co-founder, Bardehle Pagenberg, Munich

Tilman Mueller-Stoy

Partner, Bardehle Pagenberg, Munich

Christof Karl

Partner, Bardehle Pagenberg, Munich

OXFORD
UNIVERSITY PRESS

OXFORD
UNIVERSITY PRESS

Great Clarendon Street, Oxford, OX2 6DP,
United Kingdom

Oxford University Press is a department of the University of Oxford.
It furthers the University's objective of excellence in research, scholarship,
and education by publishing worldwide. Oxford is a registered trade mark of
Oxford University Press in the UK and in certain other countries

First Edition published in 2015

Published in the United States of America by Oxford University Press
198 Madison Avenue, New York, NY 10016, United States of America

British Library Cataloguing in Publication Data
Data available

Library of Congress Control Number: 2015944373

ISBN 978–0–19–967920–1

PREFACE

This book is based on two dissertations: my dissertation which was revised for a publication by the Max Planck Institute, entitled "Interpreting Patent Claims: The United States, Germany and Japan," 17 *IIC Studies* (1995), and Professor Christoph Rademacher's dissertation: "Die gerichtliche Durchsetzung von Patent- und Markenrechten in Deutschland, Japan und den USA (Judicial Enforcement of Patent and Trademark Rights in Germany, Japan and the U.S.)" (2010). This book is the product of our academic collaboration and friendship over the last decade since I met Professor Rademacher in 2007 when he was a visiting PhD student at Keio University Law School, Tokyo.

From 2003 to 2012, I annually visited Waseda Law School, Tokyo, and taught a comparative patent law course and US and European patent enforcement course. Professor Rademacher made a strong first impression on me with his excellent command of Japanese but was still struggling to read Japanese legal materials for his research. Nevertheless he successfully completed his research and defended his dissertation with his commitment to pursue excellence in comparative law study. Coincidentally, Professor Rademacher was exploring options to find a teaching position in Germany as well as Japan when I was planning to return to the full-time appointment at the University of Washington School of Law (UW Law), Seattle. It was a perfect time to recommend him to take over the IP courses I was teaching at Waseda. It was my great pleasure to find him being appointed, and then promoted to Associate Professor, to teach the courses I formerly taught and to run the IP Center I had directed with my colleagues at Waseda.

We began to develop a book proposal in 2009 when Professor Rademacher was waiting for his dissertation to be published in Germany. IP scholars in Europe and Asia frequently reference my 1995 book when they learn of my scholarship. Thus, I have been keenly aware of the necessity of updating my 1995 book. To that end I considered an overhaul of the book by expanding the scope to cover both substantive and procedural law aspects of patent enforcement. The best opportunity was presented when Professor Rademacher asked me about possible options to publish his dissertation in English. I proposed to co-author a book by merging my research interests with his and he accepted my proposal with great enthusiasm.

We want our book to provide not only research resources for academics but also basic information and tools for practitioners who manage and enforce patent portfolios worldwide. Thus, we invited leading patent practitioners to join our book project. I was particularly pleased that Dr. Jan Krauss, with whom I have been teaching a patent law seminar at UW Law, and Dr. Jochen Pagenberg, my dissertation advisor and a world-renowned patent expert, agreed to join our team. Dr. Pagenberg brought Dr. Christof Karl and Dr. Tilman Müller-Stoy, to share their perspectives as experienced patent litigators. Although I was once a patent attorney and have experience in both in-house and private practice, the co-authorship with leading practitioners, Drs. Krauss, Pagenberg, Karl and Müller-Stoy directed our research focus onto legal issues and problems practitioners encounter in multinational enforcement and makes comparative studies of the current patent enforcement systems more relevant to those who act in and represent clients in the United States, Germany, and Japan.

While working on our book project, the America Invents Act (AIA) entered into force in 2011 and introduced extensive changes in patent validity and enforcement. In addition, several bills are pending in the US Congress to introduce major reforms in procedures at US district courts. Patent enforcement in Germany also expects major changes once the Unified Patent Court (UPC) begins to operate in the next few years. The book covers all developments up to April 2015 but more developments are expected. The extent of the AIA and UPC impacts on infringement case law and litigation procedure are yet to be seen. We plan to post updates and supplements reflecting these changes via a link from my UW faculty home page (http://www.law.washington.edu/Directory/Profile.aspx?ID=790) as they become evident. I hope that our best practice proposal is helpful for policy-makers and judges who introduce these changes.

Over the years, through numerous revisions to complete the manuscript, many students from my patent law courses worked as my research assistants. In particular, I am very grateful for Ms. Lisa Elizabeth ("Lili") Tamaki who is an alumnus of the 2014 JD Class at UW Law. None of us are native English-speakers and many of my co-authors are not well-experienced with American-style legal writing. With her experience at the Washington International Law Journal, Lili carefully reviewed our manuscript and provided exhaustive grammar checks and academic proofreading to clarify ambiguous expressions. I am also grateful for my current and past assistants, Ms. Kaitlyn Bunker and Mr. Slaven Svetinovic, for their assistance in formatting and proofreading the manuscript and librarians at the UW Law library for their outstanding services to provide legal research in response to my requests.

Toshiko Takenaka, PhD
Seattle, Washington, USA

CONTENTS—SUMMARY

Table of Cases xvii
Table of Legislation xlix

PART I. INTRODUCTION

1. **History** 3
2. **Patent Enforcement Institutions** 23

PART II. INFRINGEMENT

3. **Introduction** 47
4. **United States** 49
5. **Germany** 92
6. **Japan** 134

PART III. VALIDITY CHALLENGE

7. **United States** 165
8. **Germany** 213
9. **Japan** 251

PART IV. ENFORCEMENT PROCEDURE

10. **United States** 275
11. **Germany** 312
12. **Japan** 348

PART V. REMEDIES

13. **United States** 377
14. **Germany** 403
15. **Japan** 417

PART VI. BEST PRACTICE

16. **Analysis and Proposal of Best Practice** 429

Index 451

CONTENTS

Table of Cases xvii
Table of Legislation xlix

PART I. INTRODUCTION

1. History

A. The Evolution of International Institutions 1.01
1. The World Intellectual Property Organization and the World Trade Organization 1.01
2. The European Patent Organization and the European Union 1.04
3. Trilateral Patent Office Initiatives and Beyond 1.07

B. United States 1.10
1. Early Patent System: 1730–1869 1.10
2. Anti-Patent Era: 1870–1982 1.14
3. Pro-Patent Era: 1980–2012 1.20
4. American Invents Act: 2012–present 1.23

C. Germany 1.26
1. Pre-Patent Era in Germany 1.26
2. Patents in the Nazi Era 1.30
3. Post-World War II 1.35
4. The EPC and Patent Harmonization in the EU 1.39

D. Japan 1.49
1. Meiji Restoration 1.49
2. Major Developments through the Twentieth Century 1.54
3. Pro-Patent Era 1.57

2. Patent Enforcement Institutions

A. United States 2.01
1. Overview 2.01
2. Courts 2.03
3. USPTO 2.15
4. US International Trade Commission 2.17

B. Germany 2.19
1. Overview 2.19
2. Patent Offices—EPO and GPTO 2.20
3. Courts 2.28
4. Customs Office 2.56

C. Japan 2.60
1. Overview 2.60
2. Courts 2.62
3. Japan Patent Office 2.70
4. Customs Office 2.73

PART II. INFRINGEMENT

3. Introduction

4. United States

A. Acts of Infringement 4.01
1. Direct Infringement 4.01
2. Indirect Infringement 4.06
3. Patent Term and Extension 4.10
4. Extraterritorial Infringement 4.12

B. Extent of Patent Protection 4.17
1. Overview 4.17
2. Infringement Analysis 4.22
3. Claim Construction 4.32
4. Application of Construed Claims to Accused Embodiment 4.83
5. Doctrine of Equivalents 4.91

5. Germany

A. Acts of Infringement 5.01
1. Direct Infringement 5.01
2. Indirect Infringement 5.25
3. Extraterritorial Infringement 5.41
4. Exemptions to Patent Infringement 5.51
5. Patent Term and Extension 5.56

B. Extent of Patent Protection 5.61
1. Overview 5.61
2. Infringement Analysis 5.63
3. Claim Construction 5.68
4. Application of Construed Claims to Accused Embodiment 5.107
5. Doctrine of Equivalents 5.110

6. Japan

A. Acts of Infringement 6.01
1. Direct Infringement 6.01
2. Indirect Infringement 6.13
3. Patent Term and Extension 6.20
4. Extraterritorial Infringement 6.23

B. Extent of Patent Protection 6.25
1. Overview 6.25
2. Infringement Analysis 6.29
3. Claim Construction 6.38
4. Application of Construed Claims to Accused Embodiment 6.69
5. Doctrine of Equivalents 6.72

PART III. VALIDITY CHALLENGE

7. United States

A. Introduction 7.01

B. Fundamental Rules 7.04
1. Claim Construction 7.04
2. Burden of Proof 7.08
3. Doctrines to Preclude an Invalidity Defense 7.10
4. Amendment 7.12
5. Measures to Prevent Conflicting Validity Decisions 7.18
6. Estoppel 7.24

C. Non-Court Patent Validity Procedures at the USPTO 7.26
1. *Ex Parte* Re-examination 7.26
2. *Inter Partes* Review 7.35
3. Post-grant Review 7.44
4. Special Post-grant Review for Business Methods 7.49
5. Interference Proceedings 7.52
6. Derivation Proceedings 7.56
7. Submission of Prior Art 7.62
8. Reissue 7.63
9. Patentability Validity Defenses in Civil Actions 7.67
10. Other Type of Defenses 7.106

8. Germany

A. Out-of-Court Invalidation Procedures 8.05
1. Opposition at the GPTO 8.05
2. Opposition at the EPO 8.18
3. Limitation Proceedings at the GPTO and EPO 8.30

B. Court Invalidation Procedures 8.35
1. Handling of a Defense Based on Lack of Validity Raised in a German Infringement Court 8.35
2. Invalidity Litigation ("Nullity Suit") at the German Patent Court 8.36

C. Patentability and Validity Challenges 8.46
1. Challenges Regarding Patentability—Filing of Third-party Observations 8.54
2. Patent Eligibility (Not an Invention, Excluded Inventions) 8.66
3. Lack of Novelty (Article 54 EPC) 8.74
4. Lack of an Inventive Step (Obviousness) (Article 56 EPC) 8.87
5. Lack of Industrial Applicability (Article 57 EPC) 8.99
6. Lack of Enablement (Sufficiency) 8.113
7. Inadmissible Broadening 8.124
8. Derivation (Entitlement) 8.137
9. Scope of the Validity Challenge—Nullity Proceedings 8.140

D. Other Defenses in Litigation Proceedings 8.142
1. Derivation/Lack of Entitlement 8.143
2. (Co-)Ownership in Cases of Inventions by Employees 8.144
3. License 8.145
4. Patent Misuse 8.146
5. Laches and Estoppels, in Particular Prosecution History Estoppels 8.147
6. Double Patenting 8.152
7. Prior Right and Prior Use Right 8.157
8. Compulsory License for Technology Standard 8.160
9. Experimental Use Exemption 8.161
10. Exhaustion 8.162

9. Japan

A. Introduction 9.01

B. Patent Invalidation Procedures 9.04
1. Overview 9.04
2. Correction of Claims 9.13
3. Opposition Procedure 9.15
4. Comparison with Invalidity Defense at Infringement Procedure 9.16
5. Measures to Prevent Delay and Conflicting Validity Decisions 9.23

C. Patentability Invalidity Defenses 9.28
1. Comparison between Grounds for Rejection and Invalidity 9.28
2. Frequently Cited Invalidity Grounds 9.30
3. Inventorship and Ownership 9.34

D. Other Types of Defenses 9.38
1. Private Use and Experimental Use Exception 9.38
2. Prior User Right and Intervening Right 9.42
3. Employee Inventions: Shop Right 9.47
4. Licenses 9.50
5. Exhaustion 9.53

PART IV. ENFORCEMENT PROCEDURE

10. United States

A. Jurisdiction 10.01
1. Subject Matter Jurisdiction 10.02
2. Venue 10.03
3. International Jurisdiction 10.09

B. Parties 10.13
1. Standing to Sue 10.14
2. Defendants 10.18

C. Costs 10.22
1. Court Fees and Other Costs 10.23
2. Attorney's Fees 10.25

D. Procedure 10.26
- 1. Procedure Overview and Pending Time 10.26
- 2. Pleading Standard 10.28
- 3. Evidence Collection 10.31
- 4. Jury Trial 10.52
- 5. Border Measures/ITC Proceedings 10.57
- 6. Pre-trial Proceedings 10.72
- 7. Appeals 10.78

E. Other Types of Actions 10.87
- 1. Declaratory Judgment Action 10.87
- 2. Preliminary Injunction 10.90

11. Germany

A. Jurisdiction and Venue 11.01
- 1. Subject Matter Jurisdiction 11.01
- 2. Venue 11.04
- 3. International Jurisdiction 11.08

B. Parties 11.11
- 1. Standing to Sue 11.12
- 2. Defendants 11.20

C. Costs 11.23
- 1. Court Fees 11.23
- 2. Customary Costs for Legal Representation 11.31

D. Procedure 11.37
- 1. Procedural Overview and Pending Time 11.37
- 2. Evidence Procedure 11.47
- 3. Border Measures 11.77
- 4. Pre-trial Measures 11.100

E. Other Important Proceedings 11.114
- 1. Declaratory Judgment Action 11.114
- 2. Preliminary Injunction 11.123

12. Japan

A. Jurisdiction 12.01
- 1. Subject Matter Jurisdiction and Venue 12.01
- 2. International Jurisdiction 12.02
- 3. Results of Judicial Reform 12.09

B. Parties 12.13
- 1. Standing to Sue 12.13
- 2. Defendants 12.15

C. Costs 12.17
- 1. Court Fees 12.18
- 2. Attorneys' Fees 12.20

D. Procedure 12.22
1. Procedure Overview and Pending Time 12.22
2. Evidence Collection 12.26
3. Border Measures 12.44
4. Pre-trial Proceedings 12.49

E. Other Important Proceedings 12.55
1. Declaratory Judgment Action 12.55
2. Preliminary Injunction 12.59

PART V. REMEDIES

13. United States

A. Claim for Injunctive Relief 13.01
1. Requirements 13.02
2. Scope of Injunction Order 13.19
3. Execution of Injunction Order 13.23

B. Exclusion Order 13.26

C. Claim for Damages 13.38
1. Requirements 13.39
2. Methods of Calculation 13.42
3. Increased Damages and Attorney Fees 13.71

D. Claim for Destruction 13.83

14. Germany

A. Claim for Injunctive Relief 14.02
1. Requirements 14.02
2. Scope of the Claim 14.05
3. Compulsory Enforcement 14.08

B. Claim for Damages 14.11
1. Requirements 14.11
2. Calculation of Damages 14.14

C. Claim on Account of Unjust Enrichment 14.30

D. Claims for Destruction, Recall, and Removal from Distribution Channels 14.31
1. Claim for Destruction 14.31
2. Claims for Recall and Removal from Distribution Channels 14.33

E. Claim for Information 14.38
1. Patent Act Information Disclosure Claim 14.39
2. Civil Code Information Disclosure Claim 14.43

15. Japan

A. Injunctive Relief 15.01
1. Requirements 15.01
2. Scope 15.02
3. Compulsory Enforcement 15.04

B. Damages 15.06
1. Requirements 15.07
2. Calculation of the Amount of Damages 15.09
C. Unjust Enrichment 15.25
D. Claim for Destruction 15.26

PART VI. BEST PRACTICE

16. Analysis and Proposal of Best Practice
A. Comparative Analysis 16.01
1. Introduction 16.01
2. Extent of Patent Protection 16.03
3. Defenses 16.15
4. Validity Challenge Procedures 16.19
5. Enforcement Procedure 16.26
6. Remedies 16.31
B. Proposal of Best Practice 16.37
1. Introduction 16.37
2. Extent of Patent Protection 16.40
3. Defenses 16.43
4. Validity Challenges 16.45
5. Procedure 16.50
6. Remedies 16.55

Index 451

TABLE OF CASES

Please note that American and British cases only are filed in alphabetical order; all other cases are in chronological order according to timing of decision.

EUROPEAN UNION

Lenzing v Germany (ECHR, Application No. 39025/97), September 9, 1999 . . . . 2.27
Glasser v MISAT (C-116/02), decision of December 9, 2003 . . . . 11.121
GAT v LuK (C-4/03), decision of July 13, 2006 . . . . 11.159
Pharmacia Italia (C-31/03), Judgment of the Court (Fifth Chamber) of October 19, 2004 . . . . . . 6.22
Turner v Grovit (C-159/03), decision of April 27, 2004 . . . . 11.121
Monsanto Technology v Cefetra (Case C-428/08), Court of Justice
of the European Union, 6 July 2010 . . . . 5.24, 8.112
Massachusetts Institute of Technology (C-431/04),
Judgment of the Second Chamber), May 4, 2006 . . . . 6.22
Phillips (C-446/09), decision of December 2, 2011 . . . . 11.85
Nokia (C-495/09), decision of December 2, 2011 . . . . 11.85
Brüstle (Case C-34/10), decision of October 18, 2011, ECR I-0000 . . . . 8.71, 8.72
Solway v Honeywell (C-616/10), decision of July 12, 2012 . . . . 11.159
Kingdom of Spain and Italian Republic v Council of the European Union
(C-274/11 and C 295/11), Judgment of the Grand Chamber on April 16, 2013 . . . . 1.47
Huawei Technologies Co Ltd v ZTE Corp (Case C-170/13), (July 16, 2015) 16.57

NATIONAL

Germany

Supreme Courts other than BGH

RGZ 39, 132 (decision of March 31 1897) 5.13
GRUR (1959): 435 (BVerwGE 8.350) 2.31
Klinische Versuche (BVerfG GRUR 2001, 43) 8.161

BGH (Bundesgerichtshof), Federal Court of Justice

Mülltonne (BGH GRUR 1951, 452,454) 5.16
Bäckereimaschine (BGR GRUR 1955, 87, 89) 5.05
Kabelschelle (BGH GRUR 1955, 573, 574) 5.89
Repassiernadel (BGH GRUR 1955, 244) 5.75, 5.81
Taeschner (BGH I ZR 39/55, GRUR 1957, 231) 5.08, 5.45
Taeschner/Pertussin II (BGH GRUR 57, 352, 353) 5.08
Bierhahn (BGH GRUR 1960, 546, 548) 5.75
Blockpedale (BGH GRUR 1960, 478, 480) 5.69
Metallspritzverfahren (BGH GRUR 1961, 627) 5.27
Ziegelsteine (BGH, case No. I ZR 90/59, 1961) 5.87
Diarähmchen II (BGH GRUR 1962, 509) 14.20
Drehkippbeschlag (BGH GRUR 1962, 29, 31) 5.110
Dosier- und Mischanlage (BGHZ 41, 13 - GRUR 1964, 308) 8.30
Formsand II (BGH GRUR 1964, 496) 5.27, 5.28
Rohrhalterung (BGH GRUR 1967, 586) 8.06
Faltbehälter Decision X ZR I 10/68 (BGH 26 June, 1969 X ZB 10/68) 5.106
Garmachverfahren (BGH GRUR 1968, 311, 313) 5.87
Appreturmittel (BGH GRUR 1969, 562) 8.14
Europareise (BGH GRUR 1969, 35) 5.04, 5.05

Skistiefelverschluss (BGH GRUR 1969, 534, 535) 5.110
Heißläuferdetektor (BGH GRUR 1970, 358, 360) 5.04
Imidazoline (BGHZ 58, 280, 288, BGH GRUR 1972, 541) 8.103
Trioxan (BGH GRUR 1972, 80) 5.79
Wandstekdose II (BGH GRUR 1972, 189) 14.14
Nebelscheinwerfer (BGH GRUR 1974, 53) 14.14
Gleichstromfernspeisung (BGH BIPMZ 1977 277) 8.23
Kunststoffhohlprofil I (BGH GRUR 1977, 250, 252) 14.13
Antanamid (BPatG GRUR 78, 238, 239 and BGH GRUR 1978, 238) 8.103
Stromwandler (BGH GRUR 1978, 235, 237) 5.91
Auspuffkanal für Schaltgase (GRUR 1979, 308, 309) 5.89
Farbbildröhre (BGH GRUR 1979, 461) 5.79
Schießbolzen (BGH GRUR 1979, 149, 152) 5.19, 5.103
Fullplastverfahren (BGH GRUR 1980, 38) 8.163
Tobultamid (BGH GRUR 1980, 841) 14.14
Überstromventil (BGH GRUR 1980, 219) 5.84
Heuwerbungsmaschine II (BGH GRUR 1981, 259, 260) 14.07
Rigg (BGH GRUR 1982, 165) 5.27
Offensichtlichkeitsprüfung (BGH BIPMZ 1985, 117, 118) 8.109
Zuckerzentrifuge (BGH GRUR 1985, 967) 5.82
Formstein (BGH GRUR 1986, 803, 805) 5.110, 5.128, 5.131, 6.74, 8.155
Melkstand (BGH GRUR 1986, 238, 240) 5.122
Befestigungsvorrichtung (GRUR 1987, 280) 5.91
Rundfunkübertragungssystem (GRUR 1987, 626) 5.84
Betonstahlmattenwender (BGH GRUR 1988, 757, 760) 5.89
Düngerstreuer (BGH GRUR 1988, 757, 762) 5.64, 5.89
Fluoran (BGHZ 103, 150, GRUR 1988, 447) 8.82
Ionenanalyse (BGH GRUR 1988, 896, 899) 5.112
Batteriekastenschnur (BGH GRUR 1989, 903, 904) 5.61
Decision X ZR I 19/88, December 5, 1989 .... 5.109
Ethofumesat (BGH GRUR 1990, 997, 999) 5.19
Schlüsselmühle (BGH GRUR 1990, 33, 34) 5.72
Autowaschvorrichtung (BGH GRUR 1991, 444, 447) 5.122
Befestigungsvorrichtung II (GRUR 1991, 436, 441) 5.103, 5.108, 5.119
Haftverband (BGH BIPMZ 1991, 159) 8.88
Trockenlegungs-Verfahren (GRUR 1991, 744, 746) 5.122
Beheizbarer Atemluftschlauch (BGH GRUR 1992, 40, 42) 5.27, 5.86, 5.107
Tetraploide Kamille (GRUR 1993, 651, 655) 5.79
Wandabstreifer (BGH GRUR 1993, 460, 464) 14.13
Weichvorrichtung I (BGH GRUR 1993, 886, 888) 5.87, 5.90, 8.149
Heizkörperkonsole (BGH GRUR 1994, 892) 8.15
Muffelofen (BGH GRUR 1994, 357) 5.102
Zerlegvorrichtung für Baumstämme (BGH GRUR 1994, 597, 599) 5.61, 5.75, 8.147
Abnehmerverwarnung (Customer warning), (BGH GRUR 1995, 424) 11.110
Aluminium-Trihydroxid (BGH, decision of January 10, 1995 – X ZB 11/92) 8.13
Kleiderbügel (BGH GRUR 1995, 338, 341) 5.16
Klinische Versuche (BGH GRUR 1996, 109, 113) 5.51, 5.52, 8.161
Wegfall der Wiederholungsgefahr (BGH GRUR 1996, 290, 292) 14.02
Klinische Versuche II (BGH NJW 1997, 3092, 3094) 5.53
Prospekthalter (BGH GRUR 1997, 116) 8.164
Weichvorrichtung II (BGH NJW 1997, 3377, 3380) 5.87, 5.90
Brennwertkessel (Condensing boiler), (BGH GRU 1998, 1045) 11.103
Coriolis force (BGH OJ EPO 1998, 263) 8.74
Polymermasse (BGH, decision of 3 February, 1998 – X ZB 6/97) 8.13
Regenbecken (BGH GRUR 1998, 895, 896) 5.89
Kontaktfederblock (BGH GRUR 1999, 914, 918) 5.129, 5.131

Raeumschild (BGH GRUR 1999, 977) 5.118, 11.20
Schmierfettzusammensetzung, Decision of September 30, 1999 – X ZR 168/96, GRUR 2000, 296, 297 . . . . 8.82
Spannschraube (BGH GRUR 1999, 909) 5.69, 5.70, 5.73, 5.76, 5.82, 5.84, 5.92, 5.116
Stoßwellen-Lithotripter (BGH GRUR 1999, 145, 146) 5.89
Bratgeschirr (BGH GRUR 2000, 1005, 1006) 5.115, 5.116
Extrusionskopf (Mitt 2000, 105) 5.82
Karate (BGH GRUR 2000, 299, 300) 8.162, 8.164
Berühmungsaufgabe (BGH NJW-RR 2001, 1483) 14.03
Bodenwaschanlage (BGH GRUR 2001, 223) 8.162, 8.164
Brieflocher (GRUR 2001, 232, 233) 5.66, 5.70
Gemeinkostenanteil (BGH GRUR 2001, 329) 14.16
Kabeldurchführung II (BGH GRUR 2001, 770) 5.96
Luftheizgerät (BGH GRUR 2001, 228, 231) 5.27, 5.30
Temperaturwächter (BGH GRUR 2001, 323, 324) 8.147
Custodiol I (GRUR 2002, 523, 526) 5.123
Custodiol II (GRUR 2002, 527, 531) 5.112, 5.123
Funkuhr I (BGH GRUR 2002, 599) 5.48
Kunstoffrohrteil (BGH GRUR 2002, 511) 5.86, 5.112, 8.148
Schneidmesser I (*Cutting Blade I*) (GRUR 2002, 515, 516) 5.75, 5.77, 5.112, 6.73
Schneidmesser II (*Cutting Blade II*) (GRUR 2002, 519, 521) 5.61, 5.112, 5.121, 5.122, 5.123
Snow Removal Plate, IIC 2002, 525 . . . . 11.20
Hochdruckreiniger (BGH GRUR 2003, 693, 695) 8.88
Kupplung für optische Geräte (BGH GRUR 2003, 1031, 1032) 5.04
Radio clock (IIC 2003, 432), Funkuhr, BGH GRUR 2002, 599 . . . . 11.09
Bodenseitige Vereinzelungsvorrichtung (BGH GRUR 2004, 1023, 1025) 5.83, 5.105
Drehzahlermittlung (BGH GRUR 2004, 845, 848) 5.27, 5.69
Flügelradzähler (BGH GRUR 2004, 758, 760) 5.27, 5.31, 5.33, 5.37, 6.17
Geflügelkörperhalterung (GRIR 2004, 413, 415) 5.75, 5.94
Standard-Spundfass (BGH GRUR 2004, 966) 8.160, 16.57
Vergleichsempfehlung II (Settlement recommendation II) (BGH GRUR 2005, 935) 11.16
Schweißbrennerreinigung (BGH, decision of February 1, 2005 – X ZR 214/02, GRUR 2005, 567) 8.143
Strahlungssteuerung (BGH GRUR 2005, 967), decision of July 12, 2005 X ZR 29/05 . . . . 8.22
Anbieten interaktiver Hilfe (BGH GRUR 2005, 141, 142) 5.74
Antriebsscheibenaufzug (BGH GRUR 2005, 848, 849) 5.31, 5.40, 6.17
Blasfolienherstellung (BGH GRUR 2005, 569) 14.06
Hotel-Maritime (BGH GRUR 2005, 431) 5.44
Knickschutz (BGH GRUR 2005, 754) 5.76
Staubsaugersaugrohr (BGH GRUR 2005, 41, 42) 5.71, 5.100
Unberechtigte Schutzrechtsverwarnung (Unjustified warning), Grand Panel, GRUR 2005, 882 . . . . 11.108
Unbegruendete Abnehmerverwarnung (Unfounded warning of customers), (BGH GRUR 2006, 433) 11.108
Arzneimittelwerbung im Internet (BGH GRUR 2006, 513) 5.44
Baumscheibenabdeckung (BGH GRUR 2006, 311, 313) 5.116, 14.06
Deckenheizung (BGH GRUR 2006, 839, 841) 5.35, 5.38
Detektionseinrichtung I (Detection device I) (BGH GRUR 2006, 217) 11.117
Funkuhr II (BGH GRUR 2006, 839, 841; BGH GRUR 2007, 313, 316) 5.27, 5.45
Koksofentür (BGH GRUR 2006, 316, 317) 5.106
Kunststoffbügel (BGH GRUR 2006, 927, 928) 5.04
Luftabscheider für Milchsammelanlage (BGH GRUR 2006, 923) 5.90, 5.103
Decision VIII ZR 392/03 (Decision of October 19, 2005, NJW-RR 2006, 243 . . . . 14.17
Parfümtestkäufe (BGH GRUR 2006, 504) 14.32
Rangierkatze (BGH GRUR 2006, 399, 401) 5.108, 5.109, 6.71
Seitenspiegel (BGH GRUR 2006, 131) 5.95, 5.108

Stapeltrockner (BGH GRUR 2006, 313, 315) 5.112, 5.115
Carvedilol II (BGH GRUR 2007, 404) 8.71
Haubenstrechautomat (BGH GRUR 2007, 679, 684) 5.35
Kettenradanordnung (BGH GRUR 2007, 410, 414) 5.64, 5.68, 5.91, 5.95
Pipettensystem (BGH GRUR 2007, 769, 771) 5.31, 5.33, 6.17
Rohrschweißverfahren (BGH GRUR 2007, 773, 775) 5.20, 5.27, 8.163
Schussfädentransport (BGH GRUR 2007, 309) 5.82, 5.83
Simvastatin (BGH GRUR 2007, 221, 222) 5.05, 5.06
Steckverbindungsgehäuse (BGH GRUR 2007, 431) 14.22, 14.23, 14.24
Zerfallszeitmessgerät (BGH GRUR 2007, 1059) 5.16, 5.107, 5.117
Ziehmaschinenzugeinheit (GRUR 2007, 778) 5.82, 5.89
EURO oder Schwarzgeld (EURO or illegal earnings), (GRUR 2008, 360) 11.116
Mehrgangnabe (BGH GRUR 2008, 779, 782) 5.64, 5.68, 5.95, 5.96
Tintenpatrone (BGH GRUR 2008, 896= IIC 2009, 475) 11.17, 14.43
Decision X ZR 105/06, December 9, 2008 . . . . . 5.102
Decision X ZR 107/05, 38 (BeckRS 2009, 23384, June 30, 2009) 5.85
Olanzapin, Case X ZR 89/07, GRUR 2009, 382 . . . . . 8.82, 8.88, 8.90
Fraesautomat (Milling machine), (BGH GRUR 2009, 878) 11.110
MP3 Player Import, IIC 2010, 471 (BGH GRUR 2009, 1142 . . . . . 11.20
Airbag-Auslösesteuerung (BGH, decision of April 30, 2009 – Xa ZR 56/05, GRUR 2009, 743) 8.123
Druckmaschinen-Temperierungssystem II (BGH decision of April 21, 2009 – XZR 153/04, GRUR 2009, 933) 8.123
Fischbissanzeigerdecision of 18 June 2009 – Xa ZR 138/05, GRUR 2009, 1039 . . . . . 8.90
Escitalopram, decision of 10 September 2009 – Xa ZR 130/07, GRUR 2010, 123 . . . . . 8.82
Neurale Vorläuferzellan, decision of 17 December 2009 – Xa ZR 58/07, GRUR 2010, 212 . . . . . 8.71
Bauschalungsstütze (BGH GRUR 2009, 837, 838) 5.66, 5.103
Lagerregal (BGH GRUR 2009, 390) 5.106
Motorradreiniger (BGH GRUR 2009, 515) 14.30
MP3-Player Import (BGH GRUR 2009, 1142,1144) 5.07
Orange-Book-Standard (BGH GRUR 2009, 694) 8.160, 16.57
Schmiermittel (BGH GRUR 2009, 933) 14.17, 14.19
Straßenbaumaschine (BGH GRUR 2009, 653, 654) 5.99
Nabenschaltung II (BGH, decision of March 18, 2010 – Xa ZR 74/09, GRUR 2010, 708) 8.159
Windenergiekonverter (BGH, decision of September 9, 2010 – Xa ZR 14/10, GRUR 2010, 1084) 8.136
Wiedergabe topografischer Informationen (BGH GRUR 2011, 125 – X ZR 47/07 . . . . . 8.66
Bildunterstützung bei Katheternavigation (BGH GRUR 2010, 1081, 1083) 5.104
Winkelmesseinrichtung (BGH, decision of October 21, 2010 – Xa ZB 14/98 GRUR 2011, 40) 8.136
Bordako (BGH GRUR 2010, 996) 11.164, 11.166
Gelenkanordnung (GRUR 2010, 602) 5.74, 5.86
Lichtbogenschnürung (Arc lacing) (BGH GRUR 2010, 318) 11.67
Restwertbörse (BGH GRUR 2010, 623) 14.43
Schubladenverfuegung (Concealed preliminary Injunction) (BGH GRUR 2010, 257) 11.151
Walzenformgebungsmaschine (BGH GRUR 2010, 950, 951) 5.97
Werbung des Nachrichtensenders (BGH 2010, 1090) 14.23
Integrationselement (BGH, decision of June 21, 2011 – X ZR 43/09, GRUR 2011, 1003) 8.136
Polierendpunktbestimmung (BGH, decision of July 18, 2011 – X ZB 10/10, GRUR 2012, 91) 8.159
Crimpwerkzeug IV (Crimping tool IV), (BGH GRUR 2011, 313) 5.115, 11.18
Fentanyl-TTS (BGH GRUR 2011, 129, 131) 5.77
Okklusionsvorrichtung (BGH, decision of May 10, 2011 – X ZR 16/09, GRUR 2011, 701) 5.84, 5.86, 5.124, 8.148
Diglycidverbindung (BGH GRUR 2012, 45, 47) 5.115, 5.124
MPEG-2 Videosignalcodierung (BGH GRUR 2012, 1230, 1235) 5.27, 5.31

Palettenbehälter III (BGH GRUR 2012, 1122, 1123) 5.115, 5.116
Rohrreinigungsdüse II (BGH GRUR 2012, 485) 14.06
Tintenpatrone III (BGH GRUR 2012, 753) 11.164
Patentsreitscache II (BGH decision X ZB 15/12 of March 20, 2013) 2.35
Fräsverfahren (BGH GRUR 2013, 713, 714) 5.40

Higher Regional Courts
Thrimothprim (OLG Hamburg, GRUR Int. 1991, 301) 5.45
Mehrfachkleiderbügel (OLG Düsseldorf, GRUR 1993, 818) 14.40
Surfbretter (OLG München GRUR 1995, 806) 5.84
Mehrpoliger Steckverbinder (OLG Düsseldorf, Mitt 1998, 179) 5.84
Staubsaugerfilter (OLG Düsseldorf, GRUR 2000, 599, 604) 5.92
Dünnbramme II, OLG Düsseldorf, Decision of September 4, 2003, file No. 2 U 24/02 . . . . . 11.149
Faelschungsverdacht II, Higher Regional Court of Munich, August 26, 2003, August 26, 2003 (InstGE 3, 301) 11.141
Raumkühlgeraet (*Air cooling unit*), Higher Regional Court of Düsseldorf, GRUR-RR 2003, 327 . . . . . 11.58
Unberechtigte Abnehmerverwarnung (*Unjustified warning of customers*), Higher Regional Court of Düsseldorf, GRUR 2003, 814 . . . . . 11.105
INTERPACK, Higher Regional Court of Düsseldorf, January 12, 2004 (InstGE 4, 159) 11.104
Messeangebot ins Ausland II, OLG München, September 16, 2004 (InstGE 5, 15) 5.05
Rohrschweißverfahren (OLG Düsseldorf, GRUR-RR 2004, 346, 349) 5.39
Lifter, Higher Regional Court of Düsseldorf, June 2, 2005 (InstGE 5, 251) 14.23, 14.24
Kaffee-Filterpads (OLG Düsseldorf, GRUR-RR 2006, 39, 42) 5.38
Schubladenverfügung, Higher Regional Court of Munich GRUR-RR 2006, 176 . . . . . 11.151
Permantentmagnet, Higher Regional Court of Düsseldorf, February 16, 2006 (InstGE 6, 152) 11.22
Thermocycler, Higher Regional Court of Düsseldorf, December 21, 2006 (InstGE 7, 139) 14.32
Cercho Card, Higher Regional Court of Hamburg, GRUR-RR 2007, 29 . . . . . 11.124
Schwerlastregal II, Higher Regional Court of Düsseldorf, February 15, 2007 (InstGE 7, 194) 14.24
Transglutaminase, Higher Regional Court of Hamburg, March 29, 2007 (InsGE 8, 11) 14.40
Fahrbare Betonpumpe, Higher Regional Court of Düsseldorf, June 28, 2007 (InsGE 8, 117) 14.10
Klinkerriemchen II, Higher Regional Court of Düsseldorf, September 9, 2007 (InstGE 8, 186) 11.69
Niederspannungs-Leistungsschalte r III (OLG Düsseldorf, September 20, 2007, Az. 2 U 42/06) 8.35
Thermocycler (OLG Düsseldorf, GRUR RR 2007, 259) 5.44
Schaumstoffherstellung, Higher Regional Court of Düsseldorf, February 7, 2008 (InstGE, 9, 41) 11.69
Olanzapin, Higher Regional Court of Düsseldorf, May 29, 2008 (InsGE 9, 140) 8.53, 11.134
Olanzapin II, Higher Regional Court of Düsseldorf, August 22, 2008 (InstGE 10, 60) 11.137
Druckerpatrone II, OLG Düsseldorf, October 8, 2008 (InstGE, 10, 129) 8.160
November 12, 2008,Higher Regional Court of Düsseldorf, file no. 2 U 62/08, BeckRS 2011, 16058 . . . . . 11.147
Inhalator (Inhaler), Higher Regional Court of Düsseldorf, November 13, 2008 (InstGE 10, 124) 11.140
Higher Regional Court of Cologne, NJOZ 2008, 957 . . . . . 11.151
Irreführende Berechtigungsanfrage, Higher Regional Court of Karlsruhe, GRUR-RR 2008, 197 . . . . . 11.112
SMD-Widerstand, OLG Karlsruhe, January 14, 2009 (InstGE 11, 15) 5.13
Zeitversetztes Fernsehen, OLG Düsseldorf, January 14, 2009, InstGE 10, 198 . . . . . 5.120, 11.67
Staubsaugerfilterbeutel (*Filter bag for vacuum cleaner*), Higher Regional Court of Düsseldorf, Decision dated February 2, 2009, file no. 2 U 114/08, BeckRS 2009, 09402 . . . . . 11.133

Holzhaecksler (Wood shredder), Higher Regional Court of Düsseldorf, Decision dated May 18, 2009, file no. 2 U 140/08, BeckRS 2009, 18590 .... 11.133, 11.134
VA-LCD-Fernseher, Higher Regional Court of Karlsruhe, July 8, 2009 (InstGE 11, 143) 11.134
Judgment of December 10, 2009, Case No. I-2 U 51/08 (OLG Düsseldorf, BeckRS 2010 12415) 5.46
Kaffeemaschine, Higher Regional Court of Düsseldorf, December 17, 2009 (InstGE 11, 296) 11.67, 11.134
Torpedo, Higher Regional Court of Düsseldorf, GRUR-RR 2009, 401 .... 11.122
Weissmacher (Whitener), Higher Regional Court of Düsseldorf, January 20, 2010 (InstGE 11, 298) 11.51
March 25, 2010, Higher Regional Court of Düsseldorf, file no. 2 U 61/08, BeckRS 2010, 16645 .... 11.19
Lesevorrichtung für Reliefmarkierungen, OLG Munich, April 15, 2010 (InstGE 12, 192) 11.69
Harnkatheterset, Higher Regional Court of Düsseldorf, April 29, 2010 (InstGE 12, 114) 8.53, 11.132, 11.134
Cinch-Stecker, Higher Regional Court of Düsseldorf, May 6, 2010 (InstGE 12, 88) 14.37
May 18, 2010, Higher Regional Court of Karlsruhe, file no 6W 28/10, BeckRS 2011, 18386 .... 11.54, 11.72
MP3-Standard, OLG Karlsruhe, May 26, 2010 (InstGE 12, 220) 8.160
30 November 2010, Higher Regional Court of Düsseldorf, Case No. I-2 U 82/09 .... 14.13
Case No. I-2 U 65/09 (OLG Düsseldorf, BeckRS 2010, 21760) 5.122
Patentverwertungsgesellschaft. (OLG Karlsruhe, GRUR-RR 2010, 120) 8.146
Testkauf patentverletzender DVDs—interframe dropping (OLG Düsseldorf, NJOZ 2010, 1781, 1789) 8.160, 8.163
Videosignal-Codierung I (OLG Düsseldorf, decision of January 14, 2010—I-2 U 124/08) 5.11, 5.13
Vollstreckungsverzicht im Eilverfahren (Waiver of enforcement in summary proceedings), Higher Regional Court of Cologne, GRUR-RR 2010, 448 .... 11.141
Fernsehmenü-Steuerung, OLG Düsseldorf, January 13, 2011 (InstGE 12, 261) 11.14
Lungenfunktionsmessgerät, OLG Düsseldorf, February 24, 2011 (InstGE 13, 78) 5.16
Ausgelagerter Server, Higher Regional Court of Munich, March 11, 2011 (InstGE 13, 298) 11.67
Case No. I-2 U 9/10 and 2 U 9/10 (OLG Düsseldorf, judgment of May 5, 2011 .... 5.50
Schwangerschaftstestgerät VI (Pregnancy test device VI), BeckRS 2011, 20938, (OLG Düsseldorf, decision of June 24, 2011), file no. 2 U 26/10 .... 11.13, 11.14
Gleitsattelscheibenbremse II (Sliding caliper disc brake), Higher Regional Court of Düsseldorf, GRUR-RR 2011, 81 .... 11.134
Schräg-Raffstore, Higher Regional Court of Düsseldorf, September 8, 2011 (InstGE 13, 199) 14.24
January 11, 2012, Higher Regional Court of Karlsruhe, file no. 6 U 59/11 .... 11.14
Run-Flat-Vorrichtung, OLG Düsseldorf, Case No I-2 U 134/10, February 23, 2012 .... 5.43
Az. I-2 U 58/10 (OLG Düsseldorf, decision of August 2, 2012) 8.147
20 December 2012, Higher Regional Court of Düsseldorf, Case No I-2 U 89/07, BeckRS 2013 11856 .... 14.06
May 8, 2013, Case No. 6 U 34/12 (OLG Karlsruhe) 5.20
May 15 2014, Case Number I-2 U 74/13, BeckRS 2014 14360 (OLG Düsseldorf) 14.06
July 9, 2014, 6 U 29/11 (OLG Karlsruhe) 8.148
MP2-Geräte (OLG Karlruhe, GRUR 2014, 59) 5.50

District Courts

Diazepam (District Court of Düsseldorf GRUR 1970, 550, 55) 5.43
Grasherbizid (District Court of Düsseldorf, GRUR 1987, 896) 5.14, 6.08
NMR-Kontrastmittel (District Court of Düsseldorf, GRUR 2000, 692) 8.146
Cam-Carpet (District Court of Düsseldorf, GRUR-RR 2001, 201, 204) 5.19
Dünnbramme II (*Thin Slab II*), District Court of Düsseldorf, January 10, 2002 (InstGE 2, 157) 11.149
Sohlen für Sportschuhe (District Court of Düsseldorf, February 5, 2002, case No. 4a O 33/01) 5.44
Hochdruckreiniger, District Court of Düsseldorf, December 3, 2002 (InstGE 3, 86) 11.110

Cholesterin-Test (*Cholesterol test*), District Court of Düsseldorf, December 19, 2002 (InstGE 3, 8) 11.121
Decision No. 4a O 311/02, District Court of Düsseldorf, February 28, 2003) 5.49
Fälschungsverdacht I, District Court of Munich I, May 28, 2003 (InstGE 3, 297) 11.138, 11.139, 11.141
Borstenverrundung, District Court of Frankfurt, October 29, 2003 (InstGE 6, 141) 14.24
Decision No. 7 O 412/03, District Court of Mannheim, June 25, 2004) 5.49, 5.50
Kunstharzzusammensetzung, District Court of Frankfurt, June 15, 2005 (InstGE 6, 1) 5.78
Wandverkleidung, District Court of Düsseldorf, June 23, 2005 (InstGE 5, 173) 5.39
Frachtführer, District Court of Düsseldorf, July 12, 2005 (InstGE 5, 241) 14.13
Decision No. 7 O 506/04, District Court of Mannheim, August 26, 2005) 5.49
Decision No. 4b O 198/06, District Court of Düsseldorf, August 23, 2007) 5.16
Beleghalter für Scheibenbremse, District Court of Düsseldorf, November 27, 2007 (InstGE 9, 18) 11.05
RFID-Karte II (*RFID-card II*), District Court of Düsseldorf, decision of March 27, 2008, file no. 4b O 159/07 . . . . . 11.19
Decision No. 4b O 284/08, District Court of Düsseldorf, January 16, 2009 . . . . . 11.138
Italienischer Torpedo (Italian torpedo), District Court of Düsseldorf, GRUR-RR 2009, 402 . . . . . 11.122
Arzneimittelherstellung, District Court of Munich I, October 20, 2010 (InstGE 13, 181) 11.72
Sauggreifer (*Vacuum cups*), District Court of Mannheim, October 29, 2010 (InstGE 13, 11) 11.132
SMS-Nachricht, District Court of Düsseldorf, February 24, 2011, BeckRS 2011, 20668 . . . . . 11.116
Oberflächenbehandlung, District Court of Düsseldorf, March 1, 2011 (InstGE 13, 97) 5.40
Kreissägeblatt II (*Circular saw-blade*), District Court of Düsseldorf, May 27, 2011, Decision No. 4b O 84/11 . . . . . 11.134
Später Besichtigungsantrag (*Late inspection request*), District Court of Düsseldorf, GRUR-RR 2011, 289 . . . . . 11.72
Verwendungspatent, District Court of Mannheim, Decision No. 2 O 129/09, April 17, 2012 . . . . . 11.14
Decision No. 4b O 100/11, District Court of Düsseldorf, November 20, 2012, BeckRS 2013, 14799) 14.06
Decision No. 3 U 184/10, District Court of Hamburg, April 30, 2013 (BeckRS 2013 11573) 14.06
Decision of 30 April 2013, District Court of Hamburg, Case No. 3 U 184/10, BeckRS 2013 11573 . . . . . 14.06
Seitenaufprall-Schutzeinrichtung (District Court of Mannheim, GRUR-RR 2013, 449, 451) 5.25, 5.49
Decision Number 7 O 24814/13, District Court of Munich I, July 24, 2014 (BeckRS 2014 16686) 14.06
Decision No. Az. 4a O 92/13, District Court of Düsseldorf, October 30, 2014 . . . . . 14.10

Federal Patent Court (BPatG)
Weichvorrichtung II (Mitt 1997, 364 (408) 8.149
Polyvinylalkohole, Decision of July 27, 2006 - 3 Ni 7/04 (EU), Mitt. 2007, 139 . . . . . 8.82
Antriebsvorrichtung (decision of 28 August, 2006, 9 W (pat) 16/04 . . . . . 8.15
Bearbeitungsmaschine, Decision of Nov 8, 2012 – Ni 43/10 (EP), GRUR 2013, 601 . . . . . 8.42
Dichtungsring, Decision of January 15, 2013 – 4 Ni 13/11 . . . . . 8.42

Decisions of the EPO
i) Enlarged Board of Appeal (G) and Legal Board of Appeal (J)
G 5/83 (second medical use, superseded) OJ EPO 1985, 60 . . . . . 8.70, 8.71
G 3/89, OJ EPO 1993 . . . . . 8.126, 8.127
G 9/91 and G10/91, OJ EPO 1993, 408, 420 . . . . . 8.25
G 11/91, OJ EPO 1993, 125 . . . . . 8.126, 8.127
G 3/92, OJ EPO 1994, 607 . . . . . 8.137
G 1/93, OJ EPO 1994, 541 . . . . . 8.126, 8.135
G 2/93, OJ EPO 1995, 275 . . . . . 8.114
G 3/97, OJ EPO 1999, 245 . . . . . 8.23
G 1/98 (transgenic plants), OJ EPO 2000, 111 . . . . . 8.71, 8.72

G 2/98, OJ EPO 2001, 413 . . . . 8.74, 8.84, 8.126, 8.128
G 3/98, OJ EPO 2001, 62 . . . . 8.74
G 1/03, OJ EPO 2004, 413 . . . . 8.71, 8.126, 8.128, 8.132
G 2/03 (disclaimer) OJ EPO 2004, 448 . . . . 8.71, 8.132
G 1/04 (diagnostic methods), OJ EPO 2006, 334 . . . . 8.71, 8.72
G 3/04 OJ EPO 2006, 118 . . . . 8.23
G 1/05, OJ EPO 2008, 271 . . . . 8.155
G 1/06, OJ EPO 2008, 307 . . . . 8.155
G 2/06 (stem cells), OJ EPO 2009 . . . . 1.43, 8.71, 8.72, 8.104
G 1/07 (method of treatment by surgery), OJ EPO 2011, 134 . . . . 8.71, 8.72
G 1/08 (Broccoli I), OJ EPO 2012, 206 . . . . 8.71, 8.72
G 2/08 (dosage regime), OJ EPO 2010, 456 . . . . 8.71
G 2/10 (Disclaimer/SCRIPPS), OJ EPO 2012, 376 . . . . 8.126, 8.127, 8.132
G 2/12 (Tomatoes II), of March 25, 2015 . . . . 8.71
G 2/13 (Broccoli II), of March 25, 2015 . . . . 8.71
G 3/14 (Examination of clarity objections), of March 24, 2015 . . . . 8.58
J 15/13 (Resumption of Proceedings for Grant), of May 9, 2014, unpublished 8.19

ii) Opposition Divisions and Technical Boards of Appeal (T)

T 219/85, OJ EPO 1986, 376 . . . . 8.114
T 10/86, of September 1, 1988, unpublished 8.114
T 158/91, of July 30, 1991, unpublished 8.121
Decision of Opposition Division - No-Challenge Obligation, OJ EPO 1992, 747 . . . . 8.23
T 002/92 (Queuing System), of July 6, 1994, unpublished 8.21
T 694/92 (Modifying Plant Cells), OJ EPO 1997, 408 . . . . 8.121
T 1072/92, of June 28, 1994, unpublished 8.96
T 351/93, of March 1, 1995, unpublished 8.96
T 639/95 (Biopolymers/MIT), of January 21, 1998, unpublished 8.121
T 0022/98 (Party status), OJ 2013, 582 . . . . 8.19
T 36/00 (Proteinase deficient fungi/Genencor), of October 2, 2003, unpublished 8.121
T 786/00, of December 19, 2001, unpublished 8.77
T/1081/01, of September 27, 2004, unpublished 8.75
T 1329/04 (Factor-9/John Hopkins), of June 28, 2005, unpublished 8.97, 8.99
T 1336/04 (Cellulase/NOVOZYME), of March 9, 2006, unpublished 8.109
T 898/05 (Hematopoietic receptor/Zymogenetics), of July 7, 2006, unpublished 8.102, 8.108
T 1466/05, of July 27, 2007, unpublished 8.121
T 1538/05, of August 28, 2006, unpublished 8.67, 8.99
T 608/07, of April 27, 2009, unpublished 8.119
T 1877/08 (Refrigerants/E.I. du Pont de Nemours and Company), of February 23, 2010, unpublished 8.84
T 1109/10 (Hydroxylases/lexicon), of March 13, 2014, unpublished 8.108
T 1222/11, of December 4 2012, unpublished 8.85
T 1496/11, of September 12, 2012, unpublished 8.84
T 2619/11, of February 25, 2013, unpublished 8.130
T 373/12 (Examination of Clarity Objections), OJ EPO 11/2014, A 115 . . . . 8.118
T 609/12 (AP-1 complex/Salt Institute), of October 27, 2004, unpublished 8.122
T 373/12 (Examination of Clarity Objections), OJ EPO 11/2014, A 115 . . . . 8.118

Japan

Supreme Court

December 7, 1962, Sho 36 (wo) No. 464, 16 Minshū (No. 12) 2321 . . . . 6.63
August 4, 1964 (Crude Petroleum Rotation Combustor), Sho 37 (wo) No. 871, 18 Minshū (No. 7) 1319 . . . . 6.27, 6.64
September 24, 1968, Sho 43 (O) 43 (O) No. 260, 13 Minshū (1968), 3428 . . . . 12.71
February 27, 1969, Sho 41 (O) No. 280, 23-2 Minshū (1969), 44 (*Hyakusenmu*) 12.20
October 17, 1969, 23 Minshū (No. 10) 1777 . . . . 9.43

March 10, 1976, Sho 42 (Gyo tsu) No. 28, 30 Minshū (No. 2) 79 . . . . . 9.26
October 13, 1977, 31 Minshū (No. 6) 805 . . . . . 9.35, 9.43
June 30, 1981, Sho (wo) No. 336, 35 Minshū (No. 4) 848 . . . . . 6.50
October 16, 1981, 1980 (O) No. 130, 35-7 (Minshū) 1224
(*Goto et al v Malaysian Airlines Systems*) 12.02, 12.04
October 3, 1986, 40 Minshū (No. 6) 1068 . . . . . 9.43
January 26, 1988, Sho 60 (O) No. 122,42-11 Minshū (1988), 1 (*Utaeteiki*) 12.50
March 8, 1991, Sho (Gyo Tsu) No. 3, 45 Minshū (No. 3) 123 (*Lipase*) 6.36, 9.17
July 1, 1997, Hei 7 (o) No. 1988, 51 Minshū (No. 6) 2299
(*BBS Kraftfahrzeugtechnik AG v Racimex Japan*) 6.23, 9.53, 12.45
November 11, 1997, 1993 (O) 1660, 51-10 Minshū (1997), 4055 = JAIL No. 41 (1998),
117 (*Family Co Ltd. v Shin Miyahara*) 12.02
February 24, 1998, 52 Minshū (No. 1) 113, 1630 Hanrei Jiho 32 (1998)
(*Ball Spline*) 6.28, 6.33, 6.72, 6.75, 6.76
November 10, 1998, Hei (wo) No. 1579 . . . . . 6.50
April 16, 1999, 53 Minshū (No. 4) 627 . . . . . 9.41
April 11, 2000, Hei 10 (o) No. 364, 54-4 (Minshū) 1368 (*Kilby*) 1.58, 6.27, 6.48, 6.49, 6.64, 9.02, 9.03, 12.61
November 12, 2001, Hei 11 (Kyo) No. 2,53-8 Minshū (1999), 1785 (*Bunshoteishutsumeirei*) . . . 12.36
March 3, 2002, Hei 11 (Kyo) No. 20,1708 Hanrei Jihō (2000), 115 (*Bunshoteishuttsumeirei*) . . . 12.36
April 25, 2002, Hei 13 (ju) No. 898, 56 Minshū (No. 4) 808 . . . . . 9.53
September 26, 2002, Hei 12 (Ju) No. 580, 56-7 Minshū (2002), 1551 (*Cardreader*) 6.12, 12.04
June 17, 2005, Hei 16 (uke) No. 997, 1900 Hanrei Jihō (2005), 139 = IIC 2006, 221 (*Flex X*) 12.13
April 11, 2007, Hei 18 (ju) No. 826, 61 (Minshū) 2989
(*Recycle Assist Co. Ltd v Canon, Inc*) 9.54, 9.55, 12.45
November 8, 2007, 61 Minshū (No. 8) 2989 . . . . . 6.10
April 28, 2011, Hei 21 (gyō hi) No. 326, 65 Minshū (No. 3) 1654 = 1348 Hanrei Taimuzu 102 . . . . . 6.21
June 5, 2015, Hei 24 (iyu) No. 1204 . . . . . 6.50

High Courts

IP High Court

April 25, 2001, Hei 12 (ne) No. 1266 . . . . . 6.42
September 30, 2005, Hei 17 (ne) No. 100040, Hanrei Jihō (No. 1904) 47 . . . . . 6.17
December 28, 2005, Hei 17 (wa) No. 10103 . . . . . 6.41, 6.42, 6.44, 6.58
January 19, 2006, Hei 17 (Gyo ke) Nos. 10193 . . . . . 9.36
September 25, 2006, Hei 17 (ne) 10047 (*Massage Chair*) 15.15, 15.23, 15.24
September 20, 2007 (ne) 10038, 3 (*Claim for declaratory judgment*) 12.56
May 15, 2007, Hei 17 (ne) No. 10119 . . . . . 12.53
September 12, 2007, Hei 18 (ne) No. 10080 . . . . . 12.53
May 29, 2008, Gyo(ne) No. 10037, Hanrei Jihō (No. 2018) 146 . . . . . 9.35
May 30, 2008, Hei 18 (gyō ke) No. 10563 . . . . . 2.61
July 14 2008, Hei (mu) No. 10002, No. 1003, Hanrei Taimuszu (No. 1307) 295 . . . . . 9.27
January 28, 2009, Hanrei Jiho No. 2043, 117, Hanrei Taimuzu No. 1299,
272 (*Hitachi Kasei*) 9.30
March 11 2009, Hei 19 (ne) No. 10025 . . . . . 6.66
April 23, 2009, Hei 18 (ne) No. 10075, Hanrei Taimuzu (No. 1301) 99 . . . . . 6.63
May 29, 2009, Hei 20 (gyō ke) No. 10458, 1305 Hanrei Tailmuzo 80;
2047 Hanrei Jihō 11 . . . . . 2.67, 6.21
June 29, 2009, Hei 20 (gyo ke) No.s 10427, 10428 and 10429 . . . . . 9.36
June 29, 2009, Hei 21 (ne) No. 10006, Hanrei Taimusu (No. 2077)
123 (*Hollow Golf Club Head*) 6.55, 6.60, 6.76, 6.78
August 25, 2009, Hei 20 (ne) No. 10068, Hanrei Tainmusu (No. 1319) 246 . . . . . 9.24
March 24, 2010, Hei 20 (ne) No. 10085, Hanrei Taimuzu (No. 1358) 184 . . . . . 6.12
May 27, 2010 (INAX) 9.31
July 15, 2010, Hei 21 (*Gyo-Ke*), No. 10238 . . . . . 8.97
August 25, 2010, Hei 20 (ne) no. 100068 . . . . . 9.21

September 15, 2010, Hei 22, 1340 Hanrei Times, Hei 22 (ne) No. 10001 . . . . 12.08
January 24, 2012, Hei 22 (ne) 10032 (*Golf Ball*) 15.15
January 27, 2012, Hei 19 (wa) No. 35342, Hanrei Jihō (No. 2144)
55 (*Pravastatin Sodium*) 6.51
February 1, 2013, Hei (ne) No. 10015, 1388 Hanrei Times (2013) 77
(*Waste Storage Device*) 15.16, 15.17
March 25, 2013, Heisei 24 (ne) 10059 . . . . 12.53
July 11, 2013, Hei 25 (ne) No. 10014 . . . . 6.04
May 16, 2014, Hei 25 (ne) no. 10043, Hanrei Jihō (No. 2225) 146 . . . . 16.33
Osaka High Court
May 8, 1969, Sho 42 (ne) No. 1104, 237 Hanrei Times, 201 . . . . 12.67
December 20, 1978, Sho(ne) No. 783, Hanrei Taimuzu (No. 381) 165 . . . . 6.48
January 30, 1984, 9 Sho 55 (ne) No. 2965 . . . . 9.40
February 1, 2000, Hei 10 (ne) No. 5507, Hanrei Jihō (No. 1712) 167 . . . . 6.67
May 27, 2003, Hei 15 (ne) No. 320 . . . . 9.52
July 21, 2005, Hei 15 (wa) No. 7750, 1912 Hanrei Jihō (2005), 107
(*Damage Claim for Wrongful Injunction*) 12.71
Sapporo High Court
March 27, 1974, Sho 48 (ra) No. 58, 308 Hanrei Times (1976), 227 (*Misono Azumusushi*) . . . 15.03
Tokyo High Court
March 30, 1973, Sho 44 (Kouke) No. 57, 306 Hanrei Times (1973), 269 (*Shokak*) 15.20
June 15, 1999, Hei 10 (ne) No. 2249, 1697 Hanrei Jihō (1999), 96 (*Sashitomeijiken*) 15.11
August 29, 2002, Case Number Heisei 13 (ne) 5555, 1801 Hanrei Jihō (2002)
113 (*Metallic Powder*) 12.52
September 9, 2003, Hei 14 (ne) No. 3714 . . . . 6.58
February 27, 2004, Hei 15 (ne) No. 1223, Hanrei Jihō, 1870, 84 (*Injunctive Relief*) 12.13
April 27 2004, Case No. Hei 14 (ne) 4448 . . . . 15.08
November 14, 2004, Hei 13 (ne) 107 . . . . 12.13

District Courts
Aomori District Court
May 22, 1972, Sho 46 (yo) No. 2, 4-1 Mutaishū, 313 . . . . 12.67
Gifu District Court
April 14, 1971, Sho 44 (yo) No. 53, 3-1 Mutaishū, 180 . . . . 12.67
December 18, 1991, Sho 63 (wa) No. 277, 2293 Hanrei Kōgyōshoyūkenhō
30 (*Dosha Ryushutsu Bōshiyo Hasui Filter*) 15.26, 15.27
Kyoto District Court
June 26, 1967 (yo) No. 56 . . . . 12.67
Nagoya District Court
July 25, 1974, Sho 48 (moshi) No. 707, 761 Hanrei Jihō, 99 . . . . 12.13
August 31, 1984, Sho 56 (wa) No. 558,16-2 Mutaishū (1984), 568 . . . . 12.51
May 20, 1985, Sho 59 (yo) No. 318, 17-2 Mutaishū, 239 . . . . 12.65, 12.67
March 6, 1998, Hei 4 (wa) No. 474, 1003 Hanrei Times (1998) 277 . . . . 15.17
April 28, 2005, Hei 16 (wa) No. 1307 . . . . 9.45
Osaka District Court
January 24, 1975, Sho 48 (wa) No. 3834, 323 Hanrei Times (1975), 270 (*Plastic film*) 15.01
February 10, 1976, 8 Mutaishū (No. 1) 85 . . . . 6.64
March 29, 1977, Sho 45 (wa) No. 5258, 4-1, Muteisaishu 1, 137 (*Crash Barrier*) 15.08
December 19, 1978, Sho 43 (wa) No. 3091, 10-2 Mutaishū (1978), 617 . . . . 12.51
October 31, 1980, Sho 54 (wa) No. 4824,12-2 Mutaishū (1980),
632 (*Kodomoyojōmonotaiyaa*) 15.25
October 28, 1980, 12 Muraishū 580 . . . . 6.27
April 9, 1981 (yo) No. 52 . . . . 12.65
January 28, 1982, Sho 55 (ne) No. 1928,14-1 Mutaishū (1982), 41 ff (*Kyukyu*) 15.25
October 28, 1983, Sho (wa) No. 8565, 514 Hanrei Times (1983) 303 (*Torigaakuiru*) 15.25
October 30, 1984, Sho 57 (wa) No. 7273543 Hanrei Times (1985) 263 (*Tesagebukoro*) 15.08

May 23, 1985, Sho 61 (wa) No. 3515, 18 Mutaishū (No. 2) 5 .... 6.67
April 25, 1986, Sho 55 (wa) No. 6390, 609 Hanrei Times (1986), 89 .... 12.51
March 14, 1986, Sho 59 (wad) No. 8943,617 Hanrei Times (1986), 153 (*Denkikamisori*) 15.20
October 14, 1987, Sho 59 (wa) No. 6210, 19-3 Mutaishū (1987), 389 (*Okeya*) 15.25
November 25, 1987, Sho 59 (wa) No. 712719-3 Mutaishū (1987) 34 (*Wood Work*) 15.02
April 24, 1989, Sho 60 (wa) No. 6851, 21-1 Mutaishū (1989), 279 (*Seisaki no Hanma*) 15.13
May 30, 1995, 27 27 Chisaishū (No. 2) 386 .... 9.45
October 24, 1997, Hei 8 (wa) No. 12109, Hanrei Taimuzu (No. 1081) 241 .... 6.24
October 22, 1998, Hei 5 (wa) No. 2549-1 (*Denjiyudōkanetsusōchi*) 15.20
February 22, 2000, Hei 10 (wa) No. 12235 .... 6.73
October 24, 2000, Hei 8 (wa) No. 12109, Hanrei Taimusu (No. 1081) 241 .... 6.14, 9.39
December 21, 2000, Hei 10(wa) No. 12875, Hanrei Taimuzu (No. 1104) 270 .... 6.24
December 26, 2000, Hei 10 (wa) No. 16963, Hei 11 (wa) No. 17278 .... 9.45
July 13, 2001, Hei 12 (wa) No. 4184 (*Wallpaper Glue Machine*), LEX/DB 28061576 .... 15.08
October 9, 2001, Hei 10 (wa) No. 12889 .... 6.69
December 13, 2001, Hei 12 (wa) No. 4290 .... 6.59
December 16, 2004 Hei 15 (wa) No. 6580 .... 12.53
July 28, 2005, Hei 16 (wa) No. 9318 .... 9.45
April 18, 2008, Hei 20 (mo) No. 363,1287 Hanrei Times (2008), 220 .... 12.39
November 26, 2008, Hei 20 (wa) No. 9732, 1326 Hanrei Times, 267 .... 12.08

Shizuoka District Court
1973 Mo 442 .... 12.66, 12.67

Tokyo District Court
March 16, 1955, 6 Kakyu Minshū 479 .... 9.47
March 18, 1964, Sho 36 (wa) No. 5836, 377 Hanrei Jihō 63 .... 12.13
September 14, 1969, Sho 35 (wa) No. 6935,14-9 Shitamin (1963), 1778 (*Hanso Sōchi*) 15.27
December 22, 1969, Sho 41 (wa) No. 11570 1 Mutaishū (1969), 394 .... 15.01
June 30, 1971, Sho 42 (wa) No. 9666,266 Hanrei Times (1971), 220 (*Shokuhinsetsudanki*) 15.13
March 17, 1972, Sho 45 (wa) No. 2700, 278 Hanrei Times (1972), 374 (*Fuigobaki*) 12.51
February 28, 1973, Sho 3 (wa) No. 15198, 302 Hanrei Times (1973), 305 (*Higesoriki*) 15.20
June 30, 1976, Sho 51 (mo) No. 6490,346 Hanrei Times (1976), 271 .... 12.34
May 22, 1972, Sho 44 (wa) No. 8219, 4-1 Mutaishū (1977), 294 (*Roshutsukokei*) 15.20
February 25, 1981, Sho 50 (wa) No. 9647, 13 Mutaishū (No. 1) 139,
Hanrei Jihō (No. 1007) 72 .... 6.14
January 18, 1984, Sho 58 (wa) No. 8056,1101 Hanrei Jihō (1984)
109 (*Porno Disneyland*) 15.03
October 26, 1984, Sho 55 (wa) No. 429, Hanrei Taimuzu (No. 543) 205 .... 6.42
July 10, 1987, 19 Muraishu (No. 2) 231 .... 9.40
July 10, 1987, Sho 60 (wa) No. 7463,19-2 Mutaishū (1987), 231 (*Jyosozai*) 15.28
December 9, 1988, Sho 61 (wa) No. 2964, 1295 Hanrei Jihō (1989),
121 (*Mojiwaku Koteisōchi*) 15.27
February 9, 1990, Sho 56 (wa) No. 3939, 1347 Hanji (1990) 111 .... 15.17
April 4, 1991, Sho 63 (wa) No. 7097, 24-1 Chitekishū (1992), 230 .... 12.51
October 30, 1995, Hei 1 (wa) No. 8292, 1560 Hanrei Jihō (1995),
24 (*Shisutemusaiensuhonan*) 15.27
October 18, 1996, Hei 6 (wa) No. 16290, 1585 Hanrei Jihō (1996) 106 .... 15.07
December 22, 1998, Sho 51 (ne) No. 783, Hanrei Jihō (No. 1674) 152 .... 6.48
October 7, 1998, Hei 3 (wa) No. 10687, 1657 Hanrei Jihō (1998), 122 (*Seikyūken*) 15.11
June 15, 1999, Hei 10 (ne) No. 2249 (*Heat Storage*) 15.13
September 20, 1999, Hei 11 (yo) No. 22125, 1696,1696 Hanrei Jihō (1999), 76 (*iMac*) 12.69
March 23, 2000, Hei 10 (wa) No. 11453, Hanrei Jihō (No. 1739) 122 .... 6.73
April 27, 2000, Hei (wa) No. 10545 .... 9.43
August 31, 2000,Hei 8 (wa) No. 16782 .... 9.55
September 20, 2000, Hei 12 (wa) No. 20503, Hanrei Jihō (No. 1764) 112 .... 6.12
March 30, 2001, Hei 12 (wa) No. 8204, Hanrei Taimuzo (No. 1059) 195 .... 6.67
July 17, 2001, Hei 11 (wa) No. 23013, (*Kirokushi*) (23013) 15.14

September 20, 2001, Hei 12 (wa) No. 11657, 1801 Hanrei Jihō (2001), 113 (*Jikishingōkirokuyōkinsokufunmatsu Jiken Daiishin*) 12.53
March 19, 2002, Hei 11 (wa) 23945 (*Pachinko Slot Machine*) 15.14
December 12, 2002, Hei 9 (wa) No. 24064, 1824 Hanrei Jihō, 94 . . . . 12.53
February 6, 2003, Hei 13 (wa) No. 21278, Hanrei Jihō 1870, 107. . . . . 12.13
April 14, 2003, Case No Hei 14 (wa) 9503 . . . . 15.27
October 16, 2003, Hei 14 (wa) No. 1943, 1874 Hanrei Jihō (2002) 23 (*Coral Sands*) 12.03, 12.53
December 26, 2003, Hei 14 (wa) No. 3237,1159 Hanrei Times (2004), 275 (*Liquid Filling Machine Nozzle*) 15.18
January 28, 2004, Hei 14 (wa) No. 18628, 1847 Hanrei Jihō (2004) 60 (*Mobile Software*) 12.53
April 23, 2004, Hei 16 (wa) No. 6035, Hanrei Jihō (No. 1892) 89 . . . . 6.17
August 17, 2004, Hei 16 (wa) No. 9208,1873 Hanrei Times (2004) 153 (*Overlaykōhō*) 6.11, 6.12, 12.15
August 31, 2004, Hei 14 (wa) No. 18830, 1183 Hanrei Times (2004) 320 . . . . 12.53
October 1, 2004, Hei 15 (wa) No. 28554 (*Confirmation of Absence of Damage Claims*). 12.58
January 24, 2006, Heo (wa) No. 8496, Hanrei Jihō (No. 2018) 146 . . . . 9.35
September 15, 2006, Hei 18 (mo) No. 9933, 1250 Hanrei Times, 300 . . . . 12.39
August 8, 2006 (wa) No.2006 (*Songaibaishō Seikyūken*) 12.50
February 27, 2007, Hei 15 (wa) No. 16924, Hanrei Taimuzu (No. 1253) 241 . . . . 6.24
December 14, 2007, Hei 16 (wa) No. 25576 . . . . 6.12
May 20, 2009, Hei 19 (wa) No. 8426 . . . . 6.36
February 24, 2011, Hei 20 (wa) 2944 ("*Flow Control Valve*"). 15.17
December 26, 2011, Hei 21 (wa) No. 44391). 15.16
August 26, 2011, Hei 20 (wa) Nr. 831,1402 Hanrei Times 344 (2011) (*Dōbutsu-yō hainyō shori-zai*) 15.01
November 2, 2012, Hei 22 (wa), No. 24479, 2185 Hanrei Jihō (2013) 115 . . . . 15.17
Toyama District Court
September 7, 1970, Sho 41 (wa) No. 30, 253 Hanrei Times (1970) 142 (*Meraninjusshi*) 15.25
Yamaguchi District Court
February 28, 1963, Sho 34 (wa) No. 250, 142 Hanrei Times (1963), 184 (*Bojen*). 12.13

Administrative/JPO decisions
Tokkyo Hatsumeino Hogo Han'I (The Scope of Protection for a Patented Invention) (Trial decision, 1981). 2.60

The Netherlands

Dijkstra v Saier (Hoge Raad, decision of December 22, 2006 (C05/200HR) 5.86, 8.151
Sandoz v Glaxo, January 26, 2011 . . . . 8.94

Switzerland

Swiss Federal Court of Justice
Stacker, OJ EPO 1993, 1970 . . . . 8.74

United Kingdom

Actavis UK, Ltd. v Novartis AG [2010] EWCA Civ 82 . . . . 8.93
Bristol-Myers Squibb v Baker Norton Pharmaceuticals [2001] RPC 1 (Court of Appeal) 8.70
Darcy v Allin, 74 Eng. Rep. 1131 (K.B. 1602) (Eng.). 7.01
Follicle-Stimulating Hormone II (HR 23 June 1995, HC 1998) 8.74
Kirin-Amgin, Inc. v Hoechst Marion Roussel Limited, 2004 UKHL 46 (House of Lords 2004) 6.57, 6.65, 8.150
Nestec SA v Dualit, Ltd. [2013] EWHC 923 . . . . 8.84
Pozzoli Spa v BDMO SA and anor [2007] EWCA Civ 588 (22 June 2007) 8.92
Windsurfing International Inc. v Tabur Marine (GB), Ltd. [1985] RPC 59. . . . . 8.92

United States

AT&T Corp. v Excel Communications, Inc., 172 F.3d 1352, 1355 (Fed. Cir. 1999) 10.83
A123 Systems, Inc. v Hydro-Quebec, 626 F.3d 1213, 1221 (Fed. Cir. 2010) 10.15
800 Adept, Inc. v Murex Securities, Ltd., 539 F.3d 1354, 1370 (Fed. Cir. 2008) 10.74
ABB Robotics, Inc. v GMFanuc Robotics Corp., 52 F.3d 1062, 1063–65 (Fed. Cir. 1995) 10.73
Abbott Diabetes Care Inc. v Roche Diagnostics Corp., 2007 WL 4166030, *3 (N.D. Cal. 2007) 13.51
Abbott Laboratories v Andrx Pharmaceuticals, Inc., 452 F.3d 1331, 1348 (Fed. Cir. 2006) 10.99
Abbott Laboratories v Baxter Travenol Laboratories, Inc., 676 F. Supp. 831, 832–33 . . . . 10.49
Abbott Laboratories v Dey, L.P., 287 F.3d 1097, 1105, 62 U.S.P.Q. 2d 1545 (Fed. Cir. 2002) 4.97, 4.121
Abbott Laboratories v Sandoz, Inc., 544 F.3d 1341, 1362–63 (Fed. Cir. 2008) 10.97, 10.105
Abbott Labs. v Baxter Pharm. Prods., 334 F.3d 1274, 67 U.S.P.Q. 2d 1191 (Fed. Cir. 2003) 6.62
Abbott Labs. v Sandoz, Inc., 566 F.3d 1282, 90 U.S.P.Q. 2d 1769 (Fed. Cir. 2009) 4.44, 4.74, 6.53, 7.06
ACCO Brands, Inc. v ABA Locks Mfr. Co., 501 F.3d 1307, 1311 (Fed. Cir. 2007) 10.36
ActiveVideo Networks, Inc. v Verizon Communications, Inc., 694 F.3d 1312, 1339 (Fed. Cir. 2012) 10.55
Acumed, LLC v Stryker Corp., 551 F.3d 1323 (Fed. Cir. 2008), 1330 . . . . 13.15
Adams v Burke, 84 U.S. (17 Wall.) 453 (1873) 7.137
Additive Control & Measurement Systems, Inc. v Flowdata, Inc., 29 U.S.P.Q. 2d (BNA) 1890, 1896 (S.D. Tex. 1993), modified, 32 U.S.P.Q. 2d (BNA) 1747 (S.D. Tex. 1994) 13.80
Adenta GMBH v OrthoArm, Inc., 501 F.3d 1364, 1371, 2007 U.S. App. LEXIS 22315 (Fed. Cir. 2007) 7.08
Adept, Inc. v Murex Securities, Ltd., 505 F. Supp. 2d 1327 (M.D. Fla. 2007), 1338 . . . . 13.14
Adrain v Genetec Inc., 2009 WL 3063414, *2+ (E.D. Tex. September 22, 2009) (NO. 2:08-CV-423) 10.19
Advanced Cardiovascular Systems, Inc. v C.R. Bard, Inc., 144 F.R.D. 372 (N.D. Cal. 1992) 10.46
Advanced Cardiovascular Systems, Inc. v Medtronic Vascular, Inc., 579 F. Supp. 2d 554, 560–61 (D. Del. 2008) 13.09, 13.18
Aelony v Arni, 547 F.2d 566, 192 U.S.P.Q. 486 (CCPA 1977) 7.52
Aetna Life Ins. Co. v Haworth, 300 U.S. 227, 239, (1937) 10.88
Akamai Techs., Inc. v Limelight Networks, Inc., 692 F.3d 1301 (Fed. Cir. 2012) 5.19
Akeva, LLC v Mizuno Corp., 243 F. Supp. 2d 418, 422 (M.D. N.C. 2003) 10.45
Alice Corp. Pty., Ltd. v CLS Bank Int' l, 134 S. Ct. 2347, 189 L. Ed. 2d 296, 110 U.S.P.Q. 2d 1976 (U.S. 2014) 1.25, 7.73, 7.76, 7.77, 9.32
Alldread v City of Grenada, 988 F.2d 1425, 1434 (5th Cir. 1993) 10.48
Alps South, LLC v Ohio Willow Wood Co., 787 F.3d 1379, 1382 (Fed. Cir. 2015) 10.14
Al-Site Corp. v VSI Int' l, Inc., 174 F.3d 1308, 50 U.S.P.Q. 2d 1161 (Fed. Cir. 1999) 4.41, 4.90, 7.05
Altana Pharma AG Wyeth v Teva Pharmaceuticals USA, Inc., 566 F.3d 999, 1005 (Fed. Cir. 2009); Titan Tire Corp. v Case New Holland, Inc., 566 F.3d 1372, 1375–76 (Fed. Cir. 2009) 10.93, 10.94
Altiris, Inc. v Symantec Corp., 318 F.3d 1363, 65 U.S.P.Q. 2d 1865 (Fed. Cir. 2003) 4.85
Am. Calcar, Inc. v Am. Honda Motor Co., 651 F.3d 1318, 1339, 99 U.S.P.Q. 2d 1137 (2011) . . . 4.117
Am. Med. Sys. v Biolitec, Inc., 618 F.3d 1354, 96 U.S.P.Q. 2d 1652 (Fed. Cir. 2010) 4.79, 4.80
Amado v Microsoft Corp., 517 F.3d 1353 (Fed. Cir. 2008) 7.24
Amazon.com, Inc. v Barnesandnoble.com, Inc., 239 F.3d 1343, 1359 (Fed. Cir. 2001) 10.94
American Academy of Science Tech Center, In re, 367 F.3d 1359, 70 U.S.P.Q. 2d 1827 (Fed. Cir. 2004) 7.04
American Medical Systems, Inc. v Medical Engineering Corp., 6 F.3d 1523, 1538 (Fed. Cir. 1993), cert. denied, 511 U.S. 1070, 128 L. Ed. 2d 366, 114 S. Ct. 1647 (1994) 13.40
American Standard, Inc. v Pfizer Inc., 828 F.2d 734, 745 (Fed. Cir. 1987) 10.44

Amgen, Inc. v Chugai Pharmaceutical Co., Ltd., 927 F.2d 1200, 18 U.S.P.Q. 2d 1016 (Fed. Cir. 1991) 7.94
Amgen, Inc. v Elanex Pharmaceuticals, Inc., 1996 U.S. Dist. LEXIS 22015, 1996 WL 84590, *3 (W.D. Wash. 1996) 5.07
Amgen, Inc. v F. Hoffman-La Roche, Ltd., 581 F. Supp. 2d 160, 212–26 (D. Mass. 2008), aff'd in part, vacated in part, 580 F.3d 1340 (Fed. Cir. 2009) 13.18
Amgen, Inc. v F. Hoffmann-La Roche, Ltd., 580 F.3d 1340 (Fed. Cir. 2009) 4.02
Amgen Inc. v Hoechst Marion Roussel, Inc., 314 F.3d 1313, 1351, 65 U.S.P.Q. 2d 1385 (Fed. Cir. 2003) 4.103, 4.114
Amgen v U.S. Int' l Trade Comm'n, 902 F.2d 1532, 14 USPQ2d 1734 (Fed. Cir. 1990) 5.14
Amsted Industries Inc. v Buckeye Steel Castings Co., 24 F.3d 178, 183–84 (Fed. Cir. 1994), rehearing denied, en banc suggestion declined 13.80
Anderson v City of Bessemer City, 470 U.S. 564, 573–74 (1985) 10.82
Ansul Co. v Uniroyal, Inc., 448 F.2d 872, 880, 169 U.S.P.Q. 759, 764 (2d Cir. 1971) 7.127
Apotex USA, Inc. v Merck & Co., Inc., 254 F.3d 1031, 59 U.S.P.Q. 2d 1139 (Fed. Cir. 2001) 7.95, 7.96
Apple, Inc., In re, 456 Fed. Appx. 907, 2012 WL 112893 . . . . 10.08
Apple, Inc. v Motorola, Inc., 757 F.3d 1286, 1340 (Fed. Cir. 2014) 13.10, 16.31
Apple, Inc. v Samsung Electronics Co., Ltd., 735 F.3d 1352, 1364–65 (Fed. Cir. 2013) 13.10
Apple, Inc. v Samsung Electronics Co., Ltd., 2011 WL 7036077, *20+ (N.D. Cal. 2011) (No. 11-CV-01846-LHK), aff'd in part, vacated in part, remanded by 678 F.3d 1314 (Fed. Cir. 2012) 10.96
Apple, Inc. v Samsung Electronics Co., Ltd., 2011 WL 1938154, *1–*3 (N.D. Cal. 2011) 10.101
Apple, Inc. v Samsung Electronics Co., Ltd., 2011 WL 7036077, *20+ (N.D. Cal. 2011) (No. 11-CV-01846-LHK), aff'd in part, vacated in part, remanded by 678 F.3d 1314 (Fed. Cir. 2012) 13.08, 13.10
Apple, Inc. v Samsung Electronics Co., Ltd., 2012 WL 2572037, *67 (N.D. Cal. 2012) 10.105
Apple, Inc. v Samsung Electronics Co., Ltd., 2012 WL 2576136, *8 (N.D. Cal. July 3, 2012) (No. 12-CV-00630-LHK) 13.14
Application of Deiulemar Compagnia Di Navigazione S.p.A. v M/V Allegra, 198 F.3d 473 (4th Cir. 1999) 10.32
Applied Med. Res. Corp. v U.S. Surgical Corp., 435 F.3d 1356, 1361 (Fed. Cir. 2006) 13.55, 13.67
Aquatex Industries, Inc. v Techniche Solutions, 419 F.3d 1374, 1381 (Fed. Cir. 2005) 4.67
Aria Diagnostics, Inc. v Sequenom, Inc., 2013 WL 4034379, *7 (Fed. Cir. 2013) 10.98
Ariad Pharmaceuticals, Inc. v Eli Lilly & Co., 598 F.3d 1336 (Fed. Cir. 2010) (en banc 7.12
Arlington Indus., Inc v Bridgeport Fittings, Inc., No. 3:01-CV-0485, 2010 WL 817519, *3–4 (M.D. Pa. March 9, 2010) 13.09
Aro Mfg. Co. v Convertible Top Co., 377 U.S. 476, 141 U.S.P.Q. 681 (1964) 4.03, 4.06
Aro Mfg. Co. v Convertible Top Replacement Co., 365 U.S. 336, 346, 128 U.S.P.Q. 354, 359 (1961) 7.139
Arthrocare Corp. v Smith & Nephew, Inc., 406 F.3d 1365, 1370 (Fed. Cir. 2005) 10.55
Arvin Indus., Inc., v Berns Air King Corp., 525 F.2d 182, 185, 188 U.S.P.Q. 49, 52 (7th Cir. 1975) 4.96
Asahi/America, Inc., In re, 68 F.3d 442, 445 (Fed. Cir. 1995) 10.82
Ashcroft v Iqbal, 556 U.S. 662, 678, 129 S. Ct. 1937, 1949 (2009) 10.29
Aspex Eyewear Inc. v Clariti Eyewear, Inc., 605 F.3d 1305, 1311 (Fed. Cir. 2010) 10.73
Aspex Eyewear, Inc. v Miracle Optics, Inc., 434 F.3d 1336, 1344 (Fed. Cir. 2006) 10.17
Ass'n for Molecular Pathology v Myriad Genetics, Inc., 133 S. Ct. 2107, 186 L. Ed. 2d 124, 106 U.S.P.Q. 2d 1972 (U.S. 2013) 1.25, 7.79
Astrazeneca AB v Mutual Pharmaceutical Co., Inc., 384 F.3d 1333, 72 U.S.P.Q. 2d 1726 (Fed. Cir. 2004) 4.49
Astrazeneca LP v Apotex, Inc., 633 F.3d 1042, 1050 (Fed. Cir. 2010) 10.95
AsymmetRx, Inc. v Biocare Medical, LLC, 582 F.3d 1314, 1322 (Fed. Cir. 2009) 10.16
ATD Corp. v Lydall, Inc., 159 F3d 534, 544 (Fed. Cir. 1998) 10.82
Athletic Alternatives v Prince Mfg., 73 F.3d 1573, 37 U.S.P.Q. 2d 1365 (Fed. Cir. 1996) 4.75

Atlanta Attachment Co. v Leggett & Platt, Inc., No. 1:05-CV-1071, 2007 WL 5011980, *8 (N.D. Ga. February 23, 2007) 13.17
Atlantic Thermoplastics Co., Inc v Faytex Corp., 970 F.2d 834, 23 U.S.P.Q. 2d 1481 (Fed. Cir. 1992). 4.43
Atlas Powder Co. v E.I. du Pont De Nemours & Co., 750 F.2d 1569 (Fed. Cir. 1984). 4.87, 4.88
Augustine Med., Inc. v Gaymar Indus., Inc., 181 F.3d 1291, 1301, 50 U.S.P.Q. 2d 1900, 1907 (Fed. Cir. 1999) 4.97
Autogiro Co. of Am. v United States, 181 Ct. Cl. 55, 384 F.2d 391, 155 U.S.P.Q. 697 (1967) 4.20, 4.35, 4.52, 4.101
Automated Merchandising Sys. v Crane Co., Nos. 2009–1158, 2009–1164, 2009 WL 4878643, *3 (Fed. Cir. December 16, 2009) 13.08
Aventis Pharma S.A. v Hospira, Inc., 675 F.3d 1324, 102 U.S.P.Q. 2d 1445 (Fed. Cir. 2012). 7.124
Avia Group Intern., Inc. v L.A. Gear California, Inc., 853 F.2d 1557, 1567 (Fed. Cir. 1988). 13.80
B. Braun Melsungen AG v Terumo Medical Corp., 778 F.Supp.2d 506, 525 (D. Del. 2011). . . . 13.16
Baden Sports, Inc. v Kabushiki Kaisha Molten, No. C06-210, 2007 WL 2790777, *3 (W.D. Wash. September 25, 2007) 13.17
Ballard Med. Prods. v Allegiance Healthcare Corp., 268 F.3d 1352, 1358 (Fed. Cir. 2001) 4.26
Bard Peripheral Vascular, Inc. v W.L. Gore & Associates, Inc., 682 F.3d 1003 (Fed. Cir. 2012), cert. denied, 2013 WL 141409 (U.S. January 14, 2013) (No. 12-458, 12A189). 13.77
Baxter Healthcare Corp. v Spectramed, Inc., 49 F.3d 1575, 1583, 34 U.S.P.Q. 2d 1120, 1126 (Fed. Cir. 1995) 4.122
Bayer Aktiengesellschaft v Duphar Intern. Research B.V., 738 F.2d 1237, 1242 (Fed. Cir. 1984) 13.80
Bayer Cropscience AG v Dow Agrosciences, LLC, 288 F.R.D. 84, 86 (D. Del. 2012) 10.30
Beach Aircraft Corp. v EDO Corp., 990 F.2d 1237, 26 U.S.P.Q. 2d 1572 (Fed. Cir. 1248). 7.140
Beatrice Foods Co. v New England Printing & Lith. Co., 923 F.2d 1567 (Fed. Cir. 1991) 13.71
Becton Dickinson & Co. v C.R. Bard, Inc., 922 F.2d 792, 17 U.S.P.Q. 2d 1097 (Fed. Cir. 1990). 4.72
Becton Dickinson & Co. v Tyco Healthcare Group, LP, No. 02-1694, 2008 WL 4745882 (D. Del. October 29, 2008). 13.08, 13.17
Bel Fuse, Inc. v Molex, Inc., 27 F. Supp. 3d 557, 562 (D.N.J. 2014). 10.30
Belden Techs. Inc. v Superior Essex Communs. LP, 733 F. Supp. 2d 517, 534–36 (D. Del. 2009) 13.40
Bell & Howell Document Management Products Co. v Altek Systems, 132 F.3d 701, 708 (Fed. Cir. 1997) 10.98
Bell Atlantic Corp. v Twombly, 550 U.S. 544, 555 (2007). 10.29
Bell Atlantic Network Services, Inc. v Covad Communications Group, Inc., 262 F.3d 1258, 59 U.S.P.Q. 2d 1865 (Fed. Cir. 2001) 4.54, 4.59
Bell Communications Research v Vitalink Communications Corp., 55 F.3d 615, 34 U.S.P.Q. 2d (BNA) 1816 (Fed. Cir. 1995) 4.80
Berlenbach v Anderson & Thompson, 329 F.2d 782, 785, 141 U.S.P.Q. 84, 87 (9th Cir. 1964) 7.128
Biagro Western Sales Inc. v Helena Chemical Co., 160 F. Supp. 2d 1136, 1143 (E.D. Cal. 2001). 10.15
BIC Leisure Prods. v Windsurfing Int' l Inc., 1 F.3d 1214 (Fed. Cir. 1993) 7.15, 13.48
Bicon, Inc. v Straumann Co., 441 F.3d 945, 950–51 (Fed. Cir. 2006) 4.49
Bill of Lading Transmission & Processing Sys. Patent Litig., In re, 681 F.3d 1323, 1335 (Fed. Cir. 2012). 10.30
Bilski, In re, 545 F.3d 943 (Fed. Cir. 2008) (en banc) 7.74
Bilski v Kappos, 130 S. Ct. 3218, 3227, 177 L. Ed. 2d 792,803, 95 U.S.P.Q. 2d 1001 (U.S. 2010) 7.74, 10.85
Bio-Technology General Corp. v Genentech, Inc., 80 F.3d 1553, 38 U.S.P.Q. 2d 1321 (Fed. Cir. 1996) 4.02, 4.39

Black & Decker, Inc. v Robert Bosch Tool Corp., No. 04 C 7955, 2006 WL 3446144, *5 (N.D. Ill. November 29, 2006) 13.17
Blonder-Tongue Laboratories, Inc. v University of Illinois Foundation, 402 U.S. 313, 28 L. Ed. 2d 788, 91 S. Ct. 1434 (1971) 7.20
BMC Res., Inc. v Paymentech, L.P., 498 F.3d 1373, 84 U.S.P.Q. 2d 1545 (Fed. Cir. 2007) 4.04
Bonito Boats v Thunder Craft Boats, 489 U.S. 141, 109 S. Ct. 971, 103 L. Ed. 2d 118, 9 U.S.P.Q. 2d 1847 (U.S. 1989) 1.10
Bosies v Benedict, 27 F.3d 539, 30 U.S.P.Q. 2d 1862 (Fed. Cir. 1994) 7.94
Bowman v Monsanto Co., 133 S. Ct. 1761 (2013) 7.136, 7.137, 7.139
Bristol-Myers Squibb Co. v Ben Venue Labs., Inc., 246 F.3d 1368, 1375, 58 U.S.P.Q. 2d 1508, 1513 (Fed. Cir. 2001) 4.81
Broadcom Corp. v Emulex Corp., 732 F.3d 1325, 1337–38 (Fed. Cir. 2013) 13.09
Broadcom Corp. v Qualcomm, Inc., 543 F.3d 683, 702 (Fed. Cir. 2008) 13.08, 13.12, 13.16
Brooks Furniture Mfg., Inc. v Dutailier Intern., Inc., 393 F.3d 1378, 1381 (Fed. Cir. 2005) 13.79
Brooktrout, Inc. v Eicon Networks Corp., No. 2:03-CV-59, 2007 WL 1730112 (E.D. Tex. June 14, 2007) 13.08, 13.17
Brown, In re, 459 F.2d 531, 535, 173 U.S.P.Q. 685, 688 (CCPA 1972) 7.07
Builders Concrete, Inc. v Bremerton Concrete Products Co., 757 F.2d 255, 225 U.S.P.Q. 240 (Fed. Cir. 1985) 4.107
Burroughs Welcome Co., v Barr Lab., Inc., 40 F.3d 1223, 1227–28 (Fed. Cir. 1994) 7.85
Business Objects, S.A. v Microstrategy, Inc., 393 F.3d 1366, 1375, 73 U.S.P.Q. 2d 1520 (Fed. Cir. 2005) 4.112
Buysafe, Inc. v Google, Inc., 2014 U.S. App. LEXIS 16987 . . . . . 7.76
A. C. Aukerman Co. v R. L. Chaides Construction Co., 960 F.2d 1020, 22 U.S.P.Q. 2d 1321 (Fed. Cir. 1992) (en banc) 7.129, 7.132
Calderon v U.S. Dist. Court for Northern Dist. of California, 144 F.3d 618, 621 (9th Cir. 1998) 10.32
California Table Grape Commission v RB Sandrini, Inc., 2007 U.S. Dist. LEXIS 48362 (E.D. Calif. 2007) 5.07
Callaway Golf Co. v Acushet Co., 585 F. Supp. 2d 600, 621 (D. Del. 2008), aff'd in part, vacated in part, 576 F.3d 1331 (Fed. Cir. 2009) 13.11, 13.14
Cardiac Pacemakers, Inc. v St. Jude Medical, Inc., No. IP 96-1718-C-H/K, 2002 WL 1801525, *74 (S.D. Ind. July 5, 2002), aff'd in part, rev'd in part, and remanded, 381 F.3d 1371 (Fed. Cir. 2004), vacated, 315 Fed. Appx. 273 (Fed. Cir. 2009) 13.68
Cardinal Chemical Co. v Morton Int' l, Inc., 508 U.S. 83, 98 (1993) 10.88
Cargill, Inc. v Sears Petroleum & Transport Corp., 2003 WL 22225580, *3+ (N.D.N.Y. 2003) (NO. CIVA5:03CV0530 (DEP) 10.47
Carl Zeiss Stiftung v Renishaw plc, 945 F.2d 1173, 1181, 20 U.S.P.Q. 2d 1094, 1101 (Fed. Cir. 1991) 4.39
Carnegie Mellon Univ v Hoffman-La Roche, Inc., 541 F.3d 1115, 1129 (Fed. Cir. 2008) 4.116
Carnegie Mellon University v Marvell Technology Group, Ltd., 2014 WL 1320154, *27 (W.D. Pa. 2014) 13.10
Cat Tech, LLC v TubeMaster, Inc., 528 F.3d 871, 879 (Fed. Cir. 2008) 10.88, 10.89
Catalina Mktg. Int' l, Inc. v Coolsavings.com, Inc., 289 F.3d 801, 809 (Fed. Cir. 2002) 4.80, 4.82
Caterpillar, Inc. v Detroit Diesel Corp., 961 F. Supp. 1249, 41 U.S.P.Q. 2d 1876 (N.D. Ind. 1996), aff'd, 194 F.3d 1336 (Fed. Cir. 1999) (unpublished) 4.42
Caught Fish Enters., LLC v Blaze Wharton Constr., Inc., No. 09-cv-02878-PAB-KMT, slip op. at 3 (D. Colo. February 24, 2010) 13.83
CCS Fitness, Inc. v Brunswick Corp., 288 F.3d 1359, 62 U.S.P.Q. 2d 1658 (Fed. Cir. 2002) 4.46, 4.55
Certain 3G Mobile Handsets and Components Thereof, Inv No. 337-TA-613, Order No. 42, Initial Determination (March 10, 2009) 10.70
Certain Coaxial Cable Connectors, Inv No. 337-TA-650, Remand Initial Determination, 25 (May 27, 2010) (Public Version) 10.68, 10.69

Certain Display Controllers and Prods. Containing Same and Certain Display Controllers with Upscaling Functionality and Products Containing Same, Comm'n Op. 52, Inv Nos. 337-TA-491/481 (consolidated) (February 4, 2005), 2005 WL 996252 . . . . 10.64
Certain Erasable Programmable Read-Only Memories, Components Thereof, Prods. Containing Such Memories, & Processes for Making Such Memories, USITC Pub. No. 2196, Inv No. 337-TA-276, Comm'n Op. (March 16, 1989) (EPROM Order), aff'd sub nom., Hyundai Elecs. Indus. Co. v U.S. Int' l Trade Comm'n, 899 F.2d 1204, 1209–10 (Fed. Cir. 1990) 13.31
Certain Flash Memory Chips & Prods. Containing the Same, USITC Pub. No. 2640, Complaint, 36–39 (November 17, 2008) 13.34
Certain Multimedia Display and Navigation Devices and System Components Thereof and Products Containing Same, Inv No. 337-TA-694, Comm'n Op. (July 22, 2011) (Public Version) 10.66
Certain Semiconductor Chips with Minimized Chip Package Size and Products Containing Same, Inv No. 337-TA-432, Order No. 13, Initial Determination (January 24, 2001) 10.70
Certain Zero-Mercury-Added Alkaline Batteries, Parts Thereof and Products Containing Same, Inv No. 337-TA-493, Initial Determination (June 2, 2004) 10.70
Checkpoint Systems, Inc. v US Int' l Trade Comm'n, 54 F.3d 756, 35 U.S.P.Q. 2d 1042 (Fed. Cir. 1995) 7.95
Chiron Corp. v Genentech, Inc., 363 F.3d 1247, 1254 (Fed. Cir. 2004) 8.120
Chore-Time Equipment, Inc. v Cumberland Corp., 713 F.2d 774, 781–82 (Fed. Cir. 1983) 10.24
Cias, Inc. v Alliance Gaming Corp., 504 F.3d 1356, 84 U.S.P.Q. 2d 1737 (Fed. Cir. 2007) 4.74
Classen Immunotherapies, Inc. v Shionogi, Inc., 993 F. Supp. 2d 569, 575 (D.Md. 2014) 10.30
Clement, In re, 131 F.3d 1464, 45 U.S.P.Q. 2d 1161 (Fed. Cir. 1997) 7.65
CollegeNet, Inc. v ApplyYourself, Inc., 418 F.3d 1225 (Fed. Cir. 2005) 4.39
Colonial Data Technologies Corp. v Cybiotronics, Ltd., 41 U.S.P.Q. 2d 1763, 1996 WL 875081 (D. Conn. 1996) 10.98
Comiskey, In re, 554 F.3d 967, 975 (Fed. Cir. 2009) 10.83
Commonwealth Scientific and Indus. Research Org. v Buffalo Tech., Inc. ("CSIRO"), 492 F. Supp. 2d 600, 601 (E.D. Tex. 2007) 13.12
Computer Docking Station Corp. v Dell, Inc., 519 F.3d 1366, 86 U.S.P.Q. 2d 1129 (Fed. Cir. 2008) 4.78
Conair Group, Inc. v Automatik Apparate-Maschinenbau GmbH, 944 F.2d 862, 866 (Fed. Cir. 1991) 10.102
Concept Design Electronics and Mfg., Inc. v Duplitronics, Inc., 52 F.3d 342 (Fed. Cir. 1995) 10.74
Connell v Sears, Roebuck & Co., 722 F.2d 1542, 1553 (Fed. Cir. 1983) 10.24
Conoco, Inc. v Energy & Environmental International, L.C., 460 F.3d 1349, 1364, 79 U.S.P.Q. 2d 1801 (Fed. Cir. 2006); KCJ Corp. v Kinetic Concepts, Inc., 223 F.3d 1351, 1359–60 (Fed. Cir. 2000) 4.109
Conroy v Reebok International, Ltd., 14 F.3d 1570, 29 U.S.P.Q. 2d 1373 (Fed. Cir. 1994) 4.121
Continental Paper Bag Co. v Eastern Paper Bag Co., 210 U.S. 405, 422–30, 28 S. Ct. 748, 52 L. Ed. 1122, 1908 Dec. Comm'r Pat. 594 (1908) 16.56
Continuum Co., Inc. v Incepts, Inc., 873 F.2d 801, 803, 13 Fed. R. Serv 3d 1080 (5th Cir. 1989) 10.104
Convergent Tech. Sec. Litig., In re, 108 F.R.D. 328, 336 (N. D. Cal. 1985) 10.41
Convolve, Inc. v Compaq Computer Corp., 2007 WL 4205868, *1+ (S.D. N.Y. 2007) 10.49
Cooper v Goldfarb, 154 F.3d 1321, 1998 U.S. App. LEXIS 21410, 47 U.S.P.Q. 2d (BNA) 1896 (Fed. Cir. 1998) 7.85, 7.94
Cordis Corp v Boston Scientific Corp., 2003 WL 22843072 (D. Del. 2003), aff'd, 99 Fed. Appx. 928 (Fed. Cir. 2004) 4.05, 10.99
Cornell Univ v Hewlett-Packard Co., 609 F. Supp. 2d 279 (N.D. N.Y. 2009) 13.70
Corning Glass Works v Sumitomo Electric U.S.A., Inc., 868 F.2d 1251, 1257, 9 U.S.P.Q. 2d 1962, 1966 (Fed. Cir. 1989) 4.81, 4.84, 4.85

C.R. Bard, Inc. v United States Surgical Corp., 388 F.3d 858, 73 U.S.P.Q. 2d 1011
(Fed. Cir. 2004) 4.49, 4.74
Creative Compounds, LLC v Starmark Laboratories, 65 1 F.3d 1303,
1313 (Fed. Cir. 2011) 7.56, 7.94
Cross Medical Products, Inc. v Medtronic Sofamor Danek, Inc., 424 F.3d 1293,
1301–2 (Fed. Cir. 2005) 10.103
Crucible, Inc. v Stora Kopparbergs Bergslags AB, 226 U.S.P.Q. 842,
1985 WL 2872 (W.D. Pa. 1985) 13.24
Crystal Semiconductor Corp. v TriTech Microelectronics International, Inc.,
246 F.3d 1336, 57 U.S.P.Q. 2d 1953 (Fed. Cir. 2001) 4.16
Cuno, Inc. v Pall Corp., 121 F.R.D. 198, 204 (E.D.N.Y. 1988) 10.47
Cuno Engineering Corp. v Automatic Devices Corp., 314 U.S. 84,
62 S. Ct. 37, 86 L. Ed. 58, 51 U.S.P.Q. 272 (U.S. 1941) 1.16
CVI/Beta Ventures v Tura LP, 112 F.3d 1146, 42 U.S.P.Q. 2d 1577
(Fed. Cir. 1997) 4.39, 4.57, 4.59
Cybor Corp. v FAS Techs., Inc., 138 F.3d 1448, 1454–56 (Fed. Cir. 1998) (en banc) . . . 10.56, 10.83
Datascope Corp. v Kontron Inc., 786 F.2d 398, 401 (Fed. Cir. 1986) 10.99
Deepsouth Packing Co. v Laitram Corp., 406 U.S. 518 (1972) 4.12
Deere & Co. v International Harvester Co., 710 F.2d 1561 (Fed. Cir. 1983) 13.61
Deerpoint Group, Inc. v Acqua Concepts, Inc., 2014 WL 7178210, *4 (E.D. Cal. 2014) 10.30
Delano Farms Co. v California Table Grape Comm'n, 655 F.3d 1337 (Fed. Cir. 2011) 7.123
Delta-X Corp. v Baker Hughes Production Tools, Inc., 984 F.2d 410, 413 (Fed. Cir. 1993) 10.24
Depuy Spine, Inc. v Medtronic Sofamor Danek, Inc., 469 F.3d 1005, 80 U.S.P.Q.
2d 1865 (Fed. Cir. 2006) 4.117
DePuy Spine, Inc. v Medtronic Sofamor Danek, Inc., 567 F.3d 1314,
1329–32 (Fed. Cir. 2009) 13.46
Depuy Synthes Products, LLC v Globus Medical, Inc., 2013 WL 4509655 (D. Del. 2013) 10.96
Desper Prods. v QSound Labs., Inc., 157 F.3d 1325, 48 U.S.P.Q. 2d (BNA)
1088 (Fed. Cir. 1998) 4.35
Devices for Medicine, Inc. v Boehl, 822 F.2d 1062, 1068, 3 U.S.P.Q. 2d 1288,
1293–94 (Fed. Cir. 1987) 7.147
Diamond Scientific Co. v Ambico, Inc., 848 F.2d 1220, 6 U.S.P.Q. 2d 2028
(Fed. Cir. 1988) 7.10, 7.68
Diamond v Chakrabarty, 447 U.S. 303, 100 S. Ct. 2204, 65 L. Ed. 2d 144,
206 U.S.P.Q. 193 (U.S. 1980) 1.20, 7.71
Dickinson v Zurko, 527 U.S. 150, 119 S. Ct. 1816, 144 L. Ed. 2d 143,
50 U.S.P.Q. 2d 1930 (U.S. 1999) 2.04
Display Technologies, LLC v Display Industries, LLC, 2011 WL 6188742,
*3 (S.D. N.Y. 2011) 10.97
Doble Eng'r Co. v Leeds & Northrup Co., 134 F.2d 78, 56 U.S.P.Q. 426 (1st Cir. 1943) 4.96
Dominant Semiconductors Sdn. Bhd. v OSRAM GmbH, 524 F.3d 1254, 1261
(Fed. Cir. 2008) 10.74
Donaldson, In re, 16 F.3d 1189, 29 U.S.P.Q. 2d 1845 . . . . 7.05
Dorel Juvenile Group, Inc. v Graco Children's Prods., 429 F.3d 1043,, 77 U.S.P.Q. 2d 1090
(Fed. Cir. 2005) 4.25
Douglas Dynamics, LLC v Buyers Products Co., 717 F.3d 1336, 1341 (Fed. Cir. 2013) 10.82
Doyle, In re, 293 F.3d 1355 (Fed. Cir. 2002) 7.17
DSU Medical Corp. v JMS Co., Ltd., 471 F.3d 1293, 1303, 81 U.S.P.Q. 2d 1238
(Fed. Cir. 2006) 4.07, 4.16, 6.19
Duhn Oil Tool, Inc. v Cooper Cameron Corp., 2009 WL 3381052,
*2+ (E.D. Cal. 2009) 10.49
eBay Inc. v MercExchange, LLC, 547 U.S. 388, 126 S. Ct. 1837, 164 L. Ed. 2d 641,
78 U.S.P.Q. 2d 1577 (U.S. 2006) 1.22, 10.85, 13.01, 13.03, 13.04,
13.14, 13.23, 16.31, 16.56
EchoStar Communications Corp., In re, 448 F.3d 1294, 1300 (Fed. Cir. 2006) 10.44, 10.49

Ecolab, Inc. v Envirochem, Inc., 264 F.3d 1358, 1367, 60 U.S.P.Q. 2d 1173 (Fed. Cir. 2001)....4.50
Edward Lowe Indus., Inc. v Oil–Dri Corp. of Am., No. 94–C–7568, 1995 WL 399712, *3 (N. D. Ill. July 7, 1995)....10.41
E.I. du Pont de Nemours & Co. v MacDermid, Inc., 2009 WL 3048421, *2+ (D. N.J. 2009) (NO. CIV. A. 06-3383 MLC)....10.47
E.I. du Pont de Nemours & Co. v MacDermid Printing Solutions, L.L.C., 525 F.3d 1353, 1358 (Fed. Cir. 2008)....10.94, 10.103
E-I-M Co. v Philadelphia Gear Works, Inc., 223 F.2d 36, 41–42 (5th Cir. 1955), cert. denied, 350 U.S. 933 (1956)....13.21
Eli Lilly & Co. v American Cyanamid Co., 82 F.3d 1568 (Fed. Cir. 1996)....4.02, 5.14, 6.08, 10.96
Eli Lilly & Co. v Medtronic, Inc., 496 U.S. 661, 110 S. Ct. 2683, 15 U.S.P.Q. 2d 1121 (U.S. 1990)....7.106
Emory Univ v Nova Biogenics, Inc., No. 1:06-CV-0141, 2008 WL 2945476, *4 (N.D. Ga. 2008)....13.11, 13.12, 13.17
Endress + Hauser, Inc. v Hawk Measurement Systems Pty. Ltd., 932 F. Supp. 1147, 1149 (S.D. Ind. 1996); ePlus Inc. v Lawson Software, Inc., 2013 WL 4829321 (E.D. Va. 2013)....13.24
Energy Transp. Group, Inc. v William Demant Holding A/S, 2012 U.S. App. LEXIS 21200 (Fed. Cir. October 12, 2012)....4.86
Enzo APA & Son, Inc. v Geapag A.G., 134 F.3d 1090, 1093 (Fed. Cir. 1998)....10.14, 10.17
Eolas Techs., Inc. v Adobe Sys., Inc., No. 6:09-CV-446, 2010 WL 3835762, *2 (E.D. Tex. September 28, 2010)....10.19
Eolas Techs., Inc. v Microsoft Corp., 399 F.3d 1325, 73 U.S.P.Q. 2d 1782 (Fed. Cir. 2005)....4.65
Epcon Gas Sys., Inc. v Bauer Compressors, Inc., 279 F.3d 1022, 1029, 61 U.S.P.Q. 2d 1470, 1475 (Fed. Cir. 2002)....4.82
Ethicon, Inc. v Quigg, 849 F.2d 1422 (Fed. Cir. 1988)....7.08, 7.21, 7.32, 7.34
Ethicon Endo-Surgery, Inc. v United States Surgical Corp., 937 F. Supp. 1015 (D.Conn. 1996), aff'd 135 F.3d 1456, 45 U.S.P.Q. 2d 1545 (Fed Cir. 1998), cert. denied, 525, U.S. 923 (1998), 149 F.3d 1309, 47 U.S.P.Q. 2d 1272 (Fed. Circ. 1998)....4.84, 7.81, 7.85, 7.146
Evans v Eaton, 20 U.S. 356, 7 Wheat. 356, 5 L. Ed. 472 (1822)....4.18
Evens v Eaton, 20 U.S. 356, 5 L. Ed 472, 7 Wheat 356 (1822)....1.13
Exergen Corp. v Wal-Mart Stores, Inc., 575 F.3d 1312 (Fed. Cir. 2009)....7.123
Exigent Technology, Inc. v Atrana Solutions, Inc., 442 F.3d 1301, 1312 (Fed. Cir. 2006)....10.23
EZ Gard Industries, Inc. v XO Athletic Co., 2008 WL 1827490, *5 (D. Minn. 2008), aff'd without opn., No. 2008-1384, 2008 WL 5207021 (Fed. Cir. December 15, 2008)....10.98
Feltner v Columbia Pictures Television, Inc., 523 U.S. 340, 353–55 (1998)....10.55
Festo Corp. v Shoketsu Kinzoku Kogyo Kabushiki Co., 535 U.S. 722, 122 S. Ct. 1831, 152 L. Ed. 2d 944, 62 U.S.P.Q. 2d 1705 (U.S. 2002)....1.22, 4.29, 4.105, 4.106, 4.109, 4.110, 4.112, 4.114, 4.115
Fiers v Revel, 984 F.2d 1164, 25 U.S.P.Q. 2d 1601 (Fed. Cir. 1993)....7.94
Fina Research, S.A. v Baroid, Ltd., 141 F.3d 1479, 1481 (Fed. Cir. 1998)....10.88
Fisher, In re, 427 F.2d 839....8.120
Flex-Rest, LLC v Steelcase, Inc., 455 F.3d 1351 (Fed. Cir. 2006)....7.95
Foster v Hallco Manufacturing Co., 947 F.2d 469, 20 U.S.P.Q. 2d 1241 (Fed. Cir. 1991)....7.68
Fourco Glass Co. v Transmirra Products Corp., 353 U.S. 222 (1957)....10.04
Francklyn v Guilford Packing Co., 695 F.2d 1158, 1160–61, 217 U.S.P.Q. 317, 319 (9th Cir. 1983)....7.143
Free Motion Fitness, Inc. v Cybex International, Inc., 423 F.3d 1343 (Fed. Cir. 2005)....4.68, 4.87
Freedman Seating Co. v Am. Seating Co., 420 F.3d 1350, 1359 (Fed. Cir. 2005)....4.116
Fressola, Ex parte, 27 U.S.P.Q. 2d 1608 (Bd. Pat. App. & Interferences 1993)....4.18
Fuji Photo Film Co., Ltd. v Jazz Photo Corp., 394 F.3d 1368 (Fed. Cir. 2005)....7.138
Fujifilm Corp. v Benun, 605 F.3d 1366, 2010 U.S. App. LEXIS 10827 (Fed. Cir. 2010)....7.138

Fujitsu, Ltd. v Netgear, Inc., 620 F.3d 1321, 96 U.S.P.Q. 2d 1742
(Fed. Cir. 2010). 4.06, 4.09, 6.17
Gambro Lundia AB v Baxter Healthcare Corp., 110 F.3d 1573, 42 U.S.P.Q. 2d 1378
(Fed. Cir. 1997) 7.56, 7.86
Gardiner, In re, 36 C.C.P.A. 748, 171 F.2d 313, 315–16, 80 U.S.P.Q. 99, 101 (CCPA 1948) 4.82
Garneau v Dozier, 102 U.S. 230, 12 Otto 230, 26 L. Ed. 133 (1880). 7.11
Gayler v Wilder, 51 U.S. 477, 10 How. 477, 493, 13 L. Ed. 504)(1851) 7.140
Genentech, Inc., In re, 566 F.3d 1338, 1345 (Fed. Cir. 2009) 10.07
Genentech, Inc. v United States International Trade Commission, 122 F.3d 1409, 1415
(Fed. Cir. 1997) 10.47
Genentech Inc. v Wellcome Found., 29 F.3d 1555, 31 U.S.P.Q. 2d 1161
(Fed. Cir. 1994) 4.76, 4.77
General Electric Co. v Wabash Appliance Co., 304 U.S. 364, 37 U.S.P.Q. 466 (1938) 4.32
General Foods Corp. v Studiengesellschaft Kohle mbH, 972 F.2d 1272,
23 U.S.P.Q. 2d 1839 (Fed. Cir. 1992) 7.103
General Talking Pictures Co. v Western Elec. Co., 304 U.S. 175 (1938) 7.127
Gentry Gallery v Berkline Corp., 134 F.3d 1473, 45 U.S.P.Q. 2d 1498 (Fed. Cir. 1998) 4.63
Georgia-Pacific Corp. v United States Plywood Corp., 318 F. Supp. 1116, 1120 (S.D. N.Y. 1970),
modified and aff'd, 446 F.2d 295 (2d Cir. 1971) 13.62, 13.64, 13.65, 13.66
Giese v Pierce Chemical Co., 29 F. Supp. 2d 33, 40, 49 U.S.P.Q. 2d 1498,
1504 (D. Mass. 1998) 7.131
Gillette Co. v Energizer Holdings, Inc., 405 F.3d 1367, 1370 (Fed. Cir. 2005) 10.95
Glaxo Group, Ltd. v Apotex, Inc., 64 Fed. Appx. 751 (Fed. Cir. 2003) 10.98
Glaxo Operations UK, Ltd. v Quigg, 894 F.2d 392, 394 (Fed. Cir. 1990). 6.22
Glaxo Wellcome, Inc. v Andrx Pharms., Inc., 344 F.3d 1226 (Fed. Cir. 2003) 4.88, 4.99
Glaxo Wellcome, Inc. v Eon Labs Manufacturing, Inc., 2002 U.S. Dist.
LEXIS 14923 (S.D. N.Y. 2002) 7.63
Global-Tech Appliances, Inc. v SEB S.A., 131 S. Ct. 2060, 179 L. Ed. 2d 1167,
98 U.S.P.Q. 2d 1665 (U.S. 2011) 4.07, 4.08
Golden Blount, Inc. v Robert H. Peterson Co., 438 F.3d 1354 (Fed. Cir. 2006) 13.69
Golden Trade, S.r.L. v Lee Apparel Co., 143 F.R.D. 514, 518–19 (S.D.N.Y. 1992);
Gorman v Polar Electro, Inc., 137 F. Supp. 2d 223, 227 (E.D.N.Y. 2001) 10.47
Goldenberg v Cytogen, Inc., 373 F.3d 1158, 71 U.S.P.Q. 2d 1255 (Fed. Cir. 2004);
Tex. Digital Sys. v Telegenix, Inc., 308 F.3d 1193, 1211 (Fed. Cir. 2002) 4.63
Gonnocci Trust v Three M Tool & Machine, Inc., 2006 U.S. Dist. LEXIS 21534
(E.D. Mich. 2006) 7.144
Gottschalk v Benson, 409 U.S. 63, 69 (U.S. 1972) 7.71
Gould v Control Laser Corp., 705 F.2d 1340, 217 U.S.P.Q. 985 (Fed. Cir. 1983) 7.34
Graham v John Deere Co., 383 U.S. 1, 33, 148 U.S.P.Q. 459, 473 (1966) 4.70
Grain Processing Corp. v American Maize-Products Co., 893 F. Supp. 1386,
1347 (N.D. Ind. 1995), aff'd in part, vacated in part, 108 F.3d 1392 (Fed. Cir. 1997),
further decision on remand, 979 F. Supp. 1233 (N.D. Ind. 1997), aff'd, 185 F.3d 1341
(Fed. Cir. 1999). 13.49, 13.68
Granny Goose Foods, Inc. v Brotherhood of Teamsters and Auto Truck Drivers
Local No. 70 of Alameda County, 415 U.S. 423, 433 n. 7 (1974) 10.100
Graver Tank & Mfg. Co. v Linde Air Products Co., 339 U.S. 605, 70 S. Ct. 854, 94 L. Ed.
1097, 85 U.S.P.Q. 328 (1950) 4.19, 4.93, 4.96, 4.101
Greenberg v Ethicon Endo-Surgery, 91 F.3d 1580, 39 U.S.P.Q. 2d 1783 (Fed. Cir. 1996). 4.42
Griffith v Kanamaru, 816 F.2d 624, 2 U.S.P.Q. 2d 1361 (Fed. Cir. 1987) 7.94
Gulf Oil Corp. v Gilbert, 330 U.S. 501, 508–9 (1947) 10.07
Gyromat v Champion Spark Plug Co., 735 F.2d 549 (Fed. Cir. 1984). 13.47
Hall v Aqua Queen Manufacturing Inc., 93 F.3d 1548, 39 U.S.P.Q. 2d 1925
(Fed. Cir. 1996) 7.132
Hallco Mfg. Co., Inc. v Foster, 256 F.3d 1290, 59 U.S.P.Q. 2d 1346 (Fed. Cir. 2001). 7.11
Halliburton Energy Servs. v M-I, LLC, 514 F.3d 1244, 85 U.S.P.Q. 2d 1654
(Fed. Cir. 2008) 4.75

Halliburton Oil Well Cementing Co. v Walker, 329 U.S. 1, 71 U.S.P.Q. 175 (1946) 1.17, 4.32
Hanson v Alpine Valley Ski Area Inc., 718 F.2d, 1075 (Fed. Cir. 1983) 13.61, 13.67
Hayes Microcomputer Products, Inc. Patent Litigation, In re, 766 F. Supp. 818, 823, 20 U.S.P.Q. 2d 1836 (N.D. Cal. 1991), judgment aff'd, 982 F.2d 1527, 25 U.S.P.Q. 2d 1241 (Fed. Cir. 1992) 13.24
Haynes International, Inc. v Jessop Steel Co., 8 F.3d 1573, 28 U.S.P.Q. 2d 1652 (Fed. Cir. 1993) 4.109
Hedgewick v Akers, 497 F.2d 905, 908, 182 U.S.P.Q. 167, 169 (CCPA 1974) 7.86, 7.97
Hemstreet v Spiegel, Inc., 851 F.2d 348, 7 U.S.P.Q. 2d 1502 (Fed. Cir. 1988) 7.68
Henry v A.B. Dick Co., 224 U.S. 1 (1912) 4.08
Hensley v Eckerhart, 461 U.S. 424, 433 (1983) 13.82
Hewlett-Packard Co. v Acceleron, LLC, 587 F.3d 1358, 1361 (Fed. Cir. 2009) 10.88
Hewlett-Packard Co. v Repeat-O-Type Stencil Manufacturing Corp., Inc., 123 F.3d 1445, 43 U.S.P.Q. 2d 1650 (Fed. Cir. 1997) 7.139
High Tech Medical Instrumentation, Inc. v New Image Industries, Inc., 49 F.3d 1551, 1554 (Fed. Cir. 1995) 10.92, 10.93, 10.97
Highmark, Inc. v Allcare Health Management Systems, Inc., 687 F.3d 1300, 1311 (Fed. Cir. 2012) 13.81
Highmark Inc. v Allcare Health Management System, Inc., 134 S. Ct. 1744 (2014) 10.25
Hill-Rom Co., Inc. v Kinetic Concepts, Inc., 209 F.3d 1337, 54 U.S.P.Q. 2d 1437 (Fed. Cir. 2000) 4.49
Hitzeman v Rutter, 243 F.3d 1345, 58 U.S.P.Q. 2d 1161 (Fed. Cir. 2001) 7.94
Hobbs v Beach, 180 U.S. 383, 399 (1901) 1.15
Hoechst Celanese Corp. v BP Chems., Ltd., 78 F.3d 1575, 1582 (Fed. Cir. 1996) . . . 4.88, 4.99, 13.78
Hoffmann-La Roche Inc., In re, 587 F.3d 1333, 1336–37 (Fed. Cir. 2009) 10.07
Hoffmann-La Roche Inc. v Cobalt Pharmaceuticals Inc., 2010 WL 4687839, *11–*13 (D. N.J. 2010) 10.96
Hoffmann-La Roche, Inc. v Promega Corp., 323 F.3d 1354,66 U.S.P.Q. 2d 1385 (Fed. Cir. 2003) 7.120
Holland Furniture Co. v Perkins Glue Co., 277 U.S. 245, 48 S. Ct. 474, 72 L. Ed. 868, 1928 U.S. LEXIS 686 (U.S. 1928) 1.17
Honeywell, Inc. v Metz Apparatewerke, 509 F.2d 1137, 1141, 184 U.S.P.Q. 387 (7th Cir. 1975) 4.16
Honeywell Int' l, Inv v Hamilton Sundstrand Corp., 523 F.3d 1304, 1313, 86 U.S.P.Q. 2d 1718 (Fed. Cir. 2008) 4.98, 4.113, 4.114
Honeywell Intern., Inc. v Universal Avionics Systems Corp., 397 F. Supp. 2d 537, 549 (D. Del. 2005), 515 . . . . 13.24
Honeywell International Inc. v Hamilton Sundstrand Corp., 370 F.3d 1131, 1148, 71 U.S.P.Q. 2d 1065 (Fed. Cir. 2004) (en banc) 4.39, 4.106, 4.107
Hopp Press, Inc v Joseph Freeman & Co., 323 F.2d 636, 637–38 (2d Cir. 1963) 13.21
Hotchkiss v Greenwood, 52 U.S. (11 How.) 248 (1850) 1.16
Huang, In re, 100 F.3d 135, 138 (Fed. Cir. 1996) 10.83
Hughes Aircraft Co. v United States, 140 F.3d 1470, 46 U.S.P.Q. 2d 1285 (Fed. Cir. 1998) 4.86, 4.95
Hughes v Novi American, Inc., 724 F.2d 122, 125 (Fed. Cir. 1984) 13.81
Hupp v Siroflex of America, Inc., 122 F.3d 1456, 1467–68 (Fed. Cir. 1997) 10.104
Hybritech, Inc. v Abbott Labs., 4 U.S.P.Q. 2d 1001 (C.D. Cal. 1987), aff'd, 849 F.2d 1446 (Fed. Cir. 1988) 10.98, 10.99, 13.01
Hynix Semiconductor, Inc. v Rambus, Inc., 609 F. Supp. 2d 951, 983 (N.D. Cal. 2009) 13.12
i4i Ltd. Partnership v Microsoft Corp., 670 F. Supp. 2d 568 (E.D. Tex. 2009), aff'd, 598 F.3d 831 (Fed. Cir. 2010), aff'd 131 S.Ct. 2238 (2011) 4.08, 10.98, 13.12
i4i Ltd. Partnership v Microsoft Corp., 343 F. App'x 619, 619 (Fed. Cir. 2009) (per curiam) 13.25
i4i Ltd. Partnership v Microsoft Corp., 670 F. Supp. 2d 568 (E.D. Tex. 2009), aff'd, 598 F.3d 831 (Fed. Cir. 2010), aff'd 131 S.Ct. 2238 (2011) 13.78
ICU Medical, Inc. v Alaris Medical Systems, Inc., 558 F.3d 1368, 1375 (Fed. Cir. 2009) 13.81

Ill. Tool Works Inc. v Indep. Ink, Inc., 547 U.S. 28, 126 S. Ct. 1281, 164 L. Ed. 2d 26, 77 U.S.P.Q. 2d 1801 (2006) 4.08
Illinois Tool Works, Inc. v Grip-Pak, Inc., 906 F.2d 679, 683 (Fed. Cir. 1990) 10.98
Image Technical Services Inc. v Eastman Kodak, 125 F.3d 1195, 44 U.S.P.Q. 2d 1065 (9th Cir. 1997) 7.127
Imhaeuser v Buerk, 101 U.S. 647, 25 L. Ed. 945, 11 Otto 647 (U.S. 1880) 1.19
Impax Laboratories, Inc. v Aventis Pharmaceuticals, Inc., 235 F. Supp. 2d 390, 396 (D. Del. 2002) 10.98
Independent Service Organizations Antitrust Litigation, In re, 203 F.3d 1322, 53 U.S.P.Q. 2d 1852 (Fed. Cir. 2000) 7.127
Innovative Scuba Concepts, Inc. v Feder Indus., Inc., 26 F.3d 1112, 1115, 31 U.S.P.Q. 2d (BNA) 1132, 1134 (Fed. Cir. 1994) 7.96
Innovative Therapies, Inc. v Kinetic Concepts, Inc., 2008 WL 4809104, *2 (D. Del. 2008), aff'd, 599 F.3d 1377, 1384–85 (Fed. Cir. 2010) 10.89
Inpro II Licensing, S.A.R.L. v T-Mobile USA, Inc., 450 F.3d 1350, 78 U.S.P.Q. 2d 1786 (Fed. Cir. 2006) 4.57, 4.74
Int' l Rectifier Corp. v IXYS Corp., 383 F.3d 1312, 1316 (Fed. Cir. 2004) 13.19
Integra Lifesciences I, Ltd. v Merck KGaA, 331 F.3d 860, 869 (Fed. Cir. 2003), vacated on other grounds, 545 U.S. 193 (2005) 13.67
Intel Corp v ULSI System Technology, Inc., 995 F.2d 1566, 1568 (Fed. Cir. 1993) 10.93
Intellectual Property Development, Inc. v TCI Cablevision, Inc., 248 F.3d 1333, 1345–46 (Fed. Cir. 2001) 10.14, 10.16
Interactive Gift Express, Inc. v Compuserve Inc., 256 F.3d 1323, 59 U.S.P.Q. 2d 1401 (Fed. Cir. 2001) 4.85
InterDigital Communications, LLC v International Trade Com'n, 690 F.3d 1318, 1329–30 (Fed. Cir. 2012), denying reh'g and reh'g en banc, 707 F. 3d 1295, 1298 (Fed. Cir. 2013) 10.65
International Cork Co. v New Process Cork Co., 6 F.2d 420, 422 (2d Cir. 1925) 4.35, 4.53
International Glass Co. v United States, 408 F.2d 395, 159 U.S.P.Q. 434, 161 U.S.P.Q. 116 (Ct. Cl. 1969) 7.95
International Rectifier Corp. v IXYS Corp., 361 F.3d 1363, 1376–77, 70 U.S.P.Q. 2d 1209 (Fed. Cir. 2004) 7.84
International Shoe Co. v Washington, 326 U.S. 310, 316 (1945) 10.04
International Visual Corp. v Crown Metal Manufacturing Co., Inc., 991 F.2d 768, 772, 26 U.S.P.Q. 2d 1588, 1591 (Fed. Cir. 1993) 4.123
Intra-Video Inc. v Hughes Electronics Corp., 51 U.S.P.Q. 2d 1383, 1384 (S.D.N.Y. 1999) 7.127
Jack Winter Inc. v Koratron Co., 50 F.R.D. 225 (N.D. Cal. 1970) 10.46
Jazz Photo Corp. v Int' l Trade Comm'n, 264 F.3d 1094, 1110–11 (Fed. Cir. 2001) 7.138, 7.139
Jeneric/Pentron, Inc. v Dillon Company, Inc., 205 F.3d 1377, 1384 (Fed. Cir. 2000) 10.95
John Mezzalingua Assoc., Inc. v Int' l Trade Comm'n, 660 F.3d 1322, 1327–30 (Fed. Cir. 2011) 10.68
Johns Hopkins Univ v Datascope Corp., 513 F. Supp. 2d 578 (D. Md. 2007), rev'd on other grounds and remanded, 543 F.3d 1342 (Fed. Cir. 2008) 13.12, 13.14
Johnson & Johnstone Assocs. v R.E. Serv Co., 285 F.3d 1046, 1057–58, 62 U.S.P.Q. 2d 1225 (Fed. Cir. 2002) 4.98, 4.124
Johnson Worldwide Associates, Inc. v Zebco Corp., 175 F.3d 985, 989–90, 50 U.S.P.Q. 2d 1607, 1610–11 (Fed. Cir. 1999) 4.50, 4.77
Johnston v IVAC Corp., 885 F.2d 1574, 1578 n. 3, 12 U.S.P.Q. 2d 1382, 1387 n. 3 (Fed. Cir. 1989) 4.22
Joy Technologies, Inc. v Flakt, Inc., 24 U.S.P.Q. 2d (BNA) 1150, 1151 (D. Del. 1992) 13.25
Joy Techs., Inc. v Flakt, Inc., 6 F.3d 770, 774, 28 U.S.P.Q. 2d 1378 (Fed. Cir. 1993) 4.06
Joyal Products, Inc. v Johnson Electric North America, Inc., No. 04-5172, 2009 WL 512156 (D. N.J. February 27, 2009) aff'd per curiam, 335 Fed. Appx. 48 (Fed. Cir. 2009) 13.12
Jungersen v Ostby & Barton Co., 335 U.S. 560, 69 S. Ct. 269, 93 L. Ed. 235, 80 U.S.P.Q. 32 (U.S. 1949) 1.16
Jurgens v McKasy, 927 F.2d 1552, 1561, 18 U.S.P.Q. 2d 1031, 1038 (Fed. Cir. 1991) 4.123

Kaufman Co. v Lantech Inc., 926 F.2d 1136, 1142 (Fed. Cir. 1991) 13.51
Kewanee v Bicron, 416 U.S. 470, 94 S. Ct. 1879, 40 L. Ed. 2d 315,
181 U.S.P.Q. 67 (U.S. 1974) 1.10
Key Manufacturing Group, Inc. v Microdot, Inc., 925 F.2d 1444, 1449,
17 U.S.P.Q. 2d 1806, 1810 (Fed. Cir. 1991). 4.123
Keystone Retaining Wall Sys., Inc. v Westrock, Inc., 997 F.2d 1444,
1993 U.S. App. LEXIS 15508, 27 U.S.P.Q. 2d (BNA) 1297 (Fed. Cir. 1993) 7.127
Kimberly-Clark Worldwide, Inc. v First Quality Baby Prods., LLC, 660 F.3d 1293,
1294–98 (Fed. Cir. 2011) 10.94
King Instr. Corp. v Perego, 65 F.3d 941 (Fed. Cir. 1995). 13.44
Kingsdown Medical Consultants, Ltd. v Hollister Inc., 863 F.2d 867,
9 U.S.P.Q. 2d 1384 (Fed. Cir. 1988) 7.120
Kirtsaeng v John Wiley & Sons, Inc., 133 S. Ct. 1351 (2013) 7.139
Knight v Baltimore & 0. R.R. Co., 14 F. Cas. 758, 759 (C.C. Md. 1840) 1.16
Knogo Corp. v United States, 213 U.S.P.Q. (BNA) 936 (Ct. Cl. 1980) 10.46
Knorr-Bremse Systeme Fuer Nutzfahrzeuge GmbH v Dana Corp., 383 F.3d
1337 (Fed. Cir. 2004) 10.49
Kohus v Toys R Us, Inc., 282 F.3d 1355, 1357 (Fed. Cir. 2002). 10.24
Kone Corp. v ThyssenKrupp USA, Inc., 2011 WL 4478477, *6–*8 (D. Del. 2011) 10.101
Koninklijke Philips Electronics N.V. v Cinram Intern., Inc., 2012 WL 4074419,
*4+ (S.D. N.Y. 2012) 10.49
Kori Corp. v Wilco Marsh Buggies Inc., 761 F.2d 649, 653 (Fed. Cir. 1985) 13.44
Kowalski v Mommy Gina Tuna Resources, Nos. 05-00679, 05-00787,
06-00182, 2009 WL 856006 (D. Haw. March 30, 2009), clarified,
2009 WL 1360695 (D. Haw. May 7, 2009). 13.12, 13.17
Kridl v McCormick, 105 F.3d 1446, 41 U.S.P.Q. 2d 1686 (Fed. Cir. 1997) 7.94
KSM Fastening Sys., Inc. v H.A. Jones Co., 776 F.2d 1522 (Fed. Cir. 1985) 13.20
KSR Int' l Co. v Teleflex Inc., 550 U.S. 398, 127 S. Ct. 1727, 167 L. Ed. 2d 705,
82 U.S.P.Q. 2d 1385 (U.S. 2007) 1.25, 10.85
K-Tech Telecomms., Inc. v Time Warner Cable, Inc., 714 F.3d 1277,
1286 (Fed. Cir. 2013) 10.30, 16.26
Kyocera v Int' l Trade Comm'n, 545 F.3d 1340 (Fed. Cir. 2008). . . 13.32, 13.33, 13.34, 13.35, 13.36
Laitram Corp. v Hewlett-Packard Co., Inc., 827 F. Supp. 1242, 1246 (E.D. La. 1993) 10.46
Laitram Corp. v NEC Corp., 163 F.3d 1342 (Fed. Cir. 1998) 7.13
Lane & Bodley Co. v Locke, 150 U.S. 193 (1893) 7.144
LaSalle v Carlton's Laydown Service, Inc., 680 F.2d 432, 216 U.S.P.Q. 276 (5th Cir. 1982) 4.96
LaserDynamics, Inc. v Quanta Computer, Inc., 694 F.3d 51, 75 (Fed. Cir. 2012) 13.67, 13.70
Lava Trading, Inc. v Sonic Trading Mgmt., LLC, 445 F.3d 1348,
1350, 78 U.S.P.Q. 2d 1624 (Fed. Cir. 2006) 4.25
Lear, Inc. v Adkins, 395 U.S. 653, 162 U.S.P.Q. 1 (1969) 7.68
Lear Siegler, Inc. v Aeroquip Corp., 733 F.2d 881, 889, 221 U.S.P.Q. 1025, 1031 (1984) 4.53
Leggett v Standard Oil Co., 149 U.S. 287 (1893) 7.132
Lektron, Inc. v GE Lighting, Inc., 2012 WL 1085486, *3 (N.D. Okla. March 30, 2012)
(NO. 11-CV-413-TCK-PJC). 10.19
Liebel-Flarsheim Co. v Medrad, Inc., 358 F.3d 898, 910 (Fed. Cir. 2004). 4.60
LifeScan, Inc. v Shasta Technologies, LLC, 2013 WL 1149827, *18 (N.D. Cal. 2013) 10.96
Lighting Ballast Control, LLC v Philips Elecs. North Am. Corp., 744 F.3d 1272,
109 U.S.P.Q. 2d 1969 (Fed. Cir. 2014) 2.12
Lightwave Technologies, Inc. v Corning Glass Works, 19 U.S.P.Q. 2d (BNA) 1838,
1849 (S.D. N.Y. 1991) 13.80
Limelight Networks, Inc. v Akamai Techs., Inc., 2014 U.S. LEXIS 3817,
110 U.S.P.Q. 2d 1681 (U.S. June 2, 2014) 4.04, 4.06
Liquid Dyn. Corp. v Vaughan Co., 449 F.3d 1209 (Fed. Cir. 2006) 13.78
Litecubes, LLC v Northern Light Products, Inc., 523 F.3d 1353, 1363 (Fed. Cir. 2008) 4.05
Lizardtech, Inc. v Earth Res. Mapping, Inc., 424 F.3d 1336 (Fed. Cir. 2005) 4.21, 16.18
Lonardo, In re, 119 F.3d 960, 43 U.S.P.Q. 2d 1262 (Fed. Cir. 1997). 7.28

Luck, In re, 476 F.2d 650, 177 U.S.P.Q. 523 (CCPA 1973) 4.43
Luminous Unit Co. v Freeman-Sweet Co., 3 F.2d 577 (7th. Cir. 1924) 7.22
Macronix Intern. Co., Ltd. v Spansion Inc., 4 F. Supp. 3d 797, 801 (E.D. Va. 2014) 10.30
Madey v Duke University, 307 F.3d 1351, 1361, 64 U.S.P.Q. 2d 1737
(Fed. Cir. 2002) 4.03, 7.111
Mallinckrodt, Inc. v Medipart, Inc., 976 F.2d 700, 24 U.S.P.Q. 2d (BNA)
1173 (Fed. Cir. 1992) 7.127
Mallinckrodt, Inc. v Medipart, Inc., 976 F.2d 700 (Fed. Cir. 1992) 7.137
Mane Fils, S.A. v International Flavors and Fragrances Inc., 2009 WL 1968925,
*2+ (D. N.J. 2009) 10.49
Manildra Mill. Corp. v Ogilvie Mills, Inc., 76 F.3d 1178, 1181–82 (Fed. Cir. 1996) 10.23
Marine Polymer Techs., Inc. v HemCon, Inc., 672 F.3d 1350, 102 U.S.P.Q. 2d 1161
(Fed. Cir. 2012) 4.74, 4.77, 7.66
Markman v Westview Instruments, Inc., 52 F.3d 967, 976, 34 U.S.P.Q. 2d 1321, 1326
(Fed. Cir. 1995) (en banc) 4.22, 4.23, 4.24, 4.28, 4.34, 4.46,
4.62, 4.71, 4.73, 4.112, 10.54, 10.56
Mars, Inc. v Coin Acceptors, Inc., 527 F.3d 1359, 1371 (Fed. Cir. 2008) 13.68
Mars, Inc. v Kabushiki-Kaisha Nippon Conclux 24 F.3d 1368 (Fed. Cir. 1994) 10.11
Mars Inc. v Nippon Conlux Kabushiki-Kaisha, 825 F. Supp. 73, 75–76 (D. Del. 1993) 10.11
Martek Biosciences Corp. v Nutrinova Inc., 520 F. Supp. 2d 537 (D. Del. 2007),
aff'd in part and rev'd in part, 579 F.3d 1363 (Fed. Cir. 2009) 13.09, 13.14, 13.17
Maryland Casualty Co. v Pacific Coal & Oil Co., 312 U.S. 270, 273 (1941) 10.88
Mass Engineered Design, Inc. v Ergotron, Inc., 633 F. Supp. 2d 361, 394 (E.D. Tex 2009) 13.17
Massillon-Cleveland-Akron Sign Co. v Golden State Advertising Co., 444 F.2d 425,
170 U.S.P.Q. 440 (9th Cir. 1971) 7.68
Mathis v Spears, 857 F.2d 749, 752 (Fed. Cir. 1988) 10.24
Matter of Mahurkar Double Lumen Hemodialysis Catheter Patent Litigation,
831 F. Supp. 1354 (N.D. Ill. 1993) 13.81
Mayo Collaborative Servs. v Prometheus Labs., Inc., 132 S. Ct. 1289,
182 L. Ed. 2d 321 101 U.S.P.Q. 2d 1961 (U.S. 2012) 1.25, 7.73, 7.75, 7.77, 7.78, 9.32
McCarthy v Paine Webber Group, Inc., 168 F.R.D. 448, 450 (D. Conn. 1996) 10.41
McClurg v Kingslund, 42 U.S. (1 How.) 202, 11 L. Ed. 102 (1843) 7.143
McCook Metals, LLC v Alcoa Inc., 192 F.R.D. 242, 259 (N. D. Ill. 2000) 10.45
McCoy v Mitsuboshi Cutlery, 67 F.3d 917, 36 U.S.P.Q. 2d 1289 (Fed. Cir. 1995) 7.148
McCullough Tool Co. v Well Surveys, Inc., 395 F.2d 230, 234 (10th Cir.),
cert. denied, 393 U.S. 925 (1968) 13.21
McElmurry v Arkansas Power & Light Co., 995 F.2d 1576, 1578, 27 U.S.P.Q. 2d 1129,
1131 (Fed. Cir. 1993) 7.143
McKesson Techs., Inc. v Epic Sys. Corp., 98 U.S.P.Q. 2d 1281 (Fed. Cir. 2011) 4.04
McZeal v Sprint Nextel Corp., 501 F.3d 1354, 1357 (Fed. Cir. 2007) 10.30
Medidea, LLC v Smith & Nephew, Inc., No. 2-09-cv-378-TJW, 2010 WL 1444211
(E.D. Tex. April 12, 2010) 10.08
MedImmune, Inc. v Genentech, Inc., 549 U.S. 118 (2007) 7.68, 10.85, 10.88
MEMC Electronic Materials, Inc. v Mitsubishi Materials Silicon Corp., 420 F.3d 1369
(Fed. Cir. 2005) 4.15
Mentor H/S, Inc. v Medical Device Alliance, Inc., 240 F.3d 1016, 1019 (Fed. Cir. 2001) 10.16
MercExchange, LLC v eBay, Inc., 275 F. Supp. 2d 695 (E.D. Va. 2003) 13.03
MercExchange, LLC v eBay, Inc., 401 F.3d 1323, 1338–39 (Fed. Cir. 2005) 13.03
Merck & Co. v Mediplan Health Consulting, Inc., 434 F. Supp. 2d 257,
261 (S.D. N.Y. 2006) 13.40
Merck KGAA v Integra Lifesciences I, Ltd., 545 U.S. 193 (2005) 7.108
Merrill v Yeomans, 94 U.S. 568, 4 Otto 568, 24 L. Ed. 235 (1877) 1.15, 4.18
Metallizing Engineering Co. v Kenyon Bearing & Auto Parts Co.,
153 F.2d 516, 520, 68 U.S.P.Q. 54 (C.A. 2 1946) 7.89, 7.115
Met-Coil Systems Corp. v Korners Unlimited, Inc., 803 F.2d 684, 686,
231 U.S.P.Q. 474, 476 (Fed. Cir. 1986) 7.147

Metro-Goldwyn-Mayer Studios Inc. v Grokster, Ltd., 545 U.S. 913, 935 (2005) 4.07
Metro-Goldwyn-Mayer Studios, Inc. v Grokster, Ltd., 518 F.Supp. 2d 1197, 1211 (C.D. Cal. 2007) 13.08
Meyers v Asics Corp., 974 F.2d 1304, 24 U.S.P.Q. 2d 1036 (Fed. Cir. 1992). 7.132
Micro Chemical, Inc. v Lextron, Inc., 318 F.3d 1119, 1121–25 (Fed. Cir. 2003) 13.46
Microchip Technology Inc. v Chamberlain Group, Inc., 441 F.3d 936, 942 (Fed. Cir. 2006) 10.88
Microsoft Corp., In re, 630 F.3d 1361, 1364 (Fed. Cir., 2011). 10.08
Microsoft Corp. v AT&T Corp., 550 U.S. 437 (2007) 4.12, 4.13
Microsoft Corp. v i4i Ltd. P'ship, 131 S. Ct. 1843, 179 L. Ed. 2d 770 (U.S. 2011). 7.08, 10.85
Microsoft Corp. v Multi-Tech Sys., Inc., 357 F.3d 1340, 1348 (Fed. Cir. 2004) 4.49, 4.63, 4.74
Midwest Indus. Inc v Karavan Trailers, Inc., 175 F.3d 1356, 1359 (Fed. Cir. 1999) (en banc in relevant part). 10.36
Mikohn Gaming Corp. v Acres Gaming, Inc., 165 F.3d 891, 897 (Fed. Cir. 1998) 10.74
Minnesota Min. and Mfg. Co. v Norton Co., 929 F.2d 670, 672–73 (Fed. Cir. 1991). 10.89
Minnesota Mining & Manufacturing Co. v Johnson & Johnson Orthopaedics, Inc., 976 F.2d 1559, 24 U.S.P.Q. 2d 1321 (Fed. Cir. 1992) 4.57
Mirafi, Inc. v Murphy, 928 F.2d 410 (Fed. Cir. 1991) 10.74
Modine Mfg. Co. v Allen Group, Inc., 917 F.2d 538, 543 (Fed. Cir. 1990) 13.80
Modine Mfg. Co. v United States Int' l Trade Comm'n, 75 F.3d 1545, 1550, 37 U.S.P.Q. 2d 1609, 1612 (Fed. Cir. 1996) 4.58, 4.60
Moffitt v Garr, 66 U.S. 273 (1862) 7.23
Moleculon Research Corp. v CBS, Inc., 793 F.2d 1261, 229 U.S.P.Q. 805 (1986) 4.78
Molins plc v Textron, Inc., 48 F.3d 1172, 33 U.S.P.Q. 2d 1823 (Fed. Cir. 1995) 7.119
Momenta Pharmaceuticals, Inc. v Amphastar Pharmaceuticals, Inc., 2011 WL 5882184, *1 (D. Mass. 2011) 10.105
Momenta Pharmaceuticals, Inc. v Teva Pharmaceuticals Industries, Ltd., 2011 WL 673926, *2–*3 (D. Mass. 2011). 10.101
Monolithic Power Systems, Inc. v O2 Micro Intern., Ltd., 2007 WL 801886 (N.D. Cal. 2007) 10.74
Monsanto Co. v Mycogen Plant Science, Inc., 261 F.3d 1356 (Fed. Cir. 2001) 7.94
Moore v United States, 211 U.S.P.Q. 800 (Ct. Cl. Trial Div 1981) 4.96
Morgan, In re, 990 F.2d 1230, 26 U.S.P.Q. 2d 1392 (Fed. Cir. 1993) 7.63
Morton Intern., Inc. v Cardinal Chemical Co., 5 F.3d 1464, 1468 (Fed. Cir. 1993) 10.83
Morton Salt Co. v G.S. Suppiger Co., 314 U.S. 488, 52 U.S.P.Q. 30 (1942) 7.128
Motiva, LLC v International Trade Com'n, 716 F.3d 596, 600–1 (Fed. Cir. 2013) 10.70
Motiva, LLC v Nintendo Co., Ltd., 2009 WL 1882836 (E.D.Tex. June 30, 2009) (NO. 6:08 CV 429). 10.07
MPT, Inc. v Marathon Labels, Inc., 505 F. Supp. 2d 401 (N.D. Ohio 2007), aff'd in part, rev'd in part, 258 Fed. Appx. 318 (Fed. Cir. 2007) 13.08
Mueller Brass Co. v Reading Indus., Inc., 352 F. Supp. 1357 (E.D. Pa. 1972), aff'd, 487 F.2d 1395 (3d Cir. 1973) 7.85
Muniauction, Inc. v Thomson Corp., 532 F.3d 1318, 87 U.S.P.Q. 2d 1350 (Fed. Cir. 2008); Metabolite Laboratories, Inc. v Laboratory Corporation of America Holdings, 370 F.3d 1354, 71 U.S.P.Q. 2d 1081 (Fed. Cir. 2004). 4.04
Murata Manufacturing Co., Ltd. v Bel Fuse Inc., 2005 WL 281217, *1+ (N.D. Ill. 2005). 10.47
Mycogen Plant Sci., Inc. v Monsanto Co., 243 F.3d 1316, 258 U.S.P.Q. 2d 1030 (Fed. Cir. 2001). 7.91
MyMail, Ltd. v Am. Online, Inc., 223 F.R.D. 455, 456 (E.D. Tex. 2004). 10.19
MyMail, Ltd. v Am. Online, Inc., 476 F.3d 1372, 81 U.S.P.Q. 2d (BNA) 1832 (Fed. Cir. 2007) 4.74
N. Am. Container, Inc. v Plastipak Packaging, Inc., 415 F.3d 1335, 75 U.S.P.Q. 2d 1545 (Fed. Cir. 2005) 4.64
National Hollow Brake-Beam Co. v Interchangeable Brake-Beam Co., 106 F.693 (8th Cir. 1901) 4.96
National Presto Indus. v West Bend Co., 76 F.3d 1185, 1996 U.S. App. LEXIS 1940, 37 U.S.P.Q. 2d (BNA) 1685 (Fed. Cir. 1996) 4.88

National Steel Car, Ltd. v Canadian Pacific Ry., Ltd., 357 F.3d 1319, 1325 (Fed. Cir. 2004). . . . 10.95
Nautilus, Inc v Biosig Instruments, Inc., 134 S. Ct. 2120, 189 L. Ed. 2d 37, 110 U.S.P.Q. 2d 1688 (U.S. 2014) 1.25
Nazomi Communs., Inc. v Arm Holdings plc, 403 F.3d 1364, 74 U.S.P.Q. 2d 1458 (Fed. Cir. 2005) 4.24
Neil Bros., Ltd. v World Wide Lines, Inc., 425 F. Supp. 2d 325, 330 (E.D.N.Y. 2006) 10.07
Neology, Inc. v Federal Signal Corp., 2012 WL 2308202, *17 (D. Del. 2012). 10.97
Nintendo Co., Ltd., In re, 589 F.3d 1194, 1198 (Fed. Cir. 2009). 10.07
Nintendo of America, Inc. v Lewis Galoob Toys, Inc., 16 F.3d 1032, 1036–37 (9th Cir. 1994) 10.106
Nokia Corp. v InterDigital, Inc., 645 F.3d 553, 557–59 (2d Cir. 2011) 10.106
Norian Corp. v Stryker Corp., 432 F.3d 1356 (Fed. Cir. 2005) 4.109
Novartis Vaccines and Diagnostics, Inc. v Hoffman-La Roche Inc., 597 F. Supp. 2d 706 (E.D.Tex. Feb 03, 2009) (NO. CIV.A. 2:07-CV-507 D) 10.07
Novozymes A/S v Genencor Int' l, Inc., 474 F. Supp. 2d 592, 608 (D. Del. 2007). 13.66, 13.68
NTP, Inc. v Research in Motion, Ltd., 418 F.3d 1282, 75 U.S.P.Q. 2d 1763 (Fed. Cir. 2005) 4.01, 4.03, 4.06, 4.14, 5.09, 5.46, 13.02, 13.03
Nystrom v Trex Co., Inc., 424 F.3d 1136, 1143, 76 U.S.P.Q. 2d 1481 (Fed. Cir. 2005) 4.61, 4.118
O2 Micro Int' l, Ltd. v Monolithic Power Sys., I, 467 F.3d 1355, 1365, 80 U.S.P.Q. 2d 1769 (Fed. Cir. 2006) 4.26
O2 Micro Int'l, Ltd. v Beyond Innovation Tech. Co., Ltd., 2007 WL 869576, * 3 (E.D. Tex. March 21, 2007), vacated, 521 F.3d 1351 (Fed. Cir. 2008) 4.25, 13.17
Oakley, Inc. v International Tropic-Cal, Inc., 923 F.2d 167, 170 (Fed. Cir. 1991) 10.102
Oakley, Inc. v Sunglass Hut Intern., 2001 WL 1683252 (C.D. Cal. 2001), aff'd, 316 F.3d 1331 (Fed. Cir. 2003) 10.105
Octane Fitness, LLC v ICON Health & Fitness, Inc., 134 S. Ct. 1749, 1756 (2014) 10.25, 16.59
Odetics Inc. v Storage Technology Corp., 185 F.3d 1259, 1273, 51 U.S.P.Q. 2d 1225, 1234 (Fed. Cir. 1999) 7.148
Oka v Youssefyeh, 849 F.2d 581, 7 U.S.P.Q. 2d 1169 (Fed. Cir. 1988) 7.94
Old Town Canoe Co. v Confluence Holdings Corp., 448 F.3d 1309, 78 U.S.P.Q. 2d 1705 (Fed. Cir. 2006) 4.69
Omega Eng'g, Inc. v Raytek Corp., 334 F.3d 1314, 67 U.S.P.Q. 2d 1321 (Fed. Cir. 2003) 4.63
Opprecht, In re, 868 F.2d 1264 (Fed. Cir. 1989). 7.31
O'Reilly v Morse, 56 U.S. 62, 14 L. Ed. 601, 1853 U.S. LEXIS 273, 15 How. 62 (U.S. 1854) 1.17
Ortho Pharm. Corp. v Genetics Inst., Inc., 52 F.3d 1026, 1030 (Fed. Cir. 1995) 10.16, 10.17
Ortho Pharmaceutical Corp. v Smith, WL 18681 (E.D. Pa. 1990) 10.98
Ortho-McNeil Pharm., Inc. v Mylan Labs., Inc., Nos. 04-1689, 06-757, 06-5166, 2007 WL 869545, *1 (D.N.J. March 20, 2007), aff'd in part, 520 F.3d 1358 (Fed. Cir. 2008) 13.17
Ortho-McNeil Pharmaceutical, Inc. v Mylan Laboratories, Inc., 569 F.3d 1353, 1356 (Fed. Cir. 2009) 10.24
Ortman v Stanray Corp., 371 F.2d 154, 158 (7th Cir. 1967) 10.10, 10.11
Outside the Box Innovations, LLC v Travel Caddy, Inc., 2012 U.S. App. LEXIS 19931 (Fed. Cir. September 21, 2012) 4.87
Padco, Inc. v Newell Companies, Inc., 13 U.S.P.Q. 2d (BNA) 1607, 1614 (E.D. Wis. 1988), judgment aff'd, 878 F.2d 1445 (Fed. Cir. 1989) 13.82
Paice, LLC v Toyota Motor Corp., 504 F.3d 1293, 1314–15 (Fed. Cir. 2007) 10.55
Paice, LLC v Toyota Motor Corp., No. 2:04-CV-21I-DF, 2006 WL 2385139 (E.D. Tex. August 16, 2006), *5 . . . . 13.07, 13.15
Pall Corp. v Mircon Separations Inc., 66 F.3d 1211, 1222 (Fed. Cir. 1995). 13.51
Pallin v Singer, 36 U.S.P.Q. 2d (BNA) 1050 (D. Vt. 1995) 7.116
Panduit Corp. v Band-It-Idex, Inc., 2000 WL 1121554 (N.D. Ill. 2000), aff'd, 25 Fed. Appx. 836 (Fed. Cir. 2001) 10.105
Panduit Corp. v Stahlin Bros. Fibre Works, 575 F.2d 1152 (6th Cir. 1978) 13.46, 13.49, 13.53
Paper Converting Machine Co. v Magna-Graphics Corp., 745 F.2d 11, 223 U.S.P.Q. 591 (1984) 4.04

Parallel Networks, LLC v Oriental Trading Company, Inc., et al., 6:10-cv-00474 (E.D. Texas, 2010), Memorandum Opinion and Order [Doc. 12], 3, filed March 15, 2011 . . . . 10.35
Paulik v Rizkalla, 760 F.2d 1270, 226 U.S.P.Q. 224 (Fed. Cir. 1985) 7.95
Pennock v Dialogue, 27 U.S. (2 Pet.) 1 (1829) 1.11
Pennwalt Corp. v Durand-Wayland, Inc., 833 F.2d 931, 4 U.S.P.Q. 2d 1737 (Fed. Cir. 1987), cert. denied, 485 U.S. 961, 485 U.S. 1009 (1988) 4.83, 4.93
Perkin-Elmer Corp. v Westinghouse Electric Corp., 822 F.2d 1528, 3 U.S.P.Q. 2d 1321 (Fed. Cir. 1987) 4.119
Pfaff v Wells Elecs., Inc., 525 U.S. 55, 48 U.S.P.Q. 2d 1641 (1998) 7.89, 7.93
Pfizer, Inc. v Teva Pharmaceuticals USA, Inc., 429 F.3d 1364, 77 U.S.P.Q. 2d 1257 (Fed. Cir. 2005) 4.69, 4.125, 10.93
Pfizer, Inc. v Teva Pharmaceuticals, USA, Inc., 429 F.3d 1364, 1372 (Fed. Cir. 2005) 10.105
Pfizer Inc. v Ranbaxy Labs., 457 F.3d 1284, 79 U.S.P.Q. 2d 1583 (Fed. Cir. 2006) 4.63
Philips Elecs. N. Am. Corp. v Contec Corp., 312 F. Supp. 2d 649, 652 (D. Del. 2004) 13.40
Phillips v AWH Corp., 415 F.3d 1303, 75 U.S.P.Q. 2d 1321 (Fed. Cir. 2005) 4.34, 4.36, 4.37, 4.38, 4.47, 4.49, 4.50, 4.51, 4.56, 4.57, 4.59, 4.62, 4.66, 4.70, 4.73, 4.76
PhotoCure Asa v Kappos, 603 F.3d 1372, 1376 (Fed. Cir. 2010) 6.22
Pierce v Underwood, 487 U.S. 552, 565 (1988) 10.82
Pilkington, In re, 411 F.2d 1345, 162 U.S.P.Q. 145 (CCPA 1969) 4.43
Pitney Bowes, Inc. v Hewlett-Packard Co., 182 F.3d 1298, 1314, 51 U.S.P.Q. 2d 1161 (Fed. Cir. 1999) 4.46, 4.49
Pixton v B & B Plastics, Inc., 291 F.3d 1324, 1326 (Fed. Cir. 2002) 10.02
Planet Bingo, LLC v VKGS, LLC, 2014 U.S. App. LEXIS 16412 (Fed. Cir. August 26, 2014) 7.76
Power Integrations, Inc. v BCD Semiconductor Corp., 2008 WL 5069784, *7–9 (D. Del. 2008) 10.94
Power Integrations, Inc. v Fairchild Semiconductor Int' l, Inc., No. 04-1371, 2008 WL 5210843 (D. Del. December 12, 2008) 13.08, 13.17
Power Mosfet Techs., LLC v Siemens AG, 378 F.3d 1396, 72 U.S.P.Q. 2d 1129 (Fed. Cir. 2004) 4.87
Power-One, Inc. v Artesyn Technologies, Inc., No. 2:05-CV-463, 2008 WL 1746636 (E.D. Tex. April 11, 2008), *1 n.1 . . . . 13.14, 13.17
PPG Industries, Inc. v Guardian Industries Corp., 75 F.3d 1558, 1567 (Fed. Cir. 1996) 10.99
Precision Links, Inc. v USA Products Group, Inc., 2009 WL 3076114, *8 (W.D. N.C. 2009) 10.97
Preformed Line Prod. Co. v Fanner Mfg. Co., 328 F.2d 265, 278–79, 140 U.S.P.Q. 500 (6th Cir. 1964) 7.128
Presidio Components, Inc. v American Technical Ceramics Corp., 702 F.3d 1351, 1359–62 (Fed. Cir. 2012) 13.46
Pressure Prods. Med. Supplies v Greatbatch Ltd., 599 F.3d 1308, 94 U.S.P.Q. 2d 1261 (Fed. Cir. 2010) 16.05
Primos, Inc. v Hunter's Specialties, Inc., 451 F.3d 841, 848 (Fed. Cir. 2006) 4.60
Procter & Gamble Company v Paragon Trade Brands, Inc., 989 F. Supp. 547, 610 (D. Del. 1997) 13.66
Promega Corp. v Lifecodes Corp., 1999 U.S. Dist. LEXIS 21094, *37 (D. Utah 1999) 13.66
Proveris Scientific Corp. v InnovaSystems Inc., No. 05-12424-WGY, slip op. at 3 (D. Mass. May 11, 2007) 13.83
PSC Computer Products, Inc. v Fox Conn International, Inc., 355 F.3d 1353, 69 U.S.P.Q. 2d 1460 (Fed. Cir. 2004) 4.125
Purdue Pharma L.P. v Boehringer Ingelheim GmbH, 237 F.3d 1359, 1365 (Fed. Cir. 2001) 10.94, 10.96
QBAS Co., Ltd. v C Walters Intercoastal Corp., 2010 WL 7785955, *12–*13 (C.D. Cal. 2010) 10.96
Quad/Tech, Inc. v Q.I. Press Controls B.V., 2010 WL 1292476, *9 (E.D. Pa. 2010) 10.96
Quality Tubing, Inc. v Precision Tube Holdings Corp., 75 F. Supp.2d 613, 1999 WL 1204845 (S.D. Tex. 1999) 4.15

Quanta Computer, Inc. v LG Electronics, Inc., 553 U.S. 617 (2008) 7.136, 7.137, 7.138, 10.85
Rambus Inc. v Infineon Technologies AG, 318 F.3d 1081, 1086–87 (Fed. Cir. 2003) 10.82
Reactive Metals and Alloys Corp. v ESM, Inc., 769 F.2d 1578, 1582 (Fed. Cir. 1985) 13.81
Read Corp. v Portec. Inc., 970 F.2d 816, 826–27 (Fed. Cir. 1992), superseded on other grounds 13.78
Regents of the Univ of Cal. v DakoCytomation Cal., Inc., 517 F.3d 1364, 85 U.S.P.Q. 2d 1929 (Fed. Cir. 2008) 4.114
Regents of the University of Cal., In re, 101 F.3d 1386, 1390 (Fed. Cir. 1996) 10.48
Research Corp. Techs., Inc. v Microsoft Corp., 536 F.3d 1247, 1255 (Fed. Cir. 2008) 10.36
Revision Military, Inc. v Balboa Mfg. Co., 700 F.3d 524, 525–26 (Fed. Cir. 2012) 10.95
Reynolds v American Exp. Entity One, 2009 WL 2578964, *1+ (W.D. Va. 2009) 10.32
Rheox, Inc. v Entact, Inc., 276 F.3d 1319, 61 U.S.P.Q. 2d 1368 (Fed. Cir. 2002) 4.78
Rhine v Casio, Inc., 183 F.3d 1342, 51 U.S.P.Q. 2d 1377 (Fed. Cir. 1999) 4.72
Rite-Hite Corp. v Kelley Co., 819 F.2d 1120, 1126 (Fed. Cir. 1987) 13.80
Rite-Hite Corp. v Kelley Co., Inc., 56 F.3d 1538, 1552 (Fed. Cir. 1995) (*en blanc*) 1.21, 10.16, 10.83, 10.99, 13.01, 13.44, 13.67, 13.69
Robert Bosch Healthcare Systems, Inc. v Express MD Solutions, LLC, 2012 WL 2803617, *4 (N.D. Cal. 2012) 10.30
Robert Bosch, LLC v Pylon Mfg. Corp., 659 F.3d 1142, 1154–56 (Fed. Cir. 2011) 10.96, 10.98
Robert Bosch, LLC v Snap-On Inc., 769 F.3d 1094 (Fed. Cir. 2014) 4.21
Robertson Co (H.H.). v United Steel Deck, 820 F.2d 384, 2 U.S.P.Q. 2d 1926 (Fed. Cir. 1987) 1.21
Rocform Corp. v Acitelli-Standard Concrete Wall, Inc., 367 F.2d 678, 151 U.S.P.Q. 305 (6th Cir. 1966) 7.127
Roche Products, Inc. v Bolar Pharmaceutical Co., 733 F.2d 858 (Fed. Cir. 1984) 7.110
Roche Products v Bolar Pharmaceutical, 733 F.2d 858 (Fed. Cir. 1984) 1.38, 5.54
Roper Corp. v Litton Systems, Inc., 757 F.2d 1266, 1273 (Fed. Cir. 1985) 10.97
Rosen Entm't Sys, LP v Icon Enters, Inc., 359 F. Supp. 2d 902 (C.D. Cal. 2005) 10.97
Rosuvastatin Calcium Patent Litig. v Aurobindo Pharma, Ltd.,, In re, 703 F.3d 511, 105 U.S.P.Q. 2d 1437 (Fed. Cir. 2012) 7.122
Roton Barrier, Inc. v Stanley Works, 79 F.3d 1112, 1125 (Fed. Cir. 1996) 10.83
Rowe, 112 F.3d, 479 . . . . 4.82
Rudd v Lux Products Corporation Emerson Climate Technologies Braeburn Systems, LLC, 2011 WL 148052, *2+ (N.D. Ill. January 12, 2011) (NO. CIV.A. 09-CV-6957) 10.19
Ruiz v A.B. Chance Co., 234 F.3d 654, 670 (Fed. Cir. 2000) 10.23
Ryco Inc. v Ag-Bag Corp., 857 F.2d 1418 (Fed. Cir. 1988) 13.46
Saes Getters, S.p.A. v Ergenics, Inc., 816 F. Supp. 979, 987 (D. N.J. 1992), aff'd, 989 F.2d 1201 (Fed. Cir. 1993) 10.98
Sage Prods. v Devon Indus., 126 F.3d 1420, 44 U.S.P.Q. 2d 1103 (Fed. Cir. 1997) 4.116
Salazar v Procter & Gamble Co., 414 F.3d 1342, 75 U.S.P.Q. 2d 1369 (Fed. Cir. 2005) 4.65
Sanders Brine Shrimp Co., L.C. v Bonneville Artemia Int' l, 970 F. Supp. 892 (D. Utah 1997) 4.39, 4.59
SanDisk Corp. v STMicroelectronics, Inc., 480 F.3d 1372, 1380–81 (Fed. Cir. 2007) 10.88
Sanofi-Synthelabo v Apotex, Inc., 470 F.3d 1368, 1385 (Fed. Cir. 2006) 10.105
Sanofi-Synthelabo v Apotex, Inc., 492 F. Supp. 2d 353, 397 (S.D. N.Y. 2007), aff'd, 530 F.3d 1075 (Fed. Cir. 2009) 13.18
Saxholm AS v Dynal, Inc., 164 F.R.D. 331, 337 (E.D.N.Y. 1996) 10.47
Scherer, Ex Parte, 103 U.S.P.Q. (BNA) 107 (Pat. Off. Bd. App. 1954) 7.116
Schering Corp. v Amgen, Inc., 222 F.3d 1347, 55 U.S.P.Q. 2d 1650 (Fed. Cir. 2000) 4.38
Scholle Corp. v Blackhawk Molding Co., 133 F.3d 1469, 45 U.S.P.Q. 2d 1468 (Fed. Cir. 1998) 7.132
Schwarz Pharma, Inc. v Paddock Labs., Inc., 504 F.3d 1371, 1377 (Fed. Cir. 2007) 4.113, 10.15
SciMed Life Sys., Inc. v Advanced Cardiovascular Sys., Inc., 242 F.3d 1337, 1343–44 (Fed. Cir. 2001) 4.55
Scott Paper Co. v Marcalus Mfg. Co., 326 U.S. 249, 66 S. Ct. 101, 90 L. Ed. 47, 67 U.S.P.Q. 193 (1945) 7.11

Scott v Finney, 34 F.3d 1058, 1061 (Fed. Cir. 1994) 7.93
Scott v Koyama, 281 F.3d 1243 (Fed. Cir. 2002) 7.92
Scripps Clinic & Research Foundation v Genentech, Inc., 927 F.2d 1565, 18 U.S.P.Q. 2d 1001 (Fed. Cir. 1991) 4.43
Seagate Technology, In re, LLC, 497 F.3d 1360 (Fed. Cir. 2007) (*en blanc*), denied, 552 U.S. 1230 (2008) 10.45, 10.49, 13.72, 13.75, 13.76
Sensormatic Electronics Corp. v Tag Co. U.S., 632 F. Supp. 2d 1147 (S.D. Fla. 2008) 13.08, 13.17
Senza-Gel Corp. v Seiffhart, 803 F.2d 661, 231 U.S.P.Q. 363 (Fed. Cir. 1986) 7.127
Serio-US Indus. v Plastic Recovery Techs. Corp., 459 F.3d 1311, 80 U.S.P.Q. 2d 1065 (Fed. Cir. 2006) 4.74
Serrano v Telular Corp., 111 F.3d 1578, 42 U.S.P.Q. 2d 1538 (Fed. Cir. 1997) 4.42, 4.64
Sewall v Walters, 21 F.3d 411, 415, 30 U.S.P.Q. 2d 1356, 1358 (Fed. Cir. 1994) 7.57
Shepler, Ex Parte, 102 O.G. 468 (1903) 1.15
Shockley v Arcan, Inc., 248 F.3d 1349, 58 U.S.P.Q. 2d 1692 (Fed. Cir. 2001) 7.15
Shum v Intel Corp., 629 F.3d 1360, 1366 (Fed. Cir. 2010) 10.23
Siebring v Hansen, 346 F.2d 474, 477 (8th Cir.), cert. denied, 382 U.S. 943 (1965) 13.21
Siemens Med. Solutions USA, Inc. v Saint-Gobain Ceramics & Plastics, Inc., 637 F.3d 1269, 3546, 97 U.S.P.Q. 2d 1897 (Fed. Cir. 2011) 4.88, 4.99
Singh v Brake, 317 F.3d 1334, 1340 (Fed. Cir. 2003) 7.86
Sky Technologies, LLC v SAP AG, 576 F.3d 1374, 1379 (Fed. Cir. 2009) 10.14
Slimford Mfg. Co. v Kinkead Industries, 932 F. 2d 1453, 1458 (Fed. Cir. 1991) 13.50
Slip Track Systems Inc. v Metal Lite, Inc., 159 F.3d 1337, 48 U.S.P.Q. 2d 1055 (Fed. Cir. 1998) 7.34, 7.86
Smith & Nephew, Inc. v Synthes, 466 F. Supp. 2d 978 (W.D. Tenn. 2006), 984–85 . . . . 13.14
Smith Int' l, Inc. v Hughes Tool Co., 718 F.2d 1573, 1579 (Fed. Cir. 1983) 13.25
Smithkline Beecham Corp. v Apotex Corp., 193 F.R.D. 530, 537 (N.D. Ill. 2000) 10.47
SmithKline Beecham Corp. v Apotex Corp, 439, F.3d 1312, 1318 (Fed. Circ. 2006) 7.06
SmithKline Diagnostics, Inc. v Helena Laboratories Corp., No. Civ A. B-83-10, 1989 WL 418791, *6 (E.D. Tex. June 30, 1989) 13.68
Smollar v Cawley, 31 U.S.P.Q. 2d 1506, 1507 (Bd. Pat. App. & Int'f 1993) 7.53
Sneider v Kimberly-Clark Corp., 91 F.R.D. 1, 7 (N.D. Ill. 1980) 10.46
Snellman v Ricoh Co., 862 F. 2d 283 (Fed. Cir. 1988) 13.60
Soilworks, LLC v Midwest Indus. Supply, Inc., 2008 WL 3286975, *3 (D. Ariz. 2008) 10.74
Solomon v Kimberly-Clark Corp., 216 F.3d 1372, 55 U.S.P.Q. 2d 1279 (Fed. Cir. 2000) 7.61
Solomons v United States, 137 U.S. 342, 346, 11 S. Ct. 88, 34 L. Ed. 667, 26 Ct. Cl. 620 (1980) 7.140
Solvay S.A. v Honeywell Int' l, Inc., 622 F.3d 1367 (Fed. Cir. 2010) 7.92
Sony Electronics, Inc. v Guardian Media Technologies, Ltd., 497 F.3d 1271, 1284 (Fed. Cir. 2007) 10.88
Sorensen v ITC, 427 F.3d 1375, 77 U.S.P.Q. 2d 1083 (Fed. Cir. 2005) 4.65
Spalding Sports Worldwide, Inc., In re, 203 F.3d 800, 805–6 (Fed. Cir. 2000) 10.46
Spansion, Inc. v ITC, 629 F.3d 1331 (Fed. Cir. 2010) 13.28
Speedplay, Inc. v Bebop, Inc., 211 F.3d 1245, 1249–50 (Fed. Cir. 2000) 10.14
Sperry v Florida, 373 U.S. 379, 383 (1963) 10.46
Spray Refrigeration Co. v Sea Spray Fishing, Inc., 322 F.2d 34 (9th Cir. 1963) 7.109
Spread Spectrum Screening, LLC v Eastman Kodak Co., No. 10 C 1101, 2010 WL 3516106, *2 (N.D. Ill. September 1, 2010) 10.19
SPX Corp. v Bartec USA, LLC, 247 F.R.D. 516, 525 (E.D. Mich. 2008) 10.49
SRI International v Matsushita Electric Corp. of America, 775 F.2d 1107, 227 U.S.P.Q. 577 (Fed. Cir. 1985) (en banc) 4.20, 4.101
Standard Havens Prods. v Gencor Indus., 27 U.S.P.Q. 2d 1959 (Fed. Cir. 1993) 7.22
Standard Havens Products, Inc. v Gencor Industries, Inc., 897 F.2d 511, 512 (Fed. Cir. 1990), citing Hilton v Braunskill, 481 U.S. 770, 776 (1987) 13.23, 13.24
Standard Oil Co. v Am. Cyanamid Co., 774 F.2d 448, 454 (Fed. Cir. 1985) 4.37
Standard Parts Co. v Peck, 264 U.S. 52 (1924) 7.142
Stanford, 180 L. Ed. 2d., 12 . . . . 7.140

Stanley Works v Haeger Potteries, Inc., 35 F.R.D. 551, 555 (N.D. Ill. 1964) 10.48
Stark v Advanced Magnetics, Inc., 119 F.3d 1551, 43 U.S.P.Q. 2d 1321 (Fed. Cir. 1997) 7.80
State Indus., Inc. v Mor–Flo Indus., Inc., 883 F.2d 1573, 1580 (Fed. Cir. 1989) 13.48, 13.67
State Street Bank & Trust Co. v Signature Financial Group, Inc., 149 F.3d 1368 (Fed. Cir. 1998) 7.74
Steamfeeder, L.L.M. v Sure-Feed Sys., Inc., 175 F.3d 974, 983, 50 U.S.P.Q. 2d 1515 (Fed. Cir. 1999). 4.122, 4.123
Steppan, In re, 394 F.2d 1013, 156 U.S.P.Q. 143 (CCPA 1967). 4.43
Stickle v Heublein, Inc., 590 F. Supp. 630, 635 (W.D. Wis. 1984) 13.82
Stonite Products Co v Melvin Lloyd Co., 315 U.S. 561 (1942). 10.04
Storage Tech. Corp. v Cisco Sys., Inc., 329 F.3d 823, 831 (Fed. Cir. 2003) 4.79
Streck, Inc. v Research & Diagnostic Systems, Inc., 665 F.3d 1269, 1281–84 (Fed. Cir. 2012) 10.88
Studiengesellschaft Kohle v Eastman Kodak Co., 616 F.2d 1315, 206 U.S.P.Q. 577 (5th Cir. 1980) 7.131
Summit Technology, Inc. v Nidek Co., Ltd., 435 F.3d 1371, 1374 (Fed. Cir. 2006) 10.24
Sure Plus Mfg. Co. v Korbin, 719 F.2d 1114, 1118 (11th Cir. 1983) 13.21
Swanson, In re, 540 F.3d 1368, 88 U.S.P.Q. 2d 1196 (Fed. Cir. 2008) 1.20, 7.23
SynQor, Inc v Artesyn Technologies, Inc., 2011 WL 238645, *4 (E.D. Tex. 2011) 13.15
Takeda Chemical Industries, Ltd. v Mylan Laboratories., Inc., Nos. 03-8253, 04-1966, 2007 WL 840368 (S.D. N.Y. March 21, 2007) 13.81
Takeda Chemical Industries, Ltd. v Mylan Laboratories, Inc., 549 F.3d 1381, 1390 (Fed. Cir. 2008) 13.81
Takeda Chemical. Industries, Ltd. v Mylan Laboratories., Inc., 459 F. Supp. 2d 227 (S.D. N.Y. 2006) 13.81
Tate Access Floors, Inc. v Interface Architectural Resources, Inc., 279 F.3d 1357, 61 U.S.P.Q. 2d 1647 (Fed. Cir. 2002) 4.103, 4.122
Tec Air, Inc. v Denso Mfg. Michigan, Inc., 192 F.3d 1353 (Fed. Cir. 1999) 13.69
Tec Air, Inc. v Nippondenso Mfg. U.S.A., Inc., 1996 WL 556739, *4 (N.D. Ill. 1996) 13.50
Technical, Inc. v Memorex Corp., 376 F. Supp. 828, 183 U.S.P.Q. 91 (N.D. Ill. 1974) 7.131
Technology Licensing Corp., In re, 423 F.3d 1286, 1288 (Fed. Cir. 2005) 10.55
Tegal Corp. v Tokyo Electron Am., Inc., 257 F.3d 1331, 1340–41 (Fed. Cir. 2001) 10.55
Tegal Corp. v Tokyo Electron Co., Ltd., 248 F.3d 1376, 58 U.S.P.Q. 2d 1791 (Fed. Cir. 2001) 4.07
Telemac Corp. v US/Intelicom Inc., 185 F. Supp. 2d 1084, 1101–2 (N.D. Cal. 2001) 13.66
Terlep v Brinkmann Corp., 418 F.3d 1379 (Fed. Cir. 2005) 4.67
Teva Pharm. USA, Inc. v Sandoz, Inc., 135 S. Ct. 831, 837, 190 L. Ed. 2d 719, 113 U.S.P.Q. 2d 1269, 83 U.S.L.W. 4055, 90 Fed. R. Serv 3d (Callaghan) 1244 (U.S. 2015). 4.23, 4.71, 10.83
Texas Digital Systems, Inc. v Telegenix, Inc., 308 F.3d 1193 (Fed. Cir. 2002). 4.46
Texas Instruments, Inc. v Int' l Trade Comm'n, 846 F.2d 1369, 1371–72, 6 U.S.P.Q. 2d 1886, 1889 (Fed. Cir. 1988) 4.20, 4.103
Texas Instruments, Inc. v Tessera, Inc., 231 F.3d 1325, 1328 (Fed. Cir. 2000) 10.103
Textile Productions, Inc. v Mead Corp., 134 F.3d 1481, 1484 (Fed. Cir. 1998). 10.15, 10.16, 10.17
Therasense, Inc. v Becton, Dickinson & Co., 649 F.3d 1276, 2011 U.S. App. LEXIS 10590, 99 U.S.P.Q. 2d (BNA) 1065 (Fed. Cir. 2011) 7.69, 7.120, 7.122, 7.123, 7.124
Thorpe, In re, 777 F.2d 695, 698, 227 U.S.P.Q. 964, 966 (Fed. Cir. 1985) 4.43
3M Innovative Properties Co. v Avery Dennison Corp., No. 01-1781, 2006 WL 2735499, *2 (D. Minn. September 25, 2006) 13.14
Tiber Laboratories, LLC v Hawthorn Pharmaceuticals, Inc., 527 F. Supp. 2d 1373 (N.D. Ga. 2007) 10.97
Tivo Inc. v Echostar Corp., 446 F. Supp. 2d 664, 667 (E.39 D. Tex. 2006), aff'd in part, rev'd in part, 516 F.3d 1290 (Fed. Cir. 2008) 13.08, 13.17, 13.25
Tivo Inc. v Echostar Corp., 646 F.3d 869, 98 U.S.P.Q.2d 1413 (Fed. Cir. 2011) 6.30, 13.83
Toro Co. v Deere & Co., 355 F.3d 1313, 1324, 69 U.S.P.Q. 2d 1584 (Fed. Cir. 2004). 4.84
Trading Technologies Int'l, Inc. v eSpeed, Inc., No. 04-C-5312, 2008 WL 4531371, *5 (N.D. Ill. May 22, 2008), aff'd, 595 F.3d 1340 (Fed. Cir. 2010) 4.117, 13.17

Transamerica Life Insurance Co. v Lincoln Nat' l Life Ins. Co., 625 F. Supp. 2d 702 (N.D. Iowa 2009), rev'd on other grounds sub nom., Lincoln Nat. Life Ins. Co. v Transamerica Life Ins. Co., 609 F.3d 1364 (Fed. Cir. 2010) 13.08
Transco Products, Inc. v Performance Contracting, Inc., 821 F. Supp. 537, 550 n.18, 28 U.S.P.Q. 2d 1739, 1748 n.18 (N.D. Ill. 1993), rev'd in part, vacated in part and remanded in part, 38 F.3d 551, 32 U.S.P.Q. 2d 1077 (Fed. Cir. 1994) 7.12
Transcore, LP v Electronic Transaction Consultants Corp., 563 F.3d 1271 (Fed. Cir. 2009)..... 7.145
Translogic Tech., Inc., In re, 504 F.3d 1249, 1251 (Fed. Cir. 2007)......................... 7.22
Translogic Tech., Inc. v Hitachi, Ltd., 250 F. App'x 988 (Fed. Cir. 2007) 7.22
Transocean Offshore Deepwater Drilling, Inc. v Maersk Contrs. USA, Inc., 617 F.3d 1296 (Fed. Cir. 2010) 4.15
Transparent-Wrap Mach. Corp. v Stokes & Smith, 329 U.S. 637, 72 U.S.P.Q. 148 (1947) 7.127
Trans-World Mfg. Corp. v Al Nyman & Sons, 750 F.2d 1552, 1568 (Fed. Cir. 1984) 13.55
Travel Tags, Inc. v UV Color, Inc., 2010 WL 428564, *13–*14 (D. Minn. 2010) 10.97
Tripp v United States, 406 F.2d 1066, 1070, 186 Ct. Cl. 872, 157 U.S.P.Q. 90, 161 U.S.P.Q. 115 (1969) 7.144
TruePosition, Inc. v Andrew Corp., 568 F. Supp. 2d 500, 533 (D. Del. 2008), amended in part, 2009 WL 192470 (D. Del. January 27, 2009), aff'd, 389 Fed. Appx. 1000 (Fed. Cir. 2010) 13.17
Trussell Mfg. Co. v Wilson-Jones Co., 50 F.2d 1027, 10 U.S.P.Q. 47 (2d Cir. 1931) 7.134
TS Tech USA Corp., In re, 551 F.3d 1315, 1320–21 (Fed. Cir. 2008) 10.07
TWM Manufacturing Co. Inc. v Dura Corp., 789 F.2d 895, 900 (Fed. Cir. 1986)........... 13.50
Tyco Healthcare Group LP v E-Z-EM, Inc., 2010 WL 2079920, *2+ (E.D. Tex. 2010) 10.49
Uniloc USA, Inc. v Microsoft Corp., 632 F. 3d 1292 (Fed. Cir. 2011)..................... 13.70
Unique Concepts, Inc. v Brown, 939 F.2d 1558, 19 U.S.P.Q. 2d 1500 (Fed. Cir. 1991)......... 4.58
United States Gypsum v National Gypsum, 352 U.S. 457, 112 U.S.P.Q. 340 (1957).......... 7.128
United States v Univis Lens Co., 316 U.S. 241, 53 U.S.P.Q. 404 (1942) 7.136
Universal Electronics, Inc. v Zenith Electronics Corp., 846 F. Supp. 641, 30 U.S.P.Q. 2d 1853 (N.D. Ill. 1994) 7.139
University of California v Synbiotics Corp., 29 U.S.P.Q. 2d 1463 (S.D. Calif. 1993) 7.85
University of Colorado Foundation, Inc. v American Cyanamid Co., 196 F.3d 1366, 52 U.S.P.Q. 2d 1801 (Fed. Cir. 1999) 7.80
University of Texas v Camenisch, 451 U.S. 390, 395 (1981) 10.92
USM Corp. v SPS Technologies, Inc., 694 F.2d 505, 216 U.S.P.Q. 959 (7th Cir. 1982)........ 7.127
Vaupel Textilmaschinen KG v Meccanica Euro Italia S.P.A., 944 F.2d 870, 873–76 (Fed. Cir. 1991) 10.14
VE Holding Corp. v Johnson Gas Appliance Co., 917 F.2d 1574, 1575, cert. denied, 111 S.Ct. 1315 (1991) 10.03, 10.04
Vehicular Technologies Corp. v Titan Wheel International, Inc., 212 F.3d 1377, 1380, 54 U.S.P.Q. 2d 1841, 1843 (Fed. Cir. 2000) 4.57
Vehicular Technologies Corp. v Titan Wheel Intern., Inc., 141 F.3d 1084, 1091–93 (Fed. Cir. 1998) 10.95
Verizon Services Corp. v Vonage Holdings Corp., 503 F.3d 1295 (Fed. Cir. 2007)........... 13.08
Versata Software, Inc. v Callidus Software, Inc., 771 F.3d 1368, 112 U.S.P.Q. 2d 1838 (Fed. Cir. 2014) 16.23
Virginia Panel Corp. v MAC Panel Corp., 133 F.3d 860, 45 U.S.P.Q. 2d 1225 (Fed. Cir. 1997) 7.127
Virnetx, Inc. v Cisco Systems, Inc., 767 F.3d 1308, 1326 (Fed. Cir. 2014) 13.70
Vitronics Corp. v Conceptronic, Inc., 90 F.3d 1576, 39 U.S.P.Q. 2d 1573 (Fed. Cir. 1996) 4.45, 4.53, 4.58, 4.64, 4.69
Vivid Technologies, Inc. v American Science & Engineering, Inc., 200 F.3d 795, 803, 53 U.S.P.Q. 2d 1289, 1394 (Fed. Cir. 1999) 4.24, 4.30
VLT Corp. v Unitrode Corp., 194 F.R.D. 8, 14–16 (D. Mass. 2000) 10.47
Voda v Cordis Corp 476 F.3d 887 (Fed. Cir. 2007)..................................... 10.12
Voda v Cordis Corp., 2004 WL 3392022, *1 (W.D. Okla. 2004)......................... 10.12
Voda v Cordis Corp., F.3d 1311, 1329 (Fed. Cir. 2008)................................ 13.13

Volkswagen of Am., Inc., In re, 545 F.3d 304, 315 (5th Cir. 2008) (en banc). 10.07
Volterra Semiconductor Corp. v Primarion, Inc., 2009 WL 6357679, *41 (N.D. Cal. 2009). . . . 10.94
Wald v Mudhopper Oilfield Services, Inc., No. CIV-04-1693, 2006 WL 2128851 (W.D. Okla. July 27, 2006). 13.07
Wands, In re, 858 F.2d 731, 737 (Fed. Circ. 1988) 8.120
Wang Laboratories, Inc. v Mitsubishi Electronics America, Inc., 103 F.3d 1571, 41 U.S.P.Q. 2d 1263 (Fed. Cir. 1997) 7.148
Wang Labs., Inc. v America Online, Inc., 197 F.3d 1377, 53 U.S.P.Q. 2d 1161 (Fed. Cir. 1999) 4.74
Warner Chilcott Laboratories Ireland, Ltd. v Mylan Pharmaceuticals, Inc., 2011 WL 6144301, *5 (Fed. Cir. 2011) 10.102
Warner-Jenkinson Co. v Hilton Davis Chem. Co., 520 U.S. 17, 117 S. Ct. 1040, 137 L. Ed. 2d 146, 41 U.S.P.Q. 2d 1865 (U.S. 1997). . . . 1.22, 4.19, 4.21, 4.23, 4.28, 4.29, 4.38, 4.83, 4.92, 4.93, 4.95, 4.98, 4.102, 4.105, 4.106, 4.110, 4.115, 4.116, 6.73, 7.04, 7.05
Warner-Lambert Co. v Teva Pharms. USA, Inc., 418 F.3d 1326, 75 U.S.P.Q. 2d 1865 (Fed. Cir. 2005) 4.74
Watts v XL Sys., 232 F.3d 877, 56 U.S.P.Q. 2d 1836 (Fed. Cir. 2000). 4.63
Waymark Corp. v Porta Systems Corp., 334 F.3d 1358, 1364 (Fed. Cir. 2003) 10.17
Weeks Marine, Inc. v TDM America, LLC, 2011 WL 6217799, *5–*6 (D. N.J. 2011) 10.96
Welker Bearing Co. v PHD, Inc., 550 F.3d 1090, 89 U.S.P.Q. 2d 1289 (Fed. Cir. 2008) 4.90
Welsbach Light Co. v Union Incandescent Light Co., 101 F.131, 131 (2d Cir. 1900). 4.02
Western Elec. Co. v Stewart-Warner Corp., 631 F.2d 333, 338, 208 U.S.P.Q. 183, 188 (4th Cir. 1980) 7.127
Westinghouse Electric & Mfg. Co. v Formica Insulation Co., 266 U.S. 342 (1924) 4.101
Westvaco Corp. v Int' l Paper Co., 991 F.2d 735, 26 U.S.P.Q. 2d 1353 (Fed. Cir. 1993) 7.14, 7.17, 7.66
WiAV Solutions, LLC v Motorola, Inc., 631 F.3d 1257, 1265 (Fed. Cir. 2010) 10.16
Wiegand v Dover Mfg. Co., 292 F. 255 (N.D. Ohio 1923) 7.144
Wilbur Ellis Co. v Kuther, 377 U.S. 422, 141 U.S.P.Q. 703 (1964). 7.139
Willemijn Houdstermaatschaapij BV v Apollo Computer Inc., 707 F. Supp. 1429 (D. Del. 1989). 10.47
Williamson v Citrix Online, LLC, 2015 U.S. App. LEXIS 10082, 115 U.S.P.Q.2D 1105 (Fed. Cir. June 16, 2015). 4.41
Wilson Sporting Goods Co. v David Geoffrey & Associates, 904 F.2d 677, 14 U.S.P.Q. 2d 1942 (Fed. Cir. 1990) 4.24, 4.97, 4.119, 4.123, 6.74
Wilson Sporting Goods Co. v Hillerich & Bradsby Co., 442 F.3d 1322, 1326, 78 U.S.P.Q. 2d 1382 (Fed. Cir. 2006). 4.25
Wilton v Seven Falls Co., 515 U.S. 277, 286–88 (1995) 10.89
Winans v Denmead, 56 U.S. 330, 15 How. 330, 14 L. Ed. 717(1854) 1.13, 4.19
Windsurfing Int' l v AMF, Inc., 782 F. 2d 995, 1003 (Fed. Cir. 1986). 13.14
Wireless Agents, LLC v T-Mobile, USA, Inc., 2006 WL 1540587 (N.D. Tex. 2006) 10.97
W.L. Gore & Assocs., Inc. v Carlisle Corp., 529 F.2d 614, 622, 189 U.S.P.Q. 129, 135–36 (3d Cir. 1976) 7.126
Woodcock v Parker, 30 F. Cas. 491, 1813 U.S. App. LEXIS 375, 1 Gall. 438 (C.C.D. Mass. 1813) 1.11
Wright, In Re, 999 F.2d 1557 (Fed. Cir. 1993) 4.21
York Prods. v Central Tractor Farm & Family Ctr., 99 F.3d 1568, 40 U.S.P.Q. 2d (BNA) 1619 (Fed. Cir. 1996). 4.64
z4 Techs., Inc. v Microsoft Corp., 434 F. Supp. 2d 437, 440 (E.D. Tex. 2006) . . . 13.08, 13.11, 13.15
Zenith Electronics Corp. v Exzec, Inc., 182 F.3d 1340, 1355 (Fed. Cir. 1999) 10.74
Zenith Radio Corp. v Hazeltine Research, Inc., 395 U.S. 100, 140, 161 U.S.P.Q. 577, 593 (1969). 7.126
Zenith Radio Corp. v Radio Corp. of America, 121 F. Supp. 792, 793 (D. Del. 1954) 10.46
Zimmer Holdings, Inc., In re, 609 F.3d 1378, 1381 (Fed. Cir. 2010) 10.08
Zond, Inc. v Fujitsu Semiconductor, Ltd., 990 F. Supp. 2d 50, 54 (D. Mass. 2014). 10.30

TABLE OF LEGISLATION

EUROPEAN UNION

Conventions and Treaties

Agreement on a Unified Patent Court (2013C 175/01) (UPC Agreement) 1.06, 2.44
Art 6(2) 2.46
Art 6(3) 2.45
Art 6(5) 2.45
Art 8(3) 2.45
Art 8(5) 2.45
Art 9 . . . . 2.47
Art 25 . . . . 5.01
Art 25(a) 5.02
Art 25(b) 5.02
Art 26 . . . . 5.25
Art 27 . . . . 5.51
Art 32(1)(a) 2.54
Art 32(d)–(e) 2.46
Art 33(3) 8.37
Art 33(4) 2.54
Art 36(3) 2.52
Art 48 . . . . 2.50
Art 48(2) 2.50
Art 69 . . . . 2.52
Art 71 . . . . 2.53
Agreement relating to Community Patents 89/695/EEC (Luxembourg, December 15, 1989), OJ L 401/1 (December 30, 1989)
Art 25 . . . . 5.01
Art 26 . . . . 5.25
Community Patent Convention (CPC), 1976 (never in force) 1.05, 1.41
Art 29 . . . . 5.01
Art 30 . . . . 5.25
Art 31 . . . . 5.31
Convention (EC) on Jurisdiction and the Enforcement of Judgments in Civil and Commercial Matters, 1968 . . . . 11.09
Convention for the European Patent for the Common Market 76/76/EEC (Luxembourg, December 15, 1975) . . . 1.05
Convention on International Civil Aviation
Art 27 . . . . 5.55
Convention on the Grant of European Patents, Munich, 1973 *see* European Patent Convention (EPC), 1973 (revised November 2000)
Convention on the Unification of Certain Points of Substantive Law on Patents for Inventions, 1963
Art 8(3) 5.61
European Patent Convention (EPC), 1973 (revised November 2000) 1.04, 1.05, 1.41, 2.24, 2.26, 3.04, 4.34, 7.14, 7.88, 8.30, 16.03
Art 52(2) 8.66, 8.67
Art 52(3) 7.71, 8.66
Art 52(4) (old EPC 1973) 8.104
Arts 52–57 .8.56, 8.64
Art 53 . . . . .8.68, 8.69, 8.70, 8.71, 8.72
Art 53(c) (new EPC 2000) 8.104
Art 54 . . . . 8.74–8.86
Art 54(2) 7.87
Art 54(3) 8.76, 8.83, 8.86, 8.132, 8.155
Art 54(4) 8.69, 8.78, 8.154
Art 54(5) 8.69, 8.78, 8.154
Art 55 . . . . 8.74
Art 56 . . . . 8.87–8.98, 8.109
Art 57 . . . .8.99–8.112, 8.67, 8.100, 8.102, 8.109
Art 67 . . . . 8.54
Art 67(4) 8.54
Art 69 . . . . 4.34, 5.61, 5.72, 5.80, 5.83, 5.86, 5.126, 6.38
Art 70(1) 5.61
Art 76(1) 8.56
Art 83 . . . . 8.56, 8.62, 8.64, 8.67, 8.98, 8.99, 8.109, 8.119, 8.123, 16.18
Art 84 . . . . 8.34, 8.56, 8.58–8.62, 8.98, 8.118
Art 85 . . . . 5.81
Art 87(1) 8.84
Art 88(2) 8.84
Art 88(3) 8.84
Art 97(2) 8.156
Art 99 . . . . 8.17, 8.19
Art 100 . . . . 8.19, 8.137
Art 105 . . . . 8.22, 8.63
Art 105a 5.86, 8.30, 8.33
Art 105a(2) 8.33
Art 105b(3) 8.33
Art 106 . . . . 8.34
Art 108 . . . . 8.25
Art 112 . . . . 8.29
Art 112(1)(a) 8.118
Art 112a 8.29
Art 114(2) 8.23
Art 115 . . . . .8.10, 8.55, 8.56

Art 116 . . . . 8.21
Art 117 . . . . 8.23
Art 123 . . . . 8.124, 8.125
Art 123(2) 8.34, 8.56, 8.64, 8.124, 8.125, 8.126, 8.132, 8.135
Art 123(3) 8.34, 8.125, 8.134, 8.135
Art 125 . . . . 8.156
Art 133(2) 8.20
Art 138 . . . . 8.39, 8.140
Art 153(5) 8.76
Implementing Regulations
r 14(1) 8.19
rs 26–29 . . . . 8.105
r 29(3) 8.105
r 42(1)(e) 8.109
r 42(1)(f) 8.102
r 43(1) 5.102
r 43(7) 5.106
r 79 . . . . 8.21
r 81 . . . . 8.21
r 89 . . . . 8.22
r 116(1) 8.21
Protocol on Interpretation of Art 69 . . . . 4.17, 5.86
Art 1 . . . . 4.20, 5.61, 5.64, 5.65, 5.99
Art 2 . . . . 4.20, 5.62, 5.65, 5.110
European Patent Litigation Agreement (EPLA), Draft
Art 41(4) 8.02
Lugano Jurisdiction and Enforcement Convention 11.09
Preliminary Draft Convention on a European Patent Drafted by the Patent Working Group (1962) 1.40
Treaty Establishing the European Economic Community (Treaty of Rome) 1957 (EEC Treaty) 2.56
Art 36 . . . . 1.40
Treaty on European Union (TEU) 8.23
Treaty on the Functioning of the European Union (TFEU)
Art 101 . . . . 8.23
Art 102 . . . . 8.160
Unitary Patent Protection Agreement *see under* Regulations

Directives

First Council Directive 89/104/EEC of 21 December 1988 to approximate the laws of the Member States relating to trademarks 1.45
Council Directive 93/98/EEC of 29 October 1993 harmonizing the term of protection of copyright and certain related rights 1.45
Directive 98/44/EC of the European Parliament and of the Council of 6 July 1998 on the legal protection of biotechnological inventions (Biotechnology Directive) 1.05, 1.45, 5.21, 5.23, 5.24, 8.111
Art 5 . . . . 8.105
Art 9 . . . . 8.112
Art 10 . . . . 5.51
Recital 23 . . . . 8.105
Recital 24 . . . . 8.107
Directive 98/71/EC of the European Parliament and of the Council of 13 October 1998 on the legal protection of designs 1.45
Brussels-I-Directive 44/2001 EC 11.09
Art 2 . . . . 11.158
Art 5(3) 11.158
Art 22(4) 11.159, 11.160
Art 27 . . . . 11.119, 11.121, 11.122, 11.136
Art 31 . . . . 11.158, 11.159
Directive 2001/29/EC of the European Parliament and of the Council of 22 May 2001 on the harmonization of certain aspects of copyright and related rights in the information society (Information Society Directive/EU Copyright Directive) 1.45
Directive 2001/83/EC [2001] OJ EC L311/67 on the Community Code for medicinal products for human use 1.38
Directive 2004/48/EC of the European Parliament and of the Council of 29 April 2004 on the enforcement of intellectual property rights (Enforcement Directive) 1.05, 1.45, 11.49, 14.38
Directive 2009/24/EC on the legal protection of computer programs
Art 5 . . . . 5.51
Art 6 . . . . 5.51

Regulations

Council Regulation (EEC) No. 1768/92 of June 18, 1992 concerning the creation of a supplementary protection certificate for medicinal products 1.44, 5.57
Council Regulation (EC) No. 2100/94 of July 27, 1994 on Community plant variety rights 1.44
Council Regulation (EC) No. 1610/96 concerning the creation of a supplemental protection certificate for plant protection products 5.57

Council Regulation (EC) No. 6/2002 of December 12, 2001 on Community designs 1.44
Council Regulation (EC) No. 1383/2003 Concerning Customs Action against Goods Suspected of Infringing Certain Intellectual Property Rights and the Measures to Be Taken against Goods Found to Have Infringed Such Rights [2003] OJ L 196/7. . . . . 2.57, 11.90, 11.91
Art 3(1) 11.80
Art 4(1) 11.88
Art 5(1) 11.79, 11.80
Art 5(4) 11.79
Art 5(7) 11.82
Art 8(1) 11.82
Art 8(3) 11.82
Art 9(1) 11.86
Art 9(2) 11.87
Art 9(3) 11.87
Art 10 . . . . 11.89
Art 11(1) 11.89, 11.93, 11.94
Art 11(2) 11.93
Art 13 . . . . 11.93
Art 13(1) 11.89
Art 13(1)2 . . . . 11.89
Art 13(2) 11.89
Art 14(1) 11.95
Art 14(2) 11.95
Council Regulation (EC) No. 207/2009 of February 26, 2009 on the Community Trademark 1.43
Council Regulation (EC) No. 469/2009 concerning the creation of a supplementary protection certificate for medical products 5.57
Council Regulation 1260/[2012] OJ EU L 361/89, December 31, 2012 (Unitary Patent Protection Agreement)
Art 4 . . . . 2.44
Art 9 . . . . 2.44
Recital 5 . . . . 2.44
Recital 26 . . . . 2.44
Regulation (EU) No. 1215/2012 of the European Parliament and of the Council of 12 December 2012 on jurisdiction and the recognition and enforcement of judgments in civil and commercial matters (Brussels I, revised) 1.46
Regulation on Implementing Enhanced Cooperation in the Area of the Creation of Unitary Patent Protection, Regulation 1257/[2012] OJ EU L 361/1, December 31, 2012. . . . . .1.06, 2.43
Preliminary Set of Provisions for Rules of Procedure. 2.44
r 10 . . . . 2.49
r 178 . . . . 2.48
Rules of Procedure of the Board of Appeals of the European Patent Office (RPAB)
Art 12 . . . . 8.26
Art 12(4) 8.26
Art 13(1) 8.26
Art 13(3) 8.26
Art 16 . . . . 8.28
Art 22 . . . . 8.29

INTERNATIONAL INSTRUMENTS

Agreement on Trade-related Aspects of Intellectual Property Rights (TRIPS), 1995 . . . . 1.02, 1.41, 1.56, 6.04, 7.92, 10.12, 16.01
Art 28 . . . . 3.01
Art 31 . . . . 16.56
Marrakesh Agreement Establishing the World Trade Organization, 1994 . . . . . 1.02
Annex 1C 6.04, 16.56
Paris Convention for the Protection of Industrial Property (Paris Convention), 1993 . . . . 1.01, 1.02, 1.03, 1.53, 4.10
Art 5 . . . . 5.55
Art 5A(4) 16.56
Patent Cooperation Treaty (PCT), 1970 . . . 1.03, 1.41, 1.56, 4.10, 10.12, 16.01
ss 801–805 . . . . 8.55
Patent Law Treaty (PLT), 2000 . . . . . .1.03, 1.41
Strasbourg Patent Convention, 1963 . . . . . . 1.41
Treaty between United States and Japan (January 13, 1897) 1.53
Treaty of Shipping and Trade, 1896 . . . . 1.53

NATIONAL

Austria

Patent Act
s 101b 8.55
s 163(5) 5.86

Denmark

Royal Danish Decree (November 19, 1897) 1.53

Germany

IntPatÜG
Art II, s 8 . . . . 8.156
Act regarding Patenting Costs (PatKostG)
s 2(1) 8.06, 8.13
s 3(1) 8.06

Collective wage agreement for the Reich for academically skilled employees in the chemical industry (*Reichstarifvertrag für die akademisch gebildeten Angestellten der chemischen Industrie*) 1920 . . . 1.34
Constitutional Law (*Grundgesetz*, GG)
Art 14 . . . 8.02
Art 19(4) . . . 2.31
Art 20(3) . . . 8.02
Art 22(3) . . . 8.02
Court Constitution Act (*Gerichtsverfassungsgesetz*, GVG)
s 75 . . . 11.02
s 119(1) No. 2 . . . 11.02
s 122(1) . . . 11.02
Court Fees Act (*Gerichtskostengesetz*)
s 34(1) . . . 11.24
s 39(2) . . . 11.24
s 40 . . . 11.23
s 51 . . . 11.23
Employees' Invention Law (*Gesetz über Arbeitnehmererfindungen*, ArbnErfG) 1957 . . . 1.34, 1.38
s 6 . . . 8.144
s 7 . . . 8.144
Federal Lawyer's Act (*Bundesrechtsanwaltsordnung*)
s 49b(1)1 . . . 11.34
German Code of Civil Procedure (BGB) . . . 6.74, 8.38
ss 13–35 . . . 11.04
s 17 . . . 11.04, 11.09
s 21 . . . 11.04, 11.09
s 32 . . . 11.04, 11.05, 11.09
s 35 . . . 11.05
s 78 . . . 11.37
s 91 . . . 16.58
s 93 . . . 11.106
s 114 et seq . . . 11.28
s 142 . . . 11.75
s 144 . . . 11.75
s 157 . . . 8.147
s 195 . . . 14.30
s 199 . . . 14.30
s 226 . . . 16.57
s 242 . . . 8.147, 14.38, 14.43
s 249 . . . 14.14, 14.17
s 252 . . . 14.14, 14.17
s 253 . . . 11.37, 11.38
s 256(1) . . . 11.116
s 259 . . . 14.38, 14.43
s 265(2) . . . 11.18
s 276(1)1 . . . 11.40
s 286 . . . 14.27
s 287 . . . 14.19, 14.23
s 288 . . . 14.27
s 291 . . . 14.27
s 331 . . . 11.40
s 331(3) . . . 11.40
s 432 . . . 11.15
s 485 et seq . . . 11.61, 11.70
s 491(2) . . . 11.70
s 494a . . . 11.70
s 494a(2) . . . 11.70
s 511 . . . 11.43
s 517 . . . 11.43
s 531(2) . . . 11.43
s 543 . . . 11.45
s 567 . . . 8.14, 11.69
s 580(6) . . . 11.164
s 582 . . . 11.166
s 667 . . . 14.20
s 687(2) . . . 14.20
s 707 . . . 11.147, 14.09
s 709 . . . 14.08
s 712 . . . 14.10
s 719 . . . 14.09
s 767 . . . 11.161, 11.162, 14.09
s 769 . . . 11.163
s 812(1) . . . 14.30
s 818(2) . . . 14.30
s 830(1) . . . 5.19
s 830(2) . . . 5.25
s 854 . . . 14.30
s 916 et seq . . . 11.126
s 923 . . . 11.126
s 924(3)2 . . . 11.147
s 926 . . . 11.160
s 926(2) . . . 11.70
s 929(2) . . . 11.146
s 935 . . . 11.131
s 936 . . . 11.147
s 940 . . . 11.131
s 945 . . . 11.148
s 1011 . . . 11.15
German Enforcement Act (BGBI I, 2008, 1191) . . . 14.12
German Patent Act (*Patentgesetz*, PatG, amended up to July 31 2009) . . . 1.29, 4.34, 5.09, 5.10, 5.13, 5.22, 5.26, 6.02, 6.05, 6.08, 6.23, 6.71, 7.14
pre-1981 . . . 4.27
s 1(3) . . . 8.66
ss 1–5 . . . 8.111
s 1a . . . 8.111
s 1a(1) . . . 5.23
s 2a . . . 8.70, 8.111
s 2a(1) . . . 5.55
s 2a(3) . . . 5.22
s 6 . . . 8.144
s 6 (Patent Act of 1968) . . . 5.01

s 7(2) 8.11
s 8 . . . . . 1.31, 8.143
s 9 . . . . . 5.01, 5.02, 5.04, 5.06, 5.07, 5.08, 5.10, 5.12, 6.01, 8.145, 11.08
s 9(1)–(3) 5.03
s 9(2) 6.07
s 9(3) 4.02
s 9a 5.21
s 9a(1) 5.23
s 9a(2) 5.23
s 9a(3) 5.23
s 9a–c 5.22
s 9c 5.51
s 10 . . . . . 5.19, 5.25, 5.27, 5.28, 5.31, 5.36, 8.145
s 10(1) 5.26
s 10(2) 5.26, 5.36, 6.19
s 10(3) 5.26, 5.28, 5.33, 6.15
s 11 . . . . . 5.38, 5.51, 5.52, 5.53, 5.54, 5.55
s 12 . . . . . 8.158
s 14 . . . . . 5.61, 5.72, 5.80, 5.83, 5.86, 5.126, 6.38
s 15 . . . . . 11.16
s 16 . . . . . 5.56
s 16a 5.57
s 16a(1) 5.58
s 20(3)2 . . . . . 11.13
s 21 . . . . . 8.111, 8.115
s 21(1) 8.11, 8.63, 8.64, 8.136, 8.139
s 22 . . . . . 8.39, 8.140
s 25(1) 8.06
s 27 . . . . . 8.07
s 30(3)2 . . . . . 11.12
s 33 . . . . . 8.54
s 33(1) 8.54
s 34(4) 8.123
s 35 . . . . . 2.23
s 36(2) 5.81
s 40 . . . . . 8.155
s 43(3) 8.10, 8.15, 8.55
s 49a(4) 8.09
s 58(1) 8.02
s 59(1) 8.05
s 59(2) 8.09, 8.63
s 61(1) 8.12
s 64 . . . . . 8.30, 8.32
s 64(1) 8.31
s 64(2) 8.30
s 64(3) 8.30, 8.31
s 73 . . . . . 8.13, 8.31
ss 73–80 . . . . . 8.14
s 81(2) 8.09, 8.22, 8.37
ss 81–84 . . . . . 8.38
s 82 . . . . . 8.40
s 83 . . . . . 8.40, 8.43
s 83(4) 8.41, 8.42
s 116 . . . . . 8.43
s 117 . . . . . 8.41
s 122(6) 8.159
s 123(5) 8.159
s 123(6) 8.159
s 126 . . . . . 8.06
s 126a 8.06
s 139 . . . . . 11.10, 11.12, 11.16, 11.20, 14.07, 14.30, 14.32
s 139(2) 14.14
s 140(a)(1) 14.33, 14.34
s 140(a)(3) 14.33
s 140a(4) 14.32
s 140(b) 14.38, 14.39
s 140(b)(2) 14.40
s 140(b)(3) 14.40, 14.42
s 140(b)(4) 14.41
s 140(c) 11.49, 11.51, 11.52, 11.59, 11.73, 14.42
s 140c(2) 11.49, 11.54
s 140c(5) 11.50
s 142a 2.58, 11.81, 11.82, 11.90, 11.91
s 142a(1) 11.90
s 142a(3) 11.92
s 142a(4) 11.92
s 142a(4)2 . . . . . 11.92
s 142a(4)3 . . . . . 11.92
s 142b 2.58
s 142b(3) 11.93
s 142b(4) 11.93
s 142b(6)1 . . . . . 11.82
s 143 . . . . . 2.33, 11.01, 11.03, 11.05, 11.33
s 143(1) 11.01
s 143(2) 2.33
s 144 . . . . . 11.28
s 145 . . . . . 8.154
s 242 . . . . . 14.07
ss 110–121 . . . . . 2.41
German Plant Variety Protection Act
s 10a(1) 5.54
Göring-Speer decree (*Göring-Speer-Verordnung*) 1942 . . . . . 1.34
Judicature Act (*Gerichtsverfassungsgesetz*, GVG)
s 119 . . . . . 2.36
s 184 . . . . . 2.28
Lawyer's Remuneration Act (*Rechtsanwaltsverguetungsgesetz*) 11.32, 11.35, 11.156
s 2 . . . . . 11.31, 11.34
s 3a 11.31
Regulation of the Procedure in Patent Matters before the German Patent and Trademark office
s 9(2) 5.102

Japan

Basic Law on Intellectual Property (Chiteki Zaisan Kihonhō, Law No. 122 of 2002) . . . 1.58, 2.70
Court Act (Saibanshohō, Law No. 59 of 1947)
Art 10 . . . 2.68
Art 41 . . . 2.69
Dajó Ordinance No. 105 of 1872 . . . 1.51
Enforcement Ordinance of the Patent Act, Ordinance of MITI No. 10 of March 8, 1960, as last amended by Ordinance of METI No. 35 of 2010 . . . 6.42
Independent Administrative Corporations Law (Law No. 108/2003) . . . 12.09, 12.26
Japanese Act on Costs of Civil Procedure (Law No. 40 of 1971)
s 4 . . . 12.18
s 61 . . . 12.19
Japanese Act on the Application of Laws (Law No. 10 of 1898)
s 11 . . . 12.06
s 11(1) . . . 12.06
s 11(2) . . . 12.06, 12.07
s 33 . . . 12.05
Japanese Civil Code (Law No. 89 of 1896) . . . 16.57
s 1 . . . 16.33
s 167(1) . . . 15.25
s 703 . . . 15.25
s 709 . . . 12.15, 12.51, 12.71, 15.06, 15.07, 15.09, 15.10
s 719 . . . 6.11, 12.07
Japanese Civil Provisional Remedies Act (Law No. 91 of 1989) . . . 12.61
s 12 . . . 12.62
s 23(2) . . . 12.66
s 23(4) . . . 12.68
Japanese Code of Civil Procedure (Law No. 109 of 1996) . . . 1.57, 2.62, 6.68
s 1 . . . 16.33
s 3-3(3) . . . 12.02
s 3-3(8) . . . 12.02
s 4 . . . 12.02
s 5 . . . 12.02
s 6 . . . 12.01
s 6(1) . . . 2.62
s 6-1(1) . . . 12.01
s 6-1(2) . . . 12.01
s 6(3) . . . 2.64
s 8 . . . 12.18
s 9 . . . 12.18
s 27(1)ii . . . 12.13
s 34-2 . . . 2.66
s 52-5(6) . . . 12.29
s 62 . . . 12.19
s 92-2 . . . 12.11
s 92-2–92-7 . . . 2.67
s 132-2 . . . 12.29
s 132-4 . . . 12.29
s 132-4(1)i . . . 12.29
s 132-4(1)ii . . . 12.29
s 132-4(1)iii . . . 12.29
s 132-4(1)iv . . . 12.29, 12.30
s 157 . . . 9.22, 9.26
s 163 . . . 12.31
s 167(1) . . . 15.25
s 197(1)iii . . . 12.36
s 220 . . . 12.26
s 220(iv)(a)–(d) . . . 12.37
s 220iv(b) . . . 12.36
s 220iv(c) . . . 12.36
s 223(6) . . . 12.37
s 234 . . . 12.33
s 235 . . . 12.33
s 247 . . . 12.32
s 312 . . . 2.68
s 318 . . . 2.68
s 338(1)viii . . . 9.27
s 404 . . . 15.11
Japanese Companies Act (Law No. 86 of 2005)
s 429 . . . 12.16
Japanese Customs Act (Law No. 61 of 1954)
s 69-2 . . . 2.72, 12.44
s 69-6 . . . 12.47
s 69-11 . . . 2.73, 12.44
s 69-11(2) . . . 12.47
s 69-15(1) . . . 12.47
s 69-15(2) . . . 12.47
s 69-16(1) . . . 12.47
s 69-16(2) . . . 12.47
s 69-17(1) . . . 12.47
s 69-17(4) . . . 12.47
s 89 . . . 12.47
Japanese Patent Act (Law No. 121 of 1959) . . . 4.34, 6.06, 6.35, 6.50, 7.14, 7.88, 8.30
Act of 1885 . . . 2.70
Act of 1888 . . . 1.53
Act of 1899 (Law No. 36 of 1899) . . . 1.53
Art 29 . . . 2.60
Act of 1921 (Law No. 96 of 1921) . . . 1.54
Act of 1948 (Law No. 172 of 1948) . . . 1.55
Act of 1959 (Law No. 121 of 1959) . . . 1.56
Act of 1975 (Law No. 46 of 1975) . . . 1.56
Act of 1978 (Law No. 30 of 1978) . . . 1.56
Act of 1987 (Law No. 27 of 1987) . . . 1.56
Act of 1990 (Law No. 30 of 1990) . . . 1.56
s 2(1) . . . 7.71, 9.32
s 2(3) . . . 6.01, 12.15
s 2(3) i . . . 6.02, 6.07

s 2(3) iii . . . 6.07, 6.23
s 2(3)(i) . . . 6.01
s 2(3)(ii) . . . 6.01
s 2(3)(iii) . . . 6.01
s 17-2(3) . . . 9.28
s 17-2(4) . . . 9.28
s 25 . . . 9.28, 9.34
s 29 . . . 7.87, 9.37
s 29(1) . . . 9.28, 9.47
s 29-2 . . . 7.88
s 29(2) . . . 9.28
s 29-2 . . . 9.28, 9.33
s 30 . . . 9.37
s 32 . . . 9.28
s 35 . . . 9.51
s 35(1) . . . 9.47, 9.48, 9.49
s 35(2) . . . 9.47, 9.48
s 35(3) . . . 9.48
s 35(4) . . . 9.48
s 36(1) . . . 16.18
s 36(4) . . . 6.48, 9.28
s 36(4)(1) . . . 6.42
s 36(5) . . . 6.39
s 36(6) i . . . 6.48, 6.54
s 36(6) ii . . . 6.48, 6.52
s 36(6)I, ii, and iii . . . 9.28
s 36(6)iv . . . 9.28
s 39 i-iv . . . 9.28
s 49 ii . . . 9.34
s 49 vii . . . 9.28, 9.34
s 49iii . . . 9.28
s 49vii . . . 9.34
s 67(1) . . . 6.20
s 67(2) . . . 6.20
s 67-3 . . . 6.20
s 68 . . . 6.01, 6.02, 9.38
s 69(1) . . . 9.38
s 69(2) . . . 9.38
s 69(3) . . . 9.38
s 70 . . . 4.34
s 70(1) . . . 6.25, 6.38
s 70(2) . . . 6.54
s 72 . . . 6.71
s 74 . . . 9.37
s 77 . . . 9.50
s 78 . . . 9.50
s 79 . . . 9.42, 9.51
s 80 . . . 9.51
s 81 . . . 9.51
s 83 . . . 9.51
s 92 . . . 6.72, 9.51
s 93 . . . 9.51
s 94(1) . . . 9.46, 9.49
s 94(2) . . . 9.46, 9.49
s 98(1) ii . . . 9.50
s 99 . . . 9.50
s 99(3) . . . 9.46
s 100 . . . 15.01, 15.26
s 100(2) . . . 15.02
s 101 . . . 6.10, 6.13, 12.15
s 101 iii . . . 6.05
s 101 vi . . . 6.05
s 101(1) i . . . 6.13, 6.14
s 101(1) ii . . . 6.13, 6.16
s 101(1) iii . . . 6.13
s 101(1) iv . . . 6.13, 6.14
s 101(1) v . . . 6.13, 6.16
s 101(1) vi . . . 6.13
s 102 . . . 15.06, 15.09, 15.10, 15.11, 15.20, 15.23, 15.25
s 102(1) . . . 15.13
s 102(3) . . . 15.08, 15.20, 15.22
s 102(4) . . . 15.08
s 103 . . . 15.07
s 103-4 . . . 9.27
s 104-2 . . . 12.26, 12.35
s 104-3(1) . . . 6.35
s 104-4 . . . 9.22
s 104ter . . . 9.03, 9.20
s 105 . . . 12.26, 12.27, 12.39
s 105-1 . . . 12.36
s 105-1(1) . . . 12.36
s 105-1(2) . . . 12.37
s 105-1(3) . . . 12.37
s 105-1(4) . . . 12.37
s 105-2 . . . 12.27
s 105-4 . . . 12.37
s 105-4(1) . . . 12.41
s 105-5 . . . 12.40, 12.41
s 105-7 . . . 12.43
s 113 . . . 9.15
s 114(1) . . . 9.15
s 114(3) . . . 9.15
s 114(5) . . . 9.15
s 123 . . . 9.28
s 123(1) . . . 9.04, 9.12
s 123(1)4 . . . 9.28
s 123(1)i . . . 9.28
s 123(1)ii . . . 9.28, 9.34
s 123(1)vi . . . 9.28, 9.34
s 123(1)vii . . . 9.29
s 123(1)viii . . . 9.29
s 123(2) . . . 9.36
s 123(2)iv . . . 9.28
s 125 . . . 9.12, 9.20
s 126 . . . 9.29
s 126(1) . . . 9.13, 9.14
s 126(2) . . . 9.13
s 126(5) . . . 9.13
s 126(6) . . . 9.13, 9.21
s 126(8) . . . 9.13, 9.23
s 127(1) . . . 9.14

s 128 . . . . 9.14, 9.21
s 131(1) 9.05
s 131(2) 9.04, 9.05
s 132(3) 9.14
s 133(1) 9.05
s 134(1) 9.06
s 134(2) 9.06
s 134-2(4) 9.07
s 134(3) 9.07
s 134(4) 9.08
s 134bis(5) 9.21
s 136(1) 9.05
s 137(1) 9.05
s 145(1) 9.06
s 155 . . . . 9.19
s 164-2(1) 9.09
s 167 . . . . 9.12
s 168(2) 9.24
s 176 . . . . 9.51
s 178 . . . . 2.64
s 178(1) 9.15
s 178(1)(3) 9.11
s 185 . . . . 9.12
s 200-2 . . . . 12.38
Japanese Rules of Civil Procedure (Rules of the Supreme Court) 1996
s 52-7(4) 12.30
s 53(1) 12.26
Law for Establishing the IP High Court (Law No. 109 of 2004)
Art 3 . . . . 2.64
Art 4 . . . . 2.64
Law For Partially Revising the Court Organization Law and Other Laws (Law No. 120 of 2004) 9.03
Law for Revising Part of the Civil Procedure Law (Law No. 108 of 2003)
Art 6(1) 2.62
Law for Revising Patent and Other Related Laws (Law No. 36 of 2014) 9.15
Monopoly Patent Ordinance Law (Law No. 7 of 1885) 2.70
Patent Act Implementation Ordinance
s 12 . . . . 9.18
s 14 . . . . 9.18
Patent Ordinance Law (Law No. 84 of 1888) 1.52
Protocol between Great Britain and Japan (November 20, 1897) 1.53
Recommendations of the Justice System Reform Council (2001) 2.61
Revision of Patent Act 2012 . . . . 9.50
Summary Rules of Monopoly 1871 (Ordinance No. 175 of 1871) 1.50, 1.51
Unfair Competition Prevention Act (Law No. 47 of 1993)
s 2(1)xiv 12.51
s 2(6) 12.37, 12.38
s 105(3) 12.37
s 105-7(4) 12.37

United States

Administrative Procedure Act (APA), 1946 (Pub. L. 79–404, 60 Stat. 237) 2.04
Agricultural Law (7 U.S.C.) 7.149
America Invents Act *see* Leahy-Smith America Invents Act (AIA)
American Investors Protection Act (AIPA), 1999 (Pub. L. 106–13, 113 Stat. 1501) 1.23, 7.02, 7.25
s 4303 . . . . 7.112
Code of Federal Regulations 37 C.F.R.
Pt. 1 . . . . 7.24
s 1.118 . . . . 7.12
s 1.20(c) 7.62
s 1.290(a) 7.62
s 1.290(b) 7.62
s 1.510(b)(6) 7.26
s 1.515(a) 7.29
s 1.525 . . . . 7.33
s 1.550(c) 7.30
s 1.75(e) 4.33
Pt. 5 . . . . 7.24
Pt. 10 . . . . 7.24
Pt. 11 . . . . 7.24
Pt. 41 . . . . 7.24, 7.30
s 41.208(a)(1) 7.52
Pt. 42 . . . . 7.18, 7.61
s 42.104 . . . . 7.39
s 42.105 . . . . 7.39
s 42.120–21 . . . . 7.41
s 42.15(a) 7.62
s 42.301(a) 7.50
s 42.301(b) 7.50
s 42.401 . . . . 7.58
s 42.405 . . . . 7.59
s 42.405(c) 7.59
s 42.405(b)(3)91) 7.59
Constitution 10.54
Amendment 7 . . . . 4.22
Art 1
s 8, cl 8 . . . . 1.10
Art III 10.10
s 1 . . . . 2.06
s 2 . . . . 2.07
Seventh Amendment 10.52
Copyright Law (17 U.S.C.)
s 503(b) 13.83
Evarts Act, 1891 (Ch. 517, 26 Stat. 826 of March 3, 1891) 1.14
Executive Order 9604 (August 25, 1945) . . . 1.35

Federal Circuit Rules
r 35(a) 2.12
Federal Court Improvement
Act 1982 . . . . 1.21, 10.79
Federal Food, Drug and Cosmetic Act 4.11
Federal Rules of Civil Procedure
(FRCP) 10.31
r 6(d) 10.100
r 8 . . . . 4.26
r 8(a) 10.28
r 11 . . . . 13.79, 16.59
r 20 . . . . 10.19, 10.20
r 26 . . . . 10.34
r 26(a) 10.39
r 26(b)(1) 10.45
r 26(b)(3) 10.45
r 26(f) 10.34, 10.39
r 26(f)(2) 10.39
r 26(f)(3)(C) 10.39
r 27 . . . . 10.32, 10.33
r 27(a) 10.32
r 30(a)(2)(A) 10.42
r 30(d)(1) 10.42
r 33(a)(1) 10.41
r 34 . . . . 10.32
r 35(a) 2.12
r 38 . . . . 2.07
r 38(a) 10.53
r 38(b) 10.53
r 38(d) 10.53
r 48(a) 2.07
r 52 . . . . 10.102
r 52(a) 10.82
r 53(b)(2) 2.06
r 54(d)(1) 10.23
r 61 . . . . 10.82
r 62(a) 13.23
r 62(c) 13.23
r 65 . . . . 10.100
r 65(a) 10.100
r 65(c) 10.104
r 65(d) 13.19, 13.20
r 84 . . . . 10.29, 10.30
Appendix 10.29
Federal Rules of Evidence (FRE)
r 408 . . . . 13.61
Government Organizations and
Employees (5 U.S.C.)
s 702 . . . . 2.04
Innovation Act (H.R. 3309) 16.52
Judicial Improvement and Access to
Justice Act 1988
s 1007 . . . . 10.04
Judiciary and Judicial Procedure (28 U.S.C.)
s 44 . . . . 2.11
s 631(b)(5) 2.06
s 1295 . . . . 2.10, 10.79
s 1338 . . . . 2.03, 10.02
s 1338(a) 10.53
s 1338(b) 10.53
s 1338(c) 10.53
s 1338(d) 10.53
s 1367(a) 10.10, 10.11
s 1391(c) 10.03, 10.04, 10.07
s 1400(b) 10.03, 10.04, 10.07
s 1404(a) 10.07
s 1920 . . . . 10.24
s 2201 . . . . 7.01
s 2201(a) 10.89
Lanham Act (Trademark Law, 15 U.S.C.)
s 1118 . . . . 13.83
s 1125(a)(1) 10.74
Leahy-Smith America Invents Act (AIA) 1.23,
7.52, 7.53, 7.54, 7.55, 7.56, 7.57,
7.135, 10.20, 10.21, 13.29, 16.01,
16.23, 16.45
s 3(j) 7.52
s 6 . . . . 7.02, 7.24
s 18 . . . . 1.24, 7.49
s 18(a)(1) 7.49
s 18(a)(B) 7.49
s 18(d)(1) 7.50
s 102(b)(1)(A) 7.99
s 102(b)(1)(B) 7.99
s 102(b)(2)(A) 7.99
s 102(b)(2)(B) 7.99
s 102(b)(2)(C) 7.99
s 102(c) 7.99
s 273(a)(2) 7.100
s 298 . . . . 13.74
North American Free Trade Agreement Act,
Pub. L 103-182, 107 Stat.
2057 (December 8, 1993) 7.92
North American Free Trade Agreement
(NAFTA) 7.92
Omnibus Trade and Competitiveness
Act 1988 . . . . 10.61
Patent Act, 1790 (Ch. 7, 1 Stat. 109 of
April 10, 1790) 1.10, 1.11
Patent Act, 1793 (1 Stat. 317 of
February 21, 1793) 1.11
Patent Act, 1832 (4 Stat. 162) 1.16
Patent Act, 1836 (Ch. 357, s 6, 5 Stat.
117 of July 4, 1836) 1.12, 1.13, 1.15,
1.17, 4.18
s 1 . . . . 7.01
Patent Act, 1839 (Ch. 88, s 7, Stat.
353 of March 3, 1839) 1.12
Patent Act, 1870 (Ch. 230, 16 Stat. 198–217
of July 8, 1870) 1.14, 1.15, 4.18
Patent Act, 1939 (Ch. 450, s 1, Stat. 1212 of
August 5, 1939) 1.12

Patent Law (35 U.S.C.) 5.01, 5.04, 5.06, 5.09, 6.23, 7.02, 7.70, 8.30
s 6(b) 2.16
s 6(c) 2.16
s 6(d) 2.16
s 100(a) 7.71
s 100(d) 10.14
s 101 . . . . . . 7.28, 7.49, 7.50, 7.71, 7.103, 8.101
s 102 . . . . 7.28, 7.49, 7.88
s 102(a) 7.82, 7.87, 7.91, 7.98
s 102(b) 7.57, 7.87, 7.89
s 102(d) 7.87
s 102(e) 7.87
s 102(f) 7.56, 7.82, 7.97
s 102(g) 7.87, 7.91, 7.93, 7.95
s 102(g)(2) 7.91, 7.92
s 103 . . . . 1.19, 4.37, 7.49
s 103(c) 7.88
s 111 . . . . 7.80
s 112 . . . . 7.28, 7.49, 7.53, 8.118
s 112(a) 4.21, 7.12, 8.59, 16.18
s 112(b) 4.32, 4.75, 8.59
s 112(e) 4.43
s 112(f) 1.19, 4.32, 4.40, 4.41, 4.42, 4.89, 4.90, 4.102, 4.103, 7.05, 9.32, 16.05
s 116 . . . . 7.80
s 118 . . . . 7.80
s 132 . . . . 7.12
s 135 (2006 edition) 7.52
s 135(a) 7.52, 7.53, 7.58, 7.59, 7.83
s 135(b) 7.52, 7.61, 7.83
s 135(b)(B) 7.52
s 135(c) 7.58
s 135(d) 7.61, 7.83
ss 141–44 . . . . 7.43
ss 145–46 . . . . 7.43
s 154(a)(2) 4.10
s 154(a)(3) 4.10
s 154(a) 4.01
s 154(b) 4.11
s 156 . . . . 4.11
s 156(d) 4.11
s 156(f) 6.22
ss 184–186 . . . . 7.104
s 186 . . . . 7.104
s 203 . . . . 7.149
s 251 . . . . 7.63
s 251(a) 7.64, 7.65
s 251(d) 7.12, 7.46, 7.64
s 252 . . . . 7.13, 7.65
s 252 (2006 edition) 7.16
s 252¶2 . . . . 7.15, 7.16
s 253 . . . . 7.103
s 256(a) 7.80
s 256¶2 . . . . 7.80
s 256(a) 7.81
s 256(b) 7.81
s 257 . . . . 7.69
s 257(c)(1) 7.125
s 257(e) 7.125
s 261 . . . . 7.127, 10.17
s 271 . . . . 4.04, 10.20
s 271(a) 4.01, 4.14, 5.03, 10.18
s 271(b) 4.14, 5.27, 5.37, 10.18
s 271(c) 4.08, 4.14, 5.27, 5.30, 5.31, 6.17, 10.18
s 271(d) 4.08
s 271(e) 7.106, 7.108, 9.40
s 271(e)(1) 7.108
s 271(e)(2) 7.106
s 271(f) 4.12, 4.16, 10.18
s 271(f)(1) 4.12
s 271(f)(2) 4.12
s 271(g) 4.02, 4.12, 5.03, 5.12, 6.08
s 271(g)(1) 5.13
s 273 . . . . 7.112
s 273(a)(1) 7.112, 7.113
s 273(a)(3) 7.112
s 273(b)(1) 7.112
s 273(c) 7.113
s 273(e)(1) 7.114, 9.45
s 273(e)(2) 7.114
s 273(e)(3) 7.114
s 273(e)(4) 7.114
s 273(e)(5) 7.114
s 281 . . . . 7.67, 10.14
s 282 . . . . 1.19
s 282 (2006 edition) 7.08
s 282(b) 7.67
s 283 . . . . 10.92, 13.01
s 284 . . . . 13.45, 13.59, 13.71
s 285 . . . . 13.79, 13.80
s 286 . . . . 7.133
s 287 . . . . 7.133
s 287(a) 7.134, 13.39, 13.40, 13.41
s 287(c) 7.116
s 287(c)(1) 7.117, 7.118
s 287(c)(2)(A) 7.117
s 287(c)(2)(b) 7.117
s 287(c)(2)(c) 7.117
s 291 . . . . 7.52, 7.91
s 291(a) 7.84
s 291(b) 7.84
s 292 . . . . 7.135
s 292(c) 7.135
s 299 . . . . 10.20, 10.21
s 301 . . . . 1.20
s 301 (2006 edition) 7.02
s 301(a) 7.38
s 302 . . . . 7.26, 7.27
s 303(a) 7.28

s 304 . . . . . 7.31
s 305 . . . . . 7.12, 7.30, 7.32
s 306 . . . . . 7.31
s 307 (2006 edition) 7.22
s 307(b) (2006 edition) 7.16
s 311 . . . . . 7.35
s 311(c) 7.36
s 312(3)(A)–(B) 7.39
s 312(a)(2) 7.35
s 312(a)(3) 7.39
s 312(b) 7.35
s 313 . . . . . 7.39
s 314(a) 7.29, 7.40
s 314(b) 7.40
s 315(a)(1) 7.37
s 315(a)(2) 7.37
s 315(a)(3) 7.37
s 315(b) 7.38
s 315(c) 7.38
s 315(e) 7.24, 7.25
s 316(b) 7.13
s 316(b) (2006 edition) 7.16, 7.22
s 316(d)(3) 7.12
s 317 . . . . . 7.43
s 318 (2006 edition) 7.19
s 319 . . . . . 7.43
s 321 . . . . . 1.24, 7.02, 7.44
s 321(c) 7.36, 7.44
s 322(a) 7.47
s 322(a)(2) 7.44
s 322(b) 7.44
s 324(a) 7.29, 7.47
s 324(b) 7.47
s 324(c) 7.47
s 325 . . . . . 7.37
s 325(a)(1) 7.45
s 325(a)(2) 7.45
s 325(b) 7.45
s 325(e) 7.25
s 325(f) 7.46
s 326(a) 7.47
s 326(d)(3) 7.12
s 327(a) 7.48
s 329 . . . . . 7.48
s 1295 . . . . . 1.21

Patent Pilot Program Act, 2011 (Pub. L. No. 111-349, 124 Stat. 3674) 2.08

Process Patent Amendment Act 1988 (Omnibus Trade and Competitiveness Act 1988, Pub. L. 100–418, ss. 9001–9000, 102 Stat. 1107, 1563–1567 (1988)) 1.23, 3.01, 4.02

Public Health and Welfare (42 U.S.C.) 7.149

Sherman Antitrust Act (Act of July 2, 1890) 1.18

Tariff Act of 1930 (s 337), U.S.C. Code Title 19 (s 1337) 2.01, 2.02, 10.62, 10.64, 13.26, 13.28, 13.29
s 337(d) 13.30, 13.33
s 337(d)(1) 13.27
s 1337 . . . . . 2.17
s 1337(a)(1)–(2) 10.63
s 1337(a)(1)(A) 2.01
s 1337(a)(3) 10.63
s 1337(b)(1) 10.60
s 1337(d) 2.18
s 1337(j) 10.58

Uruguay Round Agreement Act, 1994 (Pub L. 103–465, 108 Stat. 4809) 1.23, 7.92

USPTO Derivation Proceedings Final Rules
77 Fed Reg., 56069 . . . . . 7.58, 7.60
77 Fed Reg., 56074 . . . . . 7.59

USPTO Interim Guidance on Patent Subject Matter Eligibility
79 Fed Reg. 74618 . . . . . 7.79

USPTO Preliminary Examination Instructions 7.77
s 2106.01 . . . . . 7.78

Other

France
Patent Act, 1835 . . . . . 1.51
Patents Act
Art L 612 . . . . . 8.55

United Kingdom
Merchandise Marks Act, 1887 . . . . . 1.28
Patents Act
s 3 . . . . . 8.91
s 21 . . . . . 8.55
s 37 . . . . . 8.139
s 72 . . . . . 8.115
Statute of Monopolies 1623, 21 Jac. 1, c. 3
s 6 . . . . . 7.01

Part I

INTRODUCTION

1

HISTORY

A. The Evolution of International Institutions

1. The World Intellectual Property Organization and the World Trade Organization

In the field of intellectual property (IP), various aspects of IP rights procurement and enforcement have been harmonized through multilateral and bilateral international agreements. In particular, patent offices of major jurisdictions such as the United States Patent Office (USPTO), the German Patent Office, the European Patent Office (EPO), and the Japanese Patent Office (JPO) have worked with international institutions such as the World Intellectual Property Office (WIPO) and the World Trade Organization (WTO) and have taken on an important role in patent law harmonization. The efforts to harmonize patent laws began in the late nineteenth century when a diplomatic conference in Paris led to the Paris Convention for the Protection of Industrial Property (the Paris Convention).[1] None of the countries that this treatise focuses on is an original signatory country. The United States joined the Paris Convention in 1887, Germany joined in 1901, and Japan joined in 1889. The United Nations (UN) through its agency administered the Paris Convention and led the efforts on patent harmonization. WIPO took over such efforts when it was established in1967 as a self-funding agency of the UN. **1.01**

However, the harmonization efforts through the Paris Convention focused on patent procurement and did not evolve to cover protection and enforcement because of a sharp divide between the interests of developing and developed countries for enhancing patent protection. After the failure of the 1991 Diplomatic Conference on the "Basic Proposal" for patent harmonization, developed countries changed the venue for diplomatic negotiations from WIPO to the WTO so that they could negotiate with developing countries for stronger patent protection and enforcement in exchange for other trade issues that may bring benefits to developing countries. As a result, the Agreement on Trade-related Aspects of Intellectual Property Rights (TRIPS) entered into force in 1995.[2] TRIPS adopted the minimum standards of intellectual property protection, including various aspects of patent protection and enforcement. **1.02**

---

[1] Paris Convention for the Protection of Industrial Property (March 20, 1993; effective July 7, 1884, and amended June 2, 1934, and July 14, 1967) (the Paris Convention). For a history of the Paris Convention, see World Intellectual Property Organization, "International Treaties and Convention on Intellectual Property," in *WIPO Intellectual Property Handbook: Policy, Law and Use*, 241 (http://www.wipo.int/export/sites/www/about-ip/en/iprm/pdf/ch5.pdf).

[2] Agreement on Trade-related Aspects of Intellectual Property Rights, April 15, 1994, Marrakesh Agreement Establishing the World Trade Organization, Annex 1C, The Legal Texts: The Results of the Uruguay Round of Multilateral Trade Negotiations 320 (1999), 1869 U.N.T.S. 299, 33 I.L.M. 1197 (1994).

Moreover, if a member state fails to meet any standard, other WTO member states can enforce the minimum standards through a dispute settlement mechanism incorporated into the WTO system. Such a mechanism was not available in the WIPO system.

1.03 While it was unable to lead the harmonization efforts through the Paris Convention, WIPO substantially contributed to the effort by taking a leadership role in adopting the Patent Cooperation Treaty (PCT)[3] and Patent Law Treaty (PLT).[4] The PCT entered into force in 1978 with the goal of promoting international cooperation between patent offices with respect to the filing, searching, and examination of patent applications and the dissemination of patent information.[5] To achieve this goal, the PCT established an international patent application system, which enables the filing of a single patent application with a single patent office to secure the effect of an application in each of the PCT member states with the same international filing date. It provides standards for patentability in conducting an international preliminary examination of the international application. Although it is not mandatory, PCT member states have revised their patent acts to harmonize with PCT standards. The PLT also harmonized and streamlined formal procedures with respect to national and regional patent applications.

2. The European Patent Organization and the European Union

1.04 The necessity of creating a uniform market accelerated patent harmonization in Europe. European countries took a big step toward patent harmonization by adopting the European Patent Convention (EPC).[6] The EPC established a system that enables a single filing with the EPC to not only secure the application date but also lead to a bundle of patents that are effective in EPC member states. The European Patent System is operated by two organs, the EPO and the European Patent Organization (EPOrg), which has administrative and financial authority. The EPOrg is an intergovernmental organization that consists of EPC member states. The European Patent System not only created its own patent office, the EPO, but also adopted the maximal approach to harmonization in which the EPC governs not only the patentability standards during an examination but also the validity of European patents after a patent grant.[7] This approach led to the voluntary unification of substantive patent law among European countries.

1.05 Although European countries have had great success in harmonizing substantive patent laws and creating a uniform patent office, the EPO, they have not had much luck in creating a system for granting a Europe-wide unitary patent right. The first attempt to create a unitary patent system adopted the Community Patent Convention (CPC), but it was a failure because the CPC never entered into force.[8] Compared to the EPC, the European Union (EU) has so far not played a big role in patent harmonization within Europe except in the

[3] Patent Cooperation Treaty, June 19, 1970, 28 U.S.T. 7645, 1160 U.N.T.S. 231 reprinted in 9 I.L.M. 978 (1970).

[4] Patent Law Treaty, June 1, 2000, 39 I. L.M. 1047.

[5] *WIPO Intellectual Property Handbook*, 277.

[6] Convention on the Grant of European Patents, Munich, October 5, 1973, 1065 U.N.T.S. 199.

[7] Justin Pila, "The European Patent: An Old and Vexing Problem," 62 *International and Comparative Law Quarterly* (2013): 917 (http://journals.cambridge.org/action/displayFulltext?type=1&fid=9060968&jid=ILQ&volumeId=62&issueId=04&aid=9060965).

[8] Convention for the European Patent for the Common Market 76/76/EEC (Luxembourg, December 15, 1975) Agreement relating to Community Patents 89/695/EEC (Luxembourg, December 15, 1989), OJ L 401/1 (December 30, 1989).

patent protection of biotechnological inventions.[9] Currently, national courts and authorities of EPC member states decide on the infringement and validity of European patents. Unable to harmonize substantive patent laws, the EU adopted a directive for harmonizing the enforcement of intellectual property rights, including patents.[10] The directive substantially harmonized evidence-taking procedures for patent infringement procedures and the remedies available for patent infringement among EU member states.

The EU is currently taking a leadership role in creating a centralized judiciary system for deciding infringement and validity, which has led to the Agreement on a Unified Patent Court (UPC), signed by EU member states.[11] EU member states have developed regulations on unitary patent protection, which entered into force on January 20, 2013.[12] Thus the regulation will apply once the UPC enters into force. As will be discussed in Chapter 2, Patent Enforcement Institutions, the UPC may have a significant impact on patent enforcement in German courts.[13] **1.06**

3. Trilateral Patent Office Initiatives and Beyond

The EPO made a substantial contribution to patent harmonization beyond Europe. In 1983, the Trilateral Cooperation was set up by the EPO, JPO, and USPTO—the three largest offices at the time—to look into ways of solving common automation problems.[14] Through this cooperation, the JPO imported many aspects of the EPC as the best practice of substantive patent law. In particular, the EPO and JPO exchanged their examiners so they could share examination experiences and prior-art search know-how. This close interaction between examiners working in the same technical fields led to a voluntary unification of examination practices and an understanding of differences in patentability standards. Thirty years later, this exchange program still continues, and the topics covered during the exchange program include areas such as documentation, data standards, and patent information. In 2007, the cooperation expanded into the Five IP Offices (IP5) with the inclusion of the Korean Intellectual Property Office (KIPO) and State Intellectual Property Office (SIPO).[15] The Heads and Deputy Heads of the Offices meet annually to improve the quality and efficiency of patent searches and examinations. **1.07**

The trilateral initiatives also inspired the JPO to develop a work-sharing program called the "patent prosecution highway" in which patent offices mutually take advantage of examination results.[16] The leading offices' pledges to have a deeper collaboration made multilateral agreements possible with national and regional offices in Europe, North America, and South America, which led to further harmonization of substantive patent laws. **1.08**

---

[9] Directive 98/44/EC of the European Parliament and of the Council of 6 July 1998 on the legal protection of biotechnological inventions, [1998] OJ L 213/13 (Biotech Directive).

[10] Directive 2004/48/EC of the European Parliament and of the Council of 29 April 2004 on the enforcement of intellectual property rights, OJ EU L 157, April 30, 2004 (http://eur-lex.europa.eu/legal-content/EN/TXT/HTML/?uri=CELEX:32004L0048R(01)&from=EN).

[11] Agreement on a Unified Patent Court, June 20, 2013, OJ EU 56 2013/C175.

[12] Regulations Concerns Unitary Patent Protection EU/1257/2012.

[13] Ch. 2, 2.42–2.55.

[14] The Trilateral Co-operation (http://www.trilateral.net/index.html;jsessionid=hf7joj62ug1).

[15] Japan Patent Office, The Five IP Offices (http://www.jpo.go.jp/torikumi_e/kokusai_e/five_ip_offices.htm).

[16] Japan Patent Office, Patent Prosecution Highway (PPH) (http://www.jpo.go.jp/torikumi_e/t_torikumi_e/patent_highway_e.htm).

1.09 The EPO also took a leadership role in patent harmonization by sponsoring the biannual European Patent Judges' Symposium. Communication among patent judges and participation in case studies of real cases from EPC member states enhances the maximal approach to harmonization that the EPC framers adopted. Through collaboration with the JPO and USPTO, the symposium has expanded to include US judges and judges from non-EPC member states. A study conducted by the International Intellectual Property Institute revealed that ninety countries have adopted an IP specialized court.[17] The study identified the creation of subject matter expertise and the consistency and predictability of case outcomes as major benefits. Nowadays, patent professional organizations and academic institutes frequently organize patent law conferences to create a forum where patent judges from different jurisdictions can exchange views in order to cope with complex legal issues evolving from the ever-changing world of technology. As a result, as will be discussed in the following chapters, key aspects of patent enforcement under the US, German, and Japanese Patent Acts are substantially harmonized except for the unique aspects of US civil procedure and infringement remedies.

B. United States

1. Early Patent System: 1730–1869

1.10 The United States Constitution grants Congress the power to create a patent system to promote the progress of science and useful arts.[18] Historians find the origin of the US Patent System in England.[19] Prior to the ratification of the Constitution by the requisite nine states in 1788, some of the colonial states had adopted a patent system as an extension of the king's power in England through the local authority.[20] Others strongly resisted the idea of state monopolies. During the first session of the First Congress in 1789, Congress received various petitions to grant exclusive rights in works of authorship and inventions and bills to create patent and copyright systems.[21] The very first federal patent statute was adopted by the Second Congress and entered into force on April 10, 1790.[22] Even after the adoption of the first Patent Act, some states continued to grant state patents. The Congress as well as the courts acknowledged the parallel patent systems, as the Patent Act included a provision requiring inventors to surrender all patents when they obtained a US patent for the same invention.[23] The exclusivity of the legislative power of Congress to create a

[17] The International Intellectual Property Institute (IIPI) and the United States Patent and Trademark Office, *Study on Specialized Intellectual Property Courts* (2012) (http://iipi.org/wp-content/uploads/2012/05/Study-on-Specialized-IPR-Courts.pdf).

[18] US Const. Art. 1, § 8, cl. 8.

[19] Morgan Sherwood, "The Origin and Development of the American Patent System," 71 *American Scientist* (1983): 500 (http://www.jstor.org/stable/27852242).

[20] For colonial patent systems, see Oren Bracha, "Owning Ideas: A History of Anglo-American Intellectual Property," unpublished Ph.D. dissertation, Harvard Law School (June 2005), 100 (http://www.utexas.edu/law/faculty/obracha/dissertation); Camilla A. Hrdy, "Dissenting State Patent Regimes," 3:2 *IP Theory* (2013): Art. 2 (http://www.repository.law.indiana.edu/cgi/viewcontent.cgi?article=1021&context=ipt).

[21] Edward Walterscheid, "The Early Evolution of the United States Patent Act: Antecedents (Part 1)," 76 *J. Pat. & Trad. Off. Soc'y* (1994): 697.

[22] Act of April 10, 1790, Ch. 7, 1 Stat. 109.

[23] Camilla A. Hrdy, "Dissenting State Patent Regimes," 3 *IP Theory* (2013): 78, 85 (http://www.repository.law.indiana.edu/ipt/vol3/iss2/2/).

patent-like system was unclear until the Supreme Court applied the preemption doctrine and found void a Florida law granting patent-like protection to boat hulls in the 1989 *Bonito Boats* case.[24]

The very first Patent Act was replaced with the Patent Act of 1793, which introduced the four categories of patent-eligible subject matter.[25] Under both the 1790 and 1793 Acts, the three-member patent board consisting of the Secretary of State, the Secretary of War, and the Attorney General had the exclusive power to grant US patents, although the Department of State administered patents. The 1793 Act introduced fundamental requirements that are a part of all modern patent systems: novelty and sufficient disclosure of the invention in the specification.[26] The Act was unclear on whether novelty was determined under the first-to-invent priority.[27] Courts interpreted "the first and true inventor" in the novelty statute to develop the first-to-invent priority rule.[28] This rule was codified when Congress introduced in the 1836 Act a procedure to decide priority between two interfering inventors for the same invention. **1.11**

Patents were granted without examination, but defendants could assert a failure to meet these requirements as a defense when infringement of a patent was alleged against them, until the 1836 Act created a Patent Office.[29] In the 1829 *Pennock* decision, the Supreme Court introduced a fundamental doctrine, the statutory bar doctrine, to limit the first-to-invent priority.[30] To prevent unreasonable delays by inventors in filing patent applications, the Court barred inventors from obtaining a patent once an invention was publicly used.[31] The statutory bar doctrine was codified in the Patent Act of 1836.[32] The doctrine was modified by the introduction of a two-year grace period in the Patent Act of 1839[33] and further modified when the 1939 Act shortened the grace period to one year.[34] **1.12**

The 1836 Act introduced an important feature of modern patent systems: a statutory requirement of clear claiming. Although the pre-1836 Patent Act did not require inventors to specify the scope of the invention for which they claimed protection, the patent community developed a practice whereby inventors specified the part or improvement claimed as their invention.[35] This practice was endorsed in the 1822 *Evans* decision by the **1.13**

---

[24] *Bonito Boats v. Thunder Craft Boats*, 489 U.S. 141, 109 S. Ct. 971, 103 L. Ed. 2d 118, 9 U.S.P.Q. 2d 1847 (U.S. 1989). However, the Court was reluctant to find void a state law that grants a protection substantially different from the exclusive right of a patent even if the subject matter of the Patent Act and subject matter of the state law overlap. *Kewanee v. Bicron*, 416 U.S. 470, 94 S. Ct. 1879, 40 L. Ed. 2d 315, 181 U.S.P.Q. 67 (U.S. 1974).

[25] Act of February 21, 1973, 1 Stat. 317.

[26] *Chisum on Patents*, 2.

[27] *Chisum on Patents*, 4.

[28] *Woodcock v. Parker*, 30 F. Cas. 491, 1813 U.S. App. LEXIS 375, 1 Gall. 438 (C.C.D. Mass. 1813).

[29] Act of July 4, 1836, Ch. 357, § 6, 5 Stat. 117.

[30] *Pennock v. Dialogue*, 27 U.S. (2 Pet.) 1 (1829).

[31] For the statutory bar doctrine and the first-to-invent priority, see Toshiko Takenaka, "Rethinking the United States First-to-Invent Principle from a Comparative Law Perspective: A Proposal to Restructure, § 102 Novelty and Priority Provisions," 39 *Hous. L. Rev.* (2002): 621; Toshiko Takenaka, "The Best Patent Practice or Merely Compromise? A Reivew of Current Draft Patent Law Treaty and a Proposal for a First-to-Invent" Exception for Domestic Applicant," 11 *Texas Intellectual Property L.J.* (2003): 259.

[32] Act of July 4, 1836, Ch. 357, § 6, 5 Stat. 117.

[33] Act of March 3, 1839, Ch. 88, § 7, 5 Stat. 353.

[34] Act of August 5, 1939 Ch. 450, § 1, 53 Stat. 1212.

[35] For a historical perspective of claim drafting and interpretation, see Toshiko Takenaka, "Interpreting Patent Claims: The United States, Germany and Japan," 17 *IIC Studies* (1995): 6–12.

Supreme Court when it imposed a requirement of clear claiming distinct from the enablement requirement for the sufficiency of disclosure in the specification.[36] The 1836 Act's introduction of the clear claiming requirement did not cause significant changes in patent practice except that applicants began to include language such as "substantially as herein described" at the end of a claim in order to secure patent protection for minor variations of the structure or improvements identified in the claim.[37] The Supreme Court acquiesced in this claim-drafting scheme and found infringement when the accused embodiment was equivalent to the claimed invention if it used the same principle underlying the claimed invention and changed only its form.[38]

2. Anti-Patent Era: 1870–1982

1.14 The Supreme Court heard appeals of patent cases from district courts until the enactment of the Evarts Act created regional circuit courts of appeals in 1891.[39] As the number of patents appealed to the Supreme Court increased, the Court became hostile to patentees who enforced their patent claims such ambiguous language as described in the previous paragraph. The invalidity rate steadily increased after the enactment of the 1870 Act, and the invalidity rate at the Supreme Court between 1886 and 1891 was 87 percent.[40]

1.15 Despite there being only minor changes between the 1836 Act and 1870 Act to the language of the provision requiring clear claiming, some commentators began to advance their views that the ambiguous claim-drafting schemes were no longer allowed under the 1870 Act.[41] The Supreme Court and the Patent Office followed these legal commentators' interpretation of the 1870 Act and began to strike down claims drafted in ambiguous terms.[42] The Court began refusing to extend patent protection to an accused embodiment unless the embodiment was clearly described in the claims, even if the accused embodiment was disclosed in the specification, in order to protect public interests, which would be impeded by vague and indefinite descriptions of claims.[43]

1.16 Moreover, US courts invalidated many patents issued by the USPTO by applying multiple tests to negate the quality of inventions with respect to the claimed inventions in asserted patents.[44] Since the early nineteenth century, lower courts have developed an additional standard beyond novelty: the requirement of a degree of difference between the claimed invention and the prior art to demonstrate the quality of the invention.[45] In the 1850 *Hotchkiss* case, the Supreme Court acknowledged this additional requirement and invalidated the asserted patent although the 1832 Patent Act was quiet on any additional requirement beyond the novelty requirement.[46] The negative tests to deny the quality of inventions were vague and of

---

[36] *Evens v. Eaton*, 20 U.S. 356, 5 L. Ed 472, 7 Wheat 356 (1822).

[37] Warren T. Jessup, "The Doctrine of Equivalents," 54 *J. Pat. & Trad. Off. Soc'y* 248 (1994): 284.

[38] *Winans v. Denmead*, 56 U.S. (How.) 330 (1853).

[39] Act of March 3, 1891, Ch. 517, 26 Stat. 826.

[40] H. R. Mayers, "The United States Patent System in Historical Perspective," 3 *Pat. Trademark & Copy. J. Res. & Ed.* (1959): 33, 44.

[41] A. W. Deller, *Patent Claims* (2d ed., 1971), § 1; Jessup, "The Doctrine of Equivalents," 264.

[42] E.g., *Hobbs v. Beach*, 180 U.S. 383, 399 (1901); *Ex Parte Shepler*, 102 O.G. 468 (1903).

[43] *Merril v. Yeomans*, 94 U.S. (4 Otto) 568 (1876).

[44] *Chisum on Patents*, § 5.02.

[45] E.g., *Knight v. Baltimore & O. R.R. Co.*, 14 F. Cas. 758, 759 (C.C. Md. 1840). Giles S. Rich, "Thirty Years of This Judging Business," 14 *AIPLA Q.J.* (1986): 139.

[46] *Hotchkiss v. Greenwood*, 52 U.S. (11 How.) 248 (1850).

a highly abstract nature. The standard for the additional requirement developed through the negative tests was articulated by courts as an expression of "inventive effort," a "substantial invention or discovery," a "creative work in the inventive faculty," "that impalpable something," and "something new, unexpected, and exciting."[47] As the standard became as high as the requirement of a "flash of creative genius,"[48] a Supreme Court justice commented in his dissent that "the only patent that is valid is one which this Court has not been able to get its hands on."[49]

The requirement of invention was not the only grounds for the Supreme Court to invalidate patents. After the introduction of a statutory requirement of clear claiming under the 1836 Act, the Court began to strike down patents for indefinite claims and lack of enablement. In the 1854 *O'Reilly v. Morse* case, the Court struck down the validity of a claim consisting of only one element when the element was defined by its function instead of its structure.[50] Even if an asserted claim included multiple elements, the patent on the claim was invalid if the elements to distinguish the prior art were defined by their function instead of their structure.[51] In invalidating functional claims, the Court emphasized the notice function of the claim and the uncertainties introduced by functional claiming, which imposes a burden on the public to find the boundary of the exclusive right with undue experimentation on existing and after-arising technologies to perform the function recited in the claim.[52] **1.17**

Passage of the Sherman Act in 1890[53] and the growing distrust of patents as they became viewed as a kind of monopoly might be another reason for the US courts' hostile attitude towards patents.[54] The invalidity rate at the Supreme Court rose as high as 90 percent (75 percent excluding reissue patents[55]) in 1890. Compared with the Supreme Court, the invalidity rate at the circuit appeals courts was originally relatively low at 50 percent but began to rise in 1930 and was as high as 80 percent in 1940.[56] The US industry became concerned about the high invalidity rate and the legal uncertainty in enforcing patents they had invested in to secure exclusive rights. **1.18**

In 1952, Congress passed a new patent act, which is still in effect. To improve patent validity, the 1952 Act codified the additional requirement of invention as the nonobviousness requirement, eliminating all other judicially developed negative tests of inventions.[57] The Act overturned Supreme Court precedents condemning claims that defined features at the point of novelty by their function to the extent that the claims were drafted in the **1.19**

---

47 M. J. Adelman et al., *Cases and Materials on Patent Law* (1st ed., 1998), 412.

48 *Cuno Engineering Corp. v. Automatic Devices Corp.*, 314 U.S. 84, 62 S. Ct. 37, 86 L. Ed. 58, 51 U.S.P.Q. 272 (U.S. 1941).

49 *Jungersen v. Ostby & Barton Co.*, 335 U.S. 560, 69 S. Ct. 269, 93 L. Ed. 235, 80 U.S.P.Q. 32 (U.S. 1949) (Jackson, J., dissenting).

50 *O'Reilly v. Morse*, 56 U.S. 62, 14 L. Ed. 601, 1853 U.S. LEXIS 273, 15 How. 62 (U.S. 1854).

51 *Holland Furniture Co. v. Perkins Glue Co.*, 277 U.S. 245, 48 S. Ct. 474, 72 L. Ed. 868, 1928 U.S. LEXIS 686 (U.S. 1928).

52 *Halliburton Oil Well Cementing Co. v. Walker*, 329 U.S. 1, 71 U.S.P.Q. 175 (1946).

53 Act of July 2, 1890 (Sherman Antitrust Act).

54 Mayers, "The United States Patent System in Historical Perspective," 35.

55 Ibid. 44.

56 Ibid. 35.

57 35 U.S.C. § 103. For the impact of § 103 nonobviouness provision, see Edmund W. Kitch, "Graham v. John Deere Co.: New Standards for Patents," *Sup. Ct. Rev.* (1966): 293.

means-plus-function format in order to limit the scope to the embodiments disclosed in the specification and their equivalents.[58] The Act codified the presumption of validity developed through case law.[59] In spite of these efforts, the invalidity rate at US courts remained high even after the enactment of the 1952 Act.[60]

3. Pro-Patent Era: 1980–2012

1.20 The 1980 *Chakrabarty* decision marks the start of the pro-patent era with the Supreme Court announcing that "anything under the sun that is made by man" is included as statutory subject matter under the patent law.[61] The same year, Congress introduced a procedure for requesting that the USPTO re-examine a patented claim by citing patents or printed publications as the prior art (*ex parte* re-examination procedure).[62] The invalidity rate decreased to 70 percent in the late 1970s.[63] The *ex parte* re-examination procedure was created to strengthen investor confidence in the certainty of patent rights by creating an administrative procedure for the re-examination of doubtful patents.[64]

1.21 Another important development marking the pro-patent era was the creation of the US Court of Appeals for the Federal Circuit (Federal Circuit) through the enactment of the Federal Court Improvement Act of 1983.[65] After long debates over the pros and cons of specialized adjudication, Congress decided to give the Federal Circuit exclusive subject matter jurisdiction over appeals arising from a case under the patent laws.[66] The Federal Circuit developed multiple doctrines to overcome invalidity defenses.[67] The court's patentee-friendly case law led to a significant drop in invalidity rates.[68] The court also developed case law expanding the scope of patent infringement damages[69] and making it easy for patentees to request preliminary injunctions.[70]

---

58 35 U.S.C. § 112(f).

59 Ibid. § 282. The Supreme Court introduced the presumption of validity. *Imhaeuser v. Buerk*, 101 U.S. 647, 25 L. Ed. 945, 11 Otto 647 (U.S. 1880).

60 For a statistical analysis of invalidity rates at US courts, see Gloria Koenig, *Patent Invalidity: A Statistical and Substantive Analysis* (1974; 2d ed., 1980). A study indicates that the invalidity rate at the circuit appeals courts was 63.6% in 1953 and 68.5% in 1954. P. J. Fedelico, "Adjudicating Patents, 1948–1954," 38 *J. Pat. Off. Soc'y* (1956): 233. Another study examining adjudicated patents between 1953 and 1963 indicates that the average invalidity rate was 60.8%.

61 *Diamond v. Chakrabarty*, 447 U.S. 303, 100 S. Ct. 2204, 65 L. Ed. 2d 144, 206 U.S.P.Q. 193 (U.S. 1980).

62 35 U.S.C. § 301.

63 Koenig, *Patent Invalidity*, § 4.02, Table 12.

64 H.R. Rep. No. 1307, 96th Cong., 2d Sess. 3 (http://patentlyo.com/media/docs/2008/09/Legislative_History_Process_Patents.pdf) *In re Swanson*, 540 F.3d 1368, 88 U.S.P.Q. 2d 1196 (Fed. Cir. 2008).

65 Pub. L. 97–164, 96 Stat. 25 (relevant provisions codified as amended in scattered sections of 28 U.S.C.) For a general discussion on the Federal Circuit, see Rochelle Dreyfuss, "The Federal Circuit: A Case Study in Special Courts," 64 *N.U.U.L. Rev.* (1989): 1.

66 28 U.S.C. § 1295.

67 Robert W. Harris, "The Emerging Primacy of 'Secondary Considerations' as Validity Ammunition: Has the Federal Circuit Gone Too Far?," 71 *J. Pat & Trademark Off. Soc'y* (1989): 185; Jon F. Merz and Nicholas M. Pace, "Trends in Patent Litigation: The Apparent Influence of Strengthened Patents Attributable to the Court of Appeals for the Federal Circuit," 76 *J. Pat & Trademark Off. Soc'y* (1994): 579.

68 Matthew D. Henry and John L. Turner, "The Court of Appeals for the Federal Circuit's Impact on Patent Litigation," 35 *J. Legal Stud.* (2006): 85, 108, fig. 1; John R. Allison and Mark A. Lemley, "Empirical Evidence on the Validity of Litigated Patents," 26 *APILA Quarterly J.* (1998): 185.

69 *Rite-Hite Corp. v. Kelley Co.*, 56 F.3d 1538, 35 U.S.P.Q. 2d 1065 (Fed. Cir. 1995).

70 *H.H. Robertson Co. v. United Steel Deck*, 820 F.2d 384, 2 U.S.P.Q. 2d 1926 (Fed. Cir. 1987).

The tide began to turn for the pro-patent era in the final decade of the twentieth century when the Supreme Court began exercising its appellate jurisdiction over the Federal Circuit.[71] The Court emphasized the notice function and definitional function of patent claims and scrutinized the conditions for the application of the doctrine of equivalents.[72] It became difficult for patentees to get an injunction even if infringement was established.[73] 1.22

4. American Invents Act: 2012–present

By the end of the twentieth century, the US Patent Act had been through a number of revisions to harmonize its system with the rest of the world. Such revisions included the Process Patent Amendment Act of 1988,[74] the Uruguay Round Agreement Act of 1994,[75] and the American Inventors Protection Act of 1999.[76] The only major aspect that remained unique to the United States was the first-to-invent priority. This unique aspect was moved more in line with the rest of the world when President Obama signed into law the Leahy-Smith America Invents Act (AIA), which adopted the first-inventor-to-file priority.[77] Although the AIA did not completely harmonize the priority rule with the first-to-file priority under the EPC and JPA, the AIA significantly contributed to world patent harmonization by limiting the opportunity to establish pre-filing priority.[78] As will be discussed in the following chapters, the AIA also introduced a lot of ambiguity in the interpretation of the language in the novelty and priority provisions.[79] 1.23

The AIA also introduced multiple procedures for challenging the validity of a patent at the USPTO. These procedures were introduced in response to criticisms on patent quality, providing a more efficient system for challenging patents that should not have been issued and reducing litigation costs and inconsistent damage awards.[80] As the patentee win rates and the size of damage awards increased because of patentee-friendly case law, a business model to make money by asserting patent infringement in order to collect licensing royalties instead of making and selling products through practicing the patented inventions began to attract the attention of the business and legal community. A person or company who engages in the business model is called a patent troll, a non-patent practicing entity (NPE), a patent holding company (PHC), or a patent assertion entity (PAE). Patent trolls have become extremely controversial plaintiffs 1.24

---

71 Robert Merges and John Duffy, *Patent Law and Policy: Cases and Materials* (4th ed., 2007), 11.

72 *Warner-Jenkinson Co. v. Hilton Davis Chem. Co.*, 520 U.S. 17, 117 S. Ct. 1040, 137 L. Ed. 2d 146, 41 U.S.P.Q. 2d 1865 (U.S. 1997); *Festo Corp. v. Shoketsu Kinzoku Kogyo Kabushiki Co.*, 535 U.S. 722, 122 S. Ct. 1831, 152 L. Ed. 2d 944, 62 U.S.P.Q. 2d 1705 (U.S. 2002).

73 *eBay Inc. v. MercExchange, LLC*, 547 U.S. 388, 126 S. Ct. 1837, 164 L. Ed. 2d 641, 78 U.S.P.Q. 2d 1577 (U.S. 2006).

74 Omnibus Trade and Competitiveness Act of 1988, Pub. L. 100–418, §§ 9001–7, 102 Stat. 1107, 1563–67 (1988).

75 Pub. L. 103–465, 108 Stat. 4809.

76 Pub. L. 106–13, 113 Stat. 1501.

77 Leahy-Smith America Invents Act, Pub. L. 112–29, 125 Stat 284.

78 Toshiko Takenaka, "Has the United States Adopted a First-to-File System through American Invents Act? A Comparative Law Analysis of Patent Priority under First-Inventor-To-File," *GRUR Int'l* (2012): 304; Toshiko Takenaka, "A View of First-To-File Lawyer on the America Invents Act: Will the First-Inventor-To-File under America Invents Act Be the Best Practice Determining Patent Priority?" in Toshiko Takenaka (ed.), *Intellectual Property Systems in Common Law and Civil Law* (2013), 50.

79 See Ch. 7, 7.98.

80 Report on H.R. 1249, House Judiciary Committee (http://www.uspto.gov/aia_implementation/crpt-112hrpt98-pt1.pdf).

because defendants sued by patent trolls need to make a substantial investment of time and money to defend against the infringement assertion. The poor quality of patents are considered to be a source of the patent troll problem because defendants may settle a case in spite of doubtful validity in order to avoid an enormous patent litigation cost.[81] The new post-grant review aims to eliminate such doubtful patents at a cost less expensive than the litigation cost.[82] Software patents are also considered to be a major source of problems for the patent system.[83] To cope with the variety of problems relating to software patents, the AIA introduced the transitional program for covered business method patents.[84] Under the transitional program, a person who is sued or charged with infringement may petition anytime for a special post-grant review. Congress is currently reviewing multiple bills to limit patent troll activities.

1.25 The Supreme Court also responded to the criticisms on the poor quality of patents and continues interfere with the Federal Circuit's patentee-friendly case law. The Court revived some of the negative tests of inventions and weakened the tests developed by the Federal Circuit to rebut the *prima facie* obvious case in *KSR v. Teleflex*.[85] It also scrutinized the threat of patent trolls by limiting the scope of patent eligibility with respect to software inventions as well as medical inventions.[86] It also found the Federal Circuit's test for claim indefiniteness too lenient and adopted a higher standard.[87] Reflecting the Supreme Court's restrained attitude, the invalidity rate rose. The invalidity rate at district courts between 2007 and 2011 was 86 percent.[88] The invalidity rate at the Federal Circuit between 2002 and 2012 also steadily increased.[89] This trend in the courts reflects the patent allowance at the USPTO: the success rate substantially decreased from 1996 to 2005.[90] This current trend in the United States is a stark contrast to the pro-patent trend in Japan after its adoption of a national strategy to become an IP-based nation.[91]

---

[81] Geral N. Magliocca, "Blackberries and Barnyards: Patent Trolls and the Perils of Innovation," 82 *Notre Dame L. Rev.* (2007): 1809.

[82] 35 U.S.C. § 321. For more discussion, see Ch. 7, 7.44.

[83] Mark A. Lemley, "Software Patents and the Return of Functional Claiming," (October 12, 2012) *Wis. L. Rev.* (2013): 905, 928 (http://wisconsinlawreview.org/wp-content/files/1-Lemley.pdf).

[84] AIA, § 18. For more discussion, see Ch. 7, 7.49.

[85] *KSR Int'l Co. v. Teleflex Inc.*, 550 U.S. 398, 127 S. Ct. 1727, 167 L. Ed. 2d 705, 82 U.S.P.Q. 2d 1385 (U.S. 2007).

[86] *Alice Corp. Pty., Ltd. v. CLS Bank Int'l*, 134 S. Ct. 2347, 189 L. Ed. 2d 296, 110 U.S.P.Q. 2d 1976 (U.S. 2014); *Mayo Collaborative Servs. v. Prometheus Labs., Inc.*, 132 S. Ct. 1289, 182 L. Ed. 2d 321 101 U.S.P.Q. 2d 1961 (U.S. 2012); *Ass'n for Molecular Pathology v. Myriad Genetics, Inc.*, 133 S. Ct. 2107, 186 L. Ed. 2d 124, 106 U.S.P.Q. 2d 1972 (U.S. 2013).

[87] *Nautilus, Inc. v. Biosig Instruments, Inc.*, 134 S. Ct. 2120, 189 L. Ed. 2d 37, 110 U.S.P.Q. 2d 1688 (U.S. 2014).

[88] Robert Smyth, White Paper Report, United States Patent Invalidity Study 2012 (2012) (http://www.morganlewis.com/~/media/files/publication/presentation/speech/smyth_uspatentinvalidity_sept12.ashx).

[89] Ibid.

[90] Michael Carley, Deepak Hegde, and Alan Marco, *What Is the Probability of Receving a US Patent?*, USPTO Economic Working Paper No. 2013-2 (2013) (http://www.uspto.gov/ip/officechiefecon/OCE_WP_2013-2.pdf).

[91] Toshiko Takenaka, "Will Intellectual Property Policy Save Japan from Recessions? Japan's Basic Intellectual Property Policy and Its Implementation through the National Strategic Program," 35 *IIC* (2004): 877; Toshiko Takenaka, "Success or Failure? Japan's National Strategy on Intellectual Property and Evaluation of Its Impact from the Comparative Law Perspective," 8 *Wash. U. Global Studies L. Rev.* (2009): 379.

C. Germany

1. Pre-Patent Era in Germany

When looking at the history of patent laws in Germany, one first has to remember that the Federal Republic of Germany has only existed as a state since 1949. A unified German state, the *Deutsches Reich*, was founded after the Franco-Prussian War in 1871[92] and was based on the *Norddeutsche Bund*, which was dominated by Prussia. Before this time, the German territory was divided into many kingdoms and principalities that each formed a separate jurisdiction, and monopolies or privileges were granted by the local rulers. As a result, at the beginning of the nineteenth century, six different patent laws existed (and protection could be extended to nearly thirty of the jurisdictions), each of which provided a localized territorial protection.[93] At this time patents were generally kept secret, and both novel inventions and imported methods could be protected.[94] **1.26**

The discussions about unified patent protection and the advantages of such a system became more frequent during the formation of the *Deutsches Reich* (German Empire), and, for example, in 1864 the German Chambers of Commerce demanded the overall abolishment of patents, as they would be "detrimental to the general prosperity." A prominent and outspoken opponent of the patent system was Victor Boehmert,[95] who stated in an article in 1869: "Die Patente sind reif zum Fallen und werden mehr und mehr als eine faule Frucht am Baume der menschlichen Kultur erkannt" (Patents are ready to fall and are recognized more and more as a foul fruit on the tree of human culture).[96] At the time of his statement, the German industry was trailing behind the rest of Europe, especially in comparison to Great Britain, which became particularly apparent at the Vienna World Exhibition in 1873, where a conference regarding the protection of industrial products was held.[97] **1.27**

Due to the new legal structure of the *Deutsches Reich* and the beginning of mass production, some parts of German industry demanded new protective laws. Werner von Siemens, who was an industrialist, and Dr. Wilhelm André, the mayor of the Eastern German town of Chemnitz, a then hotspot of industry, founded the so-called "Association for Patent Protection" (*Patentschutzverein*).[98] The *Patentschutzverein* had Dr. André draft the new patent law. The *Patentschutzverein* was supported by the Association of German Engineers (*Verein Deutscher Ingenieure* (VDI)). Werner von Siemens was particularly dissatisfied with **1.28**

[92] Chancellor Bismarck announced the establishment of the German Empire on January 18, 1871, in Versailles, France. For an overview of history of German unification, see US Department of State, Office of the Historian, Issues Relevant to US Foreign Diplomacy: Unification of German States (https://history.state.gov/countries/issues/german-unification).

[93] Dr. Alfred Müller, *Die Entwicklung des Erfindungsschutzes und seiner Gesetzgebung in Deutschland* (1898), 8–9.

[94] For an overview see, e.g., Margrit Seckelmann, *Industrialisierung, Internationalisierung und Patentrecht im Deutschen Reich, 1871–1914* (2006).

[95] Of note, Victor Boehmert was the grandfather of the founders of the patent law firm Boehmert & Boehmert, in which I (Jan Krauss) have the privilege to be a partner.

[96] Translation by author. Victor Böhmert, "Die Erfindungspatente nach volkswirthschaftlichen Grundsätzen und industriellen Erfahrungen mit besonderer Rücksicht auf England und die Schweiz," Besonderer Abdruck aus der *Vierteljahrschrift für Volkswirthschaft und Kulturgeschichte* (1869), Vol . I.

[97] K. H. Manegold, "Der Wiener Patentschutzkongress von 1873," 38 *Technikgeschichte* (1971): 158.

[98] http://www.tu-chemnitz.de/tu/presse/1997/09.20-13.16.html.

the fact that German products were regarded as "cheap and crappy" (as was stated by the president of the Berlin Royal Technical Academy, Franz Reuleaux, at the World Exhibition in 1876 in Philadelphia).[99] Of note, the requirement for the marking "Made in Germany" was installed by the British government by the Merchandise Marks Act of 1887 in order to warn British customers of fakes and of the bad quality of German products.[100] Thus, Werner von Siemens regarded the introduction of a patent law as essential in order to strengthen and promote the German industry and the quality of its products.

1.29 On July 1, 1877, the German *Patentgesetz* (PatG) entered into force.[101] Dr. André's draft was modified only slightly and still forms the basis of today's law. One of the major differences that was newly introduced was the requirement for publication of the invention. The law was developed based on the French patent laws (which initially did not have the publication requirement), the British patent laws, and the German (such as the Saxonian and Prussian) patent laws.[102] The law was industry-friendly, and inventions were assumed to belong to the applicant.

2. Patents in the Nazi Era

1.30 Adolf Hitler stated in 1936 "Der Nationalsozialismus ist unser wertvollstes deutsches Patent" (National socialism is our most valuable patent).[103] However, the Nazi era left many German laws relating to economic issues essentially free from specific political influences; this included the patent law, which was modernized in 1936.[104]

1.31 The 1936 *Patentgesetz* included some key changes. One change that was especially important was the strengthened rights of inventors as compared to the original industry-driven law of 1877, where the rights usually directly belonged to the employer and the inventor was not even mentioned. While it is true that § 8 of the new law stipulated that the government could use an invention for purposes of military defense, such a rule was already present in earlier versions of the law.

1.32 Despite many advances, German industry tried to cease and/or invalidate certain patent rights, as they tried with other valuable property, in particular from Jewish inventors. Examples include the patents of chemist Arthur Eichengrün (who worked on the drug Aspirin®) and of engineer Josef Ganz (who designed a "Beetle" car).[105] Nevertheless, these cases do not seem to be based on actual rules found in the patent law but rather were based on legal repressions and criminal acts done by the Nazis outside of the patent law or when "applying" the laws.

---

99 Alfred Heggen, "Die Bemühungen des 'Vereins Deutscher Ingenieure' um die Reform des Erfindungsschutzes im Vorfeld des Reichspatentgesetzes von 1877," 4 *Technikgeschichte* (1973): 337–44; H. Bluhm, "Die Entstehung des ersten gesamtdeutschen Patentgesetzes," 8(9) *GRUR* (1952): 341–46; and Alfred Heggen, "Zur Vorgeschichte des Reichspatentgesetzes von 1877," 6 *GRUR* (1977): 32.

100 http://agc.gov.ms/wp-content/uploads/2011/10/Merchandise-Marks-Act.pdf.

101 http://de.wikisource.org/wiki/Patentgesetz.

102 See http://www.cdvandt.org/patent-history.htm.

103 Translation by author; Christian Dube, "Religiöse Sprache in Reden Adolf Hitlers: Analysiert an Hand ausgewählter Reden aus den Jahren 1933–1945," Dissertation Universität Kiel, Germany (2004), 238.

104 http://www.wolfgang-pfaller.de/TextPatG.1936.htm.

105 Heinz-Peter Katlewski, "Verheimlichte Herkunft," 12:10 *Zukunft* (2012) (http://www.zentralratdjuden.de/de/article/3865.html).

In 1938, the "Aryanization" of patents was mandated,[106] in that new patents could only be proposed and filed if sponsored by an Aryan German citizen, and not by dissidents, foreigners, or Jews. Existing patents held by Jews also had to be turned over to a German citizen. As one author stated in a particularly polemic paper: "Jewish commercial firms and the associated property, as well as wholesale operations and industry that are Jewish because of the degree to which they are under Jewish ownership, can be de-Jewdified. Important patents and commercial secrets must be transferred to non-Jewish control."[107] **1.33**

In 1942, the *Göring-Speer-Verordnung* (Göring-Speer decree) entered into force, to "effectively promote, exploit, and protect" inventions made by employees, in particular for military purposes.[108] The *Verordnung* was quite similar to the earlier *Reichstarifvertrag für die akademisch gebildeten Angestellten der chemischen Industrie* (Collective wage agreement for the *Reich* for the academically skilled employees in the chemical industry) of April 27, 1920,[109] and formed the basis of the post-war German *Gesetz über Arbeitnehmererfindungen* (ArbnErfG) (Employees'.Invention Law) of 1957,[110] which is essentially still in force today. **1.34**

3. Post-World War II

By 1945, World War II was over, and Germany was divided into four allied sectors. The German Patent Office had to close in 1945, and until 1951 the United States bypassed and/or confiscated virtually all German patents and trademarks. This action was based on Executive Order 9604, dated August 25, 1945,[111] in which President Harry S. Truman provided for the prompt, public, free, and general dissemination of "enemy scientific and industrial information," both in Germany and abroad, based on the *Kontrollratsgesetz* No. 5 of October 30, 1945.[112] Similar measures were undertaken by the British allies. The British and US sectors later formed the so-called "Bizone," which became the nucleus for the later Federal Republic of Germany. **1.35**

In the Russian sector of the eastern part of Germany, the *Deutsche Wirtschaftskommission* (German Trade Commission), which was installed by the Soviets, decided in September 1948 to establish an office in East Berlin for patent filings and trademark applications.[113] This office was later converted into the *Amt für Erfindungs- und Patentwesen der DDR* (Patent Office of the German Democratic Republic). **1.36**

The patent law of the German Democratic Republic (GDR) entered into force on October 1, 1950.[114] Patents were granted as a so-called *Wirtschaftspatent* (economical patent) or *Ausschliessungspatent* (exclusion patent). For inventions that were made by Eastern German "state employees," only economical patents were granted, which could be used by the **1.37**

[106] "Verordnung zur Ausschaltung der Juden aus dem deutschen Wirtschaftsleben" of November 12, 1938, RGBl. 1938 I, 1580.

[107] Max Eichler, *Du bist sofort im Bilde* (1939), 139–42.

[108] Reichsgesetzblatt I 1942, 466–67, and Reichsgesetzblatt I 1943, 257–60, entered into force July 22, 1942.

[109] Published in *GRUR* (1919): 246.

[110] Gesetz über Arbeitnehmererfindungen of 25. July 1957 BGBl. I, 756 (with later amendments).

[111] Available at http://www.trumanlibrary.org/executiveorders/index.php?month=08&year=1945.

[112] Available at http://www.verfassungen.de/de/de45-49/kr-gesetz5.htm.

[113] Decision of the 33th meeting of the secretariat of the DWK of September 15, 1948 (decision S 209/48).

[114] For the version as amended in 1984, see Hemmerling, J., "The New Patent Law of the German Democratic Republic," 23 *Industrial Property* (1984): 252.

state-run economy with compensation paid to the inventor. Other applicants could choose the type of patent they were granted, and the exclusion patent resembled a "modern" patent. Utility models, however, could not be obtained until August 1963.

1.38 Since 1963, the patent code has remained largely unchanged from its original version. While the influence of the United States on the German patent code itself has remained low (due in part to the difference in the underlying legal systems), case law from the US Supreme Court and the US Court of Appeals for the Federal Circuit has had an influence on the legal structure of both Germany and the rest of Europe. Examples can be found in the rules relating to biotechnology, computer-implemented inventions (software), pharmaceuticals (European "Bolar-Exemption"[115]), universities, and technology transfer (resulting in amendments to the *Arbeitnehmererfindergesetz* in 2002[116]).

4. The EPC and Patent Harmonization in the EU

1.39 The reasons for harmonizing intellectual property laws are clearly linked to the economy, particularly in the EU.[117] Exhaustion issues aside, in general, if a patent is governed by the particular law of one member state and its effect is limited to the territory of that state, it is an obstacle to the common market in which goods are to circulate freely.[118]

1.40 In September 1949, French Senator Henri Longchambon proposed to the Council of Europe the creation of a European Patent Office. His proposal, known as the "Longchambon plan," marked the beginning of work on a European patent law aimed at a "European patent."[119] His plan was initially found impracticable by the Council's Committee of Experts on Patents, which concluded that Article 36 of the former EEC Treaty (now EC Treaty) would not be applicable to "industrial and commercial property." Yet in a speech in 1959, German diplomat and scientist Hans von der Groeben demonstrated the necessity of creating an EC patent in parallel with the harmonization of national patent laws, principally by establishing a new patent for the whole of the "Common Market."[120] As early as 1962, the EC Commission was able to publish the Draft Agreement on a European Patent, prepared by a committee of experts from the six EC countries, under the chairmanship of the former president of the German Patent Office, Kurt Haertel, who is now considered by many as the "father" of the European Patent Organization.[121]

1.41 Nevertheless, problems associated with the integration of the system into the internal market of the EC resulted in a split of the European patent law into the European Patent

[115] Named after *Roche Products v. Bolar Pharmaceutical*, 733 F.2d 858 (Fed. Cir. 1984), it is the basis for the § 271(e)(1) exemption, or Hatch-Waxman exemption, and is found in Directive 2001/83/EC [2001] OJ EC L311/67 on the Community code for medicinal products for human use.

[116] See, e.g., Thomas Siepman, "The Global Exportation of the U.S. Bayh-Dole Act," 30 *University of Dayton Law Review* (2004): 210, and Gesetz zur Änderung des Gesetzes über Arbeitnehmererfindungen of January 18, 2002 (BGBl I, 414).

[117] Jan M. Smits and William Bul, *European Harmonisation of Intellectual Property Law: Towards a Competitive Model and a Critique of the Proposed Unified Patent Court*, Maastricht European Private Law Institute Working Paper 2012/16 (July 26, 2012) (http://ssrn.com/abstract=2117835).

[118] http://ec.europa.eu/internal_market/top_layer/goods/index_en.htm.

[119] Otto Bossung, "The Return of European Patent Law in the European Union," 27:3 *IIC* (1996).

[120] Speech by Mr. Von der Groeben on the Occasion of the Meeting on November 19, 1959 regarding the Formation of Industrial Property Law (November 19, 1959) (http://aei.pitt.edu/14935/).

[121] Preliminary Draft Convention on a European Patent Drafted by the Patent Working Group (http://aei.pitt.edu/14064/).

Convention (EPC)[122] and the Community Patent Convention (CPC),[123] the latter of which was regarded as a failure. In contrast, the more successful Strasbourg Patent Convention in 1963 had a significant impact on the EPC, national patent laws across Europe, the Patent Cooperation Treaty (PCT), the Patent Law Treaty (PLT), and the WTO's TRIPS.[124] In 1973, the Munich Diplomatic Conference for the setting up of a European System for the Grant of Patents took place, and the EPC was then enacted in Munich (sometimes referred to as the "Munich Convention"). Based on the EPC, in 1978 the European Patent Office started to examine and grant patents in Munich, Germany.

Thus, today the European system for granting patents can be regarded as "double-layered" in that both national and European patents can be granted. One of the goals of the system, as often stated by the EPO, is to keep it as harmonized as possible.[125] Nevertheless, national differences still exist, in particular with respect to the state of the art and the patentability requirements.[126] **1.42**

The EPO sometimes emphasizes its independence from the EU. The EPO and the Court of Justice for the EU (CJEU) have no institutional link, as was recently confirmed by the Enlarged Board of Appeal of the EPO in decision G2/06,[127] and hence the EPO is not obliged to implement judgments of the CJEU. Also, the EPC has been acceded by thirty-eight contracting states, while the European Union only holds twenty-eight member states. It is clear that the courts of non-EU member states such as Norway, Switzerland, and Turkey are not bound by the judgment of a CJEU decision. Nevertheless, decisions of the EPO have an immediate effect on the EU, as all EU member states are also members of the EPC. Of note, this issue could easily be addressed by creating a new EPC rule providing that the EPO Boards of Appeal have an obligation to refer questions of EU law to the CJEU and to decide in accordance with the CJEU's response with regard to the EU states' designations. **1.43**

The EU has also enacted several IP-related legal texts in the form of Council regulations, which are directly applicable, and directives, which have to be implemented into national law by the member states. Some EU harmonization based on Council regulations has occurred in trademarks,[128] designs,[129] plant varieties,[130] and supplementary protection certificates (SPCs).[131] In addition, Council Regulation (EEC) No. 2913/92 established the Community Customs Code.[132] **1.44**

---

[122] Convention on the Grant of European Patents (European Patent Convention) of 5 October 1973 (EPC).

[123] 89/695/EEC: Agreement relating to Community patents—OJ EU L 401, December 30, 1989 P. 0001–0027.

[124] G. W. Tookey, "Patents in the European Field in Council of Europe, Council of Europe Staff," *European Yearbook 1969* (1971), 76–97.

[125] E.g., in the "Tegernsee Group" (http://www.epo.org/news-issues/news/2012/20121108a.html).

[126] See, e.g., http://www.innovaccess.eu/map.php for national differences in the EU.

[127] G 2/06 of 25.11.2008—Stem cells; OJ EPO 2009, 306.

[128] Council Regulation (EC) No. 207/2009 of February 26, 2009 on the Community trademark L78, 24.3.2009, 1–48.

[129] Council Regulation (EC) No. 6/2002 of December 12, 2001 on Community designs L3, 05.01.2002, 1–24.

[130] Council Regulation (EC) No. 2100/94 of July 27, 1994 on Community plant variety rights, OJ L 227, September 9, 1994, P. 0001–0030.

[131] Council Regulation (EEC) No. 1768/92 of June 18, 1992 concerning the creation of a supplementary protection certificate for medicinal products.

[132] Council Regulation (EEC) No. 2913/92 of October 12, 1992 establishing the Community Customs Code, OJ L 302, October 19, 1992, P. 0001–0050.

1.45 Furthermore, EU directives with respect to trademarks,[133] designs,[134] biotech patents,[135] copyright (the Information Society Directive,[136] also known as the "EU Copyright Directive" (EUCD), and the Copyright Term Directive[137]), and enforcement of intellectual property rights[138] have been issued. The EU has so far failed to provide a directive for the patentability of computer-implemented inventions.

1.46 The EU has also provided the "Brussels" regime, which laid down the rules governing the jurisdiction of courts and the recognition and enforcement of judgments in civil and commercial matters in EU countries, including IP cases. A revised regulation of "Brussels I" came into force on January 9, 2013, addressing, amongst other matters, the issue of "Italian Torpedoes."[139] Recently, the Council of the European Union has published a draft regulation regarding the conditions and procedures for action by the customs authorities where goods suspected of infringing an intellectual property right are entering or are within the customs territory of the EU.[140]

1.47 The CJEU is responsible when it comes to the interpretation of EU-derived laws, and IP is no exception to this. Thus, the CJEU has decided on, for example, trademarks, copyright, the patentability of biotechnological inventions, the exhaustion of patent rights, and—last but not least—going ahead with plans for a unitary EU patent and unified patent court system in twenty-five of the twenty-eight member states of the EU despite ongoing opposition from Poland,[141] Italy, and Spain.[142]

1.48 Currently, neither a unitary patent system nor centralized patent litigation is available in the EU; thus the fact that, often, actions before different national courts are necessary to enforce an IP right or to limit or revoke the right of another is a frequent argument in favor of the harmonization of EU IP law. Litigation in a fragmented system of different national laws gives rise to inefficiencies, such as through undesirable litigation tactics like the initiation of duplicate proceedings, resulting in long delays in the enforcement of IP rights.[143]

---

[133] First Council Directive 89/104/EEC of 21 December 1988 to approximate the laws of the Member States relating to trademarks, OJ L 40, February 11, 1989, 1–7.

[134] Directive 98/71/EC of the European Parliament and of the Council of 13 October 1998 on the legal protection of designs, OJ L 289, October 28, 1998, 28–35.

[135] Directive 98/44/EC of the European Parliament and of the Council of 6 July 1998 on the legal protection of biotechnological inventions, OJ L 213, July 30, 1998, 13–21.

[136] Directive 2001/29/EC of the European Parliament and of the Council of 22 May 2001 on the harmonization of certain aspects of copyright and related rights in the information society, OJ L 167, June 22, 2001, P. 0010–0019.

[137] Council Directive 93/98/EEC of 29 October 1993 harmonizing the term of protection of copyright and certain related rights, OJ L 290, November 11, 1993, P. 0009–0013.

[138] (corrected) Directive 2004/48/EC of the European Parliament and of the Council of 29 April 2004 on the enforcement of intellectual property rights (OJ L 157, April 30, 2004), OJ L 195, June 2 2004, P. 0016–0025.

[139] Regulation (EU) No. 1215/2012 of the European Parliament and of the Council of 12 December 2012 on jurisdiction and the recognition and enforcement of judgments in civil and commercial matters, OJ L 351, 1–32.

[140] Document 5129/13 (http://register.consilium.europa.eu/pdf/en/13/st05/st05129.en13.pdf).

[141] The Polish government has actually decided to not to sign the Unitary Patent agreement until it has observed how the system is implemented in other European countries.

[142] Judgment of the Court (Grand Chamber) of April 16, 2013—*Kingdom of Spain and Italian Republic v. Council of the European Union* (Joined Cases C-274/11 and C 295/11).

[143] See M. Mejer and B. van Pottelsberghe, *Economic Incongruities in the European Patent System* (2009) (http://www.ieb.ub.edu/aplicacio/fitxers/CI09Mejer.pdf).

D. Japan

1. Meiji Restoration

Japan started to embrace patent law upon entering into the Meiji Restoration in 1868. Americans and Europeans used to consider Asian countries' lack of sufficient patent protection a so-called "cultural barrier," arguing that the concept of granting monopolies on intangibles such as technologies and ideas were foreign to Asian cultures.[144] However, as far as Japan is concerned, the pre-1868 feudal central and local governments in actuality introduced a variety of systems for granting subsidies and monopolies for technologies to promote industrial developments.[145] To substantiate the cultural barrier view, American and European scholars often cite a law prohibiting technical innovation issued by the *Tokugawa bakufu* in 1718.[146] However, the scope of this prohibition was limited to luxury products, such as silk textiles. Moreover, the *bakufu* had a system similar to a patent system, granting each local government exclusive rights for making and selling local products unique to the region, and allowed the local governments to run laboratories for improving local products.[147] **1.49**

When the Meiji government overthrew the *Edo bakufu*, it eliminated all feudal patent systems, which led to a chaotic situation in the market.[148] To maintain an orderly market, the government found it necessary to centralize a power to grant patents and was ready to adopt a modern patent system when it was pressed by foreign countries to adopt their intellectual property systems.[149] As a result, the government enacted the first set of rules as the Summary Rules of Monopoly in 1871.[150] Baron Korekiyo Takahashi, who later became the first commissioner of the Japan Patent Office (JPO) and then the prime minister of Japan, was inspired by an American scholar to whom he served as an interpreter and played a key role in introducing a patent system.[151] **1.50**

However, the Meiji government realized after a short period of time that it was not able to find Japanese engineers who were able to examine patent applications[152] and suspended the Summary Rules of Monopoly only one year after their enactment.[153] It was not until 1885 that the government, heavily relying on the French Patent Act of 1835, was able to establish the first functional Japanese patent system.[154] The system was also influenced by the US **1.51**

---

[144] Toshiko Takenaka, "Does a Cultural Barrier to Intellectual Property Trade Exist? The Japanese Example," 29 *N.Y.U. J. Int'l L. & Pol.* (1997): 153.

[145] Ibid. 154–58. For further discussion on the pre-1968 systems to promote technological developments, see Japan Patent Office, *Kōgyō Kōgyō Shoyūken Hykunen She* (1984), vol . I, and Japan Patent Office, *Moto'o Endo, 1 Nihon Shokunin Shi No Kenkyu* (1985).

[146] Shiashi Kin'shirei (Sumptuary Regulation).

[147] Japan Patent Office, *Kōgyō Kōgyō Shoyūken Hykunen She*, vol. I, 8.

[148] Ibid. 15.

[149] Ibid. 23. Takenaka, "Cultural Barrier."

[150] Senbai ryaku kisoku, Ordinance No. 175 of 1871.

[151] Korekiyo Takahashi, "Wagakuni Tokkyoseido no Ki'n (Origin of Japanese Patent System)," 1(32) *Kōgyō shoyūken Zasshi* (1908) (http://www.iip.or.jp/chizaishi/pdf/korekiyo2.pdf). For an overview in English of the fundamental role Korekiyo Takahashi played in the development of the early patent system in Japan, see Richard J. Smethurst: *From Foot Soldier to Finance Minister: Takahashi Korekiyo* (2007), 60–78.

[152] Takahashi, "Wagakuni Tokkyoseido no Ki'n," 3.

[153] Dajôkan Ordinance No. 105 of 1872.

[154] The most striking resemblances with the French Patent Act of 1835 were the exclusion of patents for pharmaceutical inventions, the recognition of improvement patents, and the nullification of a patent upon

patent system because it followed the first-to-invent principle.[155] Under this new system, an applicant could choose patent terms of five, ten, or fifteen years. Patent infringement could be pursued and injunctive relief could be requested in court, provided that products put on the market by the patentee were marked as patented. Patent infringement was also classified as a criminal offense, punishable by a term of imprisonment of between one month and one year. This second Japanese patent system proved substantially more successful than the first system in 1871, enticing 425 patent applications within its first year and 1,384 applications in its second year.[156] Because of the inability to find examiners, this first functional system did not provide for a structural examination system of applications.[157] Rather, the Ministry of Agriculture and Trade had the discretion to grant patent privileges when it deemed an invention appropriate.

1.52 Following a trip to the United States, the United Kingdom, France, and Germany by Baron Takahashi to study their respective patent systems in order to set up a patent office in Japan,[158] a thorough revision of the patent system was implemented in 1888.[159] A patent office, *Senbai Tokkyojo* (Exclusive Selling Office) was established for the examination of applications, and thus an applicant was now entitled to have a patent granted as long as the application satisfied the requirements for a patent. Modeled on the German law, a system to appeal the rejection of a patent application was introduced.[160] Finally, in addition to a claim for injunctive relief, a patentee in an infringement case could request damages.[161]

1.53 In both the 1885 and the 1888 patent law, the right to obtain patents was reserved to Japanese citizens. The first exception to this was introduced in 1896, when Japan granted German citizens the right to obtain Japanese patents.[162] Further bilateral treaties were concluded in the following years with Denmark,[163] the United Kingdom,[164] and the United States.[165] Finally, the ban against foreigners obtaining patents in Japan was lifted when Japan joined the Paris Convention in 1899.[166] However, foreign citizens still needed to have a Japanese address or a representative in Japan to be able to obtain a patent. Further

importation of the patented product by the patentee from abroad. See Christopher Heath, "Patent Law," in Wilhelm Roehl (ed.), *History of Law in Japan since 1868* (2005), 424.

155 Baron Takahashi viewed the United States as a model for Japan to become a great nation through a patent system. The USPTO extensively provided Mr. Takahashi with information and materials on patent examination. "The End of the First Century of the Patent Office," in *History of the United Patent Office*, 198 (http://www.myoutbox.net/popch31.htm). For a more detailed discussion about the first-to-invent system, see this volume, Ch. 7, 7.52.

156 Guntram Rahn, "The Role of Industrial Property in Economic Development: The Japanese Experience," *IIC* (1983): 461.

157 Takahashi, "Wagakuni Tokkyoseido no Ki'n," 3.

158 Baron Takahashi visited the United States, the United Kingdom, France, and Germany and found the US Patent System to be the most advanced. Takahashi Korekiyo, "Memory of Japan Patent Office," Speech Note at the Ceremony of 50th Anniversary of the Enactment of Patent Act (September 29, 1934) (http://www.iip.or.jp/chizaishi/pdf/korekiyo3.pdf).

159 Tokkyo Jōrei (Patent Ordinance) Law No. 84 of 1888.

160 Shinichi Aihara, "Research and Study on Patent Invalidation and Infringement," 9 *IIP Bulletin* (2000): 108.

161 Heath, "Patent Law," 426.

162 Treaty of Shipping and Trade, printed in German at RGBl. 1896, 722.

163 Royal Danish Decree of November 19, 1897.

164 Protocol between Great Britain and Japan of November 20, 1897.

165 Treaty between the United States and Japan of January 13, 1897.

166 Implemented in the course of Law No. 36/1899; Japanese version reprinted in Japan Patent Office (ed.), *Kôgyôshoyûken Seidô Hyakunen Shi* (Centennial History of Intellectual Propety) (1984), 202.

changes necessitated by the accession to the Paris Convention included the introduction of a system of seeking appeals at the Imperial Court against decisions of the patent office. The Patent Act of 1888 also introduced a bifurcated system similar to the current German system, entrusting civil courts with infringement actions and the patent office with reviewing the validity of patents.[167] The requirement of marking patented goods in order to be able to enforce the corresponding patents was abolished. The Patent Act of 1899 introduced a system of appealing JPO trial decisions to the *Daishin'in* (Great Court of Cassation), but the ground of appeal had to relate to a legal issue.[168]

2. Major Developments through the Twentieth Century

The Japanese government finally decided to abolish the first-to-invent system and replaced it with a first-to-file system during a revision of the Patent Act in 1921.[169] Somewhat similar to the situation in the United States prior to their much more recent transition to a first-to-file system, patents had almost always been granted to the first applicant. The Patent Act, as revised in 1921, modified the bifurcated system, allowing civil courts to stay infringement proceedings while the Patent Office proceeded with its review of the validity of the patent. The 1921 Act established a complaint appeal system within the JPO against JPO trial decisions and made possible appeals from complaint appeal decisions to the *Daishin'in*.[170] Pharmaceuticals, chemical substances, and articles of food remained non-patentable until well into the twentieth century. **1.54**

After the World War II, the new Japanese constitution required some revisions to the administrative provisions of the Patent Act.[171] These revisions led to a restructuring of the judicial system. The Tokyo High Court was given exclusive jurisdiction to review all appeals against decisions of the JPO, and the Supreme Court to review appeals from the Tokyo High Court. In 1950, the Tokyo High Court created a special division to review appeals from the JPO.[172] The rapid economic development of Japan after World War II required further changes to its substantive patent laws. **1.55**

The Patent Act of 1959 adopted all the basic structures of today's Patent Act.[173] For the first time, the Patent Act contained detailed provisions on infringement and remedies, including methods for calculating damages. Between 1959 and the burst of the economic bubble around 1990, the Japanese economy continued to rely increasingly on patents. By the beginning of the 1980s, the JPO handled more patent applications than any other patent office in the world. Japan had developed from a net importer into one of the largest exporters of patent rights and continued to modernize its laws to facilitate the process of obtaining patents. In 1976, the patent law was amended to allow patent protection for pharmaceutical and food-related inventions.[174] The accession to the PCT in 1978 required certain adjustments to allow for PCT applications.[175] In 1987, the Japanese patent law was amended to **1.56**

---

[167] Aihara, "Patent Invalidation," 109.
[168] Tokkyohō (Patent Act) Law No. 36 of 1899.
[169] Tokkyohō (Patent Act) Law No. 96 of 1921.
[170] Aihara, "Patent Invalidation," 109.
[171] Tokkyohō (Patent Act) Law No. 172 of 1948.
[172] Chiteki Koto Saibansho (Intellectual Property High Court), "Gaiyō · Enkaku" (Overview · History) (http://www.ip.courts.go.jp/aboutus/history/index.html).
[173] Tokkyohō (Patent Act) Law No. 121 of 1959.
[174] Tokkyohō (Patent Act) Law No. 46 of 1975.
[175] Tokkyohō (Patent Act) Law No. 30 of 1978.

allow for multiple-claim patents, namely patents featuring more than one claim.[176] Three years later, an electronic patent filing system was introduced.[177] Accession to the TRIPS Agreement in 1994 required an extension of patent terms: from fifteen years to twenty years after the filing date.[178] In 2002, computer software inventions were, for the first time, recognized as patentable, provided that the invention in question was implemented in conjunction with a hardware apparatus.

3. Pro-Patent Era

1.57 Most of the material amendments to the Japanese patent law between 1959 and the end of the twentieth century were developments and adjustments to substantive patent law. Commentators, in the meantime, continued to point out the difficulties in enforcing infringed patents due to deficiencies in procedural law. In order to strengthen the position of intellectual property and patent owners, and thereby foster innovation to enable economic revitalization, the Japanese government decided to put additional emphasis on revising intellectual property laws. To enhance the effectiveness of patent enforcement, the parliament passed a wide-ranging revision of the Civil Procedure Code, which came into effect in 1996, and a series of revisions to the Patent Act in between 1998 and 2004.[179] These revisions were mainly aimed at facilitating the process of obtaining evidence against patent infringers, entitling a patent owner to higher damages if infringement was found, and shortening the duration of the infringement procedures.[180]

1.58 The efforts of improving the standing of intellectual property were, somewhat symbolically, expressed in the Basic Law on Intellectual Property.[181] In 2005, the IP High Court, which was modeled to some degree after the US Court of Appeals for the Federal Circuit, was established as a central appellate court for patent cases and other IP cases involving technologies such computer software copyrights. While the legislature made efforts to strengthen the ability of patent owners to enforce their patents, the Supreme Court effectively undermined such efforts in the *Kilby* decision in 2000 by ordering the removal of the principle of bifurcation.[182] Allowing an alleged infringer to raise the defense of invalidity of a patent both at the JPO and in the infringement proceedings in court resulted in a significant increase in the invalidations of patents in the years after 2000, thereby effectively weakening the position of Japanese patent holders.

---

176 Tokkyohō (Patent Act) Law No. 27 of 1987; see further at Toshiko Takenaka, "Interpreting Patent Claims," 17 *IIC Studies* (1995): 48.

177 Tokkyohō (Patent Act) Law No. 30 of 1990.

178 Christopher Heath, "Continuity and Development in Japanese Intellectual Property Rights," *IIC* (1995): 901.

179 For further discussion on the judicial reform on patent enforcement, see Ch. 2, 2.62.

180 Ryu Takabayashi and Toshiko Takenaka, *Japan's IP Strategy and IP Enforcement Revisions: Improvements in Evidence Taking and Damages*, CASRIP Newsletter, Spring 2009, Vol. 16, Issue 2 (http://www.law.washington.edu/Casrip/Newsletter/default.aspx?year=2009&article=newsv16i2KiyoMunich).

181 Chiteki Zaisan Kihonhō (Basic Law on Intellectual Property) Law No. 122 of 2002. For a general discussion on the Basic IP Law and its impact, see Toshiko Takenaka and Ichiro Nakayama, "Will Intellectual Property Policy Save Japan from Recession? Japan's Basic Intellectual Property Law and its Implementation through the Strategic Program," 35:8 *IIC* (2004): 877; Toshiko Takenaka, "Success or Failure? Japan's National Strategy on Intellectual Property and Evaluation of its Impact from the Comparative Law Perspective," 8 *Wash. U. Global Studies L. Rev.* (2009): 379.

182 *Fujitsu Co. v. Texas Instruments, Inc.*, 54-4 Minshu 1368 (Sup. Ct., April 11, 2000); English versions of the decision of the Supreme Court are available at the website of the Supreme Court (http://www.courts.go.jp/app/hanrei_en/detail?id=487 and at *IIC* (2004): 91.

2

PATENT ENFORCEMENT INSTITUTIONS

A. United States

1. Overview

2.01 US patents may be enforced through negotiation and mediation or arbitration if patentees agree with the accused infringers to settle their disputes using these procedures. Without such consent, patentees have two options for enforcing their US patents: (1) file a civil action at a district court or (2) file a request for a section 337 investigation with the US International Trade Commission (ITC).[1] To choose the latter option, a patentee must satisfy the domestic industry requirement: the product infringed by the asserted patent must exist in the United States; the patentee must make a substantial investment in the facilities, labor, or capital or in the exploitation of the asserted patent; and the patentee or the licensee must practice at least one claim of the asserted patent.[2] The ITC has become a popular forum for patentees to enforce their patents because patentees have remedies similar to an injunction that are easier to obtain than those through the courts.[3]

2.02 If a patentee is unable to meet the domestic industry requirement, the only available option is to file a civil action at a district court. Until the *ex parte* re-examination was introduced in 1980, US courts enjoyed the exclusive authority to examine validity after a patent grant. Today, in order to defend a patent infringement claim by challenging the validity of an asserted patent, an alleged infringer can choose to raise a defense of invalidity in a civil action at a district court or begin one of the post-issuance procedures to challenge validity at the United States Patent and Trademark Office (USPTO).[4] A party sued at the ITC for a section 337 investigation can also raise patent invalidity as a defense.

2. Courts

(a) *Federal versus State*

2.03 The US judicial branch has two court systems: federal and state. The overwhelming majority of patent infringement actions are brought in federal district courts rather than state courts. US federal courts have limited subject matter jurisdiction and require a party to establish a statutory basis for the court's jurisdiction. Patentees can easily establish a basis because a federal statute provides original and exclusive jurisdiction over all suits arising

---

[1] 19 U.S.C. § 1337 (1930).

[2] Ibid. § 1337(a)(1)(A). For more discussion, see Ch. 10, 10.62.

[3] Ethan Horwitz and Andrea Parcelli, "ITC: Forum of Choice for Patent Litigation," *New York Law Journal* (October 25, 2010) (http://www.kslaw.com/imageserver/kspublic/library/publication/10-10nyljhorwitzpacelli.pdf).

[4] See Ch. 7, 7.26.

under any act of Congress relating to patents.[5] However, not all patent-related disputes arise under the Patent Act. Disputes on patent licensing and assignment arise under state law, and thus parties must resolve these disputes at a state district court.[6]

2.04 Unlike Germany, the US judicial branch does not have separate systems for civil and administrative proceedings. Instead, Congress enacted the Administrative Procedure Act (APA), which governs the operations of federal agencies.[7] The APA provides the US federal courts jurisdiction to directly review agency decisions.[8] Patentees can appeal a decision of the Patent Trial and Appeal Board (PTAB) to the US Court of Appeals for the Federal Circuit (Federal Circuit). The APA applies to PTAB decisions, and thus the Federal Circuit must examine the USPTO's fact-finding with the substantial review standard.[9]

(b) US District Courts

2.05 US federal district courts are courts of first instance and trial courts that have general jurisdiction to hear any type of civil or criminal cases. There are ninety-four federal judicial districts, with at least one district court located in each. Patentees can choose to file a patent infringement action among any of the district courts that meet the personal jurisdiction and venue requirements.[10] Only district courts can take evidence and find facts either by a jury trial or by a bench trial. Any additional evidence is admitted in appeal courts.

2.06 Judges in all three levels of federal courts are nominated by the president of the United States and confirmed by the Senate.[11] Unlike Japanese judges, US federal judges are appointed for a life term in the court they are appointed and thus are not transferred to any other courts. Very few judges have science backgrounds although judges in patent-heavy districts hire law clerks with science backgrounds. Judges who adjudicate patent cases at district courts include magistrate judges who are appointed by a majority vote of the active district court.[12] With the consent of the parties, magistrate judges can adjudicate civil cases, such as patent infringement cases, in the same manner as district court judges.[13] Some magistrate judges have science backgrounds and are particularly appointed to assist federal judges in patent cases. District court judges may appoint special masters to assist the judges in patent cases.[14] Special masters appointed for patent cases are almost exclusively attorneys with a high level of training and education in patent law and are responsible for overseeing the discovery process and conducting claim construction.[15] Many of the masters are partners of large firms.

---

5 28 U.S.C. § 1338. See Ch. 10, 10.02.

6 Donald S. Chisum, "The Allocation of Jurisdiction between State and Federal Courts in Patent Litigation," 46 *Wash. L. Rev.* (1971): 633, 636.

7 Administrative Procedure Act, Pub. L. 79-404, 60 Stat. 237 (1946).

8 5 U.S.C. § 702.

9 *Dickinson v. Zurko*, 527 U.S. 150, 119 S. Ct. 1816, 144 L. Ed. 2d 143, 50 U.S.P.Q. 2d 1930 (U.S. 1999).

10 See Ch. 10, 10.03–10.04.

11 Const. Art. III, § 1.

12 28 U.S.C. § 631(b)(5). For more information about magistrate judges, see Magistrate Judges Division, Office of Judges Programs, Administrative Office of the United States Courts, *The Selection, Appointment, and Reappointment of United States Magistrate Judges* (2010) (http://www.ksd.uscourts.gov/selection-appointment-reappointment-of-magistrate-judges/).

13 28 U.S.C. § 631(b)(5).

14 Fed. R. Civ. P. 53(b)(2).

15 For more information about special masters, see Jay P. Kesan and Gwendolyn G. Ball, *A Study of the Role and Impact of Special Masters in Patent Cases* (2009) (http://www.fjc.gov/public/pdf.nsf/lookup/specmapa.pdf/$file/specmapa.pdf).

They have a significant influence on the outcome of patent litigation because their reports and recommendations are almost always adopted by the court without any modifications.

In the United States, the right to trial by jury is guaranteed under the Constitution.[16] Juries have participated in patent cases since the enactment of the first Patent Act in 1970, but their participation was marginal until patentees began to request jury trials in the 1990s.[17] In the 2000s and 2010s, more than 60 percent of patent cases were tried by juries.[18] The number of jurors in civil cases must be between six and twelve.[19] Although a jury's role is limited to fact-finding, such fact-finding includes the determination of infringement and calculation of damages, and judges depend on such fact-finding to answer important patent law questions such as novelty and nonobviousness.[20] Patentees favor juries because there is a higher patentee success rate and larger damages when cases are tried by juries rather than judges.[21] **2.07**

In 2011, Congress enacted the Patent Pilot Program Act to direct patent cases to judges in selected district courts.[22] Judges in the selected district courts who volunteer are designated to participate in the program. When non-designated judges decline to hear patent and plant variety cases, which are randomly assigned, such cases are then reassigned to the designated judges. The term of this program is limited to ten years because it is an experiment to examine whether concentrating patent cases among designated judges improves efficiency by reducing the reversal rate of such cases. During the first two years of the program, one-third of the patent cases were reassigned and concentrated among the designated judges.[23] **2.08**

Most district courts selected to participate in the program have adopted their own local rules, which differ from each other with respect to the procedure for conducting discovery and *Markman* hearings.[24] Some indicate concern that these differences encourage forum shopping among the participating district courts. The impact of the Pilot Program is not yet clear, and more data is necessary to make an appropriate assessment. **2.09**

(c) US Court of Appeals for the Federal Circuit

Although cases can be filed in any district court that meets the personal jurisdiction and venue requirements, all appeals are filed with the Federal Circuit. As discussed in Chapter 1, the Federal Circuit was created in 1982. The Federal Circuit's jurisdiction consists of a broad scope beyond the exclusive jurisdiction of patent appeals. The scope includes not only appeals **2.10**

---

16 Const. Art. 3, § 2. Fed. R. Civ. P. 38.

17 Kimberly A. Moore, "Judges, Juries and Patent Cases: An Empirical Peek Inside the Back Box," 99 *Mich. L. Rev.* (2000): 366.

18 PwC, *2014 Patent Litigation Study* (2014), 8 (http://www.pwc.com/en_US/us/forensic-services/publications/assets/2014-patent-litigation-study.pdf).

19 Fed. R. Civ. P. 48(a).

20 Phillipe Signore, "On the Role of Juries in Patent Litigation," 83 *Journal of the Patent & Trademark Office Society* (2001): 791 (Part 1), 896 (Part 2) (http://www.oblon.com/content/uploads/2015/04/256.pdf).

21 Ibid. 8–9.

22 Patent Pilot Program Act, Pub. L. No. 111-349, 124 Stat. 3674 (2011). Fourteen district courts have been selected. For a list of the select district courts, see http://www.gpo.gov/fdsys/pkg/PLAW-111publ349/content-detail.html.

23 Ron Vogel, "The Patent Pilot Program: Reassignment Rates and the Effect of Local Patent Rules," *NYIPLA Bulletin* October/November 19 (2013) (http://www.fr.com/files/Uploads/Documents/Vogel.NYIPLABulletin.Pilot-Patent-Program-Reassignment-Rates-and-Effects-of-Local-Rules.OctNov2013.pdf).

24 A *Markman* hearing is a procedure to conduct claim construction. For more discussions, see Ch. 4, 4.24.

arising under the Patent Act but also appeals from the USPTO's board decisions, including cases on trademark, international trade, government contracts, certain money claims against the US government, federal personnel, veterans' benefits, and public safety officers' benefits claims.[25] Only 31 percent of the court's jurisdiction consists of intellectual property cases.[26]

2.11 The US president can appoint up to twelve judges for the Federal Circuit.[27] The judge highest in seniority among the qualified judges (active service to the court for at least one year and under the age of 65) is appointed as the Chief Judge. The Chief Judge has administrative responsibilities but does not have the power to assign cases. Instead, cases are randomly assigned to three-judge panels. Although only a few of the Federal Circuit judges have a science background, all judges are assisted by law clerks, and many of the clerks have a science and patent law background.

2.12 A party may petition for a hearing or rehearing *en banc*, where a decision is reviewed by a panel of all the active judges.[28] An *en banc* hearing or rehearing is not ordered unless (1) such hearing or rehearing is necessary to secure uniformity of the court's decisions or (2) the proceedings involve a question of exceptional importance such as an argument to overrule a binding precedent.[29] A grant of a petition for an *en banc* hearing is rare, with less than ten cases per year. Although only the court *en banc* can overrule a binding precedent, a party may argue for the overruling of a binding precedent in the Federal Circuit without petitioning for a hearing *en banc*.[30] The adjudicating panel will decide whether to ask all active judges to consider the issue *en banc*. The Federal Circuit may *sua sponte* (i.e., of its own accord) order an appeal to be initially heard or be reheard *en banc* without a petition from either party. Among decisions from the Federal Circuit, a decision resulting from an *en banc* hearing has the highest authority as a precedent because the court is particularly reluctant to overrule its own precedent in order to preserve the policies and principle of *stare decisis*.[31]

(d) US Supreme Court

2.13 The Supreme Court has the highest authority in the federal system and can freely overrule its own precedents and precedents of intermediate appellate courts. During the first three decades after the creation of the Federal Circuit, the Supreme Court's involvement in patent jurisprudence was limited because the Court seldom granted certiorari to review patent cases in the 1980s, 1990s, and 2000s.[32] The Court has recently begun to take an active role in taking up patent cases and reversing Federal Circuit decisions.

---

[25] 28 U.S.C. § 1295.

[26] CAFC, Court Jurisdiction (http://www.cafc.uscourts.gov/the-court/court-jurisdiction.html).

[27] 28 U.S.C. § 44.

[28] Fed. R. Civ. P. R. 35(a). For a discussion on the *en banc* review in the Federal Courts of Appeals, see Alexandra Sadinski, "Redefining *En Banc* Review in the Federal Courts of Appeals," 82 *Fordham L.R.* (2014): 2001 (http://ir.lawnet.fordham.edu/cgi/viewcontent.cgi?article=4965&context=flr).

[29] Fed. R. Civ. P. R. 35(a).

[30] CAFC, Federal Circuit Rules, R. 35(a) (http://www.cafc.uscourts.gov/images/stories/rules-of-practice/rules.pdf).

[31] *Lighting Ballast Control, LLC v. Philips Elecs. North Am. Corp.*, 744 F.3d 1272, 109 U.S.P.Q. 2d 1969 (Fed. Cir. 2014).

[32] Dennis Crouch, "Supreme Court Patent Cases Per Decade," *Patently-O*, July 20, 2014 (http://patentlyo.com/patent/2014/07/supreme-patent-decade.html). For a discussion on the Supreme Court–Federal Circuit relationship, see Mark D. Janis, "Patent Law in the Age of the Invisible Supreme Court," *U. Illi. L. Rev.* (2001): 387; Rochelle Cooper Dreyfuss, "What the Federal Circuit Can Learn from the Supreme

The US Supreme Court consists of the Chief Justice of the United States and eight associate justices. Currently, none of the Supreme Court justices have a science background. Supreme Court justices are assisted by law clerks, but it is rare for these law clerks to have any science or patent backgrounds. Different sectors of the patent community submit amicus curiae briefs to assist Supreme Court justices in understanding the technology and the unique features of patent law.[33] A party can file an amicus brief covering relevant subject matter that is not raised by the parties if the subject matter is of considerable help to the Court.[34] Although the rule requires the parties' consent or court approval to file an amicus brief, the Court grants leaves liberally.[35] Amicus briefs are most frequently filed by companies and industry groups.[36] In decisions by the Supreme Court, amicus briefs submitted by the US government are the most influential on the merits.[37] **2.14**

3. USPTO

The USPTO is the federal agency in the department of commerce that is in charge of granting US patents and registering trademarks and also advises the US president, the secretary of commerce, and US government agencies on intellectual property policy, protection, and enforcement.[38] Since the introduction of the *ex parte* re-examination in 1980, the USPTO has played an important role in patent enforcement by giving parties the option to have their validity challenge reviewed by administrative patent judges, who are patent law experts with relevant technological backgrounds. The USPTO's Patent Trial and Appeal Board is a quasi-judicial body that decides patent validity in post-grant *inter partes* procedures. **2.15**

Administrative patent judges are appointed by the Secretary of Commerce.[39] Administrative patent judges have both science backgrounds and law degrees, with extensive patent enforcement and/or procurement experience. Moreover, they are assisted by technical support staff. The judges review rejections by examiners and appeals of re-examinations during the *ex parte* re-examination and conduct derivation proceedings, *inter partes* reviews, and post-grant reviews.[40] The reviews and trials are conducted by at least three administrative patent judges.[41] **2.16**

4. US International Trade Commission

The International Trade Commission (ITC) is a federal agency with a quasi-judicial body to make determinations of patent infringement and other IP infringement as well as **2.17**

Court," 59 *Ame. U.L.R.* (2010): 787 (http://digitalcommons.wcl.american.edu/cgi/viewcontent.cgi?article=1015&context=aulr).

[33] Kelly Lynch, "Best Friends? Supreme Court Law Clerks on Effective Amicus Curiae Briefs," 20 *J.L. & Pol.* (2004): 33, 41.

[34] Sup. Ct. R. 37 (http://www.law.cornell.edu/rules/supct/rule_37).

[35] Reagan Simpson and Mary Vasaly, *The Amicus Brief: How to Be a Good Friend of the Court* (2d ed., 2004), 37.

[36] Colleen V. Chien, "Patent Amicus Briefs: What the Courts' Friends Can Teach Us about the Patent System," 1 *UC Irvine L.R.* (2010): 398, 411.

[37] Ibid. 425.

[38] USPTO website, "Who We Are" (http://www.uspto.gov/about/index.jsp).

[39] 35 U.S.C. § 6(d).

[40] Ibid. § 6(b).

[41] Ibid. § 6(c).

import-related claims that injure domestic industry.[42] The ITC is headed by six commissioners appointed by the president of the United States. Administrative law judges adjudicate patent infringement claims at the ITC. Like administrative patent judges at the USPTO, the administrative law judges at the ITC must be lawyers with experience in patent law and intellectual property as well as some other trade law-related practice. Once an investigation is instituted and notice of the investigation at the ITC is published, the procedure is similar to a case in a federal district court: discovery, the chance to move for summary adjudication, a hearing before a judge, and a final decision.[43]

2.18 The ITC is authorized to issue two types of remedies: exclusion orders and cease and desist orders.[44] An exclusion order directs the US Customs and Border Protection to exclude articles that infringe an asserted patent from entering the United States. A cease and desist order directs the respondent in the section 337 investigation to cease its patent infringing acts. A cease and desist order is enforced by the ITC.

B. Germany

1. Overview

2.19 As mentioned above, in Germany today there exist two separate systems that can be used by an applicant to obtain a patent with legal effect in Germany. One is the national system, administered by the German Patent and Trademark Office (GPTO),[45] and the other requires filing a patent at the European Patent Office (EPO). Nevertheless, after a grant of patent (and apart from opposition and limitation), any enforcement and/or validity challenges for patents under either system are handled exclusively by national German institutions/courts, and this chapter will briefly introduce both the systems and offices involved.

2. Patent Offices—EPO and GPTO

2.20 The first patent law of 1877 provided rules for establishing an office for the examination and grant of patents, and on July 1, 1877 the *Kaiserliche Patentamt* was established in Berlin.[46] On November 27, 1877 the first German patent was granted for a "method for producing a red ultramarine dye."[47] In 1905 the *Kaiserliche Patentamt* moved into a new building in Berlin-Kreuzberg, which is still in use today as a sub-branch of the GPTO and EPO, and in 1919 the *Kaiserliche Patentamt* was renamed *Reichspatentamt*.

2.21 In 1945 the Berlin Patent Office had to close, and about one-third of the Patent Office building in Berlin was destroyed by a heavy bombing attack on February 5 1945, but in October 1949 the German Patent Office opened in the premises of the library of the Deutsche Museum in Munich. Officially, the GPTO was moved to Munich because the technical library of the Deutsche Museum was still largely intact and some parts of the patent register had been shipped to Bavaria during the war. Nevertheless, some historians believe that the US allies wanted to

[42] 19 U.S.C. § 1337.
[43] For more discussion on the ITC procedures, see Ch. 10, 10.57 et seq.
[44] 19 U.S.C. § 1337(d).
[45] See http://www.dpma.de/amt/geschichte/index.html.
[46] Reichspatentamt (ed.), *Das Reichspatentamt 1877–1927. Rückblick auf sein Werden und Wirken* (1927).
[47] After being filed on July 1, 1877.

move the Office away from the influence of the Russians in order to keep a close eye on the technical developments in Germany.[48]

In 1951 a branch of the GPTO reopened in Berlin, and in 1959 the Office moved into its own building by the Isar River. In 1990 the GDR patent office was fused with the GPTO, and in 1998 another branch opened in Jena. The Office has officially been called the *Deutsches Patent- und Markenamt* (German Patent and Trademark Office) since 1998.[49] **2.22**

Proceedings at the GPTO are only conducted in German, and § 35 of the German Patent Act (Patentgesetz, PatG) requires a German translation after filing (which can itself be done in any language) in order to prosecute the application. The translation requirements have been relaxed with the last amendment of the PatG (*Patentrechtsnovelle*[50]). **2.23**

The 1973 diplomatic conference in Munich to discuss the introduction of a European patent grant procedure concluded with the signing of the EPC by sixteen participants. Four years later, on October 7, 1977, the EPC came into force, and the EPO in Munich began its work on June 1 1978.[51] That same year, the Office expanded to include a site in both Berlin and the former International Patent Institute in The Hague. The EPO is a patent success story: the one hundred thousandth application was filed in 1983, and in 1997 filing figures reached a million. Today, the EPO has several sites in Munich, the most prominent being the main building at the Isar River, next to the GPTO, and the Pschorr-Hoefe buildings in Bayerstrasse. The EPO works in three different official languages: English, German, and French. **2.24**

Decisions of the GPTO can be appealed, and while initially the Office handled such appeals in-house, since 1961 the Federal Patent Court has become responsible for these cases. Decisions by the EPO can be appealed as well, but these continue to be handled by their in-house Boards of Appeal. Though they are integrated into the organizational structure of the EPO, the Boards always stress their independence from the Office in their decisions.[52] **2.25**

There are currently twenty-seven technical boards of appeal (responsible for "T"-decisions), plus the Legal Board of Appeal (responsible for "J"-decisions), the Enlarged Board of Appeal (responsible for "G"-decisions), and the Disciplinary Board of Appeal (responsible for "D"-decisions). The members and chairmen are appointed for a term of five years. There is an initiative to physically move the location of the Boards out of the EPO office buildings in order to stress and ensure their independence, and this has resulted in a draft for a revision of the European Patent Convention (EPC). However, in order to implement this initiative, a diplomatic conference will be necessary, and thus far plans to find a new venue—such as The Hague—have been met with some resistance. **2.26**

The European Commission of Human Rights (now defunct) noted in *Lenzing v. Germany*[53] that "given the procedural guarantees available before the EPO, any transfer of powers to **2.27**

---

[48] An operation with a similar purpose was "Operation Paperclip," which was used by the United States to recruit scientists of Nazi Germany for employment.

[49] In order to indicate the increased importance of trademarks.

[50] BT-Drucksache 17/10308 (http://dip21.bundestag.de/dip21/btd/17/103/1710308.pdf).

[51] See http://www.epo.org/about-us/office/history.html.

[52] http://www.epo.org/about-us/boards-of-appeal.html.

[53] Application No. 39025/97 by LENZING AG against Germany (http://hudoc.echr.coe.int/eng?i=001-4410).

the EPO which led to the German courts' refusal to deal with the matter, cannot be said to be incompatible with the applicant company's rights under the Convention."[54] Although a number of national courts have held that decisions of the Boards of Appeal are not subject to national review and the court in *Lenzing* noted that the members of the Boards of Appeal are judges in all but name, this did not stop parties to the proceedings from challenging their legal status[55] and has not stopped parties from continually challenging the Board's legal authority.

3. Courts

2.28 In Germany court proceedings are held in German, and § 184 of the GVG requires this for all German courts. There is an initiative underway in parliament to make court proceedings available in English, but currently only the Cologne Higher Regional Court offers such a possibility (the decisions still have to be in German, and the parties have to agree to the English proceedings).[56] Most German judges (in particular, those involved in IP cases) speak and understand English fluently.

2.29 Nevertheless, in many instances (although this can actually quite heavily depend on the judge) proceedings in Germany still require translations of foreign documents to be filed.

(a) Federal Patent Court (Bundespatentgericht)

2.30 The Federal Patent Court is one of the larger German federal courts, with around 120 judges, of which about half are so-called technical judges—that is, judges who have a technical degree, often recruited after gaining experience as examiners at the GPTO. In technical appeal proceedings four judges decide on the case, and in nullity proceedings five judges are present. In both instances, three are technical judges. Unfortunately, at this time the Federal Patent Court has no technology in place to provide translations during oral proceedings.

2.31 As mentioned above, the *Patentamt* initially handled appeals in-house, and this structure was maintained after 1949 despite the new German Constitutional Law (*Grundgesetz* (GG)), which provides in Article 19(4) that all legal violations by the public administration must be appealable at independent courts. In 1956, a lawyer filed a complaint against a decision of the GPTO in a utility model invalidation case relating to the improvement of a hanger for a skirt (*Rockbügelhalter*).[57] The GPTO had made a decision about the costs, setting them 445.12 DM lower than requested (at that time this was quite a bit of money). After the complaint against this decision the Federal Administrative Court finally decided in 1959 that all decisions by the GPTO were indeed administrative decisions and could be appealed at administrative courts. Thus, the *Grundgesetz* had to be changed, and in 1961 the Federal Patent Court was established in Munich.

2.32 In addition to appeals against decisions of the GPTO the court also deals with appeals against decisions by the Federal Office for plant variety protection (*Bundessortenamt*).[58]

[54] See http://hudoc.echr.coe.int/sites/eng/pages/search.aspx?i=001-4410#{"itemid":["001-4410"]}.

[55] See, e.g., the file of the pending review case R 8/13 (http://www.epo.org/law-practice/case-law-appeals/eba/pending-petitions.html).

[56] http://www.rak-koeln.de/datapool/page/488/Handout_GerichtsspracheEnglisch_Vita.pdf (document in German).

[57] BVerwGE 8,350 = *GRUR* (1959): 435.

[58] http://www.bundessortenamt.de/internet30/index.php?id=3.

Furthermore, the Federal Patent Court is responsible as the court of first instance for revocation actions ("nullity proceedings").[59]

(b) District Courts (Landgerichte)

In Germany patent litigation proceedings (*Patentstreitsachen*) are civil court proceedings, and German Patent Act, § 143 requires that these cases begin at the district court level. Based on German Patent Act, § 143(2), today there are twelve German district courts that have specialized patent boards, namely Düsseldorf, Munich, Mannheim, Berlin, Braunschweig, Erfurt, Frankfurt, Hamburg, Leipzig, Nuremberg, Magdeburg, and Saarbrucken. These boards have the exclusive responsibility for IP matters, including patent litigation cases. Since patent cases are regarded as a complicated matter, the board at the district court usually consists of three judges, all of them non-technical—that is, judges with a law degree but no technical degree. **2.33**

Because of the ease of forum shopping in Germany and its general patentee-friendliness,[60] the Düsseldorf District Court handles the most patent litigation cases in Europe, and—at least according to the Ministry of Justice in the Federal State of North Rhine-Westphalia—is sometimes referred to as the "world patent court,"[61] although this title has been met with some skepticism among professionals.[62] Of the 900 or so cases in Germany each year, about 600 are filed in Düsseldorf. In an attempt to attract more cases, the Munich court recently installed the "Munich model,"[63] a streamlined procedure to shorten the proceedings from about 18 months to about 6 to 9. The German infringement courts have always been among the quickest in Europe in multiple areas of technology, including life-sciences litigation. **2.34**

Legally, "patent litigation proceedings" refers to *all* of the cases that are related to an invention, for example patent infringement proceedings, derivation cases, license agreement-related cases, and injunction-related cases. However, an action for the recovery of fees by a patent attorney is not necessarily a patent litigation procedure, particularly if no technical issues are involved.[64] **2.35**

(c) Higher Regional Courts (Oberlandesgerichte, OLGs)

According to § 119 of the Judicature Act (*Gerichtsverfassungsgesetz*, GVG), first-instance decisions of the district courts in civil matters can be appealed at the OLGs as the second instance. In patent matters, the most prominent OLGs are the ones that are responsible for the appeals against the decisions of the district courts in Düsseldorf (OLG Düsseldorf), Munich (OLG Munich), and Mannheim (OLG Karlsruhe). For historic reasons, the OLG in Berlin is called *Kammergericht*.[65] The chambers (called *Senate* (senates)) at the higher regional courts consist of three judges, all of them non-technical. **2.36**

---

[59] http://www.bpatg.de/cms/media/Das_Gericht/Veranstaltungen/Symposien/Pressemappe_BPatG.pdf.

[60] http://www.faz.net/aktuell/wirtschaft/justiz-deutschland-zieht-patentklaeger-aus-aller-welt-an-11665689.html.

[61] http://www.nrw.de/landesregierung/weltpatentgericht-duesseldorf-wird-ausgebaut-12721/.

[62] http://www.iam-magazine.com/reports/Detail.aspx?g=adfe3855-9a8f-4dd8-97a4-974716411f01.

[63] http://www.law.com/jsp/law/international/LawArticleIntl.jsp?id=1202549652407&slreturn=20130710205415.

[64] BGH Decision X ZB 15/12 of March 20, 2013—Patentstreitsache II.

[65] The court was first mentioned in 1468; its name refers to its first location in the *Kammer des Herren* (the chamber of the ruler), i.e., at the court of the Elector of Brandenburg.

2.37 The OLG usually constitutes the court of final instance for patent litigation cases. A further appeal on the points of law ("revision") to the Federal Court of Justice (BGH) is only admissible if the OLG allows it. This can only happen in cases of legal importance or where there are diverging decisions among the OLGs. A rejection of a request for revision can be appealed at the BGH (so-called *Nichtzulassungsbeschwerde*). Until the end of 2014, this required the value of the appeal to be higher than 20,000 euros, which was usually met in litigation cases.

(d) Federal Court of Justice (Bundesgerichtshof; BGH)

2.38 The Federal Court of Justice (BGH) is the highest German court for civil and criminal cases. The court was founded in 1950 and has its main seat in Karlsruhe.[66] The structure and functions of the BGH are based on the former *Reichsgericht*, which existed from 1879 to 1945 and had its seat in Leipzig. A civil matter senate at the BGH consists of five non-technical judges, and in contrast to all other judges in the lower courts, the judges at the BGH wear dark-red colored robes.

2.39 During the Nazi-Era the *Reichsgericht* played a very unfortunate role in forcing Jewish and social democratic judges to leave their jobs. After 1945 the *Reichsgericht* was dissolved by the Allies and the BGH officially ended the *Reichsgericht* on October 30 1945.[67] From August 1945 thirty-seven judges of the *Reichsgericht* were arrested by the Soviets and interned without any court proceedings. By the time of their release between January 1950 and 1955, only four judges had survived; the others had starved to death or were killed by diseases.[68] Nonetheless, some of these former judges of the *Reichsgericht* were amongst the first judges at the BGH. After the German reunification there was a proposal to move all of the BGH back to its historic location in Leipzig, but the judges in particular objected to this plan.

2.40 The tenth Senate with its current presiding judge, Peter Meier-Beck, is responsible for patent cases. In addition to handling appeals on certain points of law, including patent revocation and compulsory license cases, the tenth Senate has the responsibility of being the "regular" second-instance court, and in these cases the court makes factual findings. This structure has been in place since the introduction of patent law in 1877.

2.41 The procedural law for these cases is largely found in the German Patent Act (§§ 110–21). As the judges are not technically skilled, a court expert can be appointed. Witnesses can also be heard. To speed up proceedings, in October 2009 the procedural law at the BGH was amended, creating limitations on the introduction of new facts.[69] Subsequently the length of a typical case was reduced. According to 2012 statistics about 80 percent of patent cases were decided within twenty-four months (in 2009, about 70 percent), although the cases as a whole seemed to fall into one of two groups: those that were decided between six and twelve months and those that took longer than twenty-four months.[70]

[66] http://www.bundesgerichtshof.de/EN/Home/home_node.html.

[67] BGH NJW 1952, 937.

[68] "Das große Sterben im Reichsgericht," *Deutsche Richterzeitung* 35 (1957): 249, 250.

[69] Gesetz zur Vereinfachung und Modernisierung des Patentrechts vom 31. Juli 2009, BGBl. 2009 I No. 50, 2521.

[70] http://www.bundesgerichtshof.de/SharedDocs/Downloads/DE/DerBGH/StatistikZivil/jahresstatistikZivilsenate2012.pdf?__blob=publicationFile.

(e) The Future Unified European Patent and Patent Court System

2.42 National courts and other authorities of the contracting states of the European Patent Convention are currently competent to decide on the infringement and validity of European patents. In practice this gives rise to a number of difficulties when a patent proprietor wishes to enforce a European patent or when a third party seeks the revocation of a European patent, as they must do so in several countries, resulting in high costs, the risk of diverging decisions, and an overall lack of legal certainty. Forum shopping is also inevitable as parties seek to take advantage of the differences among national courts in their interpretation of harmonized European patent law, procedural law, speed (between "slow" and "quick" courts), and the level of damages awarded.

2.43 During the European Council of June 28–29, 2012, after a long political struggle, an agreement was reached on the provisions for a European patent with unitary effect between twenty-five of the then twenty-seven member states of the European Union. Italy and Spain decided not to take part due to the proposed language scheme, which uses English, German, and French at the exclusion of other languages. The necessary EU legislation for enhanced cooperation was approved by the European Parliament on December 11, 2012,[71] and entered into force on January 1, 2013. The provisions became effective once the related Agreement on a Unified Patent Court, signed by all EU member states except Poland and Spain, entered into force on January 1, 2014. Croatia has not yet joined the Agreement. As the first EU country, Austria ratified the Agreement, enabling a unified patent court framework to be established.[72] Belgium, France, Denmark, and Sweden subsequently joined the Agreement.[73]

2.44 The unitary patent system consists of two parts. The first is the unitary patent itself, which will coexist with national patents and with classical European patents.[74] The EPO will be generally responsible for receiving and examining unitary patents, which are similar to the already existing EPC-European patents.[75] Under the proposed reforms, post-grant opposition in the European Patent Office as well as centralized limitation proceedings will remain an option.[76] Notice of opposition has to be given within nine months of the date of grant. For unitary patents, it may be that oppositions will become less frequent because pan-European revocation will become more practical. Decisions of the EPO regarding unitary patent protection may be appealed to the Unified Patent Court.[77] The proposed

---

[71] The Regulation on Implementing Enhanced Cooperation in the Area of the Creation of Unitary Patent Protection, Regulation 1257/[2012] OJ EU L 361/1, December 31, 2012; Council Regulation 1260/[2012] OJ EU L 361/89, December 31, 2012 (Unitary Patent Protection Agreement).

[72] See http://www.bmeia.gv.at/en/foreign-ministry/news/press-releases/2013/spindelegger-neues-eu-patent-bringt-innovationsschub-fuer-die-eu.html.

[73] The ratification statuses are listed at http://ec.europa.eu/internal_market/indprop/patent/ratification/index_en.htm.

[74] Unitary Patent Protection Agreement, Recital 26. The Agreement requires member states to take the necessary measures to avoid duplication of protection by national and European patents with the unitary protection. Recital (8), Art. 4.

[75] Unitary Patent Protection Agreement, Recital 5, Art. 9.

[76] For an overview of the European uniform patent protection, The Select Committee, The Preparatory Committee, *An Enhanced European Patent System* (2014) (http://www.unified-patent-court.org/images/documents/enhanced-european-patent-system.pdf); Bardehle Pagenberg, *Unitary Patent and Unified Patent Court* (2014) (http://www.bardehle.com/fileadmin/contentdocuments/broschures/Unitary-Patent_Unified-Patent-Court.pdf).

[77] The Agreement on a Unified Patent Court, OJ EPO 2013, 287 (http://xepc.eu/node/oj2013-287), Art. 32 (Unitary Patent Court Agreement).

procedural rules for the Unified Patent Court state that a court *may* stay any proceedings (not just revocation proceedings) where a patent is subject to opposition, although a stay will not be compulsory.[78]

2.45 The second—and significantly more complicated—part is the unified patent court system. So far, there will be so-called decentralized Courts of First Instance with local, regional, and central divisions located in the member states.[79] Each contracting state is entitled to at least one local division and countries may request additional local divisions in certain defined circumstances.[80] Two or more contracting states can also join together to establish a regional division.[81] In Germany, the local divisions are expected to be located in Dusseldorf, Mannheim, and Munich,[82] and it is possible that a fourth local division will be opened in Hamburg. Austria, Italy, and Benelux are planning to open courts in Vienna, Milan, and the Netherlands (regional) or Brussels,[83] respectively. Any panel of a German local division of the Unified Patent Court (Court of First Instance) will consist of two legally qualified judges who are German nationals and one legally qualified judge who is not a German national.[84] Additionally, upon request by one of the parties to the proceedings, a technically qualified judge with qualifications and experience in the field of the technology concerned will be allocated to the relevant panel from the as-yet-to-be-established pool of judges.[85]

2.46 The central division will have its seat in Paris, where it will hear cases relating to all subject matter except chemicals, human necessities (including pharmaceutical products), and metallurgy, which have been allocated to London; and mechanical engineering, lighting, heating, weapons, and "blasting," which have been allocated to Munich.[86] Cases concerning individual revocation actions and declarations of non-infringement must be commenced in the Central Division.[87] However, where a revocation counterclaim is made in response to an infringement claim, the court will have the discretion to decide whether to hear both the infringement claim and the revocation counterclaim together or to refer the revocation counterclaim to the Central Division (which cannot be controlled by the parties) and proceed with only the infringement claim ("German-style proceedings"), which is seen as being favorable to patentees. Alternatively, by agreement of the parties, the entire case may be referred to the Central Division.[88]

2.47 The Court of Appeal will have its seat in Luxembourg, and appeal hearings will be presided over by panels consisting of three legally qualified judges and two technically qualified judges.[89] The court will be obliged to refer questions relating to issues of EU law to the

[78] Preliminary Set of Provisions for the Rules of Procedure of the Unified Patent Court (http://www.unified-patent-court.org/images/documents/draft-rules-of-procedure.pdf) (Preliminary Rules of Procedure).

[79] The Select Committee, *Enhanced European Patent System*, 11.

[80] Unitary Patent Court Agreement, Art. 6(3).

[81] Ibid. Art. 6(5).

[82] Bardehle Pagenberg, *Unitary Patent*, 13.

[83] http://www.presscenter.org/en/node/76841.

[84] For more than fifty cases per year, Unitary Patent Court Agreement, Art. 8(3).

[85] Ibid. Art. 8(5).

[86] Ibid. Art. 6(2).

[87] Ibid. Art. 32 (d)–(e); The Select Committee, *Enhanced European Patent System*, 13.

[88] Unitary Patent Court Agreement, Art. 33 (3); The Select Committee, *Enhanced European Patent System*, 11.

[89] Unitary Patent Court Agreement, Art. 9.

CJEU, although it is unclear whether substantive patent validity and infringement laws are issues of EU law and thus actually fall into the competence of the CJEU.

Procedural rules have been drafted by a group of patent experts, and the fifteenth draft of the rules was published on March 31, 2013.[90] The proposed procedure is closer in character to continental European systems of litigation than to common law systems, with the format of the proceedings closely following the current German system, such as the oral trial hearings that are intended to last a day at most and the emphasis on the parties' written submissions. In addition, the scope of the cross-examination of witnesses and the role of party expert witnesses will be limited.[91] **2.48**

The proposed rules try to speed up the proceedings by setting tight deadlines. Discovery will be available upon request by the parties, but there is no general obligation to provide requested evidence as in the United States.[92] Damages will be assessed in a separate stage from the stages deciding on liability.[93] **2.49**

The unified patent court system requires mandatory representation by either attorneys-at-law who are authorized to practice before national courts or European Patent Attorneys with the appropriate qualifications.[94] Nevertheless, what is meant by the terms "attorneys" and "appropriate qualifications" is still open to interpretation. Of course, lobbyist groups of attorneys-at-law practicing IP law before courts throughout Europe have always showed a tendency to reduce the role of patent attorneys as much as possible, arguing that only a lawyer has sufficiently broad expertise. Many lawyers suggest reducing the role of patent attorneys, but because of the considerable technical expertise that patent attorneys have, few argue in favor of completely eliminating their involvement in patent-related court proceedings.[95] A proposal has been made to qualify patent attorneys if they obtain a certificate to meet the requirement under the Uniform Patent Court Agreement.[96] **2.50**

Regarding European "bundle" patents (EPC patents), there will be a seven-year transitional period during which an action for infringement or revocation of an EPC patent may still be brought before national courts or respective national authorities.[97] Furthermore, an owner of or applicant for an EPC patent that is granted or applied for prior to the end of that transitional period may opt-out from the Unitary Patent system—and hence the exclusive competence of the Unified Patent Court—unless an action (for revocation) has already been brought before the Unified Patent Court.[98] This might prove to be an effective way to safeguard a European "bundle" patent from Europe-wide revocation. **2.51**

The European Commission calculates the fees for a unitary patent to be approximately 5,000 euros after the transition period, compared to about 32,000 euros for an EPC patent. The **2.52**

90 http://www.unified-patent-court.org/images/documents/draft-rules-of-procedure.pdf.
91 Preliminary Rules of Procedure, Rule 178.
92 Ibid. Rule 172.
93 Ibid. Rule 10.
94 Unitary Patent Court Agreement, Art. 48 UPC.
95 Which also seems to be contrary to Unitary Patent Court Agreement, Art. 48.
96 The Administrative Committee of the Unified Patent Court, Rules on the European Patent Litigation Certificate and Other Appropriate Qualifications Pursuant to Article 48(2) of the Agreement on a Unified Patent Court (http://www.unified-patent-court.org/images/documents/draft-eplc-consultation.pdf).
97 The Select Committee, *Enhanced European Patent System*, 9.
98 Ibid. 16.

savings are said to be achieved by the reduction or lack of fees for translations (which seems doubtful because of the technical and thus expensive nature of these translations), local patent offices, and local patent agents.[99] Of note, the European Commission also calculates the costs for a US patent to be in the order of 2,000 euros, which does not seem to be very realistic, as the mere filing of a US patent can already cost between 5,000 and 15,000 US dollars.[100] The court fees for infringement actions, revocation actions, and revocation counterclaims will all be calculated based on the value of the case, similar to the current German system.[101] A successful party will be able to claim its litigation costs from the losing party.[102]

2.53 The present system of European Patents has been criticized as being too expensive for small and medium-sized enterprises (SMEs).[103] This is largely due to the need to litigate a European patent in multiple jurisdictions. Nevertheless, the extent of the infrastructure and personnel required for the new unified system seems to be even greater than the current system; thus, it seems reasonable to assume that it will also be more expensive. Furthermore, according to the EU, the Unitary Patent Court will have to be self-funded.[104]

2.54 On balance, it seems that larger companies such as pharmaceutical companies—who have always needed protection in all the European jurisdictions—may find the new system more efficient. In contrast, SMEs may take the view that they only need protection in a limited home market and decide that enforcement in one or two key markets is more cost-effective. Thus, they may be more likely to only pursue national patents or European Patents with limited designations. The system certainly has a lot of advantages for patent assertion entities (PAEs), or—as they are pejoratively referred to as—"trolls."[105] The Unitary Patent's only "defense" against these trolls is the limitation on the joining of multiple defendants.[106]

2.55 However, it may be that pharmaceutical companies will also refrain from using the unified court system since British courts are known to regularly invalidate patents. This would cause companies to lose their patent in all of the states of the EU simultaneously and leave them defenseless. In view of the commercial value of having individual patents in the pharmaceutical field, the prospective cost savings are often secondary.

4. Customs Office

2.56 In 1958, France, Italy, Belgium, the Netherlands, and Germany founded the European Economic Community (EEC)[107] in order to achieve an economic region without internal

---

99 See http://ec.europa.eu/internal_market/indprop/patent/faqs/index_en.htm#maincontentSec11.

100 See http://www.ipwatchdog.com/2011/01/28/the-cost-of-obtaining-patent/.

101 Unitary Patent Court Agreement, Art. 36(3).

102 Ibid. Art. 69.

103 See http://ec.europa.eu/research/sme-techweb/newsletter/issue15/editorial_en.html.

104 Unitary Patent Court Agreement allows a natural person to apply for legal aid. Unitary Patent Court Agreement, Art. 71.

105 According to the US Federal Trade Commission (FTC)'s definition, Patent Assertion Entities (PAEs) are firms with a business model based primarily on buying patents and then attempting to generate revenue by asserting them against businesses that are already practicing the patented technologies. FTC, Patent Assertion Entities Study (http://www.ftc.gov/policy/studies/patent-assertion-entities-pae-study).

106 Unitary Patent Court Agreement, Art. 33(4). 2nd sentence: "If, however, an action for infringement as referred to in Art. 32(1)(a) between the same parties relating to the same patent has been brought before a local or a regional division, these actions may only be brought before the same local or regional division."

107 Treaty Establishing the European Economic Community, March 25, 1957, 298 U.N.T.S. 3, 4 Eur. Y.B. 412 (Treaty of Rome). The Treaty of Rome was amended to absorb the EEC into the European Union.

borders for goods. The customs union of 1968 was a step towards this goal. In 1988, a unified customs declaration replaced over 150(!) different types of documents that were being used in the member states.[108] The European internal market was established on January 1, 1993, and thus the transport of goods between the member states of the EEC is no longer controlled by customs. Nevertheless, the "classical" objectives of the customs authorities have been maintained on the borders of the EU, in harbors, and in airports. With regard to patents, today the main responsibility of the customs authorities lies in border seizures of infringing goods.

Based on EU Regulation 1383/2003, a patent holder can apply for a European Union border seizure of infringing goods that are imported directly from a non-EU member state into an EU member state (e.g., from the United States directly to Germany).[109] The European Union border seizure procedure allows for the confiscation of goods that are suspected of infringing intellectual property rights. **2.57**

As an alternative to the European border seizure, a national German border seizure is applicable if the infringing goods are imported from an EU member state into Germany. With patents, the border seizure is based on the national provisions in the German Patent Act, §§ 142a and b, which require, as opposed to the European border seizure, that the patentee show that infringement is evident. Moreover, after a detention, the applicant must provide an enforceable court decision within two weeks. **2.58**

Applications for a border seizure are free of charge and can be kept pending for up to one year. There is no rule against reapplication. In Germany, the customs authorities are part of the fiscal administration, and, after some time in Nuremberg, the "Central Division for Intellectual Property," which is responsible for respective border seizures, is now located in Munich. Since 2009, requests for border seizures (both German and European) can be filed online using "ZGR-online."[110] A European system for the exchange of relevant data on applications and border seizures called the "Application System for Action" (AFAS) is planned.[111] **2.59**

C. Japan

1. Overview

Japan is known for delegating broad authority from the legislature to bureaucrats such as those in the Ministry of Economy, Trade and Industry (METI) and the Japan Patent Office **2.60**

Treaty of Lisbon Amending the Treaty on European Union and the Treaty Establishing the European Community, December 13, 2007, [2007] OJ C 306, 1.

[108] Council Regulation (EC) No. 1383/2003 Concerning Customs Action against Goods Suspected of Infringing Certain Intellectual Property Rights and the Measures to Be Taken against Goods Found to Have Infringed Such Rights, [2003] OJ L 196/7 (http://ec.europa.eu/taxation_customs/customs/policy_issues/index_en.htm).

[109] Available at http://eur-lex.europa.eu/LexUriServ/LexUriServ.do?uri=CELEX:32003R1383:EN:HTML.

[110] See http://www.zoll.de/DE/Fachthemen/Verbote-Beschraenkungen/Gewerblicher-Rechtsschutz/Information-ZGR-online/information-zgr-online_node.html (in German).

[111] See http://ec.europa.eu/taxation_customs/resources/documents/customs/customs_controls/counterfeit_piracy/right_holders/manual_en.pdf.

(JPO).[112] Bureaucrats have taken leadership roles in law and policy development by drafting and implementing legislation and adopting broad statutory language such that details may be provided in formal agency rules and informal administrative guidance.[113] Regarding the Patent Act, the JPO has enjoyed such a leadership role. The JPO also had played a major role in patent enforcement in deciding both patent infringement and validity since the 1899 Patent Act introduced a trial procedure for certifying the scope of patent protection.[114] Until the certification trial was abolished in 1962, Japanese patentees usually commenced a certification trial in which the JPO would issue a decision to certify whether an accused embodiment fell within the patent scope. Patentees seldom filed patent infringement suits with courts because accused infringers voluntarily stopped infringement when the JPO issued a trial decision for the patentees.[115] The JPO also maintained the exclusive power to examine patent validity until the Supreme Court changed its case law and established that Japanese courts have the ability to examine patent validity in infringement litigation.[116]

2.61 Courts began to play an active role in patent law making and enforcement when the Intellectual Property High Court (IP High Court) was created in 2005.[117] Courts traditionally took a hands-off approach and endorsed the JPO's interpretation of the Patent Act in light of its legislative intent. More recent decisions indicate that the IP High Court is willing to overturn the JPO's practice and invalidate patents by applying a patentability standard different from the JPO standard, which has led to a review of the JPO's examination guidelines.[118]

2. Courts

(a) Tokyo and Osaka District Courts

2.62 In the early 2000s, there was a push for major reform of the Japanese legal system; however, the consequent reform did not significantly change the degree of deference courts gave to the JPO in interpreting ambiguous provisions in the Patent Act. The Japanese government implemented recommendations, which were published by the Judicial System Reform Council in 2001,[119] that led to major revisions in civil procedure. Patent jurisdiction was concentrated in the Osaka and Tokyo district courts, and exclusive jurisdiction of patent

---

[112] Tom Ginsburg, "Dismantling the 'Developmental State'? Administrative Procedure Reform in Japan and Korea," 4 *Am. J. Comp. L.* (2001): 585 (http://home.uchicago.edu/~/tginsburg/pdf/articles/DismantlingTheDevelopmentalState.pdf).

[113] Yukio Yanagida et al., *Law and Investment in Japan: Cases and Materials* (1994), 39.

[114] Tokkyohō (Patent Act) of 1899, Art. 29. For a discussion on the history of claim interpretation under the Japanese Patent Act, see Toshiko Takenaka, "Interpreting Patent Claims: The United States, Germany and Japan," 17 *IIC Studies* (1995): 39.

[115] Shigemitsu Matsumoto, *Tokkyo Hatsumeino Hogo Han'I (The Scope of Protection for a Patented Invention)* (1981), 78.

[116] Saikō Saibansho (Sup. Ct.) April 11, 2000, Hei 10 (o) No. 364, 54 Saikō Saibansho Minji Hanreishū (Minshū) 1368 (Japan).

[117] Toshiko Takenaka, "A Change of Leadership in Patent Policy and Law Development? The Active Role Played by Japanese Courts in Japan's Patent Term Extension Reform," in Toshiko Takenaka and John Haley (ed.), *Legal Innovations in Intellectual Property* (2014), 293.

[118] E.g., a grand panel decision of the IP High Court, May 30, 2008, Hei 18 (Gyo-Ke), No. 10563 led to a revision of the Examination Guidelines for "Amendment of Description, Claims and Drawings (New Matter)," http://www.jpo.go.jp/tetuzuki_e/t_tokkyo_e/amendment_claims_drawings_e.htm.

[119] Justice System Reform Council, *Recommendations of the Justice System Reform Council: For a Justice System to Support Japan in the Twenty-first Century*, June 12, 2001 (http://www.kantei.go.jp/foreign/judiciary/2001/0612report.html).

appeals was granted to the IP High Court.[120] The Tokyo and Osaka district courts have exclusive jurisdiction over cases involving infringement of patents, utility model rights, IC layout registration, and copyright in computer programs (all of which are called "patent cases").[121]

The Tokyo District Court has four IP special divisions to decide patent cases, and the Osaka District Court has one IP special division to decide patent cases. Approximately only 10 percent of all Japanese judges have a science background.[122] Japanese judges start their career after completing their training at the judicial institute, which is run by the Supreme Court of Japan.[123] It is relatively exceptional for judges to have careers as attorneys before their judicial appointment. Judges in the IP special divisions at the Tokyo District Court and Osaka District Court are assisted by judicial research officials who work full time for their respective courts. The Supreme Court of Japan has long adopted a policy of transferring Japanese judges from one court to another every two or three years so that judges do not develop a bias. Judges who are appointed to serve the IP special divisions are not exempt and are frequently transferred back to one of the IP special divisions and the IP High Court to further develop their patent law and technology expertise.[124] **2.63**

(b) IP High Court

On April 1, 2005, the IP High Court was developed as a semi-independent court. Under the Civil Procedure Code, the IP High Court is a special branch of the Tokyo High Court.[125] However, the court has its own administrative authority through the judicial conference and its own chief judge.[126] The IP High Court has exclusive jurisdiction to hear appeals on patent cases.[127] The court has exclusive jurisdiction over appeals of JPO decisions concerning patents and other intellectual property rights.[128] **2.64**

A third of IP High Court judges have some form of technological or science background.[129] Like the IP special divisions of the Tokyo and Osaka district courts, the IP **2.65**

---

[120] Minji Soshōhōtō No Ichibu Wo Kaisei Suru Hōritsu (Law for Revising Part of the Civil Procedure Law), Law No. 108 of 2003, Art. 6, para. 1 (amending Minji Soshōhō (Civil Procedure Law), etc. Law No. 109 of 1998).

[121] Min'ji Soshohō (Civil Procedure Code), Act No. 109 of June 26, 1996, as last amended in 2006, Art. 6(1) (Civil Procedure Code). For an overview of Japanese court systems for patent litigation, see Toshiko Takenaka, "Comparison of U.S. and Japanese Court Systems for Patent Litigation: A Special Court or Special Divisions in a General Court?" CASRIP Publication Series No. 5: Streamlining International Intellectual Property 48 (1999).

[122] Tomokatsu Tsukahara, "Intellectual Property High Court of Japan, Training Material for JPO, Asia-Pacific Industrial Property Center," *JIPII* (2013): 9 (http://www.training-jpo.go.jp/en/images_x/uploads/text_vtr/pdf/Intellectual%20Property%20High%20Court%20of%20Japan_2013.pdf).

[123] For an overview of the Japanese judiciary, see John O. Haley, "The Japanese Judiciary: Maintaining Integrity, Autonomy and the Public Trust," in Daniel Foote (ed.), *Law in Japan: A Turning Point* (2007), 99 (https://law.wustl.edu/harris/documents/2003-3HaleyJapaneseJudiciary.pdf).

[124] Toshiko Takenaka and Ichiro Nakayama, "Will Intellectual Property Policy Save Japan from Recession? Japan's Basic Intellectual Property Law and Its Implementation through the Strategic Program," 35 *Int'l Rev of Intell. Prop. & Competition Law (IIC)* (2004): 877, 887.

[125] Chiteki Zaisan Kōtōsaubansho Secchi hō (Law for Establishing the IP High Court) Law No. 109 of 2004.

[126] Ibid. Arts. 3 and 4.

[127] Civil Procedure Code, Art. 6(3). For an overview of the IP High Court's jurisdiction, see International Institute of Intellectual Property, *Study on Specialized Intellectual Property Court* (2102), 66 (http://iipi.org/wp-content/uploads/2012/05/Study-on-Specialized-IPR-Courts.pdf).

[128] Japanese Patent Act, Art. 178.

[129] Tsukahara, "Intellectual Property High Court of Japan," 9.

High Court judges have expertise in both patent law and technology. They are assisted by judicial research officials (*Saibansho chôsakan*) who have extensive experience in examining and/or preparing and pursuing patent applications as JPO appeal examiners or patent attorneys.[130] These officials give judges an explanation of the patented inventions and the prior art as well as a recommendation for a conclusion with respect to validity and infringement.[131] The report including the explanation and recommendation is not disclosed to the parties although the parties can ask research officials questions during the hearings.

2.66 Judges in the IP special divisions and IP High Court are also assisted by technical advisors (*Senmoniin*).[132] Unlike the research officials, technical advisors are not full-time employees of the IP High Court but are instead temporary employees who are appointed to assist the IP High Court judges on a case-by-case basis. The Tokyo District Court, Osaka District Court, and IP High Court each have pools of advisors in different fields of technology. When the technology involved in a patent case is so advanced and unique that research officials cannot assist the judges properly, technological advisors are selected from a pool of advisors in the patented invention's field of technology. The duty of these advisors is focused on giving an explanation of the patented invention and the prior art to the judges, instead of their own opinions.[133]

2.67 The IP High Court adopted for the first time among Japanese High Courts a grand panel system, which is applied only to patent cases.[134] Three judges, including a presiding judge, and one research official are assigned to each case.[135] Several, usually three, technical advisors are appointed to assist the judges and officials when the decision is made to appoint technical advisors due to the complexity of the technologies involved in the case.[136] When a case involves a significant patent law issue, the IP High Court hears the case by a grand panel consisting of the four presiding judges, including the chief judge and the judge-rapporteur who was originally assigned to draft the judgment of the case. The IP High Court seldom hears cases by a grand panel and granted a grand panel hearing for only nine cases during its first decade since its creation in 2005.[137] Although Japan is a civil law country and thus court decisions do not have any binding effect, Japanese judges at lower courts follow the precedents of the Supreme Court.[138] The IP High Court also follows the Court's precedents and the precedents of the Tokyo High Court, and it is likely to hear a case by a grand panel if the court overturns its precedent.[139]

[130] Ibid. 10.

[131] Ibid. 11.

[132] The 2003 revision of the Civil Procedure Code introduced the technical advisory system. Civil Procedure Code, Art. 34-2.

[133] Ibid. 16.

[134] Civil Procedure Code, Art. 92-2 through 92-7.

[135] Tsukahara, "Intellectual Property High Court of Japan," 16.

[136] Ibid.

[137] Grand panel judgments are available from the IP High Court Home Page (http://www.ip.courts.go.jp/eng/hanrei/g_panel/index.html).

[138] Shigenori Matsui, "Constitutional Precedents in Japan: A Comments on the Role of Precedent," 88 *Wash. U.L.R.* (2011): 1669 (http://digitalcommons.law.wustl.edu/cgi/viewcontent.cgi?article=1070&context=lawreview).

[139] E.g., IP High Court, May 29, 2009, Hei 20 (gyō ke) No. 10458, Saiko Saibansho Hanrei Joho (http://www.courts.go.jp/app/files/hanrei_jp/655/037655_hanrei.pdf).

(c) Supreme Court

The Supreme Court of Japan consists of the chief justice and fourteen justices.[140] It hears cases by a petty bench consisting of four or five justices and a grand bench consisting of all fifteen justices.[141] The Supreme Court must hear a *Jokoku* appeal by a grand bench if the opinions of the justices on a petty bench are divided and the case overturns the Supreme Court's own precedent and examines a violation of the constitution by a law, ordinance, rule, or disposition.[142] The justices other than the chief justice are assigned to one of three petty benches. The chief justice is nominated by the Cabinet and appointed by the emperor, but the other justices are appointed by the Cabinet and endorsed by the emperor.[143] A party has the right to a *Jokoku* appeal to the Supreme Court if the decision from the IP High Court violates a constitutional right and involves any serious procedural violations listed in the Civil Procedure Code.[144] It is very unlikely that an IP High Court decision will include one of these violations. A party may file a petition for a *Jokoku* appeal, arguing that the IP High Court made a serious mistake in its interpretation of the Patent Act as well as other laws involved in the case.[145] The Supreme Court seldom grants a petition for a *Jokoku* appeal on patent cases and has not reversed any IP High Court decision since the creation of the IP High Court except for the most recent product-by-process decision. **2.68**

Unlike judges in lower courts, Supreme Court justices can be appointed from former judges of lower courts as well as from prosecutors, attorneys, professors, and those who served the government.[146] Although it is very unlikely that they will have a science background, they are assisted by the judicial research officials. The Supreme Court judicial officials are elite judges who are appointed from the senior ranks of career judges and include at least one official who has patent and intellectual property law expertise through service as a judge for one of the IP special divisions and/or the IP High Court. **2.69**

3. Japan Patent Office

The JPO is one of three external agencies of the Ministry of Economy, Trade, and Industry (METI). The JPO was created in 1885 as part of the Ministry of Agriculture and Commerce when the very first Patent Act was enacted.[147] The JPO consists of seven departments: the General Affairs Department; the Trademark, Design and Administrative Affairs Department; First Patent Examination Department; Second Patent Examination Department; Third Patent Examination Department; Fourth Patent Examination Department; and the Appeals Department.[148] The JPO has been playing a major role in patent law making by introducing a bill to revise the Patent Act and exercising its discretion to develop rules in interpreting the Patent Act. Such bills are drafted in consultation with deliberative councils (*Shingikai*) consisting of members representing patent academics, **2.70**

140 Tsukahara, "Intellectual Property High Court of Japan," 6.
141 Ibid.
142 Saibanshohō (Court Act) Law No. 59 of 1947, Art. 10.
143 Haley, "The Japanese Judiciary," 7.
144 Civil Procedure Code, Art. 312.
145 Civil Procedure Code, Art. 318.
146 Court Act, Art. 41.
147 Senbai Tokkyo Jorei (Monopoly Patent Ordinance) Law No. 7 of 1885.
148 For more on the organization and structure of the JPO, see N. K. Joshi, *Research, Training and Awareness in the Field of Intellectual Property: Benefitting from the Experience of Japan* (2008), 11 (http://www.me.titech.ac.jp/~ytanaka/pdf/Joshi.pdf).

attorneys, and industry.[149] In 2003, the Basic IP Law was enacted to create the IP Strategy Headquarters in the Cabinet, which began to publish its annual strategy programs charging ministries and agencies, particularly the JPO and METI, to implement action plans to enhance patent protection.[150] The Basic IP Law signifies Japan's adoption of a pro-patent policy, which has enhanced the JPO's power in developing policies for patent procurement and enforcement.

2.71 In particular, the JPO plays an important role by examining patent validity challenges through the invalidation trial procedure.[151] Unlike USPTO administrative judges, JPO patent appeal examiners (PAE) usually do not have a law degree but have extensive training on the Patent Act at the JPO.[152] To be qualified as a PAE, examiners must have at least five years' experience in examining patent applications. They must receive extensive legal training on procedural laws before starting work as a PAE. A JPO patent trial board usually consists of three PAEs, including a presiding PAE, although the board may consist of five PAEs for a complex case.[153] PAEs also represent the JPO at the IP High Court in appeals from JPO trial decisions.

2.72 The JPO facilitates resolution of patent disputes by providing an advisory opinion (*hantei*) regarding whether the embodiment at dispute falls within the technical scope of the patented invention.[154] A *hantei* opinion is not enforceable at Japanese courts. A party must file for a civil action at a district court if an accused infringer does not agree to settle the case by taking a license or by stopping the infringement activities.

4. Customs Office

2.73 The Customs Act provides for bans on the importation of goods that infringe Japanese patents.[155] Patentees can make a request for the Customs Office to stop the importation of infringing goods.[156] When the Customs Office receives a request from a patentee, it will start the procedure to find infringement (*nintei*). During the *nintei* procedure, a party who plans to import or is importing allegedly infringing goods is given the opportunity to argue for non-infringement. The office bans the importation of the goods when it finds infringement through the *nintei* procedure.

2.74 The Customs Office does not start the *nintei* procedure unless it can determine infringement from the appearance of the goods.[157] Unlike the US ITC, Japan's Customs Office

---

149 Takenaka, "Change of Leadership," 306.

150 Toshiko Takenaka, "Success or Failure? Japan's National Strategy on Intellectual Property and Evaluation of Its Impact from the Comparative Law Perspective," 8 *Washington University Global Studies Law Review* (2009): 379, 380.

151 For more discussion about the invalidation trial procedure, see Ch. 9.

152 Joshi, "Training and Awareness," 21.

153 Tomoyasu Sato, "Shinpan Seido no Gaiyō to Saikin no Dok ō (Overview of Patent Trial Procedure and Recent Trends)," 63 *Patento* (2010): 93 (http://www.jpaa.or.jp/activity/publication/patent/patent-library/patent-lib/201002/jpaapatent201002_093-103.pdf).

154 For an overview of the *hantei* system, see JPO, Japanese Patent Office Hantei, Avisory Opinion on the Technical Scope of a Patented Invention (http://www.jpo.go.jp/tetuzuki_e/t_tokkyo_e/hantei.htm).

155 Kanzeihō (Customs Act) Law No. 61 of 1954, Art. 69-11.

156 Customs Act, Art. 69-2.

157 Japan Intellectual Property Association, "Tokkyoken ni motozuku Kanzeihōtō no Mizugiwasochi nituite (Measures to Stop Importation based on Patent Rights under Customs Act and other Acts)," 56 *Chizai Kanri* (2006): 1149 (http://www.jipa.or.jp/kikansi/chizaikanri/koukai/2006_08_1149.pdf).

does not have any officers who have patent law or technical expertise. If the asserted patent covers a feature that is not visible from the appearance of the goods or if it is difficult to find infringement due to the complexity of the technology, it is unlikely that the Customs Office will start the *nintei* procedure. Moreover, if a court finds no infringement or finds the asserted patent invalid in conflict with the conclusion of the *nintei* procedure, it may award the accused infringer damages resulting from the banning of importation.

Part II

INFRINGEMENT

3

INTRODUCTION

The enactment of the Trade Related Intellectual Property Systems Agreement (TRIPS Agreement)[1] substantially harmonized the definitions of acts that constitute direct infringement. The United States, Germany and Japan revised the provisions of their patent Acts to define acts of infringement to meet the requirements under Article 28 of the TRIPS Agreement. Although there are some differences in the terms used to define acts of direct infringement, the rights granted by these jurisdictions are substantially the same. Following the British tradition, US patents did not extend to a product resulting from a patented method.[2] Congress enacted the Process Patent Amendment Act in 1988 to make the exclusivity of US process patents in line with those under German and Japanese patent Acts.[3] **3.01**

In contrast, there are still major differences in the definitions of indirect infringement and exceptions to infringement. Overall, US courts are more reluctant to find a third party liable under the theory of indirect infringement. Accordingly, US courts developed detailed requirements for finding a third party liable for an act of a direct infringer. In contrast, German and Japanese courts adopt a more flexible approach to find third party liability, relying on statutory indirect infringement theories expressly provided by German and Japanese Patent Acts and joint tort theories based on a general tort under their civil codes. The scope of exceptions to infringement under the US Patent Act is more limited than the scope of exceptions under German and Japanese Patent Acts. **3.02**

Courts in all three jurisdictions follow the same rule that the claims of a patent determine the scope of the invention that defines the subject matter of examination during the patent prosecution at the patent office. The claims also determine the scope of the invention that the patentee is entitled to exclude others from working and exploting the invention during patent litigation at courts. The latter scope for exclusivity includes the scope literally defined by the claim language and the scope defined by equivalents of the claim language. This scope, the extent of patent protection, is distinguished from the scope for defining subject matter of examination because the patent office does not examine the scope of equivalents. This distinction between the scope of examination and the extent of patent protection is common to all three jurisdictions. Regardless of during the patent prosecution or patent litigation, there is always ambiguity in the words used in a claim when the claim **3.03**

---

[1] Agreement on Trade-Related Aspects of Intellectual Property Rights, April 15, 1994, Marrakesh Agreement Establishing the World Trade Organization, Annex 1C, The Legal Texts: The Results of the Uruguay Round of Multilateral Trade Negotiations 320 (1999), 1869 U.N.T.S. 299, 33 I.L.M. 1197 (TRIPS).

[2] *Keplinger v. De Young*, 23 U.S. (10 Wheat.) 358 (1825); *Chisum on Patents*, § 16.02[h].

[3] Process Patent Amendment Act was part of the Omnibus Trade and Competitiveness Act of 1988, P.L. 100–418 (Title IX, Subtitle A, sections 9001–07), 102 Stat. 1563.

is compared with an accused machine or process adopted by the accused infringer because of the difficulty in converting a machine or process into words. To clarify this ambiguity, all three courts interpret the words of asserted claims in light of the patent specification and drawing.

3.04 However, German courts' claim interpretation is influenced by the tradition of the central definition theory which the German patent system had long followed before its major revision in 1981 in order to join the European Patent Convention ("EPC").[4] German courts use the specification and drawing to take account of the knowledge of a person skilled in the art of the invention and expand the literal scope defined by the words of a claim. In contrast, US and Japanese courts tend to use the specification and drawing, as well as the record of prosecution history during the examination, to limit the literal scope of a claim. Moreover, German courts find infringement under the doctrine of equivalents more frequently than US and Japanese courts and give less significance to the words of claims than the courts in the other two jurisdictions.

[4] Convention on the Grant of European Patents, October 5, 1973, 13 I.L.M. 270. For the claim interpretation theories and history of German patent claim interpretation, see Toshiko Takenaka, "Interpreting Patent Claims: The United States, Germany and Japan," 17 *IIC Studies* (1995): 26–38.

4

UNITED STATES

A. Acts of Infringement

1. Direct Infringement

Under the US Patent System, the right conferred by a patent is to exclude others with respect to infringing acts.[1] US Patent Act, § 271(a) lists the following acts which constitute infringement if anyone engages in such acts without authority: making, using, offering to sell and selling a patented invention in the United States, and importing a patented invention into the United States.[2] If a patented invention is claimed as a device or product, all listed acts performed on the invention constitute infringement under § 271(a). In contrast, only the use of a patented invention infringes the patent if the invention is claimed as a method or process.[3] **4.01**

In addition, § 271(g) adds the following acts as infringement: importing into the United States or offering to sell, selling, or using a product within the United States if the product is made by a process patented in the United States.[4] Congress added this additional exclusivity for a product made by a patent process in 1988 through the Process Patent Amendment Act.[5] Under pre-1988 law, the purchase, use, or sale of a product made by a patented process or importing such a product into the United States did not constitute direct infringement.[6] In extending the protection to a product made by a patented process, Congress reviewed the definition of "made 'directly' from a patented process,"[7] which is used by other countries including Germany.[8] It found the definition unclear and included exceptions which are excluded from the protected product: a product which is materially changed by subsequent processes and a product which becomes a trivial and non-essential component of another.[9] The determination of whether the changes resulting from subsequent process meet the materiality requirement to remove the product is fact-specific and should focus on the structures and functions described in the asserted process claim and the specification.[10] An antibiotic drug made using an intermediate material is found to meet the materiality **4.02**

---

[1] 35 U.S.C. § 154(a).
[2] Ibid. § 271(a).
[3] *NTP, Inc. v. Research in Motion, Ltd.*, 418 F.3d 1282, 75 U.S.P.Q. 2d 1763 (Fed. Cir. 2005).
[4] 35 U.S.C. § 271(g).
[5] Process Patent Amendment Act of 1988.
[6] *Welsbach Light Co. v. Union Incandescent Light Co.*, 101 F.131, 131 (2d Cir. 1900). *Chisum on Patents*, § 16.2[6][c].
[7] David Hitchcock and Craig Nard, 3 *Fordham Intell. Prof. Media & Ent. L.J.* (1993): 441, 448.
[8] German Patent Act, § 9(3).
[9] 35 U.S.C. § 271(g).
[10] *Amgen, Inc. v. F. Hoffmann-La Roche, Ltd.*, 580 F.3d 1340 (Fed. Cir. 2009).

requirement where a patent concerns a process for making the intermediate material and thus a request for preliminary injunction is denied with respect to importation of the antibiotic made with the intermediate material.[11] In contrast, human growth hormone (hGH) made by a replicable cloning vehicle such as plasmid is found to fail to meet the materiality requirement where a patent is directed to a process for making the cloning vehicle although the property and structure of the cloning vehicle are very different.[12]

4.03 US courts interpret "selling" and "using" broadly to include any use of a patented product. Unlike German and Japanese Patent Acts, the US Patent Act does not provide immunity for private use of patented invention. Thus, US courts do not exclude private use or assignment from patent infringement.[13] The old case law suggests exclusion for using a patented invention for experimental purpose and not profit as a *de minimis* activity.[14] The Federal Circuit interprets the common law experimental exception to infringement very narrowly.[15]

4.04 Under the US Patent Act, the concept of joint infringement is limited because of the strong policy to maintain the freedom for competitors to engage in acts of making, using, and selling an invention unless these act fall into a definition of direct infringement under § 271.[16] For infringing a process patent, US courts apply the single-party rule and do not find "using" of the process if some steps in a patented process are performed by a party and other steps are performed by another party, unless one party controls the other party or directs it perform the steps that the party did not engage in.[17] This "control and direct" standard is met only when there is an agency relationship between the two parties or a contractual obligation for one party to perform the steps that the other party did not engage in.[18]

4.05 These acts of infringement must occur within the United States. A party must establish a certain fact for a US federal court to have jurisdiction over a particular cause of action. Whether an allegedly infringing act occurs within the United States is a matter on the merits rather than the threshold jurisdictional requirement.[19] The burden is on a patentee to prove that the allegedly infringing act occurred in the United States.[20]

---

[11] *Eli Lilly & Co. v. American Cyanamid Co.*, 82 F.3d 1568 (Fed. Cir. 1996).

[12] *Bio-Technology Gen. Corp. v. Genentech, Inc.*, 80 F.3d 1553 (Fed. Cir. 1996).

[13] *Aro Mfg. Co. v. Convertible Top Co.*, 377 U.S. 476, 141 U.S.P.Q. 681 (1964); *NTP, Inc. v. Research in Motion, Ltd.*, 418 F.3d 1282 (Fed. Cir. 2005).

[14] *Chisum on Patents*, § 16.3[1].

[15] *Madey v. Duke University*, 307 F.3d 1351, 1361, 64 U.S.P.Q. 2d 1737 (Fed. Cir. 2002). For more discussion on experimental use exception under the US Patent Act, see Ch. 7, 7.106 et seq.

[16] *Limelight Networks, Inc. v. Akamai Techs., Inc.*, 2014 U.S. LEXIS 3817, 110 U.S.P.Q. 2d 1681 (U.S. June 2, 2014); *Paper Converting Machine Co. v. Magna-Graphics Corp.*, 745 F.2d 11, 223 U.S.P.Q. 591 (1984) ("*no* activity other than the unauthorized making, using, or selling of the claimed invention can constitute direct infringement of a patent, *no matter* how great the adverse impact of that activity on the economic value of a patent").

[17] *Muniauction, Inc. v. Thomson Corp.*, 532 F.3d 1318, 87 U.S.P.Q. 2d 1350 (Fed. Cir. 2008); *Metabolite Laboratories, Inc. v. Laboratory Corporation of America Holdings*, 370 F.3d 1354, 71 U.S.P.Q. 2d 1081 (Fed. Cir. 2004).

[18] *McKesson Techs., Inc. v. Epic Sys. Corp.*, 98 U.S.P.Q. 2d 1281 (Fed. Cir. 2011); *BMC Res., Inc. v. Paymentech, L.P.*, 498 F.3d 1373, 84 U.S.P.Q. 2d 1545 (Fed. Cir. 2007).

[19] *Litecubes, LLC v. Northern Light Products, Inc.*, 523 F.3d 1353, 1363 (Fed. Cir. 2008).

[20] *Cordis Corp. v. Boston Sci. Corp.*, 561 F.3d 1319, 90 U.S.P.Q. 2d 1401 (Fed. Cir. 2009).

2. Indirect Infringement

Section 271 provides two types of acts which constitute indirect infringement: inducement and contributory infringement. Under US Law, indirect infringement is clearly distinguishable from direct infringement because courts examine indirect infringement only when they find direct infringement.[21] Evidence of a specific instance of direct infringement is necessary unless the asserted claim merely requires the capacity to perform a particular claimed element.[22] The patentee always has the burden to show direct infringement.[23] Because of the strong policy that competitors can engage in activities which do not constitute infringement, the US courts do not find a third party who assisted or abetted to be a direct infringer unless the party's act does not fall into the definition of inducement and contributory infringement provided in Patent Act. The US courts set a high hurdle for patentees to assert inducement and contributory infringement by requiring a patentee to show a specific knowledge held by the defendant to establish inducement and contributory infringement. **4.06**

For inducement, a patentee must establish that the defendant had (1) knowledge of the asserted patent and (2) the specific intent to induce a third party to engage in direct infringement.[24] The knowledge requirement is met with evidence of actual knowledge or willful blindness.[25] For there to be willful blindness, the defendant must subjectively believe there is a high risk that a fact (the existence of the asserted patent) exists and *must* take deliberate actions to avoid learning of the fact. With respect to the intent, intent to induce the act that constitutes direct infringement is not sufficient. Evidence to show that the defendant has a specific intent to induce infringement by another is necessary.[26] Moreover, the defendant must engage in an affirmative act which promotes and encourages infringement.[27] Instructing and advertising an infringing use are typical acts of inducement.[28] **4.07**

In contrast, contributory infringement does not require a showing of a specific intent to induce infringement. Instead, the patentee must establish the defendant had knowledge that the component sold by the defendant was specially made for infringing the asserted patent and has no substantial non-infringing use.[29] The non-infringing use should not be merely illusory, impractical, or experimental.[30] This knowledge of non-infringing use is essential for establishing contributory infringement. Under US law, a patent owner's attempt to extend the exclusivity of a patent to an unpatented component of the patented product may constitute a patent misuse or an antitrust liability.[31] Pre-1952 case law finds **4.08**

---

21 *Limelight Networks, Inc. v. Akamai Techs., Inc.*, 134 S. Ct. 2111, 189 L. Ed. 2d 52, 110 U.S.P.Q. 2d 1681 (U.S. June 2, 2014); *Aro Mfg. Co. v. Convertible Top Replacement Co.*, 365 U.S. 336, 341–2, 128 U.S.P.Q. 354 (1961).

22 *Fujitsu, Ltd. v. Netgear, Inc.*, 620 F.3d 1321, 96 U.S.P.Q. 2d 1742 (Fed. Cir. 2010).

23 *Joy Techs., Inc. v. Flakt, Inc.*, 6 F.3d 770, 774, 28 U.S.P.Q. 2d 1378 (Fed. Cir. 1993).

24 *DSU Medical Corp. v. JMS Co., Ltd.*, 471 F.3d 1293 (Fed. Cir. 2006).

25 *Global-Tech Appliances, Inc. v. SEB S.A.*, 131 S. Ct. 2060, 179 L. Ed. 2d 1167, 98 U.S.P.Q. 2d 1665 (U.S. 2011).

26 *DSU Medical Corp.*, 471 F.3d, 1304. However, the knowledge of validity is not necessary. *Commil USA, LLC v. Cisco Sys.* 135 S.Ct. 1920 (U.S. 2015).

27 *Tegal Corp. v. Tokyo Electron Co., Ltd.*, 248 F.3d 1376, 58 U.S.P.Q. 2d 1791 (Fed. Cir. 2001).

28 *Metro-Goldwyn-Mayer Studios Inc. v. Grokster, Ltd.*, 545 U.S. 913, 935 (2005).

29 35 U.S.C. § 271(c).

30 *i4i Limited Partnership v. Microsoft Corp.*, 598 F.3d 831 (Fed. Cir. 2010), *aff'd*, 131 S. Ct. 2238 (2011).

31 *Ill. Tool Works Inc. v. Indep. Ink, Inc.*, 547 U.S. 28, 126 S. Ct. 1281, 164 L. Ed. 2d 26, 77 U.S.P.Q. 2d 1801 (2006).

lawful an extension to an unpatented component only if the component has no substantial non-infringing use.[32] Congress codified the case law as a contributory infringement and introduced immunity from patent misuse for a component of a patented invention if the component has no substantial non-infringement use and thus selling of the component constitutes contributory infringement.[33] In addition to the knowledge of no substantial non-infringing use, a patentee needs to establish the defendant's actual knowledge or willful blindness with respect to the asserted patent as required for establishing inducement.[34]

4.09 Moreover, the patentee needs to establish that the component sold by the defendant is a material part of the invention. Under the current case law, the component constitutes a material part if the asserted claim recites the component. A product which is not part of the asserted claim is not a material part of the invention even if the product is used for the patented invention.[35]

3. Patent Term and Extension

4.10 A patentee enjoys the exclusivity of a patent twenty years from the earliest filing date in the United States with respect to continuation and divisional applications as well as an international application date under the Patent Cooperation Treaty and the priority date under Paris Convention.[36] If a patent is granted to an application filed in other countries claiming priority under the Paris Convention, an international patent application, or provisional application under the domestic priority system, the priority period is excluded from the twenty-year patent term.[37]

4.11 The US Patent Act allows an extension of the twenty-year term for patents on drugs and processes for making and using the drugs and medical devices which are subject to the Federal Food, Drug and Cosmetic Act.[38] A patentee must submit an application for extension before the expiration of the patent term.[39] The Act also allows an extension of the twenty-year term if an applicant lost a part of the patent term due to a delay resulting from an interference, a secrecy order, or an appellate review.[40] The extension to remedy the procedural delay is automatic by the operation of law.

4. Extraterritorial Infringement

4.12 Although the US Supreme Court emphasizes the supremacy of the territorial principle in US patent rights, the Patent Act prescribes exceptions for an act that occurs outside the United States that might infringe a US patent.[41] The Patent Act, § 271(f) provides for infringement of a US patent with respect to acts of supplying and causing to be supplied in or from the United States all or a substantial portion of the components of a patent invention if such components are uncombined, in whole or in part, to induce the combination

[32] *Henry v. A.B. Dick Co.*, 224 U.S. 1 (1912). *Chisum on Patents*, § 17.03[3].
[33] 35 U.S.C. § 271(c), (d).
[34] *Global-Tech Appliances, Inc.*, 131 S. Ct. 2060, 2068.
[35] *Fujitsu, Ltd.*, 620 F.3d 1321 (Fed. Cir. 2010).
[36] 35 U.S.C. § 154(a)(2).
[37] Ibid. § 154(a)(3).
[38] Ibid. § 156.
[39] Ibid. § 156(a)(1).
[40] Ibid. § 154(b).
[41] *Microsoft Corp. v. AT&T Corp.*, 550 U.S. 437 (2007); *Deepsouth Packing Co.* v. *Laitram Corp.*, 406 U.S. 518 (1972).

of the components outside the United States in a manner that would infringe the patent if such combination occurred within the United States.[42] It also provides for infringement of a US patent with respect to acts of supplying or causing to be supplied in or from the United States any component of a patented invention that meets the requirements of contributory infringement.[43] In other words, a US patent can be infringed even if the infringement occurred outside the United States if a component of a patented invention is supplied from the United States under the limited circumstances proscribed in § 271(f). Section 271(g) also makes clear that importing a product which is made by a process covered by a US Patent infringes the US patent even if the process is performed outside the United States.[44]

Because these provisions which provide extraterritorial effects of US patents are exceptions to the general rule (the territorial principle), the terms in these provisions must be interpreted restrictively and any doubt on an allegedly infringing act outside the United States should be resolved by the presumption against extraterritoriality [45] For example, the term "components" was interpreted to exclude software in the abstract because software cannot be combined with other components to form the patented invention unless it is expressed as a computer-readable copy.[46] Accordingly, sending the master version of software which is part of the patented invention on a disk or via electronic transmission does not constitute infringement of a US patent. **4.13**

Contrary to the extraterritorial provisions, US courts may expansively interpret the terms of direct and indirect infringement under § 271(a), (b), and (c). US courts find the use of a patented invention to be within the United States under § 271(a) even if some components of the invention are located outside the United States when the invention is claimed as a device and is patented as long as the place where control of the device is exercised and beneficial use of the device is obtained is the United States.[47] In contrast, when an invention is claimed as a process and is patented, the process is not used within the United States if some steps of the process claims are performed outside the United States.[48] **4.14**

Regarding "selling" and "offering to sell," US courts do not find sale in the United States if essential activities take place outside the United States.[49] If the defendant makes an offer to sell an allegedly infringing product in the United States, the offer infringes a US patent even if the offer is made from a foreign country.[50] In contrast, US courts may not find offering to sell in the United States even if the negotiation and execution of a contract for the sale of an allegedly infringing product takes place in the United States if the contract aims to deliver the product outside the United States.[51] **4.15**

US courts find inducement even if the act of inducement or contributory infringement took place outside the United States as long as direct infringement occurs within the United **4.16**

[42] 35 U.S.C. § 271(f)(1).
[43] Ibid. § 271(f)(2).
[44] Ibid. § 271(g).
[45] *Microsoft*, 550 U.S. 454.
[46] Ibid. 449.
[47] *NTP, Inc. v. Research in Motion, Ltd.*, 418 F.3d 1282, 75 U.S.P.Q. 2d 1763 (Fed. Cir. 2005).
[48] Ibid. 1318.
[49] *MEMC Electronic Materials, Inc. v. Mitsubishi Materials Silicon Corp.*, 420 F.3d 1369 (Fed. Cir. 2005).
[50] *Transocean Offshore Deepwater Drilling, Inc. v. Maersk Contrs. USA, Inc.*, 617 F.3d 1296 (Fed. Cir. 2010).
[51] *Quality Tubing, Inc. v. Precision Tube Holdings Corp.*, 75 F. Supp.2d 613, 1999 WL 1204845 (S.D. Tex. 1999).

States.[52] For example, the Federal Circuit found infringement of a US patent with respect to the defendant which designed and supplied from Singapore an IC chip to its customers for distribution in the United States where the chip carries out a method covered by the patent.[53] In contrast, US courts may refuse to find inducement or contributory infringement if direct infringement occurs outside the United States.[54] However, if the defendant induces or contributes to direct infringement outside the United States by supplying all or a substantial portion of components of a patented invention, as discussed above, US courts find infringement of a US patent under § 271(f).[55]

B. Extent of Patent Protection

1. Overview

4.17 Although courts in the three jurisdictions currently adopt the same rule that the claim determines the extent of patent protection, they give different significances to the language or terms of a claim. The function of a claim differs depending on whether a country subscribes to the peripheral definition theory or the central definition theory. In Europe, the United Kingdom is the paradigm of a country which follows the peripheral definition theory in contrast to pre-1981 Germany which was the paradigm of a country following the central definition theory.[56] Under the peripheral definition theory, the claim language defines the boundary of exclusive right. Courts cannot rewrite or expand the literal scope defined by the claim language. In determining the extent of patent protection, the role played by courts under the peripheral theory is limited to clarifying the meaning of disputed claim terms in light of the specification and other patent documents. In contrast, the claim merely defines the center of the extent of patent protection under the central definition theory. Thus, courts can expand the literal scope defined by the claim language in light of the specification, drawings, and general knowledge of one skilled in the art. Under the central definition theory, courts try to identify an inventive idea underlying the claim language by taking account of the technical problem and the solution provided by the inventor.

4.18 Surprisingly, the United States, which follows the common law tradition and receives influence from UK patent jurisprudence, followed the central definition theory until the mid-nineteenth century.[57] Early statutes did not impose any duty to include a claim. Early patent statutes did not provide any duty for inventors to specify their inventions. Only after the Supreme Court acknowledged the duty in *Evans v. Eaton* (1822)[58] did Congress

[52] *Honeywell, Inc. v. Metz Apparatewerke*, 509 F.2d 1137, 1141, 184 U.S.P.Q. 387 (7th Cir. 1975); *Chisum on Patents*, § 16.05[3][e].

[53] *Crystal Semiconductor Corp. v. TriTech Microelectronics International, Inc.*, 246 F.3d 1336, 57 U.S.P.Q. 2d 1953 (Fed. Cir. 2001).

[54] *DSU Medical Corp. v. JMS Co., Ltd.*, 471 F.3d 1293, 1303, 81 U.S.P.Q. 2d 1238 (Fed. Cir. 2006).

[55] 35 U.S.C. § 271(f).

[56] Protocol on the Interpretation of Article 69, EPC. The Protocol discusses two different approaches to determine the extent of patent protection under the peripheral definition theory and the central definition theory.

[57] Toshiko Takenaka, "Interpreting Patent Claims: The United States, Germany and Japan," 17 *IIC Studies* (1995): 6–12.

[58] *Evans v. Eaton,* 20 U.S. 356, 7 Wheat. 356, 5 L. Ed. 472 (1822).

codify the duty in the Patent Act of 1836.[59] Before the Supreme Court decision, the patent community developed a practice of including a statement specifying the part or improvement of a device or process to be claimed as his invention. Such a statement included terms such as "substantially as herein described" or "substantially as set forth" to extend protection to insubstantial modifications as equivalents of the embodiments disclosed in the specification and drawings.[60] A shift from the central to the peripheral definition theory began with the enactment of the 1870 Patent Act[61] and the Court's emphasis on the significance of the claim to define the extent of patent protection.[62] As a result, the central definition claim-drafting practice with terms such as "substantially as described" was on its way out by the late nineteenth century.

However, the US patent system maintained an important aspect of the central definition theory. In *Graver Tank v. Linde Air Product Co.* (1950), the Supreme Court endorsed the pre-1870 practice of extending patent protection to insubstantial modifications of the embodiments disclosed in the specification and drawings under the doctrine of equivalents.[63] The *Graver Tank* court cited *Winnans v. Denmead* (1854) in which the Court interpreted claims drafted in the central definition claim format and found infringement by the accused product which was clearly outside the literal scope of the claim language.[64] It established a two-part test for determining the extent of patent protection by examining (a) literal infringement and (b) infringement under the doctrine of equivalents. US courts retained flexibility to expand the literal scope under the peripheral theory.[65] **4.19**

The practice developed by the *Graver Tank* Court of determining the extent of patent protection is perfectly in line with the position provided in the Protocol for interpreting Article 69 of the European Patent Convention (EPC). The Protocol rejects two extreme approaches under the two theories and requires member states to take a position between the two approaches by taking account of a balance between the two competing policies: a fair protection for the patentee and a reasonable degree of legal certainty for the public.[66] The 2000 revision of the Protocol clarified the extent of patent protection under the doctrine of equivalents by requiring member states to take account of the equivalents of any elements recited in the claim.[67] US courts further refined the two-part test: (1) whether the claims read literally on the accused embodiment to determine literal infringement and (2) whether the accused embodiment performs substantially the same functions in substantially the same way to produce substantially the same result to determine infringement under the doctrine of equivalents.[68] The doctrine of equivalents can function to expand the literal **4.20**

---

59 Act of July 4, 1836, Ch. 357, § 6, 5 Stat. 117.

60 *Ex parte Fressola*, 27 U.S.P.Q. 2d 1608 (Bd. Pat. App. & Interferences 1993).

61 Act of July 8, 1870, Ch. 230, § 26, 16 Stat. 198. A. W. Deller, *Patent Claims* (2d ed., 1971), § 1; Warren Jessup, "The Doctrine of Equivalents," 54 *JPTOS* (1972): 248.

62 *Merrill v. Yeomans*, 94 U.S. 568, 4 Otto 568, 24 L. Ed. 235 (1877).

63 *Graver Tank & Mfg. Co. v. Linde Air Products Co.*, 339 U.S. 605, 70 S. Ct. 854, 94 L. Ed. 1097, 85 U.S.P.Q. 328 (1950).

64 *Winans v. Denmead*, 56 U.S. 330, 15 How. 330, 14 L. Ed. 717(1854).

65 *Warner-Jenkinson*, 520 U.S. 17 (1997), 27. The Court acknowledged the change in claim-drafting practice but rejected the accused infringer's argument that US patent system completely abandoned the central definition theory.

66 Protocol on the Interpretation of Article 69, EPC, Art. 1.

67 Ibid. Art. 2.

68 *Autogiro Co. of Am. v. United States*, 181 Ct. Cl. 55, 384 F.2d 391, 155 U.S.P.Q. 697 (1967).

scope as well as to narrow the scope.[69] The doctrine may function to limit the overly broad literal scope to cover only equivalents of the disclosed embodiments.[70] The doctrine is called the reverse doctrine of equivalents when it is used to narrow the literal scope.[71]

4.21 Under the current case law, US courts seldom apply the reverse doctrine of equivalents although the Supreme Court acknowledged the role played by the doctrine of equivalents to narrow the literal scope defined by the claim language.[72] This is because US courts can invalidate a claim with an overly broad literal scope for a violation of enablement, written description requirement,[73] and claim indefiniteness[74] and limit such scope in light of the specification, drawings, and record on patent prosecution.[75]

2. Infringement Analysis

(a) Separate Steps: Claim Construction and Application

4.22 The most unique feature in US courts' infringement analysis is the involvement of the jury. The US Constitution guarantees a right to trial by jury in suits at common law where the value of controversy exceeds 20 dollars.[76] Infringement analysis in US courts entails two separate steps: (1) construction of the patent claim by clarifying the scope and meaning of terms in the asserted claim; and (2) applying the construed claim to the accused embodiment.[77] The second step is further divided into a two-part test: (1) literal infringement if all elements in the asserted claim are found literally in the accused embodiment; and (2) infringement under the doctrine of equivalents if an equivalent element replaces any missing element in the accused embodiment.[78]

4.23 In *Markman v. Westview* (1996), the Supreme Court made clear that the ultimate question of claim construction is one of law and thus exclusively within the province of the court.[79] The Court further clarified that the question of claim interpretation may involve subsidiary factual questions when a claim uses terms which are not commonly understood.[80] Thus, district court judges construe the claim and the Federal Circuit reviews the construction with the *de novo* standard except for the subsidiary factual questions.[81] In contrast, the Supreme Court acquiesced to the Federal Circuit's holding that the jury should apply the

[69] Dennis Malone and Richard L. Schmalz, Note, *Peripheral Definition Theory v. Central Definition Theory in Patent Claim Interpretation: A Survey of the Federal Circuits*, 32 Geo Wash L Rev 609 (1364).

[70] *Texas Instruments, Inc. v. Int'l Trade Comm'n*, 846 F.2d 1369, 1371–72, 6 U.S.P.Q. 2d 1886, 1889 (Fed. Cir. 1988).

[71] *SRI International v. Matsushita Electric Corp. of America*, 775 F.2d 1107, 227 U.S.P.Q. 577 (Fed. Cir. 1985) (*en banc*).

[72] *Warner-Jenkinson Co., Inc. v. Hilton Davis Chemical Co.*, 520 U.S. 17, 41 U.S.P.Q. 2d 1865 (1997).

[73] 35 U.S.C. § 112(a). E.g., *In re Wright*, 999 F.2d 1557 (Fed. Cir. 1993)—enablement vilation; *Lizardtech, Inc. v. Eareth Res. Mapping, Inc.*, 424 F.3d 1336 (Fed. Cir. 2005)—written description violation.

[74] 35 U.S.C. § 112(a). E.g., *Robert Bosch, LLC v. Snap-On Inc.*, 769 F.3d 1094 (Fed. Cir. 2014).

[75] See Ch. 4, 4.75 "Canons Favoring Accused Infringer."

[76] US Const., Amdt. 7.

[77] *Markman v. Westview Instruments, Inc.*, 52 F.3d 967, 976, 34 U.S.P.Q. 2d 1321, 1326 (Fed. Cir. 1995) (*en banc*). The authors of this book do not distinguish construction from interpretation and use them alternatively although some scholars distinguish them.

[78] *Johnston v. IVAC Corp.*, 885 F.2d 1574, 1578 n. 3, 12 U.S.P.Q. 2d 1382, 1387 n. 3 (Fed. Cir. 1989); see *Chisum on Patents*, § 18.03[4][a].

[79] *Markman v. Westview Instruments*, 517 U.S. 370, 116 S. Ct. 1384, 134 L. Ed. 2d 577, 38 U.S.P.Q. 2d 1461 (1996).

[80] *Teva Pharm. USA, Inc. v. Sandoz, Inc.*, 135 S. Ct. 831, 837, 190 L. Ed. 2d 719, 113 U.S.P.Q. 2d 1269, 83 U.S.L.W. 4055, 90 Fed. R. Serv. 3d (Callaghan) 1244 (U.S. 2015).

[81] Ibid. 838. The subsidiary factual question is reviewed under the clearly erroneous standard.

doctrine of equivalents.[82] In other words, the second step of applying the claim to the accused embodiment is exclusively in the hands of jury.

Because of the different decision-makers, the two steps should be separate. This is in stark contrast to claim construction at German and Japanese courts where judges construe the asserted claim and apply the construed claim to the accused embodiment to determine infringement.[83] To make the two steps distinct from each other, US district courts developed the practice of construing a patent claim in a mini-hearing called a *Markman* hearing.[84] In practice, it is often difficult to distinguish the first step of claim construction from the second step of claim application.[85] To separate the two steps, US district courts are prevented from construing a claim in light of the accused embodiment to determine whether the disputed term covers or excludes an element of the accused embodiment.[86] However, courts are not completely prevented from taking account of the accused embodiment in claim construction. This is because knowledge of the accused embodiment is necessary to address the claim terms which are in dispute.[87] Moreover, US district courts need to develop evidence on the accused embodiment because, unlike German and Japanese appeal procedures, US appeals courts are unable to take any additional evidence.[88] If a party appeals from a summary judgment of non-infringement without any record of the accused embodiment, the Federal Circuit cannot fully review the non-infringement finding, including the construed claim, without knowing the operation or structure of the accused embodiment.[89] Therefore, the court acknowledges the necessity for district court judges to understand the accused embodiment and construe the disputed term with the impact of infringement finding while emphasizing the rule to construe a claim objectively in light to the patent document without resorting to the comparison with the accused embodiment.[90] **4.24**

As will be discussed below, German and Japanese judges construe a claim in light of the accused embodiment whether the disputed term excludes or includes the corresponding element of the accused embodiment. They would view the US two-step analysis as unrealistic because ambiguity in the claim term would remain unless the meaning of a claim term is clarified with respect to the accused embodiment. The ultimate question over which the parties dispute is whether a particular term of the asserted claim includes or excludes an element or step of the accused embodiment. If a claim term is construed with no knowledge of the accused embodiment, the construction given by a district court functions more like an advisory opinion.[91] Even if the parties agree that a disputed term has a common meaning, **4.25**

[82] *Warner-Jenkinson*, 520 U.S. 39.

[83] For German courts, Ch. 5, 5.63; for Japanese courts, Ch. 6, 6.29.

[84] Kimberly Moore, Paul Michel, and Timothy Holbrook, *Patent Litigation and Strategy*, 279 (3d ed, 2008), 279.

[85] Jason R. Mudd, "To Construe or Not to Construe: At the Interface between Claim Construction and Infringement in Patent Cases," 76 *Mo. L. Rev.* (2011): 709.

[86] *Wilson Sporting Goods Co. v. Hillerich & Bradsby Co.*, 442 F.3d 1322, 1326, 78 U.S.P.Q. 2d 1382 (Fed. Cir. 2006).

[87] *Vivid Technologies, Inc. v. American Science & Engineering, Inc.*, 200 F.3d 795, 803, 53 U.S.P.Q. 2d 1289, 1394 (Fed. Cir. 1999).

[88] Jeffrey C. Dobbins, "New Evidence on Appeal," 96 *Minn. L. Rev.* (2012): 2016.

[89] *Wilson Sporting Goods Co.*, 442 F.3d, 1330.

[90] *Nazomi Communs., Inc. v. Arm Holdings plc*, 403 F.3d 1364, 74 U.S.P.Q. 2d 1458 (Fed. Cir. 2005).

[91] *Wilson Sporting Goods Co.*, 442 F.3d, 1327. *Lava Trading, Inc. v. Sonic Trading Mgmt., LLC*, 445 F.3d 1348, 1350, 78 U.S.P.Q. 2d 1624 (Fed. Cir. 2006).

they dispute whether the accused device functions in the way required by the claim term.[92] If courts try to avoid an ambiguity argument and adopt a detailed construction in connection with the operation and structure of the accused embodiment, the Federal Circuit may find that the detailed construction invades the province of the trier of fact and vacate a summary judgment based on the construction.[93] In short, US district courts face the dilemma of whether to give a claim construction albeit ambiguous with respect to the accused embodiment or to adopt a claim construction with a clear coverage with respect to the accused embodiment while taking a risk of summary judgment based on the claim construction being vacated. Despite the impossible challenge of clarifying the term's meaning without the power to decide the ultimate question of infringement, US district courts are required to resolve any dispute over the patent scope by claim construction.[94] German and Japanese courts are immune from this challenge unique to the separation of power in US patent infringement analysis, and these courts' infringement analysis focuses on the accused embodiment with the coverage of the disputed term.[95] In contrast, US courts focus on the claim term by replacing the term with a clearer one.[96]

4.26 Another unique feature in US infringement analysis is the pre-trial discovery proceedings to develop evidence to support the parties' claims and defenses.[97] Unlike German and Japanese plaintiffs, US plaintiffs do not need to establish facts to support their infringement theories in their complaint because the Federal Rules of Civil Procedure requires only notice pleading.[98] The parties' infringement and defense theories, including claim construction, change as the discovery reveals facts on the accused embodiment and the priority. Although district courts are free to develop their own local rules regarding when and how to construe claims, [99] many district courts adopt a local rule to have a *Markman* hearing or a process to construe the claim during the discovery (*Markman* process).[100] This practice requires US courts to construe a claim with insufficient knowledge of the accused embodiment and may prevent parties from requesting an amendment of construction for the benefit of judicial economy.[101] Such premature claim constructions may contribute to a high reversal rate and uncertainty of claim construction.[102]

---

[92] *O2 Micro Int'l, Ltd. v. Beyond Innovation Tech. Co.*, 521 F.3d 1351, 86 U.S.P.Q. 2d 1304 (Fed. Cir. 2008).

[93] *Dorel Juvenile Group, Inc. v. Graco Children's Prods.*, 429 F.3d 1043,, 77 U.S.P.Q. 2d 1090 (Fed. Cir. 2005).

[94] *O2 Micro Int'l, Ltd.*, 521 F.3d, 1362. Dan L. Burk and Mark A. Lemley, "Fence Posts or Sign Posts? Rethinking Patent Claim Construction," 157 *U. Pa. L. Rev.* (2009): 1743.

[95] For infringement analysis at German courts, see Ch. 5, 5.63 "Infringement Analysis." For infringement analysis at Japanese courts, see Ch. 6, 6.29.

[96] Burk and Lemley, "Fence Posts or Sign Posts?," 1760.

[97] See Ch. 10, 10.31 "Evidence Collection."

[98] Fed Rules Civ. Proc. Rule 8. *O2 Micro Int'l, Ltd. v. Monolithic Power Sys., I*, 467 F.3d 1355, 1365, 80 U.S.P.Q. 2d 1769 (Fed. Cir. 2006).

[99] *Ballard Med. Prods. v. Allegiance Healthcare Corp.*, 268 F.3d 1352, 1358 (Fed. Cir. 2001).

[100] E.g., Peter S. Menell et al., *Patent Case Management Judicial Guide* (2d ed., 2012), ch. 5; Mudd, "To Construe or Not to Construe," 716. Recent statistics support a significant decrease in the Federal Circuit's reversal rate on district courts' claim construction rulings. See Jonas Anderson and Peter Menell, "Informal Deterrence: A Historical Empirical and Normative Analysis of Patent Claim Construction," 108 *Northwestern L.R.* (2014): 1.

[101] *Monolithic Power Sys.*, 467 F.3d, 1366.

[102] Mudd, "To Construe or Not to Construe," 710, Kimberly A. Moore, "*Markman* Eight Years Later: Is Claim Construction More Predictable?," 9 *Lewis & Clark L. Rev.* (2005): 231, 239, 246; Lee Petherbridge, "The Claim Construction Effect," 15 *Mich. Telecomm. & Tech. L. Rev.* (2008): 215, 228–9; David L. Schwartz, "*Practice Makes Perfect? An Empirical Study of Claim Construction Reversal Rates in Patent Cases*," 107 *Mich.*

German and Japanese courts require patentees to establish in their pleading sufficient facts to establish their infringement theories, and construe a claim to determine infringement only when patentees produce evidence concerning the accused embodiment because their analysis focuses on the embodiment.[103]

(b) Further Separate Steps in Claim Applications: Literal Infringement and Infringement under the Doctrine of Equivalents

Because the US patent system follows the peripheral definition theory, US courts are very reluctant to find infringement under the doctrine of equivalents once they find no literal infringement. Thus, determination of literal infringement is separate and distinct from the determination of literal infringement. US courts used to determine infringement under the doctrine of equivalents only when they found no literal infringement.[104] The two steps were separate and distinct to prevent courts from covering equivalents because the scope defined by equivalents is an exception to the general rule that the claim language determines the extent of patent protection. This was a stark contrast to the extent of patent protection under the pre-1981 German Patent Act in which the scope defined by equivalents was the general rule.[105] **4.27**

Warner-Jenkinson slightly modified this practice in allowing parties to present both claim construction and doctrines to limit the doctrine of equivalents in a *Markman* process.[106] The US Supreme Court acknowledged the concern from the patent community over the uncertainty introduced by the application of the doctrine of equivalents by the jury and encouraged the Federal Circuit to develop a practice of preventing the case from going to the jury to decide equivalents.[107] In response, the Federal Circuit encouraged the district courts to decide whether any doctrine applies to limit the doctrine of equivalents when they construe claims during the Markman process. If one such doctrine applies, the courts can frequently decide infringement under the doctrine of equivalents as a matter of law without jury involvement. **4.28**

Despite this modification in procedure, the distinction between literal infringement and infringement under the doctrine is clearer than the pre-*Warner-Jenkinson* practice. Because of the Supreme Court's emphasis on the public notice function of claims and the doctrines to limit the doctrine of equivalents, the chance for patentees to win a claim for infringement under the doctrine of equivalents has been significantly reduced.[108] The two presumptions of patentability-related reasons and general surrender introduced by the Court in *Warner-Jenkinson*[109]and *Festo*[110] effectively eliminate a claim of infringement under **4.29**

L. Rev. (2008): 223, 267; Michael Saunders, Note, "A Survey of Post-*Phillips* Claim Construction Cases," 22 *Berkeley Tech. L.J.* (2007): 215, 236.

[103] To collect evidence to support infringement claims, a procedure for pre-trial evidence collection is available. See Ch. 11, 11.61 "Procedure for Pre-trial Evidence Collection Art."

[104] Takenaka, "Interpreting Patent Claims," 54.

[105] Ibid. 59.

[106] *Warner-Jenkinson Co. v. Hilton Davis Chem. Co.*, 520 U.S. 17, 117 S. Ct. 1040, 137 L. Ed. 2d 146, 41 U.S.P.Q. 2d 1865 (1997).

[107] Ibid. 39, footnote 8.

[108] John R. Allison and Mark A. Lemley, "The (Unnoticed) Demise of the Doctrine of Equivalents," 59 *Stan. L. Rev.* (2007): 955, 958.

[109] *Warner-Jenkinson Co. v. Hilton Davis Chem. Co.*, 520 U.S. 17, 33 (a presumption of a substantial reason related to patentability).

[110] *Festo Corp. v. Shoketsu Kinzoku Kogyo Kabushiki Co.*, 535 U.S. 722, 740, 122 S. Ct. 1831, 152 L. Ed. 2d 944, 62 U.S.P.Q. 2d 1705 (2002) (the presumption of surrender for the scope between the original claim and amended claim).

the doctrine of equivalents unless the claim term remains as originally filed. As a result, the extent of patent protection, including the scope defined by equivalents, has become rare under the current US case law.[111] This practice is in line with the German courts' recent practice and the Japanese courts' long-established practice where courts seldom find infringement under the doctrine of equivalents.[112]

(c) Claim Construction for Validity Challenges

4.30 US courts have power to decide both infringement and validity issues. They use the same *Markman* process to construe the claim language to set the starting point for determining infringement and validity. Since the determination of validity involves factual issues such as the determination of the content of the prior art, US courts need to separate the step of claim construction and the comparison of the construed claim with the content of the prior art and thus claims should be interpreted without reference to the prior art.[113] However, US courts are not completely prevented from taking account of the prior art for the validity determination because such knowledge is necessary to limit their construction only to the claim terms in dispute.[114] Moreover, courts can take account of the prior art as part of the record of prosecution and as part of the knowledge of a person having ordinary skills in the art of the invention ("PHOSITA") for the validity determination.[115]

4.31 The USPTO applies different rules for construing claims in determining patentability during the first examination and rexamining validity in post-grant proceedings.[116] The Federal Circuit follows the same rules in reviewing the USPTO's claim construction when it reviews an appeal from a decision based on the USPTO claim construction.

3. Claim Construction

(a) Fundamental Rules

4.32 i. **Claims Defined by the Structure, Material, and Acts** US patent applicants are required to distinctively claim the subject matter which the inventor regards as the invention or a joint inventor regards as the invention.[117] To meet this requirement, the general rule is that the subject matter must be defined by the structure, material, and acts of the subject matter.[118] The shift to the peripheral definition theory led to the Supreme Court's disapproval of a claim-drafting practice in which an important element of the claimed invention is described by functional limitations as being ambiguous and overly broad.[119] For endorsing

---

[111] Many US commentators wrote about the demise of the doctrine of equivalents, e.g., Charles W. Adams, "The Doctrine of Equivalents: Becoming a Derelict on the Waters of Patent Law," 84 *Neb. L. Rev.* (2006): 1113; Lee Petherbridge, "On the Decline of the Doctrine of Equivalents," 31 *Cardozo L. Rev.* (2010): 1371, 1404; Eugene R. Quinn, "A Slow Death? Killing the Doctrine of Equivalents," 164 *Pat. World* (2004): 50 (http://ipwatchdog.com/articles/Aug-04-Closing.pdf).

[112] For the recent trend in the German courts' practice, see Ch. 5, 5.110 "Doctrine of Equivalents." For the Japanese courts' practice, see Ch. 6, 6.72 "Doctrine of Equivalents."

[113] *Chisum on Patents*, § 18.03[1][b].

[114] *Vivid Technologies, Inc. v. American Science & Engineering, Inc.*, 200 F.3d 795, 803, 53 U.S.P.Q. 2d 1289, 1394 (Fed. Cir. 1999).

[115] Ch. 4, 4.70 "Prior art."

[116] The USPTO adopts the broadest possible interpretation. For the claim constution at the USPTO, see Ch. 7, 7.04 "Claim Construction."

[117] 35 U.S.C. § 112(b).

[118] Ibid. § 112(f) provides an exception to this general rule.

[119] *General Electric Co. v. Wabash Appliance Co.*, 304 U.S. 364, 37 U.S.P.Q. 466 (1938); *Halliburton Oil Well Cementing Co. v. Walker*, 329 U.S. 1, 71 U.S.P.Q. 1 (1946).

the established practice of defining an invention by functions when the invention includes multiple elements, Congress made clear that an element of the invention can be described as a means or step for performing a function (means-plus-function claims).[120] Further, US courts developed case law to endorse a claim-drafting practice of defining an invention as a process by a product resulting from the process, instead of acts of the process (product-by-process claims). These claims drafted in special forms are controlled by rules different from those which are defined by the structure, material, and acts.[121]

US claims usually consist of three parts: the preamble, the transition phrase, and the body. The preamble comprises of a general description of the object of the sentence in the claim and recites the general use, purpose, or nature of the invention.[122] The transition phrase following the preamble signifies whether additional elements in the accused embodiment exclude a claim of infringement.[123] The transition phrase may also signify a distinction between elements in the preamble which are conventional and known in the prior art from elements which are new and improvements.[124] The body includes elements of the invention which define technical features of the invention and their interactions. A term in the body always functions as a limitation to define the scope of exclusivity.[125] In contrast, courts must decide whether a term in the preamble should function as a limitation by construing terms in the body.[126] To avoid an admission of an element as the prior art and a dispute over whether a term functions as a limitation, the preamble of US patent claims are much shorter than those of German and Japanese claims. **4.33**

Unlike the EPC, the German Patent Act, and the Japanese Patent Act,[127] the US Patent Act does not provide any rule for interpreting a claim in which the invention is defined in accordance with the general rule (regular claims). Instead, the Act only provides a special rule for a claim in which the invention is functionally defined.[128] However, US courts developed fundamental rules to determine the extent of patent protection for regular claims through case law. In *Phillips*, the *en banc* Federal Circuit discussed these fundamental rules.[129] The *Phillips* court made clear the paramount rule that the claims of a patent define the scope of exclusivity that the patentee is entitled to.[130] The written description of the specification does not define the exclusive scope.[131] However, like German and Japanese courts, US courts can interpret the language of a claim in light of the written description of the specification, drawings, and other claim interpretation aids. The *Phillips* court clarified a rule of hierarchy among these claim interpretation aids.[132] **4.34**

Japanese scholars extensively debate whether courts should be confined to the language of the claim without making reference to the specification if the disputed term is clear **4.35**

---

120 35 U.S.C. § 112(f).
121 See Ch. 4, 4.32 "Claims defined by the structure, material, and acts."
122 Martin Adelman et al., *Cases and Materials on Patent Law* (3d ed., 2009), 468.
123 For more discussion, see Ch. 4, 4.34.
124 37 C.F.R. § 1.75(e). This type of claim is called a "Jepson claim."
125 See Ch. 4, 4.83 "All Elements Rule."
126 See Ch. 4, 4.79.
127 EPC, Art. 69; Japanese Patent Act (JPA), Art. 70.
128 35 U.S.C. § 112(f).
129 *Phillips v. AWH Corp.*, 415 F.3d 1303, 1312, 75 U.S.P.Q. 2d 1321 (Fed. Cir. 2005).
130 Ibid. 1312.
131 *Markman*, 52 F.3d, 980.
132 See Ch. 4, 4.45.

and unambiguous on its face.[133] US courts view such a restrictive approach as unrealistic because they acknowledge that a clear and unambiguous claim term is rare due to the difficulty in converting a machine or process into words.[134] Moreover, an inventor can be his own lexicographer in describing an aspect of his invention because his invention is novel and thus no word exists to describe it.[135] When an inventor defines a claim term in the specification in a different manner from the common or technical meaning, courts must interpret the term in accordance with the inventor's definition.[136] Accordingly, courts must always examine the specification to determine whether the inventor has adopted a special definition for a disputed claim term.

4.36 If the written description clearly does not support an adoption of an uncommon definition by the inventor, claims should be interpreted to give claim terms the ordinary and customary meaning as understood by a PHOSITA.[137] The *Phillips* court emphasized an important role played by the perspective of a PHOSITA in claim interpretation because inventors are typically PHOSITAs; patents, particularly claims, are addressed to PHOSITAs; and the perspective of a PHOSITA gives an objective starting point to interpret the language of claim.[138] This perspective also gives another reason that courts should always look at the written description of the specification as well as drawings because PHOSITAs are deemed to read not only the particular claim including the term at dispute but also the entire patent.[139]

4.37 Despite the important role played by the perspective of a PHOSITA, US courts seldom discuss the skill level of a PHOSITA in the context of infringement analysis. This is in stark contrast to German claim interpretation in which the courts' analysis focuses on the definition and knowledge level of PHOSITAs in interpreting the claim language.[140] The US Patent Act recites PHOSITA only with respect to the assessment of obviousness.[141] US case law is unclear whether the same perspective of a PHOSITA is used for nonobviousness and infringement analysis. With respect to PHOSITAs for nonobviousness, the Federal Circuit distinguished PHOSITAs from inventors in that the latter have a creative quality while the former are not innovative and thus merely exercise conventional wisdom in the art. [142] This distinction is contrary to the *Phillips* court's notion that inventors are typically PHOSITAs.[143] According to the *Phillips* court, PHOSITAs are deemed to have knowledge of any special meaning and usage in the art of the invention.[144] Unlike German claim interpretation, the technical context of the claim understood by a PHOSITA guided by the purpose of each claim element does not play a significant role in claim interpretation.[145]

---

[133] See Ch. 4, 4.45 "Intrinsic v. Extrinsic evidence."

[134] *Autogiro Co. of America v. United States*, 384 F.2d 391, 397, 181 Ct. Cl. 55 (Ct. Cl. 1967).

[135] Ibid. 397. For more discussions on the rule that an inventor as lexicographer, see Ch. 4, 4.52.

[136] *International Cork Co. v. New Process Cork Co.*, 6 F.2d 420, 422 (2d Cir. 1925); *Desper Prods. v. QSound Labs., Inc.*, 157 F.3d 1325, 48 U.S.P.Q. 2d (BNA) 1088 (Fed. Cir. 1998).

[137] *Phillips*, 415 F.3d, 1313.

[138] Ibid.

[139] Ibid.

[140] For more discussion about German claim interpretation, see Ch. 5, 5.68.

[141] 35 U.S.C. § 103.

[142] *Standard Oil Co. v. Am. Cyanamid Co.*, 774 F.2d 448, 454 (Fed. Cir. 1985).

[143] *Phillips*, 415 F.3d, 1313.

[144] Ibid.

[145] German courts adopt a function-oriented approach to claim constution focusing on the technical context of claim guided by the purpose of each claim element. See Ch. 5, 5.69–5.71.

The meaning of a claim term understood by a PHOSITA may change as the technologies of the art of invention progress. Thus, the *Phillips* court made clear that claims should be interpreted from the perspective of a PHOSITA at the time of the invention—that is, as of the effective filing date of the patent application. [146] For example, where only one type of human alpha interferon was known at the effective filing date, the term "human alpha interferon" cannot be interpreted to include another type of human alpha interferon which was discovered after the effective filing date.[147] In short, technologies developed after the effective filing date ("after-arising technologies") do not affect the literal scope defined by the claim language. However, after-arising technologies may affect the scope defined by equivalents because US courts use the perspective of a PHOSITA at the time of infringement to determine infringement under the doctrine of equivalents.[148] **4.38**

US patents frequently include a number of independent and dependent claims. Individual claims define their own scope of exclusivity and thus a party is liable if any of these claims read on the accused embodiment.[149] US courts must examine each claim separately for infringement and validity determination.[150] Even dependent claims should be examined separately from the claims upon which they depend to give their own scope.[151] However, US courts interpret claim terms in light of other claims included in the same patent as well as related patents resulting from a parent and continuation application.[152] **4.39**

ii. Functionally Defined Claims Section 112(f) of the US Patent Act provides an exception to the paramount rule that the patent claim language defines the scope of patent exclusivity.[153] This § 112(f) exception requires US courts to limit the scope of an element of the invention to cover the structure, material, or acts described in the specification and their equivalents if the claim terms define an element of the invention by a function without reciting structure, material, or acts. In short, the specification, instead of the claim, defines the scope of patent exclusivity with respect to claims defined by functions. **4.40**

Parties frequently dispute whether claim terms define an element by a function and thus whether the § 112(f) exception applies in interpreting the claim terms. Because the § 112(f) exception allows courts to limit the scope of a disputed element to embodiments in the specification, accused infringers often argue that claim terms define an element by a function. The Federal Circuit developed an analytical framework to determine if claim terms define **4.41**

---

[146] *Phillips*, 415 F.3d, 1313.

[147] *Schering Corp. v. Amgen, Inc.*, 222 F.3d 1347, 55 U.S.P.Q. 2d 1650 (Fed. Cir. 2000).

[148] *Warner-Jenkinson*, 520 U.S., 37.

[149] *Bio-Technology General Corp. v. Genentech, Inc.*, 80 F.3d 1553, 38 U.S.P.Q. 2d 1321 (Fed. Cir. 1996); *Carl Zeiss Stiftung v. Renishaw plc*, 945 F.2d 1173, 1181, 20 U.S.P.Q. 2d 1094, 1101 (Fed. Cir. 1991).

[150] *CollegeNet, Inc. v. ApplyYourself, Inc.*, 418 F.3d 1225 (Fed. Cir. 2005).

[151] *Honeywell International Inc. v. Hamilton Sundstrand Corp.*, 370 F.3d 1131, 1148, 71 U.S.P.Q. 2d 1065 (Fed. Cir. 2004) (*en banc*) (Newman, J., dissenting) ("Each claim defines a separate invention, whether or not written in independent form; and its validity stands or falls separately: '35 U.S.C. § 282[:] Each claim of a patent (whether in independent, dependent, or multiple dependent form) shall be presumed valid independently of the validity of the other claims; dependent or multiple dependent claims shall be presumed valid even though dependent upon an invalid claim.'").

[152] *CVI/Beta Ventures v. Tura LP*, 112 F.3d 1146, 42 U.S.P.Q. 2d 1577 (Fed. Cir. 1997); *Sanders Brine Shrimp Co., L.C. v. Bonneville Artemia Int'l*, 970 F. Supp. 892 (D. Utah 1997). For a discussion of claim construction in light of other claims than the claim that the court is addressing for infringement determination, see Ch. 4, 4.59 "Terms other than the terms in dispute and the same terms as the terms in dispute in other claims."

[153] 35 U.S.C. § 112(f).

an element by a function depending on the presence or absence of the terms "means for" or "steps for" in the claim in dispute.[154] This framework is replaced with a new framework in a 2015 Federal Circuit *en banc* decision.[155] Under the new framework, the application of the § 112(f) exception depends on whether the PHOSITA understands the terms of the claim to have a sufficiently definite meaning as the name of the structure. When lack of the terms "means for" or "step for" gives rise to a presumption that the § 112(f) exception does not apply this presumption can be overcome and thus the exception applies if the challenging party demonstrates that the claim term fails to recite sufficiently definite structure or recites function without reciting sufficient structure for performing the function in the claim.[156]

4.42 Under this analytic framework, one must decide whether the disputed claim terms define an element by a function or by a structure, material, and act. However, it is often difficult to distinguish a function from a structure because many devices, such as computers, conductors, sensors, and filters are named after their function. The claim terms reciting such names should be considered as defining an element by a structure if the terms have a reasonably well understood meaning in the art.[157] It is even more difficult to distinguish a function from an act because acts in method claims are directed at obtaining a particular result through a function. The Federal Circuit applies the same test, a reasonably well-understood meaning in the art, to find an act instead of a function.[158] Because § 112(f) is an exception to the paramount rule, the court was very reluctant to find a function if a step is not drafted in the step-plus-function format.[159] It is unclear whether the Federal Circuit is more willing to apply the § 112(f) exception to method claims under the new framework adopted in the 2015 *en banc* decision.

4.43 **iii. Product-by-process Claims** As the exception under § 112(f) suggests, the principle rule is that a product must be defined by elements defined by structure or material. However, the USPTO and US courts acknowledged a practice for drafting a product defined by steps in the method or process through which the product was made.[160] A product claim that includes terms reciting steps through which the product is made is called a "product-by-process" claim. In examining patentability, the USPTO has been applying an exception to the paramount rule that the patent claim language defines the scope of patent exclusivity. Under this exception, the scope is limited by the product itself, instead of the steps in the process recited in the claim.[161] For a long time case law had been unclear whether courts should follow the same exception in determining infringement.[162]

---

154 *Al-Site Corp. v. VSI Int'l, Inc.*, 174 F.3d 1308, 50 U.S.P.Q. 2d 1161 (Fed. Cir. 1999).

155 *Williamson v. Citrix Online, LLC*, 2015 U.S. App. LEXIS 10082, 115 U.S.P.Q.2D 1105 (Fed. Cir. June 16, 2015).

156 *Williamson*, U.S. App. LEXIS 10082, 19.

157 *Greenberg v. Ethicon Endo-Surgery*, 91 F.3d 1580, 39 U.S.P.Q. 2d 1783 (Fed. Cir. 1996).

158 *Caterpillar, Inc. v. Detroit Diesel Corp.*, 961 F. Supp. 1249, 41 U.S.P.Q. 2d 1876 (N.D. Ind. 1996), *aff'd*, 194 F.3d 1336 (Fed. Cir. 1999) (unpublished).

159 *Serrano v. Telular Corp.*, 111 F.3d 1578, 42 U.S.P.Q. 2d 1538 (Fed. Cir. 1997). However, during the examination, USPTO applies the § 112(f) rule when a claim includes a non-structural generic placeholders such as "mechanism for," "module for," "device for," "unit for," "component for," "element for," "member for," "apparatus for," "machine for," or "system for." USPTO, *Manual of Patent Examining Procedure* (*MPEP*) (9th ed., 2014), § 2181 (http://www.uspto.gov/web/offices/pac/mpep/s2181.html).

160 *MPEP*, § 2173.05(p) I. *In re Luck*, 476 F.2d 650, 177 U.S.P.Q. 523 (CCPA 1973); *In re Pilkington*, 411 F.2d 1345, 162 U.S.P.Q. 145 (CCPA 1969); *In re Steppan*, 394 F.2d 1013, 156 U.S.P.Q. 143 (CCPA 1967).

161 *MPEP*, § 2113; *In re Thorpe*, 777 F.2d 695, 698, 227 U.S.P.Q. 964, 966 (Fed. Cir. 1985).

162 *Scripps Clinic & Research Foundation v. Genentech, Inc.*, 927 F.2d 1565, 18 U.S.P.Q. 2d 1001 (Fed. Cir. 1991) ("In determining patentability we construe the product as not limited by the process stated in the

In *Abbott Lab. v. Sandoz*, the Federal Circuit *en banc* clarified that the exception does not apply in determining infringement.[163] In the product claims at issue, the claim terms defined two particular crystalline forms of an antibiotic (cefdinir) in terms of steps through which the antibiotic is made. The *en banc* court found no infringement because the accused infringers used an antibiotic which was made by different steps. To remove any ambiguity, it reiterated the paramount rule that process terms in product-by-process claims serve as limitations in determining infringement.[164] It also emphasized that the exception applies to determine patentability. Instead of the steps of the process recited in the claim, the product itself resulting from the steps defines the scope of subject matter under examination.[165] As a result, US courts apply different rules in interpreting product-by-process claims when an accused infringer challenges the validity of an enforced patent.[166] **4.44**

(b) Aids for Claim Interpretation

i. Intrinsic v. Extrinsic Evidence Because of the inherent ambiguity in defining an invention by words and the freedom for inventors to define their invention by their own words, it is necessary in the United States to make reference to a variety of materials which will aid courts in clarifying claim terms, the meaning of which the parties dispute. The Federal Circuit classified such claim interpretation aids into two types: intrinsic and extrinsic evidence.[167] The intrinsic evidence includes the patent document in which the asserted claims are included and records of prosecution history. Any materials other than the patent document and prosecution history are extrinsic evidence. In interpreting the claim language, US courts give more weight to the intrinsic evidence than the extrinsic evidence. The asserted claims, other claims, written description, drawings, and any other part of the specification and records of the prosecution, are internal to the patent and available to the public, particularly competitors, in advance of patent litigation. To promote the policy for preserving the notice function of patent claims, courts should not use the extrinsic evidence to change the meaning of claim terms which are supported by the intrinsic evidence.[168] Particularly, the Federal Circuit warned against the use of expert testimonies. **4.45**

This emphasis on intrinsic evidence led to a confusion in district courts on how to deal with the evidence of expert witnesses.[169] Moreover, in the late 1990s, the Federal Circuit's emphasis on dictionary definitions led to confusion in district courts with respect to whether and how they should take account of extrinsic evidence, particularly expert testimony.[170] Unlike German and Japanese judicial systems, the US system does not have a mechanism **4.46**

---

claims. Since claims must be construed the same way for validity and for infringement, the correct reading of product-by-process claims is that they are not limited to product prepared by the process set forth in the claims."); *Atlantic Thermoplastics Co., Inc. v. Faytex Corp.*, 970 F.2d 834, 23 U.S.P.Q. 2d 1481 (Fed. Cir. 1992) ("This court already distinguishes treatment of claims for patentability before the PTO from treatment of claims for validity before the courts ...").

163 *Abbott Labs. v. Sandoz, Inc.*, 566 F.3d 1282, 90 U.S.P.Q. 2d 1769 (Fed. Cir. 2009).

164 566 F.3d, 1293.

165 566 F.3d, 1292.

166 The USPTO adopts the broadest possible interpretation. For the claim construction at the USPTO, see Ch. 7, 7.04 "Claim Construction."

167 *Vitronics Corp. v. Conceptronic, Inc.*, 90 F.3d 1576, 39 U.S.P.Q. 2d 1573 (Fed. Cir. 1996).

168 90 F.3d, 1584.

169 *Markman v. Westview Instruments, Inc.*, 52 F.3d 967, 1006, 34 U.S.P.Q. 2d 1321 (Fed. Cir. 1995) (Newman J., dissenting).

170 Martin Adelman et al., *Cases and Materials on Patent Law* (2d ed., 2003), 759.

to concentrate jurisdiction of patent cases to select district courts.[171] The overwhelming majority of judges have very little experience in hearing patent cases and feel it is necessary to resort to extrinsic evidence such as dictionaries and science treatises, particularly the assistance of experts for understanding the technology of the invention. The Federal Circuit acknowledged this necessity and endorsed the use of experts for certain purposes: to supply technological background; to understand the perspective of a PHOSITA; and to understand the patent prosecution process at the USPTO.[172] In some cases, the Federal Circuit emphasized the significance of dictionaries to understand the ordinary meaning of claim terms, which led to uncertainty over whether district courts should give more weight to the ordinary meaning supported by dictionaries than the meaning supported by the specification and prosecution history.[173]

4.47 In *Phillips* (2005), the Federal Circuit, sitting *en banc*, resolved the issue of weight given to intrinsic and extrinsic evidence in construing the claim terms.[174] The *en banc* court reiterated the basic rule that intrinsic evidence, particularly the specification, is the best claim interpretation aid and admitted that the heavy weight on extrinsic evidence such as dictionaries given by the court in some cases was inconsistent with the rule.[175] It, however, did not completely exclude the use of extrinsic evidence and acknowledged a concern that the heavy reliance on the specification may result in a scope limited to embodiments disclosed in the specification which also violates the paramount rule that the claim language should determine the scope of patent exclusivity. Nevertheless, extrinsic evidence is less reliable than intrinsic evidence because (1) unlike intrinsic evidence, it was not prepared with the view of explaining the patent's scope and meaning at the time of prosecution; (2) extrinsic evidence such as dictionaries, unlike claims, are not necessarily written for a hypothetical PHOSITA; (3) extrinsic evidence consisting of expert testimony, being prepared for litigation, is very likely to suffer from bias; (4) extrinsic evidence is, in general, less reliable, and the unbounded scope of potential extrinsic evidence makes it difficult for the court to filter useful evidence; and (5) undue reliance on extrinsic evidence undermines the public notice function of patents.

4.48 Although the *en banc* Federal Circuit emphasized the supremacy of intrinsic evidence and reiterated the rule that extrinsic evidence cannot be used for changing the meaning of patent terms supported by intrinsic evidence, courts must decide on a case-by-case basis whether intrinsic evidence fully supports the meaning of claim terms which excludes reliance on extrinsic evidence. There is no bright line to distinguish impermissible reliance on intrinsic evidence from permissible reliance: reading limitations from the written description of the specification into claim terms is impermissible; in contrast, clarifying the meaning of claim terms in light of the written description is permissible. In practice, patentees continue their attempt to persuade courts to rely more on extrinsic evidence, particularly the dictionary and technical and science treatises, to support a broad definition of the disputed claim term. In contrast, accused infringers continue their attempt to persuade courts to rely on intrinsic

---

[171] US courts started a pilot system to concentrate patent cases to a group of judges in certain district courts. See Part I of this volume.

[172] *Pitney Bowes, Inc. v. Hewlett-Packard Co.*, 182 F.3d 1298, 1314, 51 U.S.P.Q. 2d 1161 (Fed. Cir. 1999) (Rader J., additional view).

[173] *Texas Digital Systems, Inc. v. Telegenix, Inc.*, 308 F.3d 1193 (Fed. Cir. 2002); *CCS Fitness, Inc. v. Brunswick Corp.*, 288 F.3d 1359, 62 U.S.P.Q. 2d 1658 (Fed. Cir. 2002).

[174] *Phillips v. AWH Corp.*, 415 F.3d 1303, 75 U.S.P.Q. 2d 1321 (Fed. Cir. 2005).

[175] Ibid. 1318.

evidence, particularly the written description of the specification and prosecution history, to find a disclaimer from the patent scope and a special definition of the claim term.[176]

ii. Specification The most important part of intrinsic evidence is patent documents.[177] To construe the claim terms and identify the scope of exclusivity, a PHOSITA is deemed to read the entire patent including not only the claim including the terms of interest but also all other claims, the written description of the invention, and drawings in the specification.[178] US courts use various parts of the written description, including the abstract,[179] the background of the invention,[180] and the summary of the invention.[181] However, the Federal Circuit indicates that the title of invention is nearly irrelevant to claim interpretation.[182] **4.49**

Although embodiments discussed in the written description and drawings are important tools to clarify the meaning of a claim term, claims should not be construed to cover only the embodiments even if only one embodiment is disclosed in the specification.[183] Because claims are usually written to cover a scope broader than a scope which only covers embodiments disclosed in the written description of the specification, accused infringers advance a claim construction that covers only the disclosed embodiments, citing the basic rule that claim terms must be construed in light of intrinsic evidence, particularly the specification.[184] This accused infringer's attempt is restricted by the rule that courts cannot read limitations from the specification into a claim.[185] In other words, if an element of the patented invention is defined by general descriptive terms, courts should give the full meaning to the terms and cannot replace the general descriptive term with a more descriptive term with details of the element.[186] This rule applies to both structural and functional limitations.[187] **4.50**

However, as the *en banc* Federal Circuit acknowledged, there is no bright line rule for distinguishing permissible claim construction in light of specification from impermissible reading limitations from the specification.[188] There is always room for accused infringers to argue that the construction that they have advanced is merely the clarification of the claim terms in light of the specification according to the perspective of a PHOSITA. Moreover, accused infringers frequently argue that the inventor gave a special meaning to the claim terms at dispute by including a definition of the terms in the specification. **4.51**

US case law makes clear that an inventor can be his or her own lexicographer.[189] Claim drafting inherently involves the challenge of converting an apparatus or process into words. **4.52**

---

[176] For more discussions about the use of specification and prosecution history, see Ch. 4, 4.49 "Specification"; Ch. 5, 5.86 "Prosecution History."

[177] US courts most frequently rely on the specification and prosecution history for interpreting claim terms. See Anderson and Menell, "Informal Deterrence," 44.

[178] *Phillips*, 415 F.3d, 1313.

[179] *Hill-Rom Co., Inc. v. Kinetic Concepts, Inc.*, 209 F.3d 1337, 54 U.S.P.Q. 2d 1437 (Fed. Cir. 2000).

[180] *Bicon, Inc. v. Straumann Co.*, 441 F.3d 945, 950–51 (Fed. Cir. 2006).

[181] *Microsoft Corp. v. Multi-Tech Sys., Inc.*, 357 F.3d 1340, 1348 (Fed. Cir.2004); *Astrazeneca AB v. Mutual Pharmaceutical Co., Inc.*, 384 F.3d 1333, 72 U.S.P.Q. 2d 1726 (Fed. Cir. 2004); *C.R. Bard, Inc. v. United States Surgical Corp.*, 388 F.3d 858, 73 U.S.P.Q. 2d 1011 (Fed. Cir. 2004).

[182] *Pitney Bowes, Inc. v. Hewlett-Packard Co.*, 182 F.3d 1298, 51 U.S.P.Q. 2d 1161 (Fed. Cir. 1999).

[183] *Phillips*, 415 F.3d, 1323.

[184] See Ch. 4, 4.49 "Specification."

[185] *Phillips*, 415 F.3d, 1323.

[186] *Johnson Worldwide Associates, Inc. v. Zebco Corp.*, 175 F.3d 985, 989–90, 50 U.S.P.Q. 2d 1607, 1610–11 (Fed. Cir. 1999).

[187] *Ecolab, Inc. v. Envirochem, Inc.*, 264 F.3d 1358, 1367, 60 U.S.P.Q. 2d 1173 (Fed. Cir. 2001).

[188] *Phillips*, 415 F.3d, 1323.

[189] *Autogiro Co. of Am. v. United States*, 181 Ct. Cl. 55, 384 F.2d 391, 155 U.S.P.Q. 697 (1967).

A proper term to describe an element may not exist to describe an element of an invention if the invention is pioneering in the field. Thus, US courts allow inventors to be his or her own lexicographer and to develop a new term to describe the invention as long as the definition of the term is included in the specification.

4.53 This inventor's definition even overrides a common or well-established technical meaning.[190] When a claim term is clearly defined in the specification, courts cannot change the definition even if the definition is contrary to the meaning that is understood among PHOSITAs.[191] The rule protects inventors who are not familiar with terminologies in the field of the invention.[192]

4.54 This definition can be implicit.[193] Thus, infringers often rely on embodiments in the specification and argue that the inventor adopted an implicit definition of the claim term, which describes an element of the invention, because the specification discloses only a particular structure, material, or function for the element regardless of the common meaning of the claim term which describes the element generally without restricting itself to that particular structure. To prevent the claim term from being limited to a particular structure in the disclosed embodiments, patentees emphasize a competing rule that a definition contrary to the common meaning of the claim term must be clearly supported by the intrinsic evidence, particularly the specification, so that the claim term gives notice of the special meaning to PHOSITAs.[194]

4.55 Another strategy for accused infringers to limit the literal scope supported by the claim language is an argument that the specification includes a disclaimer of a particular structure, material, and function from the claim term.[195] Patentees may emphasize that a disclaimer must be clear from the specification to contradict the common meaning.[196]

4.56 In general, US courts are more willing to find a special definition or disclaimer to exclude a particular structure, material, or function if the structure, material, or function is not disclosed in the specification. The *en banc* Federal Circuit's emphasis on the supremacy of intrinsic evidence and its renouncement of a rule that claim terms are presumed to be used with a common and ordinary meaning made it easy for US courts to find a special definition or disclaimer in the specification.[197] This is a stark contrast to German courts which are very reluctant to limit a claim term which broadly describes an element of the invention. They are willing to expand the claim term to cover a structure through the function-oriented claim construction even if the structure falls outside of the scope defined by the common meaning of the claim term as long as a PHOSITA could find that the structure can provide the same function of the structure defined by the claim term.[198] US courts' willingness to limit the literal scope by the specification is more in line with the Japanese courts' approach.[199]

---

[190] *International Cork Co. v. New Process Cork Co.*, 6 F.2d 420, 422 (2d Cir. N.Y. 1925)

[191] *Vitronics Corp. v. Conceptronic, Inc.*, 90 F.3d 1576, 39 U.S.P.Q. 2d 1573 (Fed. Cir. 1996).

[192] *Lear Siegler, Inc. v. Aeroquip Corp.*, 733 F.2d 881, 889, 221 U.S.P.Q. 1025, 1031 (1984).

[193] *Bell Atl. Network Servs. v. Covad Communs. Group, Inc.*, 262 F.3d 1258, 59 U.S.P.Q. 2d 1865 (Fed. Cir. 2001).

[194] *Bell Atlantic Network Services, Inc. v. Covad Communications Group, Inc.*, 262 F.3d 1258, 59 U.S.P.Q. 2d 1865 (Fed. Cir. 2001).

[195] *SciMed Life Sys., Inc. v. Advanced Cardiovascular Sys., Inc.*, 242 F.3d 1337, 1343–44 (Fed. Cir. 2001).

[196] *CCS Fitness, Inc. v. Brunswick Corp.*, 288 F.3d 1359, 62 U.S.P.Q. 2d 1658 (Fed. Cir. 2002).

[197] *Phillips v. AWH Corp.*, 415 F.3d 1303, 1312, 75 U.S.P.Q. 2d 1321 (Fed. Cir. 2005).

[198] See Ch. 5, 5.69–5.71.

[199] See Ch. 6, 6.43–6.44.

Patent specifications originating from Europe and Japan discuss the problems of the prior art and explain the invention in terms of the technical object to solve the problems. US courts often construe patent claims in light of the problems, the solution, and the advantages resulting from the solution.[200] Although US courts do not exclude embodiments which do not achieve all the advantages from the solution,[201] if the specification emphasizes an object, solution, or problem, they may find inherent and implicit limitations if such limitations are necessary for achieving the object and solving the problem.[202] A discussion of objectives and problems may also limit the application of the doctrine of equivalents.[203] To avoid a narrow claim interpretation and an exclusion of the doctrine of equivalents, US patent attorneys advise against including an object of the invention and an explanation of the invention in terms of the prior art. **4.57**

Although the specification is used more frequently in favor of the accused infringers to limit the literal scope supported by the claim language on its face, the specification can be used in favor of the patentees. Courts are prevented from adopting a construction which excludes an embodiment disclosed in the specification under the rule that patent claims should be construed to cover all preferred embodiments.[204] The rationale for this rule is that inventors rarely define their inventions in a manner that excludes a preferred embodiment and a PHOSITA would not read the patent claim in that manner.[205] However, this rule is limited by the paramount rule that the claim language determines the patent scope. Courts cannot read a claim term to cover all preferred embodiments in the specification if some embodiments clearly fall outside the literal scope.[206] **4.58**

iii. Terms Other than the Terms in Dispute and the Same Terms as the Terms in Dispute in Other Claims Terms other than the terms in dispute in the same claim and the same terms as the terms in dispute in other claims in the same patent document are important aids for claim interpretation as intrinsic evidence.[207] US courts presume that the same terms in a patent application, both in the claims and written description of the specification, are used with the same meaning and thus a claim term used repeatedly within one claim as well as multiple claims should be construed in the same way.[208] They also give the same meaning to a claim term which appears in related applications, such as a parent and continuation applications.[209] Repeated use of a claim term in the same manner may give rise to a definition by implication under the rule of invention as lexicographer.[210] **4.59**

---

200 *CVI/Beta Ventures, Inc. v. Tura LP*, 112 F.3d 1146, 1160, 42 U.S.P.Q. 2d 1577, 1587 (Fed. Cir. 1997).

201 *Phillips v. AWH Corp.*, 415 F.3d 1303 (Fed. Cir. 2005) (*en banc*).

202 *Minnesota Mining & Manufacturing Co. v. Johnson & Johnson Orthopaedics, Inc.*, 976 F.2d 1559, 24 U.S.P.Q. 2d 1321 (Fed. Cir. 1992); *Inpro II Licensing, S.A.R.L. v. T-Mobile USA, Inc.*, 450 F.3d 1350, 78 U.S.P.Q. 2d 1786 (Fed. Cir. 2006).

203 *Vehicular Technologies Corp. v. Titan Wheel International, Inc.*, 212 F.3d 1377, 1380, 54 U.S.P.Q. 2d 1841, 1843 (Fed. Cir. 2000).

204 *Vitronics Corp.*, 90 F.3d, 1583–84.

205 *Modine Mfg. Co. v. United States Int'l Trade Comm'n*, 75 F.3d 1545, 1550, 37 U.S.P.Q. 2d 1609, 1612 (Fed. Cir. 1996).

206 *Unique Concepts, Inc. v. Brown*, 939 F.2d 1558, 19 U.S.P.Q. 2d 1500 (Fed. Cir. 1991).

207 *Phillips*, 415 F.3d, 1314–15.

208 *CVI/Beta Ventures v. Tura LP*, 112 F.3d 1146, 42 U.S.P.Q. 2d 1577 (Fed. Cir. 1997).

209 *Sanders Brine Shrimp Co., L.C. v. Bonneville Artemia Int'l*, 970 F. Supp. 892 (D. Utah 1997).

210 *Bell Atl. Network Servs. v. Covad Communs. Group, Inc.*, 262 F.3d 1258, 59 U.S.P.Q. 2d 1865 (Fed. Cir. 2001).

4.60 In contrast, US courts presume that different terms in the same claim and other claims in the same patent document have a different meaning because patentees usually include multiple claims to cover different scopes of exclusivity.[211] This rule to give different scopes to claims with different terms is called the doctrine of claim differentiation.[212] This doctrine assumes every term in a claim has significance and prevents courts from interpreting claim terms to render other terms superfluous.[213] Patentees frequently rely on the doctrine of claim differentiation to prevent courts from limiting the literal scope in light of embodiments when asserted claims use different terms from terms in the written description of the specification or other claims to identify an element of the invention. In particular, this rule prevents courts from importing terms into an independent claim from the specification if the terms in a claim dependent on the claim add a particular limitation to the independent claim.[214] To secure not only a variety of coverage but also a broad coverage for independent claims, US patents include a number of patent claims.[215]

4.61 However, the doctrine of claim differentiation has a limit. If intrinsic evidence, particularly the written description of the invention, supports multiple claims with different terms and phrases being directed to the same invention, then US courts refuse to apply the doctrine of claim differentiation.[216] The rule that claim terms should be construed in light of the specification has supremacy over the claim differentiation doctrine.

4.62 **iv. Record of Prosecution History** Unlike German courts where the prosecution history plays a very limited role for claim interpretation,[217] US courts use the record of the prosecution history as an important tool to construe claim terms.[218] This is because the prosecution history indicates how the USPTO and inventors understood the invention during the examination and how patentees explained the invention in attempting to obtain the patent.[219] US courts give varying weight to the prosecution history although the *en banc* Federal Circuit suggests that the prosecution history is less important than the written description and drawings of the specification.[220]

4.63 The prosecution history is most frequently used to reject a broad interpretation advanced by patentees. During the examination, attorneys explain the invention to distinguish the prior art. Such an explanation of the invention in terms of the prior art or an argument to highlight elements to distinguish differences between the invention and the prior art are viewed by courts as a disclaimer when a patent is issued regardless of an amendment.[221] Moreover, the explanation or argument may be used against the patentee for every claim including the

---

211 *Modine Mfg. Co. v. United States Int'l Trade Comm'n*, 75 F.3d 1545, 37 U.S.P.Q. 2d 1609 (Fed. Cir. 1996).

212 Moore, Michel, and Holbrook, *Patent Litigation and Strategy*, 270.

213 *Primos, Inc. v. Hunter's Specialties, Inc.*, 451 F.3d 841, 848 (Fed. Cir. 2006).

214 *Liebel-Flarsheim Co. v. Medrad, Inc.*, 358 F.3d 898, 910 (Fed. Cir. 2004).

215 For the average number of claims in U.S. patents issued between 1986 and 2012, see Global Patent-Innovation Quality-Measure, Apply, Profit (http://www.bustpatents.com/statistics.html). The number of claims included in European patents has significantly increased recently. Nicolas van Zeebroeck et al., *Claiming More: The Increased Voluminosity of Patent Applications and its Determinants* (March 2007), (http://dev3.cepr.org/meets/wkcn/6/6652/papers/van_Zeebroek.pdf).

216 *Nystrom v. Trex Co., Inc.*, 424 F.3d 1136, 1143, 76 U.S.P.Q. 2d 1481 (Fed. Cir. 2005).

217 See Ch. 5, 5.86 "Prosecution History."

218 *Markman*, 52 F.3d, 980.

219 *Phillips*, 415 F.3d, 1317.

220 Ibid. 1317.

221 E.g., *Gentry Gallery v. Berkline Corp.*, 134 F.3d 1473, 45 U.S.P.Q. 2d 1498 (Fed. Cir. 1998).

terms used in the explanation or argument.[222] US courts use the prosecution history of the related applications if the same terms appear in claims in the related applications resulting from the same parent application.[223] Some Federal Circuit decisions adopt the most expansive view in considering an argument made during the examination of a related application after the relevant patent is issued[224] and an argument made during the examination of a related application in a foreign country.[225] Other cases try to limit the use of the post-grant statement in claim construction and the statement made during the examination of an unrelated patent regardless of the same terms appearing in the claims at issue.[226]

Some Federal Circuit decisions, in noting that the prosecution history has a critical significance, give heavy weight to the prosecution history for interpreting claims.[227] Other decisions give less weight in requiring a finding of clear and unequivocal disavowal or disclaimer with respect to the literal scope supported by the patentee's claim interpretation.[228] The paramount rule that the claim terms determine the scope of patent exclusivity also limits a disclaimer from the prosecution history if the claim construction in light of the prosecution results in impermissible importation of limitations into the claim or impermissible altering of the claim language.[229] **4.64**

To prevent the use of prosecution history, patentees try to leave as little record as possible in the prosecution history because US courts are reluctant to draw inference against patentees as long as they are silent about the invention and the prior art.[230] An examiner's unilateral statement of a reason for allowing a patent does not give rise to a disavowal of a claim if the applicant does not respond to the statement.[231] Applicants have no duty to respond to examiners' statements with respect to a reason to allow an issuance of patent.[232] As a result, US courts' extensive use of the prosecution history for claim interpretation creates a tension in the applicant–examiner relationship. As much as applicants want to provide information about the invention and the prior art to help examiners understand the invention, whatever information provided may be used against the applicants when a patent is issued and enforced. Lack of information and response from the applicants also frustrate the USPTO examiners. To make matters worse, the use of the prosecution history in foreign countries also interferes with the good practice of giving sufficient information to the patent office in a foreign country. **4.65**

v. Dictionaries and Treatises Although the *Phillips en banc* Federal Circuit found extrinsic evidence less reliable than intrinsic evidence in interpreting claim terms, US **4.66**

222 *Watts v. XL Sys.*, 232 F.3d 877, 56 U.S.P.Q. 2d 1836 (Fed. Cir. 2000).
223 *Omega Eng'g, Inc. v. Raytek Corp.*, 334 F.3d 1314, 67 U.S.P.Q. 2d 1321 (Fed. Cir. 2003).
224 *Microsoft Corp. v. Multi-Tech Sys.*, 357 F.3d 1340, 69 U.S.P.Q. 2d 1815 (Fed. Cir. 2004).
225 *Pfizer Inc. v. Ranbaxy Labs.*, 457 F.3d 1284, 79 U.S.P.Q. 2d 1583 (Fed. Cir. 2006).
226 *Goldenberg v. Cytogen, Inc.*, 373 F.3d 1158, 71 U.S.P.Q. 2d 1255 (Fed. Cir. 2004); *Tex. Digital Sys. v. Telegenix, Inc.*, 308 F.3d 1193, 1211 (Fed. Cir. 2002),
227 *Vitronics Corp.*, 90 F.3d, 1582.
228 *N. Am. Container, Inc. v. Plastipak Packaging, Inc.*, 415 F.3d 1335, 75 U.S.P.Q. 2d 1545 (Fed. Cir. 2005).
229 *Serrano v. Telular Corp.*, 111 F.3d 1578, 42 U.S.P.Q. 2d 1538 (Fed. Cir. 1997); *York Prods. v. Central Tractor Farm & Family Ctr.*, 99 F.3d 1568, 40 U.S.P.Q. 2d (BNA) 1619 (Fed. Cir. 1996).
230 E.g., *Sorensen v. ITC*, 427 F.3d 1375, 77 U.S.P.Q. 2d 1083 (Fed. Cir. 2005).
231 *Salazar v. Procter & Gamble Co.*, 414 F.3d 1342, 75 U.S.P.Q. 2d 1369 (Fed. Cir. 2005).
232 *Eolas Techs., Inc. v. Microsoft Corp.*, 399 F.3d 1325, 73 U.S.P.Q. 2d 1782 (Fed. Cir. 2005).

courts frequently rely on dictionaries to find out the common and ordinary meaning of the term.[233] There are a number of general and technology-specific dictionaries, each of which may include a number of definitions for the disputed term. Such dictionaries are not written for a PHOSITA or in the context of disclosure in the written description of the specification and thus may stretch the meaning of the disputed term. The *en banc* court discredited the use of general dictionaries by citing a risk of improperly expanding the literal scope defined by the claim term.[234] It also warned lower courts about the risk of using technical dictionaries and treatises, which may be the same as the risk that arises from giving an improperly expansive meaning to disputed claim terms, because the terms may not be used in the same way in the patent.[235]

4.67 Because of these deficiencies, US courts are more reluctant to rely on dictionaries to find the meaning of claim terms. Nevertheless, some courts give substantial weight to both general and technical dictionaries and treatises.[236] Patentees frequently rely on dictionaries to prevent accused infringers' attempts to limit the scope of a claim term to a particular structure, material, and function of the disclosed embodiment and to try to stretch the meaning to cover accused embodiments. Patentees are more successful if intrinsic evidence, particularly the written description of the invention, includes a basis for the dictionary definition.[237]

4.68 Dictionaries present courts with unique challenges when they provide multiple definitions for the term at issue. Patentees try to rely on the broadest definition so as to stretch the scope covered by the claim term. The Federal Circuit rejected the view that a claim term is given the broadest or aggregate meaning among multiple definitions.[238] Instead, it adopted a compromise by accepting the view that the appropriate meaning should be selected from multiple definitions in light of the intrinsic evidence and judges should consult with general and technology-specific dictionaries to understand the claim term at issue before reviewing the entire patent document.[239] Some Federal Circuit judges adopt a more restrictive view that the narrowest meaning among multiple definitions should be adopted unless the specification clearly supports a meaning broader than the narrowest definition.[240]

4.69 In short, the use of dictionaries is limited in that US courts should rely on dictionary definitions only if such definitions do not contradict the specification.[241] Although courts can start with dictionary definitions to understand the claim term, it is improper to adopt the definition divorced from the context of intrinsic evidence.[242] In particular, once courts find that an inventor adopted a special meaning by including a definition in the specification under the doctrine of inventor as lexicographer, a dictionary definition cannot alter the

---

[233] *Phillips*, 415 F.3d 1303. For more discussions about the significance of extrinsic evidence compared to intrinsic evidence, see Ch. 4, 4.45 "Intrinsic v. Extrinsic Evidence."

[234] Ibid. 1322.

[235] Ibid. 1321.

[236] Anderson and Menell, "Informal Deterrence," 47.

[237] E.g., *Terlep v. Brinkmann Corp.*, 418 F.3d 1379 (Fed. Cir. 2005); *Aquatex Industries, Inc. v. Techniche Solutions*, 419 F.3d 1374, 1381 (Fed. Cir. 2005).

[238] *Free Motion Fitness, Inc. v. Cybex International, Inc.*, 423 F.3d 1343 (Fed. Cir. 2005).

[239] Ibid.

[240] Ibid, 1354 (Prost J., dissenting).

[241] *Pfizer, Inc. v. Teva Pharms. USA, Inc.*, 429 F.3d 1364, 77 U.S.P.Q. 2d 1257 (Fed. Cir. 2005).

[242] *Old Town Canoe Co. v. Confluence Holdings Corp.*, 448 F.3d 1309, 78 U.S.P.Q. 2d 1705 (Fed. Cir. 2006).

definition even if the definition is different from the ordinary and common meaning of the claim term.[243]

vi. Prior Art Prior Art is an important claim interpretation aid for US courts.[244] Prior art is intrinsic evidence if it is cited in the specification or prosecution history.[245] Such prior art is thus more important for claim construction than prior art which is not cited in the specification or prosecution history and thus constitutes extrinsic evidence. Patentees usually advance a claim construction which is broad enough to cover an accused embodiment but sustains the validity over the closest prior art. **4.70**

Although it is not mandatory, if possible, US courts try to interpret the claim language to sustain the validity.[246] This principle is based on an assumption that the patent office properly examined the patent claim and thus it is reasonable to infer that the patent is valid.[247] However, the *en banc* Federal Circuit limits the use of this principle to cases in which claim terms at issue remain ambiguous after courts have made all attempts to clarify the meaning by using all other claim interpretation aids.[248] Because the validity determination involves factual issues which should be resolved by the jury, dealing with validity issues as part of claim construction will present a conflict with the policy that all issues in claim interpretation must be resolved by the court.[249] In addition, dealing with validity may present procedural problems because accused infringers may be prevented from challenging validity for a number of reasons, such as estoppel arising from prior *interpartes* proceedings at the USPTO.[250] To avoid these possible problems, the Federal Circuit made the principle as the last resort for clarifying ambiguous patent terms. **4.71**

Moreover, courts cannot redraft a claim by reading limitations from the specification into the claim to sustain the validity.[251] The usage of the principle for sustaining validity is limited to cases where multiple plausible interpretations are possible without contradicting intrinsic evidence, particularly the claim language and specification. If the only interpretation which is consistent with intrinsic evidence renders the claim invalid, courts should declare the claim invalid.[252] **4.72**

vii. Expert and Inventor Testimonies The Federal Circuit gives a varying range of weight on expert and inventor testimonies. In *Markman* (1995), the *en banc* Federal Circuit took an extreme position in refusing to give any deference to expert and inventor testimonies in interpreting a claim term.[253] In a more recent *en banc* decision, *Phillips* (2005), the court was more willing to acknowledge the benefit of expert testimonies as long as **4.73**

---

[243] *Vitronics Corp. v. Conceptronic, Inc.*, 90 F.3d 1576, 39 U.S.P.Q. 2d 1573 (Fed. Cir. 1996). For more discussions on the rule that an inventor as lexicographer, see Ch. 4, 4.52.

[244] *Graham v. John Deere Co.*, 383 U.S. 1, 33, 148 U.S.P.Q. 459, 473 (1966).

[245] *Phillips v. AWH Corp.*, 415 F.3d 1303, 1317 (Fed. Cir. 2005) (*en banc*), *cert. denied*, 126 S. Ct. 1332 (2006).

[246] Ibid. 1327.

[247] Ibid.

[248] Ibid.

[249] *Markman v. Westview Instruments*, 517 U.S. 370, 116 S. Ct. 1384, 134 L. Ed. 2d 577, 38 U.S.P.Q. 2d 1461 (1996); However, the question of claim interpretation may involve subsidiary factual questions. *Teva Pharm. USA, Inc. v. Sandoz, Inc.*, 135 S. Ct. 831, 837, 190 L. Ed. 2d 719, 113 U.S.P.Q. 2d 1269, 83 U.S.L.W. 4055, 90 Fed. R. Serv. 3d (Callaghan) 1244 (U.S. 2015). See Ch. 4, 4.23.

[250] For estoppel arising from prior *inter partes* proceedings at the USPTO, see Ch. 7, 7.24 "Estoppel."

[251] *Becton Dickinson & Co. v. C.R. Bard, Inc.*, 922 F.2d 792, 17 U.S.P.Q. 2d 1097 (Fed. Cir. 1990).

[252] *Rhine v. Casio, Inc.*, 183 F.3d 1342, 51 U.S.P.Q. 2d 1377 (Fed. Cir. 1999).

[253] *Markman.*, 52 F.3d, 963.

the testimonies were about technologies instead of the claim term at issue.[254] The court endorsed the lower courts' reliance on expert testimony to understand the underlying technology but limited such reliance to construing a claim term at issue in exceptional cases where intrinsic evidence cannot sufficiently resolve ambiguity. In clarifying the ambiguity in such exceptional cases, expert testimony is less useful than dictionaries and prior art documents which are accessible prior to litigation and are thus objective. In contrast, expert testimony may be tainted with bias as it is prepared for litigation and should be used with the caution when it is used for construing a claim term.[255]

4.74 Despite the limited use of expert testimony for claim interpretation, the Federal Circuit gives full discretion to lower courts whether to hear expert testimony.[256] However, lower courts should discount expert testimony if the meaning of term based on the testimony contradicts with intrinsic evidence.[257] With emphasis on the significance of intrinsic evidence and warning of the risk of extrinsic evidence giving a broad construction to cover subject matter that the inventor did not invent,[258] US courts use the perspective of a PHOSITA based on the specification and the prosecution history.[259] Because judges are not PHOSITAs and thus have no ordinary skill to come up with alternative structures, materials, and actions to produce the same result, judges may find that the specification describes embodiments as the invention and limit the literal scope of a claim to cover only embodiments disclosed in the specification.[260] It is more likely for judges to find a particular feature of a preferred embodiment as the invention if the feature is discussed in the summary of the invention[261] or it is discussed as a feature of the "present invention."[262] This is in stark contrast to German claim construction which gives significant weight to the skill of a PHOSITA to take account of structures, materials, and actions to produce the same result.[263]

(c) Canons of Construction

4.75 **i. Canons Favoring Accused Infringers** While using intrinsic and extrinsic evidence as tools or aids to interpret the claim language, the Federal Circuit developed rules through its case law. Such rules are called canons of claim interpretation because rules developed by US courts for clarifying ambiguity and vagueness of a statutory language are called canons of statutory interpretation.[264] In general, these rules favor accused infringers in limiting the scope of a claim term. One such canon is that when there is an equal choice between a broad and a narrow claim construction, courts should adopt the narrow one.[265] US courts

---

[254] *Philips*, 90 F.3d, 1585, 39 U.S.P.Q. 2d, 1579.

[255] Ibid.

[256] *Serio-US Indus. v. Plastic Recovery Techs. Corp.*, 459 F.3d 1311, 80 U.S.P.Q. 2d 1065 (Fed. Cir. 2006). The Federal Circuit's use of expert evidence has decreased since *Phillips*. See Anderson and Menell, "Informal Deterrence," 47.

[257] *MyMail, Ltd. v. Am. Online, Inc.*, 476 F.3d 1372, 81 U.S.P.Q. 2d (BNA) 1832 (Fed. Cir. 2007).

[258] *Abbott Labs. v. Sandoz, Inc.*, 566 F.3d 1282(Fed. Cir. 2009).

[259] *Cias, Inc. v. Alliance Gaming Corp.*, 504 F.3d 1356, 84 U.S.P.Q. 2d 1737 (Fed. Cir. 2007).

[260] *Wang Labs., Inc. v. America Online, Inc.*, 197 F.3d 1377, 53 U.S.P.Q. 2d 1161 (Fed. Cir. 1999); *Warner-Lambert Co. v. Teva Pharms. USA, Inc.*, 418 F.3d 1326, 75 U.S.P.Q. 2d 1865 (Fed. Cir. 2005); *Inpro II Licensing, S.A.R.L. v. T-Mobile USA, Inc.*, 450 F.3d 1350, 78 U.S.P.Q. 2d 1786 (Fed. Cir. 2006).

[261] *Microsoft Corp. v. Multi-Tech Sys., Inc.*, 357 F.3d 1340, 1348 (Fed. Cir. 2004); *C.R. Bard, Inc. v. United States Surgical Corp.*, 388 F.3d 858, 73 U.S.P.Q. 2d 1011 (Fed. Cir. 2004).

[262] *Marine Polymer Techs., Inc. v. HemCon, Inc.*, 672 F.3d 1350, 102 U.S.P.Q. 2d 1161 (Fed. Cir. 2012).

[263] See Ch. 5, 5.69–5.71.

[264] Moore, Michel, and Holbrook, *Patent Litigation and Strategy*, 267.

[265] Ibid. 300; *Athletic Alternatives v. Prince Mfg.*, 73 F.3d 1573, 37 U.S.P.Q. 2d 1365 (Fed. Cir. 1996); *Halliburton Energy Servs. v. M-I, LLC*, 514 F.3d 1244, 85 U.S.P.Q. 2d 1654 (Fed. Cir. 2008).

punish patentees by choosing the narrow construction because they have drafted claims with ambiguity and violated the requirement that a claim must particularly point out and distinctly claim the patented invention.[266]

The policy for punishing patentees who introduced ambiguity dominates other canons of claim construction. When the specification includes multiple definitions for the claim term in dispute, courts should adopt the narrowest definition.[267] By adopting diverse definitions, patentees are guilty of consciously introducing ambiguity into the scope of a claim term.[268] It is likely that patentees adopted various definitions to prevent courts from finding an implicit definition by using a claim term consistently which will justify courts in limiting the scope of a claim term to embodiments disclosed in the specification. This attempt, however, conflicts with the policy that terms should be used consistently in a patent's specification and claims.[269] **4.76**

ii. Canons Favoring Patentees Under US case law, canons favoring patentees by supporting their claims of infringement are rare because patentees are guilty of drafting ambiguous claims; patentees' attempts to stretch claims to cover an accused embodiment can be viewed as introducing ambiguity in the asserted claim. One such canon is that a term used in different ways in the written description of the specification should be given broader and different meanings.[270] However, the *en banc* Federal Circuit's emphasis on the consistent claim term usage policy in *Phillips* made it difficult to override a canon favoring accused infringers that courts should adopt the narrowest definition if multiple definitions are included in a patent's specification.[271] Some federal circuit judges may find the canons for giving a broad meaning with respect to a claim term with varied usage compelling and find a claim construction based on an embodiment violating the rule that courts cannot import limitations from the specification.[272] **4.77**

The doctrine of claim differentiation[273] and the rule that claim terms should be interpreted to cover preferred embodiments[274] are also frequently cited by patentees to support a broad scope of a claim term. However, these rules are in tension with the policy that inventors are not entitled to the scope of a claim term which includes subject matter they did not invent. Thus, if the specification does not include a basis for the broad scope advanced by patentees, neither the doctrine of differentiation nor the rule for covering preferred embodiments has any force. Courts interpret claims with different terms to cover the same invention.[275] Courts adopt a claim construction to exclude a preferred embodiment when the specification or prosecution supports a disavowal of the embodiment.[276] **4.78**

---

[266] 35 U.S.C. § 112(b).
[267] *Genentech Inc. v. Wellcome Found.*, 29 F.3d 1555, 31 U.S.P.Q. 2d 1161 (Fed. Cir. 1994).
[268] Ibid. 1564.
[269] E.g., *Phillips*, 415 F.3d, 1316–17.
[270] *Johnson Worldwide Assocs. v. Zebco Corp.*, 175 F.3d 985, 50 U.S.P.Q. 2d 1607 (Fed. Cir. 1999).
[271] See *Genentech Inc.*, 29 F.3d 1555.
[272] *Marine Polymer Techs., Inc. v. HemCon, Inc.*, 672 F.3d 1350, 102 U.S.P.Q. 2d 1161 (Fed. Cir. 2012).
[273] See Ch. 4, 4.60–4.61.
[274] See Ch. 4, 4.58.
[275] *Moleculon Research Corp. v. CBS, Inc.*, 793 F.2d 1261, 229 U.S.P.Q. 805 (1986).
[276] *Rheox, Inc. v. Entact, Inc.*, 276 F.3d 1319, 61 U.S.P.Q. 2d 1368 (Fed. Cir. 2002); *Computer Docking Station Corp. v. Dell, Inc.*, 519 F.3d 1366, 86 U.S.P.Q. 2d 1129 (Fed. Cir. 2008).

4.79 Another canon which may favor patentees is that claim terms in a preamble should be construed as limitations only when the terms breathe life and meaning into the claim in which the claim terms are included. In general, claim terms in a preamble do not constitute limitations because a preamble describes an object of the sentence in the claim and sets forth the general nature of the invention.[277] These terms do not function to define the scope of patent exclusivity and thus missing such terms in the accused embodiment does not prevent infringement. [278] Two exceptions to the general rule are (1) a claim term in the preamble gives significance to a claim term in the body and (2) a claim term in the preamble is essential to particularly point out the invention defined by the claim in dispute. Courts must determine whether one of these exceptions applies depending on the facts of each case in light of the claim at issue as a whole and the written description of the specification.[279]

4.80 Despite the general rule, US courts frequently construe terms in the preamble as limitations.[280] The first exception applies if a preamble term defines a claim term in the body.[281] When a claim term in the body refers to a claim term in the preamble, the claim term in the preamble necessarily is incorporated into the body to describe the term that the preamble term refers to. However, a claim term in the preamble is not a limition to the claim scope if elements in the body constitute a complete invention and thus deletion of the term does not affect the structure or steps of the claimed invention.[282]

4.81 The second exception applies if intrinsic evidence supports that a preamble term is essential to distinguish the invention from the prior art. If the prosecution history supports that the preamble term at issue was added during the examination to distinguish the prior art, courts view the preamble term as essential to define the claimed invention with respect to the prior art and construe the term as a limitation.[283] When the written description of the invention and the prosecution history put an emphasis on a preamble term, the preamble term is construed as a limitation.[284]

4.82 In general, terms in the preamble of a Jepson-type claim, which applicants outside the United States frequently adopt, are considered to constitute limitations.[285] However, preamble terms to describe the use or purpose of the invention are not considered to constitute limitations because such terms do not function to distinguish the prior art.[286] Because a preamble term introduces a lot of uncertainty as to whether the term constitutes a limitation,

---

[277] For a discussion of the structure of claims under US practice, see Ch. 4, 4.33.

[278] *Am. Med. Sys. v. Biolitec, Inc.*, 618 F.3d 1354, 96 U.S.P.Q. 2d 1652 (Fed. Cir. 2010). Also see Moore, Michel, and Holbrook, *Patent Litigation and Strategy*, 301.

[279] *Storage Tech. Corp. v. Cisco Sys., Inc.*, 329 F.3d 823, 831 (Fed. Cir. 2003).

[280] *Chisum on Patents*, § 8.06[1][b][i].

[281] *Bell Communications Research v. Vitalink Communications Corp.*, 55 F.3d 615, 34 U.S.P.Q. 2d (BNA) 1816 (Fed. Cir. 1995).

[282] *Am. Med. Sys.*, 618 F.3d, 1359. *Catalina Mktg. Int'l, Inc. v. Coolsavings.com, Inc.*, 289 F.3d 801, 809 (Fed. Cir. 2002).

[283] *Bristol-Myers Squibb Co. v. Ben Venue Labs., Inc.*, 246 F.3d 1368, 1375, 58 U.S.P.Q. 2d 1508, 1513 (Fed. Cir. 2001).

[284] Ibid.; *Corning Glass Works v. Sumitomo Electric U.S.A., Inc.*, 868 F.2d 1251, 1257, 9 U.S.P.Q. 2d 1962, 1966 (Fed. Cir. 1989).

[285] *Rowe*, 112 F.3d, 479; *Epcon Gas Sys., Inc. v. Bauer Compressors, Inc.*, 279 F.3d 1022, 1029, 61 U.S.P.Q. 2d 1470, 1475 (Fed. Cir. 2002). For a discussion of the Jepson-type claim, see Ch. 4, 4.33.

[286] *Catalina Mrkg. Int'l v. Coolsavings com, Inc.*, 289 F.3d 801, 62 U.S.P.Q. 2d 1781 (Fed. Cir. 2001); *In re Gardiner*, 36 C.C.P.A. 748, 171 F.2d 313, 315–16, 80 U.S.P.Q. 99, 101 (CCPA 1948).

well-experienced US attorneys write a preamble as short as possible by reciting only the object of the sentence and a short description of the general nature of the object.

4. Application of Construed Claims to Accused Embodiment

(a) All Elements Rule

Once the meaning of all claim terms are clarified through claim interpretation, the construed claim terms must be compared with the accused embodiment. This comparison is considered as a question of fact and should be conducted by the jury.[287] The Supreme Court emphasized that each element in a patent claim is deemed material to define the scope of the patent right and thus courts need to find all claim elements either literally or equivalently to find infringement.[288] US courts cannot apply the doctrine of equivalents to entirely eliminate or vitiate any element of a patent claim by replacing an equivalent element with the element of the claim at issue.[289] They must examine the presence of individual elements either literally or equivalently to secure the notice function of patent claims (the element-by-element analysis).[290] They cannot apply the doctrine to the invention as a whole because such an analysis will allow the doctrine to play an overly broad role and encroach on the boundary of exclusive patent right that should be defined by the claim language. **4.83**

Although the Supreme Court emphasized the limit provided by the element-by-element analysis, the Court did not make clear what constitutes an element. An element can be interpreted as a limitation or a series of limitations (a component).[291] The Federal Circuit interprets an "element" as a "limitation" and requires lower courts to conduct a comparison between individual claim limitations and structures and acts in the accused product and process.[292] In other words, it is improper to apply the component-by-component analysis when applying the doctrine of equivalents.[293] **4.84**

However, US courts flexibly apply the all elements rule on an element-by-element basis so that the doctrine of equivalents is not confined by the claim drafting. In analyzing apparatus and product claims, courts may find infringement as long as the limitation is found somewhere in the accused product or process even if the disputed limitation is found in a component which is different from the component that includes a structure which corresponds to the disputed claim term or limitation.[294] This flexible rule also applies to method and process claims and thus courts do not require the steps to be performed in the order specified in the claim.[295] However, limitations in the steps may explicitly or implicitly require a particular action in one step being followed by an action in the previous step. For example, if a step recites a condition for triggering the action recited in a following step, courts find that the claim requires the former step to occur before the latter step.[296] To determine whether claim terms require a **4.85**

---

287 *Warner-Jenkinson*, 520 U.S. 17.

288 Ibid. The Court endorsed the view adopted by the *en banc* Federal Circuit in Pennwalt, *Pennwalt Corp. v. Durand-Wayland, Inc.*, 833 F.2d 931, 4 U.S.P.Q. 2d 1737 (Fed. Cir. 1987).

289 *Warner-Jenkinson*, 520 U.S., 39.

290 Ibid. 29.

291 *Corning Glass Works v. Sumitomo Electric U.S.A.*, 868 F.2d 1251, 1259, 9 U.S.P.Q. 2d 1962, 1968 (Fed. Cir. 1989).

292 *Ethicon Endo-Surgery, Inc. v. United States Surgical Corp.*, 149 F.3d 1309, 47 U.S.P.Q. 2d 1272 (Fed. Cir. 1998).

293 *Toro Co. v. Deere & Co.*, 355 F.3d 1313, 1324, 69 U.S.P.Q. 2d 1584 (Fed. Cir. 2004).

294 *Corning Glass Works*, 868 F.2d 1251.

295 *Interactive Gift Express, Inc. v. Compuserve Inc.*, 256 F.3d 1323, 59 U.S.P.Q. 2d 1401 (Fed. Cir. 2001).

296 *Altiris, Inc. v. Symantec Corp.*, 318 F.3d 1363, 65 U.S.P.Q. 2d 1865 (Fed. Cir. 2003).

particular order or sequence, courts apply a two-part test: (1) whether the claim terms require the steps being performed in the order specified in the claim; if no such requirement is found in the claim language (2) whether the specification directly or implicitly requires a particular order for the steps to be performed.[297] However, the construction requiring a particular order is an exception to the principle rule and thus the Federal Circuit cautions district courts by stressing that the claim scope is not limited by embodiments disclosed in the specification and courts cannot import limitations from the specification into the claims.[298]

4.86 Moreover, when an advancement of the technology after the issuance of patent obfuscates the significance of limitation at the time of amendment to include the limitation in the claim during the prosecution, courts may apply the all elements rule even more flexibly than in a case where no after-arising technologies are involved.[299] If a technological advancement makes a structure in the claim obsolete and replaces the structure with a modern equivalent so that the accused product performs substantially the same function in substantially the same way to produce substantially the same result, the replacement brings merely an insubstantial change even if the limitations related to the structure which is related to an old technology are completely missing from the accused embodiment.[300] Thus, the way in which US courts apply the doctrine of equivalents depends on the degree of technological advancement in the field of the patented invention between the time of patent prosecution and the time of infringement.

(b) Adding Elements and Improvements

4.87 Although missing an element avoids infringement, adding an element in principle also does not avoid infringement as long as the claim at issue uses an open claim transition.[301] However, parties frequently dispute whether an accused infringer merely added an element or replaced a claimed element with a different structure. When an addition of an element materially changes a structure, which the patentee asserts, to correspond to the claimed element, US courts may find the particular claimed element missing from the accused product or process.[302] When an additional element excludes the use of a claimed element, courts may also find the accused product failing to meet the all elements rule.[303] Under such circumstances, courts may simply deny infringement without examining the additional element because courts must examine a claimed element before examining an additional element.[304]

4.88 Accused embodiments are frequently improvements of patented inventions. However, an improvement or an additional function of an accused product or process does not automatically avoid either literal infringement or infringement under the doctrine of equivalents.[305]

---

[297] Ibid.

[298] Ibid.

[299] *Hughes Aircraft Co. v. United States*, 140 F.3d 1470, 46 U.S.P.Q. 2d 1285 (Fed. Cir. 1998).

[300] *Energy Transp. Group, Inc. v. William Demant Holding A/S*, 2012 U.S. App. LEXIS 21200 (Fed. Cir. October 12, 2012).

[301] E.g., *Free Motion Fitness, Inc. v. Cybex International, Inc.*, 423 F.3d 1343, 1347, 1353 (Fed. Cir. 2005). For a discussion of the open claim transition, see Ch. 4, 4.43.

[302] *Outside the Box Innovations, LLC v. Travel Caddy, Inc.*, 2012 U.S. App. LEXIS 19931 (Fed. Cir. September 21, 2012).

[303] *Atlas Powder Co. v. E.I. du Pont De Nemours & Co.*, 750 F.2d 1569 (Fed. Cir. 1984).

[304] *Power Mosfet Techs., LLC v. Siemens AG*, 378 F.3d 1396, 72 U.S.P.Q. 2d 1129 (Fed. Cir. 2004).

[305] *Atlas Powder Co.*, 750 F.2d, 1570–81.

The Federal Circuit stresses that a separate patent on an accused embodiment presents no legal or evidentiary presumption of non-infringement.[306] Whether an improvement avoids infringement depends on the particular facts.[307] However, courts may take account of separate patentability in determining the insubstantial difference for determining equivalency between the claim and the accused embodiment.[308] Although the fact of separate patentability is relevant, patentable difference does not itself tend to negate infringement.[309] As a result, the Federal Circuit found literal infringement and infringement under the doctrine of equivalents with respect to an accused product or process which are separately patented.

(c) Means-Plus-Function Elements

The all elements rule based on the element-by-element analysis applies to all forms of claims, including means-plus-function claims and product-by-process claims.[310] However, the comparison of the means-plus-function claims is modified to limit the application of the doctrine of equivalents because of the exception to the principal rule for claim interpretation; the literal scope of means-plus-function claims covers only structures, materials, and acts disclosed in the specification and their equivalents.[311] It follows that a comparison for finding all elements equivalently would be redundant if equivalents under the doctrine of equivalents are the same as literal equivalents of means-plus-function claims. **4.89**

In comparing equivalents under the doctrine of equivalents and literal equivalents under § 112(f), the Federal Circuit made it clear that the fact finder should compare the accused product or process with the claim language to find all elements equivalently only (1) if the structure or act that the patentee asserts has been infringed by an equivalent involves a technology which was developed after the issuance of patent; or (2) if the structure or act performs a function identical to that of the claimed element in respect of which the patentee asserts infringement.[312] This is because the literal equivalents under § 112(f) and equivalents under the doctrine of equivalents are the same except for (1) the timing: the literal equivalents under § 112(f) must be available at the time of patent issuance while equivalents under the doctrine of equivalents may include after-arising technologies which were developed after the patent issuance and before the time of infringement; and (2) the identity of function: the literal equivalents require strict identity between the function of the claimed element and the structure or act of the accused product or process while equivalents under the doctrine of equivalents require only substantial identity.[313] **4.90**

---

[306] *Hoechst Celanese Corp. v. BP Chems., Ltd.*, 78 F.3d 1575, 1582 (Fed. Cir. 1996).

[307] *National Presto Indus. v. West Bend Co.*, 76 F.3d 1185, 1996 U.S. App. LEXIS 1940, 37 U.S.P.Q. 2d (BNA) 1685 (Fed. Cir. 1996).

[308] *Glaxo Wellcome, Inc. v. Andrx Pharms., Inc.*, 344 F.3d 1226 (Fed. Cir. 2003).

[309] *Siemens Med. Solutions USA, Inc. v. Saint-Gobain Ceramics & Plastics, Inc.*, 637 F.3d 1269, 3546, 97 U.S.P.Q. 2d 1897 (Fed. Cir. 2011).

[310] For discussions of means-plus-function claims and product-by-process claims, see Ch. 4, 4.43 "Product-by-Process Plaims." In determining the novelty and nonobvioiusness of product-by-process claims, the USPTO does not strictly follow the all elements rule by adopting the broadest possible interpretation. See Ch. 7, 7.04 "Claim Construction."

[311] 35 U.S.C. § 112(f).

[312] *Al-Site Corp. v. VSI Int'l, Inc.*, 174 F.3d 1308, 50 U.S.P.Q. 2d 1161 (Fed. Cir. 1999); *Welker Bearing Co. v. PHD, Inc.*, 550 F.3d 1090, 89 U.S.P.Q. 2d 1289 (Fed. Cir. 2008).

[313] *Al-Site Corp.*, 174 F.3d, 1320.

5. Doctrine of Equivalents

(a) Fundamental Rules

4.91 **i. Objective Test: Insubstantial Difference** If any of the elements are missing from the accused product or process, there is no literal infringement. This will not end an infringement analysis if the patentee claims infringement under the doctrine of equivalents. US courts will examine if the missing element is replaced with a structure, material, or act which is equivalent to the missing claim element unless one of the doctrines to limit the doctrine of equivalents applies and precludes a claim of infringement under the doctrine of equivalents.[314]

4.92 In *Warner-Jenkinson*, the Supreme Court rejected the view that the doctrine of equivalents is an equitable doctrine and the application of the doctrine should be limited to cases where the accused infringer intentionally copied the patent claim or any other equity requires courts to apply the doctrine of equivalents.[315] Instead, the Court emphasized the essential nature of the doctrine is the identity between a patented invention and its equivalent. Courts should conduct an infringement analysis under the doctrine of equivalents in a similar manner as a literal infringement analysis without taking account of proof of an accused infringer's intent.

4.93 Therefore, an infringement analysis under the doctrine of equivalents should be conducted objectively on an element-by-element basis. In other words, equivalency must be shown between the claim term missing from the accused embodiment and the structure, material, or act substituted by the accused infringer, instead of equivalency between the entire claim language and the accused device as a whole. To show equivalency, patentees must establish insubstantial differences between the missing claim element and the structure in the accused embodiment.[316] Although patentees can use any factor to establish insubstantial differences objectively, the Supreme Court acknowledged that the known interchangeability between the missing claim element and the substituted structure at the time of infringement can be used as an objective test to establish insubstantial differences noted by its own precedent, *Graver Tank*.[317] US courts also frequently rely on the "triple identity" test to establish insubstantial differences by showing that the substituted structure or act performs substantially the same function in substantially the same manner to produce substantially the same result as the claimed element in the claimed product or process.[318] The Supreme Court acknowledged a concern over the triple identity test when it is applied to analyze equivalents with respect to products and processes other than mechanical devices. Nevertheless, the Court endorsed the triple identity test for establishing equivalents, emphasizing that identity or equivalency between all elements of the claim and all structures or acts in the accused product while preventing an elimination of any element entirely by the doctrine of equivalents is more important than the particular linguistic framework for establishing equivalency.[319]

---

314 For detailed discussions on these doctrines, see Ch. 4, 4.5 "Doctrines to Limit the Doctrine of Equivalents."

315 *Warner-Jenkinson*, 520 U.S., 34–35.

316 Ibid. 39.

317 *Graver Tank & Mfg. Co.* v. *Linde Air Products Co.*, 339 U.S. 605, 94 L. Ed. 1097, 70 S. Ct. 854 (1950).

318 E.g., *Pennwalt Corp. v. Durand-Wayland, Inc.*, 833 F.2d 931, 4 U.S.P.Q. 2d 1737 (Fed. Cir. 1987), *cert. denied*, 485 U.S. 961, 485 U.S. 1009 (1988).

319 *Warner-Jenkinson*, 520 U.S., 39–40.

In short, patentees can establish equivalency between a claim element and the substituted structure or act by showing one of the following elements: (1) known interchangeability, (2) triple identity, or (3) insubstantial difference with any objective evidence. This is in stark contrast to tests for establishing equivalency under German and Japanese law which require patentees to establish both (1) and (2) with additional elements.[320] Moreover, German courts require known interchangeability as of the priority date (= effective filing date), in contrast to Japanese courts which require known interchangeability at the time of infringement, as required by US courts.[321] **4.94**

Another major difference between US and German equivalents is the degree of the role played by the doctrine of equivalents. Because German courts engage in an element-by-element equivalent analysis as part of claim construction, an analysis under the doctrine of equivalents focuses on the identity between technical ideas underlying the claim language and accused embodiment and is akin to the "invention as a whole" analysis under US case law,[322] although the approach was flatly rejected by the US Supreme Court as being inconsistent with the notice function of claims.[323] **4.95**

ii. Range of Equivalents In *Graver Tank*, the Supreme Court suggested that the range of equivalents depends on the nature of invention of the claim at issue although the doctrine of equivalents applies to both pioneer inventions and improvements resulting from a combination of old elements.[324] A review of pre-Federal Circuit lower court decisions following *Graver Tank* supports the view that pioneer inventions are entitled to a more generous scope of equivalents than improvements.[325] This is because it is more difficult to draft claims and specification for pioneer inventions and the scope of such inventions are not limited by the prior art. In contrast, if an invention involves only a minor improvement in a well-established field of technology which is crowded with prior art technologies, it is entitled to a narrow range or no range of equivalents.[326] An old case supports the view that the range of equivalents varies depending on the advancement or inventive step involved in the claimed invention.[327] Moreover, when the asserted patent has never been commercialized, courts were reluctant to apply the doctrine of equivalents.[328] **4.96**

Since its creation in 1982, the Federal Circuit has been reluctant to use the notions of pioneer versus improvement inventions when it applies the doctrine of equivalents.[329] This may be because pioneer inventions are not well defined enough to be distinguished from non-pioneering improvements.[330] Although some cases support the view that the range of equivalents depends on the advancement involved in the claimed invention, it is more likely **4.97**

[320] For the tests for German doctrine of equivalents, see Ch. 5, 5.113. For the test for Japanese doctrine of equivalents, see Ch. 6, 6.72.

[321] For the timing to decide equivalency under German case law, see Ch. 5, 5.118. For the timing to decide equivalency under Japanese case law, see Ch. 6, 6.73.

[322] *Hughes Aircraft Co. v. United States*, 717 F.2d 1351, 219 U.S.P.Q. 473 (Fed. Cir. 1983).

[323] *Warner-Jenkinson*, 520 U.S., 29.

[324] *Graver Tank*, 339 U.S., 608.

[325] *Moore v. United States*, 211 U.S.P.Q. 800 (Ct. Cl. Trial Div. 1981).

[326] E.g., *LaSalle v. Carlton's Laydown Service, Inc.*, 680 F.2d 432, 216 U.S.P.Q. 276 (5th Cir. 1982); *Arvin Indus., Inc., v. Berns Air King Corp.*, 525 F.2d 182, 185, 188 U.S.P.Q. 49, 52 (7th Cir. 1975).

[327] *National Hollow Brake-Beam Co. v. Interchangeable Brake-Beam Co.*, 106 F.693 (8th Cir. 1901).

[328] *Doble Eng'r Co. v. Leeds & Northrup Co.*, 134 F.2d 78, 56 U.S.P.Q. 426 (1st Cir. 1943).

[329] *Chisum on Patents*, § 18.04[2][a][iii].

[330] *Abbott Laboratories v. Dey, L.P.*, 287 F.3d 1097, 1105, 62 U.S.P.Q. 2d 1545 (Fed. Cir. 2002).

that the range of equivalents depends on the range between the literal scope and the closest prior art.[331] This is because courts cannot apply the doctrine of equivalents to a range which is anticipated or obvious from the prior art.[332]

4.98 Even if the range of equivalents is narrow due to the prior art, such range may expand if new equivalents of claimed elements are developed after the issuance of the patent. In *Warner-Jenkinson*, the Supreme Court rejected the view that the doctrine of equivalents should not extend to an after-arising technology which was developed after the patent issuance and clarified that equivalency between a claimed element and substituted structure or act should be determined at the time of infringement.[333] The Federal Circuit is reluctant to apply the doctrine of equivalents to remedy errors made by patent attorneys. The doctrine should not be applied to equivalents foreseeable at the time of filing because attorneys could have drafted a claim which literally covers such equivalents. Instead the application of the doctrine of equivalents should focus to remedy patent attorneys' impossible task of drafting claims to cover equivalents unforeseeable at the time of filing and during the patent prosecution. To preserve the notice function of claims, the Court imposes a duty on patent drafters to draft claims to cover foreseeable equivalents.[334] Thus, the Federal Circuit is more willing to apply the doctrine of equivalents if the structure or act substituted with a claimed element was developed after the issuance of a patent and thus patent drafters were neither able to draft claims when a patent application was filed nor amend claims during the prosecution to literally cover such equivalents.

4.99 Although equivalency requires only an insubstantial difference between a claimed element and substituted element, the doctrine of equivalents may apply to accused embodiments which are covered by a separate valid patent.[335] Although US courts may take account of separate patentability of the accused embodiment against equivalency, the fact of separate patentability presents no legal or evidentiary or presumption of non-infringement and thus does not automatically preclude infringement either literally or equivalently.[336] The Federal Circuit rejected the view that obviousness for patentability is comparable to equivalence for infringement because of different analytical frameworks: for example, courts take account of objective indicia of commercial success and the level of predictability in the art for determining nonobviousness although these factors are irrelevant to an equivalence determination. The time frames for addressing nonobviousness and equivalence determinations are also different: the former is determined as of the invention date (effective filing date) in contrast to the latter being determined as of the time of infringement.[337]

---

[331] *Augustine Med., Inc. v. Gaymar Indus., Inc.*, 181 F.3d 1291, 1301, 50 U.S.P.Q. 2d 1900, 1907 (Fed. Cir. 1999).

[332] *Wilson Sporting Goods Co. v. David Geoffrey & Associates*, 904 F.2d 677, 14 U.S.P.Q. 2d 1942 (Fed. Cir. 1990). For more discussions, Ch. 4, 4.120 "Prior art limitation."

[333] *Warner-Jenkinson*, 520 U.S., 37.

[334] *Honeywell Int'l, Inv. v. Hamilton Sundstrand Corp.*, 523 F.3d 1304, 1313, 86 U.S.P.Q. 2d 1718 (Fed. Cir. 2008); *Johnson & Johnstone Assocs. v. R.E. Serv. Co.*, 285 F.3d 1046, 1057–58, 62 U.S.P.Q. 2d 1225 (Fed. Cir. 2002) (Rader, J., concurring).

[335] *Siemens Med. Solutions USA, Inc. v. Saint-Gobain Ceramics & Plastics, Inc.*, 637 F.3d 1269, 3546, 97 U.S.P.Q. 2d 1897 (Fed. Cir. 2011). For a discussion of improvement by adding elements, see Ch. 4, 4.87 "Adding Elements and Improvements."

[336] *Hoechst Celanese Corp v. BP Chems., Ltd.*, 78 F.3d 1575, 1582 (Fed. Cir. 1996); *Glaxo Wellcome, Inc. v. Andrx Pharms., Inc.*, 344 F.3d 1226 (Fed. Cir. 2003).

[337] *Siemens Med. Solutions USA, Inc*, 637 F.3d, 1282.

Although the doctrine of equivalents may apply to after-arising technologies under German law, the main role played by the doctrine of equivalents is to identify the technical scolution underlying the claim anddetermine whether the PHOSITA considers obvious modifications to produce the effect of the invention adopted by the defendant being equivalent to the solution.[338] Accordingly, German courts are not bound by the claim language as strictly as US courts and do not follow an element-by-element analysis when they apply the doctrine of equivalents. When German courts apply the doctrine of equivalents, it is irrelevant if a patent drafter fails to draft a claim to cover all foreseeable equivalents. **4.100**

iii. Reverse Doctrine of Equivalents Although the doctrine of equivalents in principle functions to expand the literal scope defined by the claim language, it may also function to limit the literal scope. The Supreme Court in *Graver Tank*,[339] cited an 1898 Supreme Court decision, *Westinghouse v. Boyden Power-Break Co.*,[340] and acknowledged that the doctrine of equivalents may be applied to exclude embodiments which do not meet the elements of equivalence although the embodiments fall into the literal scope as the claim language is being literally construed. The US Court of Claims, one of two predecessor courts of the Federal Circuit, noted the restrictive function of the doctrine in *Autogiro*[341] but did not apply the doctrine to exclude any of the accused embodiments. In one of its early cases, *SRI v. Matsushita*, the Federal Circuit, which followed the Court of Claims, adopted the doctrine by naming it "the reverse doctrine of equivalents."[342] Nevertheless, the Court declined to apply the doctrine of equivalents. **4.101**

This judicially created reverse doctrine of equivalents should be distinguished from the literal equivalents under § 112(f). Because the reverse doctrine of equivalents functions in a similar manner as the literal equivalents in limiting the literal scope to exclude non-equivalent embodiments, US courts, including the Supreme Court, often mix up the two types of equivalents.[343] However, the judicially created doctrine excludes embodiments which are not equivalents to the asserted claim; in contrast, the literal infringement excludes embodiments which are not equivalents to structures, materials, and acts explicitly disclosed in the specification. Moreover, elements to establish the two different types of equivalents differ with respect to the degree of identity in function (identical v. substantially the same) and when the equivalency was known (time of patent grant v. time of infringement).[344] **4.102**

Despite the acknowledgement, the reverse doctrine of equivalents has only marginal force as a defense of literal infringement under the Federal Circuit case law. Since *SRI*, the Federal Circuit has never applied the reverse doctrine except for a case involving infringement of literal equivalents covered by means-plus-function claims.[345] It acknowledges the presence **4.103**

[338] See Ch. 5, 5.121.

[339] *Graver Tank*, 339 U.S., 609.

[340] *Westinghouse Electric & Mfg. Co. v. Formica Insulation Co.*, 266 U.S. 342 (1924).

[341] *Autogiro Co. of Am. v. United States*, 181 Ct. Cl. 55, 66, 384 F.2d 391, 155 U.S.P.Q. 697 (1967).

[342] *SRI International v. Matsushita Electric Corp. of America*, 775 F.2d 1107, 227 U.S.P.Q. 577 (Fed. Cir. 1985).

[343] E.g., *Warner-Jenkinson*, 520 U.S., 28.

[344] See Ch. 4, 4.90.

[345] *Texas Instruments, Inc. v. U.S. Int'l Trade Comm'n*, 805 F.2d 1558, 231 U.S.P.Q. 833 (Fed. Cir. 1986). Although legal scholars frequently cite this case as a case in which the Federal Circuit applied the reverse doctrine of equivalents, the asserted claims are means-plus-function claims. Thus, the Federal Circuit applied the rule under § 112(f). However, the case law was not clear with respect to the literal equivalents and the judicially created doctrine of equivalents when *Texas Instruments v. ITC* was decided.

of the reverse doctrine of equivalents if the doctrine is raised as a defense of literal infringement but does not apply the reverse doctrine except for an exceptional circumstance where equity commands a determination of non-infringement despite literal infringement by the accused embodiment.[346] The Federal Circuit's reluctance to apply the reverse doctrine of equivalents is highlighted by its comment that the reverse doctrine is "an anachronistic exception, long mentioned but rarely applied."[347]

(b) Doctrines to Limit the Doctrine of Equivalents

4.104 **i. Prosecution History Estoppel** Because of the paramount rule that the claim language determines the scope of exclusivity and the Supreme Court's emphasis on the notice function of patent claims, the doctrines to limit the doctrine of equivalents have played a significant role in preventing patentees from claiming infringement under the doctrine of equivalents after no literal infringement is found by the court. Such limitation doctrines include (1) the prosecution history estoppel; (2) the no element vitiation rule; (3) prior art limitation; and (4) dedication to the public. If the accused infringer establishes during the *Markman* process that one of the doctrines to limit the doctrine of equivalents applies to the missing claim element that the patentee asserts was replaced with an equivalent structure or act, the court finds no infringement without giving the patentee a chance to establish equivalence between the missing claim element and the replaced structure or act.[348]

4.105 When a claim element or limitation that the patentee asserts was replaced with an equivalent structure is amended or commented upon in an argument to distinguish the prior art during the prosecution at the USPTO, the prosecution history estoppel prevents the patentee from recapturing the scope surrendered or disclaimed through the amendment or argument. In two recent decisions, *Warner-Jenkinson* (1997)[349] and *Festo* (2002),[350] the Supreme Court set conditions and an analytical framework to apply the doctrine of equivalents. The prosecution history estoppel is distinct from the traditional notion of estoppel. Like the estoppel under German law, the traditional notion of estoppel binds the party of proceedings in which a patentee made a representation giving rise to a surrender or disclaimer of the patent scope.[351] In contrast, the prosecution history estoppel applies to any party against whom the patentee asserts infringement. This is because the rationale supporting the prosecution history estoppel is NOT for the sake of equity between parties to proceedings due to reliance on a presentation but for the sake of securing the public notice function of patent claims.[352] The public should be able to rely on the claim scope surrendered during the prosecution through a record of prosecution which is publicly available before litigation. As a result, regardless of reliance, the prosecution history estoppel protects any party from a patentees' assertion of infringement under the doctrine of equivalents with respect to the scope surrendered or disclaimed during the prosecution.

[346] *Amgen Inc. v. Hoechst Marion Roussel, Inc.*, 314 F.3d 1313, 1351, 65 U.S.P.Q. 2d 1385 (Fed. Cir. 2003).

[347] *Tate Access Floors, Inc. v. Interface Architectural Resources, Inc.*, 279 F.3d 1357, 1368, 61 U.S.P.Q. 2d 1647 (Fed. Cir. 2002).

[348] See for a discussion of *Markman* process, see Ch. 4, 4.26.

[349] *Warner-Jenkinson Co., Inc. v. Hilton Davis Chemical Co.*, 520 U.S. 17, 41 U.S.P.Q. 2d 1865 (1997).

[350] *Festo Corp. v. Shoketsu Kinzoku Kogyo Kabushiki Co.*, 535 U.S. 722, 740, 122 S. Ct. 1831, 152 L. Ed. 2d 944, 62 U.S.P.Q. 2d 1705 (2002).

[351] See Ch. 4, 4.28.

[352] *Warner-Jenkinson*, 520 U.S., 41.

Prosecution history estoppel arises when an applicant makes (1) an amendment to narrow the literal scope of the claim at issue or (2) an argument to disclaim a particular type of embodiment. Regarding the amendment, an amendment to meet any statutory requirement for patentability gives rise to estoppel.[353] Both voluntary amendments and amendments in response to an office action from the USPTO examiners give rise to estoppel.[354] A narrowing amendment includes replacement of claim elements with a narrow definition as well as an addition of new elements.[355] The prosecution history estoppel applies regardless of the correctness of the USPTO's action in the prosecution history. By failing to appeal the rejection resulting from an incorrect office action, patentees cannot avoid the prosecution history estoppel because the estoppel aims to secure the notice function of patent claims which the public rely on to conduct their business.[356] **4.106**

Because US patents include many claims with different scopes, cancelling a broad claim by redrafting a dependent claim into an independent claim results in the same effect as narrowing the broad claim. Thus, US courts treat such cancellations the same as narrowing amendments and apply the prosecution history estoppel.[357] Similarly, a narrowing amendment to a term in a claim results in a narrowing amendment to any claim which includes the same term or phrase because the same term in different claims should be interpreted consistently.[358] Thus, estoppel applies to claims including the term to which a narrowing amendment is made even if the claims have never been amended during the prosecution.[359] **4.107**

US courts make sure that patentees cannot circumvent prosecution history estoppel by finding continuation applications with claims narrower than the claims included in the original patent application. When an applicant cancels broader claims in the original application and fails to prosecute the broader claims in a continuation application, courts may apply prosecution history estoppel.[360] **4.108**

In a pre-*Festo en banc* decision, the Federal Circuit made it clear that both voluntary argument and argument in response to an office action give rise to prosecution history estoppel if the argument supports surrender or disclaimer of the subject matter regardless of an amendment accompanied with the argument.[361] Because the *Festo* court only explicitly endorsed amendment-based estoppel, the Federal Circuit is cautious in applying argument-based estoppel in contrast to a narrowing amendment-based estoppel and thus requires a clear and unmistakable surrender of subject matter evidenced by an argument when no amendment is accompanied with an argument.[362] When an argument is accompanied with an **4.109**

---

353 *Festo Corp.*, 535 U.S., 740.

354 *Festo Corp. v. Shoketsu Kinzoku Kogyo Kabushiki Co.*, 234 F.3d 558, 568, 56 U.S.P.Q. 2d 1865 (Fed. Cir., 2000).

355 *Honeywell International Inc. v. Hamilton Sundstrand Corp.*, 370 F.3d 1131, 1143–44 (Fed. Cir. 2004) (*en banc*)

356 *Warner-Jenkinson*, 520 U.S., 33.

357 *Honeywell International, Inc.*, 370 F.3d, 1140.

358 See Ch. 4, 4.59 "Terms Other than the Terms in Dispute and the Same Terms as the Terms in Dispute in other Claims."

359 *Builders Concrete, Inc. v. Bremerton Concrete Products Co.*, 757 F.2d 255, 225 U.S.P.Q. 240 (Fed. Cir. 1985).

360 *Haynes International, Inc. v. Jessop Steel Co.*, 8 F.3d 1573, 28 U.S.P.Q. 2d 1652 (Fed. Cir. 1993).

361 *Festo Corp. en banc*, 234 F.3d, 568.

362 *Conoco, Inc. v. Energy & Environmental International, L.C.*, 460 F.3d 1349, 1364, 79 U.S.P.Q. 2d 1801 (Fed. Cir. 2006); *KCJ Corp. v. Kinetic Concepts, Inc.*, 223 F.3d 1351, 1359–60 (Fed. Cir. 2000).

amendment and explains the invention with respect to the effect of the amendment, the Federal Circuit is willing to apply prosecution history estoppel to prevent a patentee's assertion of infringement under the doctrine of equivalents.[363]

4.110 In *Festo*, the Supreme Court set forth an analytical framework to examine whether prosecution history estoppel prevents an assertion of infringement under the doctrine of equivalents by clarifying the burden of proof between a patentee and an accused infringer. Under this framework, if a patentee made a narrowing amendment or an amendment narrowing the patent scope, US courts presume that the amendment was made to meet a requirement of patentability under the Patent Act.[364] A patentee can rebut the presumption by explaining that the amendment was not for any patentability reason. Even if a patentee can rebut the presumption, courts presume that all scope between the original claim and amended claim is surrendered by making a narrowing amendment.[365] A patentee can rebut the second presumption by showing the presence of one of the following exceptional cases where the amendment cannot reasonably be viewed as surrendering a particular equivalent: (1) the equivalent may have been unforeseeable at the time of the amendment; (2) the rationale underlying the amendment may bear no more than a tangential relation to the equivalent in question; or (3) there may be some other reason suggesting that the patentee could not reasonably be expected to have described the insubstantial substitute in question.[366] If none of these cases apply to the claim element that infringement by equivalent is asserted, courts do not give a patentee an opportunity to establish equivalence between the claimed element and replaced structure or act.

4.111 To avoid prosecution history estoppel, patentees' arguments focus on two issues: (A) whether an amendment narrowed the scope of the patent claim and (B) whether it is one of three exceptional cases. It is unlikely that an applicant can rebut the first presumption that a narrowing amendment was made to meet a statutory requirement under the Patent Act because it is unlikely that an applicant voluntarily gives up a scope without any need to meet a statutory requirement. Moreover, the Federal Circuit made it clear that the explanation of a patentability unrelated reason for a narrowing amendment must be supported by a record of prosecution.[367] If the record reveals no reason for the amendment, US courts apply the second presumption with respect to the full-scope surrender. Because attorneys try to leave as little information as possible in the record to avoid a narrow claim interpretation in light of the prosecution history, it is unlikely for patentees to find a solid record establishing a reason for the amendment at issue.

4.112 Regarding issue (A), patentees can avoid estoppel only if they can establish that the amendment at issue was truly cosmetic or to correct an obvious omission and thus has no effect on the literal scope of patent claim.[368] They can also avoid estoppel by showing that the amendment broadened the literal scope instead of narrowing the scope.[369] Regarding issue (B),

---

[363] *Norian Corp. v. Stryker Corp.*, 432 F.3d 1356 (Fed. Cir. 2005).

[364] *Warner-Jenkinson*, 520 U.S., 33–34; *Festo Corp.*, 535 U.S., 739.

[365] *Festo Corp.*, 535 U.S., 740.

[366] Ibid. With respect to the case (1), the Supreme Court stated conflicting time frames for unforeseeable equivalent inquiry, the Federal Circuit clarified that the equivalent must be unforeseeable at the time of amendment when Festo was on remand. *Festo Corp. v. Shoketsu Kinzoku Kogyo Kabushiki Co.*, 344 F.3d 1359, 1365, FN 2, 68 U.S.P.Q. 2d 1321 (Fed. Cir. 2003) (*Festo* Remand).

[367] Ibid, 1366.

[368] *Festo Corp.*, 535 U.S., 736–37. *Conoco Inc.*, 460 F.3d, 1364.

[369] *Business Objects, S.A. v. Microstrategy, Inc.*, 393 F.3d 1366, 1375, 73 U.S.P.Q. 2d 1520 (Fed. Cir. 2005).

the Federal Circuit clarified that rebuttal for the full-scope surrender is a question of law and thus should be determined by the court.[370] Therefore, the court can decide prosecution history estoppel through the *Markman* process without involvement of a jury.

The Federal Circuit insists there is a duty on patent drafters to draft claims that literally cover foreseeable equivalents and emphasizes the goal of the doctrine of equivalents which aims to protect patentees against substitution of an equivalent structure with a claim element in an unforeseeable equivalent. To maintain the notice function of a patent claim, the court sets a high hurdle for patentees to rebut the full-scope surrender presumption. The substituted structure may be unforeseeable if the structure is not disclosed in the prior art at the time of amendment in the field of the invention.[371] However, an unforeseeable equivalent analysis does not end even if the substitute developed was not known and developed after the time of amendment because the structure is foreseeable if the solution of the after-arising structure had been known at the time of amendment in the field of the invention.[372] The Federal Circuit defines the field of invention broadly in light of the definition of an object that the invention relates to in the preamble.[373] **4.113**

The Federal Circuit views the rebuttal by the tangential relation case (2) as a very narrow exception to the prosecution history estoppel and sets an even higher hurdle for allowing patentees to rebut the full-scope surrender presumption.[374] To establish a tangential relationship to the substituted equivalent, the Federal Circuit requires the reason for amendment to be supported by a record of prosecution history.[375] With such a record, a patentee must show that the narrowing amendment was peripheral or not directly relevant to the substituted structure of the accused device in respect of which the patentee asserts equivalence between the structure and the element in the claim in dispute. The courts' inquiries on tangential relations should focus on the context in which the amendment was made.[376] Only when a record of prosecution supports that the claim element substituted with an equivalent structure was never narrowed nor at issue during the prosecution does the Federal Circuit let a patentee to successfully rebut the presumption as the reason for amendment being merely tangential to the equivalent.[377] The scope for allowing rebuttal based on case (3) is even narrower to make the exception consistent with the notice function of a patent claim. Case (3) is limited to very exceptional circumstances where the patentee could not reasonably be expected to write a claim to encompass the equivalent due to a shortcoming of language during the prosecution.[378] Because the patentee could be reasonably expected to write a claim to encompass the equivalent if the equivalent is foreseeable at the time of amendment, a chance that a patentee can rebut the full scope surrender estoppel on case (3) is very limited unless the equivalent is unforesseable. **4.114**

---

370 *Festo* Remand, 344 F.3d, 1368–69.

371 Ibid.

372 *Honeywell Int'l, Inc. v. Hamilton Sundstrand Corp.*, 523 F.3d 1304, 1313, 86 U.S.P.Q. 2d 1718 (Fed. Cir. 2008).

373 *Schwarz Pharma, Inc. v. Paddock Labs., Inc.*, 504 F.3d 1371, 1377 (Fed. Cir. 2007).

374 *Honeywell Int'l Inc.*, 523 F.3d, 1315; *Cross Med. Prods., Inc. v. Medtronic Sofamor Danek, Inc.*, 480 F.3d 1335, 1342 (Fed. Cir. 2007).

375 *Festo Remand*, 344 F.3d, 1368.

376 Ibid. 1370.

377 *Regents of the Univ. of Cal. v. DakoCytomation Cal., Inc.*, 517 F.3d 1364, 85 U.S.P.Q. 2d 1929 (Fed. Cir. 2008).

378 *Amgen, Inc. v. Hoechst Marion Roussel, Inc.*, 457 F.3d 1293, 1316 (Fed. Cir. 2006).

4.115 Because of the narrow scope of exceptional cases, the patentees' chances of winning a claim of infringement under the doctrine of equivalents is very small. The Supreme Court emphasized the public notice function of a patent claim and suggested the Federal Circuit develop a procedural remedy to limit the uncertainty resulting from a jury trial in determining equivalence. In response, the Federal Circuit developed case law to enhance the role of the prosecution history estoppel to limit the doctrine of equivalents. Thus, the doctrine of equivalents has significantly declined after *Warner-Jenkinson* and *Festo*.[379]

4.116 **ii. No Element Vitiation Rule** Regardless of an amendment or argument to meet a statutory requirement during the prosecution, courts may preclude a claim of infringement under the doctrine of equivalents if an application of the doctrine of equivalents would entirely vitiate a particular claim element.[380] The rationale of the no element vitiation rule is that the doctrine of equivalents should not change the central functions of a patent: the public notice function and the function to define subject matter under examination at the USPTO.[381] To reconcile the functions and the doctrine of equivalents, courts must examine equivalence between claimed elements and the structures in the accused embodiment on an element-by-element basis so that none of the claimed elements should be eliminated through the application of the doctrine of equivalents. In applying the no element vitiation rule, courts must consider "the totality of the circumstances of each case and determine whether the alleged equivalent can be fairly characterized as an insubstantial change from the claimed subject matter without rendering the pertinent limitation meaningless."[382]

4.117 Because the no element vitiation rule is a stretch of the all elements rule which applies commonly to literal infringement and infringement under the doctrine of equivalents, the Federal Circuit frequently rejects a patentees' assertion of equivalent with respect to a claim element that parties dispute on the meaning of the term through claim construction once the court adopts a narrow meaning for the element in favor of an accused infringer. [383] This is because an application of the doctrine of equivalents expands the meaning of the disputed term and makes the clarified meaning of the term in claim construction meaningless. Moreover, because courts have already examined and concluded that one meaning is distinct from another meaning—(1) a narrow construction excluding an accused structure and (2) a broad construction including the structure—it is unlikely that courts will find the accused structure which is excluded from the narrow meaning adopted through claim construction as merely an insubstantial variation of the claimed element.[384] These cases

[379] Lee Petherbridge, "On the Decline of the Doctrine of Equivalents," 31 *Cardozo L.R.* (2010): 1371; David L. Schwartz, "Explaining the Demise of the Doctrine of Equivalents," 26 *Berkeley Tech. L.J.* (2011): 1157.

[380] *Warner-Jenkinson*, 520 U.S., 39, FN 8. The application of the no element vitiation rule is appropriate if the patented invention has simple structures; *Sage Prods. v. Devon Indus.*, 126 F.3d 1420, 44 U.S.P.Q. 2d 1103 (Fed. Cir. 1997).

[381] *Warner-Jenkinson*, 520 U.S., 30.

[382] *Freedman Seating Co. v. Am. Seating Co.*, 420 F.3d 1350, 1359 (Fed. Cir. 2005); *Carnegie Mellon Univ. v. Hoffman-La Roche, Inc.*, 541 F.3d 1115, 1129 (Fed. Cir. 2008).

[383] *Am. Calcar, Inc. v. Am. Honda Motor Co.*, 651 F.3d 1318, 1339, 99 U.S.P.Q. 2d 1137 (2011). Some cases adopted a flexible approach for finding infringement under the doctrine of equivalent with respect to the accused feature which was distinguished from the term clarified through claim interpretation. *Depuy Spine, Inc. v. Medtronic Sofamor Danek, Inc.*, 469 F.3d 1005, 80 U.S.P.Q. 2d 1865 (Fed. Cir. 2006).

[384] E.g., *Trading Techs. Int'l, Inc. v. eSpeed, Inc.*, 595 F.3d 1340, 1355, 93 U.S.P.Q. 2d 1805 (Fed. Cir. 2010).

applying the no element vitiation rule to a claim element which was clarified though a claim construction highlights a tension between the no element vitiation rule and the doctrine of equivalents: the former prevents a finding of infringement through an elimination of an element from a patent claim; in contrast, the latter allows a finding of infringement through the replacement with an equivalent structure despite a missing element as long as the structure is an insubstantial variation of the missing element. If the no element vitiation rule applies to a construed element expansively, it will effectively eliminate a claim of the doctrine of equivalents with respect to a claim element which is disputed with respect to a structure or act of an accused product or process.

In addition, the no element vitiation rule may effectively eliminate a patentee's right of jury trial with respect to equivalence if the rule is applied expansively. The no element vitiation rule can be restated as a rule to deny a claim of infringement under the doctrine of equivalents because the accused structure or act is substantially different from the claim element.[385] Chief Judge Rader described the application of the no element vitiation rule as simply a circular application of the doctrine of equivalents and the all elements rule although the testers of insubstantial difference are different: judges for the no element vitiation rule and juries for the doctrine of equivalents.[386] Because the application of the no element vitiation rule is a question of law, courts can simply find a substantial difference between the claim element and the accused structure and issue a summary judgment of non-infringement and prevent a patentee from asserting equivalence to juries. **4.118**

In short, the no element vitiation rule extensively limits the doctrine of equivalents after *Warner-Jenkinson* and *Festo* although the rule was developed by the Federal Circuit before these Supreme Court decisions.[387] The duty for drafting claims to literally cover foreseeable equivalents also promotes the application of the no element vitiation rule if the allegedly equivalent structure or act is foreseeable at the time of claim drafting and amendment. Without any subtlety of language or complexity of technology, nor any substantial change in the state of art, a patentee should not be able to resort to the doctrine of equivalents. Under such circumstances, the no element vitiation rule should eliminate a claim of infringement under the doctrine of equivalents regardless of a surrender or disclaimer during the prosecution. **4.119**

iii. Prior Art Limitation The doctrine common to US, German, and Japanese jurisprudences is that the doctrine of equivalents cannot apply to an accused product or process which is anticipated or obvious from the prior art. It is common sense that competitors have a right to produce products or practice processes which are in the prior art and thus in the public domain. The Federal Circuit restated this common sense into a rule that a patentee cannot claim a coverage which the patentee could not lawfully have obtained with a patent by literal claims.[388] Because the prior art always limits the literal scope defined by the claim **4.120**

[385] *Chisum on Patents*, § 18.04[1][b][ii][A].

[386] *Nystrom v. Trex Co.*, 580 F.3d 1281, 1287, 92 U.S.P.Q. 2d 1060 (Fed. Cir. 2009) (Rader, J., dissenting).

[387] E.g., *Perkin-Elmer Corp. v. Westinghouse Electric Corp.*, 822 F.2d 1528, 3 U.S.P.Q. 2d 1321 (Fed. Cir. 1987). For a general discussion on the case law development on no element vitiation rule, see *Chisum on Patents*, § 18.04[1][a].

[388] *Wilson Sporting Goods Co. v. David Geoffrey & Associates*, 904 F.2d 677, 684, 14 U.S.P.Q. 2d 1942 (Fed. Cir. 1990).

language, it also limits the extent of protection, including the range of equivalents that a patentee can claim. Moreover, the extent of protection which literally covers an accused product does not need to meet enablement or written description requirements because it includes the scope of equivalents encompassing structures, materials, and acts which are developed after issuance of patent.

4.121 To examine whether the extent of patent protection asserted by a patentee including the range of equivalents is not anticipated or obvious from the prior art, courts should compare an accused product or process as a whole with the prior art under standards of patentability consistent with the Federal Circuit case law of anticipation and nonobviousness.[389] Therefore, a substitution of a structure known or obvious to one skilled in the art of the invention with a claim element does not give rise to the prior art limitation rule. Instead, such a substitution may constitute an equivalent because it is likely that such a substitution meets the known interchangeability test.[390] Nevertheless courts may refuse to apply the doctrine of equivalents under the no element vitiation rule which prevents a patentee from asserting infringement under the doctrine of equivalents with respect to equivalents which are foreseeable at the time of filing an amendment.[391]

4.122 The prior art limitation presents a procedural challenge unique to US courts due to a different burden of proof for invalidity and infringement. When the patentee asserts literal infringement and the accused infringer alleges that the accused product is anticipated or obvious from the prior art, the issue is a defense of invalidity.[392] Thus, the accused infringer bears the burden of establishing invalidity of the asserted patent claim with clear and convincing evidence.[393] In contrast, when the patentee asserts infringement under the doctrine of equivalents and the accused infringer alleges that the accused product is anticipated or obvious from the prior art, the issue is infringement with respect to the appropriate scope of protection under the doctrine of equivalents. Alternatively, a defendant may assert that the asserted claim is invalid for obviousness from the prior art, namely the defendant's product, unless the assigner estoppel and other doctrines preclude an invalidity defense from the accused infringer.[394] The accused infringer must prove the invalidity with clear and convincing evidence and cannot simply assert that the accused device is identical or obvious from the prior art to avoid infringement.[395] To avoid the high burden of proof, the accused infringer may assert the prior art limitation rule to preclude a claim of infringement under the doctrine of equivalents. Under this scenario, the accused infringer bears the burden of going forward by presenting prior art which shows that the scope of equivalents would be anticipated or obvious from the prior art.[396] Then the burden will shift to the patentee who bears the burden of persuasion for the novelty and nonobviousness of the accused product with a preponderance of evidence.

---

389 *Abbott Labs. v. Dey, L.P.*, 287 F.3d 1097, 1105, 62 U.S.P.Q. 2d 1545 (Fed. Cir. 2002); *Conroy v. Reebok International, Ltd.*, 14 F.3d 1570, 29 U.S.P.Q. 2d 1373 (Fed. Cir. 1994).

390 See Ch. 4, 4.93.

391 See Ch. 4, 4.116.

392 *Tate Access Floors, Inc. v. Interface Architectural Resources, Inc.*, 279 F.3d 1357, 61 U.S.P.Q. 2d 1647 (Fed. Cir. 2002).

393 See Ch. 7, 7.08.

394 See Ch. 7, 7.10.

395 *Baxter Healthcare Corp. v. Spectramed, Inc.*, 49 F.3d 1575, 1583, 34 U.S.P.Q. 2d 1120, 1126 (Fed. Cir. 1995).

396 *Steamfeeder, L.L.M. v. Sure-Feed Sys., Inc.*, 175 F.3d 974, 983, 50 U.S.P.Q. 2d 1515 (Fed. Cir. 1999).

To facilitate the examination of the extent of protection asserted by a patentee through the doctrine of equivalents, the Federal Circuit proposes to use a hypothetical claim which literally covers the accused product.[397] In drafting a hypothetical claim, only slight broadening of the claim at issue to literally cover the accused product is permitted.[398] However, narrowing the asserted claim to avoid prior art is not permitted. In short, all elements of the asserted claim should remain the same except for elements which distinguish the accused product. Although the Federal Circuit views the use of a hypothetical claim as helpful, it is not mandatory for courts to use a hypothetical claim to apply the prior art limitation to examine the scope asserted by a patentee under the doctrine of equivalents.[399] **4.123**

iv. Dedication to the Public Subject matter is considered as being dedicated to the public and cannot be encompassed in the scope of protection under the doctrine of equivalents if it is disclosed in the specification but is not covered by any of claims included in the asserted patent.[400] The rule of dedication to the public prevents a patentee from capturing subject matter that a patent drafter could have reasonably foreseen and drafted a claim to literally cover.[401] Moreover, the rule also prevents a patentee from circumventing a reissue procedure which allows the patentee to broaden a patent claim to literally cover disclosed but unclaimed subject matter within two years from the issuance.[402] **4.124**

The scope of the dedication to the public rule is very narrow. In applying this rule courts must identify what is disclosed in the specification. When the specification discloses both generic and specific disclosures of a claim element, it is not clear what is explicitly disclosed in the specification. A generic disclosure may not necessarily give rise to dedication of all species in the generic disclosure except for claimed species.[403] Instead, the rule denies infringement under the doctrine of equivalents if (1) a structure or act is disclosed as an alternative to a claim element in the specification but not literally covered by any asserted claims and (2) the patentee alleges equivalence between the structure and the element.[404] The rule precludes a claim of infringement under the doctrine of equivalents with respect to a structure or act only if PHOSITA can understand the unclaimed disclosed structure or act as an alternative to the claimed element upon reading the written description. **4.125**

---

397 *Wilson Sporting Goods*, 904 F.2d, 684.

398 *Steramfeeder*, 175 F.3d, 984; *Jurgens v. McKasy*, 927 F.2d 1552, 1561, 18 U.S.P.Q. 2d 1031, 1038 (Fed. Cir. 1991).

399 *International Visual Corp. v. Crown Metal Manufacturing Co., Inc.*, 991 F.2d 768, 772, 26 U.S.P.Q. 2d 1588, 1591 (Fed. Cir. 1993); *Key Manufacturing Group, Inc. v. Microdot, Inc.*, 925 F.2d 1444, 1449, 17 U.S.P.Q. 2d 1806, 1810 (Fed. Cir. 1991).

400 *Johnson & Johnston Associates Inc. v. R.E. Service Co., Inc.*, 285 F.3d 1046, 62 U.S.P.Q. 2d 1046 (Fed. Cir. 2002) (*en banc*).

401 *Johnson & Johnston Associates Inc. v. R.E. Service Co., Inc.*, 285 F.3d 1046, 1056, 62 U.S.P.Q. 2d 1046 (Fed. Cir. 2002) (*en banc*) (Rader J., concurring).

402 See Ch. 7, 7.64.

403 *PSC Computer Products, Inc. v. Fox Conn International, Inc.*, 355 F.3d 1353, 69 U.S.P.Q. 2d 1460 (Fed. Cir. 2004).

404 *Pfizer, Inc. v. Teva Pharmaceuticals USA, Inc.*, 429 F.3d 1364, 77 U.S.P.Q. 2d 1257 (Fed. Cir. 2005).

5

GERMANY

A. Acts of Infringement

1. Direct Infringement

5.01 Acts that constitute direct infringement are defined in § 9 of the German Patent Act.[1] The acts of infringement are different for patent claims directed to products and for claims directed to processes.[2] Also, for process claims, acts of infringement can be directed to the process itself or to products directly made by the patented process.

5.02 If done without consent of the owner, the following acts constitute direct infringement of a patent claim directed to a product: making, offering, putting on the market,[3] or using the product; or importing or possessing[4] the product for these purposes.[5] With regard to a process claim, infringing acts are: using the process and offering the process for use in Germany if the third party knows, or where it is obvious under the circumstances,[6] that the use of the process is prohibited without the owner's consent.[7] For products directly made by a patented process, infringing acts are: offering, putting on the market, or using the product; or importing or possessing for these purposes the product made directly by the process.[8]

---

[1] The current version of the German Patent Act was enacted on December 16, 1980, entered into force on January 1, 1981, and has been amended several times since. The wording of the exclusive rights of the patentee as defined in § 9 is identical to the wording of the exclusive rights defined in Art. 29 of the Convention for the European Patent for the Common Market (Community Patent Convention) of 1975 (76/76/EEC) and Art. 25 of its revised version of 1989 (89/695/EEC), which aimed at establishing a unitary patent for all member states of the European Community. The Community Patent Convention never entered into force because it was not ratified by a sufficient number of member states. However, in anticipation of its entry into force, a majority of the member states of the European Community at the time adopted the definitions of the exclusive rights into their respective national patent acts. As a consequence, the definitions of the acts of infringement are harmonized throughout the patent acts of major European patent jurisdictions, including Germany, France, the UK, Italy, and the Netherlands. The definitions of the directly infringing acts in Art. 25 of the Agreement on a Unified Patent Court (2013/C 175/01), which will be determinative for the European Unitary Patent to come and the national parts of European patents which are subject to the jurisdiction of the Unified Patent Court to be established, is again practically identical to the definitions in the Community Patent Convention.

[2] Prior to 1981, the German Patent Act, similar to the US Patent Act, did not differentiate between acts of infringement of product claims and method claims; see § 6 of the German Patent Act of 1968.

[3] Art. 25(a) of the Agreement on a Unified Patent Court uses the term "placing on the market."

[4] The English version of the Community Patent Convention uses the term "stocking"; the Agreement on a Unified Patent Court uses the term "storing."

[5] German Patent Act, § 9, second sentence, No. 1.

[6] Art. 25(b) of the Agreement on a Unified Patent Court uses the term "should have known."

[7] German Patent Act, § 9, second sentence, No. 2.

[8] German Patent Act, § 9, second sentence, No. 3.

Although the acts of direct infringement listed in § 9(1)–(3) of the German Patent Act are similar to the acts listed in § 271(a) and (g) of the US Patent Act, there are some noteworthy differences in the statutory language. **5.03**

First, the German Patent Act uses the term "offering" and not the term "offering for sale," as it is used by the US Patent Act. In fact, an offer under § 9 of the German Patent Act is an act which aims to facilitate completion of any deal concerning a patented product which involves the use of this product.[9] This is the case not only for deals involving the sale of the product but also for deals like leasing, licensing, lending, or gifts.[10] An "offer," therefore, is understood more expansively than in a strict legal sense. Consequently, an offer under German patent law does not require the same elements as a binding offer under German contract law,[11] but instead encompasses any statement which objectively provides the product in such a way that the acquisition of the power of disposal can be demanded,[12] or which aims at stimulating the addressee of the statement to acquire the product for use or ownership.[13] For example, a public advertisement is not a binding offer when it merely invites the recipient to make an offer, but it can nevertheless constitute patent infringement. Moreover, the product being offered does not need to exist at the time of the offer.[14] **5.04**

German courts emphasize that the act of offering, although regularly taking place prior to the act of putting on the market, is an independent act of infringement.[15] An offer of the protected product can constitute a patent infringement even if the subsequent delivery as intended under the offer does not. For example, an offer of a patented product at a trade show in Germany for delivery of the product outside of Germany would be an infringing offer.[16] As another example, an advertisement for a pharmaceutical product a few weeks prior to the expiry date of the patent protecting the product is an infringing offer even if the advertisement makes clear that the product will be available only after the expiry date of the patent.[17] **5.05**

Second, while "selling" a patented product or product made by a patented process is an infringing act under the US Patent Act, the German Patent Act instead refers to "putting on the market" as an act of infringement.[18] Linguistically, this appears to be broader than selling. In fact, a product is put on the market by any act of transferring the actual power of **5.06**

---

[9] BGH GRUR 2003, 1031, 1032—*Kupplung für optische Geräte.*

[10] Ingo Rincken and Thomas Kühnen in R. Schulte (ed.), *Patentgesetz mit EPÜ* (9th ed., 2014), § 9, Ref. 52; BGH GRUR 1970, 358, 360—*Heißläuferdetektor.*

[11] BGH GRUR 2003, 1031, 1032—*Kupplung für optische Geräte.*

[12] Rincken and Kühnen in Schulte (ed.), *Patentgesetz mit EPÜ*, § 9, Ref. 52; BGH GRUR 1970, 358, 360—*Heißläuferdetektor*; BGH GRUR 2006, 927, 928—*Kunststoffbügel.*

[13] Uwe Scharen in G. Benkard (ed.), *Patentgesetz Gebrauchsmustergesetz* (10th ed., 2006), § 9, Ref. 41.

[14] Thomas Kühnen, *Handbuch der Patentverletzung* (6th ed. 2013), Ref. 153; BGH GRUR 1969, 35—*Europareise.*

[15] Rincken and Kühnen in Schulte (ed.), *Patentgesetz mit EPÜ*, § 9, Ref. 52; Scharen in Benkard (ed.), *Patentgesetz Gebrauchsmustergesetz*, § 9, Ref. 40; BGH GRUR 2007, 221, 222—*Simvastatin*; BGH GRUR 1969, 35, 36—*Europareise*; BGH GRUR 1955, 87, 89—*Bäckereimaschine.*

[16] OLG München, InstGE 5, 15—*Messeangebot ins Ausland II.* With regard to indirect infringement, an offer made in Germany is only infringing if the recipient of the offer plans to use the offered product in Germany, see Ch. 5, 5.36.

[17] BGH GRUR 2007, 221—*Simvastatin.*

[18] German Patent Act, § 9, second sentence, Nos. 1 and 3.

disposal of the patented product from the infringer to another person. This includes delivering the product as a gift, loan, or lease item.

5.07 Third, "possessing" a patented product or a product directly made by a patented process constitutes infringement if it is done for the purpose of committing any of the other infringing acts.[19] This makes it possible to act against the recipient of a protected product even before he offers the product, passes it on, or uses it, and thus provides protection even if there is only a threat or intent that these acts will be committed, which can be established with circumstantial evidence—for example, by looking at the field of activity of a company.[20] As a general rule, warehouse keepers, forwarding agents, or shippers do not "possess" the products for the purpose of committing infringing acts.[21] In contrast, the US Patent Act does not qualify the mere possession of a patented product as constituting infringement, although also in the United States, infringement has been found in cases where the use or sale of the product was threatened or contemplated.[22]

5.08 As with "possessing," "importing" a patented product or a product directly obtained by a patented process is patent infringement only if the product is brought into Germany for the purpose of making the product, putting the product on the market, offering, or using the product. This subjective element of the "purpose" is determined objectively from the circumstances surrounding the importing act—that is, whether the imported product can be put on the market, offered for sale, or used.[23] A mere transit of patent infringing products is no such patent infringing use, and is therefore also no patent infringing import.[24]

5.09 Fourth, unlike the US Patent Act, the German Patent Act makes a distinction between products and processes which are the subject matter of the patent, and only provides the acts of "using" and "offering for use" as acts of infringement with respect to patented processes. However, although the issue was not squarely decided, the Federal Circuit has suggested that in the United States, a process is infringed only by use. The Federal Circuit also commented that it is difficult to apply the concept of "sale" or "offer to sell" to a process because it is difficult to anticipate a transfer of property through a performance of steps, and a method does not necessarily require subject matter that is capable of being transferred.[25] Therefore, in practice, German patent law actually provides one more act of infringement with respect to patented processes, namely offering for use, than US patent law.

5.10 To give rise to infringement by "offering the process for use," the German Patent Act requires two additional elements to be fulfilled: (1) the accused infringer knows or it is obvious under the circumstances that the use of the process is prohibited without the consent of the proprietor of the patent, and (2) the offer relates to a use within the territory of

---

[19] German Patent Act, § 9, second sentence, Nos. 1 and 3.

[20] Rudolf Kraßer, *Patentrecht* (6th ed., 2009), § 33 II f).

[21] Kühnen, *Handbuch der Patentverletzung*, Ref. 179; BGH GRUR 2009, 1142, 1144 MP3-Player Import.

[22] *California Table Grape Commission v. RB Sandrini, Inc.*, 2007 U.S. Dist. LEXIS 48362 (E.D. Calif. 2007); *Amgen, Inc. v. Elanex Pharmaceuticals, Inc.*, 1996 U.S. Dist. LEXIS 22015, 1996 WL 84590, *3 (W.D. Wash. 1996); *Chisum on Patents*, § 16.02[h].

[23] Denkschrift zu Art. 29 GPÜ BIPMZ 79, 332; Scharen in Benkard (ed.), *Patentgesetz Gebrauchsmustergesetz*, § 9, Ref. 47; Rincken and Kühnen in Schulte (ed.), *Patentgesetz mit EPÜ*, § 9, Ref. 69.

[24] Rincken and Kühnen in Schulte (ed.), *Patentgesetz mit EPÜ*, § 9, Ref. 69; BGHZ 23, 100, 016—*Taeschner/Pertussin I* (a trademark case); BGH GRUR 57, 352, 353—*Taeschner/Pertussin II* (a trademark case); OLG Karlsruhe GRUR 82, 295, 299.

[25] *NTP, Inc. v. Research in Motion, Ltd.*, 418 F.3d 1282, 1319, 418 USPQ 2d 1763 (Fed. Cir. 2005).

Germany.[26] The subjective element with respect to the accused infringer's knowledge or the obviousness under the circumstances is generally satisfied constructively by the publication of the patent by the patent office.[27] The objective element with respect to the place of use of a patented process limits patent infringing offers of a process to offers which relate to the use of the process within Germany.

However, the concept of offering a process for use is a matter of dispute.[28] Merely describing the performance of the patented process does not constitute infringement, as this could be drawn from the specification of the patent itself.[29] An offer for use with regard to a process is considered in two situations: first, where the offer includes a promise that the patented process will be used by the offering party itself or at its instigation; second, where the offering party is promising to sell the patented process or grant a license to the patented process for use.[30] While some authors support the first view exclusively,[31] others only support the second view,[32] and again others—including a judgment of an appeals court—seem to accept both views.[33] **5.11**

Finally, like the US Patent Act (§ 271(g)), the German Patent Act codifies an exclusive right of the patent owner to offer, put on the market, or use or possess or import for these purposes the products obtained by a patented (manufacturing) process.[34] This right extends the protection of the process patent to cases where the process is carried out abroad but the products manufactured by the process are sold or otherwise used in Germany. **5.12**

The German Patent Act requires that the product be "made directly" by the patented process. Not only a product in which a patented process results but also a product which is subjected to subsequent processes meets the "made directly" limitation if the product retains the advantageous characteristics conferred by the patented process,[35] as well as its independence[36] through the subsequent processes.[37] This is similar to the first exception of the US Patent Act for the protection of the product made by a patented process, according to which a product is not considered to be made by a process if it is materially changed by **5.13**

---

[26] German Patent Act, § 9, second sentence, No. 2.

[27] Kraßer, *Patentrecht*, § 33 III. b) 4.

[28] Kühnen, *Handbuch der Patentverletzung*, Ref. 186; Kraßer, *Patentrecht*, § 33 III. b) 3.

[29] Kühnen, *Handbuch der Patentverletzung*, Ref. 186; Kraßer, *Patentrecht*, § 33 III. b) 3.

[30] Scharen in Benkard (ed.), *Patentgesetz Gebrauchsmustergesetz*, § 9, Ref. 52; Alfred Keukenschrijver (ed.), *Busse, Patentgesetz* (7th ed., 2013), § 9, Refs. 93 and 94; Kraßer, *Patentrecht*, § 33 III. b) 3; Kühnen, *Handbuch der Patentverletzung*, Ref. 186; OLG Düsseldorf, judgment of January 14, 2010, case No. I-2 U 10/08.

[31] Keukenschrijver (ed.), *Busse, Patentgesetz*, § 9, Ref. 94; Kraßer, *Patentrecht Patentrecht*, § 33 III. b) 4.

[32] Kühnen, *Handbuch der Patentverletzung*, Ref. 186; Ulrich Krieger, *Die Benutzungsarten*, *GRUR* (1980): 687, 690.

[33] OLG Düsseldorf, judgment of January 14, 2010, case No. I-2 U 10/08; Scharen in Benkard (ed.), *Patentgesetz Gebrauchsmustergesetz*, § 9, Ref. 52.

[34] German Patent Act, § 9, second sentence, No. 3.

[35] Kraßer, *Patentrecht*, § 33 III. c) cc) 2.; Keukenschrijver (ed.), *Busse, Patentgesetz*, § 9, Ref. 107; Kühnen, *Handbuch der Patentverletzung*, Ref. 215; LG Düsseldorf, InstGE 7, 70, at III. 2. c) aa)—*Videosignal-Codierung I*; OLG Düsseldorf, decision of January 14, 2010—I-2 U 124/08, at D. 3. b).

[36] Kühnen, *Handbuch der Patentverletzung*, Refs. 200, 205, and 214; OLG Düsseldorf, decision of January 14, 2010—I-2 U 124/08, at D. 3. b).

[37] Rincken and Kühnen in Schulte (ed.), *Patentgesetz mit EPÜ*, § 9, Ref. 90; Scharen in Benkard (ed.), *Patentgesetz Gebrauchsmustergesetz*, § 9, Ref. 55; LG Düsseldorf, InstGE 7, 70, at III. 2. c) aa)—*Videosignal-Codierung I*; OLG Düsseldorf, decision of January 14, 2010—I-2 U 124/08, at D. 3. a); OLG Karlsruhe, InstGE 11, 15, at II. 5. b) (2)—*SMD-Widerstand.*

subsequent processes.[38] However, in contrast to the US Patent Act, under the German patent law a product can be considered as being "directly made" even if the product has become a trivial and nonessential component of another product.[39] Accordingly, although the US Congress examined case law in European countries with respect to the "directly made" limitation on the product that the effect of a process patent extends to before it adopted the two exceptions under § 271(g),[40] the scope of the German process patent in this respect seems broader than the one of the US process patent.

5.14 By contrast, a product patent does not extend to another product even if the product was directly obtained by a patented product.[41] If a patent is issued to a product which is an intermediary product for an end product and the essential characteristics of this intermediary product are substantially changed and transformed into another product, the end product will not fall into the scope of the patent directed to the intermediate product.[42] Thus, using the patented product abroad for making the end product and subsequently importing the end product into Germany does not constitute infringement of the product patent.[43] This interpretation is in line with US case law.[44]

5.15 In addition to statutory differences, the interpretation of the acts of direct infringement under German case law also results in some differences to US law.

5.16 In Germany, infringement of a patented product by "making" encompasses the entire activity by which the product is manufactured, from its beginning on, and is not limited to the last act which leads directly to the completion of the patented product.[45] A person who only starts the process of making, but ultimately manufactures an unfinished product, can be a direct infringer if another person finishes the product such that the finished product realizes all elements of the claim,[46] and the acts of the other person can be attributed to the person who manufactured the unfinished product.[47] For example, the manufacturer

---

[38] US Patent Act, § 271(g)(1).

[39] Cf. Kühnen, *Handbuch der Patentverletzung*, Refs. 193 and 205, arguing that a product of a patented process can be subject to the protection even if it is distributed as an integral part of a larger composition unless it has lost its existence as an object and could not be made the subject matter of a fictitious product claim any longer. However, in an older decision, the Reichsgerichtshof gave the example of nails made by a patented process which are used for building a closet. Decision of March 31, 1897, RGZ 39, 132. The court stated that in this case, the nails have lost their independence and are not protected as the product of the patented process any longer. See also Kraßer, *Patentrecht*, § 33 III. c) cc) 6, who argues that in this situation, the nails do not enjoy protection because they can be regarded as consumed.

[40] S. No. 100-83, 100th Cong., 1st Sess. (1987). Unlike in the United States, German patent law has a long history of extending the effect of a process patent to a product, see Joseph Straus, "The Scope of Protection Conferred by European Patents on Transgenic Plants and on Methods for their Production," in P. J. Nordell (ed.), *Festschrift in Honour of Marianne Levin* (2007), 639, 652.

[41] LG Düsseldorf, GRUR 1987, 896—*Grasherbizid.*

[42] Straus, "The Scope of Protection Conferred by European Patents on Transgenic Plants," 650–52.

[43] The same is true for US product patents. *Amgen v. U.S. Int'l Trade Comm'n*, 902 F.2d 1532, 14 USPQ2d 1734 (Fed. Cir. 1990). See also Ch. 4, 4.02.

[44] *Eli Lilly & Co. v. American Cyanamid Co.*, 82 F.3d 1568 (Fed. Cir. 1996). See Ch. 4, 4.02.

[45] BGH GRUR 1951, 452, 454—*Mülltonne*; BGH GRUR 1995, 338, 341—*Kleiderbügel.*

[46] Even though the term "all elements rule" is not used in Germany, direct infringement requires that (in the end) all features of the invention as defined by the claim are realized. The scope of protection does not cover a subset or a part of the combination of the features of the patent claim. BGHZ 172, 798 (at 26 et seq.)—*Zerfallszeitmessgerät.*

[47] Cf. Scharen in Benkard (ed.), *Patentgesetz Gebrauchsmustergesetz*, § 9, Ref. 32; Kraßer, *Patentrecht*, § 33 II. b) aa) 1.

of a set including all parts of a patented product commits a patent-infringing "making" of the product itself if his customer will be able to assemble the patented product from the parts of the set without any difficulties,[48] in particular if the manufacturer instructs the customer on how the parts are to be put together.[49] When the making of the unfinished product qualifies as a patent infringement, so does the offering, putting on the market, or importing or possessing the unfinished product for these purposes.[50] According to a decision of the Dusseldorf Court of Appeal, even if the product delivered to the customer does not comprise all claim elements, there is direct infringement if the missing component is a nonessential "commonplace ingredient" and the customer already has the missing ingredient or can and will certainly obtain it, in order to combine it with the delivered product so as to form the patented product.[51]

"Using" a patented product includes any use as intended. Consumption or further processing of the patented product may also constitute infringement.[52] While merely displaying a patented product is not a use of it, the demonstration of the operation of a patented product can be found to constitute infringement.[53] **5.17**

To commit direct infringement of a process patent by "using" a patented process, the defendant must perform all measures recited in the claim, in particular use any device or means necessary for performing the process in accordance with the claim.[54] However, German courts do not require all steps recited in the claim to be performed by a single entity. **5.18**

If the defendant performs only some steps recited in a process claim and another party performs the other steps, oftentimes the steps performed by the other party are attributed to the defendant as if they were performed by the defendant himself. For example, the steps performed by a joint infringer ("*Mittäter*") are attributed to the defendant.[55] Joint infringement in accordance with § 830(1) of the German Civil Code exists if the infringing acts have been committed with deliberate and intentional collaboration in realizing the claimed process.[56] In a decision of the Dusseldorf District Court, the act performed by another party was attributed to the defendant even in a case where the third party did not collaborate deliberately. The court found that the defendant had used the other party as a "tool" to perform the last act of the claimed process such that the process was predictably and inevitably finished by the other party, and independent of any knowledge of the invention by the other party.[57] Similarly, it is irrelevant if the **5.19**

---

[48] Kraßer, *Patentrecht*, § 33 II. b) aa) 4.

[49] Cf. LG Düsseldorf, decision of August 23, 2007, case No. 4b O 198/06, at III. 1. c); OLG Düsseldorf, InstGE 13, 78—*Lungenfunktionsgerät*, at II. B. 6. a).

[50] Scharen in Benkard (ed.), *Patentgesetz Gebrauchsmustergesetz*, § 9, Ref. 35.

[51] OLG Düsseldorf, InstGE 13, 78—*Lungenfunktionsgerät*.

[52] Kraßer, *Patentrecht*, § 33 II. e) 1.

[53] Kraßer, *Patentrecht*, § 33 II. e) 2.

[54] Scharen in Benkard (ed.), *Patentgesetz Gebrauchsmustergesetz*, § 9, Ref. 49.

[55] LG Düsseldorf, GRUR-RR 2001, 201, 204—*Cam-Carpet*.

[56] Kühnen, *Handbuch der Patentverletzung*, Ref. 849; Scharen in Benkard (ed.), *Patentgesetz Gebrauchsmustergesetz*, § 10, Ref. 28; BGH GRUR 1979, 149, 152—*Schießbolzen*; OLG Düsseldorf, InstGE 6, 152, at II. 1. a).

[57] LG Düsseldorf, GRUR-RR 2001, 201, 205—*Cam-Carpet*.

infringing acts are performed by the defendant himself or by a third party who acts for the defendant.[58]

5.20 In cases concerning indirect infringement, where the recipients of devices supplied by the defendant used the devices to perform only a second part of the patented process, whereas the first part was performed by other parties, German courts found that the recipients of the devices directly infringed by using the patented process, leaving open whether the recipients and the other parties acted as joint infringers or as so-called concurrent infringers ("*Nebentäter*") who infringe by independent acts without deliberate collaboration,[59] and whether the acts of the other party could be attributed to the recipients. For example, in the case underlying a decision of the Federal Court of Justice,[60] the patented process was a welding method according to which a data carrier with welding data was created in a first set of steps, which were performed by a third party, and the data carrier was used in a second set of steps, performed with the devices supplied by the defendant, for controlling the welding activity. In the case underlying a decision of the OLG Karlsruhe,[61] the process consisted of the steps of coding and decoding, building upon each other. The coding was performed (independently) by broadcasting stations, and the decoding was performed by the end customers of the defendant with the help of the devices delivered by the defendant.

5.21 The German Patent Act includes special provisions defining acts of infringement with respect to a patent which is directed to a biological material and a process using a biological material.[62] These provisions were introduced to meet the obligation under the EU Biotechnology Directive.[63]

5.22 A biological material is defined to include any material containing genetic information and capable of reproducing itself or being reproducible in a biological system.[64] Unlike an intermediate product for making an end product, a product directly obtained by biological material through propagation or multiplication will have the same characteristics as the biological material used for obtaining the end product. Thus, the German Patent Act provides additional scope for a patent directed to biological material which has specific characteristics as a result of an invention, and extends protection of such patent to any biological material derived from a patented biological material through multiplication or propagation if the derived material is in an identical or divergent form as long as the derived material has the same characteristics of the patented biological material.[65] Because the patentability of the patented biological material was based on the characteristics which are acquired through a biological process, the derived material must have the same characteristics to claim patent protection.

---

[58] BGH GRUR 1990, 997, 999—*Ethofumesat*.

[59] Hartwig Sprau, in O. Palandt, *Bürgerliches Gesetzbuch* (71st ed., 2012), § 830, Ref. 1.

[60] BGH GRUR 2007, 773—*Rohrschweißverfahren*.

[61] OLG Karlsruhe, decision of May 8, 2013, case No. 6 U 34/12.

[62] German Patent Act, § 9a.

[63] Directive 98/44/EC of the European Parliament and of the Council of 6 July 1998 on the legal protection of biotechnological inventions, OJ L 213, July 30, 1998 P. 0013–0021.

[64] German Patent Act, § 2a(3) No. 1.

[65] German Patent Act, § 9a–c.

Patent protection of a biological material extends to any biological material derived from the patented biological material through propagation or multiplication in an identical or divergent form as long as the derived material possesses the specific characteristics resulting from the invention.[66] Similarly, if a patent is granted on a process that enables a biological material to be produced possessing specific characteristics as a result of the invention, protection of such process patent extends to any biological material directly obtained through the patented process and any other biological material derived from the directly obtained biological material through propagation or multiplication in an identical or divergent form as long as the derived material possesses the specific characteristics resulting from the invention.[67] If a patent is granted to a product which contains or consists of generic information, protection of such patent extends to all material in which the product is incorporated and in which the genetic information is contained and fulfills its function, being subject to the exceptions of non-patent eligibility of the human body and the simple discovery of an element of the human body.[68] A product patent covered by the third special provision includes any product regardless of reproducible ability. To extend the protection of such patent to a material, the material must meet all three requirements of (1) inclusion of the patented product, (2) inclusion of the generic information of the patented product, and (3) performance of the "inventive" function.[69] **5.23**

Regarding the third requirement, the Court of Justice of the European Union (CJEU) made it clear that the inventive function is the function disclosed in the specification of the asserted patent to support industrial applicability because the EU Biotechnology Directive provides that a disclosure of industrial application is necessary for a product including or consisting of genetic information such as a DNA sequence to be patentable.[70] The CJEU also held that a product must perform the inventive function at the time of the alleged infringement, the actual time in which the genetic information is found, and the patent is enforced against a material which includes the patented product containing or consisting of the genetic information.[71] Whether the genetic information in the material could perform the inventive function or would be able to perform the function after the genetic information is extracted from the product is irrelevant. **5.24**

2. Indirect Infringement

Similar to US law, a defendant in Germany may be liable for patent infringement even if he himself did not directly use the patented invention. Someone who aids and abets the direct patent infringement by another is liable for patent infringement as an accessory, in the same way as the direct infringer is liable.[72] Liability as an accessory requires intent both on the **5.25**

[66] German Patent Act, § 9a(1).

[67] German Patent Act, § 9a(2).

[68] German Patent Act, § 9a(3). The German Patent Act uses the term "fulfills" (*erfüllt*) instead of the term "performs," which is used in the EU Biotechnology Directive. The exception for non-patent eligibility of the human body and the simple discovery of an element of the human body is provided in German Patent Act, § 1a(1).

[69] Straus, "The Scope of Protection Conferred by European Patents on Transgenic Plants," 649.

[70] Case C-428/08, *Monsanto Technology v. Cefetra*, Court of Justice of the European Union, 6 July 2010. See Jan Krauss and Toshiko Takenaka, "A Special Rule for Compound Protection for DNA-Sequences: Impact of the ECJ "Monsanto" Decision on Patent Practice," 93 *J. Pat. & Trademark Off. Soc'y* (2011): 189–206; Michael Kock, "Patent Protection for DNA Sequences: To Be or Not to Be?," 5 *JIPLP* (2010): 754.

[71] *Monsanto Technology v. Cefetra*, para. 45.

[72] Kraßer, *Patentrecht*, § 33 VII 1; Kühnen, *Handbuch der Patentverletzung*, Ref. 849. This type of infringement is not codified in the German Patent Act, but it is prohibited under the general tort provision of § 830(2) of the German Civil Code.

part of the direct infringer and on the part of the accessory, including knowledge of the patent and its scope of its protection.[73] However, in practice the far more relevant form of non-direct infringement is "indirect patent infringement." Whereas in the United States, the term "indirect infringement" encompasses several types of non-direct infringement, like inducement or contributory infringement, in Europe the term is used to denote the specific offense as defined in § 10 of the German Patent Act.[74]

5.26 Indirect infringement is committed by offering or supplying in Germany, without the consent of the patent owner, to any person not entitled to exploit a patented invention, means which relate to an essential element of the invention, for putting it into effect within Germany, when the third party knows, or if it is obvious under the circumstances, that these means are suitable and intended for being used for putting that invention into effect.[75] However, such offering or supplying of means does not constitute indirect infringement if the means being offered or supplied are staple products available in commerce, except where the offerer or supplier of the means induces the person supplied to engage in direct infringement.[76] Persons performing acts under the private use exemption, the experimental use exemption, the breeder's exemption, the clinical trial exemption, or the pharmacy exemption under the German Patent Act are not considered to be persons entitled to exploit the patented invention.[77]

5.27 Typical scenarios of indirect infringement include (1) the offer or supply of a device with which a protected process can be carried out (e.g. an MP3 player which performs a protected decoding method when playing back music);[78] (2) the offer or supply of a part (e.g., a memory chip) which when combined with other parts (e.g., a memory controller) realizes an overall device or system protected by the patent (e.g., a system comprising a memory chip and a memory controller);[79] or (3) the offer or supply of a machine for manufacturing a patented product (e.g., a machine for producing a patented chemical).[80] The three cases have in common that the defendant, who offers or supplies the means, does not commit direct patent infringement, but the defendant's customers do. It will often be impossible or at least economically inefficient to enforce the patent against the direct infringers, because of the sheer number of customers or the difficulty in identifying them or proving that they used the means supplied to them for direct patent infringement. German Patent Act, § 10 facilitates patent enforcement in this situation by allowing the plaintiff to sue the supplier, and therefore to "get down to the root of the trouble."[81]

---

[73] LG Mannheim, GRUR-RR 2013, 449, 451—*Seitenaufprall-Schutzeinrichtung*.

[74] German Patent Act, § 10 was introduced with the enactment of the Patent Act which entered into force on January 1, 1981. The wording of the rights of the patentee as defined in § 10 is identical to the wording of the rights defined in Art. 30 of the Community Patent Convention of 1975 and Art. 26 of its revised version of 1989 (see n. 1 above). The definition of indirect patent infringement in Art. 26 of the Agreement on a Unified Patent Court (see n. 1 above) is again practically identical to the definition in the Community Patent Convention, except that the expression "when the third party knows, or it is obvious in the circumstances" has been replaced by the expression "when the third party knows, or should have known."

[75] German Patent Act, § 10(1).

[76] Ibid. § 10(2).

[77] Ibid. § 10(3). The mentioned exemptions are discussed in Ch. 5, 5.52–5.54.

[78] Cf. Kühnen, *Handbuch der Patentverletzung*, Ref. 230. This case corresponds to the "material or apparatus for use in practicing a patented process" recited in § 271(c) of the US Patent Act.

[79] Cf. Kühnen, *Handbuch der Patentverletzung*, Ref. 231. This case corresponds to the "component of a patented machine, manufacture, combination or composition" recited in § 271(c) of the US Patent Act.

[80] Cf. Kühnen, *Handbuch der Patentverletzung*, Ref. 232.

[81] BGH GRUR 1961, 627—*Metallspritzverfahren*.

It prohibits the offer and the supply of means to an unauthorized third party which enable the third party to use the patented invention.[82] Since it aims to prevent the unauthorized use in advance, it is said to establish an offense for creating the danger of a patent infringement.[83] In fact, indirect infringement only requires that there is a danger of a direct patent infringement, but it is an offense on its own, and direct infringement is not required to show indirect infringement.[84]

Since offering or supplying a means to persons who are entitled to exploit the patented invention under the private use exemption and other exemptions can be indirect infringement,[85] the plaintiff can enforce the patent even in cases where the law does not provide a basis for preventing direct use of the invention.[86] The introduction of Patent Act, § 10 therefore effectively enlarged the reach of patent protection. **5.28**

The objective elements for finding indirect infringement are that (1) the defendant offers or supplies within Germany (2) "means" which relate to an essential element of the invention and (3) are objectively suitable to put the invention into effect (4) to a person not entitled to use the invention, and without consent of the patent owner. **5.29**

First, indirect infringement can only exist if the defendant offers or supplies a means. According to a decision of the Federal Court of Justice, "means" within the meaning of Patent Act, § 10 are physical objects.[87] However, lower-instance courts have found that the means can also be non-physical objects such as software.[88] The infringing act of "offering" is the same as the "offering" for direct infringement. A "supply" requires that the means be handed over to a third person, but the third person does not have to be identical to the person using the means in the end.[89] As a consequence of the principle of territoriality, the offer or the supply has to take place in Germany. "Making," "possessing," or "importing" the means are not acts of indirect patent infringement, which shows that these acts, unlike **5.30**

---

[82] BGH GRUR 1992, 40, 42—*Beheizbarer Atemluftschlauch.*

[83] "*Gefährdungstatbestand.*" BGH GRUR 1992, 40, 42—*Beheizbarer Atemluftschlauch*; BGH GRUR 2004, 758, 760—*Flügelradzähler*; BGH GRUR 2004, 845, 848—*Drehzahlermittlung*; BGH GRUR 2006, 839, 841; BGH GRUR 2007, 313, 316—*Funkuhr II*; BGH GRUR 2007, 773, 775—*Rohrschweißverfahren*; BGH GRUR 2012, 1230, 1235—*MPEG-2 Videosignalcodierung.*

[84] BGH GRUR 2001, 228, 231—*Luftheizgerät*; Scharen in Benkard (ed.), *Patentgesetz Gebrauchsmustergesetz*, § 10, Ref. 3; Keukenschrijver (ed.), *Busse, Patentgesetz*, § 10, Ref. 10; Rinken and Kühnen in Schulte (ed.), *Patentgesetz mit EPÜ*, § 10, Ref. 5. This was different prior to the enactment of Patent Act, § 10 in 1980. Under the old law, jurisprudence had developed a doctrine of indirect infringement under the theory of a special form of participation in (i.e., aiding and abetting) the commission of a tort by another, which is a remarkable parallel to US law prior to the enactment of the US Patent Act, §§ 271(b) and (c). As a rule, there could be no indirect infringement without direct infringement. BGH GRUR 1982, 165—*Rigg*; Kraßer, *Patentrecht*, § 33 VI a) 1. However, the defendant could be made the subject of an injunction arising from the supply of a means prior to the commission of indirect infringement, if there was a sufficient likelihood that the means would be used for direct patent infringement. Therefore, for obtaining an injunction, even under the old law the plaintiff did not necessarily have to prove direct infringement. See BGH GRUR 1964, 496—*Formsand II.*

[85] Patent Act, § 10(3).

[86] This was not true prior to the enactment of Patent Act, § 10. Since the old law required direct infringement for there to be indirect infringement (see n. 129 above), indirect infringement could be ruled out if the means supplied by the defendant was used, e.g., only for private purposes. BGH GRUR 1982, 165, 167—*Formsand II.*

[87] BGH GRUR 2001, 228, 231—*Luftheizgerät.*

[88] See decisions cited by Keukenschrijver (ed.), *Busse, Patentgesetz*, § 10, Ref. 15.

[89] Scharen in Benkard (ed.), *Patentgesetz Gebrauchsmustergesetz*, § 10, Ref. 13.

"offering" or "supplying," are not considered to pose such a great danger of a direct patent infringement that they need to be prohibited.[90]

5.31 Second, only those means come into consideration which "relate to an essential element of the invention." By virtue of their functioning, the means must be capable of resulting in interacting with the subject matter of protection,[91] otherwise there would be no danger of a (direct) patent infringement which the provisions of indirect infringement seek to prevent. In principle, every element mentioned in the patent claim is an "essential" element of the invention.[92] However, a claim element can be regarded as nonessential if it makes no contribution to the solution to the technical problem solved by the patented invention. For instance, if the invention is concerned with the improvement of a certain function of a device, a claim element related to a different function, not concerned by the invention, can be a nonessential element.[93] The "means" themselves do not have to be an element of the claimed product or an element mentioned in the claimed method. The statute only requires that the means "relate" to an essential element of the invention, which is interpreted by the Federal Court of Justice to be satisfied if the means functionally interact with such an element for the realization of the inventive concept.[94] This excludes means, such as the energy needed for the operation of a protected machine, which can be used when exploiting the invention but which contribute nothing to the realization of the technical teaching of the invention.[95] The means do not need to be adapted to the inventive concept of the patent,[96] and they can be means which were known in the prior art.[97] As a consequence, the offer or supply of means suitable for substantial non-infringing use, or means which were on sale already prior to the priority date of the patent, can constitute indirect patent infringement. This is very far-reaching, and since an absolute prohibition of the supply of such means is not the purpose of § 10, the distinction between indirect infringement and non-infringement will oftentimes need to rely on the subjective elements of indirect infringement, in particular the intended use of the means (See Chapter 5, 5.35).

5.32 Third, the means have to be objectively suitable to put the invention into effect. This is the case if, from an objective point of view, it is not against all odds that the means are used on the occasion of a direct patent infringement.[98] This will regularly already be true if the means relate to an essential element of the invention.[99]

---

[90] In the United States, contributory infringement can be committed by importing (in addition to selling and offering to sell). US Patent Act, § 271(c).

[91] Cf. BGH GRUR 2004, 758, 760—*Flügelradzähler*; BGH GRUR 2005, 848, 849—*Antriebsscheibenaufzug*; BGH GRUR 2012, 1230, 1235—*MPEG-2 Videosignalcodierung*.

[92] BGH GRUR 2004, 758, 761—*Flügelradzähler*.

[93] BGH GRUR 2007, 769, 771—*Pipettensystem*.

[94] BGH GRUR 2004, 758, 761—*Flügelradzähler*.

[95] Ibid. In BGH GRUR 2012, 1230, 1235—*MPEG-2 Videosignalcodierung*, the court found that a DVD comprising data which can be converted into video images by a patented decoding process does not relate to an essential element of the invention. The data carried by the DVD does not functionally interact with the decoding system during decoding, but forms the object and the starting point of the decoding.

[96] BGH GRUR 2004, 758, 760—*Flügelradzähler*. This is in contrast to US Patent Act, § 271(c), defining contributory infringement and requiring that the component or material or apparatus is "especially made or especially adapted for use in an infringement of such patent."

[97] BGH GRUR 2004, 758, 761—*Flügelradzähler*; BGH GRUR 2007, 769, 771—*Pipettensystem*.

[98] Scharen in Benkard (ed.), *Patentgesetz Gebrauchsmustergesetz*, § 10, Ref. 5.

[99] Kraßer, *Patentrecht*, § 33 VI b) 5. According to Scharen, the suitability of the means for putting the invention into effect is not an independent objective element of indirect infringement, but it is already examined in the context of the examination of whether the means relates to an essential element of the invention.

Finally, the person to whom the means are offered or supplied must not be entitled to exploit the invention and, of course, there must be no consent of the patent owner. For example, if the person using the means is allowed to do so under a license, then there is no indirect infringement by the supplier. A person may also be entitled to exploit the invention under one of the exemptions to patent infringement as defined in Patent Act, § 11. However, in the case of the private use exemption and a number of other exemptions, the supplier would still commit indirect patent infringement.[100] One question that often arises in this context is whether the replacement of a component which is an essential means of a patented product is only a repair or whether it constitutes a new making of the patented product. Repair is regarded as a normal use of the product, to which the purchaser of the product is entitled under the exhaustion of rights doctrine, and therefore the supplier of the component does not commit indirect infringement. On the other hand, indirect infringement exists if the result of the replacement is a new making of the patented product because the exhaustion of rights doctrine does not apply to "making." The relevant factor in distinguishing between repair and new making is whether the identity of the product is maintained in light of the specific characteristics, effects, and advantages of the invention.[101] Replacement of a wear part (i.e., a part subject to wear), which can be expected to be replaced during the lifetime of the product, is generally permissible use.[102] Exceptions exist where the effects of the invention become manifest specifically in the wear part, for instance because the invention improves the functioning or extends the service life of the wear part.[103] In this case, precisely the replacement of that part realizes the technical and economic advantages of the invention.[104] **5.33**

The subjective elements of indirect infringement are, on the part of the addressee of the offer or supply, the intention to use the means for putting the invention into effect in Germany; and on the part of the supplier, knowledge of the objective suitability and of the intended use, or that they are obvious under the circumstances. **5.34**

While actual use of the means and thus direct infringement is not required,[105] the question of whether or not there is indirect infringement hinges on the intention of the recipient of the offer or supply of the means to use the means in a way that directly infringes the patent. The subjective elements of indirect infringement must be satisfied at the time of the infringing act (offer or supply).[106] In the case of an offer, when the addressee receives the offer for the first time, he will hardly have already made a decision of how he is going to use the means.[107] Furthermore, the addressee's true intention can be difficult to prove. The subjective element is therefore already satisfied if, on an objective analysis under the circumstances from the point of view of the supplier, there is a sufficiently certain expectation that the addressee will decide to use the means offered or supplied to him in a patent infringing **5.35**

Uwe Scharen, "Die Behandlung der (so genannten) mittelbaren Patentverletzung in der Rechtsprechung des Bundesgerichtshofs," GRUR (2008): 944, 945.

[100] German Patent Act, § 10(3).

[101] BGH GRUR 2004, 758, 762—*Flügelradzähler*; BGH GRUR 2007, 772—*Pipettensystem*.

[102] Kühnen, *Handbuch der Patentverletzung*, Ref. 1548.

[103] BGH GRUR 2007, 772—*Pipettensystem*.

[104] BGH GRUR 2004, 758, 762—*Flügelradzähler*.

[105] n. 85 above.

[106] BGH GRUR 2007, 679, 684—*Haubenstrechautomat*.

[107] Scharen, "Die Behandlung der (so genannten) mittelbaren Patentverletzung in der Rechtsprechung des Bundesgerichtshofs," 947.

way.[108] If the means has no substantial non-infringing use, it will normally be obvious that the recipient will use the means for infringement.[109] If the means can be used both in an infringing way and in a non-infringing way, a sufficient level of expectation typically exists if the supplier himself has suggested or recommended the infringing use,[110] such as in the operating manual, because it can be expected that the recipient will follow the suggestions or recommendations of the supplier.

5.36 Indirect infringement requires not only that the infringing act of offering or supplying the means takes place in Germany, but also the intended use of the means.[111] This is referred to as the "double territoriality requirement"[112] and results from the purpose of indirect infringement to prevent the danger of direct patent infringement.[113] If the recipient of the means only intends to use the means abroad, there is no threat of a direct infringement in Germany.

5.37 If the means are staple commercial products, there are stricter requirements for the subjective elements.[114] In this case, it is not sufficient that the indirect infringer knows or it is obvious that the recipient intends to use the means for direct infringement. Liability exists only if the indirect infringer induces the person supplied to commit direct infringement.[115] This is similar to inducement under § 271(b) of the US Patent Act.

5.38 The rules for remedies in the case of indirect infringement have some particularities. Where there is a technically and economically sensible non-infringing use of the means, an absolute cease and desist order cannot in general be issued. Only a limited prohibition will be justified, which ensures that, on the one hand, the distribution of the means for use outside the scope of the patent is not unduly restrained and, on the other hand, infringing use by the recipients can be ruled out with sufficient certainty.[116] For example, a warning notice to the recipient that a certain use of the means constitutes a patent infringement and may not be performed without the consent of the patent owner can be suitable in certain cases to avert the threat of such use.[117] In other cases, a contractual obligation of the recipient not

[108] BGH GRUR 2006, 839, 841—*Deckenheizung*.

[109] BGH GRUR 2007, 679, 684—*Haubenstrechautomat*; Scharen, "Die Behandlung der (so genannten) mittelbaren Patentverletzung in der Rechtsprechung des Bundesgerichtshofs," 996; Kühnen, *Handbuch der Patentverletzung*, Ref. 256.

[110] BGH GRUR 2006, 839, 841—*Deckenheizung*; BGH GRUR 2007, 679, 684—*Haubenstrechautomat*; Kühnen, *Handbuch der Patentverletzung*, Ref. 257.

[111] This follows already from the formulation of German Patent Act, § 10, which prohibits offering or supplying means for putting the invention into effect within Germany.

[112] "*Doppelter Inlandsbezug*." Theo Bodewig, "Praktische Probleme bei der Abwicklung der Rechtsfolgen einer Patentverletzung—Unterlassung, Beseitigung, Auskunft," *GRUR* (2005): 632, 633; Scharen in Benkard (ed.), *Patentgesetz Gebrauchsmustergesetz*, § 10, Ref. 14; Peter Meier Beck, "Die Rechtsprechung des Bundesgerichtshofs zum Patent- und Gebrauchsmusterrecht im Jahr 2007," *GRUR* (2008): 1033, 1038.

[113] Kühnen, *Handbuch der Patentverletzung*, Ref. 249.

[114] BGH GRUR 2004, 758, 761—*Flügelradzähler*.

[115] German Patent Act, § 10(2).

[116] Kühnen, *Handbuch der Patentverletzung*, Ref. 270; BGH GRUR 2006, 839, 842—*Deckenheizung*.

[117] BGH GRUR 2006, 839, 842—*Deckenheizung*. Such a warning notice will not be effective where the recipient or end user of the means is a user whose activities are covered by any of the exemptions of German Patent Act, § 11 Nos. 1–3. In a case where the means (coffee pads) were primarily used by private users, who are covered by the private use exemption (Ch. 5, 5.52), the Dusseldorf Court of Appeal found that the defendant can be obliged to print a note on the package of the means, saying that the means are only suitable for use in a non-infringing way (only suitable for use in conventional espresso machines), even though this statement was factually wrong.

to use the means in a certain way can be justified, but normally the defendant cannot be obliged to demand from the recipients an undertaking to pay a contractual penalty to the patent owner in case they use the means in an infringing way.[118] As a minimum, the patent owner can demand that any hint on the packaging of the means be removed if it might give the user the idea that the means are suitable for infringing use.[119]

If there is substantial non-infringing use, an absolute prohibition is justified only in exceptional circumstances—for example, if neither a warning notice nor a contractual penalty agreement can offer any guarantee to be effective and the defendant can reasonably be asked to modify the means such that they are no longer suitable for infringing use,[120] or if the means can easily be modified such that they are no longer suitable for infringing use, without losing their suitability for non-infringing use.[121] This will often be the case if the means are specifically adapted for infringing use and the adaptation does not improve the suitability for non-infringing use. An unlimited cease and desist order should also be justified when the means have an optional functionality which does not necessarily have to be used, but, if this optional functionality is used, then only in an infringing way. In this case, although the overall means have non-infringing uses, the optional functionality has no non-infringing use and should therefore be removed or modified. **5.39**

The indirect infringer is liable only for the damages which are caused by directly infringing use by the recipient of the means.[122] No damages have to be paid for supplies to recipients who subsequently do not use the means for infringement, even if infringing use was originally intended. The patent owner often has difficulties in proving his damages where the means have non-infringing uses, and not even the defendant can tell which of his customers uses the means in an infringing way. The patent owner may then have to rely on witness testimony from the recipients or their employees.[123] It has been argued that in the case of mass consumer products, the court should be allowed to estimate the number of directly patent infringing users.[124] **5.40**

3. Extraterritorial Infringement

According to the principle of territoriality, a German patent can only be infringed where it accords the patent owner exclusive rights and thus, is limited geographically to the territory of Germany.[125] However, this does not mean that foreign activities are always irrelevant for finding infringement in Germany. **5.41**

[118] OLG Düsseldorf, GRUR-RR 2006, 39, 42—*Kaffee-Filterpads*; Scharen in Benkard (ed.), *Patentgesetz Gebrauchsmustergesetz*, § 10, Ref. 24; Kraßer, *Patentrecht*, § 33 VI b) 7.

[119] OLG Düsseldorf, GRUR-RR 2006, 39, 42—*Kaffee-Filterpads*. E.g., removal of the indication that the means is suitable for or compatible with certain types of coffee machines.

[120] Kühnen, *Handbuch der Patentverletzung*, Ref. 274; OLG Düsseldorf, GRUR-RR 2004, 346, 349—*Rohrschweißverfahren*.

[121] Kühnen, *Handbuch der Patentverletzung*, Ref. 275; LG Düsseldorf, InstGE 5, 173—*Wandverkleidung*; OLG Düsseldorf, case No. I-2 U 137/10.

[122] BGH GRUR 2005, 848, 854—*Antriebsscheibenaufzug*; BGH GRUR 2013, 713, 714—*Fräsverfahren*.

[123] E.g., in LG Düsseldorf, InstGE 13, 97—*Oberflächenbehandlung*, the court, after hearing witnesses, was convinced that six of the defendant's customers used the means supplied to them in a directly infringing way, but the court found that for a number of other customers, the plaintiff could not show the alleged infringing use.

[124] Kühnen, *Handbuch der Patentverletzung*, Ref. 1032.

[125] Scharen in Benkard (ed.), *Patentgesetz Gebrauchsmustergesetz*, § 9, Ref. 44.

5.42 If an activity takes place partly in Germany and this part by itself constitutes an act of infringement, the domestic activity constitutes infringement.[126]

5.43 Where an offer is made in a telephone call, a fax, a letter, an email, etc., if either the place from where the offer is sent, or the place where the offer is received is located in Germany, the offer is deemed to be made in Germany.[127] If both the person making an offer and the person initially receiving the offer are located outside of Germany, such as in a foreign trade show, infringement can exist if the initial recipient forwards the offer to a person located in Germany who is involved in making a decision about the offer.[128] However, it would be necessary to prove that the offering party could have recognized that the offer is forwarded to a location within Germany. Also, by using a disclaimer or other means, an offer being made outside of Germany can be limited to outside of Germany.

5.44 Similar considerations have to be made with regard to offers on websites. However, the mere fact that an offer can be accessed from Germany is not sufficient to constitute infringement. Instead, there has to be an economically relevant link to Germany[129]—for example, an offer in the German language,[130] the reference to a subsidiary in Germany,[131] or the acceptance of orders for supplies to locations in Germany.[132] Again, a disclaimer can be used to limit the geographical scope of the offer.[133]

5.45 A product is deemed to be put on the market or supplied in Germany even if it is sent from outside Germany to Germany (import), at least if the importer obtains power of disposal in Germany,[134] and there is no mere transit of the product.[135] A product is also deemed to be put on the market or supplied in Germany if it is sent from Germany to outside Germany (export).[136] However, exports from Germany usually do not constitute indirect infringement in Germany because even though the supply is considered to take place in Germany, the exported means are not supplied for use of the invention in Germany, as is required under the principle of double territoriality.[137] An exception to this rule was found by the Federal Court of Justice where the defendant supplied gear boxes from Germany to a manufacturer in Hong Kong, knowing that the manufacturer would integrate the gear boxes in directly patent infringing radio-controlled clocks and then distribute the clocks in Germany.[138] In this case, not only was the supply deemed to take place in Germany, it was also a supply for use of the means in the directly infringing final product in Germany.

[126] Ibid. § 9, Ref. 10.

[127] Kühnen, *Handbuch der Patentverletzung*, Ref. 164; LG Düsseldorf GRUR 1953, 285; LG Düsseldorf GRUR 1970, 550, 551—*Diazepam*.

[128] OLG Düsseldorf, case No. I-2 U 134/10—*Run-Flat-Vorrichtung*.

[129] BGH GRUR 2005, 431—*Hotel-Maritime* (a trademark case); OLG Düsseldorf, OLG-Report 2008, 672.

[130] BGH GRUR 2006, 513—*Arzneimittelwerbung im Internet* (an unfair competition case).

[131] OLG Düsseldorf, GRUR RR 2007, 259—*Thermocycler*.

[132] LG Düsseldorf, judgment of February 5, 2002, case No. 4a O 33/01—*Sohlen für Sportschuhe*.

[133] Kühnen, *Handbuch der Patentverletzung*, Ref. 174; BGH GRUR 2006, 513—*Arzneimittelwerbung im Internet*.

[134] OLG Hamburg, GRUR Int. 91, 301—*Thrimothprim*.

[135] BGH I ZR 39/55, GRUR 1957, 231—*Taeschner* (a trademark case).

[136] BGH I ZR 39/55, GRUR 1957, 231—*Taeschner* (a trademark case).

[137] See Ch. 5, 5.36.

[138] BGH GRUR 2007, 313—*Funkuhr II*.

A process claim was found to be infringed where at least one of the steps of the claimed process is performed within Germany although the other steps are performed only outside of Germany.[139] According to this decision, process steps realized by the defendant or by a third party outside Germany can be attributed to the steps realized within Germany, and therefore be treated as if they were performed in Germany, if the defendant appropriates the method steps realized abroad and takes advantage of them so that the result of infringement takes place in Germany. The activity abroad must be purposefully tailored to have an effect in Germany.[140] This case law provides the patent owner with the ability to act against an infringer who attempts to circumvent a patent by locating parts of the system abroad, particularly in the telecommunication industry. In this regard, the position of the patent owner is stronger than in the United States, where it was held that a process patent is not used within the United States unless each of the steps is performed there.[141] Under the US approach, when a part of the steps are carried out in the United States and another part is carried out in another country, there would be infringement neither in the United States nor in the other country. **5.46**

Even if the defendant's activity seemingly takes place entirely outside of Germany, courts have found infringement of German patents. **5.47**

In a case where a defendant domiciled in Hong Kong delivered patent infringing radio clocks from Hong Kong to a recipient in Germany, the Federal Court of Justice noted that it was irrelevant whether and until which moment in time the defendant was in possession or ownership of the clocks.[142] For liability of the defendant, it was sufficient that the defendant supplied the clocks with knowledge of the patent and of the country of destination, thereby knowingly and intentionally contributing to the causation of the distribution in Germany. This was true even if the defendant did not act as a joint infringer or aided and abetted the infringement by the recipient but only acted as an independent concurrent infringer[143]—that is, without deliberate collaboration with the recipient.[144] **5.48**

Based on this decision of the Federal Court of Justice, the Dusseldorf and the Mannheim District Courts found that the delivery of an infringing product outside of Germany was a direct patent infringement in Germany, where the supplier knew that the recipient would distribute in Germany at least a part of the products delivered to him outside of Germany.[145] The Mannheim District Court argued that the required link to the German territory is **5.49**

139 OLG Düsseldorf, judgment of December 10, 2009, case No. I-2 U 51/08, BeckRS 2010, 12415.

140 OLG Düsseldorf, judgment of December 10, 2009, case No. I-2 U 51/08, BeckRS 2010, 12415, at B 2. a) bb).

141 *NTP, Inc. v. Research in Motion, Ltd.*, 418 F.3d 1282, 1318 (Fed. Cir. 2005).

142 BGH GRUR 2002, 599—*Funkuhr I.*

143 "*Nebentäter*," see n. 60.

144 BGH GRUR 2002, 599—*Funkuhr I.*

145 LG Düsseldorf, judgment of February 28, 2003, case No. 4a O 311/02, at III.1; LG Mannheim, judgment of August 26, 2005, case No. 7 O 506/04, at I. However, the 7th Chamber of the Mannheim District Court, in a different composition, recently found that there is an additional requirement for the liability of the supplier in such a case: the supplier must violate a legal obligation to verify an accusation of patent infringement and to act accordingly. Such an obligation regularly comes into existence if the supplier is made aware—e.g., by a warning letter—of the possibility of a patent infringement by his recipient's distribution of the supplied products in Germany. LG Mannheim, GRUR-RR 2013, 449—*Seitenaufprall-Schutzeinrichtung.*

created by the supplier's knowingly and intentionally facilitating infringement in Germany. This broad assumption of jurisdiction by German courts provides the patent owner with the possibility of suing the foreign supplier instead of the infringer directly acting in Germany. This is useful for the patent owner if he wants to avoid suing the recipient, such as because the recipient is not only the foreign supplier's but also his own customer, as is frequently the case in the car industry.[146] Where the recipient is a large car manufacturer, the foreign supplier (and competitor of the patent owner) will practically always know that a part of the supplied products will end up being built into cars delivered to Germany.

5.50 The above-described rational was also applied by German courts in cases where the recipient only committed indirect infringement in Germany. In these cases, the defendant supplied to the recipient outside of Germany a means which the recipient subsequently distributed in Germany, where it was assembled with other parts by the end users to build a patent-infringing overall device,[147] or where it was used by the end users to carry out a patented process.[148] The courts found that the suppliers acting outside Germany were liable for indirect patent infringement in Germany. The principle of double territoriality,[149] which requires that, in indirect infringement cases, not only the intended use but also the supply of the means takes place in Germany, was satisfied because, although the defendants supplied the means outside of Germany, by doing so they knowingly and intentionally contributed to the causation of the distribution of the means in Germany.[150]

4. Exemptions to Patent Infringement

5.51 The German Patent Act codifies in § 11 a number of exemptions to patent infringement, relating to certain typically non-industrial forms of use (private use, experimental use, and use by pharmacies), and to international traffic.[151] What the different exemptions have in common is the desire of the legislator to find a balance of interests between the patent owners and the general public.[152]

---

[146] In the cases underlying LG Mannheim, judgment of June 25, 2004, case No. 7 O 412/03; LG Mannheim, case No. 7 O 506/04; LG Mannheim, GRUR-RR 2013, 449, the patent owner and the defendant were competing car suppliers, and the party acting directly in Germany was a car manufacturer.

[147] OLG Düsseldorf, judgment of May 5, 2011, case No. I-2 U 9/10 and 2 U 9/10.

[148] OLG Karlsruhe, GRUR 2014, 59—*MP2-Geräte*.

[149] Ch. 5, 5.36.

[150] OLG Düsseldorf, case No. I-2 U 9/10 and 2 U 9/10, at II.A.2; OLG Karlsruhe, GRUR 2014, 59—*MP2-Geräte*, at C.2.d). In contrast, the requirement of double territoriality was found not satisfied by the Mannheim District Court in a case where the defendant supplied to the recipient outside of Germany a means, which the recipient assembled, still outside of Germany, with other parts to realize a patent infringing overall device, which was then distributed by the recipient in Germany. LG Mannheim, case No. 7 O 412/03. In this case, like in the two cases discussed above, the acts of the defendant, had they occurred in Germany, would have constituted indirect infringement. However, unlike in the two cases discussed above, the recipient in this case acted as a direct infringer, not as an indirect infringer.

[151] The wording of the exemptions as defined in § 11 Nos. 1–6, which was introduced to the Patent Act in 1981, is identical to the wording of the exemptions defined in Art. 31 of the Community Patent Convention of 1975 and Art. 27 of its revised version of 1989 (see n. 1). The breeder's exemption of § 11 No. 2a was added 1997, and the clinical trial exception of § 11 No. 2b in 2005. Article 27 of the Agreement on a Unified Patent Court (see n. 1) lists in paras. (a)–(h) the same exemptions as German Patent Act, § 11. In addition, it lists in paras. (i) and (j) the farmer's privilege, which in the German Patent Act is codified in § 9c, and in paras. (k) and (l) the acts allowed under Arts. 5 and 6 of Directive 2009/24/EC on the legal protection of computer programs and under Art. 10 of Directive 98/44/EC on the legal protection of biotechnological inventions.

[152] BGH GRUR 1996, 109, 113—*Klinische Versuche*.

In Germany, patents are regarded as instruments of economic activity which are not meant to interfere with the private domain. Therefore, unlike in the United States, the rights conferred by a patent do not extend to acts which are done privately and for non-economic purposes.[153] Both requirements have to be fulfilled cumulatively. Acts performed for non-economic purposes but outside the private sphere—for instance, by a municipality, a school, or a church—are not exempted.[154] The same is true for acts performed within the private sphere but for purposes of profit-making, such as a medical doctor using a patented computer at home for administrative work concerning his medical practise.[155] **5.52**

One of the primary purposes of the patent system is to contribute to the development of technology. The patent system should not hinder or slow down the development. Therefore, acts done for experimental purposes relating to the subject matter of the patented invention are exempted from patent infringement.[156] The exemption is only applicable if the object of the experimental act is gaining insights about the subject matter of the invention, such as testing its usability or finding improvements or new applications.[157] Not exempted are acts in which the invention is used as an experimental tool,[158] or experiments which only serve the purpose of testing economic factors like market demand, price acceptance, and sales opportunities.[159] **5.53**

The experimental use exemption is complemented by the exemption of the use of biological material for the purpose of breeding, discovering, or developing a new plant variety,[160] which also covers acts in which the invention is used as a tool[161] but does not cover the exploitation of the new plant variety,[162] and by the exemption of studies and trials and the resulting practical requirements necessary for obtaining a marketing authorization to place a medicinal product on the market in the European Union or marketing approval for a medicinal product in any country.[163] The latter is a so-called Roche-Bolar exemption[164] and enables companies, such as generics companies, to perform all acts (not only experiments) necessary for obtaining a marketing authorization or approval for a medicinal product already during the lifetime of the patent. This enables the generics company to have the approval by the day the patent expires.[165] **5.54**

There is an exemption of instantaneous preparation of medicine in pharmacies, based on medical prescription, and acts concerning the medicine so prepared,[166] which ensures the **5.55**

---

153 German Patent Act, § 11 No. 1.

154 Scharen in Benkard (ed.), *Patentgesetz Gebrauchsmustergesetz* Benkard (ed.), *Patentgesetz Gebrauchsmustergesetz* , § 11, Ref. 4.

155 Kraßer, *Patentrecht*, § 33 IV. a).

156 German Patent Act, § 11 No. 2.

157 BGH GRUR 1996, 109, 113, 114, and 115—*Klinische Versuche I.*

158 Ibid. 114.

159 BGH NJW 1997, 3092, 3094—*Klinische Versuche II.*

160 German Patent Act, § 11 No. 2a.

161 Keukenschrijver (ed.), *Busse, Patentgesetz*, § 11, Ref. 22.

162 Scharen in Benkard (ed.), *Patentgesetz Gebrauchsmustergesetz*, § 11, Ref. 9; Keukenschrijver (ed.), *Busse, Patentgesetz*, § 11, Ref. 22; Kraßer, *Patentrecht*, § 33 IV. b) 7. Kraßer points out that the equivalent exemption in § 10a (1) No. 3 of the German Plant Variety Protection Act, which regularly also covers the exploitation of a newly bread plant, goes further in this respect.

163 German Patent Act, § 11 No. 2b.

164 Named after the US case *Roche Products Inc. v. Bolar Pharmaceutical Co.*, 733 F.2d 858 (Fed. Cir. 04/23/1984).

165 Kühnen, *Handbuch der Patentverletzung*, Ref. 1642.

166 German Patent Act, § 11 No. 3.

freedom of medical treatment and complements the exemption of methods for treatment of the human or animal body from patent protection.[167] Finally, there are exemptions for the use of patented inventions in vessels, aircrafts, land vehicles, and other means of transportation when these enter Germany on a temporary basis,[168] which protects international traffic from undue obstruction by the patent system.

5. Patent Term and Extension

5.56 According to § 16 of the German Patent Act, the term of the patent ends twenty years after the filing date of the patent. At this point in time, a claim for an injunction is no longer enforceable, and infringement proceedings would continue only for limited purposes, such as to establish legal costs and damages.

5.57 An extension of the rights conferred by the patent after the end of its term can only be achieved by means of a supplemental protection certificate ("SPC") under § 16a of the German Patent Act in accordance with European regulation (EC) No. 469/2009 (previously Council regulation (EEC) No. 1768/92) concerning the creation of a supplementary protection certificate for medical products and Council regulation (EC) No. 1610/96 concerning the creation of a supplemental protection certificate for plant protection products. SPCs are available for medical and plant protection products.[169] Supplementary protection certificates were introduced in order to encourage innovation by compensating for the long time needed to obtain regulatory approval of these products.[170] Legally, an SPC does not extend the term of the patent as such but rather affords a *sui generis* right for up to five years for a product for which a license has been obtained.[171]

5.58 The duration of an SPC is determined on the basis of the period of time between the filing of the basic patent and the granting of the first license for the product within the European Community.[172] Five years are deducted from that period of time.[173] If, for example, there is a period of ten years between the registration date and the date of issue of the license, the SPC will be valid for the maximum period of five years. Thus, there is no extension if the license for the product was granted within five years after the filling date of the patent for that product.[174] The duration starts when the patent expires.[175] However, the SPC is invalid if the basic patent ends before the end of the term expires.[176]

---

[167] Kraßer, *Patentrecht*, § 33 IV. c). The exemption from patentability is codified in German Patent Act, § 2a(1) No. 2.

[168] German Patent Act, § 11 Nos. 4 and 5, which correspond to Paris Convention, Art. 5, and § 11 No. 6, which refers to Art. 27 of the Convention on International Civil Aviation.

[169] Kühnen, *Handbuch der Patentverletzung*, Ref. 131.

[170] Christopher Brückner and Peter von Czettritz, in Christopher Brückner, *Supplementary Protection Certificates* (1st ed., 2011), Introduction, Ref. 1.

[171] Ibid.; Jürgen Schell, in Schulte (ed.), *Patentgesetz mit EPÜ*, § 16a, Ref. 6; Kühnen, *Handbuch der Patentverletzung*, Ref. 131.

[172] Brückner in Brückner, *Supplementary Protection Certificates*, Art. 13, Ref. 1.

[173] Schell in Schulte (ed.), *Patentgesetz mit EPÜ*, § 16a, Ref. 56.

[174] Brückner in Brückner, *Supplementary Protection Certificates*, Art. 13, Ref. 7.

[175] German Patent Act, § 16a(1), first sentence; Brückner in Brückner, *Supplementary Protection Certificates*, Art. 13, Ref. 2.

[176] Brückner in Brückner, *Supplementary Protection Certificates*, Art. 13, Ref. 3.

Each applicant, irrespective of the number of relevant patents, can only be issued with one supplementary protection certificate per product.[177] If several applicants have several basic patents, a supplementary protection certificate may be issued to each applicant. **5.59**

The scope of protection afforded by an SPC has to be determined by reference to the basic patent for which it is granted and its specification, but is limited to the product in respect of which the certificate has been granted.[178] If the certificate is granted for subject matter which is identical to that of the main claim, the scopes of the SPC and the basic patent are identical.[179] If the claims of the basic patent are broader, then the product for which the SPC has been granted has to replace the general term used in the basic patent.[180] **5.60**

B. Extent of Patent Protection

1. Overview

The extent of protection of a particular patent decides whether an accused product or process is covered by the exclusive rights of the patent,[181] as they are discussed above in section 1. Patents applied for prior to January 1, 1978 did not have the extent of protection specified by statute.[182] Today, the central rule for German patents is codified in § 14 of the German Patent Act, and the central rule for European patents, including the German parts of European patents, is codified in Article 69 of the European Patent Convention (EPC). The two provisions are identical in their language and state that the extent of the protection conferred by a patent or a patent application shall be determined by the claims.[183] Nevertheless, the description and drawings shall be used to interpret the claims.[184] This central rule is supplemented by the Protocol on the Interpretation of Article 69 EPC (the Protocol). It provides in its Article 1 that, on the one hand, the extent of the protection conferred by a European patent is not that defined by the strict, literal meaning of the wording used in the claims, the description and drawings being employed only for the purpose of resolving an ambiguity found in the claims.[185] On the other hand, the claims should not only serve as a guideline, and the actual protection conferred should not extend, from a **5.61**

---

[177] Brückner and von Czettritz in Brückner, *Supplementary Protection Certificates*, Introduction, Ref. 45; Schell in Schulte (ed.), *Patentgesetz mit EPÜ*, § 16a, Ref. 18.

[178] Kühnen, *Handbuch der Patentverletzung*, Ref. 132.

[179] Ibid.

[180] Ibid.; Schell in Schulte (ed.), *Patentgesetz mit EPÜ*, § 16a, Ref. 50.

[181] Kühnen, *Handbuch der Patentverletzung*, Ref. 4.

[182] Keukenschrijver (ed.), *Busse, Patentgesetz*, § 14, Ref. 2.

[183] European patent applications can be prosecuted in the English, German, or French language. Where the language of the proceedings before the European Patent Office was English or French, the text of the patent and, in particular, the claims in this language are the authentic version which determines the extent of protection in national infringement or revocation proceedings, Art. 70(1) of the European Patent Convention.

[184] EPC Art. 69 and § 14 of the German Patent Act can be traced back to Art. 8(3) of the Convention on the Unification of Certain Points of Substantive Law on Patents for Invention, signed by the Member States of the Council of Europe on November 27, 1963 at Strasbourg. According to the language of the Strasbourg Patent Convention, as it is called, the extent is determined by the "*terms of* the claims." While this language had also originally been adopted by Art. 69 of the EPC and § 14 of the German Patent Act, it was modified by the 2000 revision of the EPC and the corresponding adjustment to § 14 of the German Patent Act to now read that the extent is determined by just "the claims." The amendment was only for clarification purposes and had no impact on the practices of German courts.

[185] Protocol on the Interpretation of Article 69 EPC, Art. 1, first sentence.

consideration of the description and drawings by a person skilled in the art, to what the patent proprietor has contemplated.[186] On the contrary, a position between these extremes is to be adopted: a position combining fair protection for the patent proprietor with a reasonable degree of legal certainty for third parties.[187] According to the established case law of the Federal Court of Justice, the principles laid down in the Protocol have to be applied not only to European patents but also to German patents.[188] Therefore, the same principles and rules apply in determining the extent of protection of a German national (DE) patent and of the German part of a European (EP) patent.

5.62 The "extremes" mentioned by the Protocol are regarded as referring to, on the one hand, the former practice in the United Kingdom of strictly adhering to the wording of the claims and, on the other hand, to the German practice prior to 1978 of including a "general inventive idea" of the patent when considering its extent of protection.[189] The "general inventive idea" only had to be "derivable" from the claims, be based on the subject of the invention, be recognizable to a skilled person from the specification of the patent, and satisfy the patentability requirements.[190] The introduction of the new rules has been called "arguably [the] most consequential change [in patent law] for decades."[191] Nevertheless, even under today's German practice the extent of patent protection not only consists of embodiments which literally make use of the teaching of the patent claims (the subject matter ("*Gegenstand*") of the patent[192]), but also covers equivalents. This is in line with Article 2 of the Protocol, which was added by the 2000 revision of the EPC and provides that, for the purpose of determining the extent of protection conferred by a European patent, due account shall be taken of any element which is equivalent to an element specified in the claims. "Equivalents" recognized under today's practice[193] are much less far-reaching than embodiments covered by the "general inventive idea" under the former practice.

2. Infringement Analysis

(a) Construction and Application

5.63 Whereas in other fields of intellectual property, such as copyright, design, or trademark, the protected subject matter is determined by the work, design, or sign as such, as it is created, used, or registered, the subject of protection of (utility) patents is circumscribed by language—and language is always open to interpretation. Construction serves to capture the technical meaning behind the words of the claims and to explain the technical terms used in them.

5.64 Unlike their US colleagues,[194] the judges in German patent infringement proceedings decide all issues of the case, and there are no two different decision-makers for questions of

---

[186] Ibid. Art. 1, second sentence.

[187] Ibid. Art. 1, third sentence.

[188] BGH GRUR 1989, 903, 904—*Batteriekastenschnur*; GRUR 1994, 597, 599—*Zerlegvorrichtung für Baumstämme*; GRUR 2002, 519, 521—*Schneidmesser II.*

[189] Kraßer, *Patentrecht*, p. 707, § 32 I 3.

[190] Keukenschrijver (ed.), *Busse, Patentgesetz*, § 14, Ref. 15. See also Ch. 4, 4.17.

[191] Keukenschrijver (ed.), *Busse, Patentgesetz*, § 14, Ref. 1.

[192] Scharen in Benkard (ed.), *Patentgesetz Gebrauchsmustergesetz*, § 14, Ref. 13; Keukenschrijver (ed.), *Busse, Patentgesetz*, § 14, Ref. 19.

[193] Ch. 5, 5.111.

[194] Ch. 4, 4.17.

law and for questions of fact. Nonetheless, it is good practice and required by the Federal Court of Justice[195] to divide the infringement analysis into the steps of (1) an abstract claim construction, which is predominantly a legal exercise but may also involve fact finding, and (2) the application of the thus construed claims to the accused product or process (the "accused embodiment"), which is heavily based on the facts submitted by the parties. In the construction step, the so-called semantic content ("*Sinngehalt*"[196]) or meaning of the wording ("*Wortsinn*"[197]) of the claims is defined in an abstract manner, which helps in answering the question of whether or not the specific features of the accused embodiment can be read under the features of the patent claim, in particular in cases where the patent specification does not describe the accused embodiment as one of the preferred embodiments of the invention.[198] Although the literal scope of a patent claim is independent from the accused embodiment,[199] and at least in theory can be determined by claim construction in an absolute manner, the definition will always be given with a view to the accused embodiment.[200] This is because every embodiment may raise new issues of distinction, which need to be considered. If it was possible to provide an all-embracing definition of the protected subject matter, patents would not have to rely on claims, which practically always entail debates about their interpretation during litigation.

(b) *Further Separate Steps: Literal Infringement and DOE*

If in the application step it is determined that the accused embodiment makes use of the meaning of the wording of a claim, there is "literal" or "identical"[201] use of the patent. However, in view of the rule that the extent of protection is not that defined by the strict meaning of the wording used in the claims[202] and elements which are equivalent to elements specified in the claims have to be given due account,[203] the accused embodiment may be within the extent of protection even if it deviates from the meaning of the wording of the claim. In this case, the court has to examine in a further step if the accused embodiment makes use of the patent under the doctrine of equivalents. Unlike the subject matter (the literal scope) of the patent, the scope of equivalents cannot be determined in an absolute, exhaustive manner.[204] As a consequence, the extent of protection of a patent, which comprises its subject matter and equivalents, can only be determined with regards to a specific accused embodiment.[205] **5.65**

(c) *Claim Construction for Validity Challenges*

The subject matter of a patent claim also plays a central role in validity challenges because the validity decision-maker needs to evaluate whether the patent claim was anticipated or **5.66**

[195] Cf., e.g., BGH GRUR 2007, 410—*Kettenradanordnung*; GRUR 2008, 779, 782—*Mehrgangnabe*.
[196] Kraßer, *Patentrecht*, p. 720, § 32 III 1; Scharen in Benkard (ed.), *Patentgesetz Gebrauchsmustergesetz*, § 14, Ref. 13.
[197] The expression "*Wortsinn*" (meaning of the wording) is used in Art. 1 of the Protocol on the Interpretation of Article 69 EPC and in general is used interchangeably with the expression "*Sinngehalt*" (semantic content), see Kraßer *Patentrecht*, p. 720.
[198] Kühnen, *Handbuch der Patentverletzung*, Ref. 25.
[199] Scharen in Benkard (ed.), *Patentgesetz Gebrauchsmustergesetz*, § 14, Ref. 10.
[200] BGH, GRUR 1988, 757, 762—*Düngerstreuer*; Kühnen, *Handbuch der Patentverletzung*, Ref. 25.
[201] Kraßer, *Patentrecht*, p. 720.
[202] Protocol on the Interpretation of Article 69 EPC, Art. 1, 1st sentence.
[203] Ibid. Art. 2.
[204] Ch. 5, 5.111.
[205] Keukenschrijver (ed.), *Busse, Patentgesetz*, § 14, Ref. 18.

rendered obvious by the prior art and whether it was disclosed in the application as originally filed. For this reason, the meaning of the wording of the claim also has to be determined by way of claim construction in validity challenges.[206] In invalidation proceedings, the claim construction rules are the same as for determining infringement—that is, the same standards are applied.[207]

5.67 One particularity of the German patent litigation system is the bifurcation principle, under which infringement is assessed by the District Courts, whereas validity is challenged before the patent office (in opposition proceedings) or the Federal Patent Court (in revocation (nullity) proceedings).[208] Although, as mentioned above, the infringement court and the decision-maker in validity challenges should apply the same claim construction standards, neither of them is bound by the construction of the other. It is therefore possible for the infringement court to apply a narrower claim construction than the validity decision-maker, or vice versa. In the latter case, the defendant can fall into an "interpretation gap," where the District Court finds infringement on the basis of a broad claim construction, but the validity decision-maker construes the claim narrowly and, for this reason, finds its subject matter not anticipated or rendered obvious by the prior art. However, in practice parties also file their adversary's submissions on claim construction from the other proceedings, and in general due note is taken of them by the decision-maker. Furthermore, infringement and validity proceedings can come together in the court of last instance, the Federal Court of Justice, which ultimately guarantees uniform claim construction for the two sides of a case. Therefore, the reconciliation of interests may be complicated, but it not rendered impossible by Germany's bifurcated patent litigation system.[209]

3. Claim Construction

(a) Fundamental Rules

5.68 The starting point for the assessment of patent infringement is an analysis of the technical teaching which, from the point of view of the person skilled in the art to which the patent relates, results from the individual claim elements in their entirety. The semantic content of the patent claim in its entirety and the individual elements' contribution to the achievement of the invention are to be determined by claim construction, for which the description and the drawings have to be consulted.[210] Claim construction is a question of law and therefore subject to full review by the Federal Court of Justice, the third-instance court for patent infringement proceedings in Germany.

5.69 **i. Function-oriented Claim Construction** When construing patent claims, a meaningful understanding of their wording should be developed in order to determine what is covered by them.[211] German courts consider a purely linguistic or philological approach to claim construction as inadequate.[212] What is relevant is the technical meaning of the

[206] Cf. Keukenschrijver (ed.), *Busse, Patentgesetz*, § 14, Ref. 20. In contrast, the full extent of protection of the patent does not have to be determined because equivalents are not considered for validity challenges.

[207] BGH GRUR 2009, 837, 838—*Bauschalungsstütze*; GRUR 2001, 232, 233—*Brieflocher*.

[208] Ch. 8, 8.03.

[209] Keukenschrijver (ed.), *Busse, Patentgesetz*, § 14, Ref. 18.

[210] BGH GRUR 2007, 410—*Kettenradanordnung*; GRUR 2007, 779, 782—*Mehrgangnabe*.

[211] BGH GRUR, 2004, 1023, 1024; Scharen in Benkard (ed.), *Patentgesetz Gebrauchsmustergesetz*, § 14, Ref. 13.

[212] BGH GRUR 1999, 909—*Spannschraube*; GRUR 1960, 478, 480—*Blockpedale*; Kühnen, *Handbuch der Patentverletzung*, Ref. 66; Keukenschrijver (ed.), *Busse, Patentgesetz*, § 14, Ref. 23; n. 193 above, Scharen in Benkard (ed.), *Patentgesetz Gebrauchsmustergesetz*, § 14, Ref. 57.

features, as is understood by the unprejudiced reader when considering them in their technical context.[213]

Since the skilled reader's understanding of the terms used in a patent claim is guided by the purpose of the feature defined by them,[214] the terms should be interpreted in a way that is appropriate in view of the technical function intended to be fulfilled by the feature. This is sometimes called a "function-oriented" ("*funktionsorientiert*") approach to claim construction. It requires a profound understanding of the function of each individual claim feature in the context of the invention, which in general cannot be derived only from the claim itself but has to be determined with the help of the description and the drawings.[215] For example, a certain understanding of a feature has to be discarded if it results from a technical requirement which the only embodiment described in the specification cannot achieve.[216] **5.70**

Properly applied, the function-oriented claim construction can lead to a broader, but also to a narrower, understanding of a feature than a construction which only looks at the pure wording.[217] It is often emphasized that a specific term (e.g., a "screw") must not be unduly generalized by reducing it to its function (e.g., "detachable fixing means") because this would blur the line between literal infringement and infringement under the doctrine of equivalents.[218] However, the function-oriented claim construction as applied in practice by German courts typically leads to a broader literal scope than the practice of, for example, US courts. According to the Federal Court of Justice, the function-oriented approach is appropriate at least where the claim does not afford the reader a clear-cut understanding of its terms (e.g. the term "substantially").[219] **5.71**

ii. Problem of the Invention Prior to 1978, for a finding of infringement, courts in Germany required that the accused embodiment overcame the problem, or at least the main problem solved by the patented invention.[220] However, § 14 of the current Patent Act and Article 69 of the EPC do not mention a technical problem as a factor for determining the extent of protection, which prohibits the attachment of independent importance to it.[221] Under today's case law, an accused embodiment realizing all features of the asserted patent claim is covered even if it does not solve the problem underlying the patent. Therefore, describing in the specification the technical advantages and problems solved by the invention from the German point of view is in general not disadvantageous for the patentee.[222] **5.72**

---

213 BGH GRUR 1999, 909, 912—*Spannschraube*; BGH GRUR 2004, 845, 846—*Drehzahlermittlung*; Keukenschrijver (ed.), *Busse, Patentgesetz*, § 14, Ref. 57.

214 BGH GRUR 2001, 232, 233—*Brieflocher*; GRUR 1999, 909, 911—*Spannschraube*; Scharen in Benkard (ed.), *Patentgesetz Gebrauchsmustergesetz*, § 14, Ref. 71.

215 *Meier-Beck*, GRUR 2003, 905, 906; Kraßer, *Patentrecht*, p. 721, § 32 III c) 3.

216 Kühnen, *Handbuch der Patentverletzung*, Ref. 33; BGH GRUR 2010, 602, 604—*Gelenkanordnung*.

217 *Meier-Beck*, GRUR 2003, 905, 906; Scharen in Benkard (ed.), *Patentgesetz Gebrauchsmustergesetz*, § 14, Ref. 71.

218 *Meier-Beck*, GRUR 2003, 907; Scharen in Benkard (ed.), *Patentgesetz Gebrauchsmustergesetz*, § 14, Ref. 10, 71; Keukenschrijver (ed.), *Busse, Patentgesetz*, § 14, Ref. 22; Kühnen, *Handbuch der Patentverletzung*, Ref. 34.

219 BGH GRUR 2005, 41, 42—*Staubsaugersaurohr*.

220 Keukenschrijver (ed.), *Busse, Patentgesetz*, § 14, Ref. 72; BGH X ZR 72/67, 59.

221 Scharen in Benkard (ed.), *Patentgesetz Gebrauchsmustergesetz*, § 14, Ref. 80; cf. BGH GRUR 1990, 33, 34—*Schlüsselmühle*, explaining that a prior art gear mechanism realizing all features of a patent claim anticipates the claimed subject matter even if it does not solve the problem underlying the patent.

222 This may be different in the US, see Ch. 4, 4.57.

5.73 Nevertheless, identifying the problem solved by the invention can play an important role in determining the technical function of a claim feature, and thus in determining the extent of protection by a function-oriented claim construction. For this reason, even today German courts reiterate the formula that the claim terms are to be interpreted in consideration of the problem and the solution of the invention.[223]

5.74 In doing so, the problem may not be assessed on the basis of the subjective view of the applicant alone,[224] as is expressed by the problem mentioned in the patent specification, but may have to be determined objectively, in accordance with the actual accomplishments of the invention.[225] This seems to be the right approach because, oftentimes, at least some of the problems mentioned in the specification are not solved by the subject matter of a claim. However, the applicant's description of the problem he or she intended to solve can give clues about the problem which the skilled reader, when reading the specification, objectively understands to be solved.[226] The same is true for the description of the disadvantages of the prior art, which the invention intends to remove, or of the technical effects, advantages, or achievements of the invention.[227]

5.75 **iii. Relevant Viewpoint** The subject matter of a patent is to be determined from an objective point of view.[228] Although a patent claim defines an exclusive right and can therefore be regarded as a legal provision, unlike for other legal provisions, the subjective intent or idea of the drafter of the provision (the applicant or the inventor) is not considered for its interpretation.[229] Although not mentioned in the statute, it is recognized that the relevant viewpoint is the one belonging to the ordinary skilled person at the priority date of the patent. The skilled person ("*Fachmann*") is a fictitious person with the professional qualification and practical experience as those who, at the priority date, typically deal with the development and innovation in the industrial practice of companies active in the technical field of the invention.[230] The determination of the content of the claims, including the meaning of the terms used therein, depends on the understanding of the skilled person defined in this manner.[231] Since the terms used in the patent specification may not be given a meaning which they acquired only after the priority date—that is, due to technical development or a shift of meaning[232]—at least the literal scope of the patent will be fixed throughout the lifetime of the patent.

5.76 **iv. The Patent as its Own Dictionary** This is not to say that the terms used in a patent specification are always to be given the meaning as generally understood by the skilled person at the priority date. Due account has to be taken to the possibility that the patent

[223] BGH GRUR 1999, 909, 911—*Spannschraube.*

[224] Scharen in Benkard (ed.), *Patentgesetz Gebrauchsmustergesetz*, § 14, Ref. 81.

[225] BGH GRUR 2005, 141, 142—*Anbieten interaktiver Hilfe*; GRUR 2010, 602—*Gelenkanordnung.*

[226] Scharen in Benkard (ed.), *Patentgesetz Gebrauchsmustergesetz*, § 14, Ref. 81.

[227] Ibid.

[228] Ibid. Ref. 69; Keukenschrijver (ed.), *Busse, Patentgesetz*, § 14, Ref. 20.

[229] BGH GRUR 1960, 546, 548—*Bierhahn*; GRUR 1955, 244—*Repassiernadel*; RG GRUR 1944, 22 55; GRUR 1933, 703, 704.

[230] Kühnen, *Handbuch der Patentverletzung*, Ref. 61.

[231] BGH GRUR 1994, 597, 599—*Zerlegvorrichtung für Baumstämme*; GRUR 2002, 515, 516—*Schneidmesser I*; GRUR 2004, 413, 415—*Geflügelkörperhalterung.*

[232] Scharen in Benkard (ed.), *Patentgesetz Gebrauchsmustergesetz*, § 14, Ref. 60; BGH GRUR 1966, 312, 317.

may use a term in a way which deviates from its common meaning.[233] According to the Federal Court of Justice, patent specifications are, so to speak, their own dictionary with regard to the terms used by them. If they differ from the general (technical) language use, only the meaning which results from the patent specification is authoritative in the end.[234] For example, if the specification comprises a definition for a claim term, this definition is binding.[235] It is obvious that under this approach, a claim term can be given a narrower or a broader meaning than the general language use, or simply an entirely different meaning.

During claim construction any uncertainties are to be resolved.[236] Obvious misnomers (*falsa demonstratio*) in the claims are to be corrected, with the help of the description if necessary.[237] The same is true for potential contradictions between features within the same claim, which a sensible construction will try to eliminate whenever possible.[238] **5.77**

v. Special Types of Claims The fundamental claim construction rules outlined above are the same for all types of claims. Unlike in the US Patent Act,[239] the German Patent Act and the EPC apply the same standards to functionally defined claims as they do to claims defined by the structure, material, and acts. Therefore, functionally defined features typically lead to a broader scope than structurally defined ones. They do not only cover structures, materials, and acts which are mentioned in the description, but any structure, material, and act which satisfies the functional definition, including those which were not available at the priority date.[240] **5.78**

Like US courts, German case law has developed special rules for product-by-process claims—that is, claims which are directed to a product but at least in part circumscribe the product by a process for manufacturing it, instead of defining the product directly by its properties, like structure or material, or in a functional way. Product-by-process claims are allowable if there is no other way of adequately describing the product,[241] such as if the structural formula of a chemical substance is unknown or if the chemical substance cannot be identified by reliably determinable characteristics.[242] It is recognized that the extent of a claim using the formulation "product obtain*able* by" is not limited to products actually made by the process described in the claim but also covers products which result from other manufacturing processes, as long as they have the characteristics imparted to the product by the process described in the claim.[243] Unlike in the United States,[244] this is true not only for the assessment of validity but also for the assessment of infringement so that product-by-process claims provide a very broad protection in Germany. The discussion in **5.79**

---

233 Kühnen, *Handbuch der Patentverletzung*, Ref. 30.

234 BGH GRUR 1999, 909, 911—*Spannschraube*; GRUR 2005, 754—*Knickschutz*.

235 Cf. Kühnen, *Handbuch der Patentverletzung*, Ref. 28.

236 Scharen in Benkard (ed.), *Patentgesetz Gebrauchsmustergesetz*, § 14, Ref. 13; BGH GRUR 2002, 515, 516—*Schneidmesser I*.

237 Kühnen, *Handbuch der Patentverletzung*, Ref. 18.

238 BGH GRUR 2011, 129, 131—*Fentanyl-TTS*.

239 Ch. 4, 4.32.

240 Kühnen, *Handbuch der Patentverletzung*, Ref. 66; LG Frankfurt/Main, InstGE 6, 1—*Kunstharzzusammensetzung*.

241 BGH GRUR 1979, 461—*Farbbildröhre*; GRUR 1993, 651, 655—*Tetraploide Kamille*. See also Scharen in Benkard (ed.), *Patentgesetz Gebrauchsmustergesetz*, § 14, Ref. 46.

242 BGH GRUR 1972, 80—*Trioxan*.

243 Kühnen, *Handbuch der Patentverletzung*, Ref. 69.

244 Ch. 4, 4.44.

this jurisdiction centers around the question of whether the same broad product protection is provided by claim formulations such as "product obtain*ed* by," which is answered in the affirmative by the EPO practice[245] and also seems to be recognized by the more recent case law in Germany.[246]

(b) Aids for Claim Interpretation

5.80 **i. Intrinsic v. Extrinsic Evidence** In Germany, aids for claim interpretation are not categorized into intrinsic evidence (evidence related to the patent which can be obtained from the patent office) and extrinsic evidence (other evidence) like in the United States.[247] Rather, a distinction is drawn between documents which according to § 14 of the German Patent Act and Article 69 of the EPC can be and have to be used for determining the extent of protection, and other sources of information, which may only serve for determining the knowledge and the background of the skilled person. The former have a direct influence on claim interpretation and include the specification (description and drawings),[248] other claims,[249] possibly official publications of previous versions of the patent,[250] and prior art documents as far as they are referred to and discussed in the patent specification.[251] The latter have an indirect influence on claim construction because the claims and the specification are read through the eyes of the skilled person. They include statements made during prosecution[252] or invalidation proceedings,[253] other prior art,[254] dictionaries and science treaties,[255] and expert testimony.[256]

5.81 **ii. Specification** The German Patent Act and the EPC require that the description and drawings of the patent specification are used for interpreting the claims.[257] While the title of the invention forms part of the description and can therefore be an aid for claim construction,[258] the abstract only serves the purpose of providing technical information and may not be taken into account when interpreting the scope of protection.[259] In the past, German courts gave the description priority over the drawings in case of contradictions;[260] whether this is still true today under the claim interpretation rule provided in the second sentence of § 14 of the German Patent Act and the second sentence of Article 69 of the EPC is doubtful.[261]

---

245 EPO Guidelines for Examination, Part F, Ch. IV.4.12.

246 BGH GRUR 1993, 651, 655—*Tetraploide Kamille*; BPatG 14 W (pat) 58/93, 31; Keukenschrijver (ed.), *Busse, Patentgesetz*, § 9, Ref. 53; Kühnen, *Handbuch der Patentverletzung*, Ref. 63; Scharen in Benkard (ed.), *Patentgesetz Gebrauchsmustergesetz*, § 14, Ref. 46.

247 For the United States, see Ch. 4, 4.45).

248 Ch. 5, 5.81.

249 Ch. 5, 5.85.

250 Ch. 5, 5.86.

251 Ch. 5, 5.91.

252 Ch. 5, 5.87.

253 Ch. 5, 5.88.

254 Ch. 5, 5.91.

255 Ch. 5, 5.93.

256 Ch. 5, 5.94.

257 Ch. 5, 5.61.

258 Scharen in Benkard (ed.), *Patentgesetz Gebrauchsmustergesetz*, § 14, Ref. 23.

259 EPC, Art. 85; German Patent Act, § 36(2), first sentence; Scharen in Benkard (ed.), *Patentgesetz Gebrauchsmustergesetz*, § 14, Ref. 31.

260 BGH GRUR 1955, 244—*Repassiernadel*; RG GRUR 1942, 51, 52; Scharen in Benkard (ed.), *Patentgesetz Gebrauchsmustergesetz*, § 14, Ref. 29.

261 Scharen in Benkard (ed.), *Patentgesetz Gebrauchsmustergesetz*, § 14, Ref. 29; Keukenschrijver (ed.), *Busse, Patentgesetz*, § 14, Ref. 20.

According to this rule, the description and the drawings must always be used for claim interpretation and not only for the purpose of resolving ambiguities, mentioned in Article 1 of the Protocol.[262] Because patent specifications are their own dictionary[263] and the description oftentimes comprises definitions of terms used in the claims, even supposedly clear and understandable claims have to be read in light of the specification. This ensures that if the patent uses a particular language, this use is duly taken into account.[264] The consideration of the description and the drawings may lead to a broader understanding of the claims, but it is also possible that it will limit the claim scope to an understanding which is narrower than what the wording of the claims seems to convey on its face.[265] This is not a contradiction of the sentence that "a patent claim may not be construed below its wording,"[266] a sentence which is oftentimes quoted in Germany.[267] It means that a claim may not be given a smaller scope than what is defined by its *properly construed* wording—that is, the wording as it is understood by the skilled person in light of the specification.[268] However, a construction which results in a claim scope which is narrower than the wording of the claims seems to convey will come into consideration only in exceptional cases.[269] **5.82**

Since under § 14 of the German Patent Act and Article 69 of the EPC it is the claims which determine the extent of the protection and the specification is only to be used to interpret the claims, a broadly formulated claim may, in general, not be limited in scope to a more detailed embodiment depicted in the description or the drawings.[270] This is true even if the specification only refers to specific embodiments, in particular if a limitation to the protection of the specific embodiment is not expressed in the description.[271] For any statements made in the context of an embodiment—for example, about functions, advantages, or possible designs—it should be determined whether they only concern the particular embodiment or whether they characterize what is claimed in a broader claim.[272] In general, the detailed explanations will have to be regarded as mere example embodiments which do not limit the extent of protection. Similar principles apply to other elements of the specification which are not reflected in the claims.[273] Typically the general part of the description is considered to have priority over the parts concerning specific embodiments for claim construction.[274] **5.83**

[262] Scharen in Benkard (ed.), *Patentgesetz Gebrauchsmustergesetz*, § 14, Ref. 9, 22; Kraßer, *Patentrecht*, p. 719, § 32 III c) 1.

[263] Ch. 5, 5.76.

[264] Scharen in Benkard (ed.), *Patentgesetz Gebrauchsmustergesetz*, § 14, Ref. 22; Kühnen, *Handbuch der Patentverletzung*, Ref. 9.

[265] BGH, GRUR 1999, 909, 912—*Spannschraube*; Mitt 2000, 105—*Extrusionskopf.*

[266] *Meier-Beck*, GRUR 2003, 905, 906.

[267] E.g., in BGH GRUR 1985, 967—*Zuckerzentrifuge*; GRUR 2007, 309—*Schussfädentransport*; GRUR 2007, 778—*Ziehmaschinenzugeinheit.*

[268] Cf. *Meier-Beck*, GRUR 2003, 905, 906; BGH GRUR 2007, 309—*Schussfädentransport*, explaining in its headnote in parenthesis that the expression "wording" (*Wortlaut*) in the context of this sentence actually means "semantic content" (*Sinngehalt*).

[269] Scharen in Benkard (ed.), *Patentgesetz Gebrauchsmustergesetz*, § 14, Ref. 24; Keukenschrijver (ed.), *Busse, Patentgesetz*, § 14, Ref. 23.

[270] GRUR 2004, 1023—*Bodenseitige Vereinzelungsvorrichtung*; Kraßer, *Patentrecht*, p. 715, § 32 III. b) 3; Scharen in Benkard (ed.), *Patentgesetz Gebrauchsmustergesetz*, § 14, Ref. 51.

[271] BGH GRUR 2007, 309—*Schussfädentransport.*

[272] Scharen in Benkard (ed.), *Patentgesetz Gebrauchsmustergesetz*, § 14, Ref. 30.

[273] Kraßer, *Patentrecht*, p. 715, § 32 III. b) 3.

[274] Scharen in Benkard (ed.), *Patentgesetz Gebrauchsmustergesetz*, § 14, Ref. 23.

5.84 Another consequence of the rule that the extent of protection is determined by the claims is that a technical teaching which is only contained in the description or the drawings but has not been captured by any of the claims moves into the public domain.[275] Such a case typically arises when the claims have been limited to certain embodiments during prosecution, and the description and the drawings have not been adapted accordingly, by striking the other embodiments. The determination of whether or not an embodiment in the specification is captured by one of the claims can pose difficulties. On the one hand, the skilled person reads the claims and other parts of the patent specification as one uniform disclosure and, in case of doubt, strives to understand them in a way where no contradictions arise.[276] The embodiments described in the specification will therefore always raise the question of whether a claim construction can be found under which all variants of the invention are covered by the extent of at least one independent claim.[277] On the other hand, an example from the specification which has not found its way into the claims must not enlarge the extent of protection,[278] and the specification may be taken into account only insofar as it can be read as an explanation of the claim.[279] The difficulty lies in the circular way of determination: we are trying to find out whether an embodiment comprised by the specification is within the scope of a claim, but the claim scope is influenced by the very presence of this embodiment in the specification. As a general rule, if the claims and other parts of the specification cannot be brought in line, the claims are authoritative,[280] but this rule may be of limited help in borderline cases.

5.85 **iii. Other Claims** The principle that the skilled person reads the patent specification as one uniform disclosure is even more true for the relationship between claims. Claim interpretation therefore has to take into account the wording of other claims,[281] and it is permissible to draw inferences from the the claim's relationship to other claims.[282] Although there are no bright-line rules, the practice is to try to read a claim in a way that encompasses the subject matter of all claims dependent on it, and a claim term should be treated consistently throughout all claims in which the term is used.[283]

5.86 **iv. Prosecution History** Unlike in the United States, in Germany the prosecution history is in principle not considered for claim construction;[284] at the very least, it has no authoritative effect. Although this approach is not followed by the courts of all EPC

[275] BGH GRUR 1980, 219, 200—*Überstromventil*; GRUR 1987, 626—*Rundfunkübertragungssystem*; Kühnen, *Handbuch der Patentverletzung*, Ref. 8; Kraßer, *Patentrecht*, p. 716, § 32 III b) 3; Keukenschrijver (ed.), *Busse, Patentgesetz*, § 14, Ref. 25; Scharen in Benkard (ed.), *Patentgesetz Gebrauchsmustergesetz*, § 14, Ref. 35.

[276] BGH GRUR 2011, 701, 703—*Okklusionsvorrichtung*; OLG Düsseldorf, Mitt 1998, 179—*Mehrpoliger Steckverbinder*; Kühnen, *Handbuch der Patentverletzung*, Ref. 10; Keukenschrijver (ed.), *Busse, Patentgesetz*, § 14, Ref. 20; Scharen in Benkard (ed.), *Patentgesetz Gebrauchsmustergesetz*, § 14, Ref. 57.

[277] Kühnen, *Handbuch der Patentverletzung*, Ref. 10.

[278] OLG München GRUR 1995, 806—*Surfbretter*; Keukenschrijver (ed.), *Busse, Patentgesetz*, § 14, Ref. 25.

[279] BGH GRUR 2011, 701—*Okklusionsvorrichtung*; GRUR 1999, 909, 912—*Spannschraube*; Scharen in Benkard (ed.), *Patentgesetz Gebrauchsmustergesetz*, § 14, Ref. 22.

[280] BGH GRUR 2011, 701, 703—*Okklusionsvorrichtung*; Keukenschrijver (ed.), *Busse, Patentgesetz*, § 14, Ref. 25.

[281] Keukenschrijver (ed.), *Busse, Patentgesetz*, § 14, Ref. 20.

[282] Kühnen, *Handbuch der Patentverletzung*, Ref. 20.

[283] Cf. BGH, case No. X ZR 107/05, 38.

[284] BGH GRUR 2002, 511—*Kunstoffrohrteil*; GRUR 1992, 40, 41—*Beheizbarer Atemlufschlauch*; Scharen in Benkhard, § 14, Ref. 32; Kraßer, *Patentrecht*, p. 716, § 32 III b) 4.

member states,[285] it is reasoned by the fact that Article 69 of the EPC and the Protocol, like § 14 of the German Patent Act, do not list the prosecution file but only the claims, the description, and the drawings as instruments for determining the extent of patent protection.[286] In November 2000, the Conference for the Revision of the EPC rejected a suggestion to add a provision to the Protocol stating that due account shall be taken of the so-called "file wrapper estoppel" (prosecution history estoppel) for the purpose of determining the extent of protection.[287] Taking the prosecution file into account is considered to be problematic because what is documented in the file can never fully reflect the grounds which led to the grant of the patent.[288] As a consequence, occurrences in the prosecution proceedings—such as waivers or limitations of the extent of protection, which are not reflected by the patent specification—cannot be relied on.[289] A question which has been addressed already but left unanswered by two decisions of the Federal Court of Justice is whether any differences between the patent application and the patent as granted, or between the patent as granted and the patent as amended in limitation proceedings under Article 105a of the EPC or in opposition proceedings, can be used for interpreting the claims.[290] The differences ascertained by a comparison between the different patent publications could be revealing, particularly in cases where it is difficult to decide whether or not an embodiment disclosed in the specification is meant to be within the scope of the claims.[291] It could be argued that amendments which become apparent by such a comparison may be taken into account in claim interpretation because they are reflected in the patent specification.[292]

Even if the content of the prosecution file has no binding effect on claim interpretation, it is not entirely irrelevant. Statements made by the applicant can be an important indication on how the teaching of the patent specification was understood by the skilled person at the priority date,[293] in particular if they confirm what can already be read from the patent specification.[294] The same is true for statements by patent examiners.[295] It can be said that **5.87**

---

[285] E.g., the Supreme Court of the Netherlands arrived at the opposite result in case No. C05/200HR (2006). See also Austrian Patent Act, § 163(5), according to which the content of the prosecution file is to be considered in determining the extent of protection in a declaratory judgment of non-infringement.

[286] BGH GRUR 2002, 511, 513—*Kunstoffrohrteil*; Scharen in Benkard (ed.), *Patentgesetz Gebrauchsmustergesetz*, § 14, Ref. 32; Kühnen, *Handbuch der Patentverletzung*, Ref. 46.

[287] Ralph Nack and Bruno Phélip, "Report on the Diplomatic Conference for the Revision of the European Patent Convention," https://www.aippi.org/download/reports/DiplomaticConference.pdf; BGH GRUR 2002, 511, 514—*Kunststoffrohrteil*.

[288] Kühnen, *Handbuch der Patentverletzung*, Ref. 46; Scharen in Benkard (ed.), *Patentgesetz Gebrauchsmustergesetz*, § 14, Ref. 33.

[289] BGH, GRUR 2011, 701, 704—*Okklusionsvorrichtung*; GRUR 2002, 511, 513—*Kunstoffrohrteil*; Keukenschrijver (ed.), *Busse, Patentgesetz*, § 14, Ref. 49.

[290] BGH, GRUR 2011, 701, 704—*Okklusionsvorrichtung*; GRUR 2010, 602—*Gelenkanordnung*, 33.

[291] Ch. 5, 5.84.

[292] BGH, GRUR 2011, 701, 704—*Okklusionsvorrichtung*; Keukenschrijver (ed.), *Busse, Patentgesetz*, § 14, Ref. 49. Against this approach: Kühnen, *Handbuch der Patentverletzung*, Ref. 50.

[293] BGH GRUR 1993, 886, 888—*Weichvorrichtung I*; NJW 1997, 3377, 3380—*Weichvorrichtung II*; Scharen in Benkard (ed.), *Patentgesetz Gebrauchsmustergesetz*, § 14, Ref. 34; Keukenschrijver (ed.), *Busse, Patentgesetz*, § 14, Ref. 50; Kraßer, *Patentrecht*, p. 718, § 32 III b) 6.

[294] BGH, case No. I ZR 90/59 (1961)—*Ziegelsteine*; case No. X ZR 32/66 (1969); Scharen in Benkard (ed.), *Patentgesetz Gebrauchsmustergesetz*, § 14, Ref. 34.

[295] BGH GRUR 1968 311, 313—*Garmachverfahren*; case No. I ZR 90/59 (1961)—*Ziegelsteine*, 25; Scharen in Benkard (ed.), *Patentgesetz Gebrauchsmustergesetz*, § 14, Ref. 34; Kraßer, *Patentrecht*, p. 715, § 32 III b) 2.

the significance of the content of the prosecution file for the determination of the extent of patent protection is similar to the one of dictionaries or other extrinsic evidence.[296]

5.88 **v. Statements Made in Invalidation Proceedings** Similar rules as for statements made in prosecution proceedings apply to statements made in invalidation proceedings (opposition proceedings or revocation (nullity) proceedings), which in Germany and at the EPO are always *inter parties* proceedings and held before a different decision-maker than infringement proceedings.[297]

5.89 The reasons for a decision by which a patent is maintained are not binding on the claim interpretation of the infringement court.[298] However, they are to be treated like important statements by a skilled person and must be considered and discussed by the infringement court when it interprets the claims.[299] If the decision in the invalidation proceedings maintains the patent with amended (i.e., limited) claims, then the part of the decision which explains the reasons for the amendments replaces or supplements the description of the patent,[300] unless the description was adapted to the amended claims, in particular by striking the parts which have become superfluous.[301] The extent of protection of the amended patent is then determined by the amended claims in light of (1) the (original) description and drawings and (2) the relevant part of the invalidation decision.[302] However, this does not necessarily lead to the consequence of the infringement court adopting the claim interpretation taken in the invalidation decision.[303]

5.90 Statements made by the patent owner or the challenger in the invalidation proceedings can be treated, like statements of the applicant during prosecution proceedings, as important indications as to how the teaching of the patent specification is understood by the skilled person.[304] In addition, if the patent owner states in the invalidation proceedings that a certain embodiment is outside the scope of the claims and this statement was the basis for maintaining the patent, a subsequent complaint of the patent owner against the challenger alleging infringement by the embodiment which was subject to the statement violates good faith principles and is to be dismissed.[305] However, the statement does not limit the extent

---

[296] Kühnen, *Handbuch der Patentverletzung*, Ref. 49.

[297] Ch. 8, 8.03.

[298] BGH GRUR 1988, 444—*Betonstahlmattenwender*; GRUR 1988, 757, 760—*Düngerstreuer*. See also BGH GRUR 2007, 778, 780—*Ziehmaschinenzugeinheit*.

[299] BGH GRUR 1998, 895, 896—*Regenbecken* (with regards to EPO opposition decisions); Kühnen, *Handbuch der Patentverletzung*, Ref. 55. See also BGH GRUR 1988, 757, 760—*Düngerstreuer* (with regards to nullity decisions) and Keukenschrijver (ed.), *Busse, Patentgesetz*, § 14, Ref. 52, stating that the reasons of the decision are a "valuable aid" for claim interpretation.

[300] BGH GRUR 1955, 573, 574—*Kabelschelle*; GRUR 1979, 308, 309—*Auspuffkanal für Schaltgase*; Kühnen, *Handbuch der Patentverletzung*, Ref. 56; Scharen in Benkard (ed.), *Patentgesetz Gebrauchsmustergesetz*, § 14, Ref. 26; Keukenschrijver (ed.), *Busse, Patentgesetz*, § 14, Ref. 51.

[301] BGH GRUR 1999, 145, 146—*Stoßwellen-Lithotripter*; Kühnen, *Handbuch der Patentverletzung*, Ref. 58; Scharen in Benkard (ed.), *Patentgesetz Gebrauchsmustergesetz*, § 14, Ref. 26; Keukenschrijver (ed.), *Busse, Patentgesetz*, § 14.

[302] Scharen in Benkard (ed.), *Patentgesetz Gebrauchsmustergesetz*, § 14, Ref. 26.

[303] E.g., if the reasoning of the invalidation decision cannot be brought in line with the claims, the claims are authoritative because the reasoning of the invalidation decision is treated just like any other part of the description (BGH GRUR 2007, 778, 780—*Ziehmaschinenzugeinheit*; Keukenschrijver (ed.), *Busse, Patentgesetz*, § 14, Ref. 52; Kühnen, *Handbuch der Patentverletzung*, Ref. 56).

[304] BGH GRUR 1993, 886, 888—*Weichvorrichtung I*; NJW 1997, 3377, 3380—*Weichvorrichtung II*; BGH, GRUR case No. X ZR 32/66 (1969).

[305] BGH GRUR 1993, 886, 888—*Weichvorrichtung I*; NJW 1997, 3377, 3380—*Weichvorrichtung II*; GRUR 2006, 923—*Luftabscheider für Milchsammelanlage* (concerning a utility model); Kühnen, *Handbuch*

of protection, so the patent owner remains free to enforce the patent with its full scope against any party other than the challenger.[306]

vi. Prior Art As far as prior art documents are referred to and discussed in the patent specification, they are part of the description and must therefore be used for claim interpretation.[307] In contrast, prior art which is not acknowledged in the specification, including prior art documents only listed in the cover page,[308] cannot be used as an aid for determining the subject matter of the patent unless they belong to the common general knowledge of the skilled person.[309] **5.91**

There is no general rule that a claim needs to be construed such that its validity can be confirmed. However, the discussion of the prior art in the description of the patent gives an indication about what the skilled person understands to be the novel and the inventive aspects of its teaching.[310] The prior art mentioned in the specification can therefore lead to a claim interpretation which does not cover designs for which the patent explains that they are already known.[311] The specification may also express that the invention intends to keep a certain prior art design and the advantages associated with it.[312] However, in many cases the patent will use the acknowledged prior art only as the starting point, which does not justify the assumption that the invention wants to retain all aspects of the prior art.[313] In any event, only the prior art features discussed in the description of the patent have to be considered for claim interpretation, and the court does not have to consider all the details comprised in the referenced prior art document but not mentioned in the description of the patent.[314] The acknowledged prior art may teach the skilled person that a certain claim construction can be ruled out—for example, because the subject of the claim would not be enabled under that construction.[315] **5.92**

vii. Dictionary, Science Treatise Dictionaries and science treatises play only a minor role for claim construction in German patent litigation. They can form the starting point, to ascertain the ordinary understanding of a term by the skilled person at the priority date, but they are rarely decisive. Since the patent specification is its own dictionary with regard to the terms used by it,[316] the primary aid for interpreting the claim terms is the specification itself rather than dictionaries and science treatises.[317] However, in the absence of any hint that the specification overwrites the plain meaning of a term by using it in a different way, **5.93**

---

der Patentverletzung, Ref. 51; Keukenschrijver (ed.), *Busse, Patentgesetz*, § 14, Ref. 50; Kraßer, *Patentrecht*, p. 717, § 32 III b) 5.

306 Kühnen, *Handbuch der Patentverletzung*, Ref. 51.

307 BGH GRUR 2007, 410, 414—*Kettenradanordnung*; Kraßer, *Patentrecht*, p. 715, § 32 III b) 2; Keukenschrijver (ed.), *Busse, Patentgesetz*, § 14, Ref. 54; Scharen in Benkard (ed.), *Patentgesetz Gebrauchsmustergesetz*, § 14, Ref. 61.

308 Kraßer, *Patentrecht*, p. 719, § 32 III b) 8; Scharen in Benkard (ed.), *Patentgesetz Gebrauchsmustergesetz*, § 14, Ref. 61. However, Kühnen, *Handbuch der Patentverletzung*, Ref. 36 is of the opinion that prior art which is only mentioned on the cover sheet can be used as an aid for claim construction.

309 BGH GRUR 1978, 235, 237—*Stromwandler*; GRUR 1987, 280—*Befestigungsvorrichtung*; Scharen in Benkard (ed.), *Patentgesetz Gebrauchsmustergesetz*, § 14, Ref. 59; Kühnen, *Handbuch der Patentverletzung*, Ref. 34.

310 Kraßer, *Patentrecht*, p. 715; Keukenschrijver (ed.), *Busse, Patentgesetz*, § 14, Ref. 54.

311 Scharen in Benkard (ed.), *Patentgesetz Gebrauchsmustergesetz*, § 14, Ref. 62; Keukenschrijver (ed.), *Busse, Patentgesetz*, § 14, Ref. 54.

312 OLG Dusseldorf, GRUR 2000, 599, 604—*Staubsaugerfilter.*

313 Kühnen, *Handbuch der Patentverletzung*, Ref. 36.

314 Scharen in Benkard (ed.), *Patentgesetz Gebrauchsmustergesetz*, § 14, Ref. 61.

315 BGH GRUR 1999, 909, 911—*Spannschraube.*

316 Ch. 5, 5.76.

317 Kühnen, *Handbuch der Patentverletzung*, Ref. 30.

the ordinary understanding by the skilled person as demonstrated by the dictionary or science treatise may be relied upon.[318]

5.94 **viii. Expert Testimony** In German patent infringement or invalidation proceedings, the statements of party experts hardly enjoy any more authority than the statements of the parties themselves. The courts can appoint neutral court experts, a possibility which they make use of in less than 10 percent of the infringement proceedings, almost never in the first instance of revocation proceedings before the Federal Patent Court (where the panel includes technically qualified judges), and only occasionally in revocation appeal proceedings before the Federal Court of Justice. In particular, even a court experienced in patent cases will have to rely on the help of a court expert when there are doubts about how the skilled person understands the terms used in the claims or the description, which cannot be resolved otherwise.[319]

5.95 The primary task of the court expert is to educate the court about the knowledge of the skilled person so that the judges are in a position to correctly assess the facts. The expert is not asked to interpret the claim but to make available to the judges the technical knowledge necessary to understand the teaching of the patent and to interpret the claim themselves.[320] This includes all the information which can determine or have an influence on the understanding of the patent claim and the terms used therein, such as technical facts; the pre-existing understanding of the skilled person; the knowledge, skills, and experience of the skilled person; and his methodical approach.[321]

5.96 The information provided by the expert will support the court in its claim interpretation, which is a question of law. The judges may not leave claim interpretation to the expert or simply adopt the results of an expert opinion without further inquiry.[322] It is their responsibility to verify whether and to what extent the statements of the expert comprise information which may be of help with respect to the questions decisive for the case, which are to be answered by the court.[323]

5.97 **ix. Other Extrinsic Evidence** A disclosure only comprised in the application of a patent or in its priority document is not a valid aid for claim construction.[324] Also, the content of foreign counterparts, other family members, or parallel patents must not be taken into account.[325] German courts are of course not bound by the claim interpretation adopted by foreign courts, even if the foreign court dealt with an identical counterpart of the same European patent. However, the Federal Court of Justice requires that German courts take notice of decisions by the EPO and by courts of other EPC member states regarding the same patent. In cases where they come to a different result, the German court should discuss the grounds for the foreign decision.[326]

---

[318] Kühnen, *Handbuch der Patentverletzung*, Ref. 31; Keukenschrijver (ed.), *Busse, Patentgesetz*, § 14, Ref. 44.

[319] BGH GRUR 2004, 413—*Geflügelkörperhalterung*.

[320] BGH GRUR 2008, 779, 782—*Mehrgangnabe*.

[321] BGH GRUR 2006, 131—*Seitenspiegel*; GRUR 2007, 410, 413—*Kettenradanordnung*; GRUR 2008, 779, 782—*Mehrgangnabe*.

[322] Kühnen, *Handbuch der Patentverletzung*, Ref. 62; Kraßer, *Patentrecht*, p. 720, § 32 III c) 2; BGH GRUR 2001, 770—*Kabeldurchführung II*.

[323] BGH GRUR 2001, 770—*Kabeldurchführung II*; GRUR 2008, 779, 782—*Mehrgangnabe*.

[324] Scharen in Benkard (ed.), *Patentgesetz Gebrauchsmustergesetz*, § 14, Ref. 33.

[325] Ibid. § 14, Ref. 33, 72; Keukenschrijver (ed.), *Busse, Patentgesetz*, § 14 Ref. 53.

[326] BGH GRUR 2010, 950, 951—*Walzenformgebungsmaschine*.

(c) Canons of Claim Construction

i. Canons Favoring Accused Infringers There are very few recognized rules which are in favor of the accused infringer—that is, rules in favor of a narrow claim construction. **5.98**

One of them is the rule that in the case of an unclear claim, difficulties in the determination of the meaning of the claim should go to the detriment of the patent owner.[327] However, a patent infringement complaint may not be dismissed on the grounds that certain claim elements are so unclear that their meaning is impossible to determine;[328] in other words, the court has to attach *some* meaning to the claim, and its scope of protection may not be reduced to zero. An unclear claim feature can only be a reason to assign a limited meaning to this feature —even the narrowest possible sensible understanding, if otherwise the requirement that a reasonable degree of legal certainty for third parties should be preserved, as it is expressed in Article 1 of the Protocol, cannot sufficiently be accommodated.[329] **5.99**

Due to the unambiguity of numbers and ranges, they may be found to be more clearly limiting than verbally described features.[330] However, this does not rule out the skilled person regarding a certain variance as reconcilable with the meaning of numbers, in particular variances within the usual tolerances of the technical field in question.[331] **5.100**

Whether the order of the claim steps must be respected can only be decided on a case-by-case basis.[332] **5.101**

A European-style patent claim is typically drafted in a two-part form, having a "preamble" comprising the claim features which are known from the closest piece of prior art and a "characterizing portion" comprising the features by which the subject matter of the claim is distinguished from this closest piece of prior art; they are separated by the expression "characterized in that."[333] In determining the extent of protection, it is irrelevant whether the feature is comprised by the preamble or by the characterizing portion.[334] This is different from the US practice, where an element comprised by the preamble may have no limiting function.[335] **5.102**

ii. Canons Favoring Patentees If the purpose or the effect of a patented product is specified in the claim, the extent of protection is not limited to products used for the specified purpose or having the specified effect.[336] For example, if a "mold for molten aluminum" is claimed, even a mold which is actually used for molten steel is covered. An indication of the purpose or the effect is nevertheless a true claim limitation in that the product must be **5.103**

---

327 Scharen in Benkard (ed.), *Patentgesetz Gebrauchsmustergesetz*, § 14, Ref. 10.

328 BGH GRUR 2009, 653, 654—*Straßenbaumaschine*.

329 Ibid.

330 BGH, GRUR 2005, 41, 42—*Staubsaugersaugrohr*; Keukenschrijver (ed.), *Busse, Patentgesetz*, § 14, Ref. 45.

331 Keukenschrijver (ed.), *Busse, Patentgesetz*, § 14, Ref. 45.

332 BGH, case No. X ZR 105/06; Keukenschrijver (ed.), *Busse, Patentgesetz*, § 14, Ref. 41; Scharen in Benkard (ed.), *Patentgesetz Gebrauchsmustergesetz*, § 14, Ref. 67.

333 Rule 43(1), second sentence of the Implementing Regulations to the EPC; § 9(2) of the Regulation of the Procedure in Patent Matters before the German Patent and Trademark Office. This structure is similar to a "Jepson" claim in the United States., Ch. 4, 4.33.

334 BGH GRUR 1994, 357, 258—*Muffelofen*; Scharen in Benkard (ed.), *Patentgesetz Gebrauchsmustergesetz*, § 14, Ref. 15; Keukenschrijver (ed.), *Busse, Patentgesetz*, § 14, Ref. 29.

335 Ch. 4, 4.82.

336 BGH GRUR 1979, 149, 150—*Schießbolzen*; GRUR 1991, 436, 441—*Befestigungsvorrichtung II*; GRUR 2006, 923, 925—*Luftabscheider für Milchsammelanlage*.

formed such that it is in principle suitable for being used for the indicated purpose or for achieving the indicated effect.[337] It indirectly defines the requirements of the structure or the material of the claimed product.[338] In the example, a plastic ice-cube tray with a melting point much lower than that of aluminum would not satisfy the limitation "mold for molten aluminum."[339]

5.104 In Germany, the same rules apply to indications of purpose or effect in process claims, with the exception of use claims.[340] A "method for performing X" is realized by all methods which are in principle suitable for performing X.[341] In contrast, according to the EPO practice, a "method for performing X" is limited to methods which comprise a step of performing X.[342]

5.105 It cannot be assumed that every feature has a meaning which goes beyond a mere triviality.[343] The applicant is free to mention self-evident features when formulating the patent claim and oftentimes will do so. Therefore, the fact that under a certain interpretation a claim element would only express a triviality does not rule out this interpretation.[344] A more limiting interpretation to give the element a non-trivial meaning is not required.

5.106 Reference signs or numerals from the drawings included in a patent claim may not be construed as limiting the claim.[345] They serve to increase the intelligibility of the claim[346] but do not limit the claim scope to the embodiments corresponding to the illustrations in which the numerals are used.[347] The task of the drawings is only to illustrate the inventive idea in a diagrammatic sketch.[348] They are not to be taken as drawn to scale, so their proportions should not receive further consideration.[349] From the fact that an element is missing in a drawing, it cannot be concluded that this element must not be present.[350]

4. Application of Construed Claims to Accused Embodiment

5.107 The patent is literally infringed if and only if the accused embodiment makes use of all claim elements as construed in accordance with the principles described in the previous section. Although the term "all elements rule" is not used in Germany, the rule itself is strictly applied. The Federal Court of Justice had, for a long time, left open the question of whether under the Patent Act in force as of 1978 protection for an embodiment satisfying only a

---

337 BGH GRUR 2009, 837, 838—*Bauschalungsstütze*; GRUR 2006, 923, 925—*Luftabscheider für Milchsammelanlage*; GRUR 1979, 149, 151—*Schießbolzen*.

338 BGH GRUR 1979, 149, 151—*Schießbolzen*.

339 Example taken from the EPO Guidelines for Examination, Part F, Ch. IV.4.13.

340 Keukenschrijver (ed.), *Busse, Patentgesetz*, § 14, Ref. 31; Kühnen, *Handbuch der Patentverletzung*, Ref. 40.

341 BGH GRUR 2010, 1081, 1083—*Bildunterstützung bei Katheternavigation*.

342 EPO Guidelines for Examination, Part F, Ch. IV.4.13.

343 BGH GRUR 2004, 1023, 1025—*Bodenseitige Vereinzelungsvorrichtung*; GRUR 2010, 602, 605—*Gelenkanordnung*; Keukenschrijver (ed.), *Busse, Patentgesetz*, § 14, Ref. 28.

344 Kühnen, *Handbuch der Patentverletzung*, Ref. 14.

345 Rule 43(7), second sentence of the Implementing Regulations to the EPC.

346 Rule 43(7), first sentence of the Implementing Regulations to the EPC.

347 BGH GRUR 2006, 316, 317—*Koksofentür*; Kühnen, *Handbuch der Patentverletzung*, Ref. 26; Scharen in Benkard (ed.), *Patentgesetz Gebrauchsmustergesetz*, § 14, Ref. 16; Keukenschrijver (ed.), *Busse, Patentgesetz*, § 14, Ref. 32; Kraßer, *Patentrecht*, p. 716, § 32 III b) 3.

348 Scharen in Benkard (ed.), *Patentgesetz Gebrauchsmustergesetz*, § 14, Ref. 29.

349 BGH case No. X ZR I 10/68.

350 BGH GRUR 2009, 390—*Lagerregal*; Kühnen, *Handbuch der Patentverletzung*, Ref. 26.

subset of all claim elements may come into consideration.[351] It was answered in the negative in a decision in 2007.[352] An accused embodiment which fails to satisfy one or more claim elements either literally or equivalently is outside the extent of protection even if the skilled person recognizes that the missing element(s) are not needed for the realization of the inventive idea.[353] Even if the patent claim is more narrow than necessary in light of the prior art, competitors may trust that the protection is limited to what is specified in the claim.[354]

If an accused embodiment makes use of all claim features, it is irrelevant whether the features in the accused embodiment serve the same purpose or function or achieve the same effect as those of the patent.[355] It makes no difference whether the claim is realized only by coincidence or in a systematic, targeted manner.[356] A patent can be infringed even if the accused embodiment is, in general, used such that the properties and effects of the invention of the patent are not achieved.[357] **5.108**

Relevant for the assessment of infringement is what the claimed subject matter and the accused embodiment have in common, not how they differ.[358] A competitor generally cannot avoid infringement by adding further elements to the accused embodiment. An improved embodiment with additional advantages is within the extent of the patent as long as it makes use of all claim features.[359] The improved embodiment may itself be patentable, but it remains a dependent invention. **5.109**

5. Doctrine of Equivalents

The doctrine of equivalents is motivated by the attempt to let the inventor have his due reward in undiminished form.[360] The acceptance of the fact that it is oftentimes not feasible to recognize or foresee all possible variants of the invention and to capture them by the claim formulation supports the principle long acknowledged in Germany that embodiments in which one or more claim elements are not realized literally but by obvious "replacement means" having the same effect may be covered by the extent of patent protection.[361] This is in line with the Protocol, which now explicitly states in its Article 2 that for the purpose of determining the extent of protection conferred by a European patent, due account shall be taken of any element which is equivalent to an element specified in the claims. **5.110**

While the subject matter or literal scope of a patent claim can be determined by way of claim construction in an absolute manner and is fixed at the priority date, the boundaries of the embodiments which realize the teaching of the claim with equivalent means **5.111**

---

351 E.g. in BGH GRUR 1992, 40, 41—*Beheizbarer Atemluftschlauch.*

352 Keukenschrijver (ed.), *Busse, Patentgesetz*, § 14, Ref. 76; BGH GRUR 2007, 1059—*Zerfallszeitmessgerät.*

353 Kühnen, *Handbuch der Patentverletzung*, Ref. 124.

354 Keukenschrijver (ed.), *Busse, Patentgesetz*, § 14, Ref. 76.

355 BGH GRUR 1991, 436, 441—*Befestigungsvorrichtung II*; GRUR 2006, 131, 134—*Seitenspiegel.*

356 Kühnen, *Handbuch der Patentverletzung*, Ref. 67; Scharen in Benkard (ed.), *Patentgesetz Gebrauchsmustergesetz*, § 14, Ref. 88; BGH GRUR 2006, 399, 401—*Rangierkatze.*

357 BGH GRUR 2006, 399, 401—*Rangierkatze.*

358 BGH case No. X ZR 19/88; Keukenschrijver (ed.), *Busse, Patentgesetz*, § 14, Ref. 58.

359 BGH GRUR 2006, 399, 401—*Rangierkatze*; Keukenschrijver (ed.), *Busse, Patentgesetz*, § 14, Ref. 74; Kühnen, *Handbuch der Patentverletzung*, Ref. 126.

360 BGH GRUR 1962, 29, 31—*Drehkippbeschlag*; GRUR 1969, 534, 535—*Skistiefelverschluss*; BGH GRUR 1986, 803, 805—*Formstein*; Keukenschrijver (ed.), *Busse, Patentgesetz*, § 14, Ref. 12.

361 Scharen in Benkard (ed.), *Patentgesetz Gebrauchsmustergesetz*, § 14, Ref. 99; Kraßer, *Patentrecht*, p. 722, § 32 III d) aa); Keukenschrijver (ed.), *Busse, Patentgesetz*, § 14, Ref. 62.

cannot be drawn in a precise manner.[362] However, in the interest of legal certainty,[363] competitors should be able to recognize whether or not their products or processes are covered by the extent of a patent. These circumstances led to a series of Federal Court of Justice decisions in recent years which restricted the application of the doctrine of equivalents. Consequently, there are today only a handful of court decisions in Germany every year in which infringement is found under this doctrine. This is compensated to some extent by the function-oriented claim construction as it is practiced by German courts,[364] which may allow the inclusion of a wider range of means that have the intended function and effects already in the literal scope of protection.

(a) Fundamental Rules

5.112 After the subject matter of the claim has been determined by way of claim interpretation, any differences between the accused embodiment and an embodiment falling within the literal scope of protection can be determined.[365] In the case of an accused embodiment which deviates from the subject matter protected by the patent claims (as determined by claim interpretation), there may be infringement if the person skilled in the art could, as a result of considerations which are based on the subject matter protected by the claims, find the modified means used in the accused embodiment as having the same effect with respect to the solution of the problem underlying the invention.[366] On this basis, the Federal Court of Justice developed a three-prong test for infringement under the doctrine of equivalents which it formulated in five parallel decisions, all of which it published on the same day.[367]

5.113 According to this test, an accused embodiment which deviates from the subject matter of the claims is included in the extent of protection of the patent if (1) the embodiment solves the problem underlying the invention with means which, although modified, objectively have the same effect; (2) the expertise of the skilled person enables him to identify the modified means as having the same effect; and (3) the considerations to be applied by the skilled person are guided by the semantic content of the technical teaching protected by the patent claim in such a way that the skilled person regards the deviating embodiment with its modified means as being equivalent[368] to the solution according to the subject matter of the claim.

5.114 **i. Objective Test: Same Effect** The first prong of the German test for infringement under the doctrine of equivalents asks whether the modified means of the accused embodiment objectively have the same effect and is therefore reminiscent of the "substantially the same function" and "to produce substantially the same result" prongs of the US triple identity test.[369]

5.115 The modified means has the same effect if, first of all, the overall effect of the invention is achieved, and, secondly, the effect of the claim element which is not literally realized

[362] Scharen in Benkard (ed.), *Patentgesetz Gebrauchsmustergesetz*, § 14, Ref. 100.

[363] In the United States, this is called the "notice function" of claims, Ch. 4, 4.29.

[364] Ch. 5, 5.70.

[365] BGH GRUR 2006, 313, 315—*Stapeltrockner*.

[366] BGH GRUR 1988, 896, 899—*Ionenanalyse*.

[367] March 12, 2002: BGH GRUR 2002, 511—*Kunststoffrohrteil*; GRUR 2002, 515—*Schneidmesser I*; GRUR 2002, 519—*Schneidmesser II*; GRUR 2002, 523—*Custodiol I*; GRUR 2002, 527—*Custodiol II*.

[368] In the German language, this is called "*gleichwertig*," which literally translated means "of equal value."

[369] Ch. 4, 4.93.

is achieved as well.[370] Not all effects which the claim element in question may have when regarded in isolation are decisive,[371] but only the effects the claim element provides for the solution of the problem underlying the invention,[372]—that is, the effects the claim element is intended to bring about in the context of the invention. Effects which may objectively be associated with the claim element but which have no importance in the context of the invention are to be disregarded.[373] It therefore has to be determined which of the effects which can be achieved by the claim element have to get together for solving the underlying problem.[374]

Infringement under the doctrine of equivalents does not require that the accused embodiment achieves the effects of the invention in a perfect manner or to the same degree as embodiments covered by the literal claim scope.[375] It is in general sufficient that the effects of the invention be essentially achieved or achieved to a practically significant degree.[376] However, if the skilled person interprets the claims such that there are certain minimum requirements as to the quality or quantity of a particular effect, modified means which do not satisfy these requirements cannot be regarded as having the same effect.[377] **5.116**

If a claim element is not replaced by a modified means but is simply left off, the accused embodiment does not fall within the extent of patent protection.[378] In this case, since every claim element has one or more effects, the first prong of the test is not satisfied because no replacement means can be identified which has the same effect(s) as the missing claim element.[379] However, it is unnecessary for the accused embodiment to have the same number of elements as the claimed subject matter.[380] There can be infringement under the doctrine of equivalents even if the individual effects of several claim elements are achieved by a single replacement means or if the effect(s) of a single claim element is achieved by several replacement means together.[381] **5.117**

ii. Obviousness The accused embodiment can be within the extent of protection only if the modification having the same effect was obvious to a skilled person who knew the teaching of the patent. Therefore, the second prong of the German test for infringement under the doctrine of equivalents requires that the skilled person be able to find the modified means at the priority date on the basis of his expertise and without inventive activity.[382] He has to be able to recognize that certain claim elements can be left off and be replaced by other **5.118**

370 BGH GRUR 2011, 313, 318—*Crimpwerkzeug IV*; GRUR 2012, 1122, 1123—*Palettenbehälter III*; GRUR 2000, 1005, 1006—*Bratgeschirr*; GRUR 2006, 313, 316—*Stapeltrockner*.

371 Kühnen, *Handbuch der Patentverletzung*, Ref. 72.

372 GRUR 2000, 1005, 1006—*Bratgeschirr*; GRUR 2006, 313, 316—*Stapeltrockner*.

373 BGH GRUR 2012, 45, 47—*Diglycidverbindung*.

374 GRUR 2000, 1005, 1006—*Bratgeschirr*; GRUR 2006, 313, 316—*Stapeltrockner*.

375 Kühnen, *Handbuch der Patentverletzung*, Ref. 129; Kraßer, *Patentrecht*, p. 730, § 32 III d) dd) 1; BGH GRUR 2000, 1005, 1006—*Bratgeschirr*.

376 BGH GRUR 1999, 909, 913—*Spannschraube*; GRUR 2000, 1005, 1006—*Bratgeschirr*; GRUR 2006, 311, 313—*Baumscheibenabdeckung*.

377 BGH GRUR 2012, 1122, 1123—*Palettenbehälter III*.

378 BGH GRUR 2007, 1059—*Zerfallszeitmessgerät*; Kühnen, *Handbuch der Patentverletzung*, Ref. 93; Keukenschrijver (ed.), *Busse, Patentgesetz*, § 14, Ref. 76.

379 Scharen in Benkard (ed.), *Patentgesetz Gebrauchsmustergesetz*, § 14, Ref. 106.

380 Kühnen, *Handbuch der Patentverletzung*, Ref. 96.

381 Ibid.; Kraßer, *Patentrecht*, p. 734, § 32 III 3) bb) 2; Scharen in Benkard (ed.), *Patentgesetz Gebrauchsmustergesetz*, § 14, Ref. 106.

382 Kühnen, *Handbuch der Patentverletzung*, Ref. 74.

suitable means.[383] This includes being able to recognize that the modified means has the same effect.[384] The standard for determining whether the skilled person is able to find the modified means and identify it as having the same effect should in general be the same as for the determination of (non-)obviousness in the context of patentability assessment. Unlike for claim interpretation,[385] not only documents referenced in the patent specification but also all prior art available at the priority date can be considered for this determination.[386]

5.119 There can be infringement under the doctrine of equivalents even in cases where a particular embodiment of a modification involves an inventive step, indicated, for example, by the fact that the infringer was able to obtain a patent on the solution using the modified means. This is the case if the modified means can be understood as a specific embodiment of a more general concept which the skilled person could identify, without inventive activity, as having the same effect as the claimed feature.[387] Under these circumstances, it is irrelevant whether its specific embodiment was obvious to the skilled person or involved an inventive step.

5.120 Although in Germany the relevant moment in time for the determination of obviousness is the priority date of the patent, there seems to be agreement in legal literature that even embodiments using replacement means which were unknown at the time of filing can infringe under the doctrine of equivalents.[388] It has been suggested that cases of "after-arising technologies" can satisfactorily be dealt with by asking whether the skilled person, had he known of the after-arising technology at the priority date, would have recognized it as having the same effect.[389] While the issue has not yet been decided by the Federal Patent Court, this suggestion has been adopted in a decision of the Dusseldorf Court of Appeals.[390]

5.121 **iii. Guidance by the Subject Matter of the Claim** Not all obvious modifications of the claimed invention having the same effect fall within the extent of the patent. The third prong of the test developed by the Federal Court of Justice requires that the (hypothetical)[391] considerations for finding the modification, applied by the skilled person, be guided by the subject matter of the patent claim. The guidance must be to such a degree that the skilled person regards the deviating embodiment with its modified means as being "equivalent"[392] to the solution according to the claim. The accused embodiment needs to be sufficiently close to the claimed subject matter, which is not the case if it cannot be sensibly related to

---

[383] Scharen in Benkard (ed.), *Patentgesetz Gebrauchsmustergesetz*, § 14, Ref. 109; Keukenschrijver (ed.), *Busse, Patentgesetz*, § 14, Ref. 67.

[384] BGH GRUR 1999, 977, 981—*Räumschild*; Scharen in Benkard (ed.), *Patentgesetz Gebrauchsmustergesetz*, § 14, Ref. 110.

[385] Ch. 5, 5.91.

[386] Kühnen, *Handbuch der Patentverletzung*, Ref. 74; Scharen in Benkard (ed.), *Patentgesetz Gebrauchsmustergesetz*, § 14, Ref. 111.

[387] BGH GRUR 1991, 436—*Befestigungsvorrichtung II*.

[388] Kühnen, *Handbuch der Patentverletzung*, Ref. 116; Keukenschrijver (ed.), *Busse, Patentgesetz*, § 14, Ref. 75; Scharen in Benkard (ed.), *Patentgesetz Gebrauchsmustergesetz*, § 14, Ref. 113; Kraßer, *Patentrecht*, p. 727, § 32 III d) cc) 1.

[389] Kühnen, *Handbuch der Patentverletzung*, Ref. 116; Scharen in Benkard (ed.), *Patentgesetz Gebrauchsmustergesetz*, § 14, Ref. 113.

[390] OLG Dusseldorf, InstGE 10, 198—*zeitversetztes Fernsehen*.

[391] It is not necessary for the developer of the modified embodiment to have actually been aware of the teaching of the patent and been guided by it. Scharen in Benkard (ed.), *Patentgesetz Gebrauchsmustergesetz*, § 14, Ref. 114.

[392] For the meaning of the German expression, n. 369 above.

the claimed subject matter.[393] This third prong of the German test, which is reminiscent of the "in substantially the same manner" prong of the US triple identity test, ensures that only something which can be regarded as a variant of the invention falls within the extent of the patent, and not solutions which are detached from the patented invention and strike a different path.[394] It also serves the aim of legal certainty and sets limits to the consideration of the interests of the patentee for giving the extent of patent protection the expansion which may be justified by the achievement of the invention.[395]

For example, there may be no sufficient guidance by the claimed subject matter in cases where the main object of the invention is to avoid the use of certain means and a claim element in the accused embodiment is replaced by precisely these means;[396] where it is essential for the patented invention to achieve a certain result without additional aids and the accused embodiment uses such aids;[397] or where a claim element is replaced by its opposite.[398] The accused embodiment may also be regarded as not being equivalent where its features deviate substantially from a number or value range specified by a claim element.[399] In all these cases, there may be an overlap with the first prong of the test for infringement under the doctrine of equivalents—that is, the replacement means may already not have the same effect. **5.122**

The Federal Court of Justice also denies equivalence in cases where, from a technical point of view, the differences are not too large, so that the accused embodiment could be regarded as a technical equivalent to the claimed invention, but where formulations in the patent specification convey the impression to the skilled reader that, for the realization of the patented teaching, it is crucial that the claim element is realized literally, or at least that the full range of solutions objectively having the same effect cannot be considered.[400] In these cases, third parties do not have to expect that the use of an embodiment in which the claim element is modified could be a patent infringement.[401] **5.123**

The constellation of cases in which the Federal Court of Justice most recently denied infringement under the third prong of the test concerns cases to which the doctrine of "dedication to the public"[402] would typically be applied in the United States: if the specification discloses several alternatives for obtaining a certain technical effect, but only one of them has been included in the patent claim, then the use of the other possibilities is in **5.124**

---

393 Cf. *Meier-Beck*, GRUR 2003, 909; BGH GRUR 2002, 519—*Schneidmesser II.*

394 *Meier-Beck*, GRUR 2003, 909.

395 Ibid.

396 BGH GRUR 1991, 444, 447—*Autowaschvorrichtung*; GRUR 1991, 744, 746—*Trockenlegungs-Verfahren*; Keukenschrijver (ed.), *Busse, Patentgesetz*, § 14, Ref. 69; *Meier-Beck*, GRUR 2003, 909.

397 BGH GRUR 1986, 238, 240—*Melkstand*; Keukenschrijver (ed.), *Busse, Patentgesetz*, § 14, Ref. 69; Scharen in Benkard (ed.), *Patentgesetz Gebrauchsmustergesetz*, § 14, Ref. 114.

398 Cf. OLG Düsseldorf, case No. I-2 U 65/09, at II.2.a)(c); Keukenschrijver (ed.), *Busse, Patentgesetz*, § 14, Ref. 69; Kühnen, *Handbuch der Patentverletzung*, Ref. 103 and 105, giving the example of a "symmetrical arrangement" mentioned in the claim which is replaced by an asymmetrical arrangement.

399 E.g., in BGH GRUR 2002, 519, 523—*Schneidmesser II*, the court found that a cutting blade arranged at an angle of 25° is not regarded as equivalent to the claimed range of 10–22°; in BGH GRUR 2002, 527, 531—*Custodiol II*, a solution having 4 millimoles of magnesium chloride was not regarded equivalent to the claimed solution having 8–12 millimoles.

400 BGH GRUR 2002, 519, 523—*Schneidmesser II*; GRUR 2002, 523, 526—*Custodiol I*; GRUR 2002, 527, 531—*Custodiol II*; Kühnen, *Handbuch der Patentverletzung*, Ref. 77.

401 Scharen in Benkard (ed.), *Patentgesetz Gebrauchsmustergesetz*, § 14, Ref. 115.

402 Ch. 4, 4.124.

general not infringement by equivalent means.[403] The reader of the patent specification will have to assume that—for whatever reason—the alternatives which were disclosed but not claimed should be unprotected and left in the public domain.[404] In such a situation, even an alternative which is not disclosed in the specification may be outside the extent of protection if it does not correspond to the claimed alternative in its specific effects or if it does not differ from the disclosed alternative which has not been claimed in a similar fashion as the claimed alternative.[405]

5.125 In particular, this last group of cases makes clear that the third prong of the test, although it asks whether there is sufficient guidance by the subject matter of the claim, cannot be decided on the basis of the claim language alone. Only by reading the description and the drawings can it become apparent that literal realization of a certain claim element is regarded as indispensable or that a certain technically equivalent alternative should not be included in the extent of protection.[406] Similar to the determination of the literal scope of protection by way of claim interpretation, infringement under the doctrine of equivalents is to be decided on the basis of the claims as explained and clarified by the description and the drawings.[407]

(b) Doctrines to Limit the Doctrine of Equivalents

5.126 Although case law in Germany, like the United States, has limited the possibility of finding infringement under the doctrine of equivalents more and more,[408] the doctrine is still of practical importance. Unlike in the United States,[409] its application in practice is not limited to cases where the equivalent was unforeseeable at the time of drafting or amending a claim. This is due in part to the fact that some important US doctrines limiting the doctrine of equivalents are not recognized in Germany, in particular the prosecution history estoppel.[410] A principle that the extent of protection does not include equivalents if the claim has been amended could be regarded as contradictory to the statute because § 14 of the German Patent Act/Article 69 of the European Patent Convention and the Protocol do not distinguish between amended and unamended patents.[411]

5.127 German courts do apply a principle similar to the US "dedication to the public" doctrine, in the context of the third prong of the German test for infringement under the doctrine of equivalents, as has been discussed supra in section (a) iii. German case law also provides a "practicing the prior art" defense against an alleged infringement under the doctrine of equivalents, which will be discussed for the remainder of this section.

5.128 The so-called "*Formstein*" defense, named after a decision of the Federal Court of Justice with the same title, allows the defendant to make the argument that the embodiment which allegedly infringes the patent under the doctrine of equivalents would not have been

---

403 BGH GRUR 2011, 701—*Okklusionsvorrichtung*; GRUR 2012, 45, 47—*Diglycidverbindung*.

404 BGH GRUR 2011, 701—*Okklusionsvorrichtung*; Kühnen, *Handbuch der Patentverletzung*, Ref. 99.

405 GRUR 2012, 45—*Diglycidverbindung*.

406 Scharen in Benkard (ed.), *Patentgesetz Gebrauchsmustergesetz*, § 14, Ref. 116; Kühnen, *Handbuch der Patentverletzung*, GRUR 2013, 1086, 1087.

407 Kühnen, *Handbuch der Patentverletzung*, GRUR 2013, 1086, 1087.

408 Ch. 5, 5.111.

409 Ch. 4, 4.113.

410 Ch. 4, 4.105.

411 Scharen in Benkard (ed.), *Patentgesetz Gebrauchsmustergesetz*, § 14, Ref. 119.

patentable in light of the prior art.[412] This is the case if the combination of the claim features which are literally realized by the accused embodiment and the features which are realized in an equivalent manner is anticipated or rendered obvious by the prior art which is relevant for the patent.[413]

The rationale for this "practicing the prior art" defense, which is available only if infringement under the doctrine of equivalents is asserted but not against an assertion of literal infringement,[414] is that during examination of the patent or in opposition or revocation proceedings, patentability of the invention is only assessed with respect to the extent of the literal claim scope, and the additional extent under the doctrine of equivalents is not considered.[415] Third parties should not be denied the possibility of using non-inventive improvements of the prior art,[416] for which protection could not have been obtained by the patentee.[417] **5.129**

The test considers the features of the accused embodiment only in so far as they correspond to the subject matter of the patent claims.[418] Additional features which do not concern the protected invention are to be disregarded.[419] In practice it is advisable to use a reformulated patent claim in which the elements which are not literally realized are modified so that they read on the equivalent means. The subject matter of this hypothetical claim is then assessed with respect to novelty and inventive step.[420] **5.130**

The defendant has the full burden of proving that the accused embodiment is anticipated or rendered obvious by the prior art[421] and has to furnish the prior art documents himself. Unlike in invalidation proceedings, it is not possible for the court to examine *ex officio*.[422] Since the "practicing the prior art" defense is available only against an allegation of infringement under the doctrine of equivalents, the defendant has no reason to provide prior art and argue non-patentability of the accused embodiment if only literal infringement has been asserted by the plaintiff. Therefore, the court cannot find infringement under the doctrine of equivalents unless it has explicitly been asserted by the plaintiff and the defendant has been given the opportunity of raising the *Formstein* defense and submit suitable evidence.[423] **5.131**

---

[412] BGH GRUR 1986, 803—*Formstein*.

[413] Kühnen, *Handbuch der Patentverletzung*, Ref. 118.

[414] BGH GRUR 1999, 914, 918—*Kontaktfederblock*; Scharen in Benkard (ed.), *Patentgesetz Gebrauchsmustergesetz*, § 14, Ref. 126.

[415] Kraßer, *Patentrecht*, p. 738, § 32 III f) bb) 5.

[416] Scharen in Benkard (ed.), *Patentgesetz Gebrauchsmustergesetz*, § 14, Ref. 126.

[417] Kühnen, *Handbuch der Patentverletzung*, Ref. 118.

[418] Keukenschrijver (ed.), *Busse, Patentgesetz*, § 14, Ref. 82; see also BGH GRUR 1999, 914, 918—*Kontaktfederblock*.

[419] Keukenschrijver (ed.), *Busse, Patentgesetz*, § 14, Ref. 82.

[420] Kühnen, *Handbuch der Patentverletzung*, Ref. 119.

[421] BGH GRUR 1986, 803, 806—*Formstein*; GRUR 1999, 914, 918—*Kontaktfederblock*; Scharen in Benkard (ed.), *Patentgesetz Gebrauchsmustergesetz*, § 14, Ref. 130; Kraßer, *Patentrecht*, 737, § 32 III f) bb) 4.

[422] Kraßer, *Patentrecht*, 735, § 32 III f) aa) 3; Scharen in Benkard (ed.), *Patentgesetz Gebrauchsmustergesetz*, § 14, Ref. 130.

[423] Kühnen, *Handbuch der Patentverletzung*, Ref. 81.

6

JAPAN

A. Acts of Infringement

1. Direct Infringement

6.01 Under the Japanese Patent Act, a patent owner has the exclusive right to work the patented invention as a business.[1] Like the German Patent Act,[2] the Act classifies inventions into three categories: (1) an invention of a product; (2) an invention of a process that does not result in any product; and (3) an invention of a process that results in a product.[3] Acts constitute working an invention and thus give rise to infringement when such acts are undertaken without authority with respect to a patented invention. The scope of exclusivity differs depending on the category of invention. Regarding (1) an invention of a product, acts of working an invention include making, using, assigning, exporting, importing, and offering to assign the product.[4] Regarding (2) an invention of a process not resulting in a product, acts of working an invention are limited to use of the process.[5] Accordingly, when a patent is granted for a process to measure an object, the patent does not exclude others from working on a product made by using the patented measuring process. For example, a patent for a process to measure the efficiency of kallikrein inhibitor in human blood does not preclude others from working on a drug made by using the measuring process.[6]

6.02 The Japanese Patent Act uses the term "assigning" instead of "selling," which is used under the US Patent Act, to include any transfer of ownership of a patented product with or without compensation.[7] Acts of "assigning" under the Japanese Patent Act should be understood as comparable to "putting on the market" under the German Patent Act because the exclusive right under the Japanese Patent Act extends to acts of assigning only when the acts are performed as a business.[8] This business use requirement excludes private use, the working of an invention by a person alleged to infringe a patent and by his family members,[9] and thus is met when an assignment results in a patented product being put on the market. Acts of assigning are defined to include leasing a patented product or a product resulting from a

---

[1] Tokkyo hō (Japanese Patent Act), § 68.
[2] German Patent Act, § 9.
[3] Japanese Patent Act, § 2(3).
[4] Japanese Patent Act, § 2(3) i.
[5] Japanese Patent Act, § 2(3) ii.
[6] Japanese Patent Act, § 2(3) iii.
[7] Nobuhiro Nakayama, *Chūkai Tokkyohō (Detailed Explanation of Patent Act)* (3d ed., 2000), 35. For an overview of claim interpretation at Japanese courts, see Toshiko Takenaka, "Interpreting Patent Claims: The United States, Germany and Japan," 17 *IIC Studies* (1995): 26–38.
[8] Japanese Patent Act, § 68.
[9] Nakayama, *Chūkai Tokkyohō*, 664.

patented process.[10] Moreover, acts of offering include acts of displaying a patented product or a product resulting from a patented process if the product is displayed for the purpose of assignment and leasing.[11]

Unlike the European Patent Convention and the German Patent Act, the Japanese Patent Act makes it clear that a computer program is considered an invention of product.[12] If a patented product is a computer program, acts of assigning include providing the product through an electric telecommunication line.[13] **6.03**

Acts of offering to assign was added to comply with the obligation under Agreement on Trade-related Aspects of Intellectual Property Rights (TRIPS).[14] Like the US and German Patent Acts, the Japanese Patent Act makes it clear that an act of offering to assign is an infringing act independent from an assignment. Like the German Patent Act, the Japanese Patent Act should be interpreted as stating that an infringement arises if an act of offering occurs in Japan and before the expiration of a patent, even if an act of assigning a patented product occurs outside of Japan or after the expiration of patent. However, an act of offering must be performed in the context of an act of assigning a patented product. Merely linking to a third party's webpage advertising a patented product may be insufficient to give rise to an offering to assign if a prospective buyer needs to go through multiple links to find a patented product.[15] **6.04**

Unlike the German Patent Act, the Japanese Patent Act does not provide "possessing" as an act of direct infringement. Instead, the Act provides that an act of possessing constitutes an act of indirect infringement if a party processes a patented product or a product resulting from a patented process for the purpose of assigning or exporting as a business.[16] Moreover, an act of making, assigning, or importing such products is necessary for a party prior to an act of possessing the products. The patent owner can enforce their patents against a party who engages in the prior act as direct infringement. **6.05**

Unlike the German Patent Act, the Japanese Patent Act does not expressly require an act of "importing" to be engaged for the purpose of assigning, leading, or using a patented product or a product resulting from a patented process. It is unlikely that acts of importing unrelated to such purpose give rise to infringement because many such importing acts do not meet the business use requirement.[17] Importing and storing patented products in a warehouse may give rise to infringement even if the products are sold after the expiration of the patent. **6.06**

The Japanese Patent Act adopts the same approach as the German Patent Act in defining acts of infringement distinctively between patents directing to a product and patents **6.07**

[10] Japanese Patent Act, § 2(3) i.

[11] Ibid.

[12] Ibid.

[13] Ibid.

[14] Agreement on Trade-related Aspects of Intellectual Property Rights, April 15, 1994, Marrakesh Agreement Establishing the World Trade Organization, Annex 1C, The Legal Texts: The Results of the Uruguay Round of Multilateral Trade Negotiations, 320 (1999), 1869 U.N.T.S. 299, 33 I.L.M. 1197 (1994).

[15] Chiteki Zaisan Koto Saibansho (IP High Ct.) July 11, 2013, Hei 25 (ne) No. 10014, Saiko Saibansho Saibanrei Joho (Sup. Ct. Case Database) http://www.ip.courts.go.jp/hanrei/pdf/20130806152022.pdf.

[16] Japanese Patent Act, § 101, iii, vi.

[17] Nakayama, *Chūkai Tokkyohō*, 35.

directing to a process. Acts of offering are defined as infringement only with respect to a patented product and a product resulting from a patented process.[18] This is in stark contrast to the German Patent Act under which offering a patented process to use is explicitly provided as an infringement.[19] The Act should be read to exclude acts of offering a patented process to use from patent exclusivity.

6.08 Like German and US patents, Japanese patents directing to a process extend to the product made by a patented process. Although the Act does not require a product to be made directly from a patented process as required under the German Patent Act or provide any limitation as provided under the US Patent Act,[20] the lack of made-directly limitation should not be read as extending the exclusive right of Japanese patents to any product that is materially changed by a subsequent process. Commentators read the lack of limitation as broadly concerning products covered by a patented process so as to protect a final chemical compound resulting from a starting or intermediate material even if the structure and property of the material are materially changed.[21] However, if a subsequent step materially changes the structure or property of a product made by a patented process, the exclusivity of the process patent should not extend to the materially changed product. A starting or intermediate material and a final product are distinct from each because of the intervening process, and separate patents can be issued to them. Allowing exclusivity of a process patent for a starting or intermediate material to a final product may effectively extend the term of patent for the final product if the process patent is enforced after the expiration of the patent for the final product. This interpretation is in line with US case law[22] as well as German case law.[23]

6.09 Moreover, a Japanese process patent should be understood as extending to a product made by the process even though the product becomes a trivial and nonessential component of another product if the structure and property of the product directly made by the patented process remains the same. Thus, the exclusivity of Japanese process patent should be interpreted more broadly than those of its German and US counterparts.

6.10 To give rise to infringement by "making" with respect to a patent directing to a product, a party must complete a product that has all elements recited in the patent asserted by the patent owner. A party is not liable for direct infringement if he or she is making only a component of a patented product and the component is combined by a third party with the rest of the components to complete a patented product even though such an act may give rise to indirect infringement.[24] In contrast, a party may be liable for direct infringement by replacing or repairing a component of a patented product if such replacing or repairing gives rise to reconstruction.[25]

6.11 In principle, a party is liable for infringement by "using" a patented process only if the party engages in all steps of the process. In theory, direct infringement may arise under

[18] Japanese Patent Act, § 2(3) i and iii.
[19] German Patent Act, § 9(2). See Ch. 5, 5.04.
[20] 35 USC § 271(g). See Ch. 4, 4.02
[21] Nakayama, *Chūkai Tokkyohō*, 36.
[22] *Eli Lilly & Co. v. American Cyanamid Co.*, 82 F.3d 1568 (Fed. Cir. 1996). See Ch. 4, 4.02.
[23] LG Düsseldorf, GRUR 1987, 896—Grasherbizid. See Ch. 5, 5.14.
[24] Japanese Patent Act, § 101. For more discussion, see Ch. 6, 6.13 "Indirect Infringement."
[25] Sup. Ct. of Japan, November 8, 2007, 61 Minshū (No. 8) 2989.

the Civil Code for the joint tort of aiding and abetting if a party collaborates with another party to engage in some steps of a patented process while they perform the remaining steps.[26] However, Japanese courts are reluctant to expand the concept of direct infringement through aiding and abetting under the general joint tort theory unless an allegedly infringing act falls into the definition of acts of indirect infringement.[27]

Under exceptional circumstances, Japanese courts may rely on vicarious liability to find infringing a party who directs and controls a third party to complete the working of a patented invention. With respect to the act of "using" a patented process for the making of a product, a party may be liable for direct infringement even though a third party engages in the last step to complete the process if the allegedly infringing party used the third party as a tool to engage in the last step.[28] The Tokyo District Court found that the defendant used a third party as a tool to complete the manufacturing process when the defendant provided the third party with an unfinished product that had no use other than to engage the very last step of a patented process and completing a product.[29] Some courts found infringement of a patent claim directed to a process including multiple steps or system including multiple components even though the steps are performed by multiple parties or the components owned by different parties.[30] They distinguished the question of whether acts fall into the scope of an asserted patent claim and thus constitute infringement from the question of whether an injunction should be granted against a party. This is because the Supreme Court of Japan distinguished the nature of claims for injunctive reliefs from the nature of claims for damages to compensate infringement of intellectual property.[31] A party is liable for direct infringement of a patent directing to a process by providing access to information on a website if the party engages some steps to provide the access even though clients of the party engaged other steps of the process to get the access.[32] **6.12**

2. Indirect Infringement

Like under US and German laws, defendants may be liable even if they themselves do not engage in infringement by working on a patented invention. As discussed in the previous section, unlike German law, liability as an accessory under the general tort theory is very limited except for acts explicitly deemed as infringement ("indirect infringement") under the Japanese Patent Act. Under § 101 there are three types of acts that constitute indirect infringement: (1) acts focusing on a product that relates to the working of a patented invention (these acts are comparable to contributory infringement under US Law: "U.S.-style indirect infringement");[33] (2) acts focusing on the knowledge of an allegedly infringing party (these acts are comparable to contributory infringement under German **6.13**

[26] Minpō (Civil Code), § 719: Liability of joint tortfeasors.

[27] Tokyo Chihō Saibansho (Tokyo Dist. Ct.) August 17, 2004, Hanrei Jihō (No. 1873) 153. Makiko Takabe, *Jitsumu Shōsetsu: Tokkyo Kankei Sosho (Detailed Explanation of Practice: Patent and Related Litigations)* (2d ed., 2012), 124.

[28] Tokyo Dist. Ct., September 20, 2000, Hei 12 (wa) No. 20503, Hanrei Jiho (No. 1764) 112, Hanrei Taimuzu (No. 1094) 245.

[29] Ibid.

[30] IP High Court, March 24, 2010, Hei 20 (ne) No. 10085, Hanrei Taimuzu (No. 1358) 184, Tokyo District Court, December 14, 2007, Hei 16 (wa) No. 25576, Tokkyo Hanrei Database (http://tokkyo.hanrei.jp/hanrei/pt/7470.html).

[31] Sup. Ct. of Japan, September 26, 2002 Hei 12 (Ju) No. 580, 56 Minshū 1551.

[32] IP High Court, March 24, 2010, Hei 20 (ne) No. 10085, Hanrei Taimuzu (No. 1358) 184.

[33] Japanese Patent Act, § 101(1) i, iv.

law: "German-style indirect infringement");[34] and (3) acts of possessing a patented product or a product resulting from a patented process (these acts constitute direct infringement rather than indirect infringement under German law).[35] Regarding the acts of possessing, the patent owner must establish that an allegedly infringing party has an intent to assign or to export such products to be liable for indirect infringement.

6.14 US-style indirect infringement is further classified into two types with respect to the category of the asserted patented invention: (1) regarding a patent directing to a product, acts of making, assigning, importing, or offering for assignment with respect to any means to be used exclusively for making the patented product as a business;[36] and (2) regarding a patent directing to a process, acts of making, assigning, importing, or offering for assignment with respect to any means to be used exclusively for using the process as a business.[37] In short, the Act requires an exclusive infringing use that is comparable to non-infringing use under US law. To meet the exclusive use requirement, a patent owner must establish that the accused means, which is used for a patent invention, has no economically, commercially, or practically viable use other than an infringing use.[38] When an accused means has multiple uses and any one of these uses is non-infringing, the means fails to meet the exclusive use requirement.[39] Such means used for a patented invention include a component or unassembled components of a patented product, a machine, or material for making a patented product or for using a patented process.

6.15 Unlike US law, Japanese courts do not require a patent owner to establish direct infringement by a third party as prerequisite for US-style indirect infringement. The owner only needs to establish a *prima facie* case that the means has no non-infringing use, which will then shift the burden on the accused infringer to show a non-infringing use to rebut the *prima facie* case.[40] Japanese commentators disagree on whether direct infringement by a third party is a prerequisite for indirect infringement, in particular when the act of the third party is exempted from infringement for private use and experimental use.[41] This is a stark contrast to German law where a party is liable for indirect infringement even when a third party who engages in direct infringement is exempted from patent infringement.[42]

6.16 Patent owners frequently fail to establish US-style indirect infringement because Japanese courts interpret the exclusive use requirement restrictively. To efficiently prevent activities preparing for direct infringement, the 2002 Patent Revision introduced German-style indirect infringement by removing the exclusive use requirement. German-style indirect infringement is also classified into two types: (1) regarding a patent directing to a product, acts of making, assigning, importing, or offering for assignment with respect to any means

---

[34] Japanese Patent Act, § 101(1) ii, v.

[35] Japanese Patent Act, § 101(1) iii, vi. For German law, see Ch. 5, 5.07.

[36] Japanese Patent Act, § 101(1) i. See Takabe, *Jitsumu Shōsetsu*, 162; Ei-ichiroh Kubota, "Kansetsu Shingai ni Tsuite (Regarding Indirect Infringement)," in Toahiaki Makino et al. (eds.), *Chiteki Zaisan no Riton to Jitsumu (Theories and Practice on Intellectual Property Law)* (2007), vol. I, 198.

[37] Japanese Patent Act, § 101(1) iv.

[38] Osaka Dist. Ct., October 24, 2000, Hei 8 (wa) No. 12109, Hanrei Taimusu (No. 1081) 241. See n. 27 above.

[39] Tokyo Dist. Ct., February 25, 1981, Sho 50 (wa) No. 9647, 13 Mutaishū (No. 1) 139, Hanrei Jihō (No. 1007) 72.

[40] Ibid.

[41] Nakayama, *Chūkai Tokkyohō*, 959.

[42] German Patent Act, § 10(3).

to be used for producing the patented product and indispensable for solving the problem of the invention for the patented product as a business, knowing that the product is patented and the means is used for the working of the invention;[43] and (2) regarding a patent directing to a process, acts of making, assigning, importing, or offering for assignment with respect to any means to be used for the patented process and indispensable for solving the problem of the invention for the patented process as a business, knowing that the process is patented and the means is used for the working of the invention.[44] Like German law, if the means is a staple good that is widely distributed in Japan, making, etc. of such means does not give rise to indirect infringement.

Moreover, such means must be indispensable or essential for solving the problem of the invention for a patented product or process. This requirement is similar to the "essential element" and the "objectively suitable to put the invention into effect" requirements under German law.[45] Although German law provides these two requirements separately, courts admit that the "objectively suitable to put the invention into effect" requirement is usually met when the "essential element" requirement is met.[46] German law requires an element or means contributing to the solution of the problem that the asserted patent inventions are addressing.[47] The indispensable requirement under Japanese law is met only when the means contribute to the solution of the technical problem addressed by the invention; a means does not meet the "essential or non-dispensable" requirement if the means has been used in the prior art and does not relate to a new result even though the means is an element of the patented invention.[48] Like German law, the means includes not only elements of the patented invention but also materials or tools that are not an element of the patented invention.[49] Such means must be used directly with a patented product or directly to engage acts in a patented process.[50] This requirement is comparable to the requirement under German law that the means must interact with the patented process or product.[51] In contrast, the US Patent Act requires a component to be a material part of a patented invention to establish contributory infringement.[52] To be a material part, the component must be an element of a patented invention.[53] **6.17**

There are some major differences from German law. First, the knowledge requirement is more restrictive than knowledge under German law: an actual knowledge is necessary with respect to the asserted patent and the fact that the means is used for the working of the invention.[54] In contrast, an actual knowledge is not necessary under German law when circumstantial evidence makes it clear that the means is suitable and is intended for the **6.18**

[43] Japanese Patent Act, § 101(1) ii.

[44] Japanese Patent Act, § 101(1) v.

[45] See Ch. 5, 5.29.

[46] See Ch. 5, 5.30.

[47] BGH GRUR 2007, 769, 771—Pipettensystem.

[48] Tokyo Dist. Ct., April 23, 2004, Hei 16 (wa) No. 6035, Hanrei Jihō (No. 1892) 89. See Takabe, *Jitsumu Shōsetsu*, 163.

[49] Takabe, *Jitsumu Shōsetsu*, 163.

[50] IP High Ct., September 30, 2005, Hei 17 (ne) No. 100040, Hanrei Jihō (No. 1904) 47.

[51] Cf. BGH GRUR 2004, 758, 760—Flügelradzähler; BGH GRUR 2005, 848, 849—Antriebsscheibenaufzug; BGH GRUR 2012, 1230, 1235—MPEG-2 Videosignalcodierung.

[52] 35 U.S.C. § 271(c). See Ch. 4, 4.09.

[53] *Fujitsu, Ltd.*, 620 F.3d 1321 (Fed. Cir. 2010).

[54] See Takabe, *Jitsumu Shōsetsu*, 163.

working of the invention.[55] An actual knowledge of the asserted patent and the nature of the component or a third party's infringement is not required for establishing contributory infringement or active inducement under US law.[56]

6.19 Like German law, a patent owner does not need to establish an actual use of the means or direct infringement by a third party because the Japanese Patent Act aims to efficiently prevent preparation of direct infringement by replacing the exclusive use requirement with the essential means and knowledge equipment requirement. However, it does not aim to extend indirect infringement to inducement even though the means used for a patented process or product is a staple good and widely distributed in Japan. Under German law, a party is liable for inducement even when such means is a staple good if a patent owner establishes that a third party engages in direct infringement and such infringement resulted from the party's act of inducement.[57] US courts also find active inducement with respect to a staple good if the knowledge and intent requirements are met.[58]

3. Patent Term and Extension

6.20 The patent term is the same as under US and German laws: twenty years from the filing date, which includes the priority date under the Paris Convention and the international application date under the Patent Cooperation Treaty.[59] Like the US system, a patent term is extended by up to five years for patents on products that require an approval to market such as drugs and agricultural chemicals.[60] This patent term extension (PTE) system was introduced in 1988. Under the Japanese Patent Act, the objective of Japan's PTE system is set forth:

> Where there is a period during which the patented invention is unable to be worked because approvals prescribed by relevant Acts that are intended to ensure the safety, etc. or any other disposition designated by Cabinet Order as requiring considerable time for the proper execution of the disposition in light of the purpose, procedures, etc., of such a disposition are necessary to obtain for the working of the patented invention, the duration of the patent right may be extended, upon the filing of a request for the registration of extension of the duration, by a period not exceeding five years.[61]

To request an extension, brand name drug manufacturers must file a PTE application and may receive an extension of patent rights by a period not exceeding five years.[62] However, the Patent Act provides multiple grounds for rejecting a PTE request, including "Where the disposition designated by Cabinet Order is not deemed to have been necessary to obtain for the working of the patented invention which is under the examination for PTE."[63] When an extension is granted, the effect of the extended patent term is limited; it is effective only against such acts of working a patented invention with respect to the product that was

[55] See Ch. 5, 5.26.
[56] Evidence to establish willful blindness is sufficient. See Ch. 4, 4.07.
[57] German Patent Act, § 10(2).
[58] *DSU Medical Corp. v. JMS Co., Ltd.*, 471 F.3d 1293 (Fed. Cir. 2006). For more discussions on active inducement, see Ch. 4, 4.07.
[59] Japanese Patent Act, § 67(1).
[60] Ibid. § 67(2).
[61] Ibid. Art. 67(2).
[62] Ibid. Art. 67(2), 67-2 (2011).
[63] Ibid. Art. 67-3 (2011).

prescribed by the disposition and prohibited prior to approval by Ministry of Health, Labor and Welfare.[64]

6.21 Since the introduction of PTEs, the Japan Patent Office (JPO) has rejected PTE applications unless the patent under examination is directed to an approved drug product that contains a new active ingredient or a new use of a previously approved drug. This is because the object of the PTE system recites "considerable time" as being required for getting an execution of a disposition. The Pharmaceutical Affairs Act categorizes a drug as a new drug according to the active ingredient of the drug and categorizes use of a previously approved drug as a new use according to the "efficacy/effect" of the known drug. The IP High Court struck down the JPO's examination practice for being inconsistent with the language of the Japanese Patent Act.[65] The Supreme Court affirmed the conclusion of the IP High Court's decision.[66] To implement the IP High Court and Supreme Court's interpretation of the Japanese Patent Act, the JPO has revised the PTE examination guidelines.[67] To determine whether a previous disposition enables the patentee to practice the patented invention at issue for the drug product covered by the patent under the PTE examination—and therefore making the patent ineligible for a PTE grant—the JPO compares a drug product description from the prior disposition with the scope of the patent under PTE examination. A PTE application is rejected "if a person has obtained a disposition for a prior drug product or a prior agricultural chemical (a 'prior disposition') that satisfies the 'matters falling under the matters to define the invention (and the use)' of the drug product or the agricultural chemical that was the subject of the present disposition."[68] Under the new PTE guidelines, patentees may be entitled to a PTE for a new formulation of a previously approved drug product if a previous disposition does not allow marketing of a patented invention for the new formulation even where the active ingredient is the same.[69] The revised guidelines also limit the effect of the extended patent term to the product described in the disposition.[70]

6.22 It is interesting to note that the IP High Court interpreted the grounds for rejecting PTE applications in light of the PTE system under the US Patent Act and the Supplemental Protection Certificate in the European Union. The United States and Europe strongly enforce the active ingredient limitation and have limited PTE opportunities. The US Court of Appeals for the Federal Circuit interprets "active ingredient" broadly to mean an ingredient present in the drug being approved, including any salt or ester of such an ingredient.[71] This interpretation excludes PTEs on a new use or formulation of a drug product if the drug

---

[64] Ibid. Art. 68-2 (2011).

[65] Chiteki Zaisan Kōtō Saibansho (Intellectual Prop. High Ct.) May 29, 2009, Hei 20 (gyō ke) No. 10458, 1305 Hanrei Taimuzu 80; 2047 Hanrei Jihō 11 (Japan).

[66] Saikō Saibansho (Sup. Ct.) April 28, 2011, Hei 21 (gyō hi) No. 326, 65 Saikō Saibansho Minji Hanreishū (No. 3) 1654; 1348 Hanrei Taimuzu 102; 2115 Hanrei Jihō 32 (Japan).

[67] Japan Patent Office, Revision of the Examination Guidelines for "Patent Term Extension" (February 14, 2012), http://www.jpo.go.jp/iken_e/patent_term_rev.htm.

[68] Ibid.

[69] For a discussion of the impact of the revised PTE guidelines, see Hiroshi Kato, "A View on Patent Term Extension System" (http://www.law.nihon-u.ac.jp/publication/pdf/chizai/5/05.pdf), 8. The IP High Court struck down the new guidelines. Chiteki Zaisan Kōtō Saibansho [Intellectual Prop. High Ct.] May 30, 2014, Hei 25 (gyo ke) No. 10195, Hanrei Jiho No. 2232, 3. A petition of appeal against the IP High Court is pending at the Supreme Court of Japan.

[70] Junji Tanaka, "Revision of Patent Term Extension Examination Guidelines: Background of Revision and its Impact" (April 4, 2012) (http://ushiki-pat.com/index.php/topics-ja/3-topic/19-column2012040401).

[71] 35 U.S.C. § 156(f); *Glaxo Operations UK, Ltd. v. Quigg*, 894 F.2d 392, 394 (Fed. Cir. 1990); *PhotoCure Asa v. Kappos*, 603 F.3d 1372, 1376 (Fed. Cir. 2010).

product has the same active ingredient of a previously approved drug product. In contrast, EU Supplemental Protection Certificate (SPC) Regulation may grant multiple SPCs on drug products that have the same active ingredient under limited circumstances.[72] Because the Japanese Patent Act does not include an explicit active ingredient limitation, the IP High Court disagreed with the JPO for adopting a practice that was more in line with the US and EU PTE systems.

4. Extraterritorial Infringement

6.23 Unlike the US and German Patent Act, the Japanese Patent Act does not explicitly provide that acts of infringement must occur within the territory of Japan. The Supreme Court of Japan emphasizes the supremacy of the territorial principle with respect to the effect of patent rights and makes it clear that the effect of a patent right extends only within the country where the right is granted.[73] Like Germany, both acts of direct and indirect infringement must occur within Japan. One exception is an infringement of a process patent. Importing a product resulting from a process is infringement of a Japanese process patent where a Japanese patent is granted to the process even though the process is used outside Japan.[74]

6.24 Japanese courts also apply the "double territoriality requirement" of German courts:[75] both an act of supplying the exclusive-infringing-use means or indispensable means and the infringement act resulting from the use of the means must take place in Japan.[76] If a party exports a product that has an exclusive infringing use but the product is only used abroad, the party is not liable for indirect infringement.[77]

B. Extent of Patent Protection

1. Overview

6.25 The Japanese Patent Act provides the rule that the technical scope of a patent must be determined on the basis of its claim terms.[78] It also allows courts to clarify the meaning of a claim term in light of the specification and the drawings.[79] Because "technical scope" is a legal term used to define the extent of patent protection, the Japanese rule closely parallels the rule under EPC, Art. 69. However, this rule is relatively new in the Japanese patent system. Like Germany under its three-part theory, the original method of Japanese claiming gave little significance to the claim term in defining the extent of patent protection. However,

---

[72] Regulation (EC) No. 469/2009 of The European Parliament and of the Council of 6 May 2009 concerning the supplementary protection certificate for medicinal products, Art. 3(c)(d). C-181/95 *Biogen v. Smithkline Beecham Biologicals*; C-482/07 *AHP Manufacturing v. BIE*; C-130/11 *Neurim Pharmaceuticals*.

[73] Sup. Ct. of Japan, July 1, 1997, 51 Minshū (No. 6) 2299.

[74] Japanese Patent Act, § 2(3) iii.

[75] See Ch. 5, 5.36.

[76] Some scholars argue that only an act of supplying the exclusive infringing use or indispensable means must take place in Japan. See Takabe, *Jitsumu Shōsetsu*, 298.

[77] Osaka Dist. Ct., October 24, 1997 Hei 8(wa) No. 12109, Hanrei Taimuzu (No. 1081) 241; Osaka Dist. Ct., December 21, 2000, Hei 10(wa) No. 12875, Hanrei Taimuzu (No. 1104) 270; Tokyo Dist. Ct., February 27, 2007, Hei 15(wa) No. 16924, Hanrei Taimuzu (No. 1253) 241.

[78] Japanese Patent Act, Art. 70, para. 1.

[79] Ibid. para. 2.

unlike German courts' expansive interpretation, Japanese courts used the embodiments in the specification and drawings to limit the literal meaning of claim terms to secure room for the public to engage in further developments.[80]

The restrictive claim interpretation practice was established during the early period of the Japanese patent system, when scholars and courts developed a rule that the inventor was entitled to protection only for what he or she recognized as his/her invention regardless of the claim terms (the inventor's recognition theory).[81] As will be discussed later, this restrictive claim interpretation is similar to the purposive claim interpretation under UK case law.[82] This rule effectively functioned to limit the extent of protection to the disclosed embodiments because the disclosure in the specification and drawings constituted what was recognized by the inventor.[83] **6.26**

Further, Japanese courts developed extensive case law for giving grounds to read limitations into the claim from the specification.[84] Grounds Japanese courts frequently relied on included the disputed claim being too broad to include the prior art;[85] and the claim terms being ambiguous, thus requiring the court to resort to the specification.[86] This practice continued until the Supreme Court of Japan made it clear in the 2000 *Kilby* decision that courts in infringement litigation have jurisdiction to examine asserted patent validity.[87] **6.27**

The Supreme Court of Japan acknowledged infringement under the doctrine of equivalents for the first time in the 1998 *Ball Spline* decision.[88] Under pre-1998 case law, the inventor's recognition theory effectively prevented Japanese lower courts from finding infringement when alleged infringers did not literally copy the disclosed embodiments and the equivalents were neither disclosed in the specification nor acknowledged by the inventor.[89] Moreover, Japanese courts often found that defendants admitted to no literal infringement when patentees claimed infringement under the doctrine of equivalents. As a result, patentees' arguments focused on literal infringement by insisting on an expansive meaning of the claim terms that included equivalents producing the same function and result as the patented invention, obvious to one skilled in the art. However, courts only adopted such an expansive claim construction in exceptional circumstances where the claim is narrowly **6.28**

---

[80] For a historical review of the claiming practice in Japan, see Takenaka, "Interpreting Patent Claims," Ch. 1, § 1.04.

[81] Nakayama, *Chūkai Tokkyohō*, 705.

[82] See Ch. 6, 6.57.

[83] Regarding the scope recognized by the inventor, the majority view makes an assessment of the scope objectively from the perspective of a hypothetical person with the knowledge of the prior art and ordinary creativity. The minority view makes an assessment of the scope on the basis of the state of mind of the particular inventor.

[84] Takenaka, "Interpreting Patent Claims," Ch. 3, § 3.04[1].

[85] Judgment of Supreme Court, August 4, 1964 (Crude Petroleum Rotation Combustor), 18 Minshū (No. 7) 1319.

[86] Judgment of Osaka District Court (Diaper), October 28, 1980, 12 Mutaishū 580.

[87] Saikō Saibansho (Sup. Ct.) April 11, 2000, Hei 10 (o) No. 364, 54 Saikō Saibansho Minji Hanreishū (Minshū) 1368 (Japan) (*Kilby*).

[88] Decision of Supreme Court, February 24, 1998, 52 Minshū (No. 1) 113, 1630 Hanrei Jiho 32 (1998) (*Ball Spline*). An English translation of the decision by the author is published in Toshiko Takenaka, "The Supreme Court Affirmed the Presence of the Doctrine of Equivalents under Japanese Patent System," 5 *CASRIP Newsletter* (Winter 1998): 12 (http://www.law.washington.edu/Casrip/newsletter/newsv5i1jp1.html).

[89] Takenaka, "Interpreting Patent Claims," Ch. 3, § 3.04[2].

drafted and where failure to find infringement would result in an unreasonable hardship to the patentee.[90] They frequently rejected the use of an expansive construction by finding a disclaimer if the asserted claim literally covered the obvious equivalent.

2. Infringement Analysis

(a) Mixed Steps: Claim Construction and Application

6.29 Unlike US patent litigation, judges make factual findings. Thus, it is not necessary to distinguish between claim interpretation and the application of the claim to the accused embodiment. Contrary to US practice, the first step of infringement analysis at Japanese courts is to specify the accused embodiment.[91] This step not only defines the subject of the infringement as well as the effect of *res judicata* but also the subject matter to which an order of injunction is issued and enforced once a judgment of infringement has become final. In old practice, Japanese courts try to define the defendant's embodiment in detail as precisely as possible because an order of injunction is enforceable only with respect to the description of the embodiment. This is in stark contrast to the US courts' practice where the subject matter of the injunction is simply specified as "infringed claims" and extends the scope of the injunction to a variation of an adjudicated infringing embodiment as long as the modified embodiment is merely colorable different from the adjudicated embodiment.[92]

6.30 Under the current practice, patentees must specify the defendant's embodiment with its product number and other indications of where defendants infringe a product patent or process patent resulting in a product.[93] The pre-1998 practice required patentees to submit a document in which features of the accused embodiment were described in terms of elements of the asserted claim language. Defendants frequently disagree with the patentee's claim interpretation and application. Moreover, patentees may not have access to enough evidence to be able to specify the features of the defendant's embodiment at the beginning of litigation. The current practice allows patentees to specify the accused embodiment with its product number or ID but requires patentees to provide a claim chart as well: a document that classifies all elements of the asserted claim into components (a group of elements) and shows features of the accused embodiment corresponding to each component.

6.31 The next step is to determine whether the accused embodiment falls within the technical scope of the asserted claim.[94] In this step, the court interprets the language of the claim and defines the features of the accused embodiment by applying the claim language. Because judges are assisted by technical clerks and parties are required to produce enough

---

[90] Kousaku Yoshiguji, *Tokkyoho Gaisetsu (Outline of Patent Law)* (8th ed., 1988), 381; Yoshifuji Kosaku, "Kintouron Tekiyo Jogai Jiko wo Chūshinto Shite (Doctrine of Equvalents, Particularly Regarding the Reasons to Exlude Application of the Doctrine)," 21 *Tokkyo Kanri* (1971): 167.

[91] Makiko Takabe, "Shingaibutsu no Tokutei (Specifying Accused Products and Processes)," in Toshiaki Iimura and Ryuichi Shitara (eds.), *Chiteki zaisan kankei soshōhō (Intellectual Property Litigations)* 3 Shin saiban jitsumu taikei 1 (2008); Shinichi Koike, "Tokkyo shingai no Handan shuhō (Infringement Analysis of Patent Infringement)," in Toshiko Takenaka and Kazunori Yamagami (eds.), *Kokusai chiteki zaisan funsō shori no hōritsu sōdan (Consultation of International IP Infringement Dispute Resolution)* (2006), 335.

[92] *Tivo Inc. v. Echostar Corp.*, 646 F.3d 869, 98 U.S.P.Q.2d 1413 (Fed. Cir. 2011).

[93] Takabe, "Specifying Accused Products and Processes," 70.

[94] Ryuichi Shitara et al., "Chiteki Zaisan Kankei Soshōhō no Tetsuzuki no Ippantekina Gaiyō (Overview of IP Litigation Procedures)," in Toshiaki Iimura and Ryuichi Shitara (eds.), *Chiteki Zaisan Kankei Soshō (Intellectual Property Litigations)* 3 Legal Progressive Series (2008), 1.

documents to support their arguments, the court frequently determines the technical scope after two hearings.

During the technical scope determination, the defendant can raise any available defense, including invalidity. As will be discussed below, Japanese courts interpret claims in light of the prior art, regardless of whether a reference is cited during the examination. Because Japanese courts can make factual findings and decide legal issues, they are also eager to invalidate asserted patents. In clarifying the meaning of claim language through claim interpretation and applying the language to the accused embodiment and embodiments in the prior art, Japanese courts limit the technical scope of the asserted patent to maintain its validity or to invalidate the patent if it is necessary to read limitations into the claim in order to sustain its validity. This is a high contrast to US practice in which the court is reluctant to deal with validity issues because many of the validity issues involve factual findings, which are exclusively within the power of the jury.[95] Under the bifurcation principle, the infringing court in Germany does not have jurisdiction to deal with the validity at all.[96] **6.32**

(b) Separate Steps in Claim Application: Literal Infringement and Infringement under the Doctrine of Equivalents

During the step of determining whether the accused embodiment falls within the technical scope of the asserted claim, the court decides whether all elements of the claim correspond to features of the accused embodiment identically or equivalently. Like the US system, the Japanese Patent System follows the peripheral definition theory. Japanese courts are very reluctant to find infringement under the doctrine of equivalents and emphasize the exceptional nature of the doctrine.[97] Thus, the determination of literal infringement is clearly separate and distinct from the determination of infringement. **6.33**

In determining whether the accused embodiment falls within the technical scope, Japanese courts clarify the meaning of every claim element and find no literal infringement if any one of the claim elements is not met by a feature of the accused embodiment.[98] A finding of no literal infringement is necessary to identify the differences between the patent invention and the accused embodiment and to determine whether the differences are insignificant enough for the two to be considered as equivalent. Japanese courts utilize five tests to determine whether the missing element is replaced by an equivalent feature of the accused embodiment.[99] Unlike US courts where the court applies the negative tests and the jury applies the positive tests, Japanese courts apply all these tests to find or deny infringement under the doctrine of equivalents. Although Japanese courts may decide literal infringement and the doctrine of equivalents at the same hearing, the high hurdle presented by the five tests clearly separate literal infringement analysis from infringement analysis under the doctrine of equivalents. **6.34**

(c) Claim Construction for Validity Challenges

Like US courts but unlike German courts, Japanese courts have power to decide both infringement and validity issues. The Japanese Patent Act makes it clear that the patentee **6.35**

[95] See Ch. 4, 4.23.
[96] See Ch. 5, 5.67.
[97] Takabe, *Jitsumu Shōsetsu*, 167. Decision of Supreme Court, February 24, 1998, 52 Minshū (No. 1) 113, 1630 Hanrei Jihō 32 (1998) (*Ball Spline* case).
[98] See Ch. 6, 6.33.
[99] See Ch. 6, 6.72.

and exclusive licensees cannot enforce a patent if the court finds that the patent asserted by the patentee and exclusive licensees should be invalidated by an invalidation trial at the JPO.[100] In patent litigation, the court examines the defense of invalidity while determining whether the accused embodiment falls within the scope of the patent.[101] It is unclear whether the court should use the same rule for claim interpretation when determining infringement and validity.

6.36 Like the USPTO, the JPO uses a different rule for claim interpretation in examining the validity at invalidation trials. Under the Japanese Patent Act, the scope to define the subject matter of the examination for patent requirements at JPO trials is called "gist of invention." In contrast, the scope to define the subject matter of exclusive right in infringement procedure is called "technical scope."[102] In the 1991 *Lipase* decision, the Supreme Court of Japan held that courts should determine the gist of invention based on the claim language except for special circumstances where the court does not understand the technical significance of the claim language clearly and unambiguously or finds an obvious error in the claim language in light of the description of the invention in the specification.[103] The scope of the gist of invention should be broader than the technical scope in the infringement procedure because Japanese courts interpret claims restrictively in light of the specification and drawings as well as in light of the record of patent prosecution. When the defense of invalidity is raised at the infringement procedure, courts should apply the broader claim interpretation when examining validity, under the *Lipase* decision.[104]

6.37 In theory, Japanese courts use different rules for determining infringement and defense of invalidity. However, it is very unlikely that the different rules will result in different scopes for the same asserted claim. It is very likely that the asserted claim will be ambiguous and thus the court will not understand the gist of invention if the court needs to interpret the claim restrictively in light of the specification, drawings, and record of patent prosecution. When the special circumstances that allow the court to interpret the claim beyond the claim language exist, the court interprets the asserted claim in light of the materials beyond the claim language in determining both infringement and validity.[105]

3. Claim Construction

(a) Fundamental Rules

6.38 **i. Claims Defined by the Structure, Material and Acts** The Japanese Patent Act provides the fundamental rule that the technical scope of a patented invention shall be determined on the basis of the language of a claim.[106] In determining the technical scope, terms used in the claim must be interpreted in light of the description and drawings of the invention

---

[100] Japanese Patent Act, § 104-3(1).

[101] Shitara et al., "Chiteki Zaisan Kankei Soshōhō no Tetsuzuki no Ippantekina Gaiyō," 15.

[102] Takabe, *Jitsumu Shōsetsu*, 155.

[103] Sup. Ct. of Japan, March 8, 1991, Sho (Gyo Tsu) No. 3, 45 Minshū (No. 3) 123 (*Lipase*).

[104] Tokyo Dist. Ct., May 20, 2009, Hei 19 (wa) No. 8426, For a discussion of this case, Eiji Katayama et al., *Nich-Bei-Ō jūyō tokkyo saibanrei: meisaisho no kisai yōken kara shingairon, Songairon Made (Japan-US-Europe Leading Patent Cases: Disclosure Requirements for Patent Specification, Infringement and Damage Calculation)* (2013), 231.

[105] Misao Shimizu, "Mukō no Kōben (Defense of Invalidity)," in Toshiaki Iimura and Ryuichi Shitara (eds.), *Chiteki zaisan kankei soshōhō (Intellectual Property Litigations)* 3 Shin saiban jitsumu taikei (2008), 145.

[106] Japanese Patent Act, § 70(1).

attached to the application.[107] This rule is consistent with the rules under US case law, German Patent Act, § 14, and European Patent Convention, Article 69.

Japanese patent applicants are required to include in each claim all elements necessary to specify the invention for which the applicant requests a grant of patent.[108] Applicants can define an invention of a product by the structure, materials, property, use as well as function ("functional claims"), and the method of manufacturing the product ("product-by-process claims").[109] Unlike the US Patent Act, the Japanese Patent Act does not provide a special rule for interpreting claims that define the invention by functions.[110] The fundamental rule to determine the technical scope on the basis of the claim applies to all types of claims. **6.39**

Like US and German patent claims, Japanese claims usually consist of three parts: the preamble, the transition phrase, and the body. Like US Jepson claims, Japanese claims often use "characterized by" as the transition phrase to identify novel features in comparison with features in the prior art. However, Japanese courts view elements in the preamble as being disclosed in the embodiments, discussed as the prior art in the specification. They do not necessarily find admission with respect to elements in the preamble if the claim is compared with embodiments that are not discussed in the specification. Any element of both preamble and body constitutes limitations in determining patentability and infringement. **6.40**

Because of the *Lipase* Supreme Court decision, which allows claim interpretation in light of the specification under special circumstances,[111] Japanese scholars extensively debate whether courts should be confined to the language of the claim without making reference to the specification if the disputed term is clear and unambiguous on its face. Courts apply the *Lipase* rule only when determining the gist of invention with respect to patentability and validity in appeals from the Japan Patent Office. The Japanese Patent Act requires the invention described in the claim to be supported by the description of the invention in the specification. To understand the patented invention described in the asserted claim, courts must always interpret the terms of the claim in light of the specification and drawings, without examining whether the claim is clear and unambiguous on its face.[112] **6.41**

Moreover, courts also need to examine the specification if an ordinary or customary meaning should be given to the term in dispute when determining the technical scope. The ordinary and customary meaning is the meaning understood by those who use the term.[113] The Japanese Patent Act requires the description of the invention in the specification to comply with the Ordinance of the Ministry of Economy, Trade, and Industry.[114] Under the Ordinance, (1) when a technical term is used in the claims and specification, applicants must use the customary terms in the field of invention for the technical term; **6.42**

---

[107] Ibid.

[108] Ibid. § 36(5).

[109] Japan Patent Office, Examination Guidelines for Patent and Utility Model in Japan, Part I, Ch. 1, 2.2.2.2 (July 2013) (http://www.jpo.go.jp/tetuzuki_e/t_tokkyo_e/1312-002_e.htm).

[110] For the means-plus-function claims under the US Patent Act, see Ch. 4, 4.40 "Functionally Defined Claims."

[111] Sup. Ct. of Japan, March 8, 1991, Sho (Gyo Tsu) No. 3, 45 Minshū (No. 3) 123 (*Lipase*). For a discussion of this case, see Ch. 6, 6.36.

[112] Takabe, *Jitsumu Shōsetsu*, 157. IP High Court, December 28, 2005, Hei 17 (wa) No. 10103. For a discussion of this case, Katayama et al., *Nich-Bei-Ō jūyō tokkyo saibanrei*, 226.

[113] IP High Ct., April 25, 2001, Hei 12 (ne) No. 1266.

[114] Japanese Patent Act, § 36(4)(1).

(2) an ordinary meaning is given to a claim term and such a term must be used consistently throughout the specification; (3) if a special meaning is given to a claim term, the definition of the term must be included in the specification; (4) the description of the claims must not conflict with the description of the invention in the specification, and the terms must be used consistently between the claims and the specification.[115] It follows that claims should be interpreted to give claim terms the ordinary and customary meaning as understood by a person having ordinary skill in the art of the invention ("PHOSITA").[116] To understand the meaning of claim terms and the description of asserted claims and to understand the significance of a patented invention, courts should always examine the specification.[117]

6.43 PHOSITAs should have general knowledge and ordinary skills in the field of invention and thus should be able to find variations of the embodiments disclosed in the specification.[118] Accordingly, the perspective of a PHOSITA should allow courts to include such variations in the technical scope if the variations fall within the broadly defined claim terms, which is generalized from particular structures and materials of the disclosed embodiments. However, Japanese courts are very reluctant to use the perspective of a PHOSITA and find the technical scope to be beyond the disclosure in the specification. In the early era of the Japanese patent system, scholars and courts developed a rule that the inventor was entitled to protection only for what he or she recognized as his or her invention regardless of the claim terms (the inventor's recognition theory).[119] Under this theory, the disclosure in the specification and drawings constitutes the scope which was recognized by the inventor and prevented courts from using the perspective of a PHOSITA. As a result, older court decisions indicate the Japanese courts' heavy reliance on the disclosure in the specification, which led to a restrictive claim construction importing limitations from the specification and excluding accused embodiments which were not disclosed in the specification.[120]

6.44 The restrictive tradition under the inventor's recognition theory dies hard in Japanese courts. Even though broadly defined claim terms are used to cover variations of the embodiments disclosed in the specification, Japanese courts may find a limitation on a broadly defined term from the specification when the accused embodiment is not disclosed in the specification. For example, even when the term "a block" was used in the asserted claim, the Tokyo District Court found that natural stone blocks did not fall within the technical scope where the specification and drawings disclosed only concrete blocks and the term "concrete block" was consistently used in the specification.[121]

6.45 Case law is unclear on whether claims should be interpreted from the perspective of a PHOSITA at the time of the effective filing date of the patent application. Because of

---

[115] From No. 29, Enforcement Ordinace of the Patent Act, Ordinance of MITI No. 10 of March 8, 1960, as last amended by Ordinance of METI No. 35 of 2010.

[116] Tokyo Dist. Ct., October 26, 1984, Sho 55 (wa) No. 429, Hanrei Taimuzu (No. 543) 205.

[117] N. 113 above, IP High Court, December 28, 2005.

[118] For a comparative study of PHOSITAs used in determining the extent of patent protection under the US, UK, German, and Japanese Patent Acts, see Toshiko Takenaka, "A Person of Ordinary Skill in the Art and the Extent of Patent Protection," in D. Beier, L. Brüning-Petit, and C. Heath (eds.), *Festschrift for Jochen Pagenberg* (2006), 81.

[119] Nakayama, *Chūkai Tokkyohō*, 705.

[120] Testuya Obuchi, "A Study of Claim Construction and Validity of Patent, in Patent Litigation in the Era of the Intellectual Property Based Nation," in Japan Patent Attorneys Association Intellectual Property Study Center (ed.), *Claim Construction* (2005), 2.

[121] N. 113 above, IP High Court, December 28, 2005.

the restrictive use of the PHOSITA perspective and the influence of the inventor recognition theory, it is very likely that Japanese courts would not find literal infringement if the accused embodiment involves an after-arising technology. However, such embodiments involving after-arising technology might fall within the technical scope under the doctrine of equivalents because infringement under the doctrine of equivalents must be decided as at the time of infringement.[122]

Japanese patents include a much smaller number of independent and dependent claims than US patents. This is because the Japanese Patent System long followed the single claim tradition, which did not allow applicants to include more than one claim per patent application.[123] Under the single claim system, dependent claims did not have a technical scope that was independent and separate from the technical scope of the independent claim on which the claims depended. **6.46**

The Japanese Patent Act was revised in 1988 to introduce a US-style multiple claim system. Under the current system, both independent and dependent claims have their own technical scope. Thus a party is liable if any of its accused embodiments fall within the technical scope of any asserted claims included in the patent. However, Japanese courts have not developed the claim differentiation doctrine developed by the US case law: the doctrine assumes that claims with different terms have different technical scope.[124] **6.47**

ii. Functionally Defined Claims The Japanese Patent Act does not provide a special rule for claims that define an invention by its functions ("functional claims"), and the technical scope of functional claims should be interpreted to cover any structures, materials, and steps that perform the functions recited in the claims.[125] However, in cases before the 2000 *Kilby* decision,[126] Japanese courts interpreted the technical scope of functional claims to include only embodiments disclosed in the specification and their equivalents, when the courts found the technical scope of the asserted claims to be unreasonably broader than what was disclosed in the specification.[127] Under the Japanese Patent Act, the pre-*Kilby* and post-*Kilby* claim drafting rule remains the same. Applicants are allowed to define an invention in a claim by its functions only if all description requirements are met: the description of the claim must meet the support requirement[128] and the definiteness requirement,[129] and the description of the specification accompanied with the claim must meet the enablement requirement.[130] During the examination and trials, the JPO interprets the gist of invention for functional claims to include all structures, materials, steps, etc. that perform functions recited in the functional **6.48**

[122] The third test for establishing equivalence, obviousness of interchangeability must be decided as of the time of making, assigning, etc. of the accused product. See Ch. 6, 6.72.

[123] For a discussion of the single claim tradition and its impact on claim interpretation, see Takenaka, "Interpreting Patent Claims," 230.

[124] Ch. 4, 4.60.

[125] Ryuichi Shitara, "Kinouteki Kureimu no Kaishaku ni tsuite (Regarding Interpretation of Functional Claims)," 1 *Chiteki Zaisan no Riron to Jitsumu (Tokkyo hō 1)* (2007): 127.

[126] *Kilby*, Sup. Ct., April 11.

[127] Ryu Takabayashi, "Tokkyo Hatsumei no Gijutsuteki Han'i I (Technical Scope of Patented Invention)," in Toshiaki Iimura and Ryuichi Shitara (eds.), *Chiteki zaisan kankei soshōhō (Intellectual Property Litigations)* 3 Legal Progressive Series (2008), 84. Tokyo High Ct., December 20, 1978, Sho(ne) No. 783, Hanrei Taimuzu (No. 381) 165; Tokyo Dist. Ct., December 22, 1998, Sho 51 (ne) No. 783, Hanrei Jihō (No. 1674) 152.

[128] Japanese Patent Act, § 36(6) i.

[129] Ibid. § 36(6) ii.

[130] Ibid. § 36(4).

claim.[131] Even when the JPO found the functional claims to have met the enablement, support, and definiteness requirements and issued a patent, courts may nonetheless find that the technical scope of the functional claim is ambiguous in comparison with the accused embodiment in infringement litigation. [132] Japanese courts developed pre-*Kilby* case law to interpret ambiguous claims so as to limit the scope to cover only the embodiments disclosed in the specification because the case law did not allow courts to examine validity even though the ambiguous claims violate the description requirements and are thus invalid.[133] This restrictive claim interpretation practice frequently applied to functional claims in cases where only a few embodiments were disclosed in the specification, and thus the description of the invention in the specification did not fully support the asserted functional claims.

6.49 Under the current practice, Japanese courts have power to examine validity at the infringement procedure. However, it is unclear whether Japanese courts continue to use pre-*Kilby* restrictive claim interpretation. In theory, Japanese courts should uphold the defense of invalidity if the technical scope of an asserted claim is unreasonably broad in contrast to the disclosure in the specification and thus fails to meet any of the description requirements. However, some argue that courts should interpret the broad claims so as to limit the scope to cover only the disclosed embodiment because upholding the invalidity defense delays dispute resolution between parties.[134] Even when a claim is found to be invalid for failing to meet a description requirement, patentees can still meet this requirement by requesting a correction of their claims through trials at the JPO.[135] Once the claim is amended, the claim can be enforced against defendants as long as the accused embodiment falls within the technical scope of the amended claim.

6.50 **iii. Product-by-Process Claims** The Japanese Patent Act allows a patent applicant to define the invention of a product by a process for manufacturing the product only if there are special circumstances that make it impossible or inpractical to define the product by its structures or properties at the time of patent application.[136] A claim defining a product by its manufacturing process is called a "product-by-process" claim. In examining patentability, the JPO interprets product-by-process claims to include any product resulting from the process recited in the claim, regardless of the process of making the product.[137] In a 1980 decision, the Supreme Court of Japan applied the same rule for determining the technical scope of product-by-process claims and found infringement with respect to the accused product when the product was identical to the product resulting from the process recited in the asserted product-by-process claim, even though the accused product was made by a process different from the process recited in the claim.[138] In the 2015 *Pravastatin Sodium*

[131] Japan Patent Office, Revised Examination Guidelines on Novelty and Inventive Step, Part II, Ch. 2, 1.5.2 (http://www.jpo.go.jp/tetuzuki/t_tokkyo/shinsa/pdf/sinkisei_sinposei/sinki_sinpo01.pdf).

[132] Shitara, "Kinouteki Kureimu no Kaishaku ni tsuite," 129.

[133] For more discussion on Japanese courts'claim interpretation in light of the prior art, see Ch. 6, 6.64 "Prior Art."

[134] Shitara, "Kinouteki Kureimu no Kaishaku ni tsuite," 135.

[135] For more discussion, see Ch. 9, 9.13 "Correction of Claims."

[136] Sup. Ct., June 5, 2015, Hei 24 (jyu) No. 1204.

[137] JPO Examination Guidelines for Novelty and Inventive Step, Part I, Ch. 1.5.2.

[138] Sup. Ct., June 30, 1981, Sho (wo) No. 336, 35 Minshū (No. 4) 848; Sup. Ct., November 10, 1998, Hei (wo) No. 1579. Kazuhide Shimasue, "Purodakuto-Bai-Purosesu-Kureimu no Kaishaku ni tsuite (Regarding Interpretation of Product-By-Process Claim)," 1 Toshiaki Makino et al. (eds.), *Chiteki Zaisan no Riron to Jitsumu (Tokkyo hō 1) (Theory and Practice of Intellectual Property Law (Patent Law 1))* (2007), 138.

decision, the Court maintained the broad interpretation but remanded the case for further examination with respect to a question whether the patentee was unable to define the product by its structure or property.[139]

In the *Pravastatin Sodium* case, the Supreme Court reversed the IP High Court's Grand Panel decision. [140] The Court rejected the IP High Court's narrow claim interpretation that the technical scope of product-by-process claims includes only the products resulting from the process recited in the claim. It made clear that the technical scope of a product-by-process claim determines the structure or property of the product results from the process recited in the claim. **6.51**

The Court acknowledged the uncertainty resulting from the broad claim interpretation and a risk for a third party to infringe a product-by-process because of the lack of claim's notice function with respect to the structure or properpty which defines the technical scope. A product-by-process claim is invalid for a violation of the requirement that a claim must define the invention that the applicant seeks to obtain a patent.[141] Such a claim is valid only when there are special circumstances that make it impossible or impractical to define the product by its structures or properties at the time of patent application. The JPO has not examined the presence or absence of such special circumstances. **6.52**

The Supreme Court's broad claim interpretation is in line with the interpretation of product-by-process claims under German law.[142] However, the interpretation is contrary to the rule adopted by the *en banc* Federal Circuit in *Abbott Lab. v. Sandoz*.[143] Neither the US Federal Circuit nor the Federal Court of Justice of Germany requires special circumstances that prevent applicants from defining their inventions by the structure or property to sustain the validity of a product-by-process. **6.53**

(b) Aids for Claim Interpretation

i. Intrinsic v. Extrinsic Evidence Because the Japanese Patent Act requires an invention described in a claim to be one of the inventions as described in the detailed explanation of the invention in the specification,[144] courts must interpret the meaning of the claim language in light of the specification. The Act makes it clear that courts should interpret the claim language to determine the technical scope in light of not only the specification but also the drawings.[145] Although the Japanese Patent Act does not list the record of patent prosecution as an aid for interpreting claims, Japanese courts often examine the record of prosecution in clarifying the meaning of the claim terms in dispute. Accordingly, Japanese courts use all three types of intrinsic evidence used under US claim interpretation practice.[146] This is in stark contrast to German practice, in which courts examine only the specification and drawings to interpret claims in excluding the prosecution history from interpretation aids.[147] **6.54**

139 N. 137 above, Sup. Ct., June 5, 2015.
140 IP High Ct., January 27, 2012 (Grand Bench), Hei 19 (wa) No. 35342, Hanrei Jihō (No. 2144) 55 (*Pravastatin Sodium*).
141 Japanese Patent Act, § 36(6) ii.
142 Ch. 5, 5.79.
143 *Abbott Labs. v. Sandoz, Inc.*, 566 F.3d 1282, 90 U.S.P.Q.2d 1769 (Fed. Cir. 2009). See Ch. 4, 4.44.
144 Japanese Patent Act, § 36(6) i.
145 Ibid. § 70(2).
146 Ch. 4, 4.45 "Intrinsic v. Extrinsic Evidence."
147 Ch. 5, 5.80 "Intrinsic v. Extrinsic Evidence."

6.55 Regardless of being cited during the examination, prior art plays an important role in interpreting claims. Japanese courts give more weight to the specification than to dictionaries and adopt a special definition of the claim term in dispute when they find that the specification supports the special definition.[148] They seldom cite science treatises or other materials that might be helpful to understand technologies in the field of the asserted patent invention. Because judges in the Tokyo and Osaka District Courts and the IP High Court are assisted by judicial research officials who have extensive experience in technologies and patent law, judges can receive a tutorial from these officials on the technical terms and information necessary to understand the invention and claim terms.[149] Judges find the experts offered by parties to be less reliable than the judicial research officials and seldom give any weight to expert opinions.

6.56 Unlike US courts, Japanese courts do not distinguish intrinsic evidence from extrinsic evidence based on public policy. Although only the specification and drawings are explicitly listed as claim interpretation aids, Japanese courts have been more frequently relying on the prior art than on the specification in determining the technical scope.[150] These interpretation aids are used to limit rather than to expand the literal meaning of the claim term. The Japanese courts' use of interpretation aids is in stark contrast to German practice, where the general knowledge of a PHOSITA and the specification are used to expand the literal meaning of the claim term.[151]

6.57 **ii. Specification** Like US and German courts, the most important claim interpretation aides are patent documents, which include both asserted and unasserted claims, the specification, and drawings.[152] The tradition developed under the inventor's recognition theory dies hard. Japanese courts give more weight to the specification than the claim language in determining the technical scope. Instead of using the specification to clarify the meaning of the claim term, Japanese courts use the specification to determine the technical scope once they find a violation of the requirements for a patent grant. The Japanese courts' interpretation is influenced by the inventor's recognition theory, and the UK courts' purposive claim interpretation follows the same principle, that claim terms must be given a meaning understood by the PHOSITA regarding what the author (inventor) meant by using the claim term.[153] The PHOSITA should interpret the claim term so as to exclude embodiments that are in the prior art as well as those that are insufficiently disclosed in the specification and drawings.[154] Like UK courts, Japanese courts give claim terms a meaning that excludes embodiments that are not sufficiently disclosed or enabled by the specification, even though such an interpretation may read limitations into the claim from the specification.

[148] IP High Ct., June 29, 2009, Hei 21 (ne) No. 10006, Hanrei Taimusu (No. 2077) 123 (*Hollow Golf Club Head*). For more discussion, n. 167 below.

[149] See Ch. 2, 2.69.

[150] Masami Ichikawa, "Tokkyo Hatsui no Gijutsuteki Han'I no Kakutei ni tuite (Regarding Determination of Technical Scope of Patented Invention)," in Toshiaki Makino et al. (eds.), *Chiteki Zaisan no Riron to Jitsumu (Tokkyo hō 1) (Theory and Practice of Intellectual Property Law (Patent Law 1))* (2007), 93.

[151] This expansive claim interpretation is called the function-oriented claim construction. See Chapter 5, 5.69.

[152] Ichikawa, "Tokkyo Hatsui no Gijutsuteki Han'I no Kakutei ni tuite," 95.

[153] *Kirin-Amgin, Inc. v. Hoechst Marion Roussel Limited*, 2004 UKHL 46 (House of Lords 2004). For a comparison of UK purposive construction, see Toshiko Takenaka, "Claim Construction and the Extent of Patent Protection: A Comparative Analysis of the Phillips *en banc* Federal Circuit Decision," 1 *Journal of Intellectual Property Law & Practice* (2005): 119.

[154] *Kirin-Amgen*, 2004 UKHL 46, para. 47.

To find inherent limitations, Japanese courts often find that claims are not enabled or supported by the specification if the claims use generalized or expanded expressions of structures, properties, and steps of embodiments disclosed in the specification. The JPO's examination guidelines allow applicants to draft claims that have a literal scope broader than what is disclosed in the specification as long as the PHOSITA can expand and generalize specific structures, properties, or steps of the embodiments in the specification to the scope of the claim.[155] Even when the JPO finds all the requirements to be met and grants a patent to the claims, courts may still find that the asserted claims are not enabled or supported by the specification when the accused embodiment is not disclosed in the specification, even though the embodiment falls within the literal scope of the asserted claim.[156] When the claim includes generalized expressions of structures, properties, and steps, courts may find that the claim is directed to a technical idea obvious to the PHOSITA and thus may limit the technical scope to only the embodiments and their equivalents.[157] Courts find that the accused embodiment is an equivalent and thus falls into the technical scope only if the accused embodiment is so obvious to the PHOSITA that the PHOSITA would acknowledge that the embodiments is in effect disclosed in the specification.[158] **6.58**

Japanese courts frequently find a special meaning to the claim term in dispute when the claim term is expanded or generalized from the structures, properties, and steps of the disclosed embodiments. Like German courts, Japanese courts understand an invention to be a technical solution for attaining the object of the invention (i.e., the technical object) which produces a technical effect. Therefore, Japanese courts often take account of the object and effect to understand the invention and to decide the meaning of the terms in dispute. In particular, courts interpret claim terms to limit the technical scope, including the embodiments that are disclosed in the specification and can attain the effect discussed in the specification.[159] **6.59**

The *Hollow Golf Club Head* case highlights this restrictive claim interpretation.[160] In this leading case for affirming infringement under the doctrine of equivalents, the IP High Court defined the claim term "a suture seam material" as a material that went through multiple (at least two) holes provided in the metal surface material and had contact with the fiber reinforced plastic (FRP) surface material in at least two locations. In other words, the court could either properly find inherent limitations (has contact with the FRP surface material in multiple locations) or improperly read limitations into the claim. The court adopted this definition in light of the object and technical effect of using the suture seam material. The specification disclosed only one embodiment in which the suture material was a string that went through holes in the metal surface material so that the stiches bound the FRP surface material and the metal surface, as shown in Figure 6.1. The seam material in the accused golf club was not a string but instead was made of multiple short wedges that went through the holes provided in the contacting surface of the metal surface material to bind the metal surface material and the FRP surface material, as shown in Figure 6.2. **6.60**

155 JPO Examination Guidelines for Description and Claims, Part I, Ch. 1, 2.2.1.3.
156 N. 113 above, IP High Ct., December 28, 2005.
157 Tokyo High Ct., September 9, 2003, Hei 14 (ne) No. 3714.
158 Ibid.
159 E.g., Osaka Dist. Ct., December 13, 2001, Hei 12 (wa) No. 4290.
160 IP High Ct., June 29, 2009, Hei 21 (ne) No. 10006, Hanrei Taimusu (No. 2077) 123 (*Hollow Golf Club Head*).

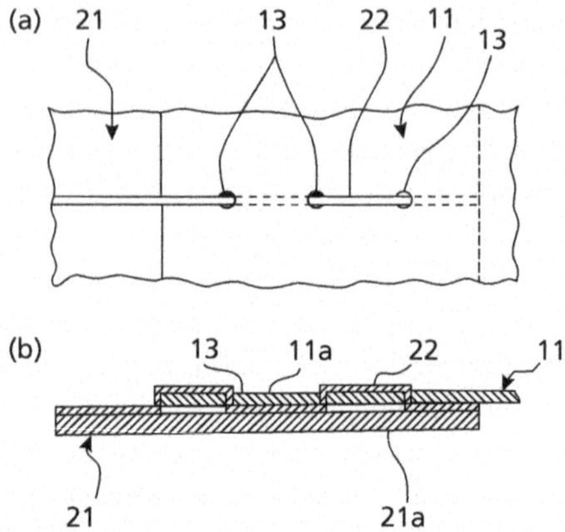

Figure 6.1. Embodiment in specification of suture seam material

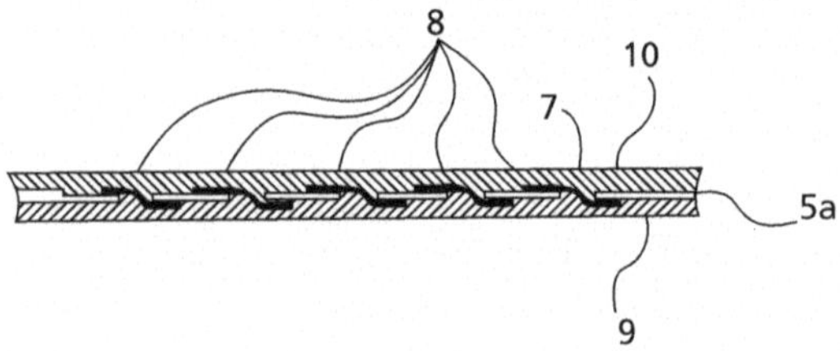

Figure 6.2. Suture seam material in accused golf club

6.61 The IP High Court found that the wedge in the accused product only went though one hole instead of multiple holes and did not fall into the definition of a suture seam material. Thus it rejected the patentee's claim of literal infringement, although it found infringement under the doctrine of equivalents.

6.62 The *Lewis Acid Inhibitor* case highlights the different approaches taken by the Federal Circuit and Japan's IP High Court. In the United States and Japan, Abbott Laboratories and Baxter Pharmaceutical Product were in dispute over whether Baxter had infringed Abbott's patents by using a selected amount of Lewis acid inhibitor in order to prevent the degradation of sevoflurane in anesthetic compositions. At the US litigation, Abbott asserted claims directed to an anesthetic composition containing a fluoroether compound and a Lewis acid inhibitor, and a method of preventing the degradation of sevoflurane anesthetics by adding an effective amount of certain specific Lewis acid inhibitors. At the US litigation, both compound and method claims were asserted.[161] The focus of the dispute was the interpretation of "an effective amount" and "a sufficient amount" of the Lewis acid inhibitor to prevent degradation of sevoflurane (commonly used as an anesthetic compound) by a Lewis acid. The United States District Court for the Northern District of Illinois limited the amount to amounts above 131 ppm of water because the prosecution history indicated a prior sale by Abbott of an anesthetic compound containing 131 ppm

[161] *Abbott Labs. v. Baxter Pharm. Prods.*, 334 F.3d 1274, 67 U.S.P.Q. 2d 1191 (Fed. Cir. 2003).

of the Lewis acid inhibitor. The Federal Circuit found this interpretation to be erroneous because disclosing to the USPTO a previous sale does not give rise to a clear disavowal of amounts lower than 131 ppm. The court interpreted the "effective amount" and "sufficient amount" in light of the specification and found that the amount depends on the specific storage conditions of the sevoflurane. In emphasizing that claims are not necessarily nor usually limited to preferred embodiments, the Federal Circuit also struck down the district court's interpretation of limiting the ranges of the amount disclosed as preferred embodiments. The Federal Circuit remanded the case to the district court to decide infringement under the proper interpretation.

In the Japanese litigation, the asserted claims were directed to a method for preserving an amount of sevoflurane by covering the inner surface of the anesthetic container with a Lewis acid inhibitor.[162] In light of the object and effect of the invention discussed in the specification, the IP High Court determined that the claim term "Lewis acid inhibitor" is met only if the PHOSITA uses general common knowledge and finds a causal nexus between neutralizing Lewis acids resulting from the containers and inhibiting degradation of sevoflurane by Lewis acids. The court found that the specification described the invention as requiring the inner surface of the container for the anesthetic composition to be in contact with the sevoflurane. The IP High Court found no infringement with respect to Baxter's method, which used epoxy resins, because Baxter's mechanism of preventing degradation of sevoflurane was different from Abbott's and thus the PHOSITA would not find a causal nexus between neutralizing Lewis acids and inhibiting degradation of sevoflurane by Lewis acids. **6.63**

iii. Prior Art As highlighted by the Japanese courts' use of the specification in interpreting claim language, the rule that courts should not read limitations into claims from the specification is not as strongly enforced in Japanese courts as in US courts. This tradition of limiting the claim language to disclosed embodiments by reading limitations from the specification was developed by pre-*Kilby* Supreme Court precedents. In a leading 1962 decision, the Supreme Court emphasized that courts should make reference to the prior art to understand a patented invention because a patent is granted only to the invention that has the novelty and inventive step in light of the state of art.[163] Although pre-*Kilby* case law did not allow Japanese courts to examine the defense of invalidity, the Supreme Court allowed Japanese courts to examine validity to the extent necessary to determine whether the technical scope of the asserted claim could be interpreted to include prior art embodiments. If the interpretation led to the inclusion of any prior art embodiment into the scope, the claim had to be interpreted to exclude such an embodiment. In another leading decision, the court established a claim interpretation allowing Japanese courts reading limitations from the specification into the asserted claim to eliminate prior art embodiments that fall into the technical scope of the patented invention.[164] In some cases, courts limited the asserted claims to include only the embodiments disclosed in the specification, regardless of the claim language, if the technical scope of such claims included a prior art embodiment.[165] **6.64**

---

[162] IP High Ct., April 23, 2009, Hei 18 (ne) No. 10075, Hanrei Taimuzu (No. 1301) 99. Katayama et al., *Nich-Bei-Ō jūyō tokkyo saibanrei*, 241.

[163] Sup. Ct., December 7, 1962, Sho 36 (wo) No. 464, 16 Minshū (No. 12) 2321. For a discussion of this case, see Takenaka, "Interpreting Patent Claims," 211.

[164] Sup. Ct., August 4, 1964, Sho 37 (wo) No. 871, 18 Minshū (No. 7) 1319.

[165] Osaka High Ct., February 10, 1976, 8 Mutaishū (No. 1) 85.

6.65 This restrictive claim interpretation was developed to prevent enforcement of an invalid patent. Since the *Kilby* decision, Japanese courts can invalidate a patent if the technical scope of the patent includes a prior art embodiment. However, the prior art still plays an important role in clarifying the claim terms in dispute.[166] Regardless of their power to examine validity, UK and US courts find inherent limitations in light of the specification.[167] Such an interpretation is a permissible claim interpretation under the US and UK case law, although these courts struggle to draw a line between permissible claim interpretation and impermissible importation of limitations into the claim from the specification. UK courts are more eager to find inherent limitations because the purposive claim contraction focuses on what the inventor meant by adopting the claim term, as understood by the PHOSITA, and thus the claim term should be understood to exclude embodiments in the prior art.[168]

6.66 Japanese courts also give claim terms a meaning that excludes embodiments in the prior art because the JPO should give patents to inventions that have the novelty and inventive step. However, under post-*Kilby* practice, Japanese courts should not read limitations into the claims if the technical scope of the asserted claims include the prior art and the claims are invalid when limitations have not been read into the claims from the specification.[169] Instead, they should uphold the defense of invalidity for lack of novelty or inventive step. In contrast, when Japanese courts find the asserted claim to be valid with respect to the prior art on which the accused infringer asserted lack of novelty and inventive step, courts refuse to interpret the claim restrictively in light of the prior art.[170]

6.67 **iv. Record of Prosecution History** Unlike German courts, but like US courts, Japanese courts use the record of prosecution history as an important tool to construe claim terms because the prosecution history indicates how the inventor recognized his invention.[171] Japanese courts interpret claim terms in light of the specification not only when the patentee expressly disclaims embodiments during the prosecution but also when the patentees amend the asserted claims to limit his or her technical scope.[172] Moreover, if the patentee makes an argument to limit the technical scope to distinguish the prior art during the examination, he or she cannot assert a technical scope that would conflict with the argument.[173] Patentees are estopped from making an argument that conflicts with the patentee's argument, made at a trial to invalidate the asserted claim, to distinguish the accused embodiment, which emphasizes the features of the patented invention.[174]

6.68 Unlike the general estoppel doctrine under the Civil Code, reliance by the party who asserts estoppel is not necessary. When a patentee amends the asserted claim to limit the technical scope, Japanese courts apply estoppel and prevent the patentee from arguing that the technical scope of the claim includes the accused embodiment regardless of whether the scope surrendered through the amendment includes the accused embodiment.[175]

---

166 Shitara, "Kinouteki Kureimu no Kaishaku ni tsuite," 81.
167 Takenaka, "Claim Construction and the Extent of Patent Protection."
168 *Kirin-Amgen*, 2004 UKHL 46, para. 47.
169 Takabe, *Jitsumu Shōsetsu*, 159.
170 IP High Ct., March 11, 2009, Hei 19 (ne) No. 10025.
171 Takabayashi, "Tokkyo Hatsumei no Gijutsuteki Han'i I," 82.
172 Osaka Dist. Ct., May 23, 1985, Sho 61 (wa) No. 3515, 18 Mutaishū (No. 2) 5.
173 Tokyo High Ct., February 1, 2000, Hei 10 (ne) No. 5507, Hanrei Jiho (No. 1712) 167.
174 Tokyo Dist. Ct., March 30, 2001, Hei 12 (wa) No. 8204, Hanrei Taimuzu (No. 1059) 195.
175 Kazuo Masui and Yoshiyuki Tamura, *Tokkyo Han'rei Gaido (Patent Case Guide)* (2d ed., 2000), 177. Some courts restrictively applied the estoppel based on the record of patent prosecution, finding that the

4. Application of Construed Claims to Accused Embodiment

Like US and German courts, Japanese courts apply the all elements rule when they compare the claim language with the accused embodiment. They define a claim term in terms of the object and effect, and if any feature of the accused embodiment does not meet the term, they find no literal infringement. The all elements rule applies to both literal infringement and infringement under the doctrine of equivalents, and the doctrine of equivalents cannot be applied to vitiate the meaning of the claim term. Moreover, if the claim term in dispute is found to be an essential element of the patented invention, courts cannot apply the doctrine of equivalents and find infringement.[176] **6.69**

In applying the claim language to the accused embodiment, Japanese courts divide claim terms into components of multiple terms. They also divide features of the accused embodiments into components of multiple features and compare claim terms in the components with the features in the components. Unlike US courts, Japanese courts apply the all elements rule on a component-by-component basis. When courts find a feature that corresponds to the claim term but is not included in the component corresponding to the component that includes the claim term, they do not find infringement. **6.70**

Because Japanese courts interpret claim terms in light of the object and effect discussed in the specification, they may find no infringement if adding an element would result in a change of the object and effect of the invention. The Japanese Patent Act makes it clear that an improvement of a prior invention will infringe a claim directed to the prior invention, and the patentee and the exclusive licensee of the improvement patent cannot work on their patented improvement invention if courts find all elements of the claim of the prior invention in the improvement invention, even though the improvement invention is separately patentable over the prior invention.[177] Patents issued to such improvement inventions are comparable to dependent inventions under the German Patent Act.[178] Under the Japanese Patent Act, the patentee and the exclusive licensee of the improvement patent can request the JPO to grant a compulsory license so that they can work on the improvement if the patentee of the prior invention refuses to give a license.[179] However, Japanese courts seldom find infringement by an improvement because separately patentable improvements are not enabled or supported by the specification. It is more likely that they will interpret the claim language to exclude patentable improvements. **6.71**

5. Doctrine of Equivalents

After finding no literal infringement, Japanese courts examine infringement under the doctrine of equivalents if the patentee asserts that the missing claim term is replaced with a feature that is equivalent to the missing element.[180] In the 1998 *Ball Spline* decision, **6.72**

---

reason for the amendment did not relate to the accused embodiment. E.g., Osaka Dist. Ct., October 9, 2001, Hei 10 (wa) No. 12889.

176 For the non-essential elements test, see Ch. 6, 6.72.

177 Japanese Patent Act, § 72.

178 Ch. 5, 5.109. BGH GRUR 2006, 399, 401—Rangierkatze.

179 Japanese Patent Act, § 92.

180 For a comparison of the doctrine of equivalents under the Japanese Patent Act and the doctrine of equivalents under the US and German Patent Acts, see Toshiko Takenaka, "The Doctrine of Equivalents in Japan," CASRIP Symposium Publication Series: Rethinking Int'l Intellectual Property, No. 6 (2001), 126 (http://www.law.washington.edu/casrip/symposium/Number6/Takenaka.pdf).

the Supreme Court of Japan set forth five tests to find infringement under the doctrine of equivalents: (1) whether the disputed claim elements are non-essential elements of the patented invention ("nonessential elements"); (2) whether the object of the patented invention can be attained even if the disputed elements are replaced with the structures in the accused embodiment, and thus the accused embodiment results in having identical functions and effects as the patented invention ("identical function and effect"); (3) if one skilled in the art would have readily conceived the interchangeability between the disputed claim elements and the replaced features in the accused embodiments as of the time of exploitation, such as the manufacturing of the accused product by the accused infringer ("obviousness of interchangeability"); (4) if the accused embodiment is novel and would not have been able to be conceived by one skilled in the art at the time the patent application for the invention was filed ("novelty and inventive step of the accused embodiment"); and (5) if the accused embodiment is something other than what the applicant intentionally removed from the technical scope of the asserted claim during the patent prosecution ("no disclaimer of the accused embodiment").[181] Japanese courts find infringement under the doctrine of equivalents only if the patentee is able to establishe that all five tests are answered affirmatively.

6.73 Japanese courts classify tests (1), (2), and (3) as positive tests establishing infringement under the doctrine of equivalents, and tests (4) and (5) as negative tests limiting infringement under the doctrine of equivalents, and place the burden of proof on the patentee with respect to the positive tests and on the accused infringers with respect to the negative tests.[182] The positive tests are very similar to the first two tests under the German doctrine of equivalents and the two tests for establishing insubstantial difference under the US doctrine of equivalents. Test (2) is a translation of the same effect test under German case law in evaluating the invention in terms of the problem or object and effect of the invention.[183] This test is also similar to the way-function-result triple identity test under US case law, which focuses on the similarity of the function and result.[184] Test (3) is a translation of the second question under German case law.[185] It is also similar to the known interchangeability test under US case law.[186] However, Japanese courts find this test to be met only if the accused embodiment is evident from the specification and is considered as equivalent to what is being disclosed or if the embodiment is a trivial and mechanical skill modification in light of the common general knowledge of the PHOSITA at the time that the accused embodiment has begun to be manufactured.[187] Moreover, they may find a disclaimer and a

---

[181] Sup. Ct., February 24, 1998, Hei 6 (wo) No. 1038, 52 Minshū (No.1) 113 (*Ball Spline*). For an English translation and case comment, see Toshiko Takenaka, "The Supreme Court Affirmed the Presence of the Doctrine of Equivalents under Japanese Patent System," 5(1) *Casrip Newsletter* (Winter 1998): 12 (http://www.law.washington.edu/Casrip/Newsletter/default.aspx?year=1998&article=newsv5i1jp1).

[182] Kei Iida, "Trends in Kin'tō ron ni Kansuru Saikin'no Saiban'rei no Keiko (Recent Decisions Relating to the Doctrine of Equivalents)," in Toahiaki Makino et al. (eds.), *Theories and Practice on Intellectual Property Law* (2007), vol. I, 177.

[183] For the same effect test, see Ch. 5, 5.114.

[184] *Warner-Jenkinson Co. v. Hilton Davis Chem. Co.*, 520 U.S. 17, 117 S. Ct. 1040, 137 L. Ed. 2d 146, 41U.S.P.Q.2d 1865 (1997). See Ch. 4, 4.93.

[185] *Schneidrmessser I (Cutting Blade I)*, 2002 11c 878.

[186] *Warner-Jenkinson Co.*, 520 U.S. 17.

[187] E.g., Osaka Dist. Ct., February 22, 2000, Hei 10 (wa) No. 12235; Tokyo Dist. Ct., March 23, 2000, Hei 10 (wa) No. 11453, Hanrei Jihō (No. 1739) 122. Iida, "Trends in Kin'tō ron ni Kansuru Saikin'no Saiban'rei no Keiko," 187.

failure to meet test (5) if a patent emphasizes the obviousness of the interchangeability in light of the specification.[188]

The negative tests are also similar to the tests limiting the doctrine of equivalents under German and US case law. Test (3) is a translation of the German courts' *Formstein* defense, which requires the accused embodiment to have the novelty and inventive step over the prior art.[189] It is also very similar to the prior art limitation under US case law, although Japanese courts do not use a hypothetical claim to literally cover the accused embodiment for deciding whether the hypothetical claim meets the novelty and inventive step requirements.[190] Test (4) includes both clear disclaimers in the specification as well as estoppel based on the record of prosecution and thus is very similar to the dedication to the public[191] and the prosecution history estoppel under US case law.[192] The prosecution history estoppel applies regardless of the reliance of a party or the JPO. This is in stark contrast to German courts, which do not examine the record of prosecution neither for claim construction nor application of the doctrine of equivalents; they find a disclaimer only based on the specification.[193] German courts do not apply the prosecution history beyond the general estoppel doctrine under its Civil Code[194] even though recent decisions from the Federal Court of Justice suggest that German courts can make reference to the differences between claims originally included in the patent application and those being issued or between claims being issued and claims amended in post-grant procedures at the European Patent Office.[195] **6.74**

Test (1) is unique to the Japanese doctrine of equivalents. Japanese courts define the essential portion as the core and as the unique portion of the technical idea, which underlies the means to solve the technical problem unique to the patented invention.[196] The nonessential elements test is added to make sure that the technical idea that underlies the patented invention and the technical idea that underlies the accused embodiment are the same because both ideas adopt the same means for solving the technical problem or attaining the technical object.[197] In other words, Japanese courts examine the equivalency between the disputed claim elements and the features of the accused embodiment on an element-by-element basis, with respect to tests (2)–(4), as well as the equivalency of the invention as a whole through a comparison of the technical solution between the patented invention and the accused embodiments in light of the prior art, with respect to test (1).[198] Japanese courts find a failure to meet the essential elements test if one of the other tests, particularly test (5), is not met.[199] **6.75**

188 Iida, "Trends in Kin'tō ron ni Kansuru Saikin'no Saiban'rei no Keiko," 189.

189 See Ch. 5, 5.128.

190 *Wilson Sporting Goods Co. v. David Geoffrey & Associates*, 904 F.2d 677, 684, 14 USPQ2d 1942 (Fed. Cir. 1990). See Ch. 4, 4.120.

191 See Ch. 4, 4.124.

192 See Ch. 4. 104.

193 See Ch. 5, 5.86.

194 See Ch. 5, 5.126.

195 See Ch. 5, 5.84.

196 The essential portion is viewed similar to the indispensable or essential requirement for establishing contributory infringement. See Ch. 6, 6.17.

197 Takabe, *Jitsumu Shōsetsu*, 168.

198 Some commentators read the *Ball Spline* decision as requiring courts to apply the essential element test on an element-by-element basis, focusing on the equivalency of technical solution between the disputed elements and features of the accused embodiment. Takabe, *Jitsumu Shōsetsu*, 168. However, it is very unlikely that the different approaches in examining the equivalency result in different conclusions.

199 Makoto Endo, "Comparative Study on Prosecution History Estoppel in the U.S. and Japan: What Can Japan Learn from the Chaos in *Warner-Jenkinson* and *Festo*?," 9(3) *CASRIP Newsletter* (Autumn

6.76 The nonessential elements test gives Japanese courts the flexibility to deny infringement under the doctrine of equivalents and presents a big hurdle for patentees to overcome.[200] As under the literal infringement analysis, Japanese courts seldom find infringement under the doctrine of equivalents unless the modification in the accused embodiment is evident to the PHOSITA.[201] The *Hollow Golf Club Head* case is one of a small number of cases in which the IP High Court found infringement under the doctrine of equivalents.[202] After adopting a definition for the claim term "a suture seam material" that excluded the multiple short wedges in the accused embodiment, the court examined tests (2) and (3) and then concluded both tests were met. It found test (1) was met being supported by the conclusion of tests (2) and (3). It also found that tests (4) and (5) were without detailed analysis once other tests were met.

6.77 First, in light of the description of the invention in the specification, the court found that the object and function/effect of the patented invention was to enhance the bond strength between the metal outer surface material and the fiber reinforced plastic (FRP) surface material. The court found that test (2) was met because the suture seam material in the asserted claim and the multiple short wedges in the accused embodiment performed the same function to produce the effect of the invention: enhancing the bond strength. Test (3) was met because the PHOSITA could have easily conceived of replacing the suture seam material with the short wedges at the time that the accused embodiment was manufactured. The court then held that the suture seam material was not an essential element and met test (1). It explained that the difference between the suture seam material, which connected the metal and FRP surface materials at multiple locations, and the multiple wedges, which connected the metal and FRP surface materials at one location, was not essential to attain the effect of the invention. At last, the court found that tests (4) and (5) were met because no evidence was introduced for either lack of novelty or inventive step or for a disclaimer with respect to the accused embodiment and the record of prosecution history.

6.78 The *Hollow Golf Club Head* case highlights the restrictive claim interpretation in light of the specification and the narrow range of the doctrine of equivalents. It is likely that US and German courts would find literal infringement with respect to the accused embodiments in cases where Japanese courts would find infringement under the doctrine of equivalents. It is very unlikely for Japanese courts to meet the obviousness of interchangeability test, test (3),

2002) (https://www.law.washington.edu/Casrip/Newsletter/2002/newsv9i3Endo.PDF); Makoto Endo, "Borusupurain Jiken Saikosai Hanketsu Igo No Kintoron No Tekiyo (Application of the doctrine of equivalents after the Supreme Court Decision in *Ball Spline* Case)," *Hanrei Taimuzu* (No. 1051) (2001): 60.

[200] Japanese courts refused to apply the doctrine of equivalents in 70 percent of cases involving a failure to meet the essential element test between 1998, after the *Ball Spline* decision, and December 31, 2006. Iida, "Trends in Kin'tō ron ni Kansuru Saikin'no Saiban'rei no Keiko," 184. See also Toshiko Takenaka, "The Essential Element Test Provides a Big Hurdle to Japanese Doctrine of Equivalents," 7(2) *CASRIP Newsletter* (Spring 2000): 13 (https://www.law.washington.edu/Casrip/Newsletter/2000/newsv7i2jp4.pdf).

[201] Between 1998 after the *Ball Spline* decision and December 31, 2006, Japanese courts found infringement under the doctrine of equivalents in less than 10% of the cases in which the patentee claimed infringement under the doctrine of equivalents. See Iida, "Trends in Kin'tō ron ni Kansuru Saikin'no Saiban'rei no Keiko," 196.

[202] IP High Ct., June 29, 2009, Hei 21 (ne) No. 10006, Hanrei Taimusu (No. 2077) 123 (*Hollow Golf Club Head*). For a discussion of literal infringement in this case, see n. 161 above. See Ch. 6, 6.60. Katayama et al., *Nich-Bei-Ō jūyō tokkyo saibanrei*, 237.

if the claim element has been replaced with an after-arising technology which was developed after the priority date and thus is not obvious from the specification, although the Supreme Court requires lower courts to apply test (3) as of the date that the accused embodiment began to be manufactured instead of the priority date, and in theory an after-arising technology can meet a claim term.

Part III

VALIDITY CHALLENGE

7

UNITED STATES

A. Introduction

The current patent system in the United States allows patent validity challenges both at the United States Patent and Trademark Office (USPTO) and in court during patent litigation. Contrary to the German and Japanese systems, courts in the United States have traditionally held exclusive power to examine the validity of a patent issued by the USPTO because the US patent system is based on the UK's Statute of Monopolies.[1] The Statute of Monopolies was originally developed to limit the power held by Queen Elizabeth I to grant patents of monopoly by giving courts the power to find a patent granted by the queen invalid if an invention covered by the patent failed to meet the novelty requirement.[2] The first US patent statute followed the UK approach by viewing the power to invalidate patents as an essential function of the court.[3] The invalidity defense in patent litigation[4] was the only option for a third party to challenge the validity of US patents outside bringing a priority contest in an interference procedure at the USPTO.[5] **7.01**

After preserving this legacy for almost two centuries since the enactment of the first patent statute, a high rate of patent invalidity in patent litigation led to a significant modification.[6] The USPTO was given the power to review patent validity for the first time in 1980 when the US Congress introduced an *ex parte* re-examination procedure.[7] The *ex parte* re-examination aims to provide competitors with an option to challenge patent validity that is less expensive than litigation by creating an administrative procedure to eliminate patents with validity that is questionable due to a reference that the USPTO did not consider at the first examination. However, the *ex parte* re-examination procedure does not effectively serve this aim because the competitors' participation as a third-party requester in the procedure is extensively limited, which lets many doubtful patents survive the validity challenge.[8] To expand **7.02**

---

1 Statute of Monopolies of 1623, 21 Jac. 1, c. 3, § 6 (Eng.).

2 *Darcy v. Allin*, 74 Eng. Rep. 1131 (K.B. 1602) (Eng.).

3 Edward Waltersheid, "The Early Evolution of the United States Patent Law," 76 *Journal of the Patent and Trademark Office Society* (1994): 697.

4 Another option to challenge validity in US courts, a declaratory action for invalidity, was created as a new remedy in 1934. 28 U.S.C. § 2201.

5 The first-to-invent party can invalidate a patent obtained by the second-to-invent party through interference procedures. These procedures for determining priority were introduced when the 1836 Patent Act created the Patent Office and introduced the examination system. Act of July 4, 1836, Ch. 357, § 1, 5 Stat. 117; for general discussion on the history of interference procedure, see *Chisum on Patents*, § 10.02.

6 Gloria K. Koenig, *Patent Validity: A Statistical and Substantive Analysis* (1974), § 5.05[4].

7 35 U.S.C. § 301 (2006); 20 House Report No. 96-1307, 96th Cong., 2d Sess. (1980) (http://www.ipmall.info/hosted_resources/lipa/patents/Legislative_History_Process_Patents.pdf).

8 Ashley Parker, "Problem Patents: Is Reexamination Truly a Viable Alternative to Litigation, 3 *N.C.J.L. & Tech.* (2002): 305.

participation by competitors, Congress added another administrative procedure, the *inter partes* re-examination procedure, in 1999.[9] The *inter partes* re-examination procedure has significantly increased the competitors' chance to invalidate patents and to at least limit the scope of patents. Competitors were still unsatisfied with the validity challenge system because the grounds for requesting both re-examination procedures are limited to prior art related grounds.[10] To provide competitors with the opportunity to take advantage of administrative procedures to re-examine patents on all grounds of validity, the most recent major patent reform, the America Invents Act (AIA), introduced a post-grant review procedure.[11] The AIA also introduced multiple administrative procedures to give the USPTO the power to examine patent validity under a variety of conditions.

7.03 Accordingly, the US Congress has significantly expanded the USPTO's role in the validity challenge. Multiple options to challenge validity through judicial and administrative procedures may lead to possible conflicting validity decisions with respect to the same patent. Moreover, the change in claim scope through an amendment during an administrative procedure at the USPTO may affect the infringement determination. The US system has included measures to avoid such conflicting validity decisions and to prevent the change in claim scope from affecting the infringement determination.

B. Fundamental Rules

1. Claim Construction

7.04 The language of the claim defines not only the extent of exclusive right but also the invention that the USPTO examines for patentability.[12] The scope of invention that USPTO examiners and administrative law judges examine is different from the extent of patent protection at infringement litigation. In interpreting claims, claims should be given the broadest reasonable interpretation consistent with the specification.[13] This is a stark contrast to the restrictive construction used for determining the extent of patent exclusivity in which claims are interpreted in light of the specification and the record of patent prosecution, with an emphasis on the claims' notice function.[14] The USPTO adopts the broadest possible interpretation to serve the public interests by preventing applicants and patentees from obtaining a scope that is broader than justified while guaranteeing a chance to amend claims and obtain appropriate coverage with clear claim language.[15] Because of the different rules for claim construction, a court in an infringement procedure may sustain the validity of a patent, but the USPTO may cancel this patent by adopting a meaning that is broader than the meaning adopted by the court in the infringement procedure and anticipated by the prior art.[16]

---

[9] American Inventor's Protection Act of 1999 (http://www.uspto.gov/patents/law/aipa/).

[10] 35 U.S.C. §§ 301, 321.

[11] Public Law 112–129 Leahy-Smith America Invents Act, Sec. 6 (http://www.gpo.gov/fdsys/pkg/PLAW-112publ29/pdf/PLAW-112publ29.pdf).

[12] *Warner-Jenkinson Co. v. Hilton Davis Chem. Co.*, 520 U.S. 17, 117 S. Ct. 1040, 41 U.S.P.Q. 2d 1865 (1997).

[13] *In re Yamamoto*, 740 F.2d 1569, 222 U.S.P.Q. 934 (Fed. Cir. 1984).

[14] See Ch. 4, 4.32 "Claim Construction."

[15] Ibid.

[16] E.g., *In re American Academy of Science Tech Center*, 367 F.3d 1359, 70 U.S.P.Q. 2d 1827 (Fed. Cir. 2004).

Moreover, the extent of patent exclusivity for determining infringement differs from the scope of invention for determining patentability and validity because the former includes the scope under the doctrine of equivalents.[17] The USPTO examines only the literal scope of a claim, and thus the scope of invention for patentability does not include equivalents if the invention is defined by structures, materials, and acts.[18] An exception applies to a claim defined by function. If the USPTO finds that an element in a claim is drafted in the means-plus-function format, it will apply § 112(f) and interpret the element to cover the structures disclosed in the specification and their equivalents.[19] In other words, the scope of invention under the examination and validity challenge is limited to the disclosed embodiments and their equivalents if the invention is defined by its function instead of structures, materials, and acts. These literal equivalents must exist at the time of patent issuance, instead of the time of infringement for equivalents under the judicially developed doctrine of equivalents.[20] **7.05**

Furthermore, the difference in scope between patentability and validity determination and infringement determination is highlighted with respect to product-by-process claims. The broadest reasonable interpretation rule requires the USPTO to interpret a product-by-process claim as covering any product resulting from the process recited in the claim regardless of the process through which the product was made.[21] In other words, patentability is determined by the product instead of the process recited in the claim. This rule applies to both examination and post-grant procedures at the USPTO as well as to an invalidity defense at infringement litigation. A product-by-process claim is valid only if the product resulting from the process recited in the claim is new and nonobvious from the prior art. **7.06**

A product-by-process claim presents a unique problem because USPTO examiners are unable to make the product and examine if the product is structurally new and nonobvious. Thus, the USPTO carries a lesser burden of proof for establishing obviousness.[22] It is unclear whether this unique problem also affects the burden of persuasion on a challenging party for establishing invalidity at infringement litigation or post-grant procedures at the USPTO. **7.07**

2. Burden of Proof

Once a patent is issued, a patent is presumed to be valid.[23] Because of the presumption of validity, invalidity must be established by clear and convincing evidence.[24] In contrast, the standard of review during all types of post-grant validity procedures at the USPTO is by a preponderance of the evidence, which means that the USPTO must issue a certificate of cancellation if the evidence establishes that the patent is more likely than not invalid.[25] The **7.08**

---

[17] Ch. 3, 3.03.

[18] Under US Patent Act the scope of claims defining the invention by functions (means-plus-function claims) includes embodiments disclosed in the written description and drawings and their equivalents. 35 U.S.C. §112(f). For more discussions, see Ch. 4, 4.40 "Functionally Defined Claims."

[19] *In re Donaldson*, 16 F.3d 1189, 29 U.S.P.Q. 2d 1845; *Al-Site Corp. v. VSI Int'l, Inc.*, 174 F.3d 1308, 50 U.S.P.Q. 2d 1161(Fed. Cir. 1999).

[20] *Warner-Jenkinson*, 520 U.S., 37.

[21] *Abbott Labs. v. Sandoz, Inc.*, 566 F.3d 1282, 90 U.S.P.Q. 2d 1769 (Fed. Cir. 2009); *SmithKline Beecham Corp. v. Apotex Corp.*, 439 F.3d 1312, 1318 (Fed. Cir. 2006).

[22] *In re Brown*, 459 F.2d 531, 535, 173 U.S.P.Q. 685, 688 (CCPA 1972).

[23] 35 U.S.C. § 282 (2006).

[24] *Adenta GMBH v. OrthoArm, Inc.*, 501 F.3d 1364, 1371, 2007 U.S. App. LEXIS 22315 (Fed. Cir. 2007).

[25] *Ethicon, Inc. v. Quigg*, 849 F.2d 1422 (Fed. Cir. 1988).

preponderance standard is lower than the clear and convincing evidence. The rationale for the difference in the evidence standard is that the USPTO, through its expertise, examined and approved patents.[26] Although the rationale may diminish with respect to prior art references that were not introduced during the first examination, the heightened standard should apply to all validity challenges at infringement and declaratory judgment (DJ) litigations regardless of whether the prior art was in fact considered during the examination.

7.09 Moreover, patentability issues are questions of law based on facts found by fact finders, frequently a jury.[27] A lay person tends to rely on the USPTO's expertise, which has already approved a challenged claim. Because of the lower standard of evidence and the broadest possible interpretation rule in combination with the expertise of USPTO administrative law judges, a party has a better chance of establishing invalidity at the USPTO than with a validity challenge at infringement litigations.

3. Doctrines to Preclude an Invalidity Defense

7.10 US courts developed equitable doctrines to prevent a party from challenging validity under special circumstances. One such doctrine is the doctrine of assignor estoppel. Assignor estoppel prevents one who has assigned their rights to a patent or patent application from later challenging the validity of the patent or the patent resulting from the application.[28] The estoppel applies to prevent any party in privity with the assignor. The rationale for the estoppel is that when an inventor/assignor has signed the oath to attest to the validity of a patent when a patent application is filed and has assigned that patent or patent application for consideration, the inventor/assignor should be estopped from defending the patent infringement claims by proving that what was assigned was worthless.

7.11 A settlement agreement between a patentee and an accused infringer may give rise to an estoppel preventing the accused infringer from challenging the validity of a patent in future suits.[29] When equitable doctrines prevent courts from examining the validity and courts find the patent invalid with respect to claims alleged to be infringed, courts may interpret claims very narrowly to exclude the accused embodiment.[30]

4. Amendment

7.12 A major benefit for patentees disputing validity at a USPTO post-grant procedure is that claims, written descriptions, and drawings can be amended to remove a ground of invalidity. Patentees can amend the scope of claims by cancelling patented claims and adding new claims. They can amend claims to enlarge the scope of the original claim by applying for a reissue of the patent within two years from the grant of the original patent.[31] Once the prescribed two-year period expires, an amendment should not enlarge the scope of

---

[26] *Microsoft Corp. v. i4i Ltd. P'ship*, 131 S. Ct. 1843, 179 L. Ed. 2d 770 (U.S. 2011).

[27] Mark A. Lemley, "Why Do Juries Decide If Patents Are Valid?" 99 *Va. L.R.* (2013): 104 (https://www.law.berkeley.edu/files/Panel_09_Lemley.pdf).

[28] *Diamond Scientific Co. v. Ambico, Inc.*, 848 F.2d 1220, 6 U.S.P.Q. 2d 2028 (Fed. Cir. 1988).

[29] *Hallco Mfg. Co., Inc. v. Foster*, 256 F.3d 1290, 59 U.S.P.Q. 2d 1346 (Fed. Cir. 2001).

[30] *Garneau v. Dozier*, 102 U.S. 230, 12 Otto 230, 26 L. Ed. 133 (1880); *Scott Paper Co. v. Marcalus Mfg. Co.*, 326 U.S. 249, 66 S. Ct. 101, 90 L. Ed. 47, 67 U.S.P.Q. 193 (1945). For a discussion of claim interpretation and the doctrine of assignor estoppel, see Toshiko Takenaka, "Interpreting Patent Claims: The United States, Germany and Japan," 17 *IIC Studies* (1995): 81–84.

[31] 35 U.S.C. § 251(d).

the claims of the patent or introduce a new matter during a reissue procedure or any of the post-grant procedures, which include *ex parte* re-examinations, *inter partes* reviews, and post-grant reviews, including the transitional post-grant review for business method patents.[32] For amendments of claims, the written description requirement prevents patentees from amending claims to capture subject matter that the inventor was not in possession of on the application date.[33] For amendments to the written description and drawings—that is, the specification other than claims—the new matter prohibition rule prevents patentees from amending claims to capture matter involving a departure from or an addition to the original disclosure on the application date.[34] An amendment does not violate the new matter prohibition (1) if it merely clarifies or makes definite matter that was expressly or inherently disclosed in the original application or (2) if it conforms to the specification of the originally disclosed drawings or claims.[35]

Although patentees can amend claims to sustain validity, amendments result in significant disadvantages on the patentees' claims of damages and cause of action. Unlike amendments of claims during post-grant procedures at the European Patent Office (EPO), German Patent Office, or Japan Patent Office (JPO), the effect of amendments or new claims that limit the scope of the original claims is not retroactive unless the scope of the amended or added claims is substantially identical.[36] It is very unlikely that a claim reissued during the post-grant validity procedures fails to meet the substantially identical requirement because the amendment was made to distinguish the claimed invention from the prior art or changing the scope of claims to meet patent eligibility, utility, and disclosure requirements. When a patent is reissued or a certificate of patentability is issued with respect to the added claims and/or amended claims, the effect of the patent on the original claim is deemed surrendered and eliminated, making any causes of action and damage claims to be invalidated. The case law makes it clear that an amended or new claim, which limited the original to sustain a prior art challenge, does not meet the substantially identical requirement necessary to get retroactive effect.[37] **7.13**

This is in stark contrast to the effect of an amendment under the European Patent Convention (EPC), German Patent Act, and Japanese Patent Act in which patentees retain a cause of action and claims of damages as long as the accused embodiment falls within the scope of the amended claim that is enforced. Under the US Patent Act, damages for infringing acts that occur before the reissue patent date are eliminated when an amended reissue claim is not identical to the original patent claim.[38] If patentees want to claim damages before the reissue date, they should sue on the original claims that were not amended. **7.14**

[32] 35 U.S.C. § 305, § 316(d)(3), § 326(d)(3).

[33] 35 U.S.C. § 112(a). *Ariad Pharmaceuticals, Inc. v. Eli Lilly & Co.*, 598 F.3d 1336 (Fed. Cir. 2010) (*en banc*).

[34] 35 U.S.C. § 132; 37 C.F.R. § 1.118.

[35] *Transco Products, Inc. v. Performance Contracting, Inc.*, 821 F. Supp. 537, 550 n.18, 28 U.S.P.Q. 2d 1739, 1748 n.18 (N.D. Ill. 1993), rev'd in part, vacated in part and remanded in part, 38 F.3d 551, 32 U.S.P.Q. 2d 1077 (Fed. Cir. 1994).

[36] 35 U.S.C. § 252, § 307(b), 316(b) (2006).

[37] *Laitram Corp. v. NEC Corp.*, 163 F.3d 1342 (Fed. Cir. 1998) (rejecting an argument that the amended or new claim simply clarifies the scope of the original claim).

[38] *Westvaco Corp. v. Int'l Paper Co.*, 991 F.2d 735, 26 U.S.P.Q. 2d 1353 (Fed. Cir. 1993).

7.15 Moreover, two types of intervening rights eliminate the patentees' causes of action against accused infringers in infringement litigation. The absolute intervening right protects from an infringement claim a specific thing such as a product made by a claimed process or that is an embodiment of a reissued apparatus claim, purchased, offered to sell, or used within the United States or imported into the United States before the reissue date.[39] This right eliminates the patentees' causes of action regardless of a party who continues to sell to others, uses, or offers to sell the specific thing.[40] The absolute intervening right extends to a thing that was made but had not been used before the reissue date.[41] It also extends to a thing that was in an infringer's inventory or had been purchased by confirmed order on the reissue date.[42]

7.16 The equitable intervening right protects a person who made, purchased, offered to sell, or used within the United States, or imported into the United States before the reissue date a thing that is an embodiment of a reissued claim.[43] It also protects a person who made, before the reissue date, substantial preparations for making, using, selling, or offering to sell within the United States a thing that is made by a process covered by a reissued process claim.[44] A court grants an equitable intervening right so that a party, including a defendant of an infringement civil action, can continue practicing the invention to the extent and under such terms as the courts deem equitable for the protection of investments made or business commenced before the grant of reissue.[45]

7.17 This procedure allows the court to decide the validity of the patent at issue and issue a judgment of invalidity, regardless of a patentee's attempt to limit the scope at a reissue or re-examination because such limitations do not affect the scope of claim considered by the court in infringement civil action. Even if the USPTO issues a reissue patent or a certificate with amended or new claims, the court can dismiss a case that deals with future infringement because the infringer's act is covered under the equitable intervening right as long as the pre-reissue activity does not infringe a valid claim of the reissue patent or re-examination certificate that was in the original patent and thus has never been changed.[46] While the decision of whether to grant an equitable intervening right is at the discretion of the district court, it is likely that an accused infringer-defendant who was engaged in one of the pre-reissue practicing activities will be protected by this right.[47]

5. Measures to Prevent Conflicting Validity Decisions

7.18 To prevent district courts from issuing a validity decision that conflicts with a decision for the same claim from the USPTO, the AIA introduced measures to prevent the institution

---

[39] 35 U.S.C. § 252¶2. *BIC Leisure Products v. Windsurfing Int'l*, 1 F.3d 1214, 27 U.S.P.Q. 2d 1671 (Fed. Cir. 1993).

[40] Although § 252¶2 recites "that person's successors in business," the absolute intervening right to a specific thing is not limited by a party who is engaging in an infringing act at the reissue date. See *Chisum on Patents*, § 15.05[2][e].

[41] Ibid. 1220–21.

[42] *Shockley v. Arcan, Inc.*, 248 F.3d 1349, 58 U.S.P.Q. 2d 1692 (Fed. Cir. 2001).

[43] 35 U.S.C. § 252¶2.

[44] Ibid.

[45] Ibid. §§ 252, 307(b), 316(b) (2006) (for a general discussion on the two types of intervening rights, see *Chisum on Patents*, § 15.05).

[46] *Westvaco Corp. v. Int'l Paper Co.*, 991 F.2d 735 (Fed. Cir. 1993).

[47] *In re Doyle*, 293 F.3d 1355 (Fed. Cir. 2002).

of a USPTO post-grant validity procedure once a civil action challenging the validity of a claim is filed and to require civil courts to stay a civil action once a party files a petition for a USPTO post-grant validity procedure.[48] The USPTO plans to complete all post-AIA *inter partes* post-grant procedures (*inter partes* reviews, post-grant reviews, transitional program for business method patent post-grant reviews, and derivation procedures) within twelve months from the date that the USPTO made the decision to initiate a procedure.[49]

The pre-AIA Patent Act did not provide for a mandatory stay of a civil action. However, district courts often exercised their discretionary powers to stay litigation while re-examination was pending at the USPTO.[50] Accordingly, even if courts did not stay their actions, it was rare for district courts to complete their actions before the USPTO made a validity decision through pre-AIA re-examination procedures.[51] **7.19**

Despite district courts' mandatory stay under the AIA, courts may issue a judgment that conflicts with a USPTO's validity decision if parties are allowed to delay filing post-grant validity procedures. US courts developed the doctrine of collateral estoppel, which prevents parties from delaying the filing of a post-grant validity procedure. Under this doctrine, the USPTO must stop any post-issuance validity procedures as soon as the courts issue a final judgment of invalidity.[52] **7.20**

Contrary to the effect of a Japanese court's final judgment of invalidity,[53] a final invalidity judgment issued by US courts binds not only the parties and non-parties of future litigation but also the USPTO.[54] Although patentees can challenge collateral estoppel by showing that they were not given a full and fair opportunity to litigate, the USPTO is not able to make such a claim. This binds the USPTO from pursuing further action until the patentee can successfully convince the court that the doctrine should not apply.[55] If the asserted claims have a ground of invalidity, patentees need to file a post-grant procedure early enough so that an amendment through the procedure is completed before a district court judgment has become final. **7.21**

The effect of cancellation certificates also urges accused infringers to file post-grant procedures early. The USPTO issues a certificate after the prescribed period for appeal has passed or once all appeals have been resolved.[56] Although the US Patent Act does not explicitly provide the effects of a cancellation certificate, courts interpret the reissue provision in parallel with the effect of amendment during the post-grant procedures—that is, a cancellation **7.22**

---

[48] See Ch. 7, 7.37.

[49] Office Patent Trial Practice Guide, 37 C.F.R., Pt. 42 (2012).

[50] 35 U.S.C. § 318 (2006). The Patent Act provides an explicit provision for staying patent litigation once an *inter partes* re-examination order has been entered. However, it does not include a similar provision for *ex parte* re-examinations. For a general discussion on requesting a stay in patent litigation while a re-examination is pending at USPTO, see David McComb, "Patent Reexamination with Litigation: Strategies and Practice Tips," 6th Annual Rocky Mountain Intellectual Property & Technology Institute (2007), 18.

[51] Toshiko Takenaka, "Merging Civil and Common Law Traditions in Patent Validity Challenge System: Japanese Experiences," in Horst-Peter Götting and Claudia Schlüter (eds.), *Nourriture de l'esprit: Festchrift für Dieter Strauder zum 70. Geburtstag* (2011), 271–92.

[52] *Blonder-Tongue Laboratories, Inc. v. University of Illinois Foundation*, 402 U.S. 313, 28 L. Ed. 2d 788, 91 S. Ct. 1434 (1971).

[53] See Ch. 9, 920.

[54] *Ethicon, Inc. v. Quigg*, 849 F.2d 1422, 7 U.S.P.Q.2D 1152 (Fed. Cir. 1988).

[55] *Ethicon, Inc.* 849 F.2d, 1429.

[56] 35 U.S.C. § 307, § 316(b) (2006).

certificate eliminates any cause of action with respect to any cancelled claim.[57] In the event that the Federal Circuit affirms a decision to cancel claims asserted by a patentee in parallel litigation, any judgment of validity and infringement issued by the district court in parallel litigation will be vacated and remanded to the district court for dismissal.[58]

7.23 Moreover, the issuance of a cancellation certificate does not have any effect on an issued final judgment of infringement, and it is not necessary for a patentee to return money received as compensation for damages.[59] The Federal Circuit emphasized that in patent disputes priority must be given to judicial decisions under the US Constitution because of the separation of powers,[60] which suggests that cancellation certificates have no effect on final judgments from the courts. There may be an exception under Rule 60(b) of the Federal Rules of Civil Procedure, where a party from prior litigation can recover damages paid under a final judgment,[61] but this is a remedy that is limited to exceptional circumstances.[62] In short, to prevent a payment of damages for invalid patents, accused infringers are urged to start a post-grant procedure early.

6. Estoppel

7.24 The US Patent Act provides a broad estoppel effect to prevent not only the parties of the first post-grant review or *inter partes* review proceedings but also the real party in interest or a privy of the party of the first procedure from re-litigating validity at any USPTO procedure or in any infringement civil action once a final written decision sustaining the validity is issued.[63] The AIA extended this estoppel effect to prevent *ex parte* re-examination requests subsequent to a final written decision in a post-grant or *inter partes* review procedure.[64] Therefore, under the US Patent Act, parties cannot adopt a strategy similar to the one available under German and Japanese practices, by which a party withholds a ground of invalidity or evidence from an *inter partes* validity procedure for use at a future invalidity procedure at the German Federal Patent Court or JPO or during an infringement civil action at Japanese courts.

7.25 Congress introduced two types of estoppel when it created the current *inter partes* review, originally called *inter partes* re-examination in 1999: (1) estoppel with respect to claims and (2) estoppel with respect to fact.[65] The AIA removed the second type of estoppel. The estoppel under the post-AIA Patent Act applies to all proceedings at the USPTO: infringement and declaratory judgment civil actions and patent infringement investigations at the International Trade Commission.[66] In these proceedings, a party to the first proceedings

---

[57] *Luminous Unit Co. v. Freeman-Sweet Co.*, 3 F.2d 577 (7th. Cir. 1924); *Standard Havens Prods. v. Gencor Indus.*, 27 U.S.P.Q. 2d 1959 (Fed. Cir. 1993).

[58] *Translogic Tech., Inc. v. Hitachi, Ltd.*, 250 F. App'x 988 (Fed. Cir. 2007); in a parallel case, *In re Translogic Tech., Inc.*, 504 F.3d 1249, 1251 (Fed. Cir. 2007), the Federal Circuit affirmed the USPTO BPAI's cancellation of all asserted claims.

[59] *Moffitt v. Garr*, 66 U.S. 273 (1862).

[60] *In re Swanson*, 540 F.3d 1368, 1379 n.5 (Fed. Cir. 2008).

[61] David McCombs, "Patent Examination: Earning its Keep in the Litigator's Toolbox," 964 *PLI/Pat* (2009): 685.

[62] *Amado v. Microsoft Corp.*, 517 F.3d 1353 (Fed. Cir. 2008).

[63] 35 U.S.C. § 315(e).

[64] AIA, Sec. 6. 37 C.F.R., Pt. 1, 5, 10, 11 and 41, Changes to Implement Miscellaneous Post Patent Provisions of the Leahy-Smith America Invents Act.

[65] America Inventor's Protection Act of 1999, Public Law 106–113.

[66] 35 U.S.C. §§ 315(e), 325(e).

and its privy can no longer challenge validity on any ground that the party not only has raised but also reasonably could have raised.[67] This estoppel effect results from only a post-grant review or an *inter partes* review when a final written decision is issued. Thus, a party can request an *ex parte* re-examination without a risk of estoppel.

C. Non-Court Patent Validity Procedures at the USPTO

1. *Ex Parte* Re-examination

Any person, including the patentees themselves and the Director of the USPTO, can request an *ex parte* re-examination (EPR) procedure.[68] Unlike post-grant review and *inter partes* review proceedings, a requester can request the USPTO to keep its identity secret.[69] Because a party and its privy of a post-grant review or an *inter partes* review are estopped from requesting an *ex parte* re-examination once a final written decision is issued, a third party in interest can use an agent to request a re-examination and keep the incident in confidence by submitting a statement to certify that the party is not estopped from filing the request.[70] **7.26**

Unlike a post-grant review and an *inter partes* review, a party can request an *ex parte* re-examination at any time.[71] The USPTO interprets "any time" as any time during the period that a patent can be enforced and limits the period to the term of a patent plus six years under the statute of limitations for bringing an infringement action.[72] If an infringement action is initiated within this statutory limitation, a party can request an *ex parte* re-examination even if the six-year statutory limitation period has expired. **7.27**

To request an *ex parte* re-examination, a requester must cite a patent or printed publication as the prior art.[73] This requirement excludes other invalidity grounds unrelated to the prior art such as patent eligibility and utility under § 101 and disclosure requirements under § 112. Such prior art must have a bearing on the patentability of at least one claim in the patent that the requester requests a re-examination of.[74] The USPTO interprets this requirement to include as proper grounds for *ex parte* re-examination not only (1) novelty and statutory bar under § 102 and (2) obviousness under § 103, but also (3) double patenting.[75] In addition to the prior art, a requesting party must submit a written statement that explains the relevance and manner of applying the prior art with respect to the claims of which the requester is requesting a re-examination.[76] **7.28**

The Director of the USPTO can only start *ex parte* re-examination proceedings upon finding a substantial new question of patentability affecting any claim of the patent concerned.[77] **7.29**

---

[67] Ibid.
[68] 35 U.S.C. § 302.
[69] Ibid.
[70] 37 C.F.R. § 1. 510(b)(6).
[71] 35 U.S.C. § 302.
[72] USPTO, *Manual of Patent Examining Procedure* (*MPEP*) (9th ed., 2014), § 2204.
[73] Ibid.
[74] Ibid.
[75] USPTO, *MPEP* (6th ed., 1995), § 2217. *In re Lonardo*, 119 F.3d 960, 43 U.S.P.Q. 2d 1262 (Fed. Cir. 1997).
[76] 35 U.S.C. § 303(a).
[77] Ibid.

This determination relates not only to the claims specified by the requester but also any claims included in the patent.[78] A substantial new question of patentability arises when a reference to the prior art cited by the requester: (1) was not considered in connection with the initial examination or any subsequent reissue or re-examination procedure, and (2) is not substantially identical to any prior art reference that was already considered at the initial examination.[79] This requirement was introduced to protect patentees from abusive re-examination requests. To determine whether to initiate *ex parte* re-examination proceedings, the USPTO needs to determine whether there is a substantial new question of patentability, not whether the cited prior art is evidence of *prima facie* unpatentability.[80] This threshold of substantial new question of patentability is higher than the threshold of reasonable likelihood to initiate an *inter partes* review and the threshold of more likely than not that at least one claim is unpatentable to initiate a post-grant review.[81]

7.30 The USPTO is required to conduct *ex parte* re-examination proceedings with "special dispatch."[82] However, the USPTO practice guideline requiring a final decision within one year from the date of initiating proceedings does not apply to *ex parte* re-examination proceedings.[83] In order to complete the examination as quickly as possible, the automatic extension provisions governing initial examination procedures do not apply to *ex parte* re-examination proceedings. A patentee can request an extension, but such a request must be filed on or before the deadline for the patentee to submit a response.[84]

7.31 During an *ex parte* re-examination, a third-party requester has the right to file a reply only when the patentee files a statement on a substantial new question of patentability that has been included in a copy of determination sent from the USPTO.[85] No more opportunities are given to a third party at the *ex parte* re-examination procedure in order to facilitate and expedite the procedures.[86] A patentee requester has a right to appeal to the Board of Trial and Patent Appeal (PTAB) at the USPTO and the Court of Appeals for the Federal Circuit (Federal Circuit) from a final decision of the Board.[87] In contrast, a third party has no right to appeal to either forum.

7.32 During *ex parte* re-examination proceedings, patentees may amend claims or add new claims as long as the amended or new claims do not enlarge the scope of the original claims.[88] Common to all post-grant proceedings at the USPTO, the standard of review during *ex parte* re-examination procedures is by a preponderance of the evidence, which means that the USPTO must issue a certificate of cancellation if the evidence establishes that the patent is more likely than not invalid.[89]

---

[78] 37 C.F.R. § 1.515(a).

[79] USPTO, *MPEP* (9th ed., 2014), § 2242 (http://www.uspto.gov/web/offices/pac/mpep/).

[80] Ibid.

[81] 35 U.S.C., §§ 314(a), 324(a).

[82] Ibid. § 305.

[83] 37 C.F.R., Pt. 41, Office Patent Trial Guide (August 2012) (http://www.uspto.gov/aia_implementation/trial_practice_guide_48756.pdf).

[84] 37 C.F.R. § 1.550(c); USPTO, *MPEP* (9th ed., 2014), § 2265.

[85] 35 U.S.C. § 304.

[86] *In re Opprecht*, 868 F.2d 1264 (Fed. Cir. 1989).

[87] 35 U.S.C. § 306.

[88] Ibid, § 305.

[89] *Ethicon, Inc. v. Quigg*, 849 F.2d 1422 (Fed. Cir. 1988).

Before the introduction of *inter partes* re-examinations in 1999, the examiner who examined the initial patent was assigned to conduct the re-examination during *ex parte* re-examination proceedings. However, the patent community criticized this practice because the examiner is very likely to be biased against a determination of invalidity. In response, the USPTO created the Central Re-examination Unit (CRU) in 2005 to effectively assign both *ex parte* and *inter partes* re-examination cases to the most appropriate examiner.[90] The CRU assigns an examiner who is different from the examiner who conducted the initial examination to conduct an *ex parte* re-examination.[91] The Unit assigns two or more examiners to join with the examiner in charge of re-examination to constitute a panel which reviews each Office action prepared by the examiner in charge.[92] **7.33**

The US Patent Act includes no explicit provision for a stay of civil action after the filing of a request for re-examination. Therefore the decision of whether to stay a parallel infringement or DJ civil action is within the discretion of the district court.[93] In principle, a party cannot appeal from an order to stay proceedings.[94] An order of stay is not reviewable by the Federal Circuit except under exceptional circumstances where the stay "effectively could put one of the appellants out of court" or if some "patent issue would escape review by a federal court if the case is stayed."[95] **7.34**

2. *Inter Partes* Review

Any party other than the patentee of the patent being challenged on its validity can request an *inter partes* review.[96] A party who requests a review must reveal all real parties in interest because estoppel applies to the parties of *inter partes* review proceedings.[97] The grounds for invalidity on which a party can request a review are limited to novelty and nonobviousness only on the basis of prior art consisting of patents and printed publication.[98] Thus, the double patenting ground, which is available when requesting an *ex parte* re-examination, is not available when requesting an *inter partes* review.[99] **7.35**

The timing for requesting an *inter partes* review is limited: after the later of either (1) the date that is nine months after the grant of a patent or the issuance of a reissue of a patent or (2) if a post-grant review is instituted, the date the post-grant review is terminated.[100] This limitation is included to prevent parallel procedures for post-grant and *inter partes* reviews during the nine-month period after a patent grant or reissue in which a party can request a post-grant review.[101] **7.36**

---

[90] Matthew Smith et al., "Recent Performance of the Central Reexamination Unit in Inter Partes Reexamination" (http://www.foley.com/files/tbl_s31Publications/FileUpload137/6778/CENTRALREEXAMINATION.pdf).

[91] 37 C.F.R., 1.525; USPTO, *MPEP* (9th ed., 2014), §§ 2236, 2636; Emily Berger, "United States Reexamination Procedures: Recent Trends, Strategies and Impact on Patent Practice," 8 *J. Marshall Rev. Intell. Prop. L.* (2009): 381.

[92] USPTO, *MPEP* (9th ed., 2014), § 2271.01.

[93] *Ethicon, Inc. v. Quigg*, 849 F.2d 1422 (Fed. Cir. 1988).

[94] *Gould v. Control Laser Corp.*, 705 F.2d 1340, 217 U.S.P.Q. 985 (Fed. Cir. 1983).

[95] *Slip Track Systems Inc. v. Metal Lite, Inc.*, 159 F.3d 1337, 48 U.S.P.Q. 2d 1055 (Fed. Cir. 1998).

[96] 35 U.S.C. § 311.

[97] Ibid. § 312(a)(2).

[98] Ibid. § 312(b).

[99] See Ch. 7, 7.28.

[100] 35 U.S.C. § 311(c).

[101] Ibid. § 321(c).

7.37 The AIA includes a mechanism to prevent conflicting decisions on validity between the review procedures at the USPTO and civil actions at US courts. If a party has filed a DJ action challenging validity at a district court, the party can no longer request an *inter partes* review.[102] However, a party who is sued for infringement can request an *inter partes* review because a counterclaim challenging the validity of a claim is not considered a DJ action preventing an *inter partes* review.[103] If a party files a DJ action on and after requesting an *inter partes* review, the DJ action is automatically stayed until either (1) the patent owner moves the court to lift the stay; (2) the patent owner files a civil action or counterclaim alleging that the petitioner or real party in interest has infringed the patent; or (3) the requesting party or real party in interest moves the court to dismiss the civil action.[104] This automatic stay provision applies to post-grant review procedures.[105] In essence, a party who wants to challenge validity must choose between a civil action at a district court and a post-grant or *inter partes* review proceedings at the USPTO.

7.38 The AIA also includes a mechanism to prevent delays in filing an *inter partes* review request and to prevent conflicting validity decisions between the USPTO and a district court. When a party is sued for infringement in a civil action and if the party, the real party in interest, or its privy wants to challenge the validity of the asserted patents at an *inter partes* review, it must request a review within one year from the date on which the complaint for the civil action was served.[106] However, this limitation does not apply to *ex parte* re-examinations, and a party can file a re-examination request at any time, even after the expiration of the one-year period from the institution of civil action.[107]

7.39 A party who requests an *inter partes* review must submit a written statement (petition) that identifies (1) claims that the party challenges, (2) the ground of invalidity that the party's challenge is based on, and (3) the evidence supporting the challenge.[108] The petition should include copies of (A) patents and printed publications that the party relies on to challenge validity and (B) affidavits or declarations of supporting evidence and opinions if the party relies on expert opinions.[109] The party must serve the petition and exhibits to the patentee so that the patentee can file a preliminary response within the period set by the USPTO Director.[110]

7.40 The USPTO Director can initiate *inter partes* review proceedings upon a finding that the information presented in the petition and responses from the requesting party show a reasonable likelihood that the petitioner would prevail with respect to at least one of the claims challenged in the petition.[111] This reasonable likelihood standard is lower than the more likely than not standard for initiating a post-grant review.[112] The Director must make the

[102] Ibid. § 315(a)(1).
[103] Ibid. § 315(a)(3).
[104] Ibid. § 315(a)(2).
[105] Ibid. § 325.
[106] Ibid, § 315(b). However, a party may join as a party to an *inter partes* review that another party initiated after the expiration of the one-year period. Ibid. § 315(c).
[107] Ibid. § 301(a).
[108] Ibid. § 312(a)(3). The USPTO also requires (1) the claim construction of the challenged claims and (2) how the construed claims are patentable under the ground of invalidity identified by the requesting party. 37 C.F.R. § 42.104.
[109] § 312(3)(A)–(B).
[110] 35 U.S.C. § 313; 37 C.F.R. § 42.105.
[111] 35 U.S.C. § 314(a).
[112] USPTO, "Changes to Implement Inter Partes Review Proceedings, Post-grant review Proceedings, and Transitional Program for Covered Business Method Patents," 77 Fed. Reg. 48,680, 48,702 (August 14,

decision within three months from (1) the receipt of a preliminary response from the patentee or (2) the last date on which a preliminary response may be filed if no response is filed.[113]

Unlike *ex parte* re-examination proceedings where an examiner re-examines the validity challenges, the PTAB conducts a trial to examine the validity of challenged claims at the *inter partes* review, post-grant review, special post-grant review for business method, and derivation proceedings.[114] The PTAB is authorized to narrow the issues for the final decision by focusing their review on the challenged claims for which the reasonable likelihood threshold standards have been met. Once the review proceedings are instituted, the patentee is given an opportunity to file a response to the petition and to propose to amend the challenged claims.[115] The petitioner is then given an opportunity to reply to the patentee's response and to oppose the proposed amendments. The patentee is given another opportunity to reply to the petitioner's reply and opposition. Discoveries by both petitioner and patentee are scheduled within the twelve-month period between the institution of review proceedings and the final written decision. **7.41**

Active participation of pre-AIA *inter partes* re-examinations by third-party requesters brought about significant improvements in eliminating questionable validity patents. Out of 964 certificates issued by the USPTO between the year 1999 and 2012, 303 (31 percent) were certificates cancelling all claims, and 593 (62 percent) were certificates confirming the patent with some changed claims.[116] Only 68 (7 percent) of all certificates confirmed the patentability of all original claims.[117] These rates are a stark contrast to the 1980–2008 rates seen at *ex parte* re-examination procedures, where 25 percent of cases result in a certificate confirming the patentability of all the original claims; 11 percent of cases result in a certificate cancelling all claims and 64 percent of cases result in certificate with claim changes.[118] The rate for confirming patentability of all the original claims at *ex parte* re-examination procedures has recently decreased: the historical rate between 1981 and 2012 is 22 per cent, which is still lower than the rate seen at *inter partes* re-examimation.[119] The rate of cases resulting in a cerficate for cancelling all claims has also increased to 11 percent. Active participation by third parties also resulted in significant delays in the patentability contest resolution. On average, the USPTO took 36.5 months to issue a certificate through *inter partes* re-examination procedures, which was approximately one year longer than the 25.4-month average for *ex parte* re-examination procedures. To eliminate the delay, the post-AIA *inter partes* review adopted a rule requiring the PTAB to enter a scheduling order when a review is instituted and to set due dates for the trial to be completed within one year.[120] The accelerated **7.42**

2012) (Response to Comment 59). But see "Message from Chief Judge James Donald Smith, Board of Patent Appeals and Interferences: USPTO Discusses Key Aspects of New Administrate Patent Trials" (http://www.uspto.gov/aia_implementation/smith-blog-extravaganza.jsp).

113 35 U.S.C. § 314(b).

114 Office Patent Trial Practice Guide, 37 C.F.R., Pt. 42 (2012). The PTAB consists of administrative judges who are lawyers with a background in science.

115 37 C.F.R. § 42. 120–21.

116 USPTO, *Inter Partes Reexamination Filing Data: June 30, 2010* (http://www.uspto.gov/sites/default/files/documents/inter_parte_historical_stats_roll_up_EOY2014.pdf).

117 Ibid.

118 USPTO, *Ex Parte Reexamination Filing Data: June 30, 2010*, http://www.uspto.gov/sites/default/files/documents/ex_parte_historical_stats_roll_up_EOY2014.pdf.

119 Ibid.

120 Office Patent Trial Practice Guide, 37 C.F.R., Pt. 42 (2012).

procedure and the major case law changes on patentability resulted in a significant increase in number of *inter partes* review requests and high rate of cases resulting in a certificate cancelling all claims: 77.5 percent with respect to all instituted claims and 65 percent with respect to all challenged claims.[121]

7.43 Both petitioner and patentee are given two options for appeal from the final written PTAB decision:[122] (1) an appeal to the United States Court of Appeals for the Federal Circuit[123] or (2) a civil action against the Director of the USPTO at the United States District Court for the Eastern District of Virginia.[124] Parties can settle their dispute over validity and can jointly request to terminate an *inter partes* review as long as the USPTO has not decided on the merits of the proceedings.[125] If a review is terminated without resulting in a final written decision, neither the petitioner, the real party in interest nor the privy of the petitioner is barred from relying on the prior art that the petitioner raised or reasonably could have raised during the *inter partes* review.[126]

3. Post-grant Review

7.44 Like an *inter partes* review, any person other than the patentee can request a post-grant review although a post-grant review applies only to claims which have effective date on and after March 16, 2013.[127] A party must file a petition which reveals all real parties in interest due to an estoppel resulting from a final written decision issued by the PTAB.[128] Unlike any other procedure at the USPTO, a party can request a review on any ground of invalidity: eligibility, utility, double patenting, novelty, nonobviousness, and disclosure requirements including enablement, written description, and definiteness of claims.[129] The timing to request a post-grant review is limited to nine months from the date of the patent grant.[130]

7.45 As discussed above, to prevent conflicting validity decisions between the USPTO and district court, the same restrictions as those for an *inter partes* review apply to a post-grant review: (1) the prohibition of a post-grant review after filing a DJ action[131] and (2) the automatic stay of a civil action, which is filed after requesting a post-grant review.[132] However the automatic stay provision does not apply to a preliminary injunction if the patent owner requesting the injunction filed an infringement action within three months from the grant of the patent even if a post-grant review was instituted against the asserted patent.[133]

---

[121] Brian Love and Shawn Ambwani, "Inter Partes Review: An Early Look at the Numbers," 81 *U. Chi. L. Rev. Dialogue* (2014): 93 (https://lawreview.uchicago.edu/sites/lawreview.uchicago.edu/files/uploads/Love_Ambwani_Dialogue.pdf).

[122] 35 U.S.C. § 319 A third-party requester did not have the right to appeal to the Federal Circuit when the *inter partes* re-examination was introduced in 1999. § 315 was revised to allow the appeal of any *inter partes* re-examination procedure that commenced prior to November 2, 2002, but only the patentee had the right to appeal to the Federal Circuit.

[123] Ibid. §§ 141–44.

[124] Ibid. §§ 145–46.

[125] Ibid. § 317.

[126] For a discussion of the estoppel, see Ch. 7, 7.24 "Estoppel."

[127] 35 U.S.C. § 321.

[128] Ibid. § 322(a)(2).

[129] Ibid. § 322(b).

[130] 35 U.S.C. § 321(c).

[131] Ibid. § 325(a)(1).

[132] Ibid. § 325(a)(2).

[133] Ibid. § 325(b).

Although the AIA allows a post-grant review against reissue patents, such reviews are available only for patents with a scope that has been broadened by a reissue procedure within two years from the patent grant of the original patent.[134] No post-grant review is available for a reissue patent if (1) the petition requests cancellation of a claim in the reissue patent that is identical or narrower than a claim in the original patent from which the reissue patent was issued and (2) the nine-month limitation prevents a request of post-grant review for the original patent.[135] 7.46

A party who requests a post-grant review—namely, the petitioner—must submit a petition including content similar to that of a petition for requesting an *inter partes* review.[136] The USPTO director can initiate a post-grant review upon a finding that the information presented in the petition supports the conclusion that it is more likely than not that at least one of the claims challenged is unpatentable.[137] The Director can also initiate a review if the information supports the conclusion that the petitioner raises a novel or an unsettled legal question that is important to other patents or patent applications.[138] The same time limit rules as those for the *inter partes* review apply to encourage a prompt decision by the USPTO Director with respect to the institution of a post-grant review.[139] 7.47

The same procedural rules apply to the *inter partes* review and the post-grant review.[140] Accordingly, a third-party petitioner is guaranteed a right to actively participate in the post-grant review procedure. Both parties can either appeal to the Federal Circuit or start a civil action against the USPTO Director at the Federal District Court for the Western District of Virginia.[141] To prevent an estoppel effect, parties who settled the validity dispute can terminate a post-grant review by jointly filing a request of termination.[142] 7.48

4. Special Post-grant Review for Business Methods

The AIA introduced a transitional program for dealing with the uncertainty in the validity of business method patents, a special post-grant review for challenging the validity of patents that claim a method, apparatus, or operation used in the practice, administration, or management of a financial product or service.[143] A party can request a post-grant review beyond the nine-month post-grant review window for challenging a covered business patent if the party, the real party in interest, or its privy has been sued for infringement of the patent or has been charged with infringement under that patent.[144] A party is entitled to request a special post-grant review when a real and substantial controversy over a business patent infringement exists such that the party would have standing to bring a declaratory judgment action in federal courts.[145] This special post-grant review is available for all claims 7.49

[134] Ibid. § 251(d). For more discussion of reissue proceedings, see Ch. 7, 7.63 "Reissue."
[135] 35 U.S.C. § 325(f).
[136] Ibid. § 322(a).
[137] Ibid. § 324(a). This standard is lower than the reasonable likelihood standard for initiating an *inter partes* review.
[138] Ibid. § 324(b).
[139] Ibid. § 324(c).
[140] Ibid. § 326(a).
[141] Ibid. § 329.
[142] Ibid. § 327(a).
[143] AIA, § 18.
[144] AIA, § 18(a)(B).
[145] For a discussion of declaratory judgment actions, see Ch. 7, 7.49 "Special Post-grant Review for Business Methods."

regardless of their effective filing dates as long as the patents are directed to a covered business method. Because a regular post-grant review is available only for patents resulting from post-AIA first-inventor-to-file applications and an *inter partes* review is limited to novelty and nonobviousness grounds under 35 U.S.C. §§ 102 and 103, the special post-grant review provides the defendant and would-be defendant of an infringement procedure with a powerful option to challenge patent validity on any grounds arising from 35 U.S.C. §§ 101 and 112. In particular, US case law has recently adopted more stringent standards for patent eligibility and disclosure requirements; business method patents issued before the adoption of the new standards are subjected to validity challenges since the new standard will apply to all patents retroactively.[146] However, when a business method patent is challenged on the grounds of novelty and nonobviousness, a party can cite only post-AIA prior art under the first-inventor-to-file.[147]

7.50 A covered business method patent is defined as a patent that claims a method or a corresponding apparatus for performing data processing or other operating apparatus for performing data processing or other operations used in the practice, administration, or management of a financial product or service, except that the term does not include patents for technological inventions.[148] To apply the technological invention exception, the USPTO must make a determination on a case-by-case basis with respect to whether the claimed subject matter as a whole recites a technological feature that is novel and nonobvious over the prior art and solves a technical problem using a technical solution.[149] The office makes clear that this definition of technological invention is used only for the purposes of the special post-grant review, and the office does not necessarily apply the same definition to other purposes such as examination of patent eligibility under § 101.[150]

7.51 A party who is sued or charged with infringement can request a special post-grant review anytime except for the nine-month period in which a regular post-grant review is available.[151] However, such a party is estopped from challenging a claim through a special post-grant review if the party or a privy of the party has challenged the claim on the ground identified in the petition at a prior *inter partes* dispute at the USPTO. In addition to the content of a petition required for a regular post-grant review, the petition for a special post-grant review must demonstrate (1) that the patent that the party requests a review of falls into the definition of a covered business method patent and (2) the petitioner is sued for or charged with infringement of the patent for which a review is sought.[152] The requirements for the institution of a review and the procedures for the regular post-grant review apply to the special post-grant review. This review is a transitional program and will cease to exist on September 16, 2020, eight years after the effective date of the special review provision.

5. Interference Proceedings

7.52 An interference procedure is unique to the pre-AIA US patent system because it determines who was the first-to-invent among multiple inventors and is available for patents granted to

---

146 For a discussion of the change in standards of patent eligibility, see Ch. 7, 7.71 "Patent Eligibility."
147 AIA, § 18(a)(1).
148 AIA, § 18(d)(1); 37 C.F.R., 42.301(a).
149 37 C.F.R., 42.301(b).
150 Ibid.
151 Ibid. 42.303.
152 Ibid. 42.304.

claims that have an effective filing date prior to March 16, 2013 (pre-FITF filing date).[153] An inventor who finds an application or a patent directed to an invention that is the same or substantially the same as her invention can request the USPTO to declare an interference to determine the priority between the inventor and the inventor of the earlier application or patent.[154] The USPTO finds the claimed inventions to be the same or substantially the same if the claimed invention of one party would, if it were prior art, have anticipated or rendered obvious the claimed invention of the other party and vice versa.[155] An interference in fact exists only if the claimed inventions are patentably indistinct.[156] A party must request interference proceedings within one year from the patent issuance date or the eighteen-month publication date for the earlier patent and application.[157] The USPTO declares an interference (1) between two or more pending applications or (2) between a patent or patents and at least one application. No interference at the USPTO is available between only issued patents.[158] Once multiple patents are issued to the same or substantially the same invention, the first-to-invent contest is available only through a civil action in which the first-to-invent party challenges the validity of the patent issued to the second-to-invent.[159] All inventions included in these patents and applications must have pre-FITF filing dates.[160] In other words, interference proceedings to challenge validity will exist until the expiration of all patents with claims that have a pre-FITF filing date.

In interference proceedings, the USPTO follows a first-to-file approach in which the date **7.53**
when an application adequately claimed the invention and met the disclosure requirement under § 112 is presumed to be the date of invention. Accordingly, the first-to-file inventor is called the senior party and presumed to be the first-to-invent, and thus parties other than the first-to-file inventor, who are called junior parties, bear the burden of going forward with evidence of an earlier invention date and the ultimate burden of persuasion on all issues of fact to establish priority.[161] When a party meets the ultimate burden and priority is awarded to her invention, and a judgment in favor of the party has become final, the claim for the interfering invention in the other patent is cancelled.[162] Due to the difficulty of meeting the burden, the pre-AIA first-to-invent system granted priority to first-to-file inventors far more frequently than to second-to-file inventors.[163]

---

153 The AIA eliminated the interference procedure and substituted it with derivation proceedings. AIA 2011, § 3(j).

154 Pre-AIA 35 U.S.C. § 135 (2006).

155 37 C.F.R. § 41.208(a)(1).

156 *Aelony v. Arni*, 547 F.2d 566, 192 U.S.P.Q. 486 (CCPA 1977). The USPTO changed its interference rules in 2004 but maintained the same patentably indistinct standard for finding interference in fact.

157 Pre-AIA 35 U.S.C. § 135(b). The 18-month publication under § 122(b) applies to applications filed on or after November 29, 2000. The content of all patent applications has been kept secret for patents resulting from an application filed prior to November 29, 2000. Even on or after November 29, 2000, an applicant can request to opt out of the 18-month publication with a certification that they will not file a corresponding application outside the United States. 35 U.S.C. § 135(b)(B). When the content of a patent application is not published through the 18-month publication, a party can file a request of interference within one year from the issuance of the patent.

158 Pre-AIA 35 U.S.C. § 135(a). For a general discussion of the requirements for an interference declaration, see *Chisum on Patents*, § 10.09[2][c][i].

159 Pre-AIA 35 U.S.C. § 291.

160 Ibid. § 135(b).

161 *Smollar v. Cawley*, 31 U.S.P.Q. 2d 1506, 1507 (Bd. Pat. App. & Int'f 1993).

162 Pre-AIA 35 U.S.C. § 135(a).

163 See Toshiko Takenaka, "A View of First-to-File Lawyer on the America Invents Act: Will the First-Inventor-to-File under America Invents Act Be the Best Practice Determining Patent Priority?," in

7.54 The first-to-invent priority and interference proceedings are viewed by the US industry and legal professionals as expensive and complex.[164] To make the US Patent System more efficient, the AIA expressly identified the elimination of interference proceedings as an important goal.[165] It also placed emphasis on the elimination of uncertainty in patentability resulting from the invention date, which is a subjective date to be determined by the USPTO in an interference procedure or a judge in civil action in contrast to the filing date, which is an objective date.[166] Unfortunately, the AIA cannot accomplish these important goals because the first-inventor-to-file rule relies on the disclosure date during the one-year grace period.[167]

7.55 The AIA needs a system to determine which inventor is the first-to-disclose if more than one inventor invents the same or substantially the same invention and files a patent application within one year from the first disclosure of the invention. Because a party cannot request interference proceedings with respect to an invention that has a post-AIA filing date, it is unclear how the first-to-disclose date is established. Since the USPTO refuses to deal with any issues other than derivation through derivation proceedings, the first-to-disclose priority issue should be dealt within post-grant review, special post-grant review, or *inter partes* review proceedings.[168]

6. Derivation Proceedings

7.56 The AIA introduced derivation proceedings that are simpler and more effective administrative proceedings than interference proceedings with the aim of guaranteeing a grant of patent only to true inventors.[169] Derivation proceedings to contest originality are part of the interference proceedings under the pre-AIA Patent Act.[170] A party can defeat the opposing party if the party can establish that the opposing party did not invent the invention but derived the invention from the party.[171] A derivation can be established with evidence of an earlier conception of the interfering invention and communication to the opposing party with respect to the conception.[172] The communication must include enough information to enable one skilled in the art to make the invention.[173]

Toshiko Takenaka (ed.), *Intellectual Property Systems in Common Law and Civil Law* (2013), 50; *Edwards v. Strazzabosco*, 58 U.S.P.Q. 2d (BNA) 1836, 1840 (Bd. Pat. App. & Interf. 2001); Charles R. B. Macedo, "First-to-File: Is American Adoption of the International Standard in Patent Law Worth the Price?," 18 Am. Intell. Prop. L.Q.J. (1989): 193, 217; Gerald J. Mossinghoff, "The US First-to-Invent System Has Provided No Advantage to Small Entities," 84 J. Pat. & Trademark Off. Soc'y (2002): 425, 427.

164 Statement of Steven W. Miller, Vice President and General Counsel, Intellectual Property, The Procter & Gamble Company, America Invents Act, Committee on House Judiciary, Subcommittee on Intellectual Property, Competition and Internet Subcommittee (March 30, 2011) (http://judiciary.house.gov/hearings/pdf/Miller03302011.pdf).

165 112th Congress, 1st Session, Report on America Invents Act ("AIA Report"), 41–42.

166 Ibid. 42.

167 For more discussion about a comparison between the first-inventor-to-file rule under AIA and the first-to-file rules under EPC and JPA, please see Takenaka, "A View of First-to-File Lawyer on the America Invents Act," 72.

168 Changes to Implement Derivation Proceedings, 77 Fed. Reg. 56068, 56079 (September 11, 2012) (hereinafter "USPTO Derivation Proceedings Final Rules").

169 AIA Report, 42.

170 For more discussion of the first-to-invent priority rule, please see Ch. 7, 7.87 "Pre-AIA Prior Art."

171 Pre-AIA 35 U.S.C. § 102(f).

172 *Creative Compounds, LLC v. Starmark Laboratories*, 65 1 F.3d 1303, 1313 (Fed. Cir. 2011).

173 *Gambro Lundia AB v. Baxter Healthcare Corp.*, 110 F.3d 1573, 42 U.S.P.Q. 2d 1378 (Fed. Cir. 1997).

Under the pre-AIA interference proceedings, the originality contest is separate and distinct from the priority contest.[174] The AIA eliminated the priority contest and made the originality contest stand alone as derivation proceedings to determine whether a party can eliminate a pre-filing disclosure or prior right from the prior art under 35 U.S.C. § 102(b).[175] It is likely that many aspects of the practice to establish derivation under pre-AIA case law will continue to apply to the determination of derivation under post-AIA derivation proceedings. **7.57**

Like pre-AIA interference proceedings, derivation proceedings are available only between multiple pending applications or between patents and at least one pending application.[176] A true inventor whose invention was derived must file a petition to institute derivation proceedings in the USPTO within one year from the first publication of a claim to an invention—that is, either the patent issuance date or the eighteen-month publication date for the earlier patent and application.[177] To request derivation proceedings, a party must be an applicant and thus have filed a patent application for her invention before filing a petition.[178] To meet this requirement, the USPTO suggests filing a patent application by copying the earlier patent or application and simultaneously requesting derivation proceedings.[179] **7.58**

The petition must set forth with particularity of the basis for finding that (1) an inventor named in an earlier application derived the claimed invention from an inventor named in the petitioner's application and (2) the earlier application was filed without authorization.[180] The USPTO adopted the pre-AIA interference rule that the claimed invention in the petitioner's application is either exactly the same or substantially the same, which corresponds to the patentably indistinct standard for interference in fact.[181] Thus, the petition must identify at least one claim in the application that is the same or substantially the same as a claim of the earlier application. The USPTO also transported the interference practice of requiring evidence of conception and communication to establish a derivation.[182] Thus, the petition must explain why a claimed invention in the earlier application is the same or substantially the same as the invention that was actually disclosed to the applicant—namely, the respondent of the early application.[183] The communication of the conception and lack of authorization for filing the earlier application must be established with sufficient evidence.[184] Such evidence includes at least one affidavit, typically a testimony by the inventor whose invention was derived by the respondent, although an inventor's own testimony on the conception and communication to the respondent should be corroborated.[185] **7.59**

---

[174] *Sewall v. Walters*, 21 F.3d 411, 415, 30 U.S.P.Q. 2d 1356, 1358 (Fed. Cir. 1994). See also *Chisum on Patents*, § 10.04[4][a].

[175] For a discussion of the exception to prior art under the post-AIA Patent Act, see Ch. 7, 7.98 "Post-AIA Prior Art."

[176] 35 U.S.C. § 135(a). If a pending application is involved in an action, the USPTO may defer the action until a patent is issued to the application: ibid. § 135(c).

[177] Ibid.; 37 C.F.R. § 42.401.

[178] 35 U.S.C. § 135(a).

[179] USPTO Derivation Proceedings Final Rules, 77 Fed. Reg., 56069.

[180] 35 U.S.C. § 135(a).

[181] 37 C.F.R. § 42.405.

[182] USPTO Derivation Proceedings Final Rules, 77 Fed. Reg., 56074.

[183] 37 C.F.R. § 42.405(b)(3)(i).

[184] Ibid. § 42.405(c).

[185] USPTO Derivation Proceedings Final Rules, 77 Fed. Reg., 56074. For more discussion of conception and corroboration, see Ch. 7, 7.94.

7.60 The derivation proceedings continues to apply the first-to-file approach in imposing the burden of proof on the second-to-file, the petitioner. The petitioner meets the burden of initiating derivation proceedings if the evidence is sufficient to support a finding that the petitioner would prevail if the respondent did not provide any rebuttal of the evidence. A respondent is given an opportunity for rebuttal. The PTAB will consider evidence submitted by both the petitioner and respondent and determine whether the petition made a *prima facie* showing of derivation. Once such a determination is made, derivation proceedings are initiated if the allegedly derived claim is in a condition for allowance.[186] To avoid costly and time-consuming derivation proceedings, the USPTO determines patentability of the allegedly derived claim before initiating proceedings.[187]

7.61 After instituting derivation proceedings, the PTAB makes a determination of derivation through the same procedural rules used in *inter partes* and post-grant review proceedings.[188] When the PTAB finds that a derivation occurred, it may correct the inventorship of the earlier application in appropriate circumstances.[189] A final decision adverse to the allegedly derived claim in an application gives rise to a final refusal on such claims.[190] If a patent has been issued to such claims, the final adverse decision gives rise to the cancellation of such claims.[191] Under the pre-AIA case law interpreting the originality requirement, US courts found a patent invalid if (1) the named inventor did not invent the claimed invention or (2) the inventorship was improper and a correction is unavailable under § 256 of the pre-AIA Patent Act.[192] Thus, it is likely to continue to apply the same case law to patents resulting from post-AIA applications.

7. Submission of Prior Art

7.62 Proceedings including *intra parte* trials such as *inter partes* reviews and post-grant reviews are very expensive, substantially more expensive than opposition proceedings at the European Patent Office and invalidation proceedings at the Japan Patent Office.[193] Even an *ex parte* examination is more expensive than EPO and JPO proceedings.[194] To save on the expensive fees for challenging the validity of an issued patent, a party can submit prior art references with comments on the relevance of the references to claims in the pending application.[195] Such references are limited to patents, published patent applications, and other printed publications. Submission must be done before: (1) the later of either (a) six months after the eighteen-month publication or (b) the date of first rejection and the date of allowance notice; and (2) the date a notice of allowance is given or mailed.[196] A party can

---

[186] USPTO Derivation Proceedings Final Rules, 77 Fed. Reg., 56069.

[187] Ibid. 56076.

[188] Office Patent Trial Practice Guide, 37 C.F.R., Pt. 42 (2012).

[189] 35 U.S.C. § 135(b). However, the AIA does not provide any details of the appropriate circumstances. See generally, *Chisum on Patents*, § 10.10[4][d][iii][A].

[190] 35 U.S.C. § 135(d).

[191] Ibid.

[192] *Solomon v. Kimberly-Clark Corp.*, 216 F.3d 1372, 55 U.S.P.Q. 2d 1279 (Fed. Cir. 2000).

[193] E.g., the fee for filing a petition to request *inter partes* review proceedings challenging up to 20 claims is $27.200 and the fee for filing a petition to request post-grant review proceedings challenging up to 20 claims is $35,800. 37 C.F.R. § 42.15(a).

[194] The fee for filing an *ex parte* re-examination is $2,520. Ibid. § 1.20(c).

[195] Ibid. § 1.290(a).

[196] Ibid. § 1.290(b).

anonymously submit references. Although there is no right for a party to communicate with examiners regarding submitted references, examiners can benefit from the interpretation of the claims under examination and the prior art that are included in the comments accompanying the prior art references. Prior art submission provides an inexpensive mechanism to weed out invalid patents.[197]

8. Reissue

The US patent system allows a patent owner to correct through a reissue process a defective patent that is, through error, deemed wholly or partly inoperable or invalid.[198] To have a patent reissued, a patent owner must establish that (1) the patent is inoperable or invalid because of (a) a defective specification or drawing or (b) a claim that covers more or less than what the inventor had a right to claim; (2) the defect resulted from an error; (3) a reissue does not introduce any new matter and is for the invention in the original patent; and (4) claims in the reissue application meet all requirements of patentability.[199] A patent owner should file a reissue application upon finding a defective patent because the USPTO reissues a patent only if the original patent has not expired before the reissuance.[200] The AIA removed the language "without any deceptive intent" from the requirements to reissue a patent.[201] However, it is likely that a reissue process remains unavailable to correct a defect resulting from a deliberate and deceptive intent.[202] **7.63**

A patent owner can file a reissue application at any time to narrow the scope of a claim in the original patent so as to avoid a ground of invalidity, as long as the original patent has not expired.[203] However, a reissue application to broaden the scope of a claim in the original patent must be filed within two years from the grant of the original patent.[204] US case law restricts the application of the doctrine of equivalents, particularly if an equivalent is disclosed but not unclaimed.[205] A patent owner should seek to reissue a patent that includes a claim literally covering a disclosed but unclaimed equivalent before the expiration of the two-year period because such an equivalent was disclosed in the original patent. A patent owner may circumvent the two-year limitation by maintaining a pending patent application in the USPTO through continuation so that the owner can amend claims to literally cover disclosed and unclaimed equivalents. **7.64**

Although a patent owner can use a reissue process to rescue an invalid patent, a reissue of a patent results in serious drawbacks to the patent owner. In filing a patent application, a patent owner must offer to surrender the original patent.[206] The surrender of the original patent occurs when the reissue patent issues.[207] Like an amendment during *inter partes* and post-grant reviews and re-examinations, a patent owner forfeits the cause of action for infringement of the original patent in a pending action unless the claims that an accused **7.65**

[197] The fee for every submission of ten references is $180. Ibid. § 1.8(p).
[198] 35 U.S.C. § 251.
[199] *Glaxo Wellcome, Inc. v. Eon Labs Manufacturing, Inc.*, 2002 U.S. Dist. LEXIS 14923 (S.D. N.Y. 2002)
[200] *In re Morgan*, 990 F.2d 1230, 26 U.S.P.Q. 2d 1392 (Fed. Cir. 1993).
[201] Pre-AIA 35 U.S.C. § 251.
[202] *Chisum on Patents*, § 15.02[10][a].
[203] 35 U.S.C. § 251(a).
[204] Ibid. § 251(d).
[205] See Ch. 4, 4.124 "Dedication to the Public."
[206] 35 U.S.C. § 251(a).
[207] *In re Clement*, 131 F.3d 1464, 45 U.S.P.Q. 2d 1161 (Fed. Cir. 1997).

embodiment infringes are reissued and the reissued claims are substantially identical to the claims in the original patent.[208] A party to the action who has been infringing the original patent obtains an equitable intervening right and can continue to manufacture, use, offer to sell, or sell the product or practice the process covered by the original patent if the product is made, purchased, offered for sale, used, or imported into the United States or substantial preparation for such acts was made before the grant of the reissue patent.[209] The scope of an intervening right is determined by the court to "the extent and under such terms as the court deems equitable for the protection made or business commenced before the grant of reissue."[210] Moreover, a reissue patent does not affect any product made, purchased, offered for sale, or used within the United States and imported into the United States before the grant of the reissue patent unless a claim that the product infringes in the original claim is substantially identical to a claim in the reissue patent.[211]

7.66 The Federal Circuit applies a strict standard for the substantial identity requirement: claims are no longer substantially identical if there is any change between the scope of the original claims and reissue claims, regardless of broadening or narrowing, unless the change merely clarifies the original claims.[212] However, a reissue does not affect the cause of action for untouched claims regardless of any arguments to narrow the scope of the original claims.[213] To maintain a cause of action and a claim for damages, it is important to keep some claims untouched.

9. Patentability Validity Defenses in Civil Actions

(a) Introduction

7.67 A patentee shall have remedy by civil action for infringement of her patent unless any of the defenses against infringement are available.[214] Such defenses include the invalidity of a patent; unenforceability of a patent; and facts and acts that give rise to a defense under the US Patent Act.[215] The most frequently asserted defense is patent invalidity. Unlike German patent infringement procedure, US civil action for patent infringement allows a party to challenge the validity of a patent asserted against that party. Moreover, a party can file for a DJ of invalidity.[216] Grounds for invalidity in infringement procedure and DJ procedure include all grounds relating to (1) conditions for patentability under §§ 101, 102, and 103, and (2) violations of (a) a requirement of disclosure under § 112 except for the failure to disclose the best mode, and (b) a requirement of reissue under § 251.[217] In the following sections, these grounds are discussed in the context of defenses in a patent infringement civil action, to be distinguished from patentability during patent prosecution.

7.68 Under Federal Circuit case law, parties to an assignment or settlement agreement and consent orders are precluded from asserting an invalidity defense or filing a DJ action. In *Lear*, the US Supreme Court indicated that the federal interest in challenging invalid patents was

---

[208] 35 U.S.C. § 252. For the effect of amendment, see Ch. 7, 7.13.
[209] 35 U.S.C. § 252.
[210] Ibid.
[211] Ibid.
[212] *Westvaco Corp. v. International Paper Co.*, 991 F.2d 735, 26 U.S.P.Q. 2d 1353 (Fed. Cir. 1993).
[213] *Marine Polymer Technologies, Inc. v. Hemcon, Inc.*, 672 F.3d 1350 (Fed. Cir. 2012) (*en banc*).
[214] 35 U.S.C. § 281.
[215] Ibid. § 282(b).
[216] For discussion of declaratory judgment actions, see Ch. 10, 10.87 "Declaratory Judgment Action."
[217] 35 U.S.C. § 282(b).

stronger than the state interest in preventing purchaser from having a right to repudiate their promises.[218] It thus eliminated the doctrine of licensee estoppel and allowed a licensee to challenge the validity of a patent.[219] A licensee can file a DJ action of invalidity without terminating a license.[220] The Court's emphasis on federal interests can be interpreted broadly to authorize an assignor of a patent a right to challenge the validity of the patent assigned. However, Federal Circuit case law distinguishes licensees from assignors and applies the doctrine of assignor estoppel to prevent assignors from asserting an invalidity defense.[221] Moreover, a party is precluded from asserting a defense of invalidity if she was a party to a consent judgment declaring the patent valid.[222] In contrast, no estoppel applies to a party of a private settlement contract that does not involve a court.[223] A settlement order in which a court's signature was required may be estopped from asserting an invalidity defense.[224]

Another major defense in civil actions is the unenforceability of a patent due to inequitable conduct during the patent procurement. This defense is unique to the US patent system. It is raised so frequently that the US legal community began to view the defense as a plague.[225] To control this plague, the Federal Circuit adopted a stringent standard to establish inequitable conduct[226] and the AIA introduced supplemental examination proceedings.[227] **7.69**

The US Patent Act and its case law provide a variety of defenses based on the acts of a party who is charged with infringement and the facts surrounding the party. A party's act may give rise to a patent misuse or an antitrust violation, resulting in a court's refusal to enforce the party's patent. The US Patent Act provides immunity to a particular class of activities and parties from infringement. Moreover, a party may obtain a license without consent from the patent owner in special circumstances under the equity theory or in the operation of law. Details of the facts and acts in such special circumstances will be discussed in the following sections. **7.70**

(b) Patent Eligibility

An invention must meet the requirements for patent eligibility by falling into one of the categories under § 101: process, machine, manufacture, and composition of matter.[228] The US Supreme Court interprets the scope of these categories by citing legislative history acknowledging that statutory subject matter includes anything under the sun that is made by man.[229] The US Patent Act uses the terms "discoveries" and "discovers" to **7.71**

---

[218] *Lear, Inc. v. Adkins*, 395 U.S. 653, 162 U.S.P.Q. 1 (1969).

[219] Ibid. Before *Lear*, licensors were precluded from a challenge of invalidity in civil actions. Federal Circuit distinguished licensees from assignors and precluded assignors from challenging patent validity. For a general discussion of licensee–assignor estoppel, see *Chisum on Patents*, § 19.02[3].

[220] *MedImmune, Inc. v. Genentech, Inc.*, 549 U.S. 118 (2007).

[221] *Diamond Scientific Co. v. Ambico, Inc.*, 848 F.2d 1220, 6 U.S.P.Q. 2d 2028 (Fed. Cir. 1988).

[222] *Foster v. Hallco Manufacturing Co.*, 947 F.2d 469, 20 U.S.P.Q. 2d 1241 (Fed. Cir. 1991).

[223] *Massillon-Cleveland-Akron Sign Co. v. Golden State Advertising Co.*, 444 F.2d 425, 170 U.S.P.Q. 440 (9th Cir. 1971).

[224] *Hemstreet v. Spiegel, Inc.*, 851 F.2d 348, 7 U.S.P.Q. 2d 1502 (Fed. Cir. 1988).

[225] Christian Mammen, "Controlling the 'Plague': Reforming the Doctrine of Inequitable Conduct," 24 *Berkeley Tech. L.J.* (2009): 1329, 1358.

[226] *Therasense, Inc. v. Becton, Dickinson & Co.*, 649 F.3d 1276, 2011 U.S. App. LEXIS 10590, 99 U.S.P.Q. 2d (BNA) 1065 (Fed. Cir. 2011).

[227] 35 U.S.C. § 257.

[228] Ibid. § 101.

[229] *Diamond v. Chakrabarty*, 447 U.S. 303, 308, 100 S. Ct. 2204, 2007–8, 65 L. Ed. 2d 144, 150, 1980 U.S.P.Q. 193 (U.S. 1980).

identify patent-eligible subject matter.[230] The terms often mislead European and Asian legal professionals into thinking that discoveries are patent eligible under the US Patent Act. It is very likely that discoveries excluded from patent eligibility as failing to meet the statutory invention requirement under the EPC and JPA are also excluded from patent eligibility under the US Patent Act because the US Supreme Court developed case law to exclude laws of nature, natural phenomena, and abstract ideas.[231] These judicially created exceptions prevent parties from obtaining a patent for discoveries of a law of nature and a natural phenomenon. Moreover, the Supreme Court made it clear that an invention is patent eligible if it comes from the application of the judicially created exceptions.[232] This requirement, which excludes exceptions as such while finding patent eligibility for applications of exceptions, are in line with the statutory invention requirement under the EPC and JPA.[233]

7.72 Patent eligibility is a ground for challenging patent validity in civil actions, in investigation procedures at the International Trade Commission, and a post-grant review with respect to patents resulting from an application filed on and after March 16, 2013 (post-AIA patents). If one of the claims included in the patent asserted by the patent owner falls into the definition of a "business method patent," a party who is sued for infringement or charged with infringement can challenge the validity of pre-AIA patents by filing a special post-grant review for business methods with respect to both pre- and post-AIA patents.[234]

7.73 Patent eligibility is frequently cited as a ground of invalidity with respect to computer-implemented inventions and biotechnological inventions. For a claim directed to one of patent-ineligible subject matter—that is, laws of nature, natural phenomena, and abstract ideas—to qualify as patent eligible, it must contains an "inventive concept" for converting the ineligible subject matter into a patent-eligible application of the subject matter.[235] Due to recent developments in US case law, many of the patents including a claim directed to computer-implemented inventions and biological inventions are expected to be subjected to validity challenge.

7.74 *In re Bilski* (2008), the Federal Circuit adopted a new test, the machine-or-transformation test, to distinguish a claim directed to a patent-ineligible abstract idea from a claim directed to a patent-eligible method or process.[236] This new test is somewhat more stringent than the practical utility test that was uniformly applied by US courts before *Biski*.[237] Under the new test, a claim is patent eligible if a process described in the claim (1) is tied to a particular machine or apparatus, or (2) transforms a particular article into a different state or

---

[230] 35 U.S.C. §§ 100(a); 101.

[231] *Diamond*, 447 U.S., 309.

[232] *Gottschalk v. Benson*, 409 U.S. 63, 69 (U.S. 1972).

[233] EPC Art. 52(3); Japanese Patent Act Art. 2(1).

[234] For more discussion of special post-grant review for business methods, see Ch. 7, 7.49 "Special Post-grant Review for Business Methods."

[235] *Mayo Collaborative Servs. v. Prometheus Labs., Inc.*, 132 S. Ct. 1289, 182 L. Ed. 2d 321, 101 U.S.P.Q. 2d 1961 (U.S. 2012); *Alice Corp. Pty., Ltd. v. CLS Bank Int'l*, 134 S. Ct. 2347, 189 L. Ed. 2d 296, 110 U.S.P.Q. 2d 1976 (U.S. 2014).

[236] *In re Bilski*, 545 F.3d 943 (Fed. Cir. 2008) (*en banc*).

[237] *State Street Bank & Trust Co. v. Signature Financial Group, Inc.*, 149 F.3d 1368 (Fed. Cir. 1998). The practical utility test found patent eligibility of a claim if a process described in the claim produced a useful, concrete, and tangible result.

thing.[238] Articles include data representing specific objects or substances.[239] The Supreme Court granted certiorari and clarified that the machine-or-transformation test is not the sole test, although it is a useful and important clue for determining whether a claim is directed to a patent-eligible process.[240] Moreover, the Supreme Court emphasized using a flexible claim-by-claim analysis to determine patent eligibility in light of its own precedent dealing with patent eligibility.[241] The post-*Bilski* patent-eligibility test applies retroactively to any patents issued, and thus many of the claims issued under the practical utility test may fail to meet the new test.

The Supreme Court also adopted a test different from the test that the Federal Circuit and USPTO had been uniformly applying to examine the patent eligibility of biological inventions. In examining biological inventions, parties' dispute focuses on whether a claim is directed to a natural phenomenon or a law of nature or its application. Under *Mayo v. Prometheus*, the Supreme Court requires an inventive application of these judicially created exceptions to convert patent-ineligible into patent-eligible subject matter.[242] If a claim recites a law of nature or a natural phenomenon, other elements in the claim must involve an "inventive concept" sufficient to ensure that the invention a claim is directed to is significantly more than a natural law as such.[243] If these elements other than a law of nature are well-understood, routine, and conventional activities, the invention does not give rise to a patent-eligible process.[244] **7.75**

In a more recent case, *Alice Corp. v. CLS Bank*, the Supreme Court refined *Mayo*'s inventive concept test in the two-step analytical framework.[245] Under this framework, the court first determines whether the claim at issue is directed to patent-ineligible subject matter, laws of nature, natural phenomena, and abstract ideas; and if so, finds an inventive concept in considering the elements of each claim individually and as an ordered combination to determine whether the additional elements transform the nature of the claim into a patent-eligible application.[246] The Court affirmed the Federal Circuit *en banc* decision finding patents invalid with respect to claims directed to a computer-implemented business method for mitigating settlement risk. After *Alice Corp.*, the Federal Circuit examines patent eligibility of a claim directed to a business method under the two-step analysis and finds a claim invalid for ineligibility even if the method is implemented by a computer unless the function performed by the computer is something more than conventional.[247] If claim elements other than an abstract idea recite conventional steps performed by a computer at a high level of generality or merely attempt to limit the use of the idea to a particular technological environment, the claim fails to meet the inventive concept requirement.[248] **7.76**

[238] Ibid. 949.
[239] Ibid. 963.
[240] *Bilski v. Kappos*, 130 S. Ct. 3218, 3227, 177 L. Ed. 2d 792,803, 95 U.S.P.Q. 2d 1001 (U.S. 2010).
[241] 130 S. Ct. 3231.
[242] *Mayo v. Prometheus Labs.*, 132 S. Ct. 1289.
[243] Ibid. 1294.
[244] Ibid. 1298.
[245] *Alice Corp. v. CLS Bank*, 134 S. Ct. 2347.
[246] Ibid. 2350.
[247] *Planet Bingo, LLC v. VKGS, LLC*, 2014 U.S. App. LEXIS 16412 (Fed. Cir. August 26, 2014).
[248] *Buysafe, Inc. v. Google, Inc.*, 2014 U.S. App. LEXIS 16987.

7.77 Because of the combination of the limited role and clear and convincing evidence applied to challenge validity in civil actions, it makes more sense for a party who is sued or is likely to be charged with infringement to challenge the validity of computer-implemented inventions at a post-grant review in which a lower level of proof, preponderance of the evidence, is applied to examine validity. Moreover, the USPTO applies the broadest reasonable interpretation standard to interpret claims, which makes it easier for a party to establish invalidity based on the abstract idea exception with respect to a claim directed to a computer-implemented invention. With respect to business method inventions which involve abstract ideas, the USPTO has incorporated *Mayo*'s two-step analytical framework in the examination guidelines by publishing a preliminary examination instruction after *Alice Corp.*[249] When examiners find that a claim is directed to an abstract idea, they must determine whether the claim includes limitations that are more than mere instructions to apply the abstract idea and thus show a patent-eligible application of the abstract idea.

7.78 With respect to biological inventions that involve a law of nature or natural phenomenon exception, the USPTO also published special rules for examining the patent eligibility of method claims in light of *Mayo v. Prometheus*.[250] Under these rules, the USPTO addresses the following questions: (1) Is the claimed invention directed to a process, defined as an act, or defined as a series of acts or steps? (2) If the first question is answered affirmatively, does the claim focus on the use of a law of nature, a natural phenomenon, or a naturally occurring relation or correlation (collectively referred to as a natural principle herein)? (3) If the second question is answered affirmatively, does the claim include additional elements/steps or a combination of elements/steps that integrate the natural principle into the claimed invention such that the natural principle is practically applied, and are sufficient to ensure that the claim amounts to significantly more than the natural principle itself? If the third question is answered affirmatively, the claimed invention is patent eligible. In addressing the third question, the USPTO will take into account the insufficient field of use and extra-solution activities to decide whether the elements or steps that are unrelated to a law of nature amount to significantly more than the law of nature itself. The rules also list multiple factors that are helpful for determining whether the invention amounts to more than a law of nature itself.[251]

7.79 With respect to product claims, the Supreme Court struck down patent eligibility of isolated DNA sequences in *Myriad*.[252] The Court found DNA sequences related to breast and ovarian cancers isolated from the human body to be a product of nature because the structural differences between these DNA sequences and the DNA sequences in the human body were merely ancillary to the breaking of the sequences from the chromosome structure of which the sequence was a part. This decision is contrary to the USPTO practice of awarding patents on isolated DNA and thus the USPTO published a revised interim guidelines in light

[249] USPTO, Preliminary Examination Instructions in View of the Supreme Court Decision in *Alice Corporation Pty., Ltd. v. CLS Bank Interantional, et al.* (http://www.uspto.gov/patents/announce/alice_pec_25jun2014.pdf).

[250] Ibid. § 2106.01.

[251] Ibid. § 2106.01.

[252] *Ass'n for Molecular Pathology v. Myriad Genetics, Inc.*, 186 L. Ed. 2d 124, 2013 US LEXIS 4540, 24 Fla. L. Weekly Fed. S 276, 2013 WL 2631062 (U.S. 2013).

of *Myriad*.[253] The patent eligibility standard in *Myriad* applies retroactively, and thus many patents including claims directed to isolated DNA that were issued prior to *Myriad* are invalid. Because patents including claims directed to isolated DNA do not fall into the definition of "covered business method patents," a party can challenge the validity of issued claims only in a civil action (either an infringement action or a DJ action of invalidity) or an ITC investigation procedure unless the claims have effective filing date on and after March 16, 2013 and thus can be challenged by filing a post-grant review.

(c) Originality—Inventorship

A patent application must be filed by a true inventor or joint inventors.[254] Contrary to the practice in Germany and Japan, the pre-AIA Patent Act required inventors to file a patent application even if the inventor was under an obligation to assign the invention to an employer.[255] The AIA harmonized US practice with Germany and Japan by making it possible for the inventors' employers and any assignors of the rights to a patent to file a patent application.[256] However, the originality requirement continues to prevent an issuance of the patent if a true inventor is not listed in the patent application.[257] If a true inventor is missing from the patent application or a person other than a true inventor is listed as an inventor, an applicant can amend the inventorship.[258] When a patent is issued with erroneous inventorship, the owner of such a patent can correct the error by requesting the USPTO to issue a certificate of an inventorship error.[259] Under the pre-AIA Patent Act, an error can be corrected only if the error occurred without any deceptive intentions. If the named inventors and their assignees intentionally omitted a true joint inventor, the patent owner cannot request an amendment or certification to correct inventorship. Unless an inventorship error is corrected, a patent is invalid.[260] However, such deceptive intent does not prevent a true inventor from requesting a correction.[261] The AIA amended the inventorship correction certificate provision and removed the requirement of the error occurring without deceptive intent.[262] However, a patent with an inventorship error continues to be invalid unless the error is corrected.[263] **7.80**

Even with a correction, it is unlikely that a patent owner will be able to enforce such a patent with erroneous inventorship resulting from deceptive intent because such misrepresentation of inventorship gives rise to inequitable conduct. Moreover, it is likely that a court will dismiss a complaint filed by the patent owner of a patent with erroneous inventorship unless the owner obtains consent for patent enforcement from a true inventor or her assignor because joint inventors each own a pro rata undivided interest in the patent and all co-owners must jointly enforce their patent.[264] **7.81**

[253] USPTO, 2014 Interim Guidance on Patent Subject Matter Eligibility, 79 Fed. Reg. 74618 (December 16, 2014) (http://www.gpo.gov/fdsys/pkg/FR-2014-12-16/pdf/2014-29414.pdf).
[254] 35 U.S.C. § 111.
[255] Pre-AIA 35 U.S.C. §§ 111 and 118.
[256] 35 U.S.C. § 118.
[257] *Chisum on Patents*, § 2.01.
[258] 35 U.S.C., § 116.
[259] Ibid. § 256(a).
[260] Pre-AIA 35 U.S.C. § 256¶2.
[261] *Stark v. Advanced Magnetics, Inc.*, 119 F.3d 1551, 43 U.S.P.Q. 2d 1321 (Fed. Cir. 1997); *University of Colorado Foundation, Inc. v. American Cyanamid Co.*, 196 F.3d 1366, 52 U.S.P.Q. 2d 1801 (Fed. Cir. 1999).
[262] 35 U.S.C. § 256(a).
[263] Ibid. § 256(b).
[264] *Ethicon, Inc. v. United States Surgical Corp.*, 937 F. Supp. 1015 (D. Conn. 1996).

7.82 Section 102(f) of the pre-AIA Patent Act provides a derivation as one of prior art and functions to prevent someone other than a true inventor from obtaining a patent.[265] A derivation is cited if an invention is kept secret as of the invention date because under § 102(a) public knowledge destroys novelty if the prior invention is publicly known as of the invention date. Accordingly, a derivation contest occurs as part of the priority contest when a true inventor finds another application or patent directed to the invention and requests the USPTO to start interference proceedings. When the USPTO finds a derivation from the true inventor for a claim included in a pending application or issued patent, the claim is cancelled or invalidated. If, within one year from the publication of an application directed to a derived invention or the issuance of a patent directed to a derived invention, a true inventor fails to file a patent application or fails to request that the USPTO declare an interference, any person can assert invalidity on the basis of derivation as long as the patent directed to a derived invention is enforced.

7.83 The AIA eliminated the derivation prior art provision from the US Patent Act. However, it is likely that derivation will continue to be a ground for rejecting and invalidating a claim directed to a derived invention.[266] A true inventor can prevent the USPTO from issuing a patent on a claim in a pending patent application or an issued patent if the claim is directed to an invention derived from her conception. The true inventor can do so, if the application and petition are filed within one year from the first publication of the claim, by filing both her own patent application and a petition.[267] When the USPTO finds a derivation, it rejects any claims directed to a derived invention in the application; if a patent is already issued, the USPTO cancels any claims directed to a derived invention.[268] When it is appropriate, the USPTO corrects inventorship, and claims may not be rejected or cancelled.[269]

7.84 If patents are issued to a true inventor and a party who derived a conception from the true inventor respectively, the AIA no longer authorizes the true inventor to request derivation proceedings. Instead, the AIA authorizes the second-to-file true inventor to challenge the validity of the patent issued to the first-to-file by filing a civil action.[270] The AIA is silent on whether the first-to-file patent owner can file a civil action to invalidate a patent issued to the second-to-file directed to a derived invention. However, the first-to-file patent owner may file a DJ action if the owner is charged with a claim of derivation by the second-to-file patent owner.[271] The derivation civil actions must be filed within one year from the issuance of the patent including a claim directed to a derived invention.[272] Although only a true inventor and her assignor can file derivation proceedings and the special civil action for derived patents, any party including a true inventor and her assignor who failed to file either derivation proceedings or a derived patent civil action within the one-year window can challenge the validity of a derived patent through a post-grant review, *inter partes* review, or *ex parte*

---

265 Pre-AIA 35 U.S.C. § 102(f).
266 See *Chisum on Patents*, § 10.10[4][b].
267 35 U.S.C. § 135(a).
268 Ibid. § 135(d).
269 Ibid. § 135(b). For further discussion, See *Chisum on Patents*, § 10.10[4][d].
270 35 U.S.C. § 291(a).
271 See *Chisum on Patents*, § 10.10[4][e].
272 35 U.S.C. § 291(b).

re-examination.[273] Such a party can also assert an invalidity defense on the basis of derivation if infringement is charged.[274]

To challenge the validity of a claim in an issued patent on the basis of errors in inventorship under pre-AIA case law, a party must establish that a person who contributed to the conception is not named in the patent or that a person who did not contribute to the conception is named in the patent. The conception is the formation, in the mind of the inventor, of a definite and permanent idea for a process or product.[275] A person who works alone to develop the means for solving a technical problem of the invention and thus has a complete conception of the invention is the sole inventor of the invention. If multiple persons collaborate and contribute to the conception of the invention, they are joint inventors.[276] A person who merely suggests a desired end result or identifies a technical problem to be solved by the invention does not qualify as a joint inventor.[277] A person who merely follows the instructions of the person who has already conceived a solution for the technical problem of the invention does not qualify as a joint inventor.[278] If a person uses her knowledge in her field of expertise and contributes in the selection of a means to solve a technical problem that another person is instructed to solve, she qualifies as a joint inventor.[279] Each joint inventor does not need to make the same type or amount of contribution or make a contribution to the invention of every claim included in the joint application.[280] **7.85**

To challenge the validity of a claim in an issued patent on the basis of derivation under pre-AIA case law, a party must establish an early conception by a true inventor and communication of the conception to the person who filed a patent application without authority.[281] The conception must be complete, including all limitations of the claim in dispute.[282] The communication between a true inventor and a person who derived the conception must be such that it can enable a person having ordinary skill in the art of the invention ("PHOSITA") to make the patented invention.[283] It is likely that the USPTO and US courts will follow pre-AIA case law to determine inventorship and derivation under the AIA. **7.86**

(d) Secret Prior Art for Lack of Novelty and Nonobviousness

i. Pre-AIA Prior Art The pre-AIA Patent Act followed the first-to-invent system and provided two types of prior art references: (1) statutory bar references that define the prior art **7.87**

---

273 See *Chisum on Patents*, § 10.10[4][d].

274 *International Rectifier Corp. v. IXYS Corp.*, 361 F.3d 1363, 1376–77, 70 U.S.P.Q. 2d 1209 (Fed. Cir. 2004).

275 *Cooper v. Goldfarb*, 154 F.3d 1321, 1998 U.S. App. LEXIS 21410, 47 U.S.P.Q. 2d (BNA) 1896 (Fed. Cir. 1998).

276 *Burroughs Welcome Co., v. Barr Lab., Inc.*, 40 F.3d 1223, 1227–28 (Fed. Cir. 1994).

277 *University of California v. Synbiotics Corp.*, 29 U.S.P.Q. 2d 1463 (S.D. Calif. 1993).

278 *Mueller Brass Co. v. Reading Indus., Inc.*, 352 F. Supp. 1357 (E.D. Pa. 1972), aff'd, 487 F.2d 1395 (3d Cir. 1973).

279 *Ethicon, Inc. v. United States Surgical Corp.*, 937 F. Supp. 1015 (D. Conn. 1996), aff'd, 135 F.3d 1456, 45 U.S.P.Q. 2d 1545 (Fed. Cir. 1998), cert. denied, 525 U.S. 923 (1998).

280 35 U.S.C. § 116.

281 *Hedgewick v. Akers*, 497 F.2d 905, 908, 182 U.S.P.Q. 167, 169 (CCPA 1974); *Gambro Lundia AB v. Baxter Healthcare Corp.*, 110 F.3d 1573, 42 U.S.P.Q. 2d (BNA) 1378 (Fed. Cir. 1997).

282 *Singh v. Brake*, 317 F.3d 1334, 1340 (Fed. Cir. 2003); *Slip Track Systems, Inc. v. Metal-Lite, Inc.*, 304 F.3d 1256, 1263 (Fed. Cir. 2002).

283 *Gambro Lundia AB v. Baxter Healthcare Corp.*, 110 F.3d 1573, 42 U.S.P.Q. 2d 1378 (Fed. Cir. 1997).

as of the date one year prior to the filing date[284] and (2) priority references that define the prior art and prior rights as of the invention date.[285] Statutory bar references function similarly to prior art references in the EPC and JPA except for the grace period.[286] During the grace period, the policy of awarding a patent to the first-to-invent prevails over the policy of encouraging inventors to file a patent as soon as the invention is ready for patenting. Pre-filing disclosures are automatically removed from the prior art during the grace period. Moreover, inventors are able to establish first-to-invent priority during the grace period if their invention was disclosed before the date of patent application.

7.88 A major difference between the pre-AIA Patent Act and the EPC and JPA is the secret prior art: the first-to-invent prior art includes multiple non-documentary references that are not publicly accessible as novelty defeating prior art.[287] Such secret prior art references include derivation, prior inventions, and inventors' secret commercial use. All of these secret prior art references can be cited for lack of nonobviousness, although there are some exceptions for derivation and prior inventions.[288] Secret prior art references are cited as a ground for invalidity in infringement litigation because the USPTO is unable to find such references during examination unless information concerning the secret prior art is provided by the public or the inventor of the invention.

7.89 Reflecting the first-to-invent policy of encouraging inventors to file a patent application when their invention is ready for patenting, US courts interpreted "public use and on sale" under § 102(b) of the pre-AIA Patent Act to include the inventor's commercial use of the invention even if the invention is kept secret.[289] For example, if an inventor or a person with the inventor's consent uses a method or machine to produce a product that is sold in the market and does not file a patent application within one year, the inventor is no longer able to file a patent application even if the method or machine was kept secret and no one could reverse-engineer the method or machine from the product.[290] Moreover, a commercial offer with respect to an invention that is ready for patenting gives rise to "on sale" under § 102(b) of the pre-AIA Patent Act even if the offer was made under a confidential relationship and thus the invention was not publicly accessible.[291]

---

[284] 35 U.S.C. §§ 102(b) and (d).

[285] Ibid. §§ 102(a), (e), and (g). Section 102(a) provides the prior art, which corresponds to the prior art under the EPC, Art. 54(2) and JPA, Art. 29; § 102(e) provides prior rights, which correspond to prior rights under the EPC, Art. 54(3) and JPA, Art. 29-2. Section 102(g) provides the priority rule, which is unique to the first-to-invent system.

[286] Toshiko Takenaka, "A View of First-to-File Lawyer on the America Invents Act: Will the First-Inventor-to-File under America Invents Act be the Best Practice Determining Patent Priority?" in Toshiko Takenaka (ed.), *Intellectual Property Systems in Common Law and Civil Law* (2013); Toshiko Takenaka, "Has the United States Adopted a First-to-File System through America Invents Act? A Comparative Law Analysis of Patent Priority under First-Inventor-to-File," 2012 *GRUR Int'l* (2012): 304; Toshiko Takenaka, "Harmony with the Rest of the World? The America Invents Act," 7 *Journal of Intellectual Property Law & Practice* (2012): 4.

[287] Pre-AIA 35 U.S.C. § 102.

[288] Ibid. § 103(c). Derivation and prior invention are excluded from the prior art for the purpose of nonobviousness where the claimed invention was made, owned by the same person, or subject to an obligation of assignment to the same person.

[289] Ibid. § 102(b). For a general discussion of secret commercial use with the inventor's consent, please see *Chisum on Patents*, § 6.02[5][b].

[290] *Metallizing Engineering Co. v. Kenyon Bearing & Auto Parts Co.*, 153 F.2d 516, 520, 68 U.S.P.Q. 54 (C.A. 2 1946).

[291] *Pfaff v. Wells Elecs., Inc.*, 525 U.S. 55, 48 U.S.P.Q. 2d 1641 (1998).

The duty of candor requires inventors to disclose secret commercial uses and commercial offers to the USPTO.[292] However, it is often unclear whether an invention is ready for patenting. An inventor may have believed in good faith that the invention was not ready for patenting when the invention was used or an offer was made and thus failed to disclose a secret commercial use and offer. Accordingly, a party discovers such a secret commercial use and offer only through discovery when the party is sued for patent infringement and cites the use or offer as evidence of lack of novelty or nonobviousness as a ground of invalidity. **7.90**

Section 102(g) of the pre-AIA Patent Act defines a prior invention that was kept secret on the invention date of the invention under examination as a reference. When a prior invention is publicly accessible on the invention date of the invention under examination, the invention is a reference under § 102(a) of the pre-AIA Patent Act. The USPTO cannot cite a secret prior invention as an interfering invention unless the inventor of such a prior invention files a patent application claiming the invention and starts interference proceedings. Even though an application is filed for the interfering prior invention, the USPTO may fail to cite the invention. If patents are issued by mistake to both prior and second-to-invent inventions, interference proceedings are no longer available.[293] Instead, the owner of an interfering prior invention can file a civil action and invalidate the patent issued to the second-to-invent invention.[294] Moreover, if a patent application was not filed for a prior invention, both the owner of the invention and a third party can cite the prior invention to establish as a ground of invalidity a lack of novelty or nonobviousness if the owner of a patent claiming the second-to-invent invention is enforcing her patent against the owner of the prior invention or a third party.[295] **7.91**

To cite a prior invention for a reference in an interference and civil action, the invention must have been made within the United States.[296] The 1993 and 1994 amendments to the pre-AIA Patent Act made it possible for inventors to establish their priority based on a prior invention made within member states of the North American Free Trade Agreement (NAFTA)[297] and Agreement on Trade-related Aspects of Intellectual Property Rights (TRIPS). The amendments did not extend the prior art effect of prior inventions made in NAFTA and WTO countries. A prior invention in a foreign country can be cited as a prior art reference if information about the invention is disclosed to a person in the United States.[298] **7.92**

The priority rule developed by pre-AIA case law and codified in the pre-AIA Patent Act defines prior inventions.[299] In principle, a prior invention is one that is first to be reduced to practice unless (1) an interfering invention is the first-to-conceive, with evidence of the **7.93**

---

[292] Ch. 7, 7.119.

[293] Interference proceedings are available for claims with the effective filing date prior to March 16, 2013. See Ch. 7, 7.52.

[294] Pre-AIA Patent Act, § 291.

[295] Ibid. § 102(g)(2); *Mycogen Plant Sci., Inc. v. Monsanto Co.*, 243 F.3d 1316, 258 U.S.P.Q. 2d 1030 (Fed. Cir. 2001).

[296] Pre-AIA Patent Act, §§ 102(g)(2), 104; *Solvay S.A. v. Honeywell Int'l, Inc.*, 622 F.3d 1367 (Fed. Cir. 2010).

[297] 1993 North American Free Trade Agreement Act, Pub. L. 103-182, 107 Stat. 2057 (December 8, 1993); 1994 Uruguay Round Agreement Act, Pub. L. 103-465, 108 Stat. 4809 (December 8, 1994).

[298] *Scott v. Koyama*, 281 F.3d 1243 (Fed. Cir. 2002). Disclosure to a person in the United States constitutes a conception.

[299] Pre-AIA 35 U.S.C. § 102(g).

inventor's reasonable diligence in reducing the invention to practice beginning from a time just prior to when the competing inventor conceived the invention; or (2) the first-to-reduce-to-practice invention is abandoned, concealed, or suppressed.[300] An actual reduction of an invention to practice can be established by constructing a product or performing a process that is read on the claim and confirming the suitability of the product or process for its intended purpose.[301] Alternatively, an invention can be reduced to practice constructively by filing a patent application with the USPTO or a foreign patent office.[302]

7.94 A first-to-conceive-with-diligence is the first exception to the first-to-reduce-to-practice rule. The conception is the formation, in the mind of the inventor, of a definite and permanent idea for a process or product.[303] The corroboration must be established by corroborating evidence: information of the invention is manifested in a written description or an oral communication with a corroborating witness and in a manner that would enable PHOSITA to make the invention.[304] The conception of the invention must be complete and show that the inventor is in possession of all the limitations of the invention.[305] For an invention in an unpredictable art such as chemical compounds and DNA sequences, an inventor must conceive a process of obtaining an invention for a prior invention[306] and utility of the invention.[307] To establish a prior invention based on a conception date, evidence of the inventor's reasonable diligence is necessary with respect to the entire period between a time just prior to the date of conception or reduction to practice by the first-to-reduce-to-practice inventor and the reduction-to-practice date of the first-to-conceive inventor.[308] Reasonable diligence does not require inventors to work on the invention every day, and short gaps in the inventors' recorded activities can be excused if a reasonable explanation is provided.[309]

7.95 The second exception is the first-to-reduce-to-practice inventor's abandonment, suppression, or concealment of her invention ("abandonment").[310] An unreasonable delay in filing a patent application after an actual reduction to practice gives rise to abandonment regardless of the inventor's lack of intent to abandon the invention.[311] An inventor can avoid abandonment by making the invention public, even if a patent application is not filed for the

[300] For a general discussion of the priority rule, see *Chisum on Patents*, § 10.03.

[301] *Scott v. Finney*, 34 F.3d 1058, 1061 (Fed. Cir. 1994).

[302] *Pfaff v. Wells Electronics*, 525 U.S. 55, 48 U.S.P.Q. 2d 1641 (1998).

[303] *Cooper v. Goldfarb*, 154 F.3d 1321, 1998 U.S. App. LEXIS 21410, 47 U.S.P.Q. 2d (BNA) 1896 (Fed. Cir. 1998).

[304] The USPTO requires a non-inventor to testify in order for the corroborating evidence to establish a prior invention. See *Chisum on Patents*, § 10.04[2].

[305] *Bosies v. Benedict*, 27 F.3d 539, 30 U.S.P.Q. 2d 1862 (Fed. Cir. 1994). An exception to the all limitations rule is the inherent limitation that specific conception is required. *Hitzeman v. Rutter*, 243 F.3d 1345, 58 U.S.P.Q. 2d 1161 (Fed. Cir. 2001).

[306] *Oka v. Youssefyeh*, 849 F.2d 581, 7 U.S.P.Q. 2d 1169 (Fed. Cir. 1988); *Amgen, Inc. v. Chugai Pharmaceutical Co., Ltd.*, 927 F.2d 1200, 18 U.S.P.Q. 2d 1016 (Fed. Cir. 1991).

[307] *Fiers v. Revel*, 984 F.2d 1164, 25 U.S.P.Q. 2d 1601 (Fed. Cir. 1993); *Kridl v. McCormick*, 105 F.3d 1446, 41 U.S.P.Q. 2d 1686 (Fed. Cir. 1997).

[308] *Creative Compounds, LLC v. Starmark Laboratories*, 651 F.3d 1303, 1312–13 (Fed. Cir. 2011).

[309] *Monsanto Co. v. Mycogen Plant Science, Inc.*, 261 F.3d 1356 (Fed. Cir. 2001). US courts are reluctant to accept an excuse for anything more than short gaps in activities to reduce the invention to practice. *Griffith v. Kanamaru*, 816 F.2d 624, 2 U.S.P.Q. 2d 1361 (Fed. Cir. 1987). See generally *Chisum on Patents*, § 10.07[4].

[310] Pre-AIA 35 U.S.C. § 102(g).

[311] *International Glass Co. v. United States*, 408 F.2d 395, 159 U.S.P.Q. 434, 161 U.S.P.Q. 116 (Ct. Cl. 1969); *Paulik v. Rizkalla*, 760 F.2d 1270, 226 U.S.P.Q. 224 (Fed. Cir. 1985); *Flex-Rest, LLC v. Steelcase, Inc.*, 455 F.3d 1351 (Fed. Cir. 2006).

invention.[312] Even though a delay in finding a patent application gives rise to an abandonment, a first-to-reduce-to-practice inventor can rely on the date of resuming activities to file a patent application after the delay if the inventor resumes the activity prior to the date of the second-to-reduce-to-practice inventor's conception or reduction to practice.[313]

In infringement litigation, a party who asserts a defense of invalidity bears the burden of establishing a prior invention with clear and convincing evidence.[314] Once a prior invention is established, the burden will shift to the patentee to produce evidence sufficient to create a genuine issue of material fact with respect to the abandonment of the prior invention. However, the ultimate burden of proving invalidity remains with the party who is challenging the validity throughout the litigation.[315] **7.96**

The pre-AIA Patent Act provides for derivation from a secret prior invention as a prior art reference.[316] A party must establish a prior conception of the patented invention and communication to the inventor(s) of the patented invention.[317] Unlike the conception for a prior invention, the prior conception for a derivation is not limited to the United States. Even if an inventor derives the conception from an activity in a foreign country, the invention is invalidated for a derivation.[318] **7.97**

ii. Post-AIA Prior Art The AIA adopted the first-inventor-to-file (FITF) priority and redefined prior art references to make it clear that the prior art and prior rights are measured from the filing date.[319] However, it is not clear whether the revision completely eliminated secret prior art because the AIA retained the pre-AIA definition of the prior art references "public use" and "on sale" even though it introduced an additional definition "otherwise available to the public." The USPTO published its own interpretation of the new definition, eliminating secret commercial use and secret commercial offer.[320] In contrast, commentators have read the pre-AIA definition and the new definition independently of each other and argue to keep "secret commercial use" and "secret commercial offer" as a part of the AIA prior art.[321] The USPTO will issue a patent because applicants have no duty to disclose a secret commercial use or offer under the USPTO interpretation and the USPTO cannot find the secret prior art without disclosure. Whether a party can cite the secret prior art **7.98**

[312] *Checkpoint Systems, Inc. v. US Int'l Trade Comm'n*, 54 F.3d 756, 35 U.S.P.Q. 2d 1042 (Fed. Cir. 1995); *Apotex USA, Inc. v. Merck & Co., Inc.*, 254 F.3d 1031, 59 U.S.P.Q. 2d 1139 (Fed. Cir. 2001).

[313] *Paulik v. Rizkalla*, 760 F.2d 1270, 226 U.S.P.Q. 224 (Fed. Cir. 1985).

[314] *Apotex USA, Inc. v. Merck & Co., Inc.*, 254 F.3d 1031, 59 U.S.P.Q. 2d 1139 (Fed. Cir. 2001).

[315] *Innovative Scuba Concepts, Inc. v. Feder Indus., Inc.*, 26 F.3d 1112, 1115, 31 U.S.P.Q. 2d (BNA) 1132, 1134 (Fed. Cir. 1994).

[316] Pre-AIA 35 U.S.C. § 102(f). Ch. 7, 7.97.

[317] The information in the communication must enable a PHOSITA to make the patented invention. See n. 68 above.

[318] *Hedgewick v. Akers*, 497 F.2d 905, 907, 182 U.S.P.Q. 167 (CCPA 1974).

[319] Post-AIA 35U.S.C. § 102(a).

[320] "Examination Guidelines for Implementing the First Inventor to File Provisions of the Leahy-Smith America Invents Act," 78 Fed. Reg. 11059, 11062 (February 14, 2013).

[321] "Comments on USPTO First to File Guidelines" by Mark Lemley, email sent October 5, 2012 to Mary C. Till, senior legal adviser, Office of Patent Legal Administration, Office of the Deputy Commissioner for Patent Examination Policy (www.uspto.gov/patents/law/comments/m-lemley_20121005.pdf). Robert Merges, "Priority and Novelty under the AIA," 27 *Berkeley Technology Law Journal* (2012): 1023; Michael O'Neill, "Secret Prior Art after America Invents Act: Are Lost Opportunities Revived?" *AIPLA Newsstand*, December 2, 2013 (http://www.lexology.com/library/detail.aspx?g=06046466-f513-4065-9ff4-53fb9d866ac1#6).

when challenging validity will remain unclear until the Federal Circuit or the Supreme Court resolves the question.

7.99 The AIA removed secret prior inventions from the prior art. However, the FITF is not a true first-to-file system because the AIA allows inventors to establish priority based on a disclosure or an invention by the disclosure.[322] The AIA provides two exceptions to the prior art and prior rights: (1) disclosures directly and indirectly derived from the inventor or joint inventor during the grace period,[323] and (2) intervening disclosures, other than the first disclosure, not derived from the inventor or joint inventor during the grace period.[324] It also provides an additional exception to prior rights: disclosures of the invention that are owned by the same person or subject to an obligation of assignment to the same person.[325]

7.100 The second exception for intervening disclosures is unique to the FITF system because the exception protects first-to-disclose inventors from any later disclosures, regardless of whether the invention in such a disclosure is independently invented by a third-party inventor, as long as the inventor files a patent application within one year from the first disclosure date.[326] The date of disclosure functions like a priority date by preventing other inventors from obtaining any rights based on their disclosure or patent filing, which is in stark contrast to the exception to the prior art under the EPC and JPA. Moreover, a first disclosure also prevents a third party from obtaining a prior-user rights defense.[327]

7.101 In other words, the AIA replaced prior inventions with prior disclosures during the grace period. Contrary to a patent filing date, which is clear from records at the USPTO, a disclosure date is similar to an invention date in that the USPTO must decide the date based on evidence outside the record of prosecution. Multiple inventors may contest who was the first-to-disclose during the grace period, based on evidence of disclosure in establishing whether the disclosure that an inventor relied on was sufficient to support the claimed invention under examination. However, the AIA does not provide any definition of the term "disclosure." The USPTO interprets disclosure expansively to include publicly accessible information that falls into the definition of the prior art and prior rights.[328] It does not provide proceedings for the first-to-disclose priority contest during the examination, and it is likely that parties will dispute disclosure dates at a post-grant review and *inter partes* review at the USPTO or a civil action for patent infringement.

7.102 A party may cite an intervening disclosure during the grace period to show lack of novelty and nonobviousness even if the disclosure is removed from the prior art in the operation of the exception. The USPTO interprets the invention in the intervening third-party disclosure as being identical to the invention in the first disclosure even though the USPTO allows minimum changes in the mode of disclosure or to the description of the invention

---

322 Paul Janicke, "A Commentary on the New Patent Law of the United States," *GRUR Intl* (2011): 887.

323 AIA, §§ 102(b)(1)(A), 102(b)(2)(A).

324 AIA, §§ 102(b)(1)(B), 102(b)(2)(B).

325 AIA, § 102(b)(2)(C). This exception applies to disclosures of an invention that was developed under a joint research agreement. AIA, § 102(c).

326 "Changes to Implementing the First Inventor to File Provisions of the Leahy-Smith America Invents Act", 78 Fed. Reg. 11065, 11066 (February 14, 2013).

327 AIA, § 273(a)(2).

328 "Changes to Implementing the First Inventor to File Provisions of the Leahy-Smith America Invents Act," 11075.

in the disclosures.[329] Neither the USPTO nor the courts have any experience in examining the identity of an invention in multiple disclosures under the pre-AIA Patent Act although they have examined the identity of a claimed invention and an invention in a disclosure. The question of what level of identity should be required for the prior art exception remains to be resolved by the Federal Circuit or the Supreme Court.

(e) Double Patenting

A party may challenge validity if a patentee received more than one patent for the same or a patentably indistinct invention.[330] The US double patenting doctrine is unique in preventing a patentee from obtaining another patent on an obvious variation of what has already been patented.[331] If a patent is issued for an obvious variation instead of the same invention, patentees can avoid a ground of invalidity by entering a terminal disclaimer.[332] **7.103**

(f) Foreign Filing

A party may challenge the validity of a patent if the patent violates a foreign filing license requirement.[333] The inventor of an invention made in the United States cannot file a patent application in a foreign country without a foreign filing license. If a patent application is filed with the USPTO, a foreign filing license is automatically issued at the expiration of six months from the filing date. A separate license is necessary to file a patent application in a foreign country without filing an application with the USPTO or before the expiration of six months from the US filing date. A foreign filing violation may result in not only patent invalidity but also criminal liability.[334] **7.104**

It is unlikely that the USPTO will find out an invention was made in the United States. Thus, a violation of a foreign filing license is asserted to challenge validity after the issuance of a patent. The ground of invalidity for the violation may be removed by a grant of retroactive license if the patentee establishes that the failure to obtain a license was through error and without deceptive intent. **7.105**

10. Other Type of Defenses

(a) 271(e) Safe Harbor

Section 271(e) of the US Patent Act provides special rules for an act of infringement unique to inventions relating to drugs, medical devices, and veterinary biological products, which require regulatory approval under federal law.[335] Applying for an abbreviated new drug application (ANDA) approval constitutes an act of infringement if the **7.106**

---

[329] Ibid. 11067. (1) There is no requirement that the mode of disclosure by the inventor or a joint inventor be the same as the mode of disclosure of an intervening disclosure (e.g., inventor discloses the invention at a trade show and the intervening disclosure is in a peer-reviewed journal); (2) there is no requirement that the disclosure by the inventor or a joint inventor be a verbatim or an *ipsissimis verbis* disclosure of an intervening disclosure in order for the exception based on a previous public disclosure of subject matter by the inventor or a joint inventor to apply; and (3) the exception applies to the subject matter of an intervening disclosure that is simply a more general description of the subject matter previously publicly disclosed by the inventor or a joint inventor.

[330] 35 U.S.C. § 101. For a general discussion of the requirement of double patenting, see *Chisum on Patents*, § 9.03.

[331] *General Foods Corp. v. Studiengesellschaft Kohle mbH*, 972 F.2d 1272, 23 U.S.P.Q. 2d 1839 (Fed. Cir. 1992).

[332] 35 U.S.C. § 253.

[333] Ibid. §§ 184–86. For a general discussion of foreign filing licenses, see *Chisum on Patents*, § 1.06.

[334] 35 U.S.C. § 186.

[335] Ibid. § 271(e)(2).

application seeks to start marketing a generic drug before the expiration of a patent covering a new drug and the application is submitted with the certification (Paragraph IV Certification) that the patent covering the new drug is invalid or not infringed.[336] As a result, a new drug manufacturer can start an ANDA patent litigation even though a generic drug manufacturer has not begun making the patented drug. Section 271(e) limits the remedies of an ANDA litigation to (1) an order to delay approval until the expiration of the new drug patent; (2) injunctive relief to prevent a commercial manufacture, use, or sale that does not fall into the activities protected by the safe harbor; (3) damages for such commercial activities; and (4) attorneys' fees if the case qualifies as an exceptional case.[337]

7.107 If a new drug manufacturer files an ANDA litigation within forty-five days from the receipt of notice from the generic drug manufacturer with respect to its ANDA application with the Paragraph IV Certification, the regulatory process is automatically stayed up to thirty months until the issues of patent validity and infringement are resolved in the litigation. To prevent generic drugs from entering into the market, new drug manufacturers almost always start an ANDA litigation.

7.108 Section 271(e) of the US Patent Act also provides a special defense: a statutory experimental exception that applies to the use of patented inventions that are reasonably related to the submission of information to the US Food and Drug Administration (FDA).[338] This exception is called a "safe harbor" because generic drug manufacturers frequently rely on this exception to shield themselves from patent infringement liability. New drug manufactures can also rely on the safe harbor because the exception exceeds pre-clinical safety studies to include information regarding, for example, the pharmacological, toxicological, pharmacokinetic, and biological qualities of a drug.[339] However the scope of the US statutory exception is narrower than that of the statutory experimental exceptions under the German Patent Act and Japanese Patent Act because the US exception applies only to uses of a patented invention that relate to the FDA regulatory process.[340]

7.109 US courts have developed a common law experimental use exception that is more broadly applicable than drugs, medical devices, and veterinary biological products. Under the common law exception, the scope of experimentation to which this is applicable is very narrow. Cases in which an accused infringer is found to be non-liable under the exception for making and/or using a patented invention are rare.[341] Experimental use arguments by defendants are frequently rejected because US courts are likely to find commercial use wherever the use is coupled with any commercial activity.[342]

---

[336] *Eli Lilly & Co. v. Medtronic, Inc.*, 496 U.S. 661, 110 S. Ct. 2683, 15 U.S.P.Q. 2d 1121 (U.S. 1990).

[337] 35 U.S.C. § 271(e)(2).

[338] Ibid. § 271(e)(1) (2006) ("it shall not be an act of infringement to...use...or import into the United States a patented invention...solely for uses reasonably related to the development and submission of information under a Federal law which regulates the...use...of drugs"); see also *Merck v. Integra*, 545 U.S. 193 (2005) (remanded as 496 F.3d 1334).

[339] *Merck KGAA v. Integra Lifesciences I, Ltd.*, 545 U.S. 193 (2005).

[340] Kevin Iles, "A Comparative Analysis of the Impact of Experimental Use Exceptions in Patent Law on Incentive to Innovate," 4 *Northwestern J. Tech. Intell. Pro.* (2005): 61 (https://law.wustl.edu/Library/Guides/Japaneselegalresearch_2010.pdf).

[341] See *Chisum on Patents*, § 16.03[1][b].

[342] See, e.g., ibid.; *Spray Refrigeration Co. v. Sea Spray Fishing, Inc.*, 322 F.2d 34 (9th Cir. 1963).

Reflecting the narrow application of the common law experimental use exception, the Federal Circuit in *Roche v. Bolar* refused to apply the exception to the use of a patented drug prior to the expiration of the term of the patent for testing geared towards FDA approval.[343] Congress enacted the statutory experimental use exception in response to the *Roche* ruling while introducing an act of infringement that occurs by applying for an ANDA application with a Paragraph IV Certificate. **7.110**

The Federal Circuit does not view the enactment of the statutory experimental use exception as indicative of Congress's intent to expand the scope of the common law experimental use exception. Instead, it continues to emphasize the narrow applicability of the exception and refuses to apply the exception unless the use was solely "for amusement, to satisfy idle curiosity, or for strictly philosophical inquiry."[344] **7.111**

(b) Prior-user Rights Defense

The AIA expanded the scope of a prior-user rights defense based on a prior commercial use of an invention to encompass any invention regardless of the field of technology or category of invention.[345] Congress first introduced a defense based on prior commercial use in the US Patent Act in 1999.[346] The defense was called the "First Inventor Defense" and is applicable only to a method of doing or conducting business.[347] This defense applies only to actions pending on and after November 29, 1999.[348] The expanded prior-user rights under the AIA apply to patents issued on or after the enactment date, September 16, 2011. Thus, the definition of a method of doing or conducting business under the pre-AIA Patent Act will continue to have significance in determining whether the defense is available until all pre-AIA patents have expired. However, the pre-AIA Patent Act did not provide any definitions for the terms "commercially used" and "commercial use" although a broad definition supports an interpretation that covers a manufacturing process for producing a product.[349] **7.112**

Under the post-AIA Patent Act, a prior-user rights defense is available if (1) a party commercially used the invention in the United States either in connection with an internal commercial use, an actual arm's length sale, or some other arm's length commercial transfer of a useful end product resulting from such a commercial use; and (2) such a use by the party occurred at least one year before the earlier of the effective filing date of the claimed invention being asserted against the party and the date on which the asserted invention was disclosed to the public in a manner that qualified for an exception from the prior art.[350] Commercial use includes experimental use for developing data for regulatory approval and use by nonprofit research laboratories and universities.[351] **7.113**

A party can assert a prior-user rights defense only if the party performed or directed the performance of the commercial use and cannot transfer the defense to another party other **7.114**

---

[343] *Roche Products, Inc. v. Bolar Pharmaceutical Co.*, 733 F.2d 858 (Fed. Cir. 1984).

[344] *Madey v. Duke Univ.*, 307 F.3d 1351, 1362 (Fed. Cir. 2002).

[345] 35 U.S.C. § 273. For a general discussion, see *Chisum on Patents*, § 16.03[4].

[346] America Inventor Protection Act (AIPA) of 1999, PL 106-113, 113 Stat. 1501, 1501A-555-557 (November 29, 1999).

[347] Pre-AIA 35 U.S.C. §§ 273(a)(3), 273(b)(1).

[348] AIPA, § 4303.

[349] Pre-AIA 35 U.S.C. § 273(a)(1).

[350] Post-AIA 35 U.S.C. § 273(a)(1).

[351] Ibid. § 273(c).

than the owner of the asserted patent without a transfer of business relating to the commercial use.[352] The defense is geographically limited to cover only the sites where the invention was commercially used.[353] A party cannot assert this defense if the invention is derived from the patentee of the asserted patent or persons in privity with the patentee.[354] The defense extends only to a specific claimed invention that a prior commercial use is established even though a party can change the quantity and volume of commercial use. A party can improve the claimed invention covered by the defense as long as the improvement does not infringe other claims that the party cannot assert a defense based on a prior commercial use.[355] The defense is no longer available if a party abandons the commercial use of the invention.[356] A party cannot assert a prior-user rights defense against universities.[357]

7.115 The first-to-invent policy encourages early patent filing and punishes the secret commercial use of an invention beyond the grace period.[358] The USPTO published a report comparing prior-user rights defenses in major countries including Japan and Germany to respond to concerns over the impact of the new defense that were indicated by legal professionals and academics.[359] Because US courts have no experience in interpreting and applying prior-users rights, US courts must clarify through case law the scope of commercial use and the parties qualified to assert the defense as well as the scope of activities covered.

(c) Medical Activities

7.116 Unlike the EPC and JPA, the US Patent Act does not exclude surgical and diagnostic methods from patent eligibility. Instead, the Patent Act provides immunity to medical practitioners from patent infringement remedies.[360] Historically, there was some reluctance in the United States to grant and enforce patents on medical treatment methods. This changed in 1954 with the *ex parte Scherer* case, in which it was determined that the USPTO would explicitly treat medical treatment methods in the same way as other technical inventions.[361] In 1996, Congress endorsed the USPTO interpretation of the Patent Act acknowledging the patentability of medical treatment methods and passed a law protecting physicians and institutions from liability for infringing medical method patents pertaining to processes such as surgical incisions.[362] Congress's action was in response to a suit in which

---

352 Ibid. § 273(e)(1).
353 Ibid.
354 Ibid. § 273(e)(2).
355 Ibid. § 273(e)(3).
356 Ibid. § 273(a)(4).
357 Ibid. § 273(a)(5).
358 *Metallizing Engineering Co. v. Kenyon Bearing & Auto Parts Co.*, 153 F.2d 516, 520, 68 U.S.P.Q. 54 (C.A. 2 1946). Commercial use by an inventor or a party with the inventor's consent constitutes a statutory bar and is public use regardless of such use being kept secret. See Ch. 7, 7.87 "Pre-AIA Prior Art."
359 USPTO, Report on the Prior User Rights Defense (January 2012) (http://www.uspto.gov/aia_implementation/20120113-pur_report.pdf).
360 35 U.S.C, § 287(c) (2006) ("With respect a medical practitioner's performance of a medical activity that constitutes an infringement under section 271(a) or (b) of this title, the provisions of sections 281, 283, 284, and 285 of this title shall not apply against the medical practitioner or against a related health care entity with respect to such medical activity").
361 *Ex parte Scherer*, 103 U.S.P.Q. (BNA) 107 (Pat. Off. Bd. App. 1954).
362 Medical Procedures Innovation and Affordability Act, S. 1334, 104th Cong. (1st Sess. 1995). For a general discussion of Medical method defense, see Jeff S. Rundle, "The Physician's Immunity Statute: A Botched Operation or a Model Procedure," 34 *Iowa J.Corp. L.* (2009): 943; Emily C. Melvin, "An Unacceptable Exception: The Ramifications of Physician Immunity from Medical Procedure Patent Infringement Liability," 91 *Minn. L. Rev.* (2007): 1088; Eric M. Lee, "35 U.S.C. § 287(c)—The Physician Immunity Statute," 79 *J. Pat. & Trademark Off. Soc'y* (1997): 701, 703.

an inventor demanded royalty payments from hospitals carrying out his patented method and sued a clinic for patent infringement.[363]

The medical method defense is available only to medical practitioners and related health care entities.[364] Medical practitioners include any licensed medical professional who can legally perform a medical activity or any person acting under the guidance of such a professional.[365] Related health care entities include all entities with which a medical practitioner may have a professional affiliation during the performance of a medical activity.[366] To assert the defense, the act performed by a medical practitioner must be a medical or surgical procedure on the body except for (1) the use of a patented machine, manufacture, or composition of matter in violation of the patent covering such subject matter, (2) the practice of a patented use of a composition of matter in violation of such a patent, or (3) the practice of a process in violation of a biotechnology patent.[367] These exceptions are in line with patent protection under the EPC, where the use of a composition of matter such as pharmaceutical compounds and an *in vitro* use of biological material for diagnostic and surgical methods are patent eligible. **7.117**

An act that qualifies for the defense is still an infringement although no infringement remedies, injunctions, or damages are available to the patentee.[368] Such remedies are available to the patentee of a medical method if the patentee sues a party for contributory infringement or inducement with respect to the medical activities performed by a medical practitioner or health care entities.[369] **7.118**

(d) Inequitable Conduct

The defense of unenforceability for inequitable conduct is unique to the US patent system. A party to an infringement litigation can assert a defense of unenforceability if the patent being asserted was fraudulently procured through inequitable conduct. This defense is a purely judge-made law and thus there is no statutory basis under the US Patent Act. Under US case law, patent applicants are under a duty of candor to deal with the USPTO throughout the examination including post-grant procedures. The duty includes a duty to not present false evidence and to disclose information that is material to patentability. This duty is applicable to any person who is involved in the patent procurement including foreign patent attorneys and agents who handle the prosecution of a corresponding foreign patent.[370] A finding of inequitable conduct with respect to a claim results in the unenforceability of all claims included in the same patent. Before the introduction of the supplemental examination under the AIA, there was no remedy for purging inequitable conduct, and thus all claims remained unenforceable, which equated to invalidity for the entire patent term. A lenient standard for establishing inequitable conduct made it possible for accused infringers to assert the defense frequently in patent litigation. As a result, the defense was often called the plague of patent litigation.[371] **7.119**

[363] *Pallin v. Singer*, 36 U.S.P.Q. 2d (BNA) 1050 (D. Vt. 1995).
[364] 35 U.S.C. § 287(c)(1).
[365] Ibid. § 287(c)(2)(b).
[366] Ibid. § 287(c)(2)(c).
[367] Ibid. § 287(c)(2)(A).
[368] Ibid. § 287(c)(1).
[369] For a general discussion on inequitable conduct, *Chisum on Patents*, § 19.03.
[370] *Molins plc v. Textron, Inc.*, 48 F.3d 1172, 33 U.S.P.Q. 2d 1823 (Fed. Cir. 1995).
[371] Christopher A. Cotropia, "Modernizing Patent Law's Inequitable Conduct Doctrine," 24 *Berkeley Tech. L.J.* (2009):723,739; Mammen, "Controlling the 'Plague': Reforming the Doctrine of Inequitable Conduct," 1358.

7.120 Responding to serious concern over the uncertainty of patent enforceability introduced by the frequently asserted defense, the Federal Circuit adopted a stringent standard for establishing inequitable conduct in its 2011 *en banc* decision, *Therasense v. Becton*.[372] A party alleging inequitable conduct must establish (1) the patentee's specific intent to deceive the USPTO and (2) the materiality of the information misrepresented or omitted by the patentee.[373] Acts found to be inequitable conduct include misrepresentation of inventorship, failures to cite prior public use or sale by the inventor or her assignees, failures to cite prior art references, and false statements in affidavits establishing the first-to-invent priority and patentability.[374] Even though pre-2011 *Therasense* case law indicated that the two requirements were separate and independent,[375] US courts frequently used a sliding scale to have a strong showing of materiality supplement a weak showing of intent.[376] This approach was clearly rejected in *Therasense*.

7.121 *Therasense* adopted a heightened standard for showing materiality: a party alleging inequitable conduct must establish the but-for materiality with respect to information that the patentee failed to disclose during examination.[377] The but-for materiality standard is met if the USPTO would not have allowed a claim had it been aware of the undisclosed prior art. In infringement litigation, district courts apply the preponderance of evidence standard and give the broadest reasonable claim construction to determine the but-for materiality. Even if a reference does not invalidate the claim at issue under the clear and convincing evidence standard, the reference may be material if it would prevent the USPTO from allowing the claim under the preponderance of evidence standard. A reference may not meet the but-for materiality even though it would establish *prima facie* unpatentability of claim if the patentee has evidence to rebut the *prima facie* case. The but-for materiality standard does not apply to cases where the patentee engaged in affirmative egregious acts such as presenting false evidence for patentability.[378]

7.122 Additionally, *Therasense* adopted a heightened standard for evidence to show the patentee's intent. Even though direct evidence is not necessary to show deceptive intent, the evidence must be sufficient to draw the single most reasonable inference of such intent.[379] Circumstantial evidence may not meet the standard if multiple inferences are drawn from the evidence.[380]

7.123 *Therasense* significantly reduced allegations of inequitable conduct by parties in patent litigation.[381] Under pre-*Therasense* case law, a pleading of inequitable conduct needed to include a sufficient allegation of underlying facts supporting a most reasonable inference with respect to the patentee's deceptive intent and knowledge that the omitted

---

372 *Therasense, Inc. v. Becton, Dickinson & Co.*, 649 F.3d 1276 (Fed. Cir. 2011) (*en banc*).

373 *Kingsdown Medical Consultants, Ltd. v. Hollister Inc.*, 863 F.2d 867, 9 U.S.P.Q. 2d 1384 (Fed. Cir. 1988).

374 For more discussions on acts giving rise to inequitable conducts, see *Chisum on Patents*, § 19.03A[2].

375 *Hoffmann-La Roche, Inc. v. Promega Corp.*, 323 F.3d 1354,66 U.S.P.Q. 2d 1385 (Fed. Cir. 2003).

376 *Therasense*, 649 F.3d, 1288.

377 Ibid. 1291–92.

378 Ibid. 1292.

379 Ibid. 1290–91. *In re Rosuvastatin Calcium Patent Litig. v. Aurobindo Pharma, Ltd.*, 703 F.3d 511, 105 U.S.P.Q. 2d 1437 (Fed. Cir. 2012).

380 *Therasense*, 649 F.3d at 1290; *In re Rosuvastatin Calcium Patent Litig.*, 703 F.3d, 520.

381 Jason Rantanen, "Recalibrating Our Empirical Understanding of Inequitable Conduct," 3 *IP Theory* (2013): 98 (http://www.repository.law.indiana.edu/ipt/vol3/iss2/3).

information was material.[382] *Therasense* did not change this reasonable inference standard for patentees.[383] Nevertheless, the pleaded facts must support a reasonable inference with respect to knowledge of the but-for materiality.

Even though the inequitable conduct defense is less frequently pleaded and even less frequently upheld by district courts after *Therasense*, the defense is still available in appropriate cases.[384] Once a district finds inequitable conduct, it is rare for the Federal Circuit to make its own ultimate conclusion.[385] To review the district courts' inequitable conduct findings, the Federal Circuit applies the clearly erroneous standard to underlying factual findings and the abuse of discretion standard to the ultimate determination of inequitable conduct.[386] As a result, the Federal Circuit must give a lot of deference to the district courts' inequitable conduct findings. **7.124**

Before asserting patent infringement, a patentee should review the patent prosecution at the USPTO and foreign offices, interview inventors and any persons involved in the US and foreign patent prosecution, and find out if any reference is being withheld from the USPTO. If a reference that may meet the but-for materiality standard is found, the patentee should resort to a supplemental examination. Once the reference is considered during the supplemental examination, inequitable conduct is purged, and a court cannot find a patent unenforceable based on that conduct.[387] However, supplemental examinations cannot cure affirmative egregious acts that give rise to fraud.[388] **7.125**

(e) Patent Misuse

A patent may not be enforceable if the patentee improperly exercises its patent contrary to the patent policy because such enforcement gives rise to patent misuse. Any acts that violate the federal antitrust law constitute misuse, but acts that do not violate the antitrust law may also constitute misuse if the acts extend the economic impact of the patent beyond the scope defined by the claim language or the patent term.[389] The patent recovers its enforceability only when the act that is found to be an inappropriate exercise is purged. **7.126**

Improper acts that courts find to be misuse per se include (1) price fixing[390] and (2) tying arrangements.[391] Acts that may give rise to misuse include (1) covenants not to deal in competing goods,[392] (2) package licensing,[393] (3) post-expiration royalties and **7.127**

---

382 *Exergen Corp. v. Wal-Mart Stores, Inc.*, 575 F.3d 1312 (Fed. Cir. 2009).

383 *Delano Farms Co. v. California Table Grape Comm'n*, 655 F.3d 1337 (Fed. Cir. 2011).

384 When a claim is invalid for a reference that the patentee withheld from the USPTO, the Federal Circuit affirms inequitable conduct if the court found a distinct intent to deceive the USPTO. *Aventis Pharma S.A. v. Hospira, Inc.*, 675 F.3d 1324, 102 U.S.P.Q. 2d 1445 (Fed. Cir. 2012).

385 Rantanen, "Recalibrating Our Empirical Understanding of Inequitable Conduct," 110.

386 *Aventis Pharma S.A. v. Hospira, Inc.*, 675 F.3d 1324, 1334 (Fed. Cir. 2012).

387 35 U.S.C. § 257(c)(1).

388 Ibid. § 257(e).

389 *Zenith Radio Corp. v. Hazeltine Research, Inc.*, 395 U.S. 100, 140, 161 U.S.P.Q. 577, 593 (1969); *W.L. Gore & Assocs., Inc. v. Carlisle Corp.*, 529 F.2d 614, 622, 189 U.S.P.Q. 129, 135–36 (3d Cir. 1976). For a general discussion of misuse, see *Chisum on Patents*, § 19.04.

390 *Ansul Co. v. Uniroyal, Inc.*, 448 F.2d 872, 880, 169 U.S.P.Q. 759, 764 (2d Cir. 1971).

391 *Senza-Gel Corp. v. Seiffhart*, 803 F.2d 661, 231 U.S.P.Q. 363 (Fed. Cir. 1986); *Virginia Panel Corp. v. MAC Panel Corp.*, 133 F.3d 860, 45 U.S.P.Q. 2d 1225 (Fed. Cir. 1997).

392 *Keystone Retaining Wall Sys., Inc. v. Westrock, Inc.*, 997 F.2d 1444, 1993 U.S. App. LEXIS 15508, 27 U.S.P.Q. 2d (BNA) 1297 (Fed. Cir. 1993).

393 *Western Elec. Co. v. Stewart-Warner Corp.*, 631 F.2d 333, 338, 208 U.S.P.Q. 183, 188 (4th Cir. 1980).

restraints,[394] and (4) royalties based on the total sales regardless of actual use of the patented product or process.[395] In principle, (1) refusals to license,[396] (2) discriminatory royalty schedules,[397] (3) territorial limitations,[398] (4) field of use limitations,[399] (5) restrictions on the use of purchased goods,[400] and (6) grant back clauses[401] do not constitute misuse.

7.128 For a patent being purged and to regain enforceability, the patentee must establish that the act giving rise to the misuse was abandoned and the consequence of the misuse was fully dissipated.[402] If the misuse relates to a provision in a license, the patent owner must cancel the provision.[403] An abandonment of the improper act with the passage of a period of time usually creates an inference of dissipation.[404] However, if the improper act results in actual adverse consequences, the patent owner must undertake steps to eliminate those consequences and show that any harmful consequences of misuse have been fully dissipated.[405]

(f) Laches and Estoppel

7.129 Once a patent owner finds infringement of her patent by a party, delays in filing a patent litigation may give rise to two types of equitable defenses, laches and estoppel, which limit the remedies the patent owner is entitled to for the infringement. Laches prevents the patent owner from recovering damages resulting from infringement that occurred prior to the filing of the suit when (1) the patent owner delays filing the suit for an unreasonable period of time without any excuse for the delay, and (2) the patent owner's delay caused material prejudice to the infringer.[406] Equitable estoppel prevents the patent owner from recovering any damages and precludes a claim of injunction when (1) the patent owner represents to the infringer that she will not press an infringement suit against the party, and (2) the party continues or expands her business in reliance on that representation. Because of the harsh consequence to the patent owner, courts are more reluctant to find an estoppel than laches.

7.130 Although these two defenses are closely based on the traditional equitable doctrines of lack of good faith and unclean hands, there is a fundamental difference. Laches results from the lapse of time that occurs after the patent owner gains knowledge of infringing activities

---

394 *Rocform Corp. v. Acitelli-Standard Concrete Wall, Inc.*, 367 F.2d 678, 151 U.S.P.Q. 305 (6th Cir. 1966); *Intra-Video Inc. v. Hughes Electronics Corp.*, 51 U.S.P.Q. 2d 1383, 1384 (S.D.N.Y. 1999).

395 *Virginia Panel Corp. v. MAC Panel Co.*, 133 F.3d 860, 869 (Fed. Cir. 1997).

396 *In re Independent Service Organizations Antitrust Litigation*, 203 F.3d 1322, 53 U.S.P.Q. 2d 1852 (Fed. Cir. 2000). But see *Image Technical Services Inc. v. Eastman Kodak*, 125 F.3d 1195, 44 U.S.P.Q. 2d 1065 (9th Cir. 1997).

397 *USM Corp. v. SPS Technologies, Inc.*, 694 F.2d 505, 216 U.S.P.Q. 959 (7th Cir. 1982).

398 35 U.S.C. § 261; *Image Technical Services Inc. v. Eastman Kodak*, 125 F.3d 1195, 44 U.S.P.Q. 2d 1065 (9th Cir. 1997).

399 *General Talking Pictures Co. v. Western Elec. Co.*, 304 U.S. 175 (1938).

400 *Mallinckrodt, Inc. v. Medipart, Inc.*, 976 F.2d 700, 24 U.S.P.Q. 2d (BNA) 1173 (Fed. Cir. 1992).

401 *Transparent-Wrap Mach. Corp. v. Stokes & Smith*, 329 U.S. 637, 72 U.S.P.Q. 148 (1947).

402 *Morton Salt Co. v. G.S. Suppiger Co.*, 314 U.S. 488, 52 U.S.P.Q. 30 (1942).

403 *Berlenbach v. Anderson & Thompson*, 329 F.2d 782, 785, 141 U.S.P.Q. 84, 87 (9th Cir. 1964).

404 *United States Gypsum v. National Gypsum*, 352 U.S. 457, 112 U.S.P.Q. 340 (1957).

405 *Preformed Line Prod. Co. v. Fanner Mfg. Co.*, 328 F.2d 265, 278–79, 140 U.S.P.Q. 500 (6th Cir. 1964).

406 *A. C. Aukerman Co. v. R. L. Chaides Construction Co.*, 960 F.2d 1020, 22 U.S.P.Q. 2d 1321 (Fed. Cir. 1992) (*en banc*).

by a party. In contrast, equitable estoppel is based on misleading conduct by the patent owner and reliance on the misrepresentation by the alleged infringer. Both doctrines require the patent owner's knowledge of the alleged infringer's activities. This requirement is met when the patent owner should have known of such activities through the exercise of due diligence.[407] The delay period for establishing laches accrues from the time that the patent owner found or should have found the infringement. Only a misleading statement or conduct with knowledge of the infringement gives rise to estoppel.

A six-year unexcused delay gives rise to a presumption of laches although courts may find laches even if the delay is less than six years.[408] This presumption shifts the burden of proof for justifying the delay to the patent owner, who should then establish adequate excuses. Such excuses include (1) the patent owner's engagement in other litigations if the patent owner gave specific notice to the infringer about those other litigations;[409] (2) the patent owner's engagement in settlement or licensing negotiations with other parties;[410] and (3) the patent owner's poverty and illness.[411] In addition to the delay, the defendant must establish either evidentiary prejudice (death of critical witnesses, the loss of documents, or economic prejudice such as the loss of monetary investments). **7.131**

Misleading conduct giving rise to an estoppel includes both affirmative statements and conduct as well as silence when the patentee's conduct creates a duty to speak.[412] Such a duty arises when the patent owner threatens to sue an alleged infringer and the alleged infringer can reasonably infer from the owner's silence that the owner waived her patent right.[413] Moreover, the alleged infringer must establish that she substantially relied on the patent owner's misleading conduct in connection with taking some action.[414] **7.132**

(g) Marking and Notice

The US patent statute provides a time limitation for recovering damages with respect to infringement committed more than six years prior to the filing of a complaint or counterclaim for infringement.[415] The statute also prevents the recovery of damages if the patent owner does not adequately mark patented products and give notice of the patent to the public.[416] The duty of patent marking applies to all patent owners as well as any person who is making or selling patented products under the authority of the patent owner. It is necessary for a patent owner to take reasonable measures to meet the marking requirement when it sells patented products through licensees. When a patented product is sold **7.133**

---

407 Ibid.

408 Ibid.

409 *Studiengesellschaft Kohle v. Eastman Kodak Co.*, 616 F.2d 1315, 206 U.S.P.Q. 577 (5th Cir. 1980). However, courts may not find an adequate excuse if a patent owner has the resources to maintain multiple infringement litigations against different infringers. *Technical, Inc. v. Memorex Corp.*, 376 F. Supp. 828, 183 U.S.P.Q. 91 (N.D. Ill. 1974).

410 *Giese v. Pierce Chemical Co.*, 29 F. Supp. 2d 33, 40, 49 U.S.P.Q. 2d 1498, 1504 (D. Mass. 1998).

411 *Leggett v. Standard Oil Co.*, 149 U.S. 287 (1893). However, the inability to obtain contingency fee counsel was found not to constitute an adequate excuse. *Hall v. Aqua Queen Manufacturing Inc.*, 93 F.3d 1548, 39 U.S.P.Q. 2d 1925 (Fed. Cir. 1996).

412 *A. C. Aukerman Co.*, 960 F.2d, 1042; *Meyers v. Asics Corp.*, 974 F.2d 1304, 24 U.S.P.Q. 2d 1036 (Fed. Cir. 1992).

413 *Scholle Corp. v. Blackhawk Molding Co.*, 133 F.3d 1469, 45 U.S.P.Q. 2d 1468 (Fed. Cir. 1998).

414 *A. C. Aukerman Co*, 960 F.2d, 1042–43.

415 35 U.S.C. § 286.

416 Ibid. § 287.

without adequate marking, the patent owner can only recover the damages resulting from the infringement that occurred after the infringer received notice of the patent infringement including the filing of the lawsuit.

7.134 The marking duty applies only if a patent owner sells the patented products directly or through licensees. If the patent owner does not sell any patented products or the patent asserted is directed to a process, no marking duty applies to the owner.[417] An adequate marking should include the word "patent" or "pat." with the patent number(s) and be fixed on the patented product in a legible manner.[418] A patent owner can choose to place "pat." with an Internet address for a website that posts the patent number(s). If the nature of the product makes it impossible to place a marking on the product, the marking can be fixed on the package or a label.

7.135 The patent statute prohibits false patent markings and false patent pending markings when no US patent covering the product has been issued or no patent application covering the product is pending at the USPTO.[419] The AIA revised the false marking statute to make sure that a patent owner is not liable for a violation of the false marking prohibition when a patent marking remains on a patented product after the expiration of its patent.[420]

(h) Exhaustion

7.136 An alleged infringer can raise the defense of patent exhaustion when a patented product is sold under the authority of the patent owner with no restrictions on the sales.[421] The basis of this defense is that an authorized sale of a patented product exhausts the patent owner's monopoly because the purpose of the patent law is fulfilled with respect to the particular product when the patent owner receives its reward by the sale of the article.[422] The exhaustion doctrine applies to self-replicating inventions such as genetically modified animals, plants, and seeds.[423]

7.137 In the United States, the exhaustion doctrine is also called the "first sale doctrine" and is intertwined with the implied license theory. The basis of the implied license theory is that an implied license to use or sell a patented product or to use a patented process arises when the patent owner sells the product without any express restrictions.[424] If the alleged infringer's defense is based on the implied license theory, a patent owner can prevent exhaustion by placing an express restriction on the use or sale of the patented product after the product has been sold under the authority of the patentee. Because the US defense is intertwined between the exhaustion doctrine and the implied license theory, it is not clear whether an express restriction on the sale of a patented product can preclude the defense of exhaustion. Federal Circuit case law supports the preclusion of the defense of exhaustion by an express

[417] Ibid. § 287(a). For a general discussion, J. M. Markarian, "Can the Marking Requirements for a Patented Article be Circumvented by Obtaining a Process Patent?" *79 J. Pat. & Trademark Off. Soc'y* (1997): 365.

[418] *Trussell Mfg. Co. v. Wilson-Jones Co.*, 50 F.2d 1027, 10 U.S.P.Q. 47 (2d Cir. 1931).

[419] 35 U.S.C. § 292.

[420] Ibid. § 292(c).

[421] *Quanta Computer, Inc. v. LG Electronics, Inc.*, 553 U.S. 617 (2008).

[422] *United States v. Univis Lens Co.*, 316 U.S. 241, 53 U.S.P.Q. 404 (1942).

[423] *Bowman v. Monsanto Co.*, 133 S. Ct. 1761 (2013).

[424] *Adams v. Burke*, 84 U.S. (17 Wall.) 453 (1873).

restriction.[425] In *Quanta Computer* (2008), the US Supreme Court found no infringement on the basis of the exhaustion doctrine, instead of the implied license theory, when a product that substantially embodies a patented invention is legally sold by a licensee of the patent owner.[426] In *Bowman v. Monsanto* (2013), the US Supreme Court suggested that an express restriction plays a role in precluding exhaustion although the Court made it clear that it was not squarely addressing a case where no express restrictions are imposed on the sales of the patented product.[427]

To raise the defense of exhaustion, an alleged infringer must establish that the patented product alleged to infringe the patentee's patent was sold in the United States under the authority of the patentee.[428] An authorized sale of a product also exhausts a product or process patent when the product substantially embodies the product patent or the exclusive use of the product is covered by the process patent.[429] There is no Supreme Court precedent squarely addressing whether the sale of a patented product outside the United States exhausts the patent covering the product. In *Kirtsaeng* (2013), the US Supreme Court applied the exhaustion of copyright internationally by upholding the defense when a copyrighted book was sold outside the United States.[430] The Court's analysis focused on the interpretation of specific language in the copyright statute and did not discuss patent exhaustion. It is unlikely that *Kirsaeng* will have a significant influence on the patent exhaustion doctrine because the patent statute does not include any language comparable to the copyright statute. **7.138**

The defense of patent exhaustion applies only to particular patented products that are legally sold. The patent exhaustion doctrine does not diminish the patent owner right's to make a patented product.[431] Accordingly, the owner of a patented product is prohibited from reconstructing the product, which is an impermissible act of making, although the owner is entitled to repair the product, which is a permissible act of using.[432] Supreme Court precedents support the expansive scope with respect to the owner of the patented product's right to repair.[433] Thus, US courts are reluctant to find infringement unless the replacement or modification of components is viewed as a true construction of the patented product so as to give rise to an entirely new product. Courts found permissible repair with respect to the replacement of worn or broken components[434] and the modification of an ink cartridge so that it may be refilled.[435] **7.139**

---

425 *Quanta Computer, Inc. v. LG Electronics, Inc.*, 553 U.S. 617 (2008).

426 *Mallinckrodt, Inc. v. Medipart, Inc.*, 976 F.2d 700 (Fed. Cir. 1992).

427 *Bowman*, 133 S. Ct. 1767, FN 3.

428 *Jazz Photo Corp. v. Int'l Trade Comm'n*, 264 F.3d 1094, 1110–11 (Fed. Cir. 2001); *Fuji Photo Film Co., Ltd. v. Jazz Photo Corp.*, 394 F.3d 1368 (Fed. Cir. 2005); *Fujifilm Corp. v. Benun*, 605 F.3d 1366, 2010 U.S. App. LEXIS 10827 (Fed. Cir. 2010).

429 *Quanta Computer, Inc. v. LG Electronics, Inc.*, 553 U.S. 617 (2008).

430 *Kirtsaeng v. John Wiley & Sons, Inc.*, 133 S. Ct. 1351 (2013).

431 *Bowman*, 133 S. Ct.,1768.

432 *Aro Mfg. Co. v. Convertible Top Replacement Co.*, 365 U.S. 336, 346, 128 U.S.P.Q. 354, 359 (1961); *Jazz Photo Corp. v. US Int'l Trade Comm'n*, 264 F.3d 1094, 1105, 59 U.S.P.Q. 2d 1907 (Fed. Cir. 2001).

433 *Aro Mfg. Co.*, 365 U.S., 364.

434 *Wilbur Ellis Co. v. Kuther*, 377 U.S. 422, 141 U.S.P.Q. 703 (1964); *Universal Electronics, Inc. v. Zenith Electronics Corp.*, 846 F. Supp. 641, 30 U.S.P.Q. 2d 1853 (N.D. Ill. 1994).

435 *Hewlett-Packard Co. v. Repeat-O-Type Stencil Manufacturing Corp., Inc.*, 123 F.3d 1445, 43 U.S.P.Q. 2d 1650 (Fed. Cir. 1997).

(i) Employee Inventions: Shop Rights

7.140 The employer of an inventor may receive a non-exclusive, non-transferable, personal license termed a "shop right" and can assert a defense if the inventor or her successors in title obtain a patent and charge the employer with infringement. In the United States, the ownership of an invention is originally vested in the inventor.[436] The US Supreme Court makes it clear that mere employment is not sufficient to transfer the ownership of an employee invention to the employer.[437] In general, the ownership of an invention belongs to the inventor and does not transfer to the employer unless the inventor expressly agrees to assign the invention.[438]

7.141 Unlike German employers, US employers are not provided with any mechanisms, by operation of law, for securing the ownership of an invention from their employee-inventors.[439] To secure ownership, employers execute a pre-invention assignment agreement as part of an employment contract, which creates a duty for employee-inventors to transfer their inventions once the invention is complete. The validity and enforceability of this agreement is controlled by state contract law.[440]

7.142 If an employer fails to execute a pre-invention assignment agreement and the employee-inventor refuses to assign the invention, common law rules provide some rights to the employer if (1) the employee was specially hired to make the particular invention (the specially hired to invent doctrine), or (2) the employee was hired to make inventions in general (the hired to invent in general doctrine).[441] The former gives rise to a duty of assignment based on the contract hiring the inventor to invent a particular subject matter.[442] Therefore, an employer secures the ownership of an employee invention under this implied license theory.

7.143 The latter gives rise to a shop right.[443] US courts rely on three distinct bases, alternatively or in combination, to support the shop right doctrine: (1) the implied license theory, (2) estoppel, and (3) equity and fairness.[444] Depending on which bases the courts rely on, a shop right arises when an employee (1) develops an invention during work hours for which the employee is compensated, (2) uses the facilities of the employer and the time of co-employees to reduce the invention to practice, or (3) allows the employer to use the invention. Courts may view the shop right doctrine as being a part of general equitable principles and may find a shop right outside of the employment relationship.[445] Whether an employee's conduct gives rise

---

436 *Stanford*, 180 L. Ed. 2d., 12. *Gayler v. Wilder*, 51 U.S. 477, 10 How. 477, 493, 13 L. Ed. 504)(1851); *Solomons v. United States*, 137 U.S. 342, 346, 11 S. Ct. 88, 34 L. Ed. 667, 26 Ct. Cl. 620 (1980); *Beach Aircraft Corp. v. EDO Corp.*, 990 F.2d 1237, 26 U.S.P.Q. 2d 1572 (Fed. Cir. 1248).

437 *Stanford*, 180 L. Ed. 2d., 14.

438 Ibid. 12.

439 For a comparative study of employee invention systems, see Toshiko Takenaka (ed.), *Employee Invention System: A Comparative Law Perspective*, Intellectual Property Systems in Common Law and Civil Law (2013), 365.

440 For more discussion about the ownership of employee inventions under the US Patent Act, see Toshiko Takenaka, "Serious Flaw of Employee Invention Ownership under the Bayh-Dole Act in *Stanford v. Roche*: Finding the Missing Piece of the Puzzle in the German Employee Invention Act," 12 *Texas Intellectual Property L.J.* (2012): 281.

441 *Chisum on Patents*, § 22.03[2][3].

442 *Standard Parts Co. v. Peck*, 264 U.S. 52 (1924).

443 *McClurg v. Kingslund*, 42 U.S. (1 How.) 202, 11 L. Ed. 102 (1843).

444 *Chisum on Patents*, § 22.03[3][a].

445 *McElmurry v. Arkansas Power & Light Co.*, 995 F.2d 1576, 1578, 27 U.S.P.Q. 2d 1129, 1131 (Fed. Cir. 1993); *Francklyn v. Guilford Packing Co.*, 695 F.2d 1158, 1160–61, 217 U.S.P.Q. 317, 319 (9th Cir. 1983).

to a shop right is fact-specific, and facts surrounding the employee-employer relationship are evaluated in the context of one or more bases supporting the shop right doctrine. The Federal Circuit upheld the shop right defense when an inventor used the alleged infringer's facility to develop the invention covered by the asserted patent, the inventor and his assignor admitted that the defendant would have shop rights, and the inventor and his assignor acquiesced in the defendant's continued use of the invention.[446]

A shop right is personal and cannot be assigned unless the right is transferred in connection with a sale or merger of the business that the shop right is originally attached to.[447] An employer who holds a shop right cannot grant licenses.[448] A shop right is non-exclusive and will exist until the expiration of the patent.[449] The scope of a shop right may vary depending on the basis that the court relies on to support the shop right doctrine. Because all three bases relate to equitable principles, the scope of shop rights depends on the facts and circumstances of each case. Such facts include the nature of the invention and the circumstances that give rise to an implied license.[450] **7.144**

(j) Licenses

A party can raise an express or implied license as a defense against a claim of infringement. A license is created when a patent owner grants a third party the right to engage in acts that would constitute infringement without the authority of the owner.[451] A patent owner's promise not to sue a party also creates a license because a non-exclusive patent license is equivalent to a covenant not to sue.[452] Thus, the doctrine of patent exhaustion applies to a patented product that was sold by a party after the patent owner agreed to an unconditional covenant not to sue the party. **7.145**

Under the US patent statute, a joint inventor can assign her right to a patent and grant a license to a third party without consent from the other joint inventors. If an allegedly infringing defendant obtained a license from a joint inventor or her assignor, an infringement lawsuit filed by the other joint inventors and their assignors would be dismissed for failure to secure consent from the joint inventor or her assignor to bring the lawsuit.[453] It is unclear whether a joint inventor or her assignor can grant a license retroactively because no case has yet squarely addressed the issue. **7.146**

An implied license arises when a patent owner sells a component designed to be used in constructing a patented product or a device designed to carry out a patented process. Under Federal Circuit case law, an allegedly infringing defendant must establish that (1) a component or device sold under the authority of the patentee has no infringing use other than the making of a patented product or the carrying out of a patented process; and (2) the **7.147**

---

[446] *McElmurry v. Arkansas Power & Light Co.*, 995 F.2d 1576, 27 U.S.P.Q. 2d 1129 (Fed. Cir. 1993).

[447] *Lane & Bodley Co. v. Locke*, 150 U.S. 193 (1893); *Gonnocci Trust v. Three M Tool & Machine, Inc.*, 2006 U.S. Dist. LEXIS 21534 (E.D. Mich. 2006).

[448] *Tripp v. United States*, 406 F.2d 1066, 1070, 186 Ct. Cl. 872, 157 U.S.P.Q. 90, 161 U.S.P.Q. 115 (1969).

[449] *Wiegand v. Dover Mfg. Co.*, 292 F. 255 (N.D. Ohio 1923).

[450] *Gonnocci Trust v. Three M Tool & Machine, Inc.*, 2006 U.S. Dist. LEXIS 38871 (E.D. Mich. 2006).

[451] *Transcore, LP v. Electronic Transaction Consultants Corp.*, 563 F.3d 1271 (Fed. Cir. 2009). For more discussion of ownership, see Ch. 7, 7.80 "Originality—Inventorship."

[452] *Transcore, LP*, 1275.

[453] *Ethicon, Inc. v. United States Surgical Corp.*, 135 F.3d 1456, 45 U.S.P.Q. 2d 1545 (Fed. Cir. 1998).

circumstances of the sale plainly indicate that a grant of a license should be inferred.[454] Anyone who purchases a patented product or device must be notified at the time of sale of any express restrictions on the use of a component or a device.[455]

7.148 An implied license may arise from involuntary sales of goods such as the purchase of a patented machine through a judicial sale and a sale pursuant to a seller's right under commercial law.[456] An implied license may arise if a patent owner inexcusably fails to timely exercise the right to exclude others and thus authorizes the public to infringe the patent.[457] Such a delay in filing a lawsuit may give rise to laches and prevent not only the recovery of damages resulting from infringement that occurred prior to the filing of the lawsuit but also an injunction against the use of the patented product made and sold during the laches period through an implied license. An implied license may occur in the context of standard essential patents. When a patent owner urges firms to adopt the technology covered by its pending applications as an industry standard and persuades an allegedly infringing defendant to adopt the technology without disclosing the owner's efforts to secure patents on the technology, the defendant may assert a defense of implied license for continued use of the technology.[458]

7.149 Unlike the German and Japanese Patent Acts, the US Patent Act does not provide a compulsory license for dependent inventions.[459] The only compulsory licenses provided under the US Patent Act are the government's march-in rights which require research institutions to grant a license to a third party with respect to federally funded inventions under the Bayh-Dole Act.[460] A license may arise when the government exercises its march-in rights with respect to inventions resulting from research funded by the federal government when the contractor of the research fails to make sufficient efforts for commercializing the invention. Outside the patent statute, federal laws provide compulsory licenses.[461]

---

[454] *Met-Coil Systems Corp. v. Korners Unlimited, Inc.*, 803 F.2d 684, 686, 231 U.S.P.Q. 474, 476 (Fed. Cir. 1986).

[455] *Met-Coil Systems Corp. v. Korners Unlimited, Inc.*, 803 F.2d 684, 231 U.S.P.Q. 474 (Fed. Cir. 1986); *Devices for Medicine, Inc. v. Boehl*, 822 F.2d 1062, 1068, 3 U.S.P.Q. 2d 1288, 1293–94 (Fed. Cir. 1987).

[456] *McCoy v. Mitsuboshi Cutlery*, 67 F.3d 917, 36 U.S.P.Q. 2d 1289 (Fed. Cir. 1995).

[457] *Odetics Inc. v. Storage Technology Corp.*, 185 F.3d 1259, 1273, 51 U.S.P.Q. 2d 1225, 1234 (Fed. Cir. 1999).

[458] *Wang Laboratories, Inc. v. Mitsubishi Electronics America, Inc.*, 103 F.3d 1571, 41 U.S.P.Q. 2d 1263 (Fed. Cir. 1997).

[459] German Patent Act, §24; Japanese Patent Act, §72.

[460] 35 U.S.C. § 203.

[461] E.g., 7 U.S.C. § 2404 (patents necessary for the nation's food supply); 42 U.S.C. § 2183 (patents necessary for national atomic energy needs).

8

GERMANY

In Germany, the validity of a granted patent, registered utility model, or supplementary protection certificate can be attacked at any time during its lifetime, sometimes even retroactively. This holds true for both granted national German patents and the German parts of granted European patents. 8.01

Furthermore, the law provides a general presumption of validity for granted patents.[1] Therefore, German patents can be enforced in a litigation action in court even if they are currently undergoing (1) a parallel out-of-court invalidation procedure (opposition or limitation) or (2) a parallel nullity suit at the Federal Patent Court. 8.02

In general, the lack of validity of the patent as granted cannot be used as a defense during litigation (of note, as explained elsewhere in this book, preliminary injunction proceedings are an exception to this principle in that the validity of the patent-in-suit must be convincingly asserted to the court). This is because the German patent system features "bifurcation"—that is, the actions for patent infringement and the counterclaims in which the patent's validity are contested are not heard by the same court at the same time in the same proceedings but are instead dealt with separately by different courts. 8.03

This chapter will first introduce the different out-of-court invalidation procedures and the grounds for invalidation, and then discuss the nullity suits at the Federal Patent Court. The second half will be directed at the different defenses that can be raised during litigation proceedings. 8.04

A. Out-of-Court Invalidation Procedures

1. Opposition at the GPTO

According to the German Patent Act (PatG), within nine months from the grant of a patent, anyone (other than the patentee) can file an opposition against the grant of said patent.[2] 8.05

---

[1] The publication of the grant (German Patent Act, § 58(1)) has a constitutive effect and is binding on the administration and the courts according to Art. 20(3) of the German Constitution. Article 22(3) reads: "(3) Die Gesetzgebung ist an die verfassungsmäßige Ordnung, die vollziehende Gewalt und die Rechtsprechung sind an Gesetz und Recht gebunden." For case law on the infringement proceedings, see, e.g., BGH GRUR 2004, 710–712, IIC 2005, 459 "Druckmaschinen-Temperierungssystem." According to Art. 14 of the German Constitution, granted patents enjoy the protection of the guarantee of ownership under constitutional law. Article 41(4) Draft EPLA, states: "The Court of First Instance shall treat the European patent as valid unless its validity is contested by the defendant."

[2] Patentgesetz (Pat G) (Patent Act), § 59(I). The most recent revision, which became effective in 2014, extended the opposition period from three months to nine months.

When there is derivation of a patent, only the actual inventor can file an opposition. Filing an opposition using a strawman is possible. The opposition has to be filed in writing and can only be based on the limited set of grounds listed in German Patent Act, § 21.[3] With the exception of derivation, it is generally possible to raise additional grounds for opposition after the expiration of the opposition period.

8.06 The opposition has to be filed in German.[4] An opposition fee (currently €200) has to be paid.[5] Despite some changes in the law in order to make electronic communication easier, the opposition writ still has to be signed by the opponent or the opponent's representative.[6] Electronic filing is possible. Representation is required if the opponent is not a German resident or does not have a seat of business in Germany.[7]

8.07 The opposition will be handled and decided by a three-member opposition division at the German Patent and Trademark Office (GPTO).[8] The division may include an additional legal member.[9] The division may be assisted by experts, but the experts will not be involved in the decision process.

8.08 After an opposition is filed, the opposition division will check for its admissibility. If the opposition is found admissible, the opposition writ is forwarded to the patentee for comments, and a response period is set (usually three months).[10] Following a response by the patentee (after which further comments may be filed by the parties), the parties are summoned to oral proceedings.[11] The opposition division may present a preliminary opinion (in particular, when new issues come up that have to be discussed).[12] The preliminary opinion does not have to be extensive, and the opposition division may only briefly mention the most important issues to be touched upon. Objections based on the late filing of documents are possible.[13]

8.09 A nullity suit cannot be filed during the opposition period or as long as an opposition is pending.[14] Similarly, a nullity suit for a supplementary protection certificate is blocked as long as a request for correction is pending.[15] In order to be able to attack a patent that is otherwise enforceable in court, an accused infringer can join the opposition proceedings even after the expiry of the opposition period.[16] This also holds true even if the accused infringer instituted proceedings for a ruling of non-infringement.[17] In these cases, a three-month period has to be observed for joining the opposition proceedings.[18]

---

[3] For further discussion see Ch. 8, 8.63.
[4] German Patent Act, § 126.
[5] German Act regarding patenting costs (PatKostG) §§ 3(1), 2(1) and schedule of official fees No. 313 600.
[6] German Patent Act, § 126, § 126a BGB, BGH GRUR 1967, 586 "*Rohrhalterung.*"
[7] German Patent Act, § 25(1).
[8] German Patent Act, § 27.
[9] German Patent Act, § 27.
[10] Einspruchsrichtlinien (2007) (currently under revision) (http://www.dpma.de/docs/service/formulare/patent/2/p2797.pdf).
[11] Ibid.
[12] Ibid.
[13] Ibid.
[14] German Patent Act, § 81(2).
[15] German Patent Act, § 49a(4).
[16] German Patent Act, § 59(2).
[17] Ibid.
[18] German Patent Act, § 59(2).

During an opposition, third parties can file observations, which may even include alleged prior public uses of the invention.[19] Nevertheless, these third parties do not become parties to the proceedings, and the handling of their observations is under the discretion of the opposition division. **8.10**

When there is a decision finding the derivation of a patent from a true inventor, the patent is revoked.[20] The actual inventor can then file a new application and claim the priority of the earlier patent.[21] The opposition proceedings, including the procedings regarding derivation, are controlled by the "Guidelines for the Opposition Proceedings at the GPTO."[22] **8.11**

The withdrawal of the opposition by the opponent terminates the opponent's position as a party to the proceedings, but it does not terminate the opposition procedure as such. The proceedings will be continued by the GPTO, and a decision will be issued.[23] **8.12**

Decisions of the opposition division can be appealed in the second instance to the Technical Boards at the Federal Patent Court.[24] In contrast to the GPTO, the Federal Patent Court cannot introduce new grounds for opposition and is bound by the requests of the parties.[25] Nevertheless, if the patentee files amended claims during appeal, this may result in the necessity to examine additional grounds for opposition.[26] The appeal has to be filed within a month from the receipt of the relevant decision (grounds can be filed later), and a fixed appeal fee has to be paid (currently €500[27]). Oral proceedings are held at the Federal Patent Court in Munich. **8.13**

The appeal proceedings at the Federal Patent Court are controlled by §§ 73–80 of the German Patent Act and the rules as applicable in regular civil proceedings.[28] **8.14**

Similar to the first instance procedure, an accused infringer can join the proceedings and can actually introduce new grounds for opposition.[29] Also, observations of third parties can be filed during the appeal stage.[30] **8.15**

The Federal Patent Court is normally the court of final instance on the substantial issues in opposition cases. In the rare cases where there are diverging decisions or legal issues to be decided further, the Federal Patent Court may allow an appeal to the BGH on the points of law ("revision"). Depending on the case, the court can also remit the proceedings back to the GPTO. **8.16**

In proceedings at the GPTO, each party usually bears its own costs. In proceedings at the Federal Patent Court, irrespective of who initiated the proceedings, the losing party **8.17**

---

[19] German Patent Act, § 43(3) or Art. 115 EPC.

[20] German Patent Act, § 21(1) No. 3.

[21] German Patent Act, § 7(2).

[22] Einspruchsrichtlinien (2007) (currently under revision) (http://www.dpma.de/docs/service/formulare/patent/2/p2797.pdf).

[23] German Patent Act, § 61(1).

[24] German Patent Act, § 73.

[25] BGH, decision of January 10, 1995—X ZB 11/92, *Aluminium-Trihydroxid.*

[26] BGH, decision of 03.02.1998—X ZB 6/97, *Polymermasse.*

[27] German Act regarding patenting costs § 2(1) and schedule of official fees No. 401 100.

[28] German code of civil procedure (ZPO) § 567 ff. (See also BGH GRUR 1969, 562—*Appreturmittel.*)

[29] BPatG, decision of 28.08.2006, 9 W (pat) 16/04—*Antriebsvorrichtung*; BGH GRUR 1994, 892—*Heizkörperkonsole.*

[30] German Patent Act, § 43(3).

will have to bear the costs. In 2012, oppositions were filed against approximately 4 percent of all granted German patents.[31] About 25 percent of these opposed patents were revoked, and 50 percent were amended or fully upheld (the rest were lapsed, settled, etc.).[32]

2. Opposition at the EPO

8.18 Although one would assume that the opposition procedures at the EPO and the national patent offices should be identical (i.e., harmonized), this is not fully the case, and they differ both in some of the formal as well as material requirements.[33]

8.19 Within nine months from the grant of a European patent, anyone (other than the patentee) can file an opposition against the grant of said patent.[34] Parties that are interested in the revocation of a patent can use a strawman in order to hide their identity.[35] The opposition has to be filed in writing and can only be based on the limited set of grounds as listed in the EPC, as will be discussed in more detail below.[36] It is possible to raise additional grounds for opposition after the expiry of the opposition period if the patentee presents new claims or if the patentee agrees to the introduction. The responsible opposition division at the EPO may allow new grounds as well.[37] Unlike the opposition at the GPTO, derivation is not a ground for opposition. The ownership of a European patent application is not checked by the EPO and cannot be challenged at the EPO. For this, national proceedings have to be initiated. If a third party provides proof to the EPO that he has opened proceedings against the applicant for the purpose of seeking a judgement that he is entitled to the grant of the European patent, the EPO will stay the proceedings for grant unless the third party communicates to the EPO in writing his consent to the continuation of such proceedings.[38]

8.20 The opposition has to be filed in English, German, or French (there are limited exceptions with respect to the language only for filing of the writ), and an opposition fee (currently €745) has to be paid. Electronic filing is possible. Representation is required if the opponent is not an EPC national or resident or if the opponent does not have a seat of business in one of the EPC member states.[39] In contrast to the German procedure, a missing signature on the opposition is an omission that can be rectified later.

8.21 The opposition will be handled and decided by the three-member opposition division at the EPO. After an opposition is filed, the opposition division will first check its admissibility. If the opposition is found admissible, the writ is then forwarded to the patentee for comments, and normally a response period of four months is set.[40] Following a response by the patentee (further comments may be filed by the parties), the parties are summoned to oral proceedings

---

[31] Art. 99 EPC.

[32] http://www.dpma.de/docs/service/veroeffentlichungen/jahresberichte/dpma_jahresbericht2012_barrierefrei.pdf.

[33] For further discussion see Ch. 8, 8.64.

[34] Art. 99 EPC.

[35] T 0022/09 (*Party status/Fischer-Tropsch Catalysts/SASOL TECHNOLOGY*) of June 21, 2013, OJ 2013, 582.

[36] Art. 100 EPC.

[37] See *Case Law of Boards of Appeal at the EPO* (7th ed., 2013), Ch. IV. D.5.3.

[38] Rule 14(1) EPC; see also, e.g., J 0015/13 (*Resumption of Proceedings for Grant*) of May 9, 2014, unpublished.

[39] Art. 133(2) EPC.

[40] Rule 79 EPC.

(if requested by one of the parties or even the EPO examiners).[41] The summons includes a preliminary opinion by the opposition division, and final comments and amendments can be filed until the fixed date (usually one month before the oral proceedings) set by the opposition division.[42] Objections against the late filing of documents are possible and are becoming more and more popular in the proceedings at the EPO. According to the decisions G 9/91 and G 10/91,[43] in principle, the opposition is to be examined only to the extent and on the grounds submitted during the period for opposition. The principles developed by the Enlarged Board with respect to new grounds also apply to late-filed facts and evidence. Thus, a document can only be filed late if it is *prima facie* relevant or if there is a reasonable excuse as to why it could not have been filed earlier, for example, in cases of substantial amendments made by the patentee.[44] Unfortunately, the actual handling of late filings can be quite different between different opposition divisions. Oral proceedings are held in Munich, The Hague, or (rarely) Berlin.

Since German Patent Act, § 81(2) is also applicable to the German parts of European **8.22** patents,[45] a German nullity suit cannot be filed during the European opposition period, a pending opposition, or an appeal. In order to provide the means to attack a patent that is otherwise enforceable in German courts, the accused infringer can join the opposition proceedings even after the expiration of the opposition period.[46] This also holds true even if the accused infringer instituted proceedings for a declaratory judgment action for non-infringement. In these cases, a three-month period has to be observed (i.e., a period shorter than the opposition period itself), and the opposition fee has to be paid.[47] The blocking of nullity suits at the Federal Patent Court by a pending opposition is a unique feature of German validity challenge proceedings (this feature actually does not relate to the bifurcated system) and is not harmonized with the rest of Europe. In cases of a pending opposition at the EPO, the effect of the proceedings on a parallel infringement case may be a stay of the main proceedings, sometimes even until a final decision has been reached by the EPO, but in most cases the courts will continue the proceedings notwithstanding the opposition.[48] This can lead to situations where the validity of a patent is challenged, in parallel, both in court and at the EPO (of course, this does not apply to Germany).

Additional differences between the German and European opposition procedures include **8.23** the following:

1. For an opposition after the expiry of a patent to be admissible in Germany, the opponent is required to have a legal interest in the revocation of the patent; nevertheless, Article 99(3) of the EPC does not require this.

---

[41] Rule 81 EPC and Art. 116 EPC.

[42] Rule 116(1) EPC.

[43] OJ EPO 1993, 408, 420.

[44] T 1002/92 (*Queueing system*) of July 6, 1994 (unpublished), and Guidelines for Examination at the EPO, ch. E.V.2.1.

[45] BGH, decision of July 12, 2005 —X ZR 29/05 *Strahlungssteuerung* GRUR 2005, 967.

[46] Art. 105 EPC.

[47] Rule 89 EPC.

[48] Malwina Mejer and Bruno van Pottelsberghe de la Potterie, "Economic Incongruities in the European Patent System", ECARES working paper 2009–003, January 2009 (https://dipot.ulb.ac.be/dspace/bitstream/2013/54115/1/RePEc_eca_wpaper_2009_003.pdf), and "International Patent Litigation Guide 2013" (http://www.cmslegal.com/relatedsites/patentswithoutborders/Documents/CMS-International-Patent-Litigation-Guide-2013.PDF).

2. At the GPTO, an opposition can be regarded as inadmissible based on a non-attack agreement (or clause) between the parties (if the non-attack agreement or clause is admissible under § 2(2) of the GWB[49] or Article 101 of the TFEU[50]); nevertheless, there are diverging opinions on this issue. At the EPO, non-attack agreements (again, if admissible as above) are not taken into account.[51]
3. At the EPO, an accused infringer who joins the appeal proceedings cannot raise new grounds for opposition;[52] this limitation does not apply to German proceedings.
4. An objection based on a late filing is possible during an opposition at the GPTO, but the opposition division always has to examine the relevance of the new documents.[53] The same holds true in the appeal phase. At the EPO, documents and also requests can be rejected as late filed.[54]
5. In contrast to the German proceedings, Article 117 of the EPC allows sworn statements in writing to be submitted as evidence.
6. The withdrawal of the opposition in the first instance at the GPTO will not end the proceedings, and a decision will be issued. At the EPO, the proceedings can be closed even without a decision. The same essentially holds true for the second instance.

8.24 Overall, about 4.5 percent of granted European patents are opposed.[55] The opposition rate before the EPO is consistently higher in the pharmaceutical sector than it is in the organic chemistry sector or in all the sectors combined (overall EPO average).[56] The costs for an opposition are rather low and usually vary between about €6,000 and €50,000 (including attorneys' fees). Many opposition cases are finalized within two years, but there is a long tail in the data. Overall, the mean is four years, and the median is about 3.5 years.[57]

8.25 Decisions of the opposition division can be appealed, and the appeals are handled in the second instance by the Boards of Appeal at the EPO. In contrast to the proceedings in the first instance, the Boards cannot introduce new grounds for opposition and are bound by the requests of the parties.[58] Notice of an appeal has to be filed within two months from the receipt of the relevant decision.[59] The notice is not deemed to be filed until a fixed appeal fee (currently €1240) is paid.[60] Grounds for appeal have to be filed within four months from the notification of the decision.[61] If requested, oral proceedings will be held at the EPO and will take place exclusively in Munich. Similar to the first instance, the accused infringer can join

[49] Gesetz gegen Wettbewerbsbeschränkungen (Kartellgesetz, GWB), republished on June 26, 2013 (BGBl. I S. 1750) last amended on July 21, 2014 (BGBl. I S. 1066).

[50] Treaty on European Union and Treaty on the Functioning of the European Union (TFEU); Official Journal of the European Union, C 115, May 9, 2008.

[51] OJ EPO 1992, 747—*No-Challenge Obligation*; and G 03/97 OJ EPO 1999, 245.

[52] See G 3/04 OJ EPO 2006, 118.

[53] BGH BlPMZ 1977, 277—*Gleichstromfernspeisung*.

[54] Art. 114(2) EPC.

[55] EPO statistics for 2012 (http://www.epo.org/about-us/annual-reports-statistics/annual-report/2012/statistics-trends/review.html).

[56] Ibid.

[57] Ibid.

[58] G 9/91, G 10/91, OJ EPO 1993, 408, 420.

[59] Art. 108 EPC.

[60] http://www.epoline.org/portal/portal/default/epoline.Scheduleoffees.

[61] Art. 108 EPC.

the proceedings but cannot introduce new grounds for opposition.[62] Also, the observations of third parties can be filed.[63]

The appeal proceedings at the Boards of Appeal are controlled by the Rules of Procedure of the Boards of Appeal (RPBA).[64] Under the RPBA, appeal proceedings shall generally be based on the notice of appeal and the statement of grounds for appeal filed as well as any written replies by the other party, any communications sent by the Board, and any answers thereto filed pursuant to the directions of the Board.[65] Any amendments to a party's case after the party has filed its grounds for appeal or its reply may be admitted and considered at the Board's discretion.[66] The discretion shall be exercised in view of, *inter alia*, the complexity of the new subject matter submitted, the current state of the proceedings, and the need for procedural economy.[67] Amendments that are submitted after the oral proceedings have been arranged shall not be admitted if they give rise to issues that the Board or the other party or parties cannot reasonably be expected to deal with without postponement of the oral proceedings.[68] Finally, it is unlikely for the Board to consider new submissions that should have been presented in the first instance proceedings.[69] **8.26**

These rules show the quite limited possibilities of amending a case that is pending in front of the Boards of Appeal. Therefore, it is important to file a complete case as soon as possible in order to avoid problems with late filing. **8.27**

In principle, each party bears its own costs for the appeal proceedings. The RPBA provides an exception to this rule and allows the Board to order a party to pay some or all of another party's costs, for example, in cases where there is an abuse of the procedure.[70] **8.28**

In the rare case where there are diverging decisions or legal problems, the Board may refer a question to the Enlarged Board of Appeals.[71] In very limited instances, any party to appeal proceedings adversely affected by a decision of the Board of Appeal may file a petition for review of the decision by the Enlarged Board of Appeal.[72] Only a very few petitions have been successful.[73] Otherwise, the appeal is the final instance. **8.29**

3. Limitation Proceedings at the GPTO and EPO

Limitation proceedings shall provide a means for patentees to deliberately limit their patents after grant (there are no limitation proceedings for SPCs). The proceedings are comparable to the reissue procedure under the US Patent Act[74] and the correction trial under the Japanese Patent Act.[75] The EPC allows patentees to request that their European patents be **8.30**

---

[62] G 9/91, G 10/91, OJ EPO 1993, 408, 420.
[63] Ibid.
[64] European Patent Office, Rules of Procedure of the Board of Appeals of the European Patent Office (RPAB) (http://www.epo.org/law-practice/legal-texts/html/caselaw/2013/e/clr_rpba.htm#CLR_RPBA).
[65] Art. 12 RPBA.
[66] Art. 13(1) RPBA.
[67] Ibid.
[68] Art. 13(3) RPAB.
[69] Art. 12(4) RPAB.
[70] Art. 16 RPAB.
[71] Art. 112 EPC; Art. 22 RPAB.
[72] Art. 112a EPC.
[73] See http://www.epo.org/law-practice/case-law-appeals/eba/decisions-petitions.html.
[74] See Ch. 7, B.8.
[75] See Ch. 9, B.2.

limited or even revoked by an amendment of the claims.[76] In Germany, the German Patent Act also provides that a patent, at the request of the patentee, may be revoked or limited with retroactive effect.[77] The GPTO examines the request for limiting the claims and decides whether the request meets the requirements for limitation.[78] In the limitation proceedings, grounds for the request have to be provided if a ground for the limitation is not obvious from the state of the art. The art then also has to be included in the request for the limitation.[79] If the patent is limited, the patent specification is adapted to the limited claims[80] and the amendment of the patent specification is also published.[81]

8.31 The limitation cannot include an examination of the patentability of the newly filed claims.[82] The office only formally examines the amended claims for clarity and their limitation of the scope of protection.[83] Decisions of the GPTO can be appealed at the Federal Patent Court.[84]

8.32 At first sight, limitation proceedings seem to be counterintuitive. Nevertheless, the procedure can be used in order to avoid nullity suits and associated costs for the patentee, in particular after new *prima facie* relevant state of the art has been identified. In contrast to the situation at the EPO, limitation is not blocked by an opposition against the patent or if a nullity suit has already been filed. A fee has to be paid for the limitation (currently €120). In practice, the number of German national limitation proceedings is very low.[85] For the patentee, it is important to realize that the effect of a limitation is *ex tunc*—that is, effective retroactively from the beginning of the patent.

8.33 Similar limitation proceedings are available at the EPO.[86] The patent can be limited with effect for all member states, and a decision to limit the European patent will issue.[87] In contrast to the GPTO proceedings, patentees do not need to include a ground for the limitation in their request. A request for limitation may not be filed while opposition proceedings with respect to the European patent are pending.[88] Nevertheless, the EPO may examine a request for limitation even if a national (e.g., German) limitation procedure or a nullity suit involving the national part of a European patent is pending.[89]

8.34 The decision about the request can be appealed by filing an appeal.[90] As in Germany, limitation is not an opportunity to re-examine the whole patent;[91] only the amended claims are

---

[76] Art. 105a EPC.
[77] German Patent Act, § 64.
[78] German Patent Act, § 64(2) and (3).
[79] German Patent Act, § 64(2) and GPTO Mitt 1958, 57.
[80] The adapted description has to be provided by the patentee as part of the request that defines the scope of the proceedings, BGHZ 41, 13 = GRUR 1964, 308 "*Dosier-* und *Mischanlage.*"
[81] German Patent Act, § 64(3).
[82] Because of German Patent Act, § 64(1) and (3).
[83] Ibid.
[84] German Patent Act, § 73.
[85] Fourteen cases in 2011 (Alfred Keukenschrijver (ed.), *Busse, Patentgesetz* (7th ed., 2013), German Patent Act, § 64, marginal number 10).
[86] Art. 105a EPC.
[87] Art. 105b(3) EPC.
[88] Art. 105a(2) EPC.
[89] As there is no rule in the EPC prohibiting this.
[90] Art. 106 EPC.
[91] European Patent Office, The Guidelines for Examination (Nov. 2014 ed.), ch. H, IV 4.2 (http://documents.epo.org/projects/babylon/eponet.nsf/0/56911A5DDF284B55C1257D81005FA359/$FILE/guidelines_for_examination_2014_part_h_en.pdf).

to be examined with regard to the requirements for amendment under the EPC[92]—that is, what should be considered is whether the requested amendments introduce a deficiency within the meaning of these provisions. Claims as granted or as maintained should not be examined anew.

B. Court Invalidation Procedures

1. Handling of a Defense Based on Lack of Validity Raised in a German Infringement Court

There is no invalidity defense in Germany due to the separation of infringement and invalidity proceedings. However, upon raising the defense in court, a German infringement court may stay the infringement proceedings in view of a pending opposition or nullity action against the patent-in-suit. The decision to stay an infringement action is at the discretion of the court and is based on a balance of the patentee's and defendant's interests. A stay of proceedings is granted only when opposition or nullity proceedings are very likely to be successful. This may be the case if, for example, new prior art is presented that is novelty destroying.[93] In consequence, the stay of an infringement action in view of a pending opposition or nullity action is quite rare in Germany. **8.35**

2. Invalidity Litigation ("Nullity Suit") at the German Patent Court

In Germany, the nullity suit (or revocation action) can be seen as a post-opposition mechanism to invalidate granted patents and/or SPCs. Thus, the procedure is essentially the same for both granted German patents and the German national parts of European patents. Of note, the third Senate of the German Patent Court is responsible for the nullity procedures for supplementary protection certificates (SPCs). **8.36**

For the nullity of unitary patents (see above), it seems likely that since Article 33(3) of the UPC Agreement allows for bifurcation, technical judges of the German Patent Court will be involved in the vaidity proceedings for these patents, in particular as part of the court of first instance. As already mentioned, according to German Patent Act, § 81(2), a nullity suit cannot be filed during the opposition period or pending an opposition or appeal. **8.37**

The German nullity suit is a "true" court procedure and is concluded by a judgment. Thus, the procedural rules for German civil court proceedings are largely applicable,[94] together with the special rules in German Patent Act, §§ 81–84. Because of the nature of the proceedings, the losing party has to bear the costs of the proceedings, in contrast to opposition procedures, where usually each party has to bear its own costs. Since the German Patent Court has the status of an appellate court (hence the appeal to the Federal Court of Justice), both the court fees and attorneys' fees to be paid and/or reimbursed can be substantial, although usually these costs are still quite low compared to the United Kingdom or the United States. **8.38**

---

[92] Art. 84 EPC; Art. 123(2) and (3) EPC.

[93] OLG Düsseldorf, Decision of September 20, 2007, Az. 2 U 42/06—*Niederspannungs-Leistungsschalter III.*

[94] German code of civil procedure, ZPO.

8.39 The nullity suit has to be filed in writing and can only be based on the limited set of grounds listed in German Patent Act, § 22 (for German patents) or in Article 138 of the EPC (for the German parts of European patents), which are nearly identical to the grounds for opposition.

8.40 In brief, after a complaint is filed at the Federal Patent Court and is found formally admissible, the complaint is served to the patentee in order to comment thereon.[95] The court will set a period of one month for the patentee to respond.[96] If the patentee files a response and intends to defend the validity of the patent, parties will be summoned for oral proceedings. The court will usually issue a preliminary opinion in order to inform the parties about the issues that need to be discussed.[97]

8.41 Importantly, the Federal Patent Court may reject the introduction of new evidence and arguments, as well as auxiliary requests if a party submits them after the expiration of the time limit set by the court, if (1) consideration of the submission results in a delay in the hearing procedure, (2) the party provides sufficient grounds for the delay, or (3) the party is instructed as to the consequence of failing to meet the time limit.[98] Once excluded, an argument or a request will stay precluded, even on appeal.[99] This can only be "repaired" by filing a new suit. However, this option may lead to the worst-case scenario for the patentee—the court may find the patent invalid.

8.42 In *Bearbeitungsmaschine*,[100] the fourth Senate of the Federal Patent Court required a balance between the arguments provided by the plaintiff and the defendant. The court rejected the plaintiff's argument that the documents were found by chance and thus had to be filed late despite all due care, but ultimately admitted the document into the proceedings, so as not to lead to an unfair situation. In *Dichtungsring*,[101] the same Senate decided on whether the court should allow the submission of new documents that are filed after the expiration of the time limit set in the preliminary opinion with respect to whether the party provided a sufficient ground for delay according to the Patent Act.[102] The decision distinguished between an amendment based on the dependent claims and an amendment based on the specification. In *Dichtungsring*, the court allowed the plaintiff to submit new prior art documents because the plaintiff did not violate the objective degree of due diligence to search prior art in advance, as required in *Bearbeitungsmaschine*, since the plaintiff was not able to foresee the specification-amended claims. Nevertheless, for the defendant it is quite important to make sure that a proper defense of the patent is established as early as possible.

8.43 German Patent Act, § 83 was amended in 2009, when new procedural rules were introduced in order to streamline and accelerate nullity suits, in particular at the appellate level.[103] Here, quite important changes have been made to the basis on which appeals can

---

95 German Patent Act, § 82.

96 Ibid.

97 German Patent Act, § 83.

98 German Patent Act, § 83(4).

99 German Patent Act, § 117.

100 BPatG Nov. 8, 2012—Ni 43/10 (EP), GRUR 2013, 601.

101 BPatG Jan. 15, 2013—4 Ni 13/11 (http://www.bpatg.de//cms/media/Entscheidungen/Eilunterrichtungen/Nichtigkeitssenat/2013/04013_11.pdf).

102 German Patent Act, § 83(4).

103 Gesetz zur Vereinfachung und Modernisierung des Patentrechts vom 31. Juli 2009 (BGBl. I S. 2521) (http://www.bmj.de/SharedDocs/Downloads/DE/pdfs/Gesetz_Patentrecht.pdf?__blob=publicationFile).

be made in nullity suits. The appeal instance at the BGH in invalidation actions has mostly been limited to the scope of the first instance.[104] Thus, the BGH will only examine requests based on facts that the BGH will use as the basis for its hearing and the decision on the appeal pursuant (i.e., legal issues).

Despite these measures, today the average length of nullity suits (both at the first instance and at the appellate level) generally remains longer than the average length of German infringement actions. It remains to be seen whether this will change in the future. **8.44**

The statistics regarding the outcome of nullity proceedings in Germany are quite surprising and show an at least partial invalidation rate of 79.08 percent for all the Senates of the German Federal Patent Court in total.[105] Most of these decisions are confirmed by the Federal Court of Justice.[106] **8.45**

C. Patentability and Validity Challenges

This chapter analyzes the grounds that can be used to challenge the patentability and/or validity of national and European patents. Furthermore, other types of defenses that can be raised by a defendant in patent litigation are discussed. Although this chapter focuses primarily on the EPC and the national situation in Germany, comparisons will also be made with the UK, France, and the Netherlands.[107] **8.46**

Although it seems obvious that a harmonization regarding the scope and effect of validity challenges and defenses is of great importance in order to provide legal security to all parties involved in patent matters in Europe, an astonishing number of differences still exist in these issues, in particular between national patent laws and case law. **8.47**

In practice, this means that the patentee of a national (e.g., German or UK) patent has to fulfill the national patentability requirements during examination and, in cases of national opposition, is challenged based on this national standard. Nevertheless, in cases of European patents, the European standard for patentability is controlling, which in a subsequent national validity challenge is maintained but then "switches" to the national interpretation of the European law. **8.48**

In order to further harmonize the differences between, for example, the EPO, Germany, the Netherlands, and the United Kingdom, the case law as provided by the leading European IP judges has taken into account foreign views and arguments more and more.[108] Having said this, there is still a long way to go. **8.49**

In general, at least some of the patentability and/or validity challenges can be raised by an opposing party at nearly any time during the life of a patent: **8.50**

1. The patentability can be challenged by filing the observations of a third party after the publication of an application.

104 German Patent Act, § 116.
105 Peter Hess, Tilman Müller-Stoy, and Martin Wintermeier, "Sind Patente nur Papiertiger?" *Mitt.* (2014): 439.
106 Ibid.
107 See, e.g., http://www.innovaccess.eu/map.php for national differences in the EU.
108 See, e.g., http://archive.epo.org/epo/pubs/oj013/04_13/special_edition_1_judges_symposium.pdf.

2. The patentability/validity can be challenged in an opposition procedure after the grant of a patent.
3. The patentability/validity can be challenged in a nullity procedure in a separate court or during infringement proceedings (after grant).
4. The validity/enforceability can be challenged during the infringement proceedings (after grant) or brought forward in a declaratory non-infringement procedure.
5. The validity/enforceability can be challenged in separate court proceedings (independent from infringement).

8.51 All of these challenges have in common the fact that not every possible ground for a lack of validity/patentability or enforceability can be raised in each of the proceedings—that is, only a limited set of grounds is usually available, as will be explained below.

8.52 As mentioned, in Germany, and in Austria as well, the validity of granted patents cannot be challenged in the infringement court since the court is bound by the fact that granted patents and supplementary protection certificates are generally presumed valid.[109] Thus, arguments must be raised in a separate nullity suit at the German Patent Court, leading to the so-called "bifurcation" system. Of note, this should not be confused with the bifurcation in the handling of liability and damages by the infringement courts, which is common in many countries, including Germany, the United Kingdom, Canada, and Japan.

8.53 As explained elsewhere in this book, in cases of preliminary injunctions, the German courts are not bound by the validity of the underlying patent, and doubts as to the validity of the said patent play an essential role in the weighing of interests to be performed and regularly exclude the presence of grounds for an injunction.[110]

1. Challenges Regarding Patentability—Filing of Third-party Observations

8.54 Although it seems that discussing validity challenges during the examination of a patent application is not required when discussing the enforcement of (granted) patents, one must keep in mind that Article 67 of the EPC and § 33(1) of the PatG allow for the enforcement of patent applications. Starting from the publication date of the application, an applicant can demand compensation appropriate to the circumstances from a person who has used the subject matter of the application although he knew or should have known that the invention used by him was the subject matter of the application.[111] Nevertheless, additional claims shall not be permitted (i.e., there is no injunctive relief available). Although in practice these cases are always stayed until the grant of the relevant patent,[112] it may be reasonable to attack the application as early as possible, especially in view of a prospective threat based on a preliminary injunction directly after grant.

8.55 At the EPO, the filing of third-party observations is controlled by Article 115 of the EPC, which specifies that observations cannot be filed until after publication of the European patent application but sets no "upper" time limit for their presentation. This means that observations can be filed during opposition proceedings, even after the expiry of the

[109] See Ch. 8, 8.03.
[110] Court of Appeals Duesseldorf InstGE 9, 140—*Olanzapin*; InstGE 12, 114—*Harnkatheterset*.
[111] Art. 67 EPC.and German Patent Act, § 33.
[112] In particular, because of Art. 67(4) EPC.

opposition period, as well as during appeal proceedings and also in nullity and limitation proceedings. Similar (but by no means identical) rules can be found in many other national European patent laws as well as in the PCT Agreement.[113] In Germany, observations can be filed based on § 43(3) of the PatG, which states that any person shall be entitled to inform the GPTO of publications that might prejudice the grant of a patent.[114] Thus, the arguments of the third party are limited to publications, which usually excludes arguments on public prior use (unless that can be shown by the publications). All observations have to be filed in writing, and the third party will not become a party to the proceedings.

(a) Scope of the Validity Challenge: Observations

Article 115 of the EPC states that a third party may file observations concerning the patentability of the invention to which the application or patent relates. Some believe that this would restrict the observations to material reasons[115] and thus would exclude formal reasons. Nevertheless, the Guidelines for Examination at the EPO in chapter E.V.3 explicitly state that third-party observations may also be directed to clarity (under Article 84 of the EPC), sufficiency of disclosure (under Article 83 of the EPC), and unallowable amendments (under Articles 76(1) and 123(2) of the EPC).[116] Legally, this makes sense, since otherwise objections under Article 84 of the EPC could not be raised by the public at all, and any third party would have to wait until opposition in order to raise objections based on Article 83 of the EPC and/or Article 123(2) of the EPC. **8.56**

If the observations at the EPO refer to a source other than a document, such as prior use, these observations will usually only be taken into account if the alleged facts either are not disputed by the applicant or proprietor or are established beyond reasonable doubt. Observations by third parties received after the conclusion of the proceedings will not be taken into account and will simply be added to the non-public part of the file.[117] **8.57**

(b) Objections Based on a Lack of Clarity and/or Support (Article 84 EPC)

Article 84 of the EPC is not a ground for opposition, and therefore it can only be raised during the examination of the application at stake. Of note, once claims are amended, for example, during opposition proceedings (i.e., when substantive amendments are made), these amended claims have to fulfill all of the requirements of the EPC and therefore also Article 84 of the EPC. Recently, this issue has been looked at by the Enlarged Board of Appeal.[118] **8.58**

Article 84 of the EPC stipulates that the claims shall define the matter for which protection is sought. They shall be clear and concise and be supported by the description. Thus, two quite different main requirements can be found in Article 84 of the EPC, namely that (a) the claims define the matter to be protected in a clear manner (i.e., that it can be understood by the person of skill) and (b) the claims are "supported by the description." These requirements are **8.59**

[113] E.g., § 101b Austrian PatG; § 21 UK Patents Act; Art. L 612 French Patent Act; §§ 801–5 of the Administrative Instructions PCT.
[114] German Patent Act, § 43(3).
[115] Arts. 52–57 EPC.
[116] Guidelines for Examination at the EPO, Ch. E.V.3.
[117] Ibid.
[118] Decision of the Enlarged Board of Appeal of March 24, 2015, G3/14 (*Examination of clarity objections*).

similar to 35 U.S.C. § 112(b)[119] ("indefiniteness") and 35 U.S.C. § 112(a)[120] ("written description requirement"), respectively.

8.60 Whereas the issue of the actual clarity of the claims has not been the focus of many recent debates (claims must be clear in themselves and define the scope in a way that the person of skill can identify whether he is working inside or outside the scope),[121] the latter issue of support in the description has become an increasingly popular objection from examiners in the context of the "raising the bar" initiative of the EPO,[122] where broad claims were generally regarded as "weak" claims and usually had to be limited. Examiners started looking for "a basis in the description for the subject-matter of every claim" and raised an objection if "the scope of the claims [was] broader than [was] justified by the extent of the description and drawings and also the contribution to the art."[123] In particular, for small and medium-sized enterprises (SMEs) and universities in the life sciences field, these new requirements cause considerable problems.[124]

8.61 As a general rule, a claim is supported by the description if, on the basis of the information given in the application as filed, the particular teaching of the description can be extended to the whole of the field claimed by using routine methods of experimentation or analysis. Support must be of a technical character. Once the examiner has set out a reasoned case that, for example, a broad claim is not supported over the whole of its breadth, the burden of proof to demonstrate that the claim is fully supported lies with the applicant.[125]

8.62 The extent to which an invention is sufficiently disclosed is also linked to the issue of support. The reasons for a failure to meet the requirements of Article 83 of the EPC may in effect be the same as those that lead to a violation of Article 84 of the EPC, namely that the invention, over the whole range claimed, extends to technical subject matter not made available to the person skilled in the art by the application as filed.[126] In other words, there can be an argument "based" on Article 84 of the EPC in opposition proceedings if the claims are so unclear and lacking in support that they also lack enablement.

(c) Challenge of Patentability—Opposition Proceedings

8.63 The patentability/validity can, furthermore, be challenged in an opposition procedure following the grant of a patent, as has been explained above at 8.05. The accused infringer can join pending opposition proceedings,[127] and the same possibility exists in German proceedings.[128] This mechanism, of course, can only be found in countries where a pending opposition blocks the possibility of challenging the validity of a patent being enforced in court (i.e., where bifurcation exists). As mentioned earlier, an interesting difference between the two proceedings

---

[119] 35 U.S.C. § 112(b) requires that the claims "particularly point out and distinctly claim the subject matter which the inventor... regards as the invention."

[120] 35 U.S.C. § 112(a) requires that "the specification shall contain a written description of the invention."

[121] *Case Law of the Boards of Appeal of the EPO*, Ch. II.A.3.1.

[122] See, e.g., http://www.epo.org/about-us/annual-reports-statistics/annual-report/2008/focus.htm l.

[123] M. Brandi-Dohrn, "Der zu weite Patentanspruch," *GRUR Int* (1995): 541, discussing the situation in Germany and the United Kingdom. This article is worth reading.

[124] See, e.g., http://www.valea.se/sites/www.valea.se/files/field_page_attachments/valea_lifesc10_r_0.pdf.

[125] Guidelines for Examination at the EPO, Ch. F.IV.6.3.

[126] Guidelines for Examination at the EPO, Ch. F.IV.6.4.

[127] Art. 105 EPC.

[128] German Patent Act, § 59(2).

in the EPO and the GPTO is that the accused infringer cannot introduce new grounds for opposition at the EPO, whereas in the GPTO this could be done. Furthermore, in the GPTO all of the grounds in German Patent Act, § 21(1) are considered as a single ground, whereas in the EPO novelty, inventive step, industrial applicability, etc. are all independent grounds for opposition. This is important for the question of if and when new grounds can be introduced into the proceedings.

(d) Scope of the Validity Challenge—Opposition Proceedings

Article 100 of the EPC provides that an opposition may only be filed on the grounds that the subject matter of the European patent is not patentable under Articles 52–57 of the EPC, the European patent lacks sufficiency,[129] and/or the subject matter of the European patent extends beyond the content of the application as filed,[130] as will be further explained later. Other grounds are not available. In contrast to the EPO, in German national opposition proceedings, derivation (*widerrechtliche Entnahme*) can be raised as a ground for opposition. In Austria, any person may file an opposition within four months after publication of the grant of the patent; in Sweden, within nine months. In the United Kingdom, there are no strict due dates for opposition proceedings (revocation), but non-entitlement is also a ground for revocation and must be raised within two years from the grant of the patent. In Italy, Spain, and France, there are no post-grant opposition procedures available against granted patents. **8.64**

Opposition at the EPO can be based exclusively on the following grounds as listed in Article 100 of the EPC: patent eligibility, lack of novelty, lack of an inventive step, lack of industrial applicability, lack of enablement, inadmissible broadening, and derivation. **8.65**

2. Patent Eligibility (Not an Invention, Excluded Inventions)

A granted European patent can be opposed if the claims thereof are directed at matter that, according to Article 52(2) of the EPC in particular, shall not be regarded as inventions. These exclusions generally relate to "non-technical teachings" such as discoveries; scientific theories and mathematical methods; aesthetic creations; schemes, rules and methods for performing mental acts, playing games, presentations of information or doing business; and programs for computers. Nevertheless, according to Article 52(3) of the EPC, the patentability of the subject matter or activities is only excluded "as such." A method of doing business is excluded from patentability even if it implies the possibility of making use of unspecified technical means or has practical utility. Nevertheless, inventions involving programs for computers can be protected in different forms of a "computer-implemented invention."[131] In practice, outside of computer programs and business models, objections based on Article 52(2) of the EPC are quite rare, and the same holds true for the German situation, where the parallel rules in German Patent Act, § 1(3) No. 3 are regarded to function only as a "course filter" for patentable subject matter.[132] Many doubtful cases are thus filtered out later when analyzing inventive step, as this criterion includes an analysis of the technical contribution over the art. **8.66**

[129] Art. 83 EPC.

[130] Art. 123(2) EPC.

[131] Guidelines for Examination at the EPO, Ch. G.II.3.5.

[132] BGH, decision of October 26, 2010, GRUR 2011, 125—X ZR 47/07 (BPatG)—*Wiedergabe topografischer Informationen.*

8.67 Analyzing whether subject matter is excluded under Article 52(2) of the EPC is usually done without any knowledge of the state of the art (including common general knowledge). If the invention makes use of both technical and non-technical means, the use of non-technical means does not detract from the technical character of the overall teaching since the invention must be assessed as a whole. Thus, if a dependent claim adds non-technical features to a prior claim, this claim is usually not invalid because of the mix of features. The EPO rejects *perpetua mobila* as lacking enablement[133] and sometimes as lacking industrial applicability.[134]

8.68 Article 53 of the EPC defines the exceptions to patentability—that is, inventions that shall not be patented for specific reasons. In doing so, Article 53 of the EPC provides three different groups of exclusions: (a) inventions that are contrary to '*ordre public*' or morality; (b)(1) plant varieties or animal species or (b)(2) biological processes for the production of plants or animals; and (c)(1) methods for treatment of the human or animal body by surgery or therapy and (c)(2) diagnostic methods practiced on the human or animal body.

8.69 Article 53 of the EPC then immediately excludes some of the exclusions, as (b)(2) microbiological processes are patentable and (c)(1) and (c)(2) do not apply to products (e.g., substances or compositions) for use in any of these methods, which opens the avenue for claims directed at medical uses.[135]

8.70 The most recent amendment to Article 53 of the EPC added the exclusion of medical methods into the list of exceptions. These methods had formerly been excluded through the legal fiction that they were not susceptible to industrial application. Since medical methods today are excluded mainly in light of public health considerations, the exclusion was consequently moved into Article 53 of the EPC. In the German PatG, the exclusion is now found in § 2a, and most countries in Europe also follow the concept of the EPO. As stated, for example, by the UK Court of Appeal: "[The exclusion] has the limited purpose of ensuring that the actual use, by practitioners, of methods of medical treatment when treating patients should not be the subject of restraint or restriction by patent monopolies. The difficulty is to decide whether the restraint concerns a method of treatment as opposed to that which is available for treatment."[136]

8.71 In oppositions outside of life sciences, Article 53 of the EPC is rarely used, but it has been the focus of quite a number of decisions by the Enlarged Board of Appeal at the EPO,[137] which are not always fully agreed to nationally. Examples include the second medical use decision,[138] which was, nevertheless, applied in German practice only slightly differently; the dosage regimen decision,[139] which has its non-identical German counterpart in

[133] Art. 83 EPC.

[134] Art. 57 EPC. See, e.g., T 1538/05 of August 28, 2006, unpublished.

[135] See Art. 54(4) and (5) EPC.

[136] UK decision *Bristol-Myers Squibb v. Baker Norton Pharmaceuticals* [2001] RPC 1 (Court of Appeal).

[137] Decisions of the Enlarged Board of Appeal: G 5/83, OJ EPO 1985, 60 (second medical use, superseded); G 1/98 (transgenic plants, OJ EPO 2000, 111); G 1/03, OJ EPO 2004, 413; G 2/03 OJ EPO 2004, 448 (disclaimer); G 1/04 (diagnostic methods, OJ EPO 2006, 334); G 2/06 (stem cells, OJ EPO 2009, 306); G 1/07 (method for treatment by surgery, OJ EPO 2011, 134); G 1/08 (Broccoli I, OJ EPO 2012, 206); G 2/08 (dosage regime, OJ EPO 2010, 456); and referrals G 2/12 (Tomatoes II of March 25, 2015), G 2/13 (Broccoli II of March 25, 2015).

[138] G 5/83, OJ EPO 1985, 60, superseded.

[139] G 2/06, OJ EPO 2009, 306.

Carvedilol II;[140] and the morality analysis in the stem cell decision,[141] which was met with criticism, particularly from the United Kingdom.[142] The CJEU later on largely followed the opinion of the Enlarged Board of Appeal in the *Brüstle* decision,[143] which responded to a referral from the German BGH regarding the interpretation of Article 6(2)(c) of the Biotech Directive, which also deals with morality issues.[144]

The main problem with the interpretation of Article 53 of the EPC is that—despite some statements to the contrary made by the Enlarged Board of Appeals, e.g. in G2/07—any exceptions to patentability should be construed narrowly. Nevertheless, during the last forty years, the case law at the EPO and in Europe has struggled—and still struggles—with defining the limits of the exclusions, in particular in the context of life sciences. Questions that are discussed in the case law but are not yet fully answered are, for example: **8.72**

"What does morality mean in the context of Article 53 of the EPC?" (discussed in G 2/06[145] and the *Brüstle* case[146])
"What are plant varieties?" (discussed in G 1/98[147])
"What are essentially biological processes?" (discussed in G 1/08[148])
"What are diagnostic methods?" (discussed in G 1/04[149])
"What is surgery?" (discussed in G 1/07[150])
"What is medical treatment and therapy?" (no decision is yet available from the Enlarged Board of Appeals at the EPO).

This chapter cannot discuss all the details of the questions above, but some tips for practical handling can be found in the Guidelines for Examination at the EPO,[151] the literature,[152] and the rather instructive "Medical guidelines" issued by the UK Patent Office.[153] **8.73**

3. Lack of Novelty (Article 54 EPC)

Together with inventive step (see below), the alleged lack of novelty is certainly one of the most commonly raised grounds in oppositions. At the EPO, the analysis of novelty is based on a "photographic" comparison of the invention (as claimed) with the "state of the art."[154] Article 54 of the EPC defines "state of the art" as comprising everything made available to the public in any way, before the date of filing of the patent application. Thus, the EPC **8.74**

[140] BGH, 19.12.2006—X ZR 236/01, GRUR 2007, 404.

[141] G 2/06, OJ EPO 2009, 306.

[142] See, e.g., S Sterckx and J Cockbain, "Assessing the Morality of the Commercial Exploitation of Inventions Concerning Uses of Human Embryos and the Relevance of Moral Complicity: Comments on the EPO's WARF Decision," 7(1) *Scripted* (2010): 83 (http://www.law.ed.ac.uk/ahrc/script-ed/vol7-1/sterckx.asp).

[143] Case C-34/10 *Brüstle* [2011] ECR I-0000.

[144] Decision of the BGH dated 17.12.2009 regarding case Xa ZR 58/07.

[145] G 2/06, OJ EPO 2009, 306.

[146] Case C-34/10 *Brüstle* [2011] ECR I-0000.

[147] G 1/98, OJ EPO 2000, 111.

[148] G 1/08, OJ EPO 2012, 206.

[149] G 1/04, OJ EPO 2006, 334.

[150] G 1/07, OJ EPO 2011, 134.

[151] Chs. G.II.4 and 5.

[152] E.g., in Duncan Bucknell (ed.), *Pharmaceutical, Biotechnology and Chemical Inventions: World Protection and Exploitation* (2011).

[153] Available at http://www.ipo.gov.uk/medicalguidelines.pdf.

[154] Also used in the context of priority, see, e.g., G2/98, OJ EPO 2001, 413.

follows the concept of absolute novelty (e.g., there are no special situations with respect to prior uses or the inventors' own publications). Although it has been discussed since the early beginnings of European patent law, there is no grace period provided in the EPC,[155] and Article 55 of the EPC only provides for very limited non-prejudicial disclosures. One non-harmonized issue is that in decision G 3/98 the Enlarged Board of Appeal decided that the priority date would not be relevant for non-prejudicial disclosures,[156] just like in Swiss and German case law,[157] which are not harmonized with, for example, Dutch case law.[158] It may be, though, that today the Hoge Raad der Nederlanden (Supreme Court of the Netherlands) would no longer follow its older ruling in order to harmonize the situation.

8.75 As summarized in decision T 1081/01, "The case law . . . accepts that information is 'available to the public' if only a single member of the public is in a position to gain access to it and understand it, and if there is no obligation to maintain secrecy."[159]

8.76 Article 54(3) of the EPC furthermore extends the content of the state of the art by also including the content of European patent applications, as filed, that were filed prior to the date referred to in paragraph 2 and that were published on or after that date. The purpose of this extension of the state of the art is to address conflicting prior rights that might otherwise, without Article 54(3), lead to more than one patent being granted to different inventors for the same invention. The extension of the definition of the state of the art under Article 54(3) is strictly limited to the assessment of novelty and does not apply to the assessment of inventive step. Article 153(5) of the EPC states that a Euro-PCT application shall be considered as comprised in the state of the art under Article 54(3) if the application is published in a language of the EPO and the filing fee is paid. The later fate of the application is then irrelevant and will not remove the document from the state of the art (so-called "petrification"). Under the old EPC 1973, the prior right effect only occurred on a designated country-by-country basis, but this approach was given up under the EPC 2000.

8.77 In T 786/00, it was stated that, when considering the question of novelty, a prior art document must be interpreted in the light of the common general knowledge available at its publication date.[160]

8.78 The function of Article 54(4) and (5) of the EPC is to provide the legal fiction establishing novelty for the first and second medical uses of known substances or compositions. The national European patent laws, such as in Germany, the United Kingdom, and the Netherlands, provide for the same fictional novelty.

8.79 Novelty assessment is done by a one-to-one comparison of the disclosure of a document (usually a printed publication, but public prior uses can also be relevant) with the matter as claimed. The disclosure of the document includes "intrinsic information," such as specifically referenced and included subject matter, and can be complemented with common

---

[155] See, e.g., the Study mandated by the Tegernsee heads of September 24, 2012 (http://documents.epo.org/projects/babylon/eponet.nsf/0/d8df66ffe4ea0dbac1257ab0004f2002/$FILE/grace_period_en.pdf).

[156] G 3/98, OJ EPO 2001, 62.

[157] Swiss Federal Court of Justice OJ EPO 1993, 170—*Stacker*; BGH OJ EPO 1998, 263—*Coriolis force.*

[158] HR 23 June 1995, IIC 1998, p. 702, *Follicle—Stimulating Hormone II.*

[159] T 1081/01 of September 27, 2004, unpublished.

[160] T 786/00 of December 19, 2001, unpublished.

general knowledge. Nevertheless, as soon as an "extrinsic" second source of information is required, this is a matter of inventive step.

At the EPO, in the context of novelty, a generic disclosure in the state of the art does not normally take away the novelty of any specific example falling within that disclosure. On the other hand, "a specific disclosure does take away the novelty of a generic claim embracing that disclosure."[161] This allows for so-called "selection inventions," which, nevertheless, still have to involve an inventive step. **8.80**

Selection inventions are of particular importance in the fields of chemistry and pharmaceuticals. Selection inventions deal with the selection of individual elements, subsets, or sub-ranges, which have not been explicitly mentioned, within a larger known set or range. According to the EPO, if a selection from two or more lists of a certain length has to be made in order to arrive at a specific combination of features, then the resulting combination of features, not specifically disclosed in the prior art, confers novelty (the "two-lists principle"). Also, a sub-range selected from a broader numerical range of the prior art or from an overlapping range can be considered novel.[162] **8.81**

Not all national courts in Europe follow the concept of novelty by selection, or at least not as strictly as the EPO. In Germany, until quite recently, the concept of invention by selection was mostly unknown.[163] Thus, in effect, if the German part of a granted European patent survived an opposition, that part could still be declared invalid in a subsequent German nullity procedure because the European patent was based on an invention by selection. Nevertheless, in more recent decisions, under specific circumstances, the German Patent Court has regarded selections as novel. Of note, all relevant decisions are based on chemical cases.[164] According to the quite famous decision *Olanzapin*,[165] based on the earlier *Schmierfettzusammensetzung*[166] and followed by *Escitalopram*[167] (for enantiomers), the disclosure of a general chemical formula does not necessarily disclose all individual compounds as covered by the formula unless additional "individualizing" information is disclosed. **8.82**

Another recent aspect of the above novelty scenarios are the effects of earlier applications by the same applicant or inventor as prior rights on later European filings, which gained popularity under the keyword "poisonous divisional applications."[168] Two novelty scenarios can be distinguished: **8.83**

(a) in a priority application, as specific example is claimed—a later second application claims the invention in more general terms (including the specific example), and the said application claims the priority of the first application; both applications are published European applications
(b) same scenario as in (a), except that the later European application is divided and the priority embodiment is claimed in the divisional application.

[161] Guidelines for Examination at the EPO, Ch. G.VI.5.
[162] Ibid. Ch. G.VI.8.
[163] Based on the decision *Fluoran*, BGHZ 103, 150.
[164] E.g., Decision of July 27, 2006—3 Ni 7/04 (EU), Mitt. 2007, 139—*Polyvinylalkohole*.
[165] BGH, Decision of December 16, 2008—X ZR 89/07, GRUR 2009, 382—*Olanzapin*.
[166] BGH, Decision of September 30, 999—X ZR 168/96, GRUR 2000, 296, 297—*Schmierfettzusammensetzung*.
[167] BGH, Decision of 10 September 2009—Xa ZR 130/07, GRUR 2010, 123—*Escitalopram*.
[168] "Poisonous EPC Divisionals," 2/11 *epi Information* (2011): 54.

The divisional application can thus be a conflicting application within the meaning of Article 54(3) of the EPC and destroys the novelty of the subject matter claimed in the parent application.

8.84 Some decisions of the EPO[169] and of the English Patents Court followed this concept and based their findings on the decision G 2/98, where the Enlarged Board of Appeal stated: "The use of a generic term or formula in a claim for which multiple priorities are claimed in accordance with Article 88(2) EPC, second sentence, is perfectly acceptable under Articles 87(1) and 88(3) EPC, provided that it gives rise to the claiming of a limited number of clearly defined alternative subject-matters."[170] This was then interpreted in the decisions of the Boards of Appeal to mean that a continuum of a numerical range of values did not correspond to distinctive alternative embodiments and that the subject matter of the contested claim as a whole was not entitled to the claimed priority date.[171] Following this case law, the Patents Court, finding that the broadened part of the claim covers a whole range of arrangements, then denied a partial priority for the specific example.[172]

8.85 Currently, the situation is unclear, and some decisions of the Boards of Appeal have expressly disagreed with T 1877/08 and similar decisions and have stated that, within the meaning of G 2/98, the specific example is specifically defined subject matter and can be distinguished from the rest of the claim, which is generic and only has the filing date as its relevant date.[173]

8.86 In view of the above, some scholars recommend the preventive withdrawal of the European priority application in order to avoid publication thereof, which would avoid the state of the art effect of Article 54(3) of the EPC.[174]

4. Lack of an Inventive Step (Obviousness) (Article 56 EPC)

8.87 In contrast to novelty, the analysis of inventive step is based on a combination of publications of the relevant state of the art. Just as in all other patent systems, the requirement for inventive step in the EPO entails adding an "inventive extra" to inventions in order to move them away from simple combinations. Nevertheless, differences exist in how this "extra" is determined for the invention at stake.

8.88 In order to identify an inventive step, the EPO has established the "problem-solution approach," which—at least in theory—allows for a rather straight-forward test. In brief, first, the "closest state of the art" is identified, usually a publication that shares most of the features with the invention or is otherwise suitable as a "promising springboard" in order to arrive at the invention. Here, the test meets criticism, for example, the German BGH regularly objects to the EPO's "intrinsic" approach that allegedly involves the invention as claimed in the analysis. This would create an ex-post analysis, which would not reflect the actual considerations of the person of skill at the time of filing.[175]

---

169 T 1496/11 of September 12, 2012, unpublished.

170 G 2/98, OJ EPO 2001, 413.

171 T 1877/08 (*Refrigerants/E.I. du Pont de Nemours and Company*) of February 23, 2010, unpublished, and *Case Law of the Boards of Appeal*, Ch. II.D.4.3.

172 *Nestec SA v. Dualit, Ltd.* [2013] EWHC 923.

173 E.g., T 1222/11 of December 4, 2012, unpublished.

174 See, e.g., http://ipkitten.blogspot.de/2013/05/poisonous-priority-how-many-ways-can.html.

175 BGH BlPMZ 1991, 159—*Haftverband*; BGH GRUR 2003, 693, 695—*Hochdruckreiniger*; BGH, GRUR 2009, 382—*Olanzapin*.

The EPO then continues to define the "objective problem" to be solved by the invention, which is based on the technical differences as identified in view of the closest state of the art. After reformulating the problem, the solution is then tested by looking for another document that adds the missing features to the invention and by asking the question of whether that document would have indeed been considered by the person of skill. If the answer is yes, the claim lacks inventive step; if not, the matter is considered inventive. **8.89**

In contrast to this, and quite similar to the situation in the United States, in Germany the "extrinsic" analysis tries to recreate the situation at the time of filing by establishing a view on the combined state of the art. Since this is quite difficult to do, in practice the German analysis often also starts with a "reasonable" document. Nevertheless, the BGH still does not approve of the "static" problem-solution approach and continues to be critical about it.[176] **8.90**

In the United Kingdom, s. 3 of the UK Patents Act states, "An invention shall be taken to involve an inventive step if it is not obvious to a person skilled in the art, having regard to any matter which forms part of the state of the art."[177] **8.91**

In determining the actual requirements for inventive step, the *Windsurfing*[178]/*Pozzoli*[179] approach is used, which comprises four steps to determine whether an invention contains an inventive step: (1)(a) identify the notional "person skilled in the art" and (1)(b) identify the relevant common general knowledge of that person; (2) identify the inventive concept of the claim of the application in question; (3) identify what, if any, differences exist between the matter cited as forming part of the "state of the art" and the inventive concept of the claim of the application in question; and (4) ask whether, when viewed without any knowledge of the alleged invention as claimed, these differences constitute steps that would have been obvious to the person skilled in the art or whether they require any degree of invention. **8.92**

In the *Actavis* case, the Court of Appeal of England and Wales discussed the differences between the problem–solution approach and the above approach, and found that step (4) could indeed be seen as different, but it would avoid the flaw of the problem–solution approach because a fully "neutral" analysis of inventive step would be performed.[180] Of note, this renders the analysis in the United Kingdom quite similar to the situation in Germany (see 8.88). Nevertheless, even when applying both tests in the case at stake, Lord Justice Jacob came to the same result, namely a lack of an inventive step.[181] **8.93**

In the Netherlands, usually the court handling both infringement and validity applies the problem–solution approach.[182] Arguments regarding inventive step can therefore focus on the selection of the closest prior art, the motivation to combine, a reasonable expectation of success, and unexpected results. **8.94**

It is also interesting to compare the functions of experts in different proceedings. In the United Kingdom, expert statements can be decisive in the case; in the Netherlands, they can **8.95**

---

176 BGH, decision of 18 June 2009—Xa ZR 138/05, GRUR 2009, 1039—*Fischbissanzeiger*, with reference to BGH—*Olanzapin*.

177 s. 3 UK Patents Act.

178 *Windsurfing International Inc. v Tabur Marine (GB), Ltd.* [1985] RPC 59.

179 *Pozzoli Spa v BDMO SA and anor* [2007] EWCA Civ 588 (22 June 2007).

180 *Actavis UK, Ltd. v Novartis AG* [2010] EWCA Civ 82.

181 Ibid.

182 E.g., in DC The Hague, *Sandoz v. Glaxo*, January 26, 2011.

be crucial. In Germany, expert statements are rare and usually play a relatively minor role. One possible explanation is the handling of the cases by technical judges in Germany—that is, the court itself is technically skilled.

8.96 The above analyses of inventive step can sometimes be supplemented (but not replaced) by so-called secondary indica, such as surprising effects, technical prejudice, long-felt need, and even commercial success. Sometimes—in particular in chemical or life science cases—it seems that the Examiners require the presence of a "surprising" effect in order to acknowledge an inventive step. Nevertheless, the case law says otherwise, as indicia can serve merely as auxiliary considerations in the assessment of inventive step.[183]

8.97 In the EPO, in contrast to other requirements, an inventive step can be supported by later-filed (also even post-published) documents and/or experimental data. Nevertheless, the verification of whether or not the claimed solution actually solves the problem—that is, whether the claimed subject matter actually provides the desired effect—must be "based" on the data in the application.[184] Post-published evidence in support of the notion that the claimed subject matter solves the problem to be solved is taken into account if it is already credible from the disclosure in the patent that the problem is indeed solved. The post-filing of data is also possible in Germany (and in, for example, China, Japan,[185] Taiwan, and Australia) although the individual situations differ between enablement (not discussed here) and data in order to support an inventive step—for example, comparative data versus data to establish an inventive effect per se. In India, applicants may submit data—for example, experimental data supporting the efficacy of an active pharmaceutical ingredient—during examination only if the Patent Office requests such data.

8.98 In an attack on a patent as granted, another important aspect of a lack of inventive step is the question whether the problem of the invention is solved over the whole range as claimed. Of note, this issue sometimes overlaps (and gets confused) with the analysis of enablement (for Article 83 of the EPC, see 8.113 "Lack of Enablement (Sufficiency)"). Also, claims that are allegedly "too broad" (which per se is not a reason for opposition) can be dealt with under this aspect, as lack of support by the description[186] is also not a ground for opposition. If the problem is not solved over the range as claimed (i.e., the claims don't fully "work"), the claims have to be limited accordingly.

5. Lack of Industrial Applicability (Article 57 EPC)

8.99 Outside of the rather rare *perpetua mobilia*[187] (although it seems to be more reasonable to handle this issue under lack of enablement, Article 83 of the EPC, as "not functioning"[188]), for a long time the lack of industrial applicability was probably the least relevant of the grounds for opposition requirements. The reason for this was the particularly generous

---

[183] See T 1072/92 of June 28, 1994, unpublished; T 351/93 of March 1, 1995, unpublished.

[184] See, e.g., T 1329/04 (*Factor-9/John Hopkins*) of June 28, 2005, unpublished.

[185] E.g., based on the judgment in the *Sunscreen* decision of July 15, 2010 by the IP high court Hei 21 (*Gyo-Ke*) No. 10238.

[186] Art. 84 EPC.

[187] See, e.g., T 1538/05 of August 28, 2006, unpublished, reason 5: "Where a method or a device is claimed that is to be operated in such a way as clearly in conflict with the established laws of physics, e.g. perpetuum mobile, such invention lacks industrial application unless the appellant can clearly and unambiguously demonstrate the contrary."

[188] See, e.g., AIPPI, Q180—Content and relevance of industrial applicability and/or utility as requirements for patentability—answer of the Dutch group (https://www.aippi.org/download/commitees/180/QS180netherlands06.pdf); and decision T 1329/07 of November 11, 2010, unpublished.

handling of this requirement by the courts, which also led to very little relevant case law in the "regular" fields of technology.

This is, of course, based on the very broad wording of Article 57 of the EPC, according to which an invention is regarded as industrially applicable "if the matter thereof can be made or used in any field of industry, including agriculture." In addition, industrial applicability can be seen as an additional filter between the technical character of the invention and the criteria with reference to the state of the art (which is not immediately relevant for Article 57 of the EPC). Thus, Article 57 of the EPC excludes very few inventions from patentability that would not already be excluded by Article 52(2) of the EPC.[189] **8.100**

When comparing the industrial applicability with the requirements according to the patent system of the United States, the "applicability" clearly finds its counterpart in the "utility" requirement of 35 U.S.C. § 101. Although still very broad, utility in Europe has to be linked to industry,[190] whereas today utility seems to be somewhat more limited in the United States. Nevertheless, this limitation has proven to be very effective in practice in that it helps to make clear that patentability has its limits. **8.101**

When strictly sticking to the wording of Article 57 of the EPC, it is sufficient if the matter of the invention can be produced or used in any kind of industry. Thus, it is sufficient to state "where" the use shall happen, and only in cases where it is not obvious from the description or the nature of the invention, according to Rule 42(1)(f) of the EPC, does it have to "explicitly" state how the invention is industrially applicable. Nevertheless, the invention must have a solid and concrete technical basis so that the use thereof can result in a practical industrial application.[191] **8.102**

In the field of chemistry, based on the decision *Imidazoline*,[192] the situation in Germany is quite liberal. The technical problem to be solved can be the "simple" provision of a compound, and the industrial applicability can be disclosed very generally with reference to a technical field (e.g., for producing a medicament). Regarding natural compounds, these are not patentable as such.[193] Nevertheless, patents can be granted that relate to yet unknown derivatives or to the isolation of such natural compounds or to synthetically produced compounds occurring in nature; these are then "new" products that are patentable as such. There is no further difference in the handling of both natural and "artificial" chemical compounds in the downstream patentability analysis. **8.103**

The medical methods mentioned in the old Article 52(4) of the EPC 1973 (which today has been moved to Article 53(c) of the EPC 2000) were treated as special with respect to their industrial applicability. This concept has apparently been given up. Industrial applicability was briefly discussed, for example, in decision G 2/06, in the context of the "commercial exploitation" of embryonic stem cells.[194] **8.104**

---

189 Guidelines for Examination at the EPO, Ch. G-III 1.

190 This was one reason why the activities of medical doctors were excluded in the old EPC of 1973.

191 T 0898/05 (*Hematopoietic receptor/Zymogenetics*) of July 7, 2006, unpublished.

192 BGHZ 58, 280, 288, BGH GRUR 1972, 541—*Imidazoline.*

193 BPatG GRUR 78, 238, 239, and BGH GRUR 1978, 238—*Antanamid.*

194 G 2/06, OJ EPO 2009, 306 (*Use of Embryos/WARF*).

8.105 Today, the criterion for industrial applicability is of particular relevance primarily for biotechnological inventions. According to the Biotech Directive,[195] a simple nucleic acid sequence without a given "function" cannot constitute a patentable invention.[196] This requirement was introduced into the EPC when Rules 26–29 of the EPC were added to the law based on the Biotech Directive. Rule 29(3) of the EPC now provides that the industrial applicability of a sequence or partial sequence of a gene must be (concretely) disclosed in the patent application. It is in doubt whether this requirement is limited only to human sequences (Article 5 of the Biotech Directive may imply this), but in practice this is of little relevance. Thus, compared with other fields of technology, Rule 29(3) of the EPC actually increases the requirements with respect to the description of an industrial applicability in cases of DNA sequences.

8.106 Historically, this special treatment comes from experience of applications from the beginning of the 1990s, where large collections of so-called "expressed sequence tags" (ESTs) were claimed without a specific use disclosed for these snippets of expressed genes. In particular, researchers in the United States were concerned that this would effectively result in a blocking of research for the human genome.[197]

8.107 Furthermore, recital 24 of the Biotech Directive requires that:

> in order to comply with the industrial application criterion it is necessary in cases where a sequence or partial sequence of a gene is used to produce a protein or part of a protein, to specify which protein or part of a protein is produced or what function it performs; in cases where the sequence is used for producing a protein or part thereof.[198]

The Guidelines for Examination at the EPO then state: "Alternatively, when a nucleotide sequence is not used to produce a protein or part of a protein, the function to be indicated could e.g. be that the sequence exhibits a certain transcription promoter activity."[199]

8.108 Since the function is identical to industrial applicability, the mere indication of a function is sufficient. Evidence is not needed or can be post-filed for the indicated function. Nevertheless, in view of the above sections of the Guidelines, which could be read as "the biological function" (whatever this may be) in cases of claims directed at a protein, the evidence could become an essential factor in how much the inventor actually knows about "his" protein and the biological function thereof. Indeed, the relevant European case law extensively discusses this issue, with T 898/05 being the most prominent:

> The function of a protein (and thus of the nucleic acid encoding it) can be seen at different levels, which include its molecular function, its cellular function and its biological function in a broad sense. The elucidation of one of these particular levels of function might result, under certain conditions, in a straightforward industrial application, even though the other levels of activity remain completely unknown or only partially characterized.[200]

---

[195] Directive 98/44/EC of the European Parliament and the Commission of July 6, 1998 on the legal protection of biotechnological inventions, OJ L 213, 30.7.1998, pp. 13–21.

[196] Biotech Directive, recital 23.

[197] See, e.g., Gary Cohen, Scott Brown, and Allen Nunnally, "Intellectual Property and Commercial Aspects of Pharmacogenomics," in Mark A. Rothstein (ed.), *Pharmacogenomics: Social, Ethical, and Clinical Dimensions* (2003).

[198] Biotech Directive, recital 24.

[199] Guidelines for Examination at the EPO, Ch. G-III 4.

[200] T 0898/05 (*Hematopoietic receptor/Zymogenetics*) of July 7, 2006, unpublished.

Nevertheless, the function as indicated must be more than purely speculative.[201]

In the field of biotechnology, problems with respect to an industrial applicability are often connected with the question of sufficiency of the invention according to Article 83 of the EPC and an inventive step according to Article 56 of the EPC. Rule 42(1)(e) of the EPC requires, in the context of sufficiency, the disclosure of at least one way of performing the invention as claimed. Nevertheless, this requirement is rather quantitative ("one" way) and refers to the content of the disclosure. Thus, the "objective" (extrinsic) industrial use of the invention, as required for Article 57 of the EPC, does not relate to Article 83 of the EPC.[202] Sometimes, Article 56 of the EPC is also cited, according to which a claim lacks an inventive step if the object of the invention is not solved over the whole range as claimed. Nevertheless, in contrast to an inventive step, normally the industrial applicability cannot be established, completed, or supported by later-filed documents.[203] **8.109**

Once the above criterion is fulfilled, patentees may enjoy compound protection for their nucleic acid sequence. **8.110**

In Germany, in particular due to political pressure at the time when the Biotech Directive was implemented, the PatG was (quite extensively) amended in order to include the rules of the Biotech Directive. With respect to the industrial applicability of DNA sequences, § 1a of the PatG was introduced, in which the industrial applicability of a sequence or partial sequence of a gene has to be "concretely" described in the application by "indicating the function that is performed by the sequence or partial sequence." This could be held valid for all "genes," irrespective of their origin. (Although the directive clearly relates to the human body, and paragraph 3 follows paragraph 2, which relates to the human being. Section 2a of the PatG then refers back to § 1a with respect to animal and plant genes.)[204] Of note, there is no explanation as to what constitutes a "gene" in this context. Then, in cases of human sequences, the use for which the industrial applicability is concretely described has to be introduced into the patent claim. As can be seen, although § 1a of the PatG is positioned in §§ 1–5 of the PatG and therefore is in the part relating to patentability (material) requirements, the introduction of the function into the claim is actually a formal requirement.[205] Since § 21 of the PatG explicitly relates to the "patentability" when referring to §§ 1–5 of the PatG, it is doubtful whether the fact that the function has not been introduced into the claim can be a ground for opposition. **8.111**

Although "officially" related to the protection of DNA sequences, the CJEU decision in *Monsanto*[206] may also have an impact on the patentability of all DNA sequences.[207] In brief, **8.112**

[201] E.g., T 1109/10 (*Hydroxylases/Lexicon*) of March 13, 2014, unpublished.

[202] For Germany, see BGH, BlPMZ 1985, 117, 118—*Offensichtlichkeitsprüfung.*

[203] See, e.g., T 1336/04 (*Cellulase/NOVOZYME*) of March 9, 2006, unpublished.

[204] E.g., R. Moufang in R. Schulte (ed.), *Patentgesetz mit Europäischem Patentübereinkommen* (8th ed., 2008), marginal number 25 for German Patent Act, § 1a; but see G. Benkard, *Patentgesetz* (10th ed., 2006), marginal number 3 for German Patent Act, § 1a.

[205] See, e.g., P. Mes, *Patentgesetz Gebrauchsmustergesetz* (3d ed., 2011), German Patent Act, § 1a: "not only a formal requirement" but without distinguishing between paras. 3 and 4.

[206] C-428/08, *Monsanto v. Cefetra* (http://curia.europa.eu/juris/liste.jsf?language=en&num=C-428/08).

[207] J. B. Krauss and T. Takenaka, "A Special Rule for Compound Protection for DNA Sequences: Impact of the ECJ 'Monsanto' Decision on Patent Practice (August 1, 2011)," 93 *Journal of the Patent and Trademark Society* (2011): 189 (University of Washington School of Law Research Paper No. 2011-18).

in *Monsanto*, transgenic (RoundUp® ready) soybeans were grown and converted into soybean meal in Argentina, where no DNA-related patent existed. The meal was then shipped to Europe (Rotterdam). Monsanto was the holder of the European patent EP 0 546 090, and the claims of this patent were (amongst others) related to "an isolated DNA sequence encoding a Class II EPSPS enzyme," which provides the RoundUp® ready effect in living plants. Monsanto consequently filed an infringement case against the import of the meal into Europe at the (responsible) Rechtbank-Gravenhage and argued that the meal contained the DNA sequence and thus would constitute infringement (only) of the DNA sequence claims. The Rechtbank-Gravenhage subsequently sent questions to the CJEU in order to find out whether the scope of protection of such claims indeed would provide a basis to block the import of the meal (in view of Article 9 of the Biotech Directive). While ultimately no infringement was found, the court stated that Article 9 of the directive would preclude the national patent legislation from offering absolute protection to the patented product as such, regardless of whether it performed its function in the material containing it. This offering could be interpreted as a requirement to (finally) limit the patentability of nucleic acids, but the decision first and foremost deals with the scope of protection as provided.

6. Lack of Enablement (Sufficiency)

8.113 Article 83 of the EPC states that an "application must disclose the invention in a manner sufficiently clear and complete for it to be carried out by a person skilled in the art." Sufficiency is considered during both examination and opposition.

8.114 This requirement must be complied with from the date of filing because a deficiency in a European patent application as filed, resulting in an insufficient identification of the subject matter claimed, cannot subsequently be cured.[208] As stated in the EPO Guidelines for Examination,[209] it must be possible to reproduce a claimed step using the original application documents without any inventive effort over and above the ordinary skills of a practitioner.[210] Where an applicant does not furnish details of the production process in the description in order to prevent the invention from being copied easily and the missing information cannot be supplied from the general knowledge of a person skilled in the art, the invention is held to be insufficiently disclosed.[211]

8.115 Insufficiency is also a ground for revocation under s. 72 of the UK Patents Act and under German Patent Act, § 21.

8.116 In practice, the ground for lack of enablement is difficult to argue—and a rather weak one. The reasons for this seem to be mainly based in the fact that enablement is a requirement of the application as such—that is, an inherent technical analysis of the matter as disclosed is required. Since the opponent has the burden of proof of showing lack of enablement, this often requires the production of experimental data (which is, of course, always disputable). Understandably, the opposition is very reluctant to discuss the "quality" of experimental data. Instead, an attack based on post-published data relating to experiences with the patented matter, preferably published by the inventor, is usually the most successful.

---

[208] E.g., G 2/93, OJ EPO 1995, 275.
[209] Guidelines for Examination at the EPO, Ch. II.C.4.1.
[210] E.g., T 10/86 of September 1, 1988, unpublished.
[211] E.g., T 219/85, OJ EPO 1986, 376.

There is no best mode requirement in Europe, and **8.117**

> an invention is in principle sufficiently disclosed if at least one way is clearly indicated enabling the person skilled in the art to carry out the invention. If this is the case, the non-availability of some particular variants of a functionally defined component feature of the invention is immaterial to sufficiency as long as there are suitable variants known to the skilled person through the disclosure or common general knowledge which provide the same effect for the invention.[212]

In addition, at the EPO, there seems to be a willingness by the Boards to accept that the person of skill is quite able to fill in the "blanks" in the description with suitable knowledge. Nationally, there is no common standard in the case law for the person of skill, in particular when it comes to any creativity in his actions.

More interestingly, "the disclosure of one way of performing an invention is only sufficient if **8.118** it allows the invention to be performed in the whole range claimed rather than only in some members of the claimed class to be obtained. Sufficiency of disclosure thus presupposes that the skilled person is able to obtain substantially all embodiments falling within the ambit of the claims."[213] This reads similar to the requirement for support (which in the United States is provided by 35 U.S.C. § 112), which is stipulated by Article 84 of the EPC. Article 84 of the EPC requires that the claims (a) shall be clear and concise and (b) be supported by the description. This ground is particularly attractive in cases where the claims are too broad,[214] as these claims may lack this support, at least partially. Nevertheless, Article 84 of the EPC is not a ground for opposition and is limited during opposition proceedings to those cases where there has been an amendment. However, when substantive amendments are made to a patent, the Opposition Division and the Boards of Appeal both have the power to deal with all the grounds and issues arising from those amendments. Regarding the mandatory examination of Article 84 of the EPC, recently a decision was issued by the Enlarged Board of Appeals.[215]

The above also results in a difficulty in effectively using a lack of enablement in cases of **8.119** overly broad claims. The EPO states: "There is a delicate balance between Article 83 and Article 84, which has to be assessed on the merits of each individual case."[216] For example, it is possible to argue, based on Article 83 of the EPC, that an ambiguity in a claim affects the scope of the said claim in such a way that it is impossible to carry out at all the invention as defined therein.[217] One example may be an ill-defined parameter, which would render the skilled person unable, on the basis of the disclosure as a whole and by using common general knowledge, to identify (without undue burden) the technical measures necessary to solve the problem underlying the application at issue.

Enablement is of particular relevance for the so-called "unpredictable arts,"[218]—that is, arts **8.120** that involve the chemical industry or the experimental sciences and other such arts where

---

212 Guidelines for Examination at the EPO, Ch. II.C.4.2.

213 Ibid. Ch. II.C.4.4.

214 See, e.g., Dr. Matthias Brandi-Dohrn, "The Unduly Broad Claim" (http://www.brandi-dohrn.de/veroeff/claim.html).

215 Case G 3/14—Decision of the Enlarged Board of Appeal under Art 112(1)a) EPC based on case T 0373/12—(*Examination of Clarity Objections*) of March 24, 2015.

216 See T 608/07 of April 27, 2009, unpublished.

217 Ibid.

218 One of the "*Wands*" factors used for the analysis of enablement in the United States, *In re Wands*, 858 F.2d 731, 737 (Fed. Cir. 1988).

the results are not easily predictable (e.g., pharmaceutical or biotech inventions).[219] Here, "the law requires an enabling disclosure for nascent technology because a person of ordinary skill in the art has little or no knowledge independent from the patentee's instruction."[220]

8.121 Although the above concept has been established by US case law, the unpredictable arts concept certainly also applies to European applications. The fact that the requirement for sufficiency of disclosure in the biotechnology field has its own chapter in the case law book at the EPO[221] may be seen as an indication for this. The case law says that:

> as for the amount of detail needed for a sufficient disclosure, this depends on the correlation of the facts of the case to certain general parameters, such as the character of the technical field and the average amount of effort necessary to put into practice a certain written disclosure in that technical field, the time when the disclosure was presented to the public and the corresponding common general knowledge, and the amount of reliable technical details disclosed in a document.[222]

In some cases, more technical details and more than one example were found necessary in order to support claims of a broad scope.

8.122 With regard to medical uses, if the description in a patent specification provides no more than a vague indication of a possible medical use for a chemical compound that is yet to be identified, more detailed evidence cannot be used later to remedy the fundamental insufficiency of the disclosure of such subject matter.[223]

8.123 In Germany, the enablement requirement is stipulated in § 34(4) of the PatG, which is identical to Article 83 of the EPC. Nevertheless, when it comes to fulfilling the enablement requirement, the case law in Germany is even more liberal than at the EPO. For working the invention, it is sufficient that the person of skill is merely pointed in the right direction.[224] Also, it is not required for a usable embodiment to be directly disclosed, and it is sufficient if a general scheme is provided for the solution of a problem. Even obvious mistakes can be recognized and overcome by the person of skill.[225]

7. Inadmissible Broadening

8.124 Article 123 of the EPC relates to amendments to a European patent application or patent and notably the conditions under which they are allowable. Article 123(2) of the EPC prohibits adding subject matter beyond the content of the application as filed, while Article 123(3) of the EPC prohibits an extension to the scope of protection by amendment after grant.

8.125 Thus, in opposition proceedings at the EPO, Article 123(2) of the EPC has to be considered, and any amended claims at the same time have to fulfill the requirements of Article 123(3) of the EPC. Of note, this is one of the very few occasions where the EPO is confronted with

[219] In *Re Fisher*, 427 F.2d, 839, and MPEP 2164.03.

[220] *Chiron Corp. v. Genentech, Inc.*, 363 F.3d 1247, 1254 (Fed. Cir. 2004).

[221] *Case Law of the Boards of Appeal at the EPO*, Ch. II.C.6.

[222] With reference to T 158/91 of July 30, 1991, unpublished; T 694/92 (*Modifying Plant Cells*) of May 8, 1996, OJ EPO 1997,408; T 639/95 (*Biopolymers/MIT*) of January 21, 1998, unpublished; T 36/00 (*Proteinase deficient fungi/Genencor*) of October 2, 2003, unpublished; and T 1466/05 (*Pyridinoline/Serex*) of July 27, 2007, unpublished.

[223] E.g., T 609/02 of October 27, 2004 (*AP-1 complex/Salt Institute*), unpublished.

[224] BGH, decision of April 30, 2009—Xa ZR 56/05, GRUR 2009, 743—*Airbag-Auslösesteuerung*.

[225] BGH, decision of April 21, 2009—X ZR 153/04, GRUR 2009, 933—*Druckmaschinen-Temperierungssystem II*.

the scope of protection of a claim. A general principle of Article 123 of the EPC is that an applicant should not be allowed any unfair advantage when amending the application (i.e., it must not be possible to "sneak in" matter after filing the application). In particular, this rule ensures legal certainty.

Article 123(2) of the EPC has become a very popular ground for opposition and is also at the core of quite a few important decisions by the Enlarged Board of Appeals.[226] The reason for its popularity is that Article 123(2) of the EPC is easy to argue and can be quite effective, in particular because of the strict standard as applied by the EPO. Since the comparison is between the patent as granted versus the application as filed, the argument is an "inherent" and very formal one, and it does not require the "external" state of the art. Furthermore, proceedings with many grounds and/or many opponents can be effectively cut short, which has made the ground very popular with the EPO. **8.126**

Which amendments are now admissible? As mentioned in both the G 3/89[227] and the G 11/91[228] decisions: **8.127**

> any amendment to parts of a European patent application or of a European patent relating to the disclosure...can therefore, irrespective of the context the amendment made, only be made within the limits of what a skilled person would derive directly and unambiguously, using common general knowledge, and seen objectively and relative to the date of filing, from the whole of these documents as filed.[229]

The more recent G 2/10 decision further emphasized:

> Whether the skilled person is presented with new information depends on how he or she would understand the amended claim, i.e. the subject-matter remaining in the amended claim and on whether, using common general knowledge, he or she would regard that subject-matter as at least implicitly disclosed in the application as filed.[230]

In practice, the EPO uses the so-called "disclosure test" (i.e., "directly and unambiguously derivable"), which corresponds to a novelty analysis of the application as granted versus the application as filed.[231] Of note, this novelty test is part of the "uniform concept of disclosure" as discussed, for example, in G 2/98[232] and G 1/03,[233] and establishes the same criteria for assessing the allowability of an amendment (relevant disclosure: application as filed), the validity of a priority claim (relevant disclosure: priority document), and novelty (relevant disclosure: prior art document). **8.128**

Thus, in order to provide a basis for an amendment, the disclosure must be essentially identical, and the EPO is quite strict about this requirement (an almost verbatim basis is required). The EPO is particularly critical of "arbitrary selections from two or more lists"[234] (i.e., no selection inventions are admissible within applications). If different specific **8.129**

---

[226] G1/93, OJ EPO 1994, 541; G3/89, OJ EPO 1993, 117; G11/91, OJ EPO 1993, 125; G2/98, OJ EPO 2001, 413; G1/03, OJ EPO 2004, 413; and G2/10, OJ EPO 2012, 376.

[227] G 3/89, OJ EPO 1993, 117.

[228] G 11/91, OJ EPO 1993, 125.

[229] *Case Law of the Boards of Appeal at the EPO*, Ch. II E 4.1.

[230] G 2/10 (Disclaimer/SCRIPPS) of August 30, 2011, OJ EPO 2012, 376.

[231] *Case Law of the Boards of Appeal at the EPO*, Ch. II D 2.1.9.

[232] G 2/98, OJ EPO 2001, 413.

[233] G 1/03, OJ EPO 2004, 413.

[234] *Case Law of the Boards of Appeal at the EPO*, Ch. II E 1.1.5.

embodiments are described, a combination of features and/or a generalization are not allowed. This is of particular relevance for chemical inventions, where general formulae are used, as well as for parameter ranges. Nevertheless, selecting a preferred embodiment from a list is not considered a selection, and a combination within multiple dependent claims is always disclosed.

8.130 In view of the criticism regarding an overly strict use of the requirement by examiners at the EPO, which was reflected in some descisions by the Boards of Appeal,[235] a new paragraph has recently been added in the section of the Guidelines for Examination at the EPO setting out the "general rules" for determining the content of the application as originally filed.[236] According to this paragraph, the focus should be placed on what is really disclosed to the skilled person by the documents as filed as directed to a technical audience. In particular, the examiner should avoid disproportionally focusing on the structure of the claims as filed to the detriment of the subject matter that the skilled person would directly and unambiguously derive from the application as a whole. It remains to be seen whether this will actually result in a less strict approach.

8.131 Of particular interest with respect to admissible amendments under the disclosure test are so-called "disclaimers." In a claim (or even the specification), a disclaimer defines excluded subject matter that shall not be claimed. A disclaimer may also introduce a negative limitation, resulting from the incorporation of a "negative" technical feature, which typically excludes specific embodiments or parts from a general feature. Thus, a disclaimer is used to either "punch a hole" into the scope of a claim or to move the whole scope of the claim towards something else (called "*aliud*"). Obviously, this can create issues with the novelty of the claimed matter.

8.132 Under the case law of the Boards of Appeal of the EPO,[237] disclaimers are allowed only in certain circumstances, as confirmed in a series of decisions. A disclaimer (which is not disclosed in the application as filed) may be allowable (a) in order to restore novelty by limiting a claim against the state of the art under Article 54(3) of the EPC (i.e., prior rights that could not be known); (b) in order to restore novelty by limiting a claim against an "accidental anticipation"—an anticipation is accidental if it is so unrelated to and remote from the claimed invention that the person skilled in the art would never have taken it into consideration when making the invention (this is rarely the case and therefore is hardly ever used); and (c) in order to disclaim subject matter that is excluded from patentability for non-technical reasons (e.g., human embryonic stem cells). It was then further decided in G 2/10 that an amendment to a claim by the introduction of a disclaimer disclaiming from it subject matter disclosed in the application as filed infringes Article 123(2) of the EPC if the subject matter remaining in the claim after the introduction of the disclaimer is not, be it explicitly or implicitly, "directly and unambiguously" disclosed in the application as filed to the skilled person using common general knowledge.[238] A case-specific "technical assessment" is necessary to decide whether this requirement has been met.

[235] E.g., T 2619/11 of February 25, 2013, unpublished; T 1906/11 of January 18, 2013, unpublished.
[236] Guidelines for Examination at the EPO, Ch. H-IV 2.3.
[237] Decisions G 1/03, OJ EPO 2004, 413; G 2/03, OJ EPO 2004, 448; and G 2/10, OJ EPO 2012, 376.
[238] G 2/10, OJ EPO 2012, 376.

The "remaining" phrase adds more uncertainty to the matter. From the detailed reasoning given in the decision, it appears that the board does not see a problem with allowing disclaimers that relate to a specific embodiment of the invention (e.g., a specific example or a specific chemical compound disclosed in the application). However, problems may arise in cases where the disclaimer results in the singling out of an individual compound or a group of compounds not specifically mentioned or at least implicitly disclosed in the application, or would lead to a particular meaning of the remaining claimed subject matter that was not originally disclosed. In the end, both disclosed and undisclosed disclaimers are permissible under specific circumstances. However, it always seems to be safer to seek an alternative, albeit potentially more restrictive, positive claim limitation. **8.133**

Article 123(3) of the EPC prohibits amending granted claims during opposition proceedings in such a way as to extend the protection conferred by a European patent. It is, for instance, not allowable to replace a technical feature of a granted claim with another technical feature that causes the claim to extend to subject matter that was not encompassed by the granted claim (*aliud*). Thus, after grant, the interests of third parties are further protected by Article 123(3) of the EPC in that the patentee's right to amend the claims is limited by the scope of the granted patent. **8.134**

As discussed, for Article 123(3) of the EPC to apply, the grant of the patent is an essential requirement. The importance of this step, which is often regarded as a mere formality for the then-patentee, cannot be overestimated, as the grant "freezes" the scope of the claims and the responsibility for any amendment always lies with the applicant.[239] If a mistake occurs, this can lead to—in a downstream opposition—the so-called "inescapable trap" situation,[240] which—in the worst-case scenario—effectively invalidates the whole patent. This happens when a European patent contains a feature that was not disclosed in the application as filed (which contravenes Article 123(2) of the EPC) and if the removal of this feature would extend the scope of protection beyond the scope conferred by the patent as granted (which contravenes Article 123(3) of the EPC). Then, in principle, the European patent has to be revoked.[241] As mentioned earlier, apart from the specific cases as mentioned, the introduction of a disclaimer is not possible. **8.135**

In Germany, the BGH did not follow this very harsh approach, and in the decision *Winkelmesseinrichtung*[242] the court decided on the question of how German law would deal with the inescapable trap.[243] In brief, the BGH allows the initially undisclosed feature to remain in the claims if it limits the scope and does not lead to claiming an *aliud*.[244] In these cases, it is not even required to introduce into the description a note or disclaimer that this feature cannot be used to derive rights therefrom. Nevertheless, in cases of an *aliud*, the BGH essentially follows the inescapable trap concept of the EPO.[245] **8.136**

239 Decision G 1/93, OJ EPO 1994, 541, Reasons, 13, last sentence.

240 Ibid.

241 Ibid.

242 BGH, decision of October 21, 2010—Xa ZB 14/09, GRUR 2011, 40—*Winkelmesseinrichtung*.

243 Art. 123 (2) and (3) EPC or German Patent Act, § 21(1) No. 4.

244 For a definition, see BGH, decision of September 9, 2010—Xa ZR 14/10, GRUR 2010, 1084—*Windenergiekonverter*.

245 BGH, decision of June 21, 2011—X ZR 43/09, GRUR 2011, 1003—*Integrationselement*.

8. Derivation (Entitlement)

8.137 At the EPO, derivation of the invention (i.e., a "wrong" inventor or applicant) is not a ground for opposition, as the list of grounds in Article 100 of the EPC is exhaustive. Derivation can be raised at any point in time during the examination of the application of interest (which practically excludes the use of the ground in post-grant opposition). The EPO does not examine derivation issues itself, and an "external" decision is required. If it is adjudged by such a decision of the court or a competent authority (within a member state) that a person other than the applicant is entitled to the grant of a European patent, the third party, within three months after the decision has become final, has three choices. First, the application can be taken over and prosecuted in place of the applicant. Second, a new European patent application can be filed with respect to the same invention (which in itself can have a lot of "unpleasant" implications if the first application was drafted poorly or has only been derived in part). Third, the true applicant can request that the application be refused. Interestingly, in a case where the application is no longer pending due to its having been withdrawn, refused, or deemed to be withdrawn, the third party can still file a new European patent application in respect of the same invention.[246]

8.138 If a third party provides proof to the EPO that she has opened proceedings against the applicant or proprietor for the purpose of seeking a judgment that she is entitled to the (grant of the) European patent, the EPO will stay the proceedings.

8.139 In the United Kingdom, the non-entitlement can actually be raised in revocation proceedings.[247] A similar situation is found in Germany, where derivation (*widerrechtliche Entnahme*) is a ground for opposition according to § 21(1) No. 3 of the PatG. The patent is revoked if the essential content thereof has been derived from another without consent. Of note, the ground cannot be raised between joint inventors in an application. Derivation requires bad faith and the presence of a patentable invention. The burden of proof generally lies with the opponent. If the opposition is successful, the opponent can file his or her own application within a month after the decision and can claim the priority of the earlier patent for this application. There are due dates to be observed, as stipulated by § 8 of the PatG.

9. Scope of the Validity Challenge—Nullity Proceedings

8.140 As explained above, nullity proceedings are national court proceedings that aim to invalidate a national patent (or the national part of a granted European patent). The post-grant invalidity proceedings thus follow the concept that, with the grant of the European patent, the patent (essentially) transforms into a bundle of national patents. According to Article 138 of the EPC, a European patent may be revoked with effect for a contracting state only on the grounds for opposition, that the protection conferred by the European patent has been extended, or that the proprietor of the European patent is not entitled to the patent. These grounds are identical to the ones listed in German Patent Act, § 22 for national German patents. No other grounds can be raised.

[246] See G 3/92, OJ EPO 1994, 607.
[247] s. 37 UK Patents Act.

Currently, bifurcation—that is, the separation of infringement and validity claims into separate court actions—is used in a few European countries, notably Austria and Germany. As discussed elsewhere in this book, staying the infringement proceedings in view of an ongoing nullity or opposition procedure is at the discretion of the court. 8.141

D. Other Defenses in Litigation Proceedings

The following paragraphs discuss the defenses that a defendant can raise when confronted with patent infringement proceedings. In brief, these defenses can be divided into three groups: defenses relating to standing to sue, the loss or waiver of the right to enforce the patent, and legal limits to the scope of protection. It has to be kept in mind that the validity of a granted patent cannot be effectively contested in a bifurcated litigation court. Of note, this is different in cases where a (non-examined) utility model is involved. 8.142

1. Derivation/Lack of Entitlement

In litigation proceedings, defendants can raise the defense of a lack of entitlement. Defendants then have to show that the features of the claim as enforced belong to their own invention. In addition to supporting the prior invention, derivation may further support a prior use right. German Patent Act, § 8 provides that derivation can only be raised within two years from the publication of the grant of the patent or within one year after the finalization of an earlier opposition procedure.[248] Nevertheless, these due dates do not apply if the derivation took place in bad faith. It is in dispute whether this due date for the derivation procedure is also applicable to the defense in infringement proceedings. 8.143

2. (Co-)Ownership in Cases of Inventions by Employees

According to § 6 of the PatG, the rights to an invention are with the inventor or successor in title. In the case of a service invention by an inventor who is an employee, all rights to the invention are transferred to the employer if the employer claims the invention. Until the 2009 amendment of the German law regarding inventions of employees (the *Gesetz über Arbeitnehmererfindungen*, ArgErfG), the employer had to specifically claim the rights to the invention within four months from the report thereof by the employee.[249] This due date was often missed and, if this happened, the rights to the service invention stayed with the inventor(s). Thus, in practice there may be quite a number of service inventions that still belong to their inventors, who could then raise the lack of a transfer as their (or their later licensees') defense. Nevertheless, as soon as the claiming was done with the correct formalities, the rights to the invention were transferred by law to the employer.[250] 8.144

[248] See, e.g., BGH, decision of February 1, 2005—X ZR 214/02, GRUR 2005, 567—*Schweißbrennerreinigung.*

[249] Of July 25, 1957, BGBl. I S. 756, last amended by Art. 7 of the "Gesetz zur Vereinfachung und Modernisierung des Patentrechts" of July 31, 2009.

[250] According to §§ 6 and 7 ArbErfG.

3. License

8.145 Since a license agreement is regarded as providing a positive right to use a patented invention,[251] the said license can be used as a defense against an alleged patent infringement.

4. Patent Misuse

8.146 This topic has gained more interest over the last few years, in particular in the following two scenarios: the patent misuse defense against litigation brought by patent trolls (non-practicing entities, NPEs) and patent misuse in cases of anti-competitive behaviour by patent holders relating to industry standards. According to PatentFreedom, a company that accesses and shares information about NPEs, based on the number of patent holdings, the top five NPEs are Intellectual Ventures, Interdigital, Round Rock Research LLC, Wisconsin Alumni Foundation, and Rockstar Consortium LLC.[252] In Germany, there is currently no specific anti-NPE case law. However, in the context of an injunction procedure, the district court in Düsseldorf[253] and recently the Appeals Court in Karlsruhe both issued critical comments stating that NPEs would constitute a special situation since the NPE would have no own marketing position worth protecting and, further, could seek damages in the main proceedings.[254]

5. Laches and Estoppels, in Particular Prosecution History Estoppels

8.147 A defense based on laches does not automatically lead to a finding of non-infringement but is instead based on the concept of good faith.[255] Laches requires a certain period of time during which the patentee knows about the infringement but does not stop infringer.[256] This ultimately leads to a form of protection on the side of the infringer regarding the infringement and, consequently, a block on injunctive relief and damages.[257] Because of the character of the patent as a time-limited right, the defense of laches is almost never successful and requires a high standard of proof.[258]

8.148 Another possibility for a defense based on laches is statements made by the patentee during the examination, which can create so-called prosecution history estoppels. In Germany, the *Okklusionsvorrichtung* (Occlusion Device) decision[259] has recently revitalized the question and discussion regarding the possibility of a limitation on the scope of protection. Nevertheless, both the case law and the literature quite strictly exclude prosecution history estoppels.[260]

---

251 See German Patent Act, §§ 9 and 10.

252 https://www.patentfreedom.com/about-npes/holdings/.

253 LG Düsseldorf, GRUR 2000, 692—*NMR-Kontrastmittel.*

254 OLG Karlsruhe, GRUR-RR 2010, 120—*Patentverwertungsgesellschaft.*

255 Good faith is referred to in § 242 BGB ("the debtor is required to perform according to the requirements of good faith, ordinary usage being taken into consideration"—translation provided by author), and by § 157 BGB ("contracts shall be interpreted according to the requirements of good faith, ordinary usage being taken into consideration"—translation provided by author).

256 E.g., see OLG Düsseldorf, decision of August 2, 2012, Az. I-2 U 58/10.

257 BGH GRUR 2001, 323, 324 right col.—*Temperaturwächter.*

258 BGH GRUR 1994, 597, 602—*Zerlegvorrichtung für Baumstämme.*

259 BGH, decision of May 10, 2011—X ZR 16/09, GRUR 2011, 701—*Okklusionsvorrichtung.*

260 T. Kühnen, "Die Erteilungsakte—Verbotenes oder gebotenes Auslegungsmittel bei der Schutzbereichsbestimmung europäischer Patente?" *GRUR* (2012): 664; BGHZ 150, GRUR 2002, 511—*Kunststoffrohrteil*; OLG Karlsruhe, decision of July 9, 2014—6 U 29/11.

In contrast, German case law recognizes the limitations in enforcing a claim because of good faith considerations in cases where the patentee acts in bad faith against statements and/or contracts between the parties. This does not lead to an actual limitation on the scope of a claim but renders the right unenforceable.[261] **8.149**

Prosecution history estoppels also do not exist in the United Kingdom: **8.150**

> The courts of the United Kingdom ... certainly discourage, if they do not actually prohibit, use of the patent office file in aid of construction. There are good reasons: the meaning of the patent should not change according to whether or not the person skilled in the art has access to the file and in any case life is too short for the limited assistance which it can provide.[262]

The courts in the Netherlands follow the opposite approach. Here, the prosecution history can be taken into account, even if the scope of the patent is clearly broader.[263] **8.151**

6. Double Patenting

Double patenting and/or double protection can occur in different scenarios. Factors to be considered are the proprietors of the rights involved, the scope of protection of the rights, and the types of rights themselves. Of note, for double protection, the grant/registration is a prerequisite. **8.152**

Double protection is not generally prohibited. Many countries in Europe allow the protection in the form of so-called "accumulation"—that is, protection based on several national rights. Examples are patents and utility models, and patents and variety protection. **8.153**

Double protection can also occur in cases where there are "overlaps" or "layers" of granted patent claims. Most prominently, such overlaps are explicitly allowed in cases of first, second, and further medical use claims, where Articles 54(4) and (5) of the EPC provide the legal fiction of novelty for these improvements. Also, patents relating to the same infringing activity must be enforced in the same proceedings.[264] This could be seen as a further indication that the law acknowledges that double protection can occur. **8.154**

In contrast, double patenting often seems to be undesired, and an indication of this can, for example, be seen in the prior right effect according to Article 54(3) of the EPC and the "internal priority" withdrawal effect based on German Patent Act, § 40. Of note, some countries in Europe (such as Austria, Denmark, and Sweden) have no double patenting prohibition. The same holds true for the EPC, which does not deal explicitly with cases of co-pending European applications of the same effective date filed by the same applicant. The Enlarged Board of Appeal published an *obiter dictum* stating that the principle behind the prohibition on double patenting is based on the notion that an applicant has no legitimate interest in the proceedings leading to the grant of a second patent for the same subject matter if the applicant already possesses one granted patent for that subject matter.[265] In the rare case in which there are two or more European applications from the same applicant designating the same states and the claims of those applications have the same filing or priority date and relate to the same invention, once one of the applications is granted, the **8.155**

[261] BGH, GRUR 1993, 886—*Weichvorrichtung I*; Mitt 1997, 364 (408)—*Weichvorrichtung II*.
[262] 2004 UKHL 46—*Kirin-Amgen/TKT*.
[263] Hoge Raad, decision of December 22, 2006 (C05/200HR)—*Dijkstra v. Saier*.
[264] German Patent Act, § 145.
[265] See G 1/05, OJ EPO 2008, 271, and G 1/06, OJ EPO 2008, 307.

other(s) will be refused.[266] Should two applications with the same effective date be received from two different applicants, each must be allowed to proceed as though the other did not exist. Thus, double patenting can be an issue in cases where the same owner has obtained two patents for the same invention, which in Europe can occur in both the EPO and/or the national level.

8.156 In Germany, double protection based on a German patent and the German part of a European patent is prohibited according to Article II § 8 of the IntPatÜG, and the overlapping scope of the German patent will be invalidated by the European patent. Only this "automatic" invalidation can be raised in German national infringement proceedings.[267]

7. Prior Right and Prior Use Right

8.157 The fact that the invention had been protected by a prior right (i.e., an older patent) can theoretically be used as a defense by an "older" user. Nevertheless, success of this defense, which is regarded by many as a "hidden" non-patentability argument, is extremely rare, at least in Germany.[268]

8.158 There are two kinds of prior use defenses, namely (a) prior use and (b) continued use after the transient expiry of the patent as enforced. In Germany, German Patent Act, § 12 provides the prior user with a defense against a patent infringement suit if it is established that the prior user commercially used or has undertaken to use, in good faith, a process, machine, manufacture, or composition of matter that is asserted to infringe the patent, before the filing date or priority date thereof.[269] Such prior users have the right to continue to use the invention, but solely for the purposes of their business.[270] The right of the prior user may further only be transferred together with the business entitled to the prior use.[271] No right based on prior use arises from the mere conception of the invention; the inventor has to show a reduction to practice or serious undertakings to do so in the very near future.[272] All European countries have such prior use rights in their laws in order to reconcile the interests of the patent owner with those of a prior user acting in good faith.

8.159 The right of continued use (*Weiterbenutzungsrecht*) allows for a similar defense after the expiry and, for example, reinstatement of a patent.[273] Rights for continued use were a particular issue in Germany after the reunification and are still relevant in cases of mistakes and/or omissions in translations of foreign patent applications (no longer relevant for granted European patents), although the German case law regarding the correction of mistakes has been relaxed.[274]

---

[266] Arts. 97(2) and 125 EPC.

[267] T. Kühnen, *Die Reichweite des Doppelschutzverbotes nach Art. II § 8 IntPatÜG* (Festschrift für König, 2003), 309; P. Mes, "Zum Doppelschutzverbot des Art. II § 8 IntPatÜG," *GRUR* (2001): 976.

[268] See, e.g., I. B. Stjerna, "Die Einrede des älteren Rechts im Patent- und Gebrauchsmusterverletzungsstreit," *GRUR* (2010): 202.

[269] German Patent Act, § 12.

[270] Ibid.

[271] Ibid.

[272] BGH GRUR 1986, 803—*Formstein.*

[273] German Patent Act, § 123(5) and (6) or Art. 122(6) EPC.

[274] BGH, decision of July 18, 2011—X ZB 10/10, GRUR 2012, 91—*Polierendpunktbestimmung* (for the filing procedure), BGH, decision of March 18, 2010—Xa ZR 74/09, GRUR 2010, 708—*Nabenschaltung II.*

8. Compulsory License for Technology Standard

Another option for the defendant is to claim abuse of the patent by the patentee in view of the antitrust rules as stipulated in Article 102 of the Treaty on the Functioning of the European Union (TFEU).[275] If an abuse is found, a license has to be granted. A particular case is the grant of a license based on "fair, reasonable and non-discriminating" (FRAND) conditions for technical standards. Everyone who invokes the FRAND defense must—in return—provide the patentee/patent pool with a concrete and reasonable offer for a license.[276] **8.160**

9. Experimental Use Exemption

Similar to the patent laws in other European countries, in Germany, the German Patent Act, § 11 lists uses of the patented invention that by law do not constitute patent infringement. Prominent uses include experimental use ("research exemption") and experiments performed for the purposes of medical registrations ("European Bolar exemption").[277] The scope of these exemptions differs between the member states of the EU and EPC. For example, in Belgium the research exemption is of a wider scope and generally includes research *on* or *with* the patented invention. For the Bolar exemption, only use with respect to gaining regulatory approval in the European Economic Area (EEA) for generic medicinal products, bioequivalents, and biosimilars are exempted in the United Kingdom, Sweden, the Netherlands, Ireland, and Belgium. The use for any application submitted for regulatory approval, both inside and outside the EU, including the first application for an innovative product, is exempted in Germany, France, Italy, Spain, Hungary, Portugal, Denmark, and Poland, as well as Switzerland. Thus, the scope of the exemption varies, from a narrower scope, such as in the United Kingdom, to a broader scope, such as in Germany. It has to be noted, however, that the case law in this field is developing quickly. **8.161**

10. Exhaustion

The patent rights can be exhausted if the patentee brings the patented product into commerce in one of the member states of the EU.[278] Thus, the EU follows the concept of union-wide exhaustion. Being a defense, the burden of proof to show that the product has been put onto the market by the patentee or a licensee lies with the defendant.[279] **8.162**

Although in theory exhaustion seems to be easy to analyze, questions often arise in practice, in particular in cases of method patents. If a device for performing a specific method is delivered to a customer by a patentee, then, in the absence of a specific agreement, this could also include an allowance to perform the method.[280] If the delivery is not clearly for a use of a patented method, for example, if a non-patented device for performing a patented method is sold, the situation is different.[281] The same is true if the patentee holds both the patent for **8.163**

275 BGH GRUR 2009, 694—*Orange-Book-Standard*; BGH GRUR 2004, 966—*Standard-Spundfass.*

276 BGH GRUR 2009, 694—*Orange-Book-Standard*; OLG Düsseldorf, InstGE 10, 129—*Druckerpatrone II*; NJOZ 2010, 1781, 1789—*Testkauf patentverletzender DVDs—interframe dropping*; OLG Karlsruhe, InstGE 12, 220—*MP3-Standard.*

277 BGH GRUR 1996, 109—*Klinische Versuche I*; BVerfG GRUR 2001, 43—*Klinische Versuche.*

278 BGH GRUR 2001, 223—*Bodenwaschanlage.*

279 BGH GRUR 2000, 299, 300—*Karate.*

280 BGH GRUR 2007, 773, 776—*Rohrschweißverfahren*; BGH GRUR 1980, 38—*Fullplastverfahren.*

281 BGH GRUR 2007, 773, 776—*Rohrschweißverfahren.*

a device for producing a compound and a separate patent for the compound as produced.[282] Also, the sale or delivery of the device does not put the patented method into commerce.[283] The patentee is free to limit the use of a device, as sold, to a specific use.[284]

8.164 If the sale by the patentee (or licensee) takes place in a member state of the EU or the EEA, exhaustion takes place.[285] It is not sufficient for the product merely to be made or produced in the EU or the EEA; it has to be introduced into commerce, even if no patent is present in the country.[286]

8.165 A special situation with respect to EU-wide exhaustion (amongst others) is parallel imports (sometimes referred to as gray market goods). As a general rule, a pharmaceutical patent is exhausted as soon as the product is marketed, which means that the manufacturer no longer has any rights over what happens to the product once it has been sold.[287] The parallel import of a medicinal product involves importing the product into one member state from another and then distributing it outside the distribution network set up by the manufacturer or its authorized distributor.

8.166 The EU Commission is of the opinion that parallel imports are a lawful form of trade within the internal market, based on the principle of the free movement of goods.[288] In the pharmaceutical sector, parallel trade benefits from the divergence in prices set by national governments to control their health care expenditure. Whilst they are legal, parallel imports of medicinal products may be restricted if they constitute a risk to the protection of human health and life, and to the protection of industrial and commercial property.[289]

[282] Ibid.

[283] Ibid.

[284] OLG Düsseldorf, NJOZ 2010, 1781, 1786—*Testkauf patentverletzender DVDs—interframe dropping*

[285] BGH, GRUR 1997, 116—*Prospekthalter*; GRUR 2001, 223—*Bodenwaschanlage;* BGH GRUR 2000, 299, 300—*Karate.*

[286] BGH GRUR 2000, 299, 300—*Karate.*

[287] Ibid.

[288] Commission Communication on parallel imports of proprietary medicinal products for which marketing authorisations have already been granted—COM(2003) 839 final.

[289] Ibid.

9

JAPAN

A. Introduction

The patent litigation in Japan has been strongly influenced by Germany, because it used a bifurcated system until the early 2000s for challenging the validity of Japanese patents, which was rooted in the separation of powers between the civil courts and administrative offices such as the JPO.[1] Early Supreme Court cases supported the view that civil courts should refrain from deciding patent validity in infringement litigation, giving the JPO exclusive jurisdiction over deciding patent validity.[2] In patent infringement litigation, accused infringers were unable to raise the defense of invalidity and were required to start separate invalidation proceedings at the JPO concurrently with the litigation. When an accused infringer started invalidation proceedings, the decision of whether to stay litigation was at the discretion of the court. To grant a stay would result in a delay in dispute resolution; however, denying a stay could result in the enforcement of an invalid patent if the JPO later found it invalid. Without the power to declare a patent invalid, Japanese courts adopted the practice of interpreting a claim to exclude the accused embodiment from the scope of the patent by reading limitations from the specification into the claim.[3] This obscure practice of claim interpretation was developed to avoid enforcing an invalid patent. **9.01**

In 2000 the Supreme Court of Japan decided *Kilby*, the case that established the ability of Japanese courts to examine patent validity in infringement litigation.[4] If a court finds a patent to be obviously invalid today, it now has the power to not enforce the patent as an abuse of right, making it unnecessary for accused infringers to start separate proceedings at the JPO to challenge the patent while in litigation. Despite these changes, the German influence remains strong because courts still do not have the power to declare a patent invalid and can only refuse to enforce a patent that they find to be invalid.[5] While a court's refusal to enforce a patent does not per se invalidate that patent, it is functionally **9.02**

---

[1] The JPO originally had exclusive jurisdiction over both validity and infringement; see Ryuichi Murabayashi, "Tokkyohō 104-jo no 3 no Seitei to Sono Kaishaku (Legislation of Patent Law Article 104ter and its Interpretation)," 63(7) *Patento* (2010): 111.

[2] For a general discussion of the validity challenge and patent infringement litigation, see Koizumi and Institute of Intellectual Property (eds.), *Tokkyo no Yukosei to Shin-gai Sosho (Validity of Patent and Infringement Litigation)* (2001), 5–7.

[3] Toshiko Takenaka, "Interpreting Patent Claims: The United States, Germany and Japan," 17 *IIC Studies* (1995): 211. Testuya Obuchi, "Two Major and Long-lasting Patent Law Issues in Japan," in Wolrad prinz su Waldeck und Pyrmont et al. (ed.), *Patents and Technological Progress in a Globalized World* (2009), 431.

[4] Saikō Saibansho (Sup. Ct.) April 11, 2000, Hei 10 (o) No. 364, 54 Saikō Saibansho Minji Hanreishū (Minshū) 1368 (Japan).

[5] Obuchi, "Two Major and Long-lasting Patent Law Issues in Japan," 434.

equivalent because an unenforced patent cannot provide any remedy for infringement.[6] A patent remains unenforceable unless all grounds for invalidity are eliminated by correction procedures. The *Kilby* decision essentially moved the Japanese validity challenge system to be more in line with the US and UK patent systems, making a defense of invalidity admissible in patent infringement litigation.[7]

9.03 The Japanese Patent Law was revised in 2004 to grant courts the power to examine patent validity, essentially codifying the *Kilby* decision.[8] This legislation reflects a demand on the part of Japanese industry for the prompt resolution of patent litigation and validity disputes.[9] The newly introduced Article 104ter gives courts the power to refuse to enforce a patent if the court finds that the patent would likely be invalidated through procedures at the JPO.[10] This codification of the *Kilby* doctrine makes it clear that courts have full power to examine all grounds for invalidity in patent litigation. However, Article 104ter does not contain the "obviousness" standard that was seen in the *Kilby* opinion, replacing it with a standard that relies on the court's judgment as to whether the patent should be invalidated. On its face, the 2004 revision expanded the scope of the *Kilby* doctrine, but experts view Article 104ter as simply codifying the *Kilby* doctrine[11] or replacing the obviousness requirement with the requirement that the JPO board would find the patent invalid if examined in invalidation procedures.[12] Regardless of the intent of the legislature, accused infringers have begun relying on the invalidity defense frequently in patent litigation, which has led to higher rates of patent invalidation by Japanese courts.[13] This high invalidation rate has scared Japanese patentees from enforcing their patents, resulting in a significant decrease in the number of patent cases filed in Japanese district courts since the introduction of Article 104ter in 2004.[14] Although invalidity rates have recently declined, the patentee win rates at

---

[6] However, a judgment upholding a defense of invalidity binds only parties and their privy. See "Merging Civil and Common Law Traditions in the Patent Vailidity Challenge System: Japanese Experiences," in H.-P. Götting and C. Schlüter (eds.), *Nourriture de l'esprit, Festschrift for Prof. Dieter Stauder* (2011), 271.

[7] Toshiko Takenaka, "Harmonizing the Japanese Patent System with its U.S. Counterpart through Judge-Made Law: Interaction between Japanese and U.S. Case Law Developments," 7 *Pac. Rim L. & Pol'y J.* (1998): 249.

[8] Saibanshohōtō no Ichibu wo Kaisei-suru Hōritsu (Law to partially revise the court organization law and other laws), Law No. 120 of 2004 (Japan).

[9] Masaaki Kondo, "Chiteki Zaisan Kōtō Saibansho Sescchi Ho (Heisei 16 nen houritu 116 go) oyobi Saibanshoho nado no Ichibu wo Kaisei-suru Hōritsu (Heisei 16 nen hōritsu 120 go) ni tsuite (Regarding a Law Establishing Intellectual Property High Court (Law No. 114 of 2004) and Law for Amendment of Court Law etc. (Law No. 120 of 2004))," 2(24) *Chizai Prism* (2004): 1.

[10] Tokkyohō (Japanese Patent Law), Art. 104ter (Japan).

[11] Obuchi, "Two Major and Long-lasting Patent Law Issues in Japan," 436.

[12] Kondo, "Chiteki Zaisan Kōtō Saibansho Sescchi Ho," 6.

[13] Institute of Intellectual Property, *Shingai Soshounado niokeru Tokkyo no Anteisei ni shisuru Tokkyo Seido Unyo ni kansuru Chousa Kenkyu Houkokusho (Establishment and Operation of a Patent System Conductive to Patent Stability in Infringement Law Suit)* (2014) (http://www.jpo.go.jp/shiryou/toushin/chousa/pdf/zaisanken/2013_12.pdf)—English summary is available at http://www.iip.or.jp/e/e_summary/pdf/detail2013/e25_06.pdf; Toshiko Takenaka, "Success or Failure? Japan's National Strategy on Intellectual Property and Evaluation of its Impact from the Comparative Law Perspective," 8 *Wash. U. Global Stud. L. Rev.* (2009): 379.

[14] Shigeo Takakura, "Review of the Recent Trend in Patent Litigation from the Viewpoint of Innovation" (2008) (http://www.rieti.go.jp/en/columns/a01_0242.html). Tomokatsu Tsukahara, "Intellectual Property High Court of Japan, Japan Patent Office: Asia-Pacific Industrial Property Center," *JIPII* (2013) (http://www.training-jpo.go.jp/en/images_x/uploads/text_vtr/pdf/Intellectual%20Property%20High%20Court%20of%20Japan_2013.pdf).

Japanese courts remain low, 23 percent on average between 2000 and 2009, which is lower than the rates at US and German courts.

B. Patent Invalidation Procedures

1. Overview

To defend an infringement claim, an alleged infringer can choose to initiate an invalidation procedure at the JPO while asserting the defense of invalidity at an infringement procedure. One can file with the JPO a request for a trial to invalidate a patent based on the following grounds for invalidity: (1) new matter through an amendment; (2) the lack of novelty or inventive step; (3) immoral inventions and inventions in conflict with public policy; (4) patent filing without consent from a co-owner of the invention; (5) a violation of the first-to-file priority; (6) lack of enablement, written description, or definite claims; (7) a violation of PCT Application Rules; (8) lack of ownership; and (9) a violation of treaty.[15] A request for an invalidation trial can be filed for a patent any time after the issuance of the patent, even during the opposition period within six months from a grant of patent[16] or after the expiration of such a patent, unless the decision to invalidate such a patent has become final. Once a decision to invalidate a patent has become final, the effect of the exclusive right will be retroactively eliminated. The final decision eliminates any cause of action or claim of damages on the basis of patent infringement. Any person can request an invalidation trial except for the grounds relating to the ownership of the claimed invention—that is, (4) patent filing without consent from a co-owner of the invention and (8) lack of ownership.[17] Only a party who has an interest in the patent being challenged can file a trial.[18] **9.04**

An invalidation trial begins with the filing of a petition to request an invalidation trial, with the petition including necessary information to identify the patent, petitioner, and patentee(s).[19] In the petition, the petitioner must identify a fact supporting a ground of invalidity and include evidence to support that fact.[20] One can request to invalidate a patent on a claim-by-claim basis.[21] When a petition is duly filed with the JPO, either three or five trial examiners are assigned to constitute a trial board.[22] The board first examines whether the petition meets all of the formality requirements and gives the petitioner an opportunity to amend the petition if any requirement is not met.[23] **9.05**

After confirming that the petition meets all of the formality requirements, the board sends a copy of the petition to the patentee and gives the patentee an opportunity to file a reply arguing in support of the patentability of the challenged claims.[24] The patentee may also **9.06**

15 Japanese Patent Act, § 123(1).
16 See Ch. 9, 9.15 "Opposition Procedure."
17 See Ch. 9, 9.32 "Inventorship and Ownership."
18 Japanese Patent Act, § 131(2). Before 2014 Patent Law Revision, anyone could file a trial.
19 Ibid. § 131(1).
20 Ibid. § 131(2).
21 Ibid. § 131(1). Japan Patent Office, "Heisei 23nen Kaisei ho ni okeru Muko Shinpan oyobi Teisei Shinpan Jitsumu no Kangaekata (Practice at Invalidation Trial and Correction Trial under 2011 Patent Law Revision)," Ch. 3, 1.1 (https://www.jpo.go.jp/shiryou/kijun/kijun2/pdf/h23_jitumu_kanngae/04_3syou.pdf).
22 Japanese Patent Act, §§ 136(1), 137(1).
23 Ibid. § 133(1).
24 Ibid. § 134(1).

file a petition to request corrections with respect to the claims, written description of the specification, and drawings.[25] After examining whether the reply and petition to request corrections meet all of the formality requirements, the board decides whether to hold an oral hearing but only when all of the formality requirements are met. In principle, the board must hold an oral hearing to decide the merits of an invalidation request.[26] However, the chief trial examiner may decide on the merits based only on submitted documents, without holding an oral hearing, at his own discretion or in response to a request from a party.[27]

9.07 If the patentee does not file a petition to request corrections, the board usually proceeds to an oral hearing without giving the petitioner an opportunity to file a rebuttal. If the patentee does file a petition to request corrections, the board should send the petitioner a copy of the reply and the petition to request corrections so that the petitioner can file a rebuttal.[28] However, if the examiner finds that the corrected claims fail to overcome the grounds for invalidity, the petitioner does not need to be given an opportunity to file a rebuttal.

9.08 Before an oral hearing, the parties receive a notice from the board. The notice includes: (1) preliminary views on the merits, including an assessment of the inadequacy of the disclosure, the definiteness of claims, or a comparison between the claimed invention and the prior art; (2) issues in dispute between the parties; and (3) if necessary, a request for an explanation of the invention and its background.[29] In response to the notice, the parties should submit a brief including a summary of oral arguments at the hearing. Because the inquisitorial principle controls oral hearings at the JPO, the chief trial examiner can ask the parties any question necessary to decide the validity of the challenged claims without being limited to the scope of invalidity grounds and arguments included in the documents filed by the parties.[30]

9.09 After both parties have been given sufficient opportunities to defend or challenge patent validity and the board is ready is to make a decision on the merits, the chief trial examiner will send the parties notice that a trial decision will be issued.[31] However, the chief trial examiner may issue a trial decision without sending notice if the patentee made it clear that notice was not needed or the board decides to issue a decision confirming the validity of all challenged claims (including corrected claims).

9.10 The notice includes the same content as a trial decision: (1) conclusions on the merits—that is, validity of the challenged claims, and (2) reasons to support the conclusion. Accordingly, the notice gives the patentee one last opportunity to file a petition to request corrections if the board finds that the challenged claims and/or corrected claims fails to overcome any ground of invalidity. If the patentee does file a petition to request corrections, the board gives the petitioner an opportunity to argue against the correction and validity. If the patentee does not file a petition to request corrections, the board issues a trial decision entering the same content included in the notice.

[25] Ibid. § 134(2).
[26] Ibid. § 145(1).
[27] Ibid. § 145(1).
[28] Ibid. §§ 134(3), 134-2(4)
[29] Japan Patent Office, "Heisei 23nen Kaisei ho ni okeru Muko Shinpan oyobi Teisei Shinpan Jitsumu no Kangaekata," Ch. 3, 9.2.
[30] Japanese Patent Act, § 134(4)
[31] Ibid. § 164-2(1).

A trial decision includes the validity or invalidity of each challenged claim, including which corrections are allowed for each claim if a petition to request corrections is filed. Within thirty days from the receipt of a trial decision, the losing party can file with the IP High Court a civil action against the trial decision.[32] The patentee can file a civil action against a trial decision on a claim-by-claim basis. The decision to invalidate a claim becomes final if a civil action against a trial decision is not filed with respect to the claim. **9.11**

Once a trial decision invalidating a patent has become final, the patent right is deemed to have never existed.[33] If a patent includes multiple claims and a trial decision invalidates only some claims but not all claims, only the exclusive right granted to the invalidated claims is retroactively eliminated.[34] The parties to a trial cannot file a petition challenging validity on the same ground and fact with respect to a claim on which a trial decision has become final.[35] **9.12**

2. Correction of Claims

If a patentee finds a prior art reference or any defects in the descriptions of the claims, specification, and drawings after a grant of patent, she may want to correct the claims, specification, and drawings to remove any defects in validity before enforcing the patent. She can initiate a correction trial to correct the claims, written description of the specification, and/or drawings any time after a patent grant.[36] A patentee can request a correction trial even after the expiration of the patent unless a trial to invalidate the patent has become final, which retroactively eliminates the exclusive right.[37] The exception to this rule is (1) the period an invalidation trial for the claims that a patentee wants to correct is pending at the JPO and (2) the period that the opposition procedure is pending at the JPO.[38] Because a patentee can correct claims during the invalidation trial and opposition procedure, she cannot request a correction trial until a trial decision resulting from the invalidation trial has become final. When a patent includes multiple claims, the patentee can request a correction trial on a claim-by-claim basis. In both a correction trial and invalidation trial, corrections are allowable only when they fall into one of the following four categories: (1) narrowing the scope of the claim; (2) correcting a typo or mistranslation of a foreign language; (3) clarifying an ambiguous statement; and (4) rewriting a dependent claim into an independent claim without changing the scope of the claim.[39] A patentee cannot introduce a new matter through a correction trial or a petition to request corrections.[40] No correction is allowable if the scope of the corrected claim is in effect broader or different from the scope of the original claims.[41] Thus, a correction of a typo or mistranslation of a foreign language in the specification is not allowable if the correction changes the scope of the claim. **9.13**

[32] Ibid. § 178(1)(3)
[33] Ibid. § 125. Exceptions to this rule are where a patent owner has lost the right to enjoy a patent under a treaty and a patent has fallen in violation of a treaty after a grant of patent.
[34] Ibid. §§ 123(1), 185.
[35] Ibid. § 167.
[36] Ibid. § 126(1).
[37] Ibid. § 126(8).
[38] Ibid. § 126(2).
[39] Ibid. § 126(1).
[40] Ibid. § 126(5).
[41] Ibid. § 126(6).

9.14 Only a patentee registered at the JPO can request a correction trial.[42] If a patent is owned by multiple parties, all co-owners must jointly request the correction trial.[43] If any exclusive or non-exclusive licenses are registered at the JPO, the patentee must obtain consent from all registered licensees.[44] The correction trial procedure is similar to the invalidation trial procedure. Either three or five trial examiners are assigned to constitute a board and examine whether the requested corrections are allowable on a claim-by-claim basis. A trial decision allowing the correction becomes final when the patentee receives the decision. Once such a decision becomes final, the correction retroactively eliminates defects from the claims, specification, and drawings of the patent.[45] Unlike amendments of claims through post-issuance procedures at the USPTO, the patentee maintains a cause of action against infringers or a claim of damages with respect to past infringement as long as their accused embodiments fall within the scope of the corrected claims. The patentee can file a civil action with the IP High Court against a trial decision denying corrections within thirty days from the patentee's receipt of the trial decision.

3. Opposition Procedure

9.15 On April 1, 2015, the JPO introduced an opposition procedure.[46] The newly introduced opposition system is similar to the *ex parte* re-examination at the USPTO: the examination is done through an *ex parte* procedure between the patentee and examiner. Unlike a trial, anyone can file an opposition within six months from a grant of patent.[47] Grounds for opposition are the same as the grounds for invalidity except that ownership and a violation of treaty are removed from the grounds for opposition.[48] The opposition procedure aims to provide a simple and quick procedure to challenge the validity of patents and thus no oral hearing is available in the opposition procedure. A panel of three or five examiners examine the patent and make a decision to cancel or maintain the patent.[49] The patentee can file a civil action with the IP High Court against a decision to cancel the patent within thirty days from the patentee's receipt of the trial decision.[50] However, no appeal is available from a decision to maintain the challenged patent.[51] Because Japanese Patent Act does not provide an estoppel, a losing party can file for a trial for invalidation on the same ground. Like a trial decision, once a decision to cancel a patent has become final, the patent right is deemed to have never existed.[52]

4. Comparison with Invalidity Defense at Infringement Procedure

9.16 Unlike invalidity challenges at the USPTO, the same burden of proof, no reasonable doubt from the perspective of an ordinary person, applies to both infringement procedures at district courts and invalidation trial procedures at the JPO. Any ground for rejecting claims

---

[42] Ibid. § 126(1).
[43] Ibid. § 132(3).
[44] Ibid. § 127(1).
[45] Ibid. § 128.
[46] Tokkyohōtōno Ichibuwo Kaiseisuru Hōritsu (Law for Revising Patent and Other Related Laws) Law No. 36 of 2014.
[47] Japanese Patent Act, § 113.
[48] For the grounds for invalidity, see Ch. 9, 9.04.
[49] Japanese Patent Act, § 114(1).
[50] Ibid. § 178(1).
[51] Ibid. § 114(5).
[52] Ibid. § 114(3).

during the examination constitutes a ground of invalidity. Although the inquisitorial system controls procedures in the JPO in contrast to the adversarial system for procedures at district courts, the difference has a very marginal effect on the outcome of validity findings between the JPO and courts.

With respect to claim construction, like the USPTO, the JPO uses a different rule for claim interpretation in examining validity at invalidation trials. As discussed in Chapter 6, B. Extent of Patent Protection,[53] under the Japanese Patent Act the scope to define the subject matter of the examination for patent requirements at the JPO during the first examination and the trials is called "gist of invention."[54] In contrast, the scope to define an exclusive right in infringement procedure is called "technical scope."[55] In theory, the scope of a gist of invention should be broader than the technical scope in an infringement procedure because Japanese courts interpret claims restrictively in light of the specification and drawings as well as in light of the record of patent prosecution. However, it is very unlikely that the different rules will result in different scopes for the same asserted claim. To avoid conflicting decisions on the validity of the same claims, the same panel at the IP High Court examines appeals from the JPO and a district court.[56] **9.17**

In an infringement procedure at a district court, the patent is examined by a panel consisting of three judges who do not have technical backgrounds, although they are assisted by judicial research officials.[57] In contrast, trial examiners who constitute a panel at the JPO have technical backgrounds, extensive training in patent law, and at least nine years of hands-on experience examining patent applications as an examiner.[58] This difference in technical backgrounds results in differing chances of success in challenging validity: judges are more willing to invalidate patents than trial examiners. After hitting its peak of 65 percent in 2008, the invalidity rate at the JPO has been steadily decreasing, with a rate of approximately 40 percent in 2012.[59] In contrast, the invalidity rate in infringement procedures at district courts between 2003 and 2012 stayed at 70–80 percent for cases in which defendants asserted an invalidity defense.[60] However, courts decide validity in infringement proceedings only in 22 percent of all cases filed. Thus, the cases in which courts found invalidity constitute only 16 percent of all cases filed with district courts. **9.18**

For accused infringers, it makes the most sense to assert a defense of invalidity while initiating an invalidation trial at the JPO if an asserted patent has any defects. The JPO makes a great effort to reduce the time pending a trial decision in an invalidation trial. The average pending period for invalidation trials is significantly shorter than the average pending period for **9.19**

---

53 Ch. 6, 6.36.

54 Sup. Ct. of Japan, March 8, 1991, Sho (Gyo Tsu) No. 3, 45 Minshū (No. 3) 123 (*Lipase*).

55 Makiko Takabe and Jitsumu Shōsetsu, *Tokkyo Kankei Sosho (Detailed Explanation of Practice: Patent and Related Litigations)* (2d ed., 2012), 155.

56 For more discussion on measures to avoid conflicting decisions, see Ch. 9, 9.23.

57 For more discussionon judicial systems for IP litigation in Japan, see Ch. 2, 2.62.

58 Patent Act Implementation Ordinance, § 12 and § 14. To become qualified as an examiner, one must have experience examining patent applications under the supervision of an examiner. Another five years of experience examining patent applications as an examiner is necessary to become qualified as a trial examiner.

59 Institute of Intellectual Property, *Shingai Soshounado niokeru Tokkyo no Anteisei ni shisuru Tokkyo Seido Unyo ni kansuru Chousa Kenkyu Houkokusho*, 53.

60 Ibid. 55.

infringement procedures at district courts.[61] To take advantage of the swift procedures at the JPO, a party should initiate an invalidation procedure as soon as possible after being sued for patent infringement. With infringement cases, 48 percent result in settlement without reaching a judgment.[62] It is very likely that these settled cases include many cases where the JPO found asserted claims to be invalid at an invalidation trial. The likelihood that the IP High Court will affirm a trial decision to invalidate claims is 70 percent.[63] A petitioner can withdraw its petition any time before a trial decision resulting from the petition has become final.[64] An accused infringer should be able to settle an infringement case in her favor at a district court when she receives a trial decision invalidating the asserted claims and offers to withdraw a petition in exchange for a license.

9.20 Failing to secure a final trial decision of invalidity may subject the winning party's contractors and customers to a risk of infringement. The most significant difference between validity challenges at the JPO and district courts is the effect of a final decision. When a trial decision becomes final and thus irrevocable, the effect of an exclusive right is retroactively eliminated as the patent is deemed to have never been granted.[65] A final decision of invalidity eliminates any past and future causes of action for infringement and prevents the patentee of the invalidated patent from suing competitors. In contrast, a judgment upholding a defense of invalidity binds only the parties of the case and their privy even if the judgment becomes final and irrevocable. Japanese civil procedure has not adopted any doctrines equivalent to the collateral estoppel doctrine, and a final judgment in litigation does not affect non-parties to that litigation with respect to future litigation or JPO procedures. In theory, a patentee may sue another accused infringer even after the court has rendered its final judgment finding a patent invalid, even though in practice it is likely that the court would again find the patent invalid and refuse to enforce it under Article 104ter.[66]

9.21 A more serious problem for failing to initiate an invalidation trial is the inability of a final judgment to stop proceedings at the JPO. A patentee who loses in an infringement procedure can initiate a trial to request corrections any time, even after a judgment of invalidity becomes final, unless a trial decision from the JPO Board invalidating the patent has become final.[67] Because amendments made through invalidation and correction procedures are retroactively effective, an amendment does not eliminate a cause of action or a claim for damages as long as the product at issue in litigation is covered by the amended claim.[68] Without any defenses or rights equivalent to the equitable intervening right, an

[61] Japan Patent Office, *Shinpan no Gaiyou (Outlines of Trials)* (2013), 18 (http://www.jpo.go.jp/torikumi/ibento/text/pdf/h25_jitsumusya_txt/09.pdf).

[62] Institute of Intellectual Property, *Shingai Soshounado niokeru Tokkyo no Anteisei ni shisuru Tokkyo Seido Unyo ni kansuru Chousa Kenkyu Houkokusho*, 51.

[63] Ibid. 53. The affirmance rate for trial decisions to uphold the validity of claims is higher, at 80%.

[64] Japanese Patent Act, § 155.

[65] Ibid. § 125.

[66] Minoru Takeda, "Tokkyocho to Saibansho no Kengen Haibun no Minaoshi (Shian): Funsou no Ikkaiteki Kaiketsu ni Mukete (Rethinking the Allocation of Power Between the Patent Office and the Courts (Proposal): Resolution of Disputes at One Forum)" (June 27, 2002) (http://www.jpo.go.jp/shiryou/toushin/shingikai/pdf/funsosyori2_gijiroku.pdf).

[67] Tokkyohō (Japanese Patent Law), Art. 126 para. 6 (Japan). A patentee cannot request limitation procedures during invalidation procedures because the patentee can limit the scope of the claim through invalidation procedures. See ibid. Art. 126 para. 2 (Japan).

[68] Ibid. Arts. 128 and 134bis para. 5 (Japan).

accused infringer is liable for future activities. The retroactive effect of amendments and the lack of an intervention right create opportunities for patentees to re-litigate a patent and cause extra delays and complexity in a patent dispute because the court must speculate as to the scope of the amended claims.[69]

Moreover, once a judgment finding infringement and awarding damages has become final, a losing party cannot request recovery of damages even if the JPO issues a trial decision invalidating the infringed claims and the trial decision becomes final and eliminates the exclusive right retroactively.[70] At the beginning of the infringement procedure, to develop a schedule of the hearings, the court asks accused infringers if they assert a defense of invalidity.[71] If a defense of invalidity is asserted, a party should assert the defense early. When a party intentionally delays asserting a defense of invalidity, in particular until the court decides infringement, the court may prevent that party from asserting the invalidity, on the basis that intentionally delaying the conclusion of the infringement dispute is an abuse of process.[72] Although it is not mandatory, parties who assert a defense of invalidity are encouraged to initiate an invalidation trial at the JPO. The parties should initiate an invalidation trial as early as possible, to prevent the infringement judgment from becoming final. **9.22**

5. Measures to Prevent Delay and Conflicting Validity Decisions

Giving Japanese courts power to decide validity in infringement procedures without adopting the collateral estoppel doctrine led to significant delays in resolving patent disputes as well as conflicting decisions between the JPO and district courts with respect to validity.[73] The scope of the asserted claims may change during patent litigation if the patentee initiates a trial to request corrections on the claims, specification, and drawings in order to defend the validity of the asserted patent claims if an accused infringer raises the defense of invalidity. A patentee can initiate a correction trial even if a judgment finding the asserted claim invalid has become final, unless a trial decision invalidating the claim has become final, because a judgment from infringement litigation has no collateral estoppel effect.[74] Even if a correction trial is already pending at the JPO, waiting for the JPO to issue a trial decision on the patentee's request for corrections may result in a significant delay in the dispute resolution. **9.23**

Although the Japanese Patent Act gives courts the discretion to stay litigation procedures if trials to invalidate and/or correct asserted claims are pending at the JPO, courts seldom exercise the discretion in order to avoid delay in dispute resolution.[75] Instead, Japanese courts allow the patentee to assert a rebuttal defense against the accused infringer's defense of invalidity.[76] This rebuttal defense is upheld and the asserted patent claims are found to be **9.24**

---

[69] Chiteki Zaisan Kōtō Saibansho (IP High Ct.), August 25, 2010, Hei 20 (ne) no. 100068.

[70] Japanese Patent Act, § 104-4. Takabe and Shōsetsu, *Tokkyo Kankei Sosho*, 215.

[71] Ryuichi Shitara et al., "Chiteki Zaisan Kankei Soshōhō no Tetsuzuki no Ippantekina Gaiyō (Overview of IP Litigation Procedures)," in Toshiaki Iimura and Ryuichi Shitara (eds.), *Chiteki Zaisan Kankei Soshō (Intellectual Property Litigations)* 3 Legal Progressive Series (2008), 1.

[72] Minji soshōhō (Code of Civil Procedure), § 157. Takabe and Shōsetsu, *Tokkyo Kankei Sosho*, 204.

[73] For more discussion, see Toshiko Takenaka, "Merging Civil and Common Law Traditions in the Patent Vailidity Challenge System: Japanese Experiences," in H.-P. Götting and C. Schlüter (eds.), *Nourriture de l'esprit, Festschrift for Prof. Dieter Stauder* (2011), 271.

[74] Japanese Patent Act, § 126(8).

[75] Ibid. § 168(2).

[76] Takabe and Shōsetsu, *Tokkyo Kankei Sosho*, 201.

infringed if (1) a trial to request corrections is initiated at the JPO; (2) the claims corrected through the trial overcome all grounds for invalidity; and (3) the accused embodiment falls within the corrected claims.[77] Under exceptional circumstances where a patentee is unable to request corrections, the court may not require the patentee to request corrections at the JPO. For example, the 2011 Patent Act Revision limits opportunities for a patentee to correct claims once an invalidation trial is initiated. Thus, courts may allow a rebuttal defense against an invalidity defense if the patentee promises to correct claims at the next available opportunity by identifying which claims and what corrections will be requested at the JPO.[78]

9.25 The Japanese courts' practice of allowing a rebuttal defense may result in a conflicting decision on the invalidity defense between the JPO and the district court that decides infringement if the JPO disagrees with the court with respect to the allowability and scope of the corrected claims. The average pending periods for both invalidation and correction trials are a couple of months shorter than the period for infringement litigation.[79] Therefore, the district court where the claims are under examination in a parallel trial is able to take advantage of the JPO decision with respect to the validity and correction of the claims, specification, and drawings, although the court is not bound by the trial decision unless the decision has become final and the patent issued in respect of the asserted claims is retroactively eliminated.

9.26 The IP High Court should be able to resolve any conflicts between the JPO trial decision and the district court judgment because appeals for both are filed at the IP High Court. When appeals from both the JPO and the district court with respect to the validity and infringement of the same claims are pending at the IP High Court, they are assigned to the same bench. The IP High Court can review claims on appeal only with respect to grounds raised during the trial at the JPO.[80] In contrast, the scope of review for an appeal from an infringement procedure is not limited, and thus parties are able to raise a new ground of invalidity and introduce new evidence. However, the IP High Court may prevent a party from asserting a new ground of invalidity or introducing new evidence if it finds that the party is abusing its right and intentionally delaying the conclusion of the appeal procedure by such assertion of a new ground or introduction of evidence.[81] A new ground of invalidity necessarily results in a significant delay because it is likely that the patentee will request corrections on the claims to overcome this ground. The IP High Court is reluctant to allow new grounds and evidence unless a party can justify the delay.

9.27 In 2011, the Japanese Patent Act was revised to minimize problems resulting from conflicting decisions when appeals were not simultaneously pending at the IP High Court. Prior to the 2011 revision, an accused infringer who lost in an infringement procedure and paid infringement damages was able to initiate a retrial to recover damages as unjust enrichment

[77] IP High Court, August 25, 2009, Hei 20 (ne) No. 10068, Hanrei Taimusu (No. 1319) 246.

[78] Takabe and Shōsetsu, *Tokkyo Kankei Sosho*, 201.

[79] JPO, *Shinpan no Gaiyou*, 8, 17. In 2011, the average pending period for correction trials was 1.9 months and the average pending period for invalidation trials was 8.4 months in contrast to the pending period for infringement procedures at district courts, which was 13.4 months.

[80] Sup. Ct. of Japan, March 10, 1976, Sho 42 (Gyo tsu) No. 28, 30 Minshū (No. 2) 79; Takabe and Shōsetsu, *Tokkyo Kankei Sosho*, 324.

[81] Code of Civil Procedure, § 157; Takabe and Shōsetsu, *Tokkyo Kankei Sosho*, 204.

if a trial decision invalidating a claim and in which the court found infringement by the infringer became final.[82] The Patent Act introduced a provision to clarify that a party cannot initiate a retrial once a judgment finding infringement and sustaining the validity of an asserted claim has become final, even if a trial decision for finding the asserted claim invalid becomes final.[83] This provision guarantees that a patentee will be entitled to damages awarded by a final judgment and prevents a losing party from recovering damages as unjust enrichment.[84] However, a final invalidation trial decision lifts any injunction orders. Any party including the losing party can freely work on the invention covered by the invalidated claim because the patentee can no longer enforce an order of injunction.[85]

C. Patentability Invalidity Defenses

1. Comparison between Grounds for Rejection and Invalidity

Conditions of patentability including patent eligibility,[86] industrial applicability,[87] first-to-file priority,[88] novelty[89] and inventive step,[90] defects on ownership,[91] and immoral inventions[92] are both grounds for rejection and grounds for a finding of invalidity. With respect to the description requirements for the claims, specification, and drawings, the enablement for the specification[93] and drawings and the definiteness and support requirements for the claims[94] are both grounds for rejection and invalidity. A new matter introduced via an amendment during the examination is also both grounds for rejection and invalidity.[95] Some insubstantial formality requirements such as the unity of invention are removed from grounds for invalidity.[96] With respect to a foreign applicant-patentee, a violation of the enjoyment of rights[97] and any provision under the Paris Convention and other international agreements[98] are both grounds for rejection and invalidity. With respect to an invention owned by multiple parties, failing to file a patent application jointly with all co-owners of the invention is both grounds for rejection and invalidity.[99] **9.28**

The Japanese Patent Act provides two grounds for invalidity that can arise after a grant of patent. One of the grounds is a new matter introduced by a correction during a correction or an invalidation trial.[100] The other ground is an exceptional circumstance where after a grant **9.29**

[82] Code of Civil Procedure, § 338(1)viii; IP High. Ct., July 14, 2008, Hei (mu) No. 10002, No. 1003, Hanrei Taimuszu (No. 1307) 295.

[83] Japanese Patent Act, § 103-4.

[84] Takabe and Shōsetsu, *Tokkyo Kankei Sosho*, 212.

[85] Ibid. 212.

[86] Japanese Patent Act, §§ 29(1), 123(1)ii.

[87] Ibid.

[88] Ibid. §§ 39 i–iv, 123(1)ii.

[89] Ibid. §§ 29(1), 29-2, 123(1)ii.

[90] Ibid. §§ 29(2), 123(1)ii.

[91] Ibid. §§ 49 vii, 123(1)vi.

[92] Ibid. §§ 32, 123(1)ii.

[93] Ibid. §§ 36(4), 123(1)4.

[94] Ibid. §§ 36(6)I,ii, and iii, 123(2)iv.

[95] Ibid. §§ 17-2(3), 123(1)i.

[96] Ibid. §§ 17-2(4), 36(6)iv, 37, 36(4)2, and 17-2(3) are removed from grounds for invalidity.

[97] Ibid. §§ 17-2(3), 123.

[98] Ibid. §§ 25, 123(1)ii.

[99] Ibid. §§ 49iii, 123(1)ii.

[100] Ibid. §§ 126, 134-2, 123(1)viii.

of patent (1) a patentee loses the right to enjoy patent protection under the Paris Convention or other international agreements; or (2) a patented invention falls in violation of a provision under the Paris Convention or other international agreements.[101]

2. Frequently Cited Invalidity Grounds

9.30 The invalidity rate at JPO invalidation trials steadily decreased from more than 60 percent in 2007 and 2008 to around 30 percent in 2011.[102] The affirmation rate for trial decisions was 70 percent in 2012. Among all the invalidity grounds, lack of inventive step is the most frequently cited to invalidate claims. The influence of US case law was significant at Japan's IP High Court in determining inventive step.[103] The IP High Court adopted a test similar to the Federal Circuit's teaching/suggestion/motivation test when the IP High Court's inventive step was under fire for its stringent standard from legal commentators who criticized its high invalidity finding on the ground of lack of inventive step.[104] In *Hitachi Kasei*,[105] the court reversed the JPO's rejection for lack of inventive step by using a general framework for making an assessment of inventive step. In this framework, it is necessary for the JPO and courts to identify the characterized elements which are essential for solving the technical problem of the invention and avoid hindsight. It also required a suggestion in the prior art that a person having ordinary skill in the art of the invention ("PHOSITA") would have arrived at the essential elements.

9.31 In *INAX*,[106] the IP High Court refined this framework for combination inventions consisting of elements from multiple references by requiring the specific understanding as required by Chief Judge Rader in *Rouffet*. After acknowledging the relatively simple structure of a claimed invention, the court commented on a risk of hindsight that is particularly associated with combination inventions consisting of old elements. To avoid this risk, the court required JPO examiners to follow an analytical framework consisting of (1) a step of identifying the difference between the claimed invention and the prior art and (2) a step of using a specific analytical process: understanding the significance of characterized elements in the context of the technical problem and the solution for the problem while supplementing teachings from the prior art to determine whether a PHOSITA would have conceived the characterized elements. Unless the examiners can give an explanation of how they reached their conclusion by following the specific analytical process, their conclusion of lack of inventive step is improper. In *INAX*, the court found that the JPO did not make it clear that it had followed the analytical process because the JPO did not give an explanation of why a PHOSITA would have conceived the characterized elements by combining the references. In short, the IP High Court uses an analytical framework and test similar to those used by the Federal Circuit to avoid hindsight.

---

[101] Ibid. § 123(1)vii.

[102] Institute of Intellectual Property, *Shingai Soshounado niokeru Tokkyo no Anteisei ni shisuru Tokkyo Seido Unyo ni kansuru Chousa Kenkyu Houkokusho*, 53.

[103] Toshiko Takenaka, "Harmonization Through Judge-made Law: Chief Judge Rader's Contribution to Comparative Patent Law," in Gomulkiewicz and Takenaka (eds.), Festschrift for Chief Judge Randall R. Rader: Judge Rader's Contribution to U.S. and Global Intellectual Property Law & Practice, 7 *Washington Law Technology and Arts Journal* (2012): 379.

[104] Shigeo Takakura, "Review of the Recet Trend in Patent Litigation from the Viewpoint of Innovation" (http://www.rieti.go.jp/en/columns/a01_0242.html).

[105] Judgment of January 28, 2009, Hanrei Jiho No. 2043, 117, Hanrei Taimuzu No. 1299, 272.

[106] Judgment of May, 27, 2010 (http://www.courts.go.jp/hanrei/pdf/20100527145701.pdf).

Regarding computer software-related inventions, petitioners frequently rely on the lack of patent eligibility in order to invalidate patent claims. The standard of patent eligibility is also similar between Japan and the United States although the JPO applies a rigorous standard for the enablement and claim definiteness requirement. Like the US Supreme Court in *Prometheus*[107] and *Alice Corp. v. CLS Bank*,[108] the key concept in distinguishing patent eligible subject matter from ineligible subject matter under the Japanese Patent Act is the utilization or application of a law of nature because the Act defines a statutory invention as a highly advanced creation of technical ideas that utilize a law of nature.[109] In examining the patent eligibility of software-implemented inventions, the JPO requires that a system or method for processing data to be concretely implemented using the hardware resources of a computer.[110] To constitute a patent-eligible invention through a sufficient application of the natural law requirement, the downloading of software into a general computer must result in a specific-use machine or an operational method in which software and hardware resources collaborate to provide an arithmetic operation or manipulation of information for a specific use. Because the Japanese Patent Act does not provide a special rule for functional claims such as 35 U.S.C. § 112(f), hardware resources disclosed in the specification are not imported into a claim even if the functions that are implemented by the hardware resources are included in the claim. Claims must include hardware resources that process data through software. **9.32**

There is no secret prior art under the Japanese Patent Act. All information must be publicly accessible on the priority date to qualify as prior art. The only exception to this rule is information in a patent application pending at the JPO on the priority date (prior rights). Any information in a pending application that is undisclosed to the public constitutes the prior art for novelty only.[111] It cannot be cited as a reason for rejecting an inventive step. **9.33**

3. Inventorship and Ownership

The Japanese Patent Act requires a patent application to be filed by the true inventor or her assignee of the right to obtain a patent for the invention and thus provide a ground of rejection and invalidity if a patent application is filed by a party other than the true inventor or her assignee of the right to obtain a patent.[112] If an invention is made by multiple joint inventors, all joint inventors and their assignees must jointly file a patent application.[113] Failing to join a true joint inventor or her assignee when filing a patent application leads to a ground for rejection and invalidation.[114] During an examination and upon finding out about a third-party application when the application is laid open after eighteen months from the application date, a true inventor may submit evidence to the JPO showing that she is the true inventor so that the examiner rejects the application by the third party.[115] In **9.34**

---

[107] *Mayo Collaborative Servs. v. Prometheus Labs., Inc.*, 132 S. Ct. 1289, 182 L. Ed. 2d 321, 101 U.S.P.Q. 2d 1961 (U.S. 2012).

[108] *Alice Corp. Pty., Ltd. v. CLS Bank Int'l*, 134 S. Ct. 2347, 189 L. Ed. 2d 296, 110 U.S.P.Q. 2d 1976 (U.S. 2014).

[109] Japanese Patent Act, § 2(1).

[110] Japan Patent Office, "Tokkyo—Jistuyō Shinn-ann Shinsa Kijun (Examination Guidelines for Patent and Utility Model)," Part VII, Ch. 1, 2 (http://www.jpo.go.jp/tetuzuki_e/t_tokkyo_e/Guidelines/7_1.pdf).

[111] Japanese Patent Act, § 29-2.

[112] Ibid. §§ 49 vii, 123(1)vi

[113] Ibid. § 25.

[114] Ibid. §§ 49 ii, 123(1)ii.

[115] Ibid. § 49 ii and vii.

practice, it is unlikely that a true inventor will find out about a third-party application during the examination and develop enough evidence to support the fact that the third-party applicant derived the invention claimed in the application from the inventor. Moreover, the very nature of disputes makes it difficult to resolve an inventorship and ownership dispute through an *ex parte* procedure.

9.35 It is likely that a true inventor will challenge inventorship and ownership of a patented invention issued to a third party through an invalidation trial. Like the US and German Patent Acts, an inventor is the original owner. In a leading case determining whether a party was a joint inventor, [116] the IP High Court cited a Supreme Court precedent and held that an invention is completed when a technical idea has been reduced to a concrete and objective idea so that one skilled in the art can repeatedly exploit that idea to attain the technical effect.[117] To qualify as an inventor, (1) a person must contribute to characteristic claim elements of the invention and (2) the contribution must be concrete and substantial in reducing a technical idea of the invention to practice so that one skilled in the art of the invention can exploit the invention.[118] Unlike US inventorship, which includes parties who contribute to the conception of any claimed elements, Japanese inventorship includes only parties who contribute to characteristic elements. In distinguishing characteristic elements from other elements, Japanese courts refer to the specification and identify the technical problem to be solved by the invention, the solution of the problem, and the effect resulting from the solution.[119] They find characteristic elements if the elements relate to the solution. In other words, a party is not a joint inventor if the contribution is to elements that are in the prior art. Moreover, a party must concretely contribute to the solution of the technical problem. A party is not an inventor or a joint inventor if (1) she identifies a technical problem and gives to other parties a general direction to solve the problem; (2) she merely collects data and conducts experiments following a direction of another party; or (3) she supports another party by providing financial support and facilities.[120]

9.36 Only a true inventor or joint inventor and her assignee can file a petition with the JPO to initiate an invalidation trial on the ground of a defect in ownership.[121] At trial, the ultimate burden of establishing ownership is on the patentee.[122] However, a true inventor must file an allegation with detailed facts and evidence showing her completion of the invention and a derivation of the invention by the patentee. The patentee must rebut the derivation

---

[116] IP High Ct., May 29, 2008, Gyo(ne) No. 10037, Hanrei Jihō (No. 2018) 146.

[117] Sup. Ct., October 13, 1977, 31 Minshū (No. 6) 805.

[118] For discussion of inventorship, see Minoru Tanabe, "Hatsumaisha no Nintei (Determination of Inventorship)," in Toshiaki Makino et al. (ed.), *Chiteki Zaisan no Riron to Jitsumu (Tokkyo hō 1) (Theory and Practice of Intellectual Property Law (Patent Law 1))* (2007), 275; Shiraki Yuichi, "Kyodo Kenkyu niokeru Hatumeishasei no Ninntei Hou ō (Determination of Inventership for Joint Research)," 65(5) *Patento* (2012): 4.

[119] IP High Ct., May 29, 2008, Hei (ne) No. 10037, Hanrei Jihō (No. 2018) 146. For more discussion on characteristic elements, see Norimasa Shimoda, "Tokkyohō niokeru 'Hatsumeisha (Kyodo Hatsumeisha)' no Igi (Significance of 'Inventor (Co-Inventor)' under Patent Act)," 62(9) *Patento* (2009): 101.

[120] Tokyo Dist. Ct., January 24, 2006, Heo (wa) No. 8496, Hanrei Jihō (No. 2018) 146.

[121] Japanese Patent Act, § 123(2).

[122] IP High Ct., January 19, 2006, Hei 17(Gyo ke) Nos. 10193; IP High Ct., June 29, 2009, Hei 20 (Gyo ke) Nos. 10427, 10428 and 10429. Tadashi Matsuhita, "Bōninnshutsugan niokeru Risshō Sekinin no Handan (Burden of Proof for Derived Invention)," 56(12) *Chizai Kanri* (2006): 1895.

allegation by introducing detailed facts and evidence such as an assignment contract stating that the patentee or his assignor is the true inventor of the patented invention.

The Japanese Patent Act was revised in 2011 to introduce an additional remedy for the true inventor whose invention was filed by a third party without an assignment of her right to obtain a patent. Under the pre-2011 Patent Act, a true inventor could not obtain a patent unless she filed a patent application within six months from the eighteen months laid-open publication of a patent application filed by a party who derived the invention from the true inventor.[123] Under the post-2011 Patent Act, a true inventor can request the transfer of a patent issued to a party who derived the patented invention from the true inventor.[124] As a result, a true inventor can either eliminate the effect of a derived patent retroactively or exercise her right to transfer the patent when the trial board finds that she is the true inventor and the patent was issued to a patent application filed by a party without the right to obtain the patent or was not filed jointly by all the inventors and their assignees. **9.37**

D. Other Types of Defenses

1. Private Use and Experimental Use Exception

Section 68 of the Japanese Patent Act provides that the exclusive right of a patent extends to working the patented invention as a business.[125] The Act also makes it clear that the exclusive right does not extend to acts of working a patented invention for experimental or research purposes.[126] The patent right does not extend to (1) vessels or aircrafts merely passing through Japan, or machines, apparatus, equipment, or other products used therefor; and (2) products existing in Japan prior to the filing of the patent application.[127] A patent granted to a product made by mixing multiple medicines or a process of making a medicine including steps for mixing multiple medicines does not extend to an act of preparing a medicine according to a prescription written by a physician or a dentist or to the medicine resulting from the preparation.[128] An accused infringer can assert as a defense that the act the patentee alleges is infringement falls within the scope of these exceptions.[129] **9.38**

Among these exceptions to the exclusivity of patent rights, the scope of private use and the scope of experimental or research use are the most controversial among Japanese legal scholars. Japanese courts interpret private use that does not meet the business use requirement restrictively to exclude only exceptional circumstances where an invention is exploited by the defendant and his or her family members.[130] Even if a patent product is covered by an exception to the exclusive right because the product is used only for private use, a party who manufactures and sells the product is liable for indirect infringement.[131] **9.39**

123 Japanese Patent Act, §§ 29 and 30.
124 Ibid. § 74.
125 Ibid. § 68.
126 Ibid. § 69(1).
127 Ibid. § 69(2).
128 Ibid. § 69(3).
129 Takabe and Shōsetsu, *Tokkyo Kankei Sosho*, 143.
130 Osaka Dist. Ct., October 24, 2000, Hei 8 (wa) No. 12109.
131 Ibid.

9.40 Case law is scarce with respect to the definition of experimental and research use.[132] However, the scope of the experimental exception is broader than the exception under § 271(e) of the US Patent Act because it extends beyond use in clinical trials. According to the limited case law and the majority view among patent law scholars, Japanese courts limit the scope by the object to be experimented and the purpose for conducting experimentation.[133] Conducting experimentation on a patented invention is permissible, but using a patented invention for conducting experimentation is not permissible. Conducting experimentation is permissible if the experimentation is conducted for the purpose of (1) examining the novelty and inventive step of a patented invention; (2) examining whether a patented invention is enabled by the disclosure of the patent; and (3) developing an improvement. The scope is similar to the scope of experimental use exceptions under the German Patent Act as well as the patent acts of many EU member states in limiting the scope of the object on which the experimentation is conducted and of the purpose for conducting experimentation.[134]

9.41 The experimental exception covers clinical trials to develop data necessary to secure market approval. The Supreme Court held that the experimental use exception covers clinical trials conducted by a generic drug manufacturer to make and use a patented drug invention before the patent expiration for the purpose of developing data necessary for market approval because finding infringement and granting an injunction result in a significant delay in the introduction of the generic drug to the market after the patent expiration.[135] The Court also made it clear that the exception does not cover the making and storing of a patented drug for the purpose of preparing to sell the drug after the patent expiration.

2. Prior User Right and Intervening Right

9.42 An accused infringer can assert the defense that she has a prior user right.[136] A party is entitled to assert the prior use defense when the following requirements are met: (1) the party is (a) a true inventor of the invention claimed in a patent application filed by the patentee and independently invented the invention without knowledge of the patentee's invention or (b) a party who derived the invention from the true inventor without knowledge of the patented invention; (2) such a true inventor or a party who derived the invention has been working the invention or preparing to work the invention in Japan at the time the patentee's application was filed; and (3) the accused embodiment falls within the scope of the invention that the true inventor or party who derived the invention has been working or preparing to work and the scope of the business of such a true inventor or party who derived the invention.[137]

9.43 To claim the prior user defense, an accused infringer must establish that she has completed an invention. An invention is completed when a technical idea has been reduced to a concrete and objective idea so that one skilled in the art can repeatedly exploit the idea to attain

132 E.g., Tokyo High Ct., January 30, 1984, 9 Sho 55 (ne) No. 2965; Tokyo Dist. Ct., July 10, 1987, 19 Muraishu (No. 2) 231.

133 Tamotsu Shouji, "Shiken Kenkyu notameno Tokkyo Hatsumei no Jisshi (Working of a Patented Invention for Experimental or Research Use)," in Toshiaki Makino *et al.* (eds.), *Chiteki Zaisan no Riron to Jitsumu (Tokkyo hō 1) (Theory and Practice of Intellectual Property Law (Patent Law 1))* (2007), 240; Takabe and Shōsetsu, *Tokkyo Kankei Sosho*, 230.

134 For discussion on the experimental use exception under German law, see Ch. 5, 5.53.

135 Sup. Ct., April 16, 1999, 53 Minshū (No. 4) 627.

136 Japanese Patent Act, § 79.

137 Takabe and Shōsetsu, *Tokkyo Kankei Sosho*, 148.

the technical effect.[138] Unlike the requirement of "reduction to practice" under the pre-AIA US case law, it is not necessary to construct a prototype.[139] The requirement is met if a party prepares any drawings or writings sufficient to enable a PHOSITA to make and use the invention.[140] Thus, the standard of invention is similar to the standard for conception or ready-for-patenting under US case law. A true inventor or party who derived the invention from the true inventor meet the working or preparing to work requirement if the true inventor or the derived party uses a contractor for making and using the invention as long as such working by the contractor is conducted on behalf of the true inventor or derived party. The contractor cannot assert the prior user defense because she did not work the invention on her own behalf.[141] The requirement of preparing to work is met if circumstantial evidence establishes that a true inventor or a party who derived the invention will start working the invention as soon as the preparation for the working is completed.[142] The working or preparing to work must be undertaken in Japan although an invention can be made outside of Japan.

It is often difficult to establish a prior user defense because a true inventor or a party who derived the invention from a true inventor worked the invention secretly. If a true inventor or a derived party worked on the invention publicly, she can raise a defense of invalidity as well as a prior user right defense at infringement procedure or initiate an invalidation trial for lack of novelty.[143] For a true inventor or a derived party to establish the completion of the invention and working on the invention at the time the patentee's patent application was filed, the JPO recommends keeping records on research activities including drawings and laboratory notes and sending records to a notary public to certify the date of such records.[144] US inventors can then use their records to establish the pre-AIA first-to-invent priority, and German inventors can use their records to calculate the employee invention calculation. **9.44**

Once the defense is available by meeting all of the requirements, a true inventor or a party who derived the invention can work on any embodiments within the scope of the invention that the inventor or the derived party worked or prepared to work at the time the patentee's application was filed.[145] A prior user defense covers any changes of the features of a product or process if the feature is not related to any claim element of the patented invention.[146] The true inventor or derived party can also replace claimed features with known equivalents.[147] A prior user defense does not cover acts of working that a true inventor or a derived party was not engaged **9.45**

[138] Sup. Ct., October 13, 1977, 31 Minshū (No. 6) 805.

[139] For discussion of the standards for the completion of invention under pre-AIA US case law, see Ch. 7, 7.80 "Originality—Inventorship."

[140] Sup. Ct., October 17, 1969, 23 Minshū (No. 10) 1777; Sup. Ct., October 3, 1986, 40 Minshū (No. 6) 1068; Tokyo Dist. Ct., April 27, 2000, Hei 10 (wa) No. 10545.

[141] Sup. Ct., October 17, 1969, 23 Minshū (No. 10) 1777.

[142] Sup. Ct., October 3, 1986, 40 Minshū (No. 6) 1068.

[143] Takahiro Ichiba, "Senshiyōken nituite (Prior User Right)," in Toshiaki Makino *et al.* (eds.), *Chiteki Zaisan no Riron to Jitsumu (Tokkyo hō 1) (Theory and Practice of Intellectual Property Law (Patent Law 1))* (2007), 232.

[144] Japan Patent Office, *Senshiyō Seido no Gaiyō (Outlines of Prior Use Right System)* (2013) (http://www.jpo.go.jp/torikumi/ibento/text/pdf/h25_jitsumusya_txt/25.pdf).

[145] Osaka Dist. Ct., December 26, 2000, Hei 10 (wa) No. 16963, Hei 11(wa) No. 17278. Hiroshi Yoshida, "Senshiyōken no han-n'I ni kansuru ichikousatsu (Study of Scope of Prior User Right)," 56(6) *Patento* (2003): 61.

[146] Osaka Dist. Ct., July 28, 2005, Hei 16 (wa) No. 9318.

[147] Osaka Dist. Ct., May 30, 1995, 27 Chisaishū (No. 2) 386.

in at the time of filing, and thus a true inventor cannot engage in acts of manufacturing if she engaged in acts of using or selling at the time of filing because the scope of the true inventor's business at the time of filing limits the scope of the defense.[148] The scope of the prior user defense is broader in Japan than the prior user defense under US law because the defense is not geographically limited to cover only the sites where the invention was commercialized.[149]

9.46 The prior user right can be transferred to a third party only where the business involving the working of the invention is also transferred, where the patentee agrees to the transfer, or where the transfer occurs as a result of general succession including inheritance.[150] A true inventor and a party derived from a true inventor do not need to register their prior user right at the JPO to assert the prior user right defense against a party to whom the original patentee assigned the patent to which the right is attached.[151] When a prior user right is transferred to a party other than the true inventor or derived party, the party must register the right to assert the defense.[152]

3. Employee Inventions: Shop Right

9.47 The Japanese Patent Act provides to employers of inventors a non-exclusive license comparable to a "shop right" under US case law so that the employers can assert a defense if the inventor or her successors in title of the invention obtain a patent and allege infringement.[153] The rule that the ownership of an invention belongs to the inventor is fundamental to the Japanese Patent Act.[154] Like the US and German systems, only a natural person can be the sole inventor or a joint inventor, thus a legal entity cannot be the original owner of an invention.[155] The Japanese Patent Act makes it clear that an invention resulting from employment belongs to the employee-inventor.[156] The ownership of an invention is assignable before or after the filing of a patent application.[157]

9.48 Unlike German employers but like US employers, Japanese employers are not provided with any mechanisms by operation of law for securing the ownership of an invention from their employee-inventor. The Japanese Patent Act makes it clear that employers can execute a pre-invention assignment as part of an employment contract or a separate assignment contract to secure ownership of inventions made by their employees while protecting inventors by making any pre-invention assignment contract void if the invention falls outside the scope of *shokumu* (service or duty) inventions.[158] To qualify as a service invention, the

---

[148] Nagoya Dist. Ct., April 28, 2005, Hei16 (wa) No. 1307, Takahiro Ichiba, "Senshiyōken nituite (Prior User Right)," in Toshiaki Makino *et al.* (eds.), *Chiteki Zaisan no Riron to Jitsumu (Tokkyo hō 1) (Theory and Practice of Intellectual Property Law (Patent Law 1))* (2007), 238.

[149] Post-AIA, § 273(e)(1). For the prior user right under US Patent Act, see Ch. 7, 7.112 "Prior-user Rights Defense."

[150] Japanese Patent Act, § 94(1).

[151] Ibid. § 94(2).

[152] Ibid. § 99(3).

[153] Ibid. § 35(1). For a discussion of the employee invention system in comparison with US and German systems, see Toshiko Takenaka and Yves Reboul, "Employ Invention System: A Comparative Law Perspective," in Toshiko Takenaka (ed.), *Intellectual Property Systems in Common Law and Civil Law* (2013), 365.

[154] Japanese Patent Act, Art. 29, para. 1. Kosaku Yoshifuji and Kenichi Kumagaya, *Tokkyoho Gaisetsu (Outlines of Patent Act)* (13th ed., 2000), 185.

[155] Judgment of Tokyo Dist. Ct., March 16, 1955, 6 Kakyu Minshu 479.

[156] Japanese Patent Act, § 35(2).

[157] Ibid. § 35(1).

[158] Ibid. § 35(2)

invention must (1) fall into a field of the employer's business activities and (2) result from an act that is performed as part of the employee's duty.[159] The Japanese Patent Act adopts an aspect of the German Employee Invention Act in limiting the freedom of contract by guaranteeing reasonable compensation for inventor-employees.[160] Once the ownership of an invention is transferred or an exclusive license is granted to an employer, the employee is entitled to a *taika* (fair price) for the transfer or grant of an exclusive license.[161] Japanese employers can adopt a method of calculating this fair price through an individual contract or a collective bargaining contract.[162] However, the Act makes it clear that the process of adopting a calculation method must be fair and reasonable and gives courts power to examine the process by taking into account (1) the appropriateness of the negotiation between employers and employees in adopting the calculation method, (2) the degree of disclosure to employees with respect to the factors to be used in the calculation, and (3) feedback from employees in support of the calculation method.[163] If a court finds the payment according to the calculation method unreasonable, it can set a fair price on a case-by-case basis by taking account of profits that the employer expects to receive, expenses and contributions that the employer has made, the employee's employment condition, and other factors.[164] Courts can also set a fair price if there is no agreement for the fair price between employers and employees.[165]

Without an express assignment contract, the Japanese Patent Act does not provide an employer with any rights in the ownership of an invention made by an employee except for a shop right, which is a royalty-free non-exclusive license.[166] An employer obtains automatically the license without a registration at the JPO when the invention meets the definition of a service invention, and the employer can assert a defense based on the license against a third party who has been assigned the patent right.[167] An employer can assign a service invention license to a third party only where the business involving the working of the invention is also transferred, where the patentee agrees to the transfer, or where the transfer occurs as a result of general succession including inheritance.[168] **9.49**

4. Licenses

A party can raise an express or implied license as a defense against a claim of infringement.[169] Under the Japanese Patent Act, licenses are also classified into (1) sole exclusive licenses called *senyō* licenses, which exclude the patentee from working the patented invention[170] and (2) licenses other than *senyō* licenses.[171] *Senyō* licenses are created when a patentee grants a third party the exclusive right to engage in acts that constitute infringement without authority from the patentee and registers the license at the JPO.[172] Licenses **9.50**

159 Ibid. § 35(1).
160 Ibid. § 35(3).
161 Ibid.
162 Ibid. § 35(4).
163 Ibid.
164 Ibid. § 35(3).
165 Ibid.
166 Ibid. § 35(1).
167 Ibid. § 94(2).
168 Ibid. § 94(1).
169 Takabe and Shōsetsu, *Tokkyo Kankei Sosho*, 146.
170 Japanese Patent Act, § 77.
171 Ibid. § 78.
172 Ibid. § 98(1) ii. 2009 Patent Act Revision introduced a preliminary *senyō* license which does not require a registration to create a Senyo exclusive license. Ibid. § 34-2.

other than *senyō* licenses are called *tsujyō* licenses and include both non-exclusive and exclusive licenses. *Tsujyō* licenses are created when a patentee grants a license without a registration at the JPO. The 2012 Revision of Patent Act made possible for a party to assert the defense of license without a registration.[173]

9.51 The Japanese Patent Act provides compulsory licenses and licenses created by operation of law. Compulsory licenses include non-exclusive licenses resulting from the non-working of a patented invention,[174] non-exclusive licenses to work on patented invention where the working of the invention infringes a third-party patent (dependent inventions),[175] and non-exclusive licenses for public interests.[176] In Japan a request for a compulsory license is very rare, and the JPO has never granted a compulsory license.[177] Statutory licenses created by operation of law include licenses or defenses based on the prior user's right,[178] service inventions under the employee invention system,[179] intervening rights resulting from a final trial decision of invalidity on the ground of double patenting,[180] intervening rights resulting from an expiration of design rights,[181] and intervening rights resulting from a retrial.[182]

9.52 To assert the defense of license, a party must establish the scope of the license and allege that the allegedly infringing act falls within the scope of the license.[183] A party is liable for patent infringement even if she has a license as long as the allegedly infringing act falls outside of the license.[184] A patentee can rebut the defense of license by alleging that the license has been terminated.[185]

5. Exhaustion

9.53 A party can raise the defense of patent exhaustion when the party has used and assigned a product assigned by a patentee or her licensee.[186] The doctrine of patent exhaustion is pure case law under the Japanese patent system.[187] In *BBS AG v. Racimex Japan*,[188] the Supreme Court held that when a patented product is assigned in Japan, the relevant patent is exhausted because the exclusive right under the patent has fulfilled its purpose, and therefore the patentee can no longer use the patent to enjoin a party from using, reassigning,

---

[173] Ibid. § 99.
[174] Ibid. § 83.
[175] Ibid. § 92.
[176] Ibid. § 93.
[177] Japan Patent Office, "Wagakuni niokeru Saitei Seido nitutie (Compulsory Licenses in Japan)" (https://www.jpo.go.jp/shiryou/toushin/shingikai/pdf/strategy_wg07/paper08.pdf).
[178] Japanese Patent Act § 79.
[179] Ibid. § 35.
[180] Ibid. § 80.
[181] Ibid. § 81.
[182] Ibid. § 176.
[183] Takabe and Shōsetsu, *Tokkyo Kankei Sosho*, 147.
[184] Osaka High Ct., May 27, 2003, Hei 15 (ne) No. 320.
[185] Takabe and Shōsetsu, *Tokkyo Kankei Sosho*, 147.
[186] Ibid. 84.
[187] For discussion on the exhaustion doctrine, see Tamotsu Shōji, "Tokkyoken no Shōjin—Saibanreini Arawareta Kokunaishoujin no Handanshuhou wo Chushin toshite (Patent Exahustion—Focuing on Standard for Determining Domestic Patent Exhaustion)," in Toshiaki Makino *et al.* (eds.), *Chiteki Zaisan no Riron to Jitsumu (Tokkyo hō 1) (Theory and Practice of Intellectual Property Law (Patent Law 1))* (2007), 256.
[188] Sup. Ct., July 1, 1997, Hei 7 (o) No. 1988, 51 Minshū (No. 6) 2299.

exporting, and importing the assigned product. The exhaustion applies even if the patented product is sold outside Japan because it is reasonable for a party who purchased the product to assume full rights with respect to the patented article, including the right to bring the article into Japan.[189] The Court therefore announced the rule of international patent exhaustion—which is in stark contrast to US case law, which requires sales of the patented product in the United States, and EU case law, which requires putting products into the EU market.[190] However, a party can prevent the international exhaustion if a restriction banning importation into Japan is noted on the patented product because the restriction prevents any expectations from a party who is assigned the patented product.[191]

The Supreme Court also clarified the scope of the exhaustion doctrine in *Recycle Assist Co., Ltd v. Canon, Inc.*[192] Even if a patented product was assigned under the authority of a patentee, a patent is not exhausted when (1) the product is reused or recycled after completing its normal lifespan and losing its effectiveness as a product (used-up products) or (2) a part of the product constituting an essential part of the patented invention is partly or completely modified or replaced by a third party (modification of essential elements) because the product results from impermissible remanufacturing instead of permissible use by the owner of the patented product. Courts must take into account the following factors in determining whether a party engaged in an impermissible remanufacture: (1) the nature of the patented product, (2) the content of the patented invention, (3) the extent of the modification and replacement of elements, and (4) trade practices. In evaluating (1) the nature of the patented product, courts should take into account the function, structure, raw materials, use, and lifespan of the product as well as the method of using the product. In evaluating (3) the extent of the modification and replacement, courts should take into account the condition of the product at the time of modification and replacement, the nature and extent of the modification, the lifespan of the replaced element, the function of the replaced element in the patented product in the context of the technical problem of the invention, and the economic value of the replaced element. The Court made it clear that a patentee can enjoin importation of a product that falls into (1) a used-up product or (2) a modification of essential elements. **9.54**

To assert the defense of exhaustion, a party must establish that the accused product was assigned by the patentee or her licensee or received from her assignee. The patentee bears the burden of rebutting the defense by establishing that the accused product is modified from the product assigned by the patentee and the modification falls within the conditions of a used-up product or a modification of essential elements in light of the factors listed by the Supreme Court in *Recycle Assist Co., Ltd v. Canon, Inc.*[193] **9.55**

---

[189] Ibid. The part of the *BBS* decision acknowledging the international exhaustion is cited by the Supreme Court in the game software copyright exhaustion case. Sup. Ct., April 25, 2002, Hei13 (ju) No. 898, 56 Minshū (No. 4) 808.

[190] For US exhaustion or first-sale doctrine, see Ch. 7, 7.136 "Exhaustion." For German exhaustion, Ch. 8, 8.162 "Exhaustion."

[191] Yoshiyuki Tamura, Heikō Yunyu to Tokkyoken (Parallel Importation and Patent Right) NBL No. 627, 29 (1997) (http://lex.juris.hokudai.ac.jp/coe/articles/tamura/casenote97c.pdf).

[192] Saikō Saibansho (Sup. Ct.) April 11, 2007, Hei 18 (ju) No. 826, 61 Saikō Saibansho Minji Hanreishū (Minshū) 2989 (Japan). An English transnlation of the decision is available at https://www.law.washington.edu/Casrip/Newsletter/default.aspx?year=2008&article=newsv15i1RecAssist.

[193] Tokyo Dist. Ct., August 31, 2000, Hei 8 (wa) No. 16782.

Part IV

ENFORCEMENT PROCEDURE

10

UNITED STATES

A. Jurisdiction

The initial question a patentee faces when seeking to enforce a patent is where to file the infringement action. The Patent Act is a federal statute, and patents have to be enforced in a federal court. While in principle every federal court can assume subject matter jurisdiction over a patent dispute, venue rules have been subject to some revisions in recent years in order to prevent unlimited forum shopping across the country. 10.01

1. Subject Matter Jurisdiction

With the exception of cases tried at the ITC, patent enforcement lawsuits can only be filed at federal district courts.[1] Each of the ninety-four federal district courts located through the United States can assume subject matter jurisdiction over a patent enforcement case as long as the respective court deems that the venue rules are satisfied. 10.02

2. Venue

A patent lawsuit, just as every other type of civil lawsuit, has to be filed at a proper venue. Patent litigation is subject to a special venue rule, which allows the patentee to enforce the patent in the district court "where the defendant resides, or where the defendant has committed acts of infringement and has a regular and established place of business."[2] The first prong of the venue statute, namely residency of the defendant, is defined in 28 U.S.C. § 1391(c),[3] which aligns the requirement of residency with the universal concept of personal jurisdiction of the district court over the defendant. 10.03

A court has personal jurisdiction over every person that is incorporated or that does business in the state in which the court is located. Generally, a person must have at least "minimum contact" with a given state for a district court located in such state to have personal jurisdiction over such person.[4] The extension of the eligible venue from the place of residence to any place where the defendant has established minimum contact has granted plaintiffs a significantly larger choice of where to file a patent infringement lawsuit. Incorporating 10.04

---

[1] 28 U.S.C. § 1338; *Pixton v. B&B Plastics, Inc.*, 291 F.3d 1324, 1326 (Fed. Cir. 2002). However, it should be noted that patent-related law suits can be filed in a state court if the infringement claim is based on a state law cause of action such as breach of a patent license contract, see, e.g., Donald S. Chisum, "The Allocation of Jurisdiction between State and Federal Courts in Patent Litigation", 46 *Wash. Law Rev.* (1971): 633.

[2] 28 U.S.C. § 1400(b).

[3] The applicability of the general provision of 28 U.S.C. § 1391(c) for patent infringement cases has been confirmed by the Federal Circuit, see *VE Holding Corp. v. Johnson Gas Appliance Co.*, 917 F.2d 1574, 1575, cert. denied, 111 S.Ct. 1315 (1991).

[4] *International Shoe Co. v. Washington*, 326 U.S. 310, 316 (1945).

Table 10.1 Popular district courts by number of patent infringement cases filed between 2000 and 2009

Rank	District	Number of patent infringement cases filed between 2000 and 2010*
1	C.D. California	2,289
2	N.D. California	1,424
3	N.D. Illinois	1,233
4	E.D. Texas	1,024
5	S.D. New York	1,018
6	D. Delaware	1,017
7	D. New Jersey	987
8	D. Minnesota	600
9	D. Massachusetts	584
10	S.D. California	519

* Source: Mark A. Lemley: "Where to File Your Patent Case," 38 *AIPLA Q.J.* (2010): 401, 405–6.

the concept of personal jurisdiction under 28 U.S.C. § 1391(c) into the determination of a patent venue has been a controversial decision, which was triggered by the Judicial Improvement and Access to Justice Act passed by Congress in 1988.[5] Its explicit application to patent law, as manifested in *VE Holding Corp.*, overwrote most of the specific rules on patent law venue which had been set forth in 28 U.S.C. § 1400(b). The second prong of 28 U.S.C. § 1400 (b), namely the place where the "defendant has committed acts of infringement and has a regular and established place of business," became basically irrelevant for the determination of patent venue, given that personal jurisdiction over a corporation is always easier to establish.[6] Therefore, the second prong of § 1400(b) remains relevant only for individual defendants which are not incorporated, and which are not impacted by 28 U.S.C. § 1391(c). However, virtually no patent lawsuits are filed against individuals.

10.05 Since the relaxation of the venue rules in the beginning of the nineties, certain patent courts became notable as patent litigation venues. As shown in Table 10.1, not only courts residing in districts that are prominent technology centers (such as the Northern and the Central District of California, the Northern District of Illinois, the Southern District of New York, etc.) but also courts located in more rural areas (most notably the District Court for the Eastern District of Texas) became prominent patent litigation venues in the last few decades.[7]

10.06 Considerations that involve plaintiff's choice of forum include factors such as speed, as well as a reputation for being patent-friendly. Applying such considerations, certain court

[5] Pub K. No. 100-702, Tit. X, § 1007, 102 Stat. 4642 (1988).

[6] See a critical review of the Federal Circuit's decision in *VE Holding Corp.* in light of earlier Supreme Court case law (*Stonite Products Co v. Melvin Lloyd Co.*, 315 U.S. 561 (1942); *Fourco Glass Co. v. Transmirra Products Corp.*, 353 U.S. 222 (1957)) by William C. Johnson, "The New Rule for Patent Venue for Corporate Defendants: Kansas Was Never Like This," 11 *Pace L. Rev.* (1991): 667.

[7] See, e.g., Yan Leychkis, "Of Fire Ants and Claim Construction: An Empirical Study of the Meteoric Rise of the Eastern District of Texas as a Preeminent Forum for Patent Litigation," 9 *Yale J.L. & Tech.* (2007): 193, 206–15.

districts such as the Eastern District of Texas, the District of Delaware, or the Eastern District of Virginia became popular choices for patentees who were looking to enforce their patent in speedy proceedings at so-called "rocket-dockets."

Obviously, the defendant will try to litigate a patent in a forum that is known to be rather defendant-friendly, or that is simply located in a more convenient location. The application of 28 U.S.C. § 1391(c) to patent law made it difficult for larger companies to dismiss a lawsuit when the plaintiff invoked 28 U.S.C. § 1400(b). The only possibility for large companies to move a lawsuit to a more convenient forum is provided for by 28 U.S.C. §1404(a).[8] District courts, including the district court for the Eastern District of Texas, have at least recently usually granted a defendant's motion to transfer cases if the defendant could show that the transferee venue is "clearly more convenient" than the venue chosen by the plaintiff.[9] One of the compelling factors in analyzing the convenience of venue[10] has been that the vast majority of evidence as well as witnesses are usually located near the defendant's place of business.[11] **10.07**

In order to maintain the litigation at the venue of choice of the plaintiff, some plaintiffs established a physical presence, for example, in the Eastern District of Texas, thereby indicating that moving the lawsuit would subject them to significant inconvenience. For a while, the E.D. Texas could be persuaded to not transfer cases by the plaintiff establishing a place of business within the district boundaries.[12] In 2010, the Federal Circuit weighed in by means of a writ of mandamus, and established that a plaintiff' physical presence in a **10.08**

---

[8] U.S.C. § 1404 (a): "For the convenience of parties and witnesses, in the interest of justice, a district court may transfer any civil action to any other district or division where it might have been brought or to any district or division to which all parties have consented."

[9] *In re Volkswagen of Am., Inc.*, 545 F.3d 304, 315 (5th Cir.2008) (*en banc*).

[10] *In re TS Tech USA Corp.*, 551 F.3d 1315, 1320–21 (Fed. Cir. 2008). The test developed by the 5th Circuit in *In re Volkswagen* (545 F.3d, 315) relies on four "private" and four "pubic" factors when assessing whether a motion to transfer should be granted. The "private" interest factors include:

(1) the relative ease of access to sources of proof;
(2) the availability of compulsory process to secure the attendance of witnesses;
(3) the cost of attendance for willing witnesses; and
(4) all other practical problems that make a trial easy, expeditious and inexpensive.

The "public" interest factors to be considered are:

(1) the administrative difficulties flowing from court congestion;
(2) the local interest in having localized interests decided at home;
(3) the familiarity of the forum with the law that will govern the case; and
(4) the avoidance of unnecessary problems of conflicts of laws [or in] the application of foreign law.

The above test comprising of private and public factors had been developed by the Supreme Court in *Gulf Oil Corp. v. Gilbert*, 330 U.S. 501, 508–9 (1947).

[11] See *In re TS Tech*, 551 F.3d., 1320–21; *In re Genentech, Inc.*, 566 F.3d 1338, 1345 (Fed. Cir. 2009) ("In patent infringement cases, the bulk of the relevant evidence usually comes from the accused infringer." (quoting *Neil Bros., Ltd. v. World Wide Lines, Inc.*, 425 F. Supp. 2d 325, 330 (E.D.N.Y. 2006)) (internal quotation mark omitted)). *In re Hoffmann-La Roche Inc.*, 587 F.3d 1333, 1336–37 (Fed. Cir. 2009), overruling the venue analysis provided by the District Court in *Novartis Vaccines and Diagnostics, Inc. v. Hoffman-La Roche Inc.*, 597 F. Supp. 2d 706 (E.D.Tex. Feb 03, 2009) (NO. CIV.A. 2:07-CV-507 D). See also *In re Nintendo Co., Ltd.*, 589 F.3d 1194, 1198 (Fed. Cir. 2009), overruling *Motiva, LLC v. Nintendo Co., Ltd.*, 2009 WL 1882836 (E.D.Tex. June 30, 2009) (NO. 6:08 CV 429); see a summary of mandamus petitions for move of venue granted by the Federal Circuit between 2008 and 2011 in Paul R. Gugliuzza, "The New Federal Circuit Mandamus," 45 *Ind. L. Rev.* 343, 381–90 (2011–2012).

[12] *Medidea, LLC v. Smith & Nephew, Inc.*, No. 2-09-cv-378-TJW, 2010 WL 1444211 (E.D. Tex. April 12, 2010), *3.

forum should only be considered as relevant if such presence is not "recent, ephemeral, and an artifact of litigation."[13] While such recent and unprecedented use of writs of mandamus to compel transfer of venue has re-established some means for a defendant to protect itself against excessive forum shopping, a defendant still needs to properly demonstrate that the venue it requests transfer to is clearly more convenient than the venue selected by the plaintiff.[14]

3. International Jurisdiction

10.09 The question of whether a US court should have jurisdiction to adjudicate not only a patent infringement dispute regarding a US patent but also disputes regarding foreign patents has been subject to significant discussion. The Federal Circuit has instructed US courts to exercise a comparatively rigid test before assuming jurisdiction over foreign patents.

10.10 In practice, patentees have asked courts to assume supplemental jurisdiction for one or more foreign patents pursuant to 28 U.S.C. § 1367(a)[15] when deciding upon the infringement of a related US patent. Before the establishment of the Federal Circuit, the Seventh Circuit permitted such practice, allowing the patentee to enforce both the US patent as well as the foreign patent, including Canadian, Brazilian, and Mexican patents in one set of proceedings.[16] The Seventh Circuit justified granting supplemental jurisdiction over the foreign patents at issue by holding that the "actions of defendant... are the result of defendant doing similar acts both in and out of the United States."[17]

10.11 In 1994, the Federal Circuit revisited this approach in *Mars, Inc. v. Kabushiki-Kaisha Nippon Conclux*.[18] The plaintiff, relying on *Ortman*, asked the district court to assume supplemental jurisdiction over a Japanese patent. The district court declined to exercise supplemental jurisdiction under § 1367(a).[19] On appeal, the Federal Circuit affirmed the decision of the district court, holding that no common nucleus of fact, being a requirement for supplemental jurisdiction, could be established. In its analysis, the court reasoned that the "respective patents are different, the accused devices are different, the alleged acts are different, and the governing laws are different."[20]

---

13 *In re Zimmer Holdings, Inc.*, 609 F.3d 1378, 1381 (Fed. Cir. 2010). See also *In re Microsoft Corp.*, 630 F.3d 1361, 1364 (Fed. Cir., 2011), holding that a request for a court to "honor connections to a preferred forum made in anticipation of litigation and for the likely purpose of making that forum appear convenient" is nothing more than "a fallacious assumption."

14 In a recent opinion, the Federal Circuit refused the defendant Apple a transfer of venue, holding that, despite the plaintiff establishing a physical presence in Texas only in anticipation of litigation, "Apple did not meet its burden of demonstrating... that the transferee venue is 'clearly more convenient,'" see *In re Apple Inc.*, 456 Fed. Appx. 907, 2012 WL 112893, *2 (Fed. Cir. 2012).

15 28 U.S.C. § 1367(a): "Except as provided in subsections (b) and (c) or as expressly provided otherwise by Federal statute, in any civil action of which the district courts have original jurisdiction, the district courts shall have supplemental jurisdiction over all other claims that are so related to claims in the action within such original jurisdiction that they form part of the same case or controversy under Article III of the United States Constitution. Such supplemental jurisdiction shall include claims that involve the joinder or intervention of additional parties."

16 *Ortman v. Stanray Corp.*, 371 F.2d 154, 158 (7th Cir. 1967).

17 Ibid.

18 24 F.3d 1368 (Fed. Cir. 1994).

19 *Mars Inc. v. Nippon Conlux Kabushiki-Kaisha*, 825 F. Supp. 73, 75–76 (D. Del. 1993).

20 *Mars*, 24 F.3d 1368, 1375 (Fed. Cir. 1994).

The most recent decision on the issue of supplemental jurisdiction was handed down in *Voda v. Cordis Corp.*[21] Here, the district court assumed supplemental jurisdiction over foreign patents issued from a common Patent Cooperation Treaty (PCT) application.[22] The Federal Circuit reversed, holding that the district court failed to properly apply factors developed in *Mars* as a guideline for determination of a common nucleus of fact.[23] While the plaintiff maintained that international patent treaties such as the PCT or the Agreement on Trade-related Aspects of Intellectual Property Rights (TRIPS) would present evidence for harmonization allowing the exercise of supplemental jurisdiction, the Federal Circuit correctly stated that "nothing in the PCT or the Agreement on TRIPS contemplates or allows one jurisdiction to adjudicate patents of another."[24] Further, the court reasoned that comity considerations would weigh against exercising supplemental jurisdiction by a US court, as the plaintiff "has not shown that foreign courts will inadequately protect his foreign patent rights."[25] The Federal Circuit's decision raised the bar for exercise of supplemental jurisdiction, in principle ordering district courts to abstain from assuming international jurisdiction for litigation involving non-US patents. **10.12**

B. Parties

Another important consideration when preparing an enforcement action is to consider which entities are entitled to bring a lawsuit. A defendant can dismiss a lawsuit or at least move to eliminate specific plaintiffs if such plaintiffs lack standing to sue. At the same time, the plaintiff needs to pay attention when naming defendants to a patent infringement lawsuit. **10.13**

1. Standing to Sue

The party filing a patent infringement lawsuit must establish that he has standing to sue. The standing of a party to sue for patent infringement derives "solely from the U.S. Patent Act,"[26] 35 U.S.C. § 281, which states that the patentee is entitled to file a lawsuit for infringement of his patent. The term patentee includes successors in title.[27] Thus, only the party which owns the patent, "either by issuance or assignment," may bring an action for patent infringement.[28] An exclusive licensee may be considered by the court as the owner of the patent, if the licensee agreement conveys all substantial rights in the patent to such licensee.[29] In such case, the exclusive licensee is considered a "virtual assignee," entitled to enforce the patent in his own name.[30] Courts have confirmed that the proper focus of the test should not be put on the name of the underlying agreement, but on "the substance of what was granted."[31] **10.14**

---

[21] 476 F.3d 887 (Fed. Cir. 2007).

[22] *Voda v. Cordis Corp.*, 2004 WL 3392022, *1 (W.D. Okla. 2004).

[23] *Voda*, 476 F.3d, 896 (Fed. Cir. 2007).

[24] Ibid. 899.

[25] Ibid. 901.

[26] *Intellectual Property Development, Inc. v. TCI Cablevision, Inc.*, 248 F.3d 1333, 1345–46 (Fed. Cir. 2001).

[27] 35 U.S.C. § 100(d).

[28] *Speedplay, Inc. v. Bebop, Inc.*, 211 F.3d 1245, 1249–50 (Fed. Cir. 2000). See also *Alps South, LLC v. Ohio Willow Wood Co.*, 787 F.3d 1379, 1382 (Fed. Cir. 2015).

[29] *Enzo APA & Son, Inc. v. Geapag A.G.*, 134 F.3d 1090, 1093 (Fed. Cir. 1998).

[30] Ibid.

[31] *Vaupel Textilmaschinen KG v. Meccanica Euro Italia S.P.A.*, 944 F.2d 870, 873–76 (Fed.Cir.1991); *Speedplay*, 211 F.3d 1245, 1250 (Fed. Cir. 2000); *Sky Technologies, LLC v. SAP AG*, 576 F.3d 1374, 1379 (Fed. Cir. 2009).

10.15 A licensee who is not entitled to all substantial rights in the patent is considered as a licensee only when assessing standing. In principle, a licensee does not have standing to sue in his own name.[32] That said, an exclusive licensee, who is not considered a virtual assignee, may act as co-plaintiff by joining a lawsuit brought by the owner of the patent. Case law allows an equitable exception to such an absolute rule, allowing an exclusive licensee to sue for infringement in their own name if "necessary to prevent an absolute failure of justice, as where the patentee is the infringer, and cannot sue himself."[33] Setting this exception aside, an exclusive licensee has standing to appeal a decision in his own name, if he was a co-plaintiff to the lawsuit in first instance, and if the patent owner has no interest in appealing the district court decision.[34]

10.16 If an exclusive licensee files a patent infringement lawsuit without the owner, courts usually do not dismiss the case for lack of standing, but rather permit or even request the patent owner to join the lawsuit,[35] thereby ensuring that the standing requirement can be met by the exclusive licensee. That said, while an exclusive licensee can join a lawsuit filed by the patent owner or initiate a lawsuit in his own name, a non-exclusive license, also referred to by case law as a "bare licensee,"[36] does not have standing to join a patent infringement lawsuit brought by the owner.[37] As a non-exclusive licensee has never acquired the right to exclude other parties from using the licensed patent, courts presume that he also does not suffer any injury if any unauthorized, infringing use occurs, and therefore does not have standing to file a lawsuit or to join an existing lawsuit brought by the patent owner.[38]

10.17 The different standing requirements make the analysis of whether a license agreement constitutes an assignment, an exclusive license, or merely a non-exclusive license highly relevant. Courts have held that while a non-exclusive license only "provide[s] a covenant not to sue," an exclusive license "makes the licensee a beneficial owner of some identifiable part of the patentee's bundle of rights to exclude others."[39] Rather than being led by the title of the licensee agreement, a court will examine the intent of the parties, as manifested in the agreement. In addition to the written agreement, courts also acknowledge oral license agreements.[40] As long as a licensor retains the right to grant other licenses to the same

[32] *Textile Productions, Inc. v. Mead Corp.*, 134 F.3d 1481, 1484 (Fed. Cir. 1998); *Biagro Western Sales Inc. v. Helena Chemical Co.*, 160 F. Supp. 2d 1136, 1143 (E.D. Cal. 2001).

[33] *Textile Productions*, 134 F.3d, 1484.

[34] *Schwarz Pharma, Inc. v. Paddock Laboratories, Inc.*, 504 F.3d 1371, 1374 (Fed. Cir. 2007); *A123 Systems, Inc. v. Hydro-Quebec*, 626 F.3d 1213, 1221 (Fed. Cir. 2010).

[35] *AsymmetRx, Inc. v. Biocare Medical, LLC*, 582 F.3d 1314, 1322 (Fed. Cir. 2009) ("A patentee that does not voluntarily join an action prosecuted by its exclusive licensee can be joined as a defendant or, in a proper case, made an involuntary plaintiff if it is not subject to service of process."); *Intellectual Prop.*, 248 F.3d, 1348; *Mentor H/S, Inc. v. Medical Device Alliance, Inc.*, 240 F.3d 1016, 1019 (Fed. Cir. 2001).

[36] *Textile Productions*, 134 F.3d, 1484.

[37] *Intellectual Property Development, Inc. v. TCI Cablevision of California, Inc.*, 248 F.3d 1333, 1345 (Fed. Cir. 2001), cert. denied, 122 S.Ct. 216 (2001); *Ortho Pharm. Corp. v. Genetics Inst., Inc.*, 52 F.3d 1026, 1030 (Fed. Cir. 1995).

[38] *Ortho*, 52 F.3d, 1031; *WiAV Solutions, LLC v. Motorola, Inc.*, 631 F.3d 1257, 1265 (Fed. Cir. 2010); *Rite-Hite Corp. v. Kelley Co., Inc.*, 56 F.3d 1538, 1552 (Fed. Cir. 1995).

[39] *Ortho*, 52 F.3d, 1032.

[40] In contrast, an assignment, including a virtual assignment, must be in writing in order to be effective under 35 U.S.C. § 261, see *Waymark Corp. v. Porta Systems Corp.*, 334 F.3d 1358, 1364 (Fed. Cir. 2003). The validity of an oral exclusive license, even an implied oral exclusive license agreement existing prior to the

intellectual property, the license cannot be considered an exclusive licensee.[41] Also, provisions such as a right or obligation by the licensors to enforce the patent or to pay patent maintenance fees are indications that the license agreement is a bare license rather than an exclusive license.

2. Defendants

Defendants in patent litigation include anybody who "without authority makes, uses or sells any patented invention."[42] Furthermore, a party who is actively inducing patent infringement[43] or who "sells a component of a patented machine, manufacture, combination or composition, or a material or apparatus for use in practicing a patented process, constituting a material part of the invention, knowing the same to be especially made or especially adapted for use in an infringement of such patent"[44], can be named as a defendant in a patent lawsuit. That said, in order to demonstrate patent inducement or contributory infringement pursuant to Article 271(b) or 271(c) of the Patent Act, the patentee must establish a *prima facie* case that the patent was directly infringed under Article 271(a) Patent Act. The range of possible defendants include parties who actively induce patent infringement outside the United States,[45] or who import a product that was manufactured outside the United States under a process covered by a US process patent.[46] **10.18**

Prior to implementation of the American Invents Act, multiple defendants were often forced to join one concentrated infringement lawsuit if infringement of the same patent was alleged. **10.19**

---

commencement of litigation, has been approved by the Federal Circuit. See, e.g., *Enzo*, 134 F.3d, 1093 (Fed. Cir. 1998); *Aspex Eyewear, Inc. v. Miracle Optics, Inc.*, 434 F.3d 1336, 1344 (Fed. Cir. 2006).

41 *Textile*, 134 F.3d, 1484.

42 35 U.S.C. § 271(a).

43 Ibid. § 271(b).

44 Ibid. § 271(c).

45 Ibid. § 271(f):

(1) Whoever without authority supplies or causes to be supplied in or from the United States all or a substantial portion of the components of a patented invention, where such components are uncombined in whole or in part, in such manner as to actively induce the combination of such components outside of the United States in a manner that would infringe the patent if such combination occurred within the United States, shall be liable as an infringer.

(2) Whoever without authority supplies or causes to be supplied in or from the United States any component of a patented invention that is especially made or especially adapted for use in the invention and not a staple article or commodity of commerce suitable for substantial noninfringing use, where such component is uncombined in whole or in part, knowing that such component is so made or adapted and intending that such component will be combined outside of the United States in a manner that would infringe the patent if such combination occurred within the United States, shall be liable as an infringer.

46 Ibid. § 271(f):

Whoever without authority imports into the United States or sells or uses within the United States a product which is made by a process patented in the United States shall be liable as an infringer, if the importation, sale, or use of the product occurs during the term of such process patent. In an action for infringement of a process patent, no remedy may be granted for infringement on account of the noncommercial use or retail sale of a product unless there is no adequate remedy under this title for infringement on account of the importation or other use or sale of that product. A product which is made by a patented process will, for purposes of this title, not be considered to be so made after—

(1) it is materially changed by subsequent processes; or
(2) it becomes a trivial and nonessential component of another product.

Permissive joinder of defendants is stipulated in Federal Rules of Civil Procedure (FRCP) 20, which states that a plaintiff may request a court to join multiple defendants if (A) a "right to relief is asserted against [multiple defendants] jointly…with respect to or arising out of the same transaction, occurrence, or series of transactions or occurrences; and (B) any question of law or fact common to all defendants will arise in the action." The purpose of this general rule is to promote judicial efficiency, and the Supreme Court encouraged courts to generously apply this joinder provision as long as a joinder is not unfair to the defending parties involved. In patent litigation, courts were split on whether joinder only required alleged infringement of the same patent,[47] or whether in addition to the infringement of the same patent a certain relation between the infringing acts and between the defendants had to be shown.[48]

10.20 The American Invents Act ended this circuit split by amending Article 299 of the Patent Act.[49] The new provision adopted the stricter test that was already applicable under FRCP 20, and clarified the requirement of "an action arising out of the same transaction" by adding that such a transaction must be related to "making, using, importing into the United States, offering for sale, or selling of the same accused product or process." The House Judiciary Committee's Report on the AIA explained that the revision of Article 299 of the Patent Act intended to solve "problems occasioned by the joinder of defendants (sometimes numbering in the dozens) who have tenuous connections to the underlying disputes in patent infringement suits."[50]

10.21 The revised provision of Article 299 came into force in September 2011. In the weeks before enactment of this portion of the AIA an unusually high number of cases, each naming dozens of defendants, were filed in courts which had supported widespread joinder in past

---

[47] Most prominently, the Eastern District of Texas followed this interpretation of FRCP 20 in *MyMail, Ltd. v. Am. Online, Inc.*, 223 F.R.D. 455, 456 (E.D. Tex. 2004); see also *Adrain v. Genetec Inc.*, 2009 WL 3063414, *2+ (E.D. Tex. September 22, 2009) (NO. 2:08-CV-423); *Lektron, Inc. v. GE Lighting, Inc.*, 2012 WL 1085486, *3 (N.D. Okla. March 30, 2012) (NO. 11-CV-413-TCK-PJC); *Eolas Techs., Inc. v. Adobe Sys., Inc.*, No. 6:09-CV-446, 2010 WL 3835762, *2 (E.D. Tex. September 28, 2010).

[48] This more strict interpretation was followed by a series of court decisions, e.g., in the Northern District of Illinois, *Rudd v. Lux Products Corporation Emerson Climate Technologies Braeburn Systems, LLC*, 2011 WL 148052, *2+ (N.D. Ill. January 12, 2011) (NO. CIV.A. 09-CV-6957); *Spread Spectrum Screening, LLC v. Eastman Kodak Co.*, No. 10 C 1101, 2010 WL 3516106, *2 (N.D. Ill. September 1, 2010).

[49] 35 U.S.C. § 299:

(a) Joinder of Accused Infringers:—With respect to any civil action arising under any Act of Congress relating to patents, other than an action or trial in which an act of infringement under section 271 (e)(2) has been pled, parties that are accused infringers may be joined in one action as defendants or counterclaim defendants, or have their actions consolidated for trial, or counterclaim defendants only if—
  (1) any right to relief is asserted against the parties jointly, severally, or in the alternative with respect to or arising out of the same transaction, occurrence, or series of transactions or occurrences relating to the **making, using, importing into the United States, offering for sale, or selling of the same accused product or process**; and
  (2) questions of fact common to all defendants or counterclaim defendants will arise in the action.

(b) Allegations Insufficient for Joinder:—For purposes of this subsection, accused infringers may not be joined in one action as defendants or counterclaim defendants, or have their actions consolidated for trial, based solely on allegations that they each have infringed the patent or patents in suit.

(c) Waiver.—A party that is an accused infringer may waive the limitations set forth in this section with respect to that party.

[50] H.R. Rep. No. 112-98, pt. 1, 55 n.61 (2011).

patent litigation.[51] Following the enactment of the AIA, one could observe that while the number of total patent infringement cases has increased, the average number of defendants per case has declined sharply.

C. Costs

Patent litigation in the United States is infamously costly. Various studies conducted in the last ten years established the average cost of enforcing a patent in court to be in excess of $400,000, and in complex and lengthy proceedings costs per party are frequently in the millions. Costs arising in the course of litigating a patent can be separated into court fees and attorney's fees. Unless a party is represented by an attorney providing services on a pro bono basis, attorney's fees are significantly higher than court fees. **10.22**

1. Court Fees and Other Costs

Reimbursement of court fees by the defeated party has been the established practice in common law for centuries.[52] In US procedure, reimbursement of court fees is stipulated in FRCP 54(d)(1), according to which the prevailing party can claim reimbursement of those costs which it incurred, other than attorney's fees. A party is considered to be a prevailing party if it invalidates a patent either as a defendant or in the course of a declaratory judgment action.[53] If a case is settled outside of court, no party is deemed to be a prevailing party.[54] **10.23**

The amount of court fees and related fees which can be claimed by the prevailing party are to be determined pursuant to 28 U.S.C. § 1920, and include (1) fees of the clerk and marshal; (2) fees for transcripts obtained for use in the case. (3) fees and disbursements for printing and witnesses; (4) costs of making copies,[55] (5) docket fees and (6) compensation of court appointed experts, compensation of interpreters, and salaries, fees, expenses, and costs of special interpretation services.[56] That said, the judge has discretion to determine the recoverable court fees, and can thereby practically deny reimbursement of court fees if such reimbursement would seem inappropriate.[57] Such reduction of the recoverable court fees requires special circumstances, which have to be substantiated by the party seeking to avoid reimbursement.[58] **10.24**

---

[51] See Charles R. Macedo, Michael J. Kasdan, and David A. Boag, "AIA's Impact on Multidefendant Patent Litigation, Part 2" (http://www.arelaw.com/downloads/ARElaw_AIAImpact2.pdf).

[52] One English statute provided for reimbursement of court fees to the prevailing party already as early as 1278 (Statute of Gloucester, 1278, 6 Edw. 1, c. 1); see Arthur L. Goodhart, "*Costs*," 38 *Yale L.J.* (1928–29): 849, 852. US courts maintained such practice after the independence of the United States, see Robert L. Harmon, *Patents and the Federal Circuit* (9th ed., 2007), 976.

[53] *Shum v. Intel Corp.*, 629 F.3d 1360, 1366 (Fed. Cir. 2010); *Ruiz v. A.B. Chance Co.*, 234 F.3d 654, 670 (Fed. Cir. 2000); *Manildra Mill. Corp. v. Ogilvie Mills, Inc.*, 76 F.3d 1178, 1181–82 (Fed. Cir. 1996).

[54] *Exigent Technology, Inc. v. Atrana Solutions, Inc.*, 442 F.3d 1301, 1312 (Fed. Cir. 2006).

[55] This does not include, e.g., expenses for production of a video for demonstration of facts, *Kohus v. Toys R Us, Inc.*, 282 F.3d 1355, 1357 (Fed. Cir. 2002); *Summit Technology, Inc. v. Nidek Co., Ltd.*, 435 F.3d 1371, 1374 (Fed. Cir. 2006).

[56] *Ortho-McNeil Pharmaceutical, Inc. v. Mylan Laboratories, Inc.*, 569 F.3d 1353, 1356 (Fed. Cir. 2009); *Chore-Time Equipment, Inc. v. Cumberland Corp.*, 713 F.2d 774, 781–82 (Fed. Cir. 1983).

[57] *Connell v. Sears, Roebuck & Co.*, 722 F.2d 1542, 1553 (Fed. Cir. 1983); *Delta-X Corp. v. Baker Hughes Production Tools, Inc.*, 984 F.2d 410, 413 (Fed. Cir. 1993); R. L. Harmon, *Patents and the Federal Circuit* (2007), 977.

[58] *Mathis v. Spears*, 857 F.2d 749, 752 (Fed. Cir. 1988).

2. Attorney's Fees

10.25 The bulk of patent litigation costs continue to be attorney's fees. While the amount of attorney's fees vary greatly from case to case, depending amongst other factors on the complexity of the technology and the duration and scope of the discovery proceedings, commentators report the average cost for attorney's fees incurred by each party to be around US$3 million to US $4 million.[59] Absent extraordinary circumstances, each party has to bear the cost of its own counsel. That said, patentees can request reasonable attorney's fees from the infringer as an element of the damage award if willfulness is found.[60] Conversely, a prevailing defendant can seek reimbursement of attorney's fees if the lawsuit filed by the patentee was later found to be frivolous, or if the patentee is found guilty of inequitable conduct. Such exceptional cases where defendants can claim reimbursement of attorney's fees used to be relatively rare. The Supreme Court, however, lowered the burden for a finding of an exceptional case in 2014, holding that an exceptional case is simply one that stands out from others with respect to the substantive strength of a party's litigating position or the unreasonable manner in which the case was litigated.[61] In a parallel case, the Supreme Court went on to give the district court greater discretion in determining whether or not a case was outstanding and thereby exceptional or not, heightening the standard of review to an abuse-of-discretion standard.[62] Both decisions aimed to empower district courts to shift attorneys' fees to prevailing defendants, in particular in frivolous cases brought by non-patent practicing entities (NPEs).[63] However, absent a finding of exceptional circumstances, the basic rule remains that each party has to pay its own lawyers.

D. Procedure

1. Procedure Overview and Pending Time

10.26 Figure 10.1 gives an overview of the different stages and actions in US patent litigation initiated by the patentee.

10.27 The average time between the filing of the complaint and the commencement of the trial varies substantially between districts.

2. Pleading Standard

10.28 A complaint in a civil litigation at a federal district court has to contain (1) a short and plain statement for the court's jurisdiction, (2) a short and plain statement of the claim showing that the pleader is entitled to relief, and (3) a demand for the relief sought.[64] In applying such a standard, complaints in patent infringement proceedings are usually very brief, often limited to identifying the asserted patent and the allegation that the defendant is directly or indirectly infringing a patent. The complaint might contain further information on the ownership of the asserted patent and a brief description of the defendant's conduct, which

[59] Michal Elmer and C. Gregory Gramenopoulos, *Global Patent Litigation* (2014), 900.
[60] See Ch. 13, 13.79.
[61] *Octane Fitness, LLC v. ICON Health & Fitness, Inc.*, 134 S. Ct. 1749, 1756 (2014).
[62] *Highmark Inc. v. Allcare Health Management System, Inc.*, 134 S. Ct. 1744 (2014).
[63] John Jurata and Amisha R. Patel, "Taming the Trolls: Why Antitrust Is Not a Viable Solution for Stopping Patent Assertion Entities," 21 *Geo. Mason L. Rev.* (2013–14): 1251, 1280–1.
[64] FRCP Rule 8(a).

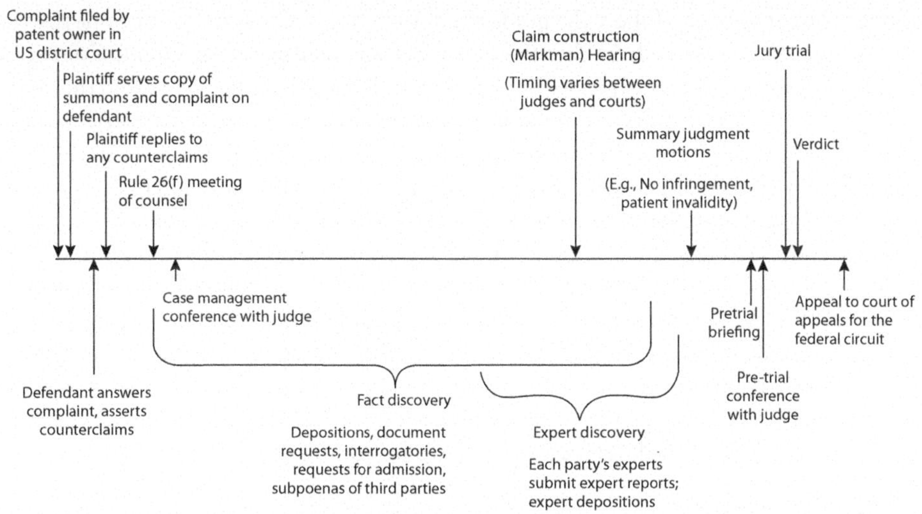

Figure 10.1 Stages and actions in US patent litigation initiated by the patentee

is alleged to be infringing. Often, the plaintiff will also attach the asserted patent, which is mandatory practice under some local court rules. However, in many cases, the defendant will not know which particular claims of the patents are being asserted, and, in cases where a concise description of the allegedly infringing act is missing, may not even know which products or processes he should be concerned about.[65]

In recent years, the appropriateness of this notice-pleading standard has increasingly been questioned. The Supreme Court has held in an antitrust case in 2007 that a "plaintiff's obligation to provide the 'grounds' of his 'entitle[ment] to relief' requires more than labels and conclusions, and a formulaic recitation of the elements of a cause of action will not do."[66] In a subsequent decision, the Supreme Court further held that such a pleading requirement is not limited to antitrust law, and reiterated that a complaint needs to "contain sufficient factual matter, accepted as true, to 'state a claim to relief that is plausible on its face."[67] It seems difficult to align such a heightened standard with the continued practice of notice-pleading in patent infringement cases, a practice that is suggested by FRCP Appendix Form 18. The direct applicability of FRCP Appendix Forms is stipulated in FRCP 84, which states that "[t]he forms in the Appendix suffice under these rules." **10.29**

During the last few years, the Federal Circuit has repeated several times that Form 18 in combination with an unrevised FRCP Rule 84 would continue to supersede the recent Supreme Court decisions, at least as far as patent law is concerned, and has directed district courts to uphold the practice of accepting complaints conforming to Form 18.[68] While the **10.30**

---

65 Peter Menell, *Patent Case Management Handbook* (2012), 2-33.

66 *Bell Atlantic Corp. v. Twombly*, 550 U.S. 544, 555 (2007).

67 *Ashcroft v. Iqbal*, 556 U.S. 662, 678, 129 S. Ct. 1937, 1949 (2009) (quoting *Twombly*, 550 U.S., 555).

68 *McZeal v. Sprint Nextel Corp.*, 501 F.3d 1354, 1357 (Fed. Cir. 2007); *In re Bill of Lading Transmission & Processing Sys. Patent Litig.*, 681 F.3d 1323, 1335 (Fed. Cir. 2012); *K-Tech Telecomms., Inc. v. Time Warner Cable, Inc.*, 714 F.3d 1277, 1286 (Fed. Cir. 2013).

majority of district courts follow the guidance of the Federal Circuit,[69] at least one district court has questioned the Federal Circuit's interpretation, holding that Supreme Court case law should be read as directly superseding Form 18 and FRCP Rule 84.[70] To avoid the risk of having a district court dismiss a complaint as insufficient, it might be good practice for patentees to offer a little more factual matter in their initial complaint than used to be the practice until a few years ago. The adequacy of providing further substantiation of facts already in the initial complaint was also admitted by the Federal Circuit in *K-Tech Telecommons* where the court held that the "adequacy of the facts pled depends on the breadth and complexity of both the asserted patent and the accused product or system and on the nature of the defendant's business activities,"[71] endorsing a pleading standard sometimes referred to as the sliding-scale standard. However, even if the Federal Circuit surrenders its use of Form 18 and follows the pleading standard suggested by the Supreme Court, the level of detail and facts that would have to supplied by a plaintiff in the initial complaint would still be significantly lower than the level required in Germany or in Japan.

3. Evidence Collection

10.31 Parties to the litigation can collect evidence not in their possession in the course of pre-trial discovery, which commences after the filing of the complaint. In addition, the FRCP also provide for a mechanism to collect evidence prior to the filing of the complaint, referred to as pre-litigation discovery.[72]

(a) Pre-litigation Discovery

10.32 Pre-litigation discovery, which is regulated by Rule 27 FRCP, can serve the purpose of verifying the basis of a lawsuit prior to its filing by securing specific evidence not in the party's possession.[73] Unlike pre-trial discovery conducted after filing of the lawsuit, pre-litigation discovery requires the petition to specify the substance of the evidence it seeks.[74] Rule 27(a) provides mainly for perpetuating witness testimony. In conjunction with Rule 34 FRCP, a party may also petition the court to order production of documents or electronically stored information, or to order inspection of the adversary's factory or other premises through pre-litigation discovery.[75] That said, the requirements for a court order under FRCP Rules 27 and 34 are relatively high. The petitioner must demonstrate that he is not yet able to file, but is either intending to file in the near future or is actively preparing to file the related

---

[69] *Bel Fuse, Inc. v. Molex, Inc.*, 27 F. Supp. 3d 557, 562 (D.N.J. 2014); *Zond, Inc. v. Fujitsu Semiconductor, Ltd.*, 990 F. Supp. 2d 50, 54 (D. Mass. 2014); *Classen Immunotherapies, Inc. v. Shionogi, Inc.*, 993 F. Supp. 2d 569, 575 (D.Md. 2014); *Bayer Cropscience AG v. Dow Agrosciences, LLC*, 288 F.R.D. 84, 86 (D. Del. 2012); *Robert Bosch Healthcare Systems, Inc. v. Express MD Solutions, LLC*, 2012 WL 2803617, *4 (N.D. Cal. 2012).

[70] *Macronix Intern. Co., Ltd. v. Spansion Inc.*, 4 F. Supp. 3d 797, 801 (E.D. Va. 2014); *Deerpoint Group, Inc. v. Acqua Concepts, Inc.*, 2014 WL 7178210, *4 (E.D. Cal. 2014); for a discussion of the effect that the recent patent reform bills would have had on the pleading requirements if they had passed as well as a discussion of local rules providing for effectively higher pleading standards, see Paul R. Gugliuzza, "Patent Litigation Reform: The Courts, Congress, and the Federal Rules of Civil Procedure," 95 *B.U.L. Rev.* (2015): 279.

[71] *K-Tech*, 714 F.3d, 1286.

[72] J. Friedenthal, M. Kane, and A. Miller, *Civil Procedure* (2005), § 7.3, 405; Lonny Sheinkopf Hoffman, "Access to Information, Access to Justice: The Role of Presuit Investigatory Discovery," 40 *U. Mich. J.L. Reform* (2007): 217, 225.

[73] Friedenthal, Kane, and Miller, *Civil Procedure*, § 7.3, 405.

[74] *Application of Deiulemar Compagnia Di Navigazione S.p.A. v. M/V Allegra*, 198 F.3d 473 (4th Cir. 1999).

[75] *Reynolds v. American Exp. Entity One*, 2009 WL 2578964, *1+ (W.D. Va. 2009).

lawsuit.[76] In addition, the petitioning party must show a high likelihood of immediate loss of evidence it is seeking to preserve.[77]

German patent procedure uses evidence collection tools prior to the filing of the lawsuit, namely the Düsseldorf procedure, which is functionally somewhat comparable to US pre-litigation discovery. However, the Düsseldorf procedure draws a large part of its relevance from the possibility of surprising the adversary by a court-issued evidence preservation order, which is enforced by the police if necessary.[78] US pre-litigation discovery does not include such an element of surprise. Rather, the adversary can defend itself again in any court-ordered pre-litigation discovery in a court hearing, notice of which has to be delivered at least twenty-one days prior to the scheduled hearing date, a process which obviously extinguishes any possible surprising element. Thus, while pre-litigation discovery theoretically provides patentees in the United States with the possibility of securing evidence prior to filing a lawsuit, in practice its use is very minor. Pre-trial discovery, available after the filing of the lawsuit, compels the adversary to provide a wider range of evidence. In addition, the initiating of an evidence preservation process under Rule 27 FRCP allows an adversary to select the litigation venue by filing a declaratory judgment action, a detrimental factor which pre-trial discovery does not include. **10.33**

(b) Pre-trial Discovery

Pre-trial discovery is usually of much greater importance to the parties than pre-litigation discovery, as it allows both the plaintiff and the defendant to obtain a wide range of information related to the lawsuit filed. The discovery process commences after the complaint is filed by the plaintiff. The process of pre-trial discovery in patent litigation is governed by Rule 26 FRCP. Accordingly, the plaintiff must initiate a discovery conference between the parties, also referred to as a Rule 26(f) meeting, at which the discovery process is discussed. The predominant purpose of this discovery conference is to prepare the case management conference with the judge. The aim of such a meeting between opposing counsel is to submit a discovery plan, which should include the parties' proposals on the subject, discovery limitations, a case management schedule, and timing deadlines for each stage of the discovery process. Also, the discovery plan should identify issues to be resolved with the judge in the case management conference. The case management conference, which is usually scheduled three weeks or more after the aforementioned Rule 26(f) meeting, sets the pace of the litigation. The judge will typically address and inquire on the following issues:[79] **10.34**

- a summary of claims and defenses raised by each party, as well as relevant background issues such as, amongst others, a general description of the identity of the accused products, whether the plaintiff asserts direct or indirect infringement, whether technology standards are involved, and whether there are third parties from which the parties will seek substantial discovery
- a summary of the market situation—that is, how the accused products relate to the defendant's business and how the patented technology relate to the patentee's business, as well as whether the parties are competitors with respect to the accused products

[76] *Deiulemar Compagnia Di Navigazione*, 473.

[77] *Calderon v. U.S. Dist. Court for Northern Dist. of California*, 144 F.3d 618, 621 (9th Cir. 1998).

[78] See the discussion of evidence collection in Germany, Ch. 11, 11.46.

[79] Menell, *Patent Case Management Handbook*, 2–82.

- if willfulness is asserted, clarification of the timing of the assertion of the claim and of the reliance on any opinion of counsel
- a discussion on the feasibility of any alternative dispute resolution (ADR)
- a decision on whether a protective order will be needed by resolving discussion on known points of contention (e.g., prosecution bar, levels of confidentiality, access by in-house lawyers) and, if applicable, conveying the court's general perspective on such issues
- a discussion on the scope of electronic discovery and consideration of the limitations on discovery
- the timing and procedures for claim construction and related summary judgment motions, and a discussion on the limits on the number of claim terms submitted for construction
- a discussion on claim construction hearing logistics, including whether live witnesses should be called, and how graphics, animations and other visual displays could aid in understanding the technology and disputed claim terms
- confirmation of whether any summary judgment issues depend on claim construction or can otherwise be resolved with little or no discovery
- a discussion on limits on the number of summary judgment motions or page limits
- a discussion on whether it would be appropriate to require damages contentions and/or an expedited damages discovery schedule, or to take other steps to facilitate the early resolution of challenges to damages-related theories or expert testimony.

10.35 The judge will determine the scope of discovery during the case management conference. Many districts have enacted special patent dispute rules[80] requiring the patentee to disclose the basis for infringement, and the defendant to disclose the basis for invalidity contentions early on in the process—that is, prior to the case management conference. Such early disclosure requirements force the parties to substantiate the claims asserted in their complaints to at least some degree early in the litigation process, and can enable a judge to filter out so-called nuisance-value claims.[81] If the judge detects a severe lack of substantive preparation and merit on the plaintiff's side, cases can be dismissed by setting early *Markman* and summary judgment hearings while staying commencement of discovery prior to ruling in these early hearings.[82]

10.36 The case management conference triggers the discovery process. That said, given the sensitive nature of information sought during discovery, disputes on the scope of discovery or concerning protective orders are frequently seen. Federal Circuit law applies only if an issue

[80] As of 2012, 18 district have local patent rules in place; these districts are the Northern District of California (revised rules effective December 1, 2009), the Southern District of California (effective November 1, 2011), the Northern District of Georgia (effective July 15, 2004), the District of Idaho (effective December 1, 2009), the Northern District of Illinois, the Southern District of Indiana (updated March 14, 2012), the District of Massachusetts (effective November 4, 2008), the District of Minnesota (effective May 9, 2011), the Eastern District of Missouri, the District of Nevada (effective August 1, 2011), the District of New Hampshire (published December 1, 2011), and the District of New Jersey (revised rules effective November 1, 2011).

[81] Ranganath Sudarshan, "Nuisance-value Patent Suits: An Economic Model and Proposal," 25 *Santa Clara Computer & High Tech. L.J.* (2008–9): 159, 161–62.

[82] E.g., *Parallel Networks, LLC v. Oriental Trading Company, Inc., et al.*, 6:10-cv-00474 (E.D. Texas, 2010), Memorandum Opinion and Order [Doc. 12], 3, filed March 15, 2011.

of patent law is central for the discovery dispute raised.[83] Otherwise, the local court rules are applied by the district court judge to resolve disputes. Finally, in some courts district court judges may choose to refer discovery disputes to other magistrate judges to avoid distraction.

(c) Scope of Discovery

Under the FRCP, both parties can request production of documents and conduct interrogatories and depositions. It is common in US patent litigation that the patentee request more than a hundred documents from the defendant, which have to be retrieved from multiple areas and departments within a company, such as product research and development, customer service and support, sales, marketing, accounting, and legal affairs. Document requests must be complied with both by collecting available hard copies and electronic data available on a party's computer system. **10.37**

Document production results in substantial costs for the parties, particularly in legal fees for collecting and processing the documents. All documents have to be reviewed to ensure that privileged documents are not submitted, and that confidentiality designations are sought for trade secrets and other confidential information. The production of documents during the discovery process can also result in severe disruption of the party's businesses, as it can take several months for the litigation counsel and the party's IP team to find the relevant documents. During this process, document custodians and often hundreds of temporary employees are employed to identify and classify documents. **10.38**

In recent years, particularly the burden of proper review, classification, and submission of electronically stored information—that is, the process referred to as electronic discovery or e-discovery—has become extremely resource-intensive, drastically increasing litigation cost. E-discovery has been recognized and specifically regulated in the FRCP since 2006. Electronically stored information (ESI) is to be particularly addressed at the outset of the discovery process. Each party's initial disclosures under FRCP Rule 26(a) must identify any ESI that it intends to use to substantiate its case. Further, pursuant to FRCP Rule 26(f)(2), the parties must "discuss any issues about preserving discoverable information; and develop a proposed discovery plan." The discovery plan produced under Rule 26(f) prior to the case management conference must address "any issues about disclosure or discovery of electronically stored information, including the form or forms in which it should be produced."[84] Often, parties to patent litigation are technology companies which have adopted electronic data systems decades ago. If faced with broad requests for submission of all ESI related to a certain product or a certain research area within the company, enormous amounts of ESI have to be produced and reviewed. **10.39**

In order to reduce the burden imposed by document production requests, the Federal Circuit Advisory Council made a concentrated attempt to limit the scope of electronic discovery by convening an eDiscovery Comittee, which adopted the Model Order Regarding EDiscovery in Patent Cases in November, 2011.[85] The model order limits email production requests to five custodians and five search terms. It intends to streamline the eDiscovery **10.40**

[83] *Midwest Indus. Inc. v. Karavan Trailers, Inc.*, 175 F.3d 1356, 1359 (Fed. Cir. 1999) (*en banc* in relevant part); *ACCO Brands, Inc. v. ABA Locks Mfr. Co.*, 501 F.3d 1307, 1311 (Fed. Cir. 2007); *Research Corp. Techs., Inc. v. Microsoft Corp.*, 536 F.3d 1247, 1255 (Fed. Cir. 2008).

[84] FRCP 26(f)(3)(C).

[85] Available at http://memberconnections.com/olc/filelib/LVFC/cpages/9008/Library/Ediscovery%20Model%20Order.pdf.

process and to allow for a tiered approach under which parties exchange core documentation regarding the technology at issue prior to producing any emails. The model order has been adopted by one of the most prominent district courts for patent litigation, the E.D. Texas in 2012, and has been employed also by other major district courts throughout the United States.

10.41 In addition to document production and production of ESI, the parties can make interrogatories and conduct depositions. An interrogatory, also sometimes referred to as a request for further information (RFI), is a set of written questions raised by one party in order to clarify matters of fact, which must be answered by the other party. The FRCP limits the number of interrogatories to twenty-five per party;[86] however, sometimes the parties jointly request the court to allow a greater number of interrogatories, especially if complex technological issues are at stake. As long as interrogatories are used in good faith by both parties, they can provide an efficient and meaningful tool to gather and streamline information. That said, litigants can also "abuse" interrogatories if they are filed before the information gained through the fact and expert discovery is properly searched and analyzed. In such case, interrogatories unnecessarily increase the responding party's efforts and costs during the process.[87]

10.42 Depositions are out-of-court oral testimony of a witness that is recorded and can be submitted in court as part of the evidence. The FRCP provides for default limitations of ten depositions in total[88] and one day per deposition,[89] unless the court grants permission for a higher number. The court will usually agree to any higher number of depositions or deposition hours if agreed upon between the parties prior to the case management conference.

(d) Limitations of Discovery

10.43 In general, any information relevant to the dispute is discoverable information and must be submitted to the other party per the lines and limitation outlined above. However, there are a few important limitations, namely privileged information and information classified as trade secrets being subject to court-issued protection orders.

10.44 **i. Attorney–Client Privilege** The attorney–client privilege is a legal concept that protects communication between the party and its attorney and keeps those communications outside the reach of discovery. It allows the party to refuse disclosing confidential communication conducted and prepared while seeking or receiving legal advice. The attorney–client privilege therefore encourages and enables "full and frank communication between a client and his attorney so that the client can make well-informed legal decisions and conform his activities to the law."[90] The attorney–client privilege extends to all types of communication, both written and oral,[91] provided that "the communication was made in confidence by clients to their lawyers for the purpose of obtaining legal advice."[92] That said, while

86 FRCP 33(a)(1).

87 *McCarthy v. Paine Webber Group, Inc.*, 168 F.R.D. 448, 450 (D. Conn. 1996); *Edward Lowe Indus., Inc. v. Oil–Dri Corp. of Am.*, No. 94–C–7568, 1995 WL 399712, *3 (N. D. Ill. July 7, 1995); *In re Convergent Tech. Sec. Litig.*, 108 F.R.D. 328, 336 (N. D. Cal. 1985).

88 Fed. R. Civ. P. 30(a)(2)(A).

89 Fed. R. Civ. P. 30(d)(1).

90 *In re EchoStar Communications Corp.*, 448 F.3d 1294, 1300 (Fed. Cir. 2006).

91 Ibid. 1301.

92 *American Standard, Inc. v. Pfizer Inc.*, 828 F.2d 734, 745 (Fed. Cir. 1987).

communication can be protected under the privilege and shielded from discovery, facts and other information being the basis for the communication with counsel do not become subject to attorney–client privilege.

ii. Work Product Immunity The work product immunity protects documents prepared by the attorney in the course of providing legal advice to its client. Different than the attorney–client privilege, such documents do not have to relate to communication between party and its counsel. The work product immunity has been codified in 1970 by FRCP 26(b)(3).[93] As stated in the FRCP, it only protects work products that have been prepared in anticipation of litigation, an anticipation that has to be specific with respect to the issue and the adversary in the litigation.[94] The work product immunity pertains both to written documents and to oral communications.[95] **10.45**

iii. Specific Issues in Patent Infringement Proceedings Application of the attorney–client privilege and the work product immunity presents a few issues specific to patent infringement proceedings. Courts have questioned in the past whether the privilege attaches not only to litigation counsel but also to patent attorneys and patent agents involved in the prosecution of the patent. Historically, US courts denied the attorney–client privilege to prosecution counsel, as patent prosecution was not considered to be legal work.[96] This conception was corrected by the Supreme Court in 1963, which held that "the preparation and prosecution of patent applications for others constitutes practice of law."[97] The Federal Circuit finally ended the discussion in 2000 on whether communication with an outside patent attorney conducting prosecution work would be fully covered by the attorney–client privilege, confirming that the invention record communicated from an inventor's patent department to a patent attorney is privileged.[98] **10.46**

An issue which is still not completely resolved is whether communication with patent agents conducted in the course of prosecution is privileged. The consensus developed in US case **10.47**

---

[93] FRCP 26(b)(3):

> Ordinarily, a party may not discover documents and tangible things that are prepared in anticipation of litigation or for trial by or for another party or its representative (including the other party's attorney, consultant, surety, indemnitor, insurer, or agent). But, subject to Rule 26(b)(4), those materials may be discovered if:
> (i) they are otherwise discoverable under Rule 26(b)(1); and
> (ii) the party shows that it has substantial need for the materials to prepare its case and cannot, without undue hardship, obtain their substantial equivalent by other means.

[94] *McCook Metals, LLC v. Alcoa Inc.*, 192 F.R.D. 242, 259 (N. D. Ill. 2000).

[95] While a few court decisions had attempted to limit the work-product immunity to written documents (e.g., in *Akeva, LLC v. Mizuno Corp.*, 243 F. Supp. 2d 418, 422 (M.D. N.C. 2003)), such limitation has been rejected by the Federal Circuit in *In re Seagate Technology, LLC*, 497 F.3d 1360, 1376 (Fed. Cir. 2007).

[96] *Zenith Radio Corp. v. Radio Corp. of America*, 121 F. Supp. 792, 793 (D. Del.1954).

[97] *Sperry v. Florida*, 373 U.S. 379, 383 (1963).

[98] *In re Spalding Sports Worldwide, Inc.*, 203 F.3d 800, 805–6 (Fed. Cir. 2000); earlier courts had sometimes refused to award the privilege to communication between patent department and patent attorney containing technical information, e.g., *Jack Winter Inc. v. Koratron Co.*, 50 F.R.D. 225 (N.D. Cal. 1970); *Sneider v. Kimberly-Clark Corp.*, 91 F.R.D. 1, 7 (N.D. Ill. 1980). This limited protection of patent prosecution work has been referred to as the "conduit theory." The majority of courts have rejected the conduit theory even before *In re Spalding*, and have awarded the attorney–client privilege to communication with prosecution counsel, e.g., *Knogo Corp. v. United States*, 213 U.S.P.Q. (BNA) 936 (Ct. Cl. 1980); *Advanced Cardiovascular Systems, Inc. v. C.R. Bard, Inc.*, 144 F.R.D. 372 (N.D. Cal. 1992); *Laitram Corp. v. Hewlett-Packard Co., Inc.*, 827 F. Supp. 1242, 1246 (E.D. La. 1993).

law indicates that communication with patent agents is privileged if that patent agent was supervised by and acted upon instruction of a patent attorney.[99] In the case of foreign patent agents prosecuting patent applications outside the United States, courts tend to award attorney–client privilege to communication with such foreign patent agents, even without supervision by an attorney.[100] Here, the courts recognize the differences between legal systems—that is, that most countries don't have patent agents and patent attorneys, but only one category of professionals admitted to the patent bar representing parties in the patent prosecution process, such as European patent attorneys admitted to practice at the European Patent Office or Japanese patent attorneys (*benrishi*) admitted to practice at the JPO.[101]

10.48 One of the constitutional requirements of the attorney–client privilege is that the communication is confidential. If a party chooses to lift the confidentiality and discloses privileged information, the party usually forfeits the privilege both to the disclosed material and all other communication on the same subject.[102] There is one recognized exception, referred to as the commonality of interest doctrine, under which parties can share privileged communication with third parties without losing the privilege, as long as such third parties share a common interest. Sample cases include parties being accused of infringing the same patent, or an exclusive licensor and licensee of a patent-in-suit.[103] In other cases, courts have upheld the attorney–client privilege in cases of inadvertent disclosure—that is, where disclosure had occurred accidentally despite reasonable safeguards in place.[104]

10.49 The context of a waiver of the attorney–client privilege has in the last years been most intensely discussed in the context of the reliance on opinion of counsel for the purpose of countering allegations of willfulness. A finding of willful infringement poses the risk of enhanced damages. For many years the only feasible defense against a willfulness allegation was to obtain an opinion of outside counsel holding that no infringement has occurred and/or that the patent-in-suit is invalid. However, in order to use such opinion of counsel in litigation, the alleged infringer had to disclose the opinion to the court and to the other party, a situation described by one court as a "cruel dilemma for one accused of willful infringement."[105] The Federal Circuit addressed this issue in a series of decisions between 2004 and 2007,[106] gradually modifying the standard for willful infringement and easing the dilemma

---

[99] *Golden Trade, S.r.L. v. Lee Apparel Co.*, 143 F.R.D. 514, 518–19 (S.D.N.Y. 1992); *Gorman v. Polar Electro, Inc.*, 137 F. Supp. 2d 223, 227 (E.D.N.Y. 2001); *Saxholm AS v. Dynal, Inc.*, 164 F.R.D. 331, 337 (E.D.N.Y. 1996); *Willemijn Houdstermaatschaapij BV v. Apollo Computer Inc.*, 707 F. Supp. 1429 (D. Del. 1989); *Cuno, Inc. v. Pall Corp.*, 121 F.R.D. 198, 204 (E.D.N.Y. 1988); *Cargill, Inc. v. Sears Petroleum & Transport Corp.*, 2003 WL 22225580, *3+ (N.D.N.Y. 2003) (NO. CIVA5:03CV0530 (DEP)); *E.I. du Pont de Nemours & Co. v. MacDermid, Inc.*, 2009 WL 3048421, *2+ (D. N.J. 2009) (NO. CIV. A. 06-3383 MLC).

[100] E.g., *Smithkline Beecham Corp. v. Apotex Corp.*, 193 F.R.D. 530, 537 (N.D. Ill. 2000); *Golden Trade, S.r.L. v. Lee Apparel Co.*, 143 F.R.D. 514, 523–24 (S.D.N.Y. 1992)

[101] See *VLT Corp. v. Unitrode Corp.*, 194 F.R.D. 8, 14–16 (D. Mass. 2000), a decision that was acknowledged in other proceedings, e.g., *Murata Manufacturing Co., Ltd. v. Bel Fuse Inc.*, 2005 WL 281217, *1+ (N.D. Ill. 2005).

[102] *Genentech, Inc. v. United States International Trade Commission*, 122 F.3d 1409, 1415 (Fed. Cir. 1997).

[103] The commonality of interest doctrine was upheld in a licensor/licensee relation in, e.g., *In re Regents of the University of Cal.*, 101 F.3d 1386, 1390 (Fed. Cir. 1996); *Stanley Works v. Haeger Potteries, Inc.*, 35 F.R.D. 551, 555 (N.D. Ill. 1964).

[104] *Alldread v. City of Grenada*, 988 F.2d 1425, 1434 (5th Cir. 1993).

[105] *Abbott Laboratories v. Baxter Travenol Laboratories, Inc.*, 676 F. Supp. 831, 832–33.

[106] *Knorr-Bremse Systeme Fuer Nutzfahrzeuge GmbH v. Dana Corp.*, 383 F.3d 1337 (Fed. Cir. 2004); *In re EchoStar Communications Corp.*, 448 F.3d 1294 (Fed. Cir. 2006); and *In re Seagate Technology, LLC*, 497 F.3d 1360 (Fed. Cir. 2007).

for the accused infringer. The most substantial review of the standard of burden of proof for willfulness as well as of reliability of the attorney–client privilege in this process occurred through *In re Seagate* in 2007, which held that submitting an opinion of counsel on invalidity or non-infringement would not result in a waiver of the attorney–client privilege for communication with the trial counsel.[107]

iv. Protective Orders Information requested in the course of discovery often involves sensitive information that parties do not want to share with competitors, such as technical data pertaining to product development or business information such as profit calculation for specific products and markets. In the vast majority of patent infringement cases, the disclosing party will request the court to issue a protective order for information classified as trade secret. To ensure that such information is not used by the other party outside the scope of litigation, the parties will request the court to issue a protective order. In most cases, the court will simply adopt the protective order in the form as negotiated by the parties and submitted to the court prior to the case management conference. **10.50**

A protective order will usually provide for two or more tiers of confidentiality. More sensitive information will be classified as "Attorney's Eyes Only," meaning that the information will only be disclosed to the adversary's attorneys, while the adversary itself may not get access to the information. The parties can agree on more detailed provisions in the protective order, such as specifying the names of the attorneys who may review certain information, or on keeping information in a locked room at the attorney's office with a log kept of persons accessing the information. Also, protective orders usually provide for the destruction or return of information disclosed, and for the prohibition of using the information in other proceedings. **10.51**

4. Jury Trial

In the court of first instance—namely, the district court proceedings—either of the parties to a patent enforcement action can insist on a jury trial. The right to a jury trial in a civil action is maintained by the Seventh Amendment to the US Constitution, which states: **10.52**

> In Suits at common law, where the value in controversy shall exceed twenty dollars, the right of trial by jury shall be preserved, and no fact tried by a jury shall be otherwise re-examined in any Court of the United States, than according to the rules of the common law.

The jury is usually established by twelve jurors. Verdicts have to be reached unanimously. As pointed out in the Seventh Amendment, juries are used to decide questions of fact, while legal questions are to be decided by the judge presiding over the trial.

(a) Right of Jury Trial

The right of a party to a jury trial is again stipulated in Rule 38(a) FRCP,[108] which confirms that the Seventh Amendment right is available to a party to a federal civil action. Rule 38(b) **10.53**

[107] *In re Seagate*, 1374–75. The ruling of the *Seagate* court was applied, e.g., in *Duhn Oil Tool, Inc. v. Cooper Cameron Corp.*, 2009 WL 3381052, *2+ (E.D. Cal. 2009); *Mane Fils, S.A. v. International Flavors and Fragrances Inc.*, 2009 WL 1968925, *2+ (D. N.J. 2009); *Koninklijke Philips Electronics N.V. v. Cinram Intern., Inc.*, 2012 WL 4074419, *4+ (S.D. N.Y. 2012); *Convolve, Inc. v. Compaq Computer Corp.*, 2007 WL 4205868, *1+ (S.D. N.Y. 2007); *Tyco Healthcare Group LP v. E-Z-EM, Inc.*, 2010 WL 2079920, *2+ (E.D. Tex. 2010); *SPX Corp. v. Bartec USA, LLC*, 247 F.R.D. 516, 525 (E.D. Mich. 2008).

[108] 28 U.S.C. § 1338(a).

FRCP clarifies, however, that a party which requests a jury has to explicitly demand it by both serving the other party as well as the court with such request.[109] Rule 38(d) FRCP further specifies that failure to request a jury trial is considered as a waiver of such party's right to a jury trial.[110] A party may limit its request for a jury trial to some particular issues of fact. In such case, the other party can request a jury trial for some or all other remaining factual issues. If a party request a jury trial pursuant to Rule 38(b) FRCP, but fails to specify which factual issues it demands a jury trial for, the court will assume that the requesting party demanded a jury trial for all issues of fact arising during the proceedings.[111]

(b) Legal Issues v. Factual Issues

10.54 The Supreme Court prominently addressed the question of whether an issue arising in a patent enforcement action should be considered as a question of law or as a question of fact in the *Markman* decision issued 1996.[112] The court held that when distinguishing between questions of law and facts, analogies should be sought in common law as it was practiced by English courts prior to enactment of the US Constitution in 1791.[113]

10.55 The Markman court briefly stated that "[t]here is no dispute that infringement cases today must be tried before a jury."[114] That said, the Federal Circuit distinguished the Supreme Court's statement in a later decision, holding that no jury trial should be invoked to determine infringement in an action where only injunctive relief and no damages are claimed by the plaintiff.[115] That said, questions of infringement and damages are both considered to be questions of fact that can be tried before a jury.[116] Somewhat surprisingly, the Federal Circuit decided in this context that the amount of post-verdict royalty payments in cases where the court found infringement but denied injunctive relief should be considered as a question of law rather than as a question of fact.[117]

10.56 The important question which was resolved in *Markman* was whether claim construction of a patent should be considered as a question of law or as question of fact. Here, the Supreme Court held that claim construction is a question of law, thus to be decided by the judge.[118] Claim construction of the patent-in-suit means the interpretation of what the words used in patent claims meant, resorting to (i) the written description accompanying the patent claims, (ii) the documentation of the history of the patent as it went through the application, (iii) standard dictionaries of English and (iv) if all else fails, expert testimony from experts "skilled in the art" at issue.

---

[109] Ibid. § 1338(b).

[110] Ibid. § 1338(d).

[111] Ibid. § 1338(c).

[112] *Markman v. Westview Instruments, Inc.*, 517 U.S. 370 (1996).

[113] Ibid. 376–77.

[114] Ibid. 377.

[115] *Tegal Corp. v. Tokyo Electron Am., Inc.*, 257 F.3d 1331, 1340–41 (Fed. Cir. 2001); similar *Arthrocare Corp. v. Smith & Nephew, Inc.*, 406 F.3d 1365, 1370 (Fed. Cir. 2005); *In re Technology Licensing Corp.*, 423 F.3d 1286, 1288 (Fed. Cir. 2005).

[116] The US Supreme Court confirmed this issue once more and in greater detail after *Markman* for statutory damage claims sought for copyright infringement in *Feltner v. Columbia Pictures Television, Inc.*, 523 U.S. 340, 353–55 (1998).

[117] *Paice, LLC v. Toyota Motor Corp.*, 504 F.3d 1293, 1314–15 (Fed. Cir. 2007). Confirmed, e.g., in *ActiveVideo Networks, Inc. v. Verizon Communications, Inc.*, 694 F.3d 1312, 1339 (Fed. Cir. 2012).

[118] *Markman*, 517 U.S. 370, 384–91 (1996); acknowledged by the Federal Circuit in *Cybor Corp. v. FAS Techs., Inc.*, 138 F.3d 1448, 1454–56 (Fed. Cir. 1998) (*en banc*).

5. Border Measures/ITC Proceedings

The International Trade Commission (ITC) is a quasi-judicial agency entrusted to carry out border measures. Similar to the customs authorities in Germany or Japan, the ITC provides assistance in seizing imported goods potentially infringing upon intellectual property of rights. That said, while its counterparts in Germany and Japan leave to the regular courts the determination of whether the imported goods really infringe, the ITC provides its own dispute resolution venue separate and independent from US district courts. Proceedings at the ITC are subject to a set of different rules than district courts. Also, if the plaintiff is successful at the ITC, he has access to a different type of remedy.[119] As shown in Figure 10.2, the number of proceedings at the ITC increased significantly over the last decade, reaching a peak in 2010. **10.57**

Proceedings at the ITC are governed by section 337. To initiate a complaint, the patentee has to provide the information as listed in ITC Rule 210.12,[120] which requires more details regarding the infringement than a complaint in district court proceedings. Within thirty days after the complaint is submitted, the ITC has to decide whether or not to initiate an investigation for patent infringement. If an investigation is initiated, it is assigned to an administrative law judge (ALJ). The ALJ presides over the hearings, conducts the prehearing case management including discovery issues, decides on summary motions, and makes an initial determination (ID) whether an infringement has occurred or not. The ITC employs six ALJ, all of whom are widely recognized as having profound expertise in patent law and a wide array of experience in technology.[121] The ID is reviewed by the International Trade Commission consisting of six commissioners.[122] Decisions of the ITC are subject to a presidential review period of sixty days, during which the White House can vacate a decision of the ITC for policy reasons.[123] Presidential reviews are rarely invoked.[124] If the ITC investigation results in a finding of patent infringement and issues an exclusion order, the respondent can appeal to the Federal Circuit. **10.58**

Proceedings at the ITC differ in various ways from those at district courts. The four most significant differences are (1) the speed of the ITC, (2) the comparatively high experience of the judges, combined with the absence of a jury trial, (3) the additional requirement of the plaintiff to satisfy a domestic industry requirement, and (4) the absence of a claim for damages or attorneys' fees. **10.59**

---

[119] See Ch. 13, 13.26.

[120] 19 CFR 210.12.

[121] For a brief introduction of the ITC see also Ch. 2, 2.17.

[122] Commissioners at the ITC are appointed by the president and have to be confirmed by the Senate, while no more than three commissioners may belong to the same party. Each commissioner is appointed for a term of 9 years.

[123] 19 USC § 1337(j).

[124] The most noted exception in the recent past was the presidential review of a final determination in a case involving enforcement of standard-essential patents of Samsung against Apple (Certain Electronic Devices, Including Wireless Communication Devices, Portable Music and Processing Devices, and Tablet Computers, Inv. No. 337-TA-794, Notice of the Commission's Final Determination Finding a Violation of Section 337; Issuance of a Limited Exclusion Order and a Cease-and-Desist Order; Termination of the Investigation, June 4, 2013). The presidential review was published under https://ustr.gov/sites/default/files/08032013%20Letter_1.PDF.

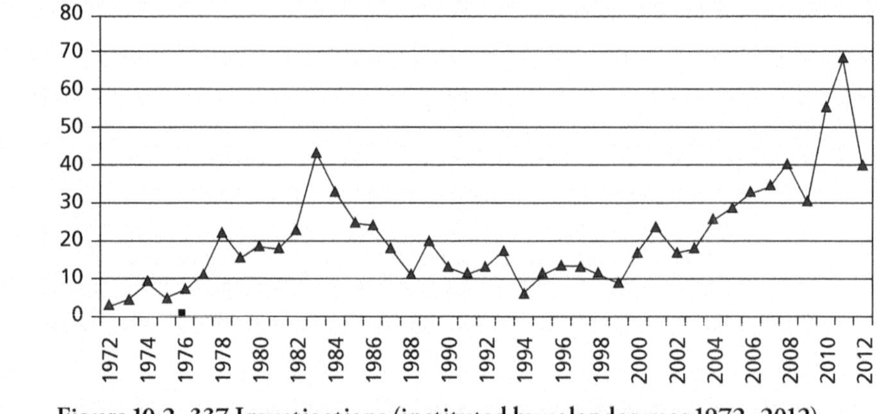

Figure 10.2 337 Investigations (instituted by calendar year 1972–2012)

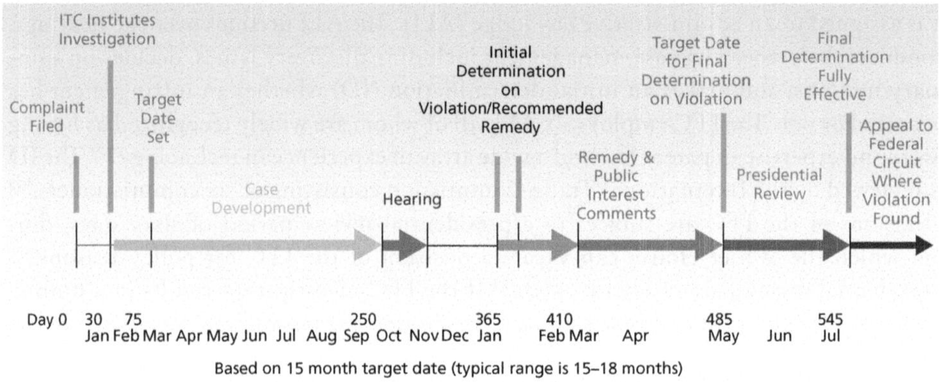

Figure 10.3 Timeline of ITC proceedings

10.60 The speed of ITC proceedings is regulated by section 337, according to which an investigation must be concluded within one year from the date of publication of the notice of the complaint. In "complicated" cases, the permissible period can be extended to eighteen months (see Figure 10.3).[125] This is considerably faster than most district court proceedings. The enhanced speed puts substantial pressure on the respondent, who has to react to the complaint significantly faster than to a district court complaint. At the same time, ITC proceedings also can create a time crunch for the complainant, who will have less time to react to discovery requests by the respondent. Thus, ITC proceedings tend to consume more resources and result in higher costs than proceedings at the district court, but produce a more instant result, which obviously can be of great value for the patentee.

[125] 19 USC § 1337(b)(1), as amended in 1994 by Pub. L. 103–465, § 321(a)(1)(B).

10.61 Congress abolished the right of the parties to a jury at ITC proceedings in 1988.[126] While the ITC also hears cases on other international trade issues, the docket of ALJs focuses to a large degree on patent cases. Due to this concentration, ALJs at the ITC are widely recognized as having more experience and a deeper understanding of the technology than an average district court judge, who has to preside over a much greater variety of legal areas.[127]

10.62 The existence of the domestic industry requirement set forth in section 337 does not discriminate between US companies and foreign companies. It merely requires the existence of an industry in the United States, which can also be owned and controlled by a foreign company. There has been significant discussion as to whether the requirement bars non-practicing entities from enforcing their patents at the ITC. Recent case law, however, confirmed that non-practicing entities can satisfy the domestic industry requirement, for example, by showing the existence of an established, operating, and economically relevant licensing program.

10.63 A complainant must show the existence of an industry in the United States, or that such an industry is in the process of being established. Section 337 requires satisfaction of both a technical and an economic prong.[128] The technical prong can be satisfied by showing that the "industry practices at least one claim of the patent at issue."[129] The economic prong can be satisfied by showing a significant investment in plant and equipment, a significant employment of labor or capital, or a substantial investment in its exploitation, including engineering, research and development, or licensing.[130]

10.64 The current economic prong of the domestic industry requirement is a result of congressional action taken in 1988. Prior to 1988, section 337 required a plaintiff to show "systematic activity which significantly employs use of American land, labor, and capital for the creation of value."[131] Such requirements made it difficult for non-manufacturing owners of intellectual property rights such as universities and movie studios to seek enforcement of infringed intellectual property rights at the ITC. Legislative change was triggered by the decision of the ITC in *Certain Products with Gremlin Character Descriptions*,[132] in which the ITC found that the complainant, Warner Brothers, Inc. Licensing Company of America, did not meet the then-existing domestic industry requirement because licensing could not form the basis of a domestic industry.[133] Due to the interpretation that the domestic

---

126 Omnibus Trade and Competitiveness Act of 1988, Pub. L. No. 100-418, § 1342, 102 Stat. 1107, 1212–16, codified at 19 U.S.C. § 1337 (1988).

127 Please note that also district courts are aiming for a higher degree of concentration of patent cases by increasingly assigning patent cases to judges who participate in the patent pilot program. See, e.g., Randall R. Rader, "Addressing the Elephant: The Potential Effects of the Patent Cases Pilot Program and Leahy-Smith America Invents Act," 62 *Am. U.L. Rev.* (2012–13): 1105, 1106–9; Etan S. Chatlynne, "On Measuring the Expertise of Patent-Pilot Judges: Encouraging Enhancement of Claim-Construction Uniformity," 12 *J. Marshall Rev. Intell. Prop. L.* (2012–13): 309.

128 19 U.S.C. § 1337(a)(1)–(2) (2000).

129 *Certain Display Controllers and Prods. Containing Same and Certain Display Controllers with Upscaling Functionality and Products Containing Same*, Comm'n Op. 52, Inv. Nos. 337-TA-491/481 (consolidated) (February 4, 2005), 2005 WL 996252.

130 19 U.S.C. § 1337(a)(3).

131 H.R. Rep. No. 100-40, 157.

132 *Certain Products with Gremlin Character Descriptions, Inv., Comm'n Op.*, No. 337-TA-201 (1986).

133 *Certain Digital Processors and Digital Processing Systems, Components Thereof and Products Containing Same*, Inv. No. 337-TA-559, Initial Determination, 89 (May 11, 2007) (citing 132 CONG. REC. H1782 (April 10, 1986) 99th Cong. (2nd Sess. 1986).

industry requirement would be too strict, Congress amended section 337 and introduced the currently applied disjunctive three-factor test for satisfaction of the economic prong.

10.65 The interpretation of the last factor, the "substantial investment in [the patent's] exploitation, including engineering, research and development, or licensing" requirement, had been the subject of recent debate, as the interpretation of this factor determines whether the ITC can serve as a venue for non-practicing patent holders who cannot satisfy either of the first two factors. The interpretation that licensing activities suffice to show a domestic industry has been for the first time unambiguously confirmed by the Federal Circuit in 2012.[134]

10.66 The requirements for establishing a domestic industry by a substantial investment in licensing of one or multiple patents have been clarified by the Commission, for example, in its decision in *Certain Multimedia Display and Navigation Devices*,[135] in which it reversed the initial determination by ALJ Charneski and found that the complainant, the Japanese company Pioneer, and its US subsidiary, failed to establish domestic industry for the asserted patents through its domestic licensing activities of its patent portfolio containing both asserted and unasserted patents. The Commission held that in order to demonstrate the required nexus between the substantial investment and the asserted patent through the licensing of a patent portfolio, a complainant must show the relative importance of the asserted patent within the portfolio by providing evidence that the asserted patent:[136]

- has been explicitly discussed in the course of license negotiations
- has been successfully litigated
- relates to a technology industry standard
- is a base patent or a pioneering patent
- is infringed or practiced in the United States
- the value of the asserted patent is recognized by the market in some other way.

10.67 The Commission reiterated that the complainant has the burden of proof to show the required nexus between the asserted patents and complainant's licensing activities amounts to a substantial investment. In particular, the Commission rejected fund allocation in the course of licensing investments equally among patents in a portfolio as insufficient to establish substantial investment, and further held that the nexus between asserted patents and substantial investment must be established based on a fact-focused and case-specific basis.[137]

10.68 A different notion of the "substantial investment through licensing activities" test was clarified in *Coaxial Cable*[138] in which the ITC had to decide whether costs incurred in patent litigation activities and related to licensing could be considered a substantial investment in the patent's exploitation sufficient to show existence of domestic industry. The Commission held that litigation activities related to licensing may satisfy the economic prong, but

[134] *InterDigital Communications, LLC v. International Trade Com'n*, 690 F.3d 1318, 1329–30 (Fed. Cir. 2012), denying reh'g and reh'g *en banc*, 707 F. 3d 1295, 1298 (Fed. Cir. 2013).

[135] *Certain Multimedia Display and Navigation Devices and System Components Thereof and Products Containing Same*, Inv. No. 337-TA-694, Comm'n Op. (July 22, 2011) (Public Version).

[136] Ibid. 10–11.

[137] Ibid. 13.

[138] *John Mezzalingua Assoc., Inc. v. Int'l Trade Comm'n*, 660 F.3d 1322, 1327–30 (Fed. Cir. 2011).

that litigation expenses on their own and not directly related to licensing, engineering or research and development activities would not be sufficient to show a domestic industry.[139]

At the same time, the Commission held that if a complainant could show litigation costs connected to a patentee deriving revenue from a license, such litigation costs could constitute a "substantial investment" into exploitation of the patent. A complainant would have to ensure, however, that any and all costs associated with the litigation were well documented and linked to the specific patent asserted in the ITC complaint. Also, the investments made by the patent owner by bringing the litigation would have to be substantial as required in the statute. Whether an investment could be regarded as substantial would require a factual inquiry and be dependent upon the industry in question and the complainant's relative size. For example, on remand in *Coaxial Cable* the ITC found that 79.4 attorney work hours resulting in litigation costs of $27,506 spent on licensing and settlement efforts attributable to the specific patent were not sufficient to establish a domestic industry.[140] The reasons considered for the finding of an absence of domestic industry included the facts that the complainant had:[141] **10.69**

- received only one license for the technology, of which only a portion was actually related to the asserted patent
- no established licensing program whatsoever
- made no other efforts to send cease and desist letters with offers to license the asserted patent
- not engaged in other licensing offers or talks with any persons or entities other than those involved with the single license to the patent.

Although finding no domestic industry for the infringement of the specific patent in question, the Commission's opinion received some criticism as it explicitly stated that litigation expenses incurred in relation to licensing could satisfy the economic prong of the domestic industry requirement test.[142] The role of litigation expenses in the domestic industry test was somewhat qualified by the Federal Circuit in 2013, which held that litigation targeted purely at financial gains and not at encouraging adoption of the patentee's technology would not be sufficient to satisfy the economic prong of the test.[143] **10.70**

There are other differences between ITC proceedings and patent litigation at district courts. District courts operate in accordance with the FRCP and local rules for the respective federal court district. Proceedings at the ITC are governed by section 337, the ITC Rules of Practice and Procedure, and a set of ground rules issued by the ALJ presiding over the case. However, other than the major differences introduced above, the ITC Rules of Practice and Procedure largely resemble the FRCP. **10.71**

---

[139] Ibid.

[140] *Certain Coaxial Cable Connectors*, Inv. No. 337-TA-650, Remand Initial Determination, 25 (May 27, 2010) (Public Version).

[141] Ibid. 25.

[142] In this context, however, it should be noted that even in earlier cases complainants had already satisfied the domestic industry test by a mere showing of licensing activities, see, e.g., *Certain Semiconductor Chips with Minimized Chip Package Size and Products Containing Same*, Inv. No. 337-TA-432, Order No. 13, Initial Determination (January 24, 2001); *Certain Zero-Mercury-Added Alkaline Batteries, Parts Thereof and Products Containing Same*, Inv. No. 337-TA-493, Initial Determination (June 2, 2004); *Certain 3G Mobile Handsets and Components Thereof*, Inv. No. 337-TA-613, Order No. 42, Initial Determination (March 10, 2009).

[143] *Motiva, LLC v. International Trade Com'n*, 716 F.3d 596, 600–1 (Fed. Cir. 2013).

6. Pre-trial Proceedings

(a) *Warning Letters*

10.72 Also in the United States, it is standard practice for a patentee to send the alleged infringer a warning letter prior to initiating a lawsuit. Warning letters are sent not only to the manufacturer but also to importers and commercial retail outlets distributing and selling the product. While there can be situations where the risk of sending a warning letter outweigh the potential benefits, a warning letter may be a first step in resolving the patent dispute without having to go through a lawsuit, and may also be a first step towards the parties agreeing on a license agreement or another form of joint commercialization of the patent. Another evident benefit of a warning letter is that it provides notice of the alleged infringement, making it easier to claim enhanced damages for willful patent infringement.[144]

10.73 Sending a warning letter without careful consideration poses multiple risks for the patentee. The biggest risk is that the warning letter triggers a declaratory judgment action, in which the alleged infringer can assert non-infringement and invalidity of the patents claimed as infringed in the warning letter. The patentee may find itself as a defendant in legal action in a non-desirable forum with significantly lower chances of being able to enforce its patents. A patentee who sends a warning letter without filing a subsequent infringement action for an extended period of time risks that the defendant can invoke an equitable estoppel claim against the infringement action. This principle was confirmed by the Federal Circuit in 2010, which ruled that a silence of three and a half years after sending a warning letter created an equitable estoppel of enforcing the patent claim.[145]

10.74 Another risk which patentees can face in the United States is that a wrongful warning letter may trigger a damage claim by the alleged infringer. Such claim can be invoked either under § 43(a) of the Lanham Act[146] as the federal statute for unfair competition law or, as the case may be, under state law. However, the hurdle for the alleged infringer to bring such a damage claim is very high,[147] as he has to show that the patentee acted both objectively and subjectively in bad faith when sending the warning letter.[148] To meet the subjective bad faith standard, the alleged infringer must show that the patentee sent a warning letter despite believing that the patent would be invalid or not infringed.[149] There are very few cases in which a court held that the patentee acted in bad faith when trying to enforce its patents.[150] Unlike, for example, in Germany where a patentee is presumed to be liable if he

---

[144] See Ch. 13, 13.72.

[145] *Aspex Eyewear Inc. v. Clariti Eyewear, Inc.*, 605 F.3d 1305, 1311 (Fed. Cir. 2010). In an earlier decision, the Federal Circuit had affirmed an equitable estoppel when the patentee had waited for five years after sending the first warning letter, see *ABB Robotics, Inc. v. GMFanuc Robotics Corp.*, 52 F.3d 1062, 1063–65 (Fed. Cir. 1995).

[146] 15 U.S.C. § 1125(a)(1).

[147] *800 Adept, Inc. v. Murex Securities, Ltd.*, 539 F.3d 1354, 1370 (Fed. Cir. 2008).

[148] *Mikohn Gaming Corp. v. Acres Gaming, Inc.*, 165 F.3d 891, 897 (Fed. Cir. 1998); *Dominant Semiconductors Sdn. Bhd. v. OSRAM GmbH*, 524 F.3d 1254, 1261 (Fed. Cir. 2008).

[149] E.g., *Mirafi, Inc. v. Murphy*, 928 F.2d 410 (Fed. Cir. 1991).

[150] One rare exception can be found in *Concept Design Electronics and Mfg., Inc. v. Duplitronics, Inc.*, 52 F.3d 342 (Fed. Cir. 1995). That said, there are a few decisions where courts denied the patentee's motion to dismiss the unfair competition counterclaims, e.g., *Zenith Electronics Corp. v. Exzec, Inc.*, 182 F.3d 1340, 1355 (Fed. Cir. 1999); *Soilworks, LLC v. Midwest Indus. Supply, Inc.*, 2008 WL 3286975, *3 (D. Ariz. 2008); *Monolithic Power Systems, Inc. v. O2 Micro Intern., Ltd.*, 2007 WL 801886 (N.D. Cal. 2007). There are significantly more opinions where courts dismissed unfair competition claims due to a lack of bad faith.

sends a warning letter which later turns out to be wrong,[151] the patentee's risk of liability for sending warning letters in the US is very low.

(b) Where and When to Sue (Forum Shopping)

As pointed out above, the most significant risk associated with sending any form of warning letter in the United States is that the alleged defendant moves for a declaratory judgment in one of the jurisdictions known as not favorable to patent holders. **10.75**

Various characteristics can be interpreted as being favorable or not favorable for a patentee. A widely noted study by Stanford Law School Professor Mark Lemley published in 2010[152] claimed that statistically the Middle District of Florida, the Eastern District of Virginia, and the District of Delaware are the most patentee-friendly jurisdiction in the United States.[153] This result was derived from a review of the outcome of all patent infringement cases filed in the United States between 2000 and 2010, analyzing district courts by general win rates, the rate of patentees getting a lawsuit to trial, and speed—namely, average time to resolution and the average time to trial. The study indicated the Eastern District of Wisconsin, the Southern District of Ohio, and the District of Columbia to be the least patent-friendly jurisdictions,[154] suggesting these jurisdictions to be favorable for an alleged infringer seeking a declaratory judgment. **10.76**

The variation in popularity triggers a dynamic sometimes referred to as a "race to the courthouse" between the patentee and the alleged infringer. As discussed above, the defendant can request the court to transfer the case to a more convenient forum.[155] While the Federal Circuit has encouraged courts in the past to consider motions for transfer more seriously, forum shopping continues to be an important strategic tool in US patent enforcement. **10.77**

7. **Appeals**

Patent infringement cases are litigated at the district court level. The losing party can appeal the decision of the district courts at the Court of Appeals for the Federal Circuit (often addressed simply as the "Federal Circuit"). If a party is dissatisfied with the appellate decision of the Federal Circuit, it can request the US Supreme Court to grant certiorari to review the decision of the Federal Circuit. **10.78**

(a) Court of Appeals for the Federal Circuit

The Federal Circuit was established in 1982 as a central appellate court to review all district court decisions in the area of patent law.[156] The aim in establishing such central review body for first instance appeals was to achieve more uniformity in patent law. During the 1970s, patent infringement cases were appealed to regional circuit courts, which had developed diverging standards in their jurisprudence. Such divergence and the resulting legal uncertainty became significant enough to be perceived as a threat to the patent system as **10.79**

[151] See Ch. 11, 11.108.
[152] See Mark A. Lemley, "Where to File Your Patent Case," 38 *AIPLA Q.J.* (2010): 401.
[153] Ibid. 418–21.
[154] Ibid.
[155] See Ch. 10, 10.07.
[156] 28 U.S.C. § 1295.

a tool to foster innovation as a whole.[157] In response, Congress passed the Federal Court Improvements Act in 1982,[158] establishing the Federal Circuit.

10.80 Other than reviewing patent infringement cases appealed from district courts, the Federal Circuit is the appellate court for decisions of the ITC and the USPTO. In addition, it is entrusted to hear appeals for certain money claims against the United States government, federal personnel, veterans' benefits, and public safety officers' benefits claims. Roughly half of the cases heard by the Federal Circuit are patent cases.[159]

10.81 The court is composed of twelve judges, who hear cases in panels of three. In addition, the Federal Circuit has six judges serving as senior judges, which is a form of semi-retirement in the US federal court system. In case the court is split on a particular issue, it has the opportunity to resolve issues *en banc*.

10.82 The Federal Circuit is entitled to review questions of law *de novo*, a standard of review which grants no deference to the finding of the district court and enables the Federal Circuit to undertake a full and independent review.[160] Questions of fact may only be reviewed if the district court judge in a fact-finding instance acted "clearly erroneously."[161] If the facts were determined by a jury, as usually the case in patent infringement proceedings, the FRCP provide for the "substantial evidence standard," under which the Federal Circuit cannot reverse a factual determination by a jury as long as "a reasonable mind might accept the evidence as adequate to support a conclusion."[162] An additional standard of review is the abuse of discretion standard, the standard giving most deference to the decision of the district court. This standard is usually applied when the Federal Circuit is asked to review issues related to trial management and supervision by the district court. If the Federal Circuit applies the abuse of discretion standard, it rarely overturns the district court.[163] Such established case law principles are rooted in FRCP Rule 61, which provides that an "error in admitting or excluding evidence... is [no] ground for granting a new trial." The decision of whether or not to admit certain evidence is a classic example of a trial management decision made by the district court.

10.83 In patent infringement proceedings, case law has developed a fairly comprehensive canon of decisive elements being either categorized as questions of fact or questions of law. The question of infringement, both literal and pursuant to the doctrine of equivalents, was held to be a question of fact to be reviewed only under a clearly erroneous or the substantial evidence

[157] Rochelle Cooper Dreyfuss, "*The Federal Circuit: A Case Study in Specialized Courts*," 64 *N.Y.U. L. Rev.* (1989): 1, 6–8.

[158] Pub. L. No. 97-164, 96 Stat. 25.

[159] See case statistics at the website of the of Federal Circuit at http://www.cafc.uscourts.gov/the-court/statistics.html.

[160] E.g., *Douglas Dynamics, LLC v. Buyers Products Co.*, 717 F.3d 1336, 1341 (Fed. Cir. 2013); *Rambus Inc. v. Infineon Technologies AG*, 318 F.3d 1081, 1086–87 (Fed. Cir. 2003); *In re Asahi/America, Inc.*, 68 F.3d 442, 445 (Fed. Cir. 1995).

[161] FRCP 52(a). The standard of a "clearly erroneous" determination of facts has been further defined by the US Supreme Court as follows: "A finding is 'clearly erroneous' when although there is evidence to support it, the reviewing court on the entire evidence is left with the definite and firm conviction that a mistake has been committed"; see *Anderson v. City of Bessemer City*, 470 U.S. 564, 573–74 (1985).

[162] *Pierce v. Underwood*, 487 U.S. 552, 565 (1988).

[163] *ATD Corp. v. Lydall, Inc.*, 159 F3d 534, 544 (Fed. Cir.1998).

standard.[164] The determination of damage claims by the district court judge or the jury is also considered to be a question of fact.[165] The method a district court applied in reaching a certain damage amount is reviewed under the abuse of discretion standard.[166] The interpretation of the language of the patent claim is a question of law, subject to *de novo* review by the Federal Circuit.[167] So in reviewing the district court's decision regarding the validity of the patent-in-suit, the Federal Circuit applies different standards, depending on the relevant question. The factual determination underlying a decision regarding non-obviousness of patent, for example, would be considered a question of fact.[168] In contrast, the review of whether a patent conforms to the subject matter eligibility requirements of § 101 of the Patent Act is considered a review of a question of law, subject to the *de novo* standard.[169]

During the last ten years, on average 400–450 patent infringement cases were filed at the Federal Circuit.[170] In roughly 35 percent of these cases, the Federal Circuit reversed the decision of the district court, most frequently on matters of claim construction, but often also through a review of other issues and by applications of standards other than the *de novo* standard.[171] In light of this comparatively high rate of reversal, the Federal Circuit is sometimes criticized as being overly active in deciding patent cases and framing patent law. At the same time, in light of the fact that appellate cases come from virtually every district court of the United States, which all operate under different sets of local court rules and which are equipped which judges having greatly varied experience in patent law, the high rate of reversion may well be considered as necessary to ensure at least some degree of uniformity within the US patent enforcement system. **10.84**

(b) US Supreme Court

If a party does not prevail at the Federal Circuit level, it can ask the US Supreme Court to consider reviewing the case. It is unlikely that the Supreme Court will grant a writ of certiorari, and thus will refuse to review the case.[172] For a long time, this was particularly true in patent law. One reason for Congress to establish the Federal Circuit was the lack of guidance in patent law from the Supreme Court. After the Federal Circuit was established in 1982, the Supreme Court showed even less of a desire to decide patent law questions, as the **10.85**

---

[164] *Roton Barrier, Inc. v. Stanley Works*, 79 F.3d 1112, 1125 (Fed. Cir. 1996); *Morton Intern., Inc. v. Cardinal Chemical Co.*, 5 F.3d 1464, 1468 (Fed. Cir. 1993).

[165] *Cybor Corp. v. FAS Techs., Inc.*, 138 F.3d 1448, 1461 (Fed. Cir. 1998) (*en banc*).

[166] *Rite-Hire Corp. v. Kelley Co.*, 56 F.3d 1538, 1543–44 (Fed. Cir. 1995) (*en banc*).

[167] See Ch. 10, 10.54; however, please note that according to recent Supreme Court case law, resolutions of factual disputes required for claim construction is to be reviewed as a factual finding subject to a clearly erroneous standard, see *Teva Pharm. USA, Inc. v. Sandoz, Inc.*, 135 S.Ct. 831, 838 (2014).

[168] *In re Huang*, 100 F.3d 135, 138 (Fed. Cir. 1996). The final decision, whether the patent is nonobvious or not, however, is reviewed *de novo*.

[169] E.g., *In re Comiskey*, 554 F.3d 967, 975 (Fed. Cir. 2009); *AT&T Corp. v. Excel Communications, Inc.*, 172 F.3d 1352, 1355 (Fed. Cir. 1999). A detailed list of review standards in patent law can be found in Kevin Casey, Jade Camara, and Nancy Wright, "Standards of Appellate Review in the Federal Circuit: Substance and Semantics," 11 *Fed. Cir. B.J.* (2001–2): 279, 361–75.

[170] See http://www.cafc.uscourts.gov/images/stories/the-court/statistics/Caseload_Patent_Infringement_2003-2012.pdf.

[171] See, e.g., a study of Federal Circuit reversal rates prepared by Ted L. Field, "Judicial Hyperactivity in the Federal Circuit: An Empirical Study," 46 *U.S.F. L. Rev.* (2011–12): 721, 725.

[172] E.g., during the fiscal year 2005, the Supreme Court granted certiorari to less than 1% of the all certiorari petitions, see David C. Thompson and Melanie F. Wachtell, "An Empirical Analysis of Supreme Court Certiorari Petition Procedures: The Call for Response and the Call for the Views of the Solicitor General," 16 *Geo. Mason L. Rev.* (2008–9): 237, 241.

task of ensuring a uniform application of patent law was now taken care of by the Federal Circuit.[173] However, for the last ten or so years the Supreme Court has shown an increased interest in patent law, and has accepted a number of cases every year where it felt the necessity to correct or adjust central questions in patent law. Recent Supreme Court case law thus has significantly impacted patent enforcement procedure in the United States, for example:

- making the claim for injunctive relief subject to the four *eBay* factors[174]
- lowering the threshold for filing a declaratory judgment action[175]
- limiting the applicability of the Circuit's application of the "teaching-suggestion-motivation" (TSM) test and therefore lowering the threshold to invalidate a patent as obvious[176]
- affirming the validity of the patent exhaustion doctrine[177]
- limiting the applicability of the machine-or-transformation test for the subject matter eligibility review[178]
- affirming that an invalidity defense has to be proven by clear and convincing evidence and not only by a preponderance of the evidence.[179]

10.86 That said, while the Supreme Court has weighed into patent law more frequently in recent years than ever before, the Court will normally not be available as a review instance in patent enforcement actions, and instead will serve to adjust fundamental questions of substantial importance for the patent system as a whole.

E. Other Types of Actions

1. Declaratory Judgment Action

10.87 In a declaratory judgment action (DJA), the parties switch sides. The alleged infringer becomes the plaintiff, seeking the court to declare that either no infringement has occurred, or that the patent of the patentee is invalid, or both. The patentee becomes the defendant and will argue for infringement of a valid patent. Acting as a plaintiff brings the advantage of being able to select the venue of the litigation. In addition, the plaintiff may be able to draw some advantage from the rules of primacy and recency, allowing the plaintiff to make the first and the last impression on the jury in the district court trial.

(a) Actual Controversy

10.88 In order to be able to file for a DJA, one party must have been accused of infringing a patent. That said, the severity of allegations which are necessary to classify a party as an alleged infringer has been subject to some revision over the last years. Prior to the Supreme Court's decision in *Medimmune*, the Federal Circuit applied a two-prong standard, requiring both "an explicit threat or other action by the patentee that creates a reasonable apprehension on the part of the declaratory plaintiff that it will face an infringement suit"; and "present activity [of the declaratory plaintiff] that could constitute infringement or concrete steps taken

[173] Between 1982 and 1999, the Supreme Court decided only six cases concerning patent law questions.
[174] *eBay Inc. v. MercExchange, LLC*, 547 U.S. 388 (2006).
[175] *MedImmune, Inc. v. Genentech, Inc.*, 549 U.S. 118 (2007).
[176] *KSR Int'l Co. v. Teleflex, Inc.*, 550 U.S. 398 (2007).
[177] *Quanta Computer, Inc. v. LG Electronics, Inc.*, 553 U.S. 617 (2008).
[178] *Bilski v. Kappos*, 130 S. Ct. 3218 (2010).
[179] *Microsoft Corp. v. i4i Limited Partnership*, 131 S. Ct. 2238 (2011).

with the intent to conduct such activity"[180] for initiating a DJA. The Supreme Court, however, held in 2007 that the requirement to show a reasonable apprehension of an infringement action collided with old Supreme Court case law.[181] The Federal Circuit responded to the *Medimmune* decision by amending its standard, only requiring the declaratory plaintiff to show that "the facts alleged, under all the circumstances, show that there is a substantial controversy, between parties having adverse legal interests, of sufficient immediacy and reality to warrant the issuance of a declaratory judgment."[182] This flexible standard, which grants district courts significant discretion in deciding whether or not to admit a DJA, has been consistently applied and confirmed by the Federal Circuit in the last years.[183]

(b) Discretion of the Court

While *MedImmune* and subsequent Federal Circuit case law provide for an already flexible standard for allowing a DJA, the standard is made even more flexible by the Declaratory Judgment Act,[184] which "confers on federal courts unique and substantial discretion in deciding whether to declare the rights of litigants."[185] The Federal Circuit has confirmed that wide discretion of district courts still exists as to whether or not to grant declaratory judgment in the aftermath of the *MedImmune* decision.[186] Typical reasons leading the district court to dismiss DJAs include the court's belief that the patentee will not file a patent infringement lawsuit, or that the court would lack subject matter jurisdiction to hear the DJA.[187] Also, the Federal Circuit has given examples in which it would consider the application of broad discretion justified: "(1) when the judgment will serve a useful purpose in clarifying and settling the legal relations in issue, and (2) when it will terminate and afford relief from the uncertainty, insecurity, and controversy giving rise to the proceeding."[188] **10.89**

2. Preliminary Injunction

In some major patent jurisdictions like Germany or the Netherlands, it is quite common for a patentee to seek a preliminary injunction, preventing the infringer from continuing **10.90**

[180] *Fina Research, S.A. v. Baroid, Ltd.*, 141 F.3d 1479, 1481 (Fed. Cir. 1998); also *Microchip Technology Inc. v. Chamberlain Group, Inc.*, 441 F.3d 936, 942 (Fed. Cir. 2006).

[181] *MedImmune, Inc. v. Genentech, Inc.*, 549 U.S. 118 (2007), 132:

> The reasonable-apprehension-of-suit test also conflicts with our decisions in *Maryland Casualty Co. v. Pacific Coal & Oil Co.*, 312 U.S. 270, 273... (1941), where jurisdiction [was] obtained even though the collision-victim defendant could not have sued the declaratory-judgment plaintiff-insurer without first obtaining a judgment against the insured; and *Aetna Life Ins. Co. v. Haworth*, 300 U.S. 227, 239,... (1937), where jurisdiction [was] obtained even though the very reason the insurer sought declaratory relief was that the insured had given no indication that he would file suit. It is also in tension with *Cardinal Chemical Co. v. Morton Int'l, Inc.*, 508 U.S. 83, 98... (1993), which held that appellate affirmance of a judgment of noninfringement, eliminating any apprehension of suit, does not moot a declaratory judgment counterclaim of patent invalidity.

[182] *SanDisk Corp. v. STMicroelectronics, Inc.*, 480 F.3d 1372, 1380–81 (Fed. Cir. 2007); *Cat Tech, LLC v. TubeMaster, Inc.*, 528 F.3d 871, 879 (Fed. Cir. 2008).

[183] See, e.g., *Hewlett-Packard Co. v. Acceleron, LLC*, 587 F.3d 1358, 1361 (Fed. Cir. 2009); *Sony Electronics, Inc. v. Guardian Media Technologies, Ltd.*, 497 F.3d 1271, 1284 (Fed. Cir. 2007). *Streck, Inc. v. Research & Diagnostic Systems, Inc.*, 665 F.3d 1269, 1281–84 (Fed. Cir. 2012).

[184] 28 U.S.C.A. § 2201(a).

[185] *Wilton v. Seven Falls Co.*, 515 U.S. 277, 286–88 (1995).

[186] *Cat Tech, LLC v. TubeMaster, Inc.*, 528 F.3d 871, 883–84 (Fed. Cir. 2008).

[187] *Innovative Therapies, Inc. v. Kinetic Concepts, Inc.*, 2008 WL 4809104, *2 (D. Del. 2008), aff'd, 599 F.3d 1377, 1384–85 (Fed. Cir. 2010).

[188] *Minnesota Min. and Mfg. Co. v. Norton Co.*, 929 F.2d 670, 672–73 (Fed. Cir. 1991).

the infringing conduct until a court comes to a decision in the main proceedings.[189] In the United States, preliminary injunctions were very rare before the establishment of the Federal Circuit. Since then, patentees have increasingly tried to obtain preliminary injunctions. In particular in the biotech and pharmaceutical area, where the market entry of an infringing generic drug can significantly impact on market conditions, patentees continue to seek preliminary injunction relief at the district courts.

(a) Jurisdiction

10.91 A court that is competent to hear the main proceedings is also competent to hear the preliminary proceedings.

(b) Claim for Preliminary Injunction

10.92 A patentee may seek a preliminary injunction under § 283 of the Patent Act.[190] Limiting the scope of remedies available through preliminary proceedings to injunctive relief is also in line with the Supreme Court's guidance that the purpose of a preliminary injunction to "merely to preserve the relative positions of the parties until a trial on the merits can be held."[191] Thus, damage claims cannot be enforced in the course of preliminary proceedings.

(c) Requirements

10.93 Generally, the requirements for seeking a preliminary injunction in a patent infringement action are no different from the requirements for preliminary relief in other areas of law.[192] A preliminary injunction is not routinely granted, but only upon the patentee showing extraordinary circumstances justifying preliminary relief.[193] While district courts enjoy wide discretion as to whether to award a preliminary injunction, they must apply the following four factors: (1) that the plaintiff is likely to succeed on the merits, (2) that the plaintiff is likely to suffer irreparable harm in the absence of preliminary relief, (3) that the balance of equities tips in the plaintiff's favor, and (4) that an injunction is in the public interest.[194]

10.94 **i. Success on the Merits** Typically, the alleged infringer will also assert invalidity of the patent during the preliminary proceedings. Here, the Federal Circuit has stated that, unlike during the main trial, the alleged infringer does not carry the burden of having to show invalidity by clear and convincing evidence.[195] Instead, the defendant must merely raise a substantial question concerning infringement or validity.[196] Multiple cases have held

---

[189] See Ch. 11, 11.123, for a discussion of the preliminary injunction proceedings in Germany. For a discussion of the Dutch proceedings, see e.g. Jan J. Brinkhof, "The Enforcement of Patent Rights in the Netherlands," 31 *IIC* (2000): 706, 776.

[190] While § 283 of the Patent Act does not explicitly address preliminary relief, a patentee's right to seek a preliminary injunction to enjoin alleged infringement of its patent while the main infringement suit is pending. See *High Tech Medical Instrumentation, Inc. v. New Image Industries, Inc.*, 49 F.3d 1551, 1554 (Fed. Cir. 1995).

[191] *University of Texas v. Camenisch*, 451 U.S. 390, 395 (1981).

[192] *High Tech Medical Instrumentation*, 49 F.3d 1551, 1554 (Fed. Cir. 1995).

[193] *Intel Corp. v. ULSI System Technology, Inc.*, 995 F.2d 1566, 1568 (Fed. Cir. 1993).

[194] *Altana Pharma AG Wyeth v. Teva Pharmaceuticals USA, Inc.*, 566 F.3d 999, 1005 (Fed. Cir. 2009); *Titan Tire Corp. v. Case New Holland, Inc.*, 566 F.3d 1372, 1375–76 (Fed. Cir. 2009); *Pfizer, Inc. v. Teva Pharmaceuticals*, USA, Inc., 429 F.3d 1364, 1372 (Fed. Cir. 2005).

[195] *Kimberly-Clark Worldwide, Inc. v. First Quality Baby Prods., LLC*, 660 F.3d 1293, 1294–98 (Fed. Cir. 2011); *Altana Pharma AG Wyeth*, 566 F.3d 999, 1005–6 (Fed. Cir. 2009); *Amazon.com, Inc. v. Barnesandnoble.com, Inc.*, 239 F.3d 1343, 1359 (Fed. Cir. 2001).

[196] *Kimberly-Clark Worldwide*, 660 F.3d 1293, 1294–98 (Fed. Cir. 2011); *E.I. du Pont de Nemours & Co. v. MacDermid Printing Solutions, L.L.C.*, 525 F.3d 1353, 1358 (Fed. Cir. 2008).

that such a substantial question is raised if the USPTO has rejected claims asserted as infringed in pending reexamination proceedings.[197] While it is easier for the defendant to attack validity during the preliminary proceedings than at trial, he still has to demonstrate persuasive evidence of invalidity. Otherwise, the patentee may rely on the presumption of validity of the patent in order to show a substantial likelihood of success.[198]

The plaintiff seeking a preliminary injunction does not have to prove ultimate success on the merits at the preliminary proceedings stage. Instead, he only has to demonstrate a reasonable likelihood of success.[199] Accordingly, the absence of an objective likelihood of success should compel the court to deny a preliminary injunction.[200] In order to demonstrate likelihood of success, the plaintiff has to "demonstrate that it will likely prove infringement of one or more claims of the patents-in-suit, and that at least one of those same allegedly infringed claims will also likely withstand the validity challenges presented by the accused infringer."[201] In case the patentee can only assert equivalent infringement of the patent, the court will most likely not find a reasonable likelihood of success at the preliminary stage, mostly due to the complex factual inquiries required when analyzing the infringement.[202] **10.95**

ii. Irreparable Harm The plaintiff must show that he is already or will immediately be incurring irreparable harm unless a preliminary injunction is issued. In case irreparable harm is only a speculative possibility, no preliminary injunction should be awarded.[203] Similar to the irreparable injury test applied when assessing whether or not to grant a permanent injunction, the likelihood that the defendant doesn't have the financial resources to compensate the plaintiff for the infringement strongly favors a showing of irreparable harm.[204] Another factor frequently invoked to show irreparable harm is to present a loss of market share, making it impossible to calculate a damage award appropriate to compensate for the loss of the patentee.[205] However, when relying on a loss of market share, the patentee has to show a "nexus" between the alleged infringement and the particular harm or the injunction will be denied. To show such a nexus, the patentee must demonstrate that the irreparable harm is directly tied to the infringing conduct. If the patentee can only assert some form of brand dilution or market confusion due to the ongoing sale of a competing product, but **10.96**

---

[197] *Volterra Semiconductor Corp. v. Primarion, Inc.*, 2009 WL 6357679, *41 (N.D. Cal. 2009); *Power Integrations, Inc. v. BCD Semiconductor Corp.*, 2008 WL 5069784, *7–9 (D. Del. 2008).

[198] *Purdue Pharma L.P. v. Boehringer Ingelheim GmbH*, 237 F.3d 1359, 1365 (Fed. Cir. 2001).

[199] *Revision Military, Inc. v. Balboa Mfg. Co.*, 700 F.3d 524, 525–26 (Fed. Cir. 2012).

[200] *National Steel Car, Ltd. v. Canadian Pacific Ry., Ltd.*, 357 F.3d 1319, 1325 (Fed. Cir. 2004).

[201] *Astrazeneca LP v. Apotex, Inc.*, 633 F.3d 1042, 1050 (Fed. Cir. 2010); *Gillette Co. v. Energizer Holdings, Inc.*, 405 F.3d 1367, 1370 (Fed. Cir. 2005).

[202] *Jeneric/Pentron, Inc. v. Dillon Company, Inc.*, 205 F.3d 1377, 1384 (Fed. Cir. 2000); *Vehicular Technologies Corp. v. Titan Wheel Intern., Inc.*, 141 F.3d 1084, 1091–93 (Fed. Cir. 1998).

[203] *Weeks Marine, Inc. v. TDM America, LLC*, 2011 WL 6217799, *5–*6 (D. N.J. 2011); *Quad/Tech, Inc. v. Q.I. Press Controls B.V.*, 2010 WL 1292476, *9 (E.D. Pa. 2010).

[204] *Robert Bosch, LLC v. Pylon Mfg. Corp.*, 659 F.3d 1142, 1154–56 (Fed. Cir. 2011); *LifeScan, Inc. v. Shasta Technologies, LLC*, 2013 WL 1149827, *18 (N.D. Cal. 2013); at the same time, the court may be convinced that a damage claim can be satisfied by the defendant, e.g., if the defendant's parent company agrees to pay a damage claim on behalf of the defendant (see, e.g., *Eli Lilly and Co. v. American Cyanamid Co.*, 82 F.3d 1568, 1579 (Fed. Cir. 1996)) or if the court can compel the defendant from removing assets which may become necessary to satisfy a damage claim later on.

[205] *Purdue Pharma L.P.*, 237 F.3d 1359, 1367–68 (Fed. Cir. 2001); *QBAS Co., Ltd. v. C Walters Intercoastal Corp.*, 2010 WL 7785955, *12–*13 (C.D. Cal. 2010); *Hoffmann-La Roche Inc. v. Cobalt Pharmaceuticals Inc.*, 2010 WL 4687839, *11–*13 (D. N.J. 2010).

cannot tie such injury directly to the infringing function of such product, the irreparable harm prong is not satisfied.[206]

10.97 Another fact which would support the court's analysis that no irreparable harm will be incurred would be past licensing activities of the patentee, especially if the patentee has granted non-exclusive licenses to the patent it asserts as infringed.[207] Somewhat connected would be the inquiry into whether the patentee actually practiced the invention or not.[208] Finally, another important factor which would weigh against irreparable harm would be any form of undue delay by the patentee in seeking preliminary relief.[209] While there is no clear and uniform rule of how long a patentee can wait until it will forfeit a claim for preliminary relief, courts have held that waiting for a period of seven months to initiate the lawsuit after learning of the infringing conduct was enough to deny an assertion of irreparable harm.[210] That said, in other instances courts have found irreparable harm and granted preliminary injunctions despite waiting periods of one and a half years by the patentee.[211]

10.98 **iii. Balance of Interests** When deciding whether or not to grant a preliminary injunction, the court must also weigh the hardship a plaintiff would incur from the denial of the preliminary injunction against the hardship that the defendant would incur if the injunction were granted.[212] In the most severe circumstances, one of the parties' economic survival may depend on issuance or denial of the preliminary injunction.[213] Under such rare circumstances, the balance of interests inquiry tips in favor of the party which clearly would rely more on the decision of the court. At the same time, the balancing of interests is performed closely in line with the other relevant inquiries. Patentees often argue that the limited life of its patent infringing competition would be a particular hardship they would incur if a preliminary injunction is not granted. On the other side, a defendant may argue that a preliminary injunction would be detrimental to its right to compete in the market and to its business. The Federal Circuit has held in the past that neither of these two arguments would be of significant weight when balancing the interests.[214] Another factor, the size of the two parties, has been referred to when balancing interests,[215] while the Federal Circuit has also

[206] *Apple, Inc. v. Samsung Electronics Co., Ltd.*, 678 F.3d 1314, 1323–28 (Fed. Cir. 2012); *Depuy Synthes Products, LLC v. Globus Medical, Inc.*, 2013 WL 4509655 (D. Del. 2013).

[207] *High Tech Medical Instrumentation, Inc. v. New Image Industries, Inc.*, 49 F.3d 1551, 1557 (Fed. Cir. 1995); *Wireless Agents, LLC v. T-Mobile, USA, Inc.*, 2006 WL 1540587 (N.D. Tex. 2006)

[208] *Abbott Laboratories v. Sandoz, Inc.*, 544 F.3d 1341, 1362–63 (Fed. Cir. 2008); *Roper Corp. v. Litton Systems, Inc.*, 757 F.2d 1266, 1273 (Fed. Cir. 1985).

[209] *High Tech Medical Instrumentation, Inc.*, 49 F.3d 1551, 1557 (Fed. Cir. 1995); *Neology, Inc. v. Federal Signal Corp.*, 2012 WL 2308202, *17 (D. Del. 2012); *Display Technologies, LLC v. Display Industries, LLC*, 2011 WL 6188742, *3 (S.D. N.Y. 2011).

[210] *Neology, Inc. v. Federal Signal Corp.*, 2012 WL 2308202, *17 (D. Del. 2012); in other cases, courts denied irreparable harm after a delay of one year (*Wireless Agents, LLC*, 2006 WL 1540587 (N.D. Tex. 2006)), of seventeen months (*Tiber Laboratories, LLC v. Hawthorn Pharmaceuticals, Inc.*, 527 F. Supp. 2d 1373 (N.D. Ga. 2007)) or of three years (*Travel Tags, Inc. v. UV Color, Inc.*, 2010 WL 428564, *13–*14 (D. Minn. 2010)). In another case, the court denied irreparable harm where the plaintiff waited for a filing for preliminary relief for five months after filing the infringement action (*Precision Links, Inc. v. USA Products Group, Inc.*, 2009 WL 3076114, *8 (W.D. N.C. 2009).

[211] *Rosen Entm't Sys, LP v. Icon Enters, Inc.*, 359 F. Supp. 2d 902 (C.D. Cal. 2005).

[212] *Hybritech, Inc. v. Abbott Laboratories*, 849 F.2d 1446, 1457 (Fed. Cir. 1988).

[213] E.g., *Aria Diagnostics, Inc. v. Sequenom, Inc.*, 2013 WL 4034379, *7 (Fed. Cir. 2013).

[214] *Illinois Tool Works, Inc. v. Grip-Pak, Inc.*, 906 F.2d 679, 683 (Fed. Cir. 1990).

[215] *Robert Bosch, LLC v. Pylon Mfg. Corp.*, 659 F.3d 1142, 1156 (Fed. Cir. 2011); *i4i, Ltd. Partnership v. Microsoft Corp.*, 598 F.3d 831, 862–63 (Fed. Cir. 2010).

held in the past that looking at the size of the parties should be of relevance only when trying to assess irreparable injury.[216] Other factors which courts have included in their analysis when balancing the interests of the parties include whether an infringer acted willfully,[217] whether he had established a practice of conducting patent clearance searches or not,[218] and whether the infringing product was already available on the market or not.[219]

iv. Public Interest When assessing whether to grant an injunction or not, courts should also consider the effect of their decision on the interest of the general public.[220] The effect on the public interest is usually not decisive. On the one hand, a patent system enabling the patentee to enforce his patents and exclude other parties from using the protected invention is favored by public policy.[221] On the other hand, courts focus on the inquiry into whether any critical public interest exists that would be undermined by the preliminary injunction.[222] Public interest factors usually only become decisive in denying preliminary relief if the injunction would interrupt the supply of necessary medical procedures, drugs, or devices.[223] **10.99**

(d) Procedure

Preliminary proceedings in federal district courts are governed by Rule 65 FRCP. For example, Rule 65(a) FRCP stipulates that no preliminary injunction may be issued without notice to the other party. Accordingly, unlike in German patent proceedings, it is impossible to obtain an *ex parte* injunction order against a patent infringer, no matter how urgent the case may be. This fundamental procedure requirement—to provide notice and to hear the defendant in preliminary proceedings—is derived from the due process clause set forth in the Fourteenth Amendment of the US Constitution. Relying on Rule 6(d) FRCP, the minimum notice period for a hearing a court can set in preliminary proceedings has been held to be five business days.[224] **10.100**

In addition to ensuring that the defendant receives notice, another requirement for a preliminary injunction is a statement of reasons. Usually, both parties will not have completed discovery by the time they are required to provide evidence supporting the grant or denial of the preliminary injunction. Nevertheless, each party will have to provide some evidence to **10.101**

---

[216] *Bell & Howell Document Management Products Co. v. Altek Systems*, 132 F.3d 701, 708 (Fed. Cir. 1997).

[217] *EZ Gard Industries, Inc. v. XO Athletic Co.*, 2008 WL 1827490, *5 (D. Minn. 2008), aff'd without opn., No. 2008-1384, 2008 WL 5207021 (Fed. Cir. December 15, 2008); *Saes Getters, S.p.A. v. Ergenics, Inc.*, 816 F. Supp. 979, 987 (D. N.J. 1992), aff'd, 989 F.2d 1201 (Fed. Cir. 1993).

[218] *Colonial Data Technologies Corp. v. Cybiotronics, Ltd.*, 41 U.S.P.Q. 2d 1763, 1996 WL 875081 (D. Conn. 1996).

[219] This factor is of particular importance in the pharmaceutical and biotech industries; see *Glaxo Group, Ltd. v. Apotex, Inc.*, 64 Fed. Appx. 751 (Fed. Cir. 2003); *Impax Laboratories, Inc. v. Aventis Pharmaceuticals, Inc.*, 235 F. Supp. 2d 390, 396 (D. Del. 2002); *Ortho Pharmaceutical Corp. v. Smith*, WL 18681 (E.D. Pa. 1990).

[220] *Rite-Hite Corp. v. Kelley Co., Inc.*, 56 F.3d 1538, 1547 (Fed. Cir. 1995).

[221] *Abbott Laboratories v. Andrx Pharmaceuticals, Inc.*, 452 F.3d 1331, 1348 (Fed. Cir. 2006); *PPG Industries, Inc. v. Guardian Industries Corp.*, 75 F.3d 1558, 1567 (Fed. Cir. 1996).

[222] *Cordis Corp. v. Boston Scientific Corp.*, 99 Fed. Appx. 928, 935–36 (Fed. Cir. 2004).

[223] Sample cases where court denied preliminary relief considering public interest factors include *Hybritech Inc. v. Abbott Laboratories*, 849 F.2d 1446, 1458 (Fed. Cir. 1988); *Datascope Corp. v. Kontron Inc.*, 786 F.2d 398, 401 (Fed. Cir. 1986); *Cordis Corp. v. Boston Scientific Corp.*, 2003 WL 22843072 (D. Del. 2003), aff'd, 99 Fed. Appx. 928 (Fed. Cir. 2004).

[224] *Granny Goose Foods, Inc. v. Brotherhood of Teamsters and Auto Truck Drivers Local No. 70 of Alameda County*, 415 U.S. 423, 433 n. 7 (1974).

prevail in preliminary proceedings. Therefore, both the patentee and the alleged infringer will usually request the court to grant expedited discovery, usually encompassing a period of roughly three months. A motion for expedited discovery is often filed by the patentee together with the motion for preliminary relief. Sometimes, courts require some proof of irreparable harm by the patentee before they grant the motion for expedited discovery.[225]

10.102 The district court is the sole fact-finding instance during the preliminary proceedings. Rule 52 FRCP provides that the district court has to make findings of fact sufficient to support the granting of a preliminary injunction. Thus, different from the main trial, no jury is involved in determining questions of fact. In case the district court fails to engage in proper fact finding, the Federal Circuit cannot meaningfully review the preliminary injunction, and therefore would have to vacate it. In such a case, failure to perform proper fact finding would be assessed as an error of law.[226]

10.103 The decision of the district court, whether it grants or denies the preliminary injunction, can be appealed. Unless the appellate court questions the fact-finding capacity of the district court, a district court's decision will be reviewed under the abuse of discretion standard.[227] In some cases, the district court may have decided whether or not to award a permanent injunction before the appellate court has reviewed the district court's preliminary injunction. In such a scenario, the preliminary injunction merges into the permanent injunction.[228]

(e) Damages for unjustified Preliminary Injunction

10.104 Another requirement stipulated in Rule 65(c) FRCP is that the plaintiff seeking preliminary relief must post a security bond. Unlike questions of patent law, which are usually governed by Federal Circuit law, questions related to the determination and posting of the security bond are governed by regional circuit law.[229] The Court of Appeals for the Fifth Circuit has explained the function of the security bond as follows:

> (1) it assures the enjoined party that it may readily collect damages from the funds posted or the surety provided in the event that it was wrongfully enjoined, without further litigation and without regard to the possible insolvency of the assured, and (2) it provides the plaintiff with notice of the maximum extent of its potential liability, since the amount of the bond "is the limit of the damages the defendant can obtain for a wrongful injunction . . . provided the plaintiff was acting in good faith.[230]

In making the security a necessary element prior to the enforcement of a preliminary injunction, the court may discourage the enforcement of frivolous claims through preliminary proceedings.

225 E.g. *Apple Inc. v. Samsung Electronics Co., Ltd.*, 2011 WL 1938154, *1–*3 (N.D. Cal. 2011); *Momenta Pharmaceuticals, Inc. v. Teva Pharmaceuticals Industries, Ltd.*, 2011 WL 673926, *2–*3 (D. Mass. 2011); *Kone Corp. v. ThyssenKrupp USA, Inc.*, 2011 WL 4478477, *6–*8 (D. Del. 2011).

226 E.g., *Conair Group, Inc. v. Automatik Apparate-Maschinenbau GmbH*, 944 F.2d 862, 866 (Fed. Cir. 1991); *Oakley, Inc. v. International Tropic-Cal, Inc.*, 923 F.2d 167, 170 (Fed. Cir. 1991); *Warner Chilcott Laboratories Ireland, Ltd. v. Mylan Pharmaceuticals, Inc.*, 2011 WL 6144301, *5 (Fed. Cir. 2011).

227 *Texas Instruments, Inc. v. Tessera, Inc.*, 231 F.3d 1325, 1328 (Fed. Cir. 2000); *E.I. du Pont de Nemours & Co. v. MacDermid Printing Solutions, LLC*, 525 F.3d 1353, 1358 (Fed. Cir. 2008).

228 *Cross Medical Products, Inc. v. Medtronic Sofamor Danek, Inc.*, 424 F.3d 1293, 1301–2 (Fed. Cir. 2005).

229 *Hupp v. Siroflex of America, Inc.*, 122 F.3d 1456, 1467–68 (Fed. Cir. 1997).

230 *Continuum Co., Inc. v. Incepts, Inc.*, 873 F.2d 801, 803, 13 Fed. R. Serv. 3d 1080 (5th Cir. 1989).

District courts have considerable discretion in determining the amount of the bond. That said, the court should set the bond at an amount of estimated costs and damages the defendant would be likely to incur from the preliminary injunction.[231] The defendant requesting that a certain amount of bond be posted must demonstrate that the requested amount is appropriate by demonstrating the costs and damages it would be subjected to by the preliminary injunction.[232] Thus, while the burden of proof lies with the enjoined party, appellate courts have advised that the district court should, when determining the amount of the bond, rather err on the high side than on the low side, as the bond only provides a cap to the amount of damages which can be claimed in case the preliminary injunction turns out to be wrongful.[233] Given the high economic stakes which can be involved, especially in patent infringement actions between pharmaceutical companies, courts have repeatedly set security bonds in the range of two or three digit million-dollar amounts.[234] **10.105**

To recover damages incurred due to a wrongful preliminary injunction, the party must prove the amount of damages that were proximately caused by the injunction. To execute against the bond, the wrongfully enjoined party must obtain a final judgment by the competent court. That said, the enjoined party may benefit from the presumption of being entitled to recover its damages, according to which it may assess the damages it believes to have been incurred,[235] whereupon the party which had moved for the preliminary injunction carries the burden of proof to challenge such damage assessment. Recovery in excess of the bond posted is only possible if the enjoined party can show that the preliminary injunction was sought in bad faith. **10.106**

---

[231] *Sanofi-Synthelabo v. Apotex, Inc.*, 470 F.3d 1368, 1385 (Fed. Cir. 2006).

[232] *Oakley, Inc. v. Sunglass Hut Intern.*, 2001 WL 1683252 (C.D. Cal. 2001), aff'd, 316 F.3d 1331 (Fed. Cir. 2003).

[233] *Panduit Corp. v. Band-It-Idex, Inc.*, 2000 WL 1121554 (N.D. Ill. 2000), aff'd, 25 Fed. Appx. 836 (Fed. Cir. 2001).

[234] See, e.g., *Abbott Laboratories v. Sandoz, Inc.*, 544 F.3d 1341, 1363 (Fed. Cir. 2008): US$200 million; *Sanofi-Synthelabo v. Apotex, Inc.*, 470 F.3d 1368, 1385 (Fed. Cir. 2006): US$400 million; *Pfizer, Inc. v. Teva Pharmaceuticals, USA, Inc.*, 429 F.3d 1364, 1372 (Fed. Cir. 2005): US$200 million; *Momenta Pharmaceuticals, Inc. v. Amphastar Pharmaceuticals, Inc.*, 2011 WL 5882184, *1 (D. Mass. 2011): US$100 million. See also *Apple, Inc. v. Samsung Electronics Co., Ltd.*, 2012 WL 2572037, *67 (N.D. Cal. 2012): US$95,637,141.60.

[235] This presumption of entitlement, which also governs outside patent law, has been confirmed in the area of patent law, e.g., in *Nintendo of America, Inc. v. Lewis Galoob Toys, Inc.*, 16 F.3d 1032, 1036–37 (9th Cir. 1994); *Nokia Corp. v. InterDigital, Inc.*, 645 F.3d 553, 557–59 (2d Cir. 2011).

11

GERMANY

A. Jurisdiction and Venue

1. Subject Matter Jurisdiction

11.01 German law provides for different types of jurisdiction. While, for example, administrative disputes are exclusively handled by administrative courts and criminal disputes are handled by criminal courts, disputes concerning patent infringement are civil law cases and are handled by German civil courts. According to § 143(1) of the Patent Act, this competence applies to all disputes related to claims arising out of legal relationships based on patents. Consequently, all disputes relating to claims for inventions[1] are civil law cases under the competence of German civil courts.[2]

11.02 In first-instance proceedings, German district courts (*Landgerichte*) are competent to hear such cases. A panel at a district court consists of three legally trained judges:[3] one presiding judge, one reporting judge, and one associate judge. The judges usually do not have any technical background, but often have years of experience in patent law. If a decision of the district court is appealed, the second instance is heard by the competent higher regional court (*Oberlandesgericht*).[4] A panel of a higher regional court also consists of three legally trained judges, again one presiding judge, one reporting judge, and one associate judge.[5]

11.03 Due to the fact that patent cases usually require very specific legal and technical knowledge, the German legislature, seeking to ensure a uniform patent judiciary, limited the competence to hear patent cases to twelve district courts.[6] The most prominent and experienced courts for patent litigation are Düsseldorf, Mannheim, and Munich.

---

[1] Such as infringement disputes, entitlement actions, and preliminary injunction requests as well as disputes in connection with license agreements.

[2] The authors thank German attorneys-at-law Nadine Heiartz and Thomas Schachl for helping with the manuscript. R. Kraßer, *Patentrecht (Patent Law)* (6th ed., 2009), 878 et seq., § 36Ia; P. Mes, *Patentgesetz (Patent Act)* (3d ed., 2011), § 143 of the Patent Act, margin no. 4, 9; T. Kühnen in R. Schulte (ed.), *Patentgesetz (Patent Act)* (8th ed., 2008), § 143 of the Patent Act, margin no. 9.

[3] § 75 Court Constitution Act; A. Keukenschrijver in J. Pagenberg and W. R. Cornich (eds.), *Interpretation of Patents in Europe* (2006), margin no. DE7.

[4] § 119(1) No. 2 of the Court Constitution Act.

[5] Ibid. § 122(1); Keukenschrijver in Pagenberg and Cornich, *Interpretation of Patents in Europe*, margin no. DE7.

[6] The following district courts are competent to hear patent and utility model infringement cases in the first instance: Berlin, Brunswick, Düsseldorf, Erfurt, Frankfurt/Main, Hamburg, Leipzig, Magdeburg, Mannheim, Munich I, Nuremberg-Fuerth, and Saarbrucken. See § 143 of the Patent Act in combination with the respective laws of the German states, and in further detail BIPMZ 2007, 92; Keukenschrijver in Pagenberg and Cornich, *Interpretation of Patents in Europe*, margin no. DE5; Mes, *Patentgesetz*, § 143 of the Patent Act, margin no. 15; Kühnen in Schulte, *Patentgesetz*, § 143 of the Patent Act, margin no. 21.

2. Venue

The admissibility of a patent infringement complaint before a district court depends on which specific district court is territorially competent to hear the individual case. Civil procedure law provides for various rules concerning the determination of the proper district court for a specific case.[7] The most relevant provisions are §§ 17, 21, and 32 of the Code of Civil Procedure. According to §§ 17 and 21 of the Code of Civil Procedure, the proper district court is where the registered office (§ 17) or the branch (§ 21) of the defendant is located. **11.04**

According to § 32 of the Code of Civil Procedure, also the district court located in the judicial district where the unlawful act, such as a sale of an infringing device, occurred is competent. In practice, § 32 of the Code of Civil Procedure is the provision most frequently applied by plaintiffs for determining the competence of the district court in patent enforcement.[8] Since many companies offer products and services all over Germany, for example, by displaying products on the internet, infringement often occurs in the whole territory of Germany and therefore also in every judicial district. Thus, in most cases, any of the competent district courts can hear the case,[9] and the plaintiff may invoke § 32 of the Code of Civil Procedure to freely choose the most convenient district court to file the complaint.[10] Section 32 of the Code of Civil Procedure is also applicable in case of a mere threat of infringement—that is, in case of a significant risk of an infringement occuring in the judicial district of a district court. However, the plaintiff has the burden of proof to show the court that such risk of infringement in Germany and in the specific judicial district of Germany exists. Such significant risk can, for example, exist in cases where a foreign defendant is offering his (infringing) products and/or services in a trade fair in Germany, provided that such a trade fair is not only local in its character.[11] In such cases, offering the (infringing) product in a trade fair in one judicial district also constitutes a risk of infringement in the whole territory of Germany, enabling the plaintiff to freely choose between competent courts.[12] **11.05**

In practice, the plaintiff usually chooses the venue according to strategic considerations, such as the court's technical experience, timing, practice of allowing a stay of infringement proceedings with regard to parallel opposition or nullity proceedings concerning the patent-in-suit, requirements in preliminary injunction proceedings, tendency of the court to commission a court expert, etc. **11.06**

Although there are twelve district courts in Germany potentially competent to hear patent and utility model-related cases, there are in fact only a few courts which are regularly chosen by plaintiffs. The most frequently chosen district courts are the Düsseldorf, Mannheim, and Munich I District Courts.[13] Each of the district courts has its own specific advantages **11.07**

[7] See §§ 13–35 of the Code of Civil Procedure.

[8] T. Kühnen, *Handbuch der Patentverletzung (Handbook of Patent Infringement)* (5th ed., 2011), margin no. 645.

[9] Ibid. margin no. 646.

[10] § 35 of the Code of Civil Procedure.

[11] Mes, *Patentgesetz*, § 143 of the Patent Act, margin no. 16.

[12] District Court of Düsseldorf InstGE 9, 18/20 et seq.—*Beleghalter fuer Scheibenbremse* (*Lining holder for disc brakes*).

[13] Keukenschrijver in Pagenberg and Cornich, *Interpretation of Patents in Europe*, margin no. DE5.

and disadvantages. The Düsseldorf court is the most experienced patent court in Germany and Europe. The Mannheim District Court is known for its high speed, as it currently renders decisions in main proceedings in about ten months after filing the complaint, whereby the Düsseldorf District Court requires at least twelve to fifteen months to render a decision in the main proceedings. The District Court of Munich I is currently even quicker than the Mannheim District Court and already issues its decisions within an average of eight months after the complaint has been filed. Notably, the Munich I District Court schedules, unlike other courts, two substantive hearings. A first oral hearing on the merits takes place already about three to four months after filing of the complaint and shortly after the defendant has filed his statement of defense. Thereby, the parties can get an idea of the preliminary view of the court at a very early stage. This enables the parties to focus their arguments on the relevant aspects, thus leading to organized and straightforward proceedings, and may also serve as an early settlement trigger.

3. International Jurisdiction

11.08 Since German courts are only competent to decide on patents granted for the territory of the Federal Republic of Germany, patent infringement under German patent law requires that the patent infringement is related to the territory of the Federal Republic of Germany.[14] Such infringing acts with relation to Germany, however, do not strictly require that the accused acts have taken place in the German territory. Rather it is sufficient if these acts take effect within the German territory. For example, this is the case if infringing products are shipped into Germany from abroad or if infringing products are offered on the German market from a location outside Germany (e.g., through the internet[15]). However, deliveries abroad have also been regarded as a contribution to patent infringement in Germany if the foreign supplier was aware that the foreign distributor intended to import the accused products into Germany.[16]

11.09 In patent infringement cases involving foreign parties, it is not always apparent whether German courts are competent to hear and decide on such cross-border disputes. The international competence of German courts to hear such patent cases is subject to the Code of Civil Procedure[17] and applicable bilateral or multilateral treaties. The most relevant treaties are the Brussels-I-Directive 44/2001 EC (applicable to almost all member states of the European Union), the 1968 EC Convention on Jurisdiction and the Enforcement of Judgments in Civil and Commercial Matters (applicable to Denmark only) and the Lugano Jurisdiction and Enforcement Convention (applicable to Switzerland, Iceland, and Norway).[18] These treaties contain provisions similar to §§ 17, 21, and 32 Code of Civil Procedure and attribute competence to those German district courts where the unlawful act has occurred in cross-border disputes involving foreign defendants.[19]

[14] See Kühnen in Schulte, *Patentgesetz*, § 9 of the Patent Act, margin nos. 95 et seq.; cf. Kraßer, *Patentrecht*, 798, § 33Vc2.

[15] Kühnen, *Handbuch der Patentverletzung* (5th ed.), margin no. 145.

[16] Federal Court of Justice IIC 2003, 432—*Radio clock* (GRUR 2002, 599—*Funkuhr*); cf. Kraßer, *Patentrecht*, 761, § 33IIc2; Mes, *Patentgesetz*, § 9 of the Patent Act, margin no. 19.

[17] See Ch. 11, 11.01 "Subject Matter Jurisdiction" and 11.04 "Venue."

[18] Cf. Kühnen, *Handbuch der Patentverletzung* (5th ed.), margin no. 651.

[19] See R. Rogge and K. Grabinski in G. Benkard (ed.), *Patentgesetz (Patent Act)* (10th ed., 2006), § 139 of the Patent Act, margin no. 101b.

There is no bilateral or multilateral treaty governing international jurisdiction with regard to defendants who are citizens or companies of Japan or the United States. Consequently, only German civil procedural law is applicable for German courts when deciding on jurisdiction to hear disputes against Japanese or United States citizens or companies.[20] In most cases, German courts are competent to hear patent-related cases if the infringement took place in Germany, irrespective of whether the defendant is German or of foreign origin. **11.10**

B. Parties

The courts are only entitled to grant an injunction if the plaintiff is entitled to sue the defendant and if the defendant is also liable for the asserted unlawful acts. **11.11**

1. Standing to Sue

In general, the owner of the patent is entitled to assert claims against the infringer of the patent.[21] This relates to all claims under the Patent Act (e.g., cease and desist, damages, rendering of accounts, destruction, and recall from the distribution chains) and all related claims. In addition, it is also required that the patent owner is registered as such in the German patent register (§ 30(3)2 of the Patent Act).[22] **11.12**

Problems may arise when the patent is assigned to a new owner. According to the prevailing opinion, § 20(3)2 of the Patent Act is decisive for the authorization of the plaintiff to file a complaint. By limiting the standing to sue to the registered patent owner, the courts are released from possibly complex determination of whether an assignment had been effective or not.[23] **11.13**

As long as the assignment has not yet been recorded in the German patent register, only the former (and still registered) patent owner may assert claims for patent infringement although he is, in fact, no longer the legitimate owner of the patent. That said, as soon as the assignment has been registered, which may also happen during the lawsuit, only the registered new patent owner may assert the claims, irrespective of the effectiveness of the assignment.[24] This is, at least, the prevailing opinion with regard to claims to cease and desist, rendering of accounts, recall, and destruction (those claims being directed towards the future). As far as damage claims (being directed towards the past) are concerned, standing is assessed inconsistently. While some courts decided that the entry in the German patent register is decisive for damage claims as well,[25] other courts take a different view.[26] **11.14**

---

[20] See Rogge and Grabinski in Benkard (ed.), *Patentgesetz*, § 139 of the Patent Act, margin no. 101a.

[21] Kühnen, *Handbuch der Patentverletzung* (5th ed.), margin no. 694.

[22] Ibid; Mes, *Patentgesetz*, § 139 of the Patent Act, margin no. 95.

[23] Kühnen, *Handbuch der Patentverletzung* (5th ed.), margin no. 697 et seq.; Higher Regional Court of Düsseldorf, decision of June 24, 2011, file no. 2 U 26/10—*Schwangerschaftstestgerät VI* (*Pregnancy test device VI*), BeckRS 2011, 20938.

[24] A. Verhauwen, "Wer darf klagen?—Noch einmal: zur Aktivlegitimation im Patentverletzungsverfahren (Who is authorized to sue? Again: on the standing to sue in patent infringement proceedings)" *GRUR* (2011): 116; Kühnen, *Handbuch der Patentverletzung* (5th ed.), margin no. 697.

[25] Kühnen, *Handbuch der Patentverletzung* (5th ed.), margin no. 698; Higher Regional Court of Düsseldorf InstGE 12, 261—*Fernsehmenue-Steuerung* (*TV menu control*); Higher Regional Court of Düsseldorf, decision of June 24, 2011, file no. 2 U 26/10—*Schwangerschaftstestgeraet VI* (*Pregnancy test device VI*), BeckRS 2011, 20938.

[26] Higher Regional Court of Karlsruhe, decision of January 11, 2012, file no. 6 U 59/11 and District Court of Mannheim, Decision of April 17, 2012, file no. 2 O 129/09, reference in Kühnen, *Handbuch der Patentverletzung* (6th ed., 2013), margin no. 812.

11.15 Patents which are owned by more than one patent owner can be asserted in infringement complaints by each of the owners independently and without the participation of the other patent owner(s).[27] However, in such a situation the liability of an infringer is limited to making a payment for the aggregate damages to one patent owner. Thus, a co-owner of the patent may, vice versa, only demand payment on behalf of all of the owners of the patent,[28] but is not entitled to request payment of damages to his own account only.

11.16 Exclusive licensees are also entitled to assert claims against the infringer of the patent.[29] For asserting such claims in court it is not required that the exclusive license is registered in the German patent register. Since the exclusive licensee plaintiff has the burden of proof with regard to his exclusive license (if challenged by the defendant), the plaintiff may have to provide to the court the license agreement or a confirmation document of the patent owner confirming that an exclusive license has been granted. If an exclusive license has been granted, the patent owner is only entitled to assert claims for patent infringement against the infringer if the exclusive license agreement explicitly provides for it, or if the patent owner remains affected by the infringement, for example, by receiving lower license payments due to the infringement.[30] Absent an explicit authorization in the license agreement, the patent owner should not be entitled to assert claims for patent infringement if he has already received a lump sum royalty payment, because the infringement would no longer affect the patent owner's pecuniary interest.

11.17 A non-exclusive licensee is not entitled to assert claims for patent infringement against an infringer unless he is authorized by the patent owner or the exclusive licensee to file an infringement action.[31] Courts accept such authorizations only if the non-exclusive licensee can demonstrate its own economic interest in asserting claims for patent infringement against the infringer. Such economic interest exists, for example, if the infringement detrimentally affects the business of the non-exclusive licensee in Germany.[32]

11.18 The patent owner may assign the patent to a third party even if infringement proceedings are pending. In such a case, the former patent owner remains the plaintiff in the infringement proceedings (§ 265(2) of the Code of Civil Procedure).[33] However, potential damages for the time after the assignment of the patent have to be paid to the new patent owner, provided that the complaint requesting, damages, and rendering of accounts have to be amended accordingly.[34] The original patent owner can only be replaced by the new patent owner as plaintiff if all parties to the proceedings, especially the defendant, agree on such a change of parties.

[27] Kühnen, *Handbuch der Patentverletzung* (5th ed.), margin no. 707.

[28] Cf. §§ 1011, 432 of the Civil Code.

[29] Kühnen in Schulte, *Patentgesetz*, § 15 of the Patent Act, margin no. 33, 37; Kühnen, *Handbuch der Patentverletzung* (5th ed.), margin no. 708.

[30] Federal Court of Justice GRUR 2005, 935—*Vergleichsempfehlung II* (*Settlement recommendation II*); IIC 2009, 475—*Ink cartridge* (GRUR 2008, 896—*Tintenpatrone*); cf. Mes, *Patentgesetz*, § 139 of the Patent Act, margin no. 97.

[31] Kühnen, *Handbuch der Patentverletzung* (5th ed.), margin no. 713.

[32] Ibid. margin no. 715.

[33] Federal Court of Justice GRUR 2011, 313—*Crimpwerkzeug IV* (*Crimping tool IV*); Kühnen, *Handbuch der Patentverletzung* (5th ed.), margin no. 704.

[34] Kühnen, *Handbuch der Patentverletzung* (5th ed.), margin no. 704.

A new patent owner is entitled to claim damages for infringing acts which occurred before the patent had been assigned to the new patent owner only if the former patent owner had assigned such claims for past damages to the new patent owner. A patent assignment does not automatically provide for such authorization. Rather, the right to claim past damages must be explicitly provided for in the transfer or assignment agreement.[35] Since the plaintiff has the burden of proof with regard to the assignment of past damage claims, it is strongly recommended to document a patent assignment in writing. **11.19**

2. Defendants

Direct offenders and persons supporting patent infringement can be named as defendants in patent infringement proceedings. While direct and intentional infringers are in most cases liable for infringement, it is more difficult to determine liability for supporting activities. According to the case law of the Federal Court of Justice, supporting activities are relevant and result in liability for patent infringement if these activities contribute to the infringement of a third party and this contribution could have been avoided by the supporting party.[36] This extends to shipping companies which are not generally obliged to examine the shipped goods, but have the duty to gather information and to examine the goods if they have concise indications of an infringement of intellectual property rights. If they fail to comply with these obligations, the importation of infringing goods can result in liability for patent infringement for the shipping company.[37] **11.20**

If corporations are named as defendants for patent infringement, not only are they subject to claims for the infringement, but also their representative officers can become personally liable if such representatives were aware of the infringing activities.[38] **11.21**

Due to the concept of limited liability of shareholders, an infringer's parent company is usually not liable for patent infringements committed by a fully-owned subsidiary.[39] German courts only impose liability on the parent company if it exercised direct control over the culpable actions of the subsidiary. However, the plaintiff has the burden of proof to show such exercise of control by the parent company.[40] **11.22**

C. Costs

1. Court Fees

Court proceedings are subject to the payment of court fees. The amount of court fees that has to be paid depends on the value of litigation (*Streitwert*). Said value of litigation is determined by the court at its discretion[41] based on the economic value of the specific case—namely, the **11.23**

[35] Higher Regional Court of Düsseldorf, decision of March 25, 2010, file no. 2 U 61/08, BeckRS 2010, 16645; District Court of Düsseldorf, decision of March 27, 2008, file no. 4b O 159/07—*RFID-Karte II (RFID-card II)*.

[36] Federal Court of Justice IIC 2002, 525—*Snow Removal Plate* (GRUR 1999, 977—*Raeumschild*); Kühnen, *Handbuch der Patentverletzung* (5th ed.), margin no. 731.

[37] Federal Court of Justice IIC 2010, 471 (GRUR 2009, 1142)—*MP3 Player Import*; Mes, *Patentgesetz*, § 139 of the Patent Act, margin no. 102.

[38] Kühnen, *Handbuch der Patentverletzung* (5th ed.), margin no. 743.

[39] Higher Regional Court of Düsseldorf InstGE 6, 152—*Permantentmagnet* (*Permanent magnet*); Kühnen, *Handbuch der Patentverletzung* (5th ed.), margin no. 730.

[40] Higher Regional Court of Düsseldorf InstGE 6, 152—*Permantentmagnet* (*Permanent magnet*).

[41] See § 51 of the Court Fees Act.

objective economic interest of the plaintiff.[42] The decisive point in time to evaluate the value of litigation is the time when the complaint is filed. In other words, the value of litigation is determined according to the circumstances given at that time.[43] In order to enable the court to evaluate the economic value of the dispute between the parties, the parties are obliged to provide correct and sufficient information to the court related to the economic value of the dispute, such as information on turnover and market shares which reveal the extent of possible damages resulting from the patent infringement for the remaining term of the patent-in-suit.[44] Furthermore, damage claims that arose prior to filing the complaint have to be taken into consideration.

11.24 Based on the specific value of litigation of the individual case, the court fees are calculated in accordance with the table on court fees provided by the Court Fees Act. The lowest value of litigation provided for by the Court Fees Act is €300 and the highest is €30 million.[45] Although the court determines the value of litigation at its discretion, in patent infringement proceedings the value of litigation usually is typically somewhere between €500,000 and €5,000,000. In rare cases of particularly low economic value, the value of litigation might be €250,000, while it can reach up to €30 million for very important and economically high profitable subject matter, such as mobile telecommunication or pharmaceuticals. On average, the value of litigation for most cases is set between €1 million and €5 million.

11.25 The plaintiff must estimate the value of litigation of the case when filing the complaint and must also advance the relevant court fees for first-instance proceedings. Until the court fees have been paid by the plaintiff, the court will not take any action and will, in particular, not serve the complaint on the defendant. Without service, the proceedings will not start. If the defendant's main place of business or residence is abroad and no German counsel has been appointed by the defendant, the complaint may have to be served abroad where German is not the official language. Under those circumstances, the plaintiff must pay the cost of translating the complaint as well as the cost of serving the complaint abroad.

11.26 The costs for second instance proceedings exceed the first-instance court fees by roughly one-third. The court fees for third-instance proceedings—if the filing of a third instance appeal to the Federal Court of Justice is admitted—are almost twice as high as the fees for the first instance.

11.27 Although the court fees have to be paid by the plaintiff in advance when filing the complaint, the plaintiff is entitled to claim reimbursement of such fees from the defendant if the plaintiff wins the case. However, the plaintiff bears the risk of bankruptcy of the defendant.

11.28 If the plaintiff cannot afford to pay the court fees, it is possible to apply for legal aid before filing the complaint[46] or to apply for a reduction of the value of litigation.[47]

---

[42] P. Hartmann, *Kostengesetze (Cost Legislation)* (42d ed., 2012), § 51 Gerichtskostengesetz (Court Fees Act), margin no. 4.

[43] See § 40 of the Court Fees Act.

[44] Kühnen, *Handbuch der Patentverletzung* (5th ed.), margin no. 2136.

[45] §§ 34(1), 39(2) of the Court Fees Act.

[46] §§ 114 et seq. of the Code of Civil Procedure.

[47] § 144 of the Patent Act.

Table 11.1 Statutory court fees

Litigation value (in EUR)	First-instance court fees (in EUR)	Second-instance court fees (in EUR)
250,000	5,268	7,024
500,000	8,868	11,824
1,000,000	13,368	17,824
2,000,000	22,368	29,824
5,000,000	49,368	65,824
10,000,000	94,368	125,824
20,000,000	184,368	245,824
30,000,000	274,368	365,824

In case of a settlement and/or withdrawal of the complaint, it is possible to obtain a reduction of the court fees incurred at the pending instance. Court fees for completed instances (e.g., first-instance proceedings in a pending appeal) may not be reduced. **11.29**

A list of statutory court fees due in first- and second-instance proceedings pursuant to some sample values is shown in Table 11.1. **11.30**

2. Customary Costs for Legal Representation

There are in general two methods for determining the attorney's fees in Germany. The first method is the calculation in accordance with the Lawyer's Remuneration Act ("*Rechtsanwaltsverguetungsgesetz*") which contains the statutory minimum fees that attorneys have to charge under the bar rules. The Lawyer's Remuneration Act also determines the maximum amount that can be claimed by the prevailing party from the losing party for fees for legal representation during the trial by providing rules for determining attorney's fees on the basis of the value of litigation of the individual case.[48] In case of patent litigation, parties often agree on lawyer's fees based on time-charge.[49] **11.31**

The Lawyer's Remuneration Act determines the attorney's fees in accordance with the value of litigation of the dispute and the extent of work done by the attorney. With regard to the extent of the attorney's work, there are—roughly speaking—two major stages in each court instance for which the Lawyer's Remuneration Act provides separate statutory attorney's fees. The first stage is the pre-trial stage, where parties prepare and carry out the initial litigation (e.g., checking the fact pattern of the case, advising the client, drafting and filing briefs). The fee related to this stage is the procedural fee (*Verfahrensgebuehr*). The second stage relevant for statutory remuneration is the oral hearing at the court, for which a hearing fee (*Termingebuehr*) can be claimed. Once one of these stages has begun, the related statutory fees are due in full. Also, the related fees are due only once per instance. In this regard, it does not matter whether the attorney has only filed one brief with the court or **11.32**

[48] A lawyer is a legally trained attorney, having a degree in law; a patent attorney has a technical background but no or not necessarily a law degree.

[49] Hartmann, *Kostengesetze*, § 3a of the Rechtsanwaltsverguetungsgesetz (Lawyer's Remuneration Act), margin no. 26—Zeithonorar (Time fee); see H. Klees and J. Teubel in H.-J. Mayer and L. Kroiß (eds.), *Rechtsanwaltsverguetungsgesetz (Lawyer's Remuneration Act)* (5th ed., 2012), § 2 of the Lawyer's Remuneration Act, margin no. 7; § 3a of the Lawyer's Remuneration Act, margin nos. 125 et seq., 188 et seq.

dozens, or whether there was only one oral hearing or several. The statutory attorney's fees are calculated for each court instance separately. Expenses (travel costs, accommodation, translations, telecommunication, copying costs, etc.) are not included in these statutory fees and have to be paid separately.

11.33 In patent infringement proceedings, it is required by law that such proceedings are handled by an attorney-at-law. However, it is common practice in Germany that patent litigation proceedings are handled by an attorney-at-law and a patent attorney jointly.[50] It is established case law that in cases in which a patent attorney is also involved, both attorneys (attorney-at-law and patent attorney) are entitled to claim statutory attorney's fees separately.[51]

11.34 In Germany, most law firms representing clients in patent litigation matters calculate attorney's fees on an hourly basis. Such a calculation requires an agreement between the attorney and the client in order to be valid.[52] As in other jurisdictions, fees charged by law firms vary significantly, depending on the complexity of the case and the hourly rates charged. Estimates suggest that the average fees invoiced for representation in infringement proceedings as well as in parallel nullity proceedings amount to US$100,000 to US$500,000.[53] If the attorney and client do not enter into such a payment agreement, the law firm can only request payment in accordance with the Lawyer's Remuneration Act. Even if attorney and client agree upon an hourly rate, the attorney is not allowed by law to charge less than the minimum fees prescribed by the Lawyer's Remuneration Act.[54] The attorney's fees which would accrue according to the Lawyer's Remuneration Act form the minimum amount the attorney has to invoice, even if the hourly rate calculation would be lower. Furthermore, it has to be emphasized that the winning party can only claim reimbursement of attorney's fees from the losing party according to the statutory fees calculated in accordance with the Lawyer's Remuneration Act. If the fees calculated on an hourly basis exceed the statutory fees, the remaining amount has to be borne by the winning party. Also, the winning party can only claim reimbursement of the attorney's fees for one attorney-at-law and one patent attorney (even if several other attorneys are involved in the case).

11.35 Table 11.2 shows some examples of statutory attorney's fees due to one attorney for representing one client in first- and second-instance proceedings in accordance with the Lawyer's Remuneration Act (including a procedural fee and hearing fee but excluding additional expenses).

11.36 Notably, foreign plaintiffs may—at the request of defendant and subject to a decision of the court—have to post a security bond safeguarding the defendant's possible cost reimbursement claim early on in the litigation.

[50] Kraßer, *Patentrecht*, 884.

[51] Mes, *Patentgesetz*, § 143 of the Patent Act, margin no. 48.

[52] See Klees in H.-J. Mayer and L. Kroiß (eds.), *Rechtsanwaltsverguetungsgesetz (Lawyer's Remuneration Act)* (5th ed., 2012), § 2 of the Lawyer's Remuneration Act, margin no. 7.

[53] Michal Elmer and C. Gregory Gramenopoulos, *Global Patent Litigation* (2014), 900.

[54] Hartmann, *Kostengesetze*, § 4 of the Rechtsanwaltsverguetungsgesetz (Lawyer's Remuneration Act), margin no. 7; § 49b(1)1 of the Bundesrechtsanwaltsordnung (Federal Lawyer's Act).

Table 11.2 Statutory attorney's fees

Litigation value (in EUR)	First-instance fees (in EUR)	Second-instance fees (in EUR)
250,000	5,130	5,745.60
500,000	7,490	8,388.80
1,000,000	11,240	12,588.80
2,000,000	18,740	20,988.80
5,000,000	41,240	46,188.80
10,000,000	78,740	88,188.80
20,000,000	153,740	172,188.80
30,000,000	228,740	256,188.80

D. Procedure

1. Procedural Overview and Pending Time

In order to initiate patent infringement proceedings, the plaintiff has to file a complaint with the relevant district court. This has to be done by an attorney-at-law admitted to the German bar, otherwise the filing of the complaint is not legally effective.[55] 11.37

Due to procedural rules, all facts known to the plaintiff which are required or helpful to substantiate the infringement have to be included in the initial complaint brief.[56] Omitting to state known facts in the initial complaint may cause preclusion issues and should thus be avoided. Therefore, it usually takes significant time for the attorney to gather all information from the client and to prepare a complaint in order to meet the procedural requirements.[57] 11.38

After the complaint has been filed with the court and the court fees have been paid by the plaintiff, the court serves the complaint on the defendant. Service within Germany is usually completed by the court within one calendar week. However, if the plaintiff does not indicate a residence or branch address of the defendant in Germany but only a foreign address, the complaint has to be served to such foreign address which generally leads to a much longer delivery period. Furthermore, if the complaint has to be served on a defendant located in a place where German is not the official language, the complaint and the exhibits to the complaint must be translated prior to delivery, which usually results in further delay. Therefore, international service can take a few weeks, up to a year, or even longer, depending on the country where the complaint has to be served. 11.39

After the complaint has been served on the defendant, the defendant is ordered to file a notice of defense with the court within a deadline of two weeks.[58] If such notice of defense is not filed or is not filed in due time, the court can render a judgment by default (if requested by the plaintiff).[59] After filing a notice of defense, the defendant is ordered 11.40

[55] § 78 of the Code of Civil Procedure; see also R. Greger in R. Zoeller (ed.), *Zivilprozessordnung (Code of Civil Procedure)* (29th ed., 2012), § 253 Code of Civil Procedure, margin nos. 4 et seq., 12a.

[56] Cf. Greger in Zoeller (ed.), *Zivilprozessordnung*, § 253 Code of Civil Procedure, margin no. 12a.

[57] It should be noted that the requirements for substantiating facts in the initial complaint are substantially higher in Germany than, e.g., under the notice-pleading standard practiced in the United States, see Ch. 12, 12.28.

[58] § 276(1)1 of the Code of Civil Procedure.

[59] Ibid. § 331(3); Herget in Zoeller (ed.), *Zivilprozessordnung*, § 331 Code of Civil Procedure, margin nos. 5, 12.

to file a statement of defense setting out his arguments within a deadline of another few weeks or months (determined by and depending on the court). After the statement of defense has been filed with the court and served on the plaintiff, the plaintiff can answer this brief by filing a reply and the defendant can subsequently file a further rejoinder. After that—usually—a (main) oral hearing takes place before the court. In some cases, also the parties are ordered by the court to attend this hearing personally (in addition to the attorney whose attendance is mandatory). The hearing usually takes about one or two hours, in complex cases several hours, but not longer than a day. It is common practice for the courts not to discuss all legal and factual aspects of the case but only the aspects which need further clarification in view of the court. Therefore, oral hearings are extremely focused. At the end of the oral hearing, the court announces a date for rendering a decision. The decision to be rendered by the court can be a final decision completing the instance, or can be a decision to take evidence by appointing a court expert or by requesting testimony of a witness, etc., if certain factual aspects need to be further clarified to render a final decision. That said, a court decision to take further evidence after the main oral hearing is quite rare in German practice.

11.41 Depending on the first-instance court where the complaint has been filed, there may be an additional early first hearing (applicable to Düsseldorf and Munich) which is held before (Düsseldorf) or shortly after (Munich) the statement of defense has been filed by the defendant. This first hearing is summoned by the court in order to clarify formalities of the proceedings like deadlines of further briefs, etc. (Düsseldorf and Munich), and to discuss the subject matter of the proceedings on the merits to the extent it is considered relevant by the court (Munich only).[60]

11.42 The length of patent infringement proceedings also depends—amongst other things—on the specific practice rules of the court in question. In general, first-instance proceedings in Düsseldorf take twelve to eighteen months, in Munich six to nine months and in Mannheim nine to twelve months. Furthermore, the duration of the proceedings can be influenced, for example, by the court appointing a court expert to render an opinion on certain technical aspects. The length of the proceedings may also be extended when the court needs to take evidence by questioning a witness about certain factual issues. Such additional circumstances can prolong the duration of proceedings by about six to twelve months.

11.43 After a decision has been rendered by the first-instance court, the losing party can file an appeal within one month after the written decision has been served on the losing party.[61] The subjects of appeal proceedings are mainly legal controversies; the court of appeal normally does not fully review the facts of the case but carries out a legal revision of the first-instance judgment.[62] The filing of new facts is only admitted if specific requirements are satisfied.[63] The process of filing briefs with the court of appeal is similar to that of first-instance proceedings. After the grounds for appeal have been filed, the respondent can file a response brief followed by a reply of the appellant which can again be answered by the respondent with a rejoinder. After all briefs have been filed, the oral hearing in the appeal proceedings

60 See Ch. 11, 11.04 "Venue."
61 § 517 of the Code of Civil Procedure.
62 H.-J. Heßler in Zoeller (ed.), *Zivilprozessordnung*, before § 511 Code of Civil Procedure, margin no. 1.
63 § 531(2) of the Code of Civil Procedure.

takes place. The duration of such hearing is similar to that in first-instance proceedings and usually takes between one and two hours.

Appeal proceedings usually take about twelve to eighteen months. However, the same circumstances that can prolong first-instance proceedings such as including testimony of a court-appointed expert may also prolong the duration of appeal proceedings. **11.44**

A court ruling rendered by a Higher Regional Court may generally only be appealed ("appeal on the law") to the Federal Court of Justice if the Higher Regional Court has permitted such further appeal in its decision. If the Higher Regional Court has refused to permit a further appeal, it is possible to file a request for admittance of a legal appeal directly with the Federal Court of Justice. However, such request is only successful if the underlying legal issues of the case are of general importance or a decision of the Federal Court of Justice is required to develop the law or to assure a uniform application of the law.[64] If admitted, the duration of further appeal proceedings at the Federal Court of Justice will last two to three years. **11.45**

Thus, while the vast majority of German patent infringement cases will not be heard at the Federal Court of Justice, it should be noted that an appeal at the Federal Court of Justice in Germany is still much more likely to occur than having a comparable case heard by the US Supreme Court or the Japanese Supreme Court, both of which hear in average no more than five patent infringement cases per year.[65] **11.46**

2. Evidence Procedure

The success of patent infringement proceedings strongly depends on the facts and evidence available to the plaintiff. The petitioner bears the burden of presentation and proof that an infringement of the patent-in-suit has occurred and that the defendant is legally responsible for such infringement. The petitioner has to provide and prove all facts that are relevant for the infringing action (e.g., offer for sale) and that are necessary to show the application of all features of the asserted patent claim by the device or process alleged as infringing. According to procedural law, the court will not *ex officio* conduct any investigations as to the facts of the case, but will decide solely on the basis of the facts presented by the parties. Generally, the defendant is not obliged to "support" the petitioner in establishing his case. **11.47**

However, it may happen in practice that the petitioner objectively cannot gather the required information and/or evidence to establish patent infringement, because insufficient information relevant to the infringement is available. This can, for example, be the case if the allegedly infringing device or process is kept confidential and used exclusively on the premises of the alleged infringer to which the petitioner or other third parties have no access (e.g., manufacturing devices or processes). In such cases—that is, if there is not enough information about the infringement available nor can it be procured without undue burden—courts and the legislator have provided measures in order to obtain evidence in separate proceedings or even in the context of the infringement proceedings themselves and thus to help the patent owner to gather evidence in order to effectively enforce his patent rights. **11.48**

---

[64] Ibid. § 543.

[65] Ch. 10, 10.85, Ch. 12, 12.01. The U.S. Supreme Court began to hear more than five cases in the last decade. See, Damon C. Andrews, *Promoting the Progress: Three Decades of Patent Jurisprudence in the Court of Appeals for the Federal Circuit*, 76 Mo. L. Rev. 839 (2011).

(a) *Claim for Inspection*

11.49 Based on Directive 2004/48/EC (Enforcement Directive) of April 29 2004, effective as of September 1, 2008, and reflecting evidence-collection procedure developed by the Düsseldorf courts,[66] a provision was incorporated into the Patent Act (§ 140c) granting the patent owner the right to request that the respondent provides documents, allows the inspection of devices which are in the possession of the respondent, or allows the inspection of processes that are subject of the patent-in-suit if the requested provision of documents or the requested inspection is necessary to substantiate the patent owner's claims. Such claim for inspection is subject to the condition that there is a sufficient likelihood that the patent claim is infringed. Furthermore, asking the respondent to provide documents or to allow the inspection of devices or processes must be proportionate in light of the given circumstances.[67]

11.50 An inspection claim can be asserted by the owner of patent rights and any other party which has standing to sue.[68] The claim is directed against the presumed patent infringer.[69] It is not required that infringement has already occurred; rather a sufficient likelihood that an infringement could occur in the future is sufficient.[70]

11.51 However, there must be specific indications as to the presumed patent infringement and a mere suspicion of patent infringement is not enough to support the claim. Sufficient indications may result from the arrangement of parallel products of the possible patent infringer that are sold abroad, from an industry standard that is expected to be generally complied with, or from the fact that individual features of the device or process are known, for example, from advertising.[71] As § 140c of the Patent Act only requires the sufficient likelihood of a patent infringement, doubts regarding the facts of the case as well as doubts regarding the legal assessment of the situation[72] do not preclude an inspection claim.[73] In practice, the hurdle of a sufficient likelihood of patent infringement is not overly high.

11.52 Another prerequisite of a request according to § 140c of the Patent Act is that the patent owner/petitioner would otherwise not be reasonably able to obtain further information and facts required for substantiating the patent infringement. In this context, it is not required that it is absolutely impossible to obtain the required information through other means; rather, it is sufficient to show that there are no other reasonable possibilities to obtain such information and evidence. An inspection is not necessary if the requested information is readily available to the public and can be obtained without much effort, for example because the presumably infringing product can be freely purchased on the market. In order to show that an inspection is necessary, the petitioner should explain previous efforts to evaluate the alleged patent infringement (e.g., research on the internet, review of

---

66 In particular the German practice with respect to the inspection of devices or processes at the respondent's premises had been introduced under the supervision of Judge Thomas Kühnen, at that time presiding judge at the Düsseldorf district court, and is therefore also referred to as the "Düsseldorf procedure."

67 § 140c(2) of the Patent Act.

68 See Ch. 11, 11.12.

69 Kühnen in Schulte, *Patentgesetz*, § 140c of the Patent Act, margin no. 11.

70 Cf. § 140c(5) of the Patent Act.

71 Kühnen, *Handbuch der Patentverletzung* (5th ed.), margin nos. 270 et seq.

72 Namely the question whether the presumed acts of the alleged patent infringer in fact are to be considered as patent infringement.

73 Higher Regional Court of Düsseldorf InstGE 11, 298—*Weissmacher* (*Whitener*).

advertising materials concerning the presumably infringing product or process, purchase of a sample, etc.) in his request.

It should be noted that it is not necessary that the petitioner seeks to file an infringement complaint against the respondent to the inspection claim. Rather, it is possible that the petitioner in an inspection claim seeks to prepare an infringement complaint against a third party (such as the manufacturer), as long as it is likely that the petitioner also has a claim for patent infringement against the respondent.[74] **11.53**

Finally, an inspection must be proportionate.[75] If it is not, the claim for inspection can be denied entirely or with regard to individual measures. It would, for example, be disproportionate and thus inadmissible to search the respondent's entire IT system for evidence of the presumed patent infringement.[76] Factors that have to be taken into consideration while weighing the conflicting interests of the petitioner (patent owner) and the respondent (presumed patent infringer) include:[77] the intensity of use of the patented invention; whether there are significant doubts to the validity of the patent-in-suit; the degree of likelihood of infringement of the patent-in-suit; the usefulness of the inspection measure in order to show and prove the presumed patent infringement; the extent of materials to be provided through the inspection claim; the significance of the impact of the inspection on the device or process to be inspected (e.g., possible damage to the product to be inspected or significant loss due to an interruption of operation of a device to be inspected); the potential business secrets that would be revealed during inspection; and the degree of culpability of the respondent. However, there is a tendency decide in favor of the petitioner; the petitioner's interest regarding an infringement of IP rights usually outweighs the respondent's interest in protection business secrets in light of a likelihood of an infringing use of the patented invention. **11.54**

In principle, all kinds of objects that presumably infringe the patent or are being used for the presumed patent infringement and which are therefore necessary to substantiate the presumed patent infringement claim can be the subject of an inspection. Suitable objects of an inspection include, for example, devices, procedures, means for carrying out a process, products of the process, substances, substance mixtures, and intermediate products as well as corresponding documents, such as especially design drawings, user manuals, installation plans, and measurement charts. **11.55**

A request for an inspection has to specify the object of inspection as precisely as possible, including reasons why the specified object may be suitable to substantiate the presumed patent infringement claim. If the object of the inspection cannot be identified, the court cannot grant an inspection order. **11.56**

Furthermore, principally all measures that are expedient and necessary to verify and/or prove the presumed patent infringement can be applied. Once the inspection is granted, the inspection can be carried out by a close examination of the objects. According to judicial practice, a close examination is allowed in addition to "palpable" or "visual" perception. An **11.57**

---

[74] Kühnen, *Handbuch der Patentverletzung* (5th ed.), margin no. 284.
[75] § 140c(2) of the Patent Act.
[76] Higher Regional Court of Karlsruhe, decision of May 18, 2010, file no. 6 W 28/10, BeckRS 2011, 18386.
[77] Kühnen, *Handbuch der Patentverletzung* (5th ed.), margin nos. 287 et seq.

inspected product can be measured, weighed, touched, or a process can be carried out. If it is necessary to use additional technical aids for determining relevant features (e.g., using a microscope as a technical aid), the petitioner is allowed to do so. In some cases, altering of the substance, removal of components or, if necessary, even destruction of the object or taking samples is also permitted if it is required for examining the object and evaluating infringement of the patent claim. Documents may have to be produced by temporarily handing them over to the petitioner or an independent third party so that copies of the documents can be taken.[78] The request should specify the necessary measures of the inspection, including whether and explaining why visual or palpable perception is insufficient to carry out the inspection. Placing this information in the initial request may prevent possible objections from the respondent when carrying out the inspection.

11.58 Although the right to an inspection does not automatically grant a direct right to search nor a right to access the respondent's business premises, it is possible to obtain a related court order to enforce access to such premises if it is required to inspect the relevant objects, and if the respondent refuses to grant access. If necessary, the search order can be enforced with the help of police officers. In this context, it is not yet determined in case law whether the respondent of the inspection has to assist the inspection, for example by disclosing the location of the objects concerned, or by turning on and operating machines, or by typing in passwords.[79] Judicial practice so far has been reluctant to order the respondent to take affirmative measures in facilitating the search; however, a reasonable approach might be that the respondent has to assist as far as it is required to ensure efficient inspection.

11.59 An inspection pursuant to § 140c of the Patent Act provides the petitioner with multiple advantages. Because the claim for an inspection can be enforced in preliminary injunction proceedings,[80] it can be enforced rather quickly and without requiring extensive efforts. The inspection can be ordered within only a couple of days after filing the request. Further, the inspection can be ordered *ex parte*—that is, without hearing the respondent. Therefore, the inspection order can "surprise" the respondent, which prevents the risk of manipulation or destruction of evidence by the respondent. The information obtained from the inspection can be used as evidence in subsequent infringement proceedings. Finally, inspection proceedings may trigger settlement negotiations because, if an inspection is ordered and an expert opinion is released to the petitioner, the court may, to at least some extent, presume that the patent is in fact infringed. However, the release of an expert opinion does not mean that the court is bound by such an opinion, and the court can still decide otherwise in the infringement proceedings.[81]

11.60 The claim for inspection can be enforced by obtaining a court order. This is possible in the infringement proceedings themselves through the course of a multi-stage complaint: in the first stage, requesting the grant of an inspection and, in the second stage, filing a complaint for patent infringement. Alternatively, an inspection claim can be enforced in separate

[78] Tilman Mueller-Stoy, *Nachweis und Besichtigung des Verletzungsgegenstandes im deutschen Patentrecht (Evidence and Inspection of the Infringing Object under German Patent Law)* (2008), margin no. 147.

[79] See, e.g., Higher Regional Court of Düsseldorf GRUR-RR 2003, 327—*Raumkühlgeraet* (*Air cooling unit*).

[80] See Ch. 13, 13.61.

[81] Kühnen, *Handbuch der Patentverletzung* (5th ed.), margin no. 345.

proceedings, usually by means of a preliminary injunction, either before an infringement complaint is filed or during the infringement proceedings are pending.

(b) Procedure for pre-trial Evidence Collection

An inspection is usually requested and granted in "independent proceedings for taking evidence"[82] before filing an infringement complaint. Such independent evidence proceedings are usually combined with a preliminary injunction to tolerate the inspection. **11.61**

Although an inspection claim can also be enforced in main proceedings, it is advisable to request the inspection in preliminary injunction proceedings because they are less time consuming, and provide a surprise effect. The inspection order can be requested at any court that is competent to hear the infringement proceedings.[83] **11.62**

Inspection proceedings are usually divided into two stages. At the first stage, an inspection is ordered and carried out by a court-appointed expert. In general, the petitioner's attorneys can be present while the expert inspects the allegedly infringing product or process. Usually, the respondent is given the opportunity to call his attorney to be present as well. If confidential information may be revealed by the inspection, the court can—at its own discretion—deny the presence of the petitioner at the inspection and can order that only the court-appointed expert and the attorneys of the petitioner get access to the information, subject to the obligation not to disclose any information to the petitioner or to third parties. **11.63**

After the inspection, the expert produces a written opinion on the results of the inspection setting out the facts and information obtained in course of the inspection. If appropriate, the report may include pictures and/or video recordings. The written opinion is delivered to the court. **11.64**

In order to protect possible business secrets of the alleged infringer that might be disclosed during the inspection and in the written opinion, the petitioner does not gain access to the expert opinion, and both the expert and the petitioner's attorneys must keep the information they received during the inspection confidential. **11.65**

At the second stage, the court must determine whether the expert opinion should be released to the petitioner. At this stage, the respondent is heard and the court again has to balance the petitioner's interest in the information obtained during the inspection against the interest of the respondent to keep his business secrets confidential. If the court comes to the provisional conclusion that the patent is infringed, the petitioner's interest prevails and the report will be released. **11.66**

The alleged infringer's business secrets may be protected by redacting critical passages of the expert opinion before the report is released to the petitioner. Another way to protect the business secrets is to limit access to the expert opinion to specific outside attorneys-at-law and/or patent attorney of the petitioner, who are made subject to a court-ordered obligation to maintain confidentiality vis-à-vis their client.[84] However, the respondent has to explain **11.67**

---

[82] §§ 485 et seq. of the Code of Civil Procedure.

[83] See Ch. 11, 11.04 "Venue." See also below considerations with respect to the urgency requirements which often result in petitioners seeking jurisdiction of the Düsseldorf courts when preparing an inspection order, see Ch. 11, 11.04.

[84] Federal Court of Justice GRUR 2010, 318—*Lichtbogenschnürung* (*Arc lacing*).

and substantiate what kind of business secrets would be affected if the expert opinion was disclosed to the petitioner, and which hardship he would incur. If the respondent cannot demonstrate any specific hardship, the expert opinion has to be released to the petitioner regardless of the result of the inspection.[85] Only the business secrets remaining at the time when the court has to decide on the release of the expert opinion are relevant; information that used to constitute business secrets but have been publicly available in the meantime (e.g., because the petitioner can obtain the relevant information by other means, such as by examining the allegedly infringing device) are not to be taken into consideration.[86] In any event, an attorney's confidentiality obligation is not violated by revealing the general conclusion of the inspection—that is, whether the expert concluded the patent to be infringed or not to his client.[87] This is because the confidentiality obligation only applies to *facts*, while the result of inspection by the expert is only an *assessment* that does not affect the respondent's sphere of business secrets.

11.68 If the patent-in-suit has been revoked or invalidated in first instance proceedings,[88] the expert opinion revealing business secrets of the respondent cannot be released to the petitioner until a final decision on the validity of the patent-in-suit is issued. Since the evidence has already been secured at that stage, there is no urgent need for further measures.[89] Moreover, infringement proceedings would be stayed until a final decision in the validity proceedings in most cases.

11.69 A decision to release or not release an expert opinion to the petitioner can be appealed by way of the so-called "*sofortige Beschwerde*" (immediate appeal; § 567 of the Code of Civil Procedure).[90]

11.70 The respondent cannot appeal a court's decision granting the inspection according to §§ 485 et seq. of the Code of Civil Procedure;[91] however, the petitioner can appeal a decision denying the inspection by means of the immediate appeal. Furthermore, the respondent can request that the court sets a deadline for the petitioner to file an infringement complaint on the merits.[92] Such a court order is also not appealable. If the petitioner does not file the infringement complaint within that deadline, he must bear the costs of the inspection proceedings[93] and the court will lift the previous inspection order.[94]

11.71 If the assumption of an infringement is not confirmed in the course of the inspection proceedings, the petitioner is liable for damages incurred by the respondent as a result of the inspection, which may include economic losses caused by an interruption of the production, and costs for the legal defense against the inspection application. The reason for non-infringement is irrelevant; non-infringement can, for example, result from revocation

[85] Ibid.; Higher Regional Court of Munich InstGE 13, 298—*ausgelagerter Server* (*Relocated server*).
[86] Higher Regional Court of Düsseldorf InstGE 11, 296—*Kaffeemaschine* (*Coffee machine*).
[87] Higher Regional Court of Düsseldorf InstGE 10, 198—*zeitversetztes Fernsehen* (*Time-shift television*).
[88] See Ch. 8 for a review of the validity proceedings in Germany.
[89] Kühnen, *Handbuch der Patentverletzung* (5th ed.), margin no. 348.
[90] Higher Regional Court of Düsseldorf InstGE 8, 186—*Klinkerriemchen II* (*Brick tile II*); InstGE 9, 41—*Schaumstoffherstellung* (*Plastic foam production*); Higher Regional Court of Munich InstGE 12, 192—*Lesevorrichtung fuer Reliefmarkierungen* (*Reading device for relief markings*).
[91] § 491(2) of the Code of Civil Procedure.
[92] Ibid. § 494a.
[93] Ibid. § 494a(2).
[94] Ibid. § 926(2); Kühnen, *Handbuch der Patentverletzung* (5th ed.), margin no. 353.

or nullification of the patent-in-suit or the fact that the alleged infringing product in fact does not make use of the features of the patent claim.

Finally, it should be noted that, while preliminary injunction proceedings principally require urgency (see 11.123 "Preliminary Injunction"), German case law is divided on the question whether the petition for an inspection order also requires such urgency. Both the Munich I District Court and the Higher Regional Court of Karlsruhe held[95] that in principal inspection proceedings also require urgency, and that requirement is only relaxed in exceptional cases. In contrast, the Düsseldorf courts have repeatedly held that urgency is not required in inspection proceedings. [96] **11.72**

(c) Procedure for Evidence Collection during the Trial

Inspection proceedings according to § 140c of the Patent Act can also be instigated while patent infringement proceedings are already pending. However, this might lead to a considerable delay in the infringement proceedings. **11.73**

If the patent owner/petitioner realizes during the infringement proceedings that he lacks sufficient information and evidence to prove the alleged patent infringement, he should be able to change the proceedings to multi-stage proceedings, seeking a petition for an inspection claim at the first stage, followed by an infringement complaint at the second stage. Alternatively requesting the inspection claim though should not be admissible as the court could only decide on the alternative request for an inspection order if the related main claim concerning patent infringement would be dismissed. **11.74**

Another alternative might be to suggest that the court proceeds according to §§ 142 and 144 of the Code of Civil Procedure, which provides that the court may order the visual observation or the assessment by a court expert and for this purpose demands presentation of objects or documents. However, there is no specific legal basis in the code for such an order, but the court may decide on such a suggestion at its discretion. **11.75**

The court may also order, at the request of the petitioner, that the defendant submits documents as part of the evidence procedure, if the order can remedy a lack of evidence to support the claim. **11.76**

3. Border Measures

The harmonized law of the European Union allows for seizing patent-infringing goods when crossing the border to Germany. Compared to trademark and copyright law, border measures are rarely used in patent practice because it is much more difficult for the customs authorities—whose staff have no technical background—to identify an infringement of a patent claim, as opposed to, for example, a counterfeit of a trademark.[97] However, the German customs authorities are not indifferent to patent infringement, and welcome patentees to explain the details of the patented invention and the alleged patent infringement. **11.77**

[95] Higher Regional Court of Karlsruhe, decision of May 18, 2010—6 W 28/10; District Court of Munich I InstGE 13, 181—*Arzneimittelherstellung* (*Medicine production*).

[96] District Court of Düsseldorf GRUR-RR 2011, 289—*Spaeter Besichtigungsantrag* (*Late inspection request*). See also Higher Regional Court of Frankfurt, decision of June 10, 2010—15 U 192/09.

[97] The German customs authorities, on average, seize approximately 9,000 goods per year (not only for alleged patent infringement but also with regard to intellectual property rights in general), whereas an extraordinary amount of more than 23,000 seizures have been performed in each of 2010 and 2011.

To enable the custom authorities to assist in enforcing a patent, it is recommendable to explain the scope and subject matter of the patent in substantial detail in the application for a border seizure and to provide information about the origin of original products and the origin of alleged infringing products as well as the names of authorized and non-authorized manufacturers, distributors and/or importers (if known to the petitioner).

(a) Application and Seizure

11.78 **i. Application** There are two different systems of border seizures available under German law and harmonized European law respectively.

11.79 According to the provisions of the Regulation (EC) No. 1383/2003 of the European Union which is directly applicable to European Union member states, a patent owner can file a request with the national customs authorities to seize patent infringing goods that are imported from outside of the European Union into the European Union.[98] Despite the possibility of filing one single application for several European Union member states, as is possible for community trademarks and community design rights,[99] an application based on patent infringement has to be filed separately for each state in which the patent owner is interested in seizing infringing goods.[100]

11.80 An application in accordance with Art. 5(1) of Regulation (EC) No. 1383/2003 is not available for seizure of parallel imports of original products that are not authorized by the patent owner for import into the European Union.[101]

11.81 In order to cover such products as well as products which are imported from other European Union member states into Germany, the patent owner can file a separate application for border seizure based on the national German provisions (§ 142a of the Patent Act).[102] In this context, it has to be considered that an application based on the national provisions does not cover goods which are subject to seizures based on Regulation (EC) No. 1383/2003. Therefore, it is often recommendable to file both the EU Regulation-based application and the national law-based application, especially in case of parallel importation or infringement of utility model rights.

11.82 The application forms for border seizure can be obtained from the German customs authorities and can be filed online. However, an application is only valid after a signed original copy has been sent to the German customs authorities by surface mail. After the application has been correctly filed with the customs authorities, it usually takes up to two months before a border seizure can be performed. After approval of the application, the custom authorities will search for infringing products for an initial term of one year. Such initial term can easily be extended every year until the expiration date of the patent.[103] The application for a border seizure does not require payment of any administrative costs.[104]

---

[98] Art. 5(1) of Regulation (EC) No. 1383/2003; see Kühnen, *Handbuch der Patentverletzung* (5th ed.), margin no. 401.

[99] Art. 5(4) of Regulation (EC) No. 1383/2003.

[100] Ibid. Art. 5(1).

[101] Ibid. Art. 3(1); Kühnen, *Handbuch der Patentverletzung* (5th ed.), margin no. 397.

[102] Kühnen in Schulte, *Patentgesetz*, § 142a of the Patent Act, margin no. 4; Kühnen, *Handbuch der Patentverletzung* (5th ed.), margin no. 416.

[103] Art. 8(1), (3) of Regulation (EC) No. 1383/2003; § 142b(6)1 of the Patent Act; see Kühnen, *Handbuch der Patentverletzung* (5th ed.), margin no. 402.

[104] Art. 5(7) of Regulation (EC) No. 1383/2003; Kühnen in Schulte, *Patentgesetz*, § 142a of the Patent Act, margin no. 12.

Once the border seizure application has been approved, the German customs authorities store all information provided by the application petitioner in an electronic information system called "eAgent." All personnel at the customs authorities have access to this system and can review certain details once suspected goods have been seized when crossing the German border. **11.83**

ii. Seizure The customs authorities inspect goods arriving by all types of transportation, such as parcel services, air traffic, maritime traffic, road traffic, and rail traffic all over Germany. Due to the substantial amount of goods imported into the territory of Germany, the customs authorities can only inspect a small number of deliveries. **11.84**

Goods in transit or stored in a bounded warehouse are generally not subject to customs measures.[105] **11.85**

When the customs authorities are satisfied that the identified goods may infringe the patent, the customs authorities are entitled to seize and detain the goods.[106] Again, it should be noted that the assessment of patent infringement is conducted by the customs personnel who—in most cases—have no technical background. For this reason, it is essential to provide the customs authorities with as much technical explanations about the patent and the alleged infringing product as possible. **11.86**

When the goods have been detained, the customs authorities inform the petitioner and the importer or owner of the seized goods, and give the petitioner or his attorney the opportunity to inspect the seized goods.[107] The customs authorities can take samples and hand them over to the patent owner. In practice, the customs authorities, where possible, try to satisfy the petitioner's interest in a sample by providing him with digital photos or otherwise send a sample of the seized goods to the petitioner or his attorney for inspection. Further, the customs authorities inform the petitioner, at his request and if known, of the names and addresses of the consignee, the consignor, the importer or the owner of the goods and the origin and provenance of the goods suspected to infringe the patent.[108] **11.87**

The customs authorities are also entitled to suspend release of goods suspected of patent infringement before an application for border measures has been lodged if they have sufficient grounds for suspecting that these goods infringe a patent. In such a case, the goods can be suspended for three working days after the patent owner and the importer or the owner of the goods have been informed about the suspension. This three-day suspension period enables the patentee to submit an application for border seizure.[109] **11.88**

When goods have been detained, the patent owner has to notify the customs authorities about his further course of action—namely, that either proceedings to determine patent infringement have been initiated[110] or that the patent owner agrees to destroy the seized goods without requiring to determine patent infringement[111] within ten working days after **11.89**

[105] ECJ, decisions of December 2, 2011, file no. C-446/09—*Philips* and file no. C-495/09—*Nokia*.

[106] Art. 9(1) of Regulation (EC) No. 1383/2003.

[107] Art. 9(2) and (3) of Regulation (EC) No. 1383/2003; Kühnen, *Handbuch der Patentverletzung* (5th ed.), margin no. 405.

[108] Art. 9(3) of Regulation (EC) No. 1383/2003.

[109] Ibid. Art. 4(1).

[110] Ibid. Art. 10.

[111] Ibid. Art. 11(1).

the receipt of the notification.[112] This deadline can be extended by a maximum of ten additional working days.[113] In case of perishable goods suspected of patent infringement, the initial period shall be three working days without the possibility of an extension.[114] If the patent owner fails to properly respond to the notification by the customs authorities, the goods are released.[115] The requirement of initiating legal proceedings is satisfied if a complaint on the merits or a request for preliminary injunction has been filed with a court.[116]

11.90 **iii. Differences of the National Seizure Request (§ 142a of the Patent Act)** The procedure according to the national provisions is not identical to the procedure provided for by Regulation (EC) No. 1383/2003. While according to the Regulation is already sufficient if the goods are suspected of patent infringement, border seizure under German law requires that the accused goods obviously infringe the patent.[117] The threshold required for seizing goods is therefore much higher under national law than under the Regulation.

11.91 It should be noted that Regulation (EC) No. 1381/2003 has priority over § 142a of the Patent Act—that is, a patent owner can only refer to German law if Regulation (EC) No. 1381/2003 is not applicable.[118]

11.92 After the goods have been seized, the owner of the goods or an authorized person has to object within two weeks after service of the notification of the seizure, otherwise the goods will be destroyed by the customs authorities.[119] In case of an objection, the patent owner has the following options: (1) withdrawing the request for seizure or (2) maintaining the request for seizure and obtaining an enforceable decision of a court ordering the customs authorities to take the goods into custody.[120] These declarations have to be provided within two weeks after service of the notification of seizure and the objection of the importer/owner of the goods, respectively.[121] If the patent owner has filed a request for a judgment with the court but has not yet obtained such judgment, this deadline can be extended by two weeks.[122] If the patent owner does not providing an enforceable decision of a court ordering the customs authorities to take the goods into custody, the customs authorities will release the goods.[123]

(b) Simplified Procedure for Destruction and Declaratory Procedure

11.93 The patent owner can, within ten working days after the receipt of the notification of the seizure (maximally twenty working days, in case of perishable goods within three working days) request the customs authorities to destroy the seized goods.[124] To enable the destruction, the patent owner has to provide the customs authorities with the written consent of the importer, who is the owner or the holder of the goods for destruction. In order to enhance

[112] Ibid. Art. 13(1).
[113] Ibid. Art. 13(1)2.
[114] Ibid. Art. 13 (2).
[115] Ibid. Art. 13 (1).
[116] Kühnen, *Handbuch der Patentverletzung* (5th ed.), margin no. 407.
[117] § 142a(1) of the Patent Act.
[118] Kühnen in Schulte, *Patentgesetz*, § 142a of the Patent Act, margin no. 4.
[119] § 142a(3) of the Patent Act.
[120] Ibid. § 142a(4).
[121] Ibid. § 142a(3), (4)2.
[122] Ibid. § 142a(4)3.
[123] Ibid. § 142a(4)3.
[124] Art. 11(1) first bullet point of Regulation (EC) No. 1383/2003; § 142b(3) of the Patent Act.

the rights of the patent owner, this consent is presumed to be accepted when the importer, the holder, or the owner of the goods has not specifically objected to the destruction within the abovementioned deadlines of ten days and three days, respectively.[125] In practice, this simplification affects such cases in which the importer, the holder, or the owner of the goods has no interest in litigating the matter before court and therefore does not object to the destruction of the goods. If the destruction of the goods is opposed by the importer, the holder, or the owner of the goods the patent owner has to initiate legal proceedings in order to avoid a release of the goods.[126]

The destruction of the goods is carried out by the customs authorities at the expense and under the responsibility of the patent owner.[127] However, the customs authorities keep samples of the goods which can be used as evidence in subsequent legal proceedings if necessary.[128] **11.94**

(c) Clearance of Seized Goods

If the patent owner has initiated legal proceedings before the seized goods have been released to the importer, the holder, or the owner of the goods, the detention of the goods is continued until the court rules on infringement. However, the importer or the holder of the goods can request release of the goods on provision of a security bond which must be sufficient to protect the interests of the patent owner.[129] **11.95**

(d) Damage Claims

In case of patent infringement, the patent owner can request damages from the distributor of the infringing goods in accordance with the general legal provisions. There are no separate or special seizure-related provisions for claiming damages against the infringer. **11.96**

If the suspended goods are released to the importer without legal proceedings being initiated by the patent owner, the patent owner is—as a general rule—not responsible for any damages suffered by the importer, as the goods were in fact suspected by the customs authorities to infringe a patent and as the customs authorities are presumed to have acted within their competence. Same applies if it turns out later that the goods have not infringed the patent at all. **11.97**

If the seizure is based on the national seizure provisions, the patent owner may be responsible for damages suffered by the owner of the goods or the authorized person if three conditions are met: the patent is not infringed, the seizure was objected to, and the patent owner did not withdraw his request or did not notify the customs authorities about a requested court decision. **11.98**

Since it can be very harmful for an importer to wait until the suspended goods are released,[130] the importer may—if he is aware of potentially misleading patents—file a protective letter with the German customs authorities. This may enable him to explain to the customs **11.99**

[125] Art. 11(1) first bullet point of the Regulation (EC) No. 1383/2003; § 142b(4) of the Patent Act; see Kühnen, *Handbuch der Patentverletzung* (5th ed.), margin no. 408.

[126] Arts. 11(2), 13 of Regulation (EC) No. 1383/2003.

[127] Ibid. Art. 11(1) second bullet point.

[128] Ibid.

[129] Ibid. Art. 14(1), (2).

[130] E.g., if the goods are supposed to be used at a trade fair which takes place at a fixed time.

authorities his interpretation of the patent and to present his non-infringement arguments in order to reduce the risk that the goods are seized by the customs authorities.

4. Pre-trial Measures

11.100 Before filing an infringement complaint, the patent owner will usually consider approaching the accused infringer outside court for several reasons. If the patent owner is not in possession of all facts required to assess and/or to prove infringement, he can make contact with the alleged infringer outside court, hoping that the latter might disclose relevant information in his answer.[131] Further, a discussion outside court might be sufficient to resolve the infringement without having to go through litigation. Also, the alleged infringer can no longer claim lack of knowledge and thus lack of negligence after he has been put on notice of the alleged infringement. .

11.101 However, as in other jurisdictions, including the United States and Japan, there is no obligation for the patent owner to seek a settlement before initiating litigation. He can also directly file an infringement complaint with the court without having approached the infringer outside court.

(a) Warning Letters

11.102 A first possible approach to the alleged infringer is to send (usually via an attorney-at-law or a patent attorney) a warning letter (*Abmahnung*). A warning letter can be an inexpensive measure to stop third parties from continuing to infringe a patent.

11.103 Warning letters typically include a statement that the addressee of the letter is allegedly infringing certain claims of a patent of the patent owner. The statement can be based on all types of patent infringement under patent law and would usually include the request to cease and desist from future use of the patent.[132] In order to make sure that the addressee refrains from further patent infringement, the addressee is requested not only to cease and desist from further infringment but also to sign a cease-and-desist declaration with an underlying penalty clause—that is, an undertaking to pay a specific amount of damages to the patent owner in the event that he makes continued use of the patent.[133]

11.104 In the warning letter, the patent owner usually sets a deadline for the accused infringer to sign the declaration. This deadline has to be reasonable and has to enable the addressee to examine and verify the accusation and, if need be, to stop the objected acts and take necessary countermeasures.[134] In most cases, the deadline is set at two to four weeks, but—depending on the circumstances of the specific case—can also be only a few days,

[131] Keukenschrijver in Pagenberg and Cornich, *Interpretation of Patents in Europe*, margin no. DE4.

[132] Kühnen, *Handbuch der Patentverletzung* (5th ed.), margin no. 521.

[133] Since the mere declaration not to infringe a patent—according to the case law of the Federal Court of Justice, see Federal Court of Justice GRU 1998, 1045—*Brennwertkessel* (*Condensing boiler*) with further references—is not sufficient to make sure that no further infringements occur, the declaration has to be penalized so that in case of further infringements the signatory to the declaration has to pay the agreed penalty to the patent owner. The amount of the penalty in most cases is already determined in the cease-and-desist declaration. The amount depends on the relevance of the infringing act and has to be sufficiently high to effectively deter the infringer from further infringement. In order to simplify the signing of such a declaration, it is common practice for the patent owner's attorney to attach a draft cease-and-desist declaration to the warning letter which *inter alia* includes the amount of the penalty. See Kühnen in Schulte, *Patentgesetz*, § 139 of the Patent Act, margin no. 43.

[134] Kühnen, *Handbuch der Patentverletzung* (5th ed.), margin no. 532.

for example, in trade-fair infringement cases.[135] In order to solve the dispute, the respondent may stop infringing the patent and sign the declaration which usually also includes the undertaking to pay the costs caused for preparing and sending the related warning letter by an attorney. Such costs are determined according to the Lawyer's Remuneration Act.[136]

The warning letter must be sent to the party infringing the patent in the territory of the **11.105**
Federal Republic of Germany. Since it is common practice in many business areas to sell products via distribution chains, all companies involved in these distribution chains which are active in Germany are potential infringers and are therefore potential addressees of a warning letter. In addition to that, the patent owner may also consider sending warning letters to customers or potential customers of the opponent, informing them about the patent infringement by the respondent's products. However, such practice could constitute an unlawful customer warning if such customers are end users or uninformed and technically inexperienced distributors who lack the knowledge to evaluate the legal implications of the warning letter.[137] In most cases it is more effective and less risky to send the warning letter to the party at the source of the distribution chain, usually the manufacturer.

There is no legal obligation to send waning letters prior to filing a complaint based on pat- **11.106**
ent infringement. However, it may happen that the respondent acknowledges the accused patent infringement in court proceedings immediately after service of the complaint. In such case, the patent owner who did not send a warning letter would usually have to pay all statutory costs and fees caused by the proceedings, unless it was clear from the beginning that the respondent would still deny patent infringement upon receipt of a warning letter.[138] If the patent owner, however, had sent a warning letter to the defendant before filing the complaint, the defendant would have to bear the costs of legal proceedings if he acknowledges the infringement after filing of the lawsuit.[139]

If the respondent ceases infringing the patent and signs a cease-and-desist declaration with **11.107**
an underlying penalty clause, the patent owner may no longer file a complaint for patent infringement against this respondent requesting an injunction, unless the respondent violates the undertaking and starts infringing the patent again. One significant risk of sending a warning letter to an alleged infringer is the risk that the latter files a complaint against the patent owner, requesting a court ruling of non-infringement, usually referred to as a negative declaratory judgment action.[140] This risk results in the fact that a warning letter is only exceptionally sent, usually only in cases where the patentee expects the alleged infringer to acknowledge the infringement upon receiving the warning letter.

(b) Claims for Unjustified Warning

The decision to send a warning letter has to be evaluated carefully. Besides risking the filing of **11.108**
a declaratory judgment action, sending a warning letter may trigger claims for injunctive relief

135 Higher Regional Court of Düsseldorf InstGE 4, 159—*INTERPACK*.

136 Kühnen, *Handbuch der Patentverletzung* (5th ed.), margin no. 552.

137 Cf. Higher Regional Court of Düsseldorf GRUR 2003, 814—*Unberechtigte Abnehmerverwarnung* (*Unjustified warning of customers*).

138 § 93 of the Code of Civil Procedure; Herget in Zoeller, *Zivilprozessordnung*, § 93 of the Code of Civil Procedure, margin no. 6—Wettbewerbsstreitigkeiten (Competition Disputes); Kühnen, *Handbuch der Patentverletzung* (5th ed.), margin no. 516.

139 Keukenschrijver in Pagenberg and Cornich, *Interpretation of Patents in Europe*, margin no. DE4.

140 See also Ch. 11, 11.114 "Declaratory Judgment Action."

and damages by the addressee of the warning letter in case the alleged patent infringement stated in the warning letter is not justified.[141] Damage claims are awarded because German case law considers unjustified warning letters as an interference with the civil law right of the alleged infringer in operating his established business (*Eingriff in den eingerichteten und ausgeübten Gewerbebetrieb*).[142] The same applies when the patent owner sends letters to customers of the alleged infringer.[143]

11.109 Therefore, the patent owner may be requested to cease and desist from sending further unjustified warning letters and—if warning letters have been sent to customers—to withdraw the warning letter sent to these customers. The respondent's damage claim may include recoverable costs for appointing an attorney-at-law and a patent attorney to evaluate the matter, as well as losses for stopping the production and sale of the accused products as well as lost orders and related damage claims of third parties.

11.110 A warning letter may be unjustified due to defects of its form or substance. Formal defects of a warning letter include, for example, if the patent (and the asserted patent claim) is not mentioned or mentioned ambiguously,[144] if the alleged infringer is not explicitly informed about the allegedly infringing act,[145] if the patent owner fails to mention pending opposition or nullity proceedings concerning the patent,[146] or if the patent owner does not disclose prior unfavorable judgments on the infringement or omits to mention that a judgment cited is currently subject to appeal proceedings.[147] Substantive defects are, for example, invalidity of the patent, lack of standing to sue, and non-infringement.[148]

(c) Request for Justification

11.111 If the patent owner is not able to sufficiently demonstrate patent infringement, he may send the alleged infringer a letter requesting information why the latter deems his conduct to be lawful in view of the existing patent rights.[149] Such inquiry letters are called a "*Berechtigungsanfrage*" (request for justification).

11.112 Other than a warning letter, a request for justification may not contain the request to cease and desist from using the alleged products, and may not indicate the intention to file an infringement action. Therefore, in turn, a request for justification generally cannot be a basis for a negative declaratory judgment action or for damage claims. However, it might be qualified as misleading advertising, for example, if the patent owner fails to mention pending opposition proceedings.[150]

---

[141] Federal Court of Justice (Grand Panel) GRUR 2005, 882—*Unberechtigte Schutzrechtsverwarnung* (*Unjustified warning*). Keukenschrijver in Pagenberg and Cornich, *Interpretation of Patents in Europe*, margin no. DE4.

[142] Alfred Keukenschrijver (ed.), in *Busse, Patentgesetz* (6th ed., 2003), § 139 of the Patent Act, margin no. 253; §§ 823, 1004 of the Civil Code.

[143] Federal Court of Justice GRUR 2006, 433—*Unbegruendete Abnehmerverwarnung* (*Unfounded warning of customers*). If the warning letter is sent to a distributer of the infringing device, the manufacturer (and all intermediate distributers) may be entitled to damage claims. See Kühnen, *Handbuch der Patentverletzung* (5th ed.), margin no. 587.

[144] See District Court of Düsseldorf InstGE 3, 86—*Hochdruckreiniger* (*High pressure cleaner*).

[145] Federal Court of Justice GRUR 2009, 878—*Fraesautomat* (*Milling machine*); see District Court of Düsseldorf InstGE 3, 86—*Hochdruckreiniger* (*High pressure cleaner*).

[146] Kühnen, *Handbuch der Patentverletzung* (5th ed.), margin no. 594.

[147] Federal Court of Justice GRUR 1995, 424—*Abnehmerverwarnung* (*Customer warning*).

[148] Kühnen, *Handbuch der Patentverletzung* (5th ed.), margin nos. 597 et seq.

[149] Kühnen, *Handbuch der Patentverletzung* (5th ed.), margin no. 631.

[150] Higher Regional Court of Karlsruhe, GRUR-RR 2008, 197—*irrefuehrende Berechtigungsanfrage* (*misleading request for justification*).

If the addressee of a request for justification answers the request for justification, the patent owner may consider taking further steps against the alleged infringer depending on the content of such answer. However, in practice requests for justification usually remain unanswered and are thus a rather inefficient strategy. **11.113**

E. Other Important Proceedings

1. Declaratory Judgment Action

As in other jurisdictions, the declaratory judgment action ("DJA" or in German "*negative Feststellungsklage*") enables an alleged infringer after having been warned by the patentee to proactively request the court to clarify whether his conduct is infringing or not. Other than in the United States, filing of a DJA under German civil procedure law does not determine the venue where the litigation is conducted. Thus, a DJA is used not so much as a strategic instrument but rather as a method of determining the substantive merits of an accusation of patent infringement. Usually, a DJA is filed upon receiving a warning letter or upon commencement of a patent enforcement action in another European jurisdiction. Therefore, in such proceedings, the patent owner (or the exclusive licensee) becomes the defendant, and the alleged infringer acts as plaintiff. **11.114**

(a) Declaratory Judgment Action under German Law

A DJA is considered as the "mirror image" of a patent infringement complaint.[151] The person who sent the warning letter—namely, the patent owner or the exclusive licensee—is named as defendant in a DJA[152] A non-exclusive licensee cannot be named as defendant in a DJA as he would not be entitled to assert own claims of patent infringement, but could only asserts claims assigned by the patent owner.[153] The value of litigation is to be determined along the same criteria as in an infringement action.[154] Therefore, the financial risk of filing a DJA depends heavily on the economic significance of the infringement for the parties. **11.115**

For the admissibility of a negative declaratory judgment action, the plaintiff must prove a legitimate interest in the clarification of a legal relationship (*Feststellungsinteresse*).[155] In patent matters, such legitimate interest typically is presumed if patent infringement is asserted through a warning letter. However, it should be noted that in case the patent owner withdraws the assertion of infringement after objections from the alleged infringer, the alleged infringer loses his legitimate interest.[156] A request for enforcement of a judgment only triggers a legitimate interest in a DJA if the requests concerns future conduct which may constitute an infringement.[157] As mentioned above, a request for justification usually **11.116**

---

[151] Therefore, the above remarks concerning jurisdiction (see Ch. 11, 11.01 "Jurisdiction and Venue") applies respectively, i.e., all district courts that are competent to hear an infringement action are also competent to hear a DJA, and all parties having standing to sue in an infringement action can be named as defendants in a DJA.

[152] Kühnen, *Handbuch der Patentverletzung* (5th ed.), margin no. 1489.

[153] Kühnen, *Handbuch der Patentverletzung* (5th ed.), margin no. 1489.

[154] Federal Court of Justice NJW 1970, 2025. See Ch. 11.23 "Court Fees."

[155] § 256(1) of the Code of Civil Procedure.

[156] District Court of Düsseldorf, decision of February 24, 2011, file no. 4b O 194/09, BeckRS 2011, 20668.

[157] Federal Court of Justice GRUR 2008, 360—*EURO oder Schwarzgeld* (*EURO or illegal earnings*).

does not establish a legitimate interest for a DJA. However, it has to be noted that a request for justification is assessed differently in other jurisdictions; for example, in Italy, a request for justification is sufficient to establish a legitimate interest. This is particularly relevant in the context of "torpedo proceedings."[158]

11.117 According to German law, the declaratory judgment action is subordinate to an infringement action (*Leistungsklage*). Therefore, the DJA becomes inadmissible if an infringement action between the same parties, concerning the same patent and the same conduct is pending at the same time, and is ready for decision.[159] Thus, if the patent owner files an infringement complaint in reaction to a DJA, the plaintiff must declare that the DJA has become moot; otherwise the DJA will be dismissed by the court. If the plaintiff declares the DJA as moot, the court only has to decide whether the complaint was admissible and justified in the first place (if so, the defendant has to bear the procedural costs).

11.118 With regard to the burden of proof, the plaintiff in a DJA has to establish that the respondent asserted patent infringement, for example, by sending a warning letter. In turn, the respondent will try to demonstrate that the plaintiff is in fact infringing his patent. Thus, the court has to decide the question of infringement when hearing a DJA in the same way as if hearing a regular infringement action.

(b) Torpedo Proceedings

11.119 Furthermore, initiating declaratory judgment actions, also known as "torpedo" proceedings, at courts known for slow judicial proceedings can be an effective strategy for delaying patent infringement proceedings in Germany. Torpedo proceedings can be initiated when an alleged infringer learns, for example by way of a warning letter, that the patent owner intends to file an infringement complaint in Germany. In this situation the alleged infringer files a declaratory judgment action for non-infringement of the German patent[160] with a foreign court known for the long duration of its proceedings, traditionally most frequently in Italy or Belgium. In this case, according to Article 27 of the Brussels-I-Directive 44/2001 EG the German court has to stay the infringement proceedings since the prior action involving the same parties and the same German patent blocks any later action concerning the same legal question between the same parties until the foreign court has decided on the negative declaratory judgment action. Even in case of a clear lack of jurisdiction of the foreign court, the decision on admissibility of the action may lead to a substantial delay of the pending German infringement proceedings.

11.120 Thus, because an alleged infringer might be induced to file a torpedo in reaction to a warning letter or in reaction to a request for justification, the patent owner should carefully consider the risk of a torpedo action before sending a warning letter or request for justification.

11.121 However, according to German case law,[161] a defendant in German infringement proceedings may not be able to rely on Article 27 of the Brussels-I-Directive 44/2001 EG, if the torpedo

---

[158] See Ch. 11, 11.119 "Torpedo Proceedings."

[159] Federal Court of Justice GRUR 2006, 217—*Detektionseinrichtung I* (*Detection device I*).

[160] Here it should be noted that the different national parts of a European patent are not considered to be one right, but as several independent national patents. Therefore, in the negative declaratory judgment action the plaintiff has to explicitly refer also to the German part of the European patent and request the declaration that the German part of the European patent is not infringed.

[161] District Court of Düsseldorf InstGE 3, 8—*Cholesterin-Test* (*Cholesterol test*).

constitutes an inadmissible exercise of right. According to the Düsseldorf District Court, this is the case if the negative declaratory judgment action was filed by the defendant for the purpose of slowing down the proceedings with a court that is obviously not competent to hear the case in Germany. According to the Düsseldorf District Court, applying Article 27 of the Brussels-I-Directive 44/2001 EG in such a case would constitute an abuse of right by the party relying on the torpedo. Such interpretation of the Brussels-I-Directive 44/2001 EG has to be aligned with the case law of the European Court of Justice, which has in the past decided that Article 27 has to be applied even if the torpedo proceedings take an unreasonably long time[162] or if the defendant only started the foreign proceedings to disturb the German proceedings.[163]

One possibility to avoid the torpedo risk might be granting an exclusive license to the patent-in-suit to a subsidiary company.[164] According to Article 27 of the Brussels-I-Directive 44/2001 EG, the German infringement proceedings only have to be stayed if "the same parties" are concerned. The German infringement proceedings do not have to be stayed if the complaint is filed by the exclusive licensee who is not "the same party" as the patent owner involved in the negative declaratory judgment action. **11.122**

2. Preliminary Injunction

In stopping a specific infringing conduct, time may be of the essence if a new infringing product is introduced on the market, especially if such infringing product is sold at low prices likely to result in market erosion and thus in damages for which the patent owner will usually not be adequately compensated. In such particularly urgent cases, the patent owner can apply for a preliminary injunction to temporarily prevent the infringer from using the patent even before initiating the main proceedings. **11.123**

(a) Jurisdiction and Venue

With regard to jurisdiction und venue, in the context of preliminary injunction proceedings the same rules apply as in main proceedings.[165] Although there are twelve district courts potentially competent to hear patent infringement cases, in most cases, preliminary injunction proceedings are brought before the District Courts of Düsseldorf, Mannheim, Munich I, Hamburg, and Frankfurt. **11.124**

(b) Claim for Preliminary Injunction

A preliminary injunction can be used to quickly obtain a cease-and-desist order prohibiting the patent infringer, for example, from showing infringing products at a trade fair in Germany or importing infringing products into Germany. If the patent infringement is particularly obvious, the petitioner can also request information on the origin of the infringing products and the parties forming the distribution channels. In order to secure the claim for destruction of the infringing products, the petitioner has the right to claim that the infringing products are to be taken into custody to prevent their sale or delivery. Damage claims and rendering of accounts in preparation for a damage claim, however, cannot be asserted in preliminary injunction proceedings.[166] **11.125**

---

162 ECJ, decision of December 9, 2003, file no. C-116/02—*Gasser vs. MISAT.*

163 ECJ, decision of April 27, 2004, file no. C-159/03—*Turner vs. Grovit.*

164 District Court of Düsseldorf GRUR-RR 2009, 402—*Italienischer Torpedo* (*Italian torpedo*); Higher Regional Court of Düsseldorf GRUR-RR 2009, 401—*Torpedo.*

165 See Ch. 11, 11.01 "Subject Matter Jurisdiction" and 11.04 "Venue."

166 Higher Regional Court of Hamburg GRUR-RR 2007, 29—*Cerebo Card.*

11.126 To stop the appearance of the infringing product in a trade fair or to ensure cost reimbursement, related measures should be considered especially if a preliminary injunction is requested against foreign infringers from countries with which Germany has no reciprocity agreement. This can be accomplished by means of attachment,[167] allowing the petitioner, for example, to seize the respondent's goods. The prospect of an attachment order might also cause the respondent to agree to an amicable settlement of the case. However, it should be noted that the respondent can prevent an attachment by depositing a specific amount being specified in the attachment order.[168]

(c) Requirements

11.127 To obtain a preliminary injunction, the petitioner has to demonstrate a claim for injunction, and grounds for an injunction.

11.128 **i. Claim for Injunction: Infringement** A preliminary injunction can only be granted if the petitioner can demonstrate a claim for injunctive relief by substantiating the facts on which his claim is based—that is, he has to demonstrate that the embodiment makes use of the asserted patent claim.

11.129 However, substantiation of his claim does not require full evidence. Rather, it is sufficient if the petitioner can show that he is highly likely to succeed on the merits.

11.130 The evidence for such a showing must be in a form allowing its presentation to the Court at an oral hearing. For example, witness testimony is only permissible in preliminary proceedings if the witness is present in the oral hearing and does not need to be summoned by the court.

11.131 **ii. Grounds for an Injunction** The second requirement for a preliminary injunction is to demonstrate grounds for an injunction. Such grounds for an injunction would be if the enforcement is urgent, as the petitioner's rights would otherwise be frustrated or at least significantly complicated[169] without an injunction and if the injunction is necessary to avoid serious disadvantages for the petitioner.[170] This condition of "urgency" is not presumed but has to be demonstrated by the petitioner.

11.132 **iii. Balance of Interests** A preliminary injunction may only be granted when a balance of the parties' interests, considering all relevant circumstances of the individual case, clearly favors the petitioner.[171]

11.133 The factors that have to be assessed by the court when balancing the conflicting interests of the petitioner and the respondent include[172] whether:

- the patent-in-suit is clearly infringed, or the question of patent infringement is difficult to be evaluated, for example, because the respondent only assesses infringement by equivalent means

[167] §§ 916 et seq. of the Code of Civil Procedure.
[168] Ibid. § 923.
[169] Ibid. § 935.
[170] Ibid. § 940.
[171] District Court of Mannheim InstGE, 13, 11—*Sauggreifer* (*Vacuum cups*); Higher Regional Court of Düsseldorf InstGE 12, 114—*Harnkatheterset* (*Urinary catheter set*).
[172] Kühnen, *Handbuch der Patentverletzung* (5th ed.), margin nos. 1547 et seq.

- the technology of the invention is easily understandable or rather difficult and complex, requiring special knowledge for which the court would have to consult an expert[173]
- the patent-in-suit has only just been granted or the opposition period has at least already lapsed to such an extent that the respondent has been able to search for relevant prior art when defending himself against the claim for a preliminary injunction[174]
- the validity of the patent-in-suit has been proven in previous opposition and/or nullity proceedings;[175] in this regard it must also be taken into account if its validity is acknowledged by competitors who may have taken a license in the patent-in-suit, or the invention of the patent-in-suit is close to the prior art so that its validity seems to be questionable
- patent infringement was already found in former infringement proceedings based on the same or comparable embodiments and on the same patent-in-suit
- the patent-in-suit is almost expired, so that the petitioner does not have sufficient time to address his claims in main proceedings but his right would be frustrated if the preliminary injunction would not be granted
- the petitioner might suffer severe disadvantages with regard to his market position due to a price erosion or predatory competition if the preliminary injunction would not be granted
- the issuance of a preliminary injunction would cause severe disadvantages for the respondent, for example, if the embodiment forms the basis of his business
- the embodiment is offered only for a short time
- the patent owner is a patent licensing agency without own market presence which only exploits the patent-in-suit by granting licenses; this might constitute a factor against the need for a preliminary injunction as the petitioner would be satisfied by receiving monetary compensation—that is, by claiming damages in the main proceedings.

11.134 In the course of the balance of interests, the question of validity of the patent-in-suit is of paramount importance. Doubts as to the validity of the patent-in-suit regularly make it impossible to obtain a preliminary injunction.[176] In order to minimize the risk of a wrong decision, the validity of the patent-in-suit can usually only be regarded as sufficiently certain if it has already been confirmed in the course of adversarial proceedings, such as opposition or nullity proceedings, at least in respective first instance proceedings[177] or if the validity of the patent-in-suit is obvious for the district court or the appeal court deciding infringement of the patent-in-suit.[178]

11.135 In this regard, it should also be noted that the dismissal of a request for a preliminary injunction due to doubts as to the validity of the patent-in-suit might also affect subsequent

[173] Higher Regional Court of Düsseldorf, decision dated February 2, 2009, file no. 2 U 114/08, BeckRS 2009, 09402—*Staubsaugerfilterbeutel* (*Filter bag for vacuum cleaner*).

[174] Kühnen, *Handbuch der Patentverletzung* (5th ed.), margin no. 1562.

[175] Higher Regional Court of Düsseldorf, decision dated May 18, 2009, file no. 2 U 140/08, BeckRS 2009, 18590—*Holzhaecksler* (*Wood shredder*).

[176] Higher Regional Court of Düsseldorf InstGE 9, 140—*Olanzapin*; InstGE 12, 114—*Harnkatheterset* (*Urinary catheter set*).

[177] Higher Regional Court of Düsseldorf InstGE 12, 114—*Harnkatheterset* (*Urinary Catheter Set*); GRUR-RR 2011, 81—*Gleitsattelscheibenbremse II* (*Sliding caliper disc brake*); Higher Regional Court of Karlsruhe InstGE 11, 143—*VA-LCD-Fernseher* (*VA-LCD television*); Higher Regional Court of Düsseldorf, decision of June 10, 2010, file no. 2 U 131/09—*Tintenpatrone (2) IV* (*Ink cartridge (2) IV*) and District Court of Düsseldorf, decision dated May 27, 2011, file no. 4b O 84/11—*Kreissaegeblatt II* (*Circular saw-blade*), both available under www.Düsseldorfer-archiv.de.

[178] Higher Regional Court of Düsseldorf, decision dated May 18, 2009, file no. 2 U 140/08, BeckRS 2009, 18590—*Holzhaecksler* (*Wood shredder*).

main proceedings. It would only be consistent to stay such main proceedings if the court is not sufficiently convinced of the validity of the patent-in-suit. Therefore, concerns with respect to validity, including the chances of success in opposition or nullity proceedings, should be carefully assessed before filing a request for a preliminary injunction.

11.136 Finally, pending torpedo proceedings[179] can also be taken into account. Article 27 of the Brussels-I-Directive 44/2001 EG does not apply in preliminary proceedings—in other words, the issuance of a preliminary injunction is in principal possible even if a pending torpedo action would prevent the filing of a main infringement action.

11.137 **iv. Urgency** Another decisive factor that has to be considered when determining whether a preliminary injunction is appropriate is "urgency." The petitioner must enforce his claim without undue delay after he gained sufficient knowledge of the patent infringement. [180]

11.138 It should be noted that the prominent infringement courts apply different rules and time frames: the District Court of Munich I usually applies a strict one-month rule to gather the necessary substantiating evidence;[181] if this is not possible and the petitioner exceeds this one-month period, he has to explain and show in detail why he was not able to meet this deadline despite his best efforts.[182] The District Court of Düsseldorf[183] decides on urgency depending on the individual case and only considers the one-month-deadline as a rough guideline. The District Court of Mannheim has no strict time limit, but grants preliminary injunctions in any event only very rarely and only in exceptional cases, as main proceedings at the District Court of Mannheim are almost as fast as preliminary injunction proceedings.

11.139 A delay in filing the request for a preliminary injunction may be justified by[184] difficulty in establishing patent infringement (e.g., that complex examination and analysis of the infringing product was necessary), or difficulty in obtaining necessary evidence. Such reasons have to be demonstrated to the court in detail.[185]

11.140 Furthermore, according to the Higher Regional Court of Düsseldorf[186] the petitioner can wait for the outcome of a pending opposition or nullity proceedings before filing a request for a preliminary injunction, without this having a negative impact on the assessment of urgency. Thus, the petitioner would not eliminate urgency if he would first file an infringement complaint in the course of main proceedings, and only after prevailing in the opposition proceedings, file an additional request for a preliminary injunction.[187]

11.141 Whether urgency is affected if the petitioner does not file the request for preliminary injunction because he initiated settlement negotiations with the respondent is not assessed

[179] See Ch. 11, 11.119 "Torpedo Proceedings."

[180] Despite some discussion, demonstrating a swift reaction is still necessary and has not become obsolete as a result of the Enforcement Directive (Directive 2004/48/EC), see Higher Regional Court of Düsseldorf InstGE 10, 60—*Olanzapin II.*

[181] District Court of Munich I InstGE 3, 297—*Faelschungsverdacht I* (*Suspicion of plagiarism I*).

[182] Ibid.

[183] District Court of Düsseldorf, decision of January 16, 2009, file no. 4b O 284/08, available under www.Düsseldorfer-archiv.de.

[184] Kühnen, *Handbuch der Patentverletzung* (5th ed.), margin no. 1576.

[185] District Court of Munich I InstGE 3, 297—*Faelschungsverdacht I* (*Suspicion of plagiarism I*).

[186] Higher Regional Court of Düsseldorf InstGE 10, 124—*Inhalator* (*Inhaler*).

[187] Kühnen, *Handbuch der Patentverletzung* (5th ed.), margin no. 1581.

uniformly. The District Court of Munich I and the Munich Higher Regional Court[188] are of the opinion that settlement negotiations cannot prolong the time frame for urgency. Other courts [189] have held that urgency is not affected if the petitioner seriously and quickly conducts settlement discussion and files a request for preliminary injunction immediately after the discussions failed.[190]

(d) Procedure for Obtaining a Preliminary Injunction

If the court deems a request for a preliminary injunction as unfounded, it usually informs the petitioner informally of such assessment and thereby gives the petitioner the chance to withdraw his request before it is served on the respondent. Withdrawal is beneficial in that it allows the petitioner to proceed without warning the respondent of a possible subsequent action, as well as resulting in considerably lower costs. **11.142**

If the court comes to the conclusion that the claim is valid, it can issue the preliminary injunction *ex parte*—that is, without hearing the respondent. However, in patent infringement matters such *ex parte* injunctions are exceptional, because the court usually cannot reliably assess the question of infringement and validity of the patent-in-suit without hearing the respondent. Basically, an *ex parte* injunction is only granted in case of trade-fair matters or if the patent-in-suit is going to expire soon. If the court grants the preliminary injunction *ex parte*, it can usually be obtained within a few days or even within several hours. If a party expects another party to request a preliminary injunction, it can file a protective letter to avoid or at least to reduce the risk of an *ex parte* injunction.[191] It should, however, be noted that filing a protective letter might increase the risk of an *ex parte* injunction as the court might assume that the respondent comprehensively presented his arguments against a preliminary injunction without being able to cast doubts of the court as to the validity of the petitioner's claim. **11.143**

If the court is not willing to render a decision after a preliminary examination, it will schedule an oral hearing in order to give the respondent the opportunity to defend himself against the alleged infringement. The oral hearing usually takes place within a period of between three weeks and three months after filing of the request, depending on the individual case. If the case is complex because it, for example, involves a technical field that is rather difficult to understand, the oral hearing may be further delayed. Usually, the court renders its decision on the same day as the hearing. **11.144**

In order to enable the court to assess patent infringement, especially in technically complex cases, it might be helpful for the petitioner to provide the court with a reliable expert opinion supporting infringement of the patent. **11.145**

---

188 District Court of Munich I InstGE 3, 297—*Faelschungsverdacht I* (*Suspicion of plagiarism I*); Higher Regional Court of Munich InstGE 3, 301—*Faelschungsverdacht II* (*Suspicion of plagiarism II*).

189 Kühnen, *Handbuch der Patentverletzung* (5th ed.), margin no. 1583; see Higher Regional Court of Cologne GRUR-RR 2010, 448—*Vollstreckungsverzicht im Eilverfahren* (*Waiver of enforcement in summary proceedings*) in case the court granted a preliminary injunction but the applicant does not (yet) enforce said injunction because of settlement talks.

190 If, however, settlement negotiations started only when the preliminary injunction proceedings were already pending, Judge *Kühnen* (presiding judge at the Higher Regional Court of Düsseldorf) is of the opinion that such pending proceedings may not be slowed down, e.g., by requesting an extension of time limit to file briefs. See Kühnen, *Handbuch der Patentverletzung* (5th ed.), margin no. 1583.

191 See Ch. 11, 11.152 "Protective Letter."

11.146 In order to enforce a preliminary injunction, the petitioner has to serve it on the respondent or his attorney of record. This has to be done within one month after the injunction has been issued.[192] However, the petitioner is not obliged to enforce the preliminary injunction. In fact, obtaining a preliminary injunction without enforcing it can be used in order to induce the respondent to observe the patent-in-suit by only informally providing the preliminary injunction to the respondent. This way liability for any damages which the respondent might suffer as a result of an enforcement of the preliminary injunction can be avoided.[193]

11.147 The losing party can appeal the district court's decision to award or deny a preliminary injunction. In practice, such appeal usually only makes sense for the respondent.[194] Such appeal proceedings usually take between three and six months, depending on the caseload of the court. It should be noted that an appeal, principally, does not prevent the enforcement of the preliminary injunction until the court has decided on the appeal. Also, although civil procedural law provides for the possibility of staying enforcement during the opposition proceedings,[195] such a request is successful only in a very few exceptional cases.[196]

(e) Damage Claims for Unjustified Preliminary Injunctions

11.148 If the preliminary injunction has been granted by the court and has been enforced by the petitioner, but is lifted at a later time,[197] the petitioner is liable for damages incurred by the respondent.[198] The petitioner is also liable if, for example, the patent-in-suit is revoked after the preliminary injunction has been granted.

11.149 The petitioner has to compensate the respondent for all damages that occurred due to the enforcement of the preliminary injunction such as such as losses due to an interruption of the production or lost orders.[199] However, if the respondent has to remove the infringing products from a trade-fair stand, expenses in connection with the booth usually are not reimbursable.[200]

(f) Extraordinary Form of Preliminary Proceedings

11.150 **i. Concealed Preliminary Injunctions (*Schubladenverfuegung*)** The term "*Schubladenverfuegung*" (concealed preliminary injunction, literally "injunction in the drawer") refers to a preliminary injunction already obtained by the petitioner *ex parte* without the respondent knowing about it. Such a concealed preliminary injunction is strategically used by serving it only after sending a warning letter to the respondent.

---

192 § 929(2) of the Code of Civil Procedure.

193 See Ch. 11, 11.148 "Damage Claims for Unjustified Preliminary Injunction."

194 The petitioner can also file an appeal if his request for a preliminary injunction has been dismissed. However, such an appeal usually is of limited success and thus of little practical importance as the preliminary effect is lost in most cases, especially in short-term trade-fair matters.

195 §§ 936, 924(3)2, and 707 of the Code of Civil Procedure.

196 See, e.g., Higher Regional Court of Düsseldorf, decision of November 12, 2008, file no. 2 U 62/08, BeckRS 2011, 16058.

197 E.g., because there was no claim for an injunction and/or no grounds for an injunction.

198 § 945 of the Code of Civil Procedure.

199 Federal Court of Justice NJW 2006, 2767.

200 District Court of Düsseldorf InstGE 2, 157—*Duennbramme II* (*Thin slab II*), according to Kühnen, *Handbuch der Patentverletzung* (5th ed.), fn 1912 confirmed by the Higher Regional Court of Düsseldorf, decision of September 4, 2003, file no. 2 U 24/02.

In such a case, the petitioner cannot claim reimbursement of the attorney's costs in respect of the warning letter.[201] As *ex parte* injunctions are very rare in patent infringement cases, concealed preliminary injunctions are almost never used. 11.151

ii. Protective Letter (*Schutzschrift*) In Germany, if a person fears being named as a respondent in a request for a preliminary injunction, he has the option of filing a protective letter (*Schutzschrift*) in anticipation of the request for a preliminary injunction.[202] Although such protective letters have no statutory basis in German law, they are widely acknowledged by case law. 11.152

In a protective letter the respondent requests that the specified request for the issuance of a preliminary injunction be dismissed and provides defense arguments, usually in particular by arguing why the patent-in-suit is not infringed and why no grounds for granting a preliminary injunction are given. 11.153

The protective letter is usually filed with all courts that are likely to receive a request for preliminary injunctions—namely, usually all twelve district courts that are competent to hear patent-related cases. They are kept at the court for several months.[203] The adversary named in the protective letter is not informed of the filing of such protective letter. The protective letter is only served if the petitioner files a request for the issuance of a preliminary injunction. 11.154

A few years ago, a central register for protective letters (*Zentrales Schutzschriftenregister*) was installed to enable possible respondents to file their protective letters electronically. When electronically filing a protective letter, a fee of EUR 45.00 has to be paid. The protective letter is preserved for ninety days, and such preservation period can be repeatedly extended for further ninety-day periods. However, so far not all of the twelve district courts hearing patent related cases participate in the central register for protective letters. Furthermore, the protective letter might not be found by the court when entering onto the search form the parameters related to the individual case. Therefore, in patent law it is advisable to still file the protective letter in hard copy with the relevant courts. 11.155

If a request for issuance of a preliminary injunction is filed and the request is dismissed, the petitioner has to reimburse the costs for preparing the protective letter. The amount of attorney's fees that has to be reimbursed is calculated based on the value of litigation according to the Lawyer's Remuneration Act (*Rechtsanwaltsverguetungsgesetz*).[204] 11.156

(g) Cross-border Preliminary Injunctions

European law also provides for the possibility of obtaining cross-border preliminary injunctions by a court in a member state of the European Union. This means that, for example, a German court may be entitled to grant a preliminary injunction for not only infringement 11.157

[201] This is because the warning letter shall contribute to avoiding court proceedings and enabling the respondent to avoid negative cost implications by immediately acknowledging the claims raised by the petitioner. This can, however, no longer be achieved if the petitioner already turned to the court and obtained a preliminary injunction. See Federal Court of Justice GRUR 2010, 257—*Schubladenverfuegung* (*Concealed preliminary Injunction*); Higher Regional Court of Munich GRUR-RR 2006, 176—*Schubladenverfuegung* (*Concealed preliminary Injunction*); Higher Regional Court of Cologne NJOZ 2008, 957.

[202] I.e., without reference to any existing and pending proceedings.

[203] The preservation periods differ between the twelve district courts.

[204] See Ch. 11, 11.31 "Customary Costs for Legal Representation."

of the German part of a European patent in Germany but also for infringement of other national parts of a European patent in their respective European countries.

11.158 According to Article 31 of Regulation (EC) No. 44/2001, requests for preliminary injunctions can be filed with the courts of a member state even if the courts of another member state have jurisdiction as to the substance of the matter. For example, even though the courts of the Netherlands principally have jurisdiction with regard to the infringing acts committed in the Netherlands and infringing the Dutch part of a European patent (Arts. 2, 5(3) of Regulation (EC) No. 44/2001), a German court can grant a preliminary injunction against the infringing acts committed in the Netherlands.

11.159 However, as soon as the validity of the patent-in-suit becomes the *object* of the proceedings in contrast to being only a preliminary question, irrespective of whether this is raised in the complaint or in a brief of the defendant,[205] Article 22(4) of Regulation (EC) No. 44/2001 applies, providing for the exclusive jurisdiction of the courts to be in the country where the patent is registered. In July 2012 the European Court of Justice held[206] that Article 22(4) of Regulation (EC) No. 44/2001 is also applicable to Article 31. However, it has not been decided yet whether the applicability of Article 22(4) results in the inadmissibility of the pending lawsuit regarding patent infringement.

11.160 If a preliminary injunction is granted, the respondent can request that the petitioner is ordered to initiate main proceedings within a deadline to be determined by the court.[207] In such main proceedings, Article 22(4) of Regulation (EC) No. 44/2001 applies again if the validity of the patent-in-suit becomes the object of the infringement proceedings. In order to avoid a significant delay due to a stay of the infringement proceedings or even risk that the infringement complaint is deemed to be inadmissible by the court, the petitioner should consider initiating main proceedings not only in Germany but also in the country where the relevant part of the European patent is registered.

(h) Action for Defense against Enforcement

11.161 The bifurcation of infringement and validity proceedings in Germany allows for the possibility that a party will be ordered by the infringement court to, for example, cease and desist the manufacturing and selling of products or services or pay damages, while the patent found to be infringed will later turn out to be actually invalid. In cases where the patentee has not yet executed the infringement verdict, the party found to be infringing can block the execution of the infringement decision by filing an action for defense against enforcement pursuant to § 767 of the Code of Civil Procedure. An action for defense against enforcement can only be filed if the asserted patent was invalidated after the conclusion of the main proceedings, resulting in a situation where such invalidation could not have been raised as a defense in the regular proceedings.

11.162 An action for defense against enforcement may be admissible not only in cases where the asserted patent has been invalidated in its entirety but also in cases where the scope of the patent has been amended in such a way that the product or process held as infringing would fall outside the narrowed scope. However, if the validity proceedings only result in

[205] ECJ, decision of July 13, 2006, file no. C-4/03—*GAT v. LuK.*

[206] ECJ, decision of July 12, 2012, file no. C-616/10—*Solvay v. Honeywell.*

[207] § 926 of the Code of Civil Procedure.

supporting a different claim construction that would have justified a different outcome in the infringement proceedings, it would not be a reason for an action for defense against enforcement under § 767 of the Code of Civil Procedure.[208]

A party seeking defense against enforcement can accelerate the proceedings by filing for temporary suspension of enforcement pursuant § 769 of the Code of Civil Procedure. Temporary suspension can be made subject to a security bond to be posted by the party seeking the suspension. **11.163**

(i) **Action for Restitution** An action for defense against enforcement will be too late in cases where the patentee has already executed the court decision. In such situations, the party against whom the decision has been executed can only file an action for restitution against the patentee, asking the infringement court to reopen the case and to reverse its own final decision.[209] Such an action for restitution finds its legal basis in an analogues application of § 580(6) of the Code of Civil Procedure, which entitles a person to an action of restitution if a "judgment of an ordinary court . . . or of an administrative court on which the judgment is based is overturned by another final and binding judgment." With an action for restitution, the person subject to the infringement decision aims for a resumption of the proceedings and will usually ask for a reimbursement of the statutory fees and a return of damages paid, if any. Also, compensation for damages incurred due to the execution of an injunction order or due to the recall and removal of goods from circulation may be claimed.[210] **11.164**

As in the action for defense against enforcement, an action for restitution may also be admissible not only in cases where the asserted patent has been invalidated in its entirety but also in cases where the scope of the patent has been amended in such a way that the product or process held as infringing would fall outside the narrowed scope. However, if the validity proceedings merely support a different claim construction that would have justified a different outcome in the infringement proceedings, it would not be a reason for an action for restitution.[211] **11.165**

The action for restitution is only available if the grounds for restitution—that is, the final ruling on invalidity of the asserted patent—could not have been raised during the ordinary proceedings.[212] Furthermore, the action for restitution is subject to certain time limitations. It can, in principle, only be filed within one month from the knowledge of the grounds for restitution.[213] A second time limitation is an absolute five-year deadline triggered by the invalidation of the patent, irrespective of knowledge or negligent lack of knowledge by the party seeking to file the action. **11.166**

---

208 T. Kühnen, *Patent Litigation Proceedings in Germany* (7th ed., 2014), margin no. 2223.

209 Federal Court of Justice GRUR 2012, 753—*Tintenpatrone III*; Federal Court of Justice GRUR 2010, 996—*Bordako*.

210 Johann Pitz, *Patentverletzungsverfahren* (2d ed., 2010), margin no. 198.

211 Kühnen, *Patent Litigation Proceedings in Germany*, margin no. 2239.

212 § 582 of the Code of Civil Procedure.

213 Knowledge of the invalidation of the patent will be assumed if the alleged infringer was also a party in the invalidation action. Otherwise, a party may also be able to file an action for restitution after the lapse of the one-month period, as the Federal Court of Justice held that a party found guilty of infringement usually has no duty to continuously confirm the validity of the patent right asserted against it; see Federal Court of Justice GRUR 2010, 996—*Bordako*.

12

JAPAN

A. Jurisdiction

1. Subject Matter Jurisdiction and Venue

12.01 In the course of the amendment of the Japanese Code of Civil Procedure in 1996, the rules on subject matter jurisdiction for patent infringement cases[1] were changed, and exclusive jurisdiction for such cases was granted to the District Courts in Tokyo and Osaka.[2] The Tokyo District Court has jurisdiction for the court districts of Tokyo, Nagoya, Sendai, and Sapporo,[3] while the Osaka District Court has jurisdiction for all court districts west of Nagoya—namely, Osaka, Hiroshima, Fukuoka, and Takamatsu.[4] To increase the technical expertise at both the Tokyo and the Osaka District Courts, special divisions within the court specializing in patent and intellectual property law were introduced in 1996.[5] All appeal cases are heard by the Intellectual Property High Court located in Tokyo. Decisions rendered by the Intellectual Property High Court can be appealed to the Supreme Court.[6]

2. International Jurisdiction

12.02 Japanese law introduced codified rules on court jurisdiction in an international context into the Japanese Code of Civil Procedure in 2011.[7] Accordingly, Japanese courts have jurisdiction over:

- actions concerning property rights as long as the subject matter of the claim is located in Japan, or where the action is to claim payment of money and any seizable property of the defendant is located in Japan[8]
- actions relating to a tort as long as the tort took place in Japan.[9]

---

[1] Besides patent infringement cases, exclusive jurisdiction was also established in the fields of utility model, topography, and software copyright infringement cases.

[2] Minjisoshōhō (Japanese Code of Civil Procedure), Law No. 109 of 1996, § 6.

[3] Japanese Code of Civil Procedure, § 6-1(1).

[4] Japanese Code of Civil Procedure, § 6-1(2).

[5] See Table 12.1.

[6] The Supreme Court has issued a number of groundbreaking decisions in the area of patent law and intellectual property law in the last few decades. That said, the Supreme Court will, in the vast majority of appeals, limit its role to formally confirming the decision of the IP High Court, functionally similar to the role the US Supreme Court assumes when denying certiorari. Since 2000, the Supreme Court has heard and issued a substantial opinion in 23 cases related to patent law.

[7] Law No. 36 of 2011.

[8] Japanese Code of Civil Procedure, § 3-3(3).

[9] Japanese Code of Civil Procedure, § 3-3(8).

While these statutes give some guidance on patent disputes, it is helpful to review the body of case law, which has developed in the last thirty years. The first major Japanese case on international court jurisdiction was the *Malaysian Airlines* case decided by the Supreme Court on October 16, 1981.[10] The court developed the doctrine of "reverse presumption," under which Japanese courts shall assume international jurisdiction as long as the same court would be competent to hear the case under the general national jurisdiction rules stipulated in Japanese Code of Civil Procedure, §§ 4 and 5. In the following years, lower courts complemented the doctrine of "reverse presumption" by assuming discretion to exceptionally decline jurisdiction in cases where a judge considered jurisdiction to be exorbitant in light of the parties' interests and the desire for expeditious proceedings.[11] Such complementary doctrine of "special circumstances" was confirmed by the Supreme Court in 1997.[12]

The Japanese standpoint on international jurisdiction in questions of patent validity had been answered by the judiciary in the *Coral Sand* case, which was decided by the Tokyo District Court in 2003.[13] A Japanese company selling and exporting health products containing coral fossil powders in the United States had asserted the invalidity of a US patent on composites including coral powder held by another Japanese company. The court held that its decision could not affect the validity of the US patent and thus could not bind the parties in the case.[14] **12.03**

The act of infringement, on the other hand, has been generally considered as a tort being subject to ordinary jurisdictional rules developed since *Malaysian Airlines*. The Supreme Court took the opportunity to review the Japanese approach to international jurisdiction in infringement cases in the *Cardreader* case, decided on September 26, 2002, which concerned a dispute between two Japanese parties on the infringement of a US patent on an FM signal demodulator.[15] The US patent was the only patent covering the invention, as no Japanese or other parallel patent existed. Presumably because both parties' habitual residence or principal place of business was in Japan,[16] the international jurisdiction of Japanese courts was not disputed, and the judges implicitly assumed international jurisdiction of Japanese courts.[17] The Supreme Court therefore moved on and decided the case, applying both Japanese and US patent law. The plaintiff had requested the Japanese court to award both: **12.04**

- injunctive relief and a claim for destruction of the defendant's products
- compensatory damages.

---

[10] Saikō Saibansho (Sup. Ct.) October 16, 1981 (O) No. 130, 35-7 Saikō Saibansho Minji Hanreishū (Minshū) (1981), 1224 = JAIL No. 26 (1983), 122—*Goto et al v. Malaysian Airlines Systems*; for a detailed English summary of the facts of the case and the court's holding, please refer to, e.g., Akihiro Hironaka, "Jurisdictional Theory Made in Japan: Convergence of U.S. and Continental European Approaches," 37 *Vand. J. Transnat'l L.* (2004): 1317, 1327–29.

[11] Yuko Nishitani, "Intellectual Property in Japanese Private International Law," 48 *Japanese Annual of International Law* (2005): 88.

[12] S. Ct. November 11, 1997 (O) 1660, 51-10 Minshū (1997), 4055 = JAIL No. 41 (1998), 117—*Family Co. Ltd. v. Shin Miyahara.*

[13] Tokyo District Court, October 16, 2003, Hei 14 (wa) No. 1943, 1874 Hanrei Jihō (2003), 23—*Coral Sands.*

[14] Ibid.

[15] S. Ct., September 26, 2002, Hei 12 (Ju) No. 580, 56-7 Minshū (2002), 1551 = JAIL No. 46 (2003), 168—*Cardreader.*

[16] Ibid. 1556.

[17] Nishitani, "Intellectual Property in Japanese Private International Law," 92.

12.05 The Supreme Court held that the claim for injunctive relief and destruction should be decided under US law, as—under the principle of reasonableness—the law of the country where the patent is registered—namely, the law of the United States—should rule. Under US patent law, the patentee could have a claim for injunctive relief for the active inducement of the US subsidiary by the Japanese parent company, the named defendant. However, the court held that extending such a claim under US law to Japan would result in an undue expansion of the effect of a US patent to Japan, which would violate Japanese public policy pursuant to the Japanese Act on the Application of Laws § 33.[18]

12.06 At the same time, the Supreme Court held that the second claim for damages raised by the plaintiff not only involved patent law questions but could also be classified as a remedy against the infringement of private property under civil law. Pursuant to the Japanese Act on the Application of Laws § 11(1)[19] such civil-law claim was to be decided under the *lex loci delicti*, being the place where the directly infringing act was committed and the result of infringement occurred. Under such standard, US law should be applied, as the defendant could be liable for inducing patent infringement when exporting its products into the United States in order to have them sold there by its subsidiary. At the same time, the court held that Japanese law should, pursuant to the Japanese Act on the Application of Laws § 11(2), cumulatively be applied in order to confirm the result derived by the application of US law. Japanese patent law does not have a provision allowing for extraterritorial application similar to the US standard for active inducement. Thus, the Japanese patent law would not support a claim for damages against the defendant, and the claim for damages was denied.

12.07 The solution adopted by the Supreme Court on international jurisdiction and applicable law received mixed reviews amongst Japanese commentators. Supreme Court Judge Masao Fujii dissented from the majority opinion and claimed that the provision of the Japanese Act on the Application of Laws § 11(2) being designed to protect Japan's public policy, should have been interpreted more widely and should not have precluded the court from awarding damages for active inducement of infringement, as active inducement can be considered a tortuous joint wrongful act pursuant to Japanese Civil Code, § 719.[20] While the rather restrictive cumulative application of Japanese patent law may indeed have been against the intention of the legislature, the result derived under such an application seems to be supported by practical considerations, as (1) it seems rather impractical to maintain separate rules for the different remedies available under the same act of infringement, and (2) in the vast majority of infringement proceedings, the defendant will raise an invalidity defense, which will have to be resolved by the court and under the laws of the country in which the patent in question is registered. While very different in its legal reasoning and

---

[18] Hōrei (Japanese Act on the Application of Laws), Law No. 10 of 1898; § 33 (prior to the laws revision in 2005) has been translated as follows: "Where a case shall be governed by a foreign law but application of those rules would be contrary to public policy (*ordre public*), those rules shall not apply."

[19] Japanese Act on the Application of Laws § 11 (as of 2002):

(1) The formation and effect of claims arising from agency by necessity (negotiorum gestio), unjust enrichment, and tort shall be governed by the law of the place where the events causing the claims occurred.

(2) The preceding paragraph shall not apply where the events that comprise the tort occurred abroad and do not constitute a tort under Japanese law.

[20] Minpō (Japanese Civil Code), Law No. 89 of 1896; see Nishitani, "Intellectual Property in Japanese Private International Law," 105.

basis, the Japanese approach to international jurisdiction and choice of law finds itself in principle, as a result, in line with the current approaches predominantly taken by courts in the United States and in Europe.

In 2010, the IP High Court explicitly confirmed for the first time that Japanese courts may also assume international jurisdiction for a foreign entity if such an entity offers a product infringing a Japanese patent through the internet even if the act of shipping and importing the product to Japan is handled by a third party.[21] In handing down its decision, the IP High Court had reversed the decision of the Osaka District Court[22] and held that an offer to transfer resulting in an act of patent infringement in Japan is to be regarded as direct patent infringement, allowing Japanese courts to assume international jurisdiction. **12.08**

3. Results of Judicial Reform

In the course of the far-reaching reforms of the Japanese intellectual property law system initiated by the former Prime Minister Koizumi in 2004, the jurisdiction rules for all intellectual property law areas were amended.[23] Most notably in the field of patent law was the enactment of the Intellectual Property High Court, a division geographically located within the Tokyo High Court, which was entrusted to hear all appeals in the area of patent law and other intellectual property laws. The Intellectual Property High Court assumed the function of the previously installed divisions at the Tokyo High Court and the Osaka High Court, which had handled appeal cases in the field of intellectual property law until 2004.[24] The Intellectual Property High Court assumed its function in April 2004 and was initially staffed with eighteen judges,[25] who were divided into five divisions.[26] Table 12.1 provides a breakdown of the number of divisions and judges established for intellectual property law disputes in Tokyo and Osaka. **12.09**

As shown in Table 12.1, the judges at the Intellectual Property High Court and the intellectual property law divisions at the Tokyo and the Osaka District Courts are supported by investigation officers, also referred to as legal research officers (*Saibansho chōsakan*), who are predominantly responsible for the analysis of technical details and backgrounds.[27] Many legal research officers are retired members of the patent examination divisions of the **12.10**

---

[21] IP High Court, September 15, 2010, Hei 22 (ne) No. 10001, 1340 Hanrei Times, 265. See in detail: Kotaru Kimura, "Hanrei to jitsumu No. 402: Kankoku hōjin ni taisuru Nipponkoku tokkyo-ken no shingai o shuchō suru uttae no kokusai saiban kankatsu ga kōtei sa reta jirei," 61(1) *Chizai Kanri* (2012): 85.

[22] Osaka District Court, November 26, 2008, Hei 20 (wa) No. 9732, 1326 Hanrei Times, 267.

[23] Law No. 108/2003.

[24] The decision to appoint the Intellectual Property High Court and thus a division of the Tokyo High Court as an exclusive appellate court in intellectual property infringement cases was—not surprisingly—greeted with little enthusiasm in Osaka, as the Osaka High Court had been home to an appellate division which became redundant after the enactment of the Intellectual Property High Court. The installation of the Intellectual Property High Court was criticized as premature and not appropriate for the Japanese judiciary system by a protest note from the Osaka Bar Association, see Nahoko Ono, "In Search of Positive Developments in International Intellectual Property Policy—Intellectual Property Litigation System Reform in Japan", *World Intellectual Property Journal* (2005): 473.

[25] Katsumi Shinohara, "Outline of the Intellectual Property High Court in Japan," *AIPPI* (2005): 131, 136; see further Masaaki Kondō and Tomoyoshi Saito, *Chitekizaisankankeinihō/Rodōshinpanhō* (2004), 17.

[26] See the website of the Intellectual Property High Court for further information on the court's structure (http://www.ip.courts.go.jp/eng/aboutus/organization/index.html).

[27] Ryu Takabayashi, "Chitekizaisankenkankeisoshō ni okeru saibanshochōsakan no yakuwari," 20 *Nihon Kōgyōshoyūken Hōgakukainenpō* (1996): 37.

Table 12.1 Japanese court divisions with subject matter jurisdiction for intellectual property law*

	Tokyo District Court			Osaka District Court			Tokyo High Court		
	Divisions for IP law	Judges	Inv. Officer	Divisions for IP law	Judges	Inv. Officer	Divisions for IP law	Judges	Inv. Officer
1997	1	8	5	1	3	3	3	10	9
1998	2	10	5	1	4	3	3	10	9
1999	3	12	7	1	5	3	3	10	9
2000	3	15	7	1	5	3	3	11	9
2001	3	15	7	1	5	3	3	12	9
2002	3	15	7	1	5	3	4	16	11
2003	3	15	7	1	5	3	4	16	11
2004	4	16	7	2	6	3	4	18	11

* Tetsuro Nakayoshi, "Chitekizaisan soshō no genjyō to Heisei 16 Nen 4 Gatsu kara no atarashii seido," 24 *Law & Technology* (2004): 42, 44; the number of divisions, judges, and legal research officers has basically remained unchanged since 2004.

Japanese Patent Office.[28] While legal research officers have been used in patent infringement proceedings for a few years,[29] the judiciary reforms increased the possibilities for them to actively influence the infringement trial.

12.11 Since the establishment of the Intellectual Property High Court in April 2004, judges can furthermore use a pool of technical advisors (*Senmoniin*) in any advisory capacity.[30] The role of the technical advisor is regulated in Japanese Code of Civil Procedure, § 92-2; accordingly, technical advisors are involved in the infringement proceedings during evidence examination as well as during mediation discussions.[31] The pool of technical advisors consists of renowned technicians, especially university professors and researchers from public institutions or private companies as well as patent attorneys.[32] Technical advisors are appointed for a term of two years. In 2006, 128 technical advisors were appointed at courts in Tokyo, and fifty-one technical advisors were appointed at the Osaka District

[28] Shinohara, "Outline of the Intellectual Property High Court in Japan," 138; as of 2006, ten of the eleven legal research officers at the IP High Court were former members of the examination divisions or the appellate divisions of the Japan Patent Office (JPO), while the remaining legal research officer was a patent attorney, see Katsumi Shinohara, "A Retrospective and a Prospective Look at the First Year of the Intellectual Property High Court," *AIPPI* (2006): 195.

[29] Noburo Nakashima, "Meisaisho no kisaifubi no ihōsei ni tsuite," in *Miyake Misao Sensei Kijuukinen* (1986), 173.

[30] Hiroyuki Matsumoto, "Grundfragen und aktuelle Probleme des Beweisrechts in Japan," *ZZP* (2008): 203, 212.

[31] Katsunori Takechi, "An Overview of the Law to Amend Part of the Code of Civil Procedure," AIPPI (2004): 175, 177; Yoichiro Komatsu, "Senmonnin—Himitsu-hojimeirei—Saiban no kokaiteishi nado no shinseido e no taiyō: Tokuchō—soshō—funsokankei no mōkadai to kongo no taiyō," 55(3) *Chizai Kanri* (2005): 323, 325.

[32] Experts appointed between April 2004 and February 2014 had the following occupations: university professor (64%), patent attorney (16%), researcher at public institutions (10%), and researcher at private institutions (10%); see the website of the IP High Court, http://www.ip.courts.go.jp/eng/documents/expert/index.html#q3.

Court.[33] The main responsibility of technical advisors is to provide an independent basis for enabling judges to understand the facts of technically complex situations in patent infringement cases by written or oral explanations. Technical advisors are usually appointed on a case-by-case basis based on their specific industry knowledge. To reduce the pressure on a single individual expert, up to three technical advisors are designated to each case.[34] The contribution of technical advisors has been requested in particular during complex cases tried at the Intellectual Property High Court.[35]

By creating special patent litigation venues and concentrating patent litigation at only two district courts, which are in addition supported by technical advisors and legal research officers, the Japanese legislature certainly has achieved a higher degree of continuity and thus made patent litigation more reliable and predictable. At the same time, the Japanese judge rotation system, which obliges even senior judges to rotate between courts and legal areas every few years (the usual period of time spent at one court is three years), undermines the concentration efforts made by the legislature, as judges who have gained experience in patent litigation matters continue to be replaced by judges inexperienced in the area of patent law, who then again require time to gain the level of experience their predecessors had. **12.12**

B. Parties

1. Standing to Sue

In patent infringement proceedings, both the patentee and the licensee to a registered exclusive license ("*senyō*-licensee")[36] have standing to claim injunctive relief and damages.[37] It used to be customary for the patentee and the *senyō*-licensee to jointly file for the patent infringement lawsuit.[38] Thus, significant confusion was caused when the Tokyo District Court in 2002 denied a patentee who had granted a registered *senyō*-license standing to sue for injunctive relief.[39] The court based its decision on the fact that a patentee who has granted a *senyō*-license is neither entitled to continued use of the patent nor entitled to grant further licenses of that patent.[40] The district court's decision, which was in line with some opinions voiced in academic literature,[41] was upheld on appeal by the Tokyo High **12.13**

[33] Shinohara, "A Retrospective and a Prospective Look at the First Year of the Intellectual Property High Court," 212.

[34] Ibid. 213.

[35] Until 2006 80% of cases in which experts were used were cases tried at the IP High Court; see ibid.

[36] A *senyō*-licence has to be registered pursuant to Tokkyo Hō (Japanese Patent Act), Law No. 121 of 1959 § 27(1)ii.

[37] Yamaguchi District Court, February 28, 1963, Sho 34 (wa) No. 250, 142 Hanrei Times (1963), 184—*Bojen*; the court concluded that the limitation of the right of a patentee and licensor to seek injunctive relief and damages could hardly be justified also after granting an exclusive license. Such a stance has been confirmed in a variety of court opinions, see Tokyo District Court, March 18, 1964, Sho 36 (wa) No. 5836, 377 Hanrei Jihō, 63 on utility models; see further Nagoya District Court, July 25, 1974, Sho 48 (moshi) No. 707, 761 Hanrei Jihō, 99 on registered designs; see in addition Shunji Miyama and Nobuo Matsumura, *Chitekizaisanken Soshō: Jitsumu kaisetsu* (2d ed., 2005), 28; Nobuo Monya, *Tokkyohō 50ko* (1998), 205.

[38] Klaus Hinkelmann, *Gewerblicher Rechtsschutz in Japan* (2004), 293.

[39] Tokyo District Court, November 28, 2002, Hei 11 (wa) No. 12382.

[40] See Shigeshi Tanaka and Noriko Itai, "Decision of the Supreme Court 17 June 2005: Exercise of Injunction Rights of Patentees who have granted Exclusive Licenses of Patent Rights," *AIPPI* (2005): 295, 298.

[41] Yoshiaki Nishida, *Chitekizaisanken: tokkyo jitsuyō shin'an ishō chosakuken shōhyō fusei kyōsō*, Minji Bengō to Saiban Jitsumu No. 8 (1998), 338.

Court.[42] However, in 2004, the Tokyo High Court had reversed its position in another proceeding and had again allowed a patentee who had granted a *senyō*-license to file for injunctive relief.[43] This later decision of the Tokyo High Court was confirmed by the Supreme Court in 2005.[44]

12.14 Case law and academics are divided over the questions of whether licensees of exclusive not-registered licenses and non-exclusive licensees have standing to sue. The spectrum of opinions include a proposed denial of standing rights for both injunctive relief and damages,[45] denial of standing rights for non-exclusive licensees while granting standing rights only for exclusive non-registered licensees,[46] grant of standing to sue only for damages and only for exclusive non-registered licensees,[47] grant of standing to sue for damages for all licensees while limiting the right to sue for injunctive relief to non-registered exclusive licensees,[48] and grant of standing to sue for both injunctive relief and for damages to all licensees.[49] Not only are academics widely divided, but case law has also over time developed different positions in assessing the question of who has standing to sue. Until a judicial reform in 1969, exclusive non-registered licensees were entitled to sue for injunctive relief. However, at present most academics and case law support the interpretation that exclusive non-registered licensees are in general entitled to sue for injunctive relief and damages, while non-exclusive licensees are not granted such right to sue.

2. Defendants

12.15 Every person that indirectly or directly conducts an unauthorized use of a patent pursuant to Japanese Patent Act, § 2(3) can be named as a defendant in a patent infringement lawsuit.[50] Persons or entities soliciting or assisting in patent-infringing conduct can be named as defendants as long as their conduct satisfies the threshold for indirect infringement pursuant to Japanese Patent Act, § 101.[51] If multiple persons or entities jointly conduct patent infringement, all infringers are in principle jointly liable in accordance with Japanese Civil Code, § 709 (*Kyōdō Fuhō Kōi*).[52] However, in light of the Tokyo District Court's decision in the *Overlaykōhō* case, joint tortfeasors may only be eligible to be named as defendants if their conduct satisfies the threshold of indirect infringement pursuant to Japanese Patent Act, § 101. Especially when considering the joint liability of network providers or other entities in situations where a rather high number of parties may have contributed in

[42] Tokyo High Court, November 14, 2004, Hei 13 (ne) 107.

[43] Tokyo High Court, February 27, 2004, Hei 15 (ne) No. 1223, Hanrei Jihō 1870, 84—affirming Tokyo District Court decision from February 6, 2003, Hei 13 (wa) No. 21278, Hanrei Jihō 1870, 107.

[44] S. Ct. June 17, 2005, Hei 16 (uke) No. 997, 1900 Hanrei Jihō (2005), 139 = IIC 2006, 221—*FlexX*; see also Hiroyuki Morisaki and Makoto Okada, "Commentary on Article 100 Patent Act," in Nobuhiro Nakayama and Naoki Koizumi (eds.), *Shin Chūkai Tokkyhō* (2011), 1425.

[45] Yoshinobu Someno, "Tokkyoshinngaisoshō ni okeru jisshisha no soshōtekikaku," in Eizo Hattori (ed.), *Kigyōhō kenkyū sōkan jisshūnen kinen ronbunshu* (1964), 205, 213.

[46] Nobuhiro Nakayama, "Tsūjō Jisshiken no shingai," in *Kokusaikōgōushoyūkenhō no shomondai: Nakamatsu Kannosuke Sensei Tsuitōronbunshū* (1976), 483.

[47] Zennosuke Nakagawa and Hajime Kaneko, *Tokkyo-Shōhyō-Shosakuken* (1972), 443.

[48] At the same time, Toyosaki suggested granting standing for a claim for injunctive relief to the licensee of a non-registered exclusive license, see Mitsue Toyosaki, *Kōgyō Shoyūkenhō* (1980), 298.

[49] Tsunekazu Kojima, "Kōgyōshoyūken to Sashitomeseikyūken," 47(4) *Hōritsu Jihō* (1975): 41, 44.

[50] Miyama and Matsumura, *Chitekizaisanken Soshō*, 38.

[51] Tokyo District Court, August 17, 2004, Hei 16 (wa) No. 9208, 1873 Jihō (2004), 153—*Overlaykōhō*.

[52] Morisaki and Okada, "Commentary on Article 100 Patent Act," 1441; Yoichi Maeda, "Shōhyōkenshingai ni tsuite—Shōhyōhō 38Jyō 1Ko Tadashigakisho ni yoru songaigakusantei oyobi Senkōsoshōnohikokuto no Kyōdōfuhōkōiseritsu ni yoru baishinsaimu no Fushinseirentaikankei ga mitomerareta jirei," 1864

some degree to patent infringement, it will be necessary to assess the precise contribution of each joint tortfeasor to determine whether such party could be named as a defendant.

In cases of patent infringement conducted by a legal entity, the construction of such an entity determines whether representatives or employees of the entity can be personally liable. In any event, the legal entity itself can be named as a defendant. Representatives of a legal entity can be personally liable pursuant to Japanese Companies Act, § 429 in cases of willful or grossly negligent conduct.[53] **12.16**

C. Costs

Patent infringement proceedings cause court and attorneys' fees. While the court fees are in general to be borne by the party losing the trial, all other costs, such as attorney's fees, travel costs, costs for experts' opinions, etc., are typically borne by the party which commissioned such costs. **12.17**

1. Court Fees

Court Fees are to be calculated pursuant to the Japanese Act on Costs of Civil Procedure, § 4[54] in connection with Japanese Code of Civil Procedure, §§ 8 and 9. As shown in Table 12.2, court fees are calculated based on the subject matter value to be determined by the court. **12.18**

The subject matter value in infringement proceedings is computed pursuant to the value of the requested injunction plus the requested claim for damages.[55] Court fees have to be paid upfront by the plaintiff.[56] However, pursuant to the Japanese Act on Costs of Civil Procedure, § 61, the losing party has to cover the court fees. Thus, if the plaintiff prevails, the losing defendant will have to reimburse the court fees to the plaintiff. Having said so, the court has authority to impose on the prevailing party those court fees that are incurred **12.19**

Table 12.2 Statutory court fees

Subject matter value	Court Fees
Up to 1,000,000 yen	1,000 yen for each 100,000 yen subject matter value
More than 1,000,000 yen	1,000 yen for each 200,000 yen subject matter value
More than 5,000,000 yen	2,000 yen for each 500,000 yen subject matter value
More than 10,000,000 yen	3,000 yen for each 1,000,000 yen subject matter value
More than 1,000,000,000 yen	10,000 yen for each 5,000,000 yen subject matter value
More than 5,000,000,000 yen	10,000 yen for each 10,000,000 yen subject matter value

Hanrei Jihō (2004): 215; see regarding joint liability in case of contributory infringement Hisao Shiomi, "Kansetsushingai ni okeru "nomi" no kaishaku to kyōdō fuhōkōi no seihi," 1083 *Jurist* (1996): 104.

[53] Kaisha-hō (Japanese Companies Act), Law No. 86 of 2005; see further Ichiro Takano, *Kaishahō Jitsumu Handobukko* (2006), 342.

[54] Minjisoshōhiyōnadō ni kansuru hōritsu (Japanese Act on Costs of Civil Procedure), Law No. 40 of 1971.

[55] David W. Hill and Shinichi Murata, "Patent Litigation in Japan," 1 *Akron Intellectual Property L.J.* (2007): 141, 160.

[56] Hironau Kaneko, *Minjisoshōhiyō no futangesoku* (1998), 3.

due to legal actions later deemed unnecessary.[57] In addition, the court can also impose court fees on the prevailing party if such party delayed the proceedings by a late submission of evidence or otherwise exceeded deadlines set by the court.[58]

2. Attorneys' Fees

12.20 A substantial cost factor other than court fees are costs incurred by the parties for advice and representation by attorneys (*bengoshi*) and patent attorneys (*benrishi*) as well as for the preparation of expert opinions. Such costs will customarily have to be borne by each party. However, in some situations the court will award the plaintiff's attorneys' fees as part of the damage award (approximately ten percent of the damages as a whole).[59] At the same time there has been a tendency for domestic companies to be hesitant to disclose their attorneys' fees and thus refrain from claiming reimbursement of their fees.[60]

12.21 Attorneys' and patent attorneys' fees are charged at an hourly rate or based on a fixed representation fee agreed upon when commencing the lawsuit. A fixed representation fee will customarily increase by 5 percent to 15 percent in case of success. Generally, Japanese companies prefer a fixed representation fee, while foreign companies prefer to be charged on a time basis. Depending on the complexity of the case, fixed representation fees range from 5 million to 20 million yen. In extraordinarily complex situations, representation fees of up to 50 million yen have been heard of. Generally, the higher the fixed representation fee is, the relatively lower the success fee will be.[61] Also, in cases of time-based representation, it is rare for attorneys' and patent attorneys' fees to exceed 50 million yen.[62]

D. Procedure

1. Procedure Overview and Pending Time

12.22 Improper accusations brought in the form of warning letters or filing of lawsuits can result in declaratory judgment actions, damage claims, and claims for litigation costs. Thus, it is recommendable to prepare the evidence analysis as far in advance as possible before initiating legal actions.

12.23 Similar to German, though different from US procedure, the initial complaint has to provide sufficient details of the alleged infringement. At the very minimum, the initial complaint has to identify the alleged product or process, and provide an infringement analysis by submitting a comparison of the elements of the alleged infringer's product or process with the elements of the asserted claim(s). To substantiate such an analysis, the patentee should provide available evidence, such as charts or structures of the product/process alleged as infringing. Further, the patentee should provide an initial estimate of the monetary damages suffered due to the infringement.[63]

---

[57] Japanese Code of Civil Procedure, § 62.

[58] Ibid.

[59] February 27, 1969, Sho 41 (O) No. 280, 23-2 Minshū (1969), 44—*Hyakusenmu*.

[60] Nodoka Nakamura, "IP Karishobun Case in Japan," Presentation 2007 (on file with author), 10.

[61] Hill and Murata, "Patent Litigation in Japan," 160.

[62] Ibid. 161; Michal Elmer and C. Gregory Gramenopoulos, *Global Patent Litigation* (2014), 710, providing an estimate of the average cost in complex cases amounting to US$300,000 to US$500,000.

[63] Mami Hino and Naho Ebata, in Eiji Katayama (ed.), *Japanese Patent Litigation* (2012), 111.

After admittance by the court, the complaint is served by the court to the defendant. Service of the complaint to a Japanese defendant usually requires a few weeks.[64] When serving the complaint, the court will also set the date of the first oral hearing, usually about four to six weeks after service. The defendant has to file a reply to the complaint by the deadline of one week before this first oral hearing. In such an initial reply, the defendant has to admit or deny facts asserted by the plaintiff. When the defendant denies facts asserted in the complaint, he should provide specific reasons for such a denial or state that there are reasonable grounds such as confidentiality concerns preventing the defendant from disclosing an analysis of his own products or processes.[65] In cases where the defendant cannot verify or deny certain facts, he should state that he is unaware of such facts. Further, the defendant should provide counterarguments in the initial reply, which may include an attack on the validity of the asserted patent. **12.24**

The infringement proceedings are conducted through a series of briefs, which are often presented at somewhat informal oral hearings.[66] Depending on the number of briefs presented, the court may schedule up to ten or more informal oral hearings. Within one year of the filing of the complaint, the court will usually render an interlocutory decision on infringement and validity. If the court finds the patent infringed and valid, additional hearings are scheduled to allow adjudication of damages. The infringement procedure is concluded with a final formal oral hearing, during which, however, no substantial issues are discussed. **12.25**

2. Evidence Collection

The plaintiff has to demonstrate infringement of a patent during the enforcement proceedings.[67] A complaint must include facts to substantiate patent infringement claims.[68] In the past, numerous observers of Japanese civil procedure have mentioned the difficulty in obtaining necessary evidence possessed or controlled only by the infringer.[69] Thus, it did not come as a surprise that an invigoration of the evidence collection process became one of the main objectives during the reform of the Japanese civil procedure system.[70] This objective resulted in extended duties of document production during litigation, which were codified in Japanese Code of Civil Procedure, § 220 as well as in Japanese Patent Act, §§ 104-2 and 105. To enable potentially infringed parties to obtain a better assessment of their legal position prior to filing a lawsuit and to foster the preparation of infringement proceedings, the **12.26**

[64] In case of serving the complaint on a non-Japanese party, the court cannot serve the complaint directly but has to go through the Ministry of Foreign Affairs or the resident embassy, which may require several months.

[65] Ryu Takabayashi, *Hyōjun tokkyo-hō (Patent Law From the Ground Up)* (5th ed., 2014), 281.

[66] Formally, such hearings are scheduled to allow for preparation of the formal hearing; thus these preparatory proceedings are not open to the general public and are held in a conference room at the court rather than in the official courtroom.

[67] Hill and Murata, "Patent Litigation in Japan," 176; see further Kuo-Chang Huang, *Introducing Discovery into Civil Law* (2003), 138.

[68] Minji soshō kisoku (Japanese Rules of Civil Procedure), Rules of the Supreme Court No. 5 of December 17, 1996, § 53(1).

[69] Christopher Heath, "Erlangung und Durchsetzung von Patentrechten in Japan," *GRUR Int.* (1998): 555, 560; Lucille M. Ponte, "Guilt by Association in United States Products Liability Cases: Are the European Commuity and Japan Likely to Develop Similar Cause-in-Fact Approaches to Defendant Identification," 15 *Loy. L.A. Int'l & Comp. L.J.* (1993): 629, 630; Morio Takeshita, "Shin Minji Shoshō Hō to Shōko Shūshū Seido," 196 *Hōgaku Kyōshitsu* (1997): 6, 10.

[70] Shoichi Okuyama and Klaus Hinkelmann, "Die neue Zivilprozessordnung in Japan—Für eine effiziente Lösung von geistige Eigentumsrechte betreffende Streitigkeiten," *Mitteilungen* (1999): 52, 57.

legislature created a procedure for "evidence collection prior to initiating a lawsuit" in the judicial reform of 2003.[71] An evidence preservation system had already been introduced during earlier reforms.

12.27 The requesting of information for the assessment of patent damages pursuant to Japanese Patent Act, § 105-2 has become common practice in Japanese patent litigation. At the same time, judges rarely order defendants to submit documents pursuant to Japanese Patent Act, § 105 to establish infringement unless the patentee himself submits evidence strongly indicating the likelihood of infringement.[72]

(a) Evidence Collection Prior to Initiating a Lawsuit

12.28 The introduction of an evidence collection system prior to initiating a lawsuit had been a conceptually fundamental change within Japanese civil procedure jurisprudence,[73] as it created a new opportunity for a party to request relevant material from its adversary prior to filing a lawsuit.[74] However, this procedure, unfortunately, has been barely used in practice, contrary to expectations at the time of its introduction.

12.29 To initiate the procedure of evidence collection prior to filing of the lawsuit, the potential plaintiff has to express the intention of filing a lawsuit to the adversary in writing pursuant to Japanese Code of Civil Procedure, § 132-2. In the written notice (*Yokokutsūchi*), the sender has to summarize the content of the legal claim and has to describe the details of the information requested.[75] The plaintiff needs to demonstrate the necessity of the requested information for the assessment and enforcement of his claim.[76] After serving the written notice, the plaintiff can request the adversary to supply information concerning facts relevant to the dispute over a period of four months and under observation of a reasonable notice period. However, the plaintiff cannot compel the adversary to supply any information requested pursuant to Japanese Code of Civil Procedure, § 132-2. If the adversary does not react or refuses to supply evidence, the plaintiff can at any time file a motion for evidence collection at a competent court pursuant to the Japanese Code of Civil Procedure, § 132-4. In order to substantiate such a motion, the plaintiff has to explain the circumstances resulting in difficulties collecting the relevant evidence.[77] After hearing the adversary, the court can:

- order the adversary to supply the evidence/documents requested[78]
- order a competent government or administrative agency to initiate a necessary investigation[79]
- request an expert to evaluate the information[80]
- request an enforcement officer to examine the condition of the object in question.[81]

[71] Law No. 108 of 2003.

[72] Mami Hino and Naho Ebata, in Eiji Katayama (ed.), *Japanese Patent Litigation* (2012), 118.

[73] Luke Nottage, "Civil Procedure Reforms in Japan: The Latest Round," *Ritsumeikan Law Review* (2005): 81, 83; rather skeptical, Carl F. Goodman, *Justice and Civil Procedure in Japan* (2004), 262.

[74] Matsumoto, "Grundfragen und aktuelle Probleme des Beweisrechts in Japan," 212.

[75] Ichiro Kasuga, in Teiichiro Nakano, Kaoru Matsūra and Masahiro Suzuki (eds.), *Shin minji soshōhō kōgi* (2d ed., 2006), 294; additional elements formally required for a notice are listed in the Japanese Rules of Civil Procedure, § 52-4(2).

[76] Kasuga, n. 75 above, 296.

[77] Japanese Rules of Civil Procedure, § 52-5(6); Kasuga, n. 75 above, 297.

[78] Japanese Code of Civil Procedure, § 132-4(1)i.

[79] Japanese Code of Civil Procedure, § 132-4(1)ii.

[80] Japanese Code of Civil Procedure, § 132-4(1)iii.

[81] Japanese Code of Civil Procedure, § 132-4(1)iv.

If the court requests examination by a court-appointed officer pursuant to Japanese Code of Civil Procedure, § 132-4(1)iv, it has to indicate to the plaintiff and to the adversary the time and the location of the examination.[82] In general, both the plaintiff and the adversary are entitled to be present during the examination.[83] 12.30

The adversary can refuse to comply with the order or the request of the court if disclosure of the evidence or examination would:[84] 12.31

- fail to fulfill any criterion stated in Japanese Code of Civil Procedure, § 163[85]
- unreasonably reveal private and secret information
- infringe upon a trade secret of the adversary.

Even if the adversary refuses to comply with the court's request without showing any of the above reasons, the current civil procedure law does not grant the courts a mechanism to enforce the court's request.[86] Having said so, a non-justified refusal to comply with the court's order for evidence production in the pre-trial phase will be considered negatively in accordance with Japanese Code of Civil Procedure, § 247 when assessing the parties' arguments and evidence provided during the trial.[87] 12.32

(b) Evidence Preservation

The evidence preservation procedure pursuant to Japanese Code of Civil Procedure, § 234 is the strongest mechanism for seizing evidence under Japanese civil procedure law. Evidence preservation can be ordered if the court is convinced that the existing circumstances could result in exacerbating the use of evidence if such evidence is not reviewed or secured before the beginning of the trial.[88] The plaintiff has to apply for the use of evidence preservation at a competent court determined in accordance with Japanese Code of Civil Procedure, § 235. Evidence preservation can be executed before or after initiating the trial.[89] In urgent cases, the plaintiff can request the court to order evidence preservation without notifying 12.33

---

[82] Japanese Rules of Civil Procedure, § 52-7(4).

[83] Kasuga, n. 75 above, 298.

[84] Ibid. 296.

[85] Japanese Code of Civil Procedure, § 163:

> A party, while the suit is pending, may specify a reasonable period and make an inquiry by means of a document to the opponent in order to request the opponent to make a response by means of a document with regard to the matters necessary for preparing allegations or proof; provided, however, that this shall not apply where the inquiry falls under any of the following items:
> (i) Inquiry that is not specific or individual
> (ii) Inquiry that insults or confuses the opponent
> (iii) Inquiry that overlaps with any previous inquiry
> (iv) Inquiry to ask opinions
> (v) Inquiry for which the opponent is required to spend unreasonable expenses or time to make a response
> (vi) Inquiry on the matters that are the same as the matters about which a witness may refuse to testify pursuant to the provisions of Article 196 or Article 197.

[86] Goodman, *Justice and Civil Procedure in Japan*, 263.

[87] Kasuga, n. 75 above, 296.

[88] It should be noted that not only the difficulties of collection evidence after filing the lawsuit but also a significant increase of costs of evidence collection after the start of the trial are traditionally regarded as reasons for the introduction of the evidence preservation process; see Shokichi Tanamachi, "Chitekizaisan no shokohozen to benrishi no yakuwari," 49(5) *Patento* (1996): 14, 16.

[89] Goodman, *Justice and Civil Procedure in Japan*, 258.

the adversary party. Thus, at least in theory, the evidence preservation mechanism would seem to be a very valuable procedural tool as it is the only way of obtaining non-public evidence which is in the possession of the adversary without giving the adversary prior notice.

12.34 In order to convince a court to order evidence preservation, a plaintiff has to show the likelihood of evidence being lost, damaged, modified, or hidden.[90] If such likelihood is not very high, the application of the evidence preservation procedure is not considered appropriate.[91] Furthermore, the impact on the adversary is evaluated by the court looking at the proportionality of the evidence preservation.[92] Thus, as the requirements for the application of evidence preservation are generally very high, it is rare to see courts ordering evidence preservation across all fields of civil law, while it practically never happens in the context of evidence collection for a patent infringement analysis. The practical difficulties still existing for patentees in collecting non-public evidence prior to initiating a lawsuit, especially in cases where a prior warning to the alleged patent infringer comes with a risk of loss or alteration of evidence, remains a significant barrier to an efficient patent enforcement procedure.

(c) Evidence Collection after Initiating a Lawsuit

12.35 **i. Obligation to Clarify the Specific Conditions Pursuant to Japanese Patent Act, § 104-2** After filing of a lawsuit, Japanese civil procedure law provides some mechanisms for obtaining evidence and information from the opposite party.[93] Other than during the pre-trial evidence collection process, there are some provisions tailored to patent law and incorporated into the Patent Act, which become applicable after filing a patent infringement lawsuit.[94] Japanese Patent Act, § 104-2[95] provides for a general obligation of the defendant to contribute to the clarification of facts by submission of products or by disclosing details regarding processes in the event of the defendant disputing the infringement claim.[96] At the same time, the second sentence of Japanese Patent Act, § 104-2 also provides for a general possibility for withholding the disclosure of information regarding

---

[90] Similar requirements apply to pre-trial witness testimony, which is only possible within the framework of the evidence preservation procedure if the witness is severely ill or about to depart from Japan; see Masahito Monguchi et al., *Minjishōkohōtaikei* (2007), vol. I, 182.

[91] Ibid.

[92] Tokyo District Court. June 30, 1976, Sho 51 (mo) No. 6490, 346 Hanrei Times 271; Monguchi et al., *Minjishōkohōtaikei 1*, 184.

[93] Kasuga, n. 75 above, 298.

[94] Goodman, *Justice and Civil Procedure in Japan*, 350; an overview of the comparable general rules of the Japanese Code of Civil Procedure can be found in Matsumoto, "Grundfragen und aktuelle Probleme des Beweisrechts in Japan," 206; see also Ichiro Kasuga, "Minji soshō-hō kaisei mondai (1): 'Dokuritsu shōko shirabe' ni tsuite", 740 *NBL* (2002): 33; Ichiro Kasuga, "Minjisoshō ni okeru Himitsuhogo (Hikōkaishinnri)—Himitsuhogo no tetsuzuki no gaiyō to konkyozuke wo chūshintoshite," in *Torihikihō no hen'yō to aratana tenkai: kawai takeshi sensei sanju kinen ronbunshū*, 2007, 358, 361; Koji Shindō, *Shinminjisoshōhō* (3d ed., 2004), 438; *Takahiro Suzuki*, "In kamera tetsuzuki to (gijutsu mataha shokugyō no himitsu (minjihō 197-1-3))," 3-1 *Sōgōseisakuronshū* (2003): 217; Makiko Takabe, "Chitekizaisankensoshō ni okeru bunsho no teishutsu," in Tatsuki Shibuya, Toshiko Takenaka, and Ryu Takabayashi (eds.), *Chizai Nenpo—Annual I.P. Report* (2006), 285.

[95] Japanese Patent Act, § 104-2:

> In litigation concerning the infringement of a patent right or an exclusive license, in order to deny the specific conditions of an article or process that a patentee or an exclusive licensee claims as one that composed an act of infringement, the adverse party shall clarify the specific conditions of his/her act; provided, however, that this shall not apply where there exist reasonable grounds preventing the adverse party from so doing.

[96] Hiroya Kawaguchi, *The Essentials of Japanese Patent Law: Cases and Practice* (2007), 123; Koichi Miki, "Tokkyokenshingaisoshō ni okeru tōjisha no jyōhōshūshūshudan no kakujyū," 1162 *Jurist* (1999): 55, 57.

the disputed facts. To do so, the defendant has to substantiate the reason for such withholding of information.[97]

ii. Order to Produce Documents Following the motion of a party, the court can order the other party to submit information or to disclose processes deemed relevant by the court for establishing infringement or for computation of damages[98] pursuant to Japanese Patent Act, § 105-1(1).[99] Having said so, the addressee of such a court order can refuse submission of information or disclosure of processes pursuant to Japanese Patent Act, § 105-1(1) if there is a valid reason for such refusal. Valid reasons for refusal of submission are generally accepted if the requested documents contain technical or other trade secrets[100] or if the said documents were prepared exclusively for internal purposes.[101] Information is considered as a trade secret if its disclosure would result in (i) a drastic reduction in value of the technology in question, (ii) difficulties in continuing the business,[102] or (iii) the risk of causing grave damages to the owner of the information or to a third party.[103] A document will be presumed to be prepared for internal purposes if certain factors developed by the Supreme Court in a non-patent case apply[104] and if disclosure of the document would threaten the owner of the document to incur unpredictable hardship.[105] **12.36**

[97] Kawaguchi, *The Essentials of Japanese Patent Law*, 123.

[98] Miki, "Tokkyokenshingaisoshō ni okeru tōjisha no jyōhōshūshūshudan no kakujyū, 58.

[99] Japanese Patent Act, § 105-1:

1. In litigation concerning the infringement of a patent right or exclusive license, the court may, upon a motion of a party, order the other party to produce documents that are required to prove the said act of infringement or to calculate the damage arising from the said act of infringement; provided, however, that this shall not apply where there are reasonable grounds for the person possessing the documents to refuse production of the said documents.
2. When the court finds it necessary for determining whether or not there are reasonable grounds as provided in the proviso to the preceding paragraph, the court may cause the person possessing the documents to present such documents. In such a case, no person may request the disclosure of the documents presented.
3. In the case of the preceding paragraph, where the court finds it necessary to hear opinions by disclosing the documents as provided in the latter sentence of the preceding paragraph to make a decision concerning the existence of reasonable grounds as provided in the proviso to paragraph (1), the court may disclose the documents to the parties, etc. (the parties (or, in the case of juridical persons, their representatives), their representatives (excluding attorneys and assistant), employees and other workers, the same shall apply hereinafter), attorneys or assistant.
4. The preceding three paragraphs shall apply mutatis mutandis to the presentation of the subject-matter of the inspection that is required to prove the act of infringement in litigation concerning the infringement of a patent right or exclusive license.

[100] Japanese Code of Civil Procedure, §§ 197(1)iii, 220 iv(b); until recently, some commentators generally denied any duty of submitting evidence if such evidence contained trade secrets: Shinya Yoshii, *Tokkyoken Shingai Soshō Taiyō* (13th ed., 1990), 191; see a contrary opinion in Yuriko Sagara, "Commentary on Article 105 Patent Act," in Nobuhiro Nakayama and Naoki Koizumi (eds.), *Shin Chūkai Tokkyohō* (2011), 1852.

[101] Japanese Code of Civil Procedure, § 220 iv(c); see also Kasuga, n. 75 above, 329; detailed also in Toshiro Mochizuku, "Baby Step or Giant Leap? Parties Expanded Access to Documentary Evidence under The New Japanese Code of Civil Procedure," 40 *Harv. Int'l. LJ* (1999): 285, 301.

[102] S. Ct., March 10, 2000, Hei 11 (Kyo) No. 20, 1708 Hanrei Jihō (2000), 115—*Bunshoteishuttsumeirei.*

[103] Ibid. 116.

[104] S. Ct., November 12, 1999, Hei 11 (Kyo) No. 2, 53-8 Minshū (1999), 1787—*Bunshoteishutsumeirei*; the Supreme Court established factors such as (1) the purpose of production of the document, (2) the content of the document, (3) the reason for the document being in possession of the adversary, etc.

[105] Ibid.; the Supreme Court asked the courts to consider whether a disclosure would violate the privacy or limit the possibility of free opinion forming of persons, associations, or societies.

12.37 **iii. In-camera Proceedings** If the party in possession of the evidence requested by the court can assert a valid reason allowing it to decline disclosure, the court can choose to examine such evidence during a non-public in-camera procedure pursuant to Japanese Patent Act, § 105-1(2).[106] The methodology of Japanese Patent Act, § 105-1(2), which was enacted on April 1, 2005, resembles the procedure under Japanese Code of Civil Procedure, § 223(6).[107] During the in-camera proceedings, the evidence in question, usually certain documents, are examined in a closed session.[108] During such session, the court determines the relevancy of the document in question for proving infringement and balances such relevancy against the reasonable interest of non-disclosure asserted.[109] Japanese Patent Act, § 105-1(3) provides for the possibility of submitting only selected parts of the requested documents or only parts of the equipment and of questioning the other party based on such partial submissions.[110] If the court acknowledges that the party who was requested to submit evidence has a valid reason for non-disclosure of specific information, it can issue a protective order (*Himitsu hoji meirei*)[111] pursuant to Japanese Patent Act, § 105-4.[112]

---

[106] Kawaguchi, *The Essentials of Japanese Patent Law*, 124; Takabe, "Chitekizaisankensoshō ni okeru bunsho no teishutsu," 293.

[107] Japanese Code of Civil Procedure, § 223(6): "The court, when it finds it necessary in order to determine which of the categories of documents set forth in Article 220(iv)(a) to (d) the document pertaining to the petition for an order to submit a document falls under, may have the holder of the document present the document. In this case, no person may request the disclosure of the document presented."

[108] Kasuga, "Minjisoshō ni okeru Himitsuhogo (Hikōkaishinnri)," 370; Komatsu, "Senmonnin—Himitsu-hojimeirei—Saiban no kokaiteishi nado no shinseido e no taiyō," 332.

[109] Kasuga, "Minjisoshō ni okeru Himitsuhogo (Hikōkaishinnri)," 370.

[110] Kawaguchi, *The Essentials of Japanese Patent Law*, 124; Takabe, "Chitekizaisankensoshō ni okeru bunsho no teishutsu," 294.

[111] Kondō and Saito, *Chitekizaisankankeinihō/Rodōshinpanhō*, 39; Takayoshi Sagae and Toshiki Yano, "Himitsuhojimeirei to himitsuishō no kankei," 59(3) *Patento* (2006): 61.

[112] Japanese Patent Act, § 105-4:

1. In litigation concerning the infringement of a patent right or exclusive license, where there is prima-facie evidence of the fact that trade secrets (refers to trade secrets as provided in Article 2(6) of the Unfair Competition Prevention Act (Law No. 47 of 1993), the same shall apply hereinafter) possessed by a party satisfy all of the following paragraphs, the court may, upon a motion of the party, order by a ruling that the parties, etc., attorneys or assistants shall neither use the trade secrets for any purpose other than those for the proceedings of the litigation nor disclose the trade secrets to any person other than those who receive the order regarding the trade secrets under this provision; provided, however, that this shall not apply where the parties, etc., attorneys or assistants have, prior to the filing of the motion, already obtained or been in the possession of the trade secrets by a method other than by reading of the briefs under item (i) or through the examination or disclosure of evidence under the said item:
   (i) where the trade secrets possessed by the party were or are contained in the briefs already submitted or to be submitted or such trade secrets were or are contained in the evidence already examined or to be examined (including documents disclosed under Article 105(3) and under Article 105-7(4)); and
   (ii) where it is necessary to restrict the use or the disclosure of the trade secrets under the preceding paragraph to prevent any possible interference with the party's business activities based on the trade secrets, that might arise if the trade secrets are used for any purpose other than those for the proceedings of the litigation or if the said trade secrets are disclosed.
2. A motion requesting the order under the preceding paragraph (hereinafter referred to as a "protective order") shall be made in writing specifying the following matters:
   (i) the person(s) to whom the protective order is to be issued;
   (ii) the facts that clearly identify the trade secrets to be protected by the protective order; and
   (iii) the facts corresponding to the reasons each of the items in the preceding paragraph is applicable.
3. Where the protective order is issued, a written ruling thereof shall be served to the person(s) to whom the protective order is issued.

iv. Protective Order If the court believes that the evidence requested is relevant but contains a trade secret within the scope of Unfair Competition Prevention Act, it will examine such evidence in-camera.[113] If the court decides to introduce the evidence into the infringement proceedings, the party who has to disclose the information can apply for a protective order binding the recipients of the confidential information.[114] A protective order directs the parties to refrain from any unauthorized use of the disclosed information within or outside the infringement proceedings.[115] Violation of a court-issued protective order can be punished by imprisonment of up to five years, a fine of up 5 million yen, or a combination of the two.[116] The court has to carefully select the individuals who will be authorized to access the confidential information and who will be bound by the protective order. That said, it can be problematic to grant a researcher of one party access to current R&D results and related know-how of the other party. While the researcher may be in a good position to evaluate the technical information and to contribute to the infringement analysis, it is easy to imagine that the confidential information obtained would become a part of his or her own future R&D activities. In such case, the researcher might be significantly restricted in future activities if such activities are related to or overlap with the content of the infringement proceedings, as he or she might be afraid of the legal consequences of violating the protective order unintentionally. To accommodate these concerns, it became common practice to limit access to confidential information and thus to limit the scope of parties bound by the protective order to the legal representatives and advisors of the party, in particular to their attorneys and patent attorneys. If the outside patent attorneys lack the technical background required to fully understand and analyze the confidential information, it has been suggested for access to be extended only to the more senior employees of the parties who would be eyeing retirement in the near future and thus would not be too restricted by the protective order.[117] 12.38

While the introduction of protective orders tailored to patent law has been subject to vigorous debate amongst legal scholars, only a few protective orders have been issued by courts in patent infringement litigations so far.[118] In cases where a court requests a defendant to disclose certain information pursuant to Japanese Patent Act, § 105, it has become established practice to conclude a non-disclosure agreement between the parties in order to ensure confidential treatment of the disclosed information and to avoid becoming subject to a court-issued protection order with its potentially harsh consequences.[119] 12.39

---

4. The protective order shall take effect as of the date the written ruling is served to the person(s) to whom the protective order is issued.
5. The decision dismissing a motion requesting the protective order shall be subject to immediate appeal.

[113] Fusei kyōsō bōshi-hō (Unfair Competition Prevention Act), Law No. 47 of 1993, § 2(6). Wataru Sueyoshi, "Himitsuhojimeirei nitsuite: Dairinin no tachiba kara no rontenseiri," 27 *Law & Technology* (2005): 19, 20.

[114] Takabe, "Chitekizaisankensoshō ni okeru bunsho no teishutsu," 289.

[115] Kasuga, "Minjisoshō ni okeru Himitsuhogo (Hikōkaishinnri)," 369.

[116] Japanese Patent Act, § 200-2.

[117] JIPA First Patent Committee, 2d Subcomittee: "Tokkyo-ken shingai kōi no risshō no yōi-ka no tame no hōritsu kaisei to kigyō no taiō," 55(3) *Chizai Kanri* (2005): 344.

[118] E.g., Tokyo District Court, September 15, 2006, Hei 18 (mo) No. 9933, 1250 Hanrei Times, 300: Osaka District Court, April 18, 2008, Hei 20 (mo) No. 363, 1287 Hanrei Times (2008), 220.

[119] *Seiji Ohno and Yoshitaka Inoue*, "Commentary on Article 105-4 Patent Act," in Nobuhiro Nakayama and Naoki Koizumi (eds.), *Shin Chūkai Tokkyohō* (2011), 1880–81.

12.40 A party bound by a protective order cannot appeal against such an order.[120] Having said so, it is possible to apply for cancellation of the protective order pursuant to Japanese Patent Act, § 105-5.

12.41 **v. Cancellation of Protective Order** To counter the disadvantages coming with the issuance of a protective order, both the party bound by the order and the party who originally applied for the issuance of the order[121] can request cancellation of the protective order pursuant to Japanese Patent Act, § 105-5.[122] A motion of cancellation of the protective order has to show that the information protected would not require further protection and that the business activities of the disclosing organization would not be endangered by cancellation of the protective order.[123]

12.42 In addition, a party should move for cancellation of the protective order if the information is within the public domain notwithstanding the protective order. Without a cancellation, the party bound by the protective order risks being fined for violation of the order.[124]

12.43 **vi. Closed Session** If the court decides to withhold access to protected information from the plaintiff, Japanese Patent Act, § 105-7 allows for non-public proceedings.[125] The court

---

[120] JIPA, "Tokkyo-ken shingai kōi no risshō no yōi-ka no tame no hōritsu kaisei to kigyō no taiō," 341.

[121] Kawaguchi, *The Essentials of Japanese Patent Law*, 127.

[122] Japanese Patent Act, § 105-5:

1. A person(s) who has filed a motion requesting a protective order or to whom a protective order is issued may file a motion with the court where the record of a case(s) is maintained (or, in the case of no such court maintaining the record of a case(s), the court issuing the protective order), requesting the rescission of the protective order on the ground that the requirements as provided in Article 105-4(1) are not met or are no longer met.
2. Where a decision on a motion requesting the rescission of a protective order is rendered, a written ruling thereof shall be served to the person who filed the motion and the adverse party in the case.
3. The decision on a motion requesting the rescission of a protective order shall be subject to immediate appeal.
4. A decision to the effect that a protective order is to be rescinded shall have no effect unless the decision becomes final and binding.
5. Where a decision to the effect that a protective order is to be rescinded is rendered, the court shall immediately notify the person(s) who, in the litigation in which the said protective order was issued, received the protective order pertaining to the trade secrets who are neither the person filing the motion requesting the rescission of the protective order nor the adverse party, if any, of the fact that the decision to the effect that the protective order is to be rescinded was rendered.

[123] JIPA, "Tokkyo-ken shingai kōi no risshō no yōi-ka no tame no hōritsu kaisei to kigyō no taiō," 343; Kondō and Saito, *Chitekizaisankankeinihō/Rodōshinpanhō*, 43.

[124] JIPA, "Tokkyo-ken shingai kōi no risshō no yōi-ka no tame no hōritsu kaisei to kigyō no taiō," 343.

[125] Japanese Patent Act, § 105-7:

1. When a party, etc., to litigation concerning the infringement of a patent right or exclusive license is to be examined as a party to the litigation, as its statutory representative or as a witness, with regard to matters that will be a basis for the determination of the existence or non-existence of the said infringement, and such matters are trade secrets possessed by a party, the court may, by a ruling, elect to hold closed examinations of such matters where the court, upon the unanimous consent of all judges, finds that the parties, etc. will be unable to make sufficient statements regarding the matters due to the obvious fact that making statements regarding the matters at an open examination will significantly interfere with the business activities of the party based on such trade secrets and that, without such statements, a proper decision on the fact of the existence or non-existence of the infringement of a patent right or exclusive license that ought to be made based on the said matters may not be made based solely on other evidence.

has to unanimously approve non-public proceedings. To allow non-public proceedings, the court must expect that the disclosure of the trade secrets would lead to severe disruption for the disclosing party and thus would not be reasonable, and the court also needs to be convinced that the examination of the evidence without the presence of the other party would result in objective findings relevant for the infringement analysis to be made by the court.[126] In addition, the court must be convinced that it would not be able to sufficiently determine infringement without the results from the non-public proceedings.[127]

3. Border Measures

The Japanese border measure system, which was originally established in 1954, has been subject to numerous amendments over the last decade as a consequence of the pro-patent policy of the Japanese government.[128] While border measures are mainly applied in the context of trademark infringement, in particular in cases of import of counterfeits,[129] it can also be a valuable tool for patentees seeking enforcement against imported infringing goods. The legal basis for the detention of infringing goods is Japanese Customs Act, § 69-11,[130] which prohibits the import of goods infringing intellectual property rights. Since 2006, the export of IP-infringing goods is also prohibited pursuant to Japanese Customs Act, § 69-2.[131] There is no specific provision in the Japanese Customs Act regulating the applicability of border measures for infringing goods in transit. In practice, the customs authorities regard transit as a combination of import and export and thus also apply border measures to goods which are only transiting through Japan.[132] **12.44**

The legal framework for parallel imports in the context of patent law has been defined in the Supreme Court's decision BBS in 1997.[133] Accordingly, the parallel importing of goods which are subject to patent protection in Japan is permissible if such imported goods have been lawfully purchased in the country of origin from the owner of the Japanese patent or a licensee and no export restriction had been agreed upon between the seller of the good and the **12.45**

2. The court shall, in rendering the ruling as provided in the preceding paragraph, hear the opinions of the parties, etc. in advance.
3. In the case of the preceding paragraph, where necessary, the court may cause the parties, etc., to present a document stating the gist of the matters to be stated. In such a case, no person may request the disclosure of the document presented.
4. When the court finds it necessary to hear opinions by disclosing the document as provided in the latter sentence of the preceding paragraph, the court may disclose the document to the parties, etc., their attorneys or assistants.
5. Where the examination on certain matters is to be closed under paragraph (1), the court shall declare such fact and reasons therefore prior to requiring the public to leave the court. Upon completion of the examination on the said matters, the court shall allow the public to re-enter the court.

[126] Kawaguchi, *The Essentials of Japanese Patent Law*, 129; Kondō and Saito, *Chitekizaisankankeinihō/Rodōshinpanhō*, 45.

[127] JIPA, "Tokkyo-ken shingai kōi no risshō no yōi-ka no tame no hōritsu kaisei to kigyō no taiō," 344.

[128] JIPA First Patent Committee, 4th Subcomittee: "Tokkyo-ken ni motodzuku kanzei teiritsu-hō-tō no misugiwa sochi ni tsuite," 56(8) *Chizai Kanri* (2006): 1149.

[129] Kazuhisa Saito, "Chitekizaisanshingaibuppin no misugiwatorishimari nitsuite," 5 *Boeki Jitsumu Digest* (2007): 1.

[130] Kanzeihō (Japanese Customs Act), Law No. 61 of 1954.

[131] See detailed examination in Yo Takeuchi, "Kanseiteiritsuhō kihontsūtatsutō no ichibun kaisei nitsuite (jou)," 4 *Chizai Purizumu* (2006): 180.

[132] JIPA, "Tokkyo-ken ni motodzuku kanzei teiritsu-hō-tō no migiwa sochi ni tsuite," 1152.

[133] S. Ct., July 1, 1997, Hei 7 (O) No. 1988, 51-6 Minshū (1997), 2299 = IIC 1998, 331—*BBS Kraftfahrzeugtechnik AG/Racimex Japan, Inc.*

importer.[134] Hence, Japan is one of the few jurisdictions following the principle of international exhaustion.[135]

(a) Application Period

12.46 To initiate border measures, the patentee has to complete an application for detention at the customs office. The customs office reports to the Japanese Ministry of Finance and conducts customs inspections at Japanese seaports and airports. Border measures are primarily enforced by IP investigators, who are stationed in Tokyo as well as in the regional customs offices in Hakodate, Kobe, Moji, Nagasaki, Nagoya, Okinawa, Osaka, and Yokohama.[136] Patentees can apply for detention at each of the nine regional customs offices. Formally, the application has to be addressed to the director of the main customs office based in Tokyo.[137] The application has to demonstrate the patentee's entitlement to use the patent and has to explain why the goods to be imported infringe the patent.[138]

(b) Detention Period

12.47 After the detaining and storing[139] of the imported goods by the customs authorities, both the applicant and the importer are notified. The notice contains a description and the quantity of the detained goods as well as the identity of the other party involved in the proceedings.[140] In addition to the notifications to the parties, the name of the parties, the content of the patent, and a description of the detained goods are published on the website of the customs authorities.[141] After receiving the notice, the patentee can issue an escrow order pursuant to Japanese Customs Act, §§ 69-15(1) and (2). Thereupon, and upon application, the patentee can inspect the detained goods pursuant to Japanese Customs Act, §§ 69-16(1) and (2). The importer is notified of the patentee's application to inspect the detained goods and can attend the inspection if desired.[142] Both parties can request the Japanese Patent Office to issue an opinion on the infringement,[143] which is supposed to be issued within thirty days.[144] If such an opinion of the JPO has been requested, the customs office usually follows such opinion. If the customs office determines that the goods are infringing a patent, it can order their destruction.[145] The decision of the customs authorities is subject to administrative appeal and thereafter can be appealed at a competent district court.[146]

---

134 Masabumi Suzuki, *Heikōyunyū to Tokkyoken, Hyakusen Tokkyohō* (2004), 218.

135 S. Ct., July 1, 1997, Hei 7 (O) No. 1988, S. Ct., November 8, 2007, Hei 18 (uke) No. 826, 61–68 Minshū, 2989—*Canon KK vs. Recycle Assist KK*; see also Scott Tobias, "No Refills: The Intellectual Property High Court Decision in Cannon v. Recycle Assist Will Negatively Impact the Printer Ink Cartridge Recycling Industry in Japan," 16 *Pac. Rim L. & Pol'y J.* (2007): 775, 781.

136 Kiyoaki Yamada, "Japan's Border Controls over Goods Infringing Intellectual Property Rights," *AIPPI* (2005): 199, 202.

137 A copy of the application form can be found in Toshio Naito, *Chitekizaisanshingaibuppin no Suisaitorishimaruseido no kaisetsu* (2007), 53.

138 Yamada, "Japan's Border Controls over Goods Infringing Intellectual Property Rights," 206; Nobuyuki Matsubara, "Border Control of Goods Infringing Intellectual Property Rights in Japan," *AIPPI* (2005): 3, 6 (with further details on application documents and required information).

139 The storage costs are charged to the applicant, who has to pay them upfront pursuant to the Japanese Customs Act, § 69-6.

140 Yamada, "Japan's Border Controls over Goods Infringing Intellectual Property Rights," 202.

141 Naito, *Chitekizaisanshingaibuppin no Suisaitorishimaruseido no kaisetsu*, 27.

142 Japanese Customs Act, § 69-16(6) of the Customs Act.

143 Ibid. Japanese Customs Act, § 69-17(1).

144 Ibid. Japanese Customs Act, § 69-17(4).

145 Ibid. Japanese Customs Act, § 69-11(2); see Naito, *Chitekizaisanshingaibuppin no Suisaitorishimaruseido no kaisetsu*, 34.

146 Japanese Customs Act, § 89.

A wrongful detention of imported goods can result in a claim for damages against the patentee.[147] Having said so, it is considered legitimate to wait for the issuance of the opinion on infringement by the JPO; thus, the patentee is not subject to a claim for damages if the detention is not extended beyond the issuance of the JPO opinion. 12.48

4. Pre-trial Proceedings

(a) Warning Letter—Practical Significance

As Japanese entities were, at least traditionally, reported to be hesitant to embark on court litigation, it only seems logical that warning letters or other out-of-court settlement approaches are an important and very relevant factor in resolving disputes. Indeed sending warning letters to manufacturers and their customers is a common and well-established practice in Japanese patent disputes.[148] 12.49

(b) Claims for Wrongful Warning Letters

i. Wrongful Warning Letters Sent to Manufacturers A wrongful warning letter sent to the manufacturer of allegedly infringing goods is generally not regarded as unlawful, as the addressee—namely, the manufacturer—is deemed capable of verifying the content of the warning letter.[149] Having said so, district court case law indicates, in at least one decision, that a wrongful warning letter sent to a manufacturer can be unlawful and thus can result in a claim for damages by the addressee.[150] The Supreme Court confirmed in 1988 that intentionally sending a wrongful warning letter to a manufacturer can trigger a claim for damages by the manufacturer.[151] However, it is almost impossible to prove the existence of such an intention in practice.[152] 12.50

ii. Wrongful Warning Letters Sent to Customers Sending a wrongful warning letter to a manufacturer's customer alleging that the manufacturer's goods infringe upon the sender's patents and urging the customer to cease purchasing or trading with the accused manufacturer's goods (*kokuchi*) can result in a claim for damages by the manufacturer against the sender pursuant to Japanese Civil Code, § 709 in combination with Unfair Competition Prevention Act, § 2(1)xiv. As a statutory requirement, such a claim for damages requires a finding of negligence on the part of the sender. Japanese jurisprudence tends to be very strict when denying negligence.[153] According to the general principles of the Japanese Code of Civil Procedure, the plaintiff has to demonstrate the defendant's negligence in court proceedings. Having said this, in cases of wrongful warning letters sent to customers, courts used to reverse such principles and shifted the burden of proof for the absence of negligence to the sender of the warning letter.[154] Until 1972, the sender of a warning letter directed 12.51

---

[147] Yamada, "Japan's Border Controls over Goods Infringing Intellectual Property Rights," 208.

[148] Also Christopher Heath, "Wrongful Patent Enforcement—Threats and Post-Infringement Invalidity in Comparative Perspective," *IIC* (2008): 307, 312.

[149] Kazufumi Dohi, "Torihikisaki ni taisuru kenrishingaikeikoku to fuseikyosōbōshihō," in *Chitekizaisanhō no ronri to gendaiteki kadai: Nakayama Nobuhiro sensei kannreki kinen Ronbunshū* (2005), 436, 440.

[150] Tokyo District Court, August 8, 2006 (wa) No. 3056, "*Songaibaishō Seikyūken*"; see Takayuki Hirose, "Chitekizaisankenshingai ni kansuru keikoku," 57(6) *Chizai Kanri* (2007): 929.

[151] S. Ct., January 26, 1988, Sho 60 (O) No. 122, 42-1 Minshu (1988), 1—*Utaeteiki.*

[152] Tokyo District Court, August 8, 2006, Hei 17 (wa) No. 3056, "*Songaibaishō Seikyūken*"; see Hirose, "Chitekizaisankenshingai ni kansuru keikoku," 929.

[153] Yoshiyuki Tamura, *Fusei kyosōhō gaisetsu* (2d ed., 2003), 442.

[154] Shigehiko Kanai, *Fusei kyosō boshihō kommentaru* (2004), 154; Tokyo District Court, March 17, 1972, Sho 45 (wa) No. 2700, 278 Hanrei Times (1972), 374—*Fuigobaki.*

to a customer of a wrongfully accused manufacturer had always been treated as negligent, without an opportunity to show an absence of negligence.[155] At the same time, the damages awarded to the claimants were not very substantial.[156] However, even after 1972, courts made it quite difficult for the sender of a warning letter to escape the presumption of negligence, holding, for example, that an opinion concluding infringement issued by a patent attorney was not sufficient in itself to show an absence of negligence.[157] The rather rare cases in which a sender of a wrongful customer warning was able to escape culpability included a few cases where the court concluded that the patentee could not reasonably have foreseen invalidation of the patent[158] and a case in which the alleged infringer had received specific insights into the intellectual property rights of the patentee through a close business relation, thus making infringement with particularly harmful consequences for the patentee highly likely.[159]

12.52 Recent case law, however, changed the assessment of sending a warning letter to the customer of an alleged infringer. In 2002, the Tokyo High Court dismissed the claim of an alleged infringer against the sender of a warning letter to the alleged infringer's customer.[160] Even though the patent was invalidated after the warning letter was sent, the court held that the patentee could not easily have been aware that there were grounds for invalidation. One important element that supported the patentee was that it had been engaged in substantial but unsuccessful discussions trying to resolve the dispute with the alleged infringer. Further, the court held that another important element was the fact that the customer addressed in the warning letter was a sophisticated company who was aware of the risk of purchasing the allegedly infringing product, and who was at the same time named as a defendant in parallel actions involving the same technology in the United States.[161]

12.53 These decisions triggered a gradual revision of the liability of a patentee in sending a warning letter to a customer. Between 2002 and 2013, courts issued multiple decisions affirming as well as denying negligence on the part of the sender of a wrongful customer warning.[162] The more forgiving approach of courts in assessing the negligence of a sender of customer warnings received both support and criticisms by prominent commentators.[163] Factors that became relevant for the assessment were external circumstances,

155 Ryuichi Shitara and Izumi Yoshikawa, "Tokkyoken ni motozuku keikosho sōfu—karishobunmeirei mōshitate," in *Shōhyō Isho Fusei Kyoso Hanrei Hyakusen* (2007), 217.

156 During the sixties, the maximum amount of damages awarded was a few hundred thousand yen; during the seventies and eighties, damage awards increased to a few million yen, see Kazufumi Dohi, "Keikokusho to fuseikyoso," in Shoen Ono and Kazunori Yamagami (eds.), *Fuseikyōsō no hōristsu sōdan* (2002), 383, 387; Nagoya District Court, February 27, 1984, Sho 52 (wa) No. 1615, 16-1 Mutaishū (1984), 91: 2,000,000 yen; Osaka District Court , May 29, 1985, Sho 58 (wa) No. 7338, 1174 Hanrei Jihō (1985), 134: 5,000,000 yen.

157 Nagoya District Court, August 31, 1984, Sho 56 (wa) No. 558, 16-2 Mutaishū, 568; Tokyo District Court, October 30, 1978, 10-2 Mutaishū (1978), 509.

158 Osaka District Court, December 19, 1978, Sho 43 (wa) No. 3091, 10-2 Mutaishū (1978), 617; Osaka District Court, April 25, 1986, Sho 55 (wa) No. 6390, 609 Hanrei Times (1986), 89.

159 Tokyo District Court, April 4, 1991, Sho 63 (wa) No. 7097, 24-1 Chitekishū (1992), 230.

160 Tokyo High Court, August 29, 2002, Hei 13 (ne) No. 5555, 1801 Hanrei Jihō (2002) 113—*Metallic Powder*.

161 Ibid.

162 Decisions finding no liability include Tokyo District Court, December 12, 2002, Hei 9 (wa) No. 24064, 1824 Hanrei Jihō, 94; Tokyo District Court, October 16, 2003, Hei 14 (wa) No. 1943, 1874 Hanrei Jihō (2002) 23; Tokyo District Court, Decision of January 28, 2004, Hei 14 (wa) No. 18628, 1847 Hanrei Jihō, 60 (*Mobile Software*); Tokyo District Court, August 31, 2004, Hei 14 (wa) No. 18830, 1183 Hanrei Times (2004) 320. On the other side, court decisions presuming and finding negligence by the sender of a customer warning include Osaka District Court, December 16, 2004, Hei 15 (wa) No. 6580; IP High Court, May 15, 2007, Hei 17 (ne) No. 10119; IP High Court, September 12, 2007, Hei 18 (ne) No. 10080.

163 Supporting, e.g., Kazufumi Dohi, "Eigyōhibōkōi toshite no kenrishinngaikeikoku," 5 *Nihon Kōgyōshoyūkenhō Gakkai Nenpō* (1982): 56, 94, arguing that a warning letter to a customer of the accused

timing of the warning letter, number of addressees, size of the affected companies, nature and importance of the relationship between the accused manufacturer and the warned customer, participation of the warned third party in the production of the allegedly infringing product, capability of the warned third party to participate in infringement proceedings, and the reaction of the warned third parties.[164] In a recent case, the IP High Court confirmed the tendency for a sender of a wrongful customer warning not to be regarded as negligent as long as it was difficult to foresee the outcome of the case and as long as the customer addressed was sufficiently sophisticated enough to understand the background of the dispute.[165]

Affected parties, especially a wrongfully accused manufacturer, always have a claim for injunctive relief against the sender of wrongful warning letters irrespective of a finding of negligence.[166] **12.54**

E. Other Important Proceedings

1. Declaratory Judgment Action

The importance of the declaratory judgment action in the Japanese patent enforcement procedure system is somehow limited, as it cannot be used as a tool for forum shopping. It becomes mostly relevant in the context of border measures. If an importer files a declaratory judgment action after the detention of the importer's goods by the customs authorities, the customs authorities tend to stay the detention until the declaratory judgment action is resolved.[167] **12.55**

The requirement for bringing a declaratory judgment action is an existing declaratory interest (*kakunin no rieki*) by the plaintiff.[168] Such interest is generally presumed if an actual controversy between the plaintiff and the defendant exists or if there is genuine uncertainty regarding the intellectual property right in question.[169] In addition to the valid interest in the declaratory judgment action, the court has to deem a declaratory judgment action as an efficient and reasonable way of resolving the dispute. **12.56**

In the context of infringement proceedings, the declaratory judgment action will typically be filed by the party explicitly or implicitly accused of infringement. The action will name **12.57**

party should not be regarded as unlawful if, in the same matter, a warning letter to the accused manufacturer had been sent but not been replied to within a reasonable period of time; see also in support Makiko Takabe, "Chitekizaisanhō no shin Chōryū (6) chiteki zaisanhō-hen (1) chiteki zaisanken o shingai suru mune no kokuchi to fusei kyōsō kōi no seihi," 1290 *Jurist* (2005): 88, 95. Opponents for revision of the strong presumption of negligence include Tamura, *Fusei kyosōhō gaisetsu*, 446, and Masabumi Suzuki, 550 *Hanrei Hyoron*, 186.

164 Tokyo District Court, September 20, 2001, Hei 12 (wa) No. 11657, 1801 Hanrei Jihō, 113—*Jikishingōkirokuyōkinsokufunmatsu Jiken Daiishin*; Tokyo District Court, October 16, 2003, Hei 14 (wa) No. 1943, 1151 Hanrei Times (2003), 109; Tamura, *Fusei kyosōhō gaisetsu*, 447.

165 IP High Court, March 25, 2013, Hei 24 (ne) No. 10059, 2013.

166 Shoen Ono, *Shin Chūkai Fusōkyosōhō* (2007), 734.

167 Makoto Hattori, "Custom Procedures for Goods Suspected of Infringing Patents," *AIPPI* (2007): 251, 263.

168 Shindō, *Shinminjisoshōhō*, 249.

169 IP High Court, September 20, 2007, Hei 19 (ne) No. 10038, *Claim for declaratory judgment*; Yoshihiko Umemoto, *Minjisoshōhō* (3d ed., 2007), 248.

the patentee as a defendant (*Shōkyokkuteki kakunin soshō*). In some cases, the patentee might file for a declaratory judgment action to confirm the validity of a patent if such validity has been questioned (*Sekkyokkuteki kakunin soshō*).[170] Different forms of declaratory judgment actions have to be filed for each of the scenarios. In any event, the court must deem an immediate resolution of the dispute by means of declaratory judgment action as objectively necessary in order to allow the action.[171]

12.58 The court will not allow a declaratory judgment action if the defendant concedes to having no claim against the plaintiff.[172] Also, no declaratory judgment action will be allowed if the underlying patent has been declared invalid at an earlier point in the proceedings. A decision by the JPO rendering parts of the underlying patent as invalid does not necessarily eliminate the interest for a declaratory judgment action as long as an administrative appeal against the JPO's decision is pursued and the possibility of at least some claim for injunctive relief cannot be excluded.[173]

2. Preliminary Injunction

12.59 Preliminary injunctions are generally considered as an important instrument to enforce patents and other intellectual property rights.[174] Preliminary injunctive relief can be very efficient in preventing further infringing activity, as it can prohibit an infringer from continuing the production or sale of an infringing good and thus can lead to substantial interruptions of the business activities of the defendant.[175]

12.60 Especially towards the end of the 1990s, court statistics and commentators showed an increase in the use of preliminary injunctions in patent enforcement, a tendency which was generally expected to continue.[176] However, as shown in Table 12.3, the number of preliminary injunctions sought has steadily decreased since 2002.

12.61 One major reason for the decreased demand for preliminary injunctions can be seen in the considerable development of the speed of the main proceedings, which is currently only slightly slower than that of the preliminary proceedings. Furthermore, the results of the *Kilby* decision,[177] leading to a higher risk of patent invalidity decisions during infringement proceedings, were another cause for the reduced demand.

(a) Jurisdiction

12.62 The competent court for a preliminary injunction has to be determined in accordance with the provisions of the Japanese Civil Provisional Remedies Act.[178,179] If the parties have

---

170 Yoshihiko Umemoto, "Shōkyokuteki kakuninnsoshō ni tsuite—Chitekizaisankenfunsō wo chūshin toshite," in Nobuhiro Nakayama (ed.), *Chiteki Zaisanhō to Gendai Shakai: Makino Toshiaki Hanji Taikan Kinen* (1999), 571, 582.

171 Hajime Kaneko, *Jōkai Minjisoshōhō* (1986), 811.

172 "Shōkyokuteki kakuninnsoshō ni tsuite—Chitekizaisankenfunsō wo chūshin toshite," 582.

173 Tokyo District Court, October 1, 2004, Hei 15 (wa) No. 28554, *Confirmation of Absence of Damage Claims.*

174 Toshiaki Iimura and Shin Sano, "Chitekizaisanjiken to Karishobun," 17 *Law & Technology* (2002): 14.

175 Toshiaki Iimura and Shin Sano, "Chitekizaisanfunsō ni okeru karishobun no katsuyō nitsuite," in Toshiaki Nagai, Kuniharu Yasue, and Sachikuni Iwasaki (eds.), *Chiteki zaisanken: Sono keisei to hogo: Akiyoshi Michihiro sensei kiju kinen ronbunshu* (2002), 34, 37.

176 Ibid. 35.

177 S. Ct., April 11, 2000, Hei 10 (O) No. 364, 54–4 Minshū, 1368—*Kilby.*

178 Minjihozenhō (Japanese Civil Provisional Remedies Act), Law No. 91 of 1989.

179 Hiroshi Segi, *Minjihozenhō* (2004), 413.

Table 12.3 Number of preliminary injunction proceedings*

	Total	Patent	Utility Model	Design	Trademark	Copyright	Software	Unfair Competition	Other
1997	410	75	30	13	40	139	–	108	5
1998	391	62	19	16	47	142	–	104	1
1999	488	62	25	10	35	275	–	79	2
2000	552	75	22	14	54	283	–	102	2
2001	522	61	15	6	40	321	–	78	1
2002	398	75	3	11	33	200	–	68	8
2003	288	30	3	11	30	160	–	53	1
2004	305	53	1	5	29	145	2	64	6
2005	269	33	3	9	38	127	2	55	2
2006	214	33	0	4	31	100	1	39	6

* Internal Court Statistics of the Supreme Court (on file with author).

already filed main proceedings or if the motion for preliminary injunction and the main proceedings are filed at the same time, the court which has jurisdiction for the main proceedings is also the competent court to decide on the preliminary injunction.[180] Also, in cases where the plaintiff files for a preliminary injunction before initiating the main proceedings, the district courts in Osaka and Tokyo have exclusive jurisdiction for preliminary proceedings in the area of patent law.[181]

During a main proceedings, a lack of jurisdiction can be excused if no party files a complaint. Deviating from the rules provided for in the Japanese Code of Civil Procedure regarding jurisdiction for the main proceedings, a court having no jurisdiction cannot decide on a preliminary injunction even if the defendant omits to complain about the lack of jurisdiction. Furthermore, it is not possible to file for a preliminary injunction in one concentrated action against multiple defendants at one court if such court lacks jurisdiction over one of the jointly named defendants.[182] **12.63**

(b) Scope of Preliminary Injunction

The purpose of a preliminary injunction is to preserve the status quo. A preliminary injunction in a patent-infringement context is typically directed towards ensuring that the defendant refrains from a certain conduct such as producing or distributing patent-infringing goods (*Sashidome no Karishobun*). **12.64**

As it is impossible for the court to retain independent expert opinions as well as to request the submission of documents or other evidence during the course of preliminary proceedings, it is often difficult to show the *prima facie* evidence of infringement required for a preliminary injunction. This is particularly true in the context of patent law, where the courts demand a preponderance of evidence corresponding to the level required in the main **12.65**

[180] Japanese Civil Provisional Remedies Act, § 12.
[181] Mamoru Hanari, *Kari sashiosae karishobun no hōritsu sōdan* (2004), 4.
[182] Iimura and Sano, "Chitekizaisanfunsō ni okeru karishobun no katsuyō nitsuite," 38.

proceedings.[183] Thus, it will only be realistic to expect a preliminary injunction in clear infringement cases where a defendant has committed literal infringement of the plaintiff's patent claims, the validity of the underlying patent is not in question,[184] no procedural complications are to be expected, and the plaintiff can demonstrate the infringement by examination of the infringing product which is in the plaintiff's possession.[185] Correspondingly, a preliminary injunction will be hard to obtain in cases of equivalent infringement or cases involving the possibility of the existence of a prior-use right or other enforcement hurdles such as the possibility of invalidity.[186]

(c) Requirement for Preliminary Injunction

12.66 Pursuant to Japanese Civil Provisional Remedies Act, § 23(2), a preliminary injunction requires a showing of immediate harm or substantial damages. To show such requirement is met, courts require the plaintiff to show the necessity (*hitsuyōsei*) of the preliminary injunction, which has to be established conducting a balance of hardships between the plaintiff and the defendant.[187] A showing of necessity is facilitated in cases of infringement likely to result in damages which would be difficult to compensate monetarily. [188] Examples are infringements of a major product line of the patentee,[189] infringements of a product designated to be sold only during a short period of time, or infringements of a product which is designated to be introduced in the distant future supported by a substantial marketing campaign. Another factor supporting the necessity of a preliminary injunction would be a possible lack of financial means of the defendant limiting the defendant's capability to compensate potential claim for damages.[190]

12.67 On the other hand, courts have denied the necessity for a preliminary injunction in cases where the injunction would have severely impacted the defendant's business, likely to result in bankruptcy, while the plaintiff only incurred slight damages by the infringement. Also, necessity has been denied in cases where the plaintiff itself had not made use of the intellectual property right in questions.[191] Other cases where the courts have followed the plaintiff's reasoning and accepted necessity include the following scenarios:

- concise preparation for the production and sale of a patent-protected product[192]
- concise marketing activities introducing the product by the patentee
- concise preparations to reintroduce a patent-protected product into the market
- showing of infringement while the patentee/plaintiff is conducting license negotiations with a third party[193]

[183] Tadayuki Mitani, "Somei (Kariosae—Karishobunseidokaisei no shomondai)," 38(20) *Hanrei Times* (1987): 30.

[184] Osaka District Court, April 9, 1981, Sho 56 (yo) No. 52, 13-1 Mutaishū, 425; Nagoya District Court, May 20, 1985, Sho 59 (yo) No. 318, 17-2 Mutaishū, 239.

[185] Iimura and Sano, "Chitekizaisanfunsō ni okeru karishobun no katsuyō nitsuite," 40.

[186] Toshiaki Iimura and Shin Sano, "Current State of Preliminary Injunction Cases Involving Intellectual Property Rights," *AIPPI* (2003): 12, 20.

[187] Shogo Nakamura, "Tokkyo jitsuyō shin'an-ken minji karishobun ni okeru 'hozen no hitsuyō-," 57(10) *Patento* (2004): 39; see also Kazuhiko Yoshida, 1062 *Hanrei Times* (2001): 59, who argues for raising the bar for accepting necessity in the context of preliminary injunctions.

[188] Iimura and Sano, "Current State of Preliminary Injunction Cases Involving Intellectual Property Rights," 19.

[189] Shizuoka District Court, November 6, 1973 (mo) No. 442, 7-1 Mutaishū, 33.

[190] Iimura and Sano, "Chitekizaisanfunsō ni okeru karishobun no katsuyō nitsuite," 41.

[191] Nagoya District Court, May 20, 1985, Sho 59 (yo) No. 318, 17-2 Mutaishū, 239.

[192] Kyoto District Court, June 26, Sho 42 (yo) No. 56, 1967 (yo) No. 56.

[193] Gifu District Court, April 14, 1971, Sho 44 (yo) No. 53, 3-1 Mutaishū, 180.

- infringement affecting the core product of the plaintiff[194]
- widespread publication of promotion material by the defendant incorrectly asserting non-infringement[195]
- infringement in a very small market with only a few participants and substitutes in which an infringement inevitably results in substantial damages for the patentee and its licensees[196]
- existence of substitute products manufactured by the defendant which are not IP-infringing
- contributory infringement by an object which can only be used for patent-infringing purposes.[197]

(d) Procedural Overview

The preliminary injunction can be decided in a trial hearing (*kōtōbenron*) or a court hearing of the defendant (*saimusha shinjin*),[198] the latter being more common in practice. The court usually grants the defendant a preparation period of three weeks until the court session.[199] Rendering a preliminary injunction without hearing the defendant is very rare and generally only possible in situations where infringement is easy to prove and where the scheduled court hearing and the accompanied warning of the defendant would obviously run against the purpose of the injunction.[200] **12.68**

A patentee will only be able to obtain a preliminary injunction against obvious infringement conduct. Thus, in a case of multiple infringement actions by one defendant, the patentee should move for preliminary injunctions only in those cases where *prima facie* evidence for an injunction can be presented. Such separation of equitable claims can also be done after filing for preliminary injunction.[201] Frequently, the defendant will not be interested in a quick resolution of the dispute. Nevertheless, he is expected to—at least in theory—contribute to an efficient and smooth resolution of the dispute and should refrain from any measures delaying the proceedings.[202] If the defendant was aware of the fact that his conduct was likely to cause infringement and had obtained expert opinion examining the legal and factual situation, he is obliged to provide the court with such expert opinions.[203] **12.69**

The patentee often moves for a preliminary injunction and files for the main proceedings at the same time.[204] In many cases, the decision regarding the preliminary injunction will be announced roughly around the time of the closing argument of the main proceedings.[205] **12.70**

194 Shizuoka District Court, November 6, 1973, Sho 48 (mo) No. 442, 7-1 Mutaishū, 33.

195 Osaka High Court, May 8, 1969, Sho 42 (ne) No. 1104, 237 Hanrei Times, 201.

196 Ibid.

197 Aomori District Court, May 22, 1972, Sho 46 (yo) No. 2, 4-1 Mutaishu, 313.

198 Japanese Civil Provisional Remedies Act, § 23(4); see also Kazuo Kato, "Shuppan-mono no insatsu, seihon, hanbai, hanpu-tō no karishobun ni yoru jizen sashidome to kenpō 21-jō 2-kō zendan ni iu ken'etsu," 41(9) *Hoso Jiho* (1989): 2621; Mamoru Hanari, *Kari sashiosae karishobun no hōritsu sōdan* (2004), 12.

199 Ibid. 39.

200 Ibid. 40; one of the rare cases of obtaining a preliminary injunction without a hearing of the defendant is described in Eiji Katayama and Takayuki Hirose, "Senryaku toshite no chizai Karishobun to kanzeitetsuzuki no yuukou katsuyou," 29 *Law & Technology* (2005): 57, 59.

201 Iimura and Sano, "Chitekizaisanfunsō ni okeru karishobun no katsuyō nitsuite," 42.

202 Iimura and Sano, "Chitekizaisanfunsō ni okeru karishobun no katsuyō nitsuite," 43.

203 Tokyo District Court, September 20, 1999, Hei 11 (yo) No. 22125, 1696, Hanrei Jihō (1999), 76—*iMac*.

204 Iimura and Sano, "Chitekizaisanfunsō ni okeru karishobun no katsuyō nitsuite," 43.

205 Ibid.

As the outcome of the preliminary injunction will heavily influence the main proceedings, especially in situations where the factual circumstances are legally and technically unambiguous, the patentee should prepare the motion for preliminary injunctive relief very carefully. In uncomplicated cases, the motion for initiating the main proceedings and the motion for the preliminary injunction can often be seen to have basically the same content.[206]

(e) Damages for Wrongful Injunctive Relief

12.71 Japanese case law allows defendants who incurred damages due to a wrongful preliminary injunction to claim compensation of such damages from the plaintiff who moved for the preliminary injunction.[207] In 2005, the Osaka High Court confirmed the applicability of such general civil law claim for damages, which is based on Japanese Civil Code, § 709, in patent law cases.[208] According to the court's decision, the defendant could claim damages for the wrongful preliminary injunction, as the underlying patent had been ruled invalid after the court issued the injunction order. The court considered the hardship for the plaintiff, who is held accountable for the examination errors of the JPO in possibly complex and unclear technical circumstances.[209] But at the same time, the court concluded that the party moving for the preliminary injunction should be in the best position of all parties, including the JPO, to provide a final evaluation of the infringement and validity situation and its underlying technical parameters. The court's decision provided a legal basis for compensating the party who might have incurred substantial and far-reaching damages caused by an unjustified preliminary injunction. Having said so, in the precedent case the court only awarded damages of 1 million yen caused by the market confusion and reputation damage incurred by the preliminary injunction, plus attorneys' fees and other costs.[210]

---

[206] Ibid.

[207] Confirmed by the Supreme Court. S. Ct., December 24, 1968, Sho 43 (O) No. 260, 22-13 Minshu (1968), 3428.

[208] Osaka High Court, July 21, 2005, Hei 15 (wa) No. 7750, 1912 Hanrei Jihō (2005), 107—*Damage Claim for Wrongful Injunction.*

[209] Ibid. 113.

[210] Ibid. 118.

Part V

REMEDIES

13

UNITED STATES

A. Claim for Injunctive Relief

Section 283 of the US Patent Act vests courts with the power to "grant injunctions in accordance with the principles of equity to prevent the violation of any right secured by patent, on such terms as the court deems reasonable."[1] Until 2006, courts routinely granted permanent injunctions after finding infringement of a valid patent. The discretion not to grant an injunction on the basis of equity was resorted to only in exceptional cases where the infringer could show that the patentee had failed to sufficiently practice the invention and thus had not served the public need.[2] Except for in the health care industry where the public relied on the availability of the infringing product, the infringer rarely met this high burden.[3] However, in 2006, the US Supreme Court reviewed the practice of granting injunctions in patent law, and held that courts must consider the principles of equity before awarding injunctive relief.[4] Consequently, it became more difficult to obtain a permanent injunction order in district court proceedings. **13.01**

1. Requirements

NTP, Inc. v. Research in Motion, Ltd., a 2005 case involving the manufacturer of the BlackBerry smart phone, sparked the discussion over the legitimacy of awarding permanent injunctions in almost every patent infringement case. The court held Research in Motion ("RIM") liable for infringing several patents related to mobile data transmission owned by the non-practicing entity (NTE).[5] To avoid an injunction that would have shut down Blackberry's messaging services in the United States, RIM reached a last-minute settlement with NTP and agreed to pay NTP US$612.5 million in damages.[6] **13.02**

While the Supreme Court had denied RIM's petition for certiorari in 2006,[7] it granted certiorari[8] to eBay in a comparable case only a few months later. In *MercExchange, LLC v. eBay, Inc.*, the District Court found eBay liable for infringing two patents owned by MercExchange.[9] The District Court conducted a rare (at the time) analysis **13.03**

---

[1] 35 U.S.C. 283.

[2] E.g., *Rite-Hite Corp. v. Kelley Co.*, 56 F.3d 1538, 1547 (Fed. Cir. 1995).

[3] E.g., *Hybritech, Inc. v. Abbott Labs.*, 4 U.S.P.Q. 2d 1001 (C.D. Cal. 1987), aff'd, 849 F.2d 1446 (Fed. Cir. 1988).

[4] *eBay Inc. v. MercExchange, LLC*, 547 U.S. 388 (2006).

[5] *NTP, Inc. v. Research in Motion, Ltd.*, 418 F.3d 1282, 1290 (Fed. Cir. 2005).

[6] Susan Decker and Rebecca Barr, "BlackBerry Maker Pays Rival $612.5M To Settle Suit," *Boston Globe*, March 4, 2006, A9.

[7] *Research In Motion, Ltd. v. NTP, Inc.*, 546 U.S. 1157 (2006).

[8] *eBay Inc. v. MercExchange, LLC*, 547 U.S. 388 (2006).

[9] *MercExchange, LLC v. eBay, Inc.*, 275 F. Supp. 2d 695 (E.D. Va. 2003).

of the appropriateness of granting permanent injunctive relief, and ultimately denied MercExchange's request for an injunction.[10] However, the Federal Circuit reopened the issue when it reversed the District Court's decision and ordered injunctive relief.[11]

13.04 In one of the first landmark Supreme Court decisions in patent law since the inauguration of the Federal Circuit, the Supreme Court unanimously overruled the Federal Circuit's opinion, and ended the practice of presuming irreparable harm in a patent infringement case.[12] Instead, the Court held that patent owners, like other non-patent litigants seeking equitable relief, must show that they are entitled to a permanent injunction under a four-factor test. Specifically, the Court concluded that the patentee must prove:[13]

(1) that the patentee has suffered an irreparable injury
(2) that remedies available at law (such as monetary damages) are inadequate to compensate for the injury
(3) that the balance of the hardships warrants a remedy in equity
(4) that the public interest would not be harmed by a permanent injunction.

13.05 One of the concurring opinions reveals that the decision was motivated in part by the Court's growing concern over the increasingly strong bargaining power of non-practicing entities ("NPEs") in patent litigation. Specifically, these NPEs would demand high damage claims from established market participants who had only infringed one of a multitude of patents contained in a complex product.[14]

13.06 After the Supreme Court handed down its *eBay* decision, district courts began routinely applying the four-factor test and accordingly began rejecting claims for injunctive relief despite infringement of a valid patent. Between 2006 and 2010, courts granted requests for injunctive relief after finding infringement in only 72 percent of all cases, down from 95 percent pre-*eBay*.[15] A very similar average injunction grant rate was reported by a more recent study reviewing decisions issued until the end of December 2013.[16] The likelihood of being able to prevail in the *eBay* test and to obtain injunctive relief depends, to a great extent, on the nature of the patentee and the competitive situation between such a patentee and the patent infringer. According to a 2012 study, the likelihood for NPEs, such as universities, research institutes, and independent inventors, to obtain a permanent injunction dropped to 54 percent[17]—that is, significantly below the average injunction grant rate. And while this number still looks rather high, a later study conducted by Colleen Chien and

[10] Ibid. 710–15.

[11] *MercExchange, LLC v. eBay, Inc.*, 401 F.3d 1323, 1338–39 (Fed. Cir. 2005).

[12] *eBay Inc. v. MercExchange, LLC*, 547 U.S. 388, 393–94 (2006).

[13] Ibid. 391.

[14] Ibid. 396–97. For further analysis, see, e.g., Miranda Jones, "Permanent Injunction, a Remedy by any other Name is Patently Not the Same: How *eBay v. MercExchange* Affects the Patent Right of Non-practicing Entities," 14 *Geo. Mason L. Rev.* 1035 (2006–7), 1037–39; Robin M. Davis, "Failed Attempts to Dwarf the Patient Trolls: Permanent Injunctions in the Patent Infringement Cases under the Proposed Patent Reform Act of 2005 and *eBay v. Mercexchange*," 17 *Cornell J. L. & Pub. Pol'y* (2007–8): 431, 443–47.

[15] Federal Trade Commission, "The Evolving IP Marketplace: Aligning Patent Notice and Remedies with Competition," March 2011 (www.ftc.gov/os/2011/03/110307patentreport.pdf) ("FTC Report"), 256.

[16] Christopher B. Seaman, "Property Rules vs. Liability Rules in Patent Litigation After eBay: An Empirical Study" (forthcoming 2015), reporting a grant rate of 72.8% (158 of 217 cases).

[17] FTC Report, 256.

Mark Lemley[18] suggests a much lower injunction grant rate of only 7 percent in litigation brought by patent assertion entities.[19] The study highlights the varying treatment that different types of NPEs receive from district courts.

(a) Irreparable Harm

In the wake of the *eBay* decision, courts tend to focus their analysis on the first two *eBay*-factors: whether (1) the patentee had suffered an irreparable injury in the course of the infringement, and (2) a damage award would be inadequate to compensate for the injury. Often, courts apply these two factors as one, reasoning that "irreparable harm" is harm that "cannot be adequately atoned for in money."[20] **13.07**

Typically, the patentee bears the burden of showing irreparable harm.[21] A central element for finding irreparable harm is a factual determination of whether the plaintiff and the defendant are competitors in the same industry. For such a determination, courts often require more than a mere assertion of competition and thus a plaintiff must produce particularized facts such as lost market share, lost customers, or price erosion.[22] One way a plaintiff can establish irreparable harm is to show the loss of "sticky" customers to an infringer's product—that is, a loss of customers who became locked into a specific hardware product due to the purchase of such a product at a critical time.[23] **13.08**

Some courts noted that a finding of lost market share, lost customers, or price erosion requires a careful determination of the relevant market. For instance, where a patentee's **13.09**

[18] Colleen V. Chien and Mark A. Lemley, "Patent Holdup, the ITC, and the Public Interest," 98 *Cornell L. Rev.* (2012): 1, 10.

[19] Ibid. 9–13.

[20] *Wald v. Mudhopper Oilfield Services, Inc.*, No. CIV-04-1693, 2006 WL 2128851 (W.D. Okla. July 27, 2006); *Paice, LLC v. Toyota Motor Corp.*, No. 2:04-CV-21I-DF, 2006 WL 2385139 (E.D. Tex. August 16, 2006), *5.

[21] See, e.g., *z4 Techs., Inc. v. Microsoft Corp.*, 434 F. Supp. 2d 437, 440 (E.D. Tex. 2006) (holding that *eBay* eliminated the irreparable harm presumption in the permanent injunction context). See also *Apple, Inc. v. Samsung Electronics Co., Ltd.*, 2011 WL 7036077, *20+ (N.D. Cal. 2011) (No. 11-CV-01846-LHK), aff'd in part, vacated in part, remanded by 678 F.3d 1314 (Fed. Cir. 2012); *Metro-Goldwyn-Mayer Studios, Inc. v. Grokster, Ltd.*, 518 F.Supp. 2d 1197, 1211 (C.D. Cal. 2007); the Federal Circuit stated in a non-precedential preliminary injunction case decided in 2009 that *eBay* removed the presumption of irreparable harm and stated that "[t]he burden is now on the patentee to demonstrate that its potential losses cannot be compensated by monetary damages." *Automated Merchandising Sys. v. Crane Co.*, Nos. 2009–1158, 2009–1164, 2009 WL 4878643, *3 (Fed. Cir. December 16, 2009). However, in an earlier case, a different panel of the Federal Circuit had held that "[i]t remains an open question whether there remains a rebuttable presumption of irreparable harm following eBay." *Broadcom Corp. v. Qualcomm, Inc.*, 543 F.3d 683, 702 (Fed. Cir. 2008).

[22] E.g., *Power Integrations, Inc. v. Fairchild Semiconductor Int'l, Inc.*, No. 04-1371, 2008 WL 5210843 (D. Del. December 12, 2008) (finding that lost market share and harm to plaintiff's reputation and goodwill provided evidence of irreparable harm); *Sensormatic Electronics Corp. v. Tag Co. U.S.*, 632 F. Supp. 2d 1147 (S.D. Fla. 2008) (future loss of market share and price erosion), aff'd in part, 367 Fed. Appx. 143 (Fed. Cir. 2010) (non-precedential opinion); *Verizon Services Corp. v. Vonage Holdings Corp.*, 503 F.3d 1295 (Fed. Cir. 2007) (lost customers and price erosion); *Becton Dickinson & Co. v. Tyco Healthcare Group, LP*, No. 02-1694, 2008 WL 4745882 (D. Del. October 29, 2008) (lost market share and customers); *Brooktrout, Inc. v. Eicon Networks Corp.*, No. 2:03-CV-59, 2007 WL 1730112 (E.D. Tex. June 14, 2007) (lost market share); *MPT, Inc. v. Marathon Labels, Inc.*, 505 F. Supp. 2d 401 (N.D. Ohio 2007) (lost market share and customer goodwill), aff'd in part, rev'd in part, 258 Fed. Appx. 318 (Fed. Cir. 2007); see FTC Report, 261–62 for further cases.

[23] *TiVo v. Echostar Commc'ns Corp.*, 446 F. Supp. 2d 664, 667 (E.39 D. Tex. 2006), aff'd in part, rev'd in part, 516 F.3d 1290 (Fed. Cir. 2008); *Transamerica Life Insurance Co. v. Lincoln Nat'l Life Ins. Co.*, 625 F. Supp. 2d 702 (N.D. Iowa 2009), rev'd on other grounds *sub nom.*, *Lincoln Nat. Life Ins. Co. v. Transamerica Life Ins. Co.*, 609 F.3d 1364 (Fed. Cir. 2010).

product and an infringing product are found to compete in a narrow market with a very low number of participants, any sale of the infringing product will almost necessarily result in a loss of the patentee's product's market share.[24] At the same time, the Federal Circuit held in *Broadcom Corp. v. Qualcomm, Inc.* that competition between a patentee and an infringer may extend beyond the scope of a product market defined by the patented technology. In that case, Broadcom successfully claimed irreparable injury even though its patents pertained only to the CDMA cell phone standard, while Qualcomm's infringing product incorporated solely WCDMA technology. The court extended the relevant market beyond CDMA technology, finding that the parties competed not only for "each consumer sale," but also for "design wins for the development and production of cell phones."[25]

13.10 The Federal Circuit heightened the standard to show irreparable harm in 2012 when it held that the patentee has to show a causal nexus between the alleged infringement and the specific harm it will suffer absent the injunction.[26] Showing such a nexus can be quite difficult in cases where products are covered by a large number of patents, out of which only a few are infringed. The Federal Circuit explained that:

> sales lost to an infringing product cannot irreparably harm a patentee if consumers buy that product for reasons other than the patented feature. If the patented feature does not drive the demand for the product, sales would be lost even if the offending feature were absent from the accused product. Thus, a likelihood of irreparable harm cannot be shown if sales would be lost regardless of the infringing conduct.[27]

Accordingly, general consumer appreciation for the overall product would not be sufficient to show the required nexus between infringement and irreparable harm. However, reliable surveys demonstrating that customers are prepared to support increased pricing for the infringed features may be sufficient to show the causal nexus.[28] The requirement to produce clear evidence for specific irreparable harm caused by the infringement has become a high obstacle for patentees requesting injunctive relief, especially in telecommunication and semiconductor cases where even selected features, which may drive customer demand, are subject to many patents other than the infringed ones.[29]

13.11 After *eBay*, a few courts also took into account additional qualitative factors, such as damage to a patentee's reputation caused by a competitor's infringing product, on the basis that

---

[24] See, e.g., *Martek Biosciences Corp. v. Nutrinova Inc.*, 520 F. Supp. 2d 537 (D. Del. 2007) (defining the market as vegetarian DHA for adult foods and beverages, in which only the plaintiff and the defendant competed, resulting in a finding of irreparable harm), aff'd in part and rev'd in part, 579 F.3d 1363 (Fed. Cir. 2009); see also *Arlington Indus., Inc. v. Bridgeport Fittings, Inc.*, No. 3:01-CV-0485, 2010 WL 817519, *3–4 (M.D. Pa. March 9, 2010) (defining the market as a narrow subset of electrical conduit fittings in line with the definition by the asserted patents); but, e.g., in *Advanced Cardiovascular Systems*, the court adopted a broader market definition, in which not only the patentee's and the infringer's product but also a number of non-infringing products competed, *Advanced Cardiovascular Systems, Inc. v. Medtronic Vascular, Inc.*, 579 F. Supp. 2d 554, 560–61 (D. Del. 2008).

[25] The relevance of "design wins" to show irreparable harm was more recently reconfirmed by the Federal Circuit in *Broadcom Corp. v. Emulex Corp.*, 732 F.3d 1325, 1337–38 (Fed. Cir. 2013).

[26] *Apple, Inc. v. Samsung Electronics Co., Ltd.*, 678 F.3d 1314, 1323–28 (Fed. Cir. 2012).

[27] Ibid. 1324.

[28] *Apple Inc. v. Samsung Electronics Co., Ltd.*, 735 F.3d 1352, 1364–65 (Fed. Cir. 2013).

[29] *Apple Inc. v. Motorola, Inc.*, 757 F.3d 1286, 1340 (Fed. Cir. 2014); *Carnegie Mellon University v. Marvell Technology Group, Ltd.*, 2014 WL 1320154, *27 (W.D. Pa. 2014).

reputational damages are difficult or impractical to quantify and, thus, impossible to be adequately compensated by money.[30]

Although an actual competitive situation in a goods market between a patentee and an infringer will be supportive when analyzing irreparable harm, the absence of such competition does not automatically bar a finding of irreparable harm. In fact, a variety of courts granted injunctions despite an absence of direct competition in a clearly defined goods market.[31] To illustrate, a permanent injunction was granted in two cases involving universities, neither of which practiced the patented invention.[32] Both universities, however, had concluded exclusive license agreements, and the respective exclusive licensees manufactured products in competition with the infringing products. Because the infringements resulted in lost sales to the licensees as well as unquantifiable damages to the reputation and market position of the patentees, the courts granted permanent injunctions.[33] In a decision involving a patent for WLAN technology held by the Australia-based Commonwealth Scientific and Industrial Research Organization ("CSIRO"), the court awarded a permanent injunction even though the patentee did not manufacture any products and had regularly granted multiple licenses to its patents.[34] Somewhat inconsistently with the prevailing interpretation of the standard for irreparable harm[35], the *CSIRO* court awarded the injunction on grounds that the conduct of the defendant, the Japanese manufacturer Buffalo, would deprive CSIRO of licensing revenue required for funding additional research projects,[36] would damage CSIRO's reputation, and would hinder CSIRO's ability to recruit leading scientists.[37] The court's decision was surprising given that monetary damages—the remedy at law—appears to have been adequate compensation for infringement in this case. Indeed, the business model of CSIRO was based on providing licenses to its WLAN technology and awarding standard reasonable and non-discriminatory ("RAND") licenses; such facts **13.12**

[30] *z4 Techs., Inc. v. Microsoft Corp.*, 434 F. Supp. 2d 437, 442 (E.D. Tex. 2006); *Callaway Golf Co. v. Acushet Co.*, 585 F. Supp. 2d 600, 621 (D. Del. 2008), aff'd in part, vacated in part, 576 F.3d 1331 (Fed. Cir. 2009); *Emory Univ. v. Nova Biogenics, Inc.*, No. 1:06-CV-0141, 2008 WL 2945476, *4 (N.D. Ga. 2008).

[31] *Broadcom Corp. v. Qualcomm, Inc.*, 543 F.3d 683 (Fed. Cir. 2008) (district court's injunction grant affirmed.); *i4i Ltd. Partnership v. Microsoft Corp.*, 670 F. Supp. 2d 568 (E.D. Tex. 2009), aff'd, 598 F.3d 831 (Fed. Cir. 2010) (affirming the grant of an injunction while modifying its effective date), aff'd 131 S.Ct. 2238 (2011); *Kowalski v. Mommy Gina Tuna Resources*, Nos. 05-00679, 05-00787, 06-00182, 2009 WL 856006 (D. Haw. March 30, 2009), clarified, 2009 WL 1360695 (D. Haw. May 7, 2009); *Joyal Products, Inc. v. Johnson Electric North America, Inc.*, No. 04-5172, 2009 WL 512156 (D. N.J. February 27, 2009) aff'd *per curiam*, 335 Fed. Appx. 48 (Fed. Cir. 2009); *Emory Univ. v. Nova Biogenics, Inc.*, No. 1:06-CV-0141, 2008 WL 2945476 (N.D. Ga. July 25, 2008); *Commonwealth Scientific and Indus. Research Org. v. Buffalo Tech., Inc.* ("*CSIRO*"), 492 F. Supp. 2d 600, 601 (E.D. Tex. 2007); *Johns Hopkins Univ. v. Datascope Corp.*, 513 F. Supp. 2d 578 (D. Md. 2007), rev'd on other grounds and remanded, 543 F.3d 1342 (Fed. Cir. 2008).

[32] *Emory Univ. v. Nova Biogenics, Inc.*, No. 1:06-CV-0141, 2008 WL 2945476 (N.D. Ga. July 25, 2008); *Johns Hopkins Univ. v. Datascope Corp.*, 513 F. Supp. 2d 578 (D. Md. 2007), rev'd on other grounds and remanded, 543 F.3d 1342 (Fed. Cir. 2008).

[33] *Emory*, 2008 WL 2945476, *5; *Johns Hopkins*, 513 F. Supp. 2d 578, 586.

[34] *Commonwealth Scientific and Indus. Research Org. v. Buffalo Tech., Inc.* ("*CSIRO*"), 492 F. Supp. 2d 600, 601 (E.D. Tex. 2007).

[35] The *CSIRO* court was not only harshly criticized, e.g., by the Northern District of California in *Hynix Semiconductor, Inc. v. Rambus, Inc.*, 609 F. Supp. 2d 951, 983 (N.D. Cal. 2009), but also by prominent commentators, e.g., Dan L. Burk and Mark A. Lemley, *The Patent Crisis and How the Courts Can Solve It* (2009), 139.

[36] *CSIRO*, 492 F. Supp. 2d, 603–8.

[37] Ibid. 604.

would usually support a finding that monetary damages—the remedy at law—would be adequate to compensate for the infringement.

13.13 Furthermore, the Federal Circuit explicitly held that NPEs not in direct competition in a goods market would be entitled to injunctive relief as long as they could demonstrate irreparable harm.[38] In reality, however, the ratio of NPEs able to obtain an injunction order after showing infringement of a valid patent is significantly smaller than the ratio of patentees practicing the invention. Between 2006 and 2010, practicing entities obtained an injunction order in 76 percent of cases after showing infringement of a valid patent, compared to only 54 percent for NPEs.[39]

(b) Balance of Hardships

13.14 A patentee also has to demonstrate that an injunction is warranted given "the balance of hardships between the plaintiff and defendant."[40] Because the hardship incurred by a plaintiff is typically analyzed when determining irreparable harm, a balance of hardship inquiry instead focuses on the hardship an injunction would impose on the defendant. In some cases where injunctive relief was awarded, courts simply dismissed the infringer's claim of hardship on the basis that a party who "elects to build a business on a product found to infringe cannot be heard to complain if an injunction against continuing infringement destroys the business."[41] In other cases where an injunction was awarded, however, courts conducted a more detailed analysis of the infringer's hardship and considered such factors as:

- the size of the defendant compared to the plaintiff[42]
- the ratio of the defendant's business consisting of infringing products[43]
- whether a minor investment was required for the defendant to develop the infringing product.[44]

13.15 On the other hand, courts often reject a request for an injunction in cases where the patentee fails to sufficiently demonstrate irreparable harm, or where an injunction would result in severe consequences for the infringer. For example, in *Paice LLC v. Toyota Motor Corp.*, the court held that shutting down the production of the "Prius" model not only would affect the defendant Toyota but also would impose grave consequences on dealers and suppliers.[45] Likewise, in *z4 Technologies, Inc. v. Microsoft Corp.*, the court held that disabling

---

[38] *Voda v. Cordis Corp.*, F.3d 1311, 1329 (Fed. Cir. 2008).

[39] FTC Report, 256; for a more detailed analysis of the injunction grant rate for NPEs after *eBay*, see the study by Chien and Lemley, "Patent Holdup, the ITC, and the Public Interest."

[40] *eBay Inc.*, 547 U.S., 391 (2006).

[41] *3M Innovative Properties Co. v. Avery Dennison Corp.*, No. 01-1781, 2006 WL 2735499, *2 (D. Minn. September 25, 2006), citing *Windsurfing Int'l v. AMF, Inc.*, 782 F. 2d 995, 1003 (Fed. Cir. 1986); other cases where courts applied the same rationale to the balance of hardship factor include *Johns Hopkins*, 513 F. Supp. 2d, 586; *Smith & Nephew, Inc. v. Synthes*, 466 F. Supp. 2d 978 (W.D. Tenn. 2006), 984–85; *Apple, Inc. v. Samsung Electronics Co., Ltd.*, 2012 WL 2576136, *8 (N.D. Cal. July 3, 2012) (No. 12-CV-00630-LHK).

[42] *Callaway Golf*, 585 F. Supp. 2d, 622; *TiVo*, 446 F. Supp. 2d, 670.

[43] *Martek*, 520 F. Supp. 2d, 559; *MPT*, 505 F. Supp. 2d, 420; 800 *Adept, Inc. v. Murex Securities, Ltd.*, 505 F. Supp. 2d 1327 (M.D. Fla. 2007), 1338.

[44] *Power-One, Inc. v. Artesyn Technologies, Inc.*, No. 2:05-CV-463, 2008 WL 1746636 (E.D. Tex. April 11, 2008), *1 n.1.

[45] *Paice*, 2006 WL 2385139, *6; however, it should be noted that the Federal Circuit has held in a more recent case that the effect of an injunction on third parties not relevant for the balance of hardship inquiry. See *Acumed, LLC v. Stryker Corp.*, 551 F.3d 1323 (Fed. Cir. 2008), 1330; see also *SynQor, Inc v. Artesyn Technologies, Inc.*, 2011 WL 238645, *4 (E.D. Tex. 2011).

the infringing activation software would create a flood of pirated software resulting in incalculable losses for the infringer Microsoft.[46]

Some courts resolve the balance of hardship by granting a grace period, lasting from two months to almost two years, before the injunction order becomes effective.[47] The duration of such a grace period is usually determined by estimating the time it would take an infringer to design around the patent in order to abrogate the infringer's hardship. **13.16**

(c) Public Interest

In recent years, only a few cases have discussed the public interest prong in detail. When granting injunctive relief, most courts reduce the analysis of the public interest by simply noting that the "public has an interest in maintaining a strong patent system. This interest is served by enforcing an adequate remedy for patent infringement."[48] **13.17**

The public interest factor is usually subject to closer scrutiny in cases involving heath care products. For instance, a court denied an injunction, basing its analysis on the fact that some cardiologists preferred the features of the infringing drug over the patented one, and was concerned that surgeries could fail if the infringing drug was no longer available.[49] In contrast, another court granted an injunction after it collected extensive evidence and found that the infringer failed to show a need for its infringing drug, as there was no evidence showing that the infringing drug provided any significant advantages over non-infringing treatments.[50] In line with the general rationale for promoting the public interest in a strong patent system, courts often grant injunctive relief despite infringers' claims that providing the market with cheaper generic drugs would serve the public interest. Courts balance the public interest in affordable drugs against the public interest in having pharmaceutical companies shouldering the substantial costs[51] required for research and development necessary before a new drug can be brought to market.[52] **13.18**

---

[46] *z4*, 513 F. Supp. 2d, 443.

[47] *Broadcom*, 543 F.3d 683, 704; *B. Braun Melsungen AG v. Terumo Medical Corp.*, 778 F.Supp.2d 506, 525 (D. Del. 2011).

[48] *TiVo*, 446 F. Supp. 2d, 670; *Funai Electronics Co., Ltd. v. Daewoo Elec. Corp.*, 593 F. Supp. 97 2d 1088, 1111 (N.D. Cal. 2009); *Kowalski*, 2009 WL 856006, *2; *Mass Engineered Design, Inc. v. Ergotron, Inc.*, 633 F. Supp. 2d 361, 394 (E.D. Tex 2009); *Becton Dickinson*, 2008 WL 4745882, *4; *Emory*, 2008 WL 2945476, *5; *Power Integrations*, 2008 WL 5210843, *1; *Power-One*, 2008 WL 1746636, *1 n.1; *Sensormatic*, 632 F. Supp. 2d, 1182; *TruePosition, Inc. v. Andrew Corp.*, 568 F. Supp. 2d 500, 533 (D. Del. 2008), amended in part, 2009 WL 192470 (D. Del. January 27, 2009), aff'd, 389 Fed. Appx. 1000 (Fed. Cir. 2010); *Trading Technologies Int'l, Inc. v. eSpeed, Inc.*, No. 04-C-5312, 2008 WL 4531371, *5 (N.D. Ill. May 22, 2008), aff'd, 595 F.3d 1340 (Fed. Cir. 2010); *Atlanta Attachment Co. v. Leggett & Platt, Inc.*, No. 1:05-CV-1071, 2007 WL 5011980, *8 (N.D. Ga. February 23, 2007); *Baden Sports, Inc. v. Kabushiki Kaisha Molten*, No. C06-210, 2007 WL 2790777, *3 (W.D. Wash. September 25, 2007); *Brooktrout*, 2007 WL 1730112, *2; *Martek*, 520 F. Supp. 2d, 558; *MPT*, 505 F. Supp. 2d, 420; *O2 Micro Int'l, Ltd. v. Beyond Innovation Tech. Co., Ltd.*, 2007 WL 869576, * 3 (E.D. Tex. March 21, 2007), vacated, 521 F.3d 1351 (Fed. Cir. 2008); *Ortho-McNeil Pharm., Inc. v. Mylan Labs., Inc.*, Nos. 04-1689, 06-757, 06-5166, 2007 WL 869545, *1 (D.N.J. March 20, 2007), aff'd in part, 520 F.3d 1358 (Fed. Cir. 2008); *Black & Decker, Inc. v. Robert Bosch Tool Corp.*, No. 04 C 7955, 2006 WL 3446144, *5 (N.D. Ill. November 29, 2006).

[49] *Advanced Cardiovascular Systems*, 579 F. Supp. 2d 554, 560–61.

[50] *Amgen, Inc. v. F. Hoffman-La Roche, Ltd.*, 581 F. Supp. 2d 160, 212–26 (D. Mass. 2008), aff'd in part, vacated in part, 580 F.3d 1340 (Fed. Cir. 2009).

[51] Industry representatives from the pharmaceutical industry have claimed that the research and development costs for one new drug in the United States costs as much as US$800 million. While this figure is generally considered as inflated, more conservative estimates predict substantial investment for research and development to be US$100 million to $300 million.

[52] *Sanofi-Synthelabo v. Apotex, Inc.*, 492 F. Supp. 2d 353, 397 (S.D. N.Y. 2007), aff'd, 530 F.3d 1075 (Fed. Cir. 2009).

2. Scope of Injunction Order

13.19 Section 283 of the Patent Act provides courts with the authority to "grant injunctions . . . on such terms as the court deems reasonable." Such broad authority is further specified by Federal Rule of Civil Procedure (FRCP) 65(d), which requires a plaintiff, in seeking an injunction, to "state its terms specifically," as well as to "describe in reasonable detail . . . the act or acts restrained or required." In interpreting this requirement, the Federal Circuit has held that injunctions prohibiting patent infringement cannot "simply prohibi[t] future infringement of patent," but must "specifically describe the infringing actions enjoined, with reference to particular products."[53]

13.20 Despite the fact that the Federal Circuit confirmed and somewhat defined the applicability of FRCP 65(d) for patent law, there is a general consensus among federal courts that a failure to meet the requirements of FRCP 65(d) does not render an injunction order void. In at least one decision, the Federal Circuit confirmed this opinion, holding that if an injunction incompliant with FRCP 65(d) is not challenged on direct appeal, it should later not be treated as void, but rather narrowly construed.[54]

13.21 The precise scope and subsequent construction of the injunction order is most relevant in contempt proceedings. According to established precedent, injunctive relief will only cover the precise product or process "previously admitted or adjudged to [the] infringer, and . . . other devices which are no more than colorably different."[55] A study by Professor John Golden revealed, however, that the scope of an injunction order is often not limited to the infringing product or process or to deviations that are no more than colorably different, but usually contains broader language, for example, ordering an infringer to generally refrain from infringing particular claims or entire patents.[56] The study analyzed every injunction order issued by district courts in 2010 available in the database Lex Machina, and found that around 57 percent of the injunctions issued contained broad language ordering the infringer to refrain from further infringing specified or unspecified patent claims or patents.[57] Indeed, every district court issuing more than one injunction included extensively broad language into at least one of its orders.

13.22 Interestingly, the study also revealed that the use of broad injunctions was substantially less frequent in cases involving the infringement of pharmaceutical and biotech related patents. Only 5 percent of the injunctions issued in such cases contained extensively broad language, and only 12 percent of the court decisions included a permissible extension of the injunction beyond the infringing product or process.[58] However, given the comparable high degree of precision in patent claim drafting and the surrounding heavy regulation of

---

[53] *Int'l Rectifier Corp. v. IXYS Corp.*, 383 F.3d 1312, 1316 (Fed. Cir. 2004).

[54] *KSM Fastening Sys., Inc. v. H.A. Jones Co.*, 776 F.2d 1522 (Fed. Cir. 1985).

[55] Ibid. 1526; see *Siebring v. Hansen*, 346 F.2d 474, 477 (8th Cir.), cert. denied, 382 U.S. 943 (1965); *Sure Plus Mfg. Co. v. Korbin*, 719 F.2d 1114, 1118 (11th Cir. 1983); *McCullough Tool Co. v. Well Surveys, Inc.*, 395 F.2d 230, 234 (10th Cir.), cert. denied, 393 U.S. 925 (1968); *Hopp Press, Inc. v. Joseph Freeman & Co.*, 323 F.2d 636, 637–38 (2d Cir. 1963); *E-I-M Co. v. Philadelphia Gear Works, Inc.*, 223 F.2d 36, 41–42 (5th Cir. 1955), cert. denied, 350 U.S. 933 (1956).

[56] John M. Golden, "Injunctions as More (or Less) than off Switches: Patent-infringement Injunctions' Scope," 90 *Tex. L. Rev.* 1399 (2011–12): 1399–472.

[57] Ibid. 1435.

[58] Ibid. 1440.

the approval process, such an exception to the general scope of injunctive relief is not that surprising.

3. Execution of Injunction Order

An injunction can be executed after fourteen days following the entry of the judgment awarding injunctive relief.[59] The defendant may, however, request the court to stay the injunction pending appeal.[60] In *Standard Havens Products*,[61] the Federal Circuit established four factors that the defendant has to establish in order to justify stay of an injunction against patent infringement pending appeal: (1) that it is likely to prevail on appeal; (2) that it will be irreparably injured if the stay is not granted; (3) that the stay will not "substantially injure other parties interested in the proceedings"; and (4) where the public interest lies. The above four factors are somewhat duplicative with the *eBay* standard, as *Standard Havens Products* had been issued fifteen years earlier than *eBay*. Nevertheless, the Federal Circuit has not amended the test of requesting stay pending appeal post-*eBay*.[62] The defendant facing execution of an injunction can request stay pending appeal both at district court and, if the district court denies such request, at the Federal Circuit.[63] **13.23**

District courts have held that an injunction should not be stayed pending appeal if the defendant clearly fails to indicate a likelihood of prevailing on appeal by merely reciting the arguments already provided at trial.[64] Showing of a "fair" or "better than negligible chance" is not sufficient to indicate a likelihood of prevailing on appeal.[65] At the same time, other courts have held that making a substantive case on the merits which doesn't need to trigger serious doubts concerning the correctness of district court decision may well be sufficient if other factors favor a stay pending appeal.[66] Especially in cases where a timely execution would cause significant hardship upon customers of the patent-infringing product or service and other third parties, courts seemed inclined to stay the injunction for a period long enough to allow the defendant to redesign the product to a degree that it would no longer infringe the patent.[67] **13.24**

However, absent such extraordinary circumstances, districts courts will usually not allow a stay pending appeal once the plaintiff succeeded in showing that an injunction is necessary.[68] And while the Federal Circuit may be more receptive to finding a likelihood of **13.25**

---

[59] FRCP 62(a).

[60] FRCP 62(c).

[61] *Standard Havens Products, Inc. v. Gencor Industries, Inc.*, 897 F.2d 511, 512 (Fed. Cir.1990), citing *Hilton v. Braunskill*, 481 U.S. 770, 776 (1987).

[62] For a suggestion of a new framework in light of eBay, see Daniel C. Tucker, "We Can't Stay This Way: Changing the Standard for Staying Injunctions Pending Appeal after eBay," 79 *Geo. Wash. L. Rev.* (2010–11): 1276.

[63] Fed. Rule App.Proc. 8(a).

[64] *Endress + Hauser, Inc. v. Hawk Measurement Systems Pty. Ltd.*, 932 F. Supp. 1147, 1149 (S.D. Ind. 1996); *ePlus Inc. v. Lawson Software, Inc.*, 2013 WL 4829321 (E.D. Va. 2013).

[65] *Honeywell Intern., Inc. v. Universal Avionics Systems Corp.*, 397 F. Supp. 2d 537, 549 (D. Del. 2005), 515 citing *Standard Havens Products*.

[66] *In re Hayes Microcomputer Products, Inc. Patent Litigation*, 766 F. Supp. 818, 823, 20 U.S.P.Q. 2d 1836 (N.D. Cal. 1991), judgment aff'd, 982 F.2d 1527, 25 U.S.P.Q. 2d 1241 (Fed. Cir. 1992); *Crucible, Inc. v. Stora Kopparbergs Bergslags AB*, 226 U.S.P.Q. 842, 1985 WL 2872 (W.D. Pa. 1985).

[67] See, e.g., *i4i Ltd. P'ship v. Microsoft Corp.*, 343 F. App'x 619, 619 (Fed. Cir. 2009) (*per curiam*).

[68] *Joy Technologies, Inc. v. Flakt, Inc.*, 24 U.S.P.Q. 2d (BNA) 1150, 1151 (D. Del. 1992); *TiVo, Inc. v. Echostar Commc'ns Corp.*, 446 F. Supp. 2d 664, 666.

prevailing on the merits than the district court, the defendant still has to meet the rather heavy burden of showing that the district court abused its discretion or committed an error of law when denying a stay.[69] Therefore, it is not surprising that the Federal Circuit does not often grant stays pending appeal that district courts have already denied.[70]

B. Exclusion Order

13.26 In addition to district courts, the International Trade Commission ("ITC") is empowered to grant exclusion orders per 19 US Code, § 1337 (section 337), which orders the US Customs and Border Protection to exclude infringing articles from importation into the United States.

13.27 According to the language of section 337 of the Tariff Act, issuance of an exclusion order is not subject to the same four-factor equitable test required to obtain injunctive relief under the Patent Act. At the same time, section 337(d)(1) of the Tariff Act provides for a public-interest qualifier, the occurrence of which may lead to a rejection of an exclusion order, depending on the exclusion order's effect upon:

(1) public health and welfare
(2) the competitive conditions in the United States economy
(3) the production of like or directly competitive articles in the United States
(4) United States consumers.

13.28 In 2010, the Federal Circuit considered whether an exclusion order under section 337 would not only require an examination of the above public-interest factors but also invoke the *eBay* factors.[71] In its analysis, the Federal Circuit focused on the legislative history of section 337, noting that the Omnibus Trade and Competitiveness Act passed by Congress in 1988[72] eliminated the previous requirement that a patentee should show irreparable harm to a domestic industry from continued importation of an infringing product.[73] In addition, the court reasoned that the absence of a monetary remedy under section 337, thus leaving an injunction as the only remedy available in ITC proceedings, served as a further indication that the *eBay* test should not apply to section 337.[74]

13.29 Even though the existence of two standards for basically the same remedy under US law is hardly ideal from a policy standpoint,[75] the Federal Circuit's interpretation of the legislative intent behind section 337 is convincing. First, the patent landscape has undergone some significant change between the passage of the Omnibus Trade and Competitiveness Act in 1988 and today. Furthermore, the considerable frustration that Congress faces when trying to update the legal framework, as evidenced by the history of the America Invents Act, highlights the significant difficulty in adapting law to changed circumstances in major

[69] *Smith Int'l, Inc. v. Hughes Tool Co.*, 718 F.2d 1573, 1579 (Fed. Cir. 1983).
[70] J. Preston Long and Allen M. Sokal, "Trial Court Procedures in Patent Litigation: Maximizing Chances of Success on Appeal: Part 2," 9 *Intell. Prop. & Tech. L.J.* (2013): 20, 25.
[71] *Spansion, Inc. v. ITC*, 629 F.3d 1331 (Fed. Cir. 2010).
[72] Pub.L. No. 100–418, 102 Stat. 1107.
[73] *Spansion*, 629 F.3d 1331, 1358–59.
[74] Ibid.
[75] See also Chien and Lemley, "Patent Holdup, the ITC, and the Public Interest," 18.

industries such as electronics or software. Nevertheless, absent a rather unlikely legislative change, the ITC will continue to apply a different standard for injunctive relief than district courts. Indeed, even Spansion, the party who argued in front of the Federal Circuit that the *eBay* standard should apply in ITC proceedings, seemed to have accepted the rationale provided by the Federal Circuit for the different standards, as it did not refer to these inconsistent standards when petitioning for a writ of certiorari from the Supreme Court.[76]

Under section 337(d), the ITC can award two different types of exclusion orders: limited exclusion orders and general exclusion orders. Limited exclusion orders ("LEO") extend only to patent-infringing products of a named respondent, whereas general exclusion orders ("GEO") extend to any product incorporating technology found to be infringing, irrespective of the product's source. Understandably, a GEO is a significantly more powerful remedy than an LEO. To obtain a GEO, a complainant has to demonstrate either (1) that the source of the infringing product is not easily identifiable, or (2) that a GEO is necessary to prevent circumvention of a LEO. **13.30**

Between 1989 and 2008, it became routine practice for the ITC to extend an LEO not only to the infringing product manufactured and imported by the named respondent but also to downstream products containing the infringing product, even if such downstream products were not manufactured by the named respondent. Such a liberal application of an LEO was granted if the complainant could show satisfaction of the so-called EPROMs factors, which were developed in the ITC decision *In Certain Erasable Programmable Read Only Memories*:[77] **13.31**

> [1.] the value of the infringing articles compared to the value of the downstream products in which they are incorporated, [2.] the identity of the manufacturer of the downstream products (i.e., are the downstream products manufactured by the party found to have committed the unfair act, or by third parties), [3.] the incremental value to complainant of the exclusion of downstream products, [4.] the incremental detriment to respondents of such exclusion, [5.] the burdens imposed on third parties resulting from exclusion of downstream products, [6.] the availability of alternative downstream products which do not contain the infringing articles, [7.] the likelihood that imported downstream products actually contain the infringing articles and are thereby subject to exclusion, [8.] the opportunity for evasion of an exclusion order which does not include downstream products, [and 9.] the enforceability of an order by Customs.[78]

In 2008, however, the Federal Circuit in *Kyocera v. International Trade Commission*[79] ended the practice of extending LEOs to parties not named as respondents. The complainant in the case, Broadcom, had obtained an LEO barring the respondent, Qualcomm, from importing a semiconductor that infringed Broadcom's patented technology.[80] Although Qualcomm was the only respondent named in the complaint, the ITC, in following its earlier practice, extended the LEO to downstream products manufactured and distributed by **13.32**

---

[76] See Appellate Petition, Motion and Filing at 2011 WL 3252818; cert. denied at 132 S. Ct. 758 (2011).

[77] *Certain Erasable Programmable Read-Only Memories, Components Thereof, Prods. Containing Such Memories, & Processes for Making Such Memories*, USITC Pub. No. 2196, Inv. No. 337-TA-276, Comm'n Op. (March 16, 1989) (EPROM Order), aff'd *sub nom., Hyundai Elecs. Indus. Co. v. U.S. Int'l Trade Comm'n*, 899 F.2d 1204, 1209–10 (Fed. Cir. 1990).

[78] Ibid. 125.

[79] *Kyocera v. Int'l Trade Comm'n*, 545 F.3d 1340 (Fed. Cir. 2008).

[80] *Certain Baseband Processor Chips & Chipsets, Transmitter & Receiver (Radio) Chips, Power Control Chips, & Prods. Containing Same*, USITC Inv. No. 337-TA-543, 2007 ITC LEXIS 621 Comm'n Op. (June 19, 2007).

sixteen customers of Qualcomm.[81] Interestingly, the ITC stressed the importance of naming all potential respondents in the action, but it explicitly refused to automatically preclude a remedy against downstream third parties on account of a complainant's failure to include such names.[82] Specifically, the ITC rejected Qualcomm's claim that Broadcom's failure to name downstream manufacturers was an attempt to mislead Qualcomm and third-party manufacturers as to the scope of the investigation and remedy requested.[83]

13.33 On appeal, however, the Federal Circuit reversed the ITC's decision[84] and found that the wording of section 337(d) did not support the ITC's practice of extending LEOs to parties not named as respondents.[85] In essence, the court found that contrary to the underlying statute, the ITC's practice had improperly blurred the lines between an LEO, which is supposed to be directed to a specific person, and a GEO, which is supposed to exclude a certain product from importation.[86]

13.34 In the direct aftermath of the Federal Circuit's decision in *Kyocera*, complainants started naming downstream manufacturers as respondents in requests for both LEOs, as well as for GEOs. For example, Spansion, in its complaint against Samsung and ten other downstream manufacturers using Samsung's semiconductors, requested a GEO citing a pattern of unauthorized use, difficulty in identifying all sources, and ease in circumvention of an LEO.[87] Despite such efforts, the higher standard required for a GEO makes it difficult for many patentees to preclude importation of an infringing product through downstream manufacturers. As mentioned earlier, to obtain a GEO a complainant has to show "exceptional circumstances," which requires at a minimum a difficulty in identifying the sources of infringing products.[88] However, as it became evident in *Kyocera*, although Broadcom did not have any difficulty naming infringing downstream manufacturers,[89] it did not want to directly sue such downstream manufacturers, as they were not only customers of Qualcomm but also either current or potential customers of Broadcom.[90]

13.35 Interestingly, after *Kyocera*, complainants at the ITC did not consequently start naming a higher number of respondents.[91] In fact, in the electronics industry, which tends to be the industry most frequently addressing the ITC, the number of named respondents per ITC filing decreased slightly.[92]

---

[81] Customers which joined Qualcomm in the appeal against the ITC's decision included wireless device manufacturers such as Kyocera Wireless Corporation, Samsung Electronics, LG Electronics, etc. and wireless network operators such as T-Mobile USA, AT&T and Sprint Nextel.

[82] Ibid. 50.

[83] Ibid. 50–51.

[84] *Kyocera v. Int'l Trade Comm'n*, 545 F.3d 1340, 1345 (Fed. Cir. 2008).

[85] Ibid.

[86] Ibid. 1356.

[87] *Certain Flash Memory Chips & Prods. Containing the Same*, USITC Pub. No. 2640, Complaint, 36–39 (November 17, 2008).

[88] *Kyocera Wireless Corp. v. Int'l Trade Comm'n*, 545 F.3d 1340, 1356 (Fed. Cir. 2008).

[89] Ibid. 1357.

[90] See also Lily Lim and Sarah E. Craven, "Injunctions Enjoined: Remedies Restructured," 25 *Santa Clara High Tech. L.J.* (2008): 787.

Santa Clara Computer & High Tech. L.J. (2008–9): 787, 810.

[91] Christopher A. Cotropia, "Strength of the International Trade Commission as a Patent Venue," 20 *Tex. Intell. Prop. L.J.* (2011–12): 1, 21–22.

[92] While prior to *Kyocera* an average of 5.31 consolidated respondents were named in electronics/computer-related technology patent dispute filings at the ITC, such numbers decreased—somewhat surprisingly—to an average of 4.87 respondents after Kyocera. Ibid. 21.

Furthermore, the number of GEOs applied for at or granted by the ITC did not increase in the three years after *Kyocera*.[93] Indeed, the ITC have granted very few GEOs since *Kyocera*. At the same time, commentators who predicted a decrease in the popularity of the ITC as a dispute resolution venue for such reason were proven wrong. **13.36**

Instead of increasing the number of named respondents, applicants continue to request LEOs against competing manufacturers and only after obtaining an LEO do they approach downstream distributors and manufacturers in out-of-court settlement negotiations. In such negotiations, the complainants request these downstream actors to either stop incorporating technology found to be infringing their patented devices, or to enter into license agreements. **13.37**

C. Claim for Damages

Damage claims are of central importance in US patent infringement litigation. Damage claim awards are granted to compensate the patentee for losses incurred due to the patent infringement. Unlike under general tort law, courts are not entitled to grant punitive damage awards under the Patent Act. However, courts can increase compensatory damages in cases of willful infringement or litigation misconduct. The determination of an appropriate damage award has developed into a science of its own, and the precise calculation of damage amounts remains considerably complex and case-specific. Unlike in Germany and Japan, damages are usually assessed in the main trial alongside the decision on infringement and validity. Therefore, the parties need to prepare and present evidence as to the amount of damages even though the court has not yet decided on infringement, adding to the complexity of the litigation. **13.38**

1. Requirements

Unlike most civil law jurisdictions, including Germany and Japan, US patent law does not generally require an infringer to engage in negligent conduct in order to award a damage claim. In fact, patent infringement has been referred to as a strict liability offense.[94] Although patent infringement is a strict liability offense, recovery of damages usually requires notice of the infringement to the infringer. Such a notice requirement is set out in § 287(a) of the Patent Act, which reads as follows: **13.39**

> Patentees, and persons making, offering for sale, or selling within the United States any patented article for or under them, or importing any patented article into the United States, may give notice to the public that the same is patented, either by fixing thereon the word "patent" or the abbreviation "pat.," together with the number of the patent, or when, from the character of the article, this cannot be done, by fixing to it, or to the package wherein one or more of them is contained, a label containing a like notice. In the event of failure so to mark, *no damages shall be recovered by the patentee* in any action for infringement, except on proof that the infringer was notified of the infringement and continued to infringe thereafter, in which event damages may be recovered only for infringement occurring after such notice. Filing of an action for infringement shall constitute such notice.[95]

---

[93] Ibid. 22–23.
[94] FTC Report, 44.
[95] 35 U.S.C. 287(a)

13.40 However, the patent statute contains one important limitation to the notice requirement: it does not apply to the recovery of damages following the infringement of a process patent.[96] Such a limitation is based on the rationale that a process, unlike a specific product covered by a patent, cannot be marked by a patentee.[97] In order to recover damages for infringement of the process portion in the case of a patent covering both a product and a process, a patentee must put the infringer on notice by marking the product.[98] Other relevant case law, however, indicates that a patentee can recover damages for infringement of a patent covering both a process and a product despite not marking the product, as long as only the process claims are asserted at trial. Yet, as some commentators have noted, such an interpretation of § 287(a) of the Patent Act would leave a patentee worse off with respect to damage recovery, by prevailing on the product claims rather than by just ignoring them in the trial.

13.41 Section 287(a) of the Patent Act states that filing an action for infringement puts an infringer on actual notice, whereas the marking of a product puts an infringer on constructive notice. Other forms of actual notice of an infringement, however, may allow a patentee to recover damages. Accordingly, patentees who fail to mark their product for any reason[99] are strongly encouraged to provide some showing of actual notice, which is often met with minimal content regarding the infringed patent and the alleged conduct.

2. Methods of Calculation

13.42 The US Patent Act provides two methods for calculating the amount of damages: a patentee can request compensation either for its lost profits or in an amount equal to a fictional reasonable royalty. Lost profits are awarded if they exceed the reasonable royalty.[100] If a court determines, however, that an infringer has acted willfully, it can award treble damages, by increasing the damages up to three times, and can also award a plaintiff reasonable attorney's fees.

13.43 US patent damages are higher than in any other jurisdiction. According to the PWC 2014 Patent Litigation Study, median damages awarded in patent cases between 2010 and 2013 amounted to US$4.3 million.[101] In the last few years, courts have awarded damages in excess of US$1 billion in five cases, with the top award exceeding US$1.5 billion.[102] When assessing damages, courts most frequently rely on the reasonable royalty analogy.[103]

---

[96] *American Medical Systems, Inc. v. Medical Engineering Corp.*, 6 F.3d 1523, 1538 (Fed. Cir. 1993), cert. denied, 511 U.S. 1070, 128 L. Ed. 2d 366, 114 S. Ct. 1647 (1994); *Philips Elecs. N. Am. Corp. v. Contec Corp.*, 312 F. Supp. 2d 649, 652 (D. Del. 2004); *Merck & Co. v. Mediplan Health Consulting, Inc.*, 434 F. Supp. 2d 257, 261 (S.D. N.Y. 2006); *Belden Techs. Inc. v. Superior Essex Communs. LP*, 733 F. Supp. 2d 517, 534–36 (D. Del. 2009).

[97] *American Medical Systems*, 6 F.3d 1523, 1538.

[98] Ibid. 1537.

[99] See a discussion on plausible reasons for failure of marking a product by Roger D. Blair and Thomas F. Cotter, "Strict Liability and Its Alternatives in Patent Law," 17 *Berkeley Tech. L.J.* (2002): 799, 806–7.

[100] 35 U.S.C. 284.

[101] Chris Barry et al., "PWC 2014 Patent Litigation Study" (http://www.pwc.com/en_US/us/forensic-services/publications/assets/2014-patent-litigation-study.pdf, 6.

[102] Ibid., 7.

[103] Ibid. 10.

(a) Lost Profits

A patentee, as well as an exclusive licensee,[104] can request compensation for all of its lost profits resulting from the infringement as long as such lost profits were a direct and foreseeable result of the infringing action.[105] **13.44**

Recovery is limited to a patentee's lost profits and does not extend to lost sales, as the damage claim is only intended to compensate the patentee and not to punish the infringer. While § 284 of the Patent Act does not entitle a patentee to recover an infringer's profits, the amount of such profits can serve as an indication of the lost profits that a patentee incurred due to the infringement. Furthermore, a patentee cannot claim lost profits in foreign markets, but can only recover such foreign lost profits by local enforcement outside the United States.[106] **13.45**

One of the most relevant tests for determining the amount of recoverable lost profits is the "but for" or Panduit test developed by the Sixth Circuit in 1978.[107] While the Panduit test is not the exclusive method for determining lost profits, it has been repeatedly deemed an acceptable test to show but-for causation.[108] The test requires a patentee to establish lost profits by showing the following four factors: (1) demand for the patented product during the period in question; (2) an absence, during that period, of acceptable non-infringing substitutes; (3) the patentee's manufacturing and marketing capability to meet or exploit that demand; and (4) a detailed computation of the amount of profits that the patentee would have made but for the infringement.[109] **13.46**

The first factor, demand for the patented product, can be demonstrated in a number of ways, but is often proven by showing a substantial number of sales by the infringer.[110] **13.47**

The second factor, an absence of an acceptable non-infringing substitute, has undergone significant adjustment by the Federal Circuit since the inception of the Panduit test. Earlier Federal Circuit case law required a narrow two-supplier market consisting of only the patentee and the infringer in order to grant lost profits. In the 1989 *State Industries v. Mor-Flo Industries, Inc.* decision, however, the court somewhat relaxed this approach by basing its analysis on the market shares of the patentee and the infringer and thus allowed for lost profits in cases involving more than two competitors in a specific market.[111] The court further refined its analysis in *BIC Leisure Products v. Windsurfing International, Inc.* by linking the first factor, demand, to the second factor.[112] In *BIC*, the plaintiff sold high-end and high-priced windsurfing boards and requested compensation for lost profits due to **13.48**

---

104 *Kori Corp. v. Wilco Marsh Buggies Inc.*, 761 F.2d 649, 653 (Fed. Cir. 1985); *Rite-Hite Corp. v. Kelley Co., Inc.*, 56 F.3d 1538, 1550 (Fed. Cir. 1995); please note that a non-exclusive licensee's recovery is limited to a reasonable royalty.

105 *King Instr. Corp. v. Perego*, 65 F.3d 941 (Fed. Cir. 1995); Robert Harmon, *Patents and the Federal Circuit* (9th ed., 2009), 993.

106 Timothy R. Holbrook, "Extraterritoriality in U.S. Patent Law," 49 *Wm. &Mary L. Rev.* (2007–8): 2119, 2130–31.

107 *Panduit Corp. v. Stahlin Bros. Fibre Works*, 575 F.2d 1152 (6th Cir. 1978).

108 *Presidio Components, Inc. v. American Technical Ceramics Corp.*, 702 F.3d 1351, 1359–62 (Fed. Cir. 2012); *DePuy Spine, Inc. v. Medtronic Sofamor Danek, Inc.*, 567 F.3d 1314, 1329–32 (Fed. Cir. 2009); *Micro Chemical, Inc. v. Lextron, Inc.*, 318 F.3d 1119, 1121–25 (Fed.Cir. 2003).

109 *Presidio Components, Inc.*, 1156; *Ryco Inc. v. Ag-Bag Corp.*, 857 F.2d 1418 (Fed. Cir. 1988).

110 *Gyromat v. Champion Spark Plug Co.*, 735 F.2d 549 (Fed. Cir. 1984).

111 *State Indus. Inc. v. Mor-Flo Indus. Inc.*, 883 F.2d 1573 (Fed. Cir. 1989).

112 *BIC Leisure Prods. v. Windsurfing Int'l Inc.*, 1 F.3d 1214 (Fed. Cir. 1993).

the infringer having marketed a similar but lower-priced board. Taking into account the price-sensitive market for windsurfing boards, the court found it unlikely that the patentee would have sold a substantial number of additional products absent the infringing product because the boards competed in different price categories and therefore, appealed to different customers.[113]

13.49 In 1999, the Federal Circuit revisited the second *Panduit* factor in *Grain Processing Corp. v. American Maize Products Co.*, when it specified what constituted an "available" non-infringing substitute. The court held that an alternative substitute does not need to be on sale during the time of infringement, but only has to be available and ready for implementation within a short period of time.[114]

13.50 An important inquiry is whether an available non-infringing substitute is acceptable or not. The analysis focuses on whether a substitute product contains the advantages of the patented product, and whether the market values and demands such particular advantages. In the damage portion of a trial, a defendant usually tries to present witness testimony to show that a non-infringing alternative product is an acceptable substitute because consumers are not specifically interested in the infringed patented features. In the 1980s, the Federal Circuit set out a list of factors that would suggest an absence of non-infringing substitutes: (1) failure of the infringer to design its own device; (2) election to infringe, despite having expended only minimal sums when notified of infringement; (3) willful infringement; (4) failure to successfully market other allegedly "acceptable" designs; (5) violation of an earlier injunction against the same or a similar form of infringement; and (6) withdrawal from the business after enforcement of such earlier injunction.[115] While reference to market share development alone is usually insufficient to prove the availability of acceptable non-infringing substitutes, the absence of any change in market share after the introduction of an infringing device tends to be highly probative of such availability.[116]

13.51 It should further be noted that the availability of non-patented product lines offered by a patentee does not warrant a finding that non-infringing substitutes are available.[117] Furthermore, while the availability of a substitute manufactured by a licensee of a patentee will in principle bar the patentee from recovering lost profits, such a bar only becomes effective upon the conclusion of a license agreement. Thus, recovery of lost profits for the period prior to the settlement and conclusion of a license agreement still remains possible.[118]

13.52 The third Panduit factor—that is, a patentee's ability to meet the market demand—can in principle only be met by those patentees selling products protected by the infringed patent. A patentee who fails to market its product bears the burden of showing a legitimate reason for not marketing its product despite having the ability. Thus, in such cases, a patentee rarely demonstrates an ability to meet the market demand. Successful commencement of production of an infringing product at a later stage does not alone provide a patentee with

---

[113] Ibid.

[114] 185 F.3d 1341, 53 (Fed. Cir. 1999).

[115] *TWM Manufacturing Co. Inc. v. Dura Corp.*, 789 F.2d 895, 900 (Fed. Cir. 1986).

[116] *Slimford Mfg. Co. v. Kinkead Industries*, 932 F. 2d 1453, 1458 (Fed. Cir. 1991); *Tec Air, Inc. v. Nippondenso Mfg. U.S.A., Inc.*, 1996 WL 556739, *4 (N.D. Ill. 1996).

[117] *Kaufman Co. v. Lantech Inc.*, 926 F.2d 1136, 1142 (Fed. Cir. 1991).

[118] *Pall Corp. v. Mircon Separations Inc.*, 66 F.3d 1211, 1222 (Fed. Cir. 1995); *Abbott Diabetes Care Inc. v. Roche Diagnostics Corp.*, 2007 WL 4166030, *3 (N.D. Cal. 2007).

sufficient evidence to show an ability to meet the demand, and thus to recoup lost profits from an earlier period of infringement. Also, the ability of a group company of the patentee to manufacture the infringed device does not necessarily demonstrate the patentee's ability to meet the demand.

Finally, a patentee must show the amount of profits the patentee would have made absent infringement by showing lost sales as well as the costs that the patentee would have incurred in generating such lost sales.[119] The patentee must present a clear and concise segregation of profits from costs, which usually requires a sophisticated economic analysis that considers, among other factors, market demand, elasticity, price erosion, increased expenses, and market share development. While the infringer has to present an accurate and complete record in order to challenge lost profits claimed by the patentee, it remains the patentee's burden to adequately separate profits, fixed costs, and variable costs. **13.53**

Once a court allows a patentee to claim lost profits, damage awards can reach very large sums. Lost profits may be derived from sales diverted to the infringer, eroded prices as a consequence of the competition, or increased expenses incurred by the patentee. **13.54**

(b) Reasonable Royalty

If a patentee fails to prove lost profits under the Panduit test, the patentee must calculate the damage award along the lines of the hypothetical and reasonable royalty. Case law defines such a reasonable royalty award as "an amount a person, desiring to manufacture, use, or sell a patented article as a business proposition, would be willing to pay as a royalty and yet be able to make a reasonable profit."[120] **13.55**

i. Established Royalty Rates In order to determine a reasonable royalty rate, courts may refer to royalty rates established in the market place for the infringed invention or for inventions comparable to the infringed invention. However, courts scrutinize any established royalty rate that may appear applicable. **13.56**

For example, the same patent may generate a significantly higher or lower royalty rate a few years after the commencement of the infringement, which would mean that the established royalty rate may deviate substantially from what a court may award as a reasonable royalty rate. Also, when the records indicate that only one license agreement with a license fee had been concluded, such a license may not regarded as setting an established royalty rate because a single license is deemed to lack general recognition. Furthermore, such licensing arrangements may contain particularly favorable terms and conditions for either the licensor or the licensee that were agreed upon for strategic and tactical reasons and thus, may differ from the pure value assigned to the patented technology. **13.57**

On the other hand, if a patentee has consistently licensed third parties to engage in conduct similar to the infringing conduct, or if a patentee possibly created a uniform license rate accepted by multiple licensees for the same technology, then such a reference rate is usually considered as an established royalty rate that can be used to calculate a damage award. **13.58**

---

[119] *Panduit Corp. v. Stahlin Bros. Fibre Works*, 575 F.2d 1152, 1156 (6th Cir. 1978).

[120] *Trans-World Mfg. Corp. v. Al Nyman & Sons*, 750 F.2d 1552, 1568 (Fed. Cir. 1984); see also *Applied Med. Res. Corp. v. U.S. Surgical Corp.*, 435 F.3d 1356, 1361 (Fed. Cir. 2006).

13.59 However, even when the market has clearly established a royalty rate, a court is still expected to verify that such an established royalty rate in fact relates to the value of the invention and thus can be deemed a reasonable royalty rate. In particular, a court determines whether the scope of an infringer's activities falls within the scope of activities contemplated and permitted under the established license terms. For example, if a royalty arrangement established in the relevant market grants the licensee permission to use certain patents as well as conveyed trademarks and other intellectual property, but the infringer only infringes the patents, then the established royalty rate will likely be considered too high to constitute a reasonable royalty rate under § 284 of the Patent Act.

13.60 Thus, while licensing terms and conditions agreed upon in the market are often referenced when determining a reasonable royalty rate, a patentee's unilateral offer to grant a license for the infringed technology or a comparable technology is generally not considered a ceiling on a reasonable royalty rate. The establishment of such a ceiling would be in the infringer's interests, but is not implemented because a party's unwillingness or lack of resources to actually litigate the patent may have significantly influenced an initial licensing offer.[121] This is the case even though the terms offered by a patentee before establishing infringement are usually different from the terms requested after establishing infringement and are often indicative of an acceptable reasonable royalty rate.

13.61 Furthermore, as a practical consideration, licensing offers made to an infringer are inadmissible under Rule 408 of the Federal Rules of Evidence ("FRE") if such offers were made in the context of a contemporaneous dispute.[122] The infringer, however, can point to either:

- licensing offers made to other infringers in separate proceedings, as long as the offers commensurate the same or a comparable technology
- terms and conditions of settlement agreements offered after establishing the infringer's liability.

13.62 **ii. Hypothetical Negotiation Framework** In many situations, courts will not have access to market-endorsed rates probative of a reasonable royalty for the technology in question. In these situations, courts will base the assessment of a reasonable royalty entirely on a hypothetical negotiation to determine the value of the infringed technology. The reasonable royalty must be in line with the amount "that a licensor (such as the patentee) and a licensee (such as the infringer) would have agreed upon (at the time the infringement began) if both had been reasonably and voluntarily trying to reach an agreement."[123]

13.63 The hypothetical negotiation framework is often perceived as counterfactual, given that the very reason for the litigation taking place is based on the fact that the parties could not come to an agreement on a reasonable royalty rate. On the other hand, the approach has been supported on the presumption that the court is better situated than the parties to overcome this lack of agreement by assessing the validity and value of the patented technology.

---

121 *Snellman v. Ricoh Co.*, 862 F. 2d 283 (Fed. Cir. 1988).

122 *Hanson v. Alpine Valley Ski Area Inc.*, 718 F.2d, 1075 (Fed. Cir. 1983); *Deere & Co. v. International Harvester Co.*, 710 F.2d 1561 (Fed. Cir. 1983).

123 *Georgia-Pacific Corp. v. United States Plywood Corp.*, 318 F. Supp. 1116, 1120 (S.D. N.Y. 1970), modified and aff'd, 446 F.2d 295 (2d Cir. 1971).

The District Court for the Southern District of New York introduced the hypothetical negotiation framework over forty years ago in its famous *Georgia-Pacific v. United States Plywood Corp.* decision. The court set forth a list of fifteen factors that should be considered by courts and parties when determining a reasonable royalty rate for patent infringement.[124] The fifteenth factor provides for the hypothetical negotiations framework, while the first fourteen factors are individual factors to be used as signposts when determining an accurate price for the (hypothetical) license. **13.64**

The US patent community viewed the increasing prominence of the *Georgia-Pacific* factors with mixed feelings. While some practitioners applauded the court for introducing a comprehensive list of factors that would grant a substantial degree of flexibility required in practice, other commentators expressed dissatisfaction over the lack of concise guidance due to the excessive catalogue of factors overwhelming parties and juries.[125] **13.65**

In order to give parties and courts a structured approach when applying the *Georgia-Pacific* factors in a reasonable royalty analysis, courts have increasingly focused on the hypothetical negotiation framework that presumes a willing licensor and willing licensee. Without such **13.66**

---

[124] *Georgia-Pacific Corp.*, 318 F. Supp. 1116, 1120 (S.D. N.Y. 1970), introducing the following fifteen factors:

1. The royalties received by the patentee for the licensing of the patent in suit, proving or tending to prove an established royalty.
2. The rates paid by the licensee for the use of other patents comparable to the patent in suit.
3. The nature and scope of the license, as exclusive or non-exclusive; or as restricted or non-restricted in terms of territory or with respect to whom the manufactured product may be sold.
4. The licensor's established policy and marketing program to maintain his patent monopoly by not licensing others to use the invention or by granting licenses under special conditions designed to preserve that monopoly.
5. The commercial relationship between the licensor and licensee, such as, whether they are competitors in the same territory in the same line of business; or whether they are inventor and promoter.
6. The effect of selling the patented specialty in promoting sales of other products of the licensee; that existing value of the invention to the licensor as a generator of sales of his non-patented items; and the extent of such derivative or convoyed sales.
7. The duration of the patent and the term of the license.
8. The established profitability of the product made under the patent; its commercial success; and its current popularity.
9. The utility and advantages of the patent property over the old modes or devices, if any, that had been used for working out similar results.
10. The nature of the patented invention; the character of the commercial embodiment of it as owned and produced by the licensor; and the benefits to those who have used the invention.
11. The extent to which the infringer has made use of the invention; and any evidence probative of the value of that use.
12. The portion of the profit or of the selling price that may be customary in the particular business or in comparable businesses to allow for the use of the invention or analogous inventions.
13. The portion of the realizable profit that should be credited to the invention as distinguished from non-patented elements, the manufacturing process, business risks, or significant features or improvements added by the infringer.
14. The opinion testimony of qualified experts.
15. The amount that a licensor (such as the patentee) and a licensee (such as the infringer) would have agreed upon (at the time the infringement began) if both had been reasonably and voluntarily trying to reach an agreement.

[125] Richard L. Stroup, "Patentee's Monetary Recovery from an Infringer," 59 *J. Pat. Off. Soc'y* (1977): 362, 388 ("One of the best decisions which enumerates and discusses the use of these and other factors is Georgia Pacific Corp."); John A. McMullen and David A. Halprin, "New Technique for Quantifying Reasonable

a conceptual framework, it would be difficult for a court to ensure that the various factors are aligned in a meaningful and integrated way. However, if a patentee can establish that treating him as an average willing licensor would be contrary to the patentee's intention at the time of the hypothetical negotiation, he can usually obtain a more favorable royalty rate. Such resistance to willingly enter into a licensing arrangement can exist in situations where the parties are competitors or where the technology at issue grants the patentee a particular competitive edge.[126] Furthermore, a patentee's resistance to license a patent to a core technology can occur in contexts where the patentee and infringer are not direct competitors, but where the patentee had an established history of not licensing any core technology or specific technology such as the infringed technology.[127]

13.67 Other significant factors influencing the outcome of a hypothetical negotiation are the timing of the negotiation and the influence that alternative technologies would have had on the behavior of the parties. The timing of the hypothetical negotiation will in many cases be essential to the outcome, as the bargaining power of a patentee increases at least proportionally with the investments made by an infringer in the manufacturing or distribution of a specific product covered by a patent.[128] The later a patentee enforces his patent, the higher the costs are for an infringer to stop using the patent by either redesigning the product or simply ceasing production. Case law places the hypothetical negotiation at the time of first infringement[129] and courts should ensure that such timing is accurate and precisely defined. However, some commentators have expressed concern over such timing, noting that the hypothetical negotiation should instead be set earlier during the phase that an infringer is designing the infringing product. Such earlier timing is to ensure that the patentee is not overcompensated by obtaining a royalty rate that accounts for the defendant's costs of redesigning the product.[130] However, numerous real license discussions begin only after a patentee discovers the existence of an allegedly infringing product and subsequently approaches the defendant to request a royalty. In these contexts, the patentee does have the enhanced bargaining power associated with increased costs for the infringer. Indeed, if one argues

Royalty from Appropriate Case Law," 75 J. *Pat. & Trademark Off. Soc'y* (1993): 843, 847 ("We were troubled by the fact that, while the Georgia Pacific case indicated relevant evidentiary factors, it did not quantify their weight or suggest a way to calculate the indicated royalty"); Daralyn J. Durie and Mark A. Lemley, "A Structured Approach to Calculating Reasonable Royalties," 14 *Lewis & Clark L. Rev.* (2010): 627, 628 ("[W]e argue that a significant part of the problem comes from the non-exclusive, fifteen-factor "Georgia-Pacific" test").

[126] Sample cases in which courts paid attention to this fifth *Georgia-Pacific* factor and approved higher royalty rates due to the competitive nature of the relation between patentee and infringer include *Novozymes A/S v. Genencor Int'l, Inc.*, 474 F. Supp. 2d 592, 608 (D. Del. 2007) and *Telemac Corp. v. US/Intelicom Inc.*, 185 F. Supp. 2d 1084, 1101–2 (N.D. Cal. 2001).

[127] This reliance on the fourth *Georgia-Pacific* factor was relevant and became part of the court's analysis in *Novozymes A/S v. Genencor Int'l, Inc.*, 474 F. Supp. 2d 592, 608 (D. Del. 2007); *Procter & Gamble Company v. Paragon Trade Brands, Inc.*, 989 F. Supp. 547, 610 (D. Del. 1997); and *Promega Corp. v. Lifecodes Corp.*, 1999 U.S. Dist. LEXIS 21094, *37 (D. Utah 1999).

[128] The Federal Circuit confirmed the relevance of the assumed timing of the hypothetical negotiations, e.g., in *Integra Lifesciences I, Ltd. v. Merck KGaA*, 331 F.3d 860, 869 (Fed. Cir. 2003), vacated on other grounds, 545 U.S. 193 (2005).

[129] *Rite-Hite Corp. v. Kelley Co.*, 56 F.3d 1538, 1545, 1554 (Fed. Cir. 1995) (*en banc*), citing *Hanson v. Alpine Valley Ski Area, Inc.*, 718 F.2d 1075, 1078 (Fed. Cir. 1983); *Applied Med. Res. Corp. v. U.S. Surgical Corp.*, 435 F.3d 1356, 1363–64 (Fed. Cir.2006); *State Indus., Inc. v. Mor–Flo Indus., Inc.*, 883 F.2d 1573, 1580 (Fed. Cir.1989); *LaserDynamics, Inc. v. Quanta Computer, Inc.*, 694 F.3d 51, 75 (Fed. Cir. 2012).

[130] E.g., Paul Alexander, "Georgia (Pacific) on My Mind," *Intellectual Property Law*, June 14, 2011, 360, (http://www.arnoldporter.com/resources/documents/Arnold&PorterLLP_IntellectualPropertyLaw360_061411.pdf).

that the timing of a hypothetical negotiation should follow that of a real negotiation, then such timing would be at the time of the infringement rather than at the time of the designing phase. On the other hand, if one argues that a reasonable royalty should be limited to a fair compensation for the incremental value of the patented technology rather than to allow for a "hold-up" of the patent infringer, then it would be reasonable to place the hypothetical negotiation at the earlier design stage.

Another debated factor is whether a reasonable royalty award should be capped at the cost incurred by an infringer to replace the patented technology with an alternative technology. The ninth *Georgia-Pacific* factor provides for consideration of an available alternative technology. Both the Federal Circuit and a number of district courts have held that the difference in cost between using the patented technology and employing an available alternative "effectively capped the reasonable royalty award," as any associated disadvantages in cost would incentivize a defendant to reject use of the patented technology.[131] In its subsequent decision in *Mars, Inc. v. Coin Acceptors, Inc.*, however, the Federal Circuit seemed to have retreated from its earlier position in *Grain Processing* when it held in dicta that an alternative technology would not effectively cap reasonable royalty awards.[132] The Federal Circuit's approach in *Mars* is not convincing, as it would be illogical to assume that an infringer, in a hypothetical negotiation, would not have walked away from the negotiation table and chosen an alternative available technology if such a choice would have put the infringer in a better financial position than if he had accepted the license and incorporated the patented technology. However, in this context an infringer faces difficulty in having to sufficiently demonstrate: **13.68**

- that an alternative technology had really been available at the time of the hypothetical negotiation
- the precise cost of an alternative technology or the profit difference between the patented technology and the alternative technology.

iii. Entire Market Value Rule Damage awards can be significantly increased by application of the entire market value rule. According to the entire market value rule, a patentee can capture the value of an entire product even though the infringement concerned only one component of the product. However, the patentee must demonstrate that the patented feature caused the relevant customer demand that resulted in the sale of the entire product. In *Rite-Hite Corp. v. Kelly Company, Inc.*, the Federal Circuit provided the current version of the entire market value rule, stating that a patentee can recapture the value of the entire product if (1) the patented feature is "the basis for customer demand" of the infringing product and (2) the patented and unpatented components together "constitute a functional unit."[133] However, courts have had trouble determining whether **13.69**

[131] See, e.g., *Grain Processing Corp. v. American Maize-Products Co.*, 893 F. Supp. 1386, 1347 (N.D. Ind. 1995), aff'd in part, vacated in part, 108 F.3d 1392 (Fed. Cir. 1997), further decision on remand, 979 F. Supp. 1233 (N.D. Ind. 1997), aff'd, 185 F.3d 1341 (Fed. Cir. 1999); see also *SmithKline Diagnostics, Inc. v. Helena Laboratories Corp.*, No. Civ.A. B-83-10, 1989 WL 418791, *6 (E.D. Tex. June 30, 1989); *Novozymes A/S v. Genencor Int'l, Inc.*, 474 F. Supp. 2d 592, 607 (D. Del. 2007); *Fresenius*, 2006 WL 1646113, *2; *Cardiac Pacemakers, Inc. v. St. Jude Medical, Inc.*, No. IP 96-1718-C-H/K, 2002 WL 1801525, *74 (S.D. Ind. July 5, 2002), aff'd in part, rev'd in part, and remanded, 381 F.3d 1371 (Fed. Cir. 2004), vacated, 315 Fed. Appx. 273 (Fed. Cir. 2009).

[132] *Mars, Inc. v. Coin Acceptors, Inc.*, 527 F.3d 1359, 1371 (Fed. Cir. 2008).

[133] *Rite-Hite Corp. v. Kelly Co.*, 56 F.3d 1538, 1550 (Fed. Cir. 1995) (*en banc*).

the patented and the unpatented components constitute a functional unit as the basis for customer demand. While the Federal Circuit qualified its test by emphasizing that lost profits cannot be extended to product components "that have essentially no functional relationship to the patented invention and that may have been sold with an infringing device only as a matter of convenience or business advantage,"[134] district courts and the Federal Circuit continue to struggle with the application of the entire market value rule. Instead of flexibly allocating a value that a patented feature contributes to an entire product, courts have followed an all-or-nothing approach when making such valuations. Illustrative decisions include *Golden Blount Inc. v. Robert H. Peterson Co.*,[135] in which the Federal Circuit granted lost profits for an artificial fireplace, where the only patented feature was a gas burner,[136] and *Tec Air, Inc. v. Denso Mfg. Michigan, Inc.*,[137] in which the court allowed damages for an entire radiator and condenser assembly because the assembly included a patented fan.[138]

13.70 In its recent *Uniloc USA, Inc. v. Microsoft Corp.*[139] decision, the Federal Circuit notably cautioned courts to review whether the patented component had in fact been essential for the market success of the entire product. The patentee Uniloc had "verified" the demanded reasonable royalty award by demonstrating that the patented component, a software registration system used to allow Microsoft software users to register product keys, would account for 2.9 percent of the gross revenue generated by Microsoft products requiring a product key.[140] The Federal Circuit, however, rejected the applicability of the entire market value rule even as a means of verifying a reasonable royalty award, holding that the infringed software registration system was not the reason for customer demand in Microsoft's products.[141] Last, patentees can further recover profits generated by "convoyed sales."

3. Increased Damages and Attorney Fees

13.71 Section 284 of the Patent Act entitles courts to "increase the damages up to three times the amount found or assessed."[142] In addition, the court can "in exceptional cases . . . award reasonable attorney fees to the prevailing party."[143] The prerequisite for both increased damages and attorney fees is a finding of willful infringement or bad faith.[144]

(a) Willful Infringement

13.72 Courts consider multiple factors when assessing whether an infringer has acted in bad faith. The standard for finding willfulness has undergone substantial revision in the last

---

134 *Rite-Hite Corp.*, 56 F.3d, 1550.

135 *Golden Blount, Inc. v. Robert H. Peterson Co.*, 438 F.3d 1354 (Fed. Cir. 2006).

136 Ibid. 1371–72.

137 *Tec Air, Inc. v. Denso Mfg. Michigan, Inc.*, 192 F.3d 1353 (Fed. Cir. 1999).

138 Ibid. 1361.

139 *Uniloc USA, Inc. v. Microsoft Corp.*, 632 F. 3d 1292 (Fed. Cir. 2011); see also *Virnetx, Inc. v. Cisco Systems, Inc.*, 767 F.3d 1308, 1326 (Fed. Cir. 2014); *LaserDynamics, Inc. v. Quanta Computer, Inc.*, 694 F.3d 51 (Fed. Cir. 2012); *Cornell Univ. v. Hewlett-Packard Co.*, 609 F. Supp. 2d 279 (N.D. N.Y. 2009).

140 *Uniloc USA, Inc. v. Microsoft Corp.*, 1318.

141 Ibid. 1318–20.

142 35 U.S.C. 284.

143 Ibid. 285.

144 *Beatrice Foods Co. v. New England Printing & Lith. Co.*, 923 F.2d 1567 (Fed. Cir. 1991).

decade, most recently in 2007, when the Federal Circuit in *In re Seagate Technology, LLC* held that in order to prove willfulness, a patentee must show by clear and convincing evidence that the (1) the accused infringer "acted despite an objectively high likelihood that its actions constituted infringement of a valid patent," and (2) the "objectively defined risk...was either known or so obvious that it should have been known to the accused infringer."[145]

The test articulated in *Seagate* created an objective prong, while in earlier willfulness tests that emphasized the infringer's "affirmative duty of due care," only the subjective knowledge and behavior of the infringer were scrutinized. Most significantly, the *Seagate* test shifted the burden of proof from the accused infringer to the patentee. Under the former standard, the accused infringer, in complying with his affirmative duty of due care, essentially had to prove lack of willfulness by immediately obtaining and disclosing a legal opinion confirming non-infringement. Such "voluntary" disclosure of a legal opinion frequently required the accused infringer to effectively waive the attorney–client privilege. **13.73**

The requirement of an *objective high likelihood of infringement*, however, shifted the burden of proof. To clarify that a lack of legal counsel did not automatically indicate willfulness, Congress introduced § 298 as a part of the American Invents Act[146] that stated that a failure to obtain an opinion by counsel cannot be relied upon when determining willfulness.[147] **13.74**

Nevertheless, *Seagate* did not end the practice of obtaining and disclosing legal opinions, as the court stated that a pre-litigation opinion concerning infringement or validity obtained by the accused infringer's counsel "may preclude the infringer's conduct from being considered reckless."[148] However, to protect the accused infringer from waiving the attorney–client privilege when asserting the advice of counsel defense, the Federal Circuit held that a disclosure of a legal opinion obtained by the accused infringer's counsel shall not extend to effectuate a waiver of the attorney–client privilege for communication with the infringer's trial counsel.[149] **13.75**

Thus, after 2007, the heightened standard for willfulness made it more difficult for the patentee to prove willfulness. According to a 2012 study by Christopher Seaman, findings of willfulness dropped from 48.2 percent prior to *Seagate* to 37.2 percent after *Seagate*.[150] Such figures, however, do not fully impart the impact of *Seagate*. A closer look reveals the substantial difference in findings of willfulness, depending on whether the finding was made by a jury or by a judge, as shown in Table 13.1. **13.76**

---

[145] *In re Seagate Tech., LLC*, 497 F.3d 1360, 1371 (Fed. Cir. 2007) (*en banc*), cert. denied, 552 U.S. 1230 (2008).

[146] Leahy-Smith America Invents Act, Pub. L. No. 112-29, § 17, 125 Stat. 284, 329 (2011).

[147] 35 U.S.C. § 298: "The failure of an infringer to obtain the advice of counsel with respect to any allegedly infringed patent, or the failure of the infringer to present such advice to the court or jury, may not be used to prove that the accused infringer willfully infringed the patent or that the infringer intended to induce infringement of the patent."

[148] *In re Seagate Tech., LLC*, 1374.

[149] Ibid.

[150] Christopher A. Seaman, "Willful Patent Infringement and Enhanced Damages after *In re Seagate*: An Empirical Study," 97 *Iowa L. Rev.* (2012): 417, 441.

Table 13.1 Findings of willfulness prior to and after *Seagate*

	% Willful	
	Before *Seagate* (Sept. 2004–Aug. 2007)	After *Seagate* (Aug. 2007–July 2010)
Jury	**60.9%** (56 of 92)	**61.9%** (52 of 84)
Judge	**53.9%** (7 of 13)	**18.5%** (5 of 27)

13.77 The difference in willfulness findings becomes particularly important in light of the more recent Federal Circuit decision in *Bard Peripheral Vascular, Inc. v. W.L. Gore & Associates, Inc.*[151] in which the Federal Circuit held that the first prong of the willfulness test—that is, whether an accused infringer acted despite an objectively high likelihood that its actions constituted infringement of a valid patent—should be treated as a question of law rather than a question of fact. The *Bard* decision is of substantial influence, as questions of law are to be reviewed by judges instead of by juries. As a review of recent decisions indicates that judges find willfulness at a substantially lower rate than juries, *Bard* is likely to result in a significant reduction in willfulness findings and thus, of enhanced damages in the coming years.

13.78 Once willfulness is determined, a court can increase the damage award up to three times. In determining the amount of enhanced damages, the court enjoys a substantial degree of discretion. The so-called *Read*-factors, which can be used to determine the amount of enhanced damages, include:

> (1) whether the infringer deliberately copied the ideas or design of another; (2) whether the infringer, when he knew of the other's patent protection, investigated the scope of the patent and formed a good-faith belief that it was invalid or that it was not infringed; (3) the infringer's behavior as a party to the litigation; (4) defendant's size and financial condition; (5) closeness of the case; (6) duration of defendant's misconduct; (7) remedial action by the defendant; (8) defendant's motivation for harm; and (9) whether defendant attempted to conceal its misconduct.[152]

13.79 Pursuant to § 285 of the Patent Act, a court may award reasonable attorney's fees to the prevailing party. Such a remedy can in principle be awarded to either prevailing party. The standard set forth in the statute is an "exceptional case." The Federal Circuit has held that a case is exceptional under § 285 "when there has been some material inappropriate conduct related to the matter in litigation, such as willful infringement, fraud or inequitable conduct

[151] *Bard Peripheral Vascular, Inc. v. W.L. Gore & Associates, Inc.*, 682 F.3d 1003 (Fed.Cir. 2012), cert. denied, 2013 WL 141409 (U.S. January 14, 2013) (No. 12-458, 12A189).

[152] *Liquid Dyn. Corp. v. Vaughan Co.*, 449 F.3d 1209 (Fed. Cir. 2006); *Read Corp. v. Portec. Inc.*, 970 F.2d 816, 826–27 (Fed.Cir.1992), superseded on other grounds as recognized in *Hoechst Celanese Corp. v. BP Chems. Ltd.*, 78 F.3d 1575, 1578 (Fed.Cir.1996); *i4i Ltd. Partnership v. Microsoft Corp.*, 598 F.3d 831, 859 (Fed. Cir. 2010).

in procuring the patent, misconduct during litigation, vexatious or unjustified litigation, conduct that violates FRCP 11,[153] or like *infractions*."[154]

In the case of a prevailing patentee seeking compensation for reasonable attorney's fees, a finding of willfulness constitutes a sufficient basis to deem a case exceptional and deserving of attorney's fees.[155] That said, a finding of willfulness does not require a court to determine the case to be exceptional under § 285.[156] **13.80**

Courts have determined cases to be exceptional and awarded attorney's fees when there is misconduct during litigation, such as hindrance of discovery.[157] Misconduct during litigation can be found against either party, and usually both parties' conduct during litigation is considered before allowing recovery of attorney's fees. Attorney's fees can also be awarded against a losing patentee for other forms of misconduct, for example, inequitable conduct during the prosecution of the patent,[158] frivolous claim construction,[159] or otherwise **13.81**

---

[153] Federal Rules for Civil Procedure 11:

(a) Every pleading, written motion, and other paper shall be signed by at least one attorney of record in the attorney's individual name, or, if the party is not represented by an attorney, shall be signed by the party. Each paper shall state the signer's address and telephone number, if any. Except when otherwise specifically provided by rule or statute, pleadings need not be verified or accompanied by affidavit. An unsigned paper shall be stricken unless omission of the signature is corrected promptly after being called to the attention of attorney or party.

(b) By presenting to the court (whether by signing, filing, submitting, or later advocating) a pleading, written motion, or other paper, an attorney or unrepresented party is certifying that to the best of the person's knowledge, information, and belief, formed after an inquiry reasonable under the circumstances, —
   (1) it is not being presented for any improper purpose, such as to harass or to cause unnecessary delay or needless increase in the cost of litigation;
   (2) the claims, defenses, and other legal contentions therein are warranted by existing law or by a nonfrivolous argument for the extension, modification, or reversal of existing law or the establishment of new law;
   (3) the allegations and other factual contentions have evidentiary support or, if specifically so identified, are likely to have evidentiary support after a reasonable opportunity for further investigation or discovery; and
   (4) the denials of factual contentions are warranted on the evidence or, if specifically so identified, are reasonably based on a lack of information or belief.

(c) If, after notice and a reasonable opportunity to respond, the court determines that subdivision (b) has been violated, the court may, subject to the conditions stated below, impose an appropriate sanction upon the attorneys, law firms, or parties that have violated subdivision (b) or are responsible for the violation.

[154] *Brooks Furniture Mfg., Inc. v. Dutailier Intern., Inc.*, 393 F.3d 1378, 1381 (Fed. Cir. 2005). Under recent Supreme Court case law, the standard for defendants being able to claim reimbursement of their attorney's fees has been significantly lowered: accordingly, a defendant can request attorney's fees if under the totality of circumstances the case brought by a patentee-plaintiff obviously lacked merit or was litigated in an unreasonable manner; see *Octane Fitness, LLC v. ICON Health & Fitness, Inc.*, 134 S. CT 1749, 1755–6 (2014).

[155] *Amsted Industries Inc. v. Buckeye Steel Castings Co.*, 24 F.3d 178, 183–84 (Fed. Cir. 1994), rehearing denied, *en banc* suggestion declined; *Modine Mfg. Co. v. Allen Group, Inc.*, 917 F.2d 538, 543 (Fed. Cir. 1990).

[156] *Rite-Hite Corp. v. Kelley Co.*, 819 F.2d 1120, 1126 (Fed. Cir. 1987); *Avia Group Intern., Inc. v. L.A. Gear California, Inc.*, 853 F.2d 1557, 1567 (Fed. Cir. 1988); *Additive Control & Measurement Systems, Inc. v. Flowdata, Inc.*, 29 U.S.P.Q. 2d (BNA) 1890, 1896 (S.D. Tex. 1993), modified, 32 U.S.P.Q. 2d (BNA) 1747 (S.D. Tex. 1994); *Lightwave Technologies, Inc. v. Corning Glass Works*, 19 U.S.P.Q. 2d (BNA) 1838, 1849 (S.D. N.Y. 1991).

[157] E.g. *Bayer Aktiengesellschaft v. Duphar Intern. Research B.V.*, 738 F.2d 1237, 1242 (Fed. Cir. 1984); *Matter of Mahurkar Double Lumen Hemodialysis Catheter Patent Litigation*, 831 F. Supp. 1354 (N.D. Ill. 1993).

[158] *Reactive Metals and Alloys Corp. v. ESM, Inc.*, 769 F.2d 1578, 1582 (Fed. Cir. 1985); *Hughes v. Novi American, Inc.*, 724 F.2d 122, 125 (Fed. Cir. 1984).

[159] *ICU Medical, Inc. v. Alaris Medical Systems, Inc.*, 558 F.3d 1368, 1375 (Fed. Cir. 2009).

objectively baseless litigation.[160] For instance, an award of attorney's fees in the amount of $16.8 million was awarded[161] and upheld[162] against a generic company that had failed to comply with certification requirements for generic companies under the Drug Price Competition and Patent Term Restoration Act.[163]

13.82 The party who seeks recovery of reasonable attorney's has to demonstrate that the amount requested is reasonable.[164] The courts tend to award a "lodestar" fee award based on a reasonable number of attorney hours multiplied by a reasonable hourly rate. While a party may use the number of hours actually billed by its counsel to determine the applicable reasonable number of attorney hours, it can rely on hourly rates compiled by sources such as the Report of the Economic Survey prepared by the *American Intellectual Property Association*, which has been used as a benchmark in actual cases.[165]

D. Claim for Destruction

13.83 Unlike patent statutes in Germany[166] and Japan,[167] or US trademark or copyright law,[168] the US Patent Act does not provide any statutory basis for requesting the destruction of patent-infringing goods or production means primarily used to manufacture infringing goods. Occasionally, injunctions compel patent infringers to destroy infringing items[169] or to permanently disable patent-infringing functions.[170] However, due to the lack of a statute or Federal Circuit case law explicitly confirming the validity of destruction orders, a claim for destruction does not play a significant role among patent infringement remedies in the United States.

---

160 *Highmark, Inc. v. Allcare Health Management Systems, Inc.*, 687 F.3d 1300, 1311 (Fed. Cir. 2012).

161 *Takeda Chem. Indus., Ltd. v. Mylan Labs., Inc.*, 459 F. Supp. 2d 227 (S.D. N.Y.2006) (determining the violation of certification requirements to constitute an exception case); *Takeda Chem. Indus., Ltd. v. Mylan Labs., Inc.*, Nos. 03-8253, 04-1966, 2007 WL 840368 (S.D. N.Y. March 21, 2007) (determining the amount of recoverable attorney's fees).

162 *Takeda Chemical Industries, Ltd. v. Mylan Laboratories, Inc.*, 549 F.3d 1381, 1390 (Fed. Cir. 2008).

163 Frequently referred to as the "Hatch-Waxman Act" (Public Law 98-417); see for a discussion of certification requirements under the Hatch-Waxman Act: Gerald J. Mossinghoff, "Overview of the Hatch-Waxman Act and Its Impact on the Drug Development Process," 54 *Food & Drug L.J.* (1999): 187.

164 Such general principle has been confirmed by the US Supreme Court in a case not related to patent damages, *Hensley v. Eckerhart*, 461 U.S. 424, 433 (1983).

165 *Padco, Inc. v. Newell Companies, Inc.*, 13 U.S.P.Q. 2d (BNA) 1607, 1614 (E.D. Wis. 1988), judgment aff'd, 878 F.2d 1445 (Fed. Cir. 1989); *Stickle v. Heublein, Inc.*, 590 F. Supp. 630, 635 (W.D. Wis. 1984).

166 See Ch.14, 14.31.

167 See Ch. 15, 15.26.

168 15 U.S.C. § 1118 (Trademark Law); 17 U.S.C. § 503(b) (Copyright Law).

169 E.g., *Proveris Scientific Corp. v. InnovaSystems Inc.*, No. 05-12424-WGY, slip op. at 3 (D. Mass. May 11, 2007); *Caught Fish Enters., LLC v. Blaze Wharton Constr., Inc.*, No. 09-cv-02878-PAB-KMT, slip op. at 3 (D. Colo. February 24, 2010).

170 *TiVo Inc. v. Echostar*, 646 F.3d 869, 890 (Fed. Cir. 2011) (*en banc*).

14

GERMANY

In the complaint, the patentee asserting infringement will usually request the court to grant a number of remedies upon finding infringement. The claim for injunctive relief is the most central remedy and is virtually always sought at the initial stage of the proceedings. Unlike in, for example, the United States, the court will not decide the amount of damages payable during the initial infringement action. If infringement is found, it will, in the initial infringement action, usually award an injunction and a claim for disclosure of information, enabling the patentee to calculate the amount that can be sought as damages. Most parties settle the amount of damages out of court, after either the district court or the appellate court awards an injunction and the claim for information. That said, if the parties cannot agree on the appropriate amount of damages, the infringed party can assert the damage claim in subsequent proceedings at the infringement court. **14.01**

A. Claim for Injunctive Relief

1. Requirements

A claim for injunctive relief against future infringements requires a risk of a first or a repeated act of infringement. In principle, a risk of repeated infringement can be assumed if the patent infringement has already occurred before the complaint was filed. In such cases, it would require exceptional circumstances to show that no risk of repeated infringement continues to exist. Generally, a risk of repeated infringement can only be removed if the infringer submits a declaration in which he or she undertakes to refrain from future infringement, with such undertaking being subject to a specific penalty payment.[1] In cases of joint patentees filing an infringement action, the submission of a declaration to undertake any of the joint patentees is considered to be effective in removing the risk of repeated infringement for the other joint patentees as well.[2] **14.02**

Unlike the risk of repeated infringement, the risk of a first infringement must be demonstrated by the patentee. The patentee must show that a tangible indication of an imminent patent infringement exists. A risk of a first infringement may, for example, be established by the defendant claiming to be entitled to manufacture or distribute certain infringing devices, either in the course of commercial communication or in the course of legal **14.03**

[1] Federal Court of Justice GRUR 1996, 290, 292—*Wegfall der Wiederholungsgefahr*.

[2] T. Kühnen, Patent Litigation Proceedings in Germany (7th ed., 2014), marginal no. 944.

proceedings.[3] If the defendant disputes that a risk of first infringement exists, the patentee has to supply concise evidence of such a risk to the court. According to the prevailing opinion, removing the risk of a first infringement is possible under requirements that are less strict than those for the risk of repeated infringement.[4]

14.04 Whether or not the defendant acted with negligence is not relevant in a claim for injunctive relief. Also, unlike in the United States[5] and other common law jurisdictions, courts do not have discretion to deny injunctive relief for equitable reasons. In order to avoid an injunction order, the defendant has to prevail with any of the substantive or procedural defenses raised in the course of the proceedings.

2. Scope of the Claim

14.05 The claim for injunctive relief regarding the protective right is directed against every form of patent infringement and therefore against every form of patent use according to the literal meaning of the claimed invention as well as against any equivalent forms. In cases of contributory patent infringement, an injunction is targeted against every specific means relating to an essential element of the invention.

14.06 Commentators and courts have engaged in considerable debate over whether the claim for injunctive relief can be extended to the literal meaning of the claimed invention or whether it should be further limited by the specific form of embodiment of the infringing device or process. The Federal Court of Justice decided in 2005 that the plaintiff's request for an injunction should name and describe the specific form of infringement against which the injunction order is sought.[6] The plaintiff can provide a description of the specific form of infringement by submitting photographs of the infringing product.[7] The Patent Senate of the Federal Court of Justice confirmed in 2012, however, that such a description of the concise form of infringement against which the injunction is sought would not bar the patentee from enjoining other forms of use that also fall within the scope of the patent.[8] While most lower courts seem to follow the approach of the Federal Court of Justice,[9] the Düsseldorf courts reject it and continue to hold that the injunction should merely be limited by the literal reading of the infringed claim.[10] In any event, there is no dispute that the scope of the injunction order should not be unreasonably broad, for example, by covering "similar acts of infringement." Requesting such an overly broad injunction may result in the request for injunction becoming inadmissible.

---

3 Federal Court of Justice NJW-RR 2001, 1483—*Berühmungsaufgabe.*

4 Ibid.

5 See for the United States Ch. 13, 13.04.

6 Federal Court of Justice GRUR 2005, 569—*Blasfolienherstellung*; see also R. Kraßer, *Patentrecht (Patent Law)* (6th ed. 2009), § 36 IV.

7 Federal Court of Justice GRUR 2006, 311—*Baumscheibenabdeckung.*

8 Federal Court of Justice GRUR 2012, 485—*Rohrreinigungsdüse II.*

9 See, e.g., District Court of Munich I, Decision of 24.07.2014, Case Number 7 O 24814/13, BeckRS 2014 16686; District Court of Hamburg, Decision of 30.04.2013, Case Number 3 U 184/10, BeckRS 2013 11573.

10 See, e.g., Higher Regional Court of Düsseldorf, Decision of 15.05.2014, Case Number I-2 U 74/13, BeckRS 2014 14360; Higher Regional Court of Düsseldorf, Decision of 20.12.2012, Case Number I-2 U 89/07, BeckRS 2013 11856; District Court of Düsseldorf, Decision of 20.11.2012, Case Number 4b O 100/11 U, BeckRS 2013 14799.

In principle, it is also possible for courts to allow certain grace periods, during which the infringer is allowed to sell goods already produced and covered by the injunction order or during which infringing articles can be modified and re-designed to fall outside the scope of the patent. The legal basis for grace periods is derived from the principle of good faith set out in § 242 of the German Civil Code (BGB). While such grace periods are primarily found in out-of-court case settlements, they can also be applied to court proceedings.[11] Courts consider grace periods if the infringer would incur disproportionate hardship due to the injunction taking immediate effect. Furthermore, grace periods for the distribution of infringing devices may be considered in cases where an immediate injunction would cause unreasonable disturbance to the general public. That said, such cases occur rather rarely in patent infringement proceedings.[12] **14.07**

3. Compulsory Enforcement

Other than, for example, in Japan,[13] an injunctive order can, in principle, be enforced against the infringer upon a decision by the first instance court even while the appeal is ongoing. However, in such a case, the infringed party initiating compulsory enforcement of the injunction order based on the first-instance decision has to post a security bond pursuant to § 709 of the Civil Procedure Code. Such a security bond is usually determined in light of the litigation value of the infringement action.[14] Injunction orders confirmed by a Higher Regional Court can be enforced without payment of a security bond. **14.08**

The defendant can request provisional suspension of compulsory enforcement of a first-instance decision subject to an ongoing appeal in case the underlying decision is obviously incorrect.[15] A decision could be considered as obviously incorrect, for example, in cases where the underlying patent has been revoked in the invalidity proceedings after the district court issued the injunction order.[16] **14.09**

A defendant may request protection against compulsory enforcement (*Vollstreckungsschutz*) pursuant to § 712 of the Civil Procedure Code against posting of a security bond. In patent law, a defendant would need to provide concise evidence of the fact that compulsory enforcement of an injunction order would probably cause the insolvency of the defendant in order to convince a court to grant protection against enforcement.[17] **14.10**

---

[11] The general permissibility of such grace periods in patent infringement proceedings was admitted in Federal Court of Justice GRUR 1981, 259, 260—*Heuwerbungsmaschine II.*

[12] R. Rogge and K. Grabinski in G. Benkard (ed.), *Patentgesetz (Patent Act)* (10th ed., 2006), § 139 of the Patent Act, margin no. 136a.

[13] It should be noted that also in Japan, preliminary injunctions can be enforced while an appeal is pending. Only injunctions awarded by a court in a main action cannot be enforced prior to the outcome of the appeal. See Ch. 15, 15.04.

[14] Kühnen, *Patent Litigation Proceedings in Germany*, marginal no. 1997.

[15] §§ 719 and 707 of the Civil Procedure Code.

[16] Kühnen, *Patent Litigation Proceedings in Germany*, marginal no. 2025; in this case, the party threatened with an injunction order would usually consider filing an action for defense against enforcement under § 767 Civil Procedure Code; see further details in Ch. 11, 11.162–11.165.

[17] Higher Regional Court of Düsseldorf InstGE 8, 117—*Fahrbare Betonpumpe*; the same court decision held that claiming the economically harmful interruption of production and distribution or the loss of jobs is not sufficient to justify protection against enforcement; see also District Court of Düsseldorf, Decision of 30.10.2014, Case Number Az. 4a O 92/13.

B. Claim for Damages

1. Requirements

14.11 Damage claims for patent infringement require that the infringer acted with negligence or intent. Negligence is presumed upon a finding of infringement. To rebut such a presumption, infringers have to show that they objectively could not have assumed that their conduct infringed a third-party patent. Case law grants patent infringers an examination period of one month after the publication of the patent application, during which negligence would not be presumed.[18]

14.12 Before 2008, normal negligence and slight negligence were treated differently, as slight negligence would result in reduced damages. Therefore, the degree of negligence would already have been discussed when determining infringement. The possibility of reducing damages in cases of slight negligence was removed with the implementation of the Enforcement Act in 2008.[19]

14.13 Generally, courts impose a high burden for rebutting the presumption of negligence. Under the standard of the Federal Court of Justice, every merchant and company that conducts commercial activities has a duty to investigate whether or not such activities infringe third-party patents prior to the commencement of such activities.[20] That said, the standard imposed is, comparatively speaking, stricter for manufacturers and specialized importers than for forwarding agents and general retailers who can operate with less profound technical knowledge and expertise and who may, therefore, be able to rebut the presumption of negligence.[21] Also, a certain likelihood of the patent being held as invalid in a parallel nullification action or even a first-instance invalidation decision is not sufficient to rebut the presumption of negligence, as the infringer has to seriously consider the possibility of the patent being held valid by the appellate court.[22]

2. Calculation of Damages

14.14 Patentees are entitled to compensation for infringement of their patent rights in line with § 249 of the German Civil Code; that said, patentees should be put in the position in which they would have been but for the infringement. Statutory provisions and case law[23] provide for three different calculation approaches to determine the amount of damages: (1) compensation of specific damage incurred due to lost profits,[24] (2) compensation of objective damage by calculating an appropriate royalty,[25] and (3) compensation in the amount of the profits generated by the infringer.[26]

---

[18] Kühnen, *Patent Litigation Proceedings in Germany*, marginal no. 1017.

[19] BGBl I 2008, 1191.

[20] Federal Court of Justice GRUR 1977, 250, 252—*Kunststoffhohlprofil I*; Federal Court of Justice GRUR 1993, 460, 464—*Wandabstreifer*.

[21] E.g., District Court of Düsseldorf InstGE 5, 241—*Frachtführer*.

[22] Higher Regional Court of Düsseldorf, Decision of 30.11.2010, Case Number I-2 U 82/09.

[23] Federal Court of Justice GRUR 1972, 189—*Wandsteckdose II*; Federal Court of Justice GRUR 1974, 53—*Nebelscheinwerfer*; Federal Court of Justice GRUR 1980, 841—*Tobultamid*.

[24] § 252 of the German Civil Code.

[25] German Patent Act, § 139(2), third sentence.

[26] German Patent Act, § 139(2), second sentence.

In principle, the infringed party has a right to freely choose between the three aforementioned methods of calculation. Combining the three methods of calculation is generally not admissible. The decision as to which method of calculation the infringed party chooses can be made at any time during the proceedings until satisfaction of the damage claim or until there is confirmation, in a final and binding decision, of a specific damage amount calculated pursuant to one of the three methods. **14.15**

Traditionally, the calculation of damages by means of a reasonable royalty was by far the most relevant method, being applied in approximately 95 percent of all damage cases.[27] The Federal Court of Justice triggered a change in the ranking of the three methods' popularity when it modified the method of calculating the infringer's profits in 2001.[28] Since the decision, using the infringer's profits has become the most popular method of calculating damages.[29] **14.16**

(a) Lost Profits

According to the principles of §§ 249 and 252 of the German Civil Code, the infringed party can always request compensation in the amount of lost profits due to the infringement. The party can compute the lost profits according to an abstract or a concrete method.[30] The abstract calculation is based on the assumption that a certain number of transactions generating profits will occur in the usual course of trade. Under the concrete method, the patentee has to show that the infringement prevented the patentee from making specific transactions that would have generated profits.[31] When using the abstract method, the patentee does not have to show that specific transactions that were otherwise certain were missed due to the infringement; however, the patentee still has to show that transactions were missed that would have occurred with a certain likelihood but for the infringement. Upon a showing of such likelihood, the infringer can try to rebut such assumed profits by showing that the transactions were consumed for reasons other than the infringement.[32] **14.17**

Requesting compensation for lost profits requires disclosure of the infringed party's relevant cost calculation in order to back the calculation of profits, which can be unappealing since specific information related to profit margins and product-specific costs are often considered to be confidential information. Furthermore, it may not be possible to provide a reliable assumption of lost turnover transactions, particularly in markets with multiple participants offering somewhat similar competing products. **14.18**

However, the German Federal Court of Justice is attempting to be more lenient when it comes to presenting lost profits. While a reliable inference cannot be made, it may be permissible to rely on the infringer's sales, at least as a starting point, in the calculation of lost **14.19**

[27] S. Rojahn, "Praktische Probleme bei der Abwicklung der Rechtsfolgen einer Patentverletzung," *GRUR* (2005): 623, 625.

[28] Federal Court of Justice GRUR 2001, 329—*Gemeinkostenanteil*, English translation published in 33 IIC 900, 902 (2002); for an English review of the decision see, e.g., P. Meier-Beck, "Damages for Patent Infringement... Law: Basic Principles, Assessment and Enforcement," *IIC* (2004): 113.

[29] K. Grabinski, "Gewinnherausgabe nach... Jahre nach dem 'Gemeinkostenanteil'-Urteil des BGH," *GRUR* (2009): 260, 262.

[30] Kühnen, *Patent Litigation Proceedings in Germany*, marginal no. 2356.

[31] Federal Court of Justice NJW-RR 2006, 243.

[32] Federal Court of Justice NJW-RR 2006, 243; Federal Court of Justice GRUR 2009, 933—Schmiermittel.

profits.[33] Initially, the infringed party merely has to show that it is more likely than not[34] that the infringement resulted in a loss of profit. Upon such an initial showing, it becomes the responsibility of the infringer to provide counter-evidence showing a lack of causality between the patent infringement and the differences in terms of profit or revenues made by the patentee. Lost profits as a result of low sales prices being forced on the patentee as a consequence of patent infringement may be claimed in addition to abstract or concrete lost sales. That said, such economic harm caused by price deterioration is also often difficult to prove, particularly in markets with multiple participants and divergent price structures.

(b) Infringer's Profits

14.20 Calculation of damages by accounting for the infringer's profits has been the most significant method for calculating damages in patent infringement proceedings in recent years. Considering the infringer's profits when calculating damages is dogmatically based on the civil law principles of agency without authority set forth in §§ 687(2) and 667 of the German Civil Code,[35] as well as on customary law. It is irrelevant whether the plaintiff would have been able to generate revenues on the same scale.[36] Calculating patent damages on the basis of the infringer's profits was codified in the course of implementing the Enforcement Directive by modifying German Patent Act, § 139(2). That said, while the language of the statute could be understood as mentioning the infringer's profits as a mere factor supporting the calculation of the patentee's lost profits, the ministerial bill published in the course of the enactment of the Enforcement Act clearly explained that the infringer's profits are an equal alternative for calculating a damage claim.[37]

14.21 The starting point for the calculation of the infringer's profits is the revenue generated by the patent-infringing activity of the defendant. In addition, revenues generated through the sale of "peripheral devices" or consumables that were not covered by the patent but sold only due to the fact that the defendant could sell the infringing device may also have to be included as relevant revenue.[38]

14.22 The infringer's profits became significantly more relevant for patent damage calculations due to a shift in determining deductible costs. Before 2001, it was possible for the infringer to deduct not only the variable costs directly related to the revenue generated by the infringing activities but also, somewhat arbitrarily, the allocated parts of the overhead costs, thereby often resulting in the infringer's profits becoming unattractively low. Such a method of calculation was criticized by a number of commentators[39] and modified in the Federal Court of Justice decision *Gemeinkostenanteil* in 2001, which held that only such overhead

[33] Federal Court of Justice GRUR 2009, 933—Schmiermittel.

[34] Such reference to a mere preponderance stems from § 287 of the German Code of Civil Procedure, according to which a plaintiff may only have to demonstrate a mere probability of a particular course of events having occurred.

[35] Kraßer, *Patentrecht*, § 35 IV d 2.

[36] Federal Court of Justice GRUR 1962, 509—*Diarähmchen II.*

[37] Government Draft Bill for the Act to Improve Enforcement of Intellectual Property Rights to Implement Directive 2004/48/EC (*Entwurf eines Gesetzes zur Verbesserung der Durchsetzung von Rechten des geistigen Eigentums zur Umsetzung der Richtlinie 2004/48/EG*) as of January 24, 2007 (published as BT-Drs. 64/07), 87.

[38] Kühnen, *Patent Litigation Proceedings in Germany*, marginal no. 2293.

[39] See, e.g., M. Lehmann, "Juristisch-ökonomische Kriterien zur Berechnung des Verletzergewinns bzw. des entgangenen Gewinns," *BB* (1988): 1680; E. Körner, *FS Steindorff* (1990), 886; H. von der Osten, "Zum Anspruch auf Herausgabe des Verletzergewinnes im Patentrecht," *GRUR* (1998): 286.

costs directly related to the infringing products remained deductible.[40] Deductible items continued to include variable or direct cost items such as the actual cost of materials and of the manufacturing of infringing products. The Federal Court of Justice in 2007 introduced another critical element to the calculation of the infringer's profits by establishing a legal fiction that the infringed party operates a business that could have carried out the same production and distribution as the infringer had.[41] Only the costs that would have been incurred by the infringed party in such fictional operations are deductible from the revenue generated by the infringer. Therefore, the deductible costs are only those that have been incurred by the infringer and those that would also have been incurred in the fictional operations of the infringed party. In turn, costs that would have been incurred by the infringer irrespective of the infringing operations or costs that would not have been incurred in the fictional operations of the infringed party are not deductible from the infringer's revenue. In the last few years, courts have decided on specific deductible and non-deductible costs, as shown in Table 14.1.[42]

The infringer has to demonstrate the costs that he or she desires to subtract from the revenue.[43] After determining the relevant revenue and cost items, the court has to determine the degree of causation between the infringer's profits and the infringed patent. In cases where the patent covers all the essential elements of the products or services with which the infringer generated profits, the requirements for demonstrating causation are very low.[44] The situation is different if the patent covers only a part of the device sold by the infringer. Other exceptional circumstances that can impede the causation between the infringed patent and the infringer's profits include an exceptionally strong brand reputation under which the infringing product is sold or the infringing product having particular technical features not covered by the infringed patent that are driving customer demand. In such situations, it will be more difficult for the patentee to claim that the infringer's entire profits are attributable to the infringement of the patent. Pursuant to § 287 of the Civil Procedure Code, the infringed party has to provide an estimate on the amount and share of the profits attributable to the infringed patent. If the infringer disputes such an estimate, the court has to determine the degree of causation by evaluating to what extent the patented features caused the infringer's customers to purchase the infringing goods.[45] **14.23**

(c) License Analogy

Due to the difficulties in demonstrating lost profits and the wide range of deductible cost items, prior to 2001 most damage awards used to be calculated based on a license analogy. As with the infringer's profits, the fictional license analogy is not a specific method but rather is an objective method of calculating compensation for patent infringement, following the concept that the party whose patent has been infringed should receive compensation for the objective market value of the unauthorized use of the patent. Resorting to a license analogy is supported by the established concept that the infringed party should not be worse off than if the party had granted the infringer the right to use the relevant patent **14.24**

40 N. 29 above.
41 Federal Court of Justice GRUR 2007, 431—*Steckverbindungsgehäuse*.
42 For a more complete list, see Kühnen, *Patent Litigation Proceedings in Germany*, marginal nos. 2311–32.
43 Federal Court of Justice GRUR 2007, 431—*Steckverbindungsgehäuse*.
44 Federal Court of Justice GRUR 2010, 1090—*Werbung des Nachrichtensenders*.
45 Higher Regional Court of Düsseldorf InstGE 5, 251—*Lifter*.

Table 14.1 Deductible and non-deductible cost positions

Deductible costs	Non-deductible costs
Actual cost of materials and manufacturing cost for production and assembly of infringing products[i]	Costs for staff hired and employed as well as for the production or distribution of non-infringing products[ii]
Cost of waste materials[iii]	Rent for production facilities and warehouses used as well as for the production or distribution of non-infringing products[iv]
Cost of acquiring machinery that has been used exclusively for the manufacture of infringing products[v]	General marketing cost[vi]
Costs for staff hired and employed only for the production or distribution of infringing products[vii]	License fees paid for additional third-party IP[viii]
Cost of energy consumed in production of infringing products[ix]	Costs incurred in the course of developing infringing products[x] or in the course of training staff in the manufacture or distribution of infringing products[xi]
Rent for production facilities and warehouses used only for the production or distribution of infringing products[xii]	Legal costs incurred in the course of defending the infringer's position in patent litigation[xiii]
Packaging and freight costs incurred only in the course of production or distribution of infringing products[xiv]	Production costs for products manufactured that cannot be sold, e.g., due to the injunction order obtained by the patentee[xv]
Sales commissions that became due only because of the sales of infringing products[xvi]	Costs for recalling and destroying infringing products

[i] Federal Court of Justice GRUR 2007, 431—*Steckverbindungsgehäuse*; Higher Regional Court of Düsseldorf InstGE 7, 194—*Schwerlastregal II*.
[ii] Federal Court of Justice GRUR 2007, 431—*Steckverbindungsgehäuse*.
[iii] District Court of Frankfurt InstGE 6, 141—*Borstenverrundung*.
[iv] Federal Court of Justice GRUR 2007, 431—*Steckverbindungsgehäuse*.
[v] Ibid.
[vi] Ibid.
[vii] Ibid.
[viii] District Court of Frankfurt InstGE 6, 141—*Borstenverrundung*.
[ix] Federal Court of Justice GRUR 2007, 431—*Steckverbindungsgehäuse*.
[x] Such costs were held to be non-deductible, as they would not have been incurred in the fictional operations of the infringed party, ibid.
[xi] Higher Regional Court of Düsseldorf InstGE 13, 199—*Schräg-Raffstore*.
[xii] Federal Court of Justice GRUR 2007, 431—*Steckverbindungsgehäuse*.
[xiii] Higher Regional Court of Düsseldorf InstGE 5, 251—*Lifter*; Higher Regional Court of Düsseldorf InstGE 7, 194—*Schwerlastregal II*.
[xiv] Federal Court of Justice GRUR 2007, 431—*Steckverbindungsgehäuse*; Higher Regional Court of Düsseldorf InstGE 7, 194—*Schwerlastregal II*.
[xv] Federal Court of Justice GRUR 2007, 431—*Steckverbindungsgehäuse*.
[xvi] Higher Regional Court of Düsseldorf InstGE 7, 194—*Schwerlastregal II*.

under a license agreement. The royalty should be derived in light of what reasonable parties would have agreed on given the objective value of the infringed patent at the time when the infringement commenced.[46] The basis for a reasonable royalty could be either a blanket license with a one-time lump sum payment or a per-unit royalty based on the number of units sold, or a combination of both. Most reasonable royalty damage awards decided by

[46] Kühnen, *Patent Litigation Proceedings in Germany*, marginal no. 2247.

German courts are calculated on the basis of a per-unit royalty, in which case the per-unit revenue or the list selling price of the infringer serves as a basis for the calculation. In cases of assembled facilities or production processes of which only a part infringes the patent, the same concerns regarding causation between the infringer's revenue and attribution to the infringed patent that arise in the context of calculating the infringer's profit arise. Again, the courts have to base their decision in light of the economic relevance of the infringed patent for the sold product.

As a second step, the court has to determine a reasonable royalty rate. In determining the royalty, courts initially use the rates customary in the market for comparable patents as a reference as long as such comparable market data is available. Adding an infringer's surcharge in order to impose something along the lines of a fictional contractual penalty or in order to simply add a deterring factor has been discussed in literature in the past but has not found support in case law, and as such a surcharge would have no foundation in patent statutes. **14.25**

In order to determine the amount of the royalty customary in the market, the infringed party may refer to comparable license agreements concluded in the past. Typical license rates vary greatly according to the industry and complexity of the technology. In addition to the typical market rates, further factors that arise due to the fact that no actual license was concluded could be taken into consideration in individual cases. Such factors may include the economic results caused by a lack of geographic market allocation or the no-challenge provisions not infrequently found in license and distribution agreements, which could increase the reasonable royalty. On the other hand, lack of access to the patentee's know-how beyond the disclosure and teaching of the patent could effectively reduce the license rate. Therefore, in principle, it is assumed that the above-mentioned advantages and disadvantages offset one another and only affect the license royalty rate in exceptional cases. **14.26**

Ultimately, the infringer must pay interest on the royalties for the period during which the patent was infringed, pursuant to §§ 286, 288, and 291 of the German Civil Code. **14.27**

(d) Damages Resulting from Market Confusion

Furthermore, the patentee can claim compensation for damages resulting from market confusion such as a loss of reputation or losses caused by the confusion in the market caused by the patent infringement. A damage award compensating for a loss of reputation is calculated by considering the costs of specific counteractions such as customer letters or advertising campaigns directed to remedy the loss of reputation. Such countermeasures have to be closely related to the act of infringement, both in terms of subject matter, customers addressed, and timing. **14.28**

In principle, damages due to market confusion have relatively little importance and are only granted in a very few cases due to the high requirements concerning evidence. **14.29**

C. Claim on Account of Unjust Enrichment

Theoretically, an infringed party may also base compensation claims on unjust enrichment pursuant to §§ 818(2) and 812(1), first sentence of the German Civil Code. That said, unjust enrichment claims are of practical interest only in either the rare case where **14.30** a damage claim under German Patent Act, § 139 is excluded due to a lack of infringer's negligence or a case where the damage claim is time-barred due to the statute of limitations.[47] A claim for the disgorgement of profits obtained through unjust enrichment will usually be less attractive than a damage claim for the infringer's profits under German Patent Act, § 139, as the decisions of the Federal Court of Justice limiting the deduction of overhead and direct costs have not yet been confirmed as being applicable to unjust enrichment claims. That said, courts have confirmed that the amount of unjust enrichment claims can be based on a reasonable royalty award.[48]

D. Claims for Destruction, Recall, and Removal from Distribution Channels

1. Claim for Destruction

14.31 German Patent Act, § 140a entitles the infringed party to a claim for the destruction of the infringing products. The purpose of such a claim for destruction is to ultimately remove the infringing products from the market. The claim for destruction was introduced for the purpose of deterring potential infringers. It extends not only to the patent-infringing products but also to the materials and equipment that have been predominantly used for the manufacture of such products.

14.32 The first prerequisite for a claim for destruction is an infringement of a patent, within the meaning of German Patent Act, § 139, that results in the infringed party making a claim for injunctive relief. Negligence of the infringer is not required. Furthermore, the infringing products have to be directly or indirectly possessed or owned by the infringer. To extend the claim for destruction to materials or equipment, the plaintiff has to show ownership by the infringer. Possession is not sufficient. Finally, all the products, devices, or equipment for which destruction is requested have to be located in Germany. The claim for destruction cannot be granted if the destruction is found to be disproportionately harsh for the possessor or owner.[49] Destruction may be disproportionately harsh if the infringing features of the products can be modified to render the product non-infringing by means other than destruction. If, however, the infringer or a third-party would be able to relatively easily reconfigure or otherwise modify the product by again adding the infringing features, the claim for destruction will usually have to be granted.[50] Furthermore, the claim for destruction may be considered disproportionately harsh if the interests of the defendant or the subsequent proprietor, who may be different from the infringer, clearly outweigh the infringed party's interests in destruction. Here, the court will review the degree of culpability of the infringer[51] as well as the number and the economic value of the items to be destroyed.[52] The infringer bears the burden of proof that the destruction would be disproportionately harsh.

---

[47] While damage claims are time-barred three years after the act of infringement, subject to knowledge of such infringement or lack of such knowledge due to gross negligence (§§ 195, 199 of the Civil Code), unjust enrichment claims are time-barred only after ten years, subject to the unjustly enriched having acted with negligence (§ 854 of the Civil Code).

[48] Federal Court of Justice GRUR 2009, 515—*Motorradreiniger* (trademark case).

[49] German Patent Act, § 140a(4).

[50] Higher Regional Court of Düsseldorf InstGE 7, 139—*Thermocycler*.

[51] Federal Court of Justice GRUR 2006, 504—*Parfümtestkäufe*.

[52] Higher Regional Court of Düsseldorf InstGE 7, 139—*Thermocycler*.

2. Claims for Recall and Removal from Distribution Channels

The claim for recall of infringing goods and their respective removal from distribution channels was newly established in German patent law in 2008[53] in line with the requirements of the Enforcement Directive. In Europe, the recall claim was first introduced in the Netherlands and was then implemented across Europe by means of the Enforcement Directive. It provides the infringed party with a basis to request the infringer to recall infringing products from commercial possessors or procure their removal from distribution channels, irrespective of whether they are still in Germany or not. That said, the claim for recall and removal from distribution channels cannot be enforced against a defendant located outside of Germany. Unlike the claim for destruction under German Patent Act, § 140(a)(1), it is not necessary for the infringer to still have the power of disposal over the infringing goods. Also, unlike the claim for destruction, the claim for recall does not extend to materials and equipment that are used for the production of the infringing goods. **14.33**

The claim for recall and removal from distribution channels is also subject to the proportionality qualifier of German Patent Act, § 140(a)(4). Accordingly, a request for recall would be considered disproportionate if the recalled product is perishable and the validity date has expired, justifying the assumption that the product will no longer be used in an infringing manner.[54] Another situation in which a recall may be considered disproportionate is if the products have been exported to a location so far away from Germany that the cost of reimporting them to Germany would be exceedingly high, making it economically prohibitive and therefore very unlikely that the products would again be used in an infringing manner in Germany in the future.[55] Furthermore, a recall claim would be barred if the infringed party waives its right for destruction under German Patent Act, § 140(a)(1).[56] **14.34**

To comply with a recall claim, the infringer has to make a serious demand to any known commercial possessor,[57] requesting that they keep the infringing product and no longer distribute it. If an undertaking to no longer distribute the infringing products would be insufficient to remedy the possibility of further infringement, the possessor should be requested to voluntarily return the products to the infringer. **14.35**

The recall should be worded as a serious request. Thus, the infringer has to provide an explanation for the request, including the legal consequences of further distribution. Furthermore, the infringer has to offer a refund of the purchase price[58] and payment of transportation or shipping costs. The infringer does not have to offer any further compensation or indemnification payments to cover, for example, lost profits incurred by the possessor due to the return of the infringing product. **14.36**

The claim for removal from distribution channels may in some cases cover different fact patterns than the recall claim. Therefore, asking for a voluntary recall may not be enough to satisfy the claim for final removal from distribution channels.[59] To comply with a claim **14.37**

---

[53] § 140(a)(3) of the German Patent Act.

[54] Kühnen, *Patent Litigation Proceedings in Germany*, marginal no. 1240.

[55] Ibid. marginal no. 1242.

[56] Ibid. marginal no. 1243.

[57] The recall claim does not include a duty to identify unknown possessors.

[58] The offer for a refund could be scaled in order to reflect the duration of use of the product. Alternatively, the infringer may offer to provide the possessor with a substitute product.

[59] Higher Regional Court of Düsseldorf InstGE 12, 88—*Cinch-Stecker*.

for final removal from distribution channels, the infringer should also actively enforce the return of the infringing products where the infringer is legally and actually able to do so, or have the infringing products destroyed at the premises of the possessor. Again, the infringer only has to request known commercial possessors to remove the products from distribution channels.

E. Claim for Information

14.38 The claim for information and rendering of accounts was enhanced in 2008, during the implementation of the Enforcement Directive, by introducing the current version of German Patent Act, § 140(b). Some categories of information related to infringing acts that occurred prior to 2008 may not be requested on the basis of German Patent Act, § 140(b), but they may possibly be requested based on a separate civil law claim for rendering accounts under §§ 242 and 259 of the German Civil Code.

1. Patent Act Information Disclosure Claim

14.39 German Patent Act, § 140(b) grants the infringed party the right to obtain information related to the origin and the distribution channels of the infringing products. Since 2008, the claim for information also requires disclosure of detailed purchase and sales prices as well as details with respect to the sales outlets. The claim for information is usually enforced in order to enable an infringed party to calculate the amount of damages, either to prepare for out-of-court settlement of the damage claims or to enable the infringed party to enforce the damage claims in subsequent court proceedings. The claim may also be enforced in order to prepare for subsequent actions against third parties who were not named as defendants in the initial enforcement action.

14.40 Under certain circumstances, the claim for information may also be directly enforced against third parties who were not named as defendants in the initial enforcement action.[60] Such an extension of the claim for information requires a certain personal and subject matter relation between the third party and the defendant. To have a subject matter relation, the patent infringement must be obvious,[61] or, alternatively, the patent enforcement action directed to confirm an infringement must be pending. Those with a personal relation are listed in German Patent Act, § 140(b)(2), according to which the claim for information can be enforced against any commercially active (1) former proprietor of the infringing products, (2) user of the patent-infringing services, (3) provider of services that contributed to the infringement, and (4) person who was mentioned by any of the entities listed in numbers (1)–(3) as being involved in the manufacture, production, or distribution of the infringing product or in the generation of the infringing service or process.[62]

---

[60] German Patent Act, § 140(b)(3).

[61] A patent infringement is obvious if both the factual circumstances and the legal assessment are so clear that a finding of non-infringement appears to be out of the question (Higher Regional Court of Hamburg InstGE 8, 11—*Transglutaminase*). In addition, the validity of the patent may not be in doubt (Higher Regional Court of Düsseldorf GRUR 1993, 818).

[62] When assessing the testimony of the entities listed in numbers (1)–(3), the reliability of such testimony has to be established. If there are doubts about the knowledge of the testifying party, its statements seem to be out of context, or the testimony seems otherwise implausible, the information claim under number (4) should not be granted.

The claim for information is subject to the same proportionality qualifier set forth in German Patent Act, § 140(b)(4) as the claim for destruction and the claim for recall. That said, there will be few cases in which the defendant's interest in keeping the requested information confidential will prevail over the infringed party's interest in obtaining access to the information, especially if there are material damage claims for the precise calculation of which the infringed party requires access to the defendant's information. 14.41

The defendant has to disclose all such information listed in German Patent Act, § 140(b)(3).[63] That said, the disclosure obligation only extends to information that is known to it by reference to its business documents and files. If there are any doubts with respect to the accuracy or completeness of the information, the defendant has to make further inquiries, for example, by contacting the relevant business partner. The information has to be disclosed immediately after the claim is granted. That said, the meaning of the term "immediate" is equivalent to "without culpable delay" and therefore depends on the amount of data to be prepared, reviewed, and disclosed. While German Patent Act, § 140(c)(5) stipulates a damage claim for the disclosure of incorrect or insufficient data in response to a claim for information, there is no damage claim for a late response. 14.42

2. Civil Code Information Disclosure Claim

Also, prior to enactment of the patent act claim for disclosure of information, German civil law provided the plaintiff with the ability to file a claim requesting a defendant to render accounts if such information would be necessary to calculate the amount of compensation or damages the plaintiff was entitled to. Such claim for information is based on the civil law principle of good faith pursuant to §§ 242 and 259 of the Civil Code. The claim requires that the plaintiff lacks access to the requested information and cannot reasonably be expected to obtain such access without disclosure by the defendant.[64] To satisfy the civil law claim for information, the defendant has to disclose all such details needed by the infringed party to establish the relevant claim for performance and to conduct a rough verification of the details provided.[65] If the civil law claim for information is asserted in order to enable the infringed party to calculate the damage award, the defendant has to disclose the following:[66] 14.43

- quantities and timing of products manufactured
- relevant supplies with a breakdown of the supplied quantities, times, and supply prices, as well as the names and addresses of the suppliers

---

[63] German Patent Act, § 140(b)(3):

The person required to provide information must specify

1. the names and addresses of the manufacturers, suppliers, and other previous possessors of the products or users of the services as well as the commercial customers and sales outlets, for which said products were intended, and
2. the quantities of products manufactured, delivered, received, or ordered as well as the prices paid for the respective products or services.

[64] Federal Court of Justice GRUR 2010, 623—*Restwertbörse*.

[65] Federal Court of Justice GRUR 2008, 896—*Tintenpatrone*; Kühnen, *Patent Litigation Proceedings in Germany*, marginal no. 1174.

[66] Kühnen, *Patent Litigation Proceedings in Germany*, marginal nos. 1177–82.

- relevant sales with a breakdown of the sold quantities, times, and prices, as well as the names and addresses of the customers; in addition, all offers for sale, including the prices quoted and the names and addresses of customers to whom quotations were made
- the extent of advertising carried out for the infringing products or services, including a breakdown of the media used for the advertisements, its circulation, its duration, and territories targeted by the advertisements
- production costs and corresponding profits generated.

15

JAPAN

A. Injunctive Relief

1. Requirements

Pursuant to Japanese Patent Act, § 100,[1] a claim for injunctive relief requires a showing of a current infringement or a likelihood of a future infringement.[2] In cases where the claim is based on a likelihood of future infringement, the court has to recognize an objective likelihood that the infringing conduct will occur in the future, which has to be supported by specific factual evidence.[3] Such likelihood of infringing conduct is assumed by the courts if the defendant has the ability to resume the infringing conduct, which can be demonstrated, for example, by showing that the defendant has the know-how to resume manufacturing the infringing product or by the fact that the defendant disputes that the allegedly infringing products fall within the scope of the invention protected by plaintiff's patent.[4] Also, a likelihood of infringing conduct will be assumed by the courts if the defendant declares that there will be resumption of the conduct if the case prevails in court.[5] The claim for injunctive relief does not require any degree of fault by the defendant.[6] **15.01**

2. Scope

The party entitled to a claim for injunctive relief can request the defendant to cease the infringing conduct (*kyōgi no sashitome seikyūken*) and to refrain from such conduct in the future (*yobō*). In addition, the plaintiff can request the defendant, pursuant to Japanese Patent Act, § 100(2), to destroy the equipment used to produce the patent-infringing goods.[7] To declare the claim for destruction of the equipment, the court needs to specify the nature of the patent-infringing goods and of the infringing conduct. Thus, the details of the infringing conduct have to be investigated and recorded, and the product names, product details, technical drafts, and serial numbers have to be confirmed by the courts.[8] **15.02**

---

[1] Tokkyo Hō [Japanese Patent Act], Law No. 121 of 1959.

[2] Tatsuki Shibuya, *Chitekizaisanhō kōgi 1* (2d ed., 2006), 188.

[3] Tokyo District Court, August 26, 2011, Hei 20 (wa) Nr. 831, 1402 Hanrei Times 344 (2011)—"*Dōbutsu-yō hainyō shori-zai.*"

[4] Osaka District Court, January 24, 1975, Sho 48 (wa) No. 3834, 323 Hanrei Times (1975), 270—"*Plastic film.*"

[5] Tokyo District Court, December 22, 1969, Sho 41 (wa) No. 11570, 1 Mutaishū (1969), 394.

[6] Yun Komatsu, *Tokkyohō Jitsuyo shinanhō* (2005), 146; Masayoshi Sumida and Naohiko Tatsumi, *Chitekizaisanhō* (2006), 133.

[7] Shunji Miyama and Nobuo Matsumura, *Chitekizaisanken Soshô: Jitsumu kaisetsu* (2d ed., 2005), 493; Sumida and Tatsumi, *Chitekizaisanhō*, 134.

[8] Osaka District Court, November 25, 1987, Sho 59 (wa) No. 7127, 19-3 Mutaishū (1987) 434—"*Wood Work.*"

15.03 The claim for injunctive relief typically encompasses only the infringing conduct identified by the court. Accordingly, the injunction orders issued by the courts are usually concise and very specific. The patentees need to enforce their patent again if the defendants modify their conduct but nevertheless still infringe the same patent.[9]

3. Compulsory Enforcement

15.04 In order to seek enforcement of the injunction, a prevailing plaintiff can request the court to order compulsory enforcement of the decision. That said, a permanent injunction issued by a district court cannot be enforced against the infringer if the infringer has filed an appeal at the IP High Court and such an appellate procedure is still ongoing. In this case, the claim for permanent injunctive relief can be enforced after it has been confirmed by the IP High Court.

15.05 After prevailing at the district court level, the plaintiff can request a declaration of provisional execution (*karishikkōsengen*), which in principle would entitle the plaintiff to enforce the permanent injunction before conclusion of the appellate proceeding. However, the defendant can stop the provisional execution by posting a security bond in an amount set by the court.

B. Damages

15.06 The patentee or the exclusive licensee can request from the infringer compensation for damages incurred as a consequence of the infringing conduct pursuant to Japanese Civil Code, § 709.[10] The provision in Japanese Patent Act, § 102 serves to facilitate the computation of the damage claim.

1. Requirements

15.07 A damage claim pursuant to Japanese Civil Code, § 709 always requires fault—that is, intent or negligence—by the tortfeasor.[11] Japanese Patent Act, § 103 provides, however, for a presumption of negligence by the infringer upon establishment of infringement.[12] Accordingly, the infringer has to show the absence of negligence in order to avoid being held liable for damages. The presumption of negligence requires publication of the infringed patent in the patent gazette at the time of infringement.[13] Thereafter, showing an absence of negligence is practically very difficult and will only be possible in a very limited number of circumstances.[14] If the court has followed the plaintiff and found infringement, it will only in very exceptional cases deny all damage claims by finding an absence of any negligence.[15]

[9] Tokyo District Court, January 18, 1984, Sho 58 (wa) No. 8056, 1101 Hanrei Jihō (1984) 109—"*Porno Disneyland*"; Sapporo High Court, March 27, 1974, Sho 48 (ra) No. 58, 308 Hanrei Times (1976), 227—"*Misono Azumusushi*"; Yoshiyuki Tamura, "Chitekizaisanshingaisoshōni okeru kajyôsashitome to chūshôteki sashitome (Ge)," 1125 *Jurist* (1997): 129, 130.

[10] Minpō [Japanese Civil Code], Law No. 89 of 1896.

[11] Tokyo District Court, October 18, 1996, Hei 6 (wa) No. 16290, 1585 Hanrei Jihō (1996) 106; Shibuya, *Chitekizaisanhō kōgi*, 192; Miyama and Matsumura, *Chitekizaisanken Soshô*, 500; Masamichi Okuda and Yoshio Shiomi, *Hōgaku Kōgi Minpō* (2005), vol. VI, 111.

[12] Japanese Patent Act, § 103 states: "An infringer of a patent right or exclusive license of another person is presumed negligent in the commission of the said act of infringement."

[13] If the patent had not been published at the time of the patent infringement and if the infringer can show the undertaking of a formal patent search, the presumption of negligence pursuant to Japanese Patent Act, § 103 is not applied; see Shibuya, *Chitekizaisanhō kōgi*, 194.

[14] Yutaka Koike, "Damages Caused by Intellectual Property Infringement, and Subjective Element on the Part of Infringers: Active Use of Article 102, Paragraph 4 of the Japanese Patent Law," *AIPPI* (2004): 357, 364.

[15] Ibid.; Yoshiyuki Tamura, *Chitekizaisanken to Songaibaishō* (2d ed., 2004), 3.

An example of exculpatory evidence would be proof that a formal examination of the patent registry did not render any results—that is, there was an error by the JPO in maintaining its records.[16] A non-infringement opinion from a patent attorney prepared before beginning the infringing conduct will not be sufficient to demonstrate an absence of negligence.[17] While it is very difficult to show a total absence of negligence, convincing the court that only a slight degree of negligence was exercised may, at least in theory, be helpful for the defendant.[18] Pursuant to Japanese Patent Act, § 102(4), courts can lower the damage award if the defendant shows a lower degree of negligence. Commentators have suggested that slight negligence might be considered in cases where the technical evaluation of the factual circumstances, and thus the evaluation of whether a conduct constitutes infringement or not, would be extraordinarily difficult and complex[19] or in cases where the defendant is a non-specialist distributor or retailer who does not need to have detailed knowledge of the technical features of the goods distributed.[20] That said, while commentators have suggested cases where a reduction of damages could be applied due to a finding of slight negligence, there have been no recent patent infringement court decisions reported that have found a reduced liability for the infringer under Japanese Patent Act, §102(4).[21] Other commentators have therefore suggested removing Japanese Patent Act, § 102(4) altogether, given the courts' obvious reluctance in applying it.[22] **15.08**

2. Calculation of the Amount of Damages

Japanese Civil Code, § 709 constitutes the general civil law obligation of a negligent tortfeasor to compensate an infringed party for all damages incurred. However, the specification of "damages incurred" as a consequence of a patent infringement and the calculation of such damages is subject to regulations outlined in the Japanese Patent Act. Following a revision of the Japanese Patent Act implemented in 1998,[23] Japanese Patent Act, § 102[24] provides for **15.09**

[16] Originally decided in the context of a utility model infringement by the Osaka District Court, March 29, 1977, Sho 45 (wa) No. 5258, 4-1, Muteisaishu 1, 137—"*Crash Barrier*"; in the context of patent law see Osaka District Court, July 13, 2001, Hei 12 (wa) No. 4184—"*Wallpaper Glue Machine*".

[17] Osaka District Court, October 30, 1984, Sho 57 (wa) No. 7273. 543 Hanrei Times (1985) 263—"*Tesagebukoro.*"

[18] Koike, "Damages Caused by Intellectual Property Infringement, and Subjective Element on the Part of Infringers," 368.

[19] E.g., in cases of equivalent patent infringement. See ibid. 365.

[20] Ibid. 368; Tamura, *Chitekizaisanken to Songaibaishō*, 328.

[21] That said, in some cases the court realized that the infringer, being a small company with little technical expertise, could not have recognized whether certain conduct would have constituted patent infringement or not, and the court did not invoke Japanese Patent Act, § 102(4) but nevertheless limited the damage award to a reasonable royalty under Japanese Patent Act, § 102(3). See, e.g., Tokyo High Court, 27.4.2004, Hei 14 (ne) No. 4448.

[22] Kei Iida, "Commentary on Article 102 Patent Act," in Nobuhiro Nakayama and Naoki Koizumi (eds.), *Shin Chūkai Tokkyohō* (2011), 1737.

[23] On regulations prior to 1998 see Toshiko Takenaka, "Patent Infringement Damages in Japan and the United States: Will Increased Patent Infringement Damage Awards Revive the Japanese Economy," 2 *Wash. U.J.L. & Pol'y* (2000): 309, 312.

[24] Japanese Patent Act, § 102 states (unofficial translation published by the Japanese Ministry of Justice (http://www.japaneselawtranslation.go.jp/?re=02):

1. Where a patentee or an exclusive licensee claims against an infringer compensation for damage sustained as a result of the intentional or negligent infringement of the patent right or exclusive license, and the infringer assigned articles that composed the act of infringement, the amount of damage sustained by the patentee or the exclusive licensee may be presumed to be the amount of profit per unit of articles which would have been sold by the patentee or the exclusive licensee if there had been no such act of infringement, multiplied by the quantity (hereinafter referred to in this paragraph as the "assigned quantity") of articles assigned by

Table 15.1 Calculation method/average damage award 1999–2013*

Basis for claim	Number of cases	Average damage award
Lost profits	39	537 million yen
Infringer's profits	56	133 million yen
Royalty	59	59 million yen

* See JIPA Patent Damage Study 2014, published in 64(10) *Chizai Kanri* (2014): 1548.

three methods of computing damages: (1) lost profits, (2) accounting for infringer's profits, and (3) accounting for a reasonable royalty fee. The infringed party can freely select the computation method to be used. As shown in Table 15.1, most damages awards in the last fifteen years have been calculated based on infringer's profits or reasonable royalty. While the number of cases in which damages were calculated based on lost profits are fewer, such cases tend to result in higher damage awards.

15.10 Prior to 1998, both objective damage calculation methods—that is, accounting for the infringer's profits and accounting for a reasonable royalty rate—had already been stipulated in Japanese Patent Act, § 102. A claim for compensation based on lost profits, however, had to be based on the general principles of Japanese Civil Code, § 709.

15.11 To claim damages under general civil law, the plaintiff could not rely on the presumption of negligence but had to prove negligence and show causation between the infringement and the damages incurred. Therefore, lost profits were virtually never claimed in patent cases before 1998.[25] However, a calculation based on lost profits as a basis for the award of damages was added to Japanese Patent Act, § 102 in 1998,[26] and since then has usually served as the basis for higher damage amounts awarded in Japan in recent years. The damage award calculated pursuant to Japanese Patent Act, § 102 is subject to an interest rate

the infringer, the maximum of which shall be the amount attainable by the patentee or the exclusive licensee in light of the capability of the patentee or the exclusive licensee to work such articles; provided, however, that if any circumstances exist under which the patentee or the exclusive licensee would have been unable to sell the assigned quantity in whole or in part, the amount calculated as the number of articles not able to be sold due to such circumstances shall be deducted.

2. Where a patentee or an exclusive licensee claims against an infringer compensation for damage sustained as a result of the intentional or negligent infringement of the patent right or exclusive license, and the infringer earned profits from the act of infringement, the amount of profits earned by the infringer shall be presumed to be the amount of damage sustained by the patentee or exclusive licensee.
3. A patentee or an exclusive licensee may claim against an infringer compensation for damage sustained as a result of the intentional or negligent infringement of the patent right or exclusive license, by regarding the amount the patentee or exclusive licensee would have been entitled to receive for the working of the patented invention as the amount of damage sustained.
4. The preceding paragraphs shall not prevent any relevant party from claiming compensation for damage in an amount exceeding the amount provided for therein. In such a case, where the infringer committed the infringement of the patent right or exclusive license without intent or gross negligence, the court may take these circumstances into consideration in determining the amount of damages.

[25] Takenaka, "Patent Infringement Damages in Japan and the United States," 320.

[26] Ryu Takabayashi, "Tokkyohōdai 102 jōni motozuku songaibaishōnitsuite," 59(1) *Patent* (2006): 71.

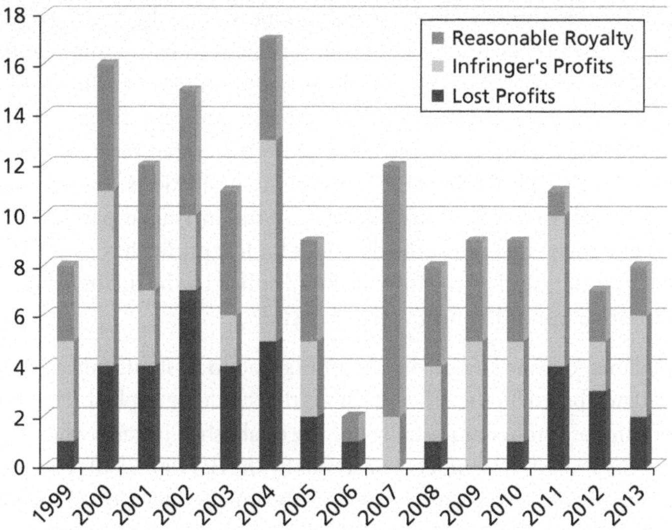

Figure 15.1 Bases chosen for calculating patent damages between 1999–2013

of 5 percent over the duration of the infringing conduct pursuant to Japanese Code of Civil Procedure, § 404.[27]

The chart in Figure 15.1 provides an overview of the bases chosen by infringed parties to calculate damages in both patent and utility model disputes between January 1, 1999 and June 30, 2013.[28] **15.12**

(a) Lost Profits

A claim for compensation in the amount of lost profits requires that the patentee or the exclusive licensee actually commercialized the infringed patent by manufacturing the protected invention or by using the protected process.[29] Pursuant to Japanese Patent Act, § 102(1), plaintiffs can request compensation for the hypothetical profits they would have made from the products that they could not sell due to the patent infringement.[30] Following the 1998 revision of the Japanese Patent Act, the requirements for establishing causation between the infringement and the non-sale were lowered. To show causation, the infringed party has to demonstrate substitutability between the patent-protected product and the infringing product manufactured and sold by the defendant.[31] Prior to the 1998 revision, establishing damages based on lost profits was considerably more difficult.[32] **15.13**

[27] Tokyo District Court, October 7, 1998, Hei 3 (wa) No. 10687, 1657 Hanrei Jihō (1998), 122—"*Seikyūken*"; Tokyo High Court, June 15, 1999, Hei 10 (ne) No. 2249, 1697 Hanrei Jihō (1999), 96—"*Sashitomeijiken.*"

[28] 64(10) *Chizai Kanri* (2014): 1548.

[29] Tamura, *Chitekizaisanken to Songaibaishō*, 310; Tokyo District Court, June 30, 1971, Sho 42 (wa) No. 9666, 266 Hanrei Times (1971), 220—"*Shokuhinsetsudanki*"; Osaka District Court, April 24, 1989, Sho 60 (wa) No. 6851, 21-1 Mutaishū (1989), 279—"*Seisaki no Hanma*"; there has been at least one decision in which a district court awarded lost profits for products peripheral to the patented products in a situation where the infringed party only commercialized the peripheral products and not the patented products, Tokyo High Court, June 15, 1999, Hei 10 (ne) No. 2249—"*Heat Storage.*"

[30] Shibuya, *Chitekizaisanhō kōgi*, 196.

[31] Tamura, *Chitekizaisanken to Songaibaishō*, 311; Toshiko Takenaka, "Tokkyokenshingai no songaibaishōno santei," in Hatsumei Kyokai (ed.), *Chiteki Zaisankenhō no gendaiteki Kadai: Monya Nobuo Kyōju Kanreki Kinen* (1998), 103, 107.

[32] Kaoru Kamata, "Tokkyokenshingai to songaibaishō—Kogyôshoyūken Shinkikai tôshin to Tokkyohōtōkaisei ni tsuite," 79 *CIPIC* (1998): 1, 17.

15.14 When determining the number of plaintiff's products not sold due to the infringement, courts have to take production and distribution capacities into account. Having said so, the infringed party does not have to show that the unsold products causing lost profits were in fact manufactured.[33] Rather, the infringed party has to indicate that it would have had the capability of supplying the amount of infringing products that were sold by the infringer. The infringer has to provide evidence to substantiate objections or doubts regarding the production and distribution capacities claimed by the infringed party.[34] If the infringer cannot substantiate such objections, the damages for lost profits has to be calculated as follows: number of products sold by the infringer multiplied by the infringed party's contribution margin (list price minus the unit variable cost).[35]

15.15 As pointed out, damage awards based on lost profits tend to be significantly higher than damage awards calculated based on the other methods that could be applied. That said, sound evidence for significant lost profits can usually only be established in cases where a small number of competing products exist. A number of decisions by the IP High Court have established that the amount of lost sales can also be influenced by substitute products other than the infringing product, the infringer's marketing efforts and selling power, other features of the infringing product that triggered customer demand, as well as the pricing of the infringing product.[36] In cases where such other factors have to be considered, the court has to establish a contribution rate—that is, a percentage of the value of the product constituted by the infringed patent.

(b) Accounting for the Infringer's Profits

15.16 Infringer's profits have, in recent years, yielded the second highest amount within the three methods of damage claim calculation. Until recently, an infringed party could only account for the infringer's profits as long as the infringed party had actually sold or marketed the product or service covered by the patent in Japan. This principle was overturned by the grand panel of the IP High Court in 2013, which decided that accounting for the infringer's profits is possible as long as circumstances exist that suggest the patentee could have made profits based on the patent if no patent infringement had been conducted.[37]

15.17 When accounting for the infringer's profits, the calculation is based upon the number of infringing products sold by the infringer, which has to be multiplied by the per unit profit generated by the infringer. Courts used to be rather lenient in allowing infringers to deduct variable costs as well as portions of their overheads to reduce the amount of the infringer's profits.[38]

---

33 Tokyo District Court, July 17, 2001, Hei 11 (wa) No. 23013—"*Kirokushi*" (23013).

34 Tamura, *Chitekizaisanken to Songaibaishō*, 316.

35 The margins claimed by the infringed party can be adjusted upwards if the infringed party can show that his margins would have increased through production of a higher number of products that were not produced and not sold due to the infringement. Tokyo District Court, March 19, 2002, Hei 11 (wa) 23945—"*Pachinko Slot Machine.*"

36 IP High Court, September 25, 2006, Hei 17 (ne) No. 10047—"*Massage Chair*"; IP High Court, January 24, 2012, Hei 22 (ne) No. 10032—"*Golf Ball.*"

37 IP High Court, February 1, 2013, Hei (ne) No. 10015, 1388 Hanrei Times (2013) 77—"*Waste Storage Device*"; an English translation of this important decision is available at the website of the IP High Court at http://www.ip.courts.go.jp/eng/vcms_lf/10015_zen.pdf; the lower court (Tokyo District Court, December 26, 2011, Hei 21 (wa) No. 44391) had decided that the patentee, a UK-based company that had licensed the infringed patent to a Japanese distributor, could only recoup damages based on reasonable royalties of 18.14 million yen. The IP High Court reversed and awarded damages of 134.61 million yen based on the infringer's profits.

38 Tokyo District Court, February 9, 1990, Sho 56 (wa) No. 3939, 1347 Hanji (1990) 111; Nagoya District Court, March 6, 1998, Hei 4 (wa) No. 474, 1003 Hanrei Times (1998) 277; Tamura, *Chitekizaisanken to Songaibaishō*, 321

That said, recent decisions seems to scrutinize the deductibility of cost items more strictly, allowing only a deduction of clearly related variable cost items such as material purchase costs or variable manufacturing costs.[39] As a consequence, infringer's profits are more frequently calculated based on the gross profit margin of the infringer. In any event, infringers have to substantiate the cost items that they desire to deduct from their revenues.

The amount of damages can be reduced if the significance of the infringed patent is considered as rather minor for the value and functionality of the sold product.[40] The court can request the infringer to produce evidence in order to verify individual items of the cost calculations provided by the infringer in the proceedings. **15.18**

Commentators used to regard substantial damage awards based on the infringer's profits as being difficult to receive due to the practical difficulties of challenging the cost positions provided by the defendant.[41] However, the recent trend toward more strict questioning of cost items presented by infringers and the resulting higher damage amounts have begun to make it more attractive to account for the infringer's profits. **15.19**

(c) Reasonable Royalty

The third method of damage computation available under § 102 of the Japanese Patent Act is to account for a reasonable royalty.[42] The calculation of the award is based on the number of infringing products sold by the infringer.[43] In 1998, the wording of Japanese Patent Act, § 102(3) was amended; prior to 1998, courts had to base the calculation on a "normal license fee." After the 1998 amendment, the word "normal" was deleted from the statute, thus authorizing the infringement court to apply a reasonable or hypothetical license fee established in consideration of the circumstances of the specific case.[44] To account for a reasonable royalty, it is not required for the plaintiff to have commercialized or used the infringed patent. To determine a royalty rate applicable to the case, courts will primarily consider industry-specific and factually comparable license agreements but will also consider factors such as industry-specific costs for research and development, the current and historic marketability of the products involved, and the ability to license the infringed patent as well as the revenue generated by the infringer.[45] In earlier decisions, courts frequently relied on a nationwide average royalty rate, which was derived either from the rates suggested by the Japan Institute of Invention and Innovation or from rates applied to government-owned patents. As a result, the royalty rate applied in almost all the cases between 1959 and 1995 was 3 percent.[46] To provide a better protection of patent rights, the rates applied since 1998 were determined by considering the actual royalty rates negotiated **15.20**

---

39 IP High Court, February 1, 2013, Hei (ne) No. 10015, 1388 Hanrei Times (2013) 77—"*Waste Storage Device*"; Tokyo District Court, November 2, 2012, Hei 22 (wa), No. 24479, 2185 Hanrei Jihō (2013) 115; Tokyo District Court, February 24, 2011, Hei 20 (wa) No. 2944—"*Flow Control Valve.*"

40 Tokyo District Court, December 26, 2003, Hei 14 (wa) No. 3237, 1159, December 26, 2003, Hei 14 (wa) No. 3237, 1159 Hanrei Times (2004), 275—"*Liquid Filling Machine Nozzle*"; Takabayashi, "Tokkyohōdai 102 jōni motozuku songaibaishōnitsuite," 73.

41 *Tamura, Chitekizaisanken to Songaibaishō*, 322.

42 Japanese Patent Act, §102(3).

43 Tamura, *Chitekizaisanken to Songaibaishō*, 251.

44 Ichiro Kasuga, "Tokkyoshingaisoshōni okeru songaigaku no nintei," 1162 *Jurist* (1999): 43.

45 Shibuya, *Chitekizaisanhō kōgi*, 210.

46 Tokyo District Court, February 28, 1973, Sho 43 (wa) No. 15198, 302 Hanrei Times (1973), 305—"*Higesoriki*"; Tokyo District Court, May 22, 1972, Sho 44 (wa) No. 8219, 4-1 Mutaishū (1977), 294—"*Roshutsukokei*";

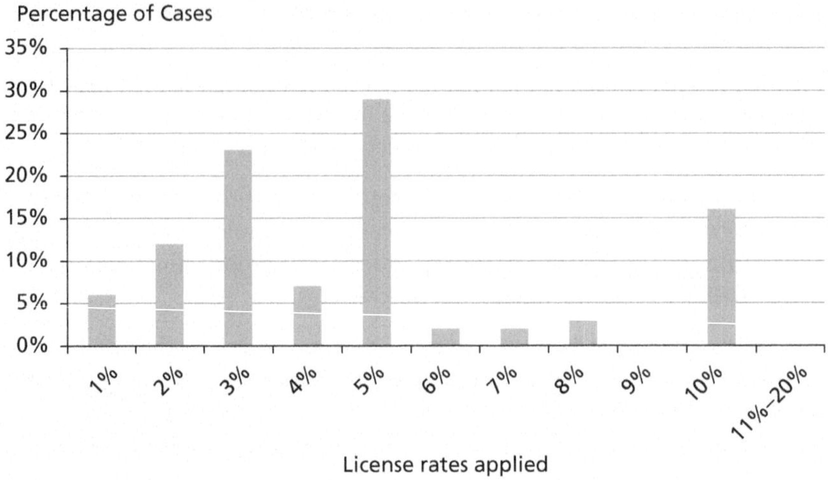

Figure 15.2 License rates applied to cases since 1998

for licenses for comparable products. This revised practice resulted in a noteworthy increase of the applied royalty rates in recent years.[47] See Figure 15.2.

15.21 The second factor of the reasonable royalty is, of course, the applicable sales amount. In cases where the infringed patented feature constitutes the sole driver for customer demand of the product or service sold, the plaintiff can base the reasonable royalty on the entire revenue generated by the infringing product. However, similar to the case when accounting for the infringer's profits or lost profits, the defendant can argue that factors other than the patented features were the vital drivers of customer demand. Especially in cases involving more complex products that are also subject to non-infringed patents, the court will have to establish a contribution rate, and the underlying sales figure will be adjusted accordingly.

15.22 Irrespective of the gradual increase in license rates, damage awards calculated pursuant to Japanese Patent Act, § 102(3) continue to result in the lowest damage amounts amongst the three calculation methods available.

(d) Selection of Calculation Method

15.23 After proving infringement, the plaintiff can, pursuant to Japanese Patent Act, § 102, freely select one of the damage award computation methods introduced above.[48] Unlike in the United States, it is not possible to combine the calculation methods—that is, to claim lost profits for sales the infringed party can prove to have lost due to the infringement plus reasonable royalties for additional sales made by the infringer.[49]

Tokyo High Court, March 30, 1973, Sho 44 (Kouke) No. 57, 306 Hanrei Times (1973), 269—"*Shokaki*"; Osaka District Court, October 22, 1998, Hei 5 (wa) No. 2549-1—"*Denjiyudōkanetsusōchi*"; Osaka District Court, March 14, 1986, Sho 59 (wad) No. 8943, 617 Hanrei Times (1986), 153—"*Denkikamisori.*"

[47] See breakdown of license rates applied for calculation of reasonable awards between January 1, 1999, and March 31, 2013, available in 64(2) *Chizai Kanri* (2014): 221.

[48] Tamura, *Chitekizaisanken to Songaibaishō*, 257.

[49] Thomas F. Cotter, *Comparative Patent Remedies* (2013), 317, citing IP High Court Hei, September 25, 2006, Hei 17 (ne) 10047—"*Massage Chair.*"

Typically, the calculation method will only be selected after the court has issued the interlocutory decision and confirmed that the defendant's conduct infringed upon the patent in question. It is fairly common for the plaintiff to initially request compensation pursuant to multiple calculations methods and select the method yielding the highest damage award.[50] 15.24

C. Unjust Enrichment

The provisions on unjust enrichment (*futōritoku*), governed by Japanese Civil Code, § 703, are sometimes applied when seeking patent enforcement, in particular when damage claims pursuant to Japanese Patent Act, § 102 are not enforceable due to the shorter statutory limitation periods. The statutory limitation for damage claims pursuant to Japanese Patent Act, § 102 is three years, while Japanese Civil Code, § 167(1) provides for a limitation period of ten years for unjust enrichment claims.[51] Also, as under German law, an unjust enrichment claim does not depend on the infringer's negligence but is available even in the rare case when infringement is found and the infringer can completely rebut the presumption of negligence.[52] The unjust enrichment award can be a reasonable royalty fee or the profits generated by the infringer.[53] However, similar to German practice, there is no presumption of negligence in computing an unjust enrichment award.[54] The absence of such regulations usually makes it very difficult for the infringed party to demonstrate the causation between the infringement and the infringer's profits. Therefore, unjust enrichment awards are almost always calculated on the basis of a reasonable royalty.[55] 15.25

D. Claim for Destruction

A claim for destruction can only be granted upon awarding a claim for injunctive relief pursuant to Japanese Patent Act, § 100. Usually the plaintiff will simultaneously request the court to issue an injunction order and to order destruction of the patent-infringing products.[56] In addition, the plaintiff can request the court to issue an order for destruction of the materials and equipment that have been used in the production of the infringing products.[57] 15.26

---

[50] IP High Court, September 25, 2006, Hei 17 (ne) No. 10047—"Massage Chair." Koichiro Suda, "Kaikei shuhō kara mita chiteki zaisan-hō-jō no songai baishō-gaku o santei shita hanrei kenkyū (sono 4)," 56(2) *Patento* (2003): 47.

[51] Miyama and Matsumura, *Chitekizaisanken Soshô*, 524; Shibuya, *Chitekizaisanhō kōgi*, 319.

[52] Shibuya, *Chitekizaisanhō kōgi*, 319.

[53] Shibuya, *Chitekizaisanhō kōgi*, 318.

[54] Osaka District Court, October 31, 1980, Sho 54 (wa) No. 4824, 12-2 Mutaishū (1980), 632—"*Kodomoyojōmonotaiyaa*"; Osaka High Court, January 28, 1982, Sho 55 (ne) No. 1928, 14-1 Mutaishū (1982), 41 ff.—"*Kyukyu*"; different Osaka District Court, October 14, 1987, Sho 59 (wa) No. 6210, 19-3 Mutaishū (1987), 389—"*Okeya*"; Fumio Umase, "Tokkyo no mudanjitsuyôka to futôritoku," in *Futoritoku—Jimukanri no kenkyū: Taniguchi Tomohei Kyôjyu Kanreki kinen* (1970), 245, 273.

[55] Toyama District Court, September 7, 1970, Sho 41 (wa) No. 30, 253 Hanrei Times (1970) 142—"*Meraninjusshi*"; Osaka District Court, October 28, 1983, Sho (wa) No. 8565, 514 Hanrei Times (1983) 303—"*Torigaakuiru*"; Tamura, *Chitekizaisanken to Songaibaishō*, 266.

[56] Minoru Takeda, *Chiteki zaisanken shingai yôron: tokkyo ishōshôhyôhen* (5th ed., 2007), 152.

[57] Gifu District Court, December 18, 1991, Sho 63 (wa) No. 277, 2293 Hanrei Kōgyōshoyūkenhō 30—"*Dosha Ryuhin*."

15.27 The scope of the claim for destruction had been unclear for some time. Pursuant to old case law, the entire infringing product was subject to the claim for destruction even if only one distinguishable element within the product infringed on the patent and such an infringing element could be separated.[58] However, pursuant to more recent case law and influential commentators, only those parts of the product that are infringing and that cannot be separated from the non-infringing parts of the product are subject to the claim for destruction.[59]

15.28 Usually, the scope of the claim for destruction granted by the courts is comparably wider for patent-infringing products in the chemical and pharmaceutical industry as long as the products in question are still in the process of obtaining the required government permits. In these cases, the claim for destruction would not only include the infringing products but also typically extends to include manufacturing equipment irrespective of whether such equipment can be used to produce other products or not.[60] In other industries, an extension of the claim for destruction to the manufacturing equipment is usually denied, especially in cases where the injunction order is based only on the reasonable likelihood of a future infringement rather than on past infringing conduct. Such limitation is usually derived from the required balance of hardships between the defendants, who would be burdened by not being able to manufacture non-infringing products, and the plaintiffs, who desire complete protection of their patent.[61]

[58] Tokyo District Court, September 14, 1969, Sho 35 (wa) No. 6935, 14-9 Shitamin (1963), 1778—"*Hanso Sōchi*": Gifu District Court, December 18, 1991, Sho 63 (wa) No. 277, 2293 Hanrei Kōgyōshoyūkenhō, 30—"*Dosha Ryushutsu Bōshiyo.*"

[59] E.g., Tokyo District Court, December 9, 1988, Sho 61 (wa) No. 2964, 1295 Hanrei Jihō (1989), 121—"*Mojiwaku Koteisōchi*"; Tokyo District Court, October 30, 1995, Hei 1 (wa) No. 8292, 1560 Hanrei Jihō (1995), 24—"*Shisutemusaiensuhonan*"; Tokyo District Court, April 14, 2003, Hei 14 (wa) No. 9503; Yoshiyuki Tamura, "Tokkyokenshingai ni okeru sashitomei," 1062 *Hanrei Times* (2001): 64, 69; Hiroyuki Morisaki and Makoto Okada, "Commentary on Article 100 Patent Act," in Nobuhiro Nakayama and Naoki Koizumi (eds.), *Shin Chūkai Tokkyohō* (2011), 1437.

[60] Tokyo District Court, July 10, 1987, Sho 60 (wa) No. 7463, 19-2 Mutaishū (1987) 231—"*Jyosozai*"; Tamura, "Tokkyokenshingai ni okeru sashitomei," 76; Kazui Masui and Yoshiyuki Tamura, *Tokkyo Hanrei Gaido* (2d ed., 2000), 242.

[61] Tomoji Yamada, "Tokkyoshingai yobôseikyū no 'Shingai suru osore' to Haikiseikyū no 'Yobōni hitsuyôna koui'," 1062 *Hanrei Times* (2001): 81, 84.

Part VI

BEST PRACTICE

16

ANALYSIS AND PROPOSAL OF BEST PRACTICE

A. Comparative Analysis

1. Introduction

What will be the future of patent litigation? Because of obligations under patent-related international agreements such as the Agreement on Trade-related Aspects of Intellectual Property Rights (TRIPS) and Patent Cooperation Treaties, substantive law aspects of patent enforcement have been extensively harmonized. Moreover, the America Invents Act (AIA) substantially changed invalidity defenses under the US Patent Act and harmonized them with those under the German and Japanese Patent Acts. In contrast, influences from the common law and civil law traditions remain strong with respect to procedural aspects. In particular, the different weights the common law and civil law traditions give to injunctions as patent infringement remedies are highlighted in cases involving patent assertion entities and inventions in IT industries in which thousands of patents cover different functions of a single product. **16.01**

Nevertheless, the patent enforcement system in Japanese courts conceptually suggests a bright future for patent enforcement by blending the best aspects of the common law and civil law traditions. The following sections will discuss major differences in the three jurisdictions and features of Japanese patent enforcement that blend influences from the United States and Germany. **16.02**

2. Extent of Patent Protection

(a) *Claim Interpretation*

Japan was once extensively criticized for its narrow claim interpretation and absence of the doctrine of equivalents. However, over the last two decades, the US Supreme Court's emphasis on the notice and definitional functions of patent claims has encouraged US courts to adopt a claim interpretation supported by patent documents and prosecution records, making it rare for US courts to apply the doctrine of equivalents. In addition, the strong policy of harmonization among European Patent Convention (EPC) member states, in particular of harmonizing with the practice of UK courts, has encouraged German courts to be more willing to stick to the claim language and has made them reluctant to apply the doctrine of equivalents as well. As a result, in general, the extent of the patent scope resulting from claim interpretation and the application of the doctrine of equivalents in the three jurisdictions is much more in line than it used to be two decades ago when one of the co-authors of this book conducted a comparative study.[1] **16.03**

---

[1] Toshiko Takenaka, "Interpreting Patent Claims: The United States, Germany and Japan," 17 *IIC Studies* (1995): 26–38.

16.04 However, there are significant differences in the infringement analysis between the German practice and the US and Japanese practices. Germany remains the most patentee-friendly jurisdiction because German courts have adopted a function-oriented approach for claim interpretation.[2] It is more likely that the literal scope which results from the function-oriented claim interpretation is broader than the literal scope which results from the claim interpretation in US or Japanese courts.[3] This is because German courts define the disputed claim term in more abstract terms than the literal meaning and find literal infringement if a feature allegedly corresponding to the disputed claim term performs the function that a person having ordinary skill in the art of the invention ("PHOSITA") would understand as being what the inventor intended for the claimed term to perform.[4] The function-oriented claim interpretation makes it possible for German courts to continue to compare the accused embodiment with the technical teaching of the patented invention underlying the claim language instead of the claim terms as such. Thus, the object and result or advantage of the invention play a very important role in finding both literal and equivalent infringement because German courts focus on the question of whether the accused embodiment uses the technical teaching either identically or equivalently, instead of simply finding every claim element in the accused embodiment.

16.05 This practice is in stark contrast to US claim interpretation in which claim terms are clarified in light of the discussions of embodiments in the specification. US applicants avoid including in the specification a discussion of an object, solution, or problem in comparison with the prior art because US courts may find inherent and implicit limitations if such limitations are necessary for achieving the object and solving the problem.[5] Although an appointment of an expert is rare in German patent infringement proceedings, testimony by a court-appointed expert on the function and the solution of the accused embodiment may play an important role in German claim interpretation.[6] Such testimony has no role in US and Japanese claim interpretation. In US claim interpretation, expert testimony is extrinsic evidence and plays a very limited role in claim interpretation.[7] Regarding means-plus-function claims, although equivalents of the disclosed embodiments fall within the literal scope of means-plus-function claims under § 112(f), the question of what structures constitute equivalents to the structure disclosed to perform the function recited in the claim is a question of fact for the jury.[8]

16.06 In Japan, courts discuss the invention and interpret a disputed term in the context of the solution of the invention. Japanese courts often use the object and technical effect of the invention to limit a disputed claim term to cover only the disclosed embodiments when the claim term is expanded or generalized from the structures, properties, and steps of these disclosed embodiments.[9] Expert testimony plays a very limited role, if any, in claim interpretation at Japanese courts. This is in stark contrast to the function-oriented claim

[2] Ch. 5, 5.71.
[3] Ch. 5, 5.71.
[4] Thomas Kühnen, *Patent Litigation Proceedings in Germany: A Handbook for Practitioners* (7th ed., 2015), marginal no. 73–74.
[5] Ch. 4. 4.57.
[6] Ch. 5. 5.94.
[7] Ch. 4, 4.73.
[8] *Pressure Prods. Med. Supplies v. Greatbatch Ltd.*, 599 F.3d 1308, 94 U.S.P.Q. 2d 1261 (Fed. Cir. 2010).
[9] See Ch. 8, 8.59.

interpretation at German courts, which includes variations to perform the intended function and thus uses a technical teaching.

Another unique feature that makes German practice more patentee-friendly than US and Japanese practices is the limited scope of the prior art available for claim interpretation. German courts can take account of only the prior art references disclosed in the patent specification. If a prior art reference is not discussed in the specification, German courts can take account of such a reference only if it is established as being part of the general knowledge of a PHOSITA.[10] In contrast, US and Japanese courts can take account of any prior art regardless of whether it is cited during the examination. They often find claims invalid over newly found prior art references or interpret claims narrowly to maintain validity over the prior art.[11] Moreover, it is unlikely for patentees to assert an overly broad claim interpretation that will subject the asserted claim to an invalidity defense. **16.07**

Because infringement and validity are examined at separate proceedings in Germany, patentees may advance a broad claim interpretation at district courts and a narrow claim interpretation at the EPO or the Federal Patent Court. This problem resulting from the bifurcation system is referred to as the Angora Cat approach: claims are as small as a wet cat with its fur smoothed down when validity is challenged; in contrast, claims are as big as an expanded cat with its fur dry and fluffy when the patentee asserts infringement.[12] At least in theory, the EPO or the Patent Court's claim interpretation and reasons for sustaining validity do not bind German courts at infringement proceedings.[13] Although the patentees' statements on the extent of patent protection in the opposition and nullity suits are relevant to claim interpretation in the infringement procedure, such statements merely indicate the perspective of a PHOSITA and seldom give rise to a disclaimer or surrender of the extent of patent protection unless the asserted claims are amended in the parallel opposition and nullity suits.[14] As a result, German courts take account of the arguments made by the patentee during the opposition and nullity suit only under very limited circumstances.[15] Such statements are binding only between the patentee and the parties in the opposition or nullity suit. **16.08**

In practice, it is unlikely for patentees to take the Angora Cat approach because the defendants would argue that the interpretation conflicts with the interpretation in the parallel proceedings. It is unlikely for district courts to take account of the statements for interpreting claims made at the EPO or Patent Court because infringement courts reach an infringement conclusion much faster than the validity conclusion can be reached in the opposition and nullity suits.[16] The EPO and Patent Court may reject a narrow claim interpretation that **16.09**

---

[10] Ch. 5, 5.91.

[11] Ch. 6, 6.64 "Prior Art."

[12] Dictionary of Intellectual Property Law (http://dictionaryofiplaw.blogspot.com/2012/08/angora-cat-problem.html). Lord Justice Jacob cited this approach in *European Central Bank v. DSS* [2008] EWCA Civ 192 (Court of Appeal for England and Wales, 19 March 2008). For a discussion of differing claim interpretations between infringement and validity proceedings, see Charleen Fei, "Justice Delayed Is Denied? The Principle of Bifurcation in the German Patent Litigation System," 14 *Wake Forest J. Business & Intellectual Property* (2014): 619 (http://ipjournal.law.wfu.edu/files/2015/01/JBIPL-Vol-14-Issue-4-Fei.pdf).

[13] Ch. 5, 5.89.

[14] Kühnen: *Patent Litigation*, marginal no. 67.

[15] Ibid. marginal no. 68.

[16] Katrin Cremers et al., "Invalid but Infringed? An Analysis of Germany's Bifurcated Patent Litigation System," Center for European Economic Research Discussion Paper No. 14-072, 8 (http://ftp.zew.de/pub/zew-docs/dp/dp14072.pdf).

conflicts with a broad claim interpretation advanced by the patentee at the infringement proceedings. Appeal courts may also prevent conflicting claim interpretations if defendants file an appeal from the infringement judgment. Finally, any conflicts in claim interpretation should be resolved at the Federal Court of Justice. However, many defendants choose to settle their disputes once district courts find infringement because an injunction is enforced against the defendant even if an appeal is filed.[17] If the defendants choose to file an appeal and to continue to challenge validity, they must bear the costs of redesign or remove their products from the German market during the period of the injunction, until a finding of invalidity.[18]

16.10 These different approaches present a serious challenge in procuring and enforcing patents in the three jurisdictions: discussions on the invention in the context of the prior art, such as the object and technical effect of the invention, help during expansive claim interpretation at German courts; in contrast, such discussions allow US and Japanese courts to find disclaimers of certain embodiments and to read limitations from the specification. Patentees thus face the dilemma of whether they should include in the specification discussions on the invention in the context of the prior art, such as the object and technical effect of the invention. Since US courts may use prosecution records from foreign patent offices, patentees may not be able to avoid a narrow claim interpretation in US courts by preparing different specifications respective to US, German, and Japanese patent applications.[19]

(b) The Doctrine of Equivalents

16.11 In all three jurisdictions, finding infringement under the doctrine of equivalents has become less frequent. In the United States, the Federal Circuit developed multiple doctrines to limit the doctrine of equivalents.[20] Since disputed terms are frequently added or amended to distinguish the prior art and for other patentability reasons, an expansive application of the prosecution history estoppel effectively prevents patentees from asserting infringement under the doctrine of equivalents unless a disputed claim term was included in the original claim and has never been changed. Even without any amendments or arguments of disclaimer, the claim element vitiation rule prevents the application of the doctrine of equivalents if the doctrine changes the claim term that was clarified through claim interpretation.[21] US courts give more weight to the policy of securing legal certainty for third parties than to the policy of guaranteeing fair protection for patentees and thus impose on inventors and their attorneys a duty to draft claims that cover all foreseeable equivalents. In Japan, the courts' reluctance to find infringement beyond the disclosed embodiments also makes it very rare to find infringement under the doctrine of equivalents.

16.12 In contrast, German courts acknowledge the fact that it is often difficult for inventors and patent attorneys to foresee all of the modifications and variations developed by competitors and thus do not require them to draft claims literally covering the variations.[22] Although the function-oriented claim interpretation has already expanded the literal scope of a disputed claim term to cover modifications seen as an alternative means for the solution of the

[17] Ch. 14, 14.08.
[18] Ch. 14, 14.08.
[19] Ch. 4, 4.63.
[20] Ch. 4, 4.104.
[21] Ch. 4, 4.116.
[22] Ch. 5, 5.110.

invention, the doctrine of equivalents comes to rescue patentees if the foreseeable equivalents do not fit into the literal scope expanded by the function-oriented claim interpretation.

However, finding infringement under the doctrine of equivalents has become less frequent in Germany because of the necessity of improving legal certainty by giving notice of patentees' exclusive rights to competitors.[23] To determine whether the technical teaching is used equivalently, German courts use a three-prong test in evaluating the solution between the accused embodiment and the patented invention.[24] Since German courts will have already addressed the first prong of the equivalent test though the function-oriented claim interpretation, they are unlikely to find infringement under the doctrine of equivalents if they determine that a feature modified from the claim term cannot perform the function intended for the claim term, and thus the courts will refuse to adopt a claim interpretation to cover the accused embodiment literally through the function-oriented claim interpretation. If a feature of the accused embodiment cannot perform the intended function of the disputed claim term, it is unlikely that a PHOSITA will adopt the feature to solve the technical problem to be solved by the patented invention, and thus the accused embodiment will also fail to meet the obviousness requirement. Only when the patented claim adopts a narrow definition and a feature of the accused embodiment is unable to fit into the definition even though the feature performs the intended function to solve the technical problem, may the courts find infringement under the doctrine of equivalents. However, if the asserted patent claim adopts a narrow definition, a PHOSITA may not find the accused embodiment to be equivalent to the claimed invention, and the claim may fail to meet the third prong of the equivalent test. As a result, German courts are unlikely to find infringement under the doctrine of equivalents once they find no literal infringement through the function-oriented claim interpretation. **16.13**

The German courts' three-prong test is similar to the US courts' insubstantial difference test. The German test is more difficult to meet than the US test because US patentees only need to establish either (1) substantial similarity of function, way, and result OR (2) known interchangeability, which is very similar to obviousness.[25] Japanese courts use a test similar to the German test, requiring both the same effect and obviousness.[26] Despite a significant decrease in the number of infringement findings under the doctrine of equivalents, a lack of prosecution history estoppel and other doctrines to limit the doctrine of equivalents makes it possible for German patentees to assert infringement under the doctrine of equivalents if German courts refuse to find literal infringement. The doctrine of practicing prior art, the *Formstein* defense, plays the most important role in preventing German courts from finding infringement under the doctrine of equivalents.[27] Unlike claim interpretation, German courts are able to take account of prior art references disclosing or rendering the accused **16.14**

[23] Ch. 5, 5.111.

[24] The three prongs applied in German practice are: (1) same/identical effect by alternative means; (2) obviousness of alternative means; and (3) technical equivalence to the teaching in question (parity). For further background and details, please refer to Ch. 5, 5.113.

[25] Ch. 4, 4.94. For a comparison of the tests for the doctrine of equivalents under US, German, and Japanese Patent Acts, see Toshiko Takenaka, "Extent of Patent Protection in the United States, Germany and Japan: Two Types of Equivalents and their Patent Policy Implications," in Annette Kur et al. (eds.), *Patent Law on the Move: Festschrift for Gert Kolle and Dieter Stauder* (2005), 135.

[26] Ch. 6, 6.72.

[27] Ch. 5, 5.128.

embodiment obvious regardless of whether the references are cited during the examination or discussed in the specification. However, when multiple references are cited, the accused infringer must establish that the combination of the references is obvious to a PHOSITA. Moreover such a combination may support the patentee's assertion of equivalents in meeting the second prong of the equivalent test. As a result, this defense is seldom successful as a doctrine to limit the doctrine of equivalents at German courts.[28]

3. Defenses

16.15 Although TRIPS and other patent-related international agreements greatly enhanced the harmonization of conditions for patentability and grounds for validity challenges in member states, secret prior art, which is unique to the pre-AIA first-to-invent system, provided multiple grounds for challenging invalidity at interference proceedings at the United States Patent Office (USPTO) and civil actions at US courts.[29] Such secret prior art includes derivation, prior inventions, and inventors' secret commercial use. These grounds are not examined at the USPTO and may continue to apply to patents resulting from pre-AIA patent applications filed before March 16, 2013.[30] Moreover, secret commercial use may remain as secret prior art under post-AIA law and provide an additional ground to challenge patents for lack of novelty and nonobviousness.[31] Because the AIA removed the geographical limitation and thus expanded the scope of secret commercial use, patents may be invalidated on the grounds of anticipation or nonobviousness if an invention is commercially exploited or is the subject of an offer abroad one year prior to the filing date, regardless of the confidentiality of such an invention. This unique defense based on secret commercial use presents a lot of challenges for multinational companies who develop a patent/trade secret protection strategy.

16.16 The exception to novelty under the first-inventor-to-file system also leads to a lot of uncertainty with respect to the availability of the invalidity defense. A patent may not be invalidated even if the patented invention of the asserted patent was independently invented and disclosed by a third party prior to the filing date of the patent if the invention was disclosed by the inventor of the asserted patent prior to the third-party disclosure.[32] Since details of the substantive and procedural rules for the new first-to-disclose priority rule are not yet well developed, it is difficult to anticipate how frequently patentees will assert this priority rule for protection against the invalidity defense. The unique case law removing from prior art all public use of the invention having an experimental purpose also remains to introduce legal uncertainty.[33]

16.17 In contrast, conditions for patentability and validity challenges are fully harmonized between the German and Japanese patent systems except for the grace period and the sufficiency of disclosure requirement. Japanese Patent Act blended US feature of grace period and expanded the scope of activities covered by the exception of lack of novelty.[34] Because the scope of lack of novelty under EPC is very narrow, a disclosure by an inventor

[28] Ch. 5, 5.128, Kühnen, *Patent Litigation*, marginal no. 156.
[29] Ch. 7, 7.87 "Pre-AIA Prior Art."
[30] Ch. 7, 7.98 "Post-AIA Prior Art."
[31] Ch. 7, 7.98.
[32] Ch. 7, 7.99.
[33] Ch. 7. 7.109.
[34] JPA, § 30(2).

may give rise to a ground of invalidity under EPC but may not give rise to a ground of invalidity under US Patent Act and Japanese Patent Act if a patent application is filed within six months from the disclosure.

In the United States and Japan, the sufficiency of disclosure is called the written description requirement and is a condition for patentability as well as a ground for challenging validity.[35] Under the EPC, the sufficiency of disclosure requirement is only a condition for patentability.[36] Japanese and US courts may find a claim invalid due to a violation of the written description requirement if the accused embodiment falls within the scope of the claim but the specification does not show the possession of the accused embodiment by the inventor at the time of the application.[37] Since German courts take account of a PHOSITA's general knowledge in interpreting claims, they are willing to find literal infringement as long as the accused embodiment uses the technical teaching and produces advantages expected for the patented invention. This difference regarding the grounds of challenging validity may also result in a difference in the extent of patent protection between, on the one hand, the United States and Japan and, on the other hand, Germany. **16.18**

4. Validity Challenge Procedures

The unique feature in German patent litigation is its bifurcation system. Defendants of patent infringement proceedings in German courts are prevented not only from asserting patent invalidity but also from advancing claim interpretation in light of the prior art, which is not discussed in the specification.[38] The separation of power between infringement courts and the Federal Patent Court enables judges in infringement proceedings to focus only on the legal issues in the claim interpretation and infringement analysis, greatly contributing to a quick dispute resolution.[39] However, the German bifurcation system is criticized for its disproportional advantages for patentees.[40] Because nullity procedures are frequently filed to defend an assertion of patent infringement in infringement proceedings and take longer as the court must examine all claims and proposed amendments in light of newly found prior art references, the conclusion of opposition and nullity suits follow the conclusion of infringement with a significant delay.[41] **16.19**

German bifurcation also discourages parties from filing unnecessary nullity suits that rely on a weak invalidity ground because of the extra cost.[42] Some may view this aspect as an advantage in promoting judicial economy, but others may view it as being unfairly disadvantageous for those who want to challenge validity. Only strong cases are brought to challenge validity at the Federal Patent Court and appealed to the Federal Court of Justice (BGH). A recent study conducted by one of the co-authors of this book reviewing validity **16.20**

[35] 35 U.S.C. § 112(a); JPA, § 36(1).

[36] EPC, Art. 83.

[37] *LizardTech, Inc. v. Earth Res. Mapping, Inc.*, 424 F.3d 1336, 76 U.S.P.Q. 2d 1724 (Fed. Cir. 2005).

[38] Ch. 5, 5.91.

[39] R. M. Hilty and M. Lamping, "Trennungsprinzip—Quo vadis, Germania?" in *50 Jahre Bundespatentgericht—Festschrift zum 50-jährigen Bestehen des Bundespatentgerichts am 1. Juli 2011* (2011), 255–73.

[40] K. Cremers et al., "Invalid but Infringed? An Analysis of Germany's Bifurcated Patent Litigation System" (https://www.law.berkeley.edu/files/Helmers_Christian_IPSC_paper_2014.pdf), 26.

[41] Cremaers et al., "Invalid but Infringed?," 18.

[42] Ibid. 12.

decisions issued between 2010 and 2013 indicates high invalidity rates at both courts: the rate for fully or partially invalidated patents at the German Federal Patent Court is almost 80 percent.[43] Such rates are even higher for software and telecommunication patents. In 75.25 percent of cases where the Federal Patent Court found the patent to be invalid, the Federal Court of Justice affirmed the invalidity decision; in 73.34 percent of cases where validity was sustained by the Federal Patent Court, the Federal Court of Justice reversed the decision.[44]

16.21 German bifurcation unfairly gives disproportionate advantages to patentees because German district courts grant injunctions that are immediately enforceable with a deposit of bond[45] even though many of the patents being found infringed are later invalidated through opposition and nullity procedures. Although defendants can file motions trying to suspend execution of the injunction orders, German courts seldom grant such motions absent extraordinary circumstances.[46] Between competitors who practice patents and sell products, the harm resulting from a grant or denial of an injunction often balance out between the parties. Such parties are also often motivated to settle their disputes by, for example, cross-licensing their patents. In contrast, the threat of a readily enforceable injunction gives non-practicing patentees unfair bargaining power to negotiate royalties. A grant of an injunction may result in irreparable harm to the defendant's market share while a denial of an injunction would only result in marginal harm such as a lack of bargaining power for the non-practicing patentee. It is unlikely for a losing defendant to file an appeal and to keep the infringement proceedings pending until an invalidity decision is issued unless the defendant has a very strong case at the nullity procedure.

16.22 Another serious problem with German bifurcation is its ineffectiveness when claims are amended during the opposition and nullity procedures. Because of the infringement and validity time lag, it is very likely that by the time a claim is found partially invalid and thus is amended during the opposition or nullity procedure, the infringement court will have already completed its infringement analysis. If the infringement proceedings are still pending, then the infringement court must interpret the amended claim and conduct its infringement analysis again. However, if the infringement proceedings have concluded and the decision to find infringement has been executed, the defendant must file an action for restitution.[47] In restitution proceedings, the court must not only re-examine whether the accused embodiment infringes the amended claim but also make an assessment of the amount to be paid to recompense the defendant if the embodiment does not infringe the amended claim. In most cases a defendant cannot be fully recompensed if it lost a significant market share because of the enforcement of an injunction. In essence, the high risk of a restitution action due to the infringement and validity time lag introduces not only a significant legal uncertainty and but also a delay in the dispute resolution.

16.23 In contrast, both US and Japanese validity challenge procedures incorporate measures to prevent the time lag between infringement and validity proceedings. In US procedures,

[43] Peter Hess, Tilman Mueller-Stoy, and Martin Wintermeier, "Are Patents Merely 'Paper Tigers'?" *Mitt.* (2014): 439 (http://www.bardehle.com/uploads/files/Patent_Papiertiger.pdf).

[44] Cremaers et al., "Invalid but Infringed?," 27.

[45] Ch. 16, 16.08.

[46] Ch. 16, 16.10.

[47] Ch. 11, 11.164.

post-grant review, and *inter partes* review proceedings must conclude within one year.[48] It is very likely that these review proceedings will conclude earlier than infringement proceedings even if the district courts refuse to stay their proceedings. US judges are willing to stay infringement proceedings if they know that waiting for a validity decision from the USPTO will not unreasonably delay dispute resolution. In particular, the AIA sets forth special factors that district courts should take account of when deciding whether to grant a stay when the requested stay relates to a special post-grant review for a business method.[49] The Federal Circuit interprets these factors in the AIA as encouraging district courts to grant stays when the request for the stay is filed early, prior to the completion of discovery or trial scheduling, even if the issues in the infringement proceedings do not completely overlap with the issues in the related post-grant review proceedings.[50]

Moreover, the US system has incorporated measures to avoid conflicting validity **16.24** decisions.[51] The US system completely prevents any inefficiencies resulting from amendments of claims at USPTO proceedings on infringement analysis because the effect of an amendment or a new claim limiting the scope of the original claim though an amendment is not retroactive unless the scope of the amended or added claim is substantially identical.[52] An issuance of a certificate of patentability with the amended claims results in the surrender of the patent on the original claims and eliminates any causes of action and damages relating to the original claims.[53] It is not necessary for the courts to decide whether an accused embodiment infringes the amended claim because they can deny injunctions by granting an equitable intervening right to the defendant if the accused embodiment infringes.

In contrast, Japanese courts also face the same dilemma German courts face resulting **16.25** from amendments of claims at the Japanese Patents Office (JPO). Because the effect of an amendment is retroactive, patentees retain their cause of action and claim of damages if the accused embodiment infringes any of the amended claims. To avoid delay, Japanese courts allow the patentee to assert a rebuttal defense against the accused infringer's defense of invalidity.[54] However, this practice may result in a conflicting decision on the invalidity of the patent if the JPO disagrees with the court with respect to the scope of the amended claims. Unlike German courts, it is more likely that the JPO will conclude its validity and correction proceedings prior to the conclusion of the district court infringement proceedings. If there are any delays, conflicting decisions should be resolved at the IP High Court, which has exclusive jurisdiction over appeals from both proceedings. As a result, the risk of conflicting decisions resulting in significant harm to the defendant is very low.

5. Enforcement Procedure

Extensive discovery makes US patent litigation extremely expensive compared to German **16.26** and Japanese patent litigation: the average cost of infringement proceedings in a US district court is US$3–4 million in contrast to US$100,000–500,000 for infringement proceedings at a German district court including parallel nullity suits for defending validity at the German

[48] Ch. 7, 7.42.
[49] Public Law 112-129 Leahy-Smith America Invents Act, § 18.
[50] *Versata Software, Inc. v. Callidus Software, Inc.*, 771 F.3d 1368, 112 U.S.P.Q. 2d 1838 (Fed. Cir. 2014).
[51] Ch. 7, 7.18 "Measures to Prevent Conflicting Validity Decisions."
[52] Ch. 7, 7.13.
[53] Ch. 7, 7.65.
[54] Ch. 9, 9.24.

Federal Patent Court and US$300,000–500,000 for infringement proceedings at either the Tokyo or Osaka District Court.[55] The scope of discovery in the United States is very broad and includes any non-privileged matter relevant to any party's infringement claim or defense, including counterclaims.[56] Because discovery provides evidence supporting the infringing claims, a complaint must include only a plausible short and plain statement of the patentee's claim showing the patentee's entitlement to relief.[57] Under the plausible statement standard, the Federal Circuit endorsed a pleading practice that follows "Form 18" in the Appendix of Forms in the Federal Rules.[58] The sample complaint in Form 18 only requires the statement and allegation of jurisdiction, patent number, date of patent, infringing activity, and relief requested. It follows that a patent owner does not need to include each element of the asserted claims or specifically to identify an accused embodiment in the complaint. This low threshold for pleading is viewed as promoting frivolous litigation, brought by patent assertion entities, which leads to unnecessary and burdensome discoveries.[59] Within a short period from the receipt of the complaint, defendants are required to respond to a request that broadly defines the object to be disclosed by using a definition such as "source code, specifications, schematics, flow charts, artwork, formulas, or other documentation sufficient to show the operation of any aspects or elements of an accused device identified by the patent owner."[60]

16.27 Such a broad scope for the document production request is not available either in Germany or Japan. The pleading threshold in German and Japanese courts is much higher than the US threshold: a complaint must include all facts known to the patent owner that are required or are helpful to substantiate the infringement claim.[61] To enable parties to meet this threshold even in circumstances where the information required for preparing an appropriate complaint are not within the public domain, the German and Japanese Patent Laws and Civil Procedure Laws provide pre-trial evidence-collection procedures.[62] In Germany, a patent owner must establish a sufficient indication of infringement in order to request, before filing a complaint, that a respondent produce documents and allow inspection of the respondent's devices and processes. Such requests are granted only when the patent owner establishes that the owner does not have access otherwise to the information necessary to show infringement. Moreover, the request must specify the object to be inspected as precisely as possible. This requirement to specify the object also applies to a document production request during the trial after filing a complaint. In short, German courts will refuse to grant a request for inspection or document production if the request broadly defines an object as is done in the general discovery requests used in the United States. Japanese courts

[55] Michal Elmer and C. Gregory Gramenopoulos, *Global Patent Litigation* (2014), 595, 710, 900. See Ch. 10, 10.25 (US), Ch. 11, 11.31 (Germany), and Ch. 12, 12.20 (Japan). It is likely that the cost of German courts includes reimbursement of court and attorney fees when a party wins the case.

[56] Ch, 10, 10.34; see also Kimberly Moore, Timothy R. Holbrook, and John E. Murphy, *Patent Litigation and Strategy* (4th ed., 2013), 196.

[57] Ch. 10. 10.28.

[58] Ch. 10, 10.30; see, e.g., *K-Tech Telecomms., Inc. v. Time Warner Cable, Inc.*, 714 F.3d 1277, 106 U.S.P.Q. 2d 1462 (Fed. Cir. 2013).

[59] Ch. 10, 10.28; see further Paual R. Gugliuzza, "Patent Litigation Reform: The Courts, Congress, and the Federal Rules of Civil Procedure," 95 *Boston U.L.R.* (2015): 279; Greg Reilly, "Linking Patent Reform and Civil Litigation Reform" (March 6, 2015) (http://ssrn.com/abstract=2568443).

[60] Local Rules of Practice for Patent Cases before the United States District Court for the Northern District of California, 3-1 (http://www.localpatentrules.com/patent-rules/california-northern/).

[61] For Germany, see Ch. 11, 11.38; for Japan, see Ch. 12, 12.23.

[62] For Germany, see Ch. 11, 11.49; for Japan, see Ch. 12, 12.25.

also impose requirements similar to Germany's on patent owners to prevent the abuse of document production requests.[63]

In addition to the limited evidence-collection procedure, in Germany the judges' expertise in patent law and technology makes the cost of German patent litigation substantially less expensive than US litigation. Judges at the patent tribunals of the district and appeal courts in Düsseldorf, Mannheim, and Munich are well experienced in construing patent claims in various technologies and seldom need the assistance of experts to understand such technologies.[64] When these judges decide to take further evidence regarding technologies, they usually appoint a court expert. The remuneration for court experts is set by a rule to keep payment at a reasonable rate. Although parties are also allowed to bring their own experts, judges are concerned about bias and tend to give less weight to testimonies given by party-appointed experts. **16.28**

Japanese judges at the IP special divisions of the Tokyo and Osaka District Courts and the IP High Court also tend to have significant expertise on patent law and technology.[65] Although Japanese judges need to deal with validity issues, they are supported by judicial research officers and technical advisors who help them understand the technologies.[66] No additional cost is incurred for research officials who are full-time court employees. An appointment of a technical advisor is rare, and the cost of appointing technical advisors is kept relatively low. **16.29**

Moreover, the bifurcation system makes German litigation less expensive than Japanese litigation by removing complex technological issues that surface in the validity challenges from the infringement proceedings. The majority of communications are conducted through the exchange of briefs. Because holding more than two hearings is rare in both district court and appeal procedures, German procedure uses its attorneys' time most effectively. Although patentees need to bear additional costs for defending validity, the 'loser pays' rule effectively discourages defendants from filing a parallel nullity suit at the Federal Patent Court. As a result, defendants file parallel nullity suits in less than one-third of infringement cases.[67] **16.30**

6. Remedies

(a) Injunctive Relief

Until the 2006 *eBay* Supreme Court decision,[68] permanent injunctions were automatic after a finding of infringement and were considered the primary remedy for patent **16.31**

---

[63] See Ch. 12, 12.24; see also Ryu Takabayashi, "Practices of Patent Litigation in Japanese Courts," 5 *CASRIP Newsletter* (Spring/Summer 1998) (http://www.law.washington.edu/Casrip/Newsletter/default.aspx?year=1998&article=newsv5i2jp2).

[64] See Ch. 11, 11.40.

[65] The rotation system essentially forces Japanese judges to move to another court, or at least to another division within the same court, every three years. Therefore, it is rare for Japanese judges to continue to hear patent cases for more than three consecutive years, and judges with very little experience in patent law constantly arrive at IP tribunals. At the same time, judges with a strong interest in IP and patent law tend to stay connected to patent law even while being on rotation at another court, and there are a number of judges who have accumulated significant experience in patent cases over the last few decades.

[66] Ch. 2, 2.15; Ch. 12, 12.10, 12.11.

[67] Cremers et al., "Invalid but Infringed?" 20.

[68] *eBay Inc. v. MercExchange, LLC*, 547 U.S. 388, 126 S. Ct. 1837 (2006).

infringement in the United States, Germany, and Japan.[69] The *eBay* decision has significantly changed the role of the permanent injunction because considerably fewer permanent injunctions have been granted at US district courts after a finding of infringement.[70] One of the factors that patentees need to establish for the grant of a permanent injunction, non-availability of adequate remedies, suggests a strong preference for monetary damages over an injunction as a remedy for patent infringement.[71] Studies confirm that the grant rate of permanent injunctions has dropped significantly post-*eBay*, with a recent study indicating that permanent injunctions are granted in only 72.8 percent of the cases in which the parties contested the grant of an injunction.[72] A decade after *eBay*, monetary damages has become the primary remedy for infringement of a patent in the United States if the patent relates to a function of products covered by the many patents owned by different parties. In recent cases, the Federal Circuit has required winning patentees to establish a causal nexus between any alleged irreparable harm and the infringement for a grant of a permanent injunction.[73] When the asserted patent covers only a part of thousands of functions covered by separate patents, it is difficult for patentees to show the nexus between the asserted harm, such as lost sales, and the infringement of that part of the functions. As a result, the rate of receiving an injunction as a remedy for patent infringement is expected to decrease in the field of information technology as products become subject to an increasing number of patents.

16.32 In contrast, permanent injunctions remain the primary remedy for patent infringement in German and Japanese courts.[74] In particular, German courts do not have any discretion to decide whether to grant a permanent injunction once the patentee establishes infringement and requests an injunction. Moreover, unlike Japan, an order of permanent injunction is enforceable upon an infringement decision from a district court even if an appeal is filed as long as the winning patentee posts a security bond.[75] In theory, the security bond in combination with the defendants' ability to sue for damages resulting from the enforcement of the injunction should discourage patentees from abusing the system. In practice, however, patentees frequently enforce or credibly threaten to enforce their permanent injunctions in order to increase their bargaining power in settlement negotiations. For companies who make and sell products, the cost of designing around their products or removing their products from the market is high, and may result in irreparable harm such as the loss of market share.[76] As a result, many defendants settle their disputes and withdraw their nullity suits after an infringement decision at the district court.[77]

[69] Ch. 13, 13.01. For a general discussion on injunctive relief, see Christoph Rademacher, "Injunctive Relief in Patent Cases in the US, Germany and Japan: Recent Developments and Outlook," in Toshiko Takenaka (ed.), *Intellectual Property in Common Law and Civil Law* (2013), 325.

[70] Ch. 13, 13.06.

[71] *eBay Inc.*, 547 U.S., 391.

[72] Christopher B. Seaman, "Property Rules vs. Liability Rules in Patent Litigation after eBay: An Empirical Study" (forthcoming 2015); see Ch. 13, 13.06, for comments on this and other studies.

[73] *Apple Inc. v. Motorola, Inc.*, 757 F.3d 1286, 110 U.S.P.Q. 2d 1695 (Fed. Cir. 2014); *Apple Inc. v. Samsung Elecs. Co.*, 735 F.3d 1352, 108 U.S.P.Q. 2d 1833 (Fed. Cir. 2013).

[74] Ch. 14, 14.02; Ch. 15, 15.01.

[75] Ch. 14, 14.08.

[76] Richard Vary, "Bifurcation: Bad for Business" (https://www.unitary-patent.eu/sites/www.unitary-patent.eu/files/nokia_vary_bifufcation.pdf).

[77] Cremers et al., "Invalid but Infringed?" 18.

Although a grant of injunctive relief is automatic upon an infringement decision as long as patentees can show present or future infringement, Japanese courts may at least in theory have slightly more flexibility than German courts in denying injunctions. Under exceptional circumstances, Japanese courts may rely on fundamental principles of civil law and deny a claim of injunction. Section 1 of the Japanese Civil Code provides for three fundamental rules: private rights must conform to the public welfare, the exercise of rights and performance of duties must be done in good faith, and no abuse of rights is permitted.[78] In a recent case involving standard essential patents, the grand panel of the IP High Court refused to grant injunctive relief due to the finding that seeking injunctive relief against a willing licensee of a patent with a fair, reasonable, and non-discriminating (FRAND) declaration constitutes an abuse of right.[79] However, this kind of decision is also extremely rare in Japan, and the primary remedy sought in patent infringement litigation continues to be permanent injunctive relief.[80] **16.33**

(b) Damage Claims

Among the three jurisdictions, damages awarded by US courts are by far the largest. The median damage award by US district courts between 2010 and 2013 was US$4.3 million.[81] The largest damage award in the United States was US$1.8 billion, in contrast to Japan's largest damage award of US$82 million and Germany's of US$1.40 million.[82] Although US courts frequently calculate damages based on reasonable royalties, the size of damages can be very large.[83] **16.34**

In Germany, damages are awarded when a party conducts infringement willfully or with negligence.[84] A presumption based on the duty to avoid infringement shifts the burden onto infringers to show a lack of negligence or intent to infringe, and infringers can rebut the presumption under special circumstances where infringers are not considered to have violated the duty.[85] Because injunctions are the primary remedy and the size of damage awards are small, in the majority of cases, parties settle their disputes after courts find infringement and grant injunctions.[86] **16.35**

Japanese courts most frequently award damages based on reasonable royalties and infringer's profits.[87] Although the Patent Act was revised to facilitate patentees in establishing causation between lost sales and infringement, patentees are reluctant to claim damages in **16.36**

---

78 Minpō (Japanese Civil Code) Law No. 89 of April 27, 1896, § 1.

79 IP High Court, May 16, 2014, Hei 25 (ne) no. 10043, Hanrei Jihō (No. 2225) 146. An English translation is available on the IP High Court website (http://www.ip.courts.go.jp/eng/vcms_lf/25ne10043full.pdf).

80 Also, German courts deny injunctive relief in cases of standard essential patents as long as they consider the defendant to be a willing licensee. Instead of following general principles of civil law, a German court would recognize a defense based on competition law. Thus, the result might not have been different in Germany. (BGH decision of May 6, 2009, KZR 39/06 2009 GRUR 801—Orange Book.)

81 PWC, 2014 Patent Litigation Study, 6 (http://www.pwc.com/en_US/us/forensic-services/publications/assets/2014-patent-litigation-study.pdf); see Ch. 13, 13.43.

82 Elmer and Gramenopoulos, *Global Patent Litigation*, 88. It should be noted that in Germany parties also agree on multi-million USD damage payments out of court.

83 PWC, 2014 Patent Litigation Study, 9.

84 Ch. 14, 14.11.

85 Ch. 14, 14.13.

86 Elmer and Gramenopoulos, *Global Patent Litigation*, 88.

87 Ch. 15, 15.10.

the form of lost profits because they must disclose their net profits per product.[88] Japanese courts inform parties of their decision on infringement before starting a discussion on damages and encourage parties to settle their disputes. As a result, the role of damage awards as a remedy for patent infringement is limited both in Germany and Japan.

B. Proposal of Best Practice

1. Introduction

16.37 Currently, both substantive and procedural aspects of patent litigation systems in the United States, Europe, and Asia are under extensive review for major reform. In the United States, multiple bills are pending in the US Congress to reduce patent litigation costs and risks.[89] Views of US economists and IP scholars are divided regarding whether such a reform is necessary.[90] In Europe, an enhanced European patent system granting European patents with unitary effect and the Unified Patent Court will come into operation in EU member states, including Germany.[91] A group of experts have been appointed to develop the procedural rules for the new court system. Over the last decade, many countries in Asia established IP specialized courts. Japan's IP High Court just celebrated its tenth anniversary in April, 2015. China started its new IP specialized courts in Beijing, Guangzhou, and Shanghai in 2014.

16.38 These developments partly result from concerns over the costs of patent litigation. US academics argue that the current patent system is in crisis because the high cost of patent litigation harms innovation.[92] It is true that patent adjudication requires subject matter expertise on the part of both judges and lawyers because patent laws and patent granting procedures are complex and the scope of protection is difficult to define. Patent litigation is substantially more expensive than other types of civil litigation because significant investment is necessary to train judges and lawyers about technology and complex patent granting procedures. It is easy to blame patent offices for their poor quality of examination when patents are invalidated. However, such conclusions are often easier to see in hindsight because patent offices are urged to complete their examinations promptly in order to give protection in a timely manner and cannot conduct a thorough search due to the unlimited number of prior art references available in the technology fields. The scope of claims considered appropriate in light of the prior art during the prosecution might be inappropriate

[88] Ch. 15, 15.11. It should be noted though that while lost profits serve as the basis for damages relatively infrequently, most damages with high amounts in recent years have been computed on the basis of lost profits.

[89] E.g., Innovation Act, H.R. 9. A collection of patent litigation reform bills introduced to the 114th Congress is available from Patent Progress (http://www.patentprogress.org/patent-progress-legislation-guides/patent-progresss-guide-patent-reform-legislation/). For a general discussion about the patent litigation reform bills, see Gugliuzza, "Patent Litigation Reform: The Courts, Congress, and the Federal Rules of Civil Procedure."

[90] Michael Risch, "Dueling Patent Reform Letters to Congress," Written Description, March 10, 2015 (http://writtendescription.blogspot.com/2015/03/dueling-patent-reform-letters-to.html).

[91] The Select Committee and The Preparatory Committee, "An Enhanced European Patent System" (http://www.unified-patent-court.org/images/documents/enhanced-european-patent-system.pdf).

[92] James Bessen and Michael J. Meurer, *Patent Failure: How Judges, Bureaucrats, and Lawyers Put Innovators at Risk* (2008); Dan L. Burk and Mark A. Lemley, *The Patent Crisis and How the Courts Can Solve It* (2009).

once it is re-examined in light of newly found prior art and accused embodiments. In short, a more realistic view is that through patent enforcement, the extent of patent protection is redefined in light of newly found prior art references and accused embodiments to give fair protection appropriate for the technical contribution attained by the patented invention.

Instead of blaming the current patent systems and patent offices, this book will conclude with a proposal of the best practice for patent enforcement for the United States, Europe, and Asia. In proposing the best practice, patent litigation reform needs to embrace more than a comparative law perspective: it needs to adopt a balancing of equity and efficiency as a key principle when evaluating its effectiveness.[93] A best-practice patent enforcement system should be well-balanced to serve equity and efficiency in light of the goals of the patent system. To serve equity, such a system should give parties equal opportunities to advance their arguments and defenses, to redefine the extent of patent protection, and to obtain access to evidence which supports their arguments and defenses. The extent of patent protection through claim interpretation should maintain a fine balance between fair protection for patent owners and a reasonable degree of legal certainty for the public. To achieve efficiency, the benefits of enforcement should be well balanced with the cost of enforcement. Remedies available for patentees should balance the level of compensation and the cost of enforcement. Although a quick and cheap enforcement system sounds attractive, such a system may not serve equity because it may fail to give parties enough opportunity for their arguments to be heard and may lead to mistakes or injustice. When considering the extent of the patent and an appropirtae remedy for its infringement, the parties and judiciary should invest sufficient time and resources to properly identify the technical contribution the particular invention brings to the state of art as well as the benefits and injury the enforcement of the patentbrings to society as a whole. **16.39**

2. Extent of Patent Protection

In all three jurisdictions, a claim is not enforced on its face. The claim is interpreted by clarifying the meaning of the disputed terms in light of specifications and other materials to define the patented invention in comparison with the accused embodiment. To serve equity, patentees should be able to advance arguments for a meaning broader than the ordinary or customary meaning of a disputed term on its face by taking account of the general knowledge of a PHOSITA as is currently done by German courts. At the same time, accused infringers should be able to advance arguments for a meaning narrower than the ordinary meaning by taking account of the embodiments that the inventors recognized and disclosed in the specification and the prior art, including references not cited during the examination. In this respect, the German claim interpretation also fails to serve equity because it prevents accused infringers from advancing arguments based on newly found prior art references. Regardless of the presumption of validity resulting from the examination at the EPO or German Patent Office, the public, including accused infringers, should be able to use technologies that are in the prior art, and the extent of patent protection should be interpreted in light of all prior art available to the public. **16.40**

US and Japanese claim construction may also fail to serve the goal of the patent system if courts place an unfairly heavy weight on the notice function at the expense of fair protection **16.41**

[93] Jonathan Wilson, *Out of Balance: Prescription for Reforming the American Litigation System* (2005), 7.

for patentees. In focusing on the notice and definitional functions of patent claims, US and Japanese courts may interpret claims to find inherent limitations and exclude from the literal scope of a claim an accused embodiment that was not expressly disclosed in the specification. A heavy reliance on the specification and prosecution history may prevent patentees from discussing the invention in comparison with the prior art. US courts should be very cautious in distinguishing a mere discussion of the invention and its embodiments from a clear disclaimer of some embodiments that fall within the literal scope of the asserted claim on its face. Patentees should not only be allowed but also be encouraged to draft a claim with a scope beyond what is disclosed in the specification by including foreseeable equivalents. A heavy burden should be imposed on a party that advances a meaning different from the ordinary and customary meaning by taking account of the general knowledge of one skilled in the art of the invention at the time of the patent application.

16.42 If a claim is interpreted expansively in light of the PHOSITA's general knowledge to include foreseeable equivalents and the accused embodiment does not fall within the literal scope, courts should deny infringement without examining infringement under the doctrine of equivalents because the expanded claim interpretation should be sufficient to serve the policy of fair protection. Thus, the extent of patent protection under the doctrine of equivalents should be exceptional. The doctrine should apply only in exceptional circumstances where the patentee was unable to draft a claim literally including the accused embodiment. Moreover, the doctrine of equivalents should not be applied to eliminate a claim term or element entirely or to recapture embodiments that are clearly disclaimed or surrendered through claim amendments. In applying the doctrine of equivalents to the expanded scope through the function-oriented claim interpretation, German courts may fail to give sufficient attention to the claim language, focusing instead on the technical solution. To guarantee a reasonable degree of certainty based on the claim language, German courts should emphasize the third prong of infringement under the doctrine of equivalents: if an accused embodiment is outside of the literal scope of the claim and thus does not infringe the claim literally, there should be strong guidance to a PHOSITA that the embodiment does not infringe the claim. In particular, when an accused embodiment is disclosed but not covered by a claim that is issued or originally covered by a claim but not covered by a claim that is issued, courts should apply a strong presumption that the embodiments were disclaimed or surrendered by the patentee. Patentees should be able to overcome the presumption only if the patentees can establish a reason why they could not reasonably be expected to have drafted a claim that literally covers the accused embodiment.

3. Defenses

16.43 Because it is a myth that a claim must be clear on its face, and because the extent of patent protection needs to be clarified and redefined in light of the specification and other materials in addition to the newly found prior art and the accused embodiment, a claim should not be invalidated for a violation of disclosure requirements. Since examiners who represent the PHOSITA were able to understand the scope of the claim being supported by the disclosure in the specification, a strong presumption should apply that the claim is in compliance with not only the enablement and description requirements but also the definiteness requirement. In particular, patentees are encouraged to draft claims to literally cover equivalents foreseeable to a PHOSITA through their general knowledge. It is difficult to draft claims to cover foreseeable equivalents while excluding non-enabled equivalent embodiments. Courts should not punish patentees by finding a violation of the enablement, written description, or claim definiteness requirements when the patentees try to argue that a claim covers an embodiment that departs from the invention and thus is not enabled or supported by the disclosure of the invention.

Since the written description and claim definiteness are grounds for rejection as well as grounds for invalidity under the US and Japanese Patent Acts, US and Japanese courts may be willing to find a violation of one of the disclosure requirements with respect to a claim including non-equivalent embodiments. They should refrain from finding a violation invalidates a claim. Instead courts should interpret the claim to find inherent limitations and redefine the extent of patent protection by excluding embodiments that are not enabled or supported by the specification. **16.44**

4. Validity Challenges

Patent offices have all of the resources and expertise necessary to examine the validity of a patent and provide patentees with remedies to amend claims if the patented claims are invalid and a ground of invalidity can be eliminated through an amendment. Accordingly, giving patent offices the first opportunity to examine validity serves both equity and efficiency. German and Japanese enforcement systems have long adopted a bifurcation system for allocating infringement and validity issues to venues that have the best resources. The AIA also moved US patent enforcement more line with Japanese and German enforcement in adopting the post-grant review and *inter partes* review. **16.45**

However, patent offices need to complete the examination quickly before courts decide on infringement. If a claim is amended, the time spent in interpreting the original claim is wasted, and courts need to interpret the amended claim again. When an injunction is granted on an invalid claim, an enforcement of the invalid patent results in a harm rather than a benefit to the society, and the interests of the public to use the prior art or non-patentable subject matter is unfairly undermined. The AIA incorporated a mechanism to coordinate review procedures with infringement procedures at district courts. Although district courts are not obligated to stay their proceedings, it is likely that they will do so if the USPTO makes a preliminary decision to meet the threshold requirement of a reasonable likelihood of non-patentability or a "more likely than not" standard and initiates an *inter partes* review or post-grant review at the early stages of the infringement procedure. **16.46**

In contrast, the German bifurcation system fails to serve equity or efficiency because infringement decisions are issued and enforced more than a year before the EPO or Patent Court decides on the validity of the asserted claims. The system gives an unfair advantage to patentees by preventing accused infringers from asserting invalidity defenses at infringement procedures. Some may argue that the current system encourages early settlements and thus appears to serve efficiency. However, equity is compromised for efficiency because justice is not well served if accused infringers are forced to settle their disputes and withdraw their validity challenge when injunctions are enforced regardless of appeals or parallel validity procedures. A system where there is a substantial risk that invalid patents will be found as infringed leads to inequity for both parties: accused infringers may suffer irreparable harm by losing market share and patentees need to defend damage claims resulting from the enforcement of the injunction. The system does not serve efficiency because parties may continue to litigate for restitution after an injunction is enforced. **16.47**

16.48 To balance equity and efficiency, accused infringers should be allowed to raise defenses based on invalidity at infringement procedures. Under the current draft rule of the Unified Patent Court, German courts are given the option of bifurcating the case when a defense of invalidity is raised at infringement procedures.[94] Because German judges have a high level of patent law and technology expertise through their experiences in deciding more cases than those handled by US and Japanese judges, they should be given full authority to examine patent validity. They have already been examining validity in deciding requests for a provisional suspension of compulsory enforcement of an injunction with respect to the question of whether the underlying decision is obviously incorrect with a substantial risk of the patent being revoked.[95] The patent community expects that German judges will refrain from bifurcating the case and decide validity in the UPC system.

16.49 To enhance efficiency, the opposition procedure at the EPO and the nullity suit at the Patent Court should be streamlined with infringement procedures at district courts. The EPO and Patent Court should accelerate the examination of claims enforced at infringement procedures and follow a tight schedule to complete examination, as is done by the USPTO with respect to post-grant reviews and *inter partes* reviews. It would be most helpful for district courts if the EPO and Patent Court make a preliminary decision regarding whether current claims are more likely than not to be invalid before starting opposition or nullity procedures. Thus, the EPO and the German Patent Court should introduce a preliminary decision system so that German district courts can take advantage of the preliminary decision and grant a provisional suspension of compulsory enforcement of an injunction. Introduction of such a system at the JPO may be also helpful for Japanese courts to make a decision on whether to stay their infringement procedures.

5. Procedure

16.50 The high costs stemming from unique features of US patent litigation are the target of criticisms from academics and the industry for giving unfair advantages to patent assertion entities.[96] The discovery-intensive litigation fails to serve equity due to the asymmetry of discovery costs: patent practicing defendants have substantially more information than small non-practicing patentees such as patent assertion entities. A variety of bills to reform patent litigation are pending in Congress to curb the costs and risks of patent litigation brought by patent assertion entities.[97] In particular, the liberal standard for pleading and the extensive discovery are identified as major sources of the problems in patent litigation. Thus, the most extensive patent litigation reform bill, the Innovation Act, addresses these issues by requiring courts to adopt a heightened pleading standard and limiting discoveries prior to claim construction.[98] In addition, the Judicial Conference Advisory Committee has proposed raising the pleading standard by eliminating the current practice of using Form 18.[99]

---

[94] 16th Draft Rules of Procedure, Draft Rules 70(3) (http://www.unified-patent-court.org/images/documents/revised-draft-rules-of-procedure.pdf).

[95] Ch. 14, 14.09.

[96] Randall Rader, Colleen Chien, and David Hricik, "Make Patent Trolls Pay in Court," *New York Times*, June 4, 2013 (http://www.nytimes.com/2013/06/05/opinion/make-patent-trolls-pay-in-court.html?_r=0).

[97] Eric Rogers and Young Jeon, "Inhibiting Patent Trolling: A New Approach for Applying Rule 11," 12 *Nw. J. Tech. & Intell. Prop.* (2014): 291 (http://scholarlycommons.law.northwestern.edu/njtip/vol12/iss4/2).

[98] Ch. 10, 10.30.

[99] Memorandam, Chair, Advisory Committee on Federal Rules of Civil Procedure, June 14, 2014 (www.uscourts.gov/file/18218/download) For the current practice, Ch. 16, 16.27. The recommended changes are currently reviewed by the Supreme Court.

The sources of these problems are not unique to patent litigation: similar problems are common to any type of US civil litigation in higher-stake cases and thus a variety of reforms have been proposed since the 1970s.[100] US scholars and the industry propose legislative reforms as well as reforms through case law and leadership of the judicial conference.[101] Many are also concerned about the possibility of unexpected negative results from substantial changes. These reforms could move US litigation more in line with German and Japanese litigation by curbing the unique features of US civil procedure that were influenced by the common law tradition. To predict the impact of these proposed reforms, the US patent community can learn from the experiences of German and Japanese patent litigation. **16.51**

Although there is some activity by patent assertion entities in Germany and Japan, problems caused by such activities are marginal outside the United States. As required by the heightened pleading standard in the Innovation Act,[102] German and Japanese patentees need to identify in their complaints each claim of each patent being asserted, the accused embodiments, acts of infringement engaged by the defendant, and an analysis regarding how each element of each asserted claim corresponds to the accused embodiments with detailed specificity.[103] In essence, patentees have the burden of substantiating their patent infringement claims in their complaint. Although pre-filing evidence-collection procedures enables German and Japanese patentees to have access to information held by defendants, they must establish the necessity for such information and sufficient likelihood of infringement.[104] This heightened pleading standard effectively prevents unnecessary litigation based on weak claims in German and Japanese courts. **16.52**

The Innovation Act proposes to limit pre-claim construction discovery to information that is necessary for the court to determine the meaning of the terms used in the patent claim.[105] The Act also instructs the Judicial Conference of the United States to develop rules and procedures to resolve the asymmetric burden and costs between patentees and accused infringers in patent litigation.[106] Moreover, the Act proposes a fundamental change in US civil procedure: a fee-shifting of the cost of producing evidence other than core documentary evidence.[107] Instead of such a fundamental change, a US academic proposes staged litigation by separating liability issues, including infringement and validity, from remedy issues, including damages and willfulness.[108] Because the liability issues are not particularly discovery-intensive, the academic anticipates a significant reduction in cost and burden on discovery by adopting staged litigation.[109] Although validity issues can be more discovery-intensive than infringement issues, such issues may be resolved at the USPTO when an *inter partes* review or post-grant review is requested early. It is very likely that district courts will grant a stay in their infringement **16.53**

---

100 Reilly, "Linking Patent Reform and Civil Litigation Reform."

101 Gugliuzza, "Patent Litigation Reform."

102 Innovation Act, H.R. 3309, 12–15 (as passed House) (https://www.congress.gov/113/bills/hr3309/BILLS-113hr3309rfs.pdf).

103 For German courts, Ch. 11, 11.38; for Japanese courts, Ch. 12, 12.23.

104 Ch. 13, 13.49; Ch. 14, 14.25–14.26.

105 Innovation Act, H.R. 3309, 12–15.

106 Innovation Act, H.R. 3309, 27.

107 Innovation Act, H.R. 3309, 27–30.

108 Reilly, "Linking Patent Reform and Civil Litigation Reform," 47.

109 Ibid. 31. (Discoveries on infringement requires the production of information on samples of accused embodiments and technical documents explaining the structure and operation of the accused embodiments and a deposition from scientists or engineers familiar with the embodiment.)

procedeedings when the USPTO initiates a review procedure at the early stages of discovery. According to recent statistics, the chance of asserted claims being fully or partially invalidated through these review procedures is very high.[110] Even without a grant of stay, it is likely that the USPTO will be able to revoke or issue a certificate before a trial on liability issues begins.

16.54 The proposed staged patent litigation is very similar to the procedure practiced in German and Japanese courts: liability is litigated first and many cases are settled once courts determine liability because of the cost and burden in establishing damages. It is likely that staged litigation will encourage parties to settle disputes after the liability stage and substantially reduce the costs and burdens unique to US patent litigation. Because the asymmetry of discovery costs and burden for fact-intensive damage and willfulness issues are particularly substantial in cases between non-practicing patentees and practicing defendants who make and sell products, it is unlikely that such defendants will continue to fight in the remedy stage when the patent assertion entities prevails on liability.

6. Remedies

16.55 Although the chance an injunction will be denied has significantly increased, US courts still grant injunctions if the winning patentees are firms who make and sell products or if they are individuals or universities.[111] Because of the high frequency with which injunctions are denied, damages have become the primary remedies for infringement of patents held by patent assertion entities. An injunction is far more effective as a remedy for patent infringement than damages: a grant of injunction gives bargaining power to patentees and thus effectively encourages settlement on the past and future royalty rates in contrast to a grant of damages in the form of reasonable royalty calculated by courts that have no information nor the experience necessary for royalty calculation. In particular, not only is the reasonable royalty calculation the most fact-intensive among any of the issues in patent litigation, but also the asymmetry in the discovery cost and burden is the most substantial between non-practicing patentees and practicing defendants. This is because such defendants must produce confidential information relating to profits resulting from the infringing products; in contrast, patentees have very little information to produce for the royalty calcuation.[112] It would be more efficient if disputes on compensation for past and future infringement could be resolved between parties who have experience and access to the necessary information instead of wasting judicial resources.

16.56 Moreover, a US academic argues that US districts courts and academics misinterpret *eBay* in denying injunctions by plaintiff type, particularly in discriminating non-practicing patentees from other types of non-practicing patentees.[113] This academic emphasizes that the equitable factors in *eBay* should be applied on a case-by-case basis. The opinion from a unanimous court instructed lower courts to use their equitable discretion consistent with the traditional principle of equity and clearly rejected the categorical approach applied by the district court to deny injunctions by classifying patentees based on whether they are willing to license or

[110] Over the two years since the introduction of the *inter partes* review on September 16, 2012, the USPTO has granted 77% of the petitions and found 68% of the instituted claims unpatentable. Michael Elmer and Gregory Gramenopoulos, *Annual Global Patent Litigation Report* (2015), S-39.

[111] Colleen V. Chien and Mark A. Lemley, "Patent Holdup, the ITC, and the Public Interest," *Cornell Law Review*, July 2, 2012 (Stanford Public Law Working Paper No. 2022168, http://ssrn.com/abstract=2022168).

[112] Ryan T. Holte, "The Misinterpretation of eBay v. MercExchange and Why: An Analysis of the Case History, Precedent, and Parties," 18 *Chapman Law Review* (2015): 677.

[113] Holte, *The Misinterpretation of eBay v. MercExchange and Why*, 727.

whether they are practicing their patent.[114] The Supreme Court also acknowledged a possible conflict between the district court's approach and its precedent, which rejected a categorical approach to deny injunction depending on whether patentees unreasonably decline to practice their patents.[115] Such a categorical approach that depends on whether patentees are practicing their patents may violate at least the spirit of the Paris Convention[116] and TRIPS:[117] the Paris Convention prevents a grant of compulsory licenses in cases of failure or insufficient working of a patented invention[118] and TRIPS provides detailed conditions for a grant of a compulsory license.[119]

As long as the equitable factors are applied on a case-by-case basis with an emphasis on equity between patentees and defendants, the factors function in the same manner as the fundamental principle of the Civil Code, which gives flexibility to Japanese courts in denying a claim for an injunction in cases where a patent is essential for a technology standard. Both factors and principles may preclude an abuse of right in preventing unequitable results and excessive hardship on defendants for redesigning and removing products from the market if the hardship significantly exceeds the benefit to the public interest resulting from such redesigning and removal of products. However, because the fundamental principle under the Civil Code is not the rule but the exception, Japanese courts have applied the principle of denying injunctions in very limited circumstances. The German Civil Code provides for a fundamental rule, good faith performance, similar to the rule under the Japanese Civil Code,[120] and provides defenses based on competition law and other laws to give defendants the possibility of defending themselves against enforcement of an injunction under exceptional circumstances where enforcement would be obviously problematic. The German Federal Court of Justice found such circumstances when standard essential patents are enforced.[121] The Court should find such circumstances where the enforcement of an injunction is contrary to public policy, and thus violates the general requirement of good faith.[122] **16.57**

Although a patent enforcement system using injunctions as its primary remedy is efficient, such a system may fail to serve equity unless patentees are compensated with at least the costs of patent enforcement. German courts award attorneys' fees to winning parties, giving small parties access to justice. The attorneys' fees are calculated based on the value of the disputes instead of the actual costs.[123] This fee-shifting gives German patentees access to justice if their patent infringement claim is based on a strong case. **16.58**

---

[114] *eBay Inc. v. MercExchange, LLC*, 547 U.S., 393.

[115] *Continental Paper Bag Co. v. Eastern Paper Bag Co.*, 210 U.S. 405, 422–30, 28 S. Ct. 748, 52 L. Ed. 1122, 1908 Dec. Comm'r Pat. 594 (1908).

[116] Paris Convention for the Protection of Industrial Property (March 20, 1993; effective July 7, 1884, and amended June 2, 1934, and July 14, 1967) (the Paris Convention).

[117] Agreement on Trade-related Aspects of Intellectual Property Rights, Apr. 15, 1994, Marrakesh Agreement Establishing the World Trade Organization, Annex 1C, The Legal Texts: The Results of the Uruguay Round of Multilateral Trade Negotiations 320 (1999), 1869 U.N.T.S. 299, 33 I.L.M. 1197 (1994).

[118] Paris Convention, Art. 5A(4).

[119] TRIPS, Art. 31.

[120] § 226, German Civil Code.

[121] BGH GRUR 2009, 694—*Orange-Book-Standard*; BGH GRUR 2004, 966—*Standard-Spundfass*. Also see Case C-170/13 *Huawei Technologies Co Ltd v ZTE Corp, ZTE Deutschland GmbH* (July 16, 2014).

[122] Vera Bolgar, "Abuse of Rights in France, Germany and Switzerland: A Survey of a Recent Chapter in Legal Doctrine," 35 *L.A. L. Rev.* (1975): 1015, 1027.

[123] § 91 of the German Code of Civil Procedure. For a general discussion on statutory attorney fees, see Ch. 11, 11.31–11.35.

16.59 In contrast, US patent litigation gives small patentees access to justice through contingency fee arrangements.[124] With the rise of patent assertion entities, contingent fee representation has begun to play an important role in patent litigation.[125] However, US academics have expressed concerns over contingent fees and a number of states prohibit them.[126] Such concerns include encouraging frivolous or unnecessary claims based on weak cases.[127] The Federal Rules of Civil Procedure (FRCP) prevent such claims by requiring attorneys to certify that the legal contention is warranted by existing law or by a nonfrivolous argument.[128] Moreover, US courts have been awarding attorneys' fees in exceptional cases such as in the enforcement of a patent procured through inequitable conduct.[129] Recently, the US Supreme Court liberalized the standard for finding exceptional cases and increased the district courts' discretion to award attorneys' fees.[130]

16.60 With the rise of contingent fee representations in patent litigation, US academics and industries renewed their attention to concerns over frivolous patent infringement claims brought by patent assertion entities. The Innovation Act proposes a fee-shifting rule, awarding prevailing parties reasonable fees and other expenses resulting from patent infringement.[131] The rule is expected to discourage patentees from bringing weak patent infringement claims, encourage defendants to fight against infringement claims, and increase defendants' bargaining power in license negotiations for settling their disputes.[132] The rule may serve both equity and efficiency as long as the calculation of attorneys' fees is based on a clear set of rules independent of the actual costs, as is done by German courts. Such a clear rule prevents losing parties from challenging the award of attorneys' fees and thus enhances efficiency.

[124] Ch.10, 10.25; Richard Moorhead, "'Improving Access to Justice'—Contingency Fees: A Study of their Operation in the United States" (November 17, 2008) (http://ssrn.com/abstract=1302843 or http://dx.doi.org/10.2139/ssrn.1302843).

[125] David L. Schwartz, "The Rise of Contingent Fee Representation in Patent Litigation" 64 *Alabama Law Review* (2012): 335 (http://ssrn.com/abstract=1990651 or http://dx.doi.org/10.2139/ssrn.1990651).

[126] Ibid. 344.

[127] Moorhead, "'Improving Access to Justice'—Contingency Fees," 21.

[128] The Federal Rules of Civil Procedure, R. 11

[129] 35 U.S.C. § 285.

[130] *Octane Fitness, LLC v. ICON Health & Fitness, Inc.*, 134 S. Ct. 1749 (2014). See Ch. 10, 10.25.

[131] Innovation Act, H.R. 3309, 6–7.

[132] James Bessen and Michael J. Meurer, "The Direct Costs from NPE Disputes," 99 *Cornell L. Rev.* (2014): 338, 422.

INDEX

Agreement on a Unified Patent Court (UPC), EU 1.06
Agreement on Trade-related Aspects of Intellectual Property Rights *see* **TRIPS**
attorneys
  attorney-client privilege 10.44
  fees
    Germany 11.36
    Japan 12.20–12.21
    US 10.25, 13.71–13.82
  unified patent court system 2.50

best practice, analysis and proposal of 16.01–16.60
  comparative analysis 16.01–16.36
    defenses 16.15–16.18
    enforcement procedure 16.26–16.30
    extent of patent protection 16.03–16.14
    remedies 16.31–16.36
    validity challenge procedures 16.19–16.25
  comparative analysis: extent of patent protection 16.03–16.14
    claim interpretation 16.03–16.10
    doctrine of equivalents 16.11–16.14
  comparative analysis: remedies 16.31–16.36
    damages claims 16.34–16.36
    injunctive relief 16.31–16.33
  proposal of best practice 16.37–16.60
    defenses 16.43–16.44
    extent of patent protection 16.40–16.42
    procedure 16.50–16.54
    remedies 16.55–16.60
    validity challenges 16.45–16.49
border measures *see* **enforcement procedure**

canons of construction *see* **claim construction**
central definition theory 4.17, 4.20
China: State Intellectual Property Office (SIPO) 1.07
claim construction, Germany 5.68–5.106
  aids for claim interpretation 5.80–5.97
    dictionaries and science treatise 5.93
    expert testimony 5.80, 5.94–5.96
    intrinsic v. extrinsic evidence 5.80
    other claims 5.85
    other extrinsic evidence 5.97
    prior art 5.91–5.92
    prosecution history 5.86–5.87
    record of prosecution history 4.62
    specification 5.81–5.84
    statements made in invalidation proceedings 5.88–5.90
  canons of construction 5.98–5.106
    canons favouring accused infringers 5.98–5.102
    canons favouring patentees 5.103–5.106
    claim terms in preambles 5.102
    unclear claims 5.99
  determining infringement 4.24–4.25
  fundamental rules 5.68–5.79
    function-oriented claim construction 5.69–5.71
    inventions defined by general rule (regular claims) 4.34
    patent as its own dictionary 5.76–5.77
    PHOSITAs, claim terms as understood by 4.36–4.37
    problem of the invention 5.72–5.74
    relevant viewpoint 5.75
    special types of claims 5.78–5.79
  structure of claims 5.102
claim construction, Japan 4.24–4.25, 6.38–6.68
  aids for claim interpretation 6.54–6.78
    intrinsic v. extrinsic evidence 6.54–6.56
    prior art 6.55, 6.64–6.66
    object and effect of invention 6.59–6.63, 6.71
    record of prosecution history 6.67–6.68
    specification 6.57–6.63
  determining infringement 4.24–4.25
  fundamental rules 6.38–6.53
    claim terms in preambles as limitations 6.40
    claims defined by the structure, material, and acts 6.38–6.47
    functionally defined claims 6.39, 6.48–6.49
    inventions defined by general rule (regular claims) 4.34–4.35
    inventor's recognition theory 6.43–6.45, 6.57
    multiple claim system 6.46–6.47
    PHOSITAs, claim terms as understood by 6.42–6.43, 6.45, 6.57–6.58
    product-by-process claims 6.39, 6.50–6.53
  structure of claims 6.40
  validity challenge 9.17
claim construction, US 4.32–4.82
  aids for claim interpretation 4.45–4.74
    dictionaries and treatises 4.66–4.69
    disclaimers of particular structure, material, function 4.55–4.56
    expert and inventor testimonies 4.45–4.47, 4.73–4.74
    intrinsic v. extrinsic evidence 4.45–4.48
    inventor's drafting/definition 4.52–5.54
    prior art 4.57, 4.70–4.72, 4.81, 4.82
    record of prosecution history 4.62–4.65
    specification 4.49–4.58
    terms other than disputed terms and same terms in other claims 4.59–4.61
  canons of construction 4.75–4.82
    canons favouring accused infringers 4.75–4.76
    canons favouring patentees 4.77–4.82
    claim differentiation doctrine 4.78, 6.47
    claim terms in preambles as limitations 4.79–4.82

claim construction, US (*cont.*):
fundamental rules 4.32–4.44
claims defined by the structure, material, and acts 4.32–4.39
functionally defined claims 4.34, 4.40–4.42
PHOSITAs, claim terms as understood by 4.36–4.38, 4.49, 4.58
product-by-process claims 4.34–4.44, 7.06–7.07
regular claims 4.34
separate examination of independent/dependent claims 4.39
structure of claims 4.33
validity challenges 7.04–7.07
broadest possible interpretation rule 7.04, 7.06, 7.09
product-by-process claims 7.06–7.07
scope of invention 7.05–7.06
construed claims application to accused embodiment, Germany 5.107–5.109
adding further elements 5.109
all elements rule, application of 5.107
construed claims application to accused embodiment, Japan 6.69–6.71
all elements rule 6.69–6.70
component-by-component basis 6.71
improvement inventions 6.71
construed claims application to accused embodiment, US 4.83–4.90
adding elements and improvements 4.87–4.88
all elements rule 4.83–4.86, 4.89
comparison as question of fact for jury 4.83
element-by-element analysis 4.83–4.85, 4.89
element, nature of 4.84
technological advancements 4.86
two-part test 4.85
means-plus-function elements 4.89–4.90
costs *see* **enforcement procedure**
Court of Justice of the European Union (CJEU)
interpreting EU-derived laws 1.47
no institutional link with EPO 1.43
No effect on non-EU EPC member states 1.43
unified patent court system, references from 2.47
Council of Europe 1.40
customs
Community Customs Code 1.44
customs offices
Germany 2.56–2.59
Japan 2.73–2
EU customs union 2.56

damages *see* **remedies**
declaratory judgment actions *see* **enforcement procedure**
developing countries: patent laws harmonization 1.02
doctrine of equivalents, Germany 5.110–5.131
doctrines to limit doctrine of equivalents 5.126–5.131
'dedication to the public' doctrine 5.127
Formstein defence 5.128, 6.74
practicing the prior art defense 4.120, 5.127–5.131
fundamental rules 5.112–5.125
guidance by subject-matter of claim 5.121–5.125
objective test: insubstantial difference 4.94–4.95
objective test: same effect 5.114–5.117
obviousness 5.118–5.120
three-prong test 5.112–5.113
purpose of doctrine 5.110
doctrine of equivalents, Japan 6.72–6.78
doctrines to limit doctrine of equivalents
prior art limitation 4.120, 6.74–6.75
fundamental rules 4.94–4.95
objective test: insubstantial difference 4.94–4.95
infringement under 6.33–6.34
essential portion as unique portion of technical idea 6.75
five tests for 6.72–6.75
non-essential elements test 6.75–6.76
doctrine of equivalents, US 4.20–4.21, 4.91–4.125
construed claims application to accused embodiment
adding elements and improvements 4.88
all elements rule, and 4.83
doctrine not confined by claim drafting 4.85
means-plus-function elements 4.89–4.90
doctrines to limit doctrine of equivalents 4.104–4.125
dedication to the public 4.124–4.125
no element vitiation rule 4.116–4.119
prior art limitation 4.120–4.123
prosecution history estoppel 4.101–4.115
fundamental rules 4.91–4.103
objective test: insubstantial difference 4.91–4.95
range of equivalents 4.96–4.100
reverse doctrine of equivalents 4.101–4.103
infringement under 4.27–4.29
reverse doctrine of equivalents 4.20, 4.101–4.103
creation of 4.101
limiting literal scope 4.101
marginal force as defense of literal infringement 4.103

enforcement procedure, Germany 11.01–11.166
border measures 11.77–11.99
application 11.78–11.83
clearance of seized goods 11.95
damage claims 11.96–11.99
differences of national seizure request (§ 142a Patent Act) 11.90–11.92
seizure 11.84–11.89
simplified procedure for destruction and declaratory procedure 11.93–11.94
costs 11.23–11.36
attorney fees, statutory 11.36
court fees 11.23–11.30
court fees, statutory 11.28
customary costs for legal representation 11.31–11.36
declaratory judgment actions 11.114–11.122
German law, under 11.115–11.118
torpedo proceedings 11.119–11.122
evidence procedure 11.47–11.76
claim for inspection 11.49–11.60

procedure for evidence collection during trial 11.73–11.76
procedure for pre-trial evidence collection 11.61–11.72
jurisdiction and venue 11.01–11.10
international jurisdiction 11.08–11.10
subject matter jurisdiction 11.01–11.03
venue 11.04–11.07
other important proceedings 11.114–11.166
declaratory judgment actions 11.114–11.122
preliminary injunctions 11.123–11.163
parties 11.11–11.21
defendants 11.20–11.22
standing to sue 11.12–11.19
preliminary injunctions 11.123–11.163
action for defense against enforcement 11.161–11.163
action for restitution 11.164–11.166
balance of interests 11.132–11.136
claim for injunction 11.125–11.126
claim for injunction: infringement 11.128–11.130
concealed preliminary injunctions (*Schubladenverfuegung*) 11.150–11.151
cross-border preliminary injunctions 11.157–11.160
damage claims for unjustified preliminary injunctions 11.148–11.149
extraordinary form of preliminary proceedings 11.150–11.156
grounds for injunction 11.131
jurisdiction and venue 11.124
procedure for obtaining preliminary injunction 11.142–11.147
protective letters (*Schutzschrift*) 11.152–11.156
requirements 11.127–11.141
urgency 11.137–11.141
pre-trial measures 11.100–11.113
claims for unjustified warning 11.108–11.110
request for justification 11.111–11.113
warning letters 11.102–11.107
procedure 11.37–11.113
border measures 11.77–11.99
evidence procedure 11.47–11.76
pre-trial measures 11.100–11.113
procedural overview and pending time 11.37–11.46

enforcement procedure, Japan 12.01–12.71
border measures 12.44–12.48
application period 12.46
detention period 12.47–12.48
costs 12.17–12.21
attorneys' fees 12.20–12.21
court fees 12.18–12.19
court fees, statutory 12.19
evidence collection 12.26–12.43
closed session 12.43
evidence collection after initiating lawsuit 12.35–12.43
evidence collection prior to initiating lawsuit 12.28–12.32
evidence preservation 12.33–12.34
in-camera proceedings 12.37
obligation to clarify specific conditions (Patent Act, § 104–2) 12.35
order to produce documents 12.36
protective orders 12.38–12.40
protective orders, cancellation of 12.41–12.42
jurisdiction 12.01–12.12
international jurisdiction 12.02–12.08
results of judicial reform 12.09–12.12
subject matter jurisdiction and venue 12.01
other important proceedings 12.55–12.71
declaratory judgment actions 12.55–12.58
preliminary injunctions 12.59–12.71
parties 12.13–12.16
defendants 12.15–12.16
standing to sue 12.13–12.14
preliminary injunctions 12.59–12.71
damages for wrongful injunctive relief 12.71
jurisdiction 12.62–12.63
numbers of 12.62
procedural overview 12.68–12.70
requirement for preliminary injunction 12.66–12.67
scope of preliminary injunction 12.64–12.65
pre-trial proceedings 12.49–12.54
claims for wrongful warning letters 12.50–12.54
warning letter – practice significance 12.49
wrongful warning letters sent to customers 12.51–12.54
wrongful warning letters sent to manufacturers 12.50
procedure 12.22–12.54
border measures 12.44–12.48
evidence collection 12.26–12.43
pre-trial proceedings 12.49–12.54
procedure overview and pending time 12.22–12.25

enforcement procedure, US 10.01–10.106
appeals 10.78–10.86
Court of Appeals for Federal Circuit 10.79–10.84
US Supreme Court 10.85–10.86
border measures/ITC proceedings 10.57–10.71
district courts, compared to 10.59, 10.71
domestic industry requirement 10.62–10.70
initiating complaints 10.58
jury trial 10.61
speed of 10.60
costs 10.22–10.25
attorney's fees 10.25
court fees and other costs 10.23–10.24
declaratory judgment actions 10.87–10.89
actual controversy 10.88
discretion of the court 10.89
evidence collection 10.31–10.51
attorney-client privilege 10.44
limitations of discovery 10.43–10.51
pre-litigation discovery 10.32–10.33
pre-trial discovery 10.34–10.36
protective orders 10.50–10.51
scope of discovery 10.37–10.42
specific issues in patent infringement proceedings 10.46–10.49
work product immunity 10.45

enforcement procedure, US (*cont.*):
jurisdiction 10.01–10.21
defendants 10.18–10.21
international jurisdiction 10.09–10.12
parties 10.13
standing to sue 10.14–10.17
subject matter jurisdiction 10.02
venue 10.03–10.08
jury trial 10.52–10.56
legal issues v. factual issues 10.54–10.56
right of jury trial 10.53
other types of actions 10.87–10.106
declaratory judgment actions 10.87–10.89
preliminary injunctions 10.90–10.106
preliminary injunctions 10.90–10.106
balance of interests 10.98
claim for preliminary injunction 10.92
damages for unjustified preliminary injunction 10.104–10.106
irreparable harm 10.95–10.97
jurisdiction 10.91
procedure 10.100–10.103
public interest 10.99
requirements 10.93–10.99
success on the merits 10.94–10.95
pre-trial proceedings 10.72–10.77
warning letters 10.72–10.74
where/when to sue (forum shopping) 10.75–10.77
procedure 10.26–10.86
appeals 10.78–10.86
border measures/ITC proceedings 10.57–10.71
evidence collection 10.31–10.51
jury trial 10.52–10.56
pleading standard 10.28–10.30
pre-trial proceedings 10.72–10.77
procedure overview and pending time 10.26–10.27
equivalents, doctrine of *see* **doctrine of equivalents**
European Commission of Human Rights 2.27
European Patent Convention (EPC) 1.04
amendment of claims, effect of 7.14
central/peripheral definition theories 4.20–4.21
doctrine of equivalents 4.20–4.21
claims, interpreting 4.34, 5.83
enactment of 1.41, 2.24
European Patent System, operation of 1.04
maximal approach to harmonization 1.09
member states deciding validity of European patents 1.05
patentability and validity challenges *see* European Patent Office (EPO)
procedural guarantees 2.27
revisions to, proposal for 2.26
single filings 1.04
European Patent Judges' Symposium 1.09
European Patent Office (EPO) 1.01, 1.05, 1.41
appeals from 2.25
Boards of Appeal 1.43, 2.25–2.26
independence of 2.25
not subject to national review 2.27
challenges regarding patentability: third-party observations 8.54–8.65
challenge of patentability: opposition proceedings 8.63
objections based on lack of clarity/support 8.58–8.62
scope of validity challenge: observations 8.56–8.57
scope of validity challenge: opposition proceedings 8.64–8.65
CJEU, no institutional link with 1.43
contracting states 1.43
decisions of EPO affecting EU 1.43
EU, independent from 1.43
European Patent System, operation of 1.04
exchanging examiners with JPO 1.07
filing patents 2.19
limitation proceedings at 8.33
opposition at 8.18–8.29
appeals 8.25–8.29
conduct of proceedings 8.19–8.23
patentability and validity challenges 8.46–8.141
challenges regarding patentability: filing third-party observations 8.55–8.65
derivation (entitlement) 8.137–8.139
inadmissible broadening 8.124–8.136
lack of enablement (sufficiency) 8.113–8.123
lack of industrial applicability (Article 57 EPC) 8.99–8.112
lack of inventive step (obviousness) (Article 56 EPC) 8.87–8.98
lack of novelty (Article 54 EPC) 8.74–8.86
patent eligibility (not invention, excluded inventions) 8.66–8.73
scope of the validity challenge: nullity proceedings 8.140–8.141
post-grant review procedure 7
amendment 7.13
proposal for 1.40
Trilateral Cooperation 1.07
unitary patents 2.44
decisions appealed to Unified Patent Court 2.44
European Patent Organization (EPOrg)
European Patent System, operation of 1.04
nature of 1.04
sponsoring European Patent Judges' Symposium 1.09
European Patent System
double-layered 1.42
future unified European patent/court system 2.42–2.55
maximal approach to harmonization 1.04, 1.09, 1.42
operation of 1.04
European Union
Brussels regime 1.45
centralized judiciary for deciding infringement/validity 1.06
CJEU *see* Court of Justice of the European Union (CJEU)

Community Customs Code 1.44
Community Patent Convention 1.05, 1.41
customs union 2.56
border seizure procedure 2.57
EPO independent from 1.43
EPOrg *see* European Patent Organization (EPOrg)
European patents, cost of 2.53
forum shopping on patent law 2.42
future unified European patent/court system 2.42–2.55
IP-related regulations and directives 1.44–1.45
IP rights, enforcing 1.48
origins 2.56
patent infringement procedures 1.05
patent laws harmonization *see* harmonization of patent laws
patent office *see* European Patent Office (EPO)
patent system *see* European Patent System
Unified Patent Court *see* Unified Patent Court
unified patent court system *see* unitary patents, EU
unitary patents *see* unitary patents, EU
evidence
aid to construction, as *see* claim construction
enforcement, for *see* enforcement procedure
expert/inventor testimonies
Germany 5.80, 5.94–5.96
Japan 16.06
US 4.45–4.47, 4.73–4.74, 10.56, 16.05

German Patent and Trademark Office (GPTO) 1.01, 2.19
appeals from 2.25
Federal Patent Court 2.32
language of proceedings 2.23
validity challenges *see* validity challenges, Germany
Germany
central definition theory, and 4.17
infringement *see* infringement, Germany
GPTO *see* German Patent and Trademark Office (GPTO)
legal structure, influence of US case law on 1.38
Paris Convention 1.01
patent enforcement institutions *see* Germany: patent enforcement institutions
patent enforcement procedure *see* enforcement procedure, Germany
patent protection, extent of *see* Germany: patent protection, extent of
patent system history
EPC, EU patent harmonization and 1.39–1.48
patent offices, establishment of 2.20–2.22
patents in Nazi era 1.30–1.34
post-World War II 1.35–1.38
pre-patent era 1.26–1.29
remedies *see* remedies, Germany
validity challenges *see* validity challenges, Germany
Germany: patent enforcement institutions 2.19–2.59
courts 2.28–2.55
district courts (*Landgerichte*) 2.33–2.35, 4.46
Federal Court of Justice (*Bundesgerichtshof; BGH*) 2.39–2.41
Federal Patent Court (*Bundespatentgericht*) 2.25, 2.30–2.32
future unified European patent/court system 2.42–2.55
higher regional courts (Oberlandesgerichte, OLGs) 2.36–2.37
language of proceedings 2.28
customs office 2.56–2.59
EU border seizure 2.57
German border seizure 2.58–2.59
enforcement procedure *see* enforcement procedure, Germany
overview 2.19
patent offices- EPO and GPTO 2.20–2.27
EPO, success of 2.24
remedies *see* remedies, Germany
validity challenges *see* validity challenges, Germany
Germany: patent protection, extent of 5.61–5.131
construed claims *see* construed claims application to accused embodiment , Germany
claim construction *see* claim construction, Germany
doctrine of equivalents *see* doctrine of equivalents, Germany
infringement analysis 5.63–5.67
claim construction for validity challenges 5.66–5.67
construction and application 5.63–5.64
further separate steps: literal infringement and DOE 5.65
overview 5.61–5.62

harmonization of patent laws 1.01, 1.07, 1.08
harmonization of patent laws, European 1.04–1.05, 1.09
economic reasons for harmonization 1.39
EPC 1.04, 1.07
EU patent harmonization, and 1.39–1.48
EPO 1.09, 1.42
EU
biotechnological inventions 1.05
case law 8.49–8.51
directive for harmonizing enforcement of IP rights 1.05
EU harmonization 1.44
reasons for harmonization 1.48
role of 1.05
importance of harmonization 8.47

infringement, Germany 5.01–5.131
biological material 5.21–5.24
definition 5.22
inventive function 5.24
new plant varieties 5.54
patent protection, extent of 5.23
claim construction and application 4.22–4.23, 4.34
claims of patent determine scope of invention 3.03, 4.17

infringement, Germany (*cont.*):
direct infringement 3.01, 5.01–5.24
acts constituting infringement 5.01–5.03, 5.21
biological material 5.21–5.24
concurrent infringers 5.21
exclusive rights of patent owner to products 5.12–5.13
'importing' 5.08
joint infringement 5.19–5.20
'making' 5.16
'offering' 5.04–5.05
'possessing' 5.07
products and processes 5.09–5.13
'selling' 5.06
'using' and 'offering for use' 5.09–5.11, 5.17–5.18
exemptions to patent infringement 5.51–5.55
experimental use 5.53–5.54
instantaneous preparation of medicines in pharmacies 5.55
methods for treatment of humans/animals 5.55
new plant varieties 5.54
non-economic purposes 5.52
transportation 5.55
extraterritorial infringement 5.41–5.50
activities partly in Germany 5.42
offers by email/phone/fax 5.43
principle of territoriality 5.41
process claims 5.46–5.47
products deemed to be on market 5.45
websites, offers on 5.44
indirect infringement 3.02, 5.20, 5.25–5.40
absolute prohibitions 5.39
acts constituting indirect infringement 5.26–5.28
cease and desist orders 5.38, 5.39
damages 5.40
double territoriality requirement 5.36
exemptions 5.26, 5.28
indirect patent infringement 5.25
inducement 6.19
intention of recipient of offer/supply of means 5.35
liability as accessory 5.25
limited prohibitions 5.38
means objectively suitable to put invention into effect 5.32, 6.17
means relating to 'essential element of the invention' 5.31, 6.17
no entitlement to exploit invention 5.33
objective elements of 5.29–5.33
'offers or supplies a means' 5.30
remedies 5.38–5.40
staple commercial products, means as 5.37, 6.19
subjective elements of 5.34–5.37
patent protection, extent of *see* Germany: patent protection, extent of patent term and extension 5.56–5.60
duration of patent term 5.56
extension of rights/supplemental protection certificates 5.57–5.60
specification and drawing, use of 3.04

infringement, Japan 6.01–78
claims of patent determine scope of invention 3.03, 4.17
direct infringement 3.01, 6.01–6.12
acts constituting infringement 6.01
aiding and abetting 6.11
'assigning' 6.02
computer programs 6.03
'importing' 6.06
'making' 6.10
offering to assign 6.04
'possessing' 6.05
products and processes 6.07–6.09
'using' 6.11–6.12
vicarious liability 6.12
extraterritorial infringement 6.23–6.24
'double territoriality requirement' 6.24
territorial principle 6.23
indirect infringement 3.02, 6.13–6.19
acts constituting indirect infringement 6.13
actual knowledge 6.18
essential means and knowledge equipment requirement 6.19
exclusive use requirement 6.16
inducement 6.19
liability as accessory 6.13
means must be indispensable or essential for invention 6.17
owner's prima facie case 6.15
products and processes 6.14, 6.16
patent protection, extent of *see* Japan: patent protection, extent of
patent term and extension 6.20–6.22
patent term extension 6.20–6.22
term 6.20
specification and drawing, use of 3.04

infringement, US 4.01–4.125
claims of patent determine scope of invention 3.03, 4.17
direct infringement 3.01, 4.01–4.05, 4.14
acts constituting infringement 4.01–4.05
joint infringement 4.04
jurisdiction 4.05
private use 4.03
'selling' and 'using' 4.03
single-party rule 4.04
extraterritorial infringement 4.12–4.16
expansive interpretation of direct/indirect infringement 4.14
inducement 4.16
'selling' and 'offering to sell', meaning of 4.15
territorial principle 4.12, 4.13
indirect infringement 3.02, 4.06–4.09, 4.14
acts constituting indirect infringement 4.06
component as material part of invention 4.09
contributory infringement 4.08
inducement 4.07, 6.19
inducement 4.07, 4.16
patent protection, extent of *see* US: patent protection, extent of
patent term and extension 4.10–4.11
extension 4.11
term 4.10

specification and drawing, use of 3.04
territorial principle 4.12, 4.13
injunctions
enforcement, and *see* enforcement procedure
remedy, as *see* remedies
intellectual property (IP)
EU directive for harmonizing enforcement of 1.05
TRIPS *see* TRIPS
WIPO *see* World Intellectual Property Organization (WIPO)
international institutions, evolution of 1.01–1.09
European Patent Organization and EU 1.04–1.06
trilateral patent office initiatives and beyond 1.07–1.09
WIPO and WTO 1.01–1.03
International Intellectual Property Institute 1.09
International Trade Commission *see* **US International Trade Commission (ITC)**

Japan
infringement *see* infringement, Japan
JPO *see* Japan Patent Office (JPO)
Paris Convention 1.01
patent enforcement institutions *see* Japan: patent enforcement institutions
patent enforcement procedure *see* enforcement procedure, Japan
patent protection, extent of *see* Japan: patent protection, extent of
patent system history
major developments through 20th century 1.54–1.1.56
Meiji restoration 1.49–1.53
pro-patent era 1.57–1.58
remedies *see* remedies, Japan
validity challenges *see* validity challenges, Japan
Japan: patent enforcement institutions 2.60–2.74
courts 2.62–2.69, 4.46
IP High Court 2.64–2.67
judges 2.63, 2.65–2.69, 2.71
Supreme Court 2.68–2.69
Tokyo and Osaka district courts 2.62–2.63
customs office 2.73–2
functions/role 2.73
enforcement procedure *see* enforcement procedure, Japan
JPO *see* Japan Patent Office (JPO)
overview 2.60–2.61
remedies *see* remedies, Japan
validity challenges *see* validity challenges, Japan
Japan Patent Office (JPO) 1.01
advisory opinions 2.72
composition 2.70
European Patent Judges' Symposium, and 1.09
exchanging examiners with EPO 1.07
functions/role 2.70–2.71
importing many EPC aspects 1.07
invalidation trial procedure 2.71
patent appeal examiners 2.71
'patent prosecution highway', development of 1.08
Trilateral Cooperation 1.07
validity challenges *see* validity challenges, Japan
Japan: patent protection, extent of 6.25–6.78
construed claims *see* construed claims application to accused embodiment, Japan
claim construction *see* claim construction, Japan
doctrine of equivalents *see* doctrine of equivalents, Japan
infringement analysis 6.29–6.37
claim construction for validity challenges 6.35–6.37
mixed steps: claim construction and application 6.29–6.32
peripheral definition theory 6.33
separate steps: literal infringement and doctrine of equivalents 6.33–6.34
overview 6.25–6.28
juries, US 2.07, 4.22, 4.83, 6.32, 7.09, 10.61
jury trial 10.52–10.56
legal issues v. factual issues 10.54–10.56
right of jury trial 10.53
jurisdiction *see* **enforcement procedure**

Korean Intellectual Property Office (KIPO) 1.07

Paris Convention for the Protection of Industrial Property (Paris Convention)
patent laws harmonization 1.01–1.03
priority date 6.20
patent assertion entities (PAEs/trolls) 2.54
Patent Cooperation Treaty (PCT) 1.41
aim 1.03
international application date 6.20
international patent application system established 1.03
patent enforcement institutions
Germany *see* Germany: patent enforcement institutions
Japan *see* Japan: patent enforcement institutions
US *see* US: patent enforcement institutions
patent enforcement procedures *see* **enforcement procedure**
Patent Law Treaty (PLT) 1.03, 1.41
peripheral definition theory 4.17, 4.20
PHOSITAs: claim terms as understood by
Germany 4.36–4.37
Japan 6.42–6.43, 6.45, 6.57–6.58
US 4.36–4.38, 4.49, 4.58
preliminary injunctions *see* **enforcement procedure**
prior art, Germany
aids for claim interpretation, and 5.91–5.92
doctrine of equivalents, and 5.127–5.131
prior art, Japan
aids for claim interpretation, and 6.55, 6.64–6.66
doctrine of equivalents, and 4.120, 6.74–6.75
prior art, US
aids for claim interpretation, and 4.57, 4.70–4.72
distinguishing invention from 4.81
preamble terms describing invention 4.82
doctrine of equivalents, and
limiting doctrine of equivalents 4.120–4.123
range of equivalents, and 4.96

prior art, US (*cont.*):
validity challenges 7.62
validity challenge defenses: secret prior art 7.87–7.102
post-AIA prior art 7.98–7.102
pre-AIA prior art 7.87–7.97

remedies, Germany 14.01–14.43
damages, calculation of 14.14–14.29
deductible and non-deductible costs positions 14.24
infringer's profits 14.20–14.23
licence analogy 14.24–14.27
lost profits 14.17–14.19
market confusion, damages resulting from 14.28–14.29
damages, claims for 14.11–14.29
calculation of damages 14.14–14.29
requirements 14.11–14.13
destruction, recall and removal from distribution, claims for 14.31–14.37
destruction, claims for 14.31–14.32
recall and removal from distribution channels, claims for 14.33–14.37
information, claims for 14.38–14.43
Civil Code, information disclosure claim 14.43
Patent Act information disclosure claim 14.39–14.42
injunctive relief, claims for 14.02–14.10
compulsory enforcement 14.08–14.10
requirements 14.02–14.04
scope of claims 14.05–14.07
unjust enrichment, claims on account of 14.30
remedies, Japan 15.01–15.28
damages 15.06–15.24
calculation of amount of damages 15.09–15.24
requirements 15.07–15.08
damages, calculation of amount of 15.09–15.24
accounting for infringer's profits 15.16–15.19
lost profits 15.13–15.15
reasonable royalty 15.20–15.22
selection of calculation method 15.23–15.24
destruction, claims for 15.26–15.28
injunctive relief 15.01–15.05
compulsory enforcement 15.04–15.05
requirements 15.01
scope 15.02–15.03
unjust enrichment 15.25
remedies, US 13.01–13.83
damages and attorney fees, increased 13.71–13.82
misconduct during litigation 13.81
willful infringement 13.72–13.82
damages, claims for 13.38–13.82
central importance of 13.38
increased damages and attorney fees 13.71–13.82
methods of calculation 13.42–13.70
requirements 13.39–13.41
damages, methods of calculation of 13.42–13.70
entire market value rule 13.69–13.70
established royalty rates 13.56–13.61
hypothetical negotiation framework 13.62–13.68
lost profits 13.44–13.54
reasonable royalty 13.55–13.70
destruction, claims for 13.83
exclusion orders 13.26–13.37
general exclusion orders 13.30, 13.33–13.36
limited exclusion orders 13.30–13.37
public interest qualifier 13.27
requirements 13.28
types of exclusion orders 13.30
injunctive relief, claims for 13.01–13.25
execution of injunction orders 13.23–13.25
requirements 13.02–13.18
scope of injunction orders 13.19–13.22
requirements for injunctive relief 13.02–13.18
balance of hardships 13.14–13.16
irreparable harm 13.07–13.13
public interest 13.17–13.18

Trilateral Cooperation 1.07
TRIPS 1.41
direct infringement 3.01
minimum standards of intellectual property protection 1.02

Unified Patent Court 2.43, 2.44
appeals from EPO 2.44
patent court system, unified *see* unitary patents, EU
procedural rules 2.44
self-funding 2.53
unitary patents, EU
EPO role 2.44
decisions appealed to Unified Patent Court 2.44
proposal for 2.43
Unified Patent Court *see* Unified Patent Court
unified patent court system 2.45–2.46
advantages 2.54
Central Division 2.46
CJEU, references to 2.47
cost of 2.53
Court of Appeal 2.47
Courts of First Instance, decentralized 2.45
EPC patents 2.51
fees for unitary patents 2.52
judges 2.45, 2.47
mandatory representation by authorized attorneys 2.50
multiple defendants, limitations on joining 2.54
pharmaceutical companies 2.55
procedural rules 2.48–2.49
qualifications of patent attorneys 2.50
SMEs, and 2.53–2.54
unitary patent protection 1.06, 2.44
unitary patent system, nature of 2.44–2.45
United Nations (UN) 1.01
United States (US)
central definition theory 4.18–4.20
claim construction *see* claim construction, US
infringement *see* infringement, US
ITC *see* US International Trade Commission (ITC)
Paris Convention 1.01

patent enforcement institutions *see* US: patent enforcement institutions
patent enforcement procedure *see* enforcement procedure, US
patent protection, extent of *see* US: patent protection, extent of
patent rights 4.01
patent system history
American Invents Act (2012–present) 1.23–1.25
anti-patent era (1870–1982) 1.14–1.19
early patent system: (1730–1869) 1.10–1.11
pro-patent era (1980–2010) 1.20–1.22
remedies *see* remedies, US
USPTO *see* US Patent Office (USPTO)
validity challenges *see* validity challenges, US

US International Trade Commission (ITC)
cease and desist orders 2.18
exclusion orders 2.18, 13.26–13.37
general exclusion orders 13.30, 13.33–13.36
limited exclusion orders 13.30–13.37
public interest qualifier 13.27
requirements 13.28
types of exclusion orders 13.30
functions/role 2.17
investigations by 2.01, 2.02
nature of 10.57
proceedings 10.57–10.71
district courts, compared to 10.59, 10.71
domestic industry requirement 10.62–10.70
initiating complaints 10.58
jury trial 10.61
speed of 10.60
quasi-judicial functions on patent infringement 2.17
remedies 2.18

US: patent enforcement institutions 2.01–2.18
civil actions in district courts 2.01, 2.02
courts 2.03–2.14
federal versus state 2.03–2.04
judges 2.06, 2.08, 2.11, 2.14, 2.16, 2.17
jury trials 2.07, 4.22
Patent Pilot Program 2.08–2.09
US Court of Appeals for the Federal Circuit 2.10–2.12
US district courts 2.05–2.09
US International Trade Commission 2.17–2.18
see also US International Trade Commission (ITC)
US Supreme Court 2.13–.14
USPTO 2.15–2.16
see also United States Patent Office (USPTO)
enforcement procedure *see* enforcement procedure, US
ITC investigations *see* US International Trade Commission (ITC)
mediation/arbitration by consent 2.01
overview 2.01–2.02
post-issuance procedures to challenge validity at USPTO 2.02
remedies *see* remedies, US
validity challenges *see* validity challenges, US

US Patent Office (USPTO) 1.01
European Patent Judges' Symposium, and 1.09
functions/role 2.15
patent enforcement role 2.15
Patent Trial and Appeal Board 2.15
Trilateral Cooperation 1.07
validity challenges *see* validity challenges, US

US: patent protection, extent of 4.17–4.125
construed claims *see* construed claims application to accused embodiment , US
claim construction *see* claim construction, US
doctrine of equivalents *see* doctrine of equivalents, US
infringement analysis 4.22–4.31
claim construction for validity challenges 4.30–4.31
literal Infringement and infringement under equivalents doctrine 4.27–4.29
pre-trial discovery proceedings 4.26
separate steps: claim construction and application 4.22–4.26
overview 4.17–4.21
peripheral/central definition theories 4.17, 4.20–4.21

validity challenges, Germany 8.01–8.166
court invalidation procedures 8.35–8.45
handling of defense of lack of validity in infringement court 8.35
invalidity litigation ('nullity suit') in patent court 8.36–8.45
challenges regarding patentability- filing third-party observations 8.55–8.65
challenge of patentability: opposition proceedings 8.63
objections based on lack of clarity/support (Article 84 EPC) 8.58–8.62
scope of validity challenge: observations 8.56–8.57
scope of validity challenge: opposition proceedings 8.64–8.65
general presumption of patent validity 8.02
invalidity litigation ('nullity suit') in patent court 8.36–8.45
appeals 8.43
conduct of proceedings 8.39–8.43
nature of proceedings 8.38
opposition at EPO 8.18–8.29
appeals 8.25–8.29
conduct of proceedings 8.19–8.23
opposition at GPTO 8.05–8.17
appeals 8.13–8.16
conduct of proceedings 8.07–8.12, 8.17
requirements 8.05–8.06
other defenses in litigation proceedings 8.142–8.166
compulsory license for technology standard 8.160
(co-)ownership in cases of inventions by employees 8.144
derivation/lack of entitlement 8.143

validity challenges, Germany
other defenses in litigation proceedings (*cont.*):
double patenting 8.152–8.156
exhaustion 8.162–8.166
experimental use exemption 8.161
laches and estoppels, in particular prosecution history estoppels 8.147–8.151
license 8.145
patent misuse 8.146
prior right and prior use right 8.157–8.159
out-of-court invalidation procedures 8.05–8.34
limitation proceedings at GPTO and EPO 8.30–8.34
opposition at EPO *see* European Patent Office (EPO)
opposition at GPTO 8.05–8.17
patentability and validity challenges 8.46–8.141
challenges regarding patentability: filing third-party observations 8.55–8.65
derivation (entitlement) 8.137–8.139
inadmissible broadening 8.124–8.136
lack of enablement (sufficiency) 8.113–8.123
lack of industrial applicability (Article 57 EPC) 8.99–8.112
lack of inventive step (obviousness) (Article 56 EPC) 8.87–8.98
lack of novelty (Article 54 EPC) 8.74–8.86
patent eligibility (not invention, excluded inventions) 8.66–8.73
scope of the validity challenge: nullity proceedings 8.140–8.141
post-grant review procedure
amendment 7.13, 7.14
validity challenges, Japan 9.01–9.55
courts' powers to examine patent validity 9.02–9.03
other types of defenses 9.38–9.55
employee inventions: shop right 9.47–9.49
exhaustion 9.53–9.55
licenses 9.50–9.52
prior user right and intervening right 9.42–9.46
private use and experimental use exception 9.38–9.41
patent invalidation procedures 9.04–9.27
comparison with invalidity defense at infringement procedure 9.16–9.22
corrections of fact 9.13–9.14
measures to prevent delay/conflicting validity decisions 9.23–9.27
opposition procedure 9.15
overview 9.04–9.12
patentability invalidity defenses 9.28–9.37
comparison between grounds for rejection and invalidity 9.28–9.29
frequently cited invalidity grounds 9.30–9.33
inventorship and ownership 9.34–9.37
post-grant review procedure
amendment 7.13, 7.14
validity challenges, US 7.01–7.149
biotechnological inventions 7.73, 7.75, 7.78
computer-implemented inventions 7.73, 7.76–7.77
derivation proceedings 7.56–7.61
conduct of proceedings 7.61
establishing derivations 7.56
first-to-file approach 7.60
grounds for 7.59
when available 7.58
drug inventions/medical devices 7.106–7.111
ex parte re-examination 7.02, 7.26–7.34
amendment 7.32
conduct of proceedings 7.30–7.33
estoppel 7.24–7.25
grounds for 7.28–7.29
identity, keeping secret 7.26
request made at any time 7.27
stay of parallel proceedings 7.34
fundamental rules 7.04–7.25
assignor estoppel doctrine 7.10
amendment 7.12–7.17
burden of proof 7.07, 7.08–7.09
claim construction 7.04–7.07
doctrines to preclude invalidity defense 7.10–7.11
estoppel 7.24–7.25
measures to prevent conflicting validity decisions 7.18–7.23
presumption of validity 7.08
inter partes review 7.02, 7.35–7.43
appeals 7.43
conduct of proceedings 7.39–7.41
conflicting decisions, preventing 7.37–7.38
estoppel 7.24–7.25
grounds for 7.35
timing of request limited 7.36
interference proceedings 7.52–7.55
first-to-file approach 7.53
problems with 7.54
purpose of 7.52
non-court patent validity procedures at USPTO 7.26–7.149
derivation proceedings 7.56–7.61
ex parte re-examination 7.26–7.34
inter partes review 7.35–7.43
interference proceedings 7.52–7.55
other types of defenses 7.106–7.149
patentability validity defenses in civil actions 7.67–7.105
post-grant review 7.44–7.48
reissue 7.63–7.66
special post-grant review for business methods 7.49–7.51
submission of prior art 7.62
other types of defenses 7.106–7.149
employee intervention: shop rights 7.140–7.144
exhaustion 7.136–7.139
inequitable conduct 7.119–7.125
laches and estoppel 7.129–7.132
licenses 7.145–7.149
marking and notice 7.133–7.135
medical activities 7.116–7.118
patent misuse 7.126–7.128
prior user rights defense 7.112–7.115
safe harbour (s271(e) Patent Act) 7.106–7.111

patentability validity defenses in civil actions 7.67–7.105
  double patenting 7.103
  foreign filing 7.104–7.105
  introduction 7.67–7.70
  originality-inventorship 7.80–7.86
  patent eligibility 7.71–7.79
  secret prior art for lack of novelty/ nonobviousness 7.87–7.102
post-grant review 7.02, 7.44–7.48
  amendment 7.12–7.13
  conduct of proceedings 7.47–7.48
  conflicting decisions, preventing 7.45
  grounds for 7.44
  standard of review 7.08–7.09
special post-grant review for business methods 7.49–7.51
  conduct of proceedings 7.51
  covered business method patent, definition of 7.50
  timing of request for 7.49, 7.51
USPTO powers to review patent validity 7.01–7–03

World Intellectual Property Organization (WIPO) 1.01–1.03
  patent laws harmonization 1.02, 1.03
  patent treaties, adopting 1.03
World Trade Organization (WTO) 1.01–1.03
  dispute settlement mechanism 1.02
  patent laws harmonization 1.02
  TRIPS *see* TRIPS

The manufacturer's authorised representative in the EU for product safety is Oxford University Press España S.A. of El Parque Empresarial San Fernando de Henares, Avenida de Castilla, 2 - 28830 Madrid (www.oup.es/en or product.safety@oup.com). OUP España S.A. also acts as importer into Spain of products made by the manufacturer.
Printed and bound by CPI Group (UK) Ltd, Croydon, CR0 4YY
14/09/2026
02216286-0016